Honda CR-V

Owners Workshop Manual

Jeremy Churchill and RM Jex

Models covered

(4747 - 416)

Honda CR-V 'Mk II' models

Petrol: 2.0 litre (1998cc) i-VTEC
Diesel: 2.2 litre (2204cc) i-CDTi

Does NOT cover 'Mk I' range ('97-'01) or 'Mk III' range introduced for 2007

ABCDE
FGHIJ
KLMNO

A book in the **Haynes Owners Workshop Manual Series**

ISBN **978 1 78521 315 1**

British Library Cataloguing in Publication Data
A catalogue record for this book is available from the British Library.

Printed in Malaysia

Haynes Publishing
Sparkford, Yeovil, Somerset BA22 7JJ, England

Haynes North America, Inc
861 Lawrence Drive, Newbury Park, California 91320, USA

Printed using NORBRITE BOOK 48.8gsm (CODE: 40N6533) from NORPAC; procurement system certified under Sustainable Forestry Initiative standard. Paper produced is certified to the SFI Certified Fiber Sourcing Standard (CERT - 0094271)

Contents

Contents

REPAIRS AND OVERHAUL

Engine and associated systems

Transmission

Brakes and suspension

Body equipment

Wiring diagrams

REFERENCE

Index

Whether one calls them SUVs (Sport Utility Vehicles), MPVs (Multi-Purpose Vehicles), MAVs (Multi-Activity Vehicles), or 'soft-roaders', there is no doubt that the civilised leisure 4x4, with its implied rugged dependability and versatile, go-anywhere nature, has established itself as a firm favourite with those who have families, active lifestyles or large dogs – or a combination of these. The Honda CR-V (Compact Recreational Vehicle) offers part-time four-wheel-drive with good ground clearance, a roomy and versatile interior (the boot floor converts into a picnic table, for example), and Honda brand values like quality and reliability, making it a very popular choice.

The CR-V range covered by this manual was introduced late in 2001. Although visually very similar to the model which preceded it, this CR-V was an all-new design, and was built in Honda's Swindon plant. A minor facelift arrived in 2005.

As expected of a modern design, the CR-V offered high levels of passenger safety, scoring four stars in the Euro NCAP safety tests; the CR-V also scored well for pedestrian safety. To an impact-absorbing bodyshell with side impact beams were added front airbags and seat belt tensioners, with side airbags in the front seats. All models also feature ABS with EBD and Brake Assist.

The model range was limited to just the one 5-door body style. Even the 'entry-level' SE model was well-equipped – besides the valuable safety equipment already mentioned, all have air conditioning, rolling code engine immobiliser, remote keyless entry, electric mirrors and electric front windows. The Sport model offers climate control, an electric sunroof, and cruise control in addition, while Executive models benefit from full leather upholstery.

The 2.0 litre i-VTEC petrol engine is a new, highly-efficient unit which is shared with several other Honda models. In this case, the variable valve timing VTEC feature is used to provide plenty of pulling power at low revs.

The 2.2 litre i-CTDi diesel engine was introduced to the CR-V range in 2005, having previously been used in the Accord. Honda are famous for their engine-making skills, and this, their first diesel engine, offers diesel levels of economy with petrol-engine refinement.

All models have four-wheel-drive. A five-speed manual transmission is standard on petrol-engined models, with a six-speed unit being fitted to diesels. A four-speed automatic transmission is also available on petrol-engined models, which offers even greater interior space, as the selector lever is facia-mounted, leaving a completely flat front floor. Usually, the front wheels only are driven, but if any slippage is detected, a clever hydraulically-operated four-wheel-drive system smoothly feeds power to the rear wheels also.

The front suspension is of conventional MacPherson strut type, incorporating lower arms and an anti-roll bar; at the rear, wishbones, coil springs and shock absorbers are used.

Your Honda CR-V manual

The aim of this manual is to help you get the best value from your vehicle. It can do so in several ways. It can help you decide what work must be done (even should you choose to get it done by a garage). It will also provide information on routine maintenance and servicing, and give a logical course of action and diagnosis when random faults occur. However, it is hoped that you will use the manual by tackling the work yourself. On simpler jobs it may even be quicker than booking the vehicle into a garage and going there twice, to leave and collect it. Perhaps most important, a lot of money can be saved by avoiding the costs a garage must charge to cover its labour and overheads.

The manual has drawings and descriptions to show the function of the various components so that their layout can be understood. Tasks are described and photographed in a clear step-by-step sequence.

References to the 'left' and 'right' of the vehicle are in the sense of a person in the driver's seat, facing forwards.

Acknowledgements

Thanks are due to Draper tools Limited, who provided some of the workshop tools, and to all those people at Sparkford who helped in the production of this manual.

Dedication

This manual is dedicated to the memory of its co-author, Bob Jex, who died before it was published. Bob worked enthusiastically for Haynes for 21 years. He wrote over 20 car Owners Workshop Manuals and 10 modifying manuals, and edited many more. He is much missed; his memory lives on among his colleagues and in the pages of the excellent manuals he wrote.

Working on your car can be dangerous. This page shows just some of the potential risks and hazards, with the aim of creating a safety-conscious attitude.

General hazards

Scalding

• Don't remove the radiator or expansion tank cap while the engine is hot.
• Engine oil, automatic transmission fluid or power steering fluid may also be dangerously hot if the engine has recently been running.

Burning

• Beware of burns from the exhaust system and from any part of the engine. Brake discs and drums can also be extremely hot immediately after use.

Crushing

• When working under or near a raised vehicle, always supplement the jack with axle stands, or use drive-on ramps. ***Never venture under a car which is only supported by a jack.***

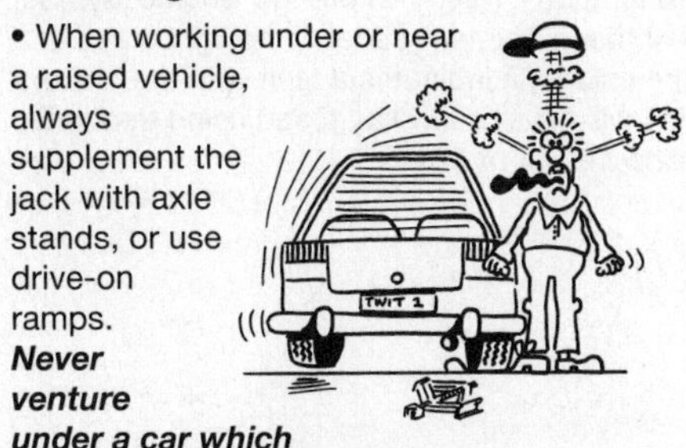

• Take care if loosening or tightening high-torque nuts when the vehicle is on stands. Initial loosening and final tightening should be done with the wheels on the ground.

Fire

• Fuel is highly flammable; fuel vapour is explosive.
• Don't let fuel spill onto a hot engine.
• Do not smoke or allow naked lights (including pilot lights) anywhere near a vehicle being worked on. Also beware of creating sparks (electrically or by use of tools).
• Fuel vapour is heavier than air, so don't work on the fuel system with the vehicle over an inspection pit.
• Another cause of fire is an electrical overload or short-circuit. Take care when repairing or modifying the vehicle wiring.
• Keep a fire extinguisher handy, of a type suitable for use on fuel and electrical fires.

Electric shock

• Ignition HT voltage can be dangerous, especially to people with heart problems or a pacemaker. Don't work on or near the ignition system with the engine running or the ignition switched on.

• Mains voltage is also dangerous. Make sure that any mains-operated equipment is correctly earthed. Mains power points should be protected by a residual current device (RCD) circuit breaker.

Fume or gas intoxication

• Exhaust fumes are poisonous; they often contain carbon monoxide, which is rapidly fatal if inhaled. Never run the engine in a confined space such as a garage with the doors shut.

• Fuel vapour is also poisonous, as are the vapours from some cleaning solvents and paint thinners.

Poisonous or irritant substances

• Avoid skin contact with battery acid and with any fuel, fluid or lubricant, especially antifreeze, brake hydraulic fluid and Diesel fuel. Don't syphon them by mouth. If such a substance is swallowed or gets into the eyes, seek medical advice.
• Prolonged contact with used engine oil can cause skin cancer. Wear gloves or use a barrier cream if necessary. Change out of oil-soaked clothes and do not keep oily rags in your pocket.
• Air conditioning refrigerant forms a poisonous gas if exposed to a naked flame (including a cigarette). It can also cause skin burns on contact.

Asbestos

• Asbestos dust can cause cancer if inhaled or swallowed. Asbestos may be found in gaskets and in brake and clutch linings. When dealing with such components it is safest to assume that they contain asbestos.

Special hazards

Hydrofluoric acid

• This extremely corrosive acid is formed when certain types of synthetic rubber, found in some O-rings, oil seals, fuel hoses etc, are exposed to temperatures above $400^{0}C$. The rubber changes into a charred or sticky substance containing the acid. *Once formed, the acid remains dangerous for years. If it gets onto the skin, it may be necessary to amputate the limb concerned.*
• When dealing with a vehicle which has suffered a fire, or with components salvaged from such a vehicle, wear protective gloves and discard them after use.

The battery

• Batteries contain sulphuric acid, which attacks clothing, eyes and skin. Take care when topping-up or carrying the battery.
• The hydrogen gas given off by the battery is highly explosive. Never cause a spark or allow a naked light nearby. Be careful when connecting and disconnecting battery chargers or jump leads.

Air bags

• Air bags can cause injury if they go off accidentally. Take care when removing the steering wheel and/or facia. Special storage instructions may apply.

Diesel injection equipment

• Diesel injection pumps supply fuel at very high pressure. Take care when working on the fuel injectors and fuel pipes.

Warning: Never expose the hands, face or any other part of the body to injector spray; the fuel can penetrate the skin with potentially fatal results.

Remember...

DO

• Do use eye protection when using power tools, and when working under the vehicle.

• Do wear gloves or use barrier cream to protect your hands when necessary.

• Do get someone to check periodically that all is well when working alone on the vehicle.

• Do keep loose clothing and long hair well out of the way of moving mechanical parts.

• Do remove rings, wristwatch etc, before working on the vehicle – especially the electrical system.

• Do ensure that any lifting or jacking equipment has a safe working load rating adequate for the job.

DON'T

• Don't attempt to lift a heavy component which may be beyond your capability – get assistance.

• Don't rush to finish a job, or take unverified short cuts.

• Don't use ill-fitting tools which may slip and cause injury.

• Don't leave tools or parts lying around where someone can trip over them. Mop up oil and fuel spills at once.

• Don't allow children or pets to play in or near a vehicle being worked on.

The following pages are intended to help in dealing with common roadside emergencies and breakdowns. You will find more detailed fault finding information at the back of the manual, and repair information in the main chapters.

If your car won't start and the starter motor doesn't turn

- ☐ Open the bonnet and make sure that the battery terminals are clean and tight.
- ☐ Switch on the headlights and try to start the engine. If the headlights go very dim when you're trying to start, the battery is probably flat. Get out of trouble by jump starting (see next page) using a friend's car.
- ☐ If it's a model with automatic transmission, the selector must be in P or N.

A Check the condition and security of the battery connections.

If your car won't start even though the starter motor turns as normal

- ☐ Is there fuel in the tank?
- ☐ Has the engine immobiliser been deactivated? This should happen automatically when the key is inserted and turned to the first position.
- ☐ Is there moisture on electrical components under the bonnet? With the ignition off, wipe off any obvious dampness with a dry cloth. Spray a water-repellent aerosol product (WD-40 or equivalent) on ignition and fuel system electrical connectors like those shown in the photos. On petrol models, pay special attention to the ignition coil wiring connectors (which are under a plastic cover).
- ☐ Is the engine management warning light (also known as the Malfunction Indicator Light) on? This is an orange 'engine' symbol, on the left-hand side of the instrument panel. If the light stays on when trying to start the engine, it indicates a fault with the fuel or ignition systems, which will have to be diagnosed using dedicated test equipment (see Chapter 4A or 4B).

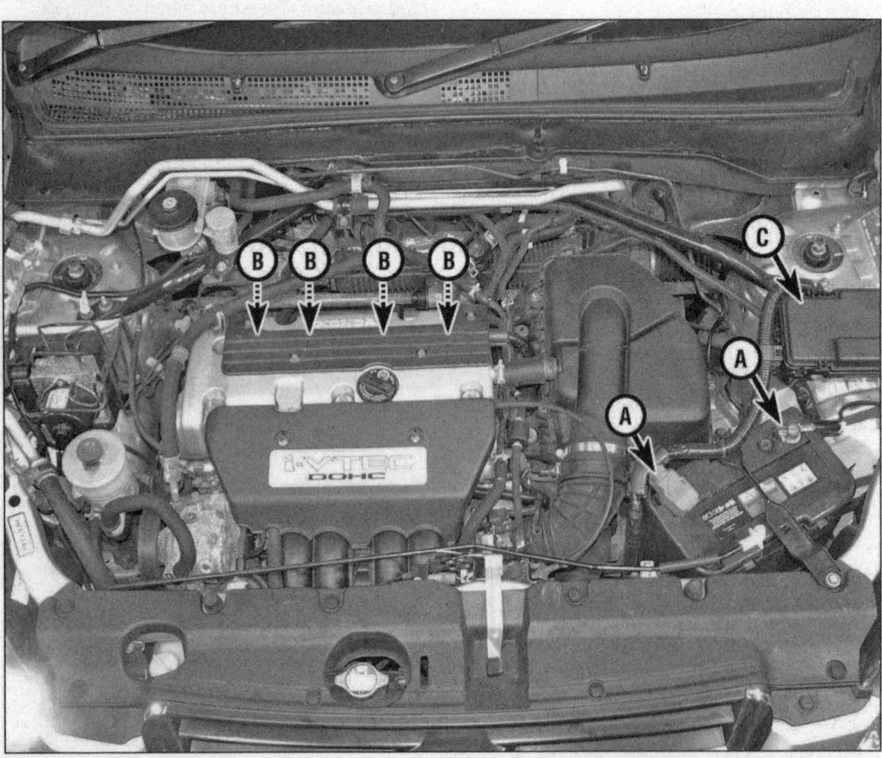

Check that electrical connections are secure (with the ignition switched off) and spray them with a water-dispersant spray like WD-40 if you suspect a problem due to damp.

B With the ignition off, check that the four ignition coils (petrol models only) are securely connected.

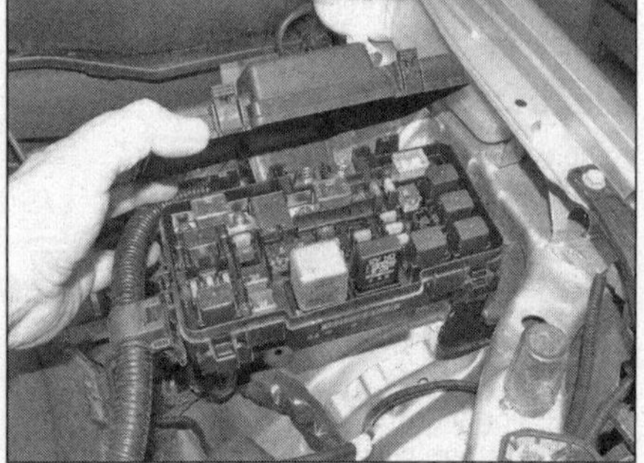

C With the ignition off, check the fuses and relays in the engine compartment fusebox.

Jump starting

When jump-starting a car using a booster battery, observe the following precautions:

- ✔ Before connecting the booster battery, make sure that the ignition is switched off.
- ✔ Ensure that all electrical equipment (lights, heater, wipers, etc) is switched off.
- ✔ Take note of any special precautions printed on the battery case.
- ✔ Make sure that the booster battery is the same voltage as the discharged one in the vehicle.
- ✔ If the battery is being jump-started from the battery in another vehicle, the two vehicles MUST NOT TOUCH each other.
- ✔ Make sure that the transmission is in neutral (or PARK, in the case of automatic transmission).

Jump starting will get you out of trouble, but you must correct whatever made the battery go flat in the first place. There are three possibilities:

1 The battery has been drained by repeated attempts to start, or by leaving the lights on.

2 The charging system is not working properly (alternator drivebelt slack or broken, alternator wiring fault or alternator itself faulty).

3 The battery itself is at fault (electrolyte low, or battery worn out).

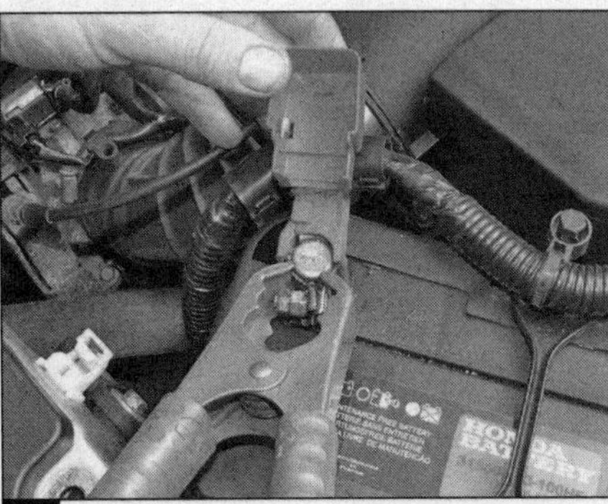

1 Connect one end of the red jump lead to the positive (+) terminal of the flat battery

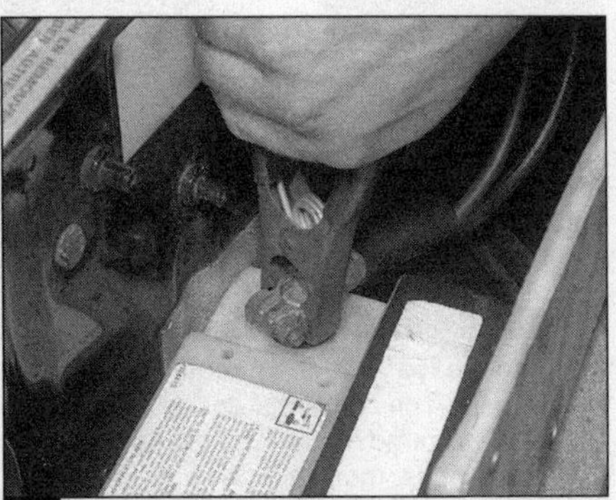

2 Connect the other end of the red lead to the positive (+) terminal of the booster battery.

3 Connect one end of the black jump lead to the negative (-) terminal of the booster battery

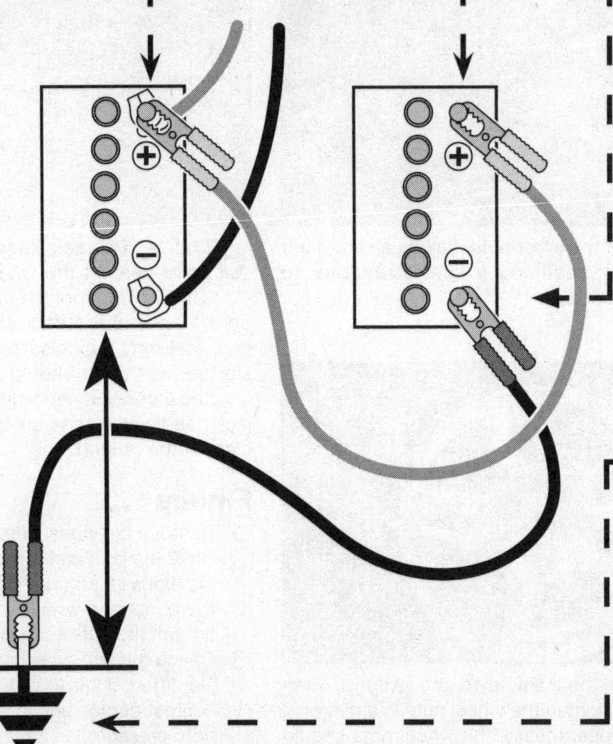

4 Connect the other end of the black jump lead to a bolt or bracket on the engine block, well away from the battery, on the vehicle to be started.

5 Make sure that the jump leads will not come into contact with the fan, drive-belts or other moving parts of the engine.

6 Start the engine using the booster battery and run it at idle speed. Switch on the lights, rear window demister and heater blower motor, then disconnect the jump leads in the reverse order of connection. Turn off the lights etc.

Wheel changing

Warning: Do not change a wheel in a situation where you risk being hit by other traffic. On busy roads, try to stop in a lay-by or a gateway. Be wary of passing traffic while changing the wheel – it is easy to become distracted by the job in hand.

Preparation

- ☐ When a puncture occurs, stop as soon as it is safe to do so.
- ☐ Park on firm level ground, if possible, and well out of the way of other traffic.
- ☐ Use hazard warning lights if necessary.
- ☐ If you have one, use a warning triangle to alert other drivers of your presence.
- ☐ Apply the handbrake and engage first or reverse gear (or P on automatic transmission).
- ☐ Chock the wheel diagonally opposite the one being removed – a couple of large stones will do for this.
- ☐ If the ground is soft, use a flat piece of wood to spread the load under the jack.

Changing the wheel

1 The vehicle jack and tools are on the right-hand side of the luggage compartment. The tools are behind a cover – turn the handle anti-clockwise to release it. The jack is mounted vertically at the rear – turn its end fitting anti-clockwise to slacken it for removal.

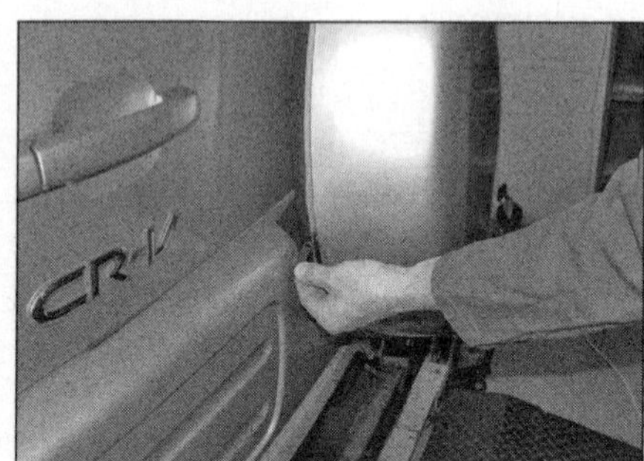

2 The spare wheel is mounted on the tailgate. The soft cover unzips from below, while to remove the hard cover, pull it out at the base, then lift it off.

3 On alloy wheels, remove the centre cap. Undo the spare wheel nuts with the wheelbrace. On steel wheels, with the nuts removed, take off the wheel trim.

4 Use the wheelbrace to slacken each wheel nut by half a turn.

5 One of the wheelnuts may be an anti-theft design, requiring a special adapter to unscrew it.

6 Locate the jack head into the jacking point nearest the wheel to be changed. The jacking points are elongated tabs on the base of the door sills at the front and rear, that may be indicated by an arrow – the slotted jack head should locate on the tab. Use the extension and wheel brace to turn the jack handle clockwise until the wheel is raised clear of the ground.

7 Remove the nuts (take off the wheel trim on steel-wheel models), and lift the punctured wheel clear. Fit the spare wheel (and steel-wheel trim). Refit the wheel nuts, and tighten moderately with the wheelbrace.

8 Lower the vehicle to the ground, then finally tighten the wheel nuts in a diagonal sequence. Ideally, the wheel nuts should be slackened and retightened to the specified torque at the earliest opportunity.

Finally . . .

- ☐ Remove the wheel chocks.
- ☐ Stow the jack and tools in the correct locations in (and on) the vehicle. If refitting the punctured wheel to the tailgate, tighten the nuts securely.
- ☐ Check the tyre pressure on the wheel just fitted. If it is low, drive slowly to the nearest garage and inflate the tyre to the right pressure.
- ☐ Have the damaged tyre or wheel repaired as soon as possible.

Identifying leaks

Puddles on the garage floor or drive, or obvious wetness under the bonnet or underneath the car, suggest a leak that needs investigating. It can sometimes be difficult to decide where the leak is coming from, especially if the engine bay is very dirty already. Leaking oil or fluid can also be blown rearwards by the passage of air under the car, giving a false impression of where the problem lies.

Warning: Most automotive oils and fluids are poisonous. Wash them off skin, and change out of contaminated clothing, without delay.

The smell of a fluid leaking from the car may provide a clue to what's leaking. Some fluids are distinctively coloured. It may help to clean the car carefully and to park it over some clean paper overnight as an aid to locating the source of the leak.
Remember that some leaks may only occur while the engine is running.

Sump oil

Engine oil may leak from the drain plug...

Oil from filter

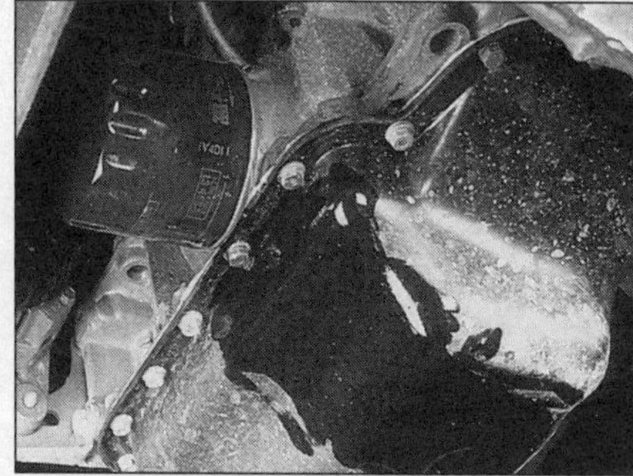

...or from the base of the oil filter.

Gearbox oil

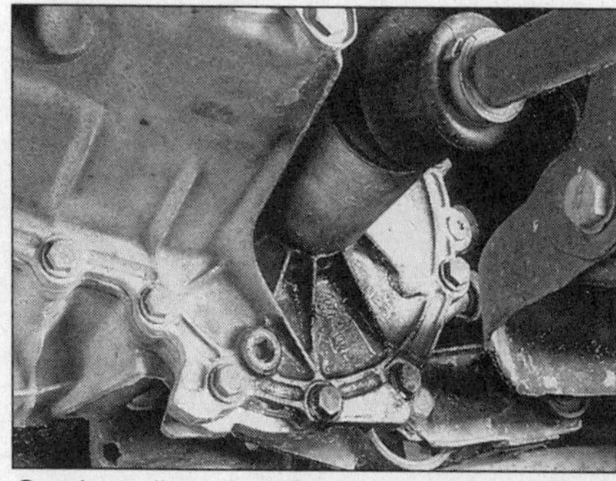

Gearbox oil can leak from the seals at the inboard ends of the driveshafts.

Antifreeze

Leaking antifreeze often leaves a crystalline deposit like this.

Brake fluid

A leak occurring at a wheel is almost certainly brake fluid.

Power steering fluid

Power steering fluid may leak from the pipe connectors on the steering rack.

Towing

When all else fails, you may find yourself in need of rescue. Honda stress that, due to the likelihood of damage to the CR-V's four-wheel-drive system, an immobilised CR-V should **only** be moved on a flatbed transporter.

Warning: If you do have to call a breakdown recovery service or vehicle rescue organisation, be sure to tell the operator exactly what sort of vehicle it is that you have. The vehicle should not be towed for recovery with two wheels (front or rear) off the ground (suspended tow), nor should it be raised on slings that attach to suspension components, thus ruling out wheel-lift or sling-type towing equipment.

If you are using your CR-V to tow another vehicle, observe the following points:

☐ Use a proper tow-rope – they are not expensive. Attach the rope only to a properly-mounted towbar – wrapping a tow-rope around any suspension components, for example, will result in damage. Similarly, the tie-down points (two at the front, one at the rear) are for lashing the CR-V down on a transporter; they are NOT strong enough for towing. The vehicle being towed must display an ON TOW sign in its rear window.

☐ Always turn the ignition key to the first position on the vehicle being towed, so that the steering lock is released, and that the direction indicator and brake lights will work.

☐ Also on the vehicle being towed, release the handbrake and select neutral on the transmission.

☐ Note that greater-than-usual pedal pressure will be required to operate the brakes, since the vacuum servo unit is only operational with the engine running.

☐ The driver of the car being towed must keep the tow-rope taut at all times to avoid snatching.

☐ Make sure that both drivers know the route before setting off.

☐ Only drive at moderate speeds and keep the distance towed to a minimum. Drive smoothly and allow plenty of time for slowing down at junctions.

Introduction

There are some very simple checks which need only take a few minutes to carry out, but which could save you a lot of inconvenience and expense.

These *Weekly checks* require no great skill or special tools, and the small amount of time they take to perform could prove to be very well spent, for example:

☐ Keeping an eye on tyre condition and pressures, will not only help to stop them wearing out prematurely, but could also save your life.

☐ Many breakdowns are caused by electrical problems. Battery-related faults are particularly common, and a quick check on a regular basis will often prevent the majority of these.

☐ If your car develops a brake fluid leak, the first time you might know about it is when your brakes don't work properly. Checking the level regularly will give advance warning of this kind of problem.

☐ If the oil or coolant levels run low, the cost of repairing any engine damage will be far greater than fixing the leak, for example.

Underbonnet check points

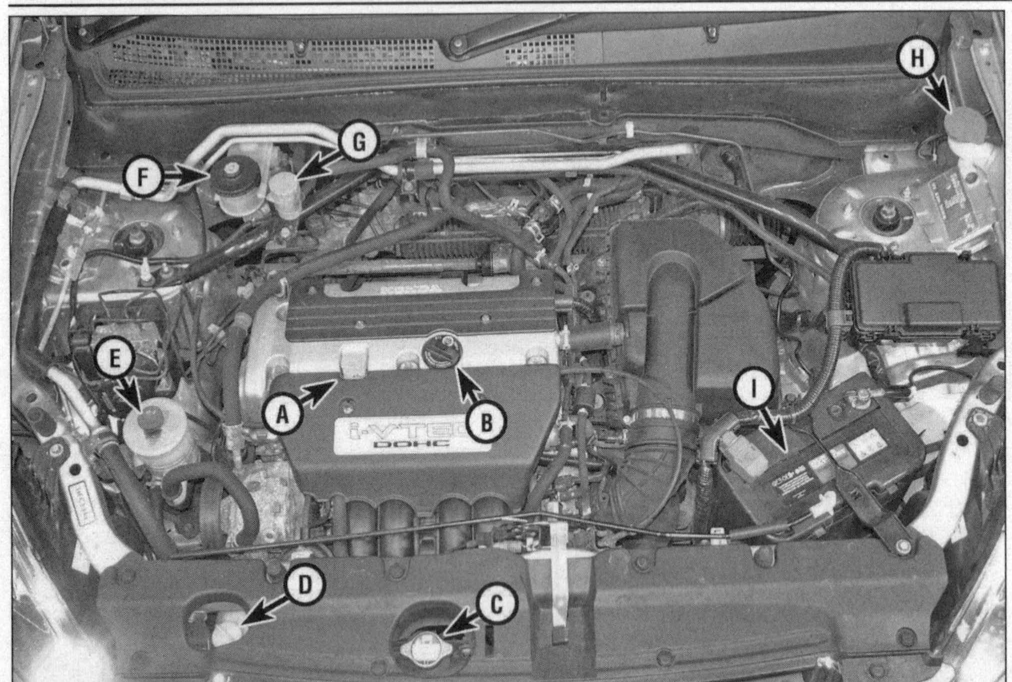

◀ **Petrol engine**

A *Engine oil level dipstick*
B *Engine oil filler cap*
C *Radiator cap*
D *Expansion tank filler cap*
E *Power steering fluid reservoir*
F *Brake fluid reservoir*
G *Clutch fluid reservoir*
H *Screen washer fluid reservoir filler*
I *Battery*

◀ **Diesel engine**

A *Engine oil level dipstick*
B *Engine oil filler cap*
C *Expansion tank filler cap*
D *Power steering fluid reservoir*
E *Brake fluid reservoir*
F *Clutch fluid reservoir*
G *Screen washer fluid reservoir filler*
H *Battery*

Engine oil level

Before you start

✔ Make sure that the vehicle is on level ground.

✔ On petrol-engined models, check the oil level when the engine is fully warmed-up; switch the engine off and wait a few minutes before checking the oil level.

✔ On diesel-engined models, check the oil level DAILY, when the engine is cold.

If the oil is checked immediately after driving the vehicle, some of the oil will remain in the upper engine components, resulting in an inaccurate reading on the dipstick.

The correct oil

Modern engines place great demands on their oil. It is very important that the correct oil for your car is used (see *Lubricants and fluids*).

Vehicle care

● If you have to add oil frequently, you should check whether you have any oil leaks. Remove the engine undershield, place some clean paper under the vehicle overnight, and check for stains in the morning. If there are no leaks, the engine may be burning oil (see *Fault finding*).

● Always maintain the level between the upper and lower dipstick marks (see photo 2). If the level is too low, severe engine damage may occur. Oil seal failure may result if the engine is overfilled by adding too much oil.

1 The dipstick is on top of the engine at the front, and has a yellow or orange handle (see *Underbonnet check points* for exact locations). Pull out the dipstick.

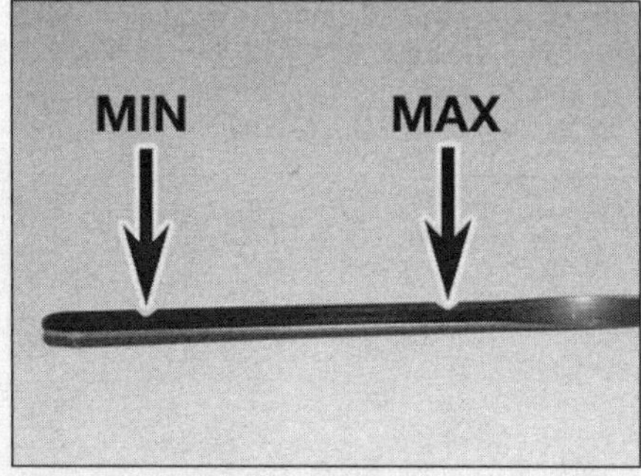

2 Using a clean rag or paper towel, wipe all the oil from the dipstick. Insert the clean dipstick into the tube as far as it will go, then withdraw it again. Note the oil level on the end of the dipstick, which should be between the lower and upper marks.

3 Oil is added through the filler cap on top of the engine. Unscrew the filler cap, then top-up the level – use a funnel to reduce spillage. Add the oil in small amounts to raise the level from the lower to the upper mark, checking the level on the dipstick often – allow a minute or so for the oil added to reach the sump. Take care not to overfill.

Power steering fluid level

Before you start

✔ The level should be checked when the engine is cold (ie, before the vehicle is driven), with the wheels pointing straight-ahead.

For the check to be accurate, the steering must not be turned once the engine has been stopped.

Safety first!

● The need for frequent topping-up indicates a leak, which should be investigated immediately.

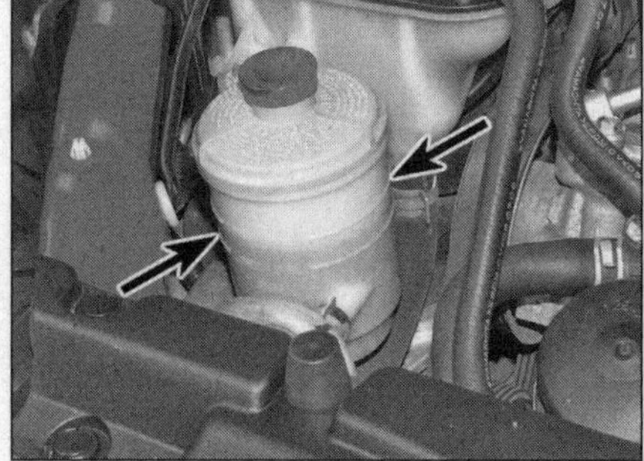

1 The power steering fluid reservoir is in the front corner of the engine compartment on the driver's side, and has a red cap. The fluid level is visible through the reservoir body, and should be up to the UPPER LEVEL mark.

2 If topping-up is required, wipe clean the area around the top of the reservoir, and unscrew the filler cap. When topping-up, use the specified type of fluid, and do not overfill the reservoir. When the level is correct, securely refit the cap.

Coolant level

Warning: DO NOT attempt to remove the radiator cap nor the expansion tank cap when the engine is hot, as there is a very great risk of scalding. Only check the level when the system is cold, after the vehicle has been standing for several hours (preferably, after being left overnight). Do not leave open containers of coolant about, as it is poisonous.

Vehicle care

- Adding coolant should not be necessary on a regular basis. If frequent topping-up is required, it is likely there is a leak. Check the radiator, all hoses and joint faces for signs of staining or wetness, and rectify as necessary.
- It is important that antifreeze is used in the cooling system all year round, not just during the winter months. Don't top-up with water alone, as the antifreeze will become too diluted; use a 50/50 mixture of neat antifreeze and water. Genuine Honda antifreeze comes pre-mixed, ready to use.

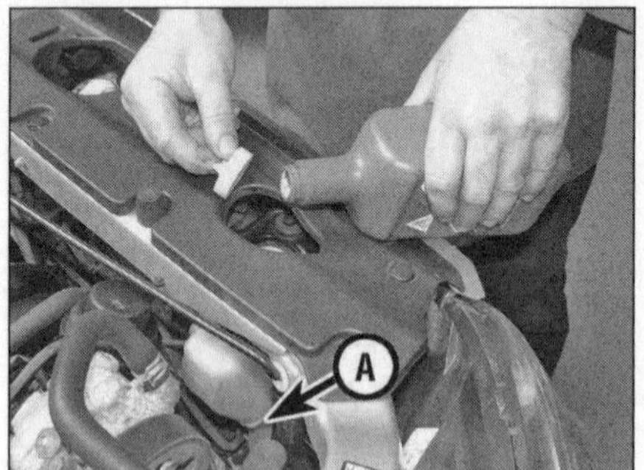

1 The level of coolant in the system is checked at the expansion tank. On petrol models, the tank is at the front, next to the radiator. When the engine is cold, the level should be between the MAX and MIN marks. When the engine is hot, the level may rise slightly above the MAX (A) mark.

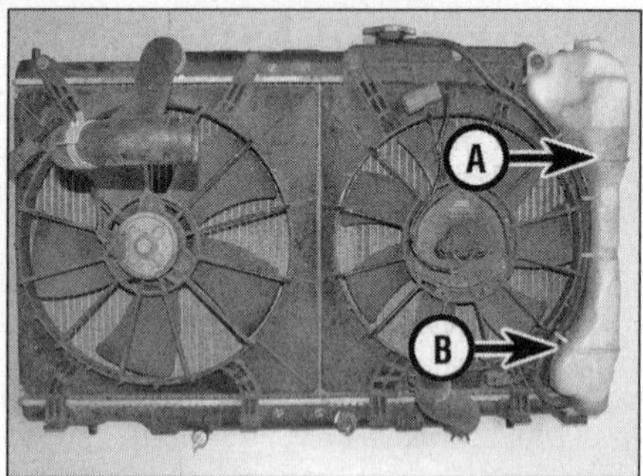

2 If topping-up is necessary, wait until the engine is cold, then remove the cap on the expansion tank. Add genuine Honda antifreeze until the coolant is up to the MAX mark, then refit the cap securely. Both marks are difficult to see, the MIN (B) mark especially so; it is nearly at the bottom of the radiator.

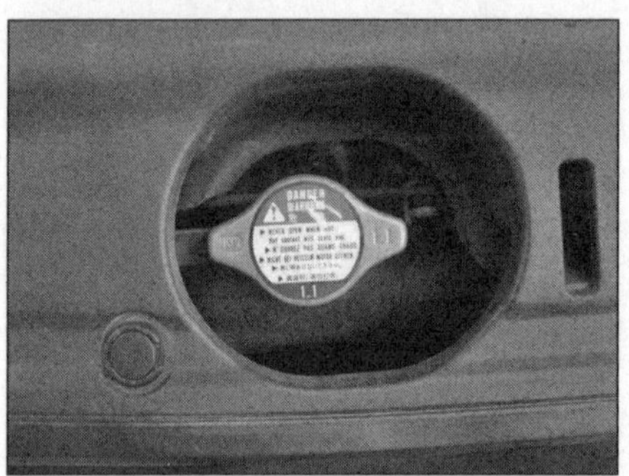

3 On petrol models only, if the expansion tank is empty or below the MIN mark the level in the radiator itself should be checked first, and for this, the engine must be cold. Turn the radiator cap anti-clockwise to the first stop, then press down and continue turning to remove it. The level should be up to the base of the filler neck – top-up if necessary, using genuine Honda antifreeze. Refit the cap securely on completion, then top-up the expansion tank and check carefully for leaks when the engine is restarted.

4 On diesel models, the expansion tank is on the driver's side of the engine bay. When the engine is cold, the level should be between the MAX (A) and MIN (B) marks. When the engine is hot, the level may rise slightly above the MAX (A) mark. If topping-up is necessary, with the engine cold, turn the expansion tank cap anti-clockwise to the first stop, then press down and continue turning to remove it. Add genuine Honda antifreeze until the coolant is up to the MAX mark, then refit the cap securely.

Wiper blades

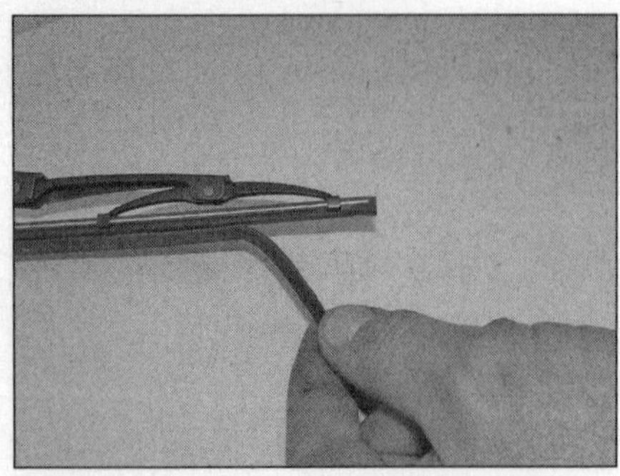

1 Check the condition of the wiper blades; if they are cracked or show any signs of deterioration, or if the glass swept area is smeared, renew them. For maximum clarity of vision, wiper blades should be renewed annually, as a matter of course.

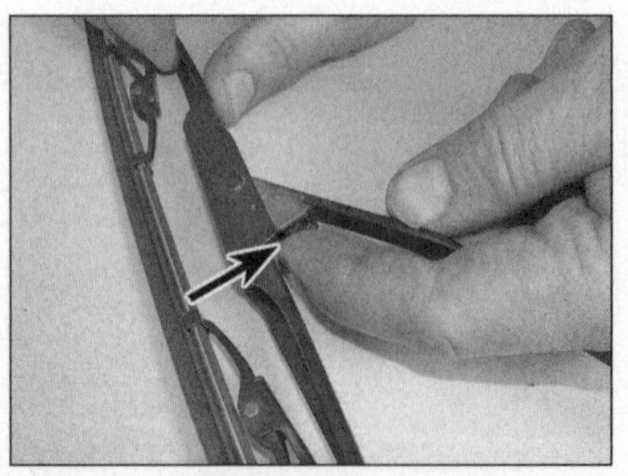

2 To remove a windscreen wiper blade, pull the arm fully away from the screen until it locks. Swivel the blade through 90°, then depress the locking clip at the base of the mounting block, and slide the blade out of the hooked end of the arm.

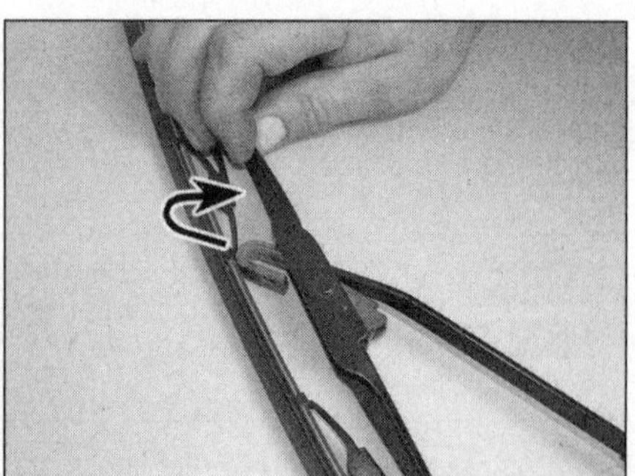

3 Don't forget to check the tailgate wiper blade as well, which unclips from the arm the same way as the front blades.

Brake and clutch fluid levels

Warning: Brake fluid can harm your eyes and damage painted surfaces, so use extreme caution when handling and pouring it. Do not use fluid that has been standing open for some time, as it absorbs moisture from the air, which can cause a dangerous loss of braking effectiveness.

Safety first!

- If the reservoirs require repeated topping-up, this is an indication of a fluid leak somewhere in the brake or clutch system, which should be investigated immediately. If a leak is suspected, the vehicle should not be driven until the braking system has been checked. Never take any risks where brakes are concerned.
- The fluid level in the brake fluid reservoir will drop slightly as the brake pads wear down (the same applies to the clutch fluid level as the friction plate wears), but the fluid level must never be allowed to drop below the MIN mark for either.

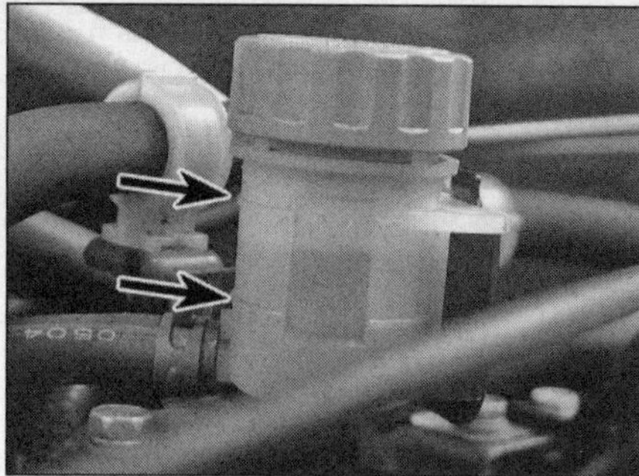

1 The two reservoirs are located next to each other, at the rear of the engine bay on the driver's side. The clutch fluid reservoir is mounted on the front suspension strut brace.

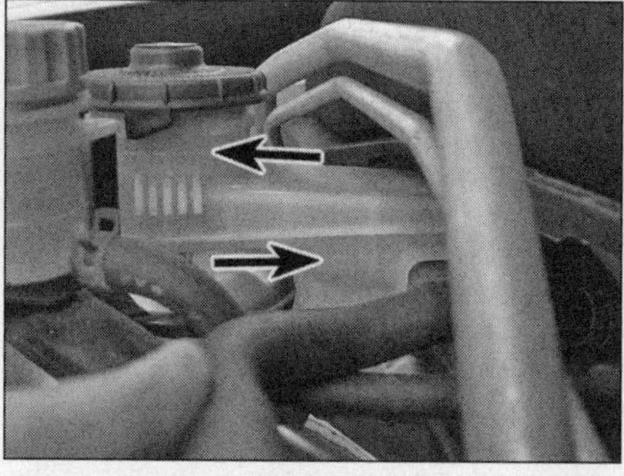

2 The larger of the two is the brake reservoir. Both reservoirs have MAX and MIN level marks – the fluid level must be kept between these two marks.

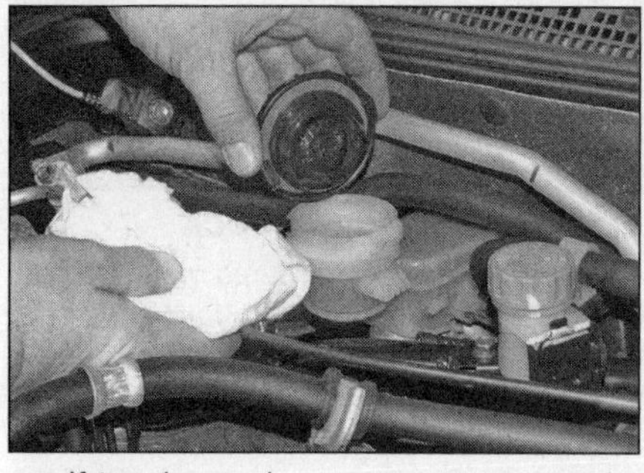

3 If topping-up is necessary, unscrew the cap, then take out the plastic inner cap and the black rubber seal (rest them on a clean piece of paper towel). If the fluid in the reservoir is dark or dirty, it should be changed. Wipe up any spilt fluid.

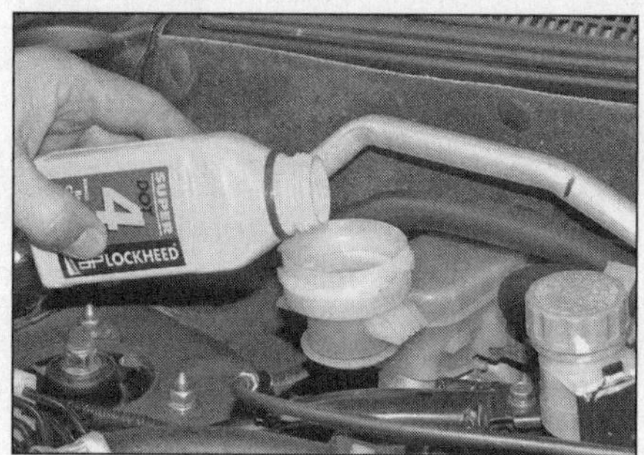

4 Carefully add fluid, avoiding spilling it on surrounding paintwork. Use only the specified hydraulic fluid. After filling to the correct level, refit the cap securely, and wipe off any spilt fluid.

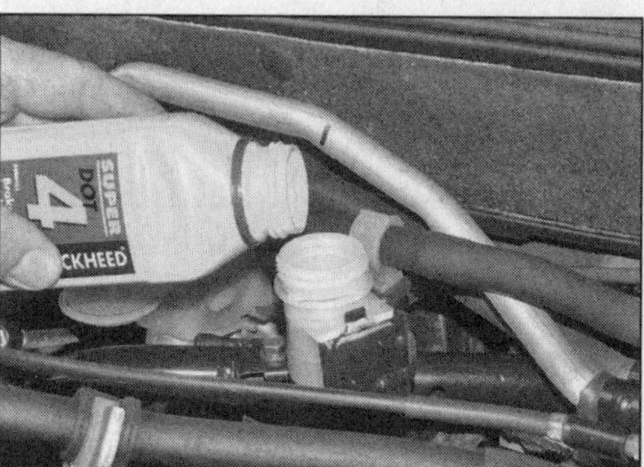

5 Topping-up the clutch fluid level is the same as the brake reservoir – on completion, refit the rubber seal, then the inner cap, then tighten the outer cap securely.

Screen washer fluid level

- Screenwash additives not only keep the windscreen clean during bad weather, they also prevent the washer system freezing in cold weather – which is when you are likely to need it most. Don't top-up using plain water, as the screenwash will become diluted, and will freeze in cold weather.

Caution: On no account use engine coolant antifreeze in the screen washer system – this may damage the paintwork.

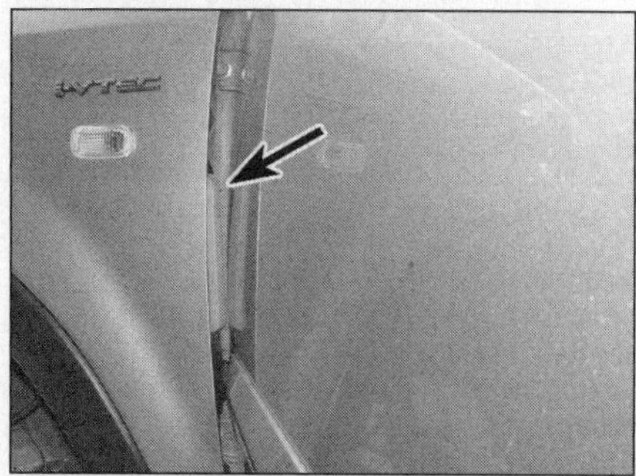

1 To check the washer fluid level, open the front passenger door, and look between the door edge and the inside of the wing. The reservoir lower level mark is just visible above the door's check strap – if the level is below this mark (which means that there is 0.5 litre of fluid remaining), topping-up is needed.

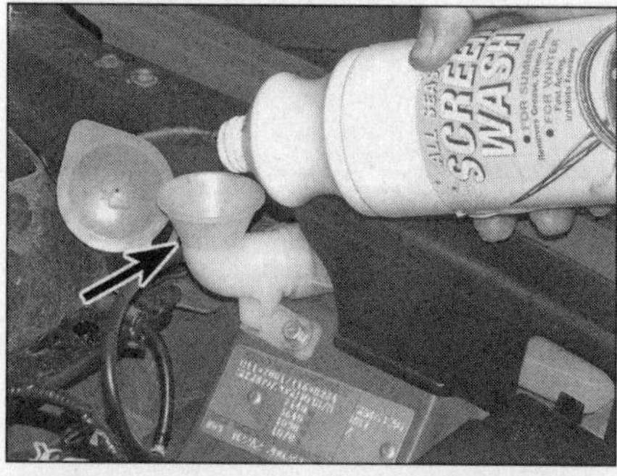

2 The washer fluid reservoir filler neck has a blue cap, and is located at the rear of the engine compartment, on the passenger side. Unclip and remove the cap. When topping-up the reservoir, a screenwash additive should be added in the quantities recommended on the bottle. The reservoir can safely be filled right to the top of the filler neck.

Tyre condition and pressure

It is very important that tyres are in good condition, and at the correct pressure - having a tyre failure at any speed is highly dangerous. Tyre wear is influenced by driving style - harsh braking and acceleration, or fast cornering, will all produce more rapid tyre wear. As a general rule, the front tyres wear out faster than the rears. Interchanging the tyres from front to rear ("rotating" the tyres) may result in more even wear. However, if this is completely effective, you may have the expense of replacing all four tyres at once!

Remove any nails or stones embedded in the tread before they penetrate the tyre to cause deflation. If removal of a nail does reveal that the tyre has been punctured, refit the nail so that its point of penetration is marked. Then immediately change the wheel, and have the tyre repaired by a tyre dealer.

Regularly check the tyres for damage in the form of cuts or bulges, especially in the sidewalls. Periodically remove the wheels, and clean any dirt or mud from the inside and outside surfaces. Examine the wheel rims for signs of rusting, corrosion or other damage. Light alloy wheels are easily damaged by "kerbing" whilst parking; steel wheels may also become dented or buckled. A new wheel is very often the only way to overcome severe damage.

New tyres should be balanced when they are fitted, but it may become necessary to re-balance them as they wear, or if the balance weights fitted to the wheel rim should fall off. Unbalanced tyres will wear more quickly, as will the steering and suspension components. Wheel imbalance is normally signified by vibration, particularly at a certain speed (typically around 50 mph). If this vibration is felt only through the steering, then it is likely that just the front wheels need balancing. If, however, the vibration is felt through the whole car, the rear wheels could be out of balance. Wheel balancing should be carried out by a tyre dealer or garage.

1 ***Tread Depth - visual check***

The original tyres have tread wear safety bands (B), which will appear when the tread depth reaches approximately 1.6 mm. The band positions are indicated by a triangular mark on the tyre sidewall (A).

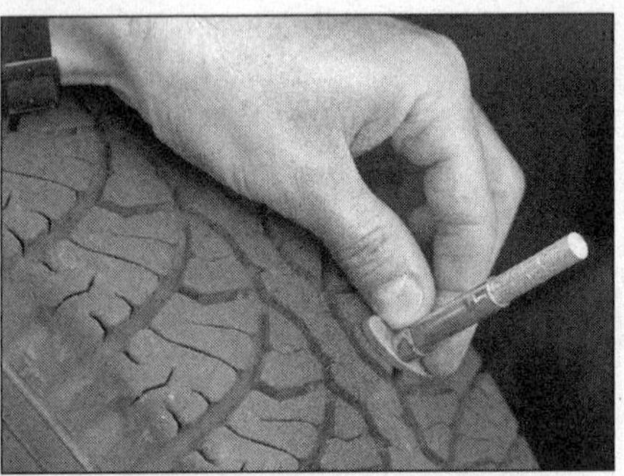

2 ***Tread Depth - manual check***

Alternatively, tread wear can be monitored with a simple, inexpensive device known as a tread depth indicator gauge.

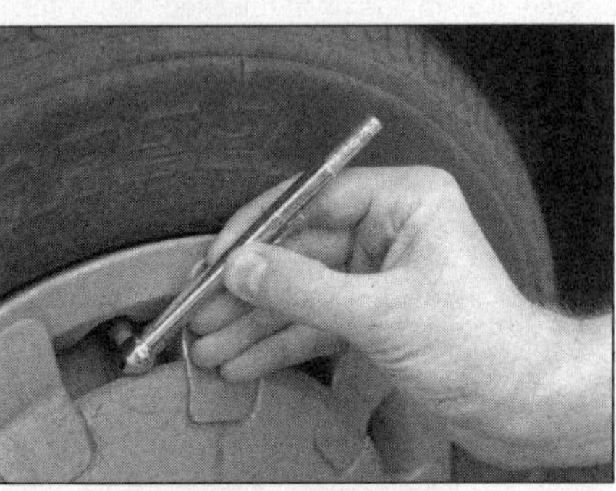

3 ***Tyre Pressure Check***

Check the tyre pressures regularly with the tyres cold. Do not adjust the tyre pressures immediately after the vehicle has been used, or an inaccurate setting will result.

Tyre tread wear patterns

Shoulder Wear

Underinflation (wear on both sides)
Under-inflation will cause overheating of the tyre, because the tyre will flex too much, and the tread will not sit correctly on the road surface. This will cause a loss of grip and excessive wear, not to mention the danger of sudden tyre failure due to heat build-up.
Check and adjust pressures
Incorrect wheel camber (wear on one side)
Repair or renew suspension parts
Hard cornering
Reduce speed!

Centre Wear

Overinflation
Over-inflation will cause rapid wear of the centre part of the tyre tread, coupled with reduced grip, harsher ride, and the danger of shock damage occurring in the tyre casing.
Check and adjust pressures

If you sometimes have to inflate your car's tyres to the higher pressures specified for maximum load or sustained high speed, don't forget to reduce the pressures to normal afterwards.

Uneven Wear

Front tyres may wear unevenly as a result of wheel misalignment. Most tyre dealers and garages can check and adjust the wheel alignment (or "tracking") for a modest charge.
Incorrect camber or castor
Repair or renew suspension parts
Malfunctioning suspension
Repair or renew suspension parts
Unbalanced wheel
Balance tyres
Incorrect toe setting
Adjust front wheel alignment
Note: *The feathered edge of the tread which typifies toe wear is best checked by feel.*

Battery

Caution: Before carrying out any work on the vehicle battery, read the precautions given in 'Safety first!' at the start of this manual.

✔ Make sure that the battery tray is in good condition, and that the clamp is tight. Corrosion on the tray, retaining clamp and the battery itself can be removed with a solution of water and baking soda. Thoroughly rinse all cleaned areas with water. Any metal parts damaged by corrosion should be covered with a zinc-based primer, then painted.

✔ Periodically (approximately every three months), check the charge condition of the battery as described in Chapter 5A.

✔ If the battery is flat, and you need to jump start your vehicle, see *Roadside Repairs*.

✔ The original-equipment battery is described as 'maintenance-free', but some have removable cell covers, and the electrolyte level can be seen inside. If the level in any cell is obviously low, there is no harm in topping-up with a little distilled water.

Battery corrosion can be kept to a minimum by applying a layer of petroleum jelly to the clamps and terminals after they are reconnected.

1 The battery is located at the front of the engine compartment, on the passenger's side. The battery should be inspected periodically for damage such as a cracked case. Honda batteries have a condition indicator window (arrowed), which should show either blue or green if all is well.

2 Check the tightness of the battery cable clamps to ensure good electrical connections. You should not be able to move them. Also check each cable for cracks and frayed conductors.

3 If corrosion (white, fluffy deposits) is evident, remove the cables from the battery terminals, clean them with a small wire brush, then refit them. Automotive stores sell a tool for cleaning the battery post . . .

4 . . . as well as the battery cable clamps.

Electrical systems

✔ Check all external lights and the horn. Refer to the appropriate Sections of Chapter 12 for details if any of the circuits are found to be inoperative.

✔ Visually check all accessible wiring connectors, harnesses and retaining clips for security, and for signs of chafing or damage.

If you need to check your brake lights and indicators unaided, back up to a wall or garage door and operate the lights. The reflected light should show if they are working properly.

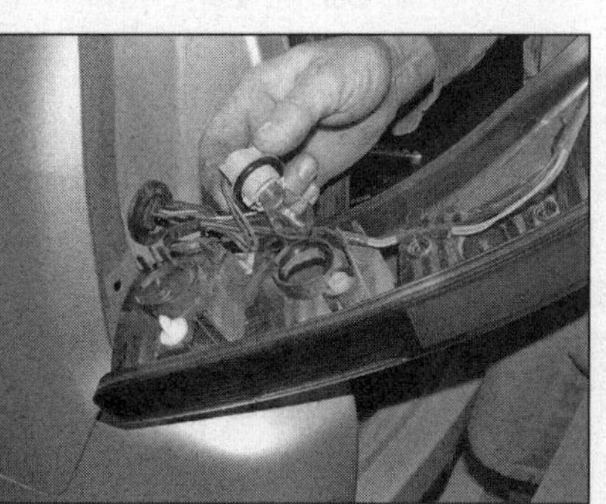

1 If a single indicator light, brake light or headlight has failed, it is likely that a bulb has blown and will need to be renewed. Refer to Chapter 12 for details. If both brake lights have failed, it is possible that the stop-light switch, operated by the brake pedal, is to blame. Refer to Chapter 9 for details.

2 If more than one indicator light or headlight has failed, it is likely that either a fuse has blown, or that there is a fault in the circuit (see Chapter 12). Half the fuses are mounted underneath the steering column – pull out the fuse panel's cover using the handle provided.

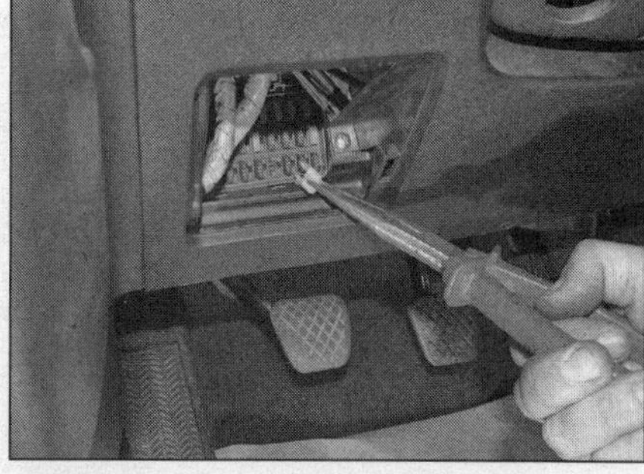

3 The fuse list is shown inside the lid. If the circuit isn't shown, the fuse will be in the engine compartment fuse/relay box. To renew a fuse, first ensure the ignition is switched off (take out the key). Remove the fuse using the plastic tool provided (if applicable). Fit a new fuse of the same rating. It is important that you find the reason that the fuse blew (see *Electrical fault finding* in Chapter 12).

Lubricants and fluids

Engine	
Petrol	Premium-grade detergent engine oil, viscosity SAE 0W-20, 0W-30, 0W-40, 5W-20, 5W-30, 5W-40, 10W-30, 10W-40 or 15W-40, to specification API SJ or SL or better
Diesel	Synthetic engine oil, viscosity 0W-30, to specification ACEA A5/B5 or better
Cooling system	Honda All Season Antifreeze/Coolant Type 2 (pre-mixed 50% antifreeze, 50% water)
Manual gearbox (including transfer case)	Honda Manual Transmission Fluid (MTF)
Automatic transmission (including transfer case)	Honda automatic transmission fluid ATF-Z1
Final drive*	Honda Dual Pump System Fluid (DPSF)
Brake and clutch systems	Honda Brake Fluid, or hydraulic fluid to specification DOT 3 or DOT 4
Power steering system	Honda Power Steering Fluid (type V, II or S)

* **Note:** *A moaning/groaning noise when manoeuvring on full lock can be due to premature degradation of the final drive fluid. This may be easily misdiagnosed as a steering rack problem, and may lead to unnecessary repairs. If this is suspected, the first course of action is to renew the final drive fluid as described in Chapter 1A or 1B.*

Tyre pressures (cold)

Note: *Pressures apply to original-equipment tyres only, and may vary if any other make or type of tyre is fitted; check with the tyre manufacturer or supplier for correct pressures if necessary. The pressures are given on the sticker attached to the driver's door pillar. Tyre pressures should be checked when the tyres are cold; do not forget to check the spare.*

2001 to 2004 models	**Front**	**Rear**
Typical normal use – two passengers plus luggage	26 psi (1.8 bar)	26 psi (1.8 bar)
Maximum load – five passengers plus luggage	26 psi (1.8 bar)	29 psi (2.0 bar)
Towing	26 psi (1.8 bar)	35 psi (2.4 bar)
2005-on models	**Front**	**Rear**
Typical normal use	30 psi (2.1 bar)	29 psi (2.0 bar)
Towing	30 psi (2.1 bar)	32 psi (2.2 bar)

The tyre pressures are given on a sticker on the driver's door pillar

Chapter 1 Part A: Routine maintenance and servicing – petrol models

Contents

Degrees of difficulty

Easy, suitable for novice with little experience

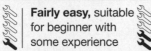

Fairly easy, suitable for beginner with some experience

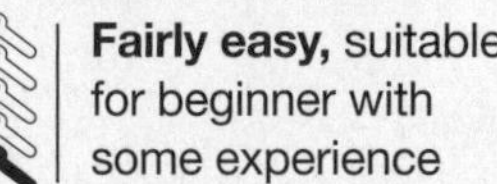

Fairly difficult, suitable for competent DIY mechanic

Difficult, suitable for experienced DIY mechanic

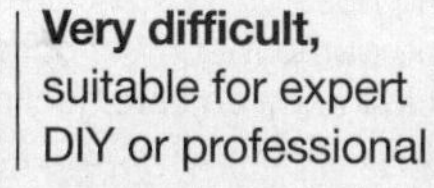

Very difficult, suitable for expert DIY or professional

Lubricants and fluids .... Refer to *Lubricants and fluids* on page 0•16

Capacities*

	Change	Total
Engine oil (including oil filter)	4.2 litres	5.3 litres
Cooling system:		
Manual gearbox	5.4 litres	7.1 litres
Automatic transmission	5.3 litres	7 litres
Manual gearbox (includes transfer case)	1.9 litres	2.3 litres
Automatic transmission (includes transfer case)	3.1 litres	7.2 litres
Final drive:		
2001 to 2004 models	1 litre	1.2 litres
2005-on models	1.2 litres	1.4 litres
Power steering fluid:		
Reservoir	0.26 litres	N/App.
System overhaul	N/App.	0.72 litres
Washer fluid reservoir	N/App.	4.5 litres
Fuel tank:		
Overall	N/App.	58 litres
Low fuel indicator lights at	10.4 litres	N/App.

* *All capacities are approximate.*

Engine

Valve clearances (engine cold):	
Intake	0.21 to 0.25 mm
Exhaust	0.28 to 0.32 mm
Idle speed (not adjustable):	
No load	650 ± 50 rpm
Full load – air conditioning fully on, rear window and headlamps on.	700 ± 50 rpm

Cooling system

Coolant type .... Refer to *Lubricants and fluids* on page 0•16

Auxiliary drivebelt

Automatic tensioner arrow and line align at .... 27 to 36 Nm (20 to 27 lbf ft)

Ignition system

Spark plugs type and electrode gap	NGK ZFR6K-11	1.0 to 1.1 mm
	Denso KJ20DR-M11	1.0 to 1.1 mm

Brakes

	2001 to 2004 models	2005-on models
Friction material minimum thickness:		
Front brake pads	1.6 mm	1.6 mm
Rear brake pads	1.0 mm	1.6 mm
Disc minimum thickness:		
Front disc	21.0 mm	23.0 mm
Rear disc	7.0 mm	8.0 mm
Handbrake adjustment	Locked @ 5 to 9 clicks	

Torque wrench settings

	Nm	lbf ft
Air cleaner cover retaining bolts	3	2
Automatic transmission fluid drain plug	49	36
Auxiliary drivebelt tensioner mounting bolts	22	16
Auxiliary drivebelt tensioner pulley bolt	55	41
Braking system bleed nipples	See Chapter 9	
Clutch slave cylinder bleed nipple	See Chapter 6	
Cylinder head cover nuts	12	9
Engine oil (sump) drain plug	45	33
Final drive fluid filler/level and drain plugs	47	35
Ignition coil cover nuts	9.8	7
Ignition coil retaining bolts	12	9
Intake manifold cover bolts	12	9
Manual gearbox fluid drain plug	39	29
Manual gearbox fluid filler/level plug	44	32
Roadwheel nuts	108	80
Spark plugs	18	13
Steering hose clamp-to-cylinder head cover bolt	12	9
Steering pump mounting bolts	22	16
Valve clearance adjuster locknuts:		
Intake	20	15
Exhaust	14	10

This servicing schedule is based on the one specified by the vehicle manufacturer, with additional recommendations based on practical experience, on the assumption that you, not the dealer, will be carrying out the work. The service intervals are applicable to vehicles used in normal conditions; vehicles used in adverse conditions (eg, driven in dusty areas or in extremes of climate, used full-time for towing, or driven frequently at slow speeds (idling in traffic) or on short journeys, or used for taxi work) may need servicing more frequently. These are the minimum maintenance intervals recommended by us for vehicles driven daily. If you wish to keep your vehicle in peak condition at all times, you may wish to perform some of these procedures more often. We encourage frequent maintenance, because it enhances the efficiency, performance and resale value of your vehicle.

When the vehicle is new, it should be serviced by a dealer service department (or other workshop recognised by the vehicle manufacturer as providing the same standard of service) in order to preserve the warranty. The vehicle manufacturer may reject warranty claims if you are unable to prove that servicing has been carried out as and when specified, using only original-equipment parts, or parts certified to be of equivalent quality.

Every 250 miles or weekly

☐ Refer to *Weekly checks*

Note: *If the air conditioning system is not regularly used, it should be operated at least once a week, all year round, for at least 10 minutes at a time to circulate the lubricating oil around its components.*

Monthly

☐ Check the automatic transmission fluid level (Section 3).

Every 6250 miles or 6 months, whichever comes first

☐ Rotate the tyres (Section 4).
☐ Change the engine oil and filter (Section 5).

Note: *Frequent oil and filter changes are good for the engine, so we recommend halving Honda's specified interval, which is 12 months or 12 500 miles.*

Every 12 500 miles or 12 months, whichever comes first

Carry out all checks listed under previous interval headings, then complete the following:

☐ Check the braking system (Section 6).
☐ Check the suspension and steering components for condition and security (Section 7).
☐ Check the condition of the driveshaft gaiters (Section 8).
☐ Check the condition of the hoses and lines (Section 9).
☐ Check the manual gearbox fluid level (Section 10).
☐ Check the final drive fluid level (Section 11).
☐ Check the condition of the exhaust system (Section 12).
☐ Carry out a road test (Section 13).
☐ Check the expiry date of the puncture repair bottle and renew if expired.

Every 25 000 miles or 2 years, whichever comes first

Carry out all checks listed under previous interval headings, then complete the following:

☐ Check the auxiliary drivebelt, and renew if necessary (Section 14).
☐ Renew the pollen filter elements (Section 15).

Note: *Renew the pollen filter elements annually if the vehicle is used primarily in urban or dusty areas.*

Every 25 000 miles

Carry out all checks listed under previous interval headings, then complete the following:

☐ Check, and if necessary adjust, the valve clearances (Section 16).
☐ Renew the air filter element (Section 17).
☐ Renew the spark plugs (Section 18).

Note: *This interval applies only if standard-type spark plugs are fitted.*

Every 3 years, regardless of mileage

☐ Change the brake fluid (Section 19).

Every 75 000 miles or 6 years, whichever comes first

Carry out all checks listed under previous interval headings, then complete the following:

☐ Renew the fuel filter (Section 20).
☐ Check the engine idle speed (Section 21).

Every 75 000 miles or 8 years, whichever comes first

Carry out all checks listed under previous interval headings, then complete the following:

☐ Change the manual gearbox fluid (Section 22).
☐ Change the automatic transmission fluid* (Section 23).
☐ Change the final drive fluid** (Section 24).

*** Note:** *This should be changed once only at this interval, at its* ***first*** *occurrence. Subsequently, Honda's renewal interval drops to every 50 000 miles or 4 years, whichever comes first.*

**** Note:** *This should be changed once only at this interval, at its* ***first*** *occurrence. Subsequently, Honda's renewal interval drops to every 37 500 miles or 4 years, whichever comes first.*

Every 75 000 miles

Carry out all checks listed under previous interval headings, then complete the following:

☐ Renew the spark plugs (Section 18).

Note: *This interval applies only if platinum or iridium spark plugs are fitted.*

Every 120 000 miles or 10 years, whichever comes first

Carry out all checks listed under previous interval headings, then complete the following:

☐ Change the coolant (Section 25).

Note: *This renewal interval should be observed once only, at its* ***first*** *occurrence. Subsequently, the recommended renewal interval drops to every 60 000 miles or 5 years, whichever comes first.*

Component location – petrol models

Underbonnet view (ignition coil and intake manifold covers removed)

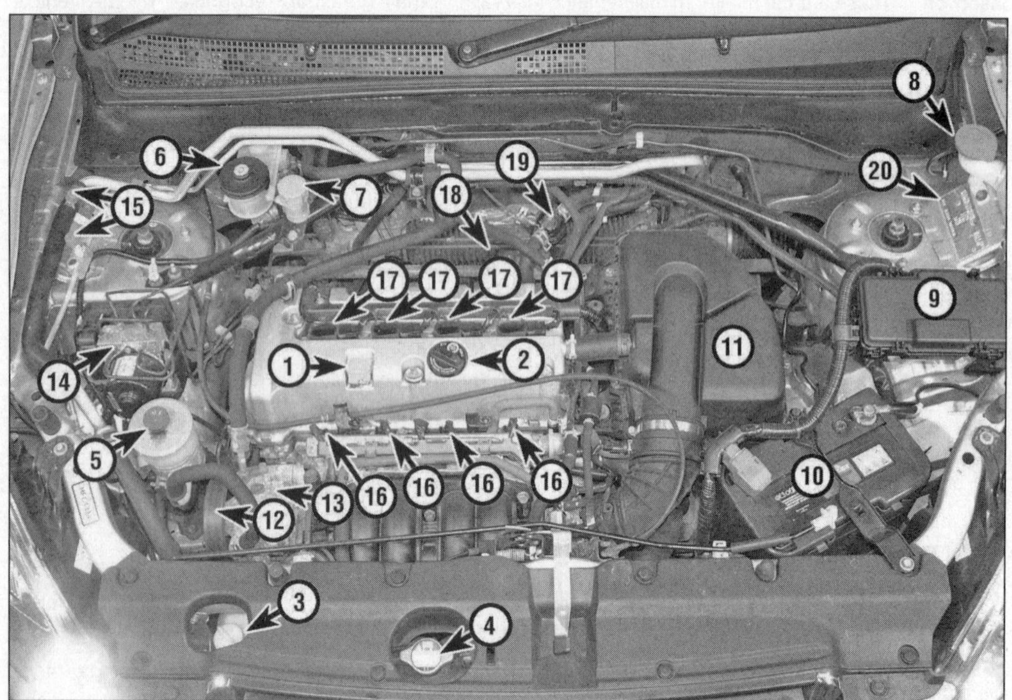

1 *Engine oil level dipstick*
2 *Engine oil filler cap*
3 *Expansion tank filler cap*
4 *Radiator cap*
5 *Power steering fluid reservoir*
6 *Brake fluid reservoir*
7 *Clutch fluid reservoir*
8 *Screen washer fluid reservoir filler*
9 *Engine compartment main fuse/relay box*
10 *Battery*
11 *Air cleaner*
12 *Auxiliary drivebelt*
13 *Power steering pump*
14 *ABS modulator-control unit*
15 *Air conditioning system sight glass and service valves*
16 *Fuel injectors*
17 *Ignition HT coils*
18 *Steering rack*
19 *Heater system valve*
20 *Vehicle identification plate*

Front underbody view

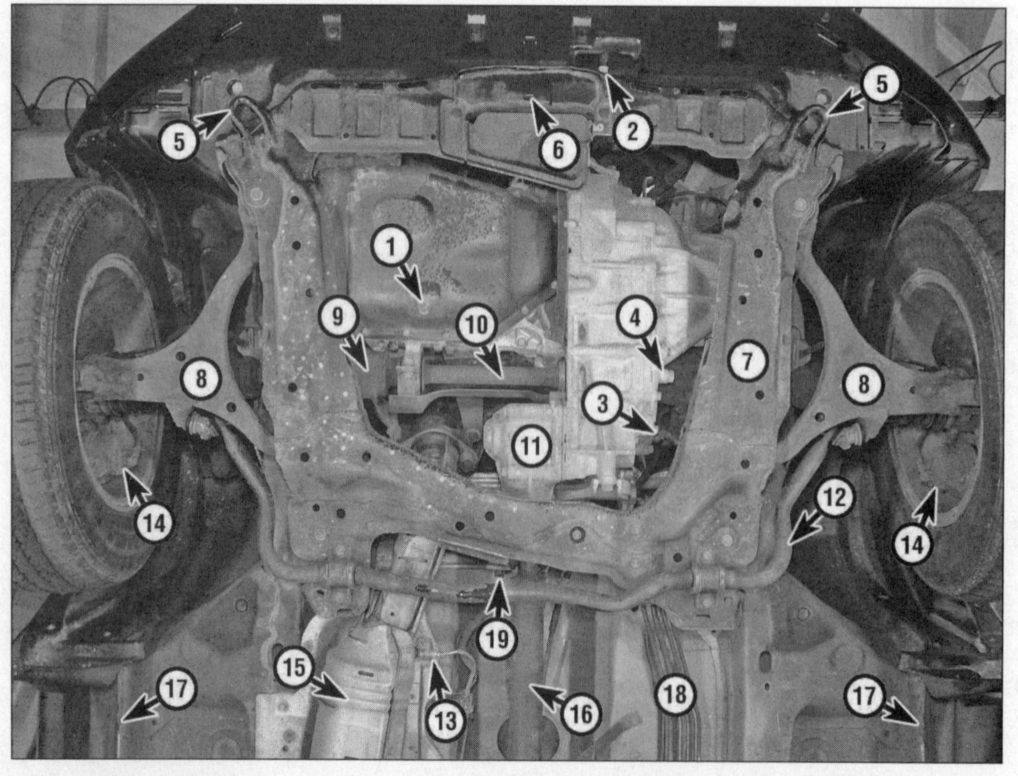

1 *Engine oil drain plug*
2 *Radiator drain tap*
3 *Gearbox fluid filler/level plug*
4 *Gearbox fluid drain plug*
5 *Transporter tie-down points (NOT for towing)*
6 *Front jacking point*
7 *Front suspension subframe*
8 *Front suspension lower arms*
9 *Right-hand driveshaft inboard joint*
10 *Right-hand driveshaft inboard (intermediate) shaft*
11 *Transfer case*
12 *Anti-roll bar*
13 *Oxygen sensor*
14 *Front brake calipers*
15 *Catalytic converter*
16 *Propeller shaft*
17 *Front door sill jacking/ support points*
18 *Braking system pipes*
19 *Air conditioning system evaporator drain tube*

Rear underbody view

1 *Final drive fluid drain plug (filler/level plug above)*
2 *Final drive (Dual Pump section)*
3 *Final drive (rear differential section)*
4 *Driveshaft inboard joints*
5 *Driveshaft CV joint gaiters*
6 *Rear hub carriers*
7 *Rear wheel toe-adjusting bolts*
8 *Anti-roll bar*
9 *Rear jacking point*
10 *Rear suspension subframe*
11 *Rear suspension trailing arms*
12 *Rear suspension struts*
13 *Exhaust rear silencer*
14 *Charcoal canister assembly*
15 *Fuel tank*
16 *Trailing arm front mountings*
17 *Final drive front mounting*
18 *Propeller shaft*
19 *Exhaust pipe*
20 *Rear door sill jacking/support points*
21 *Handbrake cable*

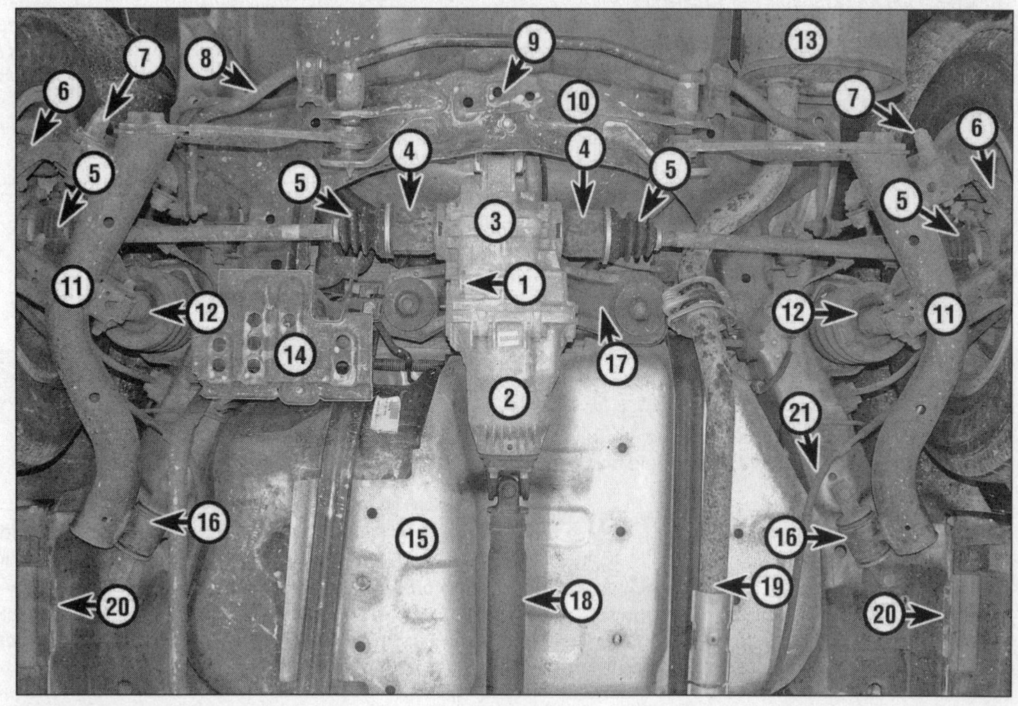

Maintenance procedures

1 General information

1 This Chapter is designed to help the home mechanic maintain his/her vehicle for safety, economy, long life and peak performance.

2 The Chapter contains a master maintenance schedule, followed by Sections dealing specifically with each task in the schedule. Visual checks, adjustments, component renewal and other helpful items are included. Refer to the accompanying illustrations of the engine compartment and the underside of the vehicle for the locations of the various components.

3 Servicing your vehicle in accordance with the mileage/time maintenance schedule and the following Sections will provide a planned maintenance programme, which should result in a long and reliable service life. This is a comprehensive plan, so maintaining some items but not others at the specified service intervals, will not produce the same results.

4 As you service your vehicle, you will discover that many of the procedures can be grouped together, because of the particular procedure being performed, or because of the proximity of two otherwise-unrelated components to one another. For example, if the vehicle is raised for any reason, the exhaust can be inspected at the same time as the suspension and steering components.

5 The first step in this maintenance programme is to prepare yourself before the actual work begins. Read through all the Sections relevant to the work to be carried out, then make a list and gather all the parts and tools required. If a problem is encountered, seek advice from a parts specialist, or a dealer service department.

2 Regular maintenance

1 If, from the time the vehicle is new, the routine maintenance schedule is followed closely, and frequent checks are made of fluid levels and high-wear items, as suggested throughout this manual, the engine will be kept in relatively good running condition, and the need for additional work will be minimised.

2 It is possible that there will be times when the engine is running poorly due to the lack of regular maintenance. This is even more likely if a used vehicle, which has not received regular and frequent maintenance checks, is purchased. In such cases, additional work may need to be carried out, outside of the regular maintenance intervals.

3 If engine wear is suspected, a compression test (refer to Chapter 2A) will provide valuable information regarding the overall performance of the main internal components. Such a test can be used as a basis to decide on the extent of the work to be carried out. If, for example, a compression test indicates serious internal engine wear, conventional maintenance as described in this Chapter will not greatly improve the performance of the engine, and may prove a waste of time and money, unless extensive overhaul work is carried out first.

4 The following series of operations are those most often required to improve the performance of a generally poor-running engine:

Primary operations

a) Clean, inspect and test the battery (refer to Weekly checks).
b) Check all the engine-related fluids (refer to Weekly checks).
c) Check the condition and tension of the auxiliary drivebelt (Section 14).
d) Renew the spark plugs (Section 18).
e) Check the condition of the air filter, and renew if necessary (Section 17).
f) Check the condition of all hoses, and check for fluid leaks (Section 9).
g) Check the valve clearances (Section 16).
h) Renew the fuel filter (Section 20).

5 If the above operations do not prove fully effective, carry out the following secondary operations:

Secondary operations

All items listed under *Primary operations*, plus the following:

a) Check the charging system (refer to Chapter 5A).

b) Check the ignition system (refer to Chapter 5B).

c) Check the fuel system (refer to Chapter 4A).

Maintenance Required indicator

6 Some models are fitted with a 'Maintenance required' indicator in the tachometer which reminds the driver of when scheduled maintenance is required for the vehicle.

7 Whenever scheduled maintenance is complete by a dealer, the indicator will be reset. The indicator can be reset as follows:

a) Switch off the ignition.

b) Press and hold the 'Select/Reset' button in the lower right corner of the instrument panel.

c) Switch on the ignition and hold the 'Select/Reset' button until the indicator resets (which will take approximately ten seconds).

Every month

3 Automatic transmission fluid level check

Note: *The transfer case shares the same lubricant as the transmission.*

1 The level of the automatic transmission fluid should be carefully maintained. Low fluid level can lead to slipping or loss of drive, while overfilling can cause foaming, loss of fluid and transmission damage.

2 The transmission fluid level should only be checked with the vehicle parked on level ground.

3 Start the engine, warm it up to operating temperature (wait until the radiator cooling fan comes on, and cuts out), then switch it off.

4 Remove the dipstick – it is found beside the battery, and can be identified by the yellow loop on top **(see illustration)**. Note that this yellow loop must point in the direction of the transmission breather tube on the top of the transmission casing.

5 Wipe the fluid from the dipstick with a clean rag, and re-insert it until the cap seats on the transmission casing. Ensure that the dipstick sealing plug is pressed all the way into the transmission casing and that the handle loop points towards the breather tube.

3.4 Automatic transmission fluid level dipstick has a yellow top

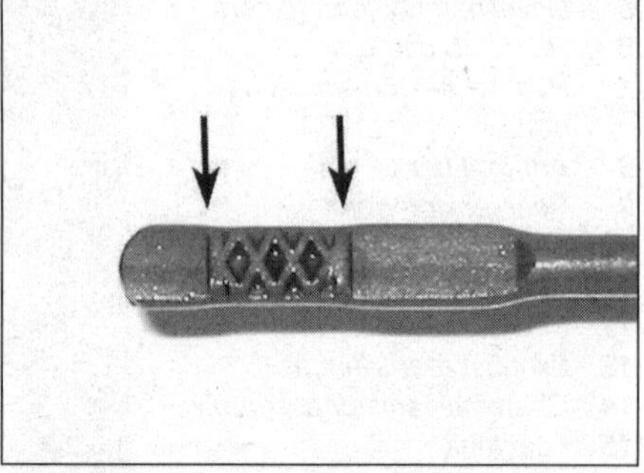

3.6 Fluid level should be between upper and lower marks on dipstick

6 Pull the dipstick out again and note the fluid level, which should be between the upper and lower marks on the dipstick **(see illustration)**. If the level is low, add the specified automatic transmission fluid through the dipstick opening, using a funnel, to fill the transmission to the proper level.

7 Add the specified fluid a little at a time and keep checking the level until it is correct.

8 The condition of the fluid should be checked as well as its level. If the fluid at the end of the dipstick is black or a dark reddish brown colour, or if it emits a burned smell, the fluid should be changed (see Section 23). If you are in doubt about the condition of the fluid, purchase some new fluid and compare the two for colour and smell.

Every 6250 miles or 6 months

4 Tyre rotation

1 The tyres should be rotated at the specified intervals and whenever uneven wear is noticed. Since the vehicle will be raised and the tyres removed anyway, check the brakes (see Section 6) at this time.

2 Radial tyres must be rotated in a specific pattern **(see illustrations)**. Most models are equipped with non-directional tyres, but some models may have directional tyres, which have a different rotation pattern. When rotating tyres, examine the sidewalls. Directional tyres have arrows on the sidewall that indicate the direction they must turn. The left and right side tyres must not be rotated to the other side.

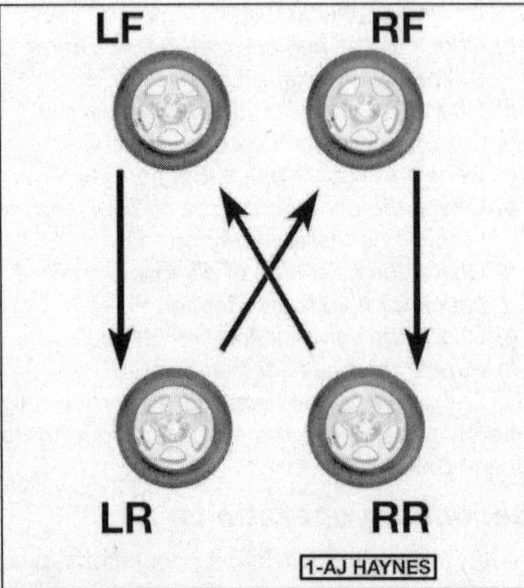

4.2a Wheel/tyre rotation pattern (not including spare) – non-directional radial tyres

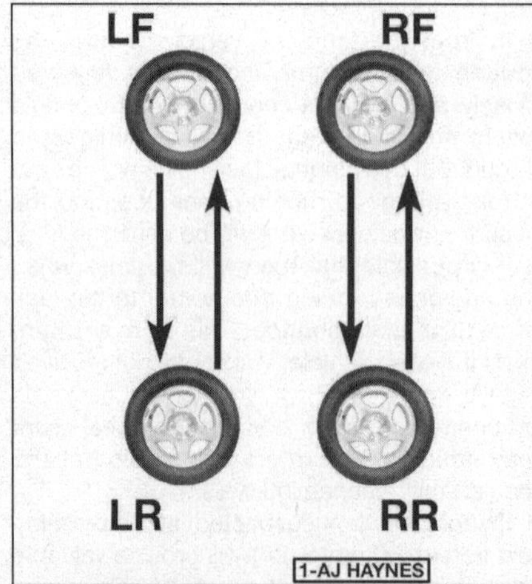

4.2b Wheel/tyre rotation pattern (not including spare) – directional radial tyres

3 Refer to the information in *Jacking and vehicle support* at the back of this manual for the proper procedures to follow when raising the vehicle and changing a tyre. If the brakes are to be checked, do not apply the handbrake as stated. Make sure the wheels are chocked to prevent the vehicle from moving.

4 Preferably, the entire vehicle should be raised at the same time. This can be done on a hoist or by jacking up each corner and then lowering the vehicle onto axle stands placed under the jacking/support points. Always use four axle stands and make sure the vehicle is firmly supported.

5 After rotation, check and adjust the tyre pressures as necessary and be sure to check the wheel nut tightness. Ideally, wheel nuts should be tightened to the torque listed in this Chapter's Specifications, and rechecked after 25 miles of driving.

Caution: The ABS and VSA systems base their operation on precise comparison of wheel speeds. Tyres of different size and

construction to those fitted as original equipment may affect wheel speeds, causing these systems to function erratically. Always fit tyres of the recommended size and type (see Chapter 10, and the tyre information label on the driver's door pillar). If possible, it is best to renew all four tyres at the same time; if this is not possible or necessary, renew just the two fronts or the two rears as a matched pair. Renewing just one tyre with one of a significantly different size, due to wear, will affect the operation of these systems, not to mention the negative consequences for the vehicle's handling and roadholding.

5 Engine oil and filter renewal

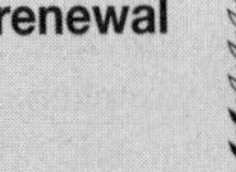

Note: *In addition to the oil and filter, a new drain plug sealing washer will be required.*

1 Frequent oil and filter changes are the most important preventative maintenance procedures which can be undertaken by the DIY owner. As engine oil ages, it becomes diluted and contaminated, which leads to premature engine wear.

2 Before starting this procedure, gather together all the necessary tools and materials. Also make sure that you have plenty of clean rags and newspapers handy, to mop-up any spills. Ideally, the engine oil should be warm, as it will drain more easily, and more built-up sludge will be removed with it. Take care not to touch the exhaust or any other hot parts of the engine when working under the vehicle. To avoid any possibility of scalding, and to protect yourself from possible skin irritants and other harmful contaminants in used engine oils, it is advisable to wear gloves when carrying out this work.

3 Firmly apply the handbrake, then jack up the front of the vehicle and support it securely on axle stands (see *Jacking and vehicle support*).

4 Remove the oil filler cap.

5 Using a spanner, or preferably a suitable socket and bar, slacken the drain plug (at the rear of the sump) about half a turn **(see illustration)** Position the draining container under the drain plug, then remove the plug completely and discard the sealing washer – this must be renewed as a matter of course whenever it is disturbed.

5.5 Unscrewing engine oil (sump) drain plug

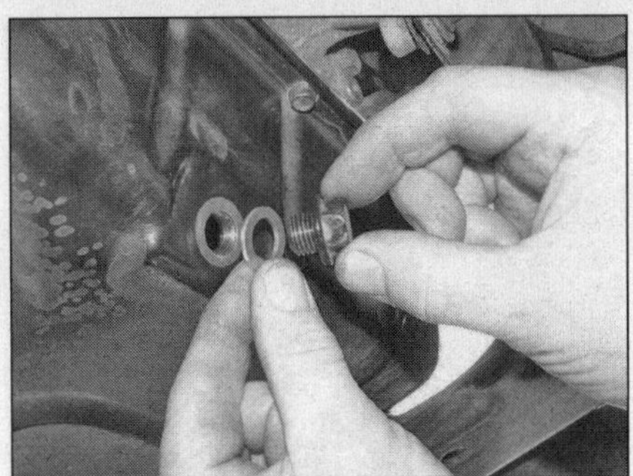

5.7a Fit new sealing washer . . .

5.7b . . . and tighten drain plug to specified torque wrench setting

5.9 Using a filter removal tool to unscrew oil filter

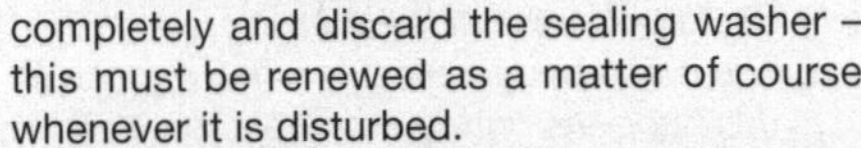

6 Allow some time for the oil to drain, noting that it may be necessary to reposition the container as the oil flow slows to a trickle.

7 After all the oil has drained, wipe the drain plug with a clean rag and fit the new sealing washer. Clean the area around the drain plug opening, and refit the plug complete with washer and tighten it to the specified torque **(see illustrations)**.

8 Move the container into position under the oil filter, which is on the back of the engine, at the timing chain end.

Warning: The oil filter is located very close to the exhaust and care must be taken to prevent burns when removing it. If necessary, leave the vehicle to cool completely before touching the oil filter.

9 Use an oil filter removal tool to slacken the filter initially, then unscrew it by hand the rest of the way **(see illustration)**. Empty the oil from the old filter into the oil drain container; puncture the filter dome in two places and allow any remaining oil to drain through the punctures. Check the filter to make sure the filter sealing ring has come off with it – if not, it may still be stuck to the engine, and should be removed.

10 Use a clean rag to remove all oil, dirt and sludge from the filter sealing area on the engine. Wipe up any oil spilt on the back of the engine and on the subframe.

11 Apply a light coating of clean engine oil to the sealing ring on the new filter, then screw the filter into position on the engine. Tighten the filter firmly by hand only – **do not** use any tools – following the instructions on the filter or its packaging; typically it must be tightened by hand until the filter sealing ring

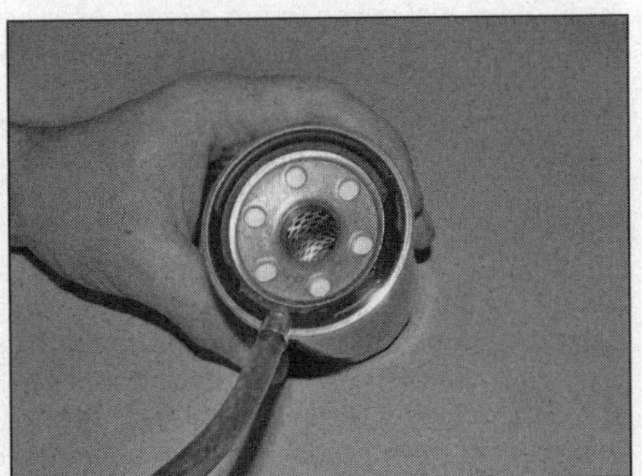

5.11a Lubricate filter sealing ring with clean engine oil . . .

5.11b . . . and fit to engine

5.11c Numbers marked on genuine filter base . . .

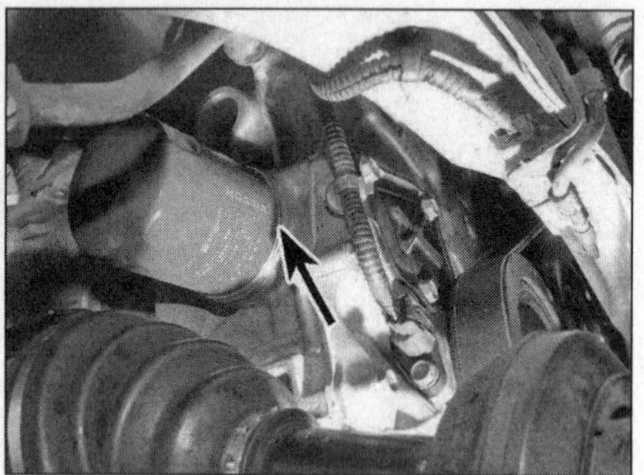

5.11d . . . to assist in accurate tightening of filter onto engine

contacts the sealing area on the engine, then tightened by a further three-quarters of a turn **(see illustrations)**. If a genuine Honda filter is used, numbered marks are made around the outside of the filter base which can be used as a guide to accurate tightening as follows:

a) *If numbers 1 to 4 (or one to four arrows) are found, tighten the filter by hand until the filter sealing ring contacts the sealing area on the engine, then note which number is at the bottom (or next to any convenient fixed point of reference) and tighten the filter by turning it clockwise three numbers or marks (three-quarters of a turn) from the one noted. For example, if the number 2 was at the bottom, tighten the filter until the number 1 is at the bottom – if number 4, tighten the filter until number 3 aligns.*

b) *If numbers 1 to 8 are found, tighten the filter by hand until the filter sealing ring contacts the sealing area on the engine, then note which number is at the bottom (or next to any convenient fixed point of reference) and tighten the filter by turning it clockwise seven numbers or marks (seven-eighths of a turn) from the one noted. For example, if the number 2 was at the bottom, tighten the filter until the number 1 is at the bottom – if number 4, tighten the filter until number 3 aligns.*

12 Remove the old oil and all tools from under the vehicle, then lower the vehicle to the ground.

13 Fill the engine through the oil filler hole, using the correct grade and type of oil (refer to *Weekly checks* for details of topping-up). Pour in half the specified quantity of oil first, then wait a few minutes for the oil to drain into the sump. Continue to add oil, a small quantity at a time, until the level is up to the lower mark on the dipstick.

14 Start the engine and run it for a few minutes, while checking for leaks around the oil filter seal and the sump drain plug. Note that there may be a delay of a few seconds before the low oil pressure warning light goes out when the engine is first started, as the oil circulates through the new oil filter and the engine oil galleries before the pressure builds-up.

15 Stop the engine, and wait a few minutes for the oil to settle in the sump once more. With the new oil circulated and the filter now completely full, recheck the level on the dipstick, and add more oil as necessary.

16 Dispose of the used engine oil safely with reference to *General repair procedures*. It should be noted that used oil filters should not be included with domestic waste. Most used oil 'banks' also have filter disposal points alongside.

Every 12 500 miles or 12 months

6 Braking system check

Warning: The dust created by the brake system may be harmful to your health. Never blow it out with compressed air and don't inhale any of it. An approved filtering mask should be worn when working on the brakes. Do not, under any circumstances, use petroleum-based solvents to clean brake parts. Use brake system cleaner only.

1 In addition to the specified intervals, the brakes should be inspected every time the roadwheels are removed or whenever a defect is suspected.

2 Any of the following symptoms could indicate a potential brake system defect:

a) *The vehicle pulls to one side when the brake pedal is depressed.*

b) *The brakes make squealing or dragging noises when applied (this might also be the pad wear indicators – see below).*

c) *Brake pedal travel is excessive.*

d) *The brake pedal pulsates when applied (if this happens during emergency braking only and can be felt through the pedal, this is most likely to be due to ABS operation and is not a cause for concern if that is the case).*

e) *Brake fluid leaks, usually onto the inside of the tyre or roadwheel.*

3 Slacken the roadwheel nuts.

4 Raise the vehicle and support it securely on axle stands (see *Jacking and vehicle support*).

5 Remove the roadwheels.

Brake pads, discs and hoses

6 There are two pads (outboard and inboard) in each caliper. On the front calipers, the inboard pads are visible through an inspection hole in the caliper body, while the outboard pad is best checked looking at the caliper from the outside **(see illustrations)**. On the rear calipers, both pads are visible through an inspection hole in the caliper body. The inboard pad in each caliper has a wear indicator tab attached to it; when the friction material is worn down to the point at which pad renewal is required, the tab rubs against the brake disc when the brakes are applied and produces a distinctive metallic 'screeching' sound. If the pads are not renewed, the wear indicators will finally screech all the time. This 'screeching' is meant to be clearly audible and different from the squeals or squeaks that sometimes occur in normal brake operation. If in any doubt about the cause of such noises, remove all four roadwheels in turn, swing up or remove the caliper body and withdraw the pads for cleaning and inspection, as described in Chapter 9.

7 If the thickness of remaining friction material is less at any point than the minimum listed in this Chapter's Specifications, renew the pads – all four together, irrespective of the condition of the others. **Note:** *Keep in mind that the friction material is bonded to a metal backing plate – this metal plate is not included in the measurement.*

6.6a Friction material on front brake inboard pads (and both rear pads) can be checked though inspection hole

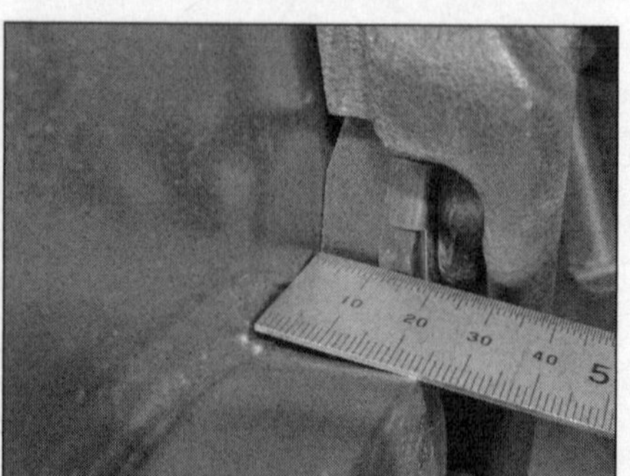

6.6b Measuring friction material remaining on front brake outboard pads

HAYNES HiNT ***Always renew brake components in axle sets, where applicable – this means renewing brake pads, shoes, etc, on BOTH sides, even if only one set of pads is worn. In the instance of uneven brake wear, the cause should be investigated and fixed (the most likely causes being caliper bodies sticking on their guide pins or sticking caliper pistons).***

6.10a Measuring front brake disc thickness with a micrometer

8 If it is difficult to determine the exact thickness of the remaining pad material by the above method, or if you are at all concerned about the condition of the pads, remove all four roadwheels in turn, swing up or remove the caliper body and withdraw the pads for further inspection (refer to Chapter 9).

9 Once the pads are removed from the calipers, clean them with brake cleaner and measure them with a ruler or a vernier caliper. Ensure they are greased, and that the caliper body slides smoothly and easily on its guide pins before reassembling.

10 Measure the disc thickness with a micrometer to make sure that it still has service life remaining **(see illustrations)**. If any disc is thinner than the specified minimum thickness, renew it (refer to Chapter 9). Even if the disc has service life remaining, check its condition. Look for scoring, gouging and burned spots. If these conditions exist, remove the disc and have it resurfaced (see Chapter 9).

11 Before installing the roadwheels, check all brake pipes and hoses for damage, wear, deformation, cracks, corrosion, leakage, bends and twists, particularly in the vicinity of the rubber hoses at the calipers **(see illustration)**.

12 Make sure that all hoses and pipes are clear of sharp edges, moving parts and the exhaust system. If any of the above conditions are noted, repair, reroute or renew the pipes and/or fittings as necessary (see Chapter 9).

Brake servo check

13 Sit in the driver's seat and perform the following sequence of tests.

14 With the brake fully depressed, start the engine – the pedal should move down a little when the engine starts.

15 With the engine running, depress the brake pedal several times – the travel distance should not change.

16 Depress the brake, stop the engine and hold the pedal in for about 30 seconds – the pedal should neither sink nor rise.

17 Restart the engine, run it for about a minute and turn it off. Then firmly depress the brake several times – the pedal travel should decrease with each application.

18 If the brakes do not operate as described, the brake servo or its vacuum hose may have failed. Refer to Chapter 9.

6.10b Brake disc minimum thickness is marked on disc

Handbrake

19 Slowly pull on the handbrake and count the number of clicks you hear until the handle is at the end of its travel. The adjustment is correct if you hear between 5 and 9 clicks. If you hear more clicks, the handbrake needs adjusting (see Chapter 9); fewer clicks, and the cables may have seized, or the brakes are dragging (not releasing).

7 Suspension and steering check

Roadwheel nut tightness check

1 Work around each roadwheel in turn, and check the tightness of the roadwheel nuts using a torque wrench.

2 If you suspect that the nuts have been overtightened, slacken and then tighten each nut (one at a time) to the specified torque.

Front suspension and steering

3 Raise the front of the vehicle, and securely support it on axle stands (see *Jacking and vehicle support*).

4 Visually inspect the balljoint dust covers and the steering rack-and-pinion gaiters for splits, chafing or deterioration **(see illustration)**. Any wear of these components will cause loss of lubricant, together with dirt and water entry, resulting in rapid deterioration of the balljoints or steering gear.

5 Check the suspension strut for signs of fluid leakage from the damper – if evident, this indicates that the damper has failed (the vehicle would fail an MoT in this condition). **Note:** *Suspension units should always be renewed in pairs on the same axle.*

7.4 Check balljoint dust covers for splits, chafing or deterioration

6.11 Bend flexible hoses close to unions to check for signs of cracking or splitting

6 Grasp the roadwheel at the 12 o'clock and 6 o'clock positions, and try to rock it **(see illustration)**. Very slight free play may be felt, but if the movement is appreciable, further investigation is necessary to determine the source. Continue rocking the wheel while an assistant depresses the footbrake. If the movement is now eliminated or significantly reduced, it is likely that the hub bearings are at fault. If the free play is still evident with the footbrake depressed, then there is wear in the suspension joints or mountings.

7 Now grasp the roadwheel at the 9 o'clock and 3 o'clock positions, and try to rock it as before. Any movement felt now may again be caused by wear in the hub bearings or the track rod balljoints. If the outer balljoint is worn, the visual movement will be obvious. If the inner joint is suspect, it can be felt by placing a hand over the rack-and-pinion rubber gaiter and gripping the track rod. If the wheel is now rocked, movement will be felt at the inner joint if wear has taken place.

8 Using a large screwdriver or flat bar, check for wear in the suspension mounting bushes by levering between the relevant suspension component and its attachment point. Some movement is to be expected, as the mountings are made of rubber, but excessive wear should be obvious. Also check the condition of any visible rubber bushes, looking for splits, cracks or contamination of the rubber.

9 With the vehicle standing on its wheels,

7.6 Grasp roadwheel at 12 o'clock and 6 o'clock positions and try to rock it, to check for wheel bearing wear

8.1 Check driveshaft CV joint gaiters for signs of cracking, splits or deterioration

have an assistant turn the steering wheel back-and-forth, about an eighth of a turn each way. There should be very little, if any, lost movement between the steering wheel and roadwheels. If this is not the case, closely observe the joints and mountings previously

Check for a chafed area that could fail prematurely.

Check for a soft area indicating the hose has deteriorated inside.

Overtightening the clamp on a hardened hose will damage the hose and cause a leak.

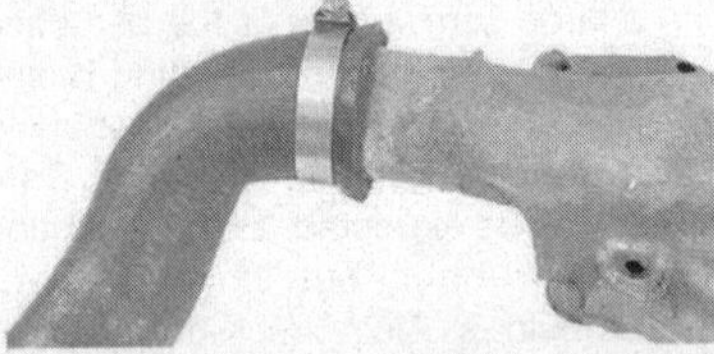

Check each hose for swelling and oil-soaked ends. Cracks and breaks can be located by squeezing the hose.

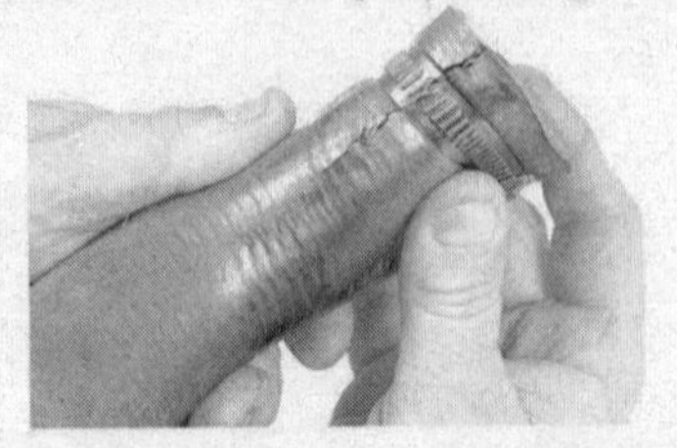

9.3 Hoses, like drivebelts, have a habit of failing at the worst possible moment – to avoid the inconvenience of a cooling system failure at the roadside, inspect hoses carefully as shown here

8.4 Don't forget to check inboard joints also

described. In addition, check the steering column universal joints for wear, and also check the rack-and-pinion steering gear itself.

10 Check the power steering fluid hoses for chafing or deterioration, and the pipe and hose unions for fluid leaks. Also check for signs of fluid leakage under pressure from the steering gear rubber gaiters, which would indicate failed fluid seals within the steering gear.

11 The efficiency of the dampers may be checked by bouncing the vehicle at each corner. Generally speaking, the body will return to its normal position and stop after being depressed. If it rises and returns on a rebound, the strut is probably suspect.

Rear suspension

12 Chock the front roadwheels, then jack up the rear of the vehicle and support securely on axle stands (see *Jacking and vehicle support*).

13 Working as described previously for the front suspension, check the rear hub bearings, the suspension bushes and the struts/dampers for wear.

8 Driveshaft CV joint gaiter check

1 With the front of the vehicle raised and securely supported on stands, turn the steering onto full lock, then slowly rotate the roadwheel. Inspect the condition of the outboard constant velocity (CV) joint rubber gaiters while squeezing the gaiters to open out the folds **(see illustration)**.

2 Check for signs of cracking, splits or deterioration of the rubber, which may allow the grease to escape and water and grit to get into the joint.

3 Check the security and condition of the retaining clips.

4 Repeat these checks on the inboard CV joints **(see illustration)**.

5 Lower the front of the vehicle to the ground, and chock the front roadwheels. Jack up the rear of the vehicle, and securely support it on axle stands (see *Jacking and vehicle support*).

6 With the transmission in neutral (or N), slowly turn each rear roadwheel, and check the condition of the rear driveshaft gaiters (inboard and outboard).

7 As with the front gaiters, check for perished rubber or loose/missing retaining clips.

8 In either case, if any damage or deterioration is found, the gaiters should be renewed as described in Chapter 8.

9 Hose and fluid leak check

1 Visually inspect the engine joint faces, gaskets and seals for any signs of water or oil leaks. Pay particular attention to the areas around the cylinder head cover, cylinder head, oil filter and sump joint faces. Bear in mind that, over a period of time, some very slight seepage from these areas is to be expected – what you are really looking for is any indication of a serious leak. Should a leak be found, renew the offending gasket or oil seal by referring to the appropriate Chapters in this manual.

2 Also check the security and condition of all the engine-related pipes and hoses, all braking system pipes and hoses, and the fuel lines. Ensure that all cable-ties or securing clips are in place, and in good condition. Clips which are broken or missing can lead to chafing of the hoses, pipes or wiring, which could cause more serious problems in the future.

3 Carefully check the radiator hoses and heater hoses along their entire length **(see illustration)**. Renew any hose which is cracked, swollen or deteriorated. Cracks will show up better if the hose is squeezed. Pay close attention to the hose clips that secure the hoses to the cooling system components. Hose clips can pinch and puncture hoses, resulting in cooling system leaks. If spring-type hose clips are used, it may be a good idea to substitute Jubilee clips.

4 Inspect all the cooling system components (hoses, joint faces, etc) for leaks.

5 Where any problems are found on cooling system components, renew the component or gasket with reference to Chapter 3.

6 With the vehicle raised, inspect the fuel tank and filler neck for punctures, cracks and other damage. The connection between the filler neck and tank is especially critical **(see illustration)**. Sometimes a rubber filler neck or connecting hose will leak due to loose retaining clamps or deteriorated rubber.

9.6 Check fuel tank filler hose at both ends

10.2 Manual gearbox fluid filler/level plug

10.3 Using an Allen key as a dipstick to check level in relation to edge of hole

10.4 Topping-up manual gearbox fluid

7 Carefully check all rubber hoses and metal fuel lines leading away from the fuel tank. Check for loose connections, deteriorated hoses, crimped lines, and other damage. Pay particular attention to the vent pipes and hoses, which often loop up around the filler neck and can become blocked or crimped. Follow the lines to the front of the vehicle, carefully inspecting them all the way. Renew damaged sections as necessary. Similarly, whilst the vehicle is raised, take the opportunity to inspect all underbody brake fluid pipes and hoses (see Section 6).

8 From within the engine compartment, check the security of all fuel, vacuum and brake hose attachments and pipe unions, and inspect all hoses for kinks, chafing and deterioration.

9 Where applicable, check the condition of the automatic transmission fluid pipes and hoses.

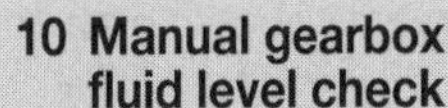

10 Manual gearbox fluid level check

Note: *The transfer case shares the same lubricant as the gearbox. In addition to the fluid that may be needed, a new filler/level plug sealing washer will be required.*

1 To check the fluid level, the gearbox should ideally be at normal operating temperature (after a run of 5 miles or more). The vehicle should be parked so that it is absolutely level from front-to-rear and from side-to-side; switch off the ignition and apply the handbrake firmly. Direct access is from the side, behind the left-hand roadwheel – but if the vehicle has to be jacked up for access (see *Jacking and vehicle support*), be careful to keep it level.

2 The fluid level is checked by removing the filler/level plug, which is located in the left-hand side of the gearbox, behind the left-hand driveshaft inboard joint – turning the steering fully to the left or right may improve access **(see illustration)**.

3 Remove all traces of dirt from around the filler/level plug, unscrew the plug, and recover the sealing washer; discard the original washer, which should be renewed whenever it is disturbed. Be prepared for a small amount of fluid to leak out when the plug is removed; if fluid pours out, refit the filler/level plug and check very carefully that the vehicle is level from front-to-rear as well as from side-to-side. Remove the plug again and allow any surplus to drain off. If the fluid level is correct, it should be up to the lower edge of the hole; it may be easier to use an Allen key as a dipstick to see where the level is in relation to the edge of the hole **(see illustration)**.

4 If the fluid level is too low, add more through the filler/level hole. There being insufficient access to use a funnel, the fluid can be added only by inserting the flexible tube equipping most transmission fluid bottles – the bottle can then be squeezed from almost any angle. Stop filling when fresh fluid begins to run out of the hole and allow any surplus to drain off **(see illustration)**.

In practice, access is very restricted and it is not always easy to check the level accurately. For most, the simplest solution will usually be to remove the filler/level plug and, assuming that the level is not found to be too high, to squeeze in a little fresh fluid at a time until it starts to run out of the filler/level hole. If a lot of fluid has had to be added, refit the filler/level plug and take the vehicle for a short drive to distribute the new fluid around the gearbox components, then on your return, allow time for the fluid level to settle before removing the filler/level plug and allowing the surplus to drain off.

5 Refit the plug with a new sealing washer and tighten it securely to the specified torque wrench setting. Drive the vehicle a short distance, then check for leaks.

11 Final drive fluid level check

Note: *In addition to the fluid that may be needed, a new filler/level plug sealing washer will be required.*

1 The final drive does not have a dipstick. To check its fluid level, the final drive should ideally be at operating temperature (after a run of 5 miles or more). The vehicle should be parked on level ground – if it has to be jacked up for access (see *Jacking and vehicle support*), try to keep the vehicle as level as possible.

2 The filler/level plug is directly in front of the left-hand rear driveshaft, and a square key will be needed – we found that the 3/8-inch square fitting on a socket handle or extension bar will fit **(see illustration)**.

3 Unscrew the plug, recover the washer and discard it – it should be renewed whenever it is disturbed. If the lubricant level is correct, it should be up to the lower edge of the hole; it may be easier to use an Allen key as a dipstick to see where the level is in relation to the edge of the hole **(see illustrations)**. Be prepared for a small amount of lubricant to leak out when the plug is removed; if lubricant pours out, refit the filler/level plug and check very carefully that the vehicle is level from front-to-rear as well as from side-to-side. Remove the plug again and allow any surplus to drain off.

11.2 Final drive fluid filler/level plug needs a square key

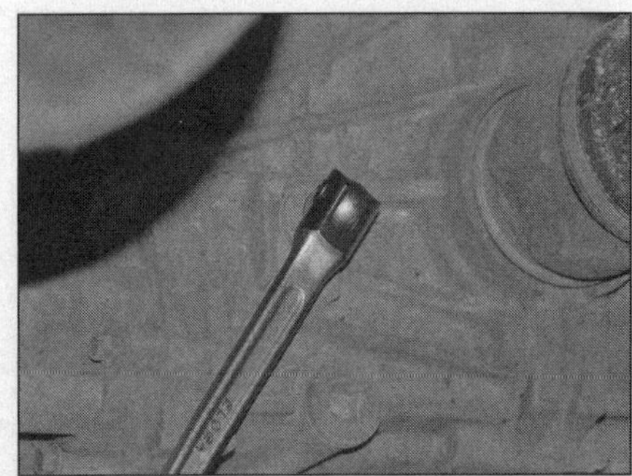

11.3a Unscrew filler/level plug . . .

11.3b . . . recover sealing washer and discard it – fit a new washer

11.3c Using an Allen key as a dipstick to check level in relation to edge of hole

4 If the lubricant level is too low, add more through the filler/level hole. If there is sufficient access, a funnel can be used, but most transmission fluid bottles have a flexible tube attached – by squeezing the bottle, fluid can be added from almost any angle. Stop filling when fresh lubricant begins to run out of the hole. Note that the final drive uses a specific lubricant, different to that in the other transmission components (refer to *Lubricants and fluids*, at the end of *Weekly checks*), and that Honda specifically state that automatic transmission fluid (ATF) must NOT be used in the final drive.

5 Refit the plug and tighten it to the specified torque wrench setting. Drive the vehicle a short distance, then check for leaks.

12 Exhaust system inspection

1 With the engine cold (at least three hours after the vehicle has been driven), check the complete exhaust system from the engine to the end of the tailpipe. Ideally, the inspection should be done with the vehicle on a hoist to permit unrestricted access. If a hoist isn't available, raise the vehicle and support it securely on axle stands (see *Jacking and vehicle support*).

2 Check the exhaust pipes and connections for evidence of leaks, severe corrosion and damage. Make sure that all brackets and hangers are in good condition and tight **(see illustrations)**.

3 At the same time, inspect the underside of the body for holes, corrosion, open seams, etc, which may allow exhaust gases to enter the passenger compartment. Seal all body openings with silicone or body filler.

4 Rattles and other noises can often be traced to the exhaust system, especially the mounts and hangers. Try to move the pipes, silencer and catalytic converter. If the components can come in contact with the body or suspension parts, secure the exhaust system with new mounts.

12.2a Check exhaust system connections . . .

12.2b . . . and mountings for condition and security

13 Road test

Instruments and electrical equipment

1 Check the operation of all instruments and electrical equipment.

2 Make sure that all instruments read correctly, and switch on all electrical equipment in turn, to check that it functions properly.

Steering and suspension

3 Check for any abnormalities in the steering, suspension, handling or road 'feel'.

4 Drive the vehicle, and check that there are no unusual vibrations or noises.

5 Check that the steering feels positive, with no excessive sloppiness or roughness, and check for any suspension noises when cornering and driving over bumps.

Drivetrain

6 Check the performance of the engine, clutch, transmission and driveshafts.

7 Listen for any unusual noises from the engine, clutch and transmission.

8 Make sure that the engine runs smoothly when idling, and that there is no hesitation when accelerating.

9 Check that, where applicable, the clutch action is smooth and progressive, that the drive is taken up smoothly, and that the pedal travel is not excessive. Also listen for any noises when the clutch pedal is depressed.

10 Check that all gears can be engaged smoothly without noise, and that the gear lever action is smooth and not abnormally vague or 'notchy'.

11 On automatic transmission models, make sure that all gearchanges occur smoothly, without snatching, and without an increase in engine speed between changes. Check that all of the gear positions can be selected with the vehicle at rest. If any problems are found, they should be referred to a Honda dealer or specialist.

12 Listen for a metallic clicking sound from the front of the vehicle, as the vehicle is driven slowly in a circle with the steering on full lock; repeat the check on full-left and full-right lock. This noise may also be apparent when pulling away from a standstill with lock applied. If a clicking noise is heard, this indicates wear in the outboard constant velocity joints (see Chapter 8). If vibration, consistent with roadspeed, is felt through the vehicle when accelerating, there is a possibility of wear in the inboard constant velocity joints. The principle is the same for the rear driveshafts, but obviously more difficult to distinguish. If in doubt raise the vehicle and carry out a physical examination of all four driveshafts and the propeller shaft, looking for signs of play in joints as the components of each shaft are rotated against each other and as the shaft is pulled and pushed up-and-down and from side-to-side. Refer to Chapter 8 for details of removal, refitting and overhaul (where possible) of the various shafts.

13 Listen for any unusual noises from the rear axle – these may be more evident when the vehicle is coasting (on the overrun). A whining noise may indicate wear (or a low final drive lubricant level). However, note that some brands of tyre (especially 'all-terrain' tyres) may generate a whining sound at certain speeds. If there is any doubt about the correct operation of the Real Time four-wheel-drive system, especially in the switching in and out of four-wheel-drive by the Dual Pump arrangement, the vehicle must be taken to a Honda dealer for the system to be checked, a process that involves the use of a rolling road and workshop lifts that allow all four wheels to be driven while the vehicle is raised off the ground.

Braking system

14 Make sure that the vehicle does not pull to one side when braking, and that the roadwheels do not lock when braking hard.

15 Check that there is no vibration through the steering when braking.

16 Check that the handbrake operates correctly, without excessive movement of the lever, and that it holds the vehicle stationary on a slope.

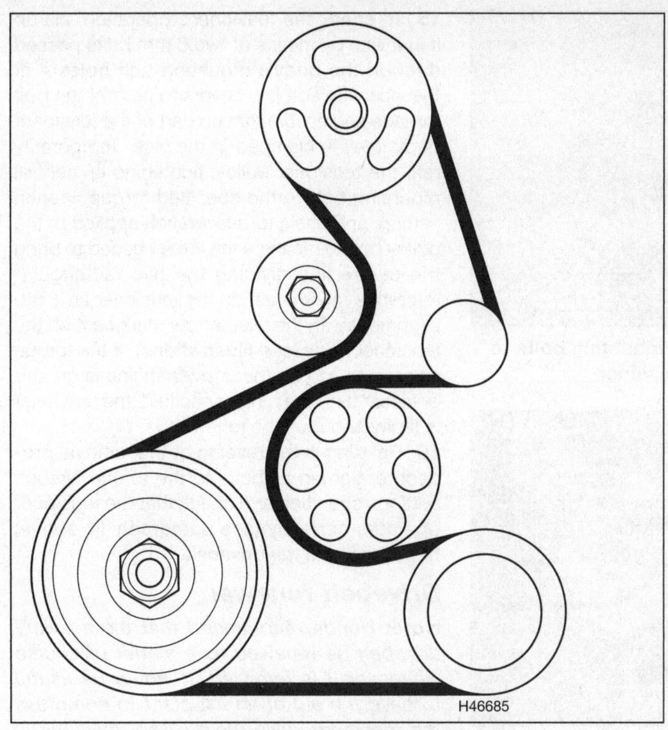

14.1 Routing of auxiliary drivebelt

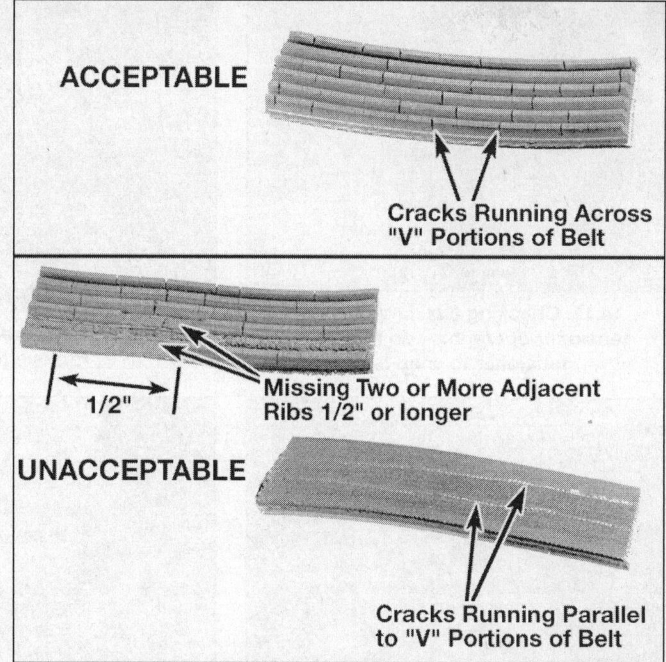

14.5 Here are some of the more common faults found on multi-ribbed auxiliary drivebelts – check very carefully and renew in good time to prevent the inconvenience of a roadside breakdown

Every 25 000 miles or 2 years

14 Auxiliary drivebelt check and renewal

General

1 The auxiliary drivebelt is of the flat, multi-ribbed (or 'polyvee') type, and is located on the right-hand end of the engine. It drives the alternator, water pump, steering pump and the air conditioning compressor from the engine's crankshaft pulley **(see illustration)**.

2 The good condition and proper tension of the auxiliary drivebelt are critical to the operation of the engine. An automatic spring-loaded tensioner eliminates any need for drivebelt maintenance beyond a periodic check of its condition.

3 Because of their composition and the high stresses to which they are subjected, drivebelts wear and deteriorate as they get older. They must, therefore, be regularly inspected.

Drivebelt condition check

4 With the engine switched off (take out the key), open and support the bonnet. For improved access to the right-hand end of the engine, first slacken the right-hand front roadwheel nuts, then jack up the front right-hand side of the vehicle and support it securely on an axle stand (see *Jacking and vehicle support*). Remove the roadwheel, then release the two securing clips and prise back the wheel arch liner section of the engine compartment undershield as necessary to reach the crankshaft pulley and bolt. Unclip the steering fluid reservoir and secure it to one side without disconnecting or straining its hoses.

5 Using an inspection light or an electric torch, and rotating the engine when necessary with a spanner applied to the crankshaft pulley bolt, check the whole length of the drivebelt for cracks in the rubber, separation of the belt plies, and torn or worn ribs **(see illustration)**. Also check for fraying and glazing, which gives the drivebelt a shiny appearance. Check the pulleys for nicks, cracks, distortion and corrosion.

6 Both sides of the drivebelt should be inspected, which means you will have to twist the drivebelt to check the ribbed surface. Use your fingers to feel the drivebelt where you can't see it.

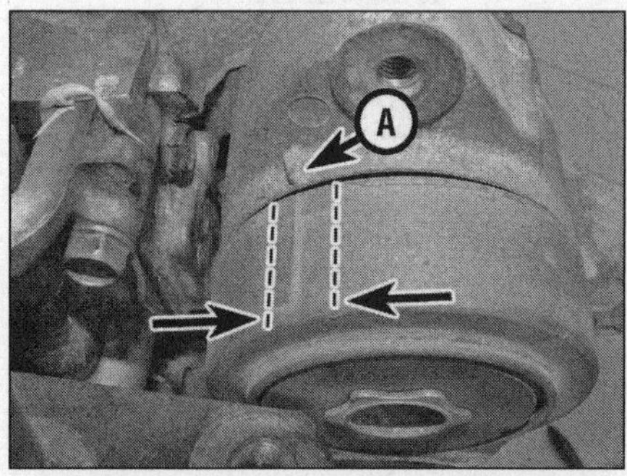

14.7 Tensioner body fixed arrow mark (A) should be within range marked by long and short rectangular reference marks on tensioner arm

7 Check the state of wear of the drivebelt as follows. With the engine stopped, the fixed arrow mark cast on the tensioner body should be somewhere in the range marked by the long and the short rectangular reference marks cast on the tensioner arm (visible just underneath the steering feed hose union on the steering pump) **(see illustration)**. If the fixed arrow mark indicates beyond the short rectangular mark, then the drivebelt is worn out and must be renewed.

8 If you are in any doubt as to the condition of the drivebelt, renew it as described below.

Drivebelt tension (and tensioner) check

9 The auxiliary drivebelt is tensioned by an automatic tensioner.

10 If you suspect that the drivebelt is slipping and/or running slack, or that the tensioner is otherwise faulty, check the operation of the tensioner as follows. With the engine stopped, the fixed arrow mark cast on the tensioner body should be somewhere in the range marked by the long and the short rectangular reference marks cast on the tensioner arm (see paragraph 7 above). Have an assistant start the engine, but be careful to keep your hands and clothing well clear of the drivebelt. If the rectangular marks move in relation to the fixed arrow mark as the engine is started, or if their position varies as the engine is idling, then

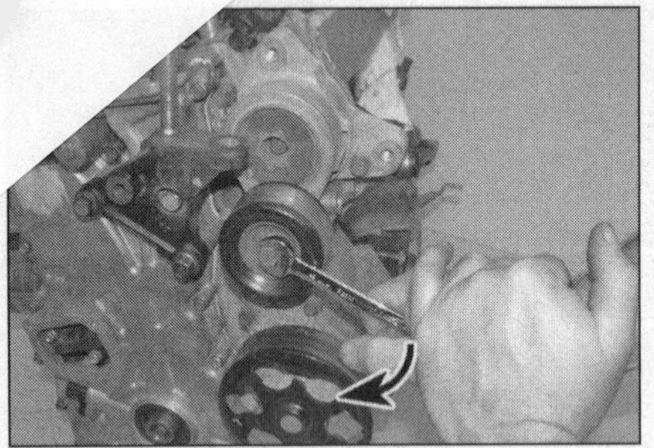

14.11 Checking auxiliary drivebelt tensioner operation – do NOT allow tensioner to snap back

14.15a Use a torque wrench to measure the force needed. . .

the tensioner is faulty and must be renewed. Listen for abnormal noises (whistling, whining, grinding or screeching) from the tensioner pulley; if any such sounds are heard, the pulley bearings are worn and it must be renewed. To remove either the tensioner and/or the pulley and to check further the tensioner's operation, first remove the drivebelt as described in paragraphs 17 to 20 below.

11 With a long spanner (or two shorter spanners used together) applied to the tensioner pulley bolt, move the tensioner pulley and arm clockwise as far as possible, then release them slowly and carefully; do NOT allow the tensioner arm to snap back against spring pressure – it will break **(see illustration)**. Check that the tensioner works properly, with strong spring pressure being felt when its pulley and arm are rotated clockwise,

14.19 Using two spanners together to move tensioner pulley and arm clockwise until drivebelt can be slipped off pulleys. Note tensioner body fixed arrow mark (A)

14.14 Unscrew three mounting bolts to remove tensioner

14.15b . . . to align centre line of tensioner arm reference marks with tensioner body fixed arrow mark (diesel version shown)

and a smooth return to the limit of its travel when released. Listen carefully for abnormal noise and check that there is no sign of jerkiness in the tensioner's movement; if it is noisy or jerky in operation, the tensioner is faulty and must be renewed.

12 Unscrew its two mounting bolts and dismount the steering pump; move it to one side and secure it out of the way without disconnecting or straining its hoses.

13 Unscrew its central mounting bolt and remove the tensioner's pulley.

14 Unscrew its three mounting bolts and remove the tensioner **(see illustration)**.

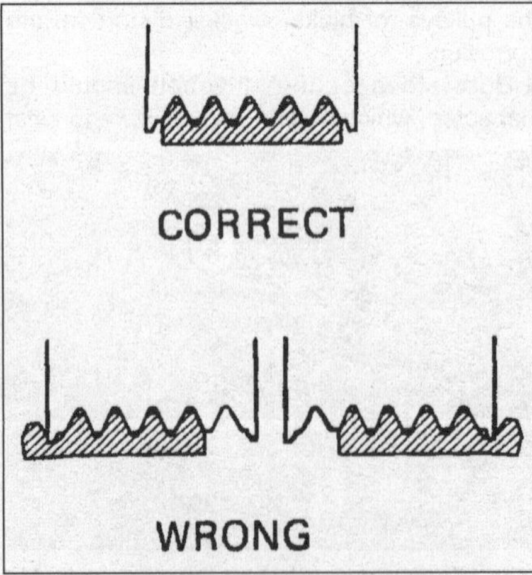

14.22 When installing an auxiliary drivebelt, make sure it is centred on pulleys – it must not overlap to either side

15 To check the tensioner's operation, clamp it in a vice by means of two 8 mm bolts passed through the body's mounting bolt holes – fit the vice with soft jaw covers to protect the bolt threads and ensure that no part of the tensioner body itself is clamped in the vice. Temporarily refit the tensioner pulley, tightening its central mounting bolt to the specified torque wrench setting, and use a torque wrench applied to the pulley bolt to measure the force needed to bring the centre line dividing the two rectangular reference marks cast on the tensioner arm into alignment with the fixed arrow mark cast on the tensioner body **(see illustrations)**. If the torque needed to line up the arrow and line is greater or lesser than the range specified, the tensioner is faulty and must be renewed.

16 Refitting is the reverse of the removal procedure; tighten all bolts to the torque wrench settings specified and check that the tensioner operates correctly (see paragraph 11 above) before refitting the drivebelt.

Drivebelt renewal

Note: *Honda recommend that the auxiliary drivebelt be renewed as a matter of course whenever it is removed. It would be useful to have the aid of an assistant to compress the tensioner while the auxiliary drivebelt is slipped on and off the pulleys. Be very careful to avoid the risk of personal injury through trapped fingers, etc.*

17 Gain access to the drivebelt as described in paragraph 4.

18 If the existing drivebelt is to be refitted, mark it, or note the maker's markings on its flat surface, so that it can be installed the same way round.

19 With a long spanner (or two shorter spanners used together) applied to the tensioner pulley bolt, move the tensioner pulley and arm clockwise until the drivebelt can be slipped off the first pulley, then release them slowly and carefully; do NOT allow the tensioner arm to snap back against spring pressure – it will break **(see illustration)**.

20 Working from the wheel arch or engine compartment as necessary, and noting its routing, slip the drivebelt off the remaining pulleys and withdraw it.

21 Check all the pulleys, ensuring that their grooves are clean, and removing all traces of oil and grease. Clean any rust, dirt or rubber deposits from the working surfaces of the water pump and tensioner pulleys.

22 If the original drivebelt is being refitted, use the marks or notes made on removal to ensure that it is installed to run in the direction as it was previously. To fit a drivebelt, arrange it on the pulleys so that it is centred in their grooves **(see illustration)**, and not overlapping their raised sides (note that the flat surface of the drivebelt is engaged on the water pump and tensioner pulleys) and routed correctly. When it is installed on all but one pulleys, move the tensioner pulley and arm clockwise, slip the drivebelt onto the final pulley and release the tensioner pulley and arm.

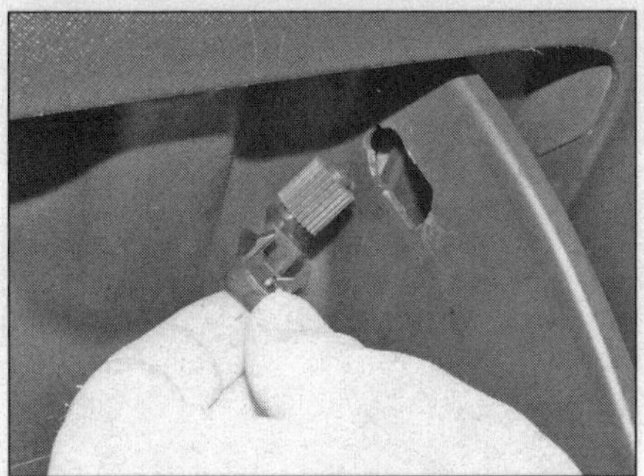

15.2a Press forwards to release, then remove hooks . . .

15.2b . . . then allow glovebox to swing fully open . . .

15.3a . . . press pollen filter cover locking tab sideways to release . . .

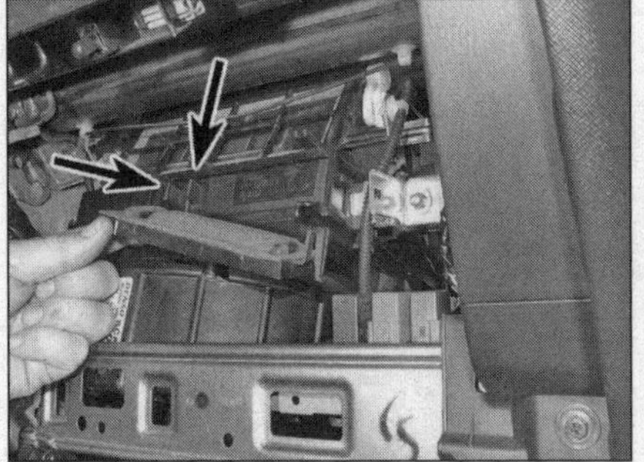

15.3b . . . and remove cover. Note filter section grip tabs (arrows)

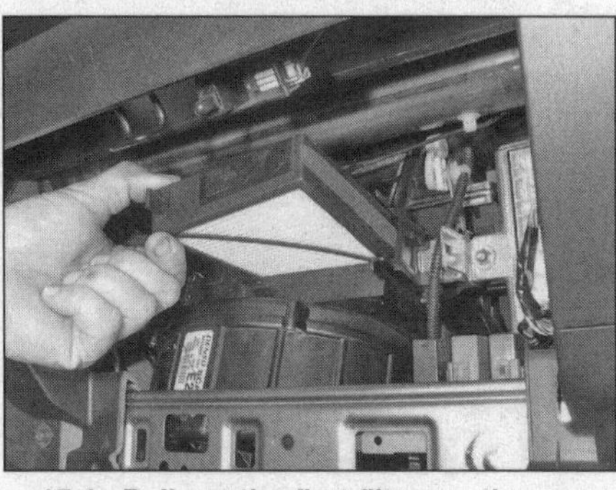

15.4a Pull out the first filter section . . .

15.4b . . . then slide across and pull out second filter section

23 Using a spanner applied to the crankshaft pulley bolt, rotate the crankshaft through at least two full turns clockwise to settle the drivebelt on the pulleys, then check that the drivebelt is properly installed.

24 Refit the components removed for access, then (where applicable) lower the vehicle to the ground. If the right-hand roadwheel was removed, tighten the wheel nuts to the specified torque.

15 Pollen filter element renewal

1 All models are equipped with a filter behind the passenger side of the facia that cleans the air entering the vehicle through the ventilation system. If this filter is allowed to get blocked, the air output will be greatly reduced and the ventilation system's efficiency, whether heating, cooling or demisting, will be significantly reduced.

2 Open and empty the glovebox. Press the two hooks, one on either side of the glovebox, forwards to release the stops, remove both hooks and allow the glovebox to swing down further **(see illustrations)**.

3 Unclip the pollen filter cover by pressing the locking tab on one side inwards, then pull the cover towards you **(see illustrations)**.

4 The pollen filter is in two sections, side-by-side in the filter housing. Pull out the first one by gripping the small tab protruding from its frame. The other section of the filter can also be seen – grip its tab and slide it sideways so that it too can be withdrawn from the filter housing **(see illustrations)**.

5 Remove each filter element from its frame, noting how it fits.

6 Observing the direction-of-fitting markings on the side of each element (the airflow arrows should point downwards), fit the new elements to their frames **(see illustration)**.

7 As far as possible, wipe clean the inside of the housing.

8 Establish which section of the new filter goes in first, and which way up it should be (the airflow arrows should point downwards, and the grip tabs should be side-by-side, facing into the vehicle's interior). Insert it into the housing, and slide it across. Check that the second section is also correctly aligned, then slot it home too **(see illustrations)**.

9 Clip the filter cover back in place, and secure with the locking tab on the side.

10 Swing the glovebox back into place, refit the hooks and close it to complete.

15.6 Fit new elements to frames so that airflow arrows point downwards . . .

15.8a . . . and ensure airflow arrows on frames point downwards . . .

15.8b . . . when refitting pollen filter sections

16.4a Unbolt and withdraw plastic cover over intake manifold . . .

16.4b . . . withdraw engine oil level dipstick, then plug opening

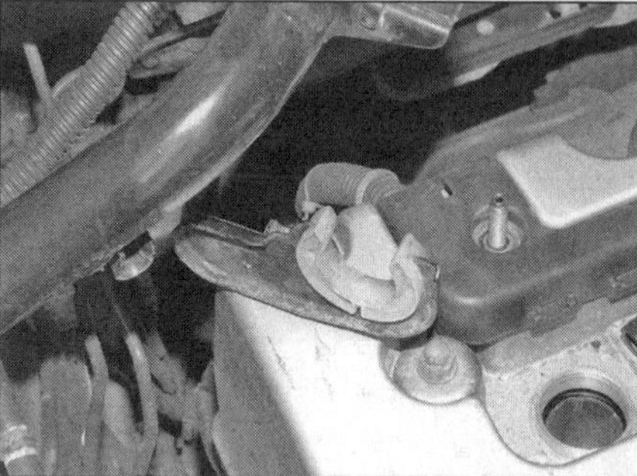

16.5a Unbolt steering hose clamp from rear right-hand end of cylinder head cover . . .

16.5b . . . and disconnect breather hose from cover's left-hand end

16.5c Release throttle cable from its guide bracket . . .

16.5d . . . and lift wiring conduit from its mountings; be careful not to lose spacer from each mounting stud

Every 25 000 miles

16 Valve clearance check and adjustment

Note: *Liquid gasket (Honda Part No. 08C70-K0234M, 08C70-K0334M, 08C70-X0331S or 08718-0001 or equivalent) must be available on reassembly, in addition to any other items (gaskets, seals, etc) found to be in need of renewal during the procedure.*

1 It is necessary for a clearance to exist between the tip of each valve stem and the valve operating mechanism, to allow for the expansion of the various components as the engine reaches normal operating temperature. This means that these valve clearances (also known as 'tappet' clearances) must be checked and adjusted regularly. If the clearances were allowed to be too slack, the engine would be very noisy, its power output would suffer and its fuel consumption would increase. If the clearances were allowed to be too tight, as will occur naturally and gradually as the valve seats wear and the valves recess up into the cylinder head, the engine's power output would be reduced and the valves and their seats could be severely damaged.

2 The valve clearances must be checked and adjusted with the engine cold.

3 Remove all four ignition coils and the spark plugs as described in Section 18. The standard-type spark plugs are due to be renewed at this interval, so unless the valve clearances are being checked for any other reason, obtain a new set of plugs for refitting.

16.6a Extract seals around spark plug tubes if leaking . . .

16.6b . . . obtain new ones . . .

4 Unbolt and withdraw the plastic cover over the intake manifold. Withdraw the engine oil level dipstick; plug its opening to prevent dirt or other objects from dropping into the engine **(see illustrations)**.

5 Unbolt the steering hose clamp from the rear right-hand end of the cylinder head cover and disconnect the breather hose from the cover's left-hand end. Where applicable, release the throttle cable from its guide bracket and lift the large square-section black plastic wiring conduit from its mountings; be careful not to lose the spacer from each mounting stud. Secure cable and conduit clear of the cylinder head cover **(see illustrations)**.

6 Unscrew the retaining nuts and remove the cylinder head cover. Check the condition of the cover gasket, the seals around the spark plug tubes and the sealing washers under each of the cover retaining nuts and renew any that are damaged **(see illustrations)**.

7 Apply the handbrake, jack up the front of the vehicle and securely support it on axle stands (see *Jacking and vehicle support*). Release the two securing clips and prise back the wheel arch liner section of the engine compartment undershield as necessary to reach the crankshaft pulley and bolt, then rotate the crankshaft clockwise until the single notch (usually painted orange) in the inboard rim of the crankshaft pulley aligns exactly with the arrow mark cast on the timing chain case **(see illustrations)**. Nos. 1 and 4 cylinders are now at TDC, one of them on the compression

16.6c . . . and fit using hammer and tubular drift . . .

16.6d . . . to drive home until seated in cover

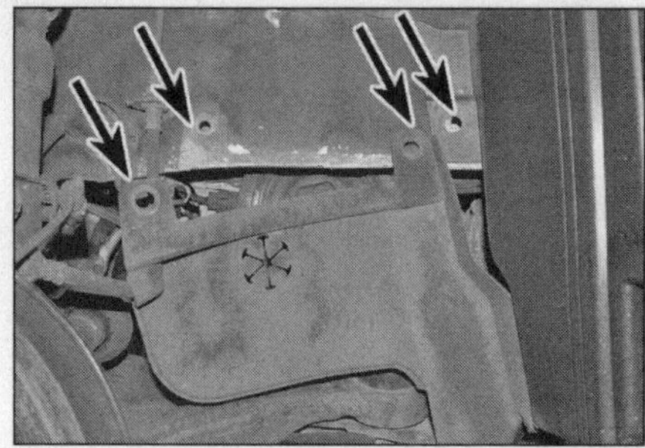

16.7a Release two securing clips and prise back wheel arch liner section of engine compartment undershield . . .

16.7b . . . so that TDC notch in inboard rim of crankshaft pulley can be seen aligning with arrow mark cast on timing chain case

16.8 No. 1 cylinder is at TDC on compression stroke when punch marks and arrow mark (A) are both at the top, while lines (B) point inwards towards each other and align exactly with cam follower assembly support-bearing cap mating surface

stroke (refer to Section 3 of Chapter 2A for further information).

8 To establish whether it is No. 1 or No. 4 cylinder that is on the compression stroke check the valve positions and the timing marks on the exhaust camshaft sprocket and intake camshaft sprocket/Variable Timing Control (VTC) actuator. No. 1 cylinder is correctly positioned if all four cam lobes are pointing away from No. 1 cylinder's valves and the punch marks on the rims of the camshaft sprockets and the arrow mark stamped on the VTC actuator are all at the top (twelve o'clock position), while the lines stamped in both sprocket rims point inwards towards each other and align exactly with the mating surface of the No. 1 cam follower assembly support and its bearing cap **(see illustration)**. If not, rotate the crankshaft one full turn (360°) clockwise until the pulley notch and timing marks align as described. No. 1 cylinder will then be at TDC on the compression stroke.

9 With the engine in this position, the four valves for No. 1 cylinder can be checked and adjusted **(see illustration)**.

10 Start with the intake valve clearances at the front of the engine. Insert a feeler gauge of the correct thickness (see this Chapter's Specifications) between the first valve's stem and its follower adjuster screw's tip. Withdraw it, and you should feel a slight drag. If there's no drag or a heavy drag, slacken the locknut and undo the adjuster screw. Carefully tighten the adjuster screw until you can feel a slight drag on the feeler gauge as you withdraw it **(see illustration)**.

11 Hold the adjuster screw with a screwdriver to stop it turning and securely tighten the locknut. Do not overtighten the locknut – this will merely distort the threads and make future adjustments very difficult; use a torque wrench to ensure that the locknuts are correctly tightened, but note that intake and exhaust valve locknuts have different torque settings

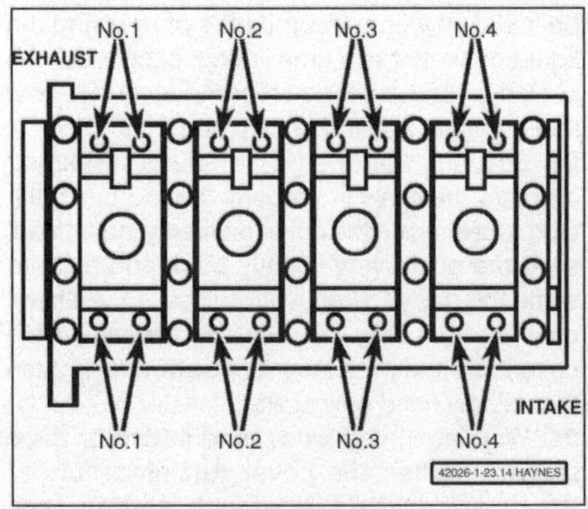

16.9 Valve layout

16.10 Checking the clearance of an intake valve

16.11 Overtightening locknuts will distort threads and make adjustment difficult

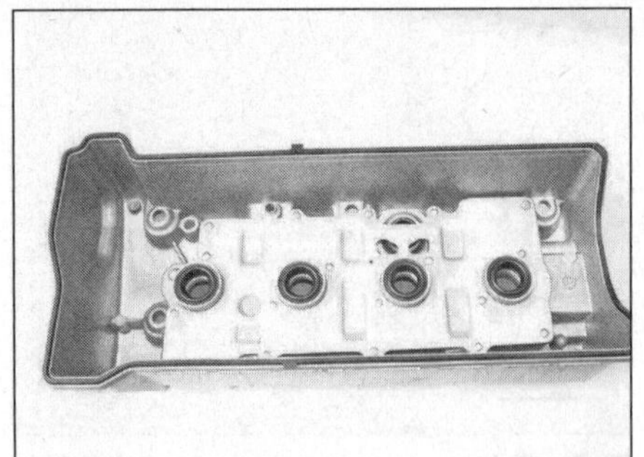

16.18a Ensure that gasket is correctly seated in cylinder head cover grooves . . .

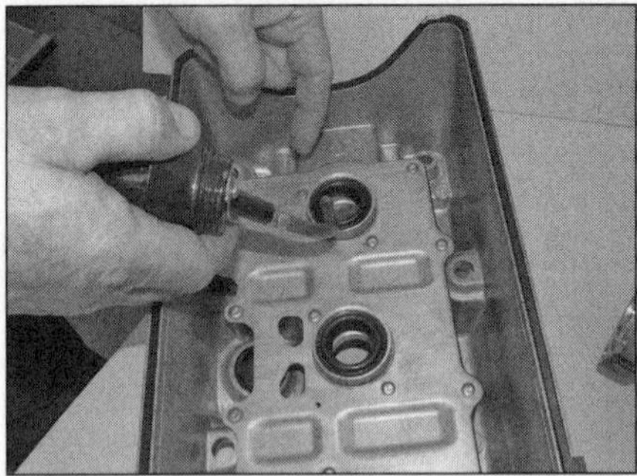

16.18b . . . and apply smear of clean engine oil to lips of spark plug tube seals

16.19a Apply liquid gasket to cylinder head cover/timing chain case/cylinder head intersections (arrows) . . .

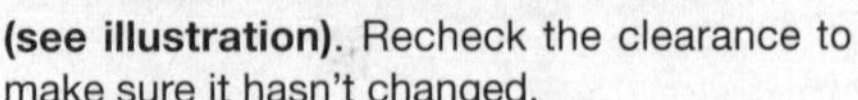

16.19b . . . and to edges (arrows) of No. 5 cam follower assembly support

16.20a Refit cylinder head cover . . .

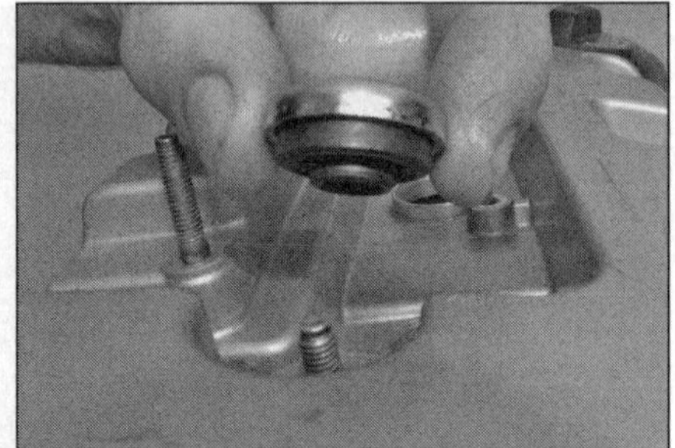

16.20b . . . then refit sealing washers, ensuring that they are located correctly in cover

(see illustration). Recheck the clearance to make sure it hasn't changed.

12 Repeat the check-and-adjust procedure on the remaining No. 1 cylinder intake valve, then on the two exhaust valves.

13 Rotate the crankshaft pulley 180° clockwise (the camshaft sprockets will move through 90°) until No. 3 piston is at TDC on the compression stroke. The punch mark on the rim of the exhaust camshaft sprocket will be at the three o'clock position, and its line will point straight down, while the punch mark and arrow mark stamped on the intake camshaft sprocket/VTC actuator will be at the three o'clock position, and its line will be at the top. Check and adjust No. 3 cylinder's valves.

14 Rotate the crankshaft pulley 180° further clockwise until No. 4 piston is at TDC on the compression stroke. The punch mark on the rim of the exhaust camshaft sprocket will now be at the six o'clock position, and its line will be at nine o'clock, while the punch mark and arrow mark stamped on the intake camshaft sprocket/VTC actuator will be at the six o'clock position, and its line will be at three o'clock. Check and adjust No. 4 cylinder's valves.

15 Rotate the crankshaft pulley 180° clockwise again to bring No. 2 piston to TDC on the compression stroke. The punch mark on the rim of the exhaust camshaft sprocket will now be at the nine o'clock position, and its line will be at the top, while the punch mark and arrow mark stamped on the intake camshaft sprocket/VTC actuator will be at the nine o'clock position, and its line will be at six o'clock. Check and adjust No. 2 cylinder's valves.

16 Though there should be no real need, the engine can be turned again to bring No. 1 back to TDC on the compression stroke, and the clearances can be re-checked. If the engine is then turned further in sequence, the clearances for the remaining three cylinders can be re-checked.

17 On completion, thoroughly clean the mating surfaces of the cylinder head and cover. Clean any oil or old gasket material and sealant from the cover groove. Thoroughly clean the spark plug wells in the cover and cylinder head. Be very careful not to allow dirt and debris to fall into the combustion chambers.

18 Ensure that the cylinder head cover gasket is correctly seated in the cover grooves and apply a smear of clean engine oil to the lips of the seals around the spark plug tubes **(see illustrations).**

19 Apply liquid gasket to the points shown, to ensure that there are no oil leaks from the cylinder head cover/timing chain case/cylinder head intersection or from around the edges of the No. 5 cam follower assembly support **(see illustrations)**. The cylinder head cover must be installed within five minutes of applying the liquid gasket; if this time limit is exceeded, the sealant must be wiped off completely and new liquid gasket applied in its place.

20 Ensuring that the gasket is not dislodged and that the seals fit properly around the spark plug tubes, place the cover on the cylinder head, slide the cover very slightly back-and-forth to settle the gasket, then refit the sealing washers, ensuring that they are located correctly in the cover, and the nuts **(see illustrations)**. Tighten the nuts by hand only at first.

21 Working in sequence, and in two or three stages, tighten the cover retaining nuts to the specified torque wrench setting **(see illustration)**.

22 Refit the wiring conduit to its mountings

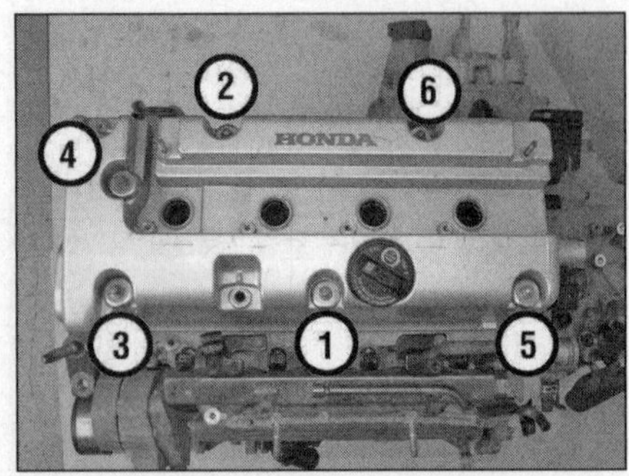

16.21 Cylinder head cover retaining nuts tightening sequence

16.22 Do not forget to refit spacer under each mounting stud of wiring conduit

and refit the coil cover spacers on their mounting studs **(see illustration)**. Unplug its opening and refit the engine oil level dipstick.

23 Reconnect the breather hose, reposition the throttle cable in its guide bracket (where applicable), then refit the steering hose clamp to the rear of the cylinder head cover and the plastic cover to the intake manifold. Tighten the manifold cover bolts and steering hose clamp retaining bolt to their specified torque wrench settings. Reconnect any other wiring or hoses that were disconnected on removal.

24 Complete spark plug servicing as described in Section 18.

25 When Honda's own liquid gasket has been used to seal a joint, note the following:

a) Where applicable, wait at least 30 minutes before filling the engine with oil.

b) Do not run the engine for at least three hours.

17 Air filter element renewal

1 Disconnect the breather hose from the cover, then remove the five bolts around the edge of the air cleaner cover **(see illustrations)**. Lift the cover to one side for access to the filter element.

2 Lift the cylindrical element out of the housing, and wipe out the inside of the air cleaner housing with a clean rag.

3 While the air cleaner cover is off and the element is removed, be careful not to drop anything down into the engine's air intake tract.

4 Fit the new element into the air cleaner housing, making sure it seats properly, and observing any direction-of-fitting markings **(see illustration)**.

5 Refit the air cleaner cover, ensuring that its edges seat correctly, and secure with the five bolts. Tighten them carefully, so as not to damage or distort the housing and cover; note the specified torque wrench setting.

18 Spark plug renewal

1 Good spark plug performance is vital to the correct running and efficiency of the engine. It is essential that the plugs fitted are appropriate for the engine; the recommended types are specified at the beginning of this Chapter, or in the vehicle's handbook. If the correct type is used and the engine is in good condition, the spark plugs should not need attention between scheduled renewal intervals. Spark plug cleaning is rarely necessary, and should not be attempted unless specialised equipment is available, as damage can easily be caused to the firing ends.

2 Ensure that the ignition is switched off (take out the key).

17.1a Disconnect the breather hose from the cover . . .

17.1b . . . then unscrew . . .

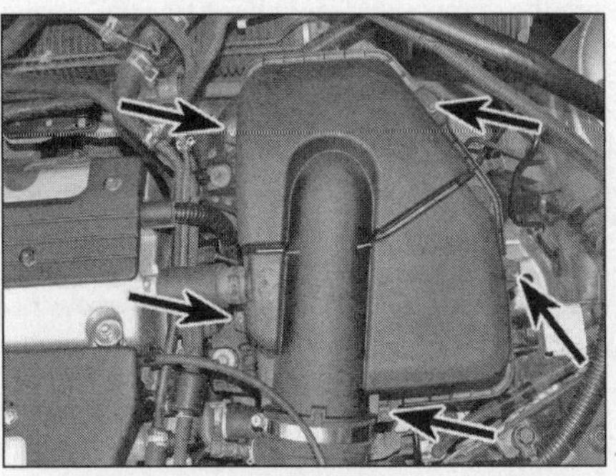

17.1c . . . the five air cleaner cover retaining bolts

17.4 Fit the new element into air cleaner housing, and ensure it seats properly

3 Unscrew the four nuts securing the ignition coil cover on top of the engine. Lift off the cover; be careful not to lose the separate spacer from each rear mounting stud **(see illustrations)**.

4 Cleanliness is vital from this point on to prevent anything from falling into the combustion chambers when the spark plugs are removed. Wipe or brush around the coils and the top of the engine as necessary – if an airline is available, blow away any particles of dirt, etc, that have gathered (taking care to avoid any risk of eye injury), and mop-up any oil or water. It is essential that dirt and debris does not enter the engine.

5 Unscrew the bolt securing each ignition coil to the cylinder head cover. On coils Nos. 2 and 4, a deep socket (or a spanner) will be needed, as their bolts have studs on top for securing the coil cover **(see illustration)**.

6 Lift the first coil slightly to detach it from the spark plug, but note that it is still plugged in at this point. Check that there is no build-up of dirt, dust, etc, under the coil's sealing rubber; wipe away anything that is found.

7 Press the locking tab on the coil's wiring

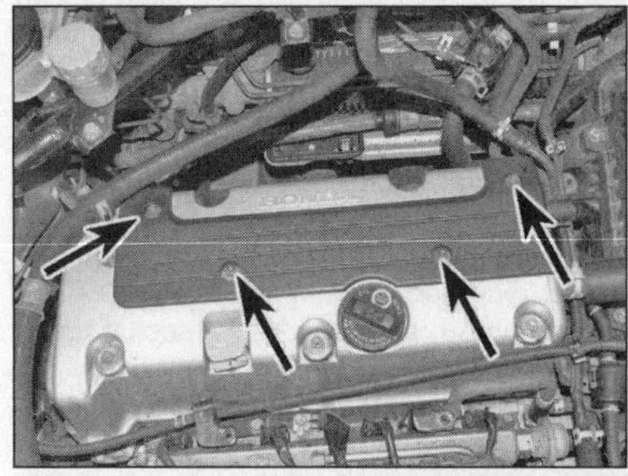

18.3a Unscrew four nuts securing ignition coil cover on top of engine

18.3b Lift off cover; be careful not to lose spacer from each rear mounting stud

18.5 Unscrew ignition coil mounting bolts, noting studs fitted to coils 2 and 4 . . .

18.7 ... then disconnect coil wiring plugs

18.8 Clean away any dirt before lifting coils off spark plugs ...

18.10 ... use a slim spark plug socket and a long extension to unscrew spark plugs

connector, and slide the connector back to disconnect the coil **(see illustration)**.

8 Lift out the coil **(see illustration)**. If possible, it is advisable to work on one coil and plug at a time, to avoid mixing them up, although the coils do appear to be identical. Thoroughly clean the coil, carefully wiping off any dirt or corrosion with a clean rag. Check for signs of tracks (arcing) on the coil's body – especially if engine misfiring has been experienced or a multiple-misfire fault code has been logged; sometimes these can be erased by polishing with a clean cloth, but it may be necessary to renew the coil if it is damaged or faulty. Check the condition of the sealing rubber under the coil's head and renew it if it is damaged.

9 Using an electric torch if necessary, check inside the spark plug well to see whether there is an accumulation of dirt or moisture which might fall into the combustion chamber when the spark plug is unscrewed. Use whatever means necessary to remove any such foreign matter; an airline is best, provided that suitable eye protection is worn, but a fine long-handled paintbrush and kitchen towel, used carefully, will do the job.

10 Using a slim (5/8-inch/16 mm) spark plug socket, unscrew and remove the first spark plug **(see illustration)**. The spark plugs are deeply recessed, so a long extension will be necessary. A proper spark plug socket has a rubber insert fitted, which is very useful for gripping the plug during removal and refitting – the spark plug will drop out of an ordinary deep socket. As each spark plug is removed, cover or plug its well with clean rag or similar to prevent dirt or other objects from dropping into the combustion chambers; be very careful to keep this in place all the time the spark plugs are removed so as not to allow dirt and debris to fall into the engine.

11 Examination of the spark plugs will give a good indication of the condition of the engine. As each plug is removed, inspect it as follows:

12 The ceramic insulator should show no signs of cracks – especially around the centre electrode – and should be clean; light brown or rusty staining just above the metal body may be corona staining, which is a natural phenomenon that is caused by electrical stress in the air around the spark plug. The metal body should be free from damage, especially to the threads and gasket, and the electrodes should be clean and unworn (ie, have sharp, square edges). If the insulator nose is covered with light tan to greyish-brown deposits, then the mixture is correct and it is likely that the engine is in good condition.

13 If the insulator nose of the spark plug is clean and white, with no deposits, this is indicative of a weak mixture or too hot a plug (a 'hot' plug transfers heat slowly away from the electrode and therefore runs 'hotter' than a 'cold' plug, which transfers heat away quickly).

14 If the tip and insulator nose are covered with hard black-looking deposits, then this is indicative that the mixture is too rich. Should the plug be black and oily, then it is likely that the engine is fairly worn, as well as the mixture being too rich.

15 Where multi-electrode and/or iridium plugs are fitted, the electrode gaps are all preset, and **no** attempt should be made to bend the electrodes – fit the plugs straight out of the packet.

16 If standard single-electrode plugs are fitted, the spark plug electrode gap is of considerable importance. If the gap is too large or too small, the size of the spark and its efficiency will be seriously impaired and it will not perform correctly under all engine speed and load conditions. The gap specified at the start of this Chapter is that recommended for the plugs listed, but may not be if other makes of plug are used. Do NOT attempt to adjust the gap of iridium spark plugs.

17 To set the gap, measure it with a feeler blade or spark plug gap gauge and then carefully bend the outer electrode until the correct gap is achieved **(see illustrations)**. The centre electrode should never be bent, as this may crack the insulator and cause plug failure, if nothing worse. If using feeler blades, the gap is correct when the appropriate-size blade is a firm sliding fit.

18 Special spark plug electrode gap adjusting tools are available from most motor accessory shops, or from some spark plug manufacturers.

19 Before fitting the spark plugs, check that the threaded connector sleeves on top are tight, and that the plug exterior surfaces and threads are clean. A little copper grease applied to the plug threads will make the plugs easier to remove next time **(see illustration)**. Thoroughly clean the spark plug wells – both the tubes in the cylinder head cover and the seatings in the cylinder head. Be very careful not to allow dirt and debris to fall into the combustion chambers.

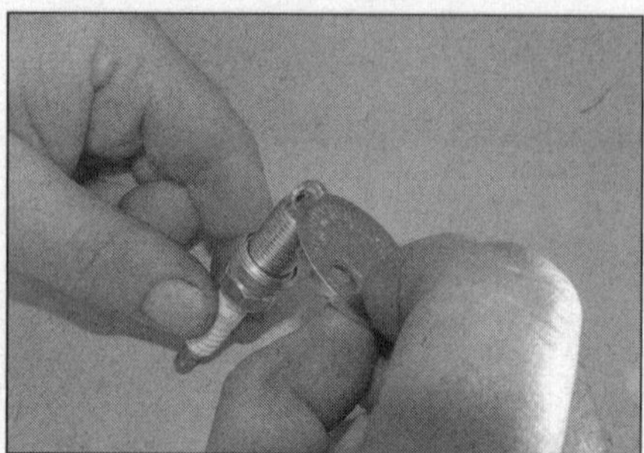

18.17a Measuring spark plug electrode gap with special spark plug electrode gap adjusting tool

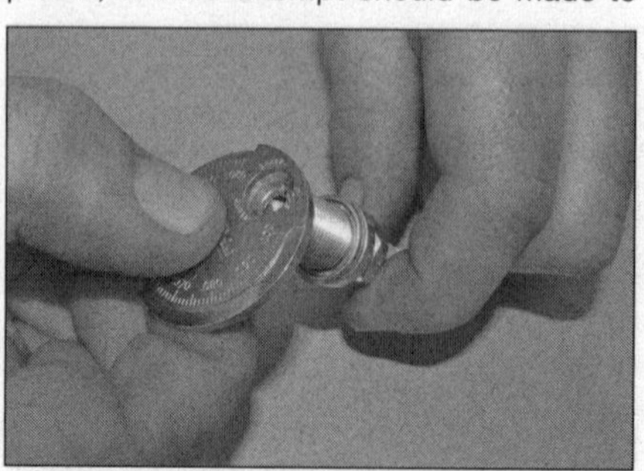

18.17b Adjust gap (non-iridium standard single-electrode plugs only) by bending earth electrode

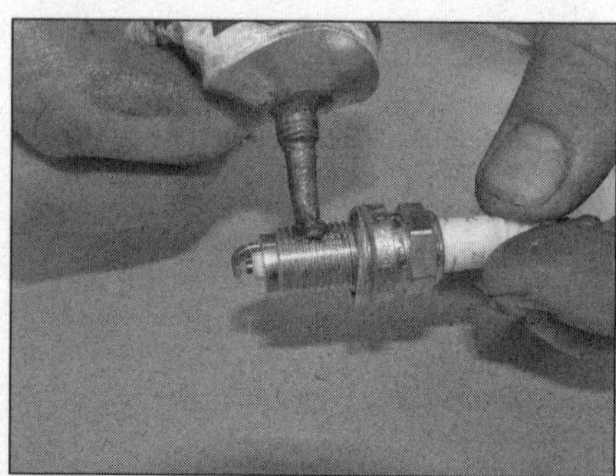

18.19 Apply copper grease to spark plug threads to ease future removal

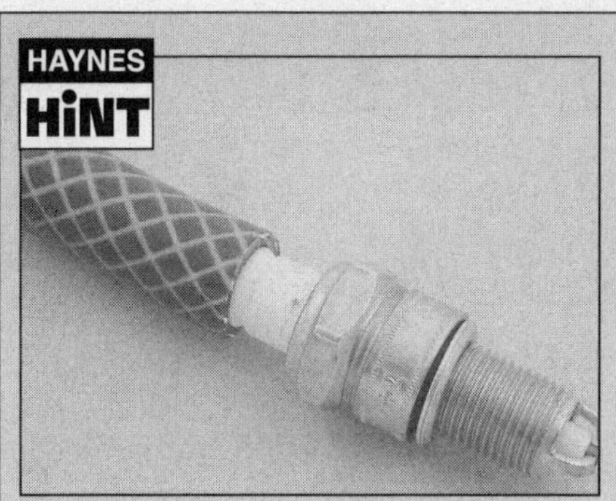

It's often difficult to insert spark plugs into their holes without cross-threading them. To avoid this possibility, fit a short piece of hose over the end of the plug. The flexible hose acts as a universal joint, to help align the plug with the plug hole. Should the plug begin to cross-thread, the hose will slip on the spark plug, preventing thread damage to the aluminium-alloy cylinder head.

20 Remove the material covering or plugging the well, fit the new plug into the spark plug socket, then offer it into the engine with the long extension – do not just drop it in.

21 Tighten the plug initially by hand – this way, it is possible to feel whether the plug is going in correctly (there should be little or no effort needed), or whether it is misaligned and is cross-threading **(see Haynes Hint)**. After several turns, the plug will be felt to 'seat' (contact the cylinder head).

18.22 Do not overtighten spark plugs – use a torque wrench to ensure correct tightening

22 Using a torque wrench, tighten the plug to the specified torque setting **(see illustration)**. If a torque wrench is not available – and this is one case where the use of a torque wrench is highly recommended – tighten the plug by no more than half to three-quarters of a turn (180 to 270°) after it seats. If refitting used spark plugs, their already-compressed gasket will require less force; one-twelfth to one-eighth (30 to 45°) of a turn after seating will suffice. Do not overtighten spark plugs, or the threads in the aluminium-alloy cylinder head will be damaged.

18.23 Do not forget sealing rubber when refitting coils; press coil firmly down onto its sealing rubber and onto spark plug

23 Refit the ignition coil, reconnect the coil wiring plug, ensuring that a good connection is made, then press the coil firmly down onto its sealing rubber and onto the plug **(see illustration)**. Fit the coil mounting bolt, and tighten it to the specified torque setting.

24 Repeat the procedure for the remaining spark plugs and coils.

25 On completion, refit the cover over the coils, and secure with the four nuts; do not overtighten the nuts – note the specified torque setting.

Every 3 years

19 Brake fluid renewal

Warning: Brake hydraulic fluid can harm your eyes and damage painted surfaces, so use extreme caution when handling and pouring it. Do not use fluid that has been standing open for some time, as it absorbs moisture from the air. Excess moisture can cause a dangerous loss of braking effectiveness.

Note: *On manual transmission models, we recommend the renewal of the clutch hydraulic fluid at the same time as the brake fluid.*

1 The procedure is similar to that for the bleeding of the hydraulic system as described in Chapter 9.

2 Working as described in Chapter 9, open the first bleed nipple in the sequence, and pump the brake pedal gently until nearly all the old fluid has been emptied from the master cylinder reservoir. Top-up to the MAX level with new fluid, and continue pumping until only the new fluid remains in the reservoir, and new fluid can be seen emerging from the bleed nipple. Tighten the nipple, and top the reservoir level up to the MAX level line.

3 Work through all the remaining bleed nipples in the sequence until new fluid can be seen at all of them. Be careful to keep the master cylinder reservoir topped-up to above the MIN level at all times, or air may enter the system and greatly increase the length of the task.

Old hydraulic fluid is invariably much darker in colour than the new, making it easy to distinguish the two.

4 When the operation is complete, check that all bleed nipples are securely tightened, and that their dust caps are refitted. Wash off all traces of spilt fluid, and recheck the master cylinder reservoir fluid level.

5 Check the operation of the brakes before taking the vehicle on the road.

Every 75 000 miles or 6 years

20 Fuel filter renewal

Note: *The fuel filter is not a conventional externally-mounted canister-type filter – it is a gauze component clipped to the base of the in-tank fuel pump/gauge sender unit. Not only is it part of Honda's maintenance schedule to renew the filter at this interval, but Honda also state that the filter should be renewed when the fuel pressure drops below the value quoted in Chapter 4A Specifications.*

Note: *The fuel pump/gauge sender unit locking ring and sealing ring must be renewed as a matter of course whenever they are disturbed.*

Warning: The following procedure requires the opening of the petrol tank and the removal of components containing petrol, which will result in fuel spillage. Before carrying out any operation on the fuel system, refer to the precautions given in Safety first! at the beginning of this manual, and follow them implicitly. Petrol is a highly-dangerous and volatile liquid, and the precautions necessary when handling it cannot be overstressed.

1 Remove the fuel pump/gauge sender unit as described in Chapter 4A.

2 With the assembly drained of fuel and removed to a clean working area, dismantling can begin.

3 Disconnect the fuel level sender unit upper

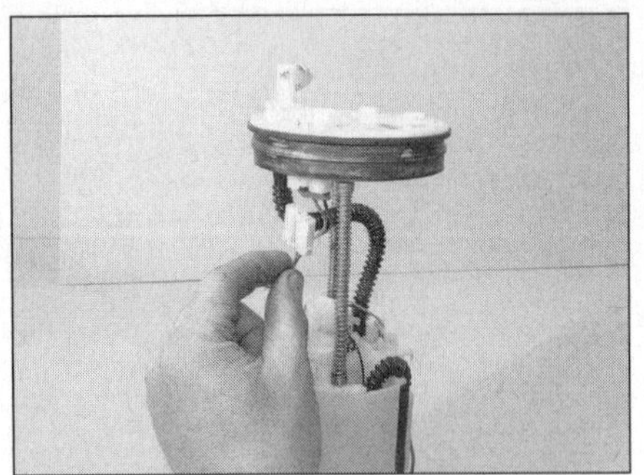
20.3a Disconnect fuel level sender unit upper wiring plug . . .

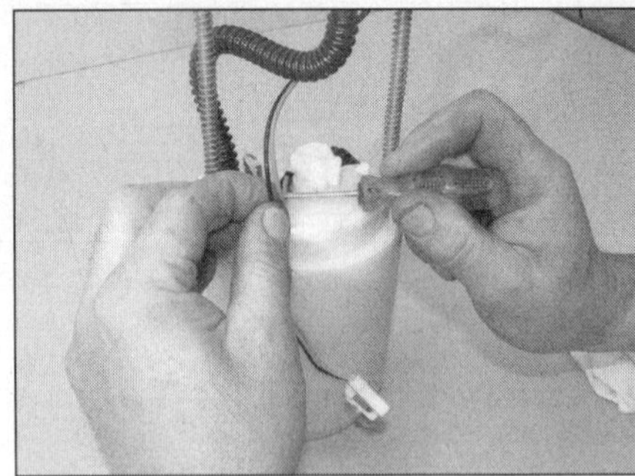
20.3b . . . and release wiring from top of tank unit

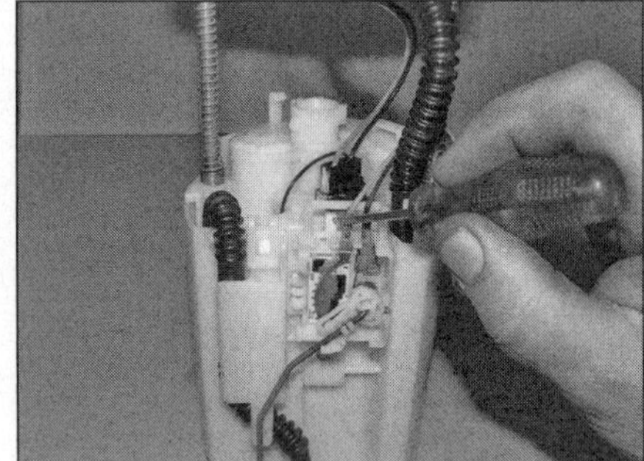
20.4a Depress locating tab . . .

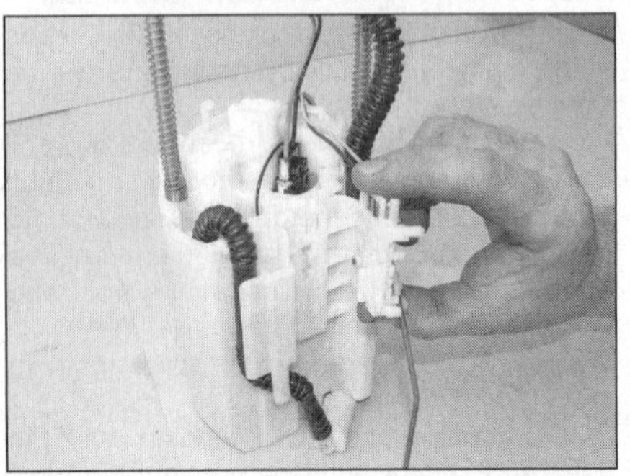
20.4b . . . and remove sender unit from side of assembly

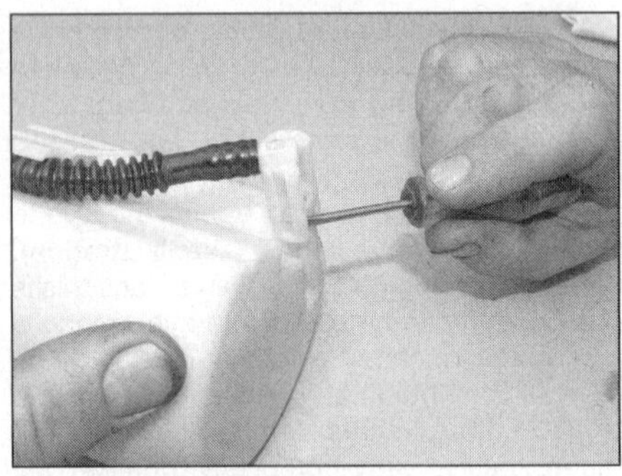
20.5a Release fuel hose connection from base of sediment bowl . . .

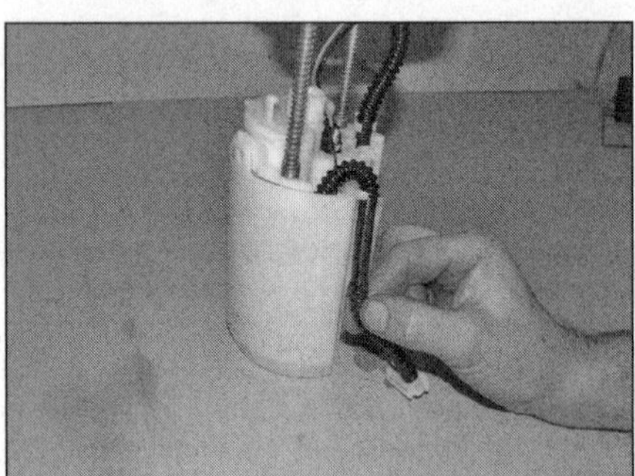
20.5b . . . and unclip hose from side of bowl

wiring plug and release the wiring from the top of the tank unit **(see illustrations)**.

4 Using a small screwdriver, depress the locating tab and remove the sender unit from the side of the assembly **(see illustrations)**.

5 Release the fuel hose connection from the base of the sediment bowl and unclip it from the side of the bowl **(see illustrations)**.

6 Release the three securing tabs, and slide off the sediment bowl **(see illustrations)**.

7 Release the three securing tabs to release the pump lower cover. Recover the seat which fits between the pump and its cover, noting how it fits **(see illustrations)**.

8 Extract the clip and discard it – it must be

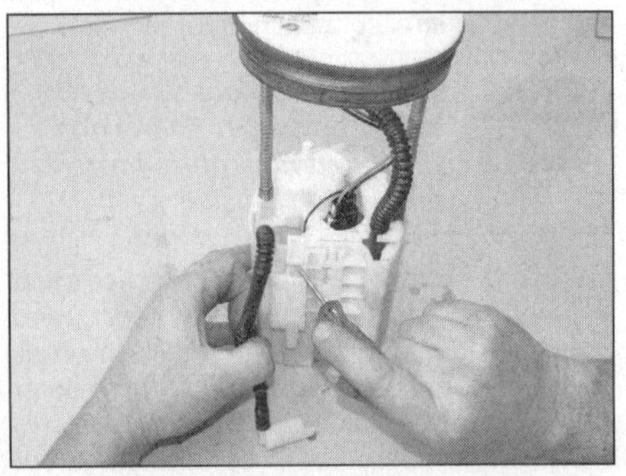
20.6a Use a screwdriver to release securing tab on one side . . .

20.6b . . . release two securing tabs opposite . . .

20.6c . . . and remove sediment bowl

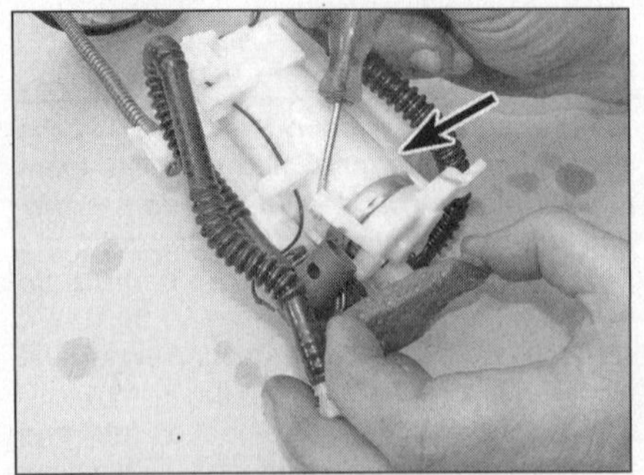
20.7a Use a screwdriver to release securing tabs . . .

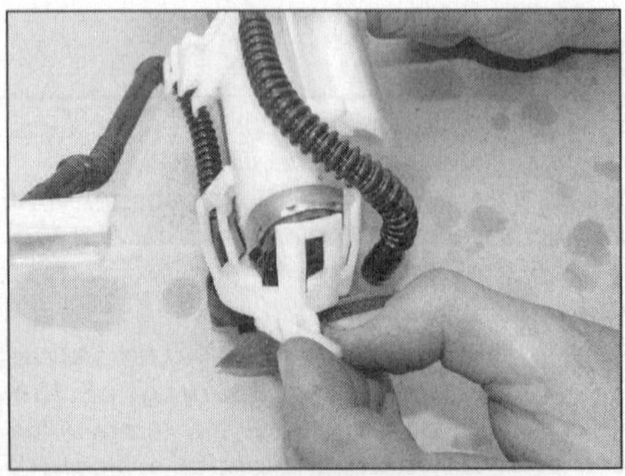
20.7b . . . and withdraw pump lower cover . . .

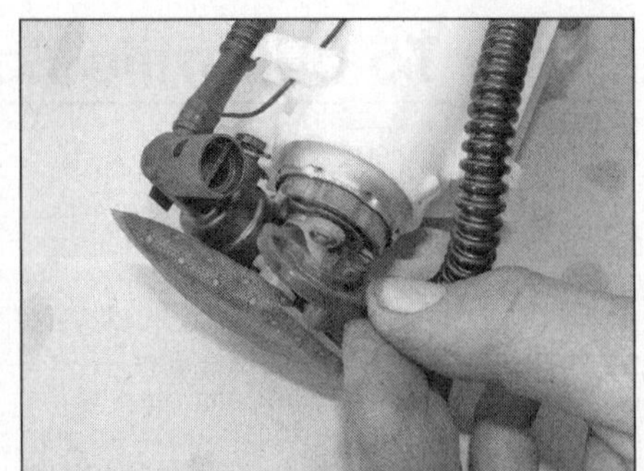
20.7c . . . then remove seat

renewed whenever it is disturbed (a new clip should be included with the new filter gauze). Prise the filter gauze off the bottom of the pump **(see illustrations)**.

9 Press the new filter gauze firmly onto the pump's union and locating peg, taking care not to damage the filter. Fit the new clip and press it firmly and evenly into place **(see illustrations)**.

10 Refit the seat to the base of the pump and clip the pump lower cover back into place **(see illustrations)**. Ensure that the filter gauze and pump lower cover are correctly located and securely fastened.

11 Refit the sediment bowl, clipping it firmly into place and making sure the tabs engage properly. Clip the hose connection back onto the side and base of the bowl **(see illustration)**.

12 Clip the sender unit back onto the side of the assembly, route its wiring securely and reconnect its wiring plug **(see illustration)**.

13 Refit the fuel pump/gauge sender unit as described in Chapter 4A, using a new sealing ring and locking ring **(see illustration)**.

21 Idle speed check

1 Engine idle speed is the speed at which the engine runs when it is fully warmed-up to normal operating temperature, with no throttle applied, when the vehicle is completely stopped and all electrical systems are switched off. Note that it is normal for the idle speed to be held up for a second or two, before dropping to base idle – most vehicles will also run above idle while rolling to a stop, or when coasting downhill. The speed is critical to the performance of the engine itself, as well as many sub-systems.

2 The idle speed is under the control of the engine management system's Electronic Control Unit (ECU) and is not adjustable manually. If the idle speed is significantly different from that specified, in the first

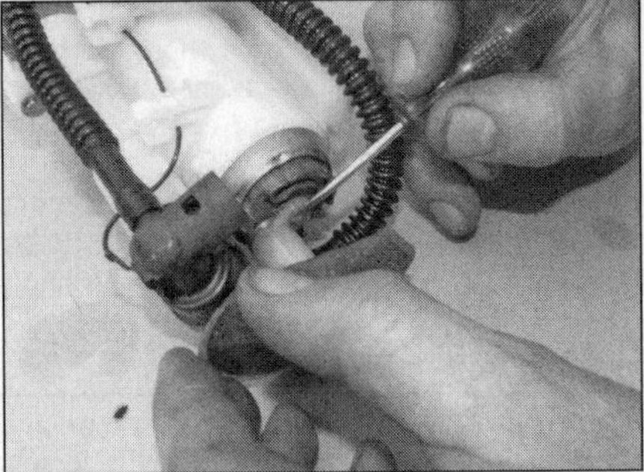

20.8a Use a screwdriver to extract filter securing clip . . .

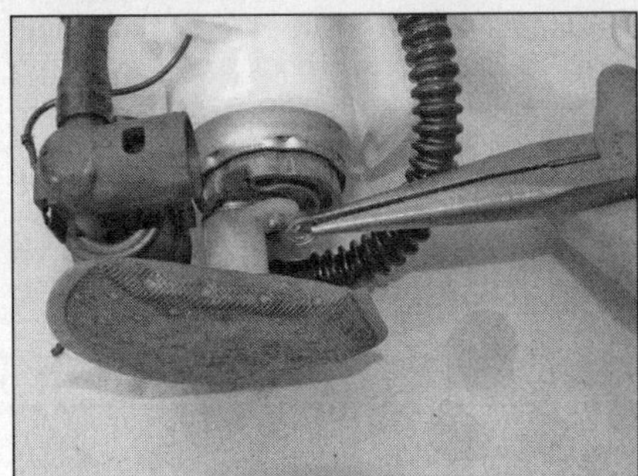

20.8b . . . then withdraw and discard clip . . .

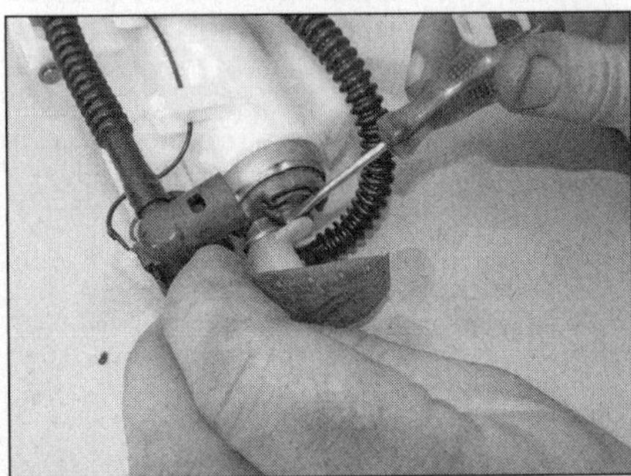

20.8c . . . and prise filter off pump base

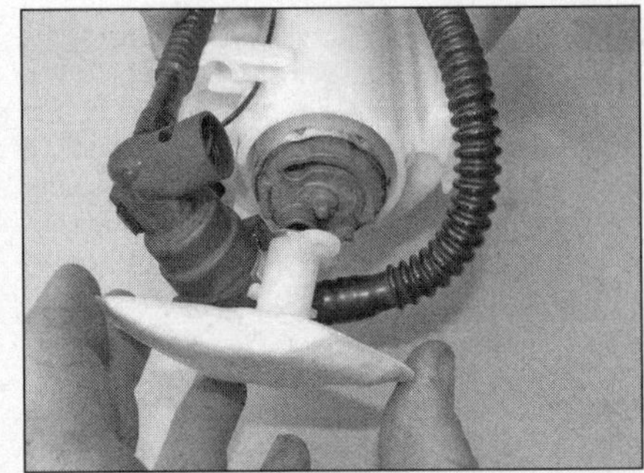

20.9a Press new filter gauze firmly onto pump union and locating peg

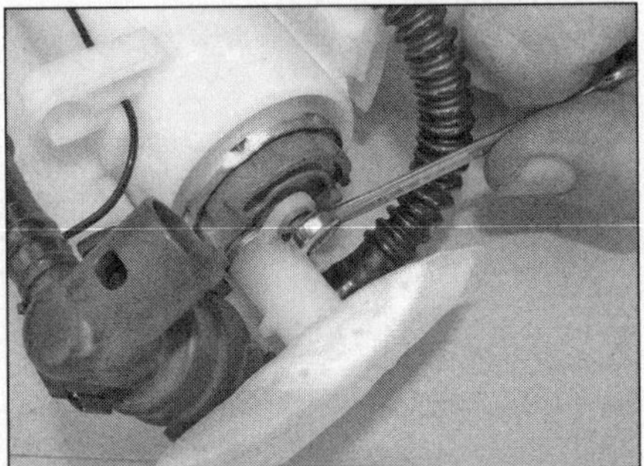

20.9b Fit new clip and press it firmly and evenly into place

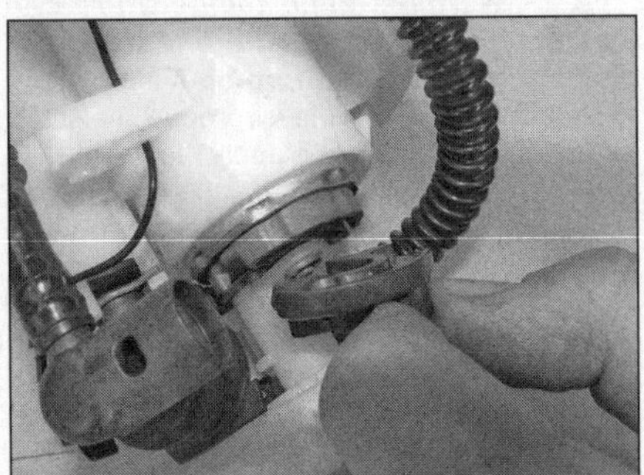

20.10a Refit seat to base of pump . . .

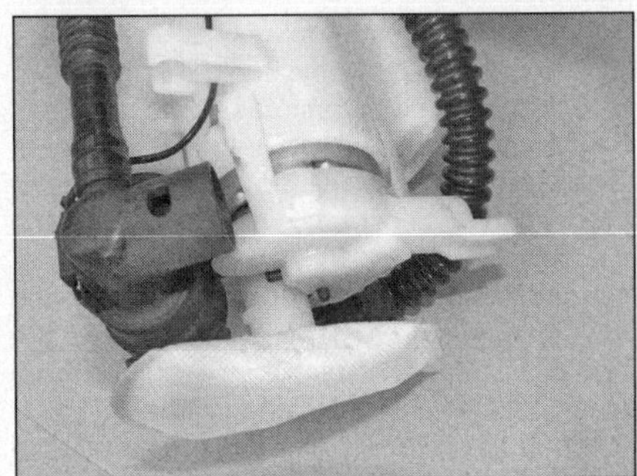

20.10b . . . and clip pump lower cover back into place

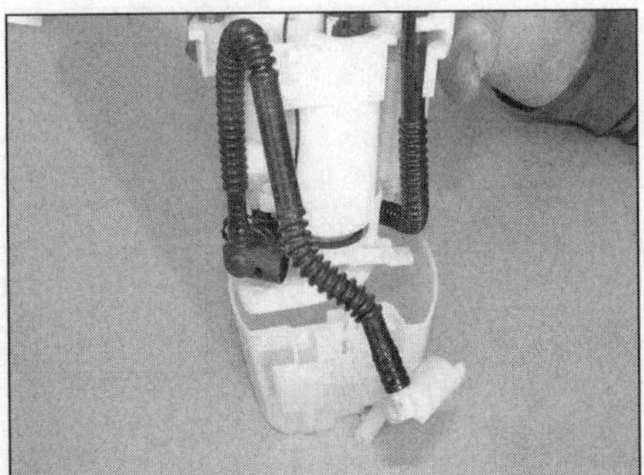

20.11 Refit sediment bowl, making sure tabs engage properly

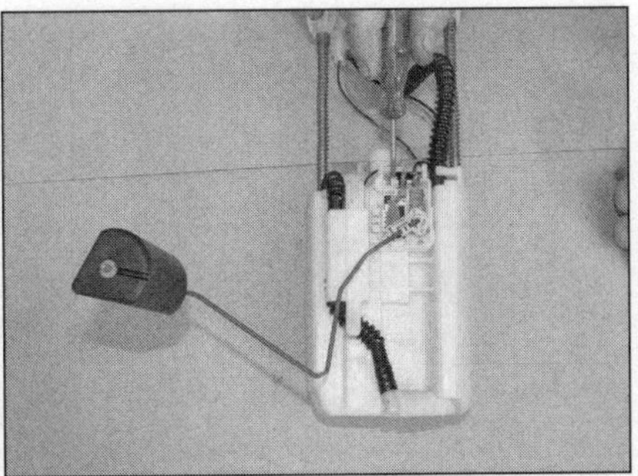

20.12 Clip sender unit back onto side of assembly

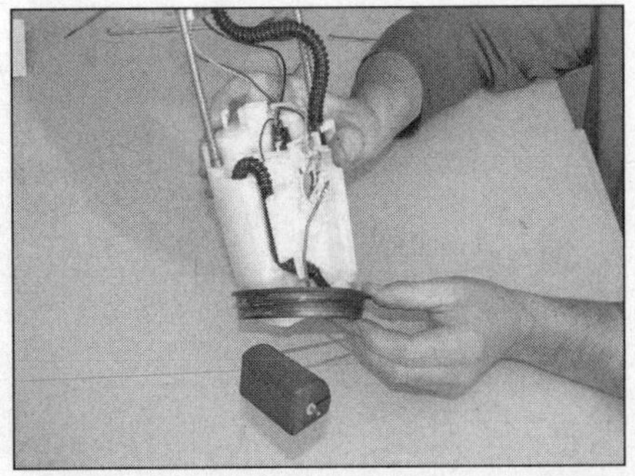

20.13 Always renew sealing ring and locking ring when refitting sender unit

instance, check the throttle cable (where applicable) and throttle body.

3 Poor idle quality could be due to poor maintenance – change the engine oil, and carry out the primary operations listed in Section 2.

4 As a rough guide, an idle speed which is too high may be due to an air leak – the engine is sucking in excess air somewhere (perhaps from a loose or split air or vacuum hose), and the ECU is compensating for the extra air by adding fuel.

5 An engine prone to stalling could be suffering a problem with one of the engine-driven ancillaries, such as the alternator, or the problem could be low fuel pressure. Also check the stop-lamp switch and vehicle speed sensor (see Chapters 9 and 4A).

6 Ultimately, a persistent idle speed problem will have to be referred to a Honda dealer for diagnosis.

Every 75 000 miles or 8 years

22 Manual gearbox fluid renewal

Note: *The transfer case shares the same lubricant as the gearbox. In addition to the fluid that will be needed, new filler/level and drain plug sealing washers will be required.*

1 Drive the vehicle to warm the engine/gearbox up to normal operating temperature.

2 Park the vehicle on level ground, switch off the ignition and apply the handbrake firmly. For improved access, jack up the front of the vehicle and support it securely on axle stands (see *Jacking and vehicle support*). Note that the vehicle must be lowered to the ground and level, to ensure accuracy, when refilling and checking the fluid level.

3 Remove all traces of dirt from around the filler/level plug, unscrew the plug and recover the sealing washer (see Section 10).

4 Position a suitable container under the drain plug which is also situated on the left-hand side of the gearbox, underneath the driveshaft inboard joint.

5 Unscrew the drain plug – a square key will be needed, for which a 3/8-inch socket extension can be substituted – and allow the fluid to drain completely into the container **(see illustrations)**. If the fluid is hot, take precautions against scalding. Clean both the filler/level and the drain plugs, being especially careful to wipe any metallic particles off the magnetic inserts (where fitted). Discard the original sealing washers; they should be renewed whenever they are disturbed.

6 When the fluid has finished draining, clean the plug threads of the gearbox casing, fit a new sealing washer and refit the drain plug, tightening it to the specified torque **(see illustration)**. It the vehicle was raised for the draining operation, now lower it to the ground.

7 Refilling the gearbox is an awkward operation (see Section 10). Refill the gearbox with the exact amount of the specified type of fluid (see *Lubricants and fluids*) then check the fluid level as described in Section 10.

8 When the level is correct, refit the filler/level plug with a new sealing washer and tighten it to the specified torque.

23 Automatic transmission fluid renewal

Note: *The transfer case shares the same lubricant as the transmission. In addition to the fluid that will be needed, a new drain plug sealing washer will be required.*

1 The fluid should be drained when hot, preferably immediately after the vehicle has been driven on a journey of sufficient length to warm the engine/transmission up to normal operating temperature.

Warning: Fluid temperature can exceed 120°C in a hot transmission. Wear protective gloves.

2 Park the vehicle on level ground, select P, switch off the ignition and apply the handbrake firmly. For improved access, jack up the front of the vehicle and support it securely on axle stands (see *Jacking and vehicle support*). Note that the vehicle must be lowered to the ground and level, to ensure accuracy, when refilling and checking the fluid level.

3 Move the tools and drain pan under the vehicle, being careful not to touch any of the hot exhaust components.

4 Place the drain pan under the transmission and remove the drain plug – a square key, for which a 3/8-inch socket extension can be substituted, will be needed to undo it. If the fluid is hot, take precautions against scalding. Clean the drain plug, being especially careful to wipe any metallic particles off the magnetic insert (where fitted). Discard the original sealing washer; this should be renewed whenever it is disturbed.

5 Once the fluid is drained, clean the plug threads of the transmission casing, fit a new sealing washer and refit the drain plug, tightening it to the specified torque. Lower the vehicle to the ground.

6 Pull out the dipstick, then add new fluid to the transmission through the dipstick tube. Use a funnel to prevent spills. It is best to add a little fluid at a time, continually checking the level with the dipstick (see Section 3). The engine should be left switched off at this stage.

7 When the fluid level reaches the upper mark on the dipstick, start the engine and slowly shift the selector into all positions, then shift into P and apply the handbrake. Let the engine warm up to operating temperature (wait until the radiator cooling fan has come on, and gone off).

8 Turn off the engine and check the fluid level as described in Section 3.

24 Final drive fluid renewal

Note 1: *In addition to the fluid that will be needed, new filler/level and drain plug sealing washers will be required.*

Note 2: *A moaning/groaning noise when manoeuvring on full lock can be due to premature degradation of the final drive fluid. The first course of action is to renew*

22.5a Unscrewing manual gearbox fluid drain plug

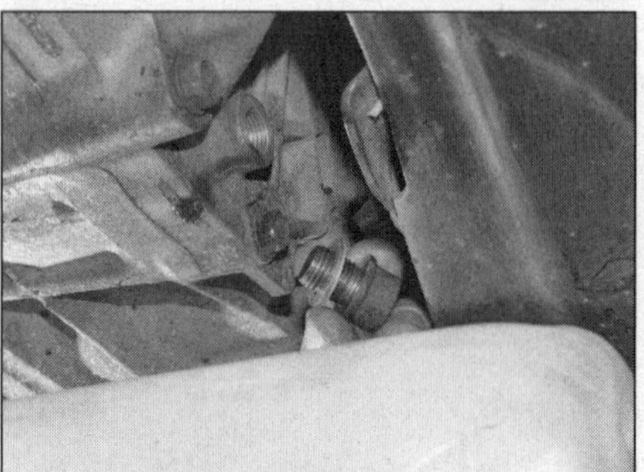

22.5b Allow fluid to drain. Renew drain plug sealing washer

22.6 Tighten drain plug to specified torque wrench setting

the fluid as described below, using the latest specification of Honda Dual Pump II (DPF II) fluid.

1 The fluid should be drained when hot, preferably immediately after the vehicle has been driven. Park the vehicle on level ground to begin with.

2 If necessary, raise the rear of the vehicle and place it on axle stands for access to the final drive drain plug (see *Jacking and vehicle support*).

3 Remove all traces of dirt from around the filler/level plug, unscrew the plug and recover the sealing washer (see Section 11).

4 Position a suitable container under the drain plug – it's located on the left-hand side of the final drive, directly below the filler/level plug, and a square key will be needed – on our vehicle, a 3/8-inch socket extension fitted **(see illustration)**.

5 Unscrew the drain plug and allow the fluid to drain completely into the container. Once the fluid is drained, clean and refit the drain plug, using a new sealing washer and tightening it to the specified torque. If the vehicle was raised, lower it to the ground, and make sure that it is level.

6 Refilling the final drive is an extremely awkward operation (see Section 11). Refill the final drive with the exact amount of the specified type of fluid (see *Lubricants and fluids*) then check the fluid level as described in Section 11.

7 When the level is correct, refit the filler/level plug with a new sealing washer and tighten it to the specified torque.

24.4 Unscrewing final drive fluid drain plug

Every 120 000 miles or 10 years

25 Coolant renewal

Note: *This renewal interval should be observed once only, at its **first** occurrence. Subsequently, even if the system is refilled with Honda's specified coolant, the recommended renewal interval drops to every 60 000 miles or 5 years, whichever comes first. If any antifreeze other than Honda's is to be used, the coolant must be renewed at regular intervals to provide an equivalent degree of protection; the conventional recommendation is to renew the coolant every three years.*

Warning: Refer to Chapter 3 and observe the warnings given. In particular, never remove the radiator cap or expansion tank filler cap when the engine is running, or has just been switched off, as the cooling system will be pressurised and hot, and the consequent escaping steam and scalding coolant could cause serious injury. If the engine is hot, the electric cooling fan may start rotating even if the engine is not running, so be careful to keep hands, hair and loose clothing well clear when working in the engine compartment.

Cooling system draining

Warning: Wait until the engine is cold before starting this procedure.

1 Switch on the ignition and turn the heater temperature control to the maximum heat position. Switch off the ignition.

2 To drain the system, first remove the radiator cap. Place a thick cloth over the radiator cap, then turn the cap anti-clockwise as far as the first stop and wait for any pressure to be released, then depress it and turn it further anti-clockwise to remove it. Similarly, remove the expansion tank cap.

3 If additional working clearance is required, apply the handbrake, then jack up the front of the vehicle and support it on axle stands (see *Jacking and vehicle support*).

4 If required, remove the engine compartment undershield (see Chapter 11), but the radiator drain can be reached through the access hole provided **(see illustrations)**. Place a large drain tray underneath, and slacken the radiator drain tap. Allow the coolant to drain into the tray. On completion, retighten the drain tap securely.

5 Move the drain tray to the rear of the engine, underneath the oil filter. Above and to the right of the oil filter is the cylinder block coolant drain plug **(see illustration)** – unscrew the plug and allow the rest of the system contents to drain into the tray.

6 When the block has been drained of coolant, and the system has been flushed (if required), refit the drain plug with a little liquid gasket applied to its threads. Tighten the drain plug securely **(see illustrations)**. Where necessary, lower the vehicle to the ground.

7 Honda also stipulate that the contents of the expansion tank should be drained when renewing the coolant. Unless suitable syphoning equipment is available (and remember, antifreeze is poisonous), or a

25.4a Radiator drain tap can be reached through access hole in engine compartment undershield . . .

25.4b . . . but access to hose connections, if required, is easier with undershield removed

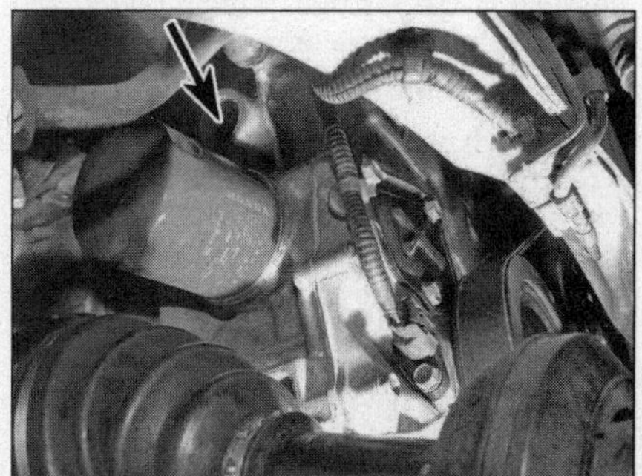

25.5 Cylinder block coolant drain plug is located in recess above oil filter

25.6a Apply smear of liquid gasket to threads of cylinder block coolant drain plug . . .

25.6b . . . and tighten carefully on refitting

pressure-testing kit can be fitted to the expansion tank filler neck to pressurise it and blow the coolant out of the bottom, up the tube and out at the radiator filler neck, this will mean removing the radiator and tank to pour out the contents. To remove the radiator and tank, refer to Chapter 3.

Cooling system flushing

8 If coolant renewal has been neglected, or if the antifreeze mixture has become diluted, then in time, the cooling system may gradually lose efficiency, as the coolant passages become restricted due to rust, scale deposits, and other sediment. The cooling system efficiency can be restored by flushing the system clean.

9 The radiator should be flushed independently of the engine, to avoid unnecessary contamination.

Radiator flushing

10 Disconnect the top and bottom hoses and any other relevant hoses from the radiator, with reference to Chapter 3.

11 Insert a garden hose into the radiator top inlet. Direct a flow of clean water through the radiator, and continue flushing until clean water emerges from the radiator bottom outlet.

12 If after a reasonable period, the water still does not run clear, the radiator can be flushed with a good proprietary cleaning agent. It is important that the manufacturer's instructions are followed carefully. If the contamination is particularly bad, remove the radiator, insert the hose in the radiator bottom outlet, and reverse-flush the radiator.

Engine flushing

13 Remove the thermostat as described in Chapter 3 then, if the radiator top hose has been disconnected from the engine, temporarily reconnect the hose.

14 With the top and bottom hoses disconnected from the radiator, insert a garden hose into the radiator top hose. Direct a clean flow of water through the engine, and continue flushing until clean water emerges from the radiator bottom hose.

15 On completion of flushing, refit the thermostat and reconnect the hoses with reference to Chapter 3.

Antifreeze mixture

16 Honda's own coolant is pre-mixed at 50/50 strength, and is therefore ready to use. If you are using any other type of antifreeze, to give the recommended mixture ratio, 50% (by volume) of neat antifreeze must be mixed with 50% of clean, soft water; however, always note the antifreeze manufacturer's instructions.

17 Before adding antifreeze, the cooling system should be completely drained, preferably flushed, and all hoses checked for condition and security. Fresh antifreeze will rapidly find any weaknesses in the system.

18 After filling with antifreeze, a label should be attached to the expansion tank, stating the type and concentration of antifreeze used, and the date installed. Any subsequent topping-up should be made with the same type and concentration of antifreeze.

Cooling system filling

19 Before attempting to fill the cooling system, make sure that all hoses and clips are in good condition, and that the clips are tight and the cylinder block drain plug (if disturbed) has been correctly tightened. If removed, refit the radiator and expansion tank.

20 Check that the heater temperature control has not been moved from the maximum heat position. If there is a chance it has been disturbed, temporarily switch on the ignition and set the control to maximum heat, then switch the ignition off once more.

21 Slowly fill the system through the radiator filler aperture until the coolant level reaches the base of the radiator filler neck. Wait a few minutes for the level in the radiator to stabilise.

22 Without fitting the radiator cap, start the engine and let it run for about 30 seconds, then switch it off.

23 Recheck the coolant level in the radiator, and if necessary, fill it to the base of the filler neck.

24 Fill the expansion tank until the level reaches the MAX mark, then refit the expansion tank cap. Fit the radiator cap, but only tighten it to its first stop.

25 Start the engine, and run it at idle until the engine reaches normal operating temperature, as indicated by the radiator cooling fan cutting in and out at least twice.

26 Switch off the engine, then check the level in the radiator and top-up if necessary to the base of the radiator filler neck.

27 Start the engine again, and run it at 1500 rpm until the radiator cooling fan comes on again.

28 Switch off the engine, and again check the level in the radiator and top-up if necessary. Fit the radiator cap and tighten it fully.

29 Check the coolant level in the expansion tank and top-up to the MAX mark if necessary. Fit the expansion tank cap and tighten it fully.

30 Make a careful check of all disturbed components, hose unions, etc, checking that all are securely fastened and that there is no sign of coolant leakage anywhere. Use clean water to flush away any spilt coolant, so that any leaks that may occur in the future are easier to spot. Refit all components removed for access.

Airlocks

31 If, after draining and refilling the system, symptoms of overheating are found which did not occur previously, then the fault is almost certainly due to trapped air at some point in the system, causing an airlock and restricting the flow of coolant; usually, the air is trapped because the system was refilled too quickly.

32 If an airlock is suspected, first try gently squeezing all visible coolant hoses. A coolant hose which is full of air feels quite different to one full of coolant, when squeezed. After refilling the system, most airlocks will clear once the system has cooled, and been topped-up.

33 While the engine is running at operating temperature, switch on the heater and heater blower, and check for heat output. Provided there is sufficient coolant in the system, any lack of heat output could be due to an airlock in the system.

34 Airlocks can have more serious effects than simply reducing heater output – a severe airlock could reduce coolant flow around the engine. Check that the radiator top hose is hot when the engine is at operating temperature – a top hose which stays cold could be the result of an airlock (or a non-opening thermostat).

35 If the problem persists, stop the engine and allow it to cool down **completely**, before unscrewing the radiator and expansion tank caps or slackening the hose clips and squeezing the hoses to bleed out the trapped air. In the worst case, the system will have to be at least partially drained (this time, the coolant can be saved for re-use) and flushed to clear the problem.

Radiator cap check

36 Clean the radiator cap, and inspect the seal inside the cap for damage or deterioration. If there is any sign of damage or deterioration to the seal, fit a new pressure cap. If the cap is old, it is worth considering fitting a new one for peace of mind – they are not expensive. If the pressure cap fails, excess pressure will be allowed to develop in the system, which may result in the failure of hoses, the radiator, or the heater matrix.

Chapter 1 Part B:
Routine maintenance and servicing – diesel models

Contents

Degrees of difficulty

Easy, suitable for novice with little experience 	**Fairly easy,** suitable for beginner with some experience	**Fairly difficult,** suitable for competent DIY mechanic	**Difficult,** suitable for experienced DIY mechanic	**Very difficult,** suitable for expert DIY or professional 

Servicing specifications – diesel models

Lubricants and fluids	Refer to *Lubricants and fluids* on page 0•16	
Capacities*	**Change**	**Total**
Engine oil (including oil filter)	5.9 litres	6.5 litres
Cooling system	6.8 litres	8.0 litres
Gearbox (includes transfer case)	2.5 litres	3.1 litres
Final drive	1.2 litres	1.4 litres
Power steering fluid:		
Reservoir	0.26 litres	N/App.
System overhaul	N/App.	0.72 litres
Washer fluid reservoir	N/App.	4.5 litres
Fuel tank:		
Overall	N/App.	58 litres
Low fuel indicator lights at	10.4 litres	N/App.

* *All capacities are approximate.*

Engine

Engine code	See Chapter 2B
Idle speed – no load (not adjustable)	850 ± 50 rpm

Cooling system

Coolant	Refer to *Lubricants and fluids* on page 0•16

Auxiliary drivebelt

Automatic tensioner arrow and line align at	50 to 61 Nm (37 to 45 lbf ft)

Brakes

Brake pad friction material minimum thickness – front and rear	1.6 mm
Disc minimum thickness:	
Front disc	23.0 mm
Rear disc	8.0 mm
Handbrake adjustment	Locked @ 5 to 9 clicks

Torque wrench settings

	Nm	lbf ft
Acoustic engine cover retaining nuts	12	9
Air cleaner cover retaining bolts	3	2
Auxiliary drivebelt idler pulley bolt (where fitted)	44	32
Auxiliary drivebelt tensioner mounting bolts	22	16
Auxiliary drivebelt tensioner pulley bolt	120	89
Braking system bleed nipples	See Chapter 9	
Clutch slave cylinder bleed nipple	See Chapter 6	
Cooling system bleed nipple	10	7
Cooling system expansion tank mounting bolts	10	7
Cooling system radiator drain tap	2	1
Cylinder block coolant drain plug	39	29
Engine compartment undershield access flap securing bolt	10	7
Engine oil (sump) drain plug	39	29
Engine oil filter cap	25	18
Final drive fluid filler/level and drain plugs	47	35
Fuel filter:		
Nominal tightening torque	17 ± 3	13 ± 2
Using Honda service tool (see text)	16	12
Fuel filter water level switch:		
Nominal tightening torque	5 ± 1	4 ± 1
Using Honda service tool (see text)	5	4
Gearbox fluid drain plug	39	29
Gearbox fluid filler plug	44	32
Gearbox fluid level plug	12	9
Roadwheel nuts	108	80
Steering pump mounting bolts	22	16

This servicing schedule is based on the one specified by the vehicle manufacturer, with additional recommendations based on practical experience, on the assumption that you, not the dealer, will be carrying out the work. The service intervals are applicable to vehicles used in normal conditions; vehicles used in adverse conditions (eg, driven in dusty areas or in extremes of climate, used full-time for towing, or driven frequently at slow speeds (idling in traffic) or on short journeys, or used for taxi work) may need servicing more frequently. These are the minimum maintenance intervals recommended by us for vehicles driven daily. If you wish to keep your vehicle in peak condition at all times, you may wish to perform some of these procedures more often. We encourage frequent maintenance, because it enhances the efficiency, performance and resale value of your vehicle.

When the vehicle is new, it should be serviced by a dealer service department (or other workshop recognised by the vehicle manufacturer as providing the same standard of service) in order to preserve the warranty. The vehicle manufacturer may reject warranty claims if you are unable to prove that servicing has been carried out as and when specified, using only original-equipment parts, or parts certified to be of equivalent quality.

Every 250 miles or weekly

☐ Refer to *Weekly checks*

Note: *If the air conditioning system is not regularly used, it should be operated at least once a week, all year round, for at least 10 minutes at a time to circulate the lubricating oil around its components.*

Every 6250 miles or 6 months, whichever comes first

Carry out all Weekly checks, then complete the following:

☐ Rotate the tyres (Section 3).
☐ Change the engine oil and filter element (Section 4).

Note: *Frequent oil and filter changes are good for the engine, so we recommend halving Honda's specified interval, which is 12 months or 12 500 miles.*

Every 12 500 miles or 12 months, whichever comes first

Carry out all checks listed under previous interval headings, then complete the following:

☐ Drain any water from the fuel filter (Section 5).
☐ Check the braking system (Section 6).
☐ Check the suspension and steering components for condition and security (Section 7).
☐ Check the condition of the driveshaft gaiters (Section 8).
☐ Check the condition of the hoses and lines (Section 9).
☐ Check the gearbox fluid level (Section 10).
☐ Check the final drive fluid level (Section 11).
☐ Check the condition of the exhaust system (Section 12).
☐ Carry out a road test (Section 13).
☐ Check the expiry date of the puncture repair bottle and renew if expired.

Every 25 000 miles or 2 years, whichever comes first

Carry out all checks listed under previous interval headings, then complete the following:

☐ Check the auxiliary drivebelt, and renew if necessary (Section 14).
☐ Renew the pollen filter elements* (Section 15).
☐ Renew the fuel filter (Section 16).

* **Note:** *Renew the pollen filter elements annually if the vehicle is used primarily in urban or dusty areas.*

Every 25 000 miles

Carry out all checks listed under previous interval headings, then complete the following:

☐ Renew the air filter element (Section 17).

Every 3 years, regardless of mileage

☐ Change the brake fluid (Section 18).

Every 62 500 miles or 5 years, whichever comes first

Carry out all checks listed under previous interval headings, then complete the following:

☐ Change the coolant (Section 19).

Note: *This renewal interval should be observed once only, at its* ***first*** *occurrence. Subsequently, even if the system is refilled with Honda's specified coolant, the recommended renewal interval drops to every 37 500 miles or 3 years, whichever comes first.*

Every 75 000 miles or 6 years, whichever comes first

Carry out all checks listed under previous interval headings, then complete the following:

☐ Check the engine idle speed (Section 20).

Every 75 000 miles or 8 years, whichever comes first

Carry out all checks listed under previous interval headings, then complete the following:

☐ Change the gearbox fluid (Section 21).
☐ Change the final drive fluid* (Section 22).

* **Note:** *This should be changed once only at this interval, at its* ***first*** *occurrence. Subsequently, Honda's renewal interval drops to every 37 500 miles or 4 years, whichever comes first.*

Component location – diesel models

Underbonnet view (acoustic engine cover removed)

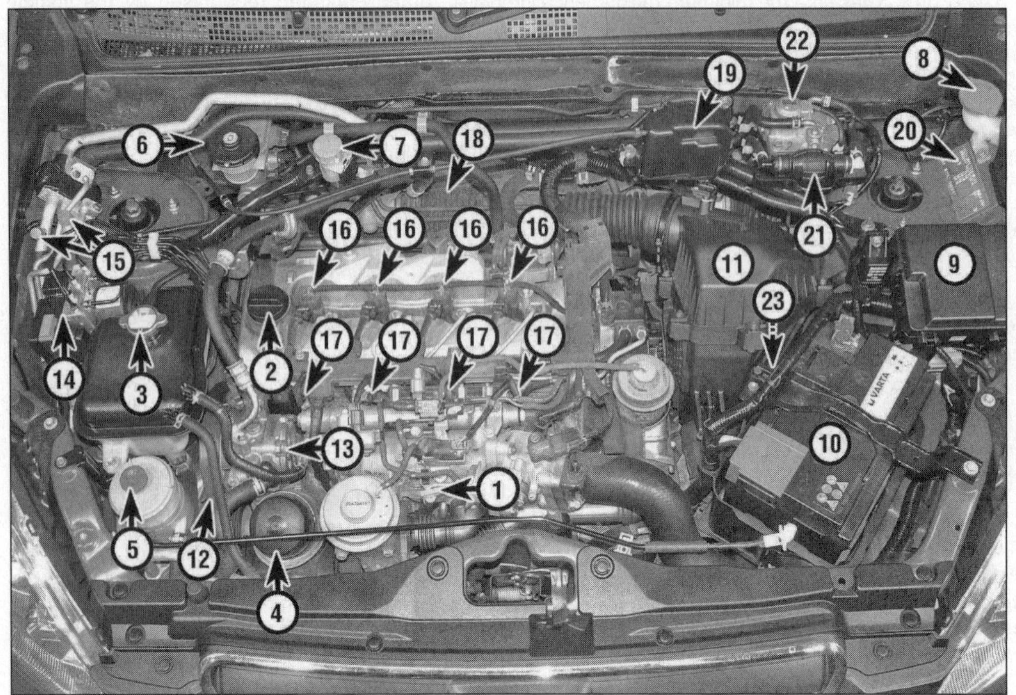

1 Engine oil level dipstick
2 Engine oil filler cap
3 Expansion tank filler cap
4 Engine oil filter
5 Power steering fluid reservoir
6 Brake fluid reservoir
7 Clutch fluid reservoir
8 Screen washer fluid reservoir filler
9 Engine compartment fuse/ relay box
10 Battery
11 Air cleaner
12 Auxiliary drivebelt
13 Power steering pump
14 ABS modulator-control unit
15 Air conditioning system sight glass and service valves
16 Fuel injectors
17 Glow plugs
18 Steering rack
19 Throttle cable quadrant/ accelerator pedal position sensor assembly
20 Vehicle identification plate
21 Fuel system hand primer
22 Fuel filter assembly
23 Location of gearbox fluid filler plug

Front underbody view (engine compartment undershield removed)

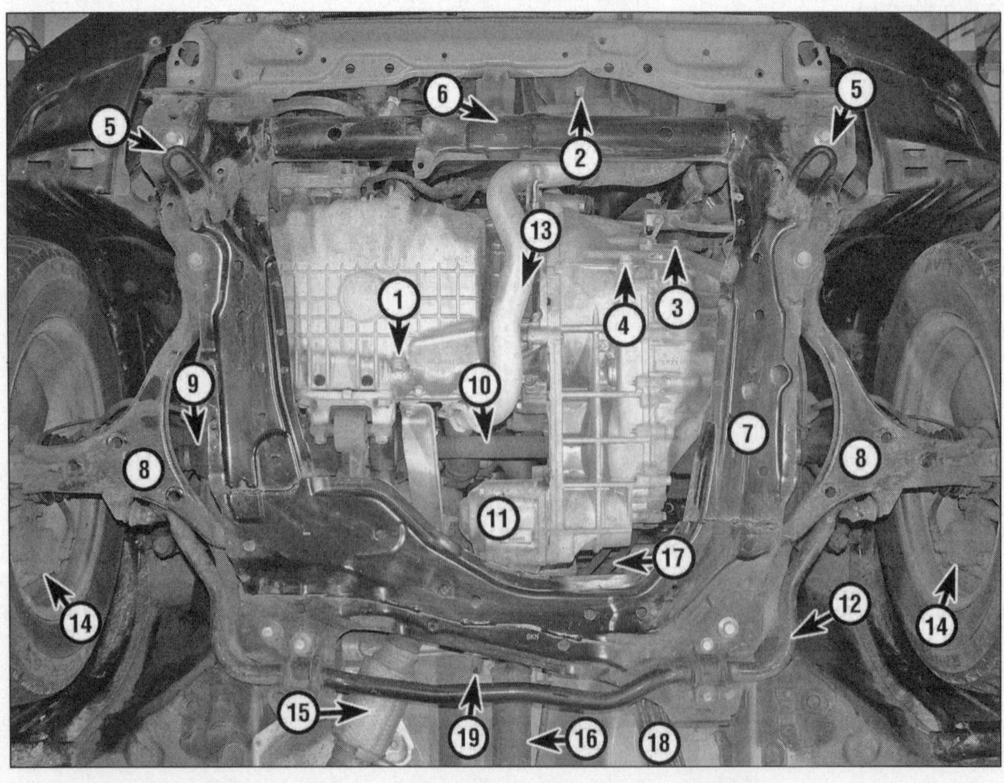

1 Engine oil drain plug
2 Radiator drain tap
3 Gearbox fluid level plug
4 Gearbox fluid drain plug
5 Transporter tie-down points (NOT for towing)
6 Front jacking point
7 Front suspension subframe
8 Front suspension lower arms
9 Right-hand driveshaft inboard joint
10 Right-hand driveshaft inboard (intermediate) shaft
11 Transfer case
12 Anti-roll bar
13 Turbocharger-to-intercooler pipe
14 Front brake calipers
15 Exhaust system flexible section
16 Propeller shaft
17 Gearchange cables
18 Braking system pipes
19 Air conditioning system evaporator drain tube

Rear underbody view

1 *Final drive fluid drain plug (filler/level plug above)*
2 *Final drive (Dual Pump section)*
3 *Final drive (rear differential section)*
4 *Driveshaft inboard joints*
5 *Driveshaft CV joint gaiters*
6 *Rear hub carriers*
7 *Rear wheel toe-adjusting bolts*
8 *Anti-roll bar*
9 *Rear jacking point*
10 *Rear suspension subframe*
11 *Rear suspension trailing arms*
12 *Rear suspension struts*
13 *Exhaust rear silencer*
14 *Fuel tank filler tube*
15 *Fuel tank*
16 *Trailing arm front mountings*
17 *Final drive front mounting*
18 *Propeller shaft*
19 *Exhaust pipe*
20 *Rear door sill jacking/support points*
21 *Handbrake cable*

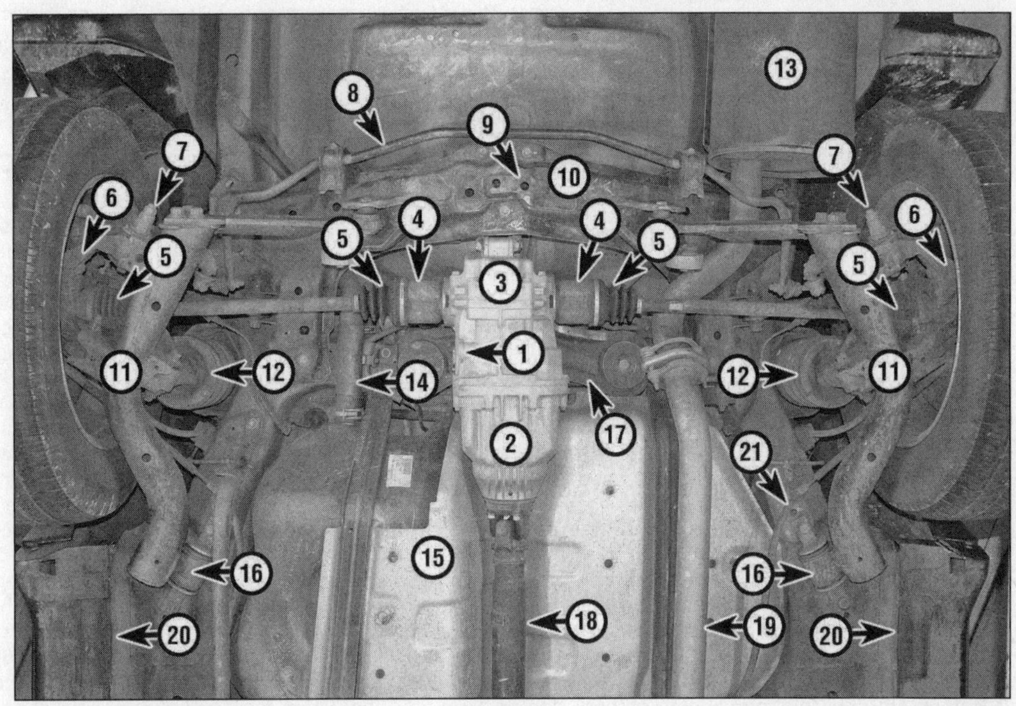

Maintenance procedures

1 General information

1 This Chapter is designed to help the home mechanic maintain his/her vehicle for safety, economy, long life and peak performance.

2 The Chapter contains a master maintenance schedule, followed by Sections dealing specifically with each task in the schedule. Visual checks, adjustments, component renewal and other helpful items are included. Refer to the accompanying illustrations of the engine compartment and the underside of the vehicle for the locations of the various components.

3 Servicing your vehicle in accordance with the mileage/time maintenance schedule and the following Sections will provide a planned maintenance programme, which should result in a long and reliable service life. This is a comprehensive plan, so maintaining some items but not others at the specified service intervals, will not produce the same results.

4 As you service your vehicle, you will discover that many of the procedures can be grouped together, because of the particular procedure being performed, or because of the proximity of two otherwise-unrelated components to one another. For example, if the vehicle is raised for any reason, the exhaust can be inspected at the same time as the suspension and steering components.

5 The first step in this maintenance programme is to prepare yourself before the actual work begins. Read through all the Sections relevant to the work to be carried out, then make a list and gather all the parts and tools required. If a problem is encountered, seek advice from a parts specialist, or a dealer service department.

2 Regular maintenance

1 If, from the time the vehicle is new, the routine maintenance schedule is followed closely, and frequent checks are made of fluid levels and high-wear items, as suggested throughout this manual, the engine will be kept in relatively good running condition, and the need for additional work will be minimised.

2 It is possible that there will be times when the engine is running poorly due to the lack of regular maintenance. This is even more likely if a used vehicle, which has not received regular and frequent maintenance checks, is purchased. In such cases, additional work may need to be carried out, outside of the regular maintenance intervals.

3 If engine wear is suspected, a compression test (refer to Chapter 2B) will provide valuable information regarding the overall performance of the main internal components. Such a test can be used as a basis to decide on the extent of the work to be carried out. If, for example, a compression test indicates serious internal engine wear, conventional maintenance as described in this Chapter will not greatly improve the performance of the engine, and may prove a waste of time and money, unless extensive overhaul work is carried out first.

4 The following series of operations are those most often required to improve the performance of a generally poor-running engine:

Primary operations

a) Clean, inspect and test the battery (refer to Weekly checks).
b) Check all the engine-related fluids (refer to Weekly checks).
c) Check the condition and tension of the auxiliary drivebelt (Section 14).
d) Check the condition of the air filter, and renew if necessary (Section 17).
e) Check the condition of all hoses, and check for fluid leaks (Section 9).
f) Renew the fuel filter (Section 16).

5 If the above operations do not prove fully effective, carry out the following secondary operations:

Secondary operations

All items listed under *Primary operations*, plus the following:

a) Check the charging system (refer to Chapter 5A).
b) Check the fuel system (refer to Chapter 4B).

Maintenance Required indicator

6 Some models are fitted with a 'Maintenance required' indicator in the tachometer which reminds the driver of when scheduled maintenance is required for the vehicle.

7 Whenever scheduled maintenance is complete by a dealer, the indicator will be reset. The indicator can be reset as follows:

a) *Switch off the ignition.*

b) *Press and hold the 'Select/Reset' button in the lower right corner of the instrument panel.*

c) *Switch on the ignition and hold the 'Select/Reset' button until the indicator resets (which will take approximately ten seconds).*

Every 6250 miles or 6 months

3 Tyre rotation

Refer to Chapter 1A, Section 4.

4 Engine oil and filter element renewal

Note: *In addition to the oil and filter, a new drain plug sealing washer and filter sealing O-rings will be required.*

1 Frequent oil and filter changes are the most important preventative maintenance procedures which can be undertaken by the DIY owner. As engine oil ages, it becomes diluted and contaminated, which leads to premature engine wear.

2 Before starting this procedure, gather together all the necessary tools and materials. Also make sure that you have plenty of clean rags and newspapers handy, to mop-up any spills. Ideally, the engine oil should be warm, as it will drain more easily, and more built-up sludge will be removed with it. Take care not to touch the exhaust or any other hot parts of the engine when working under the vehicle. To avoid any possibility of scalding, and to protect yourself from possible skin irritants and other harmful contaminants in used engine oils, it is advisable to wear gloves when carrying out this work.

3 Unscrew the four retaining nuts and remove the acoustic engine cover **(see illustrations)**. Remove the oil filler cap.

4 Firmly apply the handbrake, then jack up the front of the vehicle and support it securely on axle stands (see *Jacking and vehicle support*).

5 Working underneath the vehicle, unscrew its securing bolt and remove the access flap in the engine compartment undershield that provides access to the engine oil (sump) drain plug **(see illustrations)**.

6 Using a spanner, or preferably a suitable socket and bar, slacken the drain plug (at the rear of the sump) about half a turn. Position the draining container under the drain plug, then remove the plug completely and discard the sealing washer – this must be renewed as a matter of course whenever it is disturbed. Allow some time for the oil to drain, noting that it may be necessary to reposition the container as the oil flow slows to a trickle.

7 After all the oil has drained, wipe the drain plug with a clean rag and fit the new sealing washer **(see illustration)**. Clean the area around the drain plug opening, and refit the plug complete with washer and tighten it to the specified torque. Refit the access flap and tighten its bolt securely; note the specified torque wrench setting. Remove the draining container with the old oil and all tools from under the vehicle and lower the vehicle to the ground.

8 Place clean rag around the oil filter, which is located at the front right-hand end of the engine, to prevent old oil from being spilt on to surrounding components, particularly the auxiliary drivebelt. Use an oil filter removal tool to slacken the filter cap, then unscrew it by hand the rest of the way **(see illustration)**. The Honda service tool for this task is Part No. 04151-RBD-305; either acquire the use of one of these or find its commercial equivalent.

9 Carefully lift out the filter assembly; place it immediately in a drip tray or other suitable container and do not allow oil to drip on other components. Very carefully wipe out the filter chamber using kitchen towel or clean rag; remove all traces of old oil and any other

4.3a Unscrew four retaining nuts . . .

4.3b . . . and lift off acoustic engine cover

4.5a Unscrew securing bolt . . .

4.5b . . . and withdraw engine compartment undershield flap to reach engine oil (sump) drain plug

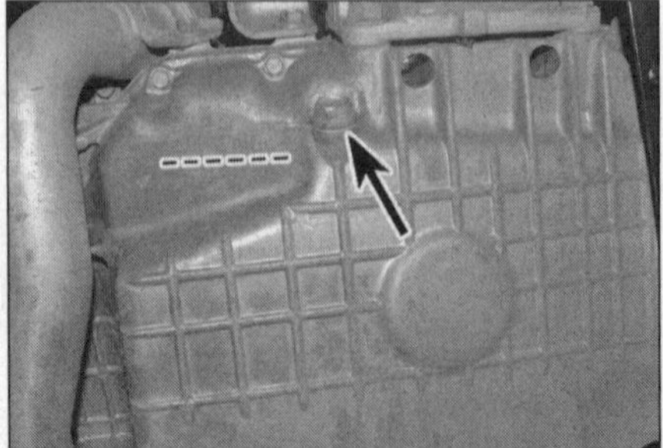

4.5c Helpful inscription in sump shows location of engine oil drain plug, in case there is any doubt

4.7 Fit new sealing washer and tighten engine oil (sump) drain plug to specified torque wrench setting

4.8 Using a filter removal tool to unscrew oil filter cap

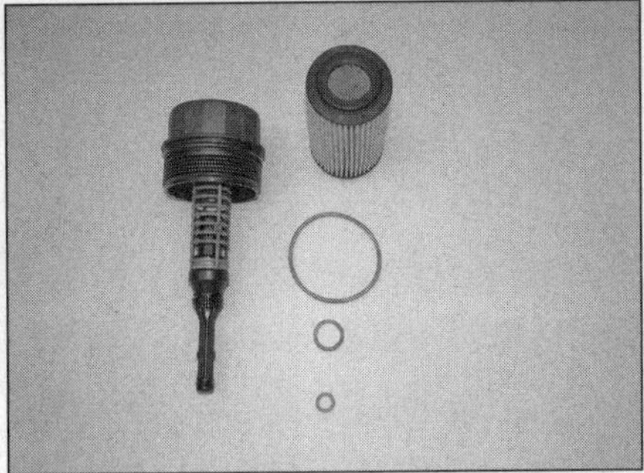

4.11a Components of engine oil filter assembly

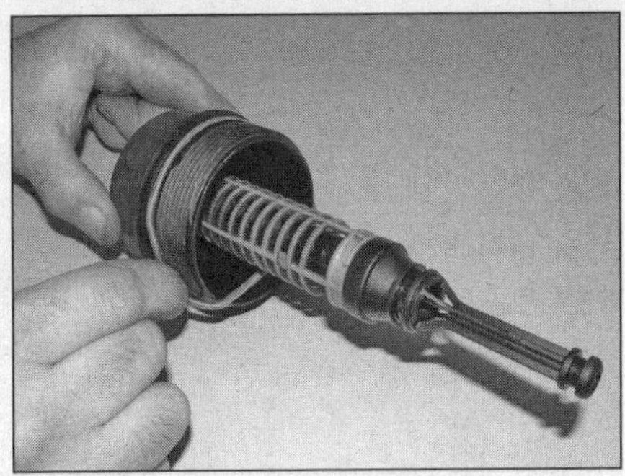

4.11b Fit largest O-ring to cap . . .

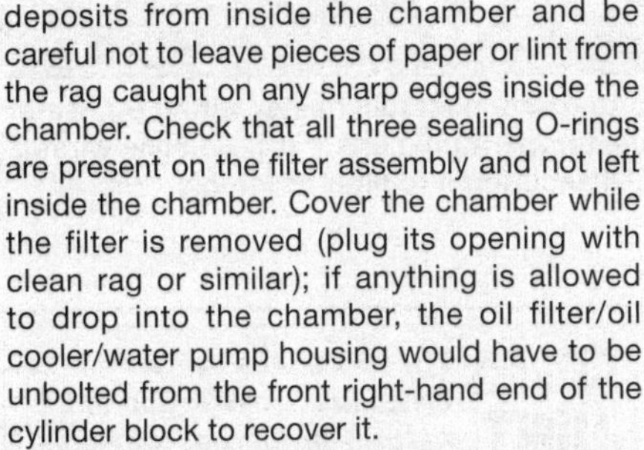

deposits from inside the chamber and be careful not to leave pieces of paper or lint from the rag caught on any sharp edges inside the chamber. Check that all three sealing O-rings are present on the filter assembly and not left inside the chamber. Cover the chamber while the filter is removed (plug its opening with clean rag or similar); if anything is allowed to drop into the chamber, the oil filter/oil cooler/water pump housing would have to be unbolted from the front right-hand end of the cylinder block to recover it.

10 Remove the old filter element and all three sealing O-rings from the filter cap. Wash the filter cap in solvent and clean it with a brush, then wipe it dry. The filter cap and chamber must be scrupulously clean before reassembly can commence.

11 Fit the large sealing O-ring to the groove in the cap, then the medium-sized O-ring to the mid-point of the filter cap's stem and the smallest O-ring to the groove at its tip. Carefully fit the new filter element to the cap's stem, ensuring that the seals at either end of the element are not dislodged or damaged, then lubricate the O-rings with clean engine oil before fitting the filter assembly to the chamber **(see illustrations)**.

12 Tighten the filter cap to the specified torque wrench setting. Do NOT overtighten the cap; it is made of synthetic material and will break or distort if over-stressed **(see illustration)**. Refit the acoustic engine cover and tighten securely its retaining nuts.

13 Fill the engine through the oil filler hole, using the correct grade and type of oil (refer to *Weekly checks* for details of topping-up). Pour in half the specified quantity of oil first, then wait a few minutes for the oil to drain into the sump. Continue to add oil, a small quantity at a time, until the level is up to the lower mark on the dipstick.

14 Start the engine and run it for a few minutes, while checking for leaks around the oil filter seal and the sump drain plug. Note that there may be a delay of a few seconds before the low oil pressure warning light goes out when the engine is first started, as the oil circulates through the new oil filter and the engine oil galleries before the pressure builds-up.

15 Stop the engine, and wait a few minutes for the oil to settle in the sump once more. With the new oil circulated and the filter now completely full, recheck the level on the dipstick, and add more oil as necessary.

16 Dispose of the used engine oil safely with reference to *General repair procedures*. It should be noted that used oil filters should not be included with domestic waste. Most used oil 'banks' also have filter disposal points alongside.

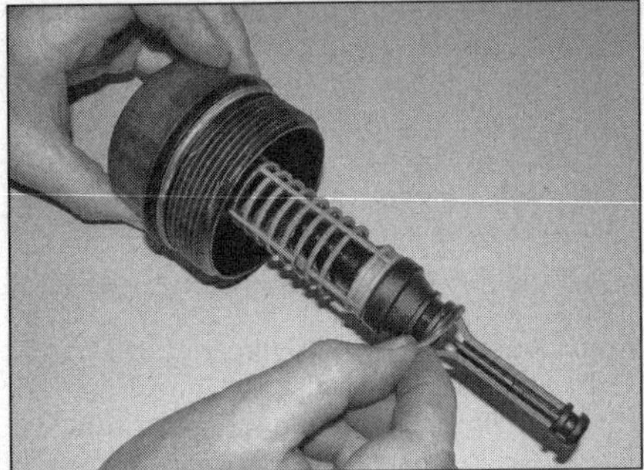

4.11c . . . medium sized O-ring to cap stem middle groove . . .

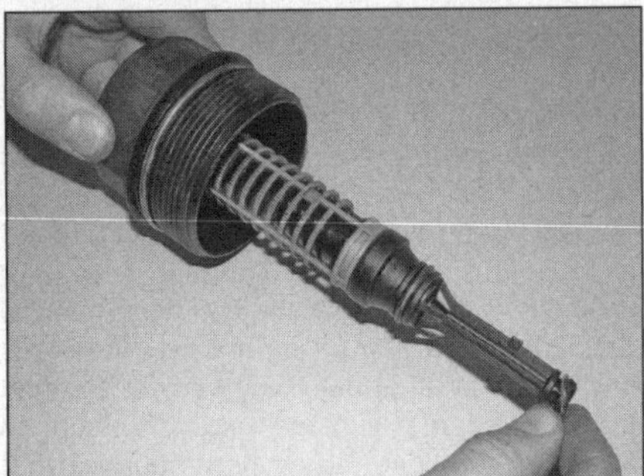

4.11d . . . and smallest O-ring to groove at cap tip

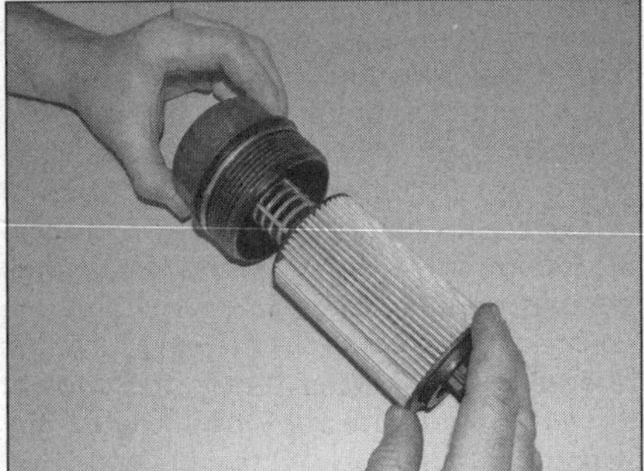

4.11e Take care not to dislodge or damage seals when fitting new filter element to cap

4.11f Lubricate filter sealing O-rings with clean engine oil . . .

4.11g . . . and fit filter assembly to the filter chamber

4.12 Tighten engine oil filter cap to specified torque wrench setting

5.3 Unclip hand primer, then undo primer bracket mounting bolts (A) and unclip wiring (B) from bracket

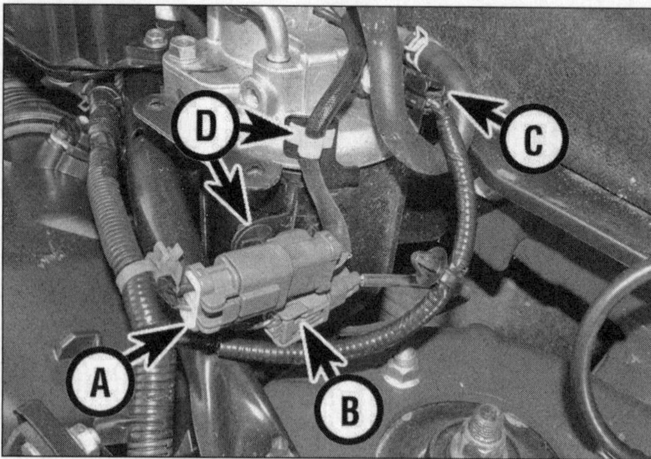

5.4 Unplug connectors to disconnect fuel heater wiring (A), water level switch (B) and fuel temperature sensor (C). Release wiring from clips (D) securing it to filter assembly

Every 12 500 miles or 12 months

5 Fuel filter water draining

Caution: Before starting any work on the fuel filter, wipe clean the filter assembly and the area around it; it is essential that no dirt or other foreign matter is allowed into the system. Obtain a suitable clean container into which the filter can be drained and place rags or similar material around and under the filter assembly to catch any spillages. Do not allow diesel fuel to leak into the clutch bellhousing or it will contaminate the clutch friction plate material which will cause severe clutch slip which can be cured only by the renewal of the clutch plate and the degreasing of all fouled surfaces. Similarly, diesel fuel should never be allowed to contaminate components such as the steering rack, the alternator and starter motor, the coolant hoses and engine mountings, and any wiring.

1 The Water in Diesel Filter Indicator lamp in the instrument panel illuminates when the ignition is switched on as a check of its function (have the vehicle checked by a Honda dealer if it does not, at any time). If the lamp lights while the vehicle is being driven, this shows that an unacceptable amount of water is present in the fuel filter and that this must be drained out at the earliest possible moment to prevent water from getting any further into the injection system and provoking misfiring and uneven engine performance. If you do not do the job yourself, the vehicle MUST be taken to a Honda dealer or diesel injection specialist as soon as possible for the water to be drained out and any resulting fault diagnosis and repair to be carried out. If water is allowed to reach the common-rail injection system's fuel pump or injectors these components will be damaged and will be very expensive indeed to repair. To prevent this situation from ever arising in the first place, the fuel filter must be drained once a year (or more often, if there is any doubt at all about the quality of the fuel that has been put in the vehicle's tank), to flush out any water and other impurities that may have gathered there.

5.5a Use brake hose clamps to prevent escape of diesel fuel and entry of dirt into fuel system when disconnecting fuel supply hoses

5.5b Use plenty of clean rag to catch spilt diesel fuel when disconnecting fuel supply hoses from fuel filter pipes

The presence of water in diesel fuel tanks is due to the natural properties of diesel fuel, which make moisture-related problems more likely than with petrol tanks. Diesel fuel's lower volatility allows air and moisture to infiltrate the diesel fuel in both vehicle and bulk storage tanks much faster than petrol. The longer the fuel is stored, the larger the problems of water condensation become. The best way of avoiding this is to buy fuel only from outlets that sell high-quality brands of fuel and/or have a high turnover, so that the storage tanks are more likely to be properly-maintained and there is less chance of the fuel containing significant amounts of water.

2 The filter has a drain cock in its base, but this is inaccessible (unless it can be reached from underneath, via the steering rack/track rod aperture in the left-hand wheel arch, or by removing the air cleaner assembly as described in Chapter 4B). The easiest way of draining the filter is to unbolt and remove it, as follows:

3 Unclip the fuel system hand primer, unbolt it and release the wiring from the primer bracket **(see illustration)**.

4 Unplug their connectors to disconnect the wiring from the fuel heater, the water level switch and the fuel temperature sensor. Release the wiring from the clips securing it to the filter assembly **(see illustration)**.

5 Clamp the fuel hoses using brake hose clamps, carefully wrap each hose union in turn in clean rag, use pliers to release its spring securing clip and disconnect the hose from the filter assembly pipe. As noted above, take every possible precaution to prevent diesel fuel from spraying or dripping on to other components **(see illustrations)**. If brake hose

5.6a Unscrew two mounting bolts . . .

5.6b . . . and lift out fuel filter assembly

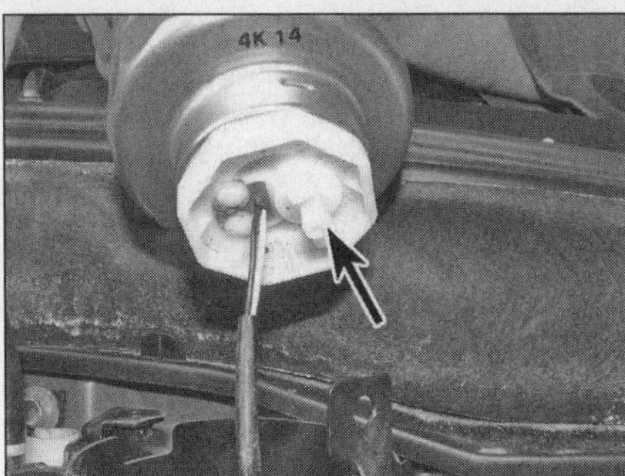
5.7a Fuel filter drain cock is located at the bottom of the filter assembly

clamps are not available, unplug each hose in turn and plug it as quickly as possible to prevent diesel fuel from contaminating other components and to prevent dirt from getting into the fuel system.

6 Unscrew the two bolts and lift out the filter assembly **(see illustrations)**.

7 Open the drain cock and allow the filter to drain into a clean container **(see illustrations)**. Close the drain cock and mop-up any spilt fuel, then check the container for signs of water or dirt in the drained fuel. **Note:** *If significant amounts of water or dirt are drained out of the fuel filter at any time, the fuel tank must be drained, flushed out and refilled. Since the fuel tank does not have a drain plug, this can be done only by removing the fuel gauge sender unit as described in Chapter 4B, and by using a hand pump to empty the contents of the tank into a container (which must be capable of holding diesel fuel safely). The tank must then be removed so that it can be rinsed out with clean diesel fuel until it is completely clean and all traces of water and dirt are removed.*

8 Refitting is the reverse of removal. Tighten securely the filter assembly mounting bolts **(see illustration)**. Ensure that the fuel hoses are correctly reconnected and securely fastened by their spring clips, and that the wiring is correctly routed and clipped into place on the filter assembly and the hand primer bracket.

9 Once the filter assembly is refitted, operate the hand primer as many times as necessary (40 or 50 strokes) until the filter and hoses are refilled with diesel fuel and the primer becomes hard. Start the engine and keep it running at a fast idle until it is running smoothly, then allow it to idle and check for signs of fuel leakage. If the engine does not start first time – do NOT operate the starter for more than 30 seconds at a time, or there is a risk of damage to the starter motor and to the common-rail injection system's fuel pump – operate the hand primer again until it becomes hard, then try again.

10 On completion, dispose safely of the drained fuel. Check carefully all disturbed components to ensure that there are no leaks (of air or fuel) when the engine is restarted.

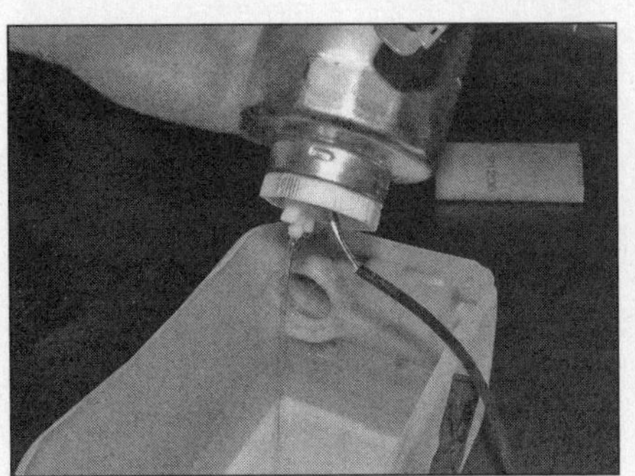
5.7b Drain filter into a clean container – you have to be able to see what's coming out, and whether there's any water, etc, in it

6 Braking system check

Refer to Chapter 1A, Section 6.

7 Suspension and steering check

Refer to Chapter 1A, Section 7.

8 Driveshaft CV joint gaiter check

Refer to Chapter 1A, Section 8.

9 Hose and fluid leak check

Refer to Chapter 1A, Section 9.

10 Gearbox fluid level check

Note: *The transfer case shares the same lubricant as the gearbox. In addition to the fluid that may be needed, new filler and level plug sealing washers will be required.*

5.8 Tighten filter assembly mounting bolts securely

1 To check the fluid level, the gearbox should ideally be at normal operating temperature (after a run of 5 miles or more). The vehicle should be parked so that it is absolutely level from front-to-rear and from side-to-side; switch off the ignition and apply the handbrake firmly. Direct access is from the front and from above – if the vehicle has to be jacked up for access (see *Jacking and vehicle support*), be careful to keep it level.

2 Remove the engine compartment undershield (see Chapter 11).

3 The fluid level is checked by removing the level plug, which is located in the front face of the gearbox **(see illustration)**. Remove all traces of dirt from around the level plug, unscrew the plug, and recover the sealing washer; discard the original washer, which should be renewed whenever it is disturbed.

10.3 Removing gearbox fluid level plug to check fluid level in gearbox – fit a new washer

10.4a Gearbox fluid filler plug is reached between battery and air cleaner . . .

10.4b . . . shown here with battery and air cleaner removed, for clarity . . .

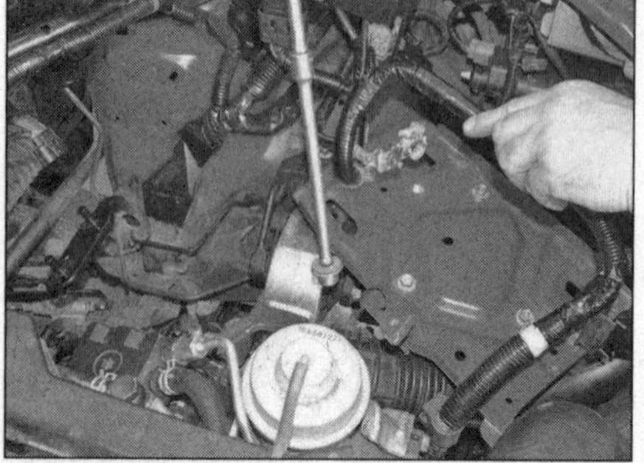
10.4c Gearbox fluid filler plug needs a square key – apply a dab of stiff grease to stick the plug to the key so it doesn't drop off and get lost

10.4d Topping-up gearbox fluid

Be prepared for a small amount of fluid to leak out when the plug is removed; if fluid pours out, refit the level plug and check very carefully that the vehicle is level from front-to-rear as well as from side-to-side. Remove the plug again and allow any surplus to drain off. If the fluid level is correct, it should be up to the lower edge of the hole; it may be easier to use an Allen key as a dipstick to see where the level is in relation to the edge of the hole.

4 If the fluid level is too low, add more through the filler hole in the top of the gearbox; this is reached using long extension bars passed down between the battery and the air cleaner assembly. The filler plug is undone using a square key – we found that the 3/8-inch square fitting on a socket extension bar will fit. The flexible tube equipping most transmission fluid bottles being too short, it will be necessary to use a funnel and hose to get fluid into the gearbox without spilling it everywhere. Stop filling when fresh fluid begins to run out of the hole and allow any surplus to drain off **(see illustrations)**.

Squeeze in a little fresh fluid at a time until it starts to run out of the level hole. If a lot of fluid has had to be added, refit the filler and level plugs and take the vehicle for a short drive to distribute the new fluid around the gearbox components, then on your return, allow time for the fluid level to settle before removing the level plug and allowing the surplus to drain off.

5 Refit both plugs with new sealing washers and tighten each securely, to its specified torque wrench setting. Drive the vehicle a short distance, then check for leaks before refitting the engine compartment undershield.

11 Final drive fluid level check

Refer to Chapter 1A, Section 11.

12 Exhaust system inspection

Refer to Chapter 1A, Section 12.

13 Road test

Refer to Chapter 1A, Section 13.

Every 25 000 miles or 2 years

14 Auxiliary drivebelt check and renewal

Note: *A shorter drivebelt may be found on some vehicles, running straight from the alternator pulley to the water pump pulley, the idler pulley having been deleted. It would appear that only the shorter drivebelt is available from Honda dealers, and that if such a drivebelt is supplied, the idler pulley, with its washers, bearing, centre bush and bolt, must be scrapped* ***(see illustration).***

14.0 Idler pulley, with its washers, bearing, centre bush and bolt, must be scrapped if shorter auxiliary drivebelt is supplied

General

1 The auxiliary drivebelt is of the flat, multi-ribbed (or 'polyvee') type, and is located on the right-hand end of the engine. It drives the alternator, water pump, steering pump and the air conditioning compressor from the engine's crankshaft pulley **(see illustration)**.

2 The good condition and proper tension of the auxiliary drivebelt are critical to the operation of the engine. An automatic spring-loaded tensioner eliminates any need for drivebelt maintenance beyond a periodic check of its condition.

3 Because of their composition and the high stresses to which they are subjected, drivebelts wear and deteriorate as they get older. They must, therefore, be regularly inspected.

Drivebelt condition check

4 With the engine switched off (take out the key), open and support the bonnet. Unscrew the four retaining nuts and remove the acoustic engine cover. For improved access to the right-hand end of the engine, first slacken the right-hand front roadwheel nuts, then jack up the front right-hand side of the vehicle and support it securely on an axle stand (see *Jacking and vehicle support*). Remove the roadwheel, then release the two securing clips and prise back the wheel arch liner section of the engine compartment undershield as necessary to reach the crankshaft pulley and bolt. Unclip the steering fluid reservoir and unbolt the cooling system expansion tank and its mounting bracket from the right-hand inner wing. Secure both reservoir and tank to one side without disconnecting or straining their hoses or spilling their contents **(see illustrations)**.

5 Using an inspection light or an electric torch, and rotating the engine when necessary with a spanner applied to the crankshaft pulley bolt, check the whole length of the drivebelt for cracks in the rubber, separation of the belt plies, and torn or worn ribs **(see illustration)**. Also check for fraying and glazing, which gives the drivebelt a shiny appearance. Check the pulleys for nicks, cracks, distortion and corrosion.

6 Both sides of the drivebelt should be inspected, which means you will have to twist the drivebelt to check the ribbed surface. Use your fingers to feel the drivebelt where you can't see it.

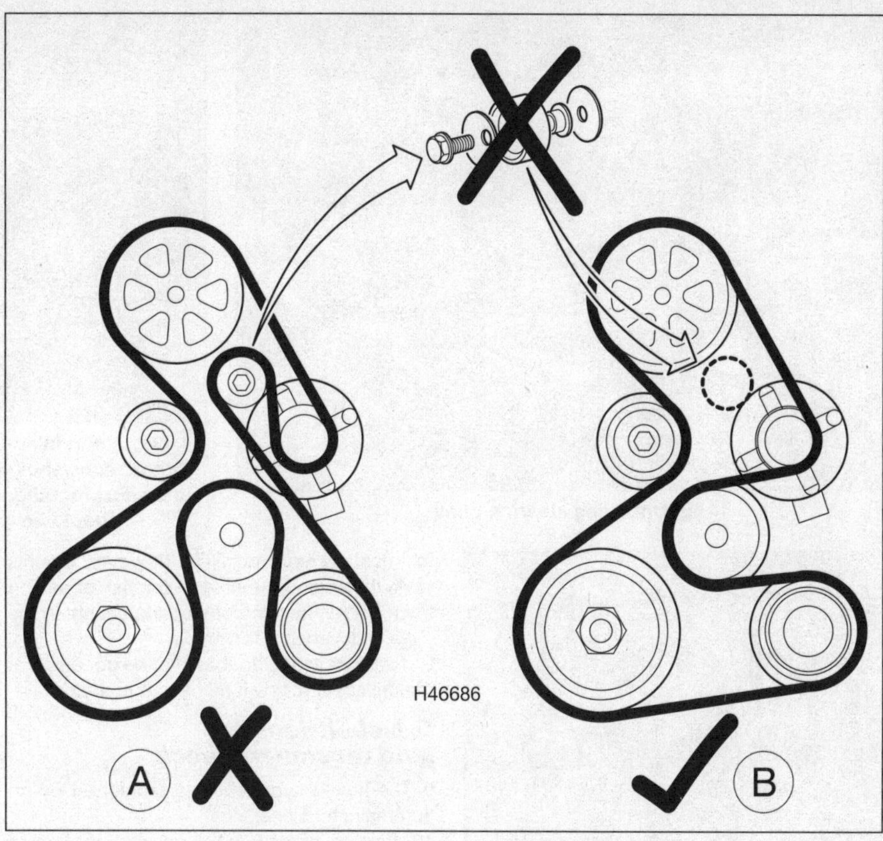

14.1 Routing of auxiliary drivebelt

A Original routing with long drivebelt and idler pulley

B Revised routing with shorter drivebelt and without idler pulley

14.4a Unclip steering fluid reservoir . . .

14.4b . . . then unscrew expansion tank mounting bracket front mounting bolt on wing . . .

14.4c . . . rear inboard mounting bolt . . .

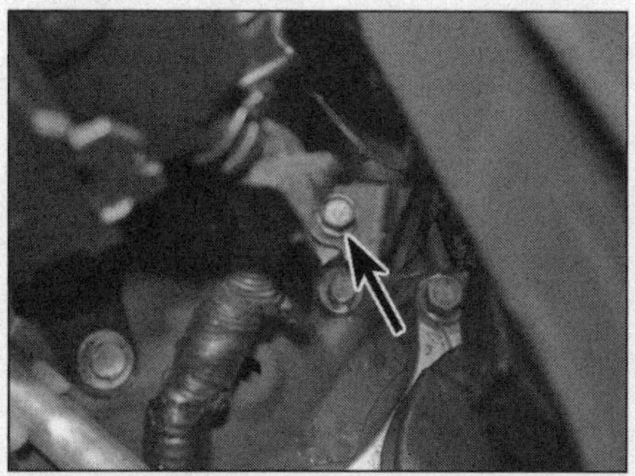

14.4d . . . and rear outboard mounting bolt to remove cooling system expansion tank

7 Check the state of wear of the drivebelt as follows. With the engine stopped, the fixed line marked on the tensioner body should be somewhere in the range marked by the long and the short rectangular reference marks cast on the tensioner arm **(see illustration 14.15b)**. If the fixed line indicates beyond the short rectangular mark, then the drivebelt is worn out and must be renewed. The marks are extremely difficult to see, being partially hidden by the

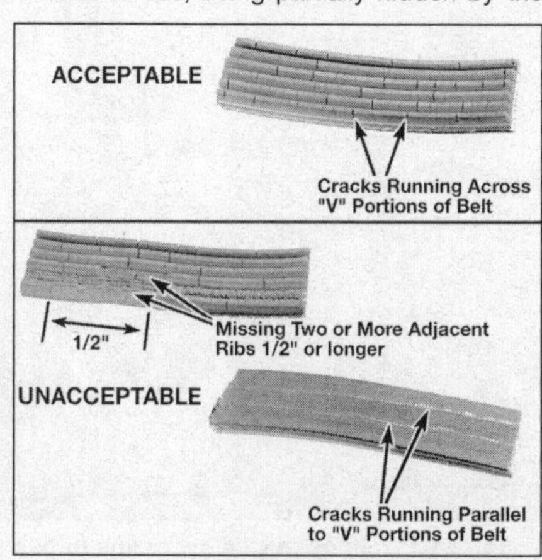

14.5 Check very carefully for some of the more common faults found on multi-ribbed auxiliary drivebelts

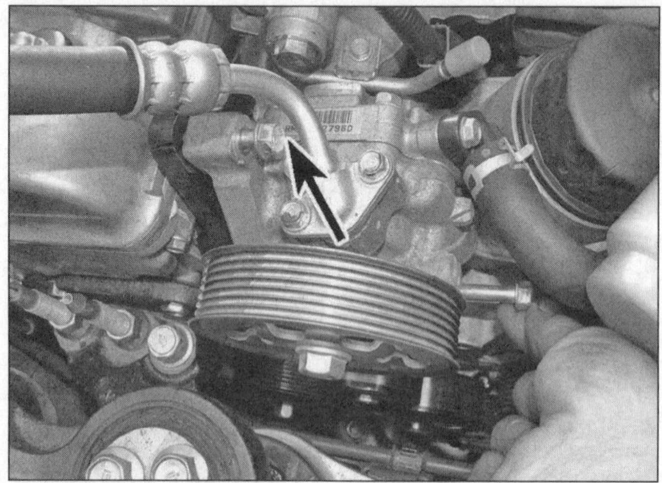
14.12 Unbolting steering pump . . .

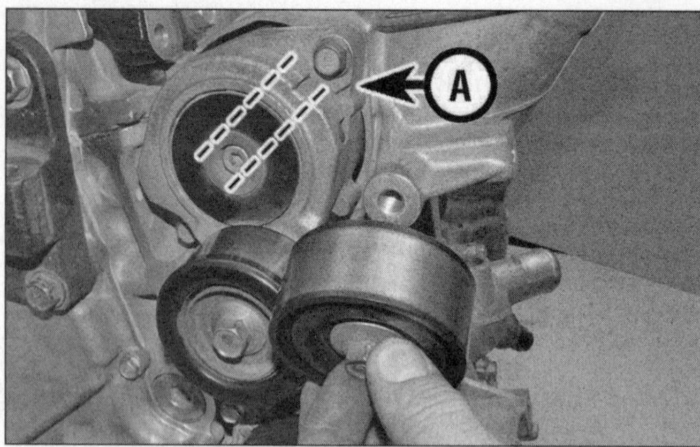

14.13 . . . and idler pulley. Note location of tensioner fixed line (A). Dotted lines show normal range marked by tensioner arm long and short rectangular reference marks – tensioner fixed line (A) should be within this range if drivebelt is unworn

14.14 Unscrew three mounting bolts to remove tensioner . . .

tensioner front mounting bolt's head, underneath the steering pump, and obscured by the steering pump fluid intake hose and by the drivebelt itself **(see illustration 14.13)**. Removing the steering fluid reservoir and cooling system expansion tank might improve matters, but an electric torch and a small mirror on a balljointed stem will be the only solution for most owners; do NOT, however, do this while the engine is running – the risk of getting torch, mirror, hair and/or clothing caught in the moving drivebelt is too great.

8 If you are in any doubt as to the condition of the drivebelt, renew it as described below.

Drivebelt tension (and tensioner) check

9 The auxiliary drivebelt is tensioned by an automatic tensioner.

10 If you suspect that the drivebelt is slipping and/or running slack, or that the tensioner is otherwise faulty, check the operation of the tensioner as follows. Unscrew the four retaining nuts and remove the acoustic engine cover. With the engine stopped, the fixed line marked on the tensioner body should be somewhere in the range marked by the long and the short rectangular reference marks cast on the tensioner arm (see paragraph 7 above). Have an assistant start the engine, but be careful to keep your hands and clothing well clear of the drivebelt. If the rectangular marks move in relation to the fixed line as the engine is started, or if their position varies as the engine is idling, then the tensioner is faulty and must be renewed. Listen for abnormal noises (whistling, whining, grinding or screeching) from the tensioner pulley; if any such sounds are heard, the pulley bearings are worn and it must be renewed. To remove either the tensioner and/or the pulley and to check further the tensioner's operation, first remove the drivebelt as described in paragraphs 17 to 20 below.

11 With a long spanner (or two shorter spanners used together) applied to the tensioner pulley bolt, move the tensioner pulley and arm clockwise as far as possible, then release them slowly and carefully; do NOT allow the tensioner arm to snap back against spring pressure – it will break. Check that the tensioner works properly, with strong spring pressure being felt when its pulley and arm are rotated clockwise, and a smooth return to the limit of its travel when released. Listen

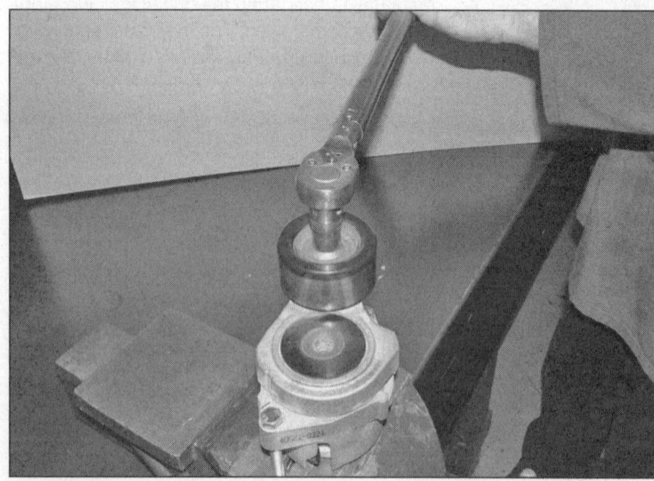
14.15a . . . clamp in vice by means of two 8 mm bolts passed through tensioner body's mounting bolt holes . . .

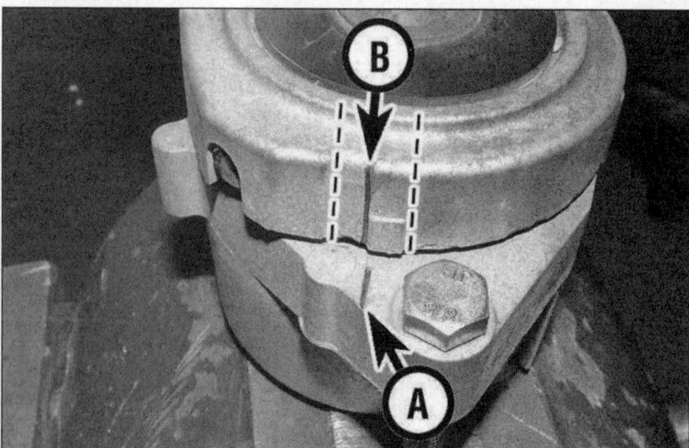

14.15b . . . and use torque wrench to measure force needed to align centre line (B) of tensioner arm reference marks with tensioner body fixed line mark (A). Dotted lines show normal range marked by tensioner arm long and short rectangular reference marks – tensioner body fixed line mark (A) should be within this range if drivebelt is unworn

14.19a Move tensioner pulley and arm clockwise until drivebelt can be slipped off pulleys. Note original routing with long drivebelt and idler pulley

14.19b Using two spanners together to move tensioner pulley and arm clockwise until drivebelt can be slipped off pulleys. Note revised routing with shorter drivebelt and without idler pulley

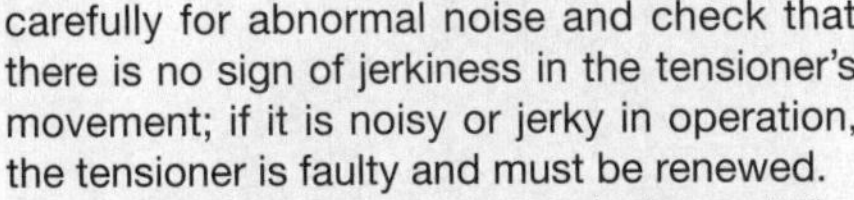

carefully for abnormal noise and check that there is no sign of jerkiness in the tensioner's movement; if it is noisy or jerky in operation, the tensioner is faulty and must be renewed.

12 Unscrew its two mounting bolts and dismount the steering pump; move it to one side and secure it out of the way without disconnecting or straining its hoses **(see illustration)**.

13 If it is still fitted, unscrew its central mounting bolt and remove the idler pulley **(see illustration)**.

14 Unscrew its three mounting bolts and remove the tensioner **(see illustration)**.

15 To check the tensioner's operation, clamp it in a vice by means of two 8 mm bolts passed through the body's mounting bolt holes – fit the vice with soft jaw covers to protect the bolt threads and ensure that no part of the tensioner body itself is clamped in the vice. Temporarily refit the tensioner pulley, tightening its central mounting bolt to the specified torque wrench setting, and use a torque wrench applied to the pulley bolt to measure the force needed to bring the centre line dividing the two rectangular reference marks cast on the tensioner arm into alignment with the fixed arrow mark cast on the tensioner body **(see illustrations)**. If the torque needed to line up the arrow and line is greater or lesser than the range specified, the tensioner is faulty and must be renewed.

16 Refitting is the reverse of the removal procedure; tighten all bolts to the torque wrench settings specified and check that the tensioner operates correctly (see paragraph 11 above) before refitting the drivebelt.

Drivebelt renewal

Note: *Honda recommend that the auxiliary drivebelt be renewed as a matter of course whenever it is removed. It would be useful to have the aid of an assistant to compress the tensioner while the auxiliary drivebelt is slipped on and off the pulleys. Be very careful to avoid the risk of personal injury through trapped fingers, etc.*

17 Gain access to the drivebelt as described in paragraph 4.

18 If the existing drivebelt is to be refitted, mark it, or note the maker's markings on its flat surface, so that it can be installed the same way round.

19 With a long spanner (or two shorter spanners used together) applied to the tensioner pulley bolt, move the tensioner pulley and arm clockwise until the drivebelt can be slipped off the first pulley, then release them slowly and carefully; do NOT allow the tensioner arm to snap back against spring pressure – it will break **(see illustrations)**.

20 Working from the wheel arch or engine compartment as necessary, and noting its routing, slip the drivebelt off the remaining pulleys and withdraw it.

21 Check all the pulleys, ensuring that their grooves are clean, and removing all traces of oil and grease. Clean any rust, dirt or rubber deposits from the working surfaces of the water pump and tensioner pulleys.

22 If the original drivebelt is being refitted, use the marks or notes made on removal to ensure that it is installed to run in the direction as it was previously. To fit a drivebelt, arrange it on the pulleys so that it is centred in their grooves **(see illustration)**, and not overlapping their raised sides (note that the flat surface of the drivebelt is engaged on the water pump and tensioner pulleys) and routed correctly. When it is installed on all but one pulleys, move the tensioner pulley and arm clockwise, slip the drivebelt onto the final pulley and release the tensioner pulley and arm. If the shorter drivebelt is supplied as a new part when the longer type was originally fitted, the idler pulley must be unbolted and discarded and the different routing must be used **(see illustration 14.1)**.

23 Using a spanner applied to the crankshaft pulley bolt, rotate the crankshaft through at least two full turns clockwise to settle the drivebelt on the pulleys, then check that the drivebelt is properly installed.

24 Refit the components removed for access, then (where applicable) lower the vehicle to the ground. If the right-hand roadwheel was removed, tighten the wheel nuts to the specified torque.

Alternator pulley check

25 The alternator pulley incorporates a one-way over-run clutch mechanism to absorb the shock loads placed on the auxiliary drivebelt which are particular to diesels – especially modern common-rail diesels. This reduces variations in tension, minimises shock loads and vibration in the drivebelt which might otherwise damage it and reduces noise from the drivebelt components. If this over-run clutch seizes it can damage the auxilliary drivebelt.

26 The operation of the alternator pulley should be checked whenever the auxiliary drivebelt is removed for servicing or during the course of other repair work, or if noise and vibrations are experienced which lead one to suspect a problem in this area.

27 To check the operation of the alternator pulley one-way clutch mechanism, prevent the alternator rotor from rotating by removing the pulley centre cap and by holding the pulley with a 17 mm Allen key or similar applied to its

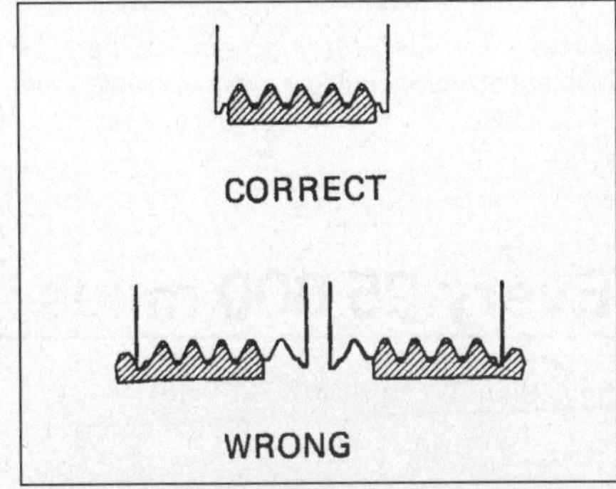

14.22 When installing an auxiliary drivebelt, make sure it is centred on pulleys – it must not overlap to either side

14.27 Pulley should rotate smoothly in one direction but lock in the other

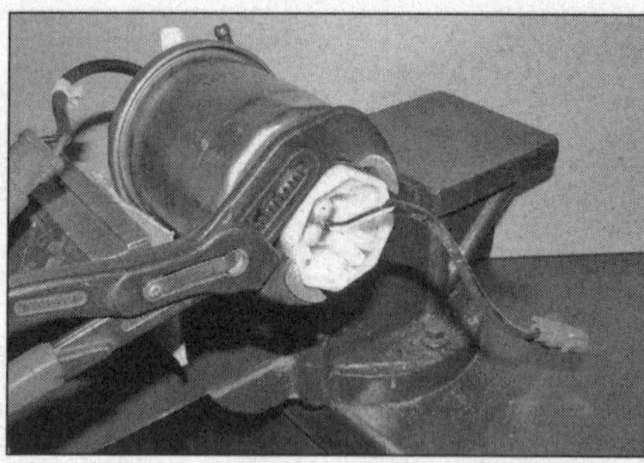

16.3a Be careful not to damage water level switch when unscrewing it from base of fuel filter . . .

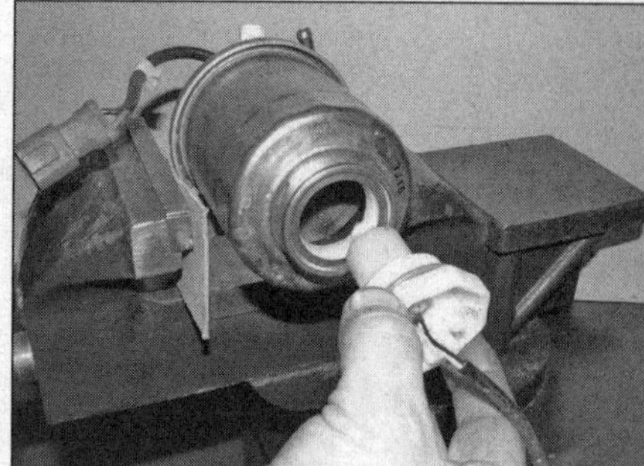

16.3b . . . remove and discard sealing O-ring; this must be renewed

16.4 Unscrewing fuel filter from filter head using standard filter removal tool

16.5a Fit new sealing O-ring to filter on reassembly . . .

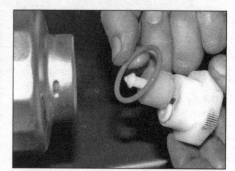

16.5b . . . and renew water level switch O-ring also

centre (or simply hold the rotor with a metal rod held against the rotor itself) and try to rotate the pulley in both directions; it should rotate smoothly in one direction, but lock immediately in the other **(see illustration)**. If the pulley rotates in both directions, or in neither, or if it is rough or jerky in operation, it must be renewed.

15 Pollen filter element renewal

Refer to Chapter 1A, Section 15.

16 Fuel filter renewal

Note: *The fuel filter assembly can be dismantled easily using readily-available tools (and a little care). Tightening the filter and water level switch correctly on reassembly, however, requires more specialised tools to prevent the risk of fuel leakage. Owners without such tools may prefer to have this work carried out by a Honda dealer or diesel injection specialist.*

1 Remove and drain the fuel filter as described in Section 5.

2 Clamp the filter head very gently in a vice fitted with soft jaw covers to protect the filter head from damage; ensure that the vice is tightened just sufficiently to prevent the filter head from rotating and that no part of the filter itself is clamped in the vice.

3 Unscrew the water level switch from the base of the filter. Recover and discard the sealing O-ring **(see illustrations)**.

4 Unscrew the filter from the filter head **(see illustration)**. Again, recover and discard the sealing O-ring.

5 On reassembly, renew the sealing O-rings on the filter itself and on the water level switch **(see illustrations)**. To tighten the filter, Honda service tool Part No. 070AA-RMAC100 is required; if this tool is available, note the torque wrench setting applicable. If a commercial cup-type equivalent is found of the sort shown in illustrations 4.8 and 4.12, the nominal torque value should be applied.

6 Similarly, to tighten the water level switch, Honda service tool Part No. 070AA-RMAC200 is required; if this tool is available, note the torque wrench setting applicable. If a commercial equivalent is found, the nominal torque value should be applied.

7 Refit the filter assembly to the vehicle, prime the fuel system and restart the engine. Check carefully for any signs of fuel leaks from the filter assembly. On completion, dispose safely of the drained fuel and the used filter; it should be noted that used filters should not be included with domestic waste. Most local authority used oil 'banks' also have used filter disposal points alongside.

Every 25 000 miles

17 Air filter element renewal

Note: *Whenever the air cleaner cover is removed, it is essential that the turbocharger air intake is packed with clean rag or similar to prevent dirt or other objects falling in.*

1 Unscrew the four bolts around the edge of the air cleaner cover. Lift the cover at the front for access to the filter element **(see illustrations)**. If the cover is to be lifted very much, or removed completely, disconnect the mass air flow sensor wiring connector first.

2 Lift the element out of the housing, and wipe out the inside of the air cleaner housing with a clean rag.

3 While the air cleaner cover is off and the element is removed, be careful not to drop anything down into the turbocharger's air intake tract.

4 Fit the new element into the air cleaner housing, making sure it seats properly, and observing any direction-of-fitting markings **(see illustration)**.

5 Refit the air cleaner cover, ensuring that its edges seat correctly, and secure with the four bolts **(see illustration)**. Tighten them carefully, so as not to damage or distort the housing and cover; note the specified torque wrench setting. Reconnect the mass airflow sensor wiring, if disturbed.

17.1a Unscrew the four air cleaner cover retaining bolts . . .

17.1b . . . and lift cover at front to withdraw filter element

17.4 Observe UP marking showing which way up new element must fit into air cleaner housing, and ensure it seats properly

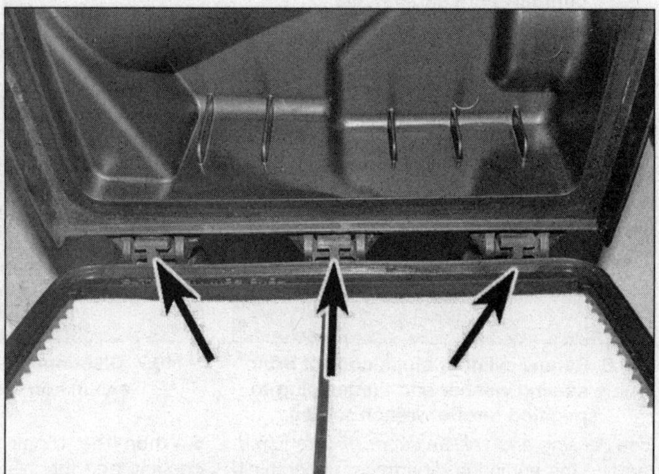

17.5 Ensure air cleaner cover is engaged correctly on hinges at rear and that its edges seat well

Every 3 years

18 Brake fluid renewal

Refer to Chapter 1A, Section 19.

Every 62 500 miles or 5 years

19 Coolant renewal

Note: *See the maintenance schedule for more information about the coolant renewal interval.*

Warning: Refer to Chapter 3 and observe the warnings given. In particular, never remove the expansion tank filler cap when the engine is running, or has just been switched off, as the cooling system will be pressurised and hot, and the consequent escaping steam and scalding coolant could cause serious injury. If the engine is hot, the electric cooling fan may start rotating even if the engine is not running, so be careful to keep hands, hair and loose clothing well clear when working in the engine compartment.

Cooling system draining

Warning: Wait until the engine is cold before starting this procedure.

Note: *In addition to the coolant and any hoses and/or hose clips that will be needed, a new cylinder block drain plug sealing washer will be required.*

1 Switch on the ignition and turn the heater temperature control to the maximum heat position. Switch off the ignition. Unscrew the four retaining nuts and remove the acoustic engine cover.

2 To drain the system, first remove the expansion tank filler cap. Place a thick cloth over the cap and turn it anti-clockwise as far as the first stop, wait for any pressure to be released (ie, wait for any hissing to stop completely before proceeding), then depress it and turn it further anti-clockwise to remove it.

3 Slacken the cooling system bleed nipple fitted to the air separation cover on the gearbox end of the cylinder head, next to the EGR valve **(see illustration 19.21)**.

4 If additional working clearance is required, apply the handbrake, then jack up the front of the vehicle and support it on axle stands

19.4a Radiator drain tap can be reached through access hole in engine compartment undershield . . .

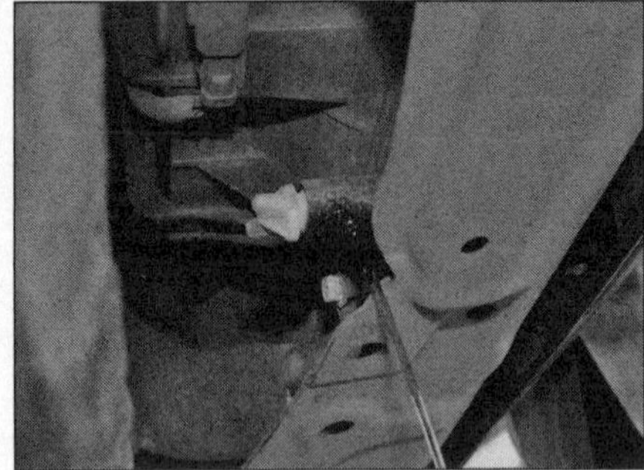
19.4b . . . but access to hose connections, if required, is easier with undershield removed

19.5 Cylinder block coolant drain plug is located behind air cleaner-to-turbocharger intake pipe's union on turbocharger

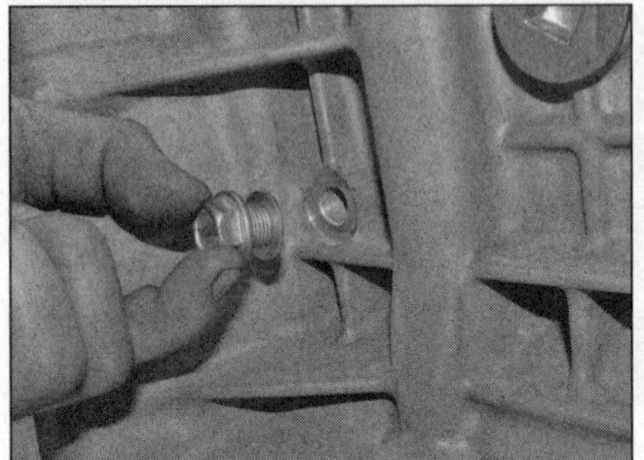
19.6 Renew cylinder block coolant drain plug sealing washer and tighten plug to specified torque wrench setting

(see *Jacking and vehicle support*). If required, remove the engine compartment undershield (see Chapter 11), but the radiator drain can be reached through the access hole provided **(see illustrations)**. Place a large drain tray underneath, and slacken the radiator drain tap. Allow the coolant to drain into the tray. On completion, retighten the drain tap securely.

5 Move the drain tray to the rear of the engine, at the gearbox end of the block. Behind the air cleaner-to-turbocharger intake pipe's union on the turbocharger is the cylinder block coolant drain plug – unscrew the plug and allow the rest of the system contents to drain into the tray **(see illustration)**. Recover the drain plug's sealing washer and discard it – a new one should be fitted on reassembly.

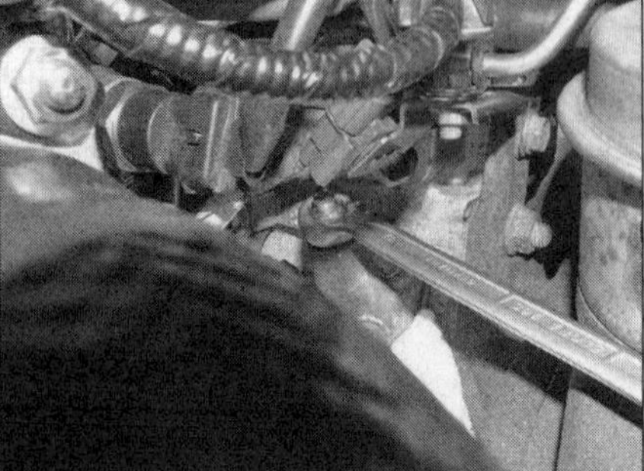
19.12 Cooling system bleed nipple is located at gearbox end of cylinder head – ensure no air bubbles can be seen in coolant before tightening nipple

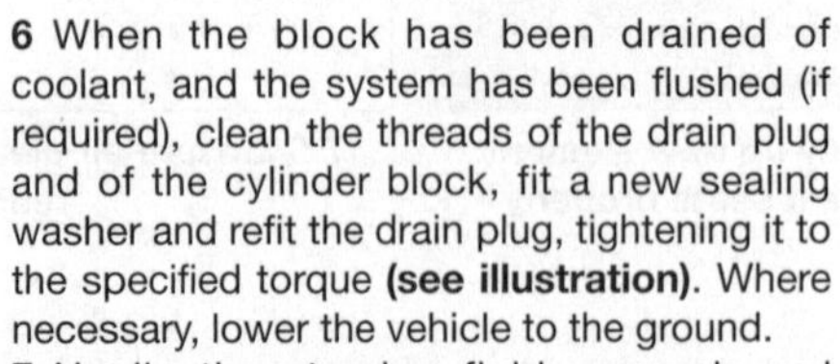
19.7 Disconnect hose from bottom of expansion tank to drain tank

6 When the block has been drained of coolant, and the system has been flushed (if required), clean the threads of the drain plug and of the cylinder block, fit a new sealing washer and refit the drain plug, tightening it to the specified torque **(see illustration)**. Where necessary, lower the vehicle to the ground.

7 Unclip the steering fluid reservoir and unbolt the cooling system expansion tank and its mounting bracket from the right-hand inner wing **(see illustrations 14.4a to 14.4d)**. Secure the fluid reservoir to one side without disconnecting or straining its hoses or spilling its contents. Release the spring clip and disconnect the hose from the bottom of the expansion tank and allow its contents to drain into a suitable container **(see illustration)**. On completion, flush out the expansion tank with clean water, then reconnect the hose and refit the expansion tank, tightening its mounting bolts to the specified torque wrench setting.

Cooling system flushing

8 Refer to Chapter 1A, Section 25.

Antifreeze mixture

9 Refer to Chapter 1A, Section 25.

Cooling system filling

10 Before attempting to fill the cooling system, make sure that all hoses and clips are in good condition, and that the clips are tight and the cylinder block drain plug (if disturbed) has been correctly tightened. If removed, refit the expansion tank.

11 Check that the heater temperature control has not been moved from the maximum heat position. If there is a chance it has been disturbed, temporarily switch on the ignition and set the control to maximum heat, then switch the ignition off once more. Check also that the cooling system bleed nipple is still slackened.

12 Slowly fill the system through the expansion tank filler aperture until the coolant level reaches the top of the translucent part of the tank. Wait a few minutes for the level in the tank to stabilise, and watch the bleed nipple carefully. When coolant flows out of the bleed nipple in a steady stream with no sign of air bubbles, tighten the bleed nipple securely, to its specified torque wrench setting **(see illustration)**.

13 Fit the expansion tank filler cap, but only tighten it to its first stop. Start the engine and let it run at idle until the engine reaches normal operating temperature, as indicated by the radiator cooling fan cutting in and out at least twice, then switch it off. The engine must be fully warmed-up for all traces of air to be purged from the coolant passages in the cylinder block and head.

14 Recheck the coolant level in the expansion tank, and if necessary, fill it to the MAX mark, then refit the expansion tank cap and tighten it fully.

15 Start the engine again, and run it at idle until the radiator cooling fan comes on again. Check for leaks.

16 Switch off the engine and check the level in the expansion tank, and top-up to the MAX mark if necessary. Refit the expansion tank cap and tighten it fully.

17 Make a careful check of all disturbed components, hose unions, etc, checking that all are securely fastened and that there is no sign of coolant leakage anywhere. Use clean water to flush away any spilt coolant, so that any leaks that may occur in the future are easier to spot. Refit all components removed for access; tighten securely the acoustic engine cover's retaining nuts.

Airlocks

18 Refer to Chapter 1A, Section 25, but note that there is also a bleed screw to slacken when removing trapped air.

Expansion tank filler cap check

19 Clean the expansion tank cap, and inspect the seal inside the cap for damage or deterioration. If there is any sign of damage or deterioration to the seal, fit a new pressure cap. If the cap is old, it is worth considering fitting a new one for peace of mind – they are not expensive. If the pressure cap fails, excess pressure will be allowed to develop in the system, which may result in the failure of hoses, the radiator, or the heater matrix.

Every 75 000 miles or 6 years

20 Idle speed check

1 Engine idle speed is the speed at which the engine runs when it is fully warmed-up to normal operating temperature, with no throttle applied, when the vehicle is completely stopped and all electrical systems are switched off. Note that it is normal for the idle speed to be held up for a second or two, before dropping to base idle – most vehicles will also run above idle while rolling to a stop, or when coasting downhill. The speed is critical to the performance of the engine itself, as well as many sub-systems.

2 The idle speed is under the control of the engine management system's Electronic Control Unit (ECU) and is not adjustable manually.

3 Poor idle quality could be due to poor maintenance – change the engine oil, and carry out the primary operations listed in Section 2.

4 An engine prone to stalling could be suffering a problem with one of the engine-driven ancillaries, such as the alternator, or the problem could be low fuel pressure. Also check the stop-lamp switch and vehicle speed sensor (see Chapters 9 and 4B).

5 Ultimately, a persistent idle speed problem will have to be referred to a Honda dealer for diagnosis.

Every 75 000 miles or 8 years

21 Gearbox fluid renewal

Note: *The transfer case shares the same lubricant as the gearbox. In addition to the fluid that will be needed, new filler, level and drain plug sealing washers will be required.*

1 This operation is much quicker and more efficient if the vehicle is first taken on a journey of sufficient length to warm the engine/gearbox up to normal operating temperature.

2 Park the vehicle on level ground, switch off the ignition and apply the handbrake firmly. Remove the engine compartment undershield (see Chapter 11). If improved access is required, jack up the front of the vehicle and support it securely on axle stands (see *Jacking and vehicle support*), but note that, since the drain plug is at the front of the gearbox housing, the vehicle must be lowered to the ground (and even raised at the rear) to ensure reasonably rapid and complete draining. Furthermore, the vehicle must be level, both front-to-rear and side-to-side, to ensure accuracy when refilling and checking the fluid level.

3 Remove all traces of dirt from around the filler and level plugs, unscrew the plugs and recover their sealing washers (see Section 10).

4 Position a suitable container under the drain plug which is also situated in the front face of the gearbox.

5 Unscrew the drain plug – a square key will be needed, for which a 3/8-inch socket extension can be substituted – and allow the fluid to drain completely into the container **(see illustrations)**. If the fluid is hot, take precautions against scalding. Clean the filler, level and drain plugs, being especially careful to wipe any metallic particles off the magnetic inserts (where fitted). Discard the original sealing washers; they should be renewed whenever they are disturbed.

6 When the fluid has finished draining, clean the plug threads of the gearbox casing, fit a new sealing washer and refit the drain plug, tightening it to the specified torque **(see illustration)**. It the vehicle was raised, now lower it to the ground.

7 Refill the gearbox as described in Section 10. Refill the gearbox with the exact amount of the specified type of fluid (see *Lubricants and fluids*) then check the fluid level as described in Section 10. Above all, allow plenty of time for the fluid level to settle properly before checking it; if in doubt, overfill the gearbox slightly, refit the filler and level plugs and take the vehicle for a short drive to distribute the new fluid around the gearbox components, then on your return, allow time for the fluid level to settle before removing the level plug and allowing the surplus to drain off. Note that the vehicle must be parked on flat level ground when checking the fluid level.

8 When the level is correct, refit the filler and level plugs with new sealing washers and tighten each to its specified torque wrench setting.

22 Final drive fluid renewal

Refer to Chapter 1A, Section 24.

21.5a Unscrewing gearbox fluid drain plug

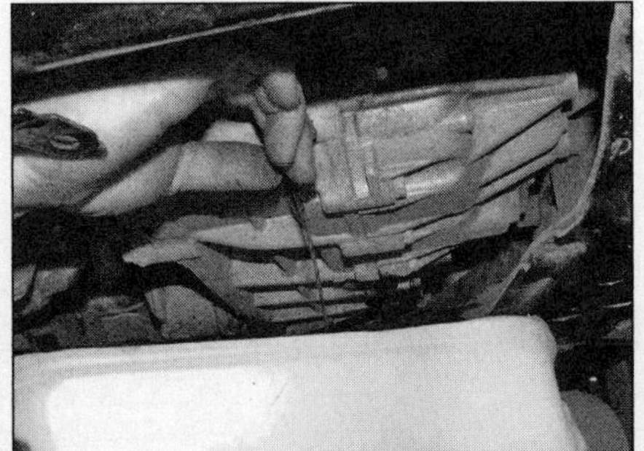

21.5b Allow fluid to drain

21.6 Renew drain plug sealing washer before tightening drain plug

Notes

Chapter 2 Part A:
Petrol engine in-car repair procedures

Contents

Degrees of difficulty

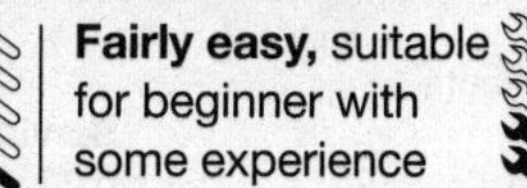

Easy, suitable for novice with little experience	**Fairly easy,** suitable for beginner with some experience	**Fairly difficult,** suitable for competent DIY mechanic	**Difficult,** suitable for experienced DIY mechanic	**Very difficult,** suitable for expert DIY or professional

Specifications

General

Manufacturer's engine code	K20A4
Bore	86 mm
Stroke	86 mm
Capacity	1998 cc
Compression ratio	9.8:1
Compression pressure @ starter motor cranking speed, engine fully warmed-up to normal operating temperature:	
Minimum	9.3 bars
Maximum variation between cylinders	2 bars
Output:	
Maximum power	110 kW @ 6500 rpm
Maximum torque	192 Nm @ 4000 rpm
Firing order	1-3-4-2 (No. 1 cylinder at timing chain end)
Direction of crankshaft rotation	Clockwise (seen from right-hand side of vehicle)

Camshaft

Endfloat:		
Standard	0.05 to 0.20 mm	
Maximum	0.40 mm	
Camshaft bearing journal-to-bearing clearance:	**Standard**	**Maximum**
No. 1 journal	0.0030 to 0.0069 mm	0.15 mm
Nos. 2, 3, 4 and 5 journals	0.0060 to 0.0099 mm	0.15 mm
Total runout:		
Standard	0.03 mm	
Maximum	0.04 mm	
Cam lobe height – standard:		
Intake primary	33.925 mm	
Intake secondary	29.638 mm	
Exhaust	34.092 mm	

Valve clearances	See Chapter 1A

Cam follower assembly and i-VTEC/VTC components

	Standard	Maximum
Cam follower pivot bore-to-shaft clearance:		
Intake	0.025 to 0.052 mm	0.08 mm
Exhaust	0.018 to 0.056 mm	0.08 mm
i-VTEC cam follower test pressure:		
Intake primary and secondary followers must be linked at	2.9 bars	
i-VTEC solenoid valve resistance – terminals 1 to 2	14 to 30 ohms	
VTC oil control solenoid valve resistance – terminals 1 to 2	6.75 to 8.25 ohms	

Flywheel

Runout of clutch plate surface:	
Nominal	0.05 mm
Maximum	0.15 mm

Balancer shafts

	Standard	Service limit
Bearing journal diameter:		
No. 1 journal (oil pump housing), front/oil pump shaft	19.938 to 19.950 mm	19.92 mm
No. 1 journal (oil pump housing), rear/driveshaft	23.938 to 23.950 mm	23.92 mm
No. 2 journal (between weights), front/oil pump and rear/driveshafts	32.949 to 32.961 mm	32.93 mm
Bearing journal maximum taper	N/App.	0.005 mm
Shaft-to-bearing clearance:		
No. 1 journal (oil pump housing), front/oil pump shaft	0.050 to 0.082 mm	0.10 mm
No. 1 journal (oil pump housing), rear/driveshaft	0.050 to 0.082 mm	0.10 mm
No. 2 journal (between weights), front/oil pump and rear/driveshafts	0.060 to 0.120 mm	0.15 mm
Bearing bore diameter:		
No. 1 journal (oil pump housing), front/oil pump shaft	20.000 to 20.020 mm	20.03 mm
No. 1 journal (oil pump housing), rear/driveshaft	24.000 to 24.020 mm	24.03 mm
No. 2 journal (between weights), front/oil pump and rear/driveshafts	33.021 to 33.069 mm	33.09 mm
Shaft endfloat	0.070 to 0.135 mm	0.15 mm

Lubrication system

Oil pump displacement @ 6000 engine rpm	54.3 litres per minute	
Oil pump:	**Standard**	**Service limit**
Inner-to-outer rotor tip clearance	0.02 to 0.16 mm	0.20 mm
Pump housing-to-outer rotor clearance	0.15 to 0.21 mm	0.23 mm
Pump housing-to-rotor axial clearance (rotor endfloat)	0.02 to 0.07 mm	0.12 mm
Minimum oil pressure – with oil @ 80°C:		
At idle speed	0.7 bars	
At 3000 engine rpm	3.4 bars	

Torque wrench settings

	Nm	lbf ft
Baffle plate-to-lower crankcase/main bearing ladder bolts	12	9
Balancer assembly upper-to-lower half clamp bolts:		
6 mm – including baffle plate bolts	12	9
8 mm – oil threads	27	20
Balancer/oil pump assembly mounting bolts:		
8 mm	22	16
10 mm	44	32
Balancer/oil pump drive chain:		
Driven sprocket retaining bolt – oil threads	44	32
Tensioner mounting bolts	12	9
Camshaft bearing cap bolts/cam follower assembly support mounting bolts:		
6 mm	12	9
8 mm	22	16
Connecting rod big-end bearing cap bolts – oil threads:		
Stage 1	20	15
Stage 2	Angle-tighten a further 90°	
Crankshaft pulley bolt – oil threads and under head	245	181
Cylinder head bolts – oil threads and under heads:		
Stage 1	39	29
Stage 2	Angle-tighten a further 90°	
Stage 3	Angle-tighten a further 90°	
Stage 4 – new bolts only	Angle-tighten a further 90°	
Driveplate mounting bolts	74	55
Engine bellhousing-to-gearbox/transmission bolts	64	47
Engine bellhousing (flywheel/torque converter) cover plate bolts	12	9
Engine management/fuel and exhaust system component fasteners	See Chapter 4A	
Engine oil filter threaded mounting stub	49	36

Torque wrench settings (continued)	Nm	lbf ft
Engine oil (sump) drain plug	See Chapter 1A	
Engine right-hand (timing end) mounting fasteners:		
Bracket-to-timing chain case/cylinder head and block bolts	44	32
Earth lead-to-mounting clamp bolt	12	9
Intermediate bracket-to-mounting centre nut (tighten last)	54	40
Intermediate bracket-to-timing chain case bracket nut and bolt (tighten first)	54	40
Engine/transmission front mounting fasteners:		
Mounting-to-automatic transmission bolts	64	47
Mounting-to-cylinder block and bellhousing bolts (manual gearbox)	64	47
Mounting-to-front suspension subframe through-bolt* and nut	64	47
Engine/transmission left-hand mounting fasteners:		
Bracket-to-gearbox/transmission nuts and bolt (tighten first)	54	40
Mounting-to-bracket through-bolt (tighten last)	54	40
Engine/transmission rear mounting fasteners:		
Bracket-to-gearbox/transmission bolts	54	40
Bracket-to-mounting through-bolt	64	47
Mounting-to-front suspension subframe bolts	59	44
Exhaust camshaft sprocket-to-camshaft retaining bolt – oil threads	72	53
Flywheel mounting bolts	122	90
Ignition system component fasteners	See Chapter 5B	
Intake camshaft sprocket/VTC actuator-to-camshaft retaining bolt – oil threads	113	83
i-VTEC camshaft position sensor retaining screw	12	9
i-VTEC oil pressure switch	22	16
i-VTEC solenoid valve assembly cover/mounting bolts:		
Early models – 6 mm bolts	10	7
Later models	12	9
i-VTEC/VTC cylinder head oil gallery sealing plug	20	15
Lower crankcase/main bearing ladder-to-cylinder block bolts:		
8 mm	22	16
10 mm (main bearing cap bolts):		
Stage 1	29	21
Stage 2	Angle-tighten a further 56°	
Oil pressure relief valve threaded plug	39	29
Oil pump housing mounting bolts	12	9
Positive Crankcase Ventilation (PCV) valve assembly	See Chapter 4C	
Roadwheel nuts	See Chapter 1A	
Spark plugs	See Chapter 1A	
Sump-to-lower crankcase/main bearing ladder nuts and bolts	12	9
Timing chain case retaining bolts	12	9
Timing chain front run fixed guide mounting bolts	12	9
Timing chain tensioner:		
Blade pivot bolt	22	16
Cover plate bolts	12	9
Mounting bolts	12	9
Timing chain top run fixed guide mounting bolts	22	16
VTC actuator/intake camshaft sprocket-to-camshaft retaining bolt – oil threads	113	83
VTC oil control solenoid valve mounting bolt	12	9
Water outlet-to-cylinder head bolts	12	9
Water pump housing-to-cylinder block bolts and nuts	44	32
Wiring harness-to-cylinder block/crankcase retaining bolt	12	9
Vacuum pipe support bracket-to-cylinder head bolts	12	9

** Use new fasteners.*

1 General information

How to use this Chapter

This Part of Chapter 2 is devoted to those repair procedures for the petrol engine that can reasonably be carried out while the engine remains in the vehicle. All procedures concerning engine removal and refitting, and engine block/cylinder head overhaul can be found in Chapter 2C.

Most of the operations included in this Part are based on the assumption that the engine is still fitted in the vehicle. Therefore, if this information is being used during a complete engine overhaul, with the engine already removed, many of the steps included here will not apply.

The Specifications included in this Part of Chapter 2 apply only to the procedures contained in this Chapter. Chapter 2C contains the Specifications necessary for cylinder head and engine block rebuilding.

Engine description

The engine is a water-cooled four-stroke spark-ignition (petrol) unit, of four-cylinder in-line DOHC (Double OverHead Camshaft) layout with four valves per cylinder, mounted transversely at the front of the vehicle, with the clutch and transmission on its left-hand end.

With the exception of the pressed-steel sump, all major engine housings and covers are castings of aluminium alloy. Cast-iron cylinder liners are cast into the open-deck cylinder block/crankcase.

The crankshaft runs in five shell-type main bearings, thrustwashers to control crankshaft endfloat being fitted on each side of No. 4 main bearing's upper half. Instead of individual caps securing each of the main bearings, a single large cast aluminium alloy lower crankcase/main bearing ladder is bolted to the underside of the cylinder block/crankcase. The connecting rods rotate on horizontally-split bearing shells at their big-ends.

The pistons are attached to the connecting rods by gudgeon pins which are secured by circlips in the connecting rod small-end eyes. The aluminium alloy pistons are fitted with three piston rings: two compression rings and an oil control ring.

The intake and exhaust valves – two of each per cylinder – are closed by coil springs; they operate in guides which are shrink-fitted into the cylinder head, as are the valve seat inserts.

The two camshafts are driven from the crankshaft by the same timing chain, each operating eight valves via pivoting followers; a roller in each follower minimises losses due to friction. Routine checking and adjustment of the valve clearances is made by a screw-and-locknut adjuster bearing on each valve stem. Each camshaft rotates in five bearings that are line-bored directly in the follower assembly supports and their (bolted-on) bearing caps; this means that the bearing caps are not available separately from the follower assembly supports and must not be interchanged with caps from another engine. The entire length of the timing chain is supported by fixed guides along its front and top runs and it is tensioned by a pivoting tensioner blade on its rear run. A tensioner assembly acting on the tensioner blade's free end uses the lubrication system's hydraulic pressure to automatically tension the chain, while a spring-loaded ratchet prevents the tensioner plunger from retracting when the engine is switched off and oil pressure is relaxed.

The Lanchester harmonic balancer assembly mounted in the sump uses two bobweights on each of two counter-rotating shafts mounted below and equidistant from the crankshaft axis which rotate at twice crankshaft speed to cancel out the unbalanced secondary inertia forces inherent in any in-line four-cylinder engine. Driven from the crankshaft right-hand end by a chain, the rear shaft drives the front by gear teeth to ensure that the two are always correctly timed in relation to the movement of the crankshaft and pistons. The oil pump is mounted on the right-hand end of the front (driven) shaft. The shafts rotate in bearings machined in the oil pump housing at their right-hand ends and in horizontally-split bearing shells located between their bobweights. The balancer/oil pump drive chain is supported along its rear run by a fixed plastic guide and tensioned by a spring-loaded tensioner via a plastic-faced tensioner blade along its front run.

The water pump is mounted in a housing bolted to the right-hand end of the cylinder block and is driven with the steering pump, alternator and air conditioning compressor by an auxiliary drivebelt from the crankshaft pulley. An automatic spring-loaded tensioner eliminates any need for drivebelt maintenance beyond a periodic check of its condition.

Lubrication system

The forced, wet-sump lubrication system uses an eccentric-rotor trochoid pump, which is mounted on the right-hand end of the front (driven) balancer shaft and draws oil through a strainer located in the sump. The pump forces oil through an externally-mounted filter. From the filter, the oil is pumped into a main gallery in the cylinder block/crankcase, from where it is distributed to the crankshaft (main bearings) and cylinder head. Pressure is controlled by a spring-loaded pressure relief valve located in the pump housing.

The big-end bearings are supplied with oil via internal drillings in the crankshaft.

The cylinder head is provided with extensive oil galleries to ensure constant oil supply to the camshaft bearings and cam followers and to the components of the i-VTEC and VTC systems; the latter have small wire-mesh filter screens to catch impurities that might hinder their correct operation.

While the crankshaft, camshaft and balancer shaft bearings and the cam followers (particularly the intake) receive a pressurised supply, the camshaft lobes and valves are lubricated by splash, as are all other engine components.

The i-VTEC and VTC systems

Honda first introduced its VTEC (Variable Valve Timing and Lift, Electronic Control) technology in 1989, producing an engine that had the ability to operate on two completely different cam profiles, eliminating a major compromise in engine design. One profile designed to operate the valves at low engine speeds provided good road manners, low fuel consumption and low emissions. The second was a high-lift, long-duration profile and came into operation at high engine speeds to provide an increase in power output. Since then, VTEC systems have been further developed in various forms to improve engine performance.

i-VTEC ('intelligent' VTEC) incorporates a variation of VTEC, which effectively alters the lift, timing and opening duration of the intake valves to help the engine produce both good low-speed torque and good high-speed power, with VTC (Variable Timing Control), which continuously varies relative valve overlap to best match the current engine load, and IMRC (Intake Manifold Runner Control), a variable-length intake manifold for increased torque in the low and medium engine speed ranges. These systems work under the control of the engine management system to optimise engine efficiency, reducing fuel consumption and minimising exhaust emissions while providing a substantial performance increase across a broad power band.

This version of VTEC uses one roller cam follower per intake valve. During low-speed operation, the two followers for the valves of each cylinder are separate and follow different cam lobes so that the opening of the intake valves is staggered and their lift asymmetric – creating a very strong swirl effect within the combustion chambers to maximise combustion efficiency. At higher speeds, engine oil pressure (controlled by the i-VTEC solenoid valve mounted on the rear right-hand end of the cylinder head) is used to force across a piston in the primary follower, against spring pressure, into the secondary follower, thus locking both together and causing both intake valves of each cylinder to open for the same lift and duration (following the primary lobe's higher-lift, longer-duration profile), substantially increasing airflow into that cylinder and boosting performance.

VTC provides continuously-variable camshaft phasing throughout the engine's speed range, taking engine load into consideration. This improves charging efficiency and combustion, produces higher torque, reduced intake resistance and improved efficiency of exhaust gas recirculation. As engine speed increases, a VTC actuator – controlled by the engine management system's control unit that monitors cam position, ignition timing, exhaust-gas oxygen content and throttle position – advances or retards the intake cam through a 50-degree range, optimising engine output and reducing emissions. The VTC actuator – a hydraulically-driven, compact vane-type pump combined with the camshaft sprocket on the intake camshaft's right-hand end – uses engine oil pressure (controlled by the VTC oil control solenoid valve mounted in the timing chain case) to vary the intake camshaft position relative to that of the exhaust camshaft, so advancing or retarding the opening of the intake valves. During periods of high engine load, VTC ensures a relatively small degree of valve overlap which provides the best output, the valve opening angle utilising the inertia of the intake air. In situations where the engine is not under heavy load but is running at high speeds (for example during motorway cruising), there is much greater valve overlap to reduce pumping losses, maximise the exhaust gas recirculation effect for reduced NOx levels and provide the best balance between fuel consumption and output. At idle and low engine speeds during light load conditions, intake valve opening is retarded for minimal overlap, generating strong swirl and therefore stable combustion.

Made from resin for light weight, the intake manifold features IMRC – a variable length intake tract controlled by a rotary valve, the IMT (Intake Manifold Tuning) actuator valve, which is itself opened and closed via a solenoid valve. At low engine speeds, the speed of the airflow into the combustion chamber is increased by closing the valve to direct the air through a longer path (540 mm) with limited cross-sectional area. This provides optimum airflow inertia, enabling more efficient cylinder filling, and boosts torque. Above 4700 rpm, when the engine load increases, the valve is opened to direct the air through the shorter (270 mm) and larger path so that a greater amount of air can enter the combustion chamber, so increasing power.

Operations with engine in vehicle

The following operations can be carried out without having to remove the engine from the vehicle:

a) Removal and refitting of the timing chain, sprockets and tensioner components.
b) Removal and refitting of the i-VTEC and VTC components.
c) Removal and refitting of the camshafts and cam follower assembly.
d) Removal, refitting and overhaul of the cylinder head.
*e) Removal and refitting of the sump.**
*f) Removal and refitting of the oil pump, drive chain, sprockets and tensioner components.***
*g) Removal and refitting of the balancer shafts.***
h) Renewal of the crankshaft oil seals.
*i) Removal and refitting of the pistons and connecting rods.***
j) Renewal of the engine mountings.
k) Removal and refitting of the flywheel/driveplate.

** Removal of the sump with the engine in the vehicle requires first the removal of the front suspension subframe. Depending on the skills and equipment available and the nature of the work being undertaken, the home mechanic may prefer to consider removing the engine/transmission complete and then removing the sump, in the interests of improved safety, cleanliness and improved access.*

*** These operations can be carried out after removal of the sump, but as mentioned above it is better for the engine to be removed.*

2 Compression and leakdown tests – description and interpretation

Compression test

Note: *A compression tester will be required for this test, as will the aid of an assistant.*

1 When engine performance is down, or if misfiring occurs which cannot be attributed to a fault in the ignition or fuel systems, a compression test can provide diagnostic clues as to the engine's condition. If the test is performed regularly it can give warning of trouble before any other symptoms become apparent.

2 A compression tester will be required. The tester is either connected to an adapter which screws into the spark plug hole or is pressed tight to the spark plug hole and held there for the duration of the test; the first type of tester is preferred. It is unlikely to be worthwhile buying such a tester for occasional use, but it may be possible to borrow or hire one – if not, have the test performed by a garage.

3 Observe the following points:

a) The battery must be in a good state of charge.
b) The air filter must be clean.
c) The engine must be at normal operating temperature.

4 Switch off the ignition.

5 Relieve the pressure in the fuel system as described in Chapter 4A.

6 Remove all four ignition coils and spark plugs (see Chapter 1A).

7 Fit the compression tester to the No. 1 cylinder spark plug hole.

8 Have the assistant hold the throttle wide open and crank the engine on the starter motor. After one or two revolutions, the compression pressure should build-up to a maximum figure and then stabilise. Record the highest reading obtained.

9 Repeat the test on the remaining cylinders, recording the pressure in each.

10 All cylinders should produce very similar pressures, greater than the minimum specified. The actual compression pressures measured are not as important as the balance between cylinders; a difference of more than 2 bars between any cylinder(s) and the others indicates a fault. Note that the compression should build-up quickly in a healthy engine; low compression on the first stroke, followed by gradually-increasing pressure on successive strokes, indicates worn piston rings. A low compression reading on the first stroke, which does not build-up during successive strokes, indicates leaking valves or a blown head gasket (a cracked head could also be the cause). Deposits on the undersides of the valve heads can also cause low compression.

11 If the pressure in any cylinder is significantly low, introduce a teaspoonful of clean oil into that cylinder through its spark plug hole and repeat the test.

12 If the addition of oil temporarily improves the compression pressure, this indicates that bore or piston wear is responsible for the pressure loss – the oil having provided a temporary seal. No improvement suggests that leaking or burnt valves, or a blown head gasket, may be to blame.

13 A low reading from two adjacent cylinders is almost certainly due to the head gasket having blown between them and the presence of coolant in the engine oil will confirm this.

14 If the compression reading is unusually high, the combustion chambers are probably coated with carbon deposits.

15 On completion of the test, refit the spark plugs and ignition coils (see Chapter 1A), and refit the fuel pump fuse.

Leakdown test

16 A leakdown test measures the rate at which compressed air is lost that has been fed into the cylinder. It is an alternative to a compression test and in many ways it is better, since the escaping air provides easy identification of where pressure loss is occurring (piston rings, valves or head gasket).

17 The equipment needed for leakdown testing is unlikely to be available to the home mechanic. If poor compression is suspected, have the test performed by a suitably-equipped garage.

3 Top Dead Centre (TDC) for No. 1 piston – locating

General

1 Top Dead Centre (TDC) is the highest point in its travel up-and-down its cylinder bore that each piston reaches as the crankshaft rotates. Each piston reaches TDC both at the top of the compression stroke and again at the top of the exhaust stroke. For the purpose of timing the engine, TDC refers to the No. 1 piston position at the top of its compression stroke.

2 It is useful for several servicing procedures to be able to position the engine at TDC.

3 No. 1 cylinder is at the right-hand (timing chain) end of the engine. Note that the crankshaft rotates clockwise when viewed from the right-hand side of the vehicle.

Locating TDC

4 Unless the starter motor is to be used to turn the engine, disconnect the battery negative (earth) lead (refer to *Disconnecting the battery*).

5 Apply the handbrake, then jack up the front of the vehicle and support it securely on axle stands (see *Jacking and vehicle support*). If the engine is to be turned using the right-hand front roadwheel with top gear engaged, it is only necessary to raise the right-hand front roadwheel off the ground.

6 Either release the two securing clips and prise back the wheel arch liner section of the engine compartment undershield as necessary to reach the crankshaft pulley and bolt, or (depending on the work about to be undertaken) remove the undershield completely (Chapter 11).

7 Remove all four ignition coils and spark plugs (see Chapter 1A) to enable the engine to be turned easily. It is best to rotate the crankshaft using a spanner applied to the crankshaft pulley bolt; however, it is possible also either to select top gear and to turn the engine via the right-hand front roadwheel, or to use the starter motor to bring the engine close to TDC, then finish with a spanner. If

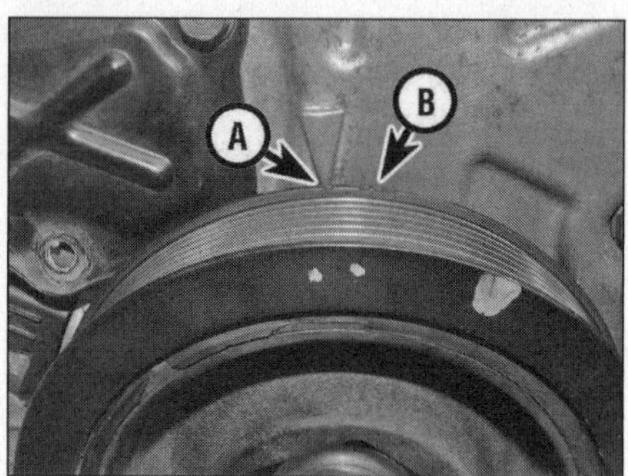

3.8 TDC mark (A) – single notch usually painted orange. Centre notch (B), painted red, of three closely-grouped notches is 8º BTDC mark for checking ignition timing

the starter is used, be sure to disconnect the battery negative (earth) lead immediately the starter is no longer required.

8 Rotate the crankshaft clockwise until the notches in the inboard rim of the crankshaft pulley approach alignment with the arrow mark cast on the timing chain case. First are the three closely-grouped notches, the centre one of which is painted red and represents the 8º BTDC mark for checking the ignition timing, while the next, the single notch usually painted orange, is the TDC mark **(see illustration)**.

9 With the TDC notch in the crankshaft pulley aligned exactly with the cast arrow on the timing chain case, Nos. 1 and 4 cylinders are now at TDC, one of them on the compression stroke. The only way of establishing which is to remove the cylinder head cover (see next Section) so that the cam lobe positions, and/or the timing marks on the exhaust camshaft sprocket and intake camshaft sprocket/VTC actuator, can be seen. If all four cam lobes are pointing away from No. 1 cylinder's valves (or if the timing marks align as described in Section 6, paragraph 4), then it is No. 1 cylinder that is correctly positioned. If not, rotate the crankshaft one full turn (360º) clockwise until the pulley notch aligns again. No. 1 cylinder will then be at TDC on the compression stroke.

10 Once No. 1 cylinder has been positioned at TDC on the compression stroke, TDC for any of the other cylinders can then be located by rotating the crankshaft clockwise 180º at a time and following the firing order (see Specifications).

5.4 Bolt a strap between flywheel and cylinder block/crankcase to prevent crankshaft rotation while pulley bolt is slackened

4 Cylinder head cover – removal and refitting

Note: *Liquid gasket (Honda Part No. 08C70-K0234M, 08C70-K0334M, 08C70-X0331S or 08718-0001 or equivalent) must be available on reassembly, in addition to any other items (gaskets, seals, etc) found to be in need of renewal during the procedure.*

Removal

1 Proceed as described in Chapter 1A, Section 16, paragraphs 3 to 6.

Refitting

2 Proceed as described in Chapter 1A, Section 16, paragraphs 17 to 25.

5 Crankshaft pulley – removal and refitting

Note: *The crankshaft pulley retaining bolt is extremely tight; the aid of an assistant will be required. Be very careful to avoid the risk of personal injury through trapped fingers, etc.*

Note: *It is good practice to renew highly-stressed fasteners such as the crankshaft pulley retaining bolt as a matter of course, irrespective of their apparent condition, whenever they are disturbed.*

Removal

1 Bring the engine to TDC as described in Section 3 (it does not matter whether No 1 or No 4 is on the compression stroke).

2 Depending on the work about to be undertaken, remove the right-hand or both front roadwheels, and remove the undershield (Chapter 11).

3 Remove the auxiliary drivebelt (Chapter 1A).

4 Slacken the crankshaft pulley retaining bolt. This is extremely tight; first, ensure that the vehicle is securely supported. Only use good-quality, close-fitting tools for this job – if something slips, it may result in injury. For extra leverage, use a long-handled breaker bar, or a length of substantial tubing slipped over the socket handle, to extend it. If an extension bar is fitted on the socket, rest the outer end of the extension bar on another axle stand, to keep it horizontal – this improves leverage, and reduces the chance of the socket slipping off under load. Use one of the following methods to prevent crankshaft rotation:

a) *The Honda service tools for this task are a pulley holder (Part No. 07JAB-0010400) which has a 50 mm hexagon to engage with the centre of the pulley, a long handle (Part No. 07JAB-0010200) to fit over the holder and a deep 19 mm socket (Part No. 07JAA-0010200) slim enough to fit through the holder. Either acquire these tools or find their commercial equivalents.*

b) *Remove the starter motor (Chapter 5A) and have an assistant insert a wide-bladed screwdriver in the teeth of the starter ring gear.*

c) *Unbolt the bellhousing cover plate and bolt a strap between the flywheel and the cylinder block/crankcase* ***(see illustration)****.*

5 Unscrew the pulley bolt and washer, then remove the pulley from the crankshaft. Note the locating key; if this is loose in its crankshaft keyway, remove it and keep it with the pulley.

Refitting

6 Fit the locating key to the crankshaft keyway **(see illustration)**. Wipe clean the lips of the crankshaft right-hand oil seal, then thoroughly clean the boss on the pulley's inboard face which passes through the oil seal

5.6a Fit crankshaft pulley locating key to crankshaft keyway . . .

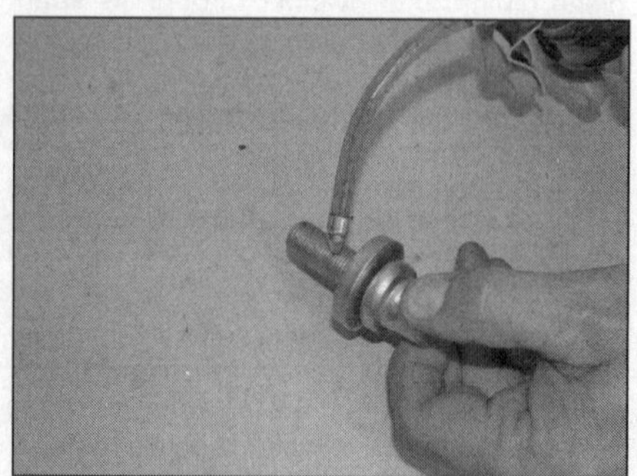

5.6b . . . apply a film of clean oil to threads . . .

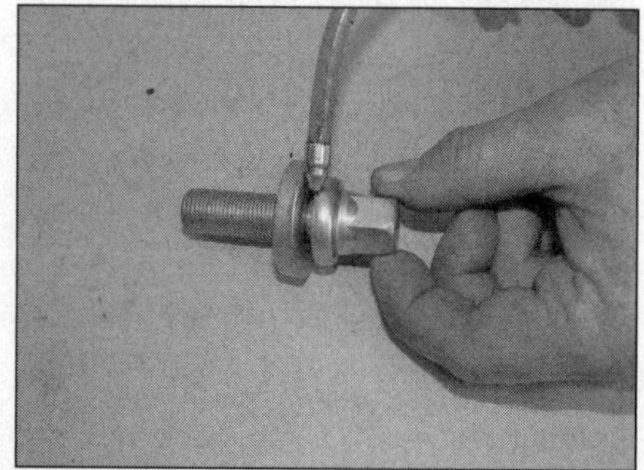

5.6c . . . and under head of pulley retaining bolt

5.7a Fit pulley to crankshaft, aligning pulley keyway with locating key – take care not to damage oil seal lips as pulley enters . . .

5.7b . . . fit pulley retaining bolt and washer . . .

5.8 . . . and tighten to specified torque setting

6.4 No. 1 cylinder is at TDC on compression stroke when punch marks and arrow mark (A) are both at the top, while lines (B) point inwards towards each other and align exactly with cam follower assembly support-bearing cap mating surface

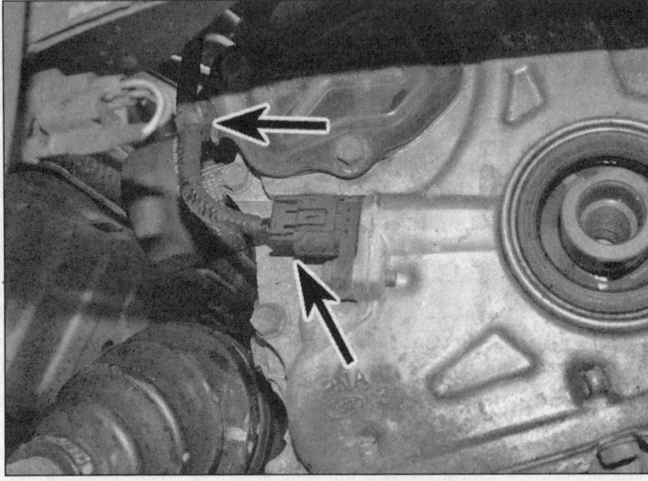

6.7a Disconnect crankshaft position sensor wiring and release wiring from tensioner cover . . .

lips; polish away any burrs or raised edges which might damage the seal lips. Clean the pulley retaining bolt thread in the crankshaft right-hand end, the pulley's central bore which fits over the crankshaft and the seating for the retaining bolt washer. Clean the washer, then apply a film of clean oil to the threads and under the head of the retaining bolt **(see illustrations)**.

7 Fit the pulley to the crankshaft, aligning the pulley keyway with the locating key and being careful not to damage the seal lips as the pulley enters them, then refit the retaining bolt and washer **(see illustrations)**.

8 Lock the crankshaft using the method used

6.7b . . . then disconnect VTC oil control solenoid valve wiring

on removal, and tighten the pulley retaining bolt to the specified torque setting **(see illustration)**. **Note:** *Honda specifically forbid the use of an impact wrench to tighten this bolt.*

9 Fit a new auxiliary drivebelt as described in Chapter 1A.

10 The remainder of refitting is a reversal of removal.

6 Timing chain case – removal and refitting

Note: *Liquid gasket (Honda Part No. 08C70-K0234M, 08C70-K0334M, 08C70-X0331S or 08718-0001 or equivalent) must be available on reassembly, in addition to a new auxiliary drivebelt.*

Removal

1 Bring the engine to TDC as described in Section 3 (it does not matter at this stage whether No 1 or No 4 is on the compression stroke).

2 Depending on the work about to be undertaken, remove the right-hand or both front roadwheels, and remove the undershield (Chapter 11).

3 Remove the cylinder head cover (Chapter 1A, Section 16, paragraphs 3 to 6).

4 If dismantling such as removal/refitting of the timing chain, valve gear and/or cylinder head is intended, position the engine with No. 1 cylinder at TDC on the compression stroke. To establish whether it is No. 1 or No. 4 cylinder that is on the compression stroke, check the cam lobe positions and the timing marks on the exhaust camshaft sprocket and intake camshaft sprocket/VTC actuator. No. 1 cylinder is correctly positioned if all four cam lobes are pointing away from No. 1 cylinder's valves. The punch marks on the rims of the camshaft sprockets and the arrow mark stamped on the VTC actuator must be at the top (twelve o'clock position), while the lines stamped in both sprocket rims must point inwards towards each other and align with the mating surface of the No. 1 cam follower assembly support and its bearing cap **(see illustration)**. If not, rotate the crankshaft one full turn (360°) clockwise until the pulley notch and timing marks align as described.

5 Remove the auxiliary drivebelt (Chapter 1A).

6 Remove the crankshaft pulley (see previous Section).

7 Disconnect the wiring for the crankshaft position sensor and the VTC oil control solenoid valve at the bottom and top, respectively, of the timing chain case **(see illustrations)**.

8 Remove the VTC oil control solenoid valve (Section 9) **(see illustration)**.

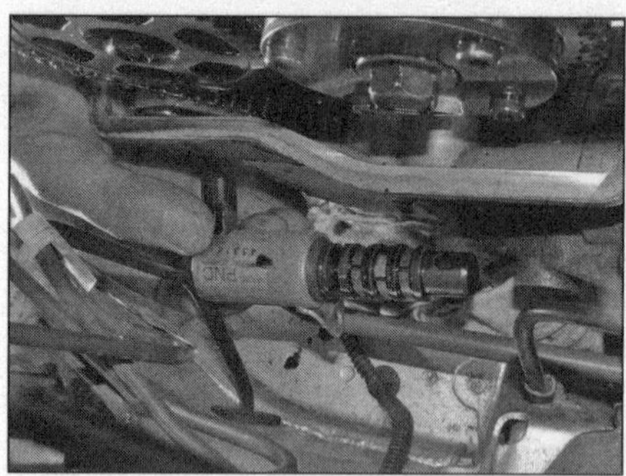

6.8 Removing VTC oil control solenoid valve

6.9 Unscrew nuts and bolt securing intermediate bracket to mounting and engine – note earth lead clamp bolt

6.10a Unscrew engine right-hand mounting's bracket from timing chain case/cylinder head and block . . .

6.10b . . . and remove bracket

6.11 Timing chain case retaining bolt locations

9 Remove the engine right-hand mounting's intermediate bracket. First support the engine using a trolley jack and block of wood beneath the sump. Make sure the engine is adequately supported, then unscrew the nuts and bolt securing the intermediate bracket to the timing chain case/cylinder head and block bracket and to the rubber mounting itself. Unbolt the earth lead and remove the bracket **(see illustration)**.

10 Unscrew the three bolts, then remove the engine right-hand mounting's timing chain case/cylinder head and block bracket **(see illustrations)**.

11 Unscrew the bolts securing the timing chain case **(see illustration)**. If any of the bolts are shouldered to locate the case as well as retaining it, note their positions.

12 Use a hammer and a block of wood or a soft-faced mallet to break the seal by tapping all around the periphery of the timing chain case, then very carefully prise it away from the cylinder head, cylinder block and the sump. It is a thin and delicate casting, easily damaged or even broken if carelessly handled, and the liquid gasket used on assembly sticks tight. Do NOT lever between the mating surfaces; these are easily scratched or gouged and will leak oil if badly marked. Leverage points are provided at the top on the end of the cylinder head and at the rear next to the oil pressure switch; insert a large flat-bladed screwdriver and gently prise the timing chain case away at these points first. At the same time, a hammer and a block of wood can be used to jar the cases apart **(see illustrations)**. As soon as the case is removed, cover the sump opening to prevent to prevent dirt and debris from falling in.

Caution: Be careful not to nick or gouge the mating surfaces of the timing chain case, the cylinder head, the cylinder block and the sump or oil leaks will result. Check the timing chain case for cracks and other damage.

13 Remove and discard the small triangular O-ring from inside the case; this must be renewed whenever it is disturbed. Renew the crankshaft right-hand oil seal (Section 19) if any oil leakage is evident.

Refitting

14 Thoroughly clean the mating surfaces of the timing chain case, the cylinder head, the cylinder block and the sump. Clean any oil or old gasket material and sealant from the mating surfaces and from the bolt holes and threads. Be very careful not to allow dirt and debris to fall into the sump. Degrease the surfaces completely before applying sealant.

15 With the new O-ring fitted to the groove inside the timing chain case, apply liquid gasket and refit the timing chain case as directed below. The timing chain case must be installed within five minutes of applying the liquid gasket – if this time limit is exceeded, it must be wiped off completely and new liquid gasket applied. A 'dry' practice run before applying liquid gasket is recommended.

16 Apply a continuous bead of liquid gasket (approximately 3 mm diameter) evenly along the length of the chain case's front, rear and bottom mating surfaces so that the bead is around the inside edges of the bolt holes **(see illustrations)**. Also apply a bead around the edge (around the outside edges of these bolt holes) of the VTC oil control solenoid

6.12a Leverage points are provided to allow timing chain case to be GENTLY prised away . . .

6.12b . . . to break grip of sealant without damaging timing chain case . . .

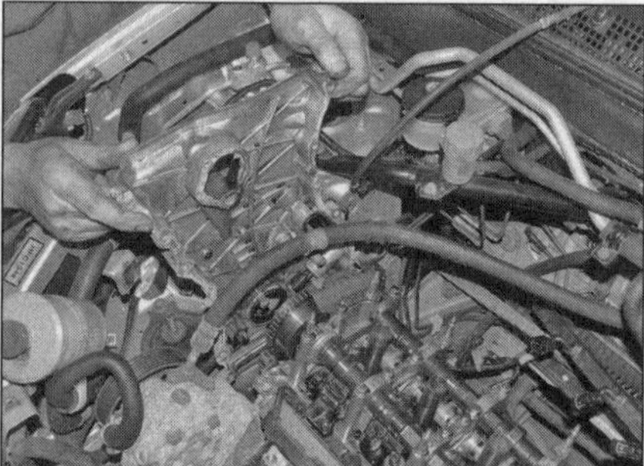

6.12c . . . so that it can be removed unmarked

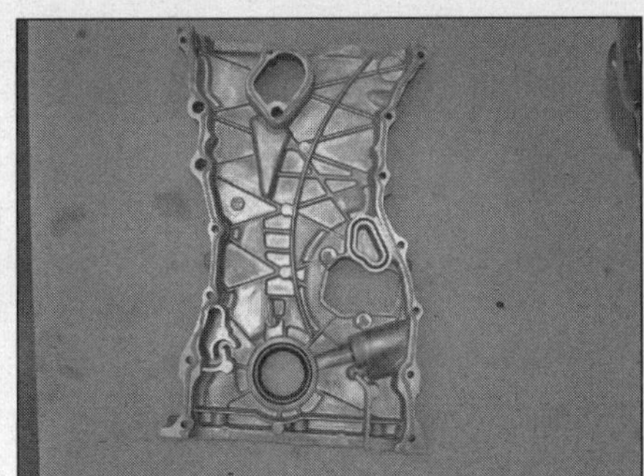

6.16a Apply a continuous 3.0 mm diameter bead of liquid gasket evenly to timing chain case's mating surfaces

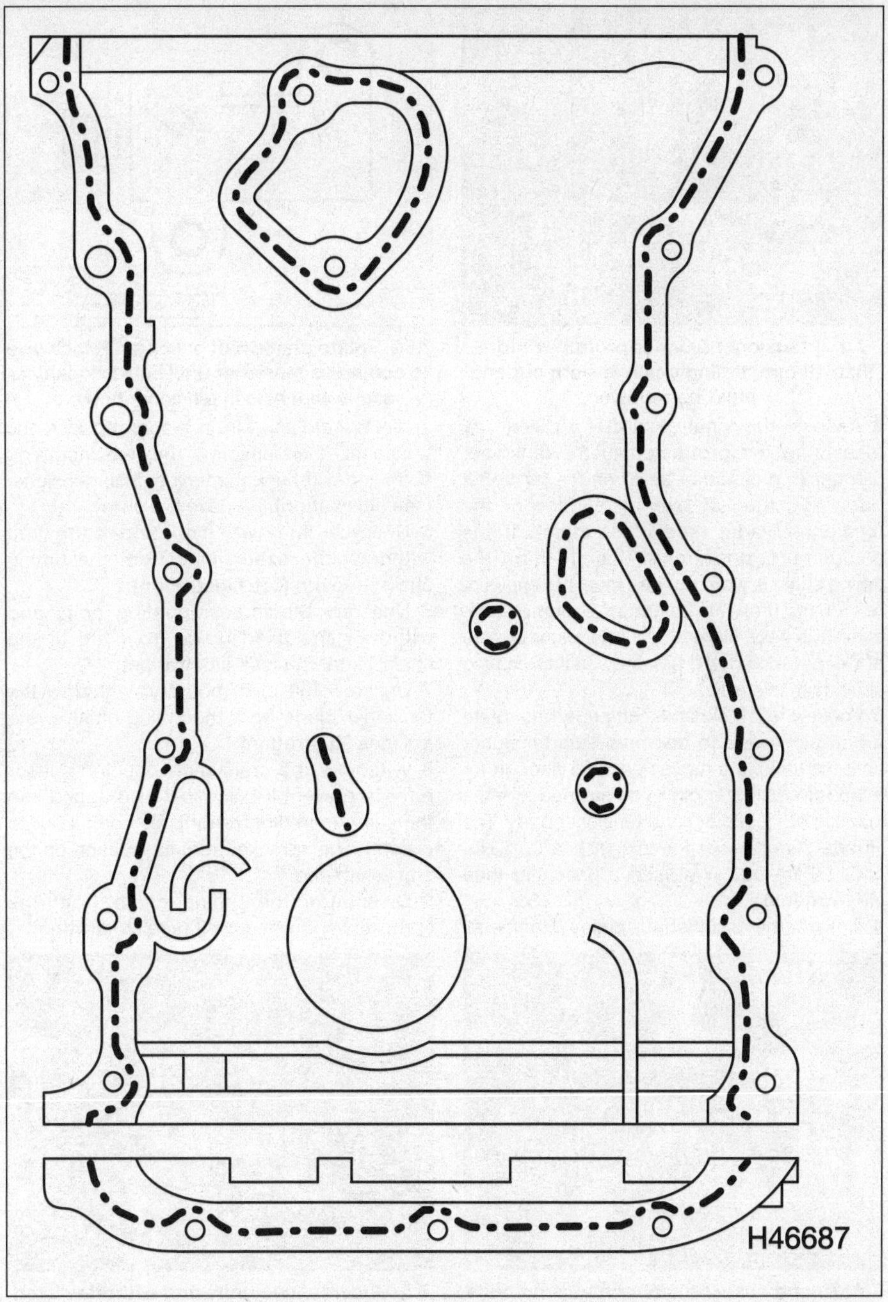

valve aperture, and to the three supporting bosses on the inside of the chain case. Apply liquid gasket to the four points on the cylinder head/block/lower crankcase mating surfaces. Apply a small blob of liquid gasket to those bolt holes in the cylinder head/block/lower crankcase which pass through to the outside and to the three bolt holes along the bottom edge of the timing chain case to ensure that there are no oil leaks from the threads. Do NOT apply sealant to blind holes in the castings.

17 Offer up the timing chain case so that the crankshaft end passes through the oil seal, and align the bottom outer edge of the timing chain case on the sump while the upper end is tilted back clear of the cylinder block. Carefully tilt the chain case into place and refit one or two bolts – for preference any that are shouldered – to hold it. **Note:** *The timing chain case should fit on the cylinder head and block without being forced. If the case is not correctly seated, remove it and investigate the problem. Do not attempt to pull it into place using the bolts as it could crack.*

18 Refit all the bolts, tightening them by hand only at first until the timing chain case is correctly settled in position. Tighten first the three bolts along the bottom edge, then, working in a diagonal sequence from the centre outwards and in two or three stages, tighten the retaining bolts to the specified torque. Wipe off any excess sealant.

19 Refit the engine right-hand mounting brackets (Section 21).

20 Refit the VTC oil control solenoid valve (Section 9).

21 Reconnect the crankshaft position sensor and the VTC oil control solenoid valve wiring.

22 Refit the crankshaft pulley (see previous Section).

23 Fit a new auxiliary drivebelt (Chapter 1A).

24 Refit the cylinder head cover (Chapter 1A).

25 The remainder of reassembly is the reverse of the removal procedure. For 2005-onwards models, Honda specify that their Honda Diagnostic System (HDS) tester must be used to clear CKP (CranKshaft Position sensor) pattern data from the engine management system ECU memory and then to run a sequence during a road test whereby the ECU can learn new CKP pattern data. This requirement is not mentioned for 2001 to 2004 models. If on restarting the engine the engine management Malfunction Indicator warning Lamp (MIL) illuminates, the vehicle must be taken to a Honda dealer or other specialist for the fault code to be erased and for the CKP pattern data to be cleared and relearned.

26 When Honda's own liquid gasket has been used to seal a joint, note the following:

a) Where applicable, wait at least 30 minutes before filling the engine with oil.

b) Do not run the engine for at least three hours.

H46687

6.16b Apply liquid gasket evenly along timing chain case's front, rear and bottom mating surfaces, around inside edges of bolt holes – also to supporting bosses shown and around outside edges of bolt holes of VTC oil control solenoid valve aperture

7 Timing chain – removal, inspection and refitting

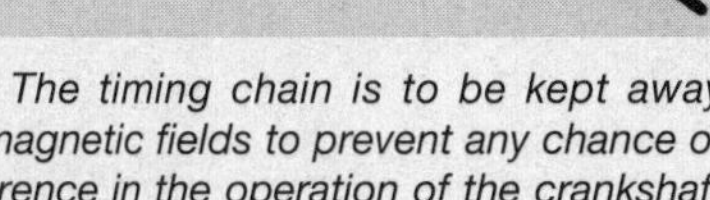

Note: *The timing chain is to be kept away from magnetic fields to prevent any chance of interference in the operation of the crankshaft position sensor.*

Removal

1 Remove the timing chain case (see previous Section).

7.2 If tensioner plunger protrudes more than 16 mm, timing chain is worn out and must be renewed

2 Assess the chain's state of wear by measuring the protrusion of the tensioner plunger (the distance between the tensioner body and the flat bearing surface of the tensioner blade) **(see illustration)**. If the plunger protrudes more than 16 mm, the timing chain is worn out and must be renewed. Assuming that the balancer/oil pump drive chain will have suffered an equivalent degree of wear, it too should be renewed if the timing chain fails this test.

3 Loosely refit the crankshaft pulley and rotate it anti-clockwise to compress the tensioner until the lockplate moves back far enough for a 1.5 mm diameter pin to be inserted into the holes in the lockplate and tensioner body. The Honda service tool for this task is Part No. 14511-PNA-003. We used a paperclip **(see illustrations)**.

4 Rotate the crankshaft pulley clockwise again to hold the pin in place and lock the tensioner, then unscrew the two mounting bolts and withdraw the timing chain tensioner **(see illustration)**. Remove the pulley.

5 Unscrew the two mounting bolts and withdraw the fixed guide from the timing chain's top run **(see illustration)**.

6 Unscrew the three mounting bolts and withdraw the fixed guide from the timing chain's front run **(see illustration)**.

7 Unscrew the pivot bolt and withdraw the tensioner blade from the timing chain's rear run **(see illustration)**.

8 Withdraw the crankshaft position sensor rotor to prevent it being lost or dropped into the sump **(see illustration)**. Be careful not to dislodge the sprocket from its location on the crankshaft end.

9 Disengage the timing chain from the sprockets and withdraw it **(see illustration)**.

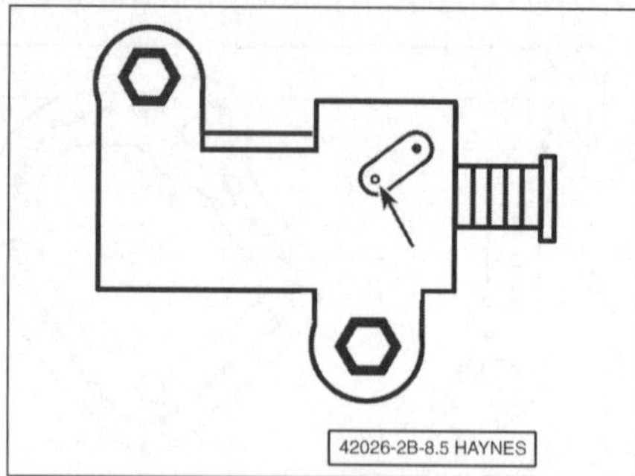

7.3a Rotate crankshaft pulley anti-clockwise to compress tensioner until hole in lockplate aligns with hole in tensioner body . . .

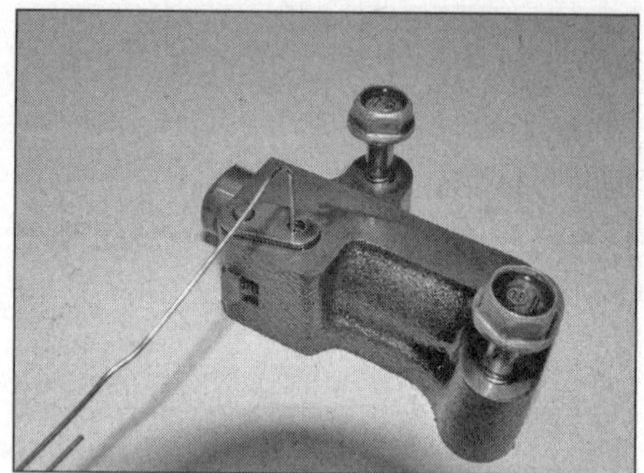

7.3b . . . then insert a 1.5 mm diameter pin through plate and into tensioner to lock it in compressed position

Inspection

10 The chain's wear should already have been checked as described in paragraph 2.

11 Inspect the links of the chain for signs of wear or damage on the plates. Look for links that are looser or tighter than the others, or kinked. If there is any sign of binding, excessive side play or kinking in the chain, it must be renewed.

12 It is a sensible precaution to renew the timing chain, regardless of its apparent condition, if the engine has covered a high mileage, or if the chain has sounded noisy with the engine running.

13 Examine the teeth on the camshaft and crankshaft sprockets for any sign of wear or damage such as chipped or hooked teeth. It is good practice to renew the chain and sprockets as a matched set.

14 Examine the chain guides and tensioner

7.4 Timing chain tensioner mounting bolts

7.5 Unscrew two bolts and withdraw fixed guide from timing chain's top run

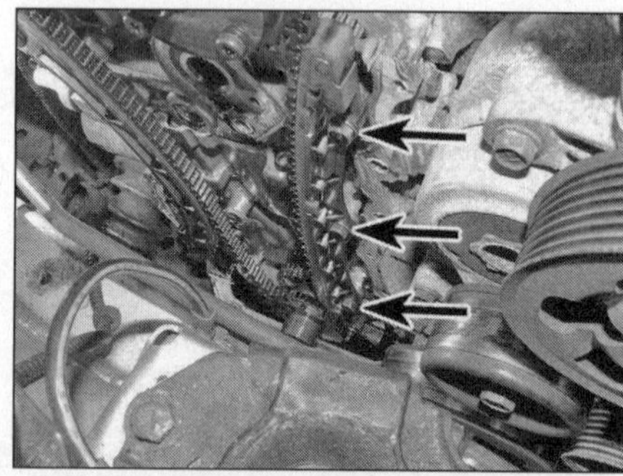

7.6 Unscrew three bolts and withdraw fixed guide from timing chain's front run

7.7 Unscrew pivot bolt and withdraw tensioner blade from timing chain's rear run

7.8 Withdraw crankshaft position sensor's rotor to prevent it being lost or dropped into the sump

7.9 Removing the timing chain

7.15a Camshafts can be rotated using a spanner as shown to align timing marks on reassembly

7.15b Crankshaft keyway and arrow mark on crankshaft drive sprocket must align with cylinder block arrow mark as shown

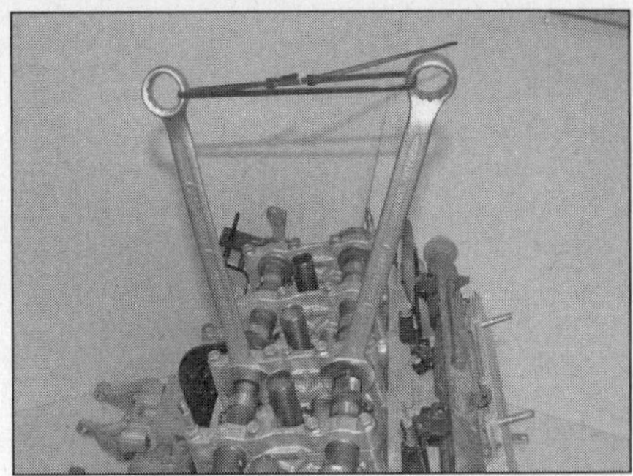
7.15c Use spanners and cable tie as shown to secure camshafts in position against valve spring pressure . . .

7.16a . . . so that timing marks align as shown and timing chain's two closest blue plates (A) fit over punch-marked teeth (B) on camshaft sprockets . . .

7.16b . . . and single blue plate fits over punch-marked tooth on crankshaft drive sprocket

blade for signs of wear or damage to their plastic chain contact faces, renewing any that are badly marked.

Refitting

15 Check that No. 1 cylinder is at TDC on the compression stroke by ensuring that the timing marks on the crankshaft and camshafts are aligned as described below. Temporarily refit the crankshaft pulley, if necessary, to rotate the crankshaft; rotate the camshafts by means of an open-ended spanner applied to the hexagons formed at their mid-point **(see illustration)**. If either camshaft has to be rotated very far to bring its marks into alignment, first rotate the engine 45° backwards (anti-clockwise) using a spanner or socket on the crankshaft pulley. This positions the pistons half-way up the bores, ensuring there is no danger of accidental valve-to-piston contact. Once the camshafts are correctly positioned, return the crankshaft to TDC. The marks must be as follows:

a) *With the sprocket pressed firmly back against the shoulder on the crankshaft end so that its locating peg is engaged in the second/inboard crankshaft keyway, the arrow mark stamped on the balancer/oil pump part of the timing chain and balancer/oil pump drive chain crankshaft drive sprocket must align with the arrow mark cast on the cylinder block; the first/outboard keyway in the crankshaft end will also align with the cylinder block arrow mark* ***(see illustration)****.*

b) *The punch marks on the rims of the camshaft sprockets and the arrow mark stamped on the VTC actuator must all be at the top (twelve o'clock position), while the lines stamped in both sprocket rims must point inwards towards each other and align exactly with the mating surface of the No. 1 cam follower assembly support and its bearing cap* ***(see illustration 6.4)****. To hold the camshafts in this position against valve spring pressure while the timing chain is missing, fit a spanner to each camshaft's hexagonal section, align the marks, and secure the spanners with a cable tie* ***(see illustration)****.*

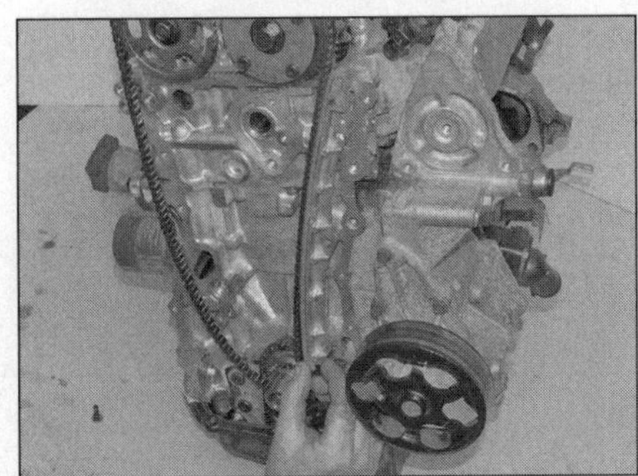
7.17a Keeping chain front run taut, refit fixed guide . . .

16 One side of the timing chain has three blue-coloured sideplates, two of which are seven links apart while the third is some distance away. Fit the timing chain to the crankshaft drive sprocket so that the single coloured sideplate fits over the punch-marked tooth, then, keeping the chain as taut as possible on its front run, fit it first to the intake camshaft sprocket, then to the exhaust, so that the coloured sideplates fit over the punch-marked teeth on each **(see illustrations)**.

17 Refit the fixed guide to the timing chain's front run. Tighten the mounting bolts to the specified torque **(see illustrations)**.

18 Refit the tensioner blade to the timing chain's rear run. Tighten the pivot bolt to the specified torque **(see illustration)**.

19 Refit the tensioner, engaging its plunger on the tensioner blade's free end. Tighten the mounting bolts to the specified torque **(see illustration 7.4)**.

20 Refit the fixed guide to the timing chain's

7.17b . . . and tighten mounting bolts to specified torque wrench setting

7.18 Refit tensioner blade to timing chain's rear run and tighten pivot bolt to specified torque wrench setting

7.20 Refit timing chain top guide and tighten bolts

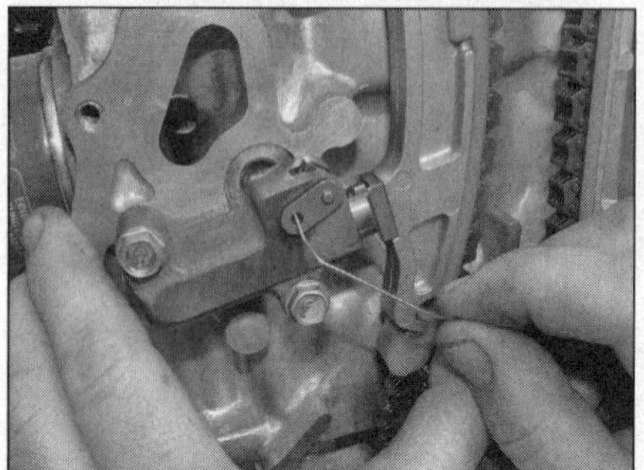
7.21a Hold tensioner blade against tensioner plunger and remove locking pin from tensioner . . .

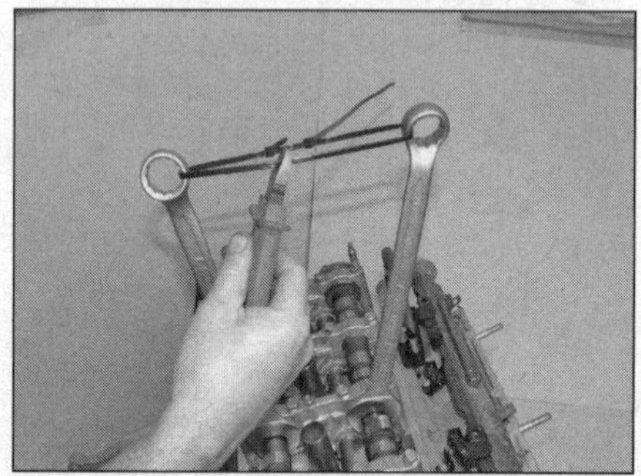
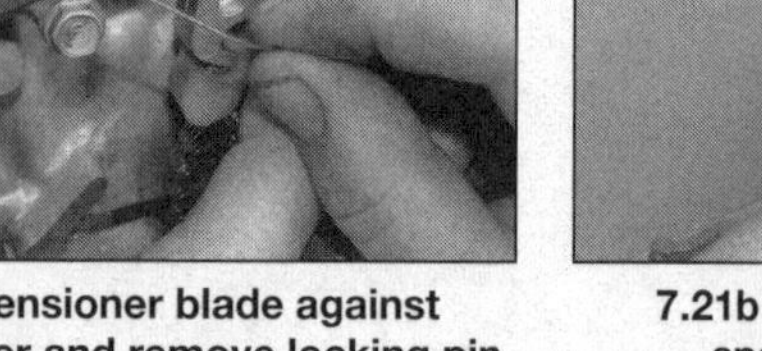
7.21b . . . cut cable tie and remove spanners from camshafts . . .

7.21c . . . then check that timing marks are all aligned and tensioner has tightened timing chain

top run. Tighten the mounting bolts to the specified torque **(see illustration)**.

21 Hold the tensioner blade against the tensioner plunger and remove the locking pin from the tensioner. Cut the cable tie and remove the spanners from the camshafts **(see illustrations)**. Check that the timing marks and coloured sideplates are correctly in place and that the tensioner plunger has taken up any slack in the chain **(see illustration)**.

22 Refit the crankshaft position sensor's rotor (if removed). Its locating key must engage in the crankshaft keyway and the OUT-SIDE marking must be visible **(see illustration)**.

23 Temporarily refit the crankshaft pulley and rotate the crankshaft two full turns (720°) clockwise and check that when the arrow mark on the balancer/oil pump part of the timing chain and balancer/oil pump drive chain crankshaft drive sprocket aligns again with the arrow mark cast on the cylinder block, that the camshaft sprocket marks align exactly, as described in paragraph 15 above. If not, repeat the procedure until the timing chain is correctly refitted.

24 Refit the timing chain case (see previous Section).

8 Timing chain tensioner and sprockets – removal, inspection and refitting

Tensioner – chain case in situ

Note: *Liquid gasket (Honda Part No. 08C70-K0234M, 08C70-K0334M, 08C70-X0331S or 08718-0001 or equivalent) must be available on reassembly.*

Removal

1 Bring the engine to TDC, No. 1 firing, as described in Section 3.

2 Unclip the crankshaft position sensor's wiring guide from the tensioner's cover plate, then unscrew its three retaining bolts **(see illustration)**.

3 Withdraw the cover plate **(see illustration)**. Use a hammer and a block of wood or a soft-faced mallet to break the seal by tapping the cover plate, then carefully prise it away from the timing chain case; the liquid gasket used on assembly sticks tight. Do NOT lever between the mating surfaces.

Caution: Be careful not to nick or gouge the mating surfaces of the tensioner cover plate and timing chain case or oil leaks will result.

4 Rotate the crankshaft pulley anti-clockwise

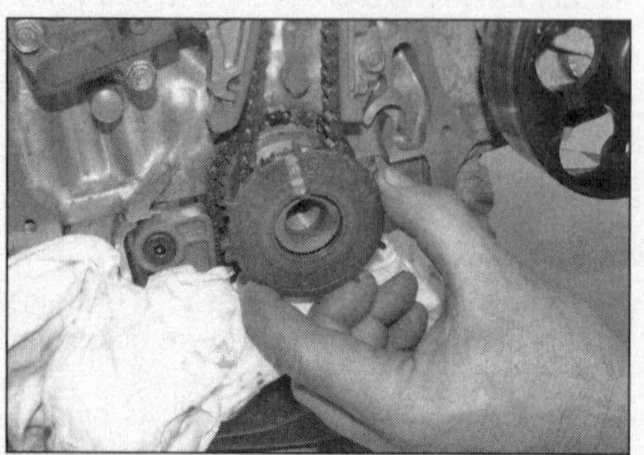
7.22 Refit crankshaft position sensor's rotor with locating key engaged in crankshaft keyway and OUT-SIDE marking visible

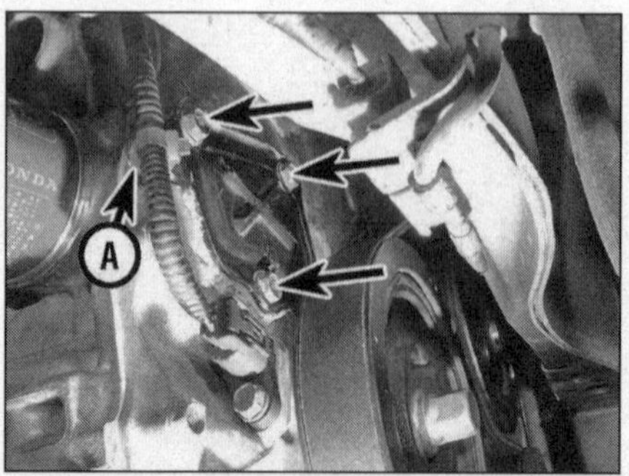

8.2 Unscrew bolts and crankshaft position sensor's wiring guide (A) . . .

8.3 . . . to withdraw timing chain tensioner's cover plate

8.4a Rotate crankshaft pulley anti-clockwise to compress tensioner until holes align . . .

to compress the tensioner until the lockplate moves back far enough for a 1.5 mm diameter pin to be inserted into the holes in the lockplate and tensioner body **(see illustrations)**. Also see Section 7.

5 Rotate the crankshaft pulley clockwise again to hold the pin in place and lock the timing chain tensioner, then unscrew its two mounting bolts and withdraw the tensioner.

Caution: Do NOT rotate the crankshaft while the tensioner is removed, or the timing chain may drop clear of the crankshaft sprocket and so lose correct valve timing. This will necessitate the removal of the timing chain.

6 Clean the mating surfaces of the timing chain case and the tensioner's cover plate. Clean any oil or old gasket material and sealant from the mating surfaces and from the bolt holes and threads. Be careful not to allow dirt and debris to fall into the engine. Degrease the surfaces completely before applying sealant.

Inspection

7 Check that the tensioner is undamaged and that its oilways are clear. Compress the plunger by hand until the locking pin can be withdrawn and press in the exposed end of the ratchet, against its spring pressure, to enable the plunger to be moved in and out through its full range of movement. It should move smoothly, with no sticking or jerkiness. Do not allow the plunger to fly out uncontrolled, or the assembly may be damaged.

8 With the ratchet released, check that the plunger can extend but cannot be compressed back into the tensioner body. Check also that there is no sign of wear along the plunger's length.

9 If there is any evidence of wear or damage, the tensioner must be renewed.

Refitting

10 Disengage the ratchet and compress the plunger as far as possible into the tensioner, then release the ratchet and fit the locking pin into the holes in the lockplate and tensioner body.

11 Refit the tensioner, engaging its plunger on the tensioner blade's free end. Tighten the mounting bolts to the specified torque.

12 Hold the tensioner blade against the tensioner plunger and remove the locking pin. Rotate the crankshaft two full turns (720°) clockwise until the pulley notch and timing marks align again. Check that the tensioner plunger has taken up any slack in the chain.

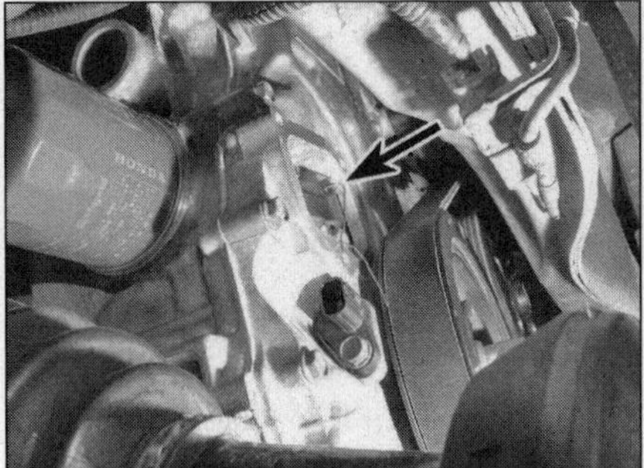

8.4b . . . then insert 1.5 mm diameter pin through plate and into tensioner to lock it in compressed position

13 Apply a continuous bead of liquid gasket (approximately 3 mm diameter) evenly around the cover plate's mating surface so that the bead is around the inside edges of the bolt holes **(see illustration)**. Also apply a small blob of liquid gasket to the bolt holes in the timing chain case to ensure that there are no oil leaks from the threads. Work carefully, but as quickly as possible; the cover plate must be installed within five minutes of applying the liquid gasket – if this time limit is exceeded, it must be wiped off completely and new liquid gasket applied in its place.

14 Refit the cover plate, tightening its bolts to the specified torque.

15 The remainder of reassembly is the reverse of the removal procedure.

16 When Honda's own liquid gasket has been used to seal a joint, note the following:

a) Where applicable, wait at least 30 minutes before filling the engine with oil.

b) Do not run the engine for at least three hours.

Tensioner – chain case removed

Removal

17 Proceed as described in Section 7, paragraphs 1 to 4.

Inspection

18 See paragraphs 7 to 9 above.

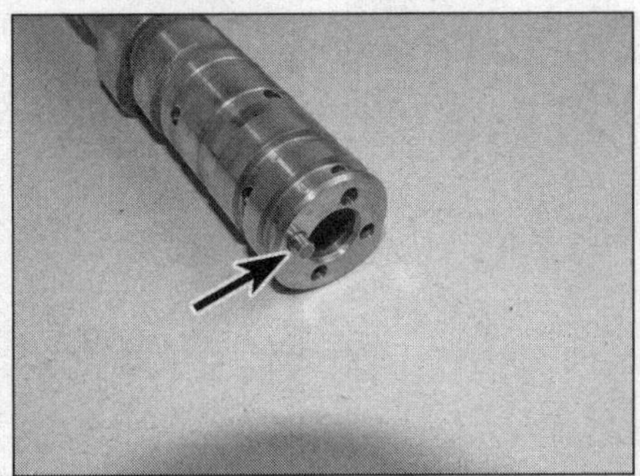

8.21 Note dowel pin locating intake camshaft sprocket/VTC actuator on camshaft end

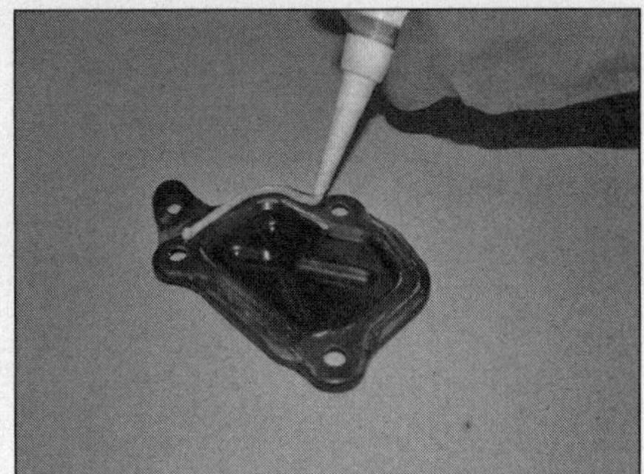

8.13 Apply bead of liquid gasket evenly around cover plate's mating surface around inside edges of bolt holes

Refitting

19 Proceed as described in Section 7.

Camshaft sprockets/ VTC actuator

Removal

20 Remove the timing chain (Section 7).

21 Hold the camshaft with an open-ended spanner on the hexagon formed at its mid-point, then slacken the sprocket retaining bolt. Unscrew the bolt and withdraw the sprocket (and VTC actuator on the intake camshaft), noting the locating dowel pin; if this is loose it should be removed and kept with the sprocket **(see illustration)**.

Inspection

22 See Section 7, paragraph 13. If applicable check the VTC actuator as described in Section 9.

Refitting

23 Refit the locating dowel pin (if removed). Fit the sprocket to the camshaft end, engaging it on the locating dowel. Apply a film of clean oil to the threads of the sprocket retaining bolt, hold the camshaft with an open-ended spanner and tighten the bolt to the specified torque **(see illustrations)**.

24 The remainder of reassembly is the reverse of the removal procedure.

Crankshaft sprocket

Caution: The removal of the timing chain and balancer/oil pump drive chain's crankshaft drive sprocket requires the

8.23a Fit sprocket/actuator to camshaft end, engaging it on locating dowel . . .

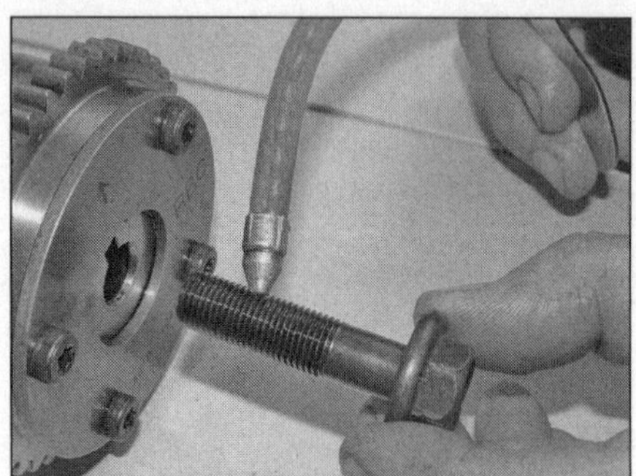

8.23b . . . apply clean oil to threads of sprocket/actuator's retaining bolt . . .

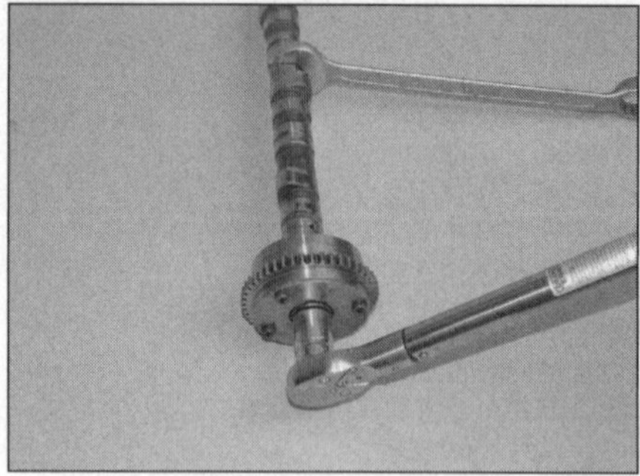

8.23c . . . hold camshaft with open-ended spanner and tighten bolt to specified torque wrench setting

removal first of the timing chain case and of the sump, the latter entailing the removal of the front suspension subframe. This leaves the engine/transmission unit hanging on the hoist in the engine compartment and located only by its left-hand mounting. The home mechanic may prefer to consider removing the engine/transmission complete and then removing the sump.

Removal

25 Remove the timing chain and the crankshaft position sensor's rotor (Section 7).

26 Support the timing chain end of the engine with an engine hoist. Bolt a lifting eye to the right-hand end of the cylinder head.

27 Remove the sump (Section 13).

28 Remove the balancer/oil pump drive chain (Section 15).

Inspection

29 See Section 7, paragraph 13.

Refitting

30 Both keyways in the crankshaft end must point straight up (twelve o'clock position), to align with the arrow mark cast on the cylinder block; temporarily refit the crankshaft pulley, if necessary, to rotate the crankshaft into position **(see illustration)**.

31 Refit the balancer/oil pump drive chain (Section 15).

32 Once the timing chain has been refitted, refit the crankshaft position sensor's rotor (Section 7).

33 The remainder of reassembly is the reverse of the removal procedure.

9 i-VTEC and VTC systems – component renewal

HAYNES HiNT ***If investigating a suspected fault in the i-VTEC and VTC systems, remember that these systems have proved themselves generally reliable; any perceived fault may be due to external factors such as low oil level, poor oil quality or clogged filters, rather than to a faulty component of the system. If a fault is encountered, especially if the vehicle's service history is in any way dubious, the first step is to perform an engine oil and filter change.***

Note: *If a fault code related to VTEC System Malfunction is logged in the engine management ECU's memory so that the engine management Malfunction Indicator warning Lamp (MIL) illuminates, the VTC system control will be disabled and it will default to fix the valve timing at full retard. The fault code must be cleared using a Honda PGM Tester or Honda Diagnostic System (HDS) tester, or equivalent, connected to the diagnostic socket under the driver's side of the facia, and the necessary action taken.*

Cam follower assembly

1 Refer to Section 11.

Camshaft position sensor

Removal

2 There are two identical camshaft position sensors fitted to the left-hand end of the cylinder head **(see illustration)**. The front sensor, detecting the position of the intake camshaft, serves the i-VTEC/VTC system.

3 Remove the air cleaner assembly (Chapter 4A).

4 Disconnect the sensor's electrical connector **(see illustration)**. Remove the retaining screw, and withdraw the sensor from the cylinder head; be prepared for slight oil loss. Remove and discard the sealing O-ring; this must be renewed.

Refitting

5 Refitting is the reverse of the removal procedure, noting the following points:

a) Apply clean engine oil to the new O-ring.
b) Locate the sensor fully in the cylinder head, and wipe off any surplus lubricant before securing it.
c) Tighten the screw securely.

Camshaft position sensor rotor

Removal

6 Remove the cylinder head cover (Chapter 1A, Section 16, paragraphs 3 to 6).

8.30 Crankshaft first/outboard keyway (A) and second/inboard keyway (B) must align with cylinder block arrow mark (C). Crankshaft drive sprocket locating peg (D) must engage with keyway (B)

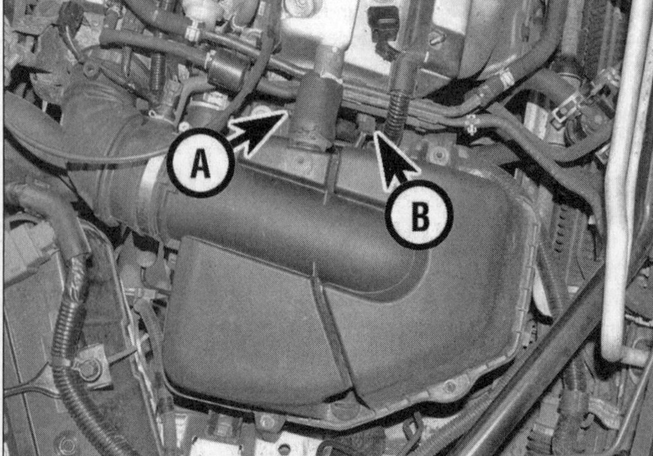

9.2 Front camshaft position sensor (A) serves i-VTEC/VTC system; rear sensor (B) is TDC sensor for engine management system

9.4 Disconnecting camshaft position sensor's electrical connector

7 Hold the camshaft with an open-ended spanner on the hexagon formed at its mid-point, then slacken the rotor retaining bolt **(see illustration)**. Unscrew the bolt and withdraw the rotor from the camshaft, noting the locating dowel pin; if this is loose it should be removed and kept with the rotor.

Inspection

8 Renew the rotor if it is marked or damaged in any way.

Refitting

9 Refit the locating dowel pin (if removed). Fit the rotor to the camshaft end, engaging it on the locating dowel. Hold the camshaft with an open-ended spanner and tighten the rotor retaining bolt securely.

10 Refit the cylinder head cover (Chapter 1A)

i-VTEC oil pressure switch

Note: *Two oil pressure switches are fitted to the engine. The switch mounted on the i-VTEC solenoid valve assembly, at the right-hand rear end of the cylinder head, serves the i-VTEC/VTC system.*

Removal

11 The switch can be removed as part of the solenoid valve assembly (see below). To remove the switch alone, proceed as follows.

12 Disconnect the battery negative (earth) lead (see *Disconnecting the battery*).

13 Unbolt the steering hose clamp from the rear right-hand end of the cylinder head cover.

14 If the black plastic-covered wiring harness prevents access to the switch, unscrew the four nuts securing the ignition coil cover on top of the engine. Lift off the cover; be careful not to lose the separate spacer from each rear mounting stud. Disconnect the ignition coils and lift the wiring conduit from its mountings. See Sections 16 and 18 of Chapter 1A for further information.

15 Disconnect the oil pressure switch connector from the top of the solenoid valve assembly.

16 Unscrew the switch and withdraw it; be prepared for slight oil loss. Remove and discard the sealing O-ring; this must be renewed.

Refitting

17 Refitting is the reverse of the removal

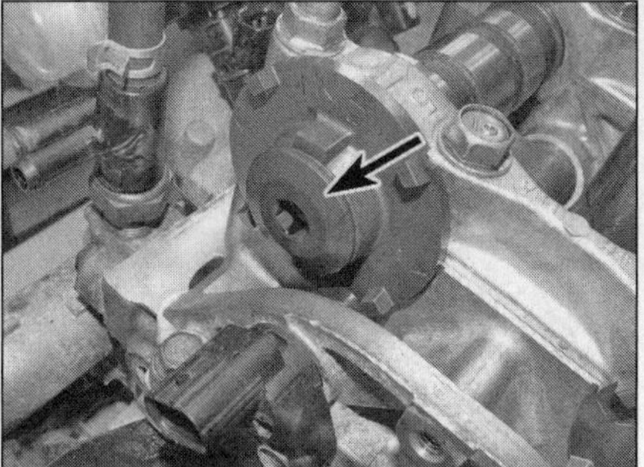

9.7 Unscrew camshaft position sensor rotor's retaining bolt to remove rotor

procedure. Use a new O-ring and tighten the switch to the specified torque.

i-VTEC solenoid valve assembly

Removal

18 The i-VTEC solenoid valve assembly is located at the right-hand rear end of the cylinder head **(see illustration)**.

19 Proceed as in paragraphs 12 to 14 above.

20 Disconnect the i-VTEC solenoid valve and oil pressure switch connectors on the top of the assembly **(see illustration)**.

21 Unscrew the three bolts from the rear and withdraw the assembly from the cylinder head; be prepared for slight oil loss. Note that a fourth bolt secures the assembly's cover **(see illustration)**.

22 Retrieve the O-ring/filter and check the filter gauze for signs of clogging **(see illustration)**. Note that on 2005-on models,

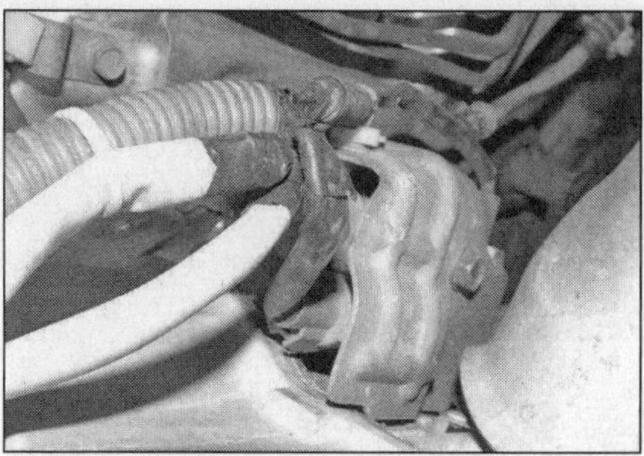

9.18 i-VTEC solenoid valve assembly is located at right-hand rear end of cylinder head

this component must be renewed as a matter of course whenever it is disturbed.

Inspection

23 The resistance of the solenoid windings can be measured. If the readings obtained differ significantly from those specified, the solenoid is faulty and the assembly must be renewed.

24 If the filter gauze is found to be clogged, Honda state that it must be renewed, and that the engine oil and filter must be changed. In this case the VTC filter on the front side of the cylinder head should be removed and cleaned as well.

25 If there is any sign of oil leakage from the assembly/cylinder head mating surface or any evidence that the O-ring is too flattened to provide an effective seal, it must be renewed.

26 Check the oilways for signs of clogging and either flush them with solvent or use an airline to blow them clear **(see illustration)**.

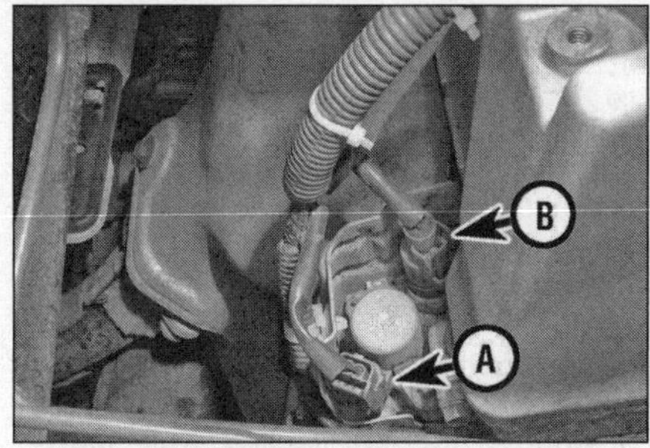

9.20 i-VTEC solenoid valve (A) and oil pressure switch (B) connectors on top of i-VTEC solenoid valve assembly

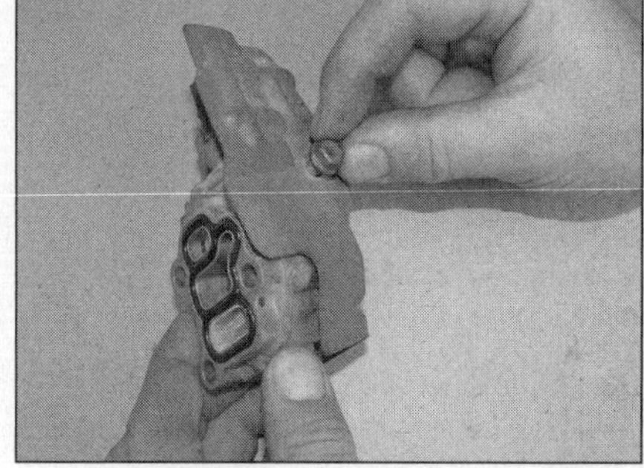

9.21 i-VTEC solenoid valve assembly's cover is secured by a fourth bolt

9.22 Check i-VTEC solenoid valve assembly's O-ring/filter gauze and clean or renew as required

9.26 Check i-VTEC solenoid valve assembly's oilways for signs of clogging and flush with solvent or blow clear as required

9.27 On refitting, fit O-ring/filter gauze (new on later models) to assembly grooves

9.33b . . . to the other. Renew actuator if movement is limited or jerky and rough

Refitting

27 Refitting is the reverse of the removal procedure. Fit the O-ring into the grooves **(see illustration)**. Tighten the mounting bolts to the specified torque.

VTC actuator

Removal

28 The actuator is removed with the camshaft sprocket (Section 8).

Inspection

29 If the camshaft sprocket teeth are worn or damaged in any way the sprocket/VTC actuator must be renewed as an assembly.

30 To check the operation of the VTC actuator it must be removed while attached the intake camshaft (Section 10). Proceed as follows.

31 Hold the camshaft and attempt to rotate the VTC actuator clockwise and anti-clockwise; if it is not locked, the sprocket/VTC actuator must be renewed.

Warning: Wear eye protection during the next step; oil will spray everywhere.

32 Wipe clean the camshaft's right-hand bearing journal. The journal has two grooves, each of which has an oilway drilled in it; the oilway furthest from the VTC actuator provides the pressurised oil supply to advance the VTC actuator. Wrap several layers of insulating tape around the camshaft, sealing these two oilways but noting the location of the advance opening. Punch a hole in the tape over this oilway, and use an airline to apply pressure (4 bars approx) to the VTC actuator **(see illustration)**.

33 With air pressure applied, it should be possible to move the VTC actuator backwards and forwards throughout its full range of travel **(see illustrations)**. If the actuator does not move, or if it is limited in travel or rough and jerky in operation, the sprocket/VTC actuator must be renewed.

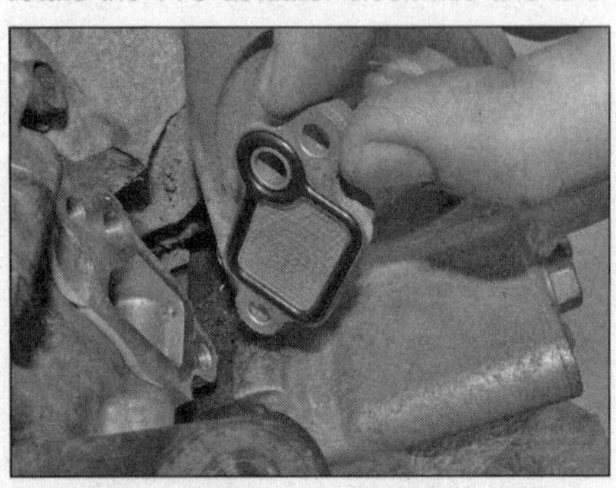

9.40a On refitting, fit O-ring/filter gauze to cover plate grooves . . .

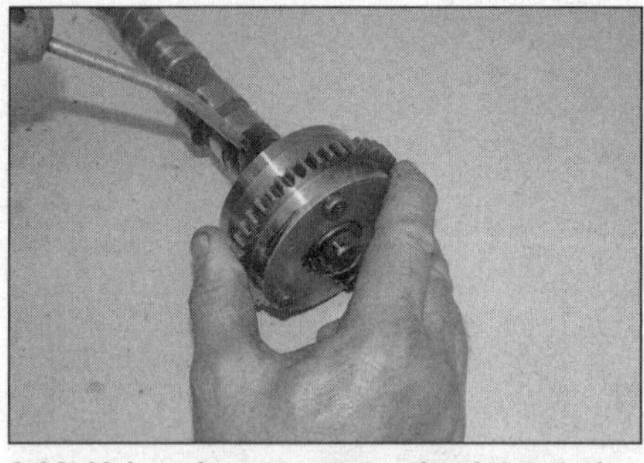

9.32 Using air pressure to check operation of VTC actuator – wear eye protection against oil spray

9.37 VTC filter is located at right-hand front end of cylinder head

9.40b . . . and tighten filter cover plate bolts securely

9.33a With air pressure applied, actuator should be free to move from one end of its movement range . . .

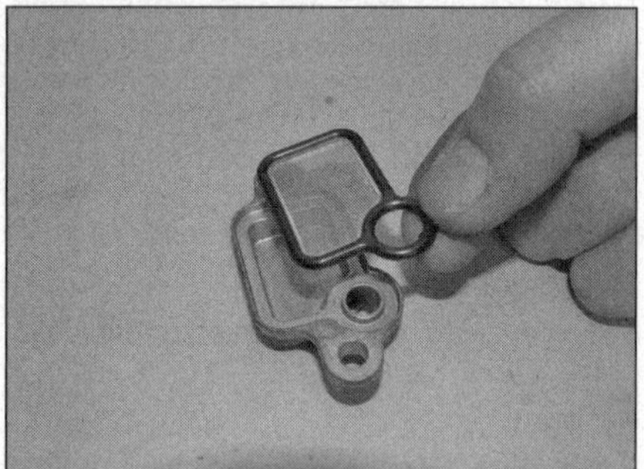

9.38 Check VTC O-ring/filter gauze and clean or renew as required

Refitting

34 Refer to Section 8.

VTC filter

Removal

35 The VTC filter is located at the right-hand front end of the cylinder head.

36 Remove the auxiliary drivebelt and its tensioner as described in Chapter 1A.

37 Unbolt the filter cover plate and withdraw it **(see illustration)**.

38 Retrieve the O-ring/filter and check the filter gauze for signs of clogging **(see illustration)**.

Inspection

39 If the filter gauze is found to be clogged, it can be cleaned with solvent and a brush. If this is necessary it is advisable to change the engine oil and filter. If there is any sign of oil leakage from the filter/cylinder head mating surface the filter must be renewed.

Refitting

40 Refitting is the reverse of the removal procedure, noting the following points:

*a) Fit the filter and sealing O-ring to the cover plate **(see illustration)**.*

*b) Tighten securely the cover plate mounting bolts **(see illustration)**.*

c) Fit a new auxiliary drivebelt as described in Chapter 1A.

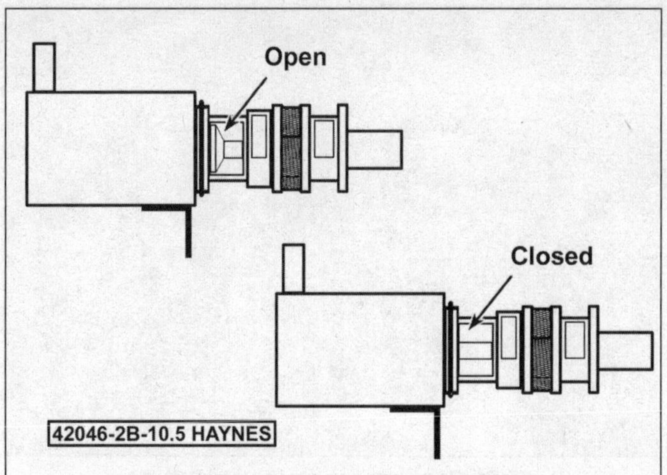

9.44a Check whether piston shoulder is visible in port nearest valve's mounting flange; with no power connected, piston should not be visible

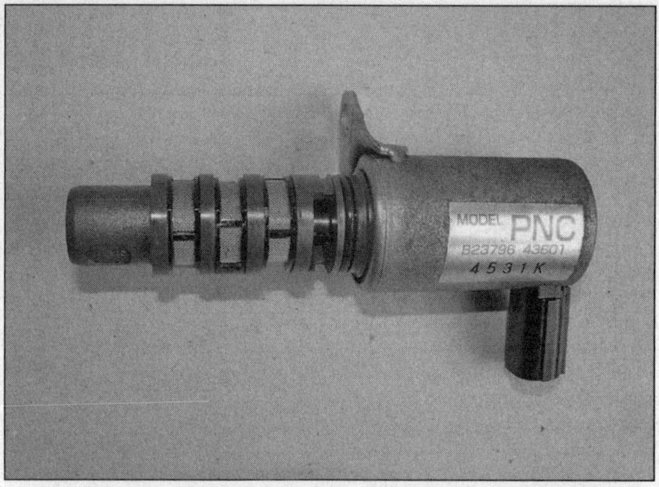

9.44b Check VTC oil control solenoid valve filter gauzes and clean or renew valve as required. Note that some models have three gauze screens, while others have only two

VTC oil control solenoid valve

Removal

41 The VTC oil control solenoid valve is located at the top of the timing chain case.

42 Disconnect the battery negative (earth) lead (see *Disconnecting the battery*).

43 Disconnect the solenoid valve's electrical connector. Remove the mounting bolt and withdraw the solenoid valve from the cylinder head; be prepared for slight oil loss. Remove and discard the solenoid valve's sealing O-ring; this must be renewed.

Inspection

44 With no power connected to the solenoid, the valve should be closed – ie, the piston shoulder should be in the closed position, flush with the solenoid body **(see illustrations)**. If the shoulder projects at all beyond the solenoid body, the valve is jammed open. When the solenoid is energised by connecting the vehicle's battery across its terminals (battery negative lead to the solenoid's No. 1 terminal), the valve should open so that the piston shoulder projects at least 1.2 mm beyond the solenoid body. If the valve does not open and close as described, it must be renewed.

45 The resistance of the solenoid windings can be measured. If the readings obtained differ significantly from those specified, the solenoid is faulty and must be renewed.

46 If the filter gauze is found to be clogged, it must be renewed. In this case the VTC filter on the front side of the cylinder head should be removed and cleaned as well, the engine oil should be changed and the filter renewed.

Refitting

47 Refitting is the reverse of the removal procedure, noting the following points:

a) Do not wear fibrous gloves when fitting the oil control solenoid valve and be careful not to contaminate the opening in the timing chain case/cylinder head.

b) Apply clean engine oil to the new O-ring when installing it ***(see illustration)****.*

c) Clean and dry the mating surfaces of the solenoid valve and cylinder head, then locate the valve fully in the cylinder head ***(see illustration)****.*

d) Tighten the bolt to the specified torque ***(see illustration)****.*

10 Camshafts – removal, inspection and refitting

Note: *If either camshaft's sprocket or position sensor rotor is to be removed, slacken its retaining bolt or screw before unbolting the camshaft bearing caps, when the camshaft is easier to hold.*

Removal

1 Bring the engine to TDC, No 1 firing, and remove the timing chain (Section 7).

2 Slacken the locknuts and completely slacken (but do not remove) the valve adjuster screws, to remove valve spring pressure from the camshafts and follower assembly components.

3 Working in sequence, slacken the camshaft bearing cap bolts/cam follower assembly support bolts two turns at a time, to relieve the pressure evenly and in several gradual stages **(see illustration)**. Unless the cam follower assembly is to be removed as well, leave the two 6 mm bolts securing No. 5 cam follower assembly support (Nos. 2 and 3 in the illustration). In this case, do not disturb No. 5 cam follower assembly support, or the complete assembly will have to be removed for the mating surface to be cleaned and for new liquid gasket to be applied.

Caution: If the bearing cap bolts are slackened carelessly, a cap might break. If any of the caps is broken, the complete

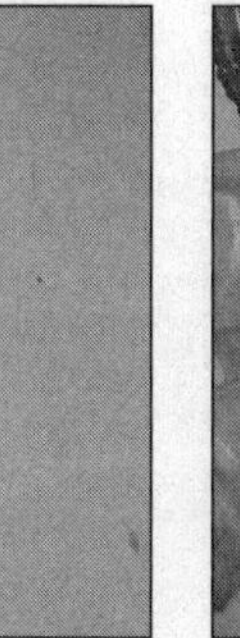

9.47a Apply clean engine oil to solenoid valve's new sealing O-ring when installing

9.47b Ensure absolute cleanliness when refitting VTC oil control solenoid valve . . .

9.47c . . . and tighten mounting bolt to specified torque wrench setting

10.3 Camshaft bearing cap bolts/cam follower assembly support mounting bolts SLACKENING sequence

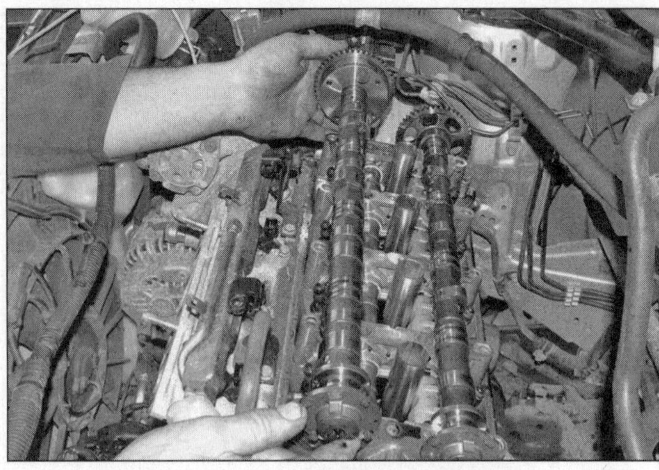

10.5a Removing the intake camshaft . . .

cam follower assembly support must be renewed, along with the cylinder head.

4 Withdraw the camshaft bearing caps, noting how they are numbered and marked with arrows pointing to the timing chain end as a guide to correct reassembly. Note also the correct fitted positions of the locating dowels. If the dowels are loose, remove them and store them with their bearing caps.

5 Lift out the camshafts **(see illustrations)**.

Inspection

6 Examine the camshaft bearing surfaces and cam lobes for signs of wear ridges and scoring. Check that the lobes are not significantly worn below the height specified; when checking the intake camshaft, note that the primary lobes are the wider ones **(see illustration)**. Renew the camshaft if any of these conditions are apparent.

7 To check camshaft runout and endfloat, first remove the cam follower assembly, as described in the following Section, remove the follower pivot shafts and followers, then refit the supports, the camshafts and their bearing caps to the cylinder head. Tighten the camshaft bearing cap bolts to the specified torque, as described below. Check the camshaft endfloat with a dial gauge bearing on the sprocket end of the camshaft. Push the camshaft fully away, then zero the gauge. Push the camshaft fully the other way, and check the endfloat. If it is beyond the service limit specified, the cylinder head must be renewed and the endfloat rechecked. If it is still excessive, then the camshaft must be renewed.

10.5b . . . and the exhaust camshaft . . .

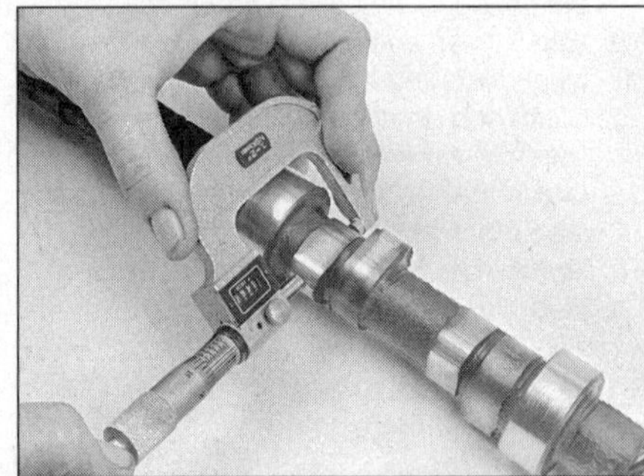

10.6 Measure camshaft lobe height with a micrometer

10.10a On refitting, clean camshaft bearing surfaces and oil liberally . . .

10.10b . . . apply lubricant (special assembly lubricant shown here) to camshaft lobes and bearing journals . . .

8 Use Plastigauge to check the camshaft bearing journal-to-bearing clearance. Unbolt the bearing caps, wipe clean the camshafts and refit them. Lay a strip of Plastigauge on each bearing journal, refit the bearing cap and tighten the camshaft bearing cap bolts to the specified torque. Unbolt the bearing caps again and measure the width of each strip at its widest point to determine the clearance. If any of the clearances are beyond the specified service limit then the worn components – either the camshaft or the cam follower/ cylinder head assembly – must be renewed.

9 Examine the condition of the bearing surfaces both on the camshaft journals and in the cam follower assembly support. If any of the bearing surfaces are worn or damaged, the components concerned will need to be renewed.

Refitting

10 Wipe clean the camshaft bearing journals and lobes and the bearing surfaces in the cam follower assembly supports. Liberally oil all bearing surfaces, the camshaft lobes and the followers **(see illustrations)**.

Caution: Failure to adequately lubricate the camshafts and related components can cause serious damage to shaft journals and bearing surfaces during the first few seconds after engine start-up.

11 Refit the camshafts to the cylinder head; the intake camshaft can be identified by having primary and secondary lobes for each cylinder. The punch marks on the rims of the camshaft sprockets and the arrow mark stamped on the VTC actuator must all be at the top (twelve o'clock position), while the lines stamped in both sprocket rims must point inwards towards each other **(see illustrations)**.

12 Refit the camshaft bearing caps, lubricating

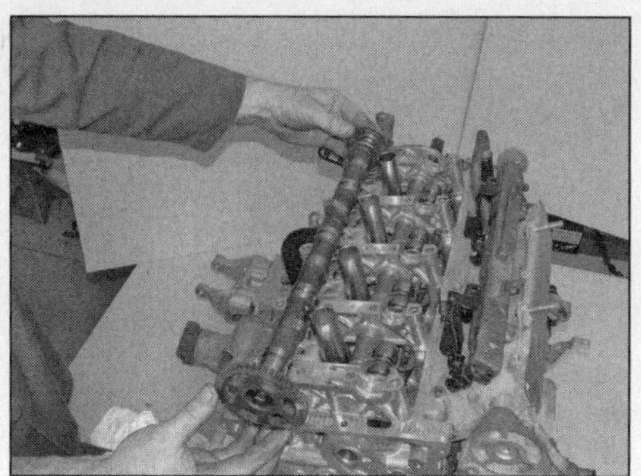

10.11a ... then refit the exhaust camshaft ...

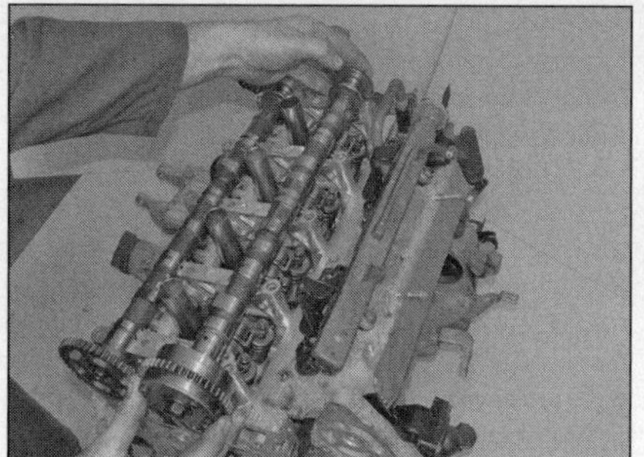

10.11b ... and the intake camshaft (with primary and secondary lobes) ...

10.11c ... and rotate so that timing marks (A) and (B) are at the top, and lines (C) point towards each other at the centre

10.12a Lubricate bearing surfaces and refit bearing caps ...

10.12b ... using arrow marks and cap numbering to ensure correct fitting

their bearing surfaces with clean engine oil and ensuring that the locating dowels are in position. Each cap is numbered 1 to 5 in ascending order from timing side to flywheel end and is marked with an arrow which must point towards the timing chain end. Tighten the bolts by hand only at this stage. Check that the locating dowels enter squarely into their bores **(see illustrations)**.

13 Working in sequence, evenly and progressively tighten the retaining bolts to draw the bearing caps and camshafts squarely down into place. Once the bearing caps are in contact with the head, go around in sequence and tighten the retaining bolts to the specified torque **(see illustration)**. As the camshafts are drawn into place, check that the sprocket timing marks remain in alignment, as shown in illustrations 6.4 and 7.16a. **Note:** *While the timing chain top run fixed guide mounting bolts will have to be unscrewed again to refit the guide when the timing chain is refitted later, they must still be tightened now, in their correct sequence, to ensure that the cam follower assembly is correctly and evenly tightened down on to the cylinder head.*

Caution: If the bearing cap bolts are carelessly tightened, a cap might break. If any of the caps is broken, the complete cam follower assembly support must be renewed, along with the cylinder head.

14 Tighten all the valve adjuster screws gently to close up the clearance between cam followers and camshaft lobes, but do not yet tighten the adjuster screw locknuts.

15 Refit the timing chain (Section 7).

16 As soon as the timing chain is correctly refitted and the crankshaft can be rotated safely, adjust the valve clearances as described in Chapter 1A.

17 Refit the timing chain case (Section 6).

11 Cam follower assembly – testing, removal, inspection and refitting

Testing

Note: *Testing the operation of the i-VTEC cam follower assembly requires an air compressor delivering at least 4 bars, plus adapters and blanking plugs that fit the various unions and threads on the engine. Owners without such tools may prefer to have this work carried out by a Honda dealer.*

1 Remove the cylinder head cover and bring the engine to TDC, No 1 firing (Chapter 1A, Section 16, paragraphs 3 to 8).

2 Check that No. 1 cylinder's intake primary and secondary followers move independently. Rotate the crankshaft pulley 180° clockwise until No. 3 piston is at TDC and check that cylinder's followers. Turn the crankshaft again to check No. 4 cylinder's followers and again to check No. 2's. If any followers are not free to move independently, the cam follower assembly must be removed for the cleaning and inspection.

3 Before proceeding to the next part of the test, check the valve clearances and adjust them if necessary; see Chapter 1A. Return the engine TDC, No 1 firing.

4 The test involves unscrewing the i-VTEC/VTC oil gallery sealing plug from the right-hand rear corner of the cylinder head and using a special air stopper to seal the relevant oilway **(see illustration)**. Bolts Nos. 15 and 23 in illustration 10.3 are then unscrewed from Nos. 2 and 3 bearing caps and are replaced by VTEC air adapters that are connected via a regulator to a compressor and a pressure of

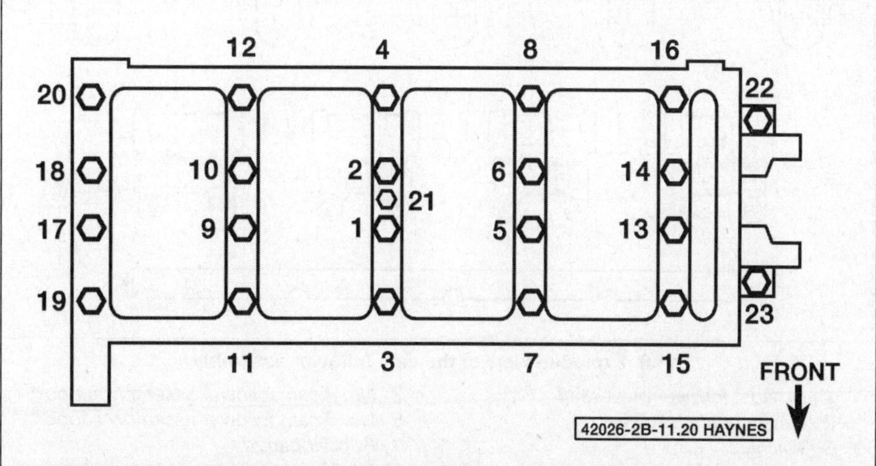

10.13 Camshaft bearing cap bolts/cam follower assembly support mounting bolts TIGHTENING sequence

11.4 i-VTEC/VTC oil gallery sealing plug

2.9 bars applied to the system. No. 1 cylinder's intake primary and secondary followers should be linked and unable to move independently; if they can still move separately, turn the crankshaft slowly clockwise to ensure that the bores in the primary and secondary followers are aligned. The test is then repeated with the crankshaft turned so bring each cylinder in turn to TDC on the compression stroke.

5 If each cylinder's intake primary and secondary followers are free to move independently with no air pressure applied, but locked instantly pressure is applied, and then released as soon as it is removed, then the cam follower assembly is functioning normally. If not, the assembly must be removed and dismantled for thorough cleaning, as described below. If any components are found to be worn or damaged, they must be renewed.

6 On completion of the test, remove the test equipment and refit the bolts and sealing plug, tightening them to their specified torques.

Removal

Note: *Liquid gasket (Honda Part No. 08C70-K0234M, 08C70-K0334M, 08C70-X0331S or 08718-0001 or equivalent) must be available on reassembly, in addition to any other items (gaskets, seals, etc) found to be in need of renewal during the procedure.*

7 With the engine positioned so that No. 1 cylinder is at TDC on the compression stroke, remove the timing chain (Section 7), then remove the camshafts (Section 10).

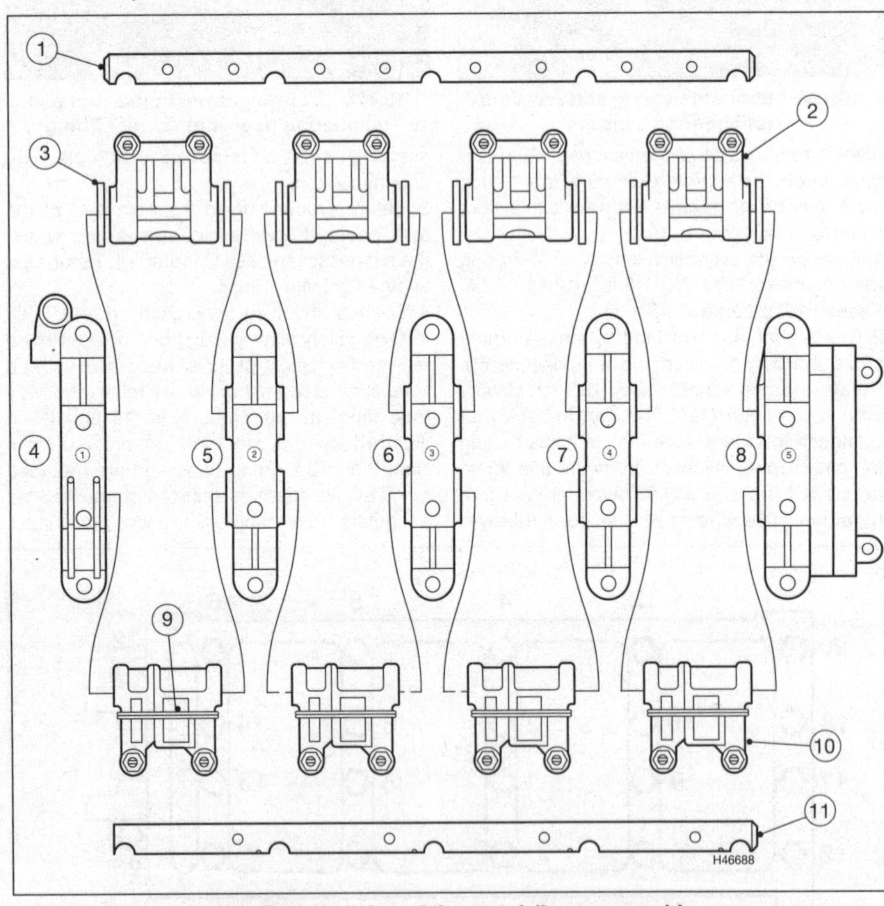

11.9 Exploded view of the cam follower assembly

1 *Exhaust follower pivot shaft*
2 *Exhaust cam followers*
3 *Washers*
4 *No. 1 cam follower assembly support*
5 *No. 2 cam follower assembly support*
6 *No. 3 cam follower assembly support*
7 *No. 4 cam follower assembly support*
8 *No. 5 cam follower assembly support*
9 *Rubber bands*
10 *Intake cam primary and secondary followers*
11 *Intake follower pivot shaft*

8 Unscrew the bolts securing the fuel feed hose, charcoal canister pipe and braking system vacuum pipe support bracket to the left-hand end of the cylinder head and No. 5 cam follower assembly support. Unscrew the two 6 mm bolts securing No. 5 cam follower assembly support to the cylinder head (Nos. 2 and 3 in illustration 10.3).

9 Before disturbing the assembly, make a careful note of its layout and the marks on the supports identifying their location **(see illustration)**. Use rubber bands to tie the intake primary and secondary followers tightly together.

10 Loosely refit the timing chain top run fixed guide mounting bolts and their counterparts in No. 5 cam follower assembly support (Nos. 6, 7, 10 and 11 in illustration 10.3) and keep them there while the assembly is removed and refitted. This will keep Nos. 1 and 5 cam follower assembly supports in place on the follower pivot shafts and prevent the whole assembly from falling apart as it is handled.

11 Tap very gently each support to release it and lift the assembly, noting the locating dowels at the front and rear bolt hole of each support **(see illustration)**.

Inspection

Caution: It is vital that all disturbed components are refitted in their original locations. Make identifying marks or notes. Absolute cleanliness is also essential.

12 Remove the retaining bolts and slip the supports and followers off the follower pivot shafts. Mark each shaft clearly to show whether it is intake or exhaust. As each follower or follower pair is removed, mark it to show which cylinder it belongs to, or place it in a separate, clearly-marked container. Note the washer clipped to each face of the exhaust cam followers.

13 Start by washing each component of the assembly in solvent and drying it. Be particularly careful to clean out all oilways, if possible with an airline (taking care to avoid any risk of eye injury), and check that all are clear before proceeding; see the Hint at the beginning of Section 9, regarding the most likely causes of faults in the i-VTEC and VTC systems.

11.11 Removing cam follower assembly – leave four bolts arrowed in place to stop assembly from falling apart

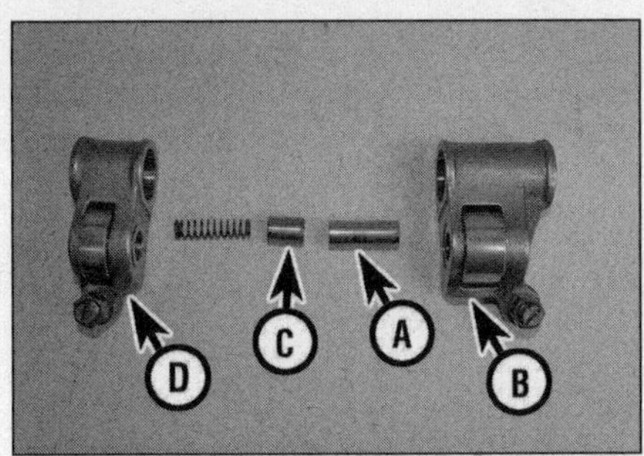

11.15 Piston (A) must slide smoothly inside primary follower (B) and piston (C) must be free to slide against spring pressure in secondary follower (D)

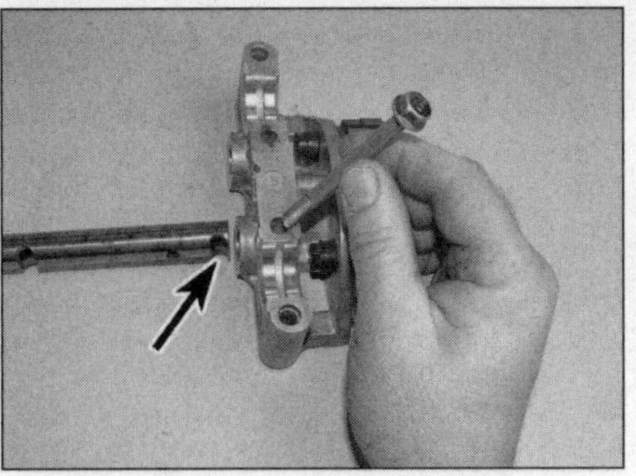
11.17a Refitting intake follower pivot shaft to No. 5 cam follower assembly support – bolt passes through cut-out in shaft

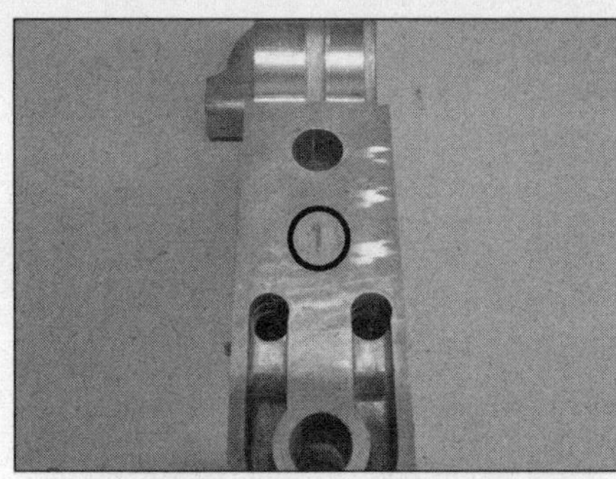
11.17b Refit cam follower assembly supports so that identifying numbers can be read from same side

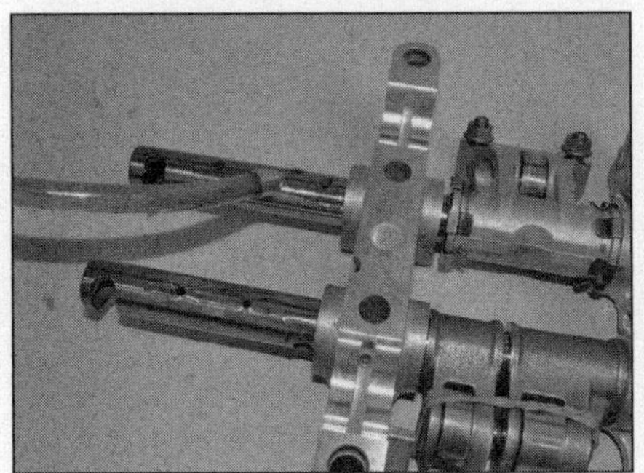
11.17c Liberally oil all bearing surfaces . . .

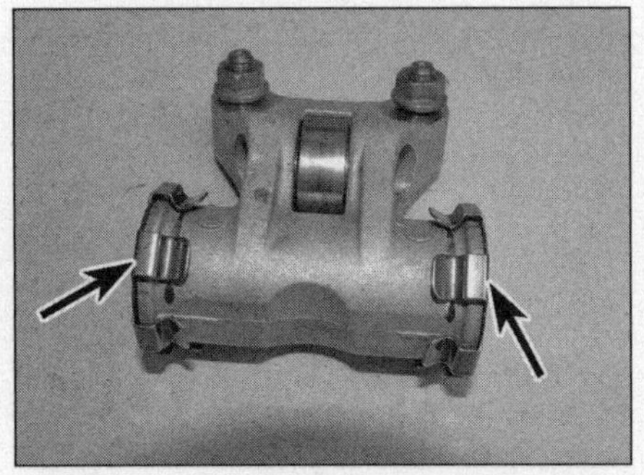
11.17d . . . ensure washers are clipped to each face of exhaust cam followers . . .

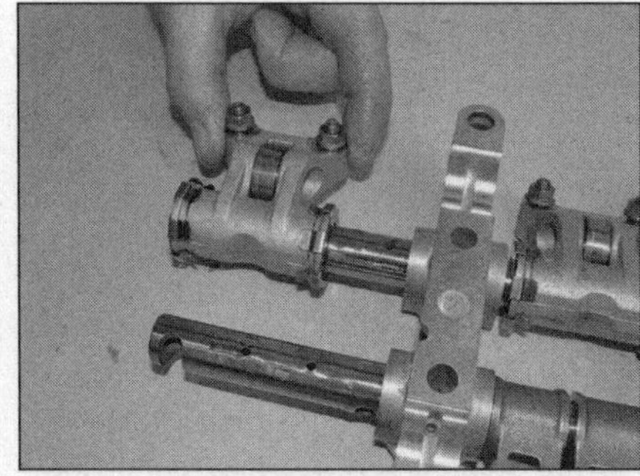
11.17e . . . before refitting to follower pivot shaft . . .

14 Examine the follower rollers and their adjuster screw tips which bear on the camshaft lobes and valve stems; look for any sign of wear and scoring, and for rollers which do not rotate easily and smoothly when spun.

15 When examining the intake primary and secondary followers, check that each piston slides smoothly in its respective bore and that the piston in the secondary follower is returned smoothly against spring pressure **(see illustration)**. If any sign of wear or damage is found on any part of the intake primary and secondary followers, the pair must be renewed complete.

16 Check the surfaces of the pivot shafts that the followers ride on, as well as the bearing surfaces inside the followers, for scoring and excessive wear. Make sure the oil holes in the shafts are not blocked.

17 On completion, assemble the components on to No. 5 cam follower assembly support – note that the follower shafts have deep cut-outs which must align with the bolt holes as the supports are refitted. The identifying numbers stamped into each support must be positioned so that they can be read from the intake side of the cylinder head. Fit the supports and followers to the follower pivot shafts, ensuring that each component is well-lubricated and goes back to the location from which it was removed. Fit the four bolts to keep the supports and followers together pending refitting **(see illustrations)**.

Refitting

18 Wipe clean the mating surfaces of the cam follower assembly supports and the cylinder head. Thoroughly clean the mating surfaces of No. 5 cam follower assembly support and the cylinder head; clean any oil or old gasket material and sealant from the mating surfaces and from the bolt holes and threads. Degrease the surfaces completely before applying sealant.

19 The liquid gasket recommended by Honda requires that the cam follower

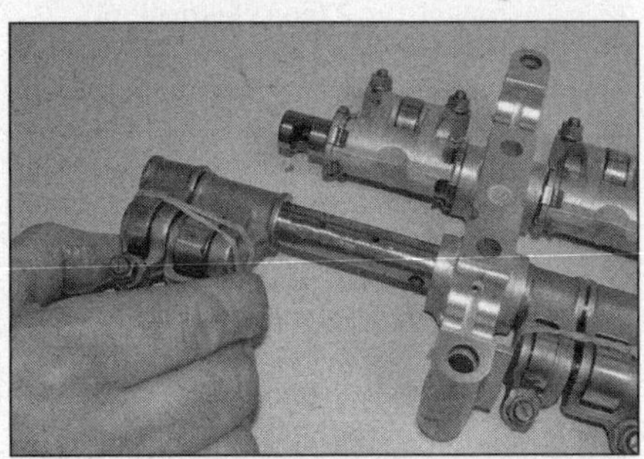
11.17f . . . use rubber bands to tie intake primary and secondary followers tightly together . . .

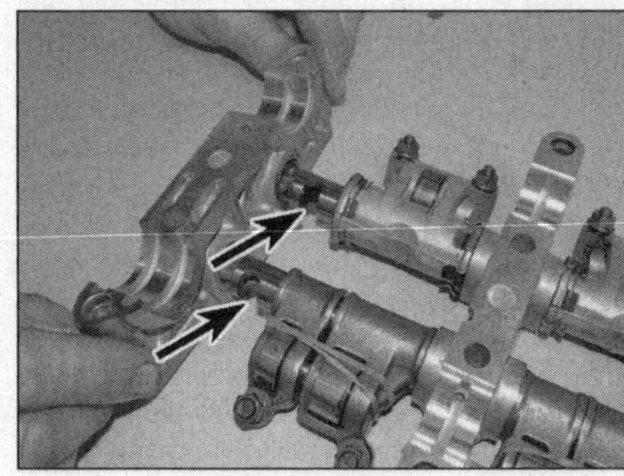
11.17g . . . align pivot shaft cut-outs to refit No. 1 cam follower assembly support . . .

11.17h . . . and refit timing chain top run guide mounting bolts . . .

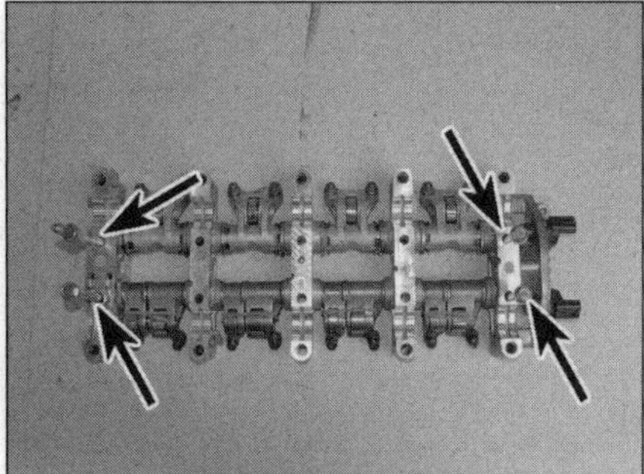
11.17i . . . to secure assembly for refitting

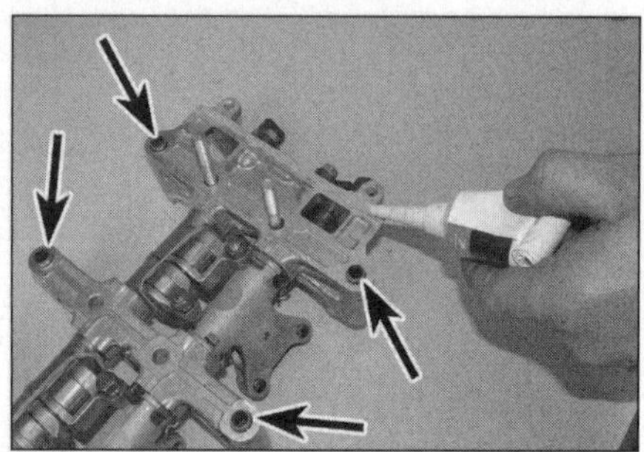

11.20 Apply bead of liquid gasket across No. 5 cam follower assembly support's mating surface so that bead is inside bolt holes – note locating dowels in supports

11.21c Tap follower assembly firmly down on to cylinder head – check carefully that locating dowels enter squarely into bores

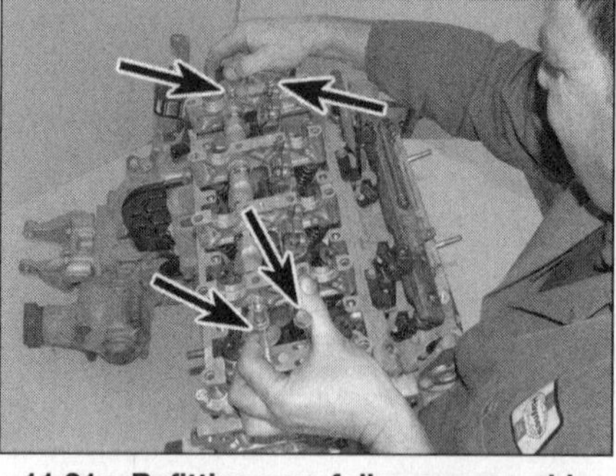

11.21a Refitting cam follower assembly – hold four arrowed bolts in place to stop assembly from falling apart . . .

11.22 Refit 6 mm bolts to No. 5 cam follower assembly support

11.21b . . . and fit assembly so that numbers stamped into supports can be read from intake side of cylinder head

11.23 Cut rubber bands from intake followers and retrieve pieces

assembly and camshafts must be installed (ie, camshaft bearing cap bolts/cam follower assembly support mounting bolts tightened) within five minutes of applying the liquid gasket – if this time limit is exceeded, the sealant must be wiped off completely and new liquid gasket applied in its place. A 'dry' practice run before applying liquid gasket is recommended.

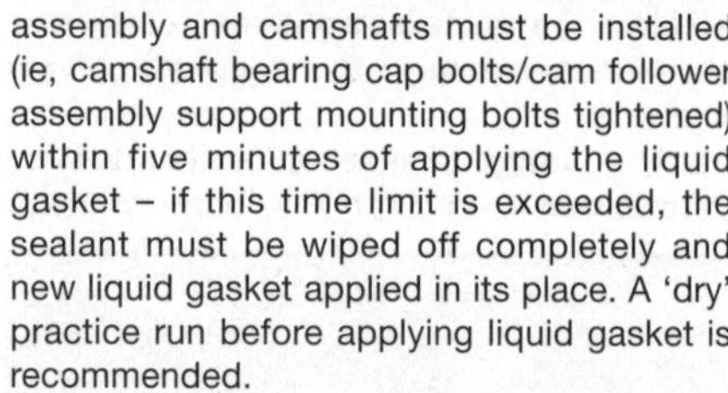

20 Apply a continuous bead of liquid gasket (approximately 3 mm diameter) evenly along the length of the support's mating surface so that the bead is inside the 6 mm bolt holes **(see illustration)**.

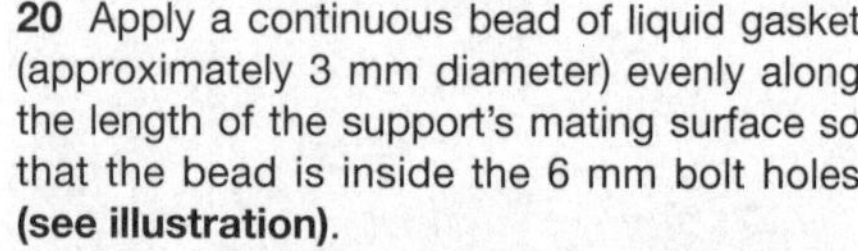

21 Ensuring that the locating dowels are in position, refit the cam follower assembly so that the identifying numbers stamped into each support can be read from the intake side of the cylinder head. Tap the assembly firmly down into contact with the cylinder head, checking that the locating dowels enter squarely into their bores **(see illustrations)**. Remove the four bolts.

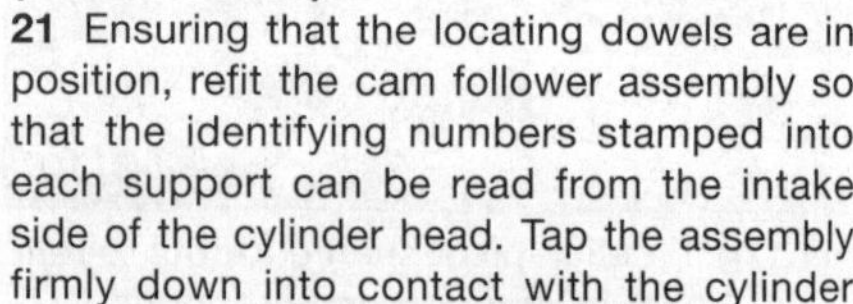

22 Refit the two 6 mm bolts securing No. 5 cam follower assembly support – Nos. 22 and 23 in illustration 10.13 **(see illustration)**.

23 Refit the camshafts (Section 10). When all the camshaft bearing cap bolts/cam follower assembly support mounting bolts have been properly tightened, wipe off any excess sealant from the mating surfaces and cut the rubber bands from the intake followers; be careful to retrieve all the pieces **(see illustration)**. Refit the vacuum pipe support bracket bolts, tightening them to the specified torque.

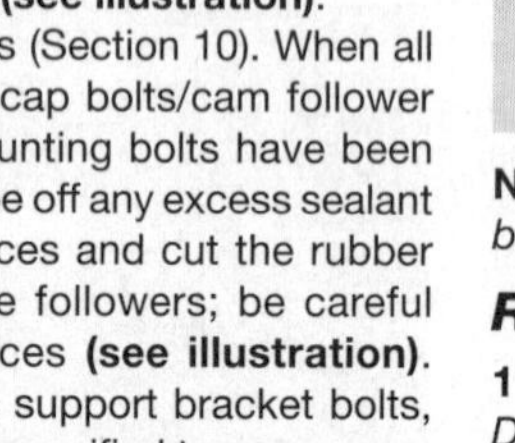

24 Refit the timing chain (Section 7), then adjust the valve clearances as described in Chapter 1A.

25 When Honda's own liquid gasket has been used to seal a joint, note the following:

a) Where applicable, wait at least 30 minutes before filling the engine with oil.

b) Do not run the engine for at least three hours.

12 Cylinder head – removal and refitting

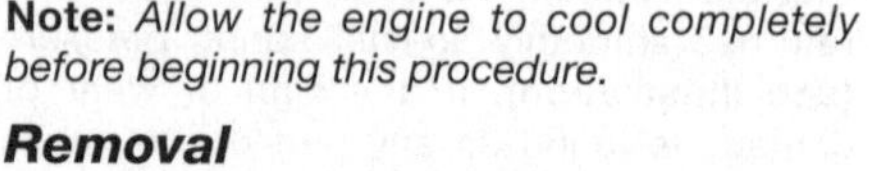

Note: *Allow the engine to cool completely before beginning this procedure.*

Removal

1 Disconnect the battery negative lead (see *Disconnecting the battery*).

2 Remove the engine compartment under-shield (Chapter 11).

3 Drain the cooling system (Chapter 1A).

4 Remove the auxiliary drivebelt (Chapter 1A).

5 Unbolt and withdraw the plastic cover over the intake manifold, then depressurise the fuel system (see Chapter 4A). Disconnect the fuel feed hose from the fuel rail; be prepared for fuel spillage **(see illustration)**.

6 Remove the outer intake manifold as described in Chapter 4A. (If no work is to be carried out on the cylinder head, the head can be removed complete with manifold once the preliminary operations have been carried out.)

7 Disconnect the cooling system hoses from the outlet at the left-hand front end of the cylinder head **(see illustration)**.

8 Remove the exhaust manifold as described in Chapter 4A. (If no work is to be carried out on the cylinder head, the head can be removed complete with manifold once the preliminary operations have been carried out.)

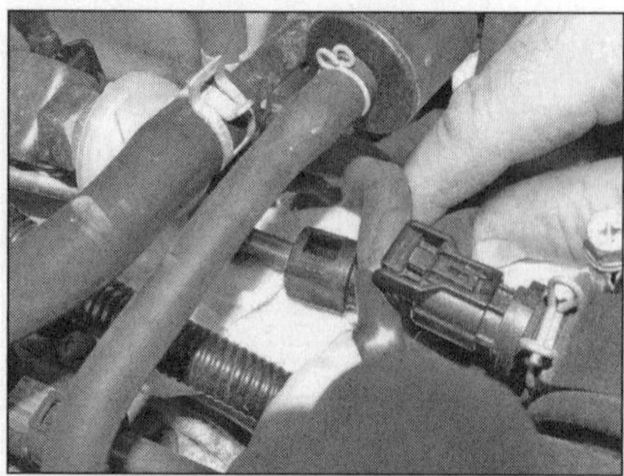

12.5 Depressurise fuel system and disconnect fuel feed hose from fuel rail; be prepared for fuel spillage

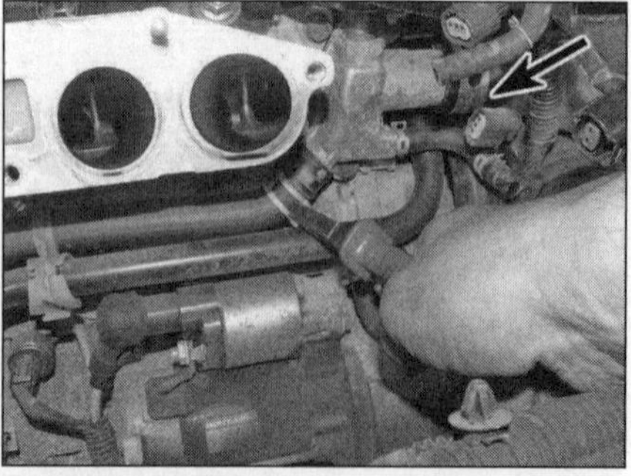

12.7 Disconnect cooling system bypass hose and radiator top hose from water outlet

12.9 Disconnect fuel injector wiring (A) and unbolt earth lead (B) from intake manifold

12.10a Disconnect wiring from engine coolant temperature sensor . . .

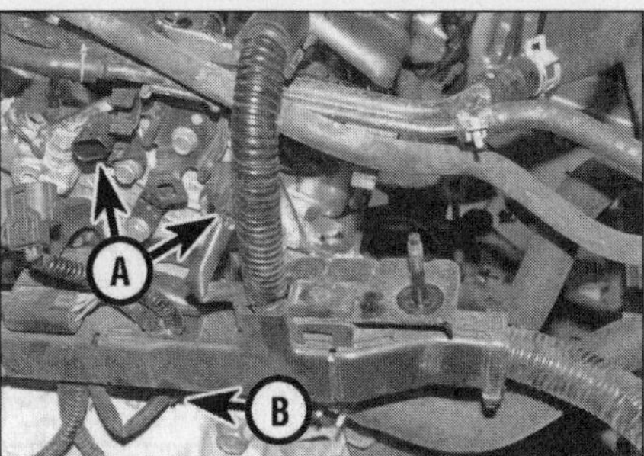

12.10b . . . and camshaft position sensors (A); engine coolant temperature sensor location shown at (B)

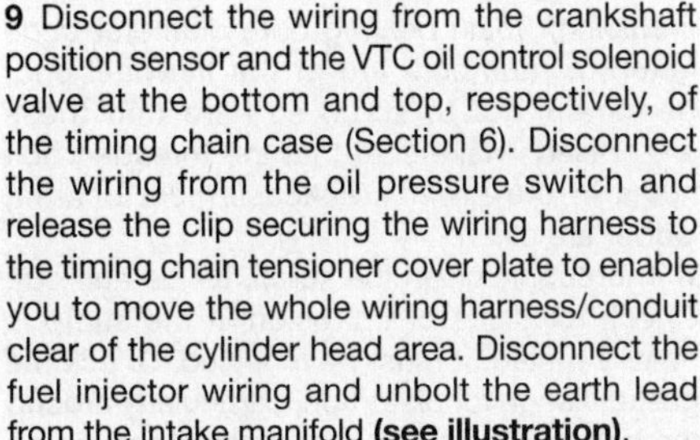

9 Disconnect the wiring from the crankshaft position sensor and the VTC oil control solenoid valve at the bottom and top, respectively, of the timing chain case (Section 6). Disconnect the wiring from the oil pressure switch and release the clip securing the wiring harness to the timing chain tensioner cover plate to enable you to move the whole wiring harness/conduit clear of the cylinder head area. Disconnect the fuel injector wiring and unbolt the earth lead from the intake manifold **(see illustration)**.

10 From the left-hand end of the cylinder head, disconnect the wiring from the engine coolant temperature sensor and both camshaft position (i-VTEC/VTC and TDC) sensors, then unclip the wiring conduit from its support bracket **(see illustrations)**.

11 Disconnect the heater hose from the union at the left-hand rear end of the cylinder head. Unscrew the bolts securing the hose and conduit brackets to the left-hand end of the cylinder head **(see illustration)**. Ensure that hoses, wiring and pipes are secured clear of the cylinder head and cannot hinder its removal.

12 Remove the cylinder head cover as described in Chapter 1A, Section 16, paragraphs 3 to 6.

13 Remove the timing chain case (Section 6).

14 Remove the timing chain (Section 7).

15 Remove the camshafts (Section 10).

16 Remove the cam follower assembly (Section 11).

17 Working in the **reverse** of the tightening sequence, progressively slacken the cylinder head bolts by a one-third of a turn at a time until all ten are fully slackened **(see illustration 12.31)**.

18 Lift the cylinder head off the engine, noting that two dowels are used at the front. If resistance is felt, don't prise between the head and block gasket mating surfaces – damage to the mating surfaces will result. Instead, try to rock the head free by inserting a blunt lever (such as a hammer handle) into the intake or exhaust ports.

19 Remove the head from the engine, and set it down on a clean, flat surface – remember at all times to avoid damage to the gasket sealing surfaces. Recover the gasket and discard it – a new one must be fitted on reassembly.

20 Cylinder head dismantling and inspection procedures are covered in detail in Chapter 2C.

Preparation for refitting

21 The mating faces of the cylinder head and cylinder block/crankcase must be perfectly clean before refitting the head. Use a hard plastic or wood scraper to remove all traces of gasket and carbon. Also clean the piston crowns. Take particular care, as the soft aluminium alloy is damaged easily. Also, make sure that the carbon is not allowed to enter the oil and water passages – this is particularly important for the lubrication system, as carbon could block the oil supply to any of the engine components. Using adhesive tape and paper, seal the water, oil and bolt holes in the cylinder block/crankcase. To prevent carbon entering the gap between the pistons and bores, smear a little grease in the gap. After cleaning each piston, use a small brush to remove all traces of grease and carbon from the gap, then wipe away the remainder with a clean cloth. Clean all the pistons in the same way.

22 Check the mating surfaces of the cylinder block/crankcase and the cylinder head for nicks, deep scratches and other damage. If the damage is light, it may be possible to have the cylinder head refaced (see Chapter 2C).

23 If warpage of the cylinder head gasket surface is suspected (especially after overheating), use a straight-edge to check it for distortion. Refer to Part C of this Chapter if necessary.

24 Clean the threads in the cylinder head bolt holes. Dirt, corrosion, sealant and damaged threads will affect torque values. Ensure that there is no water or oil in the bolt holes in the block – if this is not either sucked or blown out, the resulting hydraulic pressure when the bolts are fitted may crack the block.

25 Check the cylinder head bolts for obvious signs of wear or damage; renew them all as a set of any such signs are visible. Measure the diameter of the threads of each bolt 50 mm and 45 mm from the tip; if a bolt has stretched so that its diameter is less than 10.6 mm at either of these points, it must be renewed. Although Honda are happy to have bolts re-used as long as they pass this test, note that it is considered good practice to renew highly-stressed fasteners such as cylinder head bolts as a matter of course, irrespective of their apparent condition, whenever they are disturbed. These bolts are subject to significant pressure, and if one should fail during retightening, considerable extra expense and inconvenience will be incurred.

26 If new bolts are not being fitted, clean the threads of the old ones thoroughly.

Refitting

27 Check that the crankshaft is positioned so that Nos. 1 and 4 cylinders are at TDC.

28 The mating surfaces of the cylinder head and block must be perfectly clean. Use a clean rag soaked in gasket remover or cellulose thinners to remove any traces of oil or dirt from the mating surfaces.

29 Place a new gasket on the cylinder block, and locate it over the two dowels at the front. Check to see if there are any markings (such as TOP) on the gasket to indicate how it is to be fitted. Those identification marks must face up.

12.10c Unclip wiring conduit from its support bracket

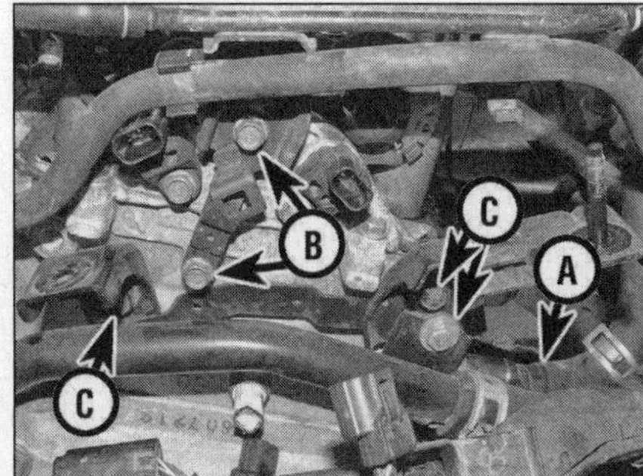

12.11 Disconnect heater hose (A) and unscrew bolts (B) and (C) to remove ancillary items from end of cylinder head

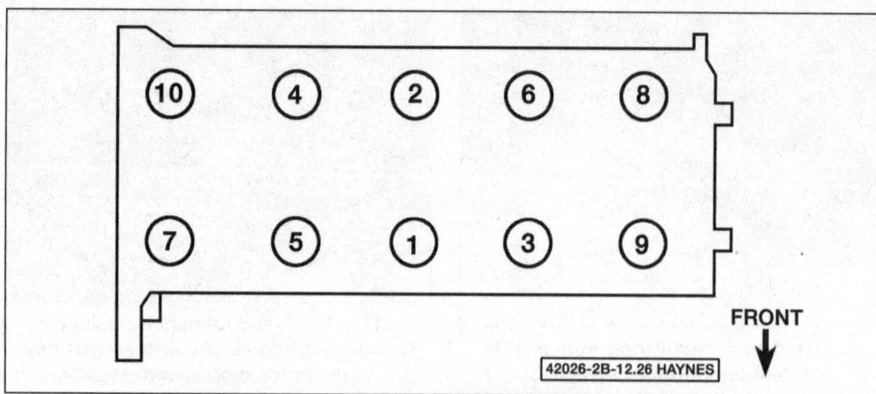

12.31 Cylinder head bolt TIGHTENING sequence

30 Place the cylinder head carefully onto the block, and locate it on the two dowels.

31 Lightly oil the threads and the underside of the heads of the cylinder head bolts, then refit them. Tighten the bolts in the recommended sequence, in stages, to the specified torque **(see illustration)**. Because of the critical function of cylinder head bolts, the manufacturer specifies the following conditions for tightening them:

a) A beam-type or dial-type torque wrench is preferable to a preset (click-stop) torque wrench. If you use a preset torque wrench, tighten slowly and be careful not to overtighten the bolts.

b) If a bolt makes any sound while you're tightening it (creaking, clicking, etc), slacken it completely and tighten it again in the specified stages.

32 Refit the cam follower assembly (Section 11).

33 Refit the camshafts (Section 10).

34 Refit the timing chain (Section 7).

35 Refit the timing chain case (Section 6).

36 Adjust the valve clearances, then refit the cylinder head cover (Chapter 1A).

37 Refit the intake manifold (where removed) or reconnect the manifold hoses and wiring (Chapter 4A). Reconnect and adjust the throttle cable.

38 Refit the exhaust manifold or reconnect the exhaust front pipe (as applicable) (Chapter 4A).

39 Refit the remaining parts in the reverse order of removal.

40 Refill the cooling system and check all fluid levels.

41 Reconnect the battery.

42 Run the engine until normal operating temperature is reached. Check for leaks and proper operation.

13 Sump – removal and refitting

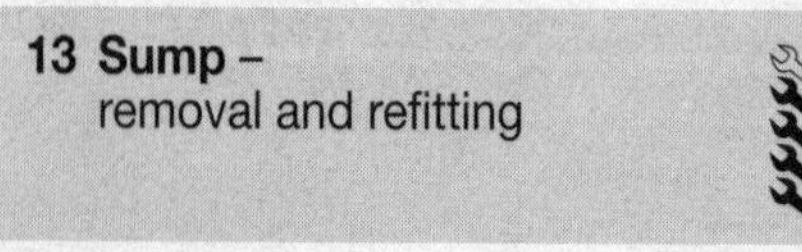

Caution: The removal of the sump requires the removal first of the front suspension subframe. Read through the procedure first to ensure that all the tools and equipment required are to hand. Depending on the skills and equipment available and the nature of the work being undertaken, the home mechanic may prefer to consider removing the engine/transmission complete and then removing the sump.

Note: *If the vehicle is very dirty underneath, wash it before starting work, especially around the edges of the sump.*

Removal

1 Drain the engine oil and remove the oil filter (Chapter 1A).

2 Remove the front suspension subframe (Chapter 10).

3 Progressively slacken and remove the fourteen bolts and two nuts securing the sump to the lower crankcase/main bearing ladder. Note that the bolts are of different lengths. Check carefully that all fasteners have been removed before trying to remove the sump.

4 Breaking the grip of the sealant used as gasket material is not easy; there are no leverage points provided and the sealant sticks very tight. Try to break the seal by striking the sump with the palm of the hand, or use a hammer and a block of wood or a soft-faced mallet and tap all around the edge of the sump. Alternatively an oil pan seal cutter tool (also referred to as seal cutters and/or RTV cutters) can be used. Such tools are hammered into the joint between the sump and the lower crankcase and then hammered to the left and right, all the way round the sump (remembering the two mounting studs), to cut the seal. Great care is required when using such a tool not to scratch or otherwise damage the mating surfaces. Do NOT jam the tool into the joint and then use it as a lever; cut the seal all the way round, then pull the sump down.

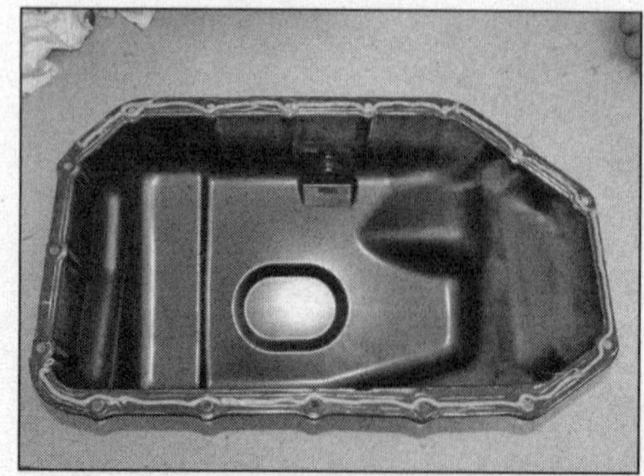

13.10 Apply a continuous 3.0 mm diameter bead of liquid gasket evenly around sump's mating surface

Preparation for refitting

5 Take the opportunity to clean the filter screen on the oil pump pick-up, using solvent and a brush.

6 Using a gasket scraper or a brass wire brush, remove all traces of sealant from the lower crankcase/main bearing ladder and the sump mating surfaces. Note that the crankshaft main bearing bore diameter code letters or numbers are at the flywheel end; be careful not to scrub so hard that these are erased. Make sure that the threaded bolt holes in the lower crankcase/main bearing ladder are clean.

7 Thoroughly clean the sump, inside and out. Check for signs of corrosion; if the sump is heavily rusted, it must be renewed. Check the gasket flange for distortion, particularly around the bolt holes. If necessary, place the sump on a flat wooden surface and use a hammer to flatten and restore the gasket surface. After this, use a straight-edge to ensure that the mating surfaces are completely flat the sump (or refit the sump 'dry' and check for gaps while holding it lightly in place).

Refitting

8 Clean the mating surfaces of the crankcase and the sump. Degrease the surfaces before applying sealant and wipe down the inside of the engine with a clean, lint-free rag to prevent any drips of oil from contaminating the new sealant on reassembly.

9 The sump must be installed within five minutes of applying the liquid gasket recommended by Honda (Honda Part No. 08C70-K0234M, 08C70-K0334M, 08C70-X0331S, 08718-0001 or equivalent) – if this time limit is exceeded, it must be wiped off completely and new liquid gasket applied. A 'dry' practice run before applying liquid gasket is recommended.

10 Apply the liquid gasket as a continuous thin bead (3 mm diameter approx) evenly around the sump's mating surface so that the bead is around the inside edges of the bolt holes **(see illustration)**. Also apply a small blob of liquid gasket to those bolt holes in the lower crankcase/main bearing ladder which pass through to the outside and to the three bolt holes along the bottom edge of the timing chain case to ensure that there are no oil leaks from the threads. Do NOT apply sealant to blind holes in the castings. Do not apply excess sealant, as this will end up inside the engine.

11 Offer up the sump and carefully fit it into place without sliding. Refit one or two bolts to hold it **(see illustration)**.

12 Refit all the bolts and the two nuts,

tightening them by hand only at first until the sump is correctly settled in position. Working in a diagonal sequence from the centre outwards and in two or three stages, tighten the retaining bolts and nuts to the specified torque. Check that an even bead of sealant is visible all the way round the edge of the sump; wipe off any excess from the mating surfaces.

13 Refit the front suspension subframe as described in Chapter 10.

14 Fit a new oil filter. Wait at least 30 minutes (or as stated on the sealant packaging), then refill the engine with oil.

15 Wait at least three hours (or as stated on the sealant packaging), then start the engine and check for leaks.

14 Oil pump – removal, inspection and refitting

Removal

1 Remove the cylinder head cover and bring the engine to TDC, No 1 firing (Chapter 1A, Section 16, paragraphs 3 to 8).

2 Remove the sump (Section 13).

3 Unscrew the three bolts and withdraw the balancer/oil pump drive chain tensioner assembly.

4 Prevent the balancer shafts from rotating by inserting a 6 mm diameter pin through the hole provided in the underside of the balancer/oil pump assembly and into the hole in the rear shaft **(see illustration)**. The Honda service tool for this task is Part No. 07744-0010500; a pin punch is the best substitute (a drill bit is not recommended, as it might shear off, while a 6 mm bolt might bend). Unscrew and remove the balancer/oil pump sprocket retaining bolt, then remove the locking pin. Wipe the chain and look for the blue-coloured sideplates (there should be two on adjacent links and one at the other end of the chain); note where they are in relation to the sprocket's timing mark to ensure correct balancer shaft timing on reassembly.

5 Unscrew the four bolts and withdraw the balancer/oil pump assembly, noting the two locating dowels. Withdraw the sprocket from the rear balancer shaft, disengaging it from the drive chain. Note the locating dowel pin; if this is loose it should be removed and kept with the sprocket.

6 Note the oil control orifice fitted into the lower crankcase/main bearing ladder between Nos. 3 and 4 main bearings. This must be removed and cleaned.

Inspection

7 Undo the oil pump housing mounting bolts, withdraw the housing from the balancer assembly, and dismantle the oil pump. Note any marks identifying either surface of the outer rotor; if none can be seen, make your own. Thoroughly clean and inspect the rotors and housing.

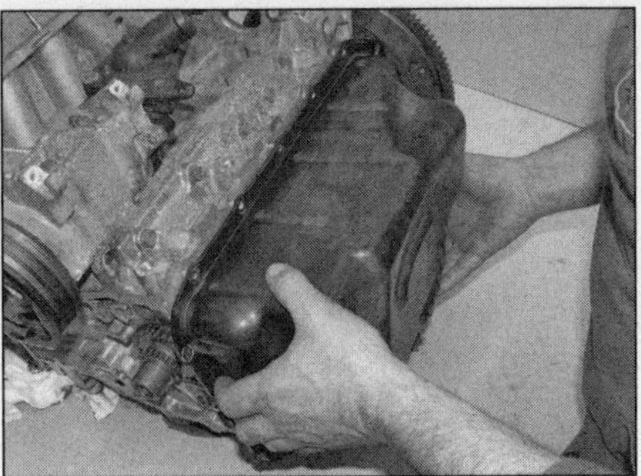

13.11 Work quickly to refit sump before sealant sets

8 Refit the rotors to the pump housing and, using feeler blades of the appropriate thickness, measure the clearance between the outer rotor and the pump housing, then between the inner rotor tip and the outer rotor.

9 Using feeler blades and a straight-edge placed across the top of the pump housing and the rotors, measure the rotor endfloat.

10 Except for the pressure relief valve components, the pump is only available as a complete assembly, including the balancer assembly housing halves. If any measurement is outside the specified limits, the complete pump assembly must be renewed.

11 Unscrew the pressure relief valve threaded plug and extract the spring and plunger from the pump housing. Check the spring for distortion and the plunger for scoring; if the plunger does not slide freely in the pump housing bore, then it must be renewed.

12 Lubricate the pump rotors with clean engine oil and refit them, using the marks made or noted on removal to ensure that the outer rotor is refitted the original way round. Check that the pump rotates freely, then prime it by injecting oil into its passages and rotating it. If not refitting the pump to the engine immediately, prime it again before installation. Packing the spaces between the rotors with petroleum jelly will also prime the pump.

13 Refit the oil pump housing to the balancer assembly, aligning it on the two locating dowels and engaging the pump inner rotor on the front balancer shaft's drive tongue, then refit the housing mounting bolts and tighten them to the torque specified. Lubricate and refit the oil pressure relief valve plunger and spring, then refit the plug, and tighten to the specified torque.

Refitting

14 Refit the oil control orifice to the lower crankcase/main bearing ladder.

15 Check that No. 1 cylinder is still exactly at TDC, No 1 firing.

16 Refit the driven sprocket locating dowel pin (if removed) to the rear balancer shaft. Rotate the balancer shafts until the dowel pin aligns with the arrow mark cast on the pump housing **(see illustration)**. Insert the 6 mm diameter pin to lock the balancer shafts in this position and secure it with a rubber band so that it stays in place while the balancer/oil pump assembly is refitted. Position the driven sprocket on the rear balancer shaft, engaging its keyway on the locating pin.

17 Refit the balancer/oil pump assembly, engaging the driven sprocket on the chain and aligning the assembly on the two locating dowels. The sprocket must be fitted to the chain so that the chain's rear run is kept as taut as possible and so that the blue-coloured sideplates are restored to the relationship with the driven sprocket timing mark that was noted on removal.

18 Tighten the four balancer/oil pump assembly mounting bolts to the torques specified.

19 Lightly oil its threads, refit the driven sprocket retaining bolt and tighten it to the specified torque. Remove the locking pin.

20 Compress the chain tensioner and insert a locking pin (we used an Allen key) into the loop in the tensioner blade to keep it compressed; new tensioner assemblies are supplied with clips for this purpose. Refit the tensioner, tighten its bolts to the specified torque and withdraw the locking pin or clip to release the tensioner against the chain **(see illustrations)**.

21 Rotate the crankshaft two full turns (720°) clockwise and check that when the pulley TDC mark aligns with the arrow mark on the timing chain case and the camshaft sprocket marks align as described in Chapter 1A, Section 16,

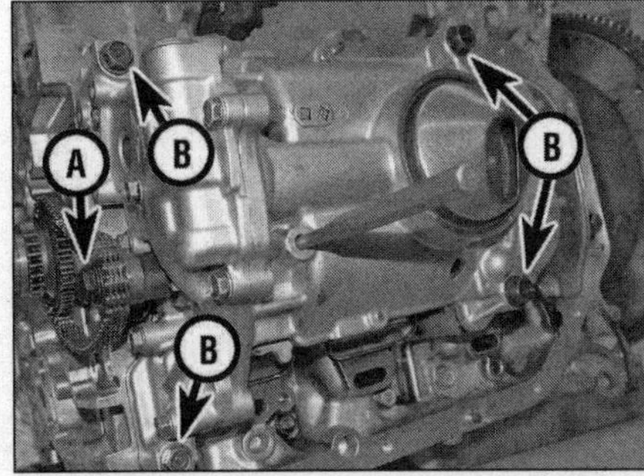

14.4 Insert locking pin to prevent balancer shafts from rotating while driven sprocket bolt (A) is slackened. Note balancer/oil pump assembly mounting bolts (B)

14.16 Driven sprocket locating dowel pin must align with arrow mark cast on pump housing

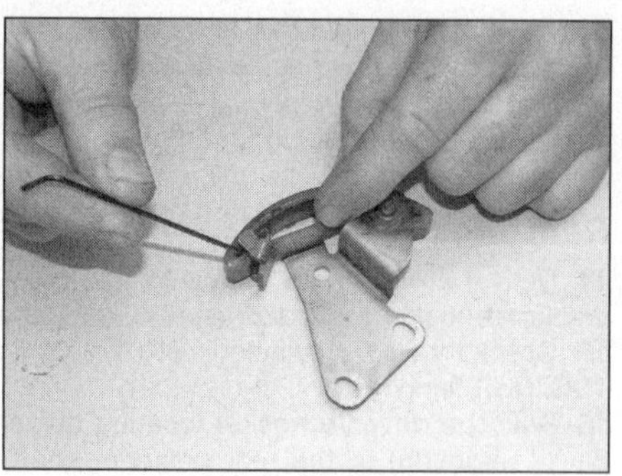

14.20a Compress tensioner blade and insert locking pin

14.20b Fit tensioner assembly, tighten bolts and withdraw locking pin to release tensioner against drive chain

paragraph 8, the balancer/oil pump driven sprocket timing mark aligns with the arrow mark cast on the pump housing. If not, repeat the procedure until the assembly is correctly timed.

22 Refit the cylinder head cover (Chapter 1A, Section 16).

23 Refit the sump (see Section 13).

15 Balancer/oil pump drive chain – removal, inspection and refitting

Caution: The removal of the timing chain and balancer/oil pump drive chain's crankshaft drive sprocket requires the removal first of the timing chain case and of the sump, the latter entailing the removal of the front suspension subframe. Depending on the skills and equipment available and the nature of the work being undertaken, the home mechanic may prefer to consider removing the engine/transmission complete and then removing the sump.

Removal

1 Remove the timing chain and the crankshaft position sensor's rotor (Section 7).

2 Support the timing chain end of the engine. This must be done from above, with an engine hoist/crane. Bolt a lifting eye to the right-hand end of the cylinder head.

3 Remove the sump (Section 13).

4 Unscrew the three bolts and withdraw the balancer/oil pump drive chain tensioner assembly, then undo the two bolts and withdraw the chain's fixed guide from its rear run **(see illustration)**.

5 Prevent the balancer shafts from rotating by inserting a 6 mm diameter pin through the hole provided (See Section 14). Unscrew and remove the balancer/oil pump driven sprocket retaining bolt.

6 Remove the balancer/oil pump drive chain with the drive and driven sprockets. As the drive sprocket slides off the crankshaft, note the locating peg on its inboard surface. As the driven sprocket slides off the rear balancer shaft, note the locating pin in the shaft.

Inspection

7 See Section 7, paragraphs 2 and 10 to 14.

Refitting

8 Both keyways in the crankshaft end must point straight up (twelve o'clock position), to align with the arrow mark cast on the cylinder block; temporarily refit the crankshaft pulley, if necessary, to rotate the crankshaft into position. Rotate the balancer shafts until the driven sprocket locating dowel pin aligns with the arrow mark cast on the pump housing **(see illustration 14.16)**. Insert the 6 mm diameter pin to lock the balancer shafts in this position and secure it with a rubber band so that it stays in place while the chain is refitted.

9 One side of the chain has three blue-coloured sideplates, two of which are adjacent while the third is some distance away. Fit the chain to the appropriate teeth of the drive sprocket so that the single coloured sideplate fits over the arrow-marked tooth, then fit it to the driven sprocket so that the coloured sideplates fit on each side of the punch-marked tooth **(see illustration)**.

10 Refit the drive chain and sprockets, keeping the chain as taut as possible on its rear run. As the drive sprocket slides on to the crankshaft, ensure that the locating peg on its inboard surface engages with the second/inboard crankshaft keyway and that the sprocket is pressed firmly back against the shoulder on the crankshaft end. Ensure also that the driven sprocket engages on its locating dowel pin, then lightly oil its threads, refit the driven sprocket retaining bolt and tighten it to the specified torque **(see illustrations)**. Remove the locking pin.

11 Refit the fixed guide to the chain's rear run. Tighten the mounting bolts securely.

12 Compress the chain tensioner and insert a

15.4 Undo screws arrowed to remove drive chain fixed guide

15.9 Fit chain to sprockets so that single coloured sideplate fits over drive sprocket's arrow-marked tooth, and two coloured sideplates fit each side of driven sprocket punch-marked tooth

15.10a Fit sprockets and chain as an assembly . . .

15.10b . . . so that timing marks align as shown on crankshaft drive sprocket . . .

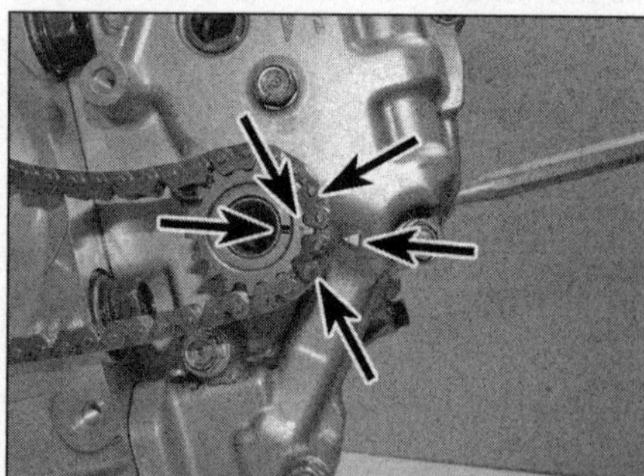

15.10c . . . and as shown on balancer/oil pump driven sprocket

locking pin (we used an Allen key) into the loop in the tensioner blade to keep it compressed; new tensioner assemblies are supplied with clips for this purpose. Refit the tensioner, tighten its bolts to the specified torque and withdraw the locking pin or clip to release the tensioner against the chain **(see illustration)**.

13 Refit the timing chain and the crankshaft position sensor's rotor (Section 7). Temporarily refit the crankshaft pulley and rotate the crankshaft two full turns (720°) clockwise, then check that all the timing marks align exactly, as described, for both chains. If not, repeat the procedure until both chains are correctly refitted.

14 The remainder of reassembly is the reverse of the removal procedure.

16 Balancer shafts – removal, inspection and refitting

Removal

1 Remove the balancer/oil pump assembly (Section 14).

Inspection

2 Mount a dial gauge so that its tip bears on the sprocket end of the rear balancer shaft. Push the shaft fully away, then zero the gauge. Push the shaft fully the other way, and check the endfloat; repeat to check the front shaft's endfloat. If the endfloat of either shaft is beyond the service limit specified, then the shaft must be renewed and the endfloat rechecked; if it is still excessive the balancer/oil pump assembly must be renewed.

3 While there is no need to remove the oil pump housing in order to dismantle the balancer assembly, there is little point in not dismantling, cleaning and checking the oil pump while the opportunity presents itself; refer to Section 14.

4 Unscrew the clamp bolts and separate the two halves of the balancer assembly, noting the two locating dowels. The bearing shells are identical, but if disturbed must be refitted in their original locations. Make identifying marks or notes before removing any of the bearing shells.

5 Clean the shafts and housing halves; check particularly the bearing surfaces on the balancer shaft bearing journals and bearing shells. If there is any obvious sign of wear or damage, the component concerned must be renewed. Note that while the shafts and bearing shells are available separately, if either of the housing halves are found to be worn or damaged, they are available only as a matched pair, with the oil pump.

6 Use Plastigauge to check the balancer shaft bearing journal-to-bearing clearance. Wipe clean the balancer shafts and refit them to the housing lower half. Lay a strip of Plastigauge on each bearing journal, refit the housing upper half and tighten the clamp bolts to the

15.10d Lightly oil its threads before refitting driven sprocket retaining bolt and tightening it

specified torque. Unbolt the housing upper half again and measure the width of each strip at its widest point to determine the clearance. If any of the clearances are beyond the specified service limit then the worn components must be renewed.

7 If the necessary equipment is available, the balancer shaft bearing journals and bearing bores can also be checked for wear by direct measurement.

8 On reassembly, clean the backs of the bearing shells and the bearing locations in both housing halves. Press the bearing shells into their locations, ensuring that each is refitted in its original location if the originals are being re-used, and that the tab on each shell engages in the notch in the housing location. Take care not to touch any shell bearing surface with your fingers.

9 Lubricate each bearing shell in the housing lower half, then match the balancer shafts together so that the punch-marked tooth on the rear shaft fits between the two punch-marked teeth on the front shaft. Lower the shafts into position **(see illustration)**.

10 Lubricate each bearing shell in the housing upper half, then lower it into place, engaging it on the two locating dowels. Lightly oil the threads of the 8 mm clamp bolts, then refit them and tighten them to the specified torque. Refit the 6 mm clamp bolts with the baffle plate and tighten them to the specified torque. If removed, refit the two locating dowels to their locations in the top surface of the balancer assembly.

11 Refit the oil pump housing to the balancer assembly as described in Section 14.

Refitting

12 Refit the balancer/oil pump assembly as described in Section 14.

17 Flywheel/driveplate – removal and refitting

Caution: The removal of the transmission also requires the removal of the front suspension subframe. Read through the procedure first to ensure that all the tools and equipment required are to hand.

15.12 Fit tensioner assembly, tighten bolts and withdraw locking pin to release tensioner against drive chain

Removal

1 Remove the transmission (Chapter 7).

2 On manual gearbox models, remove the clutch assembly (Chapter 6). Now is a good time to renew the clutch components and the crankshaft pilot bush if necessary.

3 Prevent the flywheel from turning by locking the ring gear teeth, or bolt a strap between the flywheel and the cylinder block/crankcase **(see illustration 5.4)**. Make alignment marks between the flywheel and crankshaft using paint or a suitable marker pen. Remove the bolts that secure the flywheel to the crankshaft – note that they have bi-hex heads, but any normal socket should undo them. Since the flywheel is heavy, be sure to support it while removing the last bolt.

4 Remove the flywheel from the crankshaft.

Inspection

5 Clean the flywheel to remove clutch dust, grease and oil. Inspect the surface for cracks, rivet grooves, burned areas and score marks. Light scoring can be removed with emery cloth. Check for cracked and broken ring gear teeth. Lay the flywheel on a flat surface and use a straight-edge to check for warpage. If any sign of wear or damage is found, the flywheel must be renewed.

6 Clean and inspect the mating surfaces of the flywheel and the crankshaft. If the oil seal is leaking, renew it now (see Section 19).

7 Clean the bolt threads and check their condition before re-using them. These bolts

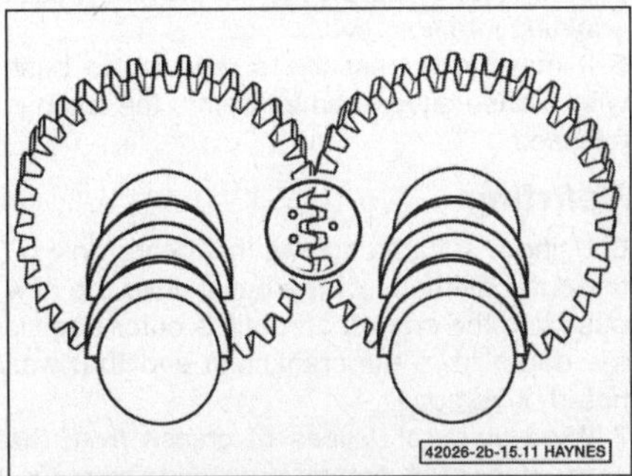

16.9 Align punch-marked tooth on rear (drive) balancer shaft between two punch-marked teeth on front (driven/oil pump) balancer shaft

are subject to significant stress, and while not specifically required by Honda, it is advisable to renew them whenever they are disturbed.

Refitting

8 Position the flywheel against the crankshaft using the marks made on removal to ensure that it is refitted in its original location. Some engines have an alignment dowel or staggered bolt holes to ensure correct refitting.

9 Prevent the flywheel from turning as described in paragraph 3. Using a diagonal pattern, tighten the bolts to the specified torque (note that the flywheel and driveplate have different torques).

10 The remainder of refitting is the reverse of the removal procedure.

18 Crankshaft pilot bush – inspection, removal and refitting

Inspection

1 The pilot bush is fitted into the end of the crankshaft, and provides support for the free end of the gearbox input shaft on manual gearbox vehicles. It can only be examined once the clutch has been removed (Chapter 6). Using an electric torch and magnifying glass, if required, check the bearing surface of the bush and check for any roughness, scoring or looseness in the bush. If any of these conditions are evident, the bush must be renewed.

Removal

2 Remove the clutch as described in Chapter 6.

3 Measure and record the depth from a straight-edge placed across the end of the crankshaft to the bush's outer edge. Pack heavy grease through the centre of the bush until the space inside the crankshaft hole is completely filled.

4 Select a rod or tubular drift which fits exactly into the centre of the bush. The idea is to tap the tool through the centre of the bush, compressing the grease and forcing the bush from the crankshaft, so the tool must be a snug fit in the bush or the grease will escape past it. Wear eye protection to prevent grease squirting into your eyes.

5 It may be necessary to repack the bush with grease several times before the bush is released.

Refitting

6 Using a suitable socket that bears only on the outer diameter of the bush, drive the new bush into the crankshaft until its outer edge is the depth from the crankshaft end that was noted on removal.

7 Wipe away all traces of grease from the crankshaft, bush and flywheel and thoroughly degrease them, using solvent and a clean rag or kitchen towel, before refitting the clutch.

8 Apply a thin smear of grease to the bearing surface of the bush and to the gearbox input shaft; Honda recommend Urea Grease UM264 (Part No. 41211-PY5-305).

9 Refit the clutch (Chapter 6).

19 Crankshaft oil seals – renewal

1 Refer to Chapter 2B, Section 17, noting the following points:

a) *For the right-hand (timing chain end) oil seal, the depth from the seal's outer edge to the timing case mating surface should be 33.0 to 33.7 mm.*

b) *For the left-hand (transmission end) oil seal, the depth from the end of the crankshaft to the seal's outer face should be 5.5 to 6.5 mm.*

20 Water pump housing – removal and refitting

Note: *Liquid gasket (Honda Part No. 08C70-K0234M, 08C70-K0334M, 08C70-X0331S or 08718-0001 or equivalent) must be available on reassembly, in addition to a new auxiliary drivebelt.*

Removal

1 Disconnect the battery negative lead (see *Disconnecting the battery*).

2 Remove the engine compartment undershield (Chapter 11).

3 Drain the cooling system (Chapter 1A).

4 Remove the auxiliary drivebelt and its tensioner (Chapter 1A).

5 Unbolt and withdraw the plastic cover over the intake manifold, then depressurise the fuel system (see Chapter 4A). Disconnect the fuel feed hose from the fuel rail; be prepared for fuel spillage.

6 Remove the outer intake manifold as described in Chapter 4A.

7 Remove the alternator (Chapter 5A). This includes removal of the Positive Crankcase Ventilation (PCV) valve.

8 Unscrew the air conditioning compressor's four mounting bolts. With the compressor unbolted, secure it clear of the working area without disconnecting or straining its wiring and pipes. The compressor clutch wiring can be disconnected, if required, to move it far enough away from the engine.

9 Referring to Chapter 3, remove the water pump and thermostat, then unbolt the thermostat housing and secure it clear of the water pump housing without damaging the coolant pipes connected to it. Recover and discard the sealing O-rings from the thermostat and the thermostat housing – new ones should be used on refitting.

10 Check that all coolant hoses, wiring harnesses and their support brackets have been removed from the water pump housing.

11 Unscrew the two bolts and two nuts securing the water pump housing to the cylinder block, then remove the housing. Remove and discard the sealing O-ring – this must be renewed whenever it is disturbed.

Refitting

12 Clean any oil, coolant or old gasket material and sealant from the mating surfaces and from the coolant passages, bolt holes and threads. Be careful not to allow dirt and debris to fall inside the engine. Degrease the surfaces completely before applying sealant.

13 With the new O-ring fitted to its groove, apply liquid gasket and refit the water pump housing as directed below. The water pump housing must be installed within five minutes of applying the liquid gasket – if this time limit is exceeded, the sealant must be wiped off and new liquid gasket applied. A 'dry' practice run before applying liquid gasket is recommended.

14 Apply liquid gasket in a continuous thin bead (3 mm diameter approx) evenly along the length of the water pump housing's mating surface so that the bead is around the inside edges of the bolt holes and around the inside of the O-ring groove. Also apply a small blob of liquid gasket to the bolt holes in the cylinder block to ensure that there are no leaks from the threads. Do NOT apply sealant to blind holes in the castings.

15 Offer up the water pump housing, taking care to avoid spreading sealant everywhere, and carefully slide it into place on its studs, ensuring that you do not smear the sealant bead.

16 Refit the two bolts and the two nuts, tightening them by hand only at first until the water pump housing is correctly settled in position. Tighten the retaining bolts and nuts to the specified torque. Wipe off any excess sealant.

17 The remainder of reassembly is the reverse of the removal procedure.

18 Wait at least 3 hours (or as directed on the liquid gasket packaging) before running the engine.

21 Engine/transmission mountings – inspection and renewal

Inspection

1 If improved access is required, raise the front of the vehicle and support it securely on axle stands (see *Jacking and vehicle support*). Unclip the steering fluid reservoir and secure it to one side without disconnecting or straining its hoses to examine the engine right-hand (timing end) mounting. Remove the engine compartment undershield (Chapter 11) to reach the front mounting. Remove the air cleaner assembly (Chapter 4A) and/or the battery tray (Chapter 5A) to reach the left-hand (upper) mounting.

2 Check the mounting rubber to see if it is

cracked, hardened or separated from the metal at any point; renew the mounting if any such damage or deterioration is evident.

3 Check that all the fasteners are securely tightened; use a torque wrench to check if in doubt.

4 Using a large screwdriver or a crowbar, check for wear in the mounting by carefully levering against it to check for freeplay; where this is not possible, enlist the aid of an assistant to move the engine/transmission back-and-forth, or from side-to-side, while you watch the mounting. While some freeplay is to be expected even from new components, excessive wear should be obvious. If excessive freeplay is found, check first that the fasteners are correctly secured, then renew any worn components as described below.

Renewal

Engine right-hand (timing end) mounting

5 Unclip the steering fluid reservoir and secure it to one side without disconnecting or straining its hoses.

6 Support the weight of the engine using a trolley jack and block of wood beneath the sump. Make sure the engine is adequately supported, then unscrew the nuts and bolt securing the intermediate bracket to the engine and to the rubber mounting itself. Unbolt the earth lead and remove the bracket **(see illustrations)**.

7 Unscrew the three bolts securing the mounting to the inner wing **(see illustration)**. Check the rubber section for signs of perishing, cracks, or deterioration of the metal-to-rubber bonding.

8 Unscrew the three bolts and remove the mounting bracket from the engine **(see illustration)**.

9 Whenever the intermediate bracket is removed, use a wire brush to scrub clean the mating surfaces of the two brackets and the earth lead mounting points. If corrosion is found, apply a smear of copper-based grease to the mating surfaces on reassembly.

10 Refitting is a reversal of removal. When refitting the intermediate bracket, note that it must engage on the locating pin projecting from the top of the mounting's centre and tighten the bracket-to-timing chain case bracket nut and bolt first, followed by the bracket-to-mounting centre nut last; do not forget to refit the engine earth lead. Tighten all nuts and bolts to the specified torques, where given.

Engine/transmission front mounting

Note: *The front mounting through-bolt must be renewed irrespective of its apparent condition whenever it is disturbed. Obtain a new bolt before starting work, but, depending on the work being undertaken, be careful at exactly which stage of the tightening procedure you fit the bolt and tighten it (see paragraphs 16 and 27 to 29 below).*

11 Remove the engine compartment under-shield (Chapter 11).

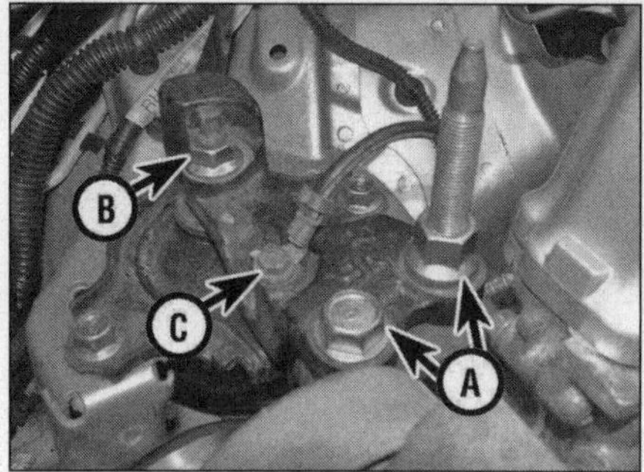

21.6a Engine right-hand (timing end) mounting intermediate bracket fasteners – tighten nut and bolt (A) first, then nut (B). Do not forget to refit earth lead bolt (C) . . .

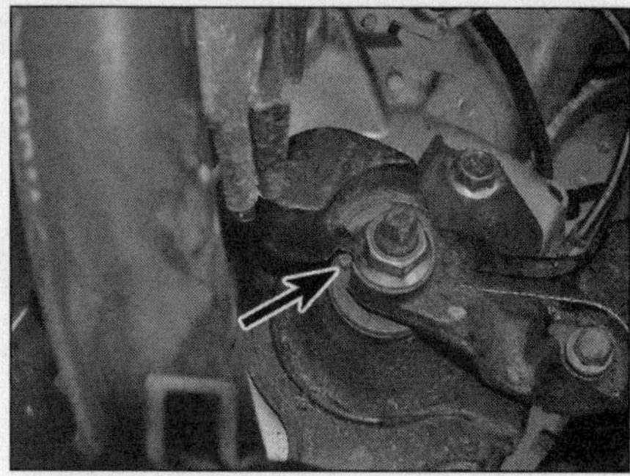

21.6b . . . intermediate bracket must engage on locating pin projecting from top of mounting's centre

21.7 Engine right-hand (timing end) mounting-to-body bolts

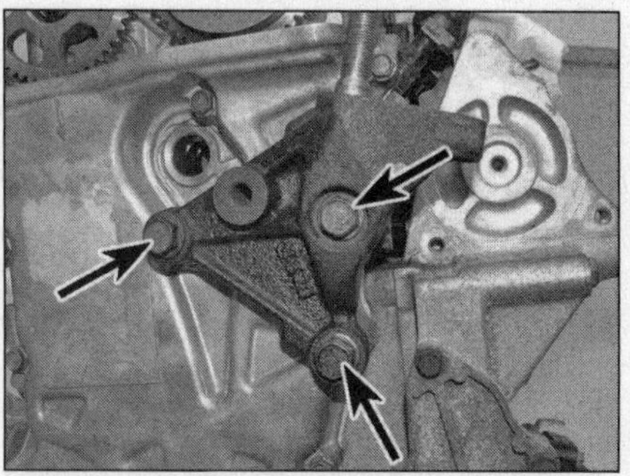

21.8 Engine right-hand (timing end) mounting bracket-to-timing chain case/ cylinder head and block bolts

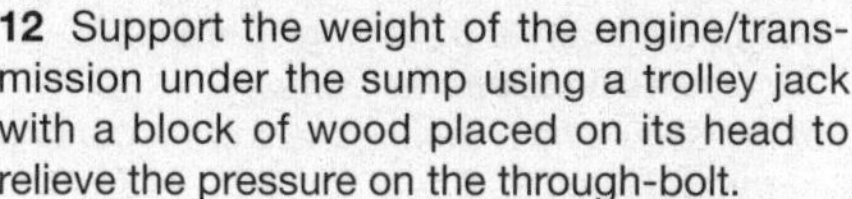

12 Support the weight of the engine/transmission under the sump using a trolley jack with a block of wood placed on its head to relieve the pressure on the through-bolt.

13 Unscrew the through-bolt from the front mounting – note that the nut is effectively 'captive', with a tab that fits inside a loop on the subframe.

14 On manual gearbox models, unscrew the three bolts securing the front mounting to the cylinder block and bellhousing, and remove it, with the wiring harness bracket **(see illustrations)**. Check the rubber section for signs of perishing, cracks, or deterioration of the metal-to-rubber bonding.

15 On automatic transmission models, unscrew the two bolts securing the front mounting to the transmission and remove it. Check the rubber section as described in the previous paragraph.

16 Refitting is a reversal of removal; tighten all the bolts to the specified torques. When refitting the through-bolt, ensure that the tab on the nut fits inside the loop on the subframe; if it is simply a matter of renewing the mounting, then discard the original bolt, fit the new one and tighten it to the specified torque. If the mounting is being tightened as part of one of the sequences outlined in paragraphs 27 to 29, use the original bolt for the preliminary tightening and only fit the new bolt on the last and final tightening.

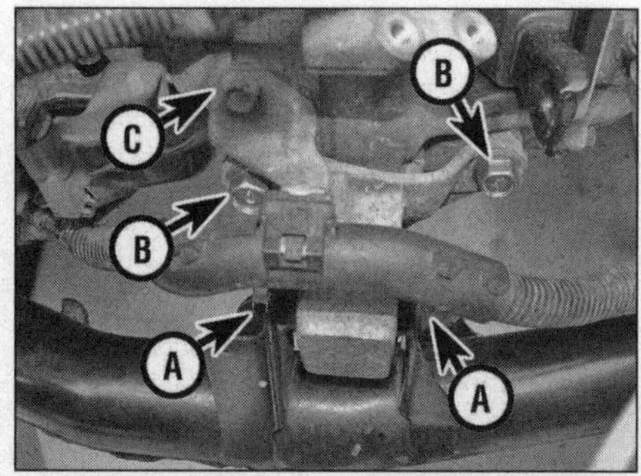

21.14a Engine/transmission front mounting bolt and nut (A), two mounting-to-cylinder block and bellhousing bolts (B) and wiring harness bolt (C)

21.14b Engine/transmission front mounting-to-cylinder block and bellhousing bolts

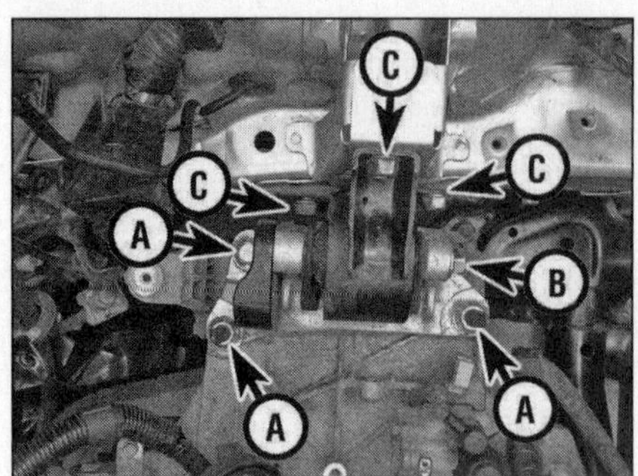

21.19 Engine/transmission left-hand mounting bracket-to-gearbox/transmission nuts and bolt (A), through-bolt (B), and mounting-to-body bolts (C)

21.20 Engine/transmission left-hand mounting-to-body bolts

21.23 Engine/transmission rear mounting-to-subframe bolts

Engine/transmission left-hand mounting

17 Remove the air cleaner assembly (Chapter 4A) and/or the battery tray (Chapter 5A).

18 Support the weight of the unit under the gearbox/transmission using a trolley jack with a block of wood placed on its head to relieve the pressure on the through-bolt.

19 Unscrew the mounting through-bolt, then unscrew the two nuts and bolt, and remove the mounting bracket from the gearbox/transmission **(see illustration)**. The damper can be unbolted from the rear of the mounting bracket if required.

20 Unscrew the three bolts securing the mounting to the inner wing **(see illustration)**. Check the rubber section including the rubber dampers for signs of perishing, cracks, or deterioration of the metal-to-rubber bonding.

21 Refitting is a reversal of removal; tighten all the fasteners to the specified torques, where given. Tighten the mounting bracket-to-gearbox/transmission nuts and bolt first, then the through-bolt. Refit the components removed for access.

Engine/transmission rear mounting

22 Support the weight of the engine/transmission under the gearbox/transmission using a trolley jack with a block of wood placed on its head to relieve the pressure on the mounting and through-bolt.

23 Unscrew the three mounting-to-front suspension subframe bolts **(see illustration)**.

24 Unscrew the mounting through-bolt and remove the mounting **(see illustration)**. Check the rubber section including the rubber dampers for signs of perishing, cracks, or deterioration of the metal-to-rubber bonding.

25 Undo the three bolts to remove the bracket from the gearbox/transmission **(see illustration)**.

26 Refitting is a reversal of removal; tighten all the bolts to the specified torques.

Engine/transmission mounting alignment

27 When refitting the engine and transmission, tighten the mounting fasteners to their specified torques in the following sequence:

a) Tighten the rear mounting-to-front suspension subframe bolts.
b) Loosely tighten the original front mounting through-bolt and nut.
c) Tighten the right-hand (timing end) mounting intermediate bracket-to-timing chain case bracket nut and bolt.
d) Tighten the left-hand mounting bracket-to-gearbox/transmission nuts and bolt.
e) Unscrew and discard the original front mounting through-bolt, fit a new one and tighten it fully.

28 When refitting the manual gearbox, tighten the mounting fasteners to their specified torques in the following sequence:

a) Tighten the rear mounting-to-front suspension subframe bolts.
b) Loosely tighten the original front mounting through-bolt and nut.
c) Tighten the left-hand mounting bracket-to-gearbox nuts and bolt.
d) Tighten the left-hand mounting-to-bracket through-bolt.
e) Unscrew and discard the original front mounting through-bolt, fit a new one and tighten it fully.

29 When refitting the automatic transmission, tighten the mounting fasteners to their specified torques in the following sequence:

a) Loosely tighten the left-hand mounting through-bolt.
b) Tighten the left-hand mounting bracket-to-transmission nuts and bolt.
c) Tighten the left-hand mounting through-bolt.
d) Tighten the rear mounting-to-front suspension subframe bolts.
e) Tighten the original front mounting through-bolt.
f) After the road test (Chapter 7B), unscrew and discard the through-bolt of the front mounting and slacken the through-bolts of the rear and left-hand mountings, then retighten them to their specified torques; tighten first the left-hand mounting through-bolt, then the rear mounting through-bolt, and finally fit and tighten a new front mounting through-bolt onto its nut.

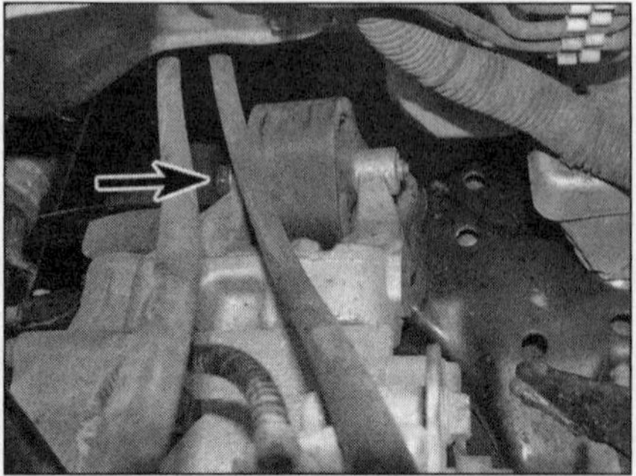
21.24 Engine/transmission rear mounting through-bolt

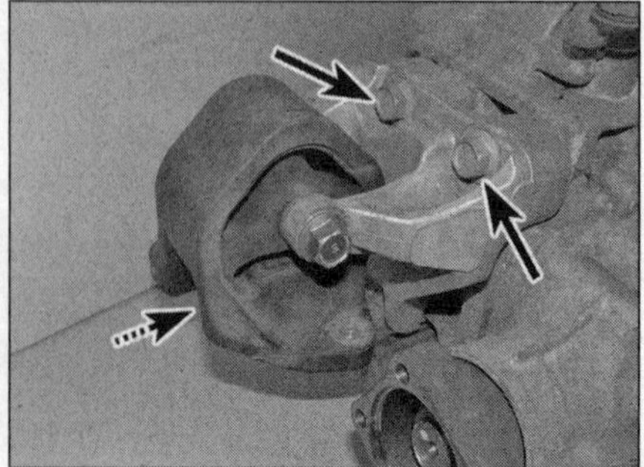
21.25 Engine/transmission rear mounting bracket-to-gearbox bolts

Chapter 2 Part B:
Diesel engine in-car repair procedures

Contents

Degrees of difficulty

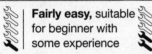

Easy, suitable for novice with little experience 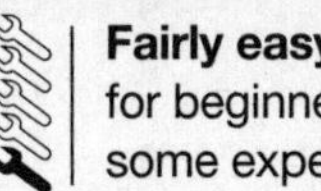	**Fairly easy,** suitable for beginner with some experience	**Fairly difficult,** suitable for competent DIY mechanic	**Difficult,** suitable for experienced DIY mechanic	**Very difficult,** suitable for expert DIY or professional 

Specifications

General

Manufacturer's engine code	N22A2	
Bore	85 mm	
Stroke	97.1 mm	
Capacity	2204 cc	
Compression ratio	16.7:1	
Compression pressure:		
Minimum	24 bars	
Maximum variation between cylinders	2 bars	
Output:		
Maximum power	103 kW @ 4000 rpm	
Maximum torque	340 Nm @ 2000 rpm	
Firing order	1-3-4-2 (No. 1 cylinder at timing chain end)	
Direction of crankshaft rotation	Clockwise (seen from right-hand side of vehicle)	

Camshaft

Endfloat:		
Standard	0.05 to 0.15 mm	
Maximum	0.16 mm	
Camshaft-to-carrier clearance:	**Standard**	**Maximum**
No. 1 journal	0.0012 to 0.0027 mm	0.08 mm
Nos. 2, 3, 4 and 5 journals	0.0020 to 0.0035 mm	0.10 mm
Total runout:		
Standard	0.03 mm	
Maximum	0.04 mm	
Cam lobe height:		
Intake A **(see illustration 9.7b)**	36.433 mm	
Intake B **(see illustration 9.7b)**	35.362 mm	
Exhaust	35.539 mm	

Flywheel

Runout on clutch plate surface – nominal	0.05 to 0.45 mm	

Balancer shafts

	Standard	Service limit
Bearing journal diameter:		
No. 1 journal (oil pump housing), rear/driveshaft	23.938 to 23.950 mm	23.92 mm
No. 2 journal (next to drive gear), front/oil pump and rear/driveshafts	23.938 to 23.950 mm	23.92 mm
No. 3 journal (between weights), front/oil pump and rear/driveshafts	32.949 to 32.961 mm	32.93 mm
Bearing journal maximum taper	N/App.	0.005 mm
Shaft-to-bearing clearance:		
No. 1 journal (oil pump housing), rear/driveshaft	0.050 to 0.082 mm	0.10 mm
No. 2 journal (next to drive gear), front/oil pump and rear/driveshafts	0.050 to 0.082 mm	0.11 mm
No. 3 journal (between weights), front/oil pump and rear/driveshafts	0.060 to 0.120 mm	0.15 mm
Bearing bore diameter:		
No. 1 journal (oil pump housing), rear/driveshaft	24.000 to 24.020 mm	24.03 mm
No. 2 journal (next to drive gear), front/oil pump and rear/driveshafts	24.000 to 24.020 mm	24.03 mm
No. 3 journal (between weights), front/oil pump and rear/driveshafts	33.021 to 33.069 mm	33.09 mm
Shaft endfloat	0.07 to 0.14 mm	0.15 mm

Lubrication system

Oil pump displacement @ 4000 engine rpm	52.2 litres per minute	
Oil pump:	**Standard**	**Service limit**
Inner-to-outer rotor tip clearance	0.02 to 0.14 mm	0.19 mm
Pump housing-to-outer rotor clearance	0.15 to 0.21 mm	0.23 mm
Pump housing-to-rotor axial clearance (rotor endfloat)	0.020 to 0.055 mm	0.10 mm
Minimum oil pressure – with oil @ 80°C:		
At 820 engine rpm	1.1 bars	
At 3,000 engine rpm	4.1 bars	
Piston-cooling oil jets open at	1.2 bars	

Torque wrench settings

	Nm	lbf ft
Air separation cover-to-cylinder head bolts	12	9
Baffle plate-to-lower crankcase/main bearing ladder bolts	12	9
Balancer assembly upper-to-lower half clamp bolts:		
6 mm	12	9
8 mm – oil threads	27	20
Balancer/oil pump assembly mounting bolts	44	32
Balancer/oil pump drive chain:		
Driven sprocket retaining bolt – oil threads	83	61
Rear run fixed guide mounting bolts	12	9
Tensioner blade pivot bolt	22	16
Tensioner mounting bolts	12	9
Camshaft bearing cap/carrier-to-cylinder head bolts:		
6 mm	12	9
8 mm	22	16
Camshaft carrier-to-cylinder head bolts	12	9
Connecting rod big-end bearing cap bolts – oil threads and under heads:		
Stage 1	20	15
Stage 2	Angle-tighten a further 90°	
Cooling system air separation cover-to-cylinder head mounting bolts	12	9
Crankshaft position sensor pulse plate bolts	9	7
Crankshaft pulley bolt – oil threads and under head:		
Stage 1 – new bolt or new crankshaft	34	25
Stage 1 – used bolt	29	21
Stage 2 – all bolts	Angle-tighten a further 90°	
Cylinder block threaded plugs/core plugs:		
28 mm x 1.5 mm thread (gearbox end)	127	94
28 mm x 1.0 mm thread (front, rear and both ends)	83	61
24 mm x 1.5 mm thread (timing chain end, lower plug)	54	40
16 mm x 1.5 mm thread (rear, beneath turbocharger oil feed union)	39	29
Oilway stopper retaining bolt (timing chain end)	12	9
Cylinder head:		
6 mm bolts	12	9
Main bolts – oil threads and under heads:		
Stage 1	49	36
Stage 2	Angle-tighten a further 100°	
Stage 3	Angle-tighten a further 100°	
Stage 4	Slacken all bolts fully and re-oil threads and under heads	
Stage 5	49	36

Torque wrench settings (continued)

	Nm	lbf ft
Cylinder head (continued):		
Main bolts (continued)		
Stages 6 to 8 – used bolts:		
Stage 6	Angle-tighten a further 90°	
Stage 7	Angle-tighten a further 90°	
Stage 8	Angle-tighten a further 90°	
Stages 6 to 8 – new bolts:		
Stage 6	Angle-tighten a further 110°	
Stage 7	Angle-tighten a further 100°	
Stage 8	Angle-tighten a further 100°	
Cylinder head cover retaining nuts	10	7
Dipstick tube mounting bolt	12	9
Engine bellhousing-to-gearbox bolts	64	47
Engine management/fuel and exhaust system component fasteners	See Chapter 4B	
Engine rear mounting fasteners:*		
Bracket-to-lower crankcase/main bearing ladder/sump bolts	54	40
Torque rod-to-bracket bolts	54	40
Torque rod-to-front suspension subframe through-bolt	103	76
Engine right-hand (timing end) mounting fasteners:		
Bracket-to-timing chain case/cylinder head and block bolts	60	44
Intermediate bracket-to-mounting centre bolt (tighten first)	64	47
Intermediate bracket-to-timing chain case bracket nuts and bolt (tighten last)*	93	69
Mounting-to-body bolts	38	28
Torque rod bolts:*		
Front (12 mm) bolts-to-intermediate bracket (tighten first)	64	47
Rear (14 mm) through-bolt-to-body (tighten last)	93	69
Engine/transmission left-hand (lower) mounting fasteners:*		
Mounting-to-gearbox bolts	74	55
Mounting-to-front suspension subframe bolts	64	47
Engine/transmission left-hand (upper) mounting fasteners:		
Bracket-to-body bolts*	93	69
Earth lead-to-mounting clamp bolt	10	7
Mounting-to-body bracket through-bolt (tighten last)*	74	55
Mounting-to-gearbox nuts and bolt (tighten first)*	93	69
Exhaust camshaft driven sprocket retaining bolt – oil threads	118	87
Exhaust camshaft drive gear retaining bolt – oil threads	78	58
Flywheel mounting bolts – oil under heads	118	87
Fuel pump driveshaft mounting bolts:		
6 mm	12	9
8 mm	22	16
Heater outlet cover-to-cylinder head mounting bolts	12	9
Intake camshaft driven gear retaining bolt – oil threads and under head	78	58
Intake camshaft position sensor rotor retaining bolt	12	9
Lower crankcase/main bearing ladder-to-cylinder block bolts:		
8 mm	22	16
10 mm (main bearing cap bolts):		
Stage 1	29	21
Stage 2	Angle-tighten a further 58°	
Oil cooler mounting bolts	12	9
Oil filter/oil cooler/water pump housing mounting bolts	44	32
Oil pressure relief valve threaded plug	39	29
Oil pump housing mounting bolts	12	9
Piston-cooling oil jet retaining bolts	22	16
Roadwheel nuts	See Chapter 1B	
Steering hose clamp-to-cylinder head cover bolt	12	9
Sump-to-lower crankcase/main bearing ladder bolts	12	9
Sump threaded access plug	39	29
Timing chain case retaining bolts	12	9
Timing chain tensioner:		
Blade pivot bolt – oil threads	22	16
Cover plate bolts	12	9
Mounting bolts	12	9
Vacuum line-to-cylinder head cover mounting bolts	12	9
Water outlet-to-cylinder block/crankcase mounting bolts	12	9
Wiring harness-to-cylinder block/crankcase retaining bolt	12	9

* *Use new fasteners.*

1 General information

How to use this Chapter

This Part of Chapter 2 is devoted to those repair procedures for the diesel engine that can reasonably be carried out while the engine remains in the vehicle. All procedures concerning engine removal and refitting, and engine block/cylinder head overhaul, can be found in Chapter 2C.

Most of the operations included in this Part are based on the assumption that the engine is still fitted in the car. Therefore, if this information is being used during a complete engine overhaul, with the engine already removed, many of the steps included here will not apply.

The Specifications included in this Part of Chapter 2 apply only to the procedures contained in this Chapter. Chapter 2C contains the Specifications necessary for cylinder head and engine block rebuilding.

Engine description

The 2.2 i-CTDi is Honda's first in-house developed diesel engine. Based on the petrol engine also described in this manual, it is light in weight, compact but strong and makes good use of several features to deliver strong performance, good fuel economy and exceptional refinement. The engine is a water-cooled four-stroke compression-ignition (diesel) unit, of four-cylinder in-line DOHC (Double OverHead Camshaft) layout with four valves per cylinder, mounted transversely at the front of the vehicle, with the clutch and transmission on its left-hand end. Pendulum-type engine mountings, an acoustic engine cover and a full engine compartment undershield minimise engine noise.

All major engine housings and covers are castings of aluminium alloy, care being taken to design an engine in which each of these components is as rigid as possible in the interests of smooth and quiet operation with minimal friction, while still being compact and light in weight. Cast-iron cylinder liners are cast into the closed-deck cylinder block/crankcase, offset in the interests of further reducing noise and vibration.

The crankshaft runs in five shell-type main bearings, thrustwashers to control crankshaft endfloat being fitted on each side of No. 4 main bearing's upper half. Instead of individual caps securing each of the main bearings, a single large cast aluminium alloy lower crankcase/bearing ladder is bolted to the underside of the cylinder block/crankcase. The connecting rods rotate on horizontally-split bearing shells at their big-ends.

High strength 'cracked' connecting rods are used in which rod and cap are forged as a single unit during the manufacturing process, and then cracked apart so that rod and cap align precisely, one way only, without the need for locating dowel pins. This minimises connecting rod weight and size, while also increasing rigidity and long-term durability thanks to increased fatigue resistance.

The pistons are attached to the connecting rods by gudgeon pins which are secured by circlips in the connecting rod small-end eyes. The aluminium alloy pistons are fitted with three piston rings: two compression rings and an oil control ring, and have low-friction coatings on the thrust faces of their skirts. After manufacture, the cylinder bores and piston skirts are measured and classified into two grades which must be carefully matched together to ensure the correct piston/cylinder clearance; oversizes are available to permit reboring.

The intake and exhaust valves – two of each per cylinder – are closed by coil springs; they operate in guides which are shrink-fitted into the cylinder head, as are the valve seat inserts. The exhaust ports in the cylinder head are siamesed, each pair of valves serving a single port. A passage in the exhaust manifold and through the cylinder head left-hand end allows exhaust gases to be fed to the EGR system components at the front of the cylinder head without using bulky external conduits and associated heat shielding. The intake ports are separate from the IMRC (Intake Manifold Runner Control) valve assembly onwards, ie, throughout the length of the intake manifold and into the cylinder head itself. However (in spite of having the same name), rather than being a version of the variable-length intake manifold used on the petrol engine, IMRC here is a continuously-variable swirl control valve. The intake manifold's lower (swirl) tract (the only one to which the EGR valve is connected) supplies air to the intake valves opened by the higher-lift A-cam lobes through ports whose tangential orientation is designed to maximise axial swirl in the combustion chamber. The intake manifold's upper (secondary) tract, supplying those intake valves opened by the milder B-cam lobes, is opened and closed by vacuum acting on the butterfly-type IMRC valve, controlled by the engine management system Electronic Control Unit (ECU) via the IMRC solenoid valve acting on information from the IMRC valve position sensor. The combination of different port geometry, dissimilar cam lobes and the enhanced swirl generated by the IMRC system provides very high swirl in the combustion chamber at low engine speeds, reducing gradually as engine speed increases to give the ideal combustion environment at all times. This, referred to by Honda as the 'intelligent combustion control system', improves combustion efficiency so that the engine can use a relatively low compression ratio (and thus escape the friction, vibration and noise penalties of higher compression pressures) while still producing power outputs comparable with sales rivals.

Driven from the crankshaft right-hand end by a single-row (simplex) roller timing chain, the exhaust camshaft drives the intake camshaft by gears on the right-hand end of each; a spring-loaded anti-backlash gear in the exhaust camshaft drive gear minimises noise due to any backlash in the gear teeth. The entire length of the timing chain is supported by fixed guides along its front and upper rear runs and it is tensioned by a pivoting tensioner blade on its lower rear run; both guide and tensioner blades incorporate plastic bearing surfaces to minimise noise. A tensioner assembly acting on the tensioner blade's free end uses the lubrication system's hydraulic pressure automatically to tension the chain, while a spring-loaded ratchet prevents the tensioner plunger from retracting when the engine is switched off and oil pressure is relaxed.

Each camshaft operates eight valves via finger followers; a roller in each follower minimises losses due to friction at the point of contact with the cam lobe. Each follower bears on the tip of the valve stem at its inner end and on a hydraulic tappet at its outer end, thus using the lubrication system's hydraulic pressure to automatically take up any free play in the components between each camshaft lobe and its respective valve stem and so eliminating the need for routine checking and adjustment of the valve clearances. Each camshaft rotates in five bearings that are line-bored directly in the camshaft carrier and the (bolted-on) bearing caps; this means that the bearing caps are not available separately from the camshaft carrier and must not be interchanged with caps from another engine. The use of a single, separate, bolted-on camshaft carrier (as opposed to five pairs of separate bearing caps) adds to the rigidity of the cylinder head assembly. Camshaft endfloat is controlled by the No. 4 bearing caps.

The Lanchester harmonic balancer assembly mounted in the sump uses two bobweights on each of two counter-rotating shafts mounted below and equidistant from the crankshaft axis which rotate at twice crankshaft speed to cancel out the unbalanced secondary inertia forces inherent in any in-line four-cylinder engine. Driven from the crankshaft right-hand end by a single-row (simplex) roller chain, the rear shaft drives the front by gear teeth to ensure that the two are always exactly correctly timed in relation to the movement of the crankshaft and pistons. The oil pump is mounted on the right-hand end of the front (driven) shaft, the load this imposes ensuring that noise due to backlash in the gear teeth is minimised. The shafts rotate in bearings machined in the oil pump housing at their right-hand ends and next to the drive gears, and in horizontally-split bearing shells located between their bobweights. Similarly to the camshaft drive/timing chain, the balancer/oil pump drive chain is supported along its rear run by a fixed plastic guide and by a plastic-faced tensioner blade along its front run. A tensioner assembly acting on the tensioner blade's free end uses the lubrication system's hydraulic pressure to tension the chain, while a spring-loaded ratchet prevents the tensioner plunger from retracting when the engine is switched off and oil pressure is relaxed.

The flywheel is of the dual-mass type, to further reduce noise and vibration in the driveline, especially during cruising and under acceleration. The assembly consists of an inner and an outer flywheel joined by high and low torsion springs to form a torsional vibration damper which protects the transmission gear teeth and synchro-rings from torque fluctuations, to which diesel engines are particularly prone.

The common-rail injection system's fuel pump is mounted on the left-hand end of the cylinder head and driven by gear from the exhaust camshaft. A spring-loaded anti-backlash gear in the camshaft drive gear minimises noise due to any backlash in the gear teeth.

The braking system vacuum pump is bolted to the left-hand face of the timing chain case, at the rear right-hand end of the cylinder block. It is driven by the timing chain from the crankshaft.

The water pump is mounted in the oil filter/oil cooler housing bolted to the front right-hand end of the cylinder block and is driven with the steering pump, alternator and air conditioning compressor by a flat 'polyvee' type auxiliary drivebelt from the crankshaft pulley. An automatic spring-loaded tensioner eliminates any need for drivebelt maintenance beyond a periodic check of its condition.

Lubrication system

The forced, wet-sump lubrication system uses an eccentric-rotor trochoid pump, which is mounted on the right-hand end of the front (driven) balancer shaft and draws oil through a strainer located in the sump. The pump forces oil through a full-flow paper element-type filter located in the oil filter/oil cooler housing bolted to the front right-hand end of the cylinder block – an oil cooler is fitted to the oil filter mounting, so that clean oil entering the engine's galleries is cooled by the main engine cooling system. From the filter, the oil is pumped into a main gallery in the cylinder block/crankcase, from where it is distributed to the crankshaft (main bearings) and cylinder head. Pressure is controlled by a spring-loaded pressure relief valve located in the pump housing.

The big-end bearings are supplied with oil via internal drillings in the crankshaft. Each piston crown is cooled by a spray of oil directed at its underside by a jet. These jets are fed by passages off the crankshaft oil supply galleries, with spring-loaded valves to ensure that the jets open only when there is sufficient pressure to guarantee a good oil supply to the rest of the engine components.

The cylinder head is provided with extensive oil galleries to ensure constant oil supply to the camshaft bearings and hydraulic tappets. An oil control orifice is inserted into the cylinder block's top surface, at the rear, on the timing chain end, to control the flow of oil to those components.

While the crankshaft, camshaft and balancer shaft bearings and the hydraulic tappets receive a pressurised supply, the camshaft lobes and valves are lubricated by splash, as are all other engine components.

Valve clearances – general

This engine employs hydraulic tappets which use the lubricating system's oil pressure to automatically take up the clearance in the components between each camshaft lobe and its respective valve stem. Therefore, there is no need for regular checking and adjustment of the valve clearances, but it is essential that only good-quality oil of the recommended viscosity and specification is used in the engine and that this oil is always changed at the recommended intervals.

On starting the engine from cold, there will be a slight delay while full oil pressure builds-up in all parts of the engine, especially in the tappets; the valve components, therefore, may well 'rattle' for about 10 seconds or so and then quieten. This is a normal state of affairs and is nothing to worry about, provided that all tappets quieten quickly and stay quiet.

After the vehicle has been standing for several days, the valve components may 'rattle' for longer than usual, as nearly all the oil will have drained away from the engine's top end components and bearing surfaces. While this is only to be expected, care must be taken to avoid high speed running until all the tappets are refilled with oil and operating normally. With the vehicle stationary, hold the engine at no more than a fast idle speed (maximum 2000 rpm) for 10 to 15 seconds, or until the noise ceases. *Do not run the engine at more than 3000 rpm until the tappets are fully recharged with oil and the noise has ceased.*

Operations with engine in vehicle

The following operations can be carried out without having to remove the engine from the vehicle:

a) Removal and refitting of the timing chain, sprockets and tensioner components.
b) Removal and refitting of the camshafts, cam followers and hydraulic tappets.
c) Removal, refitting and overhaul of the cylinder head.
*d) Removal and refitting of the sump.**
*e) Removal and refitting of the oil pump, drive chain, sprockets and tensioner components.***
*f) Removal and refitting of the balancer shafts.***
g) Renewal of the crankshaft oil seals.
*h) Removal and refitting of the connecting rods and pistons.***
i) Renewal of the engine mountings.
j) Removal and refitting of the flywheel.

** Removal of the sump with the engine in the vehicle requires first the removal of the front suspension subframe. Depending on the skills and equipment available and the nature of the work being undertaken, the home mechanic may prefer to consider removing the engine/transmission complete and then removing the sump, in the interests of improved safety, cleanliness and improved access.*

*** These operations can be carried out after removal of the sump, but as mentioned above it is better for the engine to be removed.*

2 Compression and leakdown tests – description and interpretation

Compression test

Note: *A compression tester specifically designed for diesel engines must be used for this test. The aid of an assistant will be required.*

1 When engine performance is down, or if misfiring occurs which cannot be attributed to a fault in the fuel system, a compression test can provide diagnostic clues as to the engine's condition. If the test is performed regularly it can give warning of trouble before any other symptoms become apparent.

2 A compression tester is connected to an adapter which screws into the glow plug hole or is fitted to the injector seating. It is unlikely to be worthwhile buying such a tester for occasional use, but it may be possible to borrow or hire one – if not, have the test performed by a garage.

3 Observe the following points:

a) The battery must be in a good state of charge.
b) The air filter must be clean.
c) The engine must be at normal operating temperature.

4 Switch off the ignition.

Warning: Before disconnecting any part of the high-pressure side of the fuel system, read the warnings concerning depressurising the fuel system given in Chapter 4B.

5 If the compression tester adapter fits the injector seatings, all four injectors must be removed; be careful to remove also the copper sealing washers (which must be renewed when the injectors are refitted), otherwise they may be blown out, and note that the high-pressure pipes must also be renewed (Chapter 4B). If the compression tester adapter screws into the glow plug holes, the glow plugs must be removed (Chapter 5C). **Note:** *In this latter case, the injectors must be disabled to prevent them spraying fuel into the combustion chamber as the test is carried out. Honda specify the use of the Honda Diagnostic System (HDS) tester to switch off the injectors and to switch them on again once the test is complete. The obvious alternative is simply to disconnect the injector wiring connectors and*

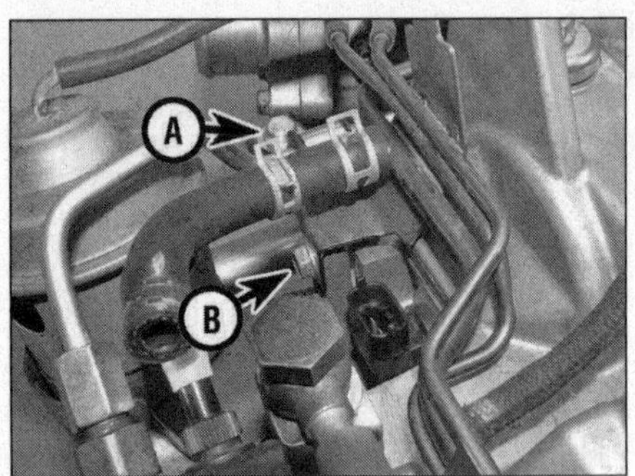

4.3a Unscrew bolt (A) securing fuel pump-to-fuel rail high-pressure pipe's clamp, then unscrew two bolts – one at front (B) . . .

to reconnect them afterwards. This, however, will almost certainly cause a fault code to be logged so that the engine management Malfunction Indicator warning Lamp (MIL) will illuminate, and/or the glow plug warning lamp will flash, until the vehicle can be taken to a Honda dealer or other specialist for the fault code to be erased.

6 With the injectors or glow plugs removed and the injectors disabled, as applicable, fit the compression tester to No. 1 cylinder.

7 Have the assistant crank the engine on the starter motor; there is no need to hold the accelerator pedal down because a diesel engine's air intake is not throttled. After one or two revolutions, the compression pressure should build-up to a maximum figure and then stabilise. Record the highest reading obtained.

8 Repeat the test on the remaining cylinders, recording the pressure in each.

9 All cylinders should produce very similar pressures, greater than the minimum specified. The actual compression pressures measured are not as important as the balance between cylinders; a difference of more than 2 bars between any cylinder(s) and the others indicates a fault. Note that the compression should build-up quickly in a healthy engine; low compression on the first stroke, followed by gradually-increasing pressure on successive strokes, indicates worn piston rings. A low compression reading on the first stroke, which does not build-up during successive strokes, indicates leaking valves or a blown head gasket (a cracked head could also be the cause). Deposits on the undersides of the valve heads can also cause low compression.

10 The cause of poor compression is less easy to establish on a diesel engine than on a petrol one. Introducing oil into the cylinders ('wet' testing) is not recommended because of the much smaller volume of the combustion chamber (risk of hydraulic lock).

11 A low reading from two adjacent cylinders is almost certainly due to the head gasket having blown between them; the presence of coolant in the engine oil will confirm this.

12 If the compression reading is unusually high, the combustion chambers are probably coated with carbon deposits.

13 On completion of the test, refit the glow plugs and re-enable the injectors or refit the injectors, using new high-pressure pipes and copper sealing washers, as applicable (Chapter 4B or 5C).

Leakdown test

14 A leakdown test measures the rate at which compressed air fed into the cylinder is lost. It is an alternative to a compression test and in many ways it is better, since the escaping air provides easy identification of where pressure loss is occurring (piston rings, valves or head gasket).

15 The equipment needed for leakdown testing is unlikely to be available to the home mechanic. If poor compression is suspected, have the test performed by a suitably-equipped garage.

3 Top Dead Centre (TDC) for No. 1 piston – locating

General

1 Top Dead Centre (TDC) is the highest point in its travel up-and-down its cylinder bore that each piston reaches as the crankshaft rotates. While each piston reaches TDC both at the top of the compression stroke and again at the top of the exhaust stroke, for the purpose of timing the engine, TDC refers to the No. 1 piston position at the top of its compression stroke.

2 No. 1 piston and cylinder are at the right-hand (timing chain) end of the engine. Note that the crankshaft rotates clockwise when viewed from the right-hand side of the car. There are no timing marks on the exterior of the engine.

Locating TDC

3 Remove the glow plugs (Chapter 5C) to make the engine easier to turn.

4 It is best to rotate the crankshaft using a spanner applied to the crankshaft pulley bolt; however, it is possible also either to select top gear and (with the front of the vehicle jacked up) to turn the right-hand front roadwheel, or to use the starter motor to bring the engine close to TDC, then finish with a spanner.

5 Remove the cylinder head cover (Section 4) so that the timing marks on the exhaust camshaft sprocket and the two camshaft drive gears can be seen. Rotate the crankshaft until the camshaft timing marks align as described in Section 6, paragraph 2. No. 1 cylinder will then be at TDC on the compression stroke.

6 TDC for any of the other cylinders can now be located by rotating the crankshaft clockwise 180° at a time and following the firing order.

4 Cylinder head cover – removal and refitting

Note: *The removal of the cylinder head cover is in itself a very simple and easy procedure. However, the fuel injectors must be removed first; not only is this difficult, but all four fuel injector high-pressure pipes and copper sealing washers must be renewed. The cover gaskets must also be renewed and liquid gasket (Honda Part No. 08C70-K0234M, 08C70-K0334M, 08C70-X0331S, 08718-0001 or equivalent) must be available on reassembly.*

Removal

1 Unscrew the four retaining nuts and remove the acoustic engine cover.

Warning: Before disconnecting any part of the high-pressure side of the fuel system, read the warnings concerning depressurising the fuel system in Chapter 4B.

2 Remove the fuel injectors (see Chapter 4B). Take precautions to prevent dirt falling into the combustion chambers.

3 From the front left-hand end of the cylinder head unscrew the bolt securing the fuel pump-to-fuel rail high-pressure pipe's clamp to the mounting bracket, then unscrew the two bolts securing the fuel return line to the cylinder head **(see illustrations)**.

4 Unbolt the turbocharger boost control solenoid valve from the left-hand end of the cylinder head cover **(see illustration)**.

5 From the rear right-hand end of the cylinder head cover unscrew the bolt securing the steering hose clamp, then unscrew the two

4.3b . . . other at rear – securing fuel return line to cylinder head . . .

4.4 . . . then unbolt turbocharger boost control solenoid valve

4.5a Unbolt steering hose clamp . . .

4.5b . . . and vacuum line assembly from rear of cylinder head cover

4.6 Disconnect breather hose from rear of cylinder head cover

bolts securing the vacuum line assembly to the rear of the cylinder head cover **(see illustrations)**.

6 Disconnect the breather hose from the rear of the cylinder head cover **(see illustration)**.

7 Release the large wiring conduit from its mountings and secure all wiring hoses and fuel lines clear of the cylinder head cover so that it can be withdrawn. Unbolt the vacuum line assembly mounting bolts and secure the assembly clear of the cover.

8 Unscrew the retaining nuts and remove the cylinder head cover **(see illustration)**. Peel off and discard the gaskets. Check the condition of the sealing washers under each of the cover retaining nuts and renew as necessary.

Refitting

9 Thoroughly clean the mating surfaces of the cylinder head and cover. Clean any oil or old gasket material and sealant from the cover grooves. Thoroughly clean the injector wells and the passages around the injector clamp mountings in the cover and the injector wells in the cylinder head. Be careful not to allow dirt and debris to fall into the combustion chambers.

10 Fit the new gaskets, ensuring that each is correctly seated in the cover grooves **(see illustration)**.

11 Apply liquid gasket to the points shown, to ensure that there are no oil leaks from the cylinder head cover/timing chain case/cylinder head intersection **(see illustration)**. The cylinder head cover must be installed within five minutes of applying the liquid gasket; if this time limit is exceeded, the sealant must be wiped off completely and new liquid gasket applied.

12 Ensuring that the gaskets are not dislodged, place the cover on the cylinder head, slide the cover very slightly back-and-forth to settle the gaskets, then refit the sealing washers and nuts. Tighten the nuts by hand only at first.

13 Working in a diagonal sequence from the centre outwards and in two or three stages, tighten the cover retaining nuts to the specified torque **(see illustration)**.

14 Refit the wiring conduit to its mountings and reconnect any wiring or hoses that were disconnected on removal.

15 Reconnect the breather hose and refit the vacuum line assembly and steering hose clamp to the rear of the cylinder head cover. Tighten the vacuum line and steering hose clamp retaining bolts to their specified torques.

16 Refit the turbocharger boost control solenoid valve. Tighten its mounting bolts to their specified torque.

17 Refit the fuel return line and high-pressure pipe clamp. Tighten the mounting bolts to their specified torques.

18 Refit the fuel injectors as described in Chapter 4B.

19 Make a final check that all hoses, pipes and wiring have been reconnected and secured. Refit the acoustic engine cover and securely tighten its retaining nuts.

20 When Honda's own liquid gasket has been used to seal a joint, note the following:

a) Where applicable, wait at least 30 minutes before filling the engine with oil.

b) Do not run the engine for at least three hours.

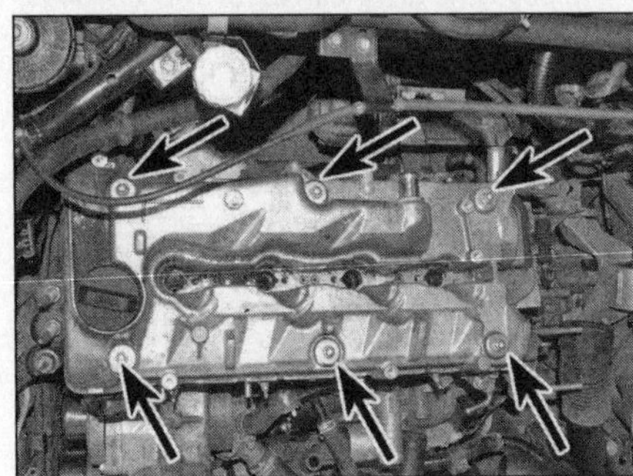

4.8 Unscrew retaining nuts to remove cylinder head cover

4.11 Apply liquid gasket to points shown and refit cover . . .

5 Crankshaft pulley – removal and refitting

Note: *The crankshaft pulley retaining bolt is extremely tight; the aid of an assistant will be required. Be very careful to avoid the risk of personal injury through trapped fingers, etc.*

Removal

1 Apply the handbrake, jack up the front of the vehicle and support it on axle stands (see *Jacking and vehicle support*). Depending on the work about to be undertaken, remove either just the right-hand front roadwheel or both front roadwheels.

2 Remove the engine compartment under-shield (Chapter 11).

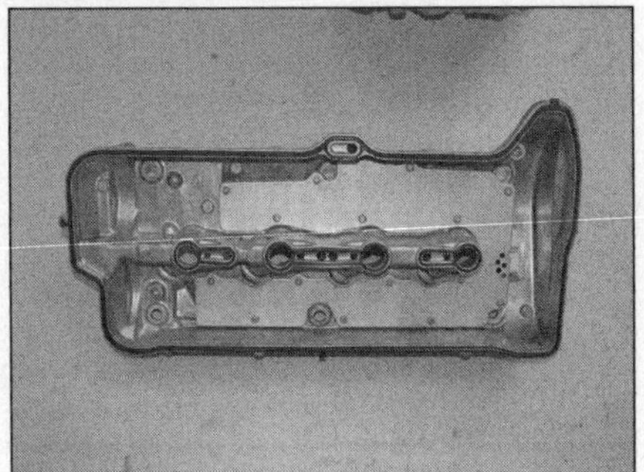

4.10 Ensure that new gaskets are correctly seated in cover grooves on refitting

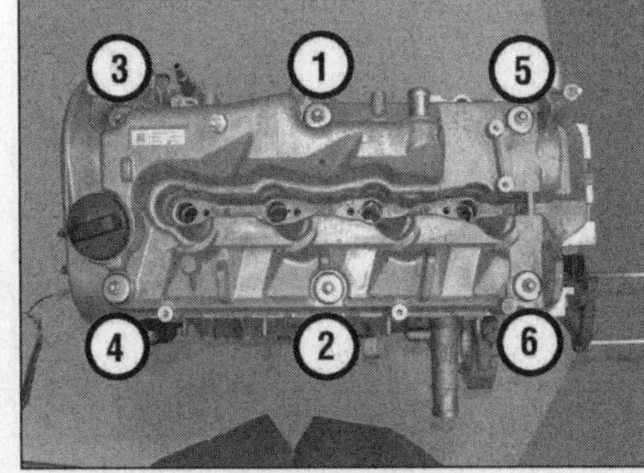

4.13 . . . tighten cover retaining nuts to specified torque setting in sequence shown

5.4 Unscrew and discard two nuts and bolt securing engine right-hand mounting

5.7 Don't disturb locating key when removing and refitting crankshaft pulley

5.8a Wipe clean lips of crankshaft right-hand oil seal, then clean the boss on pulley

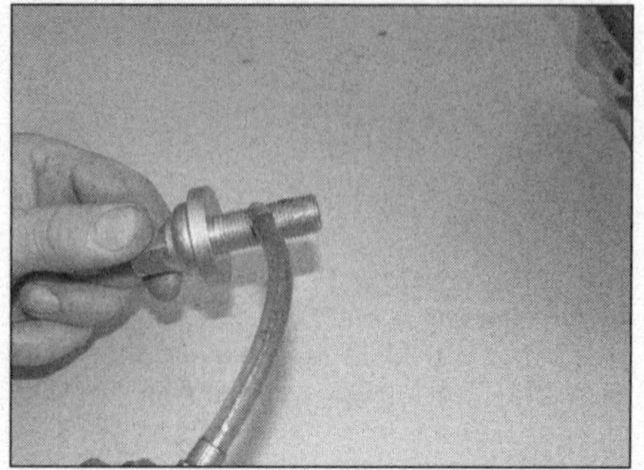

5.8b Apply a film of clean oil to threads . . .

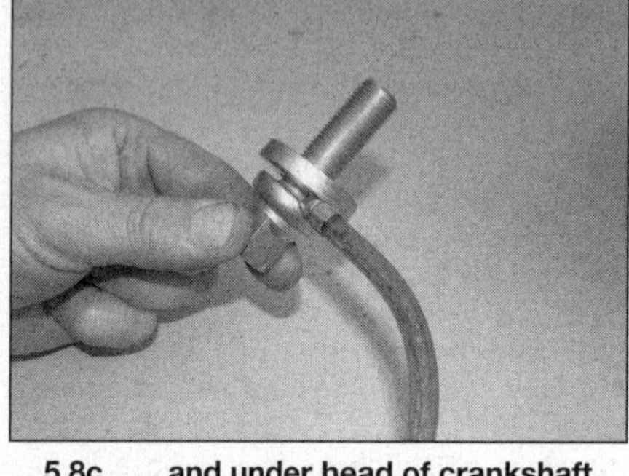

5.8c . . . and under head of crankshaft pulley bolt

3 Remove the auxiliary drivebelt (Chapter 1B).

4 The engine right-hand mounting must now be disconnected. First support the weight of the engine using a trolley jack and block of wood beneath the sump. Unscrew and discard the two nuts and the bolt securing the intermediate bracket to the timing chain case/cylinder head and block bracket **(see illustration)**.

5 Lower the engine approximately 50 mm.

6 Slacken the crankshaft pulley retaining bolt. This is extremely tight; first, ensure that the vehicle is securely supported. Only use good-quality, close-fitting tools for this job – if something slips, it may result in injury. For extra leverage, use a long-handled breaker bar, or a length of substantial tubing slipped over the socket handle to extend it. If an extension bar is fitted on the socket, rest the outer end of the extension bar on another axle stand, to keep it horizontal – this improves leverage, and reduces the chance of the socket slipping off under load. Use one of the following methods to prevent crankshaft rotation:

a) *The Honda service tools for this task are a pulley holder (Part No. 07JAB-0010400) which has a 50 mm hexagon to engage with the centre of the pulley, a long handle (Part No. 07JAB-001020B) to fit over the holder and a deep 19 mm socket (Part No. 07JAA-001020A) slim enough to fit through the holder. Either acquire these tools or find their commercial equivalents.*

b) *Remove the starter motor (Chapter 5A) and have an assistant insert a wide-bladed screwdriver in the teeth of the starter ring gear.*

c) *If the engine is removed from the vehicle, a home-made holding tool can be fabricated to lock the flywheel (see Section 15).*

7 Unscrew the pulley bolt and washer, then remove the pulley from the crankshaft. Note the locating key; this should not be loose in its keyway, as it also locates the camshaft drive/timing chain and balancer/oil pump drive chain drive sprocket **(see illustration)**. Be careful not to dislodge it as the pulley is removed.

Refitting

Note: *The engine right-hand mounting nuts and bolt must be renewed, as must the auxiliary drivebelt. It is also considered good practice to renew highly-stressed fasteners such as the crankshaft pulley retaining bolt.*

8 Check that the locating key is firmly in place in the crankshaft keyway. Wipe clean the lips of the crankshaft hand oil seal, then clean the boss on the pulley's inboard face which passes through the oil seal lips; polish away any burrs or raised edges which might damage the seal lips **(see illustration)**. Similarly clean the pulley retaining bolt thread in the crankshaft, the pulley's central bore which fits over the crankshaft and the seating for the retaining bolt washer in the pulley's outboard face. Clean the retaining bolt washer's seating face, then apply a film of clean oil to the threads and under the head of the retaining bolt **(see illustrations)**.

9 Fit the pulley to the crankshaft, aligning the pulley keyway with the locating key and being careful not to damage the seal lips as the pulley enters them, then refit the retaining bolt and washer.

10 Lock the crankshaft using the method used on removal, and tighten the pulley retaining bolt to the specified first stage torque.

11 Once the bolt has been tightened to the Stage 1 torque, tighten it through its specified Stage 2 angle, using a socket and extension bar **(see illustrations)**.

12 Raise the engine on the jack until the engine right-hand mounting's intermediate bracket is lifted back into full contact with the timing chain case/cylinder head and block bracket. Tighten the mounting's new nuts and bolt to their specified torque.

13 Fit a new auxiliary drivebelt (Chapter 1B).

14 The remainder of refitting is a reversal of removal.

5.11a Tighten pulley bolt to Stage 1 setting, then make two paint marks 90° apart and tighten . . .

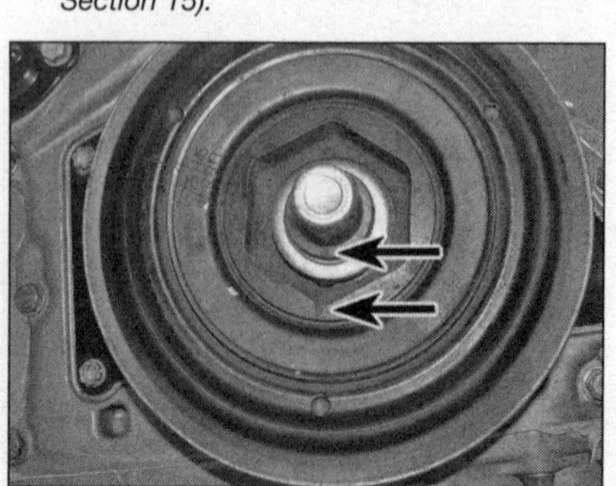

5.11b . . . until marks align as shown

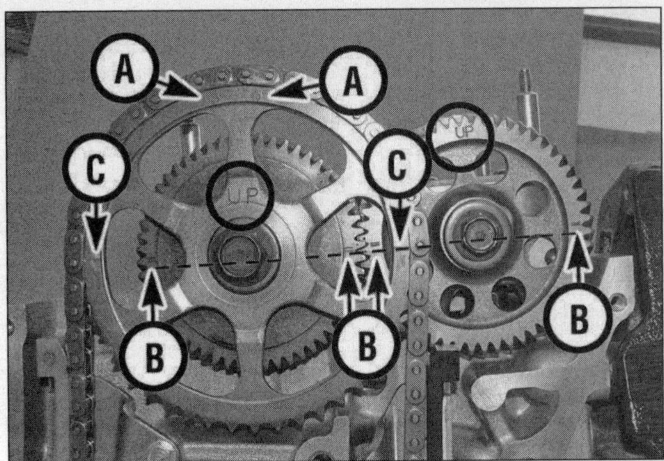

6.2 No. 1 cylinder is at TDC on compression stroke when UP marks and punch marks (A) are both at the top, while double-line marks (B) and lines (C) are aligned through bolt centres

6.5a Unscrew and discard bolts and remove engine right-hand mounting torque rod . . .

6 Timing chain case – removal and refitting

Note: *Liquid gasket (Honda Part No. 08C70-K0234M, 08C70-K0334M, 08C70-X0331S or 08718-0001 or equivalent) must be available on reassembly.*

Removal

1 Remove the cylinder head cover (Section 4).

2 If further dismantling, such as removal/refitting of the timing chain, valve gear and/or cylinder head, is intended, bring the engine to TDC, No 1 firing. No. 1 cylinder is correctly positioned when all four cam lobes are pointing away from No. 1 cylinder's valves and when the UP marks on the exhaust camshaft sprocket and the intake camshaft driven gear are both in the twelve o'clock position. The four double-line marks etched in both drive gear rims must be lined up through the drive gear retaining bolt centres, with, at the centre, the punch-marked tooth on the exhaust camshaft drive gear aligned exactly between the two punch-marked teeth on the intake camshaft driven gear. The two punch marks in the rim of the exhaust camshaft sprocket must also be in the twelve o'clock position **(see illustration)**. Rotate the crankshaft clockwise (see Section 3) until the marks align as described.

3 If not already done, jack up the front of the vehicle and support it securely on axle stands (see *Jacking and vehicle support*). Depending on the work about to be undertaken, remove the right-hand or both front roadwheels. Remove the engine compartment undershield (Chapter 11).

4 Remove the auxiliary drivebelt (Chapter 1B).

5 The engine right-hand mounting must now be disconnected. Support the weight of the engine using a trolley jack and block of wood beneath the sump. Unscrew and discard the three bolts securing the torque rod to the body and mounting and remove the torque rod. Unscrew and discard the two nuts and the bolt securing the intermediate bracket to the timing chain case/cylinder head and block bracket, then unscrew the intermediate bracket-to-mounting centre nut and remove the intermediate bracket **(see illustrations)**.

6 Remove the crankshaft pulley (Section 5).

7 Unscrew the four bolts, then remove the engine right-hand mounting's timing chain case/cylinder head and block bracket **(see illustration)**.

8 Unscrew the seventeen bolts – three along the bottom, five up the front edge and nine up the rear edge – securing the timing chain case **(see illustration)**. Note that certain bolts are shouldered to locate the case as well as retaining it.

9 Remove the timing chain case **(see illustration)**. Use a hammer and a block of wood or a soft-faced mallet to try and break the seal by tapping all around the edge of the timing chain case, then carefully prise it away. It is a thin and delicate casting, easily damaged or even broken if carelessly handled, and the liquid gasket used on assembly sticks tight. Do not lever between the mating surfaces; these are easily scratched or gouged and will leak oil if badly marked. Leverage points are provided at the top and bottom of the front

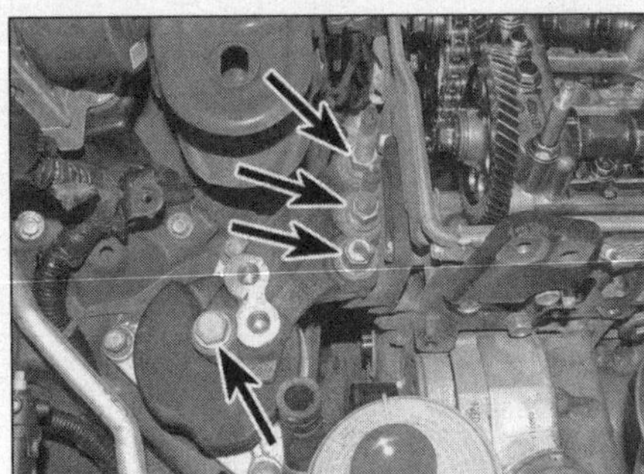

6.5b . . . then unbolt mounting intermediate bracket

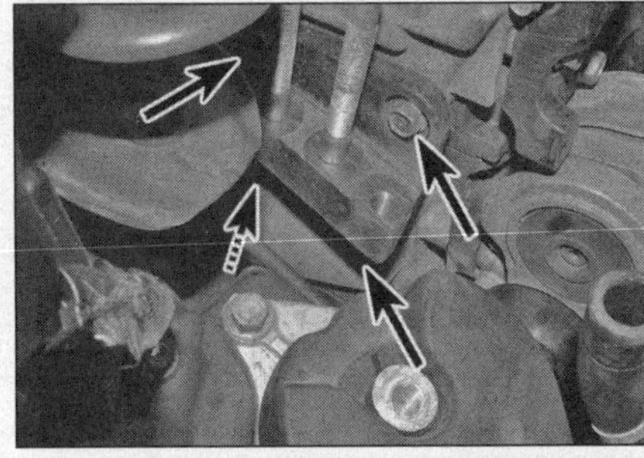

6.7 Unbolt engine right-hand (timing end) mounting timing chain case/cylinder head and block bracket

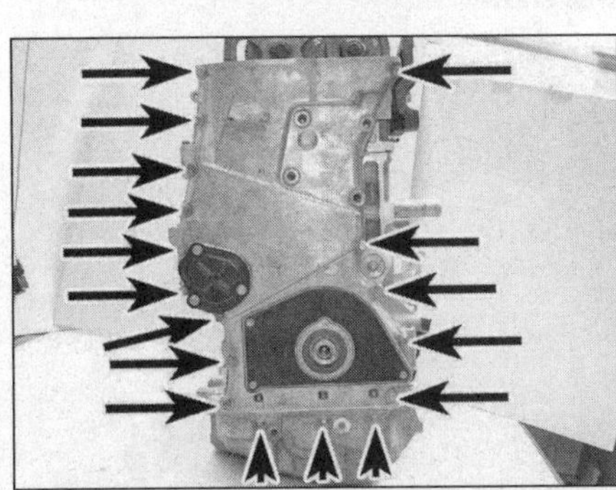

6.8 Timing chain case retaining bolt locations

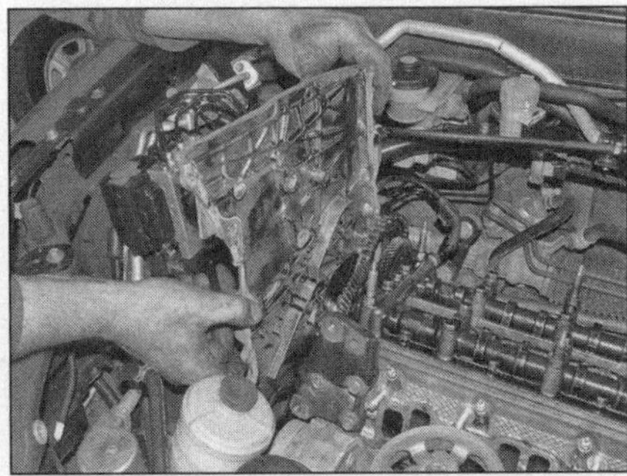

6.9 Removing timing chain case

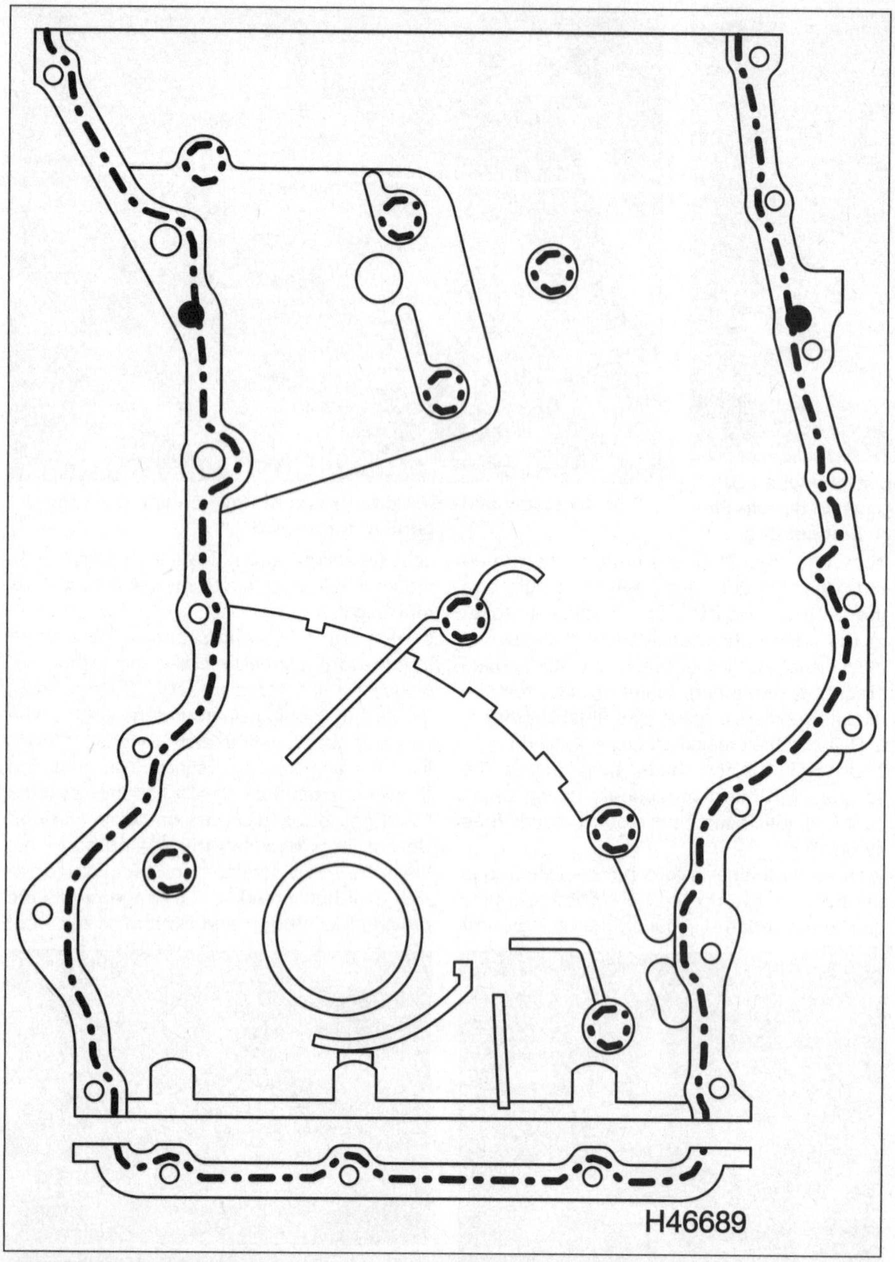

edge and at the rear next to the turbocharger oil feed union and braking system vacuum pump. Insert a large flat-bladed screwdriver and gently prise the timing chain case away at these points first. At the same time, a hammer and a block of wood can be used to jar the cases apart. As soon as the case is removed, cover the sump opening to keep dirt out.

10 Renew the crankshaft right-hand oil seal (Section 17) if any oil leakage is evident.

Refitting

11 Thoroughly clean the mating surfaces of the timing chain case, the cylinder head, the cylinder block and the sump. Clean any oil or old gasket material and sealant from the mating surfaces and from the bolt holes and threads. Be careful not to allow dirt to fall into the sump. Degrease the surfaces completely before applying sealant.

12 The timing chain case must be installed within five minutes of applying the liquid gasket – if this time limit is exceeded, the sealant must be wiped off completely and new liquid gasket applied. A 'dry' practice run before applying liquid gasket is recommended.

13 Apply liquid gasket in a continuous thin bead (3 mm diameter approx) evenly along the length of the chain case's front, rear and bottom mating surfaces so that the bead goes around the inside edges of the bolt holes **(see illustration)**. Also apply a bead to the eight supporting bosses on the inside of the chain case. Also apply liquid gasket to the four points on the cylinder head/block/lower crankcase mating surfaces. Apply a small blob of liquid gasket to those bolt holes in the cylinder head/block/lower crankcase which pass through to the outside, and to the three bolt holes along the bottom edge of the timing chain case, to ensure that there are no oil leaks from the threads. Do not apply sealant to blind holes in the castings.

14 Offer up the timing chain case so that the crankshaft end passes through the oil seal and align the bottom outer edge of the timing chain case on that of the sump while the upper end is tilted back clear of the cylinder block and head to avoid spreading sealant everywhere. Carefully tilt the chain case into place and refit the shouldered bolts to hold it **(see illustrations)**. **Note:** *The timing chain case should fit on the cylinder head and block without being forced. If the case is not correctly seated, remove it and investigate the problem. Do not attempt to pull it into place using the bolts as it could crack.*

15 Refit all the bolts, tightening them by hand only at first until the timing chain case is correctly settled in position. Tighten first the three bolts along the bottom edge, then, working in a diagonal sequence from the centre outwards and in two or three stages, tighten the retaining bolts to the specified torque **(see illustration)**. Wipe off any excess sealant from the sump and chain case mating surfaces.

16 Refit the engine right-hand mounting's

6.13 Apply a continuous 3.0 mm diameter bead of liquid gasket evenly along timing chain case's front, rear and bottom mating surfaces, around inside edges of bolt holes – also to supporting bosses shown

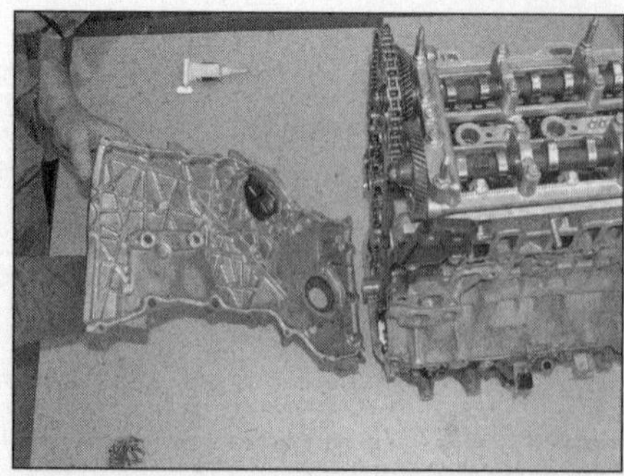

6.14a Carefully refit timing chain case as shown to avoid smearing sealant . . .

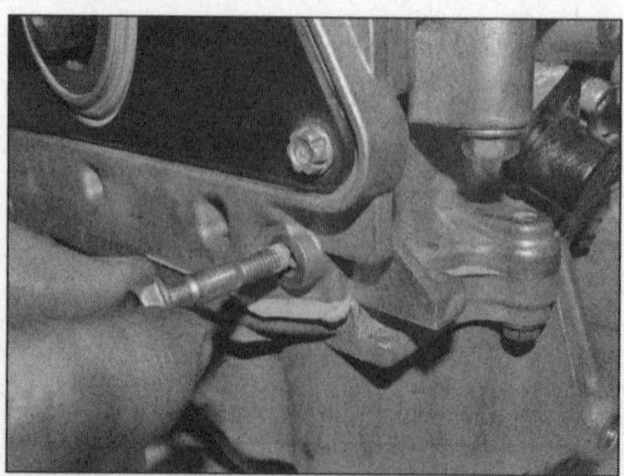

6.14b . . . and fit shouldered bolts to locate case

timing chain case/cylinder head and block bracket, tightening the four bolts to the specified torque.

17 Refit the crankshaft pulley (Section 5).

18 Refit the engine right-hand mounting intermediate bracket and torque rod as described in Section 20, using new nuts and bolts where specified and tightening the bolts and nuts to the torques specified. **Note:** *This requires the slackening and retightening of some of the engine/transmission left-hand (upper) mounting's fasteners.*

19 Fit a new auxiliary drivebelt (Chapter 1B).

20 Refit the cylinder head cover (Section 4).

21 The remainder of reassembly is the reverse of the removal procedure.

22 When Honda's own liquid gasket has been used to seal a joint, note the following:

a) Where applicable, wait at least 30 minutes before filling the engine with oil.

b) Do not run the engine for at least three hours.

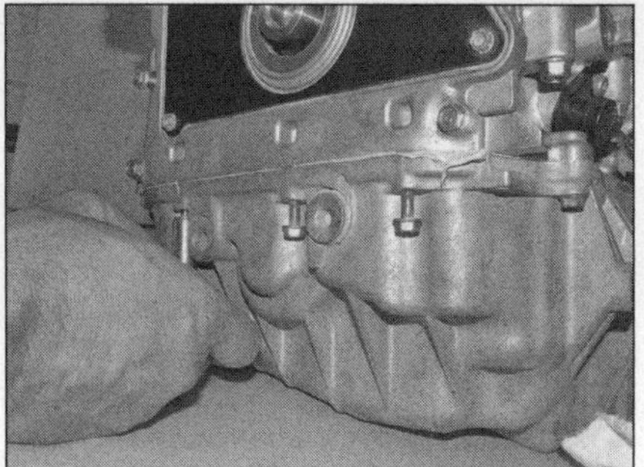

6.15 Don't forget three bolts along bottom edge – tighten these first to pull case down on to sump, then tighten remaining bolts

7 Timing chain – removal, inspection and refitting

Note: *The timing chain is to be kept away from magnetic fields to prevent any chance of interference in the operation of the crankshaft position sensor.*

Removal

1 Remove the timing chain case (see previous Section).

2 Loosely refit the crankshaft pulley and rotate it anti-clockwise to compress the tensioner until the lockplate moves back far enough for a 2.5 mm diameter pin to be inserted into the holes in the lockplate and tensioner body. We used a Torx key **(see illustrations)**.

3 Rotate the crankshaft pulley clockwise again to hold the pin in place and lock the tensioner, then unscrew its two mounting bolts and withdraw the timing chain tensioner. Remove the pulley.

4 Unscrew the pivot bolt and withdraw the tensioner blade **(see illustration)**.

5 Disengage the timing chain from the sprockets and withdraw it **(see illustration)**.

6 If the cylinder head is to be removed, the timing chain's fixed guides must first be removed from its upper rear (two bolts) and front (two bolts) **(see illustration)**.

Inspection

7 Make a careful examination of the links of the chain, looking for signs of wear or damage on the sideplates as well as on the rollers. Check the whole length of the chain looking for links that are looser or tighter than the others, or kinked. If there is any sign of binding, excessive side play or kinking in the chain, it must be renewed.

8 Renew the timing chain regardless of its apparent condition if the engine has covered a high mileage, or if the chain has sounded noisy with the engine running. It is good practice to renew the chain and sprockets as a matched set.

9 Examine the teeth on the camshaft and crankshaft sprockets for any sign of wear or damage such as chipped or hooked teeth. If there is any such sign on any of the sprockets, all sprockets and the timing chain should be renewed as a set.

10 Examine the chain guides and tensioner blade for signs of wear or damage to their contact faces, renewing any that are badly marked.

Refitting

11 If removed, refit the timing chain's fixed guides. Tighten the mounting bolts securely **(see illustrations)**.

12 Check that No. 1 cylinder is at TDC on the compression stroke by ensuring that the timing marks are aligned as described below. Temporarily refit the crankshaft pulley, if necessary, to rotate the crankshaft; rotate

7.2a Rotate crankshaft pulley anti-clockwise to compress timing chain tensioner until hole in lockplate aligns with hole in tensioner body . . .

7.2b . . . then insert a 2.5 mm diameter pin through plate and into tensioner to lock it in compressed position

7.4 Unscrew pivot bolt and withdraw tensioner blade

7.5 Removing the timing chain

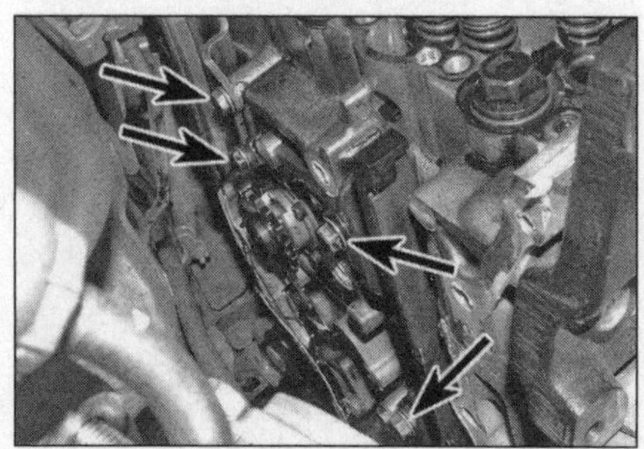

7.6 Unscrew two bolts each to withdraw fixed guides from timing chain's front and upper rear runs

7.11a Refitting timing chain's fixed guides to upper rear . . .

7.11b . . . and front runs – tighten bolts securely

7.12 Punch mark on crankshaft sprocket must align with mark cast on block; keyway in crankshaft end (arrow) will point straight up, in twelve o'clock position

7.13a Refit timing chain so that, with chain front run taut . . .

7.13b . . . single-coloured sideplate fits over punch-marked tooth on crankshaft drive sprocket . . .

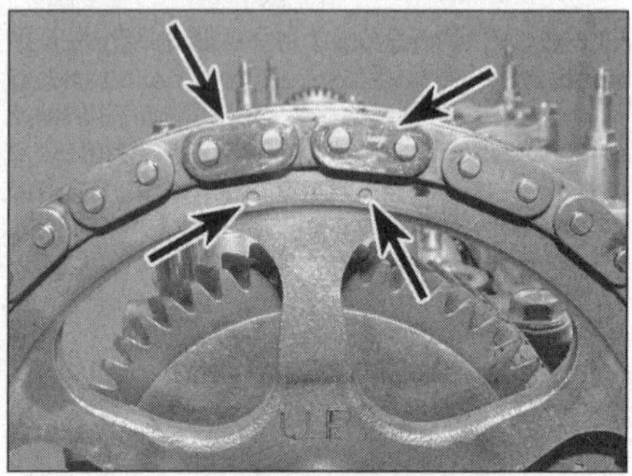

7.13c . . . and two-coloured sideplates fit over punch-marked teeth on exhaust camshaft sprocket

7.14 Oil pivot bolt threads on refitting timing chain tensioner blade

the camshafts by means of an open-ended spanner applied to the hexagons formed between the lobes of Nos. 1 and 4 cylinders. If either camshaft has to be rotated very far to bring its marks into alignment, first rotate the engine 45° backwards (anti-clockwise) using a spanner or socket on the crankshaft pulley. This positions the pistons half-way up the bores, ensuring there is no danger of accidental valve-to-piston contact. Once the camshafts are correctly positioned, return the crankshaft to TDC. The marks must be as follows:

a) *The punch mark stamped on the crankshaft sprocket must align with the arrow mark cast on the cylinder block; the keyway in the crankshaft end will point straight up, in the twelve o'clock position* ***(see illustration).***

b) *The timing marks on the camshaft sprockets and gears must align as described in Section 6, paragraph 2.*

13 One side of the timing chain has three gold-coloured sideplates, two of which are on adjacent links while the third is some distance away. Fit the timing chain to the crankshaft sprocket so that the single coloured sideplate fits over the punch-marked tooth, then, keeping the chain taut on its front run, fit it first to the exhaust camshaft sprocket, so that the coloured sideplates fit over the punch-marked teeth, then to the braking system vacuum pump sprocket **(see illustrations)**.

14 Refit the tensioner blade to the timing chain's lower rear run. Apply a film of clean oil to the threads of the blade's pivot bolt, then tighten the pivot bolt to the specified torque **(see illustration)**.

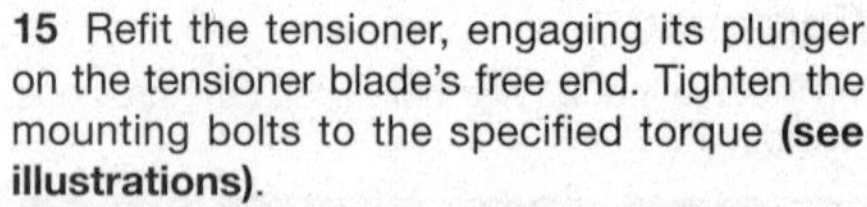

15 Refit the tensioner, engaging its plunger on the tensioner blade's free end. Tighten the mounting bolts to the specified torque **(see illustrations)**.

16 Hold the tensioner blade against the tensioner plunger and remove the locking pin from the tensioner **(see illustration)**. Check that the timing marks and coloured sideplates are correctly aligned and that the tensioner plunger has taken up any slack in the chain.

17 Temporarily refit the crankshaft pulley and rotate the crankshaft two full turns (720°) clockwise and check that the crankshaft and camshaft timing marks come back into alignment as previously described. If not, repeat the procedure until the timing chain is correctly refitted.

18 Refit the timing chain case (Section 6).

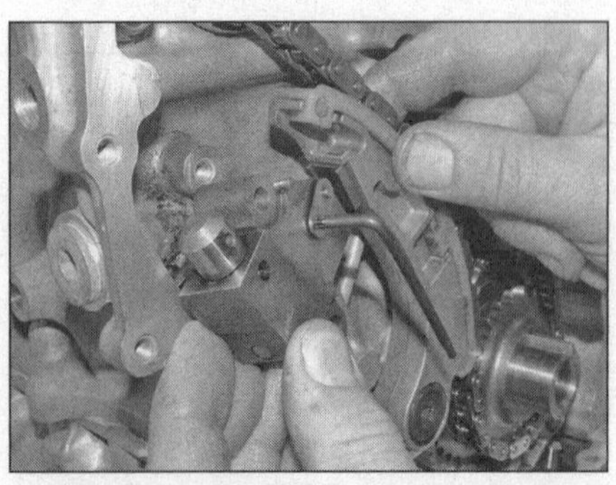

7.15a Engage tensioner plunger on blade . . .

7.15b . . . then refit and tighten mounting bolts

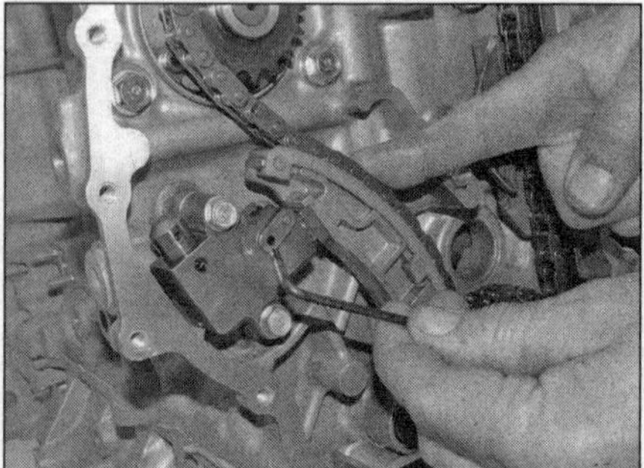

7.16 Hold tensioner blade against tensioner plunger and remove locking pin to release tensioner

8 Timing chain tensioner and sprockets – removal, inspection and refitting

Tensioner – chain case in situ

Note: *Liquid gasket (Honda Part No. 08C70-K0234M, 08C70-K0334M, 08C70-X0331S or 08718-0001 or equivalent) must be available on reassembly.*

Removal

1 Jack up the front of the vehicle and support it securely on axle stands (see *Jacking and vehicle support*). Release the two securing clips and prise back the wheel arch liner section of the engine compartment undershield to reach the timing chain tensioner cover plate.

2 In theory, the tensioner can be removed without disturbing any component other than its cover plate. However, in practice, it would be best to remove the cylinder head cover and bring the engine to TDC, No 1 firing (see Section 6, paragraph 2) before removing the tensioner. This permits checking on reassembly that the valve timing has not jumped a tooth while the tensioner has been removed.

3 Unscrew its three retaining bolts and withdraw the tensioner's cover plate **(see illustration)**. Use a hammer and a block of wood or a soft-faced mallet break the seal by tapping the cover plate, then carefully prise it away from the timing chain case; the liquid gasket used on assembly sticks tight. Do not lever between the mating surfaces; these are easily scratched or gouged and will leak oil if badly marked.

4 Rotate the crankshaft pulley anti-clockwise to compress the tensioner until the lockplate moves back far enough for a 2.5 mm diameter pin to be inserted into the holes in the lockplate and tensioner body **(see illustration)**.

5 Rotate the crankshaft pulley clockwise again to hold the pin in place and lock the timing chain tensioner, then unscrew its two mounting bolts and withdraw the tensioner **(see illustration)**.

Caution: Do not rotate the crankshaft while the tensioner is removed, or the timing chain may drop clear of the crankshaft sprocket and so lose correct valve timing. This will necessitate the removal of the timing chain.

6 Thoroughly clean the mating surfaces of the timing chain case and the tensioner's cover plate. Clean any oil or old gasket material and sealant from the mating surfaces and from the bolt holes and threads. Be careful not to allow dirt and debris to fall into the engine. Degrease the surfaces completely before applying sealant.

Inspection

7 Refer to Chapter 2A, Section 8, paragraphs 7 to 9.

Refitting

8 Disengage the ratchet and compress the plunger as far as possible into the tensioner, then release the ratchet and fit the locking pin into the holes in the lockplate and tensioner body.

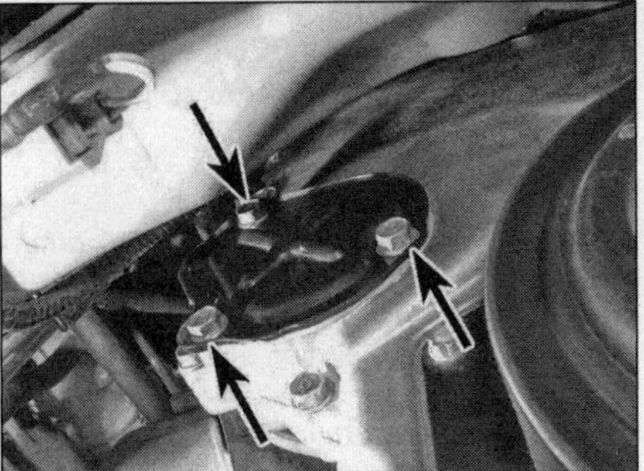

8.3 Unscrew three retaining bolts to withdraw timing chain tensioner's cover plate

9 Carefully release the plunger to hold the pin in place and lock the tensioner.

10 Refit the tensioner, engaging its plunger on the tensioner blade's free end.

11 Tighten the mounting bolts to the specified torque.

12 Hold the tensioner blade against the tensioner plunger and remove the locking pin from the tensioner. Rotate the crankshaft two full turns (720°) clockwise until the timing marks align again. Check that the timing marks are correctly aligned as described in Section 7 and that the tensioner plunger has taken up any slack in the chain.

13 Apply a continuous thin bead of liquid gasket evenly around the cover plate's mating surface so that the bead is around the inside edges of the bolt holes. Also apply a small blob of liquid gasket to the bolt holes in the timing chain case to ensure that there are no oil leaks from the threads. The cover plate must be installed within five minutes of applying the liquid gasket – if this time limit is exceeded, the sealant must be wiped off completely and new liquid gasket applied.

14 Refit the cover plate, tightening its bolts to the specified torque.

15 The remainder of reassembly is the reverse of the removal procedure.

16 When Honda's own liquid gasket has been used to seal a joint, note the following:

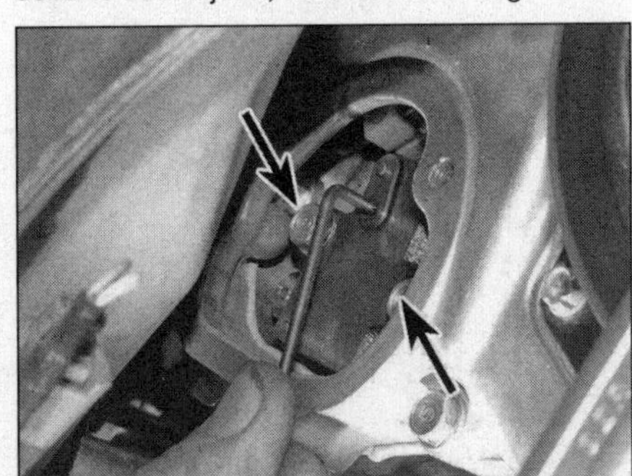

8.5 Unscrew mounting bolts to remove timing chain tensioner

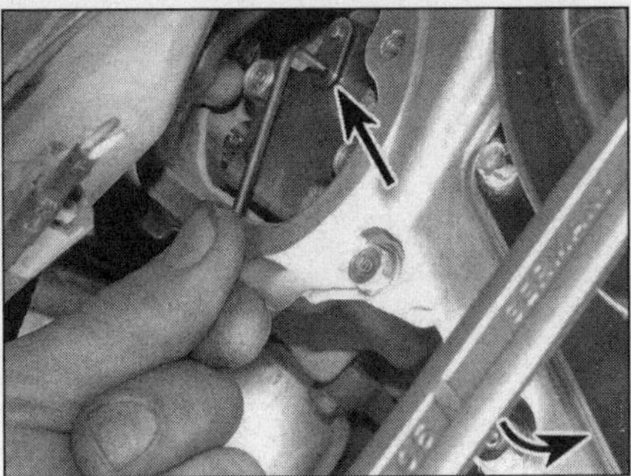

8.4 Rotate crankshaft pulley anti-clockwise to compress timing chain tensioner until hole in lockplate aligns with hole in tensioner body

a) *Where applicable, wait at least 30 minutes before filling the engine with oil.*
b) *Do not run the engine for at least three hours.*

Tensioner – chain case removed

Removal

17 Proceed as described in Section 7, paragraphs 1 to 3.

Inspection

18 Refer to Chapter 2A, Section 8, paragraphs 7 to 9.

Refitting

19 Proceed as described in Section 7.

Exhaust camshaft sprocket

Note: *Great care must be taken to keep the timing chain taut during this procedure. If it is allowed to drop clear of the crankshaft sprocket, valve timing will be lost and it will be necessary to remove the timing chain case in order to restore it.*

Removal

20 Remove the cylinder head cover (Section 4).

21 Jack up the front of the vehicle and support it securely on axle stands (see *Jacking and vehicle support*). Depending on the work about to be undertaken, remove the right-hand or both front roadwheels. Remove the engine compartment undershield (Chapter 11).

22 Bring the engine to TDC, No. 1 firing. See Section 6, paragraph 2.

23 Use a marker pen to mark the timing chain's sideplate that fits over either (or both) of the punch-marked teeth at the top of the exhaust camshaft sprocket.

24 Remove the tensioner as described in paragraphs 3 to 6 above.

25 Hold the camshaft by means of an open-ended spanner applied to the hexagons formed between the lobes of Nos. 1 and 4 cylinders, then slacken the sprocket retaining bolt. Unscrew the bolt and withdraw the sprocket from the camshaft, noting the locating Woodruff key; this should not be slack, as it still locates the camshaft drive gear, but if loose it should be secured with sticky tape.

26 Use a length of wire to fix the timing chain on to the sprocket, and secure the sprocket

8.38 Crankshaft drive sprocket locating key has a tapered end which must point inwards

and chain to an adjacent component to hold the sprocket out of the way and the timing chain taut, especially on the front run, to prevent it from dropping off the crankshaft sprocket.

Inspection

27 See Section 7, paragraph 9.

Refitting

28 If the timing chain was separated from the sprocket, refit it so that the marked sideplate(s) fit(s) over the punch-marked teeth. Fit the sprocket to the camshaft end, engaging it on the key and keeping the timing chain's front run as taut as possible. Check that the valve timing marks are aligned as described in Section 6, paragraph 2.

29 Apply a film of clean oil to the threads and under the head of the sprocket retaining bolt. Hold the camshaft with an open-ended spanner and tighten the bolt to the specified torque.

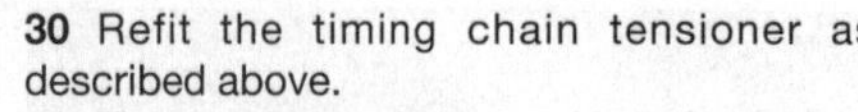

30 Refit the timing chain tensioner as described above.

31 The remainder of reassembly is the reverse of the removal procedure.

Crankshaft sprocket

Caution: The removal of the timing chain and balancer/oil pump drive chain's crankshaft drive sprocket requires the removal first of the timing chain case and of the sump, the latter entailing the removal of the front suspension subframe. This leaves the engine/transmission unit hanging on the hoist in the engine compartment and located only by its left-hand mounting. The home mechanic may prefer to consider removing the engine/transmission complete and then removing the sump.

Removal

32 Remove the timing chain (Section 7).

33 Bolt a lifting eye to the right-hand end of the cylinder head. Support the timing chain end of the engine from above, with an engine hoist or crane.

34 Remove the sump (Section 11).

35 Remove the balancer/oil pump drive chain (Section 13). As the drive sprocket slides off the crankshaft, note the locating key; remove this it and keep it with the sprocket.

Inspection

36 See Section 7, paragraph 9.

Refitting

37 The keyway in the crankshaft end must point straight up, in the twelve o'clock position; temporarily refit the crankshaft pulley, if necessary, to rotate the crankshaft into position.

38 Refit the balancer/oil pump drive chain (Section 13). As the drive sprocket slides on to the crankshaft, ensure that the locating key is refitted with its tapered end pointing inwards and that the sprocket is pressed firmly back against the shoulder on the crankshaft end **(see illustration)**.

39 The remainder of reassembly is the reverse of the removal procedure.

9 Camshafts, followers and hydraulic tappets – removal, inspection and refitting

Camshafts, followers and hydraulic tappets

Note 1: *If the exhaust camshaft sprocket, either camshaft's drive gear or the camshaft position sensor rotor is to be removed, minimise the risk of damage by slackening its retaining bolt before unbolting the camshaft bearing caps, when the camshaft is easier to hold.*

Note 2: *In theory it is possible to proceed by removing the exhaust camshaft sprocket (Section 8) and then removing the camshafts. However, such a method carries a high risk of losing the valve timing if the timing chain comes off the crankshaft sprocket. We recommend the procedure below; although apparently longer, it is far more certain of correct reassembly.*

Removal

1 Remove the timing chain (Section 7).

2 Working in the **reverse** of the tightening sequence, slacken the camshaft bearing cap bolts two turns at a time, to relieve the pressure evenly and in several gradual stages **(see illustration 9.18)**.

Caution: If the bearing cap bolts are slackened carelessly, a cap might break. If any of the caps is broken, the complete cam carrier assembly must be renewed, with the cylinder head; the caps are matched to the carrier, which is not available separately from the cylinder head.

3 Withdraw the camshaft bearing caps, noting how they are numbered (intake or exhaust and bearing number) and marked with arrows pointing to the timing chain end. Note also the correct fitted positions of the locating dowels. If the dowels are loose, remove them and store them with their bearing caps.

4 Carefully lift out the camshafts.

5 Unscrew the four retaining bolts (intake camshaft side) and withdraw the camshaft carrier from the cylinder head. Again, note the correct fitted positions of the locating dowels.

6 Obtain sixteen small, clean plastic containers, and label them for identification. Alternatively, divide a larger container into compartments. Withdraw each follower and hydraulic tappet in turn and place it in its respective container, which should then be filled with clean engine oil **(see illustration)**.

9.6 Withdraw each follower and hydraulic tappet in turn and place it in a marked container filled with clean engine oil

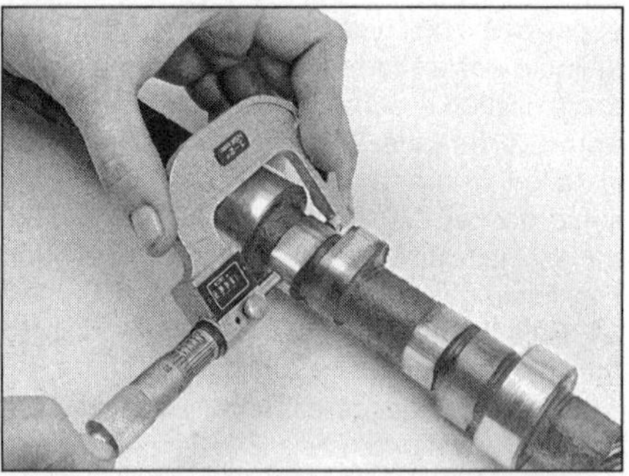

9.7a When measuring camshaft lobe height . . .

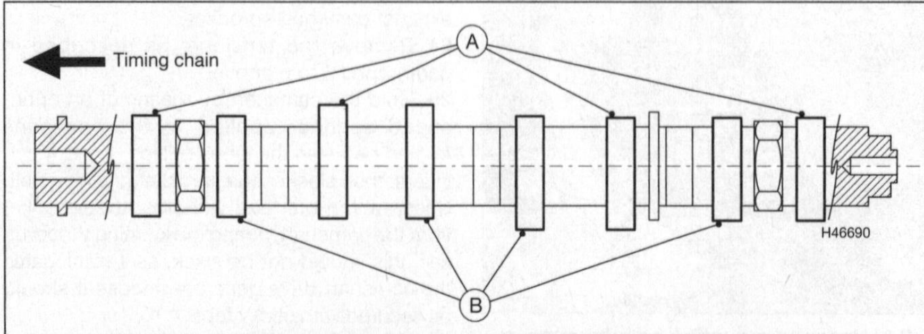

9.7b . . . note that intake camshaft A and B lobes are of different profiles

Do not interchange the followers and tappets, and do not allow the hydraulic tappets to lose oil, or they will take a long time to refill with oil on restarting the engine.

Inspection

7 Examine the camshaft bearing surfaces and cam lobes for signs of wear ridges and scoring. Check that the lobes are not significantly worn below the height specified; when checking the intake camshaft, note the locations of the higher-lift A-cam lobes and the milder B-cam lobes **(see illustrations)**. Renew the camshaft if any of these conditions are apparent.

8 To check camshaft runout and endfloat, first remove the camshaft carrier assembly, remove the followers and hydraulic tappets, then refit the carrier, the camshafts and their bearing caps to the cylinder head. Tighten the camshaft bearing cap bolts to the specified torque, as described below. Check the camshaft endfloat with a dial gauge bearing on the sprocket end of the camshaft. Push the camshaft fully away, then zero the gauge. Push the camshaft fully the other way, and check the endfloat; Honda state that if it is beyond the service limit specified, the cylinder head must be renewed and the endfloat rechecked. If it is still excessive, then the camshaft must be renewed.

9 Use Plastigauge to check the camshaft bearing journal-to-bearing clearance. Unbolt the bearing caps, wipe clean the camshafts and refit them. Lay a strip of Plastigauge on each bearing journal, refit the bearing cap and tighten the camshaft bearing cap bolts to the specified torque. Unbolt the bearing caps again and measure the width of each strip at its widest point to determine the clearance. If any of the clearances are beyond the specified service limit then the worn components – either the camshaft or the camshaft carrier/cylinder head assembly must be renewed.

10 Examine the condition of the bearing surfaces both on the camshaft journals and in the camshaft carrier. If any of the bearing surfaces are worn or damaged, the components concerned will need to be renewed.

11 Examine the follower rollers and their tips which bear on the camshaft lobes and valve stems; look for any sign of wear and scoring, and for rollers which do not rotate easily and smoothly when spun. Check the hydraulic tappets and their bores in the cylinder head for signs of wear or damage. If the engine's valvegear has sounded noisy, particularly if the noise persists after initial start-up from cold, then there is reason to suspect a faulty hydraulic tappet. If any hydraulic tappet is thought to be faulty or is visibly worn it should be renewed.

Refitting

12 On reassembly, disengage each tappet from its follower, place the tappet in a container of clean engine oil of the recommended viscosity and specification and pass a slim rod through the hole in its ball end. Press down on the check ball in the tappet's valve assembly, then release; carry on pumping until no more air bubbles (or dirty oil) emerge and the tappet is fully-charged with clean engine oil **(see illustration)**.

9.12 Hydraulic tappets must be primed in clean engine oil before refitting

9.13 Liberally oil hydraulic tappets and cam followers on refitting

13 Carefully refit the tappet to its follower, liberally oil the cylinder head tappet bore and the follower and refit them; some care will be required to enter the tappets squarely into their bores **(see illustration)**. Ensuring that each tappet is refitted to its original bore and is the correct way up, repeat on the remaining tappets to charge and refit all the tappets and followers to the cylinder head.

14 Refit the locating dowels (if removed), and refit the camshaft carrier to the cylinder head, engaging it on the dowels and noting the arrow mark which must point to the timing chain end. Refit the four retaining bolts and tighten them to the specified torque **(see illustrations)**.

15 Wipe clean the camshaft bearing journals and lobes and the bearing surfaces in the cam follower assembly supports. Liberally oil all bearing surfaces, the camshaft lobes and the followers **(see illustration)**. If any components were removed from either camshaft, they should now be refitted; their retaining bolts should be tightened fully only once the camshaft has been bolted down securely.

Caution: Failure to adequately lubricate the camshafts and related components can cause serious damage to shaft journals and bearing surfaces during the first few seconds after engine start-up.

9.14a Refitting camshaft carrier to cylinder head – ensure that locating dowels fit correctly . . .

9.14b . . . and that arrow mark points to timing chain end . . .

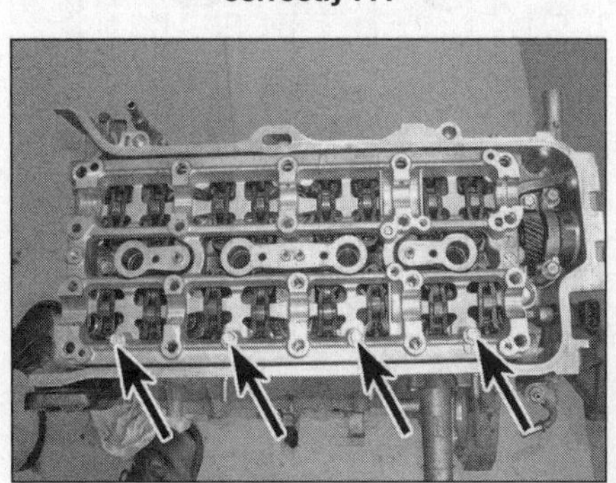

9.14c . . . then tighten camshaft carrier-to-cylinder head bolts

9.15 Camshaft bearing journals and lobes MUST be properly lubricated on reassembly – special assembly paste shown here

9.16a When refitting camshafts . . .

9.16b . . . note identifying IN or EX marks to ensure correct location and . . .

9.16c . . . align punch-marked tooth on exhaust camshaft drive gear between two punch-marked teeth on intake camshaft driven gear, with UP marks and punch marks at top

9.17a Lubricate bearing surfaces and do not forget locating dowels (A) when refitting camshaft bearing caps . . .

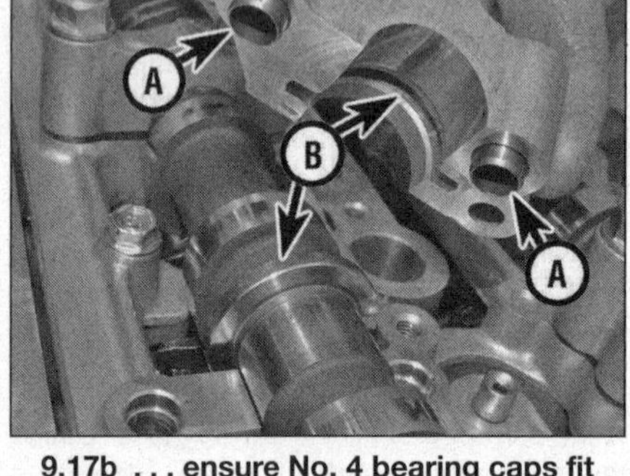

9.17b . . . ensure No. 4 bearing caps fit over endfloat-controlling flange (B) on camshafts . . .

9.17c . . . and use identifying marks and arrows to ensure correct location of bearing caps

16 Refit the camshafts to the cylinder head; the camshafts are clearly identified by being marked IN or EX, as appropriate **(see illustrations)**. The UP marks on the exhaust camshaft sprocket and the intake camshaft driven gear must both be in the twelve o'clock position, while the four double-line marks etched in both drive gear rims must line up through the drive gear retaining bolt centres, with, at the centre, the punch-marked tooth on the exhaust camshaft drive gear aligned exactly between the two punch-marked teeth on the intake camshaft driven gear; two punch marks in the rim of the exhaust camshaft sprocket must also be in the twelve o'clock position **(see illustration)**.

17 Lubricating their bearing surfaces with clean engine oil and ensuring that the locating dowels are in position, refit the camshaft bearing caps and their bolts, tightening the bolts by hand only at this stage. Check carefully that the locating dowels enter squarely into their respective bores. Each intake camshaft cap is numbered I1 to I5 in ascending order from timing side to flywheel end, the exhaust camshaft caps are similarly numbered E1 to E5 and each cap is marked with an arrow which must point towards the timing chain end **(see illustrations)**.

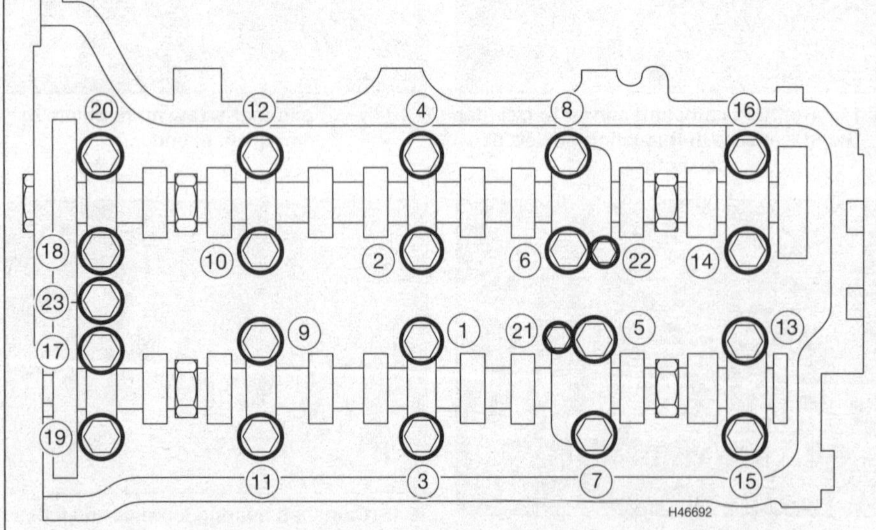

9.18 Camshaft bearing cap/carrier-to-cylinder head bolts TIGHTENING sequence

18 Working in sequence, evenly and progressively tighten the retaining bolts to draw the bearing caps and camshafts squarely down into place. Once the bearing caps are in contact with the head, go around in sequence and tighten the retaining bolts to the specified torque **(see illustration)**. As the camshafts are drawn down into place, check that the sprocket/driven gear timing marks remain in alignment. Once the camshaft bearing cap/carrier bolts are all fully and correctly tightened, tighten the bolts securing the exhaust camshaft sprocket, either camshaft's drive and driven gears and the camshaft position sensor rotor (as applicable).

Caution: If the bearing cap bolts are carelessly tightened, a cap might break.

19 Refit the timing chain (Section 7).

Camshaft drive gears

Removal

20 Remove the cylinder head cover (Section 4).

21 Hold the camshaft with an open-ended spanner, then slacken the drive gear retaining bolt **(see illustration)**.

22 Remove the camshafts, as described above. Remove the drive gear (and the

sprocket, in the case of the exhaust camshaft right-hand gear). Recover the Woodruff key if applicable.

Inspection

23 Renew the drive gear if its teeth are marked or damaged in any way. Do not attempt to dismantle the exhaust camshaft drive gears in the event of suspected wear or damage to the spring-loaded anti-backlash mechanism; they are available only as a complete components.

Refitting

24 Refit the drive gear to the camshaft end.
25 Refit the camshafts, as described above. Once the camshaft bearing cap/carrier bolts are all fully and correctly tightened, apply a film of clean oil to the threads and under the head of the drive gear retaining bolt, hold the camshaft with an open-ended spanner and tighten the bolt to the specified torque. Proceed with refitting the timing chain (Section 7).
26 Refit the cylinder head cover (Section 4).

Fuel pump driveshaft

Removal

27 Remove the fuel pump (Chapter 4B).
28 Remove the camshafts, as described above.
29 Unscrew the three mounting bolts and withdraw the driveshaft assembly, noting the arrow mark pointing to the timing chain end **(see illustrations)**.

Inspection

30 Renew the driveshaft if its teeth are marked or damaged in any way or if its bearing shows signs of free play or rough and jerky rotation when spun. Do not attempt to dismantle the driveshaft; it is available only as a single component.

Refitting

31 Refit the driveshaft assembly to the cylinder head so that the arrow mark points towards the timing chain end. Tighten the mounting bolts to the specified torques.
32 Refit the camshafts, as described above.
33 Refit the fuel pump (Chapter 4B).

Intake camshaft position sensor rotor

Removal

34 Remove the cylinder head cover (Section 4).
35 Hold the camshaft by means of an open-ended spanner applied to the hexagon formed over No. 4 cylinder, then slacken the rotor retaining bolt **(see illustration)**. Unscrew the bolt and withdraw the rotor from the camshaft, noting the locating key.

Inspection

36 Renew the rotor if it is marked or damaged in any way.

Refitting

37 Refit the rotor to the camshaft end, engaging its locating key in the camshaft keyway. Hold the camshaft with an open-ended spanner and tighten the rotor retaining bolt to the specified torque.
38 Refit the cylinder head cover (Section 4).

9.21 Hold camshaft with open-ended spanner to unscrew exhaust camshaft left-hand drive gear bolt

9.29a Noting arrow mark pointing to timing chain end, unscrew three bolts . . .

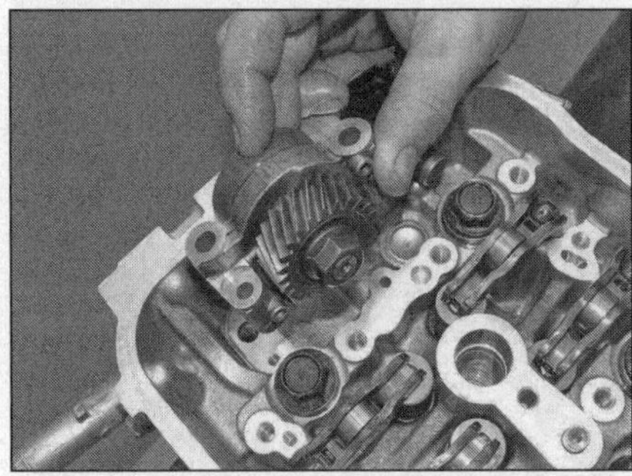

9.29b . . . to withdraw fuel pump driveshaft assembly

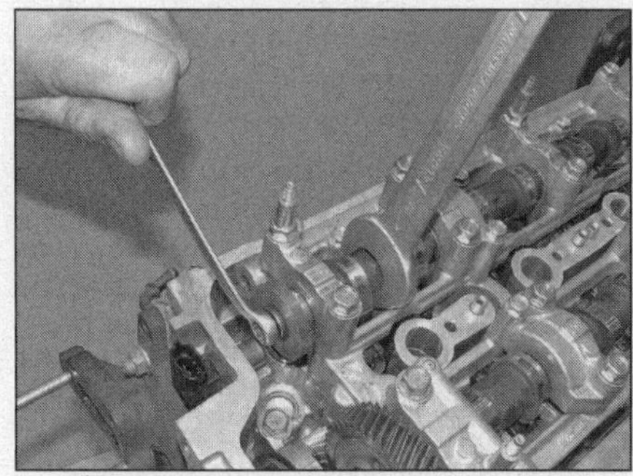

9.35 Hold camshaft with open-ended spanner to unscrew intake camshaft position sensor rotor bolt

10 Cylinder head – removal and refitting

Note: *Allow the engine to cool completely before beginning this procedure.*

Removal

1 Disconnect the battery negative lead, and position the lead away from the battery (also see *Disconnecting the battery*).
2 Unscrew the four retaining nuts and remove the acoustic engine cover.
3 Remove the air cleaner assembly (Chapter 4B).
4 Remove the engine compartment undershield (Chapter 11).
5 Drain the cooling system (Chapter 1B).
6 Remove the auxiliary drivebelt (Chapter 1B).
7 From the rear right-hand end of the cylinder head cover unscrew the bolt securing the steering hose clamp **(see illustration)**. Unscrew its two mounting bolts and dismount the steering pump; move it to one side and secure it out of the way.
8 Disconnect the fuel feed hose from the fuel pump. Plug the hose and cap the pump union to prevent the loss of fuel and the entry of dirt **(see illustrations)**.
9 From the rear left-hand end of the cylinder head cover disconnect the fuel return hose; again plug the hose and cap the pipe union.

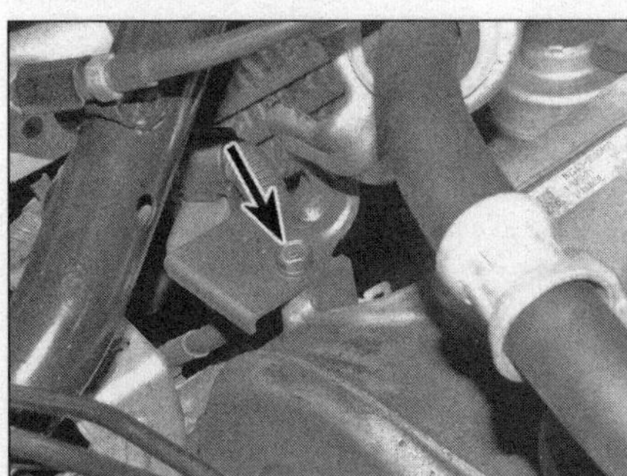

10.7 Unscrew bolt securing steering hose clamp to cylinder head cover

10.8a Disconnect fuel feed hose from fuel pump . . .

10.8b . . . then plug hose and cap pump union to prevent entry of dirt into system

10.9a Disconnect fuel return hose . . .

10.9b . . . and braking system vacuum servo hose from vacuum line assembly

10.10 Disconnect radiator top hose

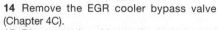

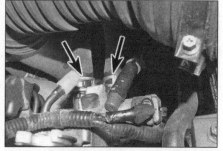

10.11 Mark heater hoses and unions so that they are reconnected correctly, and not swapped over, on refitting

Disconnect the braking system vacuum servo hose from the vacuum line assembly to the rear of the cylinder head cover **(see illustrations)**.

10 Disconnect the radiator top hose from the outlet at the left-hand front of the cylinder block **(see illustration)**.

11 From the rear left-hand end of the cylinder head cover disconnect the heater hoses **(see illustration)**. Mark the hoses and unions so that they can be reconnected correctly.

12 Remove the intake manifold (Chapter 4B). (If no work is to be carried out on the cylinder head, the head can be removed complete with manifold once the preliminary operations have been carried out.)

13 Remove the exhaust manifold (Chapter 4B). (If no work is to be carried out on the cylinder head, the head can be removed complete with manifold once the preliminary operations have been carried out.)

14 Remove the EGR cooler bypass valve (Chapter 4C).

15 Disconnect its wiring and unbolt the fuel pump (Chapter 4B).

16 From the left-hand end of the cylinder head, disconnect the wiring from the engine coolant temperature sensor and the camshaft position sensor, then disconnect the wiring from the turbocharger boost control solenoid valve **(see illustrations)**.

17 Unbolt the vacuum line assembly mounting bolts from the left-hand end and rear of the cylinder head and cover **(see illustration)**. Ensure that hoses, wiring and pipes are secured clear of the cylinder head and cannot hinder its removal.

18 Remove the cylinder head cover (Section 4).

19 Remove the timing chain case (Section 6).

20 Remove the timing chain (Section 7).

21 Remove the camshafts, followers and hydraulic tappets (Section 9).

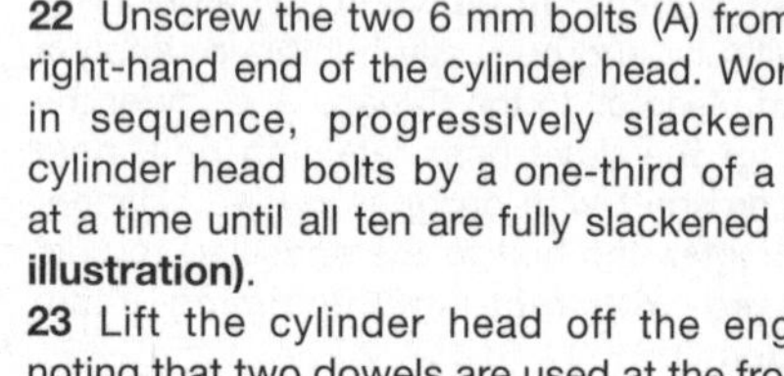

22 Unscrew the two 6 mm bolts (A) from the right-hand end of the cylinder head. Working in sequence, progressively slacken the cylinder head bolts by a one-third of a turn at a time until all ten are fully slackened **(see illustration)**.

23 Lift the cylinder head off the engine, noting that two dowels are used at the front. If resistance is felt, don't prise between the head and block gasket mating surfaces. Instead, try to rock the head free, by inserting a blunt lever (such as a hammer handle) into the intake or exhaust ports **(see illustration)**.

24 Remove the head from the engine, and set it down on a clean, flat surface, supported on two wooden blocks so that the gasket surface does not touch – remember at all times to avoid damage to the gasket sealing surfaces and to the protruding valves and glow plug tips **(see illustrations)**. Recover the gasket but do not discard it yet – a new one must be fitted on reassembly and the original will serve to check that the correct thickness gasket has been supplied. Recover also the oil control orifice from the cylinder block's top surface, at the rear. Remove and discard its sealing O-ring – a new one must be fitted on reassembly.

25 Cylinder head dismantling and inspection procedures are covered in detail in Chapter 2C.

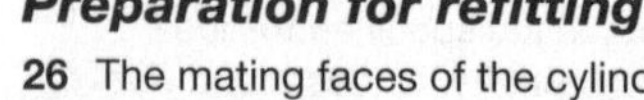

Preparation for refitting

26 The mating faces of the cylinder head and cylinder block/crankcase must be perfectly clean before refitting the head. Use a hard plastic or wood scraper to remove all traces

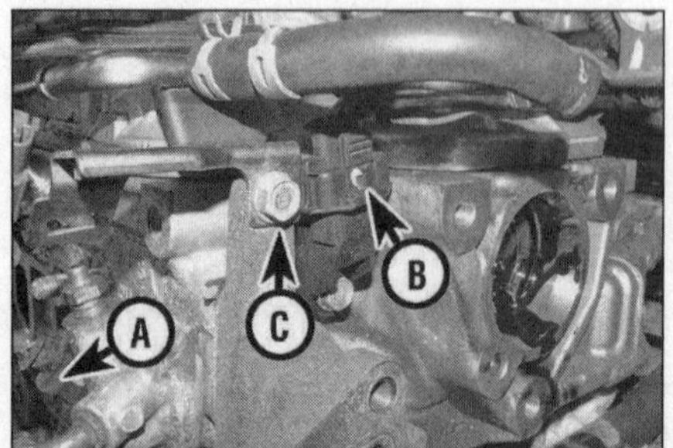

10.16a Undo coolant temperature sensor (A) and camshaft position sensor (B), then undo vacuum line assembly mounting bolt (C) . . .

10.16b . . . and disconnect wiring from turbocharger boost control solenoid valve

10.17 Undo vacuum line assembly mounting bolt on rear of cylinder head

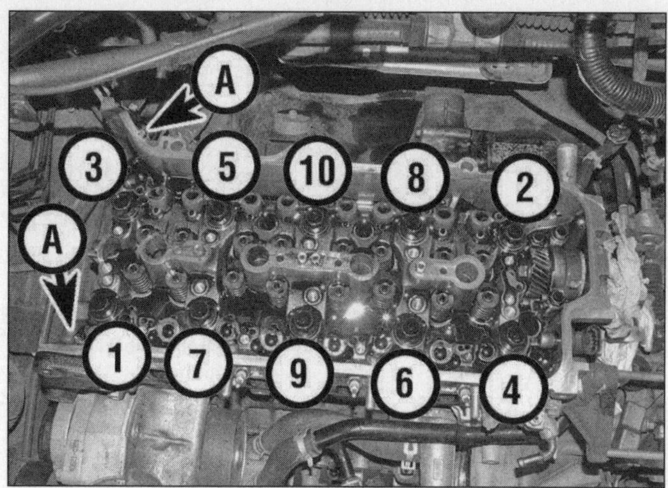

10.22 Cylinder head bolt SLACKENING sequence. Note 6 mm bolts (A)

10.23 Oil filter/oil cooler/water pump housing and steering pump bracket provide good leverage points when removing cylinder head

of gasket and carbon. Also clean the piston crowns. Take particular care, as the soft aluminium alloy is damaged easily. Also, make sure that the carbon is not allowed to enter the oil and water passages – this is particularly important for the lubrication system, as carbon could block the oil supply to any of the engine components. Using adhesive tape and paper, seal the water, oil and bolt holes in the cylinder block/crankcase. To prevent carbon entering the gap between the pistons and bores, smear a little grease in the gap. After cleaning each piston, use a small brush to remove all traces of grease and carbon from the gap, then wipe away the remainder with a clean cloth. Clean all the pistons in the same way.

27 Check the mating surfaces of the cylinder block/crankcase and the cylinder head for nicks, deep scratches and other damage. If the damage is light, it may be possible to have the cylinder head refaced (see Chapter 2C).

28 If warpage of the cylinder head gasket surface is suspected, use a straight-edge to check it for distortion.

29 Clean the threads in the cylinder head bolt holes. Dirt, corrosion, sealant and damaged threads will affect torque values. Ensure that there is no water or oil in the bolt holes in the block – if this is not either sucked up or blown out, the resulting hydraulic pressure when the bolts are fitted may crack the block.

30 Check the cylinder head bolts for obvious signs of wear or damage; renew them all as a set if any such signs are visible. Measure the diameter of the threads of each bolt 50 mm and 55 mm from the tip; if a bolt has stretched so that its diameter is less than 12.5 mm at either of these points, it must be renewed **(see illustrations)**. Although Honda are happy to have bolts re-used as long as they pass this test, it is good practice to renew highly-stressed fasteners such as cylinder head bolts as a matter of course, irrespective of their apparent condition, whenever they are disturbed. These bolts are subject to significant pressure, and if one should fail during retightening, considerable extra expense and inconvenience will be incurred.

31 If new bolts are not being fitted, clean the threads of the old ones thoroughly.

Cylinder head gasket selection

32 On this engine, the cylinder head-to-piston clearance is controlled by fitting different thickness head gaskets. The piston protrusion is represented by the identifying letter and/or number of notches in the gasket next to the timing chain area **(see illustrations)**. Select the new gasket which has the same thickness/ letter/number of notches as the original, unless new piston and connecting rod assemblies have been fitted or either gasket surface has been machined. In that case, the correct thickness of gasket required is selected by measuring the piston protrusions as follows.

33 Mount a dial test indicator securely on the block so that its pointer can be easily pivoted between the piston crown and the block mating surface.

34 Ensure the piston is at exactly TDC, then zero the dial test indicator on the gasket surface of the cylinder block. Carefully move the indicator over No. 1 piston. Measure the piston protrusion on both the left- and right-hand sides **(see illustration)**. Repeat this procedure on No. 4 piston.

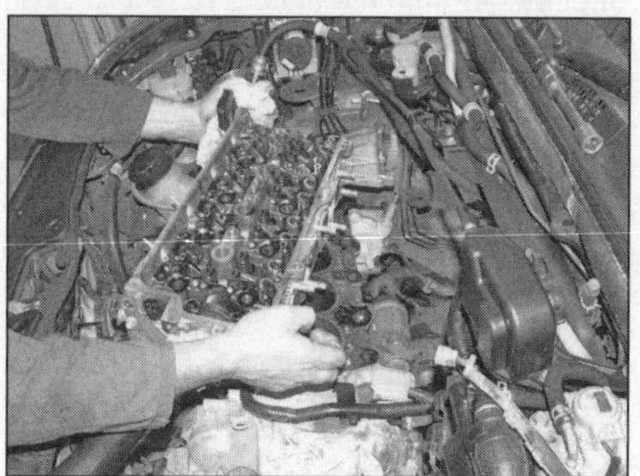
10.24a Remove cylinder head from engine . . .

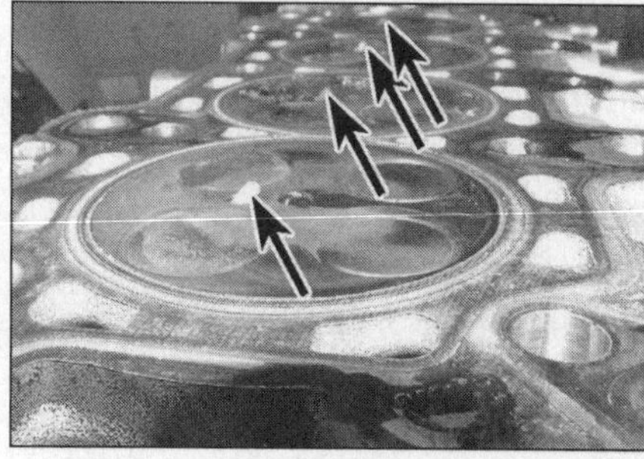
10.24b . . . but be careful of protruding valves and glow plug tips when setting it down

10.30a Measure diameter of threads of each cylinder head bolt 50 mm . . .

10.30b . . . and 55 mm from tip – renew if stretched to diameter of 12.5 mm or less

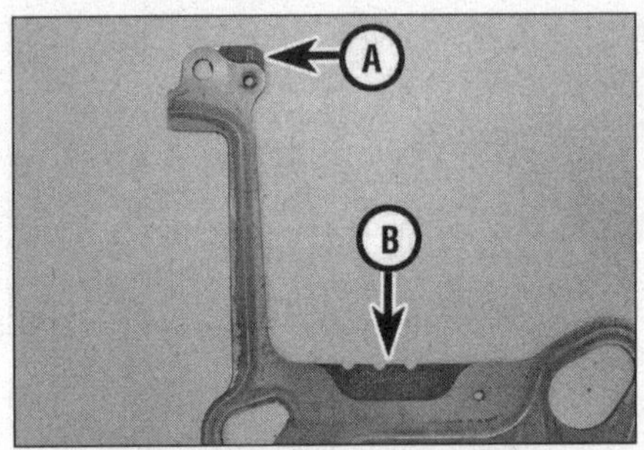

10.32a Cylinder head gasket thickness is shown by identifying letter (A) and/or number of notches at (B) . . .

10.32b . . . record original gasket letter . . .

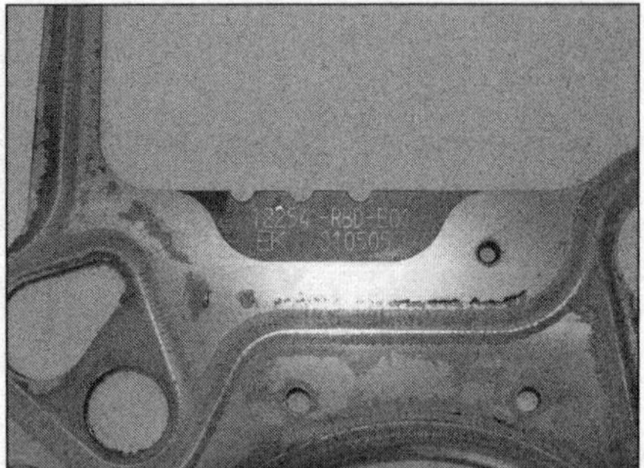

10.32c . . . with number of notches and part number

10.34 Measuring piston protrusion

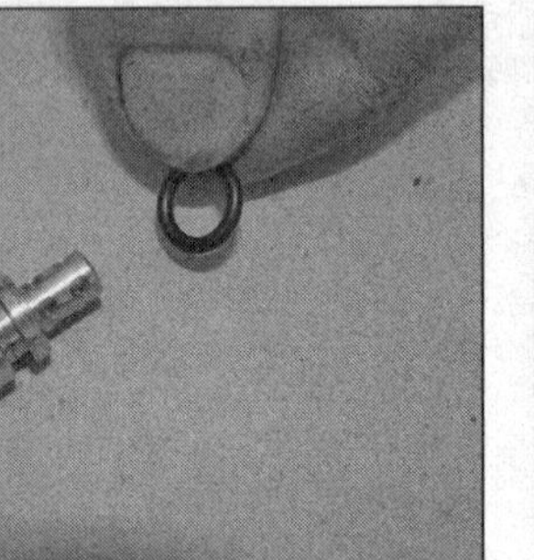

10.38a Fit new sealing O-ring to cleaned oil control orifice . . .

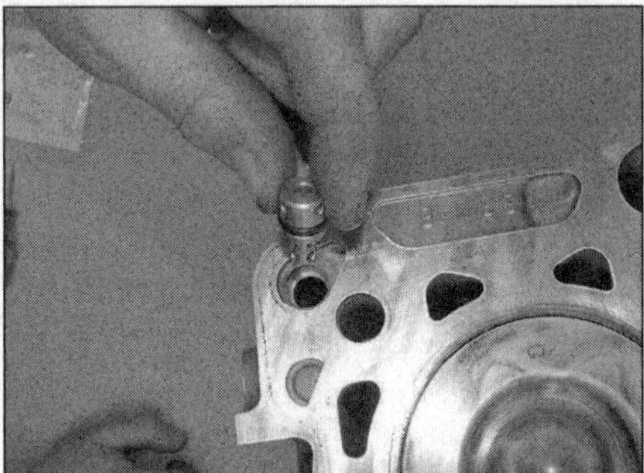

10.38b . . . and refit to location in cylinder block

35 Rotate the crankshaft 180° to bring Nos. 2 and 3 pistons to TDC. Measure the protrusions of Nos. 2 and 3 pistons, again taking two measurements for each piston. Once both pistons have been measured, rotate the crankshaft 180° to bring Nos. 1 and 4 pistons back to TDC.

36 Take the average of each piston's measurements and record the highest average protrusion found. Use the table below to select the appropriate gasket.

Refitting

37 Check that the crankshaft is positioned so that Nos. 1 and 4 cylinders are at TDC.

38 Use a clean rag soaked in gasket remover or cellulose thinners to remove any traces of oil or dirt from the mating surfaces. Clean carefully the oil control orifice and refit it, with a new sealing O-ring, to its location in the cylinder block's top surface, at the rear, on the timing chain end **(see illustrations)**.

39 Place a new gasket on the cylinder block, and locate it over the two dowels at the front **(see illustration)**. The gasket will fit only one way.

40 Place the cylinder head onto the block, and locate it on the two dowels.

41 Lightly oil the threads and the underside of the heads of the cylinder head bolts, then refit them. Tighten the bolts in the recommended sequence, in stages, to the torque listed in this Chapter's Specifications **(see illustrations)**. Because of the critical function of cylinder head bolts, the manufacturer specifies the following conditions for tightening them:

a) A beam-type or dial-type torque wrench is preferable to a preset (click-stop) torque wrench. If you use a preset torque wrench, tighten slowly and be careful not to overtighten the bolts.

b) If a bolt makes any sound while you're tightening it (creaking, clicking, etc), slacken it completely and tighten it again in the specified stages.

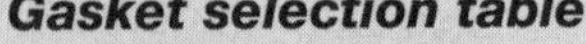

Gasket selection table

Largest piston protrusion	Gasket letter	Notch in gasket	Gasket Part No.
0.485 to 0.535 mm	A	One	12251-RBD-E01
0.535 to 0.585 mm	B	Two	12252-RBD-E01
0.585 to 0.635 mm	C	None	12253-RBD-E01
0.635 to 0.685 mm	D	Three	12254-RBD-E01
0.685 to 0.735 mm	E	Four	12255-RBD-E01

10.39 Fit new cylinder head gasket over locating dowels (arrows)

10.41a Refit cylinder head and TIGHTEN bolts in sequence shown

10.41b Oil threads . . .

42 Refit the hydraulic tappets, followers and camshafts (Section 9).
43 Refit the timing chain (Section 7).
44 Refit the timing chain case (Section 6).
45 Refit the cylinder head cover (Section 4).
46 Refit the EGR system components (Chapter 4C), and the fuel pump, exhaust manifold and turbocharger (as applicable) (Chapter 4B).
47 Refit the intake manifold (where removed) or reconnect the manifold hoses and wiring (Chapter 4B).
48 Refit the remaining parts in the reverse order of removal.
49 Refill the cooling system and check all fluid levels.
50 Reconnect the battery negative.
51 Run the engine until normal operating temperature is reached. Check for leaks and proper operation.

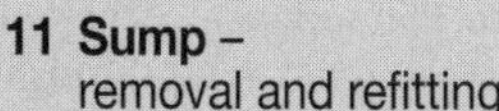

11 Sump – removal and refitting

Caution: The removal of the sump requires the removal of the front suspension subframe. Read through the procedure first to ensure that all the tools and equipment required are to hand. Depending on the skills and equipment available and the nature of the work being undertaken, the home mechanic may prefer to consider removing the engine/transmission complete and then removing the sump.

Note: *If the vehicle is very dirty underneath, wash it as soon as the engine compartment undershield is removed, especially around the edges of the sump, so that you can be sure of unscrewing all of the sump fasteners and so that dirt does not get into the engine while the sump is removed.*

Removal

1 Drain the engine oil and remove the oil filter (Chapter 1B).
2 Disconnect the battery (see *Disconnecting the battery*).
3 Remove the engine compartment undershield (Chapter 11).
4 Remove the auxiliary drivebelt (Chapter 1B).

11.5 Unbolt air conditioning compressor – if top bolts cannot be reached, alternator must be removed first

10.41c . . . and under heads of cylinder head bolts . . .

10.41e . . . and use angle-tightening gauge for succeeding stages of tightening

5 Unscrew the air conditioning compressor's four mounting bolts **(see illustration)**. If necessary remove the alternator to improve access (Chapter 5A). With the compressor unbolted, secure it clear of the working area without disconnecting or straining its wiring and pipes.
6 Remove the front suspension subframe (Chapter 10).
7 Slacken the hose clamps at each end and unbolt the turbocharger-to-intercooler pipe. Pack the turbocharger opening with clean rag to prevent anything falling in.
8 Unscrew the dipstick tube mounting bolt and withdraw the dipstick and tube. Recover and discard the sealing O-ring – a new one must be fitted on reassembly.
9 Unbolt the engine rear mounting bracket from the lower crankcase/main bearing ladder/sump.
10 Unbolt the air conditioning compressor mounting bracket from the lower crankcase/main bearing ladder/sump.
11 Unscrew the two engine bellhousing-to-gearbox bolts which pass through the sump **(see illustrations)**.
12 Progressively slacken and remove the eighteen bolts securing the sump to the lower crankcase/main bearing ladder. Check that all sump retaining bolts have been removed before trying to prise the sump down.
13 Breaking the grip of the sealant used as gasket material is not easy; the liquid gasket used on assembly sticks very tight. Try to break the seal by tapping all around the edge of the sump with a hammer and a block of wood or a soft-faced mallet, then use the three leverage points provided, two at the front and one at the rear, to prise the sump off the lower crankcase/main bearing ladder and carefully pull it down **(see illustrations)**. Do not try to tap the sump forwards or backwards; it is

11.11a Unscrew engine bellhousing-to-gearbox bolts which pass through sump at front . . .

10.41d . . . then tighten to first stage with torque wrench . . .

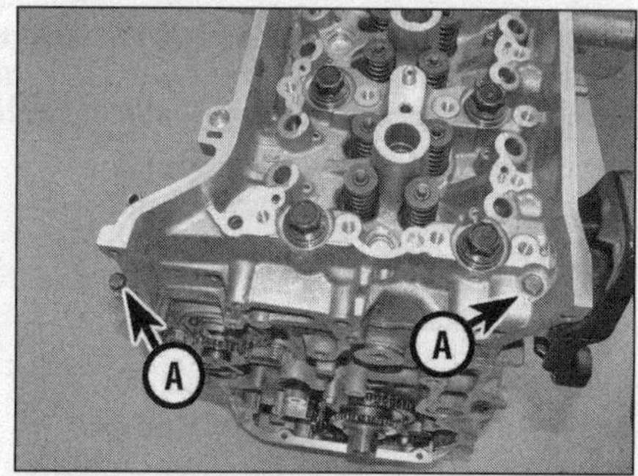

10.41f When main cylinder head bolts are fully-tightened, tighten 6 mm bolts (A)

11.11b . . . and rear of engine

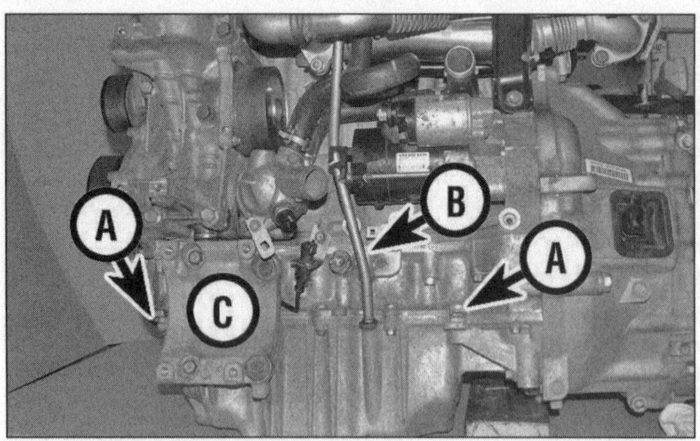

11.13a Two leverage points (A) are provided at front of sump/block joint. Dipstick tube (B) and air conditioning compressor mounting bracket (C) must be unbolted from cylinder block/sump

11.13b Leverage point – under engine rear mounting bracket which must be unbolted – provided at rear of sump/block joint

located by a large dowel at the front, next to the gearbox. Do not lever between the mating faces with metal tools or force a blade into the gap as a starting point for levering, as this will damage the mating faces.

Preparation for refitting

14 Whenever the sump is removed, take the opportunity to clean the filter screen on the oil pump pick-up using solvent and a brush **(see illustration)**. Also check the balancer/oil pump drive chain for wear or damage (Section 13).

15 Thoroughly clean the sump, inside and out. Check the drain plug threads for signs of damage. Check the mating surface for distortion, particularly around the bolt holes, using a straight-edge to ensure that the mating surface is completely flat before refitting the sump.

16 Using a gasket scraper and/or a brass wire brush, remove all traces of old sealant from the lower crankcase/main bearing ladder and the sump mating surfaces; be very careful not to mark or scratch either surface. Note that the crankshaft main bearing bore diameter code letters or numbers are marked on the bottom surface of the lower crankcase/main bearing ladder at the rear of the flywheel end; be careful not to scrub so hard that these are erased.

Refitting

17 Thoroughly clean the mating surfaces of the lower crankcase/main bearing ladder and the sump. Clean any oil or old sealant from the mating surfaces and from the bolt holes and threads. Degrease the surfaces completely before applying sealant and wipe down the inside of the engine with a clean, lint-free rag to prevent any drips of oil from contaminating the new sealant on reassembly.

18 The liquid gasket recommended by Honda requires that the sump be installed within five minutes of applying the liquid gasket – if this time limit is exceeded, the sealant must be wiped off completely and new liquid gasket applied. A 'dry' practice run before applying liquid gasket is recommended.

19 Apply liquid gasket in a continuous thin bead (3mm diameter approx) evenly around the sump's mating surface so that the bead goes around the inside edges of the bolt holes **(see illustration)**. Also apply a small blob of liquid gasket to those bolt holes in the lower crankcase/main bearing ladder which pass through to the outside and to the three bolt holes along the bottom edge of the timing chain case to ensure that there are no oil leaks from the threads. Do not apply sealant to blind holes in the castings. Do not apply excess sealant, as this will end up inside the engine.

20 Offer up the sump and carefully, ensuring that you do not smear the sealant bead by sliding it, fit the sump into place on its locating dowel, press it into position and refit one or two bolts to hold it **(see illustration)**.

21 Refit all the bolts, tightening them by hand only at first until the sump is correctly settled in position. Working in a diagonal sequence from the centre outwards and in two or three stages, tighten the retaining bolts to the specified torque **(see illustration)**. Check that an even bead of sealant is visible all the way round the edge of the sump; wipe off any excess.

22 The remainder of refitting is a reversal of removal, noting the following points:

a) Use a new O-ring on the dipstick tube.

b) Wait at least 30 minutes (or as instructed by the sealant manufacturer) before filling the engine with oil.

c) Do not run the engine for at least three hours (or as instructed by the sealant manufacturer).

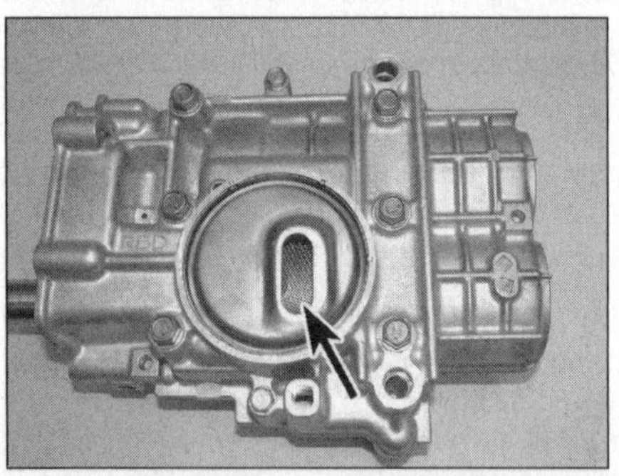
11.14 Clean oil pump pick-up filter screen whenever sump is removed

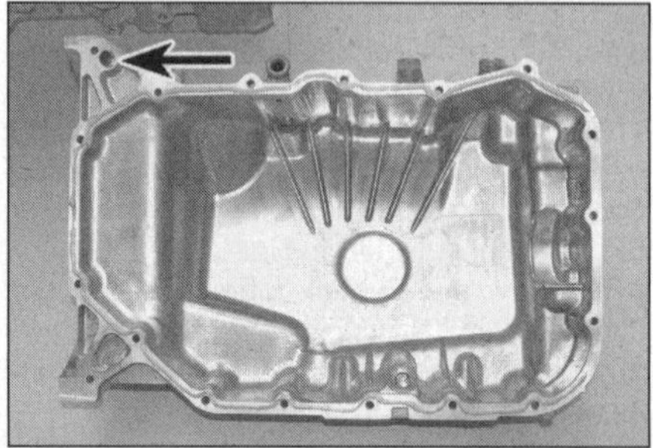
11.19 Apply a continuous bead of liquid gasket evenly around sump's mating surface. Note locating dowel

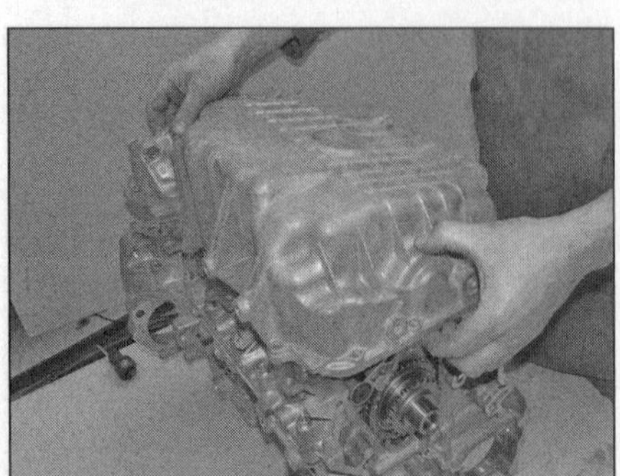
11.20 Work quickly to refit sump before sealant sets . . .

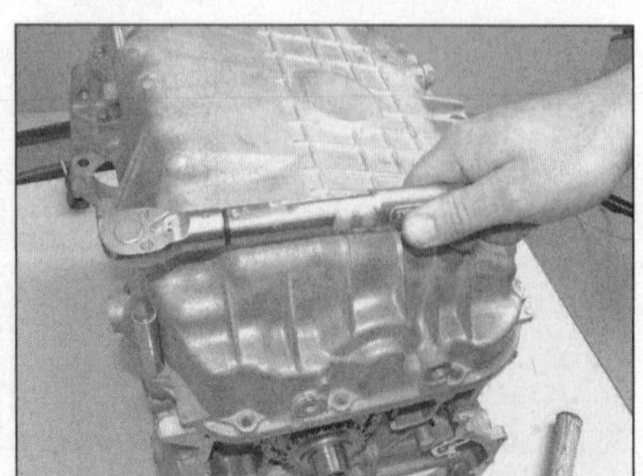
11.21 . . . and tighten sump bolts to specified torque setting

12.3a Prevent balancer shafts from rotating by inserting 8 mm diameter locking pin . . .

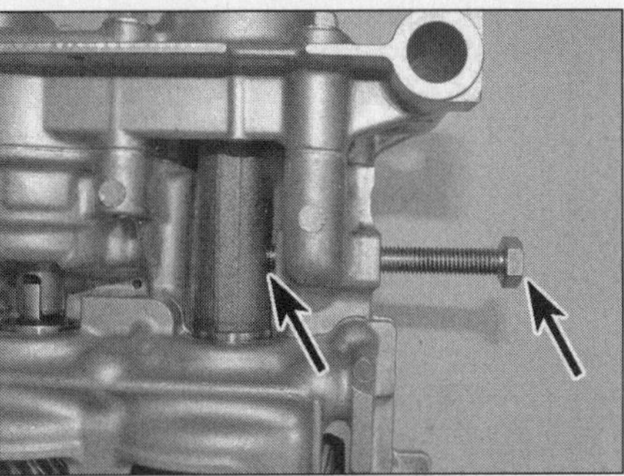

12.3b . . . and into hole in rear balancer shaft

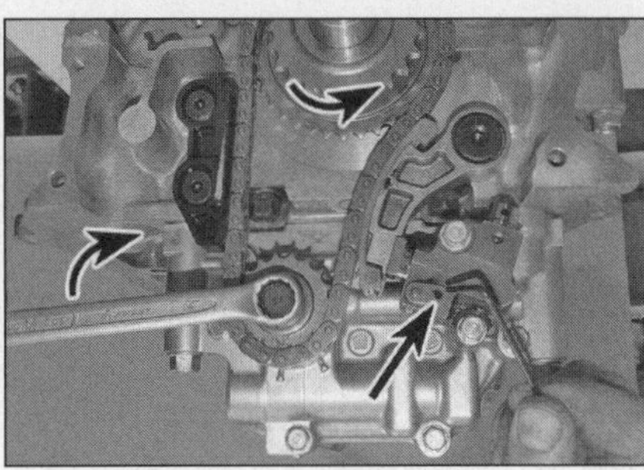

12.4 Rotate crankshaft anti-clockwise (or rear balancer shaft clockwise, as here) to compress chain tensioner so 2.5 mm locking pin can be inserted

12 Oil pump – removal, inspection and refitting

Removal

1 Bring the engine to TDC, No 1 firing.

2 Remove the sump (Section 11).

3 Prevent the balancer shafts from rotating by inserting an 8 mm diameter pin punch (or equivalent) through the hole in the rear of the balancer/oil pump assembly and into the hole in the rear balancer shaft. A pin punch is the best tool for the job (a drill bit might be too brittle and shear off, while a cheap 8 mm bolt might bend), but we found a high-tensile bolt which made a good substitute **(see illustrations)**.

4 Rotate the crankshaft pulley anti-clockwise to compress the balancer/oil pump drive chain tensioner until the lockplate moves back far enough for a 2.5 mm diameter pin to be inserted into the holes in the lockplate and tensioner body **(see illustration)**.

5 Rotate the crankshaft pulley clockwise again to hold the pin in place and lock the tensioner, then unscrew the two bolts and withdraw the balancer/oil pump drive chain tensioner.

6 Unscrew and remove the driven sprocket retaining bolt. Wipe the chain and look for the gold-coloured sideplates (there should be two on adjacent links and one at the other end); note where they are in relation to the sprocket's timing marks.

7 Unscrew the four bolts and withdraw the balancer/oil pump assembly, noting the two locating dowels, and withdraw the sprocket from the rear balancer shaft, disengaging it from the drive chain **(see illustration)**. Note the locating Woodruff key; if this is loose it should be removed and kept with the sprocket.

Inspection

8 Undo the oil pump housing mounting bolts, withdraw the housing from the balancer assembly, noting the two locating dowels, and dismantle the oil pump. Note any marks identifying either surface of the outer rotor; if none can be seen, make your own **(see illustrations)**. Thoroughly clean the rotors and housing. If there is any obvious sign of wear or damage, the pump must be renewed. Note that, except for the pressure relief valve components, the pump is only available as a complete assembly, including the balancer assembly housing halves.

9 Refit the rotors to the pump housing and, using feeler blades of the appropriate thickness, measure the clearance between the outer rotor and the pump housing, then between the inner rotor tip and the outer rotor **(see illustrations)**.

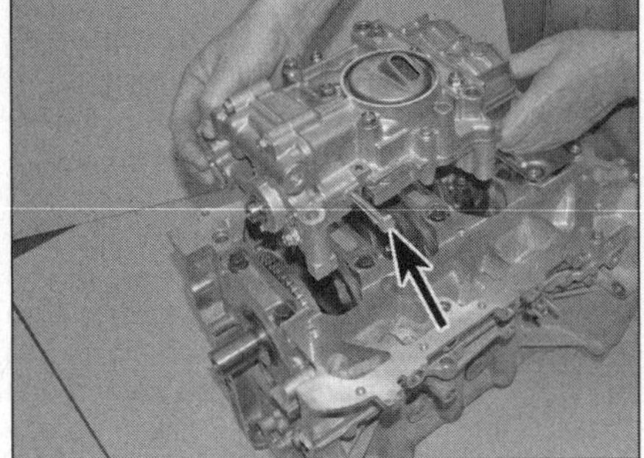

12.7 Withdrawing balancer/oil pump assembly – note locking pin (arrowed)

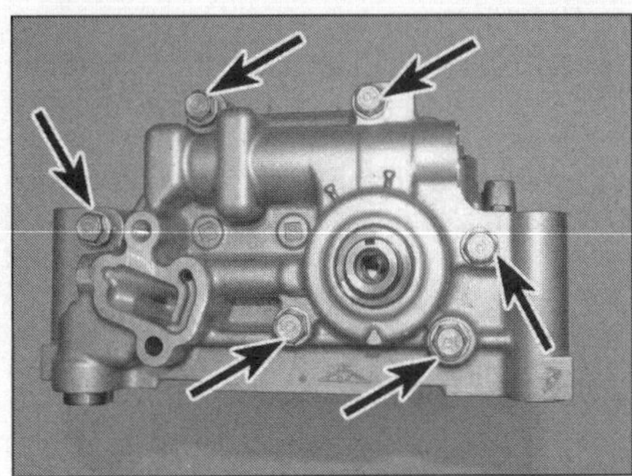

12.8a Undo oil pump housing mounting bolts . . .

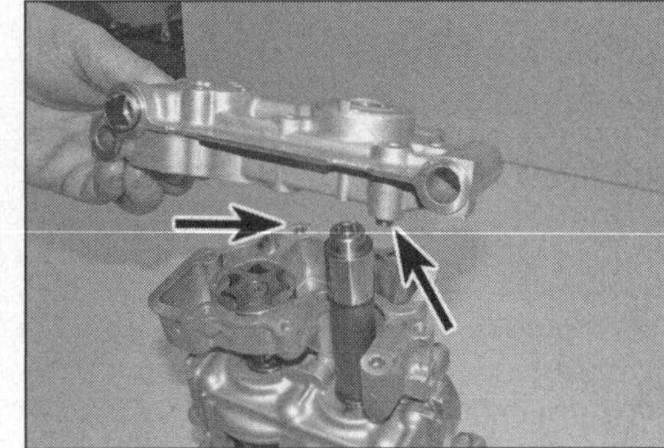

12.8b . . . and withdraw housing from balancer assembly, noting two locating dowels (arrowed)

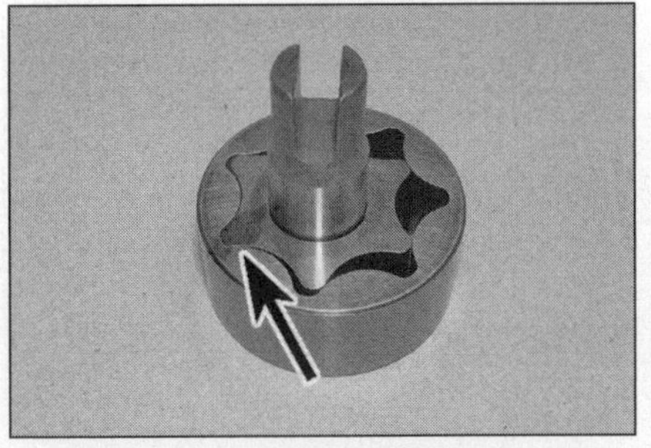

12.8c Mark one surface of outer rotor with felt-tip pen or similar so that it can be refitted same way round

12.9a Measuring pump housing-to-outer rotor clearance

12.9b Measuring inner-to-outer rotor tip clearance

12.10 Measuring pump housing-to-rotor axial clearance (rotor endfloat)

12.12a Unscrew threaded plug . . .

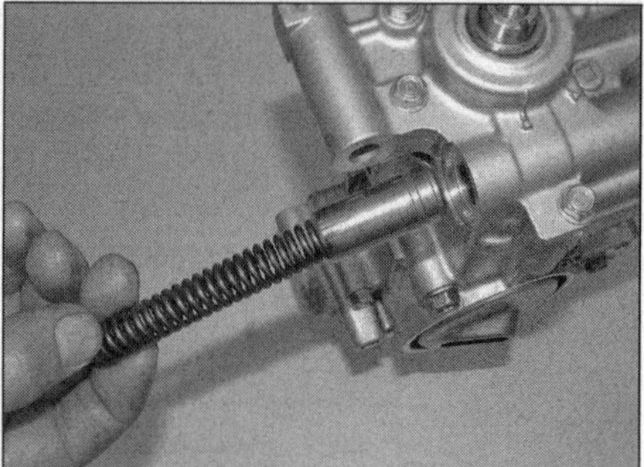

12.12b . . . and remove oil pressure relief valve spring and plunger

12.14a Refitting oil pump inner rotor

12.14b Ensure oil pump outer rotor is refitted original way round

10 Using feeler blades and a straight-edge placed across the top of the pump housing and the rotors, measure the rotor endfloat **(see illustration)**.

11 If any measurement is outside the specified limits, the complete pump assembly must be renewed.

12 Unscrew the pressure relief valve threaded plug and extract the spring and plunger from the pump housing **(see illustrations)**. Check the spring for distortion and the plunger for scoring; if the plunger does not slide freely in the pump housing bore, then it must be renewed.

13 Check the oil pump drive chain, sprocket and tensioner as described in Section 13.

14 Lubricate the pump rotors with clean engine oil and refit them, using the marks made or noted on removal to ensure that the outer rotor is refitted the original way round **(see illustrations)**. Check that the pump rotates freely, then prime it by injecting oil into its passages and rotating it. If a long time elapses before the pump is refitted to the engine, prime it again before installation. Packing the spaces between the rotors with petroleum jelly will also prime the pump.

15 Refit the oil pump housing to the balancer assembly, aligning it on the two locating dowels and engaging the pump inner rotor on the front balancer shaft's drive tongue, then refit the housing mounting bolts and tighten them to the torque specified. Lubricate and refit the oil pressure relief valve plunger and spring, then refit the plug, and tighten to the specified torque.

Refitting

16 Check again that No. 1 cylinder is at TDC on the compression stroke.

17 Rotate the balancer shafts until the keyway in the rear balancer shaft aligns with the single arrow mark cast on the pump housing **(see illustration)**. Insert the 8 mm diameter pin into the hole in the rear of the balancer/oil pump assembly to lock the balancer shafts in this position and secure it with a rubber band or similar. Position the driven sprocket on the rear balancer shaft, engaging it on the Woodruff key; note that the two punch-marked teeth will align with the arrow marks cast on the pump housing.

18 Refit the balancer/oil pump assembly, engaging the driven sprocket on the chain and aligning the assembly on the two locating dowels. The sprocket must be fitted to the chain so that the chain's rear run is kept taut and so that the gold-coloured sideplates are restored to the relationship with the sprocket timing marks noted on removal.

19 Tighten the four balancer/oil pump assembly mounting bolts to the torque specified **(see illustration)**.

20 Lightly oil its threads, refit the driven sprocket retaining bolt and tighten it to the specified torque. Remove the locking pin.

21 Refit the chain tensioner, engaging its plunger on the tensioner blade's free end. Tighten its bolts to the specified torque, then hold the tensioner blade against the tensioner plunger and withdraw the locking pin to release the tensioner against the chain **(see illustration)**. Check that the timing marks and coloured sideplates are correctly aligned and that the tensioner plunger has taken up any slack in the chain.

22 Rotate the crankshaft two full turns (720°) clockwise and check that when the camshaft

12.17 Keyway in rear balancer shaft must align with single arrow mark cast on pump housing

12.19 Tightening four balancer/oil pump assembly mounting bolts

12.21 Hold tensioner blade against tensioner plunger and withdraw locking pin to release tensioner

13.4 If tensioner plunger protrudes more than 8 mm, balancer/oil pump drive chain is worn out and must be renewed

sprocket TDC marks align again, the balancer/oil pump sprocket timing marks align again with the arrow marks cast on the pump housing. If not, repeat the procedure until the balancer/oil pump assembly is correctly timed.

23 Refit the cylinder head cover (Section 4).

24 Refit the sump (Section 11).

13 Balancer/oil pump drive chain – removal, inspection and refitting

Caution: The removal of the timing chain and balancer/oil pump drive chain's crankshaft drive sprocket requires the removal of the timing chain case and of the sump, the latter entailing the removal of the front suspension subframe. Depending on the skills and equipment available and the nature of the work being undertaken, the home mechanic may prefer to consider removing the engine/transmission complete and then removing the sump.

Removal

1 Remove the timing chain (Section 7).

2 Support the timing chain end of the engine from above, with an engine hoist or crane. Bolt a lifting eye to the right-hand end of the cylinder head.

3 Remove the sump (Section 11).

4 Before proceeding any further, assess the chain's state of wear by measuring the protrusion of the tensioner plunger from the tensioner body **(see illustration)**. If the tensioner plunger protrudes more than 8 mm, the balancer/oil pump drive chain is worn out and must be renewed. Because the timing chain will have suffered an equivalent degree of wear, it too must be renewed if the balancer/oil pump drive chain fails this test.

5 Prevent the balancer shafts from rotating by inserting an 8 mm diameter pin punch (see Section 12). Unscrew and remove the sprocket retaining bolt.

6 Rotate the crankshaft anti-clockwise and insert a locking pin into the chain tensioner (see Section 12).

7 Rotate the crankshaft pulley clockwise again to hold the pin in place, then unscrew the two bolts and withdraw the tensioner assembly.

8 Undo the two bolts and withdraw the fixed guide from its rear run.

9 Unscrew the pivot bolt and withdraw the tensioner blade.

10 Remove the chain with the drive and driven sprockets. Note the locating keys as the drive sprocket slides off the crankshaft and as the driven sprocket slides off the rear balancer shaft; if either key is loose it should be removed and kept with its sprocket.

Inspection

11 Chain wear assessment was described in paragraph 4. Also see Section 7, paragraphs 7 to 10. Check the tensioner as described in Chapter 2A, Section 8, paragraphs 7 to 9 **(see illustrations)**.

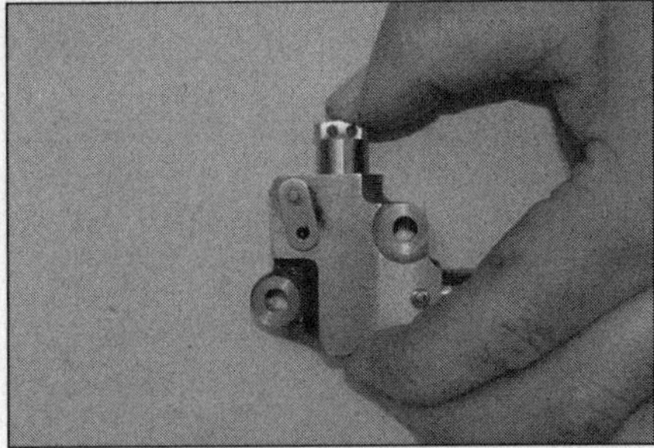

13.11a When checking balancer/oil pump drive chain tensioner, don't allow plunger to fly out . . .

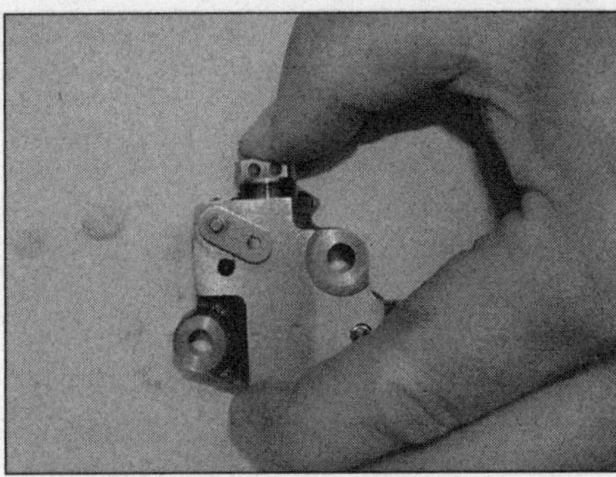

13.11b . . . check plunger moves smoothly through full range of movement . . .

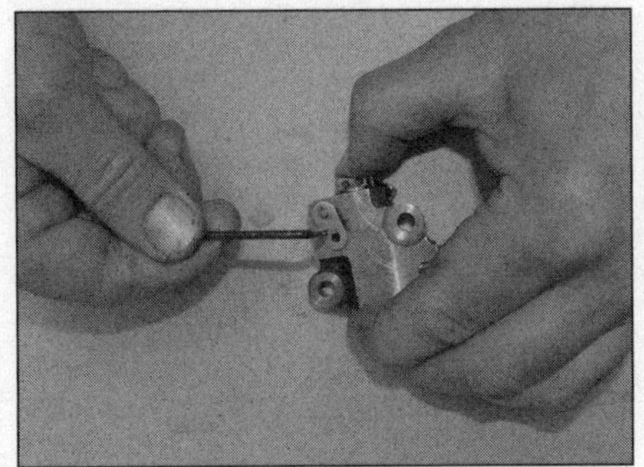

13.11c . . . then compress plunger and re-insert locking pin for refitting

13.12 Keyway must point straight up, so punch mark on drive sprocket aligns with arrow mark cast on cylinder block

Refitting

12 The keyway in the crankshaft end must point straight up (twelve o'clock position), so that the punch mark stamped on the drive sprocket aligns with the arrow mark cast on the cylinder block **(see illustration)**. Check that the locking pin is still in place in the balancer shaft assembly.

13 Fit the balancer/oil pump drive chain to the drive sprocket so that the single-coloured sideplate fits over the punch-marked tooth, then fit it to the driven sprocket so that the links with the coloured sideplates fit on each of the punch-marked teeth **(see illustrations)**.

14 Refit the drive chain and sprockets, keeping the chain taut on its rear run. As the sprockets slide on, ensure that the keyway of each sprocket engages with its key and that the crankshaft drive sprocket is pressed firmly

13.13a Fit drive chain to crankshaft sprocket so that single-coloured sideplate fits over punch-marked tooth

13.13b Fit drive chain to rear balancer shaft driven sprocket so that two coloured sideplates fit over punch-marked teeth . . .

13.14a . . . then ensure that sprocket keyway, coloured sideplates and timing marks align correctly

13.14b Ensure driven sprocket Woodruff key is fitted as shown . . .

13.14c . . . and tapered end of crankshaft drive sprocket locating key points inwards

13.15a Tighten driven sprocket retaining bolt to specified torque wrench setting . . .

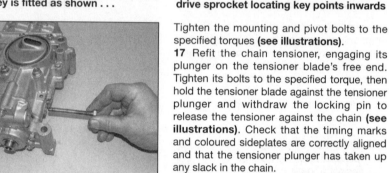

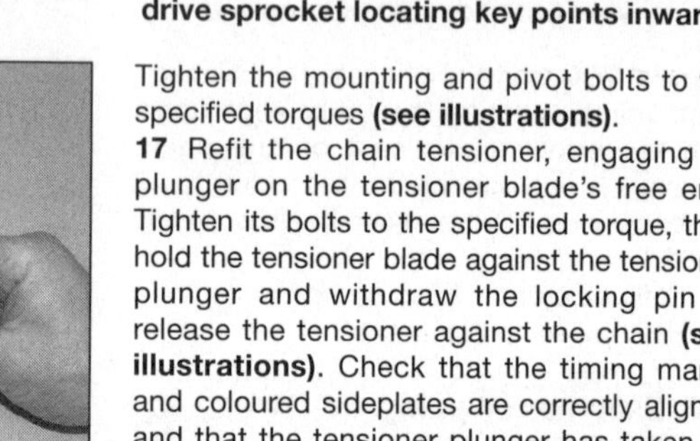
13.15b . . . then remove locking pin

back against the shoulder on the crankshaft end. Note also that the crankshaft drive sprocket locating key is fitted with its tapered end pointing inwards **(see illustrations)**.

15 Lightly oil its threads, refit the driven sprocket retaining bolt and tighten it to the specified torque. Remove the locking pin **(see illustrations)**.

16 Refit the fixed guide to the chain's rear run and the tensioner blade to the front run. Tighten the mounting and pivot bolts to the specified torques **(see illustrations)**.

17 Refit the chain tensioner, engaging its plunger on the tensioner blade's free end. Tighten its bolts to the specified torque, then hold the tensioner blade against the tensioner plunger and withdraw the locking pin to release the tensioner against the chain **(see illustrations)**. Check that the timing marks and coloured sideplates are correctly aligned and that the tensioner plunger has taken up any slack in the chain.

18 Refit the timing chain (Section 7). Temporarily refit the crankshaft pulley and rotate the crankshaft two full turns (720°) clockwise, then check that all the timing marks align exactly, as described, for both chains. If not, repeat the procedure until both chains are correctly refitted.

19 The remainder of reassembly is the reverse of the removal procedure.

13.16a Check locating key, coloured side-plates and timing marks are all aligned . . .

13.16b . . . then refit fixed guide to drive chain's rear run . . .

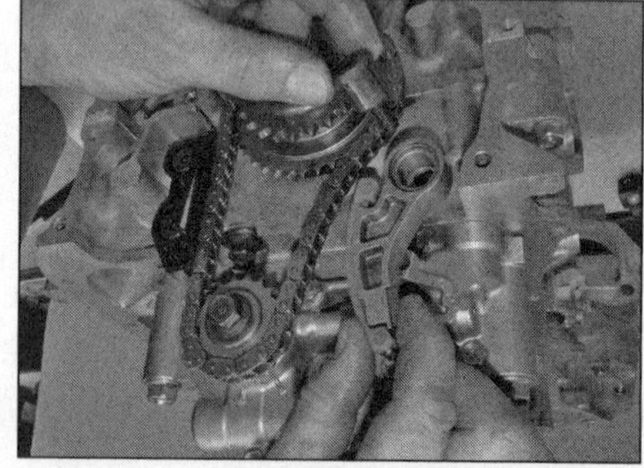
13.16c . . . and tensioner blade to front run . . .

13.17a . . . refit locked tensioner to tensioner blade . . .

13.17b . . . refit longer bolt as shown . . .

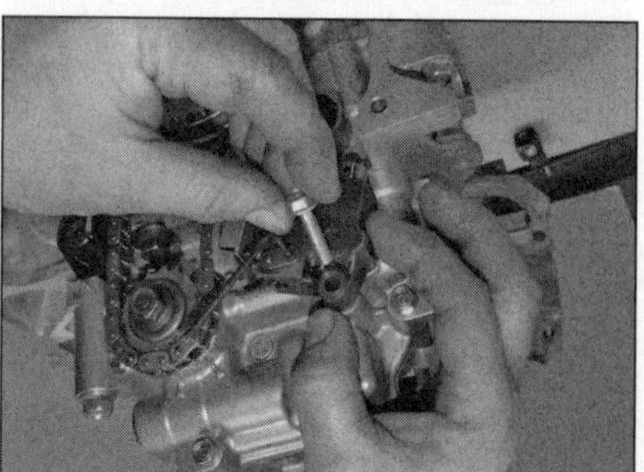
13.17c . . . then refit tensioner shorter mounting bolt

14 Balancer shafts – removal, inspection and refitting

1 See Chapter 2A, Section 16, but use the specifications from this Chapter.

15 Flywheel – removal and refitting

Caution: The removal of the transmission also requires the removal of the front suspension subframe. Read through the procedure first to ensure that all the tools and equipment required are to hand.

Removal

1 Raise the vehicle and support it on axle stands (see *Jacking and vehicle support*), then remove the gearbox (Chapter 7A).

2 Remove the clutch assembly (Chapter 6).

3 Prevent the flywheel from turning by locking the ring gear teeth with a similar arrangement to that shown **(see illustration)**. Alternatively, bolt a strap between the flywheel and the cylinder block. Make alignment marks between the flywheel and crankshaft using paint or a marker pen.

4 Remove the bolts that secure the flywheel to the crankshaft – note that they have bi-hex heads, but any normal socket should undo them. **Note:** *Honda specifically forbid the use of an impact wrench to slacken or tighten these bolts because of the likelihood of damage to the flywheel.* Since the flywheel is heavy, be sure to support it while removing the last bolt. Remove the flywheel from the crankshaft **(see illustration)**.

Inspection

Note: *Due to the amount of work necessary to remove and refit flywheels and clutch components, it is worth considering the renewal of the clutch components on a preventative basis if the engine and/or transmission have been removed for some other reason. Also note that it is sometimes recommended to renew the dual-mass flywheel at the same time as the clutch. This, however, is an extremely expensive course of action; seek expert advice if in doubt.*

5 Most problems with dual-mass flywheels will be evident from the sudden onset of knocking or rattling noises when the engine is idling, from the development of juddering, jerkiness and noise on taking up the drive and pulling away, and from difficulties with gear selection, etc. The fact that it may be possible to stop or change the noise and other symptoms by depressing and releasing the clutch pedal may lead one to suspect the clutch. Early symptoms of a failing dual-mass flywheel may be similar to a slipping clutch. In such cases, the only way to be sure is to remove the gearbox and clutch so that the clutch and flywheel can be physically checked for signs of wear or damage.

15.3 Homemade tool fabricated to lock flywheel

6 Clean the flywheel to remove clutch dust, grease and oil. Try to rotate the outer rim against the inner; while it should be possible to rotate one against the other for a short distance, the movement should be smooth and well-controlled by the torsion springs. If there is any sign of free play, of jerkiness or roughness in the motion or if any undue noises are heard, the flywheel is faulty and must be renewed. Check also that there is no sign of axial movement between the inner and outer parts of the flywheel. If any sign of wear or damage is found, the flywheel must be renewed.

7 Inspect the surface for cracks, rivet grooves, burned areas and score marks. Light scoring can be removed with emery cloth. Check for cracked and broken ring gear teeth. Lay the flywheel on a flat surface and use a straight-edge to check for warpage. If any sign of wear or damage is found, the flywheel must be renewed.

8 Clean and inspect the mating surfaces of the flywheel and the crankshaft. If the oil seal is leaking, renew it before refitting the flywheel (see Section 17).

9 Check the pilot bearing as described in Section 16.

10 Clean the bolt threads and check their condition before re-using them. These bolts are subject to significant stress, and it is good practice to renew them whenever they are disturbed.

15.12a Lightly oil under heads of flywheel mounting bolts . . .

15.4 Note alignment of flywheel on crankshaft before removing – make your own marks if none can be seen

Refitting

11 Position the flywheel against the crankshaft using the marks made on removal to ensure that it is refitted in its original location. Some engines have an alignment dowel or staggered bolt holes to ensure correct refitting.

12 Prevent the flywheel from turning. Lightly oil under the bolt heads and refit the flywheel mounting bolts, then working in a diagonal pattern and in several stages, tighten the bolts to the specified torque **(see illustrations)**. Wipe away any surplus oil.

13 The remainder of refitting is the reverse of the removal procedure.

16 Crankshaft pilot bearing – inspection, removal and refitting

Inspection

1 The pilot bearing is fitted into the flywheel, and provides support for the free end of the gearbox input shaft. It can only be examined once the clutch (Chapter 6) has been removed. The bearing should rotate smoothly and quietly and should be firmly fixed in the flywheel. Check the bearing by rotating its inner race and feeling for rough or jerky rotation and any signs of free play, also of any looseness of its fit in the flywheel. If any of these conditions are evident, the bearing must be renewed.

15.12b . . . then refit flywheel and tighten bolts in criss-cross sequence to specified torque wrench setting

17.2 Measure fitted depth to mating surface as shown . . .

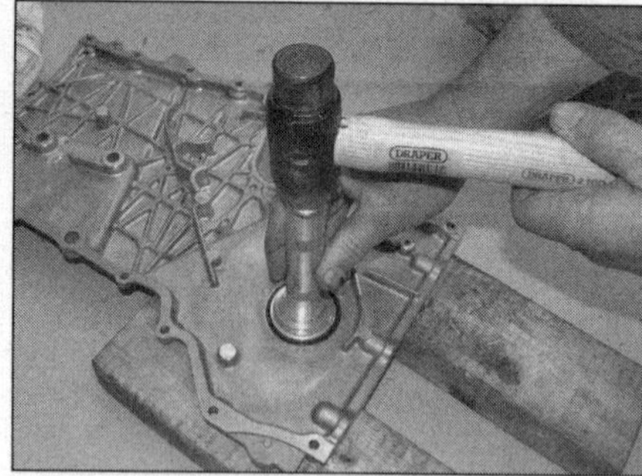
17.3 . . . then drive seal out of timing chain case housing

17.5 Driving new seal into timing chain case housing

Removal

2 Remove the flywheel as described in Section 15.

3 Measure and record the depth from a straight-edge placed across the face of the flywheel to the bearing's outer edge. Drive out the bearing using a hammer and suitable drift.

Refitting

4 Smear a thin coat of oil on the bearing outer race. Using a suitable socket that bears only on the outer diameter of the bearing, drive the new bearing squarely into the flywheel until its outer edge is the depth from the flywheel face that was noted on removal. Wipe away all traces of oil from the bearing and flywheel.

5 Refit the flywheel as described in Section 15.

6 Degrease the flywheel friction surface, using solvent and a clean rag.

7 Apply a thin smear of grease to the inner race of the bearing and to the gearbox input shaft; Honda recommend Urea Grease UM264 (Part No. 41211-PY5-305), before refitting the gearbox as described in Chapter 7A.

17 Crankshaft oil seals – renewal

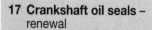

Right-hand (timing chain end)

1 Remove the crankshaft pulley as described in Section 5.

2 Measure and record the depth from a straight-edge placed across the boss on the timing chain case surrounding the oil seal to the seal's outer edge. If the timing chain case is removed from the engine, measure the depth from the seal's outer edge to a straight-edge placed across the case mating surface **(see illustration)**; this should be in the range 17.3 to 18.0 mm.

3 Carefully punch or drill two small holes opposite each other in the oil seal. Screw a self-tapping screw into each and pull on the screws with pliers to extract the seal. If the timing chain case is removed from the engine, either drive the seal out or lever it out using a screwdriver or similar; take care not to scratch the seal housing **(see illustration)**.

4 Clean the seal housing and polish off any burrs or raised edges which may have caused the seal to fail in the first place.

5 Lubricate the lips of the new seal with clean engine oil and ease it into position in the timing chain case, ensuring that the seal lips face inwards. Press the seal squarely into position as far as possible by hand. Use a suitable tubular drift, such as a socket, which bears only on the hard outer edge of the seal to tap the seal into position to the depth noted on removal **(see illustration)**.

6 Wash off any traces of oil, then refit the crankshaft pulley as described in Section 5, taking great care not to damage the seal lips during fitting.

Left-hand (transmission end)

7 Remove the flywheel (see Section 15).

8 Measure and record the depth from a straight-edge placed across the boss on the cylinder block and lower crankcase/main bearing ladder surrounding the oil seal to the seal's outer edge.

9 Carefully punch or drill two small holes opposite each other in the oil seal. Screw a self-tapping screw into each and pull on the screws with pliers to extract the seal.

10 Clean the seal housing and polish off any burrs or raised edges which may have caused the seal to fail in the first place.

11 Apply a film of clean oil to the crankshaft seal journal and the lip of the new seal, and carefully tap the seal into place with a seal driver. If a seal driver isn't available, use a large socket or piece of pipe, with an outside diameter which bears only on the hard outer edge of the seal, to tap the seal into position until it seats on the shoulder in the seal housing; check that this corresponds to the depth noted on removal **(see illustrations)**.

12 The remaining steps are the reverse of removal.

17.11a Apply a film of clean oil to crankshaft seal journal and lip of new crankshaft left-hand seal . . .

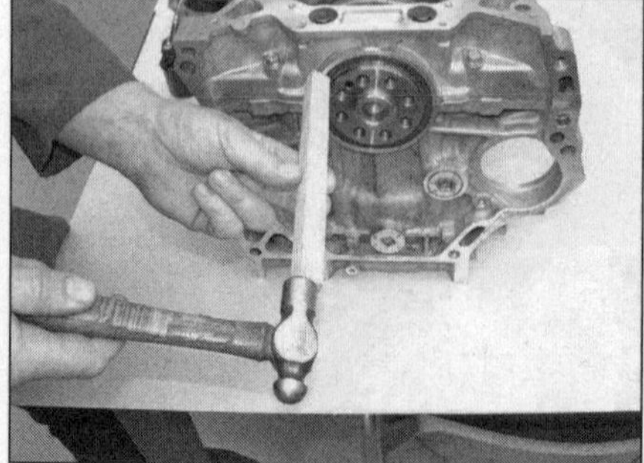
17.11b . . . then tap into place as shown until seated – ensure seal remains square in housing

18 Oil cooler – removal and refitting

Note: *The oil cooler is mounted on the front of the engine, behind the alternator and underneath the EGR equipment. Access is extremely awkward; short of removing the intake manifold and all the EGR equipment (see Chapters 4B and 4C), the most direct access is therefore from underneath, as detailed below.*

Removal

1 Drain the engine coolant, engine oil, and remove the oil filter element (Chapter 1B).

2 Remove the engine compartment undershield (Chapter 11).

3 Remove the thermostat housing (Chapter 3).

4 Unscrew the four bolts and remove the oil cooler from the oil filter/oil cooler/water pump housing **(see illustration)**. Be prepared for fluid spillage. Recover and discard the sealing O-rings – new ones must be fitted on reassembly.

Refitting

5 Ensure the mating surfaces of the oil cooler

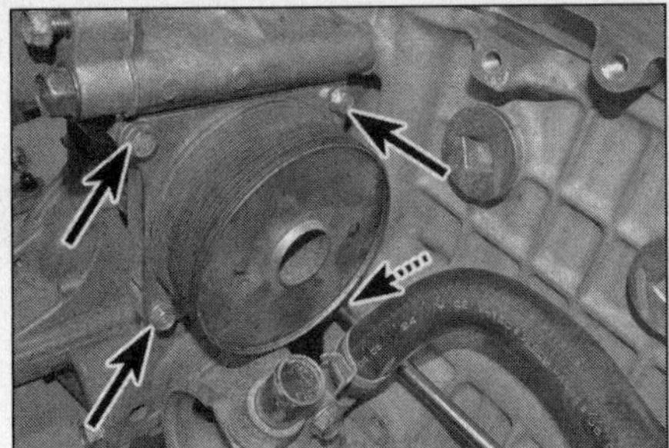
18.4 Unscrew four bolts and remove oil cooler from oil filter/oil cooler/water pump housing

18.5a Renew all four sealing O-rings on reassembly . . .

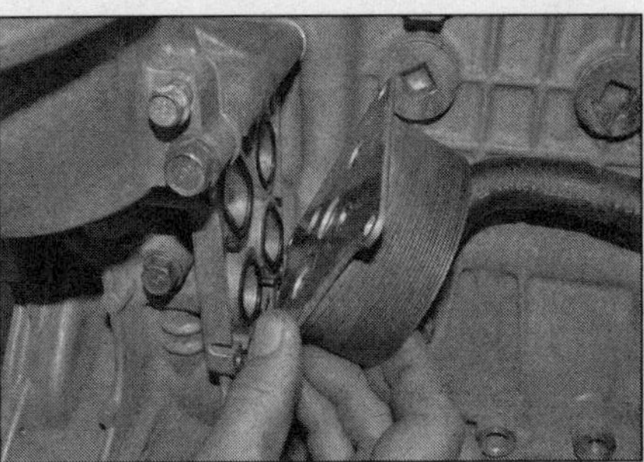
18.5b . . . and ensure mating surfaces of oil cooler and oil filter/oil cooler/water pump housing are clean and dry

and housing are clean and dry. Using new sealing O-rings, fit the cooler to the housing **(see illustrations)**. Tighten the bolts to the specified torque.

6 Refit the thermostat housing (Chapter 3).

7 Replenish the engine coolant, fit a new oil filter element, and fill the engine with new engine oil.

8 Refit the components removed for access.

19 Oil filter/oil cooler/ water pump housing – removal and refitting

Note: *The housing is mounted at the front right-hand end of the engine; the alternator must be removed and the air conditioning compressor must be unbolted to reach it. The most direct access is therefore from the front, as detailed below. When carrying out this procedure, be careful not to damage the radiator and air conditioning condenser by leaning on them; they are very delicate.*

Removal

1 Disconnect the battery negative lead (see *Disconnecting the battery*).

2 Remove the engine compartment undershield (Chapter 11).

3 Drain the cooling system (Chapter 1B).

4 Drain the engine oil and remove the oil filter element (Chapter 1B).

5 Remove the auxiliary drivebelt and its tensioner (Chapter 1B).

6 Remove the alternator (Chapter 5A).

7 Unscrew the air conditioning compressor's four mounting bolts. With the compressor unbolted, secure it out of the way without disconnecting or straining its wiring and pipes.

8 Remove the thermostat, the thermostat housing and the water pump (Chapter 3).

9 Remove the oil cooler as described in the previous Section.

10 Check that all coolant hoses, wiring harnesses and their support brackets have been removed from the housing.

11 Unscrew the bolts securing the housing to the cylinder block, then remove the housing; note the two locating dowels. Remove and discard the sealing O-rings – these must be renewed **(see illustration)**.

Refitting

12 Thoroughly clean the mating surfaces of the housing and the cylinder block. Clean any oil, coolant or sealant from the mating surfaces and from the oil and coolant passages, bolt holes and threads. Be careful not to allow dirt and debris to fall inside the engine. Degrease the surfaces completely before reassembly.

13 With the new O-rings fitted to their grooves, refit the housing, engaging its two locating dowels in their respective bores, then tighten the bolts to the specified torque **(see illustrations)**.

14 The remainder of reassembly is the reverse of the removal procedure.

20 Engine/transmission mountings – inspection and renewal

Inspection

1 Raise the front of the vehicle and support it securely on axle stands (see *Jacking and vehicle support*). Remove the engine compartment undershield (Chapter 11) to reach the engine rear mounting, the cooling system expansion tank to reach the engine right-hand (timing end) mounting, and the air cleaner assembly (Chapter 4B) and/or the battery and battery tray (Chapter 5A) to reach the engine/transmission left-hand (upper) mounting.

2 Check the mounting rubber to see if it is cracked, hardened or separated from the metal at any point; renew the mounting if any such deterioration is evident.

3 Check that all the mountings' fasteners are securely tightened.

4 Using a large screwdriver or a crowbar, check for wear in the mounting by carefully levering against it to check for freeplay; where this is not possible, enlist the aid of an assistant to move the engine/transmission back-and-forth, or from side-to-side, while you watch the mounting. While some freeplay is to be expected even from new components, excessive wear should be obvious. If excessive freeplay is found, check first that the fasteners are correctly secured, then renew any worn components as described below.

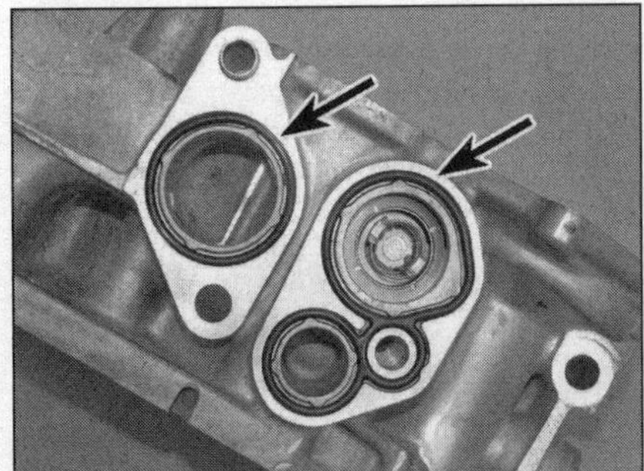
19.11 Remove and discard sealing O-rings from oil filter/oil cooler/water pump housing mating surface grooves

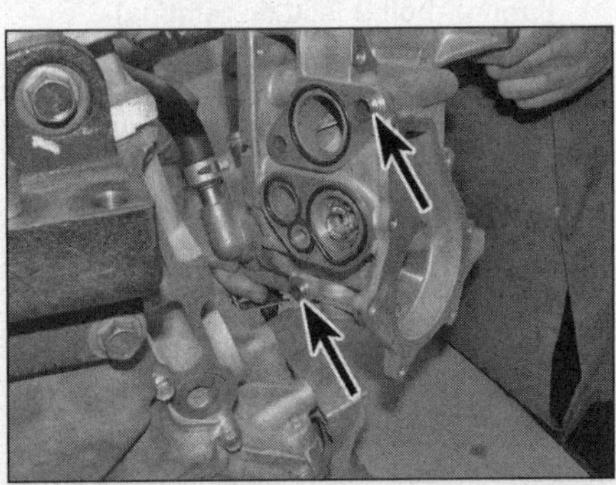
19.13a Fit new O-rings on refitting housing to cylinder block – note locating dowels

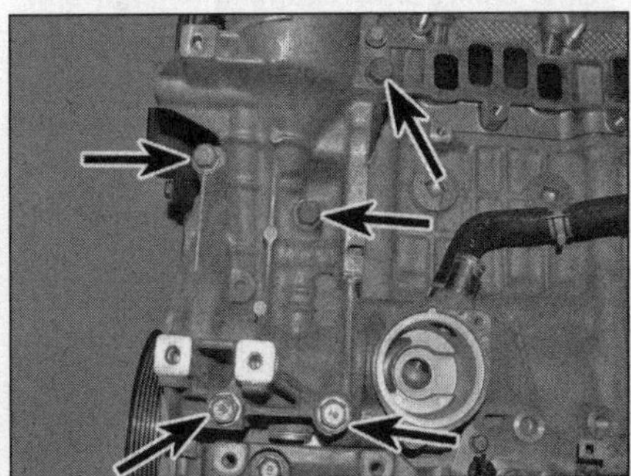
19.13b Tighten oil filter/oil cooler/water pump housing bolts to specified torque wrench setting

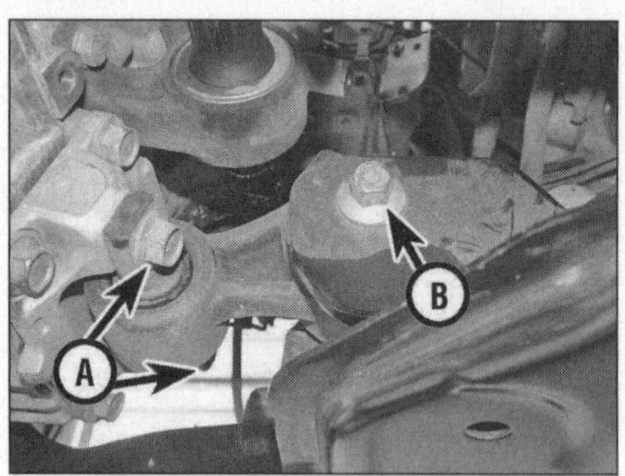

20.7a Rear mounting bracket bolts (A) and torque rod-to-subframe through-bolt (B) . . .

20.7b . . . and withdraw rear mounting torque rod

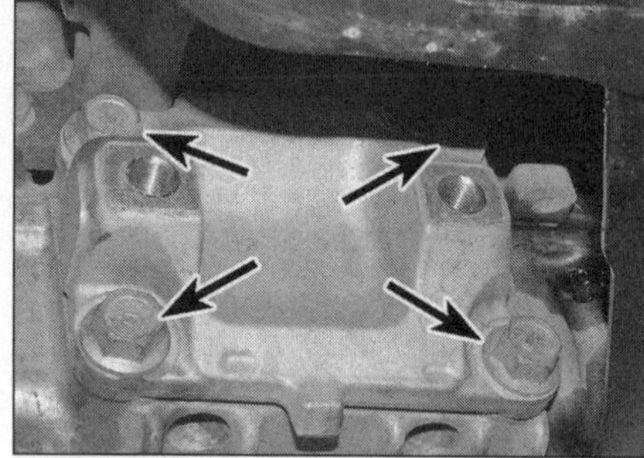

20.8 Engine mounting bracket-to-lower crankcase/main bearing ladder/sump bolts

Renewal

Note: *Before slackening any of the engine/transmission mounting bolts and nuts, note that the majority must be renewed whenever they are disturbed (see Specifications) and that a specific sequence must be followed to ensure correct alignment upon refitting.*

Engine rear mounting

Note: *All the mounting's bolts must be renewed whenever they are disturbed. Obtain new bolts before starting work, but, depending on the work being undertaken, be careful at exactly which stage of the tightening procedure you fit the new through-bolt and tighten it (see paragraphs 10 and 27 to 29 below).*

5 Remove the engine compartment undershield (Chapter 11).

6 Support the weight of the engine/transmission under the sump using a trolley jack with a block of wood placed on its head to relieve the pressure on the through-bolt.

7 Unbolt the engine rear mounting torque rod from the front suspension subframe and from the bracket on the engine and withdraw the torque rod **(see illustrations)**. Check the torque rod's rubber sections for signs of perishing, cracks, or deterioration of the metal-to-rubber bonding.

8 Unbolt the bracket from the engine **(see illustration)**.

9 On reassembly, refit the bracket to the engine, fit the new bolts and tighten them to the torque specified.

10 Refit the engine rear mounting torque rod to the bracket on the engine and the front suspension subframe, fitting the through-bolt loosely; tighten the new torque rod-to-bracket bolts to the torque specified, then remove the jack. When refitting the through-bolt, if it is simply a matter of renewing the mounting, then fit the new bolt and tighten it to the specified torque. If the mounting is being tightened as part of the sequences outlined in paragraphs 27 to 29, either use the original bolt for the preliminary tightening and only fit the new bolt on the final tightening, or fit the new bolt but be careful to tighten it only loosely until the final tightening.

11 Refit the engine compartment undershield (Chapter 11). Lower the vehicle to the ground and slacken the right-hand (timing end) mounting torque rod through-bolt-to-body to allow any stress in the mounting to be relieved **(see illustration)**. Tighten the through-bolt to the torque specified. While the through-bolt must be renewed whenever it is disturbed, Honda do not specify that this should be done in this instance, if it has merely been slackened and then retightened.

Engine right-hand (timing end) mounting

Note: *Most of the mounting's nuts and bolts must be renewed whenever they are disturbed. Obtain new nuts and bolts before starting work, but, depending on the work being undertaken, be careful at exactly which stage of the tightening procedure you fit the new torque rod through-bolt and tighten it (see paragraphs 17 and 27 to 29 below).*

12 Unclip the steering fluid reservoir and unbolt the cooling system expansion tank and its mounting bracket from the right-hand inner wing. Secure both reservoir and tank to one side without disconnecting or straining their hoses or spilling their contents.

13 Support the weight of the engine/transmission under the sump using a trolley jack with a block of wood placed on its head. Make sure the engine is adequately supported, then unscrew the three bolts securing the torque rod to the body and mounting; remove the torque rod **(see illustrations)**.

14 Unscrew and discard the two nuts and the bolt securing the intermediate bracket to the bracket on the engine, then unscrew the bolt securing the intermediate bracket to the mounting centre and withdraw the bracket **(see illustrations)**.

15 Unscrew the three bolts securing the mounting to the inner wing **(see illustration)**.

20.11 Slacken then retighten engine right-hand (timing end) mounting through-bolt

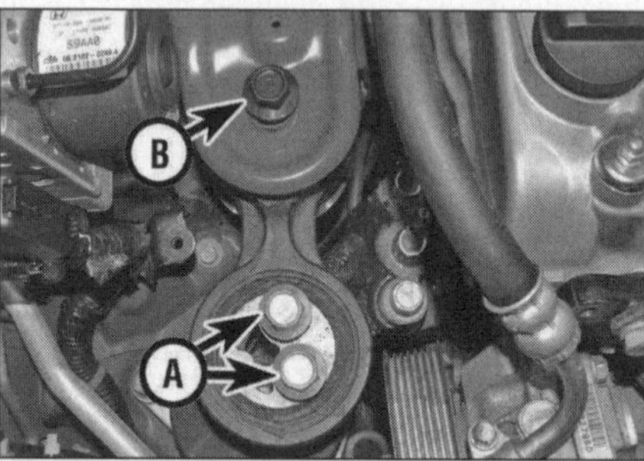
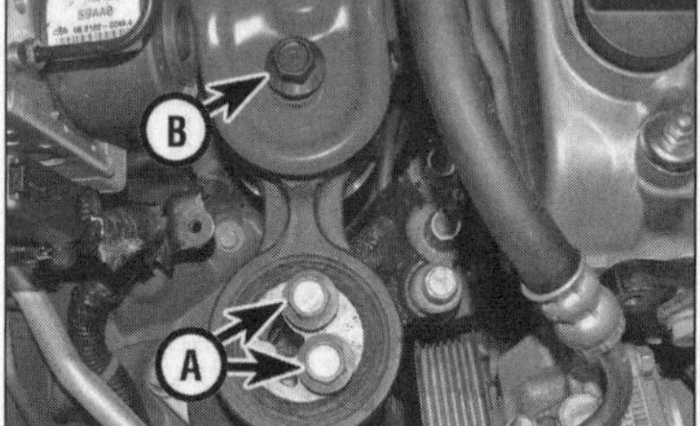

20.13a Right-hand mounting torque rod bolts (note bolts A must be tightened first, through-bolt B last, on refitting) . . .

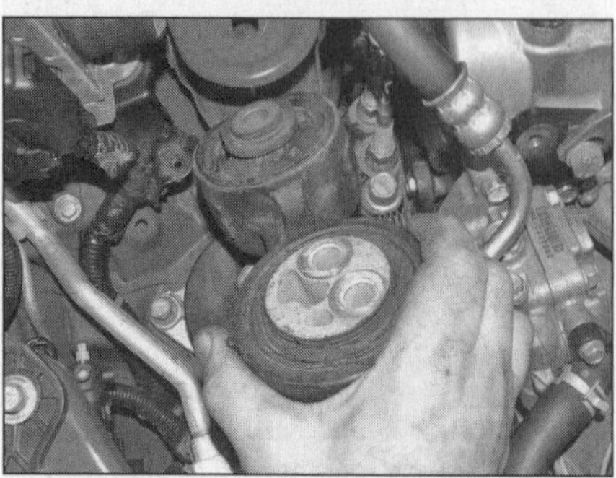

20.13b . . . and withdraw the torque rod

20.14a Unscrew and discard nuts and bolt . . .

20.14b . . . then unscrew bolt securing intermediate bracket to mounting centre

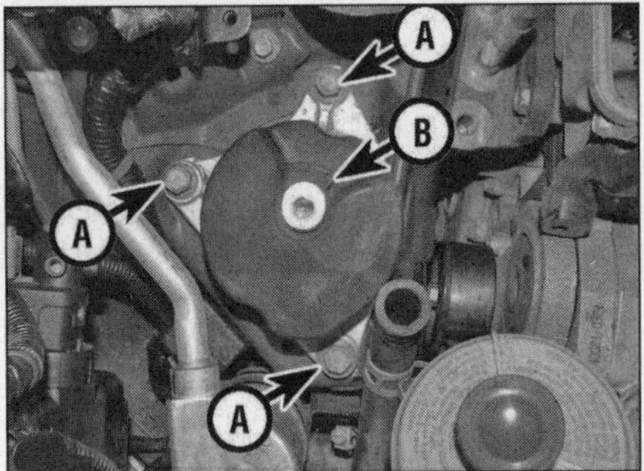

20.15 Engine right-hand (timing end) mounting-to-body bolts (A). Note locating peg (B)

20.16 Removing engine right-hand (timing end) mounting timing chain case/cylinder head and block bracket

Check the rubber section (and those of the torque rod) for signs of perishing, cracks, or deterioration of the metal-to-rubber bonding.

16 Unscrew the four bolts and remove the bracket from the engine **(see illustration)**.

17 On reassembly renew the nuts, bolts and through-bolt as described; tighten all nuts and bolts securely, to the specified torques. Proceed as follows:

a) *When refitting the intermediate bracket, note that it must engage on the locating peg projecting from the top of the mounting's centre.*
b) *Tighten loosely the new intermediate bracket-to-timing chain case bracket nuts and bolt, then tighten loosely the bracket-to-mounting centre bolt.*
c) *Remove the air cleaner assembly (Chapter 4B) and/or the battery and the battery tray (Chapter 5A).*
d) *Slacken the engine/transmission left-hand (upper) mounting-to-body bracket through-bolt and the two nuts and the bolt securing the mounting to the gearbox.*
e) *Remove the jack to let the weight settle on the partially-fastened mountings.*
f) *Tighten to their specified torques first the right-hand (timing end) mounting's intermediate bracket-to-mounting centre bolt, then the new intermediate bracket-to-timing chain case bracket nuts and bolt last.*
g) *Tighten to their specified torques first the nuts and the bolt securing the engine/transmission left-hand (upper) mounting to the gearbox, then the mounting-to-body bracket through-bolt. While the nuts, bolt and through-bolt must be renewed whenever they are disturbed, Honda do not specify that this should be done in this instance, if they have merely been slackened and then retightened.*
h) *When refitting the right-hand (timing end) mounting's torque rod, tighten the new front bolts-to-intermediate bracket first, followed by the new rear through-bolt-to-body last.*
i) *Refit the components removed for access.*

Engine/transmission left-hand (lower) mounting

18 Direct access is from the side, behind the left-hand roadwheel – turning the steering fully to the left or right may improve matters. There is no need to support the engine/transmission if only this mounting is being removed, but taking the weight of the unit using a trolley jack with a block of wood placed on its head under the gearbox will ease the task.

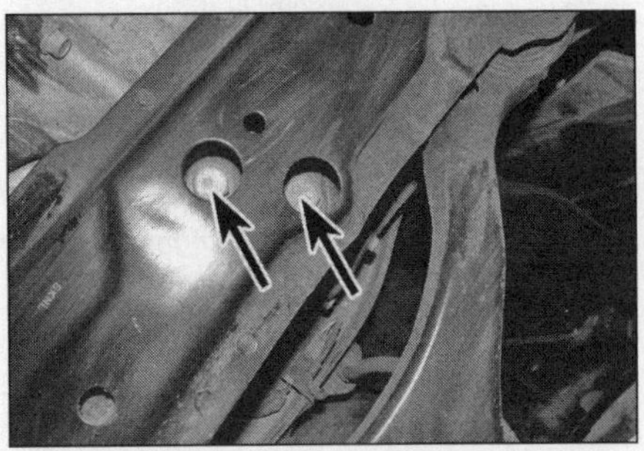

20.19 Unscrew and discard two engine/transmission left-hand (lower) mounting-to-front suspension subframe bolts . . .

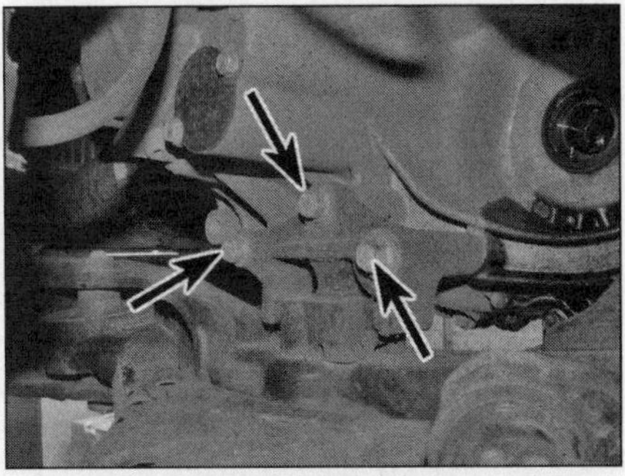

20.20 . . . then unbolt mounting from gearbox and discard bolts

19 Unscrew the two mounting-to-front suspension subframe bolts **(see illustration)**.

20 Undo the three bolts to remove the mounting from the gearbox **(see illustration)**. Check the mounting's rubber section for signs of perishing, cracks, or deterioration of the metal-to-rubber bonding.

21 Refitting is a reversal of removal; tighten all the new bolts to the specified torques.

Engine/transmission left-hand (upper) mounting

22 Remove the air cleaner assembly (Chapter 4B) and/or the battery and the battery tray (Chapter 5A).

23 Support the weight of the unit under the gearbox using a trolley jack with a block of wood placed on its head to relieve the pressure on the through-bolt.

24 Make sure the gearbox is adequately supported, then unscrew the mounting-to-body bracket through-bolt and the three bolts securing the mounting's bracket to the inner wing. Withdraw the mounting bracket **(see illustration)**.

25 Unscrew the earth lead-to-mounting clamp bolt. Unscrew the two nuts and the bolt securing the mounting to the gearbox **(see illustration)**. Remove the mounting. If necessary, unscrew the two studs from the top of the gearbox using a deep socket applied to the hexagon on their upper ends. Check the mounting's rubber section for signs

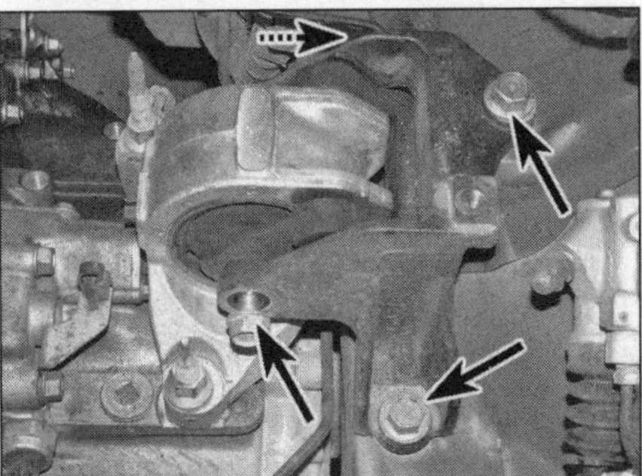

20.24 Unscrew and discard through-bolt and three bolts securing mounting's bracket to inner wing

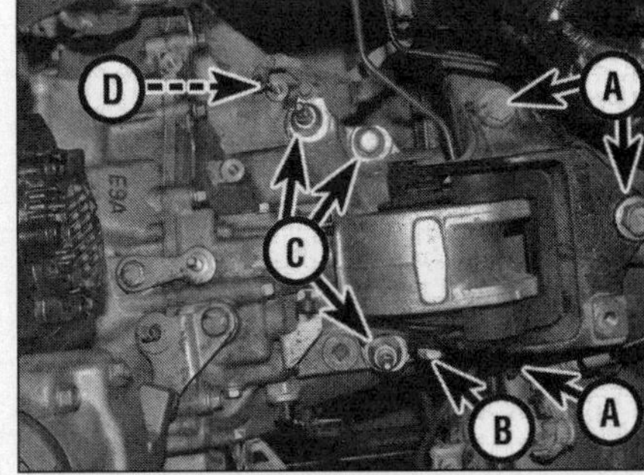

20.25 Engine/transmission mounting bolts (A), through-bolt (B), gearbox nuts and bolt (C) and earth lead clamp bolt (D)

of perishing, cracks, or deterioration of the metal-to-rubber bonding.

26 On reassembly renew the nuts, bolts and through-bolt as described; tighten all nuts and bolts to the specified torques. Proceed as follows:

a) *Tighten securely the studs (if unscrewed), then fit the mounting to the gearbox. Tighten loosely the new nuts and the bolt, and reconnect and secure the earth lead.*
b) *Refit the bracket to the body and mounting. Tighten to their specified torque the new bracket-to-inner wing bolts, then fit the new through-bolt, tightening it only loosely.*
c) *Remove the jack to let the weight settle on the partially-fastened mounting.*
d) *Tighten to their specified torques first the two nuts and the bolt securing the mounting to the gearbox, then the mounting-to-body bracket through-bolt.*
e) *Refit the components removed for access.*

Engine/transmission mounting alignment

Note: *Before slackening any of the engine/transmission mounting bolts and nuts, note that the majority must be renewed whenever they are disturbed (see Specifications and text above) and that a specific sequence must be followed to ensure correct alignment upon refitting.*

27 When refitting the engine/gearbox unit, tighten the mountings in the following sequence:

a) *With the engine and gearbox suspended on a hoist, refit the new right-hand (timing end) mounting intermediate bracket-to-timing chain case bracket nuts and bolt; tighten them loosely.*
b) *Refit the left-hand (upper) mounting to the gearbox, fit new nuts and bolt; tighten them loosely. Refit the earth lead and tighten its bolt.*
c) *Refit the left-hand (upper) mounting bracket to the body, fit new bolts and tighten them to the specified torque, then fit the new through-bolt, tightening it loosely.*
d) *Remove the hoist, raise the vehicle and refit the rear mounting torque rod. Fit new torque rod-to-bracket bolts and tighten them to the specified torque, then fit the new through-bolt, tightening it loosely.*
e) *Lower the vehicle and tighten the right-hand (timing end) mounting intermediate bracket-to-mounting centre bolt to the specified torque.*
f) *Tighten the right-hand (timing end) mounting intermediate bracket-to-timing chain case bracket nuts and bolt to the specified torque.*
g) *Tighten the left-hand (upper) mounting-to-gearbox nuts and bolt to the specified torque.*
h) *Tighten the left-hand (upper) mounting through-bolt to the specified torque.*
i) *Raise the vehicle and tighten the rear mounting through-bolt to the specified torque.*
j) *Fit new left-hand (lower) mounting-to-front suspension subframe bolts and tighten them to the specified torque.*
k) *Lower the vehicle. Refit the right-hand (timing end) mounting torque rod and fit new bolts. Tighten the two front bolts first, then the rear bolt, all to their specified torques.*

28 When refitting the gearbox, tighten the mountings in the following sequence:

a) *With the gearbox supported on a transmission jack and the engine bellhousing-to-gearbox bolts fully tightened, refit the left-hand (upper) mounting to the gearbox and screw in the two studs, tightening them securely.*
b) *Refit the original through-bolt to the left-hand (upper) mounting, tightening it loosely.*
c) *Refit the original left-hand (upper) mounting-to-gearbox nuts and bolt; tighten them to the specified torque. Refit the earth lead and tighten its bolt.*
d) *Tighten the original left-hand (upper) mounting through-bolt to the specified torque.*
e) *Refit the subframe (Chapter 10).*
f) *Refit the left-hand (lower) mounting, fit new bolts and tighten them to the specified torques.*
g) *Refit the rear mounting torque rod. Fit new torque rod-to-bracket bolts and tighten them to the specified torque, then fit the new through-bolt, tightening it loosely.*
h) *Refit the driveshafts, connect the front suspension lower arms to the swivel hubs and reconnect the anti-roll bar drop links (Chapters 8 and 10), then remove the engine hoist and transmission jack and allow the engine/transmission unit to settle on its mountings.*
i) *Carry out the engine/transmission mounting positioning procedure detailed in paragraph 29 below, renewing the fasteners where indicated.*

29 This procedure is to be carried out on refitting the gearbox and whenever increased noise, vibration and harshness leads to the suspicion that the engine and transmission might not be settled correctly on their mountings:

a) *Support the engine/transmission under the sump using a trolley jack with a block of wood placed on its head.*
b) *Unbolt and remove the right-hand (timing end) mounting torque rod.*
c) *Slacken the left-hand (upper) mounting through-bolt and the mounting-to-gearbox nuts and bolt.*
d) *Slacken the rear mounting torque rod-to-front suspension subframe through-bolt. Remember that the bolt must be renewed (but this will not be necessary if the bolt has already been renewed and merely tightened loosely, as described in paragraph 28 above).*
e) *Unscrew the old left-hand (upper) mounting-to-gearbox nuts and bolt, fit new ones and tighten them to the specified torque.*
f) *Unscrew the old left-hand (upper) mounting through-bolt, fit a new one and tighten it to the specified torque.*
g) *Unscrew the old rear mounting torque rod-to-front suspension subframe through-bolt, fit a new one and tighten it to the specified torque; if the through-bolt has already been renewed and only loosely tightened, simply tighten it fully.*
h) *Refit the right-hand (timing end) mounting torque rod and fit new bolts. Tighten the two front bolts first, then the rear bolt, all to their specified torques.*

Chapter 2 Part C:
Engine removal and overhaul procedures

Contents

Degrees of difficulty

Easy, suitable for novice with little experience 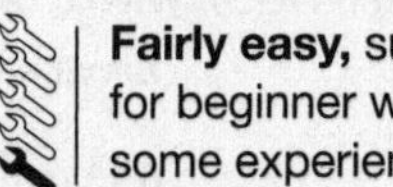	**Fairly easy,** suitable for beginner with some experience	**Fairly difficult,** suitable for competent DIY mechanic	**Difficult,** suitable for experienced DIY mechanic	**Very difficult,** suitable for expert DIY or professional 

Specifications

Petrol engine

Cylinder head

Height	103.95 to 104.05 mm	
Gasket surface maximum warpage	0.05 mm	
Maximum resurfacing limit – to minimum height of 104 mm	0.2 mm	
Valves	**Standard**	**Service limit**
Valve head diameter:		
Intake	34.85 to 35.15 mm	N/Av.
Exhaust	29.85 to 30.15 mm	N/Av.
Valve overall length:		
Intake	108.7 to 109.5 mm	N/Av.
Exhaust	108.3 to 109.1 mm	N/Av.
Valve stem diameter:		
Intake	5.475 to 5.485 mm	5.445 mm
Exhaust	5.450 to 5.460 mm	5.420 mm
Valve stem-to-guide clearance – by wobble method:		
Intake	0.06 to 0.11 mm	0.16 mm
Exhaust	0.11 to 0.16 mm	0.22 mm
Valve stem-to-guide clearance – by direct measurement:		
Intake	0.030 to 0.055 mm	0.08 mm
Exhaust	0.055 to 0.080 mm	0.11 mm
Valve seat width – intake and exhaust	1.25 to 1.55 mm	2.00 mm
Valve stem installed height:		
Intake	40.8 to 41.0 mm	N/App.
Exhaust	54.6 to 54.8 mm	N/App.
Valve spring free length:		
Intake	47.61 mm	N/Av.
Exhaust:		
Nippon Hatsujo springs	49.64 mm	N/Av.
Chuo Hatsujo springs	49.63 mm	N/Av.
Valve guide bore diameter – intake and exhaust	5.515 to 5.530 mm	5.55 mm
Valve guide installed height:		
Intake	15.2 to 16.2 mm	N/App.
Exhaust	15.5 to 16.5 mm	N/App.

Cylinder block	Standard	Service limit
Gasket surface maximum warpage	0.07 mm max.	0.10 mm
Cylinder bore diameter:*		
Bore diameter class A or I	86.01 to 86.02 mm	86.07 mm
Bore diameter class B or II	86.00 to 86.01 mm	86.07 mm
0.25 mm oversize	86.25 to 86.26 mm	N/Av.
Cylinder bore maximum taper – difference between first and third measurements	0.05 mm	
Reboring limit	0.25 mm	

* **Note:** *6 mm from block top surface, in middle of bore and 6 mm from bottom of bore. Bore diameter class letters stamped on top surface of block, at front, timing chain end.*

Pistons	Standard	Service limit
Skirt diameter:*		
Piston diameter class A, or unmarked	85.98 to 85.99 mm	85.93 mm
Piston diameter class B	85.97 to 85.98 mm	85.92 mm
Oversize piston	86.23 to 86.24 mm	N/Av.
Clearance in cylinder – cylinder bore diameter minus piston diameter	0.020 to 0.040 mm	0.05 mm
Oversizes available	+0.25 mm	
Ring groove width:		
Top ring	1.220 to 1.230 mm	1.250 mm
Second ring	1.220 to 1.230 mm	1.250 mm
Oil control ring	2.005 to 2.025 mm	2.050 mm
Gudgeon pin diameter	21.961 to 21.965 mm	21.953 mm
Gudgeon pin-to-piston clearance	-0.005 to +0.002 mm	0.005 mm

* **Note:** *11 mm from bottom of skirt, at 90° to gudgeon pin axis. Piston diameter class letter stamped on each piston crown.*

Piston rings	Standard	Service limit
Ring-to-groove clearance:		
Top ring – T or 1R mark on top surface	0.035 to 0.060 mm	0.13 mm
Second ring – 2T or 2R mark on top surface	0.030 to 0.055 mm	0.13 mm
Oil control ring	N/Av.	N/Av.
Ring width:		
Top ring – T or 1R mark on top surface	1.2 mm	N/Av.
Second ring – 2T or 2R mark on top surface	1.2 mm	N/Av.
Ring radial thickness:		
Top ring – T or 1R mark on top surface	3.1 mm	N/Av.
Second ring – 2T or 2R mark on top surface	3.4 mm	N/Av.
Ring end gap – installed (15 to 20 mm from bottom of bore):		
Top ring – T or 1R mark on top surface	0.20 to 0.35 mm	0.60 mm
Second ring – 2T or 2R mark on top surface	0.40 to 0.55 mm	0.70 mm
Oil control ring	0.25 to 0.65 mm	0.75 mm

Connecting rods	Standard	Service limit
Gudgeon pin-to-rod clearance	0.005 to 0.015 mm	0.020 mm
Small-end bore diameter	21.970 to 21.976 mm	N/Av.
Big-end bore diameter:*		
Nominal	48.0 mm	N/App.
Bore diameter class 1 or I	48.000 to 48.006 mm	N/App.
Bore diameter class 2 or II	48.006 to 48.012 mm	N/App.
Bore diameter class 3 or III	48.012 to 48.018 mm	N/App.
Bore diameter class 4 or IIII	48.018 to 48.024 mm	N/App.
Endfloat – installed on crankshaft	0.15 to 0.30 mm	0.40 mm

* **Note:** *Bore diameter class marking stamped across each connecting rod and bearing cap.*

Crankshaft	Standard	Service limit
Main bearing journal diameter:		
Nos. 1, 2, 4 and 5 journals	54.984 to 55.008 mm	N/Av.
No. 3 journal	54.976 to 55.000 mm	N/Av.
Main bearing shell-to-journal clearance:		
Nos. 1, 2, 4 and 5 journals	0.017 to 0.041 mm	0.050 mm
No. 3 journal	0.025 to 0.049 mm	0.055 mm
Big-end bearing journal diameter	44.976 to 45.000 mm	N/Av.
Big-end bearing shell-to-journal clearance	0.021 to 0.049 mm	0.060 mm
Big-end and main bearing journal taper	0.005 mm max.	0.010 mm
Big-end and main bearing journal ovality	0.005 mm max.	0.010 mm
Endfloat	0.10 to 0.35 mm	0.45 mm
Runout	0.03 mm max.	0.04 mm

Note: *Main bearing bore diameter code numbers stamped on flange on bottom surface of main bearing ladder, at rear, flywheel end. Crankshaft main and big-end bearing journal diameter codes etched on crankshaft web, flywheel end.*

Torque wrench settings	Refer to Chapter 2A Specifications	

Diesel engine

Cylinder head		
Height	114.95 to 115.05 mm	
Gasket surface maximum warpage	0.05 mm (resurfacing permissible)	

Valves	Standard	Service limit
Valve head diameter:		
Intake	27.85 to 28.15 mm	N/Av.
Exhaust	25.85 to 26.15 mm	N/Av.
Valve overall length:		
Intake	100.4 to 100.9 mm	N/Av.
Exhaust	100.1 to 100.6 mm	N/Av.
Valve stem diameter:		
Intake	5.48 to 5.49 mm	5.45 mm
Exhaust	5.45 to 5.46 mm	5.42 mm
Valve stem-to-guide clearance – by wobble method:		
Intake	0.04 to 0.10 mm	0.16 mm
Exhaust	0.10 to 0.16 mm	0.22 mm
Valve stem-to-guide clearance – by direct measurement:		
Intake	0.02 to 0.05 mm	0.08 mm
Exhaust	0.05 to 0.08 mm	0.11 mm
Valve seat width – intake and exhaust	1.26 to 1.56 mm	2.00 mm
Valve stem installed height – intake and exhaust	40.2 to 40.4 mm	N/App.
Valve spring free length – intake and exhaust	43.54 mm	N/Av.
Valve guide bore diameter – intake and exhaust	5.51 to 5.53 mm	5.55 mm
Valve guide installed height – intake and exhaust	14.5 to 15.5 mm	N/App.

Cylinder block	Standard	Service limit
Gasket surface maximum warpage	0.07 mm max.	0.07 mm
Cylinder bore diameter – 50 mm from block top surface:*		
Bore diameter class A or I:		
X axis measurement along crankshaft axis	84.997 to 85.027 mm	85.050 mm
Y axis measurement at 90° to crankshaft axis	84.986 to 85.016 mm	85.050 mm
Bore diameter class B or II:		
X axis measurement along crankshaft axis	84.987 to 85.017 mm	85.050 mm
Y axis measurement at 90° to crankshaft axis	84.976 to 85.006 mm	85.050 mm
Oversize pistons	Oversize piston diameter +0.050 to 0.070 mm	

*** Note:** *Bore diameter class letters stamped on top surface of block, at rear, timing chain end.*

Pistons	Standard	Service limit
Skirt diameter:*		
Piston diameter class A	84.95 to 84.98 mm	84.92 mm
Piston diameter class B	84.94 to 84.97 mm	84.91 mm
Oversize piston	85.20 to 85.23 mm	N/Av.
Clearance in cylinder – cylinder bore diameter minus piston diameter (Y axis measurement):		
Original pistons	0.006 to 0.066 mm	0.066 mm
Oversize pistons	0.050 to 0.070 mm	0.070 mm
Oversizes available	+0.25 mm	
Ring groove width:		
Top ring	1.805 to 1.835 mm	1.865 mm
Second ring	2.060 to 2.080 mm	2.100 mm
Oil control ring	3.020 to 3.040 mm	3.070 mm
Gudgeon pin diameter	29.995 to 30.000 mm	29.985 mm
Gudgeon pin-to-piston clearance	0.005 to 0.016 mm	0.026 mm

*** Note:** *14 mm from bottom of skirt, at 90° to gudgeon pin axis. Piston diameter class letter stamped on each piston crown.*

Piston rings	Standard	Service limit
Ring-to-groove clearance:		
Top ring – T mark on top surface	0.07 to 0.11 mm	0.12 mm
Second ring – 2T mark on top surface	0.04 to 0.08 mm	0.10 mm
Oil control ring	0.02 to 0.06 mm	0.08 mm
Ring end gap – installed (15 to 20 mm from bottom of bore):		
Top ring – T mark on top surface	0.15 to 0.25 mm	0.47 mm
Second ring – 2T mark on top surface	0.50 to 0.65 mm	0.87 mm
Oil control ring	0.20 to 0.40 mm	0.62 mm

Connecting rods	Standard	Service limit
Gudgeon pin-to-rod clearance	0.012 to 0.025 mm	0.035 mm
Small-end bore diameter	30.012 to 30.020 mm	N/Av.
Big-end bore diameter:*		
Nominal	53.0 mm	N/App.
Bore diameter class 1 or I	53.000 to 53.006 mm	N/App.
Bore diameter class 2 or II	53.006 to 53.012 mm	N/App.
Bore diameter class 3 or III	53.012 to 53.018 mm	N/App.
Bore diameter class 4 or IIII	53.018 to 53.024 mm	N/App.
Endfloat – installed on crankshaft	0.15 to 0.30 mm	0.40 mm

* **Note:** *Bore diameter class marking stamped across each connecting rod and bearing cap.*

Crankshaft	Standard	Service limit
Main bearing journal diameter:		
Nos. 1, 2, 3 and 4 journals	59.976 to 60.000 mm	N/Av.
No. 5 journal	59.972 to 59.996 mm	N/Av.
Main bearing shell-to-journal clearance	0.021 to 0.045 mm	0.050 mm
Big-end bearing journal diameter	49.976 to 50.000 mm	N/Av.
Big-end bearing shell-to-journal clearance	0.021 to 0.051 mm	0.060 mm
Big-end and main bearing journal taper	0.005 mm max.	0.006 mm
Big-end and main bearing journal ovality	0.005 mm max.	0.006 mm
Endfloat	0.10 to 0.35 mm	0.45 mm
Runout	0.03 mm max.	0.03 mm

Note: *Main bearing bore diameter code numbers stamped on flange on bottom surface of main bearing ladder, at rear, flywheel end. Crankshaft main and big-end bearing journal diameter codes etched on crankshaft web, flywheel end.*

Torque wrench settings	Refer to Chapter 2B Specifications

1 General information

Included in this Part of Chapter 2 are details of removing the engine/transmission from the vehicle and general overhaul procedures for the cylinder head, cylinder block and all other engine internal components.

The information given ranges from advice concerning preparation for an overhaul and the purchase of new parts, to detailed step-by-step procedures covering removal, inspection, renovation and refitting of engine internal components.

After Section 6, all instructions are based on the assumption that the engine has been removed from the vehicle. For information concerning in-vehicle engine repair, as well as the removal and refitting of those external components necessary for full overhaul, refer to Chapter 2A or 2B. Ignore any preliminary dismantling operations that are no longer relevant once the engine has been removed from the vehicle.

Apart from torque wrench settings, which are given in Chapters 2A and 2B, all specifications relating to engine overhaul are at the beginning of this part of Chapter 2.

2 Engine overhaul – general information

It is not always easy to determine when, or if, an engine should be completely overhauled, as a number of factors must be considered.

High mileage is not necessarily an indication that an overhaul is needed, while low mileage does not preclude the need for an overhaul. Frequency of servicing is probably the most important consideration. An engine which has had regular and frequent oil and filter changes, as well as other required maintenance, should give many thousands of miles of reliable service. Conversely, a neglected engine may require an overhaul very early in its life.

Excessive oil consumption is an indication that piston rings, valve seals and/or valve guides are in need of attention. Make sure that oil leaks are not responsible before deciding that the rings and/or guides are worn. Perform a compression test, as described in the relevant Part of this Chapter, to determine the likely cause of the problem.

Check the oil pressure with a gauge fitted in place of the oil pressure switch, and compare it with that specified. If it is extremely low, the main and big-end bearings, and/or the oil pump, are probably worn out.

Loss of power, rough running, knocking or metallic engine noises, excessive valve gear noise, and high fuel consumption may also point to the need for an overhaul, especially if they are all present at the same time. If a complete service does not remedy the situation, major mechanical work is the only solution.

An engine overhaul involves restoring all internal parts to the specification of a new engine. During an overhaul, the pistons and the piston rings are renewed. New main and big-end bearings are generally fitted; if necessary, the crankshaft may be renewed, to restore the journals. The valves are also serviced as well, since they are usually in less-than-perfect condition at this point. While the engine is being overhauled, other components, such as the starter and alternator, can be overhauled as well. The end result should be an as-new engine that will give many trouble-free miles. **Note:** *Critical cooling system components such as the hoses, thermostat and water pump should be renewed when an engine is overhauled. The radiator should be checked carefully, to ensure that it is not clogged or leaking. Also, it is a good idea to renew the oil pump whenever the engine is overhauled.*

Before beginning the engine overhaul, read through the entire procedure, to familiarise yourself with the scope and requirements of the job. Overhauling an engine is not difficult if you follow carefully all of the instructions, have the necessary tools and equipment, and pay close attention to all specifications. It can, however, be time-consuming. Plan on the vehicle being off the road for a minimum of two weeks, especially if parts must be taken to an engineering works for repair or reconditioning. Check on the availability of parts and make sure that any necessary special tools and equipment are obtained in advance. Most work can be done with typical hand tools, although a number of precision measuring tools are required for inspecting parts to determine if they must be renewed. Often the engineering works will handle the inspection of parts and offer advice concerning reconditioning and renewal. **Note:** *Always wait until the engine has been completely dismantled, and until all components (especially the cylinder block and the crankshaft) have been inspected, before deciding what service and repair operations must be performed by an engineering works. The condition of these components will be the major factor to consider when determining whether to overhaul the original engine, or to buy a reconditioned unit. Do not, therefore, purchase parts or have overhaul work done on other components until they have been* *thoroughly inspected. As a general rule, time is the primary cost of an overhaul, so it does not pay to fit worn or sub-standard parts.*

As a final note, to ensure maximum life and minimum trouble from a reconditioned engine, everything must be assembled with care, in a spotlessly-clean environment.

3 Engine removal – methods and precautions

If you have decided that the engine must be removed for overhaul or major repair work, several preliminary steps should be taken.

Locating a suitable place to work is extremely important. Adequate work space, along with storage space for the vehicle, will be needed. If a workshop or garage is not available, at the very least, a flat, level, clean work surface is required.

Cleaning the engine compartment and engine/transmission before beginning the removal procedure will make the work more pleasant.

An engine hoist or A-frame will be necessary. Make sure the equipment is rated in excess of the combined weight of the engine and transmission. Safety is of primary importance, considering the potential hazards involved.

If this is the first time you have removed an engine, an assistant should be available. Advice and aid from someone more experienced would also be helpful. There are many instances when one person cannot simultaneously perform all of the operations required when lifting the engine out of the vehicle.

Plan the operation ahead of time. Before starting work, arrange for the hire of or obtain all of the tools and equipment you will need. Some of the equipment necessary to perform engine/transmission removal and installation safely and with relative ease (in addition to an engine hoist) is as follows: a heavy duty trolley jack, complete sets of spanners and sockets, wooden blocks, and plenty of rags and cleaning solvent for mopping-up spilled oil, coolant and fuel.

Always be extremely careful when removing and refitting the engine/transmission. Serious injury can result from careless actions. Plan ahead and take your time, and a job of this nature, although major, can be accomplished successfully.

4 Petrol engine and transmission unit – removal, separation and refitting

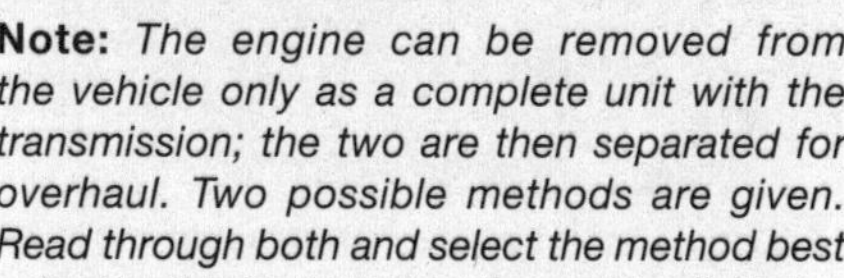

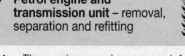

Note: *The engine can be removed from the vehicle only as a complete unit with the transmission; the two are then separated for overhaul. Two possible methods are given. Read through both and select the method best suited to the tools and equipment available.*

4.5a Unscrew terminal nuts to disconnect battery leads from engine compartment main fuse/relay box . . .

4.5b . . . and release wiring harness from retaining brackets

4.6a Open glovebox and disconnect main engine wiring harnesses . . .

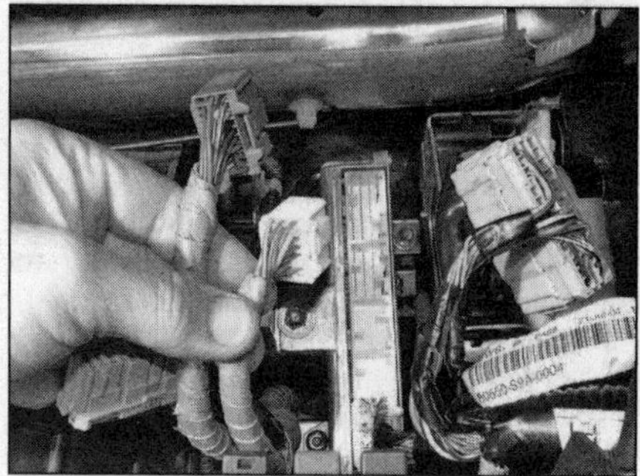

4.6b . . . and disconnect wiring from ECU . . .

Removal

Note: *The following procedure involves raising and lowering the vehicle and taking the weight of the engine/transmission unit with an engine hoist so that the front of the vehicle can be supported high enough for the front suspension subframe to be removed and the engine/transmission unit to be lowered to the ground. As well as good jacks and axle stands, and an adequate engine hoist, an engine dolly will be required so that you can move the engine/transmission around on the ground. The aid of at least one assistant will be required.*

1 Remove the bonnet (Chapter 11).

2 Unbolt and withdraw the plastic cover over the intake manifold, then depressurise the fuel system (Chapter 4A). Disconnect the fuel feed hose from the fuel rail; be prepared for fuel spillage.

3 Disconnect the battery negative lead (see *Disconnecting the battery*).

4 Remove the air cleaner assembly and intake air duct, then disconnect the throttle cable (2001 to 2004 models only) (Chapter 4A).

5 Unscrew the terminal nuts and disconnect the battery leads from the main fuse/relay box **(see illustrations)**. Disconnect the wiring to the sub fuse/relay box(es) and unbolt the earth strap from the front of the bellhousing.

6 Working inside the passenger compartment, open the glovebox and unplug the connectors to disconnect the wiring from the engine management system Electronic Control Unit (ECU) and the main engine wiring harnesses. Returning to the engine compartment, unplug the large circular rubber grommet from the bulkhead, disconnect the wiring from the accelerator pedal position sensor (where fitted) and release the wiring from any retaining clamps or ties, then pull the main engine wiring harness through the bulkhead **(see illustrations)**. Secure the wiring harness out of the way on the engine.

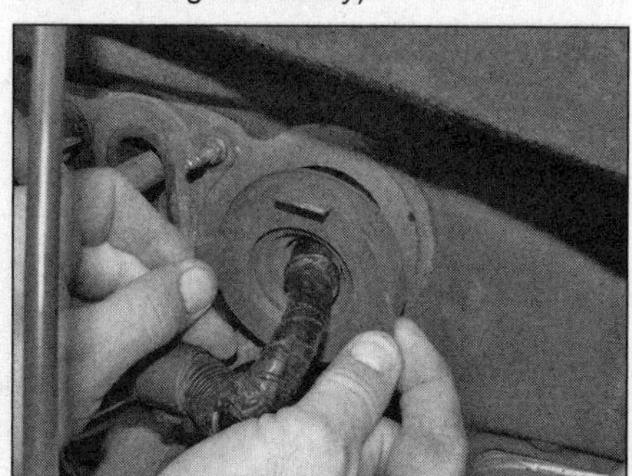

4.6c Unplug large grommet from engine compartment bulkhead . . .

4.6d . . . and pull main engine wiring harness through bulkhead to release

4.15 Disconnect propeller shaft from transfer case flange and secure clear of subframe

7 Disconnect the charcoal canister and braking system vacuum hoses from their unions at the left-hand end of the cylinder head.

8 On models with manual gearboxes, unbolt the clutch hydraulic pipe support brackets. Unbolt the clutch slave cylinder without disconnecting its hydraulic pipe and move it aside (Chapter 6).

9 On models with manual gearboxes, disconnect the gearchange cable ends from the gearbox levers (Chapter 7A). Unscrew the three bolts securing the gearchange cable bracket to the top of the gearbox, then secure the whole assembly to one side.

10 Remove the auxiliary drivebelt (Chapter 1A).

11 Unscrew its two mounting bolts and dismount the steering pump; move it to one side and secure it out of the way.

12 Remove the radiator cap and the expansion tank cap. Jack up the front of the vehicle and support it securely. Remove both front roadwheels and the engine compartment undershield (Chapter 11).

13 With reference to Chapter 1A, drain the cooling system, engine oil, and transmission fluid.

14 Disconnect the wiring from the oxygen sensors. Remove the exhaust front pipe and catalytic converter (Chapter 4A).

15 Mark the relationship of the propeller shaft front universal joint to the transfer case flange. Unscrew the Torx bolts, and move the propeller shaft to one side (Chapter 8). Support the shaft once separated – do not let it hang down **(see illustration)**.

4.30 Lowering engine/transmission unit clear of vehicle to remove it from underneath

16 Remove both front driveshafts and the intermediate shaft (Chapter 8).

17 On models with automatic transmission, disconnect the selector cable (Chapter 7B). Secure the cable clear of the transmission and subframe.

18 Disconnect the radiator bottom hose (if not already done).

19 On models with automatic transmission, unscrew the fluid filter mounting bolt, then release the hose clips and disconnect the fluid hoses from the metal pipes at the front of the transmission. Anticipate some fluid spillage as this is done – keep the hose ends turned upwards to reduce this, and plug or tape over the open connections.

20 Lower the vehicle and disconnect the heater hoses from the unions at the left-hand rear end of the cylinder head, then disconnect the radiator top hose from the cylinder head.

21 Support the weight of the engine/transmission using an engine hoist and lifting chains or straps attached to a lifting eye bolted to the right-hand end of the cylinder head and to the lifting eye bolted to the top of the transmission.

22 Ensuring that the unit is securely supported, unscrew the nuts and bolt securing the left-hand mounting bracket to the transmission.

23 Unscrew the nut and bolt securing the right-hand mounting intermediate bracket to the timing chain case/cylinder head and block bracket.

24 Jack up the front of the vehicle again, raising the engine hoist at the same time, and support it securely so that it is high enough for the engine/transmission to be removed from underneath.

25 Unscrew the three rear mounting-to-front suspension subframe bolts.

26 Unscrew the through-bolt from the front mounting.

27 Remove the front suspension subframe (Chapter 10).

28 Unscrew the air conditioning compressor's four mounting bolts. With the compressor unbolted, secure it clear of the working area without disconnecting or straining its pipes; the clutch wiring can be disconnected if required.

29 Check round the engine/transmission to make sure that everything has been disconnected from it. Slowly lower the unit about 6 inches (150 mm) and check again that nothing is fouling or still connected.

30 With the help of an assistant, manoeuvre the engine and transmission down and out of the engine compartment and lower it clear of the vehicle, then remove it from underneath **(see illustration)**.

Removal – alternative procedure

Note: *The following procedure still involves raising and lowering the vehicle to disconnect various components, but in this case the engine/transmission unit is lifted out of the vehicle. This avoids having to remove the front suspension subframe, but requires more preliminary dismantling. The aid of at least one assistant will be required.*

31 To follow this procedure, work as described above, but note the following differences:

a) *Remove the battery and the battery tray (Chapter 5A).*
b) *Remove the radiator and cooling fan assembly (Chapter 3), the outer intake manifold (Chapter 4A) and the alternator (Chapter 5A)* ***(see illustration)****.*
c) *Unscrew the air conditioning compressor's four mounting bolts. With the compressor unbolted, secure it clear of the working area without disconnecting or straining its pipes; the clutch wiring can be disconnected if required* ***(see illustrations)****.*
d) *Ensuring that the engine is securely*

4.31a Alternator (mounting bolts and connection arrowed) is easier to reach with plastic intake manifold removed first

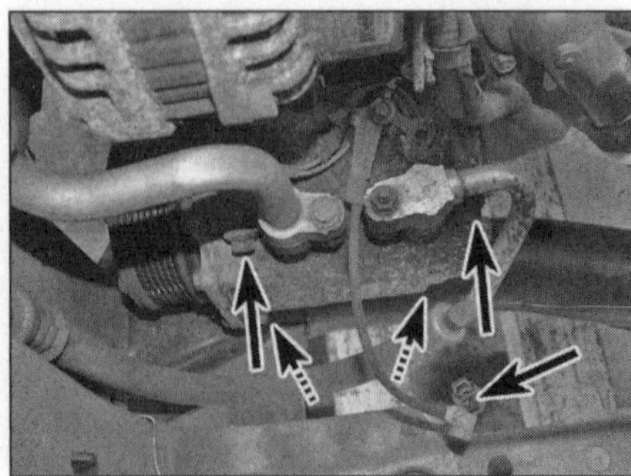
4.31b Unbolt air conditioning compressor and disconnect wiring (arrows) . . .

4.31c . . . and secure compressor clear of engine

4.31d Unscrew engine/transmission through-bolt and unbolt from inner wing

4.31e Unscrew engine/transmission rear mounting through-bolt

4.31f Lifting engine/transmission unit out of vehicle

supported by the engine hoist, unscrew the left-hand mounting through-bolt, then unscrew the three bolts and remove the mounting from the inner wing ***(see illustration)****.*

e) *Unscrew the nuts and bolt securing the right-hand mounting intermediate bracket to the timing chain case/cylinder head and block bracket and to the rubber mounting itself. Unbolt the earth lead and remove the bracket completely.*

f) *Unscrew the through-bolt from the rear mounting* ***(see illustration)****.*

g) *Unscrew the through-bolt from the front mounting.*

h) *Check round the engine/transmission that everything has been disconnected from it.*

i) *With the help of an assistant to manoeuvre the engine and transmission forwards to clear the bulkhead, lift the unit out of the engine compartment and remove it from the vehicle* ***(see illustration)****.*

Separation

32 Support the engine/transmission assembly on blocks of wood, on a workbench (or failing that, on a clean area of the workshop floor).

33 On models with manual gearboxes:

a) *Unbolt and remove the flywheel cover plate.*

b) *Unscrew the bellhousing-to-gearbox bolts.*

c) *Carefully pull the gearbox away from the engine, ensuring that the weight of the transmission is not allowed to hang on the input shaft while it is still engaged with the clutch. If necessary, carefully prise the gearbox away at first, to release the alignment dowels.*

34 On models with automatic transmission:

a) *Unbolt and remove the torque converter cover plate.*

b) *Mark the relationship of the torque converter to the driveplate.*

c) *Unscrew and remove the eight torque converter-to-driveplate bolts, turning the engine to bring each of the bolts into view.*

d) *Unbolt and remove the stiffener fitted between the engine and transmission.*

e) *Unscrew the bellhousing-to-transmission bolts.*

f) *Carefully pull the transmission away from the engine until the transmission is clear of the locating dowels. If necessary, push the torque converter back into the transmission – take care that it does not fall out as the transmission is lowered.*

g) *Either remove the torque converter or devise a method of keeping it inside the housing (such as bolting a metal strip across the bellhousing).*

35 Recover the two locating dowels, noting their fitted locations.

Reassembly

36 On models with manual gearboxes:

a) *If removed, fit the clutch components and grease the input shaft splines (see Chapter 6).*

c) *Make sure the two locating dowels are installed in the bellhousing mating face.*

d) *Slide the gearbox onto the engine so that the gearbox shaft enters the clutch. It may be necessary to 'wiggle' the gearbox slightly, to align the shaft splines with those of the clutch – if difficulty is experienced, it may mean that the clutch friction plate has not been centred (see Chapter 6). With the splines aligned, the gearbox should slide onto the two dowels, and fully up to the engine.*

e) *While an assistant holds the gearbox in place, insert two or three bellhousing-to-gearbox bolts and tighten them by hand.*

f) *Insert and tighten all the bellhousing-to-gearbox bolts to the specified torque, then refit the flywheel cover plate.*

37 On models with automatic transmission:

a) *If the torque converter was removed, refit it using a new O-ring seal. Have an assistant ready to keep the converter pressed into the housing as the transmission is refitted.*

b) *Make sure the two locating dowels are installed in the transmission mating face.*

c) *Slide the transmission onto the engine so that the torque converter seats against the driveplate; align the marks made on removal. It may be necessary to 'wiggle' the transmission slightly to align the two dowels with their locations in the engine bellhousing – with the dowels aligned, the transmission should slide fully up to the engine.*

d) *While an assistant holds the transmission in place, insert two or three bellhousing-to-transmission bolts and tighten them by hand.*

e) *Insert and tighten all the bellhousing-to-transmission bolts to the specified torque, then refit the stiffener and the torque converter cover plate.*

Refitting

38 Reconnect the lifting tackle to the lifting eyes.

39 With the aid of an assistant, carefully lift the unit into position in the engine compartment, taking care not to trap or damage any components. Raise the unit until the studs of the left- and right-hand mountings engage with their respective brackets.

40 Refit the compressor to the bracket, reconnect the clutch wiring and tighten the bolts to the specified torque.

41 Refit the front suspension subframe (if removed) as described in Chapter 10 **(see illustration)**.

42 To ensure that the unit is correctly settled on its mountings, tighten the engine/transmission mounting fasteners as described in Chapter 2A.

43 Remove the lifting tackle.

44 The remainder of the refitting procedure is a reversal of the removal sequence, noting the following points:

a) *Ensure that all wiring is correctly routed and retained and that all connectors are correctly reconnected.*

b) *Ensure that all disturbed hoses are*

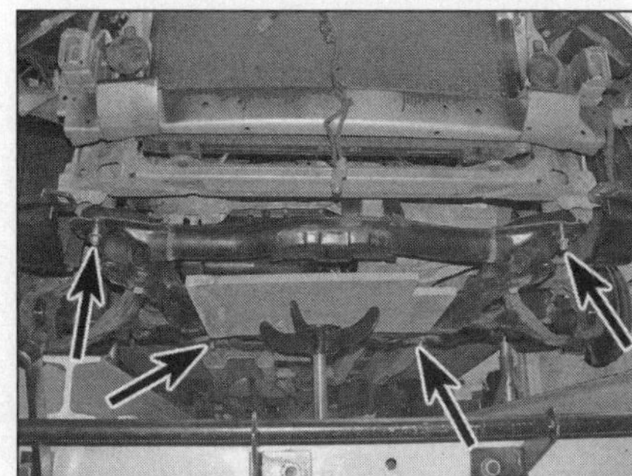
4.41 Support front suspension subframe and align on underbody, then fit new bolts (arrows) and tighten

5.4a Unscrew terminal nuts to disconnect battery leads from engine compartment main fuse/relay box . . .

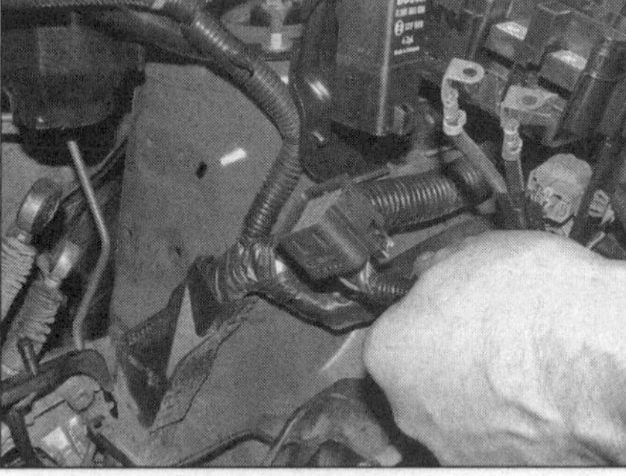

5.4b . . . disconnect glow plug control module . . .

5.4c . . . and release wiring harness from retaining brackets

5.5a Unbolt support bracket(s) securing clutch hydraulic line to battery tray mounting bracket and gearbox . . .

5.5b . . . then unbolt slave cylinder and move slave cylinder and hydraulic pipe/hose assembly clear of gearbox

correctly reconnected, and securely retained.

c) Tighten all nuts and bolts to the specified torques

d) On models with manual gearboxes, lightly grease the gearchange cable end fittings and slave cylinder pushrod end when refitting. Use new split pins and horse-shoe clips.

e) On models with automatic transmission, position the fluid hose clips 2 to 4 mm from the hose ends. Reconnect and adjust the selector cable as described in Chapter 7B.

f) Refill the gearbox/transmission with fluid (Chapter 1A).

g) Refill the engine with oil and fit a new filter (Chapter 1A).

h) Refill the cooling system (Chapter 1A).

i) Honda state that the ignition timing must be checked on refitting the engine. This is a specialist job – see Chapter 5B.

j) Honda state that the idle speed must be checked on refitting the engine. This too is a specialist job – see Chapter 1A.

k) If it is found that disconnecting the crankshaft position sensor has caused a fault code to be logged so that the engine management Malfunction Indicator warning Lamp (MIL) illuminates, the vehicle must be taken to a specialist for the fault code to be erased and for the CKP pattern data to be cleared and re-learned.

l) If the front subframe was removed, have the front wheel alignment checked.

5 Diesel engine and transmission unit – removal, separation and refitting

Note: *The engine can be removed from the vehicle only as a complete unit with the gearbox; the two are then separated for overhaul. Two methods are given. Read through both and select the method best suited to the tools and equipment available.*

Removal

Note: *The following procedure involves raising and lowering the vehicle to disconnect or refit various components so that the engine/transmission unit can be lifted out of the vehicle. The aid of at least one assistant will be required.*

1 Remove the bonnet (Chapter 11). Unscrew the four retaining nuts and remove the acoustic cover.

5.10a Remove cover under glovebox and disconnect wiring from ECU . . .

2 Remove the air cleaner assembly and intake air duct/resonator (Chapter 4B).

3 Remove the battery, battery tray and mounting bracket (Chapter 5A).

4 Unscrew the terminal nuts and disconnect the battery leads from the fuse/relay box. Disconnect the glow plug control module, unplug the two connectors to disconnect the wiring underneath the fuse/relay box and release the wiring harnesses from the retaining bracket **(see illustrations)**.

5 Unbolt the clutch hydraulic pipe support brackets. Unbolt the clutch slave cylinder without disconnecting its hydraulic pipe and move it aside (Chapter 6) **(see illustrations)**.

6 Disconnect the gearchange cable ends from the gearbox levers (Chapter 7A). Unscrew the three bolts securing the gearchange cable bracket to the top of the gearbox, then secure the whole assembly to one side.

7 Disconnect the intercooler outlet hose from the manifold air intake.

8 Disconnect the fuel feed hose from the fuel pump. Plug the hose and cap the pump union to keep fuel in and dirt out.

9 At the rear left-hand end of the cylinder head cover disconnect the fuel return hose; again, plug the hose and cap the union. Disconnect the brake vacuum servo hose from the vacuum line assembly.

10 Working inside the passenger compartment, remove the passenger's side under cover from the facia (Chapter 11) and unplug the connectors from the engine management system Electronic Control Unit (ECU). Press the two hooks on the sides of the glovebox forwards to release the stops, remove the hooks and allow the glovebox to swing down. Disconnect the main engine wiring harness, then release the harness from the two retaining brackets. Returning to the engine compartment, unplug the large circular rubber grommet from the bulkhead, disconnect the wiring from the accelerator pedal position sensor and release the wiring from any retaining clamps or ties, then unbolt the earth lead from the bodywork. Pull the wiring harness through the bulkhead **(see illustrations)**. Secure it out of the way on the engine.

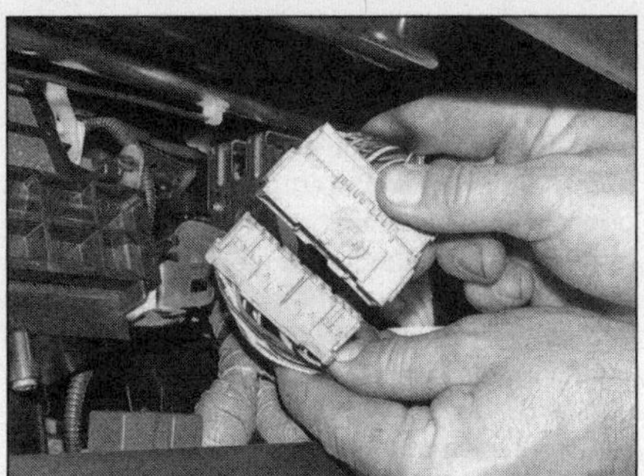

5.10b ... open glovebox and unplug connectors to disconnect wiring harness ...

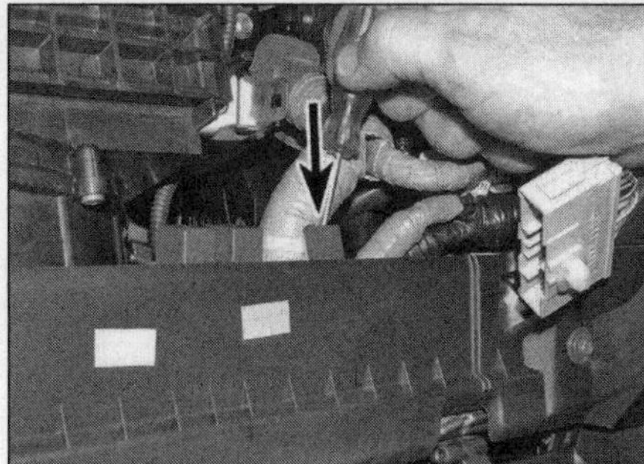

5.10c ... release wiring harness from facia support ...

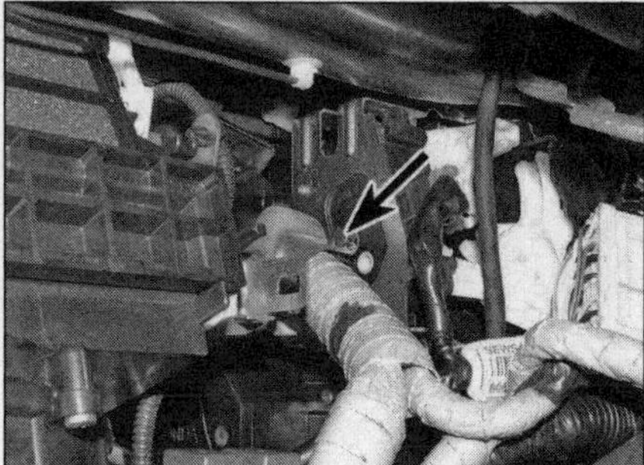

5.10d ... and from retaining bracket ...

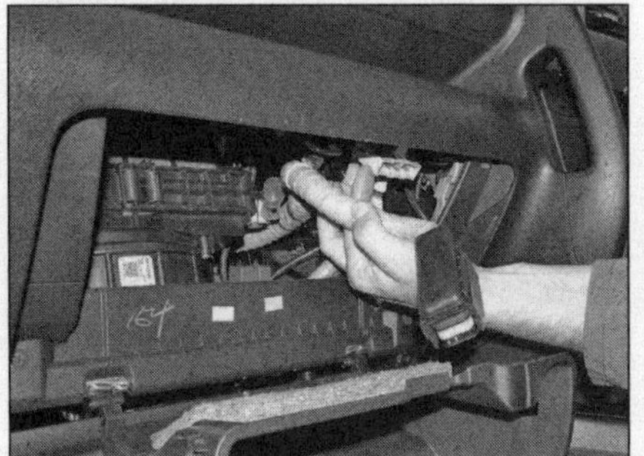

5.10e ... so that engine main wiring harness is clear ...

5.10f ... unplug large rubber grommet from bulkhead (note arrow showing correct position for refitting) ...

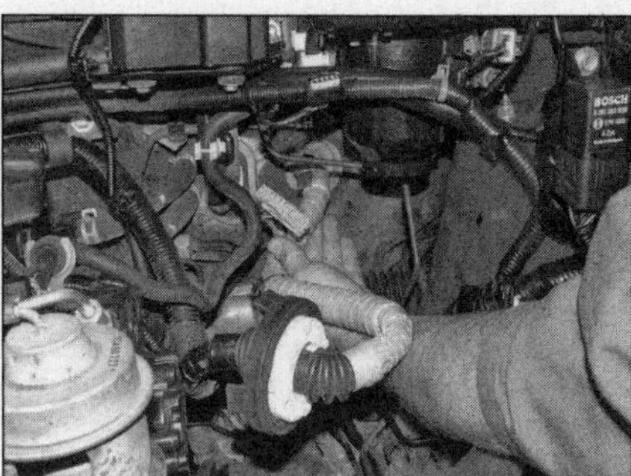

5.10g ... and pull main engine wiring harness through bulkhead to release

11 Remove the expansion tank filler cap. Jack up the front of the vehicle and support it securely on axle stands (see *Jacking and vehicle support*). Remove both front roadwheels and the engine compartment undershield (Chapter 11).

12 Drain the cooling system, engine oil, and gearbox fluid (Chapter 1B).

13 Remove both front driveshafts and intermediate shaft (Chapter 8).

14 Mark the relationship of the propeller shaft front universal joint to the transfer case flange. Unscrew the Torx bolts, and move the propeller shaft to one side (see Chapter 8). Support the shaft once separated – do not let it hang down.

15 Remove the exhaust front pipe and catalytic converter (Chapter 4B).

16 Slacken the hose clamps at each end and unbolt the turbocharger-to-intercooler pipe, then remove the turbocharger outlet hose.

17 Lower the vehicle. Remove the radiator and cooling system expansion tank (Chapter 3).

18 Remove the intercooler (Chapter 4B).

19 Remove the auxiliary drivebelt (Chapter 1B).

20 Unscrew its two mounting bolts and dismount the steering pump; move it to one side and secure it out of the way.

21 Disconnect the heater hoses from the rear left-hand end of the cylinder head cover.

22 Unscrew the air conditioning compressor's four mounting bolts. With the compressor unbolted, secure it clear of the working area without disconnecting or straining its pipes; the clutch wiring can be disconnected, if required.

23 Jack up the front of the vehicle again and support it securely.

24 Unbolt the engine rear mounting torque rod from the front suspension subframe and from the bracket on the engine and withdraw the torque rod.

25 Unscrew the two left-hand (lower) mounting-to-front suspension subframe bolts.

26 Lower the vehicle and support the weight of the engine/transmission using an engine hoist and lifting chains or straps attached to a lifting eye bolted to the right-hand end of the cylinder head and to the lifting eye bolted to the top rear of the gearbox.

27 Make sure the unit is adequately supported, then unscrew the left-hand (upper) mounting-to-body bracket through-bolt and the three bolts securing the mounting's bracket to the inner wing. Withdraw the mounting bracket.

28 Unscrew the earth lead-to-mounting clamp bolt. Unscrew the two nuts and the bolt securing the mounting to the gearbox. Remove the mounting.

29 Unscrew the three bolts securing the engine right-hand mounting torque rod to the body and mounting and remove the torque rod.

30 Unscrew the two nuts and the bolt securing the intermediate bracket to the timing chain case/cylinder head and block bracket, then unscrew the bolt securing the intermediate bracket to the mounting centre and withdraw the bracket.

31 Check that everything has been disconnected. Slowly lift the unit about 6 inches (150 mm) and check again that nothing is fouling or still connected.

5.10h Note how plastic insert fits into grommet ...

5.10i ... and ensure grommet is correctly refitted to prevent water leaks into passenger compartment

5.32 Lifting engine/transmission unit out of vehicle

32 With the help of an assistant, lift the unit out of the engine compartment and remove it from the vehicle **(see illustration)**.

Removal – alternative procedure

Note: *The procedure in Section 4 for removal and refitting of the petrol engine involves removing the front suspension subframe and lowering the engine/transmission unit to the ground to be removed from under the vehicle; the same can be done with the diesel engine. Depending on the equipment available, it may well be a simpler method than that given above. As well as good jacks and axle stands, an engine hoist will be required and an engine dolly so that you can move the engine/gearbox around on the ground.*

Separation

33 Support the assembly on suitable blocks of wood, on a workbench (or failing that, on a clean area of the workshop floor).

34 Unscrew the engine bellhousing-to-gearbox bolts.

35 Carefully withdraw the gearbox from the engine, ensuring that the weight of the gearbox is not allowed to hang on the input shaft. If necessary, carefully prise the gearbox away at first, to release the alignment dowels.

36 Recover the two locating dowels, noting their fitted locations.

Reassembly

37 If removed, fit the clutch components (Chapter 6).

38 Grease the gearbox input shaft splines (Chapter 6).

39 Make sure the two locating dowels are installed in the bellhousing mating face.

40 Raise the gearbox on a jack, then slide it onto the engine so that the gearbox shaft enters the clutch. It may be necessary to 'wiggle' the gearbox slightly, to align the shaft splines with those of the clutch – if difficulty is experienced it may mean that the clutch friction plate has not been centred (see Chapter 6). With the splines aligned, the gearbox should slide onto the two dowels, and fully up to the engine.

41 While an assistant holds the gearbox in place, insert two or three engine bellhousing-to-gearbox bolts and tighten them by hand.

42 Insert and tighten all the engine bellhousing-to-gearbox bolts to the specified torque setting.

Refitting

43 Reconnect the lifting tackle to the engine lifting eyes.

44 With the aid of an assistant, carefully lift the unit and lower it into position in the engine compartment, manipulating the hoist and lifting tackle as necessary, taking care not to trap or damage any components.

45 To ensure that the unit is correctly settled on its mountings, tighten the engine/gearbox mounting fasteners as described in Chapter 2B.

46 Remove the lifting chains and lifting eye.

47 The remainder of the refitting procedure is a reversal of the removal sequence, noting the following points:

a) Ensure that all wiring is correctly routed and retained and that all connectors are correctly reconnected.
b) Ensure that all disturbed hoses are correctly reconnected and securely retained.
c) Tighten all nuts/bolts to the specified torque.
d) Lightly grease the gearchange cable end fittings and slave cylinder pushrod end when refitting. Use new split pins and horse-shoe clips when refitting the cables.
e) Refill the gearbox with fluid (Chapter 1B).
f) Refill the engine with oil and fit a new filter (Chapter 1B).
g) Refill the cooling system (Chapter 1B).
h) Prime the fuel system when the fuel feed and return hoses have been reconnected (Chapter 4B).
i) Honda state that the idle speed must be checked on refitting the engine. This is a specialist job – see Chapter 1B.
j) If it is found that disconnecting the various system components has caused a fault code to be logged so that the engine management Malfunction Indicator warning Lamp (MIL) illuminates, the vehicle must be taken to a specialist for the fault codes to be erased.
k) If the front subframe was removed, have the front wheel alignment checked.

6 Engine overhaul – dismantling sequence

1 It is much easier to dismantle and work on the engine if it is mounted on a portable engine stand. These stands can often be hired from a tool hire shop. Before the engine is mounted on a stand, the flywheel/driveplate should be removed, so that the stand bolts can be tightened into the end of the cylinder block.

2 If a stand is not available, it is possible to dismantle the engine with it blocked up on a sturdy workbench, or on the floor. Be extra careful not to tip or drop the engine when working without a stand.

3 If you are going to obtain a reconditioned engine, many of the external components must be removed first, to be transferred to the new engine (just as they will if you are doing a complete engine overhaul yourself). These components may include the following – check carefully beforehand with the engine supplier exactly what they do and don't provide:

a) Auxiliary drivebelt, tensioner and pulleys (Chapter 1A or 1B).
b) Intake and exhaust manifolds – including EGR equipment and turbocharger (Chapter 4A or 4B).
c) Starter motor and alternator (Chapter 5A).
d) Water pump (Chapter 3).
e) Thermostat and cooling system pipes and hoses (Chapter 3).
f) Air conditioning compressor bracket.
g) Fuel system components (Chapter 4A or 4B).
h) Wiring harness and all electrical switches and sensors and their mounting brackets.
i) Engine mountings
j) Flywheel/driveplate
k) Oil cooler (diesel engines) (Chapter 2B).
l) Water pump housing (petrol engines) or oil filter/oil cooler/water pump housing (diesel engines) (Chapter 2A or 2B).

Note: *When removing the external components from the engine, pay close attention to details that may be helpful or important during refitting. Note the fitted position of gaskets, seals, spacers, pins, washers, bolts, and other small items.*

4 Some engine reconditioners may include components such as the timing chain and balancer/oil pump drive chain and related items, camshafts and cam followers and i-VTEC and VTC systems components or hydraulic tappets (as applicable), others may not. Check carefully before making your decision, and certainly before parting with any money or sending off your old engine.

5 If you are obtaining a 'short' engine (which consists of the engine cylinder block, crankshaft, pistons and connecting rods all assembled), then the cylinder head, sump, balancer assembly/oil pump, and timing and balancer assembly/oil pump drive chains will have to be removed also.

6 If you are planning a complete overhaul, the engine can be dismantled, and the internal components removed, in the order given below, referring to the relevant Part of this Chapter unless otherwise stated.

a) Intake and exhaust manifolds (Chapter 4A or 4B).
b) Timing chain, sprockets and tensioner.
c) Camshafts.
d) Cam follower assembly.
e) Cylinder head.
f) Flywheel.
g) Sump.
h) Balancer assembly/oil pump.
i) Piston/connecting rod assemblies.
j) Crankshaft.

7 Before beginning the dismantling and overhaul procedures, make sure that you have all the tools necessary.

7 Cylinder head – dismantling

Note: *New and reconditioned cylinder heads are available from the manufacturer, and from engine overhaul specialists. Be aware that some specialist tools are required for the dismantling and inspection procedures, and new components may not be readily available. It may therefore be more practical and economical for the home mechanic to purchase a reconditioned head, rather than dismantle, inspect and recondition the original head.*

1 On petrol engines remove the camshafts and cam follower assembly, then remove the cylinder head from the engine. Remove the spark plugs.

2 On diesel engines, remove the glow plugs (Chapter 5C) and injectors (Chapter 4B). Remove the camshafts, camshaft carrier and cam followers and hydraulic tappets from the cylinder head, then remove the cylinder head from the engine.

3 On all engines, using a valve spring compressor, compress each valve spring in turn until the split collets can be removed. Release the compressor, and lift off the spring retainer and spring. Using a pair of pliers, carefully extract the valve stem oil seal from the valve guide **(see illustrations)**.

4 If, when the valve spring compressor is screwed down, the spring retainer refuses to free and expose the split collets, gently tap the top of the tool, directly over the retainer, with a light hammer. This will free the retainer.

5 Pull the valve out of the head through the combustion chamber. If the valve binds in the guide (won't pull through), push it back into the head and deburr the edge of the collet groove with a fine file or fine emery cloth **(see illustration)**. It is essential that each valve is stored together with its collets, retainer, spring and spring seat. The valves should also be kept in their correct sequence, unless they are so badly worn that they are to be renewed **(see Haynes Hint)**.

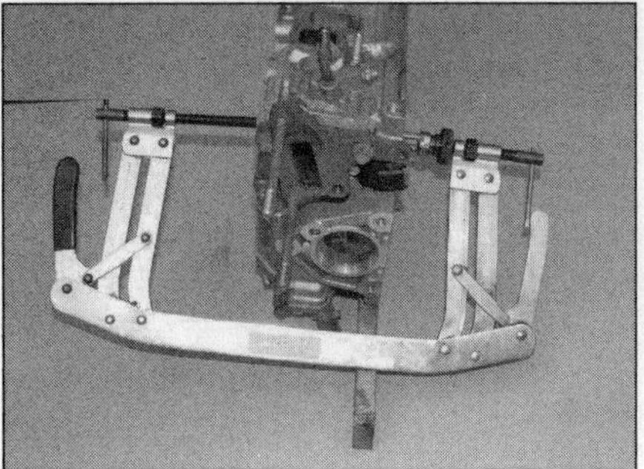

7.3a Using a valve spring compressor to compress a valve spring

7.3b Carefully remove valve stem oil seals from valve guides

7.5 If a valve won't slide easily through its guide, use fine file or emery cloth to deburr edge of collet groove

If the components are to be refitted, place each valve and its associated components in a labelled polythene bag or similar small container, and mark the bag/container with the relevant valve number to ensure that it is refitted in its original location.

8 Cylinder head and valves – cleaning and inspection

1 Thorough cleaning of the cylinder head and valve components, followed by a detailed inspection, will enable you to decide how much valve service work must be carried out during the engine overhaul. **Note:** *If the engine has been severely overheated, it is best to assume that the cylinder head is warped – check carefully for signs of this.*

Cleaning

2 Scrape away all traces of old gasket material from the cylinder head.

3 Scrape away the carbon from the combustion chambers and ports, then wash the cylinder head thoroughly with paraffin or a suitable solvent.

4 Scrape off any heavy carbon deposits that may have formed on the valves, then use a power-operated wire brush to remove deposits from the valve heads and stems.

Inspection

Note: *Be sure to perform all the following inspection procedures before concluding that the services of a machine shop or engine overhaul specialist are required. Make a list of all items that require attention.*

Cylinder head

5 Inspect the head very carefully for cracks, evidence of coolant leakage, and other damage. If cracks are found, a new cylinder head should be obtained.

6 Use a straight-edge and feeler blades to check that the cylinder head surface is not distorted **(see illustration)**. If it is, it may be possible to resurface it, provided that on petrol engines the cylinder head is not reduced to less than the minimum specified height. On diesel engines resurfacing is permissible provided that the height of the cylinder head remains within the specified range.

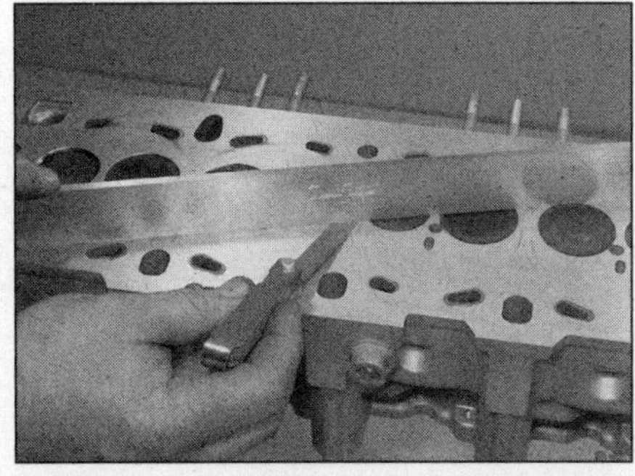

8.6 Use straight-edge and feeler blades to check cylinder head surface for distortion

7 Examine the valve seats in each of the combustion chambers. If they are severely pitted, cracked or burned, then they will need to be recut by an engine overhaul specialist. If they are only slightly pitted, this can be removed by grinding-in the valve heads and seats with fine valve-grinding compound, as described below. If any of the seats is so badly damaged or worn that it cannot be recut, the cylinder head must be renewed.

8 Check valve seat wear by inserting each valve into its relevant guide. Measure the projected height of the valve stem above the cylinder head surface **(see illustration)**. If any measurement exceeds the specified limit, repeat the check with a new valve. If the measurement still exceeds the specified limit, then the valve seat is excessively worn and the cylinder head must be renewed.

9 If the valve guides are worn (indicated by a side-to-side motion of the valve, and accompanied by excessive blue smoke in the exhaust when running) new guides must be fitted. Measure the diameter of the existing

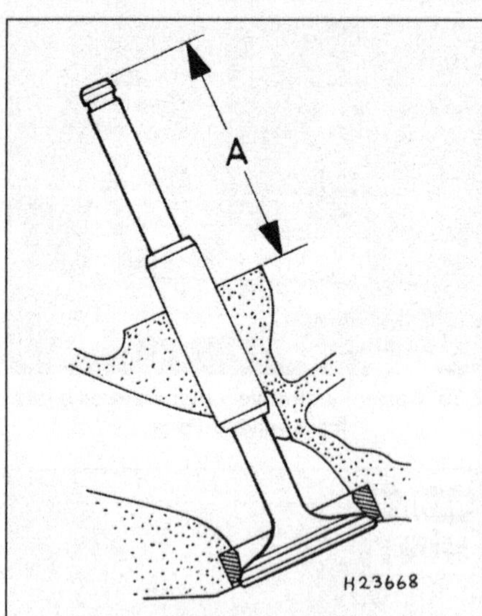

8.8 Valve stem installed height measurement (A)

valve stems (see below) and the bore of the guides, then calculate the clearance and compare the result with the specified value. If using the wobble method to assess valve stem-to-guide clearance, slide each valve out of its guide about 10 mm **(see illustration)**. If the clearance is not within the specified limits, renew the valves and/or guides as necessary.

10 The renewal of valve guides is best carried out by an engine overhaul specialist.

11 If the valve seats are to be recut this must be done only after the guides have been renewed.

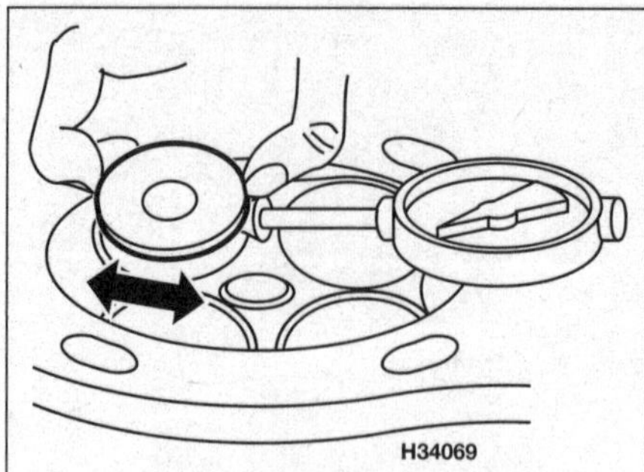

8.9 Valve stem-to-guide clearance assessed using wobble method – valve 10 mm out of guide

Valves

12 Examine the head of each valve for pitting, burning, cracks and general wear, and check the valve stem for scoring and wear ridges. Rotate the valve, and check for any obvious indication that it is bent. Look for pitting and excessive wear on the tip of each valve stem. Renew any valve that shows any such signs of wear or damage.

13 If the valve appears satisfactory at this stage, measure the valve stem diameter at several points using a micrometer **(see illustration)**. Any significant difference in the readings obtained indicates wear of the valve stem. Should any of these conditions be apparent, the valve(s) must be renewed.

14 If the valves are in satisfactory condition, they should be ground (lapped) into their respective seats, to ensure a smooth gas-tight seal. If the seat is only lightly pitted, or if it has been recut, fine grinding compound only should be used to produce the required finish. Coarse valve-grinding compound should not be used unless a seat is badly burned or deeply pitted; if it is that bad the seat should probably be recut anyway.

15 Valve grinding is carried out as follows. Place the cylinder head upside-down on a bench.

16 Smear a trace of the appropriate grade of valve-grinding compound on the seat face, and press a suction grinding tool onto the valve head. With a semi-rotary action, grind the valve head to its seat, lifting the valve occasionally to redistribute the grinding compound **(see illustration)**. A light spring placed under the valve head will greatly ease this operation.

17 If coarse grinding compound is being used, work only until a dull, matt even surface is produced on both the valve seat and the valve, then wipe off the used compound and repeat the process with fine compound. When a smooth unbroken ring of light grey matt finish is produced on both the valve and seat, the grinding operation is complete. Do not grind in the valves any further than absolutely necessary, or the seat will be prematurely sunk into the cylinder head.

18 When all the valves have been ground-in, carefully wash off all traces of grinding compound using paraffin or a suitable solvent and measure the valve stem installed heights (see paragraph 8) to ensure that none of the seats has been too deeply sunk into the cylinder head. If any of the seats is so over-ground that this measurement is excessive, the cylinder head must be renewed.

19 Examine the valve springs for signs of damage and discoloration. The condition of each spring can be judged by measuring its free length. Stand each spring on a flat surface, and check it for squareness **(see illustrations)**. If any of the springs are less than the specified free length or are damaged or distorted, obtain a complete new set of springs.

8.13 Use a micrometer to measure valve stem diameter

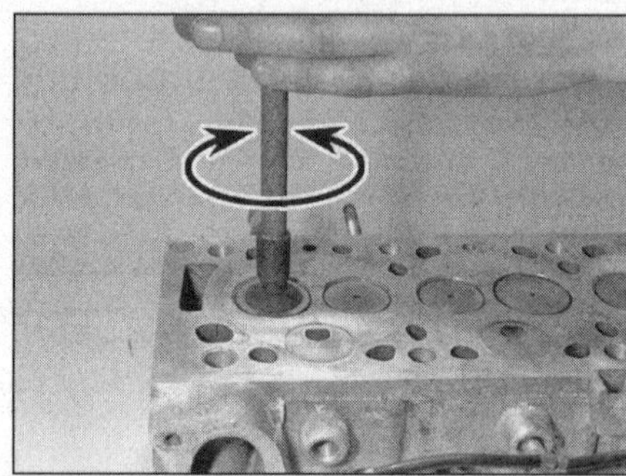

8.16 Grinding-in a valve seat

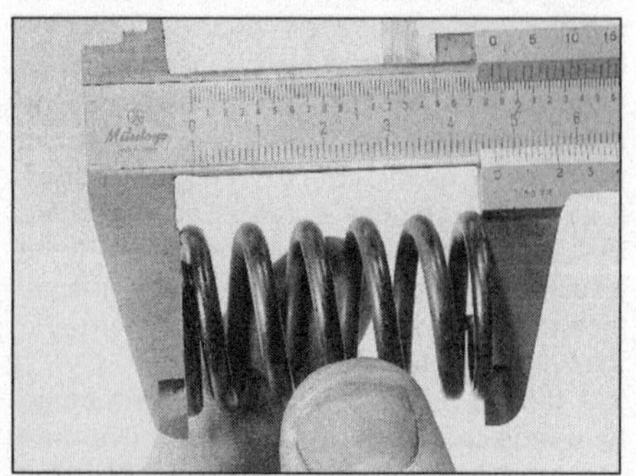

8.19a Measuring valve spring free length

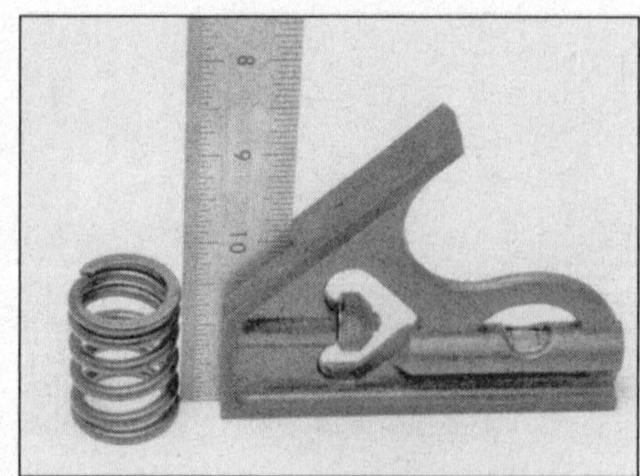

8.19b Checking valve spring squareness

9 Cylinder head – reassembly

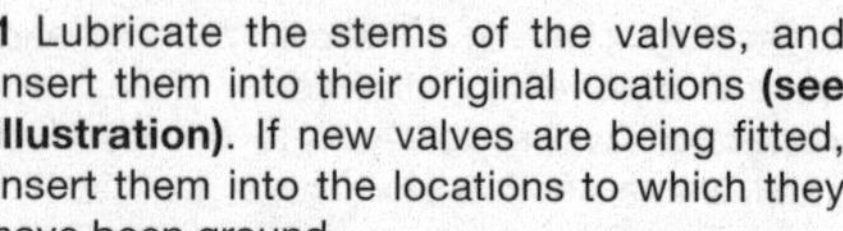

1 Lubricate the stems of the valves, and insert them into their original locations **(see illustration)**. If new valves are being fitted, insert them into the locations to which they have been ground.

2 Working on the first valve, fit the spring seat followed by the seal protector (where supplied), dip the new valve stem seal in fresh engine oil, then carefully locate it over the valve and onto the guide. The intake valve seals have white springs and the exhaust valve seals have black springs; they are not interchangeable. Take care not to damage the seal as it is passed over the valve stem. Use a

9.1 Oil valve stems and insert valves into their original locations

9.2a Fit spring seat . . .

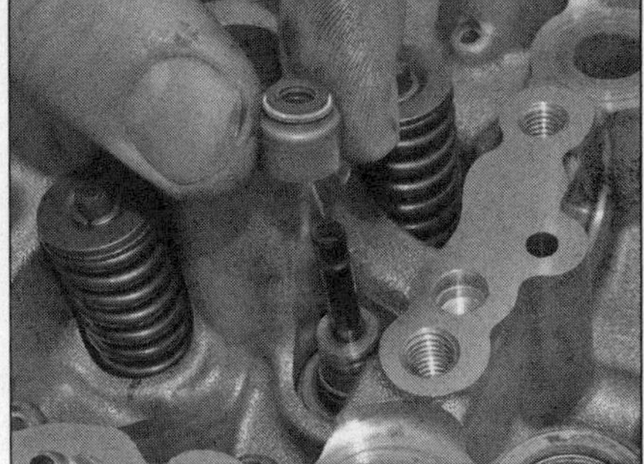

9.2b . . . then locate seal (check colour of spring) over guide . . .

9.2c . . . and using a socket (or similar) press seal into place

9.3a Fit valve spring . . .

9.3b . . . followed by retainer

suitable socket or metal tube to press the seal firmly onto the guide **(see illustrations)**.

3 Locate the spring over the seal; on petrol engines, the springs must be fitted with their closely-wound coils towards the cylinder head. Fit the spring retainer **(see illustrations)**.

4 Compress the valve spring, and locate the split collets in the recess in the valve stem **(see illustration and Haynes Hint)**. Release the compressor, then repeat the procedure on the remaining valves.

5 With all the valves installed, using a hammer and interposed block of wood, lightly tap the end of each valve stem to settle the components **(see illustration)**.

6 On petrol engines, working as described in Part A, refit the cylinder head to the engine and install the cam follower assembly and camshafts. Refit the spark plugs loosely to prevent dirt or small objects dropping into the combustion chamber (see Chapter 1A)

7 On diesel engines, working as described in Part B, refit the cylinder head to the engine and install the cam followers and hydraulic tappets, camshaft carrier, and camshafts. Refit the injectors and glow plugs as described in Chapters 4B and 5C.

10 Piston/connecting rod assembly – removal

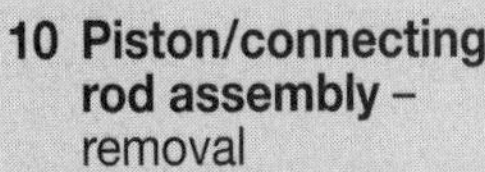

1 Referring to Part A or B of this Chapter, remove the cylinder head and sump, then unbolt the balancer assembly/oil pump from the lower crankcase/main bearing ladder.

2 Unbolt the baffle plate(s) from the lower crankcase/main bearing ladder **(see illustration)**.

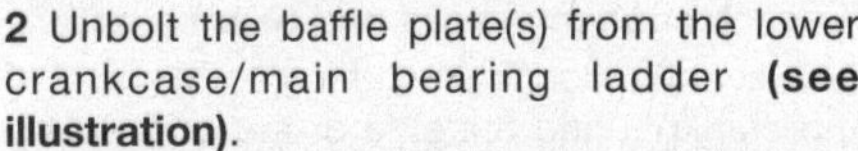

3 Remove the ridge of carbon from the top of each cylinder bore. If there is a pronounced wear ridge at the top of any bore, indicating excessive bore wear, it may be necessary to remove it with a scraper or ridge reamer, to avoid piston damage during removal **(see illustration)**.

9.4 Compress valve spring and retainer and locate collets in position

HAYNES HiNT

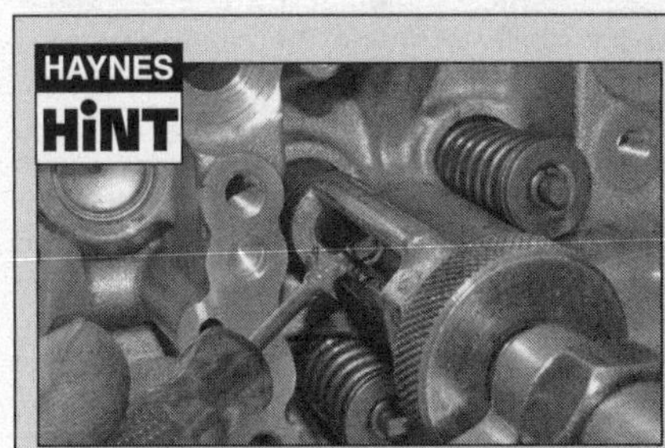

Use a dab of grease to hold the collets in position on the valve stem whilst the spring compressor is released.

9.5 Lightly tap end of each valve stem to settle components

10.2 Remove baffle plate from base of lower crankcase/main bearing ladder

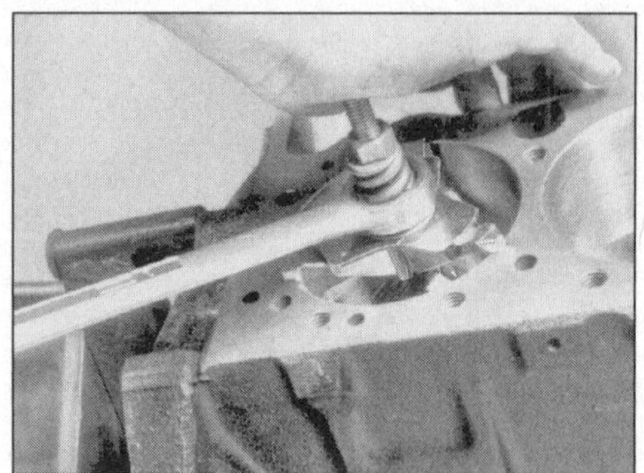

10.3 Ridge reamer being used to remove wear ridge from top of cylinder bore, before trying to remove piston/connecting rod

10.4b . . . and connecting rod big-end bearing cap with its respective cylinder number prior to removal

4 Using a hammer and centre punch, paint or similar, mark each connecting rod big-end bearing cap with its respective cylinder number on the flat, machined surface provided; make the marks in such a way that there is no possibility of fitting the caps the wrong way around on refitting **(see illustrations)**. If the engine has been dismantled before, note carefully any identifying marks made previously, but note that the number or marking etched across each connecting rod and bearing cap (and facing to the front, on the engines dismantled for the workshop project) is the big-end bearing bore diameter class marking, not a cylinder-identifying number. Note that No. 1 cylinder is at the timing chain end of the engine.

5 Turn the crankshaft to bring pistons Nos. 1 and 4 to BDC (Bottom Dead Centre).

6 Use feeler blades to measure the gap between the machined surface on the web of the crankpin and the side of the connecting rod big-end bearing **(see illustration)**. If connecting rod endfloat is greater than the specified service limit, the connecting rod or crankshaft must be renewed.

7 Unscrew and remove No. 1 big-end bearing cap bolts and withdraw the cap, complete with bearing shell, from the connecting rod. **Note:** *On petrol engines, the big-end caps are located on the connecting rods by dowels. Do not tap the caps sideways in an attempt to remove them. On diesel engines, 'cracked' connecting rods are used in which rod and cap align precisely, one way only, without the need for locating dowel pins*. If the bearing shells are to be re-used, tape the cap and the shell together. If only the bearing shells are being attended to, push the connecting rod up and off the crankpin, ensuring that the connecting rod big-ends do not mark the cylinder bore walls and that the piston-cooling oil jet (diesel engine only) is not bent or damaged, then remove the upper bearing shell **(see illustration)**. Keep the cap, bolts and bearing shells together in their correct sequence.

10.4a Use paint, or typist's correction fluid, to mark each connecting rod big-end bearing cap . . .

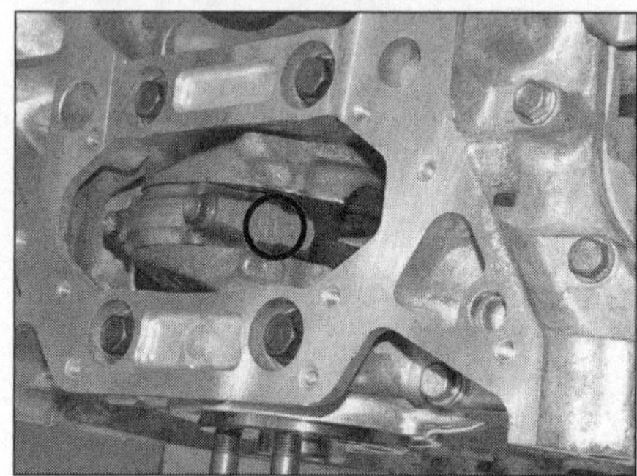

10.4c Note big-end bearing bore diameter class marking etched across front face of each connecting rod and bearing cap

10.6 Measuring connecting rod endfloat

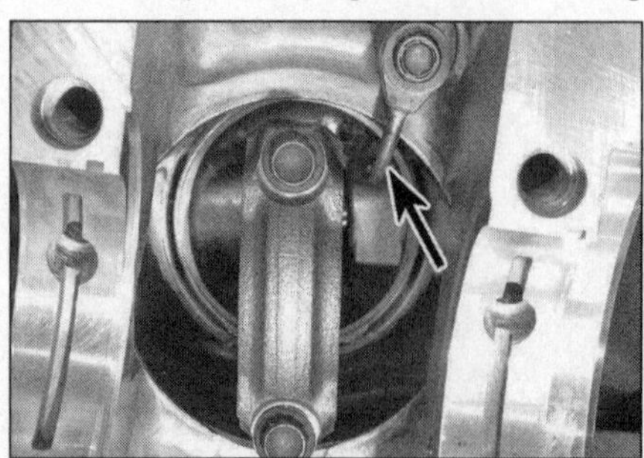

10.7 Take care not to damage piston-cooling oil jets (diesel engine only) when removing/refitting piston/connecting rod

8 To remove the piston/connecting rod assembly completely, using a hammer handle and again ensuring that the piston-cooling oil jet is not bent or damaged, push the piston up through the bore, and remove it from the top of the cylinder block. Recover the bearing shell, and tape it to the connecting rod for safekeeping.

9 Loosely refit the big-end cap to the connecting rod and secure with the bolts – this will help to keep the components in their correct locations, so that they are all kept together as a matched set.

10 Remove No. 4 piston assembly in the same way.

11 Turn the crankshaft through 180° to bring pistons Nos. 2 and 3 to BDC (Bottom Dead Centre), and remove them in the same way.

11 Crankshaft – removal

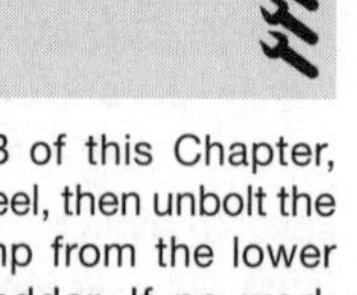

1 Referring to Part A or B of this Chapter, remove the sump and flywheel, then unbolt the balancer assembly/oil pump from the lower crankcase/main bearing ladder. If no work is to be done on the pistons and connecting rods, the cylinder head can be left in position; if they are to be removed, then the cylinder head must be removed first.

2 Unbolt the baffle plate(s) from the cylinder block.

3 Remove the piston and connecting rod assemblies as described in Section 10. If no work is to be done on the pistons and connecting rods, unbolt the caps and push the pistons far enough up the bores so that the connecting rods are clear of the crankshaft journals.

4 Check the crankshaft endfloat as described in Section 14, then proceed as follows:

5 Working in the **reverse** of the sequence shown in illustration 18.9a, progressively unscrew the lower crankcase/main bearing ladder-to-cylinder block 8 mm bolts by a turn at a time. Remove all bolts, keeping them in the correct fitted order.

6 Working in the **reverse** of the sequence shown in illustration 18.11, progressively unscrew the lower crankcase/main bearing ladder-to-cylinder block 10 mm (main bearing cap) bolts by a one-third of a turn at a time. Remove all bolts, keeping them in the correct fitted order.

7 Withdraw the lower crankcase/main bearing ladder. Note the two locating dowels at each bearing location, plus the large single dowel, and the main bearing shells, which should be removed from the ladder and stored in their correct fitted order **(see illustration)**.

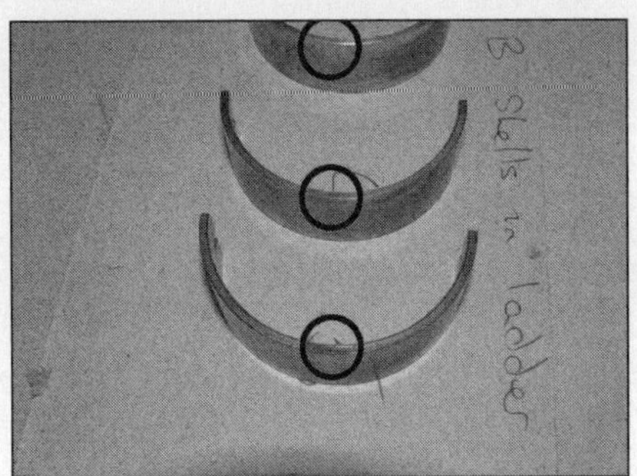

11.7 Remove bearing shells and store in their correct fitted order – note colour-coding

11.8a Remove the crankshaft

11.8b On diesel engines, crankshaft position sensor pulse plate can be unbolted if required

8 Carefully lift out the crankshaft, taking care not to displace the upper main bearing shells and being careful not to mark or damage the journals or damage the crankshaft position sensor pulse plate (diesel engines only). Remove and discard the oil seal. If necessary, the pulse plate can be unbolted **(see illustrations)**.

9 Withdraw the two thrustwashers from the No. 4 main bearing upper location. Noting the position of the grooved shells, remove the upper main bearing shells, which must be kept with their correct respective partners from the main bearing ladder so that all shells can be identified and (if necessary) refitted in their original locations.

12 Cylinder block – cleaning and inspection

Cleaning

1 Remove all external components and electrical switches/sensors from the block.

2 Remove the water pump housing (petrol engines) or the oil filter/oil cooler/water pump housing (diesel engines) – refer to Chapter 2A or 2B. Remove the water outlet.

3 Remove all oil gallery and coolant passage core plugs fitted. Most are threaded, with square- or hexagon-shaped apertures so that they can be unscrewed using the appropriate key. The plugs are usually very tight – use only good-quality tools to remove and refit them and discard the sealing washers – these must be renewed whenever the plugs are disturbed. For complete cleaning, the punched-in core plugs should also, ideally, be removed. Drill a small hole in the plug, then insert a self-tapping screw into the hole. Pull out the plug by pulling on the screw with a pair of grips, or by using a slide hammer. Carefully clean the plug threads and recesses in the casting.

4 On diesel engines, undo the retaining bolts and remove each piston-cooling oil jet from inside the cylinder block. Wash each jet thoroughly in solvent to clean its passages.

5 Check the piston-cooling oil jets **(see illustrations)**. If any has a damaged or bent nozzle, it must be renewed. Check that a 3 mm or one-eighth inch drill bit can be inserted into the oil intake (nominal diameter 3.2 mm) and that the check ball moves smoothly through a stroke of about 2 mm; if the necessary equipment is available apply air pressure and check that the check ball opens at the specified pressure (Chapter 2B Specifications). Check that a 1.5 mm or one-sixteenth inch drill bit can be inserted into the jet itself (nominal diameter 1.8 mm).

6 On all engines, thoroughly clean the mating surfaces of the cylinder block/crankcase and the lower crankcase/main bearing ladder, taking care not to damage the surfaces. Clean any oil or old sealant from the mating surfaces and from the bolt holes and threads. Note that the crankshaft main bearing bore diameter code letters or numbers are marked on the bottom surface of the lower crankcase/main bearing ladder at the rear of the flywheel end; be very careful not to scrub so hard that these are erased. Similarly, do not scrub out the cylinder bore diameter size group markings stamped on the top of the timing chain end of the cylinder block, at the front (petrol engines) or rear (diesel engines).

7 If the castings are dirty they should be steam-cleaned.

8 If the castings are not very dirty, you can do an adequate cleaning job with hot water, detergent and a stiff brush. Take plenty of time, and do a thorough job. Regardless of the cleaning method used, be sure to clean all oil holes and galleries very thoroughly, and to dry all components well. Lightly oil the cylinder bores to prevent rusting.

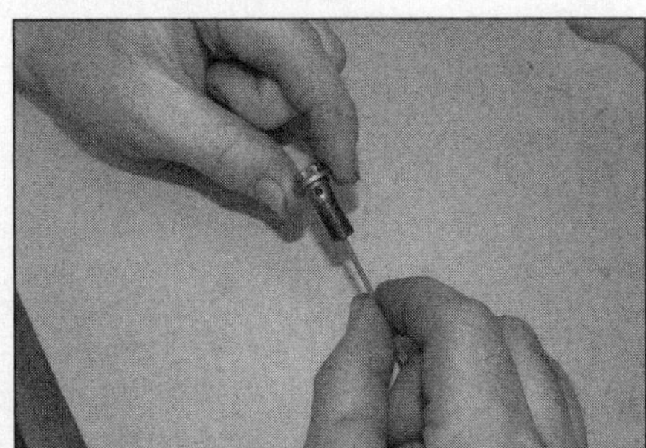

12.5a Check piston-cooling oil jets (diesel engine only) – ensure intake is clear and check ball is free to move correctly . . .

9 All threaded holes must be clean, to ensure accurate torque readings during reassembly. To clean the threads, use an old toothbrush, a small bottle brush or a small wire brush. Remove deposits of sludge and plugs and beads of old sealant using a finely-pointed instrument, but take care not to scratch the casting. If possible, use compressed air to clear the holes of debris produced by this operation. A good alternative is to inject aerosol-applied water-dispersant lubricant into each hole, using the long spout usually supplied.

Warning: Wear eye protection when cleaning out these holes in this way.

10 After the castings are returned from any resurfacing, reboring or other machining work, clean all oil holes and oil galleries one more time. Flush all internal passages with warm water until the water runs clear. Dry thoroughly, and apply a light film of oil to all mating surfaces, to prevent rusting. Also oil the cylinder bores. If you have access to compressed air, use it to speed up the drying process, and to blow out all the oil holes and galleries.

Warning: Wear eye protection when using compressed air.

11 Refit all oil gallery and coolant passage core plugs that were removed. Fit new sealing washers to the threaded plugs and tighten them securely to the torque wrench settings specified. Similarly, apply suitable sealant to new core plugs and drive them into the casting with a close-fitting tube or socket.

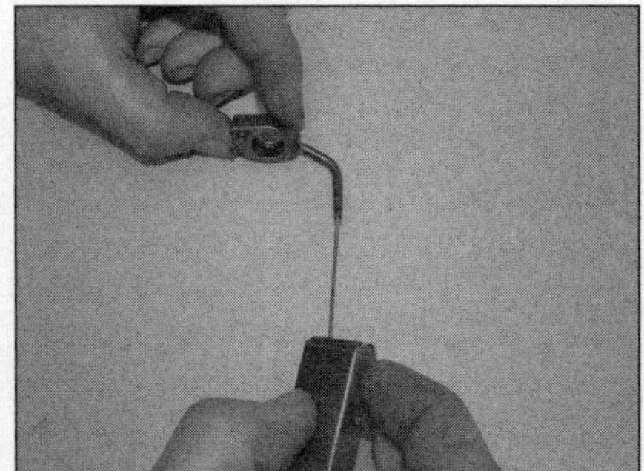

12.5b . . . and that jet nozzle is clear

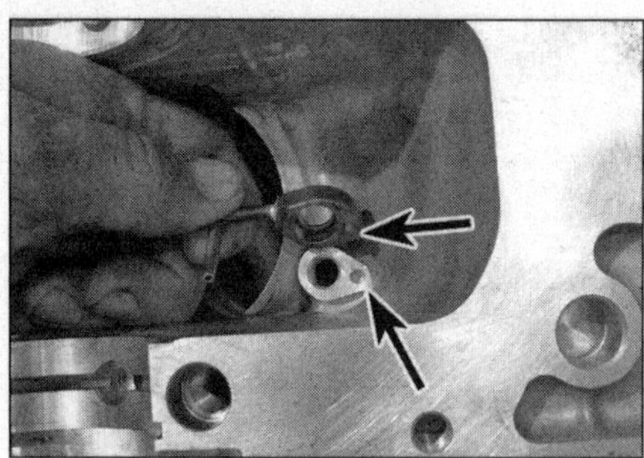

12.12 Align piston-cooling oil jet locating dowel with hole in cylinder block (diesel engine only)

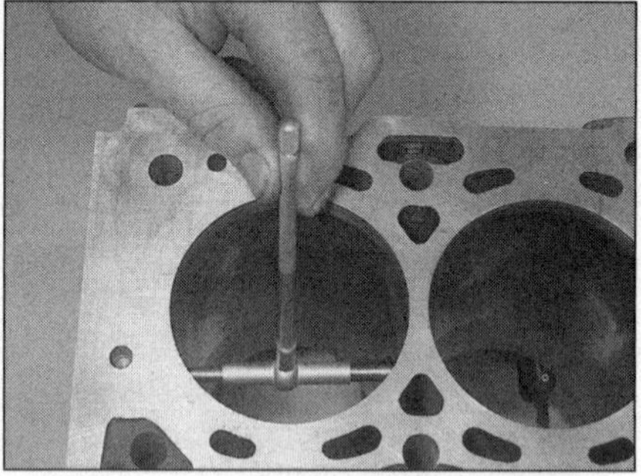

12.16a Use an internal micrometer to measure cylinder bore diameter

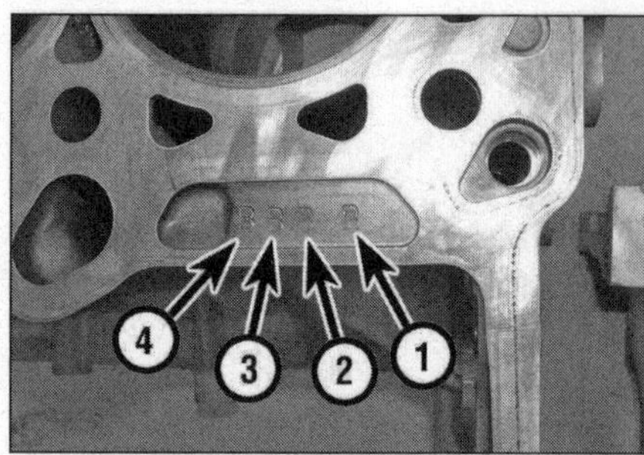

12.16b Cylinder bore diameter size group codes stamped on top of timing chain end of block

12 On diesel engines, refit the piston-cooling oil jets to the cylinder block, so that the locating peg on the jet engages in the hole in the cylinder block **(see illustration)**. Refit the retaining bolts, tightening them carefully to exactly the specified torque wrench setting.

13 If the engine is not going to be reassembled right away, cover it with a large plastic bag to keep it clean; protect all mating surfaces and the cylinder bores as described above, to prevent rusting. When you do rebuild the engine, remember to degrease completely all mating surfaces before applying sealant.

Inspection

Note: *On all engines, have the cylinder block inspected by an engine reconditioning specialist. They will be able to determine if the cylinder block is re-usable, carry out any machining work, and supply the correct new pistons, etc.*

14 Visually check the castings for cracks and corrosion. Look for stripped threads in the threaded holes. If there has been any history of internal water leakage, it may be worthwhile having an engine overhaul specialist check the cylinder block/crankcase with special equipment. If defects are found, have them repaired if possible, or renew the assembly. Damaged threads, or threads that are heavily rusted or corroded, or fouled with old thread-locking compound, must be restored by running the correct size tap into each of the holes until the thread is clear and the fastener concerned can be run in and out to its full depth by hand. Broken threads and castings are a matter for an engine reconditioning specialist.

15 Check each cylinder bore for scuffing and scoring. Check for signs of a wear ridge at the top of the cylinder, indicating that the bore is excessively worn.

16 Measure the inside diameter of each cylinder bore **(see illustration)**. Take two measurements, one parallel with the crankshaft axis and the other at right-angles to it. Compare the results with the figures given in the Specifications. Note that there are two bore diameter size groups to allow for manufacturing tolerances; the size group marking is stamped on the top of the timing chain end of the cylinder block, at the front (petrol engines) or rear (diesel engines) **(see illustration)**. No. 1 cylinder's code is the closest to the timing chain end, No. 4's closest to the flywheel.

17 Oversize pistons are available, and it should be possible to have the cylinder block rebored and fit the oversize pistons. Seek the advice of a Honda dealer or engine reconditioning specialist on the best course of action.

18 If the bores are in reasonably good condition and not worn to the specified limits, then the piston rings should be renewed. If this is the case, the bores should be honed to allow the new rings to bed in correctly and provide the best possible seal. The conventional type of hone has spring-loaded stones, and is used with a power drill. You will also need some paraffin (or honing oil) and rags. The hone should be moved up-and-down the bore to produce a crosshatch pattern, and plenty of honing oil should be used. Ideally, the crosshatch lines should intersect at approximately a 60° angle. Do not take off more material than is necessary to produce the required finish. If new pistons are being fitted, the piston manufacturers may specify a finish with a different angle, so their instructions should be followed. Do not withdraw the hone from the bore while it is still being turned – stop it first. After honing a bore, wipe out all traces of the honing oil. If equipment of this type is not available, or if you are not sure whether you are competent to undertake the task yourself, an engine overhaul specialist will carry out the work at moderate cost.

13 Piston/connecting rod assembly – inspection

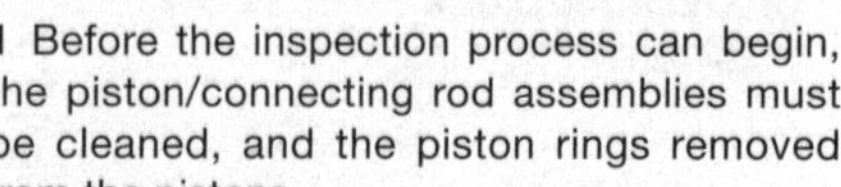

1 Before the inspection process can begin, the piston/connecting rod assemblies must be cleaned, and the piston rings removed from the pistons.

2 Carefully expand the old rings over the top of the pistons. The use of two or three old feeler blades will be helpful in preventing the rings dropping into empty grooves **(see illustration)**. Be careful not to scratch the piston with the ends of the ring. The rings are brittle, and will snap if they are spread too far. They're also very sharp – protect your hands and fingers. Note that the third (oil control) ring may consist of a spacer and two side rails, or a one-piece ring. Always remove the rings from the top of the piston. Keep each set of rings with its piston if the old rings are to be re-used.

13.2 Using a feeler blade to remove a piston ring

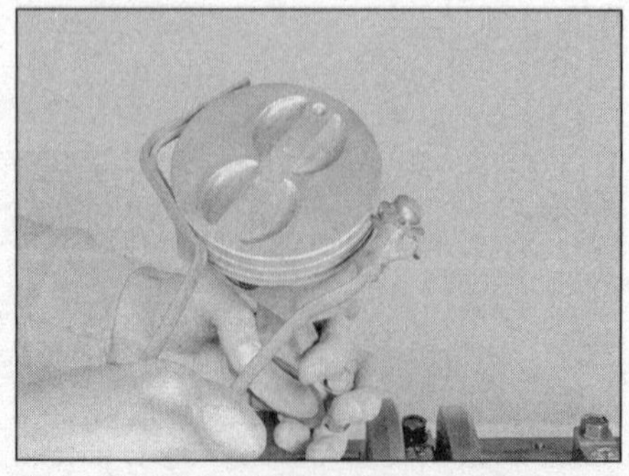

13.4a The piston ring grooves can be cleaned with a special tool, as shown here . . .

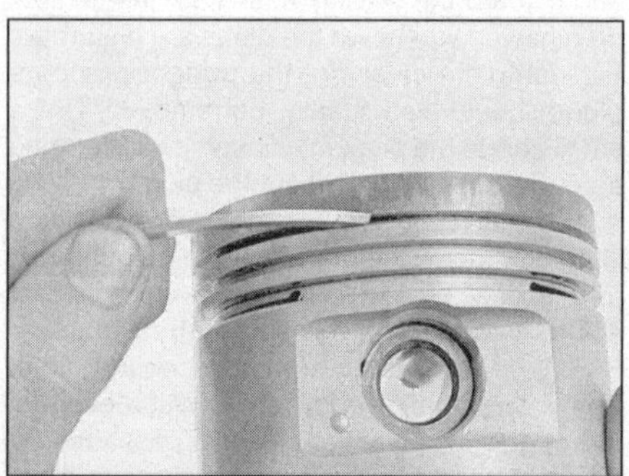

13.4b . . . or a section of a broken ring, if available

3 Scrape away all traces of carbon from the top of the piston. A hand-held wire brush (or a piece of fine emery cloth) can be used, once the majority of the deposits have been scraped away. The piston identification markings should now be visible.

4 Remove the carbon from the ring grooves in the piston, using either one of the purpose-built tools available, or an old ring **(see illustrations)**. Break the ring in half to do this (be careful not to cut your fingers – piston rings are sharp). Be careful to remove only the carbon deposits – do not remove any metal, and do not nick or scratch the sides of the ring grooves.

5 Once the deposits have been removed, clean the piston/connecting rod assembly with paraffin or a suitable solvent, and dry thoroughly. Make sure that the oil return holes in the ring grooves are clear.

6 If the cylinder bores are not damaged or worn excessively (see Section 12), check the piston/connecting rods as follows.

7 Carefully inspect each piston for cracks around the skirt, around the gudgeon pin holes, and at the piston ring lands (between the ring grooves).

8 Look for scoring and scuffing on the piston skirt, holes in the piston crown, and burned areas at the edge of the crown. If the skirt is scored or scuffed, the engine may have been suffering from overheating, and/or abnormal combustion which caused excessively high operating temperatures. The cooling and lubrication systems should be checked thoroughly. Scorch marks on the sides of the pistons show that blow-by has occurred. A hole in the piston crown, or burned areas at the edge of the piston crown, indicates that abnormal combustion (pre-ignition, knocking, or detonation) has been occurring. If any of the above problems exist, the causes must be investigated and corrected, or the damage will occur again. The causes may include incorrect ignition/injection timing (as applicable), or a faulty injector.

9 Corrosion of the piston, in the form of pitting, indicates that coolant has been leaking into the combustion chamber and/or the crankcase. Again, the cause must be corrected, or the problem may persist in the rebuilt engine.

10 Measure the piston diameter at the places given in the Specifications Section of this Chapter and compare the results **(see illustrations)**. Note that there are two piston size groups to allow for manufacturing tolerances; the size group marking is stamped on the piston crown.

11 To measure the piston-to-bore clearance, measure the bore diameter as described in Section 12. Calculate the clearance by subtracting the piston diameter from the bore measurement. Alternatively, insert each piston into its original bore, then select a feeler blade and slip it into the bore along with the piston. The piston must be aligned exactly in its normal attitude, and the feeler blade must be between the piston and bore, on one of the thrust faces, with the piston at the top, middle, and bottom of the bore. If the clearance is excessive at any point, a rebore and new pistons may be required. If the piston binds at the lower end of the bore and is loose towards the top, the bore is tapered. If tight spots are encountered as the piston/feeler blade is rotated in the bore, the bore is out-of-round.

12 Repeat this procedure for the remaining pistons and cylinder bores. Any piston which is worn beyond the specified limits must be renewed.

13 Examine each connecting rod carefully for signs of damage, such as cracks around the big-end and small-end bearings. Check that the rod is not bent or distorted. Damage is highly unlikely, unless the engine has been seized or badly overheated. Detailed checking of the connecting rod assembly can only be carried out by an engine repair specialist. Connecting rod endfloat is checked when the connecting rod is assembled on its crankshaft journal, as described in Section 10.

13.10a Measure piston diameter at right angles to gudgeon pin axis

13.10b Piston size group code is stamped on piston crown

13.15a Using a small screwdriver to remove circlips from piston . . .

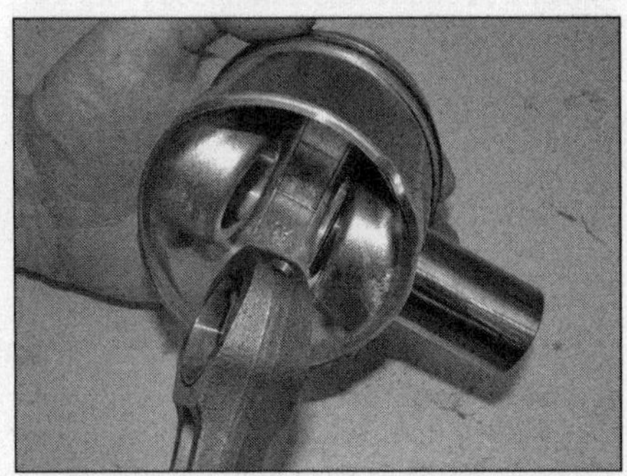

13.15b . . . and push out gudgeon pin to separate piston from connecting rod

14 Check the big-end bearings as described in Sections 14 and 15.

15 Using a small screwdriver, remove the circlips from the piston (note the location of the circlip end gaps) then push out the gudgeon pin **(see illustrations)**. Honda are careful to stress that the circlips should be oiled before being moved round to a position from which they can be removed, ie, with a free end in the cut-out in the piston boss. Hand pressure should be sufficient to remove the pin on diesel engines, but it may be necessary to heat the piston and connecting rod assembly of petrol engines to about 70°C to remove the pin. Identify the piston and rod to ensure correct reassembly. Discard the circlips – new ones must be used on refitting.

16 Inspect the connecting rod big-end bearing cap bolts closely for signs of wear or damage and check that they screw easily into the connecting rods. Renew any bolt which shows

13.16a Measure diameter of threads of each connecting rod big-end bearing cap bolt 35 mm . . .

13.16b . . . and 20 mm from underside of head, then subtract second diameter from first – renew bolt if excessively stretched

13.19 Assemble piston and connecting rod so that arrow on piston crown is pointing in same direction as embossed mark on connecting rod flank

visible signs of damage or does not screw easily into position. Measure the diameter of the threads of each bolt 35 mm (diameter A) and 20 mm (diameter B) from the underside of the head, then subtract B from A; if a bolt has stretched so that its diameter B is more than 0.1 mm less than its diameter A, it must be renewed **(see illustrations)**. Although Honda are happy to have bolts re-used as long as they pass this test, it is good practice to renew highly-stressed fasteners such as these as a matter of course, irrespective of their apparent condition, whenever they are disturbed.

17 Examine the gudgeon pin and connecting rod small-end bearing for signs of wear or damage. Wear will require the renewal of both the pin and connecting rod. If the necessary measuring equipment is available, measure the inside diameter of each piston bore and connecting rod small end eye, and the outside diameter of the gudgeon pin at the appropriate points; subtract one from the other to establish gudgeon pin-to-rod and piston clearances. Compare the results with the figures given in the Specifications.

18 Examine all components, and obtain any new parts from your Honda dealer. If new pistons are purchased, they will be supplied complete with gudgeon pins and circlips. Circlips can also be purchased individually.

19 Assemble the piston and connecting rod so that the arrow on the piston crown is pointing in the same direction as the embossed mark on the flank of the connecting rod **(see illustration)**.

20 Apply a smear of clean engine oil to the gudgeon pin and to the piston bores and connecting rod small end eye. Slide the gudgeon pin into the piston and through the connecting rod small-end; if necessary, on petrol engines, heat the piston and rod to about 70°C to allow the gudgeon pin to be refitted. Check that the piston pivots freely on the rod, then secure the gudgeon pin with two new circlips, ensuring that each circlip is correctly located in its groove in the piston. Honda state that the circlips must be turned until their end gaps are at the bottoms of the pistons, but on the engines dismantled for the project, all the end gaps were found at the tops of the pistons **(see illustration)**.

13.20 Gudgeon pin circlip end gaps should all be at bottom of piston – ensure each circlip is correctly located in its groove

14 Crankshaft – inspection

Checking crankshaft endfloat

1 If the crankshaft endfloat is to be checked, this must be done when the crankshaft is still installed in the cylinder block, but is free to move (see Section 11).

2 Check the endfloat using a dial gauge in contact with the end of the crankshaft. Push the crankshaft fully one way, and then zero the gauge. Push the crankshaft fully the other way, and check the endfloat **(see illustration)**. The result can be compared with the specified amount, and will give an indication as to whether new thrustwashers are required. Thrustwashers are supplied in one thickness only; if endfloat is excessive and new thrustwashers do not bring it back within tolerances, the crankshaft must be renewed.

3 If a dial gauge is not available, feeler blades can be used. First push the crankshaft fully towards the flywheel end of the engine, then use feeler blades to measure the gap between the web of the crankpin and the side of the thrustwasher fitted to the flywheel side of the No. 4 main bearing upper location.

Inspection

4 Clean the crankshaft using paraffin or a suitable solvent, and dry it, preferably with compressed air if available. Be sure to clean the oil holes with a pipe cleaner or similar probe, to ensure that they are not obstructed.

14.2 Check the endfloat using a dial gauge in contact with the end of the crankshaft

Warning: Wear eye protection when using compressed air.

5 Check the main and big-end bearing journals for uneven wear, scoring, pitting and cracking.

6 Big-end bearing wear is accompanied by distinct metallic knocking when the engine is running (particularly noticeable when the engine is pulling from low speed) and some loss of oil pressure.

7 Main bearing wear is accompanied by severe vibration and rumble – getting progressively worse as engine speed increases – and again by loss of oil pressure.

8 Check the bearing journal for roughness by running a finger lightly over the bearing surface. Any roughness (which will be accompanied by obvious bearing wear) indicates that the crankshaft requires regrinding (where possible) or renewal.

9 Check for burrs around the crankshaft oil holes (the holes are usually chamfered, so burrs should not be a problem unless regrinding has been carried out carelessly). Remove any burrs with a fine file or scraper, and thoroughly clean the oil holes as described previously.

10 Have the crankshaft inspected and measured by an engine overhaul specialist. They will be able to determine whether the crankshaft is re-usable or not. If the crankshaft is damaged or if it has worn beyond the specified limits, it will have to be renewed.

11 At the time of writing, it appeared that Honda do not produce undersize bearing shells. If the main or big-end bearing shell-to-journal clearances, checked using Plastigauge, are beyond the service limit specified and cannot be brought back within tolerances using new bearing shells of the same colour-coding, or shells of different thicknesses from within the range provided by Honda, then the crankshaft must be renewed. Consult an engine overhaul specialist for further information on parts availability from other sources, as this will govern whether or not the crankshaft can be reground.

12 Carefully inspect the lower crankcase/ main bearing ladder-to-cylinder block bolts (main bearing cap bolts) and renew any which show signs of damage.

15 Main and big-end bearings – inspection

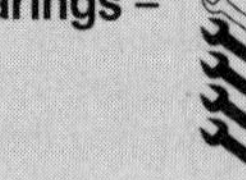

1 Even though it is normal to renew the main and big-end bearing shells during the engine overhaul, the old shells should be retained for close examination, as they may reveal valuable information about the condition of the engine.

2 Bearing failure can occur due to lack of lubrication, the presence of dirt or other foreign particles, overloading the engine, or corrosion **(see illustration)**. Regardless of the cause of bearing failure, the cause must be corrected (where applicable) before the engine is reassembled, to prevent it from happening again.

3 When examining the bearing shells, remove them from the cylinder block, the lower crankcase/main bearing ladder, the connecting rods and the connecting rod big-end bearing caps. Lay them out on a clean surface in the same general position as their location in the engine. This will enable you to match any bearing problems with the corresponding crankshaft journal. Check the colour code on the edge of each bearing shell and record them carefully; a mark of Red, Pink, Yellow, Green, Brown, Black, or Blue (in ascending order of shell thickness) should be found **(see illustration 11.7)**. On petrol engine connecting rod big-end bearings, both shells should have the same colour code; on petrol engine main bearings and both sets of bearings on diesel engines, it is possible to have two shells of different colour codes fitted to the same bearing.

4 Dirt and other foreign matter gets into the engine in a variety of ways. It may be left in the engine during assembly, or it may pass through filters or the crankcase ventilation system. It may get into the oil, and from there into the bearings. Metal chips from machining operations and normal engine wear are often present. Abrasives are sometimes left in engine components after reconditioning. Whatever the source, these foreign objects often end up embedded in the soft bearing material, and are easily recognised. Large particles will not embed in the bearing, and will score or gouge the bearing and journal. The best prevention for this cause of bearing failure is to clean all parts thoroughly, and keep everything spotlessly clean during engine assembly. Frequent and regular engine oil and filter changes are also recommended.

5 Lack of lubrication (or lubrication breakdown) has a number of interrelated causes. Excessive heat (which thins the oil), overloading (which squeezes the oil from the bearing face) and oil leakage (from excessive bearing clearances, worn oil pump or high

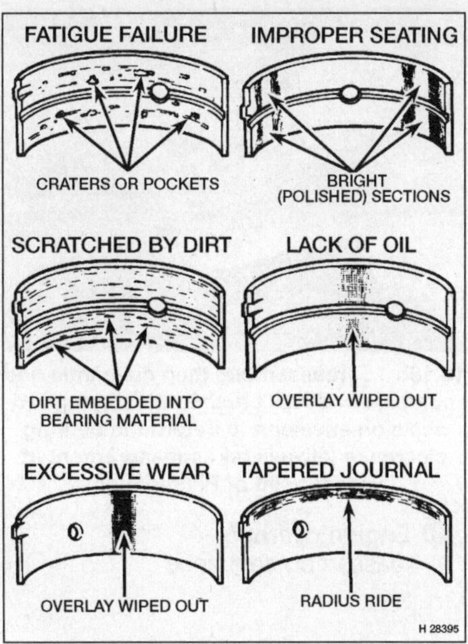

15.2 Typical bearing shell failures

engine speeds) all contribute to lubrication breakdown. Blocked oil passages, which usually are the result of misaligned oil holes in a bearing shell, will also oil-starve a bearing, and destroy it. When lack of lubrication is the cause of bearing failure, the bearing material is wiped or extruded from the steel backing of the bearing. Temperatures may increase to the point where the steel backing turns blue from overheating.

6 Driving habits can have a definite effect on bearing life. Full-throttle, low-speed operation (labouring the engine) puts very high loads on bearings, tending to squeeze out the oil film. These loads cause the bearings to flex, which produces fine cracks in the bearing face (fatigue failure). Eventually, the bearing material will loosen in pieces, and tear away from the steel backing.

7 Short-distance driving leads to corrosion of bearings, because insufficient engine heat is produced to drive off the condensed water and corrosive gases. These products collect in the engine oil, forming acid and sludge. As the oil is carried to the engine bearings, the acid attacks and corrodes the bearing material.

8 Incorrect bearing installation during engine assembly will lead to bearing failure as well. Tight-fitting bearings leave insufficient bearing running clearance, and will result in oil starvation. Dirt or foreign particles trapped behind a bearing shell result in high spots on the bearing, which lead to failure.

9 As mentioned earlier, bearing shells should be renewed as a matter of course during engine overhaul; to do otherwise is false economy.

Selection of bearing shells

10 To ensure precise bearing fits and close control of tolerances in mass production, the crankshaft, cylinder block and lower crankcase/main bearing ladder and connecting rod big-end bearings are graded into size groups, each identified by a code letter or number. Big-end bores and journal diameters are divided into four groups, or classes, as are main bearing bore diameters, while main bearing journal diameters are divided into six classes and seven thicknesses of bearing shell are provided for each bearing. Cross-referencing a bearing's bore diameter code letter or number against the journal diameter code letter or number gives the colour code of the bearing shells required for that bearing location. Where bearing shells of two colours are called for, Honda state that it does not matter which colour is used in the top or bottom shell location.

11 For crankshaft main bearings, the main bearing bore diameter code letters or numbers are marked on the bottom surface of the lower crankcase/main bearing ladder at the rear of the flywheel end **(see illustration)**. No. 1 (timing chain end) main bearing's mark is the one nearest the timing chain end, No. 5 (flywheel end) main bearing's mark is nearest the flywheel end.

12 For connecting rod big-end bearings, the connecting rod big-end bearing bore diameter code number or class marking is etched across each connecting rod and bearing cap **(see illustration)**.

13 For main and big-end bearings, the journal diameter codes are marked either on the edges of the adjacent crankshaft web, or across the face of the web nearest the flywheel **(see illustration)**. For either set of

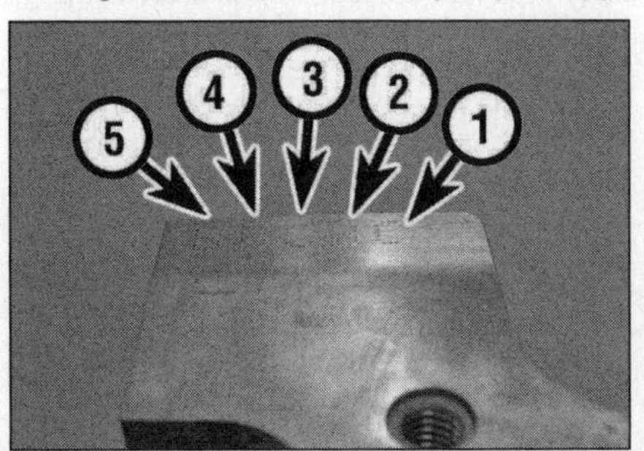

15.11 Main bearing bore diameter size group codes marked on bottom rear of flywheel end of lower crankcase/main bearing ladder

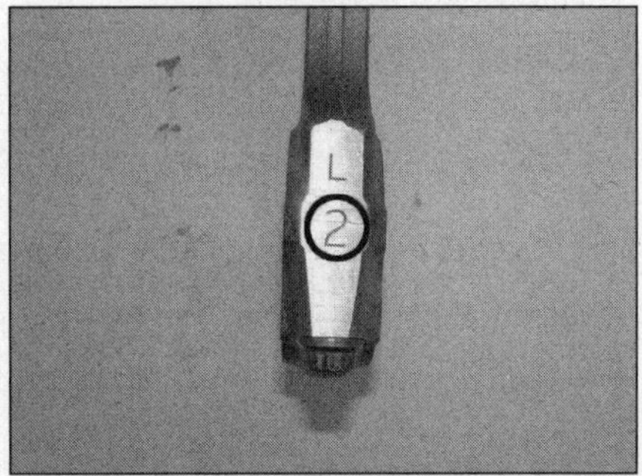

15.12 Big-end bearing bore diameter class marking etched across front face of each connecting rod and bearing cap

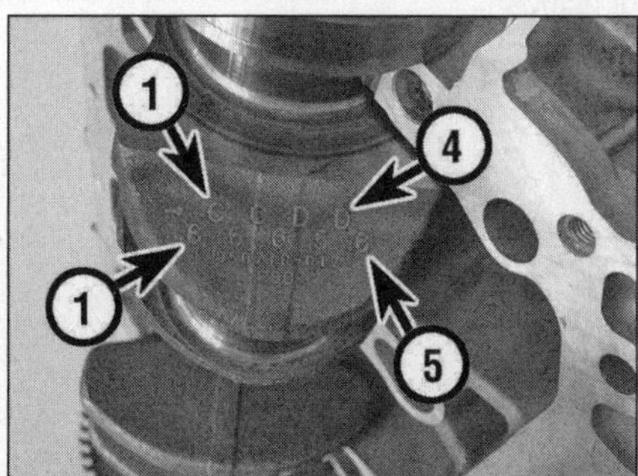

15.13 Main and big-end bearing journal diameter codes marked across face of crankshaft web nearest flywheel

15.16a To check bearing clearances, lay Plastigauge strip (arrowed) on bearing journals, parallel to crankshaft centre-line . . .

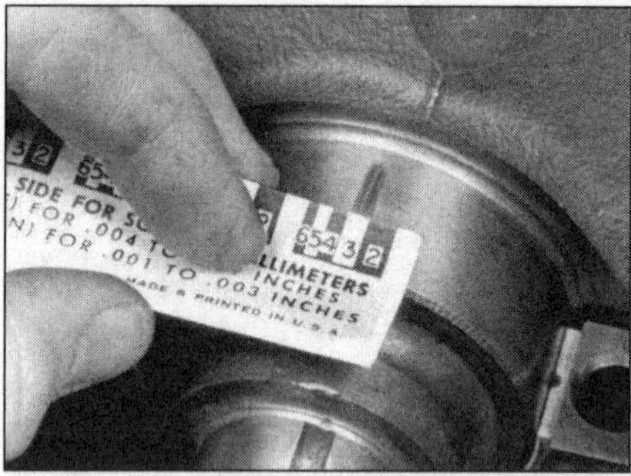

15.16b . . . reassemble, then dismantle and compare width of crushed Plastigauge to scale on envelope to determine bearing clearance (always take measurement at widest point of Plastigauge)

codes, from left to right, the codes are for No. 1 (timing chain end) on the left, through to No. 4 (big-end) or No. 5 (flywheel end main bearing).

14 Whenever new bearing shells are being ordered, or the existing ones checked, note and record all the relevant codes along with the colour codes of the existing shells, a Honda dealer or engine specialist will be able to supply correct new parts.

15 As mentioned earlier, Honda do not supply undersize bearing shells.

16 The only way of assessing the amount of wear that has taken place, if neither crankshaft journal nor bearing shells show visible signs of wear or damage, is to use Plastigauge **(see illustrations)**. If this shows any main or big-end bearing shell-to-journal clearance to be excessive, first fit new bearing shells of the same colour code(s). Recheck the clearance. If it is still incorrect, fit new shells of the next size and check the clearance again.

17 If any of the main or big-end bearing shell-to-journal clearances are beyond the service limit specified and cannot be brought back within tolerances using new bearing shells of the same colour coding, or shells of different thicknesses from within the range provided by Honda, then the crankshaft must be renewed. In that case, all new bearing shells must be ordered, cross-referencing the bearings' bore diameter code letters or numbers against the new crankshaft's journal diameter code letters or numbers.

16 Engine overhaul – reassembly sequence

1 Before reassembly begins, ensure that all new parts have been obtained, and that all necessary tools are available. Read through the entire procedure to familiarise yourself with the work involved, and to ensure that all items necessary for reassembly of the engine are at hand. In addition to all normal tools and materials, liquid gasket (Honda Part No. 08C70-K0234M, 08C70-K0334M, 08C70-X0331S or 08718-0001 or equivalent) must be available on reassembly for the joint faces that are fitted without gaskets, in addition to any other items (gaskets, seals, etc) found to be in need of renewal during the procedure.

2 In order to save time and avoid problems, engine reassembly can be carried out in the following order:

a) Crankshaft.
b) Piston/connecting rod assemblies.
c) Balancer assembly/oil pump.
d) Sump.
e) Flywheel.
f) Cylinder head.
g) Cam follower assembly.
h) Camshafts.
i) Timing chain sprockets, chain and tensioner.
j) Intake and exhaust manifolds.
k) Engine external components.

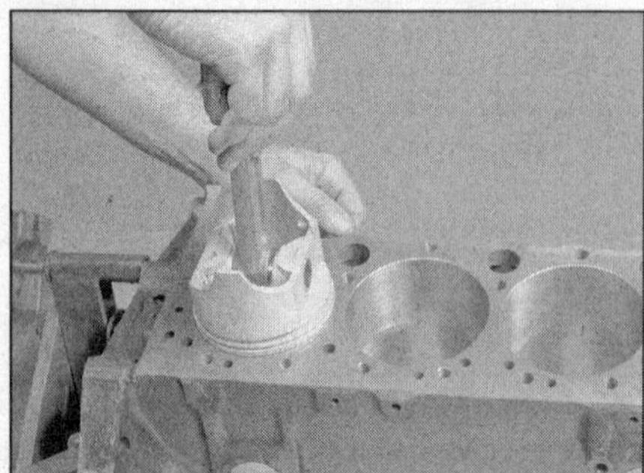

17.3 Position piston ring using piston as described in text . . .

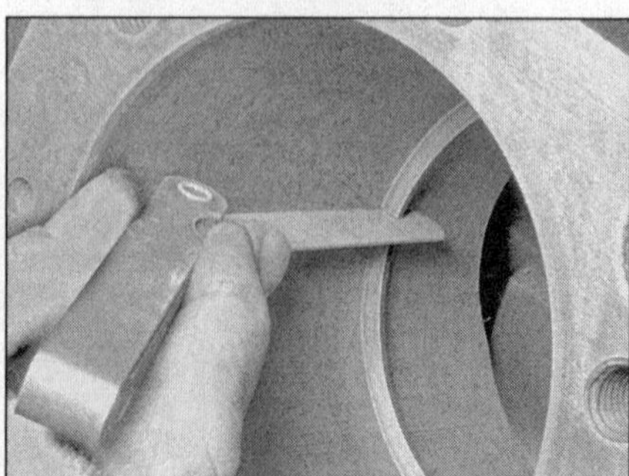

17.4 . . . then measure end gap using feeler blades

3 At this stage, all engine components should be absolutely clean and dry, with all faults repaired. The components should be laid out (or in individual containers) on a completely clean work surface.

17 Piston rings – refitting

1 Before fitting new piston rings, the ring end gaps must be checked as follows.

2 Lay out the piston/connecting rod assemblies and the new piston ring sets, so that the ring sets will be matched with the same piston and cylinder during the end gap measurement and subsequent engine reassembly.

3 Insert the top ring into the first cylinder, and push it down the bore using the top of the piston. This will ensure that the ring remains square with the cylinder walls. Push the ring down into the bore until it is positioned 15 to 20 mm from the bottom of the bore **(see illustration)**. Withdraw the piston.

4 Measure the end gap using feeler blades, and compare the measurements with the figures given in the Specifications **(see illustration)**.

5 If the gap is too small (unlikely if genuine Honda parts are used), it must be enlarged, or the ring ends may contact each other during engine operation, causing serious damage. Ideally, new piston rings providing the correct end gap should be fitted; check carefully that the correct items have been ordered and supplied. As a last resort, the end gap can be increased by filing the ring ends very carefully with a fine file. Mount the file in a vice with soft jaws, slip the ring over the file with the ends contacting the file face, and slowly move the ring to remove material from the ends. Take care, as piston rings are sharp, and are easily broken.

6 With new piston rings, it is unlikely that the end gap will be too large. If the gaps are too large, check that you have the correct rings for your engine and for the particular cylinder bore size.

7 Repeat the checking procedure for each ring in the first cylinder, and then for the rings in the remaining cylinders. Remember to keep rings, pistons and cylinders matched up.

8 Once the ring end gaps have been checked and if necessary corrected, the rings can be fitted to the pistons as follows, using the same technique as for removal.

Petrol engine

9 Fit the oil control ring expander first (it will be easier if the end gap is correctly positioned at this point), then fit the side rails, which have no identification markings and can be fitted either way up **(see illustrations)**. The second and top compression rings are of a similar cross-section but are different and can be distinguished by the identification markings

17.9a On petrol engines, fit oil control ring expander first . . .

17.9b . . . then fit side rails

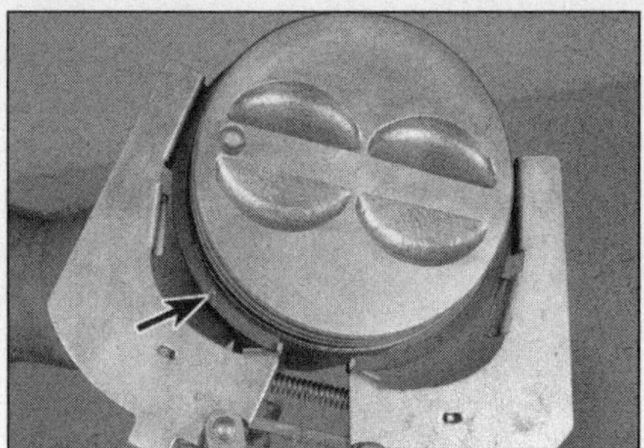

17.9c Using a special tool to fit compression rings – always ensure top surface marking (arrowed) is uppermost

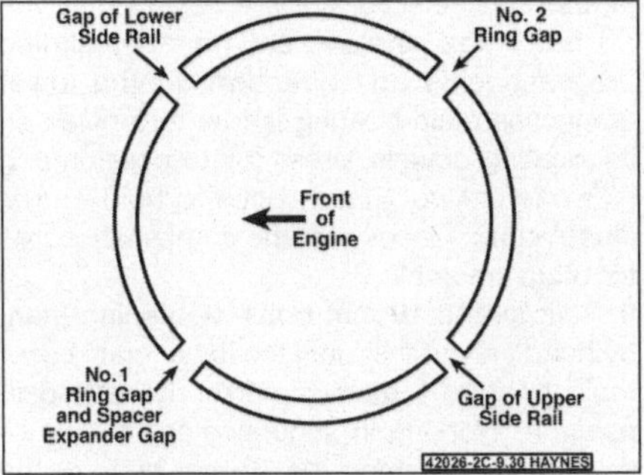

17.10 Piston ring end gap locations – petrol engines

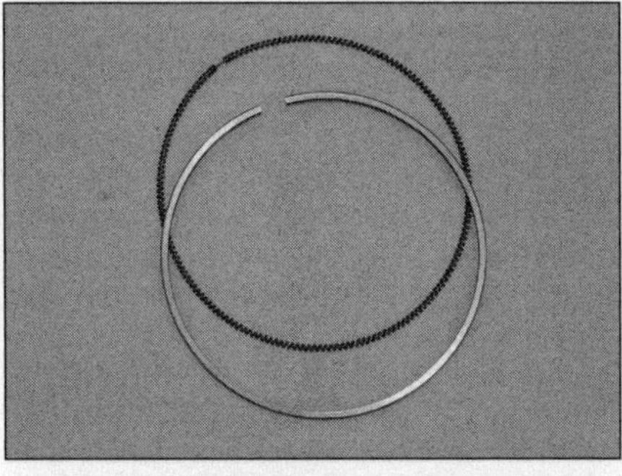

17.11a On diesel engines, oil control ring is in two pieces . . .

17.11b . . . engage oil control ring correctly over expander

on their top surfaces, near the end gaps (see Specifications); fit the rings ensuring that each ring is fitted the correct way up with its identification mark uppermost. **Note:** *Always follow any instructions supplied with the new piston ring sets – different manufacturers may specify different procedures. Do not mix up the top and second compression rings.*

10 Check that each ring is free to rotate easily in its groove, then measure the ring-to-groove clearance of each ring, using feeler blades. If the clearance is within the specified range, position the ring end gaps as shown **(see illustration)**.

Diesel engine

11 Fit the oil control ring expander first, then fit the ring to the piston; the ring has no identification marking and can be fitted either way up **(see illustrations)**.

12 The second and top rings are different (the top ring having a tapered cross-section, while the second is rectangular, with an undercut in its bottom surface) and can be distinguished by the identification markings (see Specifications) on their top surfaces, near the end gaps **(see illustrations)**. Fit the second and top compression rings ensuring that each ring is fitted the correct way up with its identification mark uppermost. **Note:** *Always follow any instructions supplied with the new piston ring sets – different manufacturers may specify different procedures. Do not mix up the top and second compression rings.*

13 Check that each ring is free to rotate easily in its groove, then measure the ring-to-groove clearance of each ring, using feeler blades. If the clearance is within the specified range, space the ring end gaps at 120° intervals. Set the top compression ring end gap 45° from the gudgeon pin axis, the second compression ring end gap 120° from that and the oil control ring end gap at 120° further round, with its expander's gap 180° away from that.

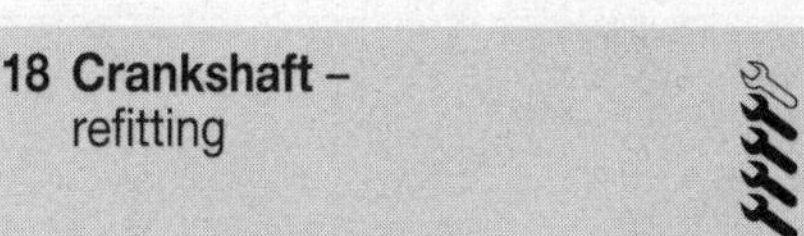

18 Crankshaft – refitting

1 If removed, fit the new crankshaft pilot bush or bearing (Chapter 2A or 2B). On diesel engines only, refit the crankshaft position sensor pulse plate, engaging it on its locating dowel; tighten its bolts to the specified torque **(see illustration)**. A drop of thread-locking compound on each bolt's threads would provide additional security against their working loose.

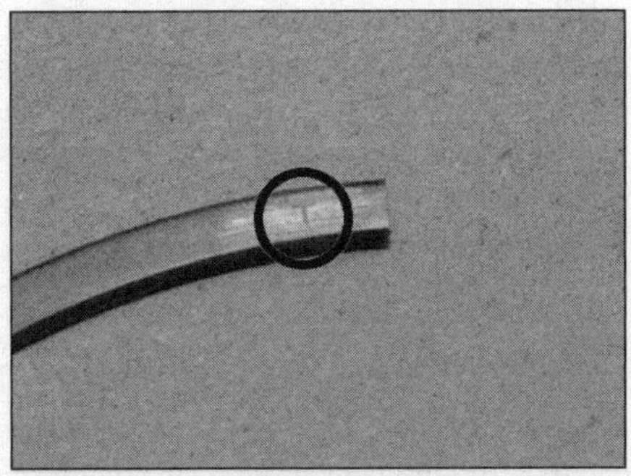

17.12a Top compression ring top surface marking

17.12b Second compression ring top surface marking

18.1 On diesel engines, crankshaft position sensor pulse plate is located on dowel

18.2 Clean backs of bearing shells and bearing locations in cylinder block and lower crankcase/main bearing ladder . . .

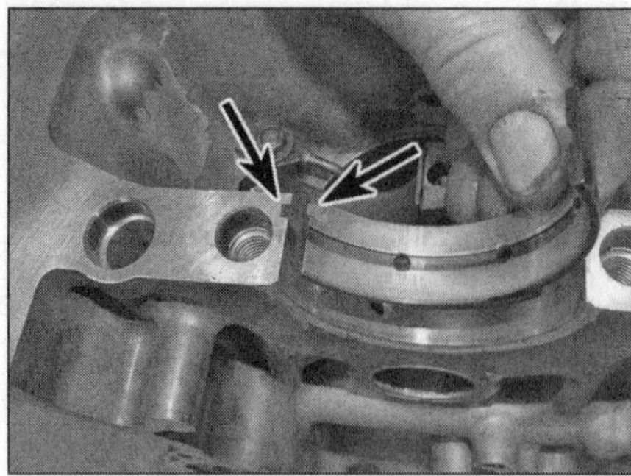

18.3 . . . press bearing shells into their locations, ensuring that tab on each shell engages in notch

Note: *Grooved main bearing shells align with oilways in cylinder block bearing locations*

2 Clean the backs of the bearing shells and the bearing locations **(see illustration)**.

3 Press the bearing shells into their locations, ensuring that the tab on each shell engages in the notch in the cylinder block or main bearing ladder **(see illustration)**. Take care not to touch any shell bearing surface with your fingers. The grooved shells must be fitted in the cylinder block bearing locations, to match the oilways in the block, while the plain shells must be fitted in the main bearing ladder. Where bearing shells of two colours are called for on any one bearing location, it does not matter which colour is used in the top or bottom location.

4 Using a little grease, stick the thrustwashers to each side of the No. 4 main bearing upper location. Ensure that the oilway grooves on each thrustwasher face outwards **(see illustrations)**.

5 Liberally lubricate each bearing shell in the cylinder block, then lower the crankshaft into position, being careful not to mark or damage the journals or damage the crankshaft position sensor pulse plate (diesel engines only) **(see illustration)**.

6 The liquid gasket recommended by Honda requires that the lower crankcase/main bearing ladder must be installed within five minutes of applying the liquid gasket – if this time limit is exceeded, the sealant must be wiped off completely and new liquid gasket applied. A 'dry' practice run before applying liquid gasket is recommended. Degrease the mating surfaces. Liberally lubricate each crankshaft main bearing journal and the lower bearing shells; apply as much oil as possible without risking drips onto the mating surfaces **(see illustration)**.

7 Apply liquid gasket in a continuous thin bead (diameter 3 mm approx) evenly along the lower crankcase/main bearing ladder's mating surface so that the bead goes around the inside edges of the front 8 mm bolt holes and around the outside edges of the rear 8 mm bolt holes **(see illustration)**. Also apply a small blob of liquid gasket to those 8 mm bolt holes in the cylinder block which pass through to the outside. Do not apply sealant to blind holes in the castings. Do not apply excess sealant, as this will end up inside the engine.

8 Offer up the lower crankcase/main bearing ladder and very carefully, ensuring that you do not smear the sealant bead by sliding the casting in any direction, fit the lower crankcase/main bearing ladder into place on its locating dowels, press it into position and refit one or two 10 mm bolts to hold it **(see illustration)**. Check that the crankshaft is free to rotate smoothly.

9 Refit all the 10 mm bolts, tightening them by hand only at first until the lower crankcase/main bearing ladder is correctly settled in position. Working in sequence and in two or three stages, tighten the 10 mm bolts to the specified Stage 1 torque **(see illustrations)**.

10 Tighten the 10 mm bolts again, in sequence, through their specified Stage 2 angle, using a socket and extension bar. It is recommended that an angle-measuring gauge is used during this stage of tightening, to ensure accuracy **(see illustration)**.

11 Refit all the 8 mm bolts, tightening them

18.4a Use grease to stick crankshaft endfloat thrustwashers in place . . .

18.4b . . . grooved surface outwards, to No. 4 main bearing upper location

18.5 Liberally lubricate each bearing shell in cylinder block, then refit crankshaft

18.6 Carefully lubricate each (plain) bearing shell in lower crankcase/main bearing ladder and check locating dowels are in place

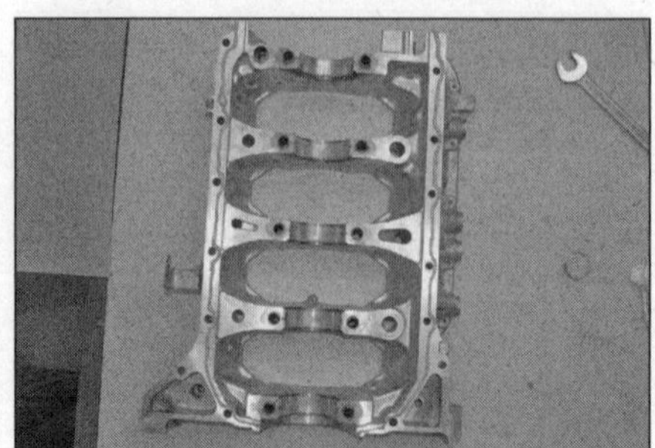

18.7 Apply sealant as shown to lower crankcase/main bearing ladder mating surface

18.8 Refitting lower crankcase/main bearing ladder – take care not to smear sealant bead

by hand only at first. Working in sequence and in two or three stages, tighten the 8 mm bolts to the specified torque **(see illustration).**

12 Check that an even bead of sealant is visible all the way round the edge of the lower crankcase/main bearing ladder; wipe off any excess.

13 Check that the crankshaft is free to rotate smoothly, without any sign of binding or tight spots; if excessive pressure is required to turn the crankshaft, investigate the cause before proceeding further.

14 Check the crankshaft endfloat as described in Section 14.

15 Refit and reconnect the piston connecting rod assemblies to the crankshaft as described in Section 19.

16 Refit the baffle plate(s) to the cylinder block. Tighten their bolts to the specified torque.

17 Working as described in Part A or B of this Chapter, carry out the following procedures in order:

a) Fit a new left-hand oil seal to the crankshaft.
b) Refit the balancer assembly/oil pump.
c) Refit the sump.
d) Refit the flywheel.

19 Piston/connecting rod assembly – refitting

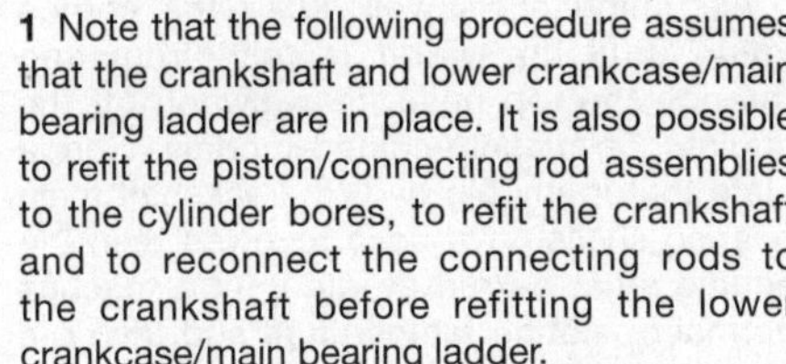

1 Note that the following procedure assumes that the crankshaft and lower crankcase/main bearing ladder are in place. It is also possible to refit the piston/connecting rod assemblies to the cylinder bores, to refit the crankshaft and to reconnect the connecting rods to the crankshaft before refitting the lower crankcase/main bearing ladder.

2 Clean the backs of the bearing shells and the bearing recesses in the connecting rods and the big-end bearing caps. Ensure that all traces of any protective grease are cleaned off using paraffin. Wipe dry the shells and connecting rods with a lint-free cloth.

3 Press the bearing shells into their locations, ensuring that the tab on each shell engages in the notch in the connecting rod or big-end bearing cap and taking care not to touch any shell's bearing surface with your fingers **(see illustration).** Where bearing shells of two colours are called for on any one bearing location (diesel engines only), it does not matter which colour is used in the top or bottom shell location.

4 Lubricate the cylinder bores, the pistons and piston rings, then lay out each piston/connecting rod assembly in its respective position.

5 Starting with assembly No. 1, make sure that the piston rings are still correctly spaced (see Section 17) then clamp them in position with a piston ring compressor **(see illustration).** Rotate the crankshaft so that No. 1 cylinder big-end bearing journal is at Bottom Dead Centre (BDC).

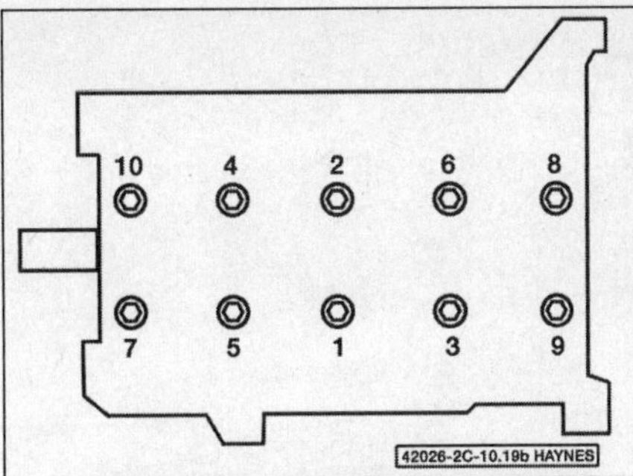

18.9a Lower crankcase/main bearing ladder 10 mm (crankshaft main bearing cap) bolts tightening sequence

18.9b Tighten 10 mm (crankshaft main bearing cap) bolts to first stage with torque wrench . . .

18.10 . . . and use angle-tightening gauge to tighten to Stage 2

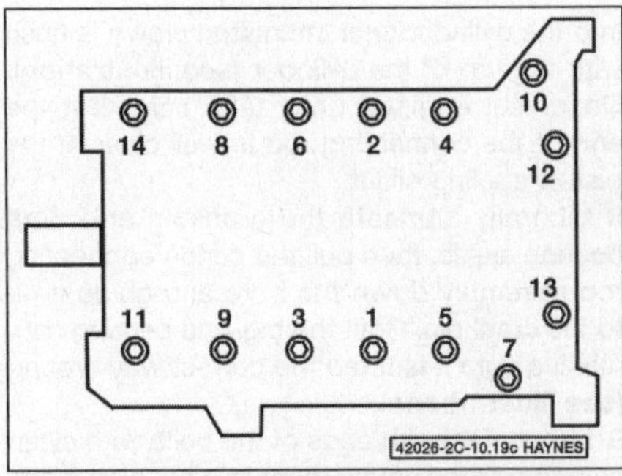

18.11 Lower crankcase/main bearing ladder 8 mm bolts tightening sequence

6 Insert the piston/connecting rod assembly into the top of cylinder No. 1, ensuring that the arrow marking on the piston crown is pointing towards the timing chain end of the engine. The big-end bearing bore diameter class number or marking etched across each connecting rod and bearing cap should face the front of the engine **(see illustration).**

7 Using a block of wood or hammer handle against the piston crown, tap the assembly

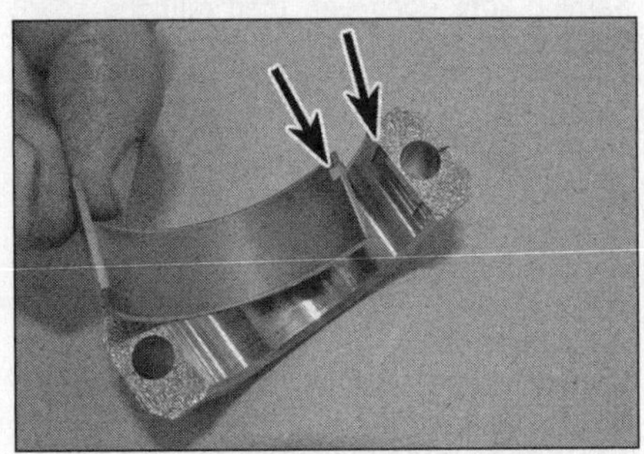

19.3 Ensure tab on each shell engages in notch in connecting rod and big-end bearing cap

19.5 Using a piston ring compressor to refit a piston/connecting rod assembly

19.6 Arrow on piston crown must point to timing belt end of engine

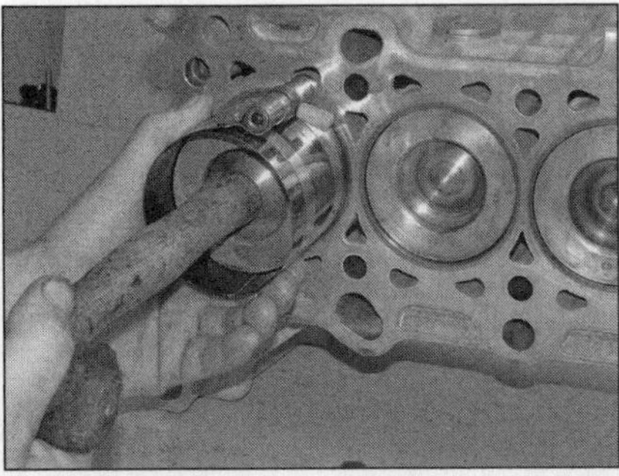

19.7 Tap piston/connecting rod assembly into cylinder . . .

19.8a . . . oil big-end bearing shells before refitting connecting rod to crankshaft . . .

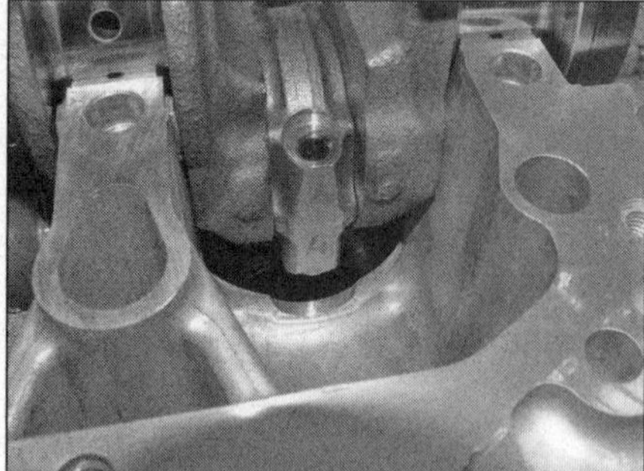
19.8b . . . refit big-end bearing cap so that marks made on removal correspond . . .

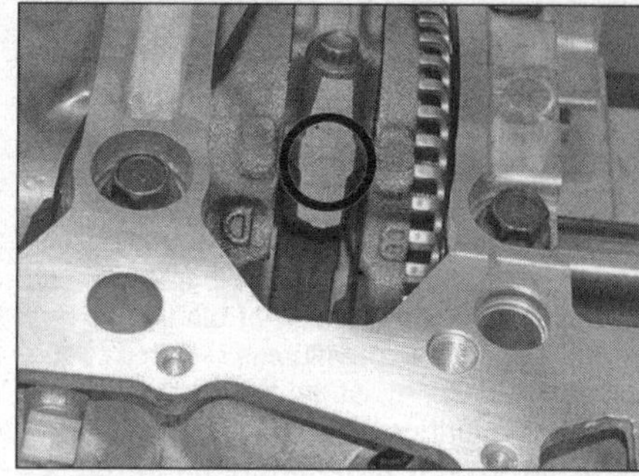
19.8c . . . and big-end bearing bore diameter class marking aligns exactly at front

into the cylinder until the piston crown is flush with the top of the cylinder **(see illustration)**. On diesel engines only, take care that the end of the connecting rod is well clear of the piston-cooling oil jet.

8 Liberally lubricate the crankpin and both bearing shells, then pull the piston/connecting rod assembly down the bore and guide it on to the crankpin. Refit the big-end bearing cap, making sure it is fitted the correct way around **(see illustrations)**.

9 Lubricate the threads of the bolts with clean engine oil then screw them into position in the connecting rod, tightening them both by hand. Evenly and progressively tighten the bolts to the specified Stage 1 torque, then tighten each bolt through the specified Stage 2 angle. It is recommended that an angle-measuring gauge is used during this stage of the tightening, to ensure accuracy **(see illustrations)**.

10 Refit the remaining three piston and connecting rod assemblies in the same way.

11 Rotate the crankshaft, and check that it turns freely, with no signs of binding or tight spots.

12 Refit the baffle plate(s) to the cylinder block. Tighten their bolts to the specified torque.

13 Working as described in Part A or B of this Chapter, carry out the following procedures in order:

a) Refit the balancer assembly/oil pump.
b) Refit the sump.
c) Refit the cylinder head.
d) Refit the cam follower assembly and camshafts (petrol engine).
e) Refit the cam followers and hydraulic tappets, camshaft carrier and camshafts (diesel engine).
f) Refit the timing chain sprockets, chain and tensioner.

20 Engine – initial start-up after overhaul

With the engine refitted in the vehicle, double-check the oil and coolant levels. Make a final check that everything has been reconnected, and that there are no tools or rags left in the engine compartment.

On petrol engined-models, disable the ignition system by removing all four ignition coils and spark plugs (Chapter 1A). Turn the engine on the starter until the oil pressure warning light goes out, then refit the spark plugs and the coils.

On diesel engined-models, if you do not have access to the Honda Diagnostic System (HDS) tester to disable the injectors, turning the engine over without starting it requires the removal of the injectors (but this requires the renewal of the copper sealing washers and the high-pressure pipes), or the disabling of the injectors by disconnecting their wiring connectors and reconnecting them afterwards. This, however, will almost certainly cause a fault code to be logged so that the engine management Malfunction Indicator Lamp (MIL) illuminates, or the glow plug warning lamp flashes while the engine is running, until the vehicle can be taken to a specialist for the fault code to be erased. Whichever method is adopted, turn the engine on the starter until the oil pressure warning light goes out, then stop and re-enable or refit the injectors, as applicable.

On all models, start the engine as normal noting that this may take a little longer than usual, due to the fuel system components having been disturbed. Prime the diesel engine fuel system if necessary (Chapter 4B).

While the engine is idling, check for fuel, water and oil leaks. Don't be alarmed if there are some odd smells and smoke from parts getting hot and burning off oil deposits.

Assuming all is well, keep the engine idling until hot water is felt circulating through the top hose, then switch off the engine. On diesel engined-models, Honda state that if any big-end or crankshaft main bearing shells have been renewed then the engine must be run at idle until it reaches normal operating temperature and then run for another 15 minutes to bed in the new components.

Allow the engine to cool then recheck the oil and coolant levels and top-up as necessary.

If new pistons, rings or crankshaft bearings have been fitted, the engine must be treated as new, and run-in for the first 500 miles. Do not operate the engine at full throttle, or allow it to labour at low engine speeds in any gear. It is recommended that the oil and filter be changed at the end of this period.

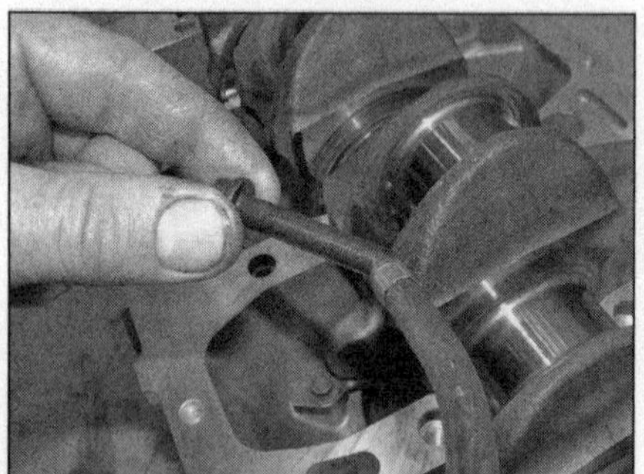
19.9a Lightly oil threads of connecting rod big-end bearing cap bolts

19.9b Tighten big-end bearing cap bolts to specified Stage 1 torque . . .

19.9c . . . and then through specified Stage 2 angle

Chapter 3
Cooling, heating and air conditioning systems

Contents

Degrees of difficulty

Easy, suitable for novice with little experience	**Fairly easy,** suitable for beginner with some experience	**Fairly difficult,** suitable for competent DIY mechanic	**Difficult,** suitable for experienced DIY mechanic	**Very difficult,** suitable for expert DIY or professional

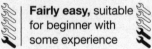

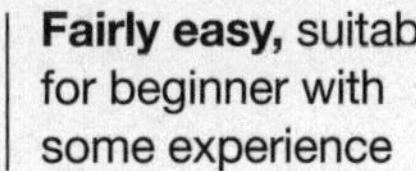

Specifications

Coolant capacity	See Chapter 1A or 1B
Coolant type	Refer to *Lubricants and fluids* on page 0•16

Radiator cooling fan

Switch-on temperature:	
Petrol-engined models	91 to 95°C
Diesel-engined models:	
First (Low) speed	91 to 95°C
Second (High) speed	98 to 102°C
Switch-off temperature – all models	3 to 8°C below actual switch-on temperature

Pressure cap rating

Petrol-engined models	0.95 to 1.25 bar
Diesel-engined models	1.12 to 1.46 bar

Thermostat

Opens at	76 to 80°C
Fully open at	90°C
Valve lift at fully open:	
Petrol-engined models	8.0 mm (minimum)
Diesel-engined models	10.0 mm (minimum)

Air conditioning system

Refrigerant type	HFC-134a (R-134a)
Refrigerant quantity:	
Petrol-engined models	480 to 530 g
Diesel engined models	450 to 500 g
Refrigerant oil:	
Petrol-engined models	Keihin SP-10 PAG
Diesel-engined models	Denso ND-Oil 8 PAG

Torque wrench settings

Torque wrench settings	Nm	lbf ft
Air conditioning compressor bracket-to-cylinder block/sump bolts	44	32
Air conditioning compressor mounting bolts	22	16
Air conditioning condenser bracket mounting bolts	10	7
Air conditioning condenser cooling fan shroud mounting bolts	7	5
Air conditioning system hose union:		
6 mm bolt and nut to compressor	10	7
6 mm bolt(s) to condenser	10	7
Air conditioning system magnet valve fasteners – diesel-engined models:		
Mounting bolts	10	7
Union bolts	10	7
Air conditioning system pipes-to-evaporator core bolt	10	7
Air conditioning system receiver line union nut – diesel-engined models	13	10
Coolant expansion tank mounting bolts – diesel-engined models	10	7
Coolant expansion tank-to-radiator mounting bolt – petrol-engined models	12	9
Coolant pipe bracket-to-air conditioning condenser cooling fan shroud bolt – diesel-engined models	7	5
Coolant temperature switch:		
Cooling fan switch-to-radiator	24	18
Cooling fan switch-to-thermostat cover – diesel-engined models	24	18
Engine coolant temperature sensor – diesel-engined models	22	16
Engine coolant temperature sensor – petrol-engined models	12	9
Cooling fan shroud-to-radiator mounting bolts	7	5
Heater blower motor housing mounting nuts and bolts	10	7
Heater control valve mounting bolt	10	7
Heater unit mounting nuts and bolts:		
On engine compartment bulkhead – 8 mm nut	12	9
In passenger compartment – 6 mm nuts and bolts	10	7
Radiator cooling fan shroud mounting bolts	7	5
Radiator top mounting bracket bolts	10	7
Radiator/bonnet lock support bracket bolts:		
Diesel-engined models	10	7
Petrol-engined models	12	9
Thermostat cover retaining bolts – diesel-engined models	12	9
Thermostat housing-to-water pump/oil filter/oil cooler housing bolts – diesel-engined models	22	16
Thermostat retaining bolts – petrol-engined models	10	7
Water pump mounting bolts	12	9

1 General information and precautions

Engine cooling system

All models covered by this manual employ a pressurised engine cooling system with thermostatically-controlled coolant circulation. The water pump is mounted in a housing bolted to the front right-hand end of the cylinder block and is driven with the steering pump, alternator and air conditioning compressor by an auxiliary drivebelt from the crankshaft pulley. The water pump pumps coolant through the engine, around each cylinder (and the engine oil cooler on diesel-engined models) and into the cylinder head. In addition to supplying the heating system, external pipes and hoses channel coolant to the turbocharger and EGR cooler (diesel-engined models), and to the throttle body and (where appropriate) the automatic transmission fluid cooler on petrol-engined models.

A thermostat controls engine coolant temperature. During warm-up, the closed thermostat prevents coolant from circulating through the radiator. As the engine nears normal operating temperature, the thermostat opens and allows hot coolant to travel through the radiator, where it is cooled before returning to the engine. The thermostat is mounted in a housing low down at the front of the engine.

The cooling system is sealed by a pressure cap, which raises the boiling point of the coolant and increases the efficiency of the radiator. On petrol-engined models, a plastic reservoir is fitted to the right-hand side of the radiator. When the engine is at normal operating temperature, the coolant expands, and the surplus is displaced past the radiator pressure cap into this expansion tank. When the system cools, the surplus coolant is automatically drawn back from the tank into the radiator. On diesel-engined models, a pressurised tank, forming an integral part of the cooling system's circulation flow, is mounted on the right-hand inner wing to act as a header tank for the radiator (providing a reserve of coolant and preventing aeration).

The operation of the cooling fans on petrol-engined models is controlled by the engine management system's Electronic Control Unit (ECU), which receives engine temperature data from the engine coolant temperature sensor, in conjunction with signals from the cooling fan switch mounted in the bottom of the radiator. At a predetermined temperature, the ECU energises the relay which operates the cooling fan. On diesel-engined models a two-speed cooling fan is fitted which has a (low-speed) cooling fan switch mounted in the bottom of the radiator and a further (high-speed) cooling fan switch mounted in the thermostat cover. At a predetermined temperature, a cooling fan control relay energises the relay which operates the cooling fan; if the higher temperature is reached, the fan motor operates at higher speed.

Heating/ventilation system

The heating system consists of a blower fan and heater matrix, the hoses connecting the heater matrix to the engine cooling system and the heater/air conditioning controls on the facia. Cold air enters the system through the grille at the rear of the engine compartment. Hot coolant is supplied to the heater control valve in the engine compartment. When the heater temperature control is turned to hot, a motor-operated flap opens to link the heater matrix chamber to the passenger compartment, and a cable opens the heater control valve. When required, a fan switch on the control panel activates the blower motor, which forces air through the matrix, increasing the supply of air. Stale air is expelled through ducts at the rear of the vehicle. A recirculation switch enables the outside air supply to be closed off.

Air conditioning system

General information

The air conditioning system enables the temperature of incoming air to be lowered; it also dehumidifies the air, which makes for rapid demisting and increased comfort. Two types of air conditioning are fitted – manual and automatic (climate control).

The cooling side of the system works in a similar way to a domestic refrigerator. Refrigerant gas is drawn into a belt-driven compressor, and passes into a condenser in front of the radiator, where it loses heat and becomes liquid. The liquid passes through an expansion valve to an evaporator, where it changes from liquid under high pressure to gas under low pressure. This change is accompanied by a drop in temperature, which cools the evaporator. The refrigerant returns to the compressor and the cycle begins again.

Air blown through the evaporator passes to the heater unit, where it is mixed with hot air to achieve the desired temperature in the passenger compartment. On models with climate control, the flap doors on the heater unit and blower motor housing are operated automatically by the system's control unit via electric motors to warm or cool the air as required and direct it wherever the controls are set. On diesel-engined models the air conditioning system is also used to provide warm air as soon as possible after starting the engine from cold, this function being governed by the magnet valve mounted beneath the right-hand headlamp, in conjunction with the engine coolant temperature sensor.

Checks

The air conditioning system should be operated at least once a week, all year round, for at least 10 minutes at a time and at full speed, to circulate the lubricating oil around those of the system's components that require it and to prevent seals from deteriorating, to dry out the system and to prevent the build-up of bacteria in the system's components that produce odours.

The following checks should be performed on a regular basis:

a) *Inspect the auxiliary drivebelt (Chapter 1A or 1B).*
b) *Inspect the system hoses. If there is any wear, damage or leakage, have them renewed.*
c) *Inspect the condenser cooling fins for leaves, insects, etc. Use a 'fin comb' or compressed air to remove debris.*
d) *If the effectiveness of the air conditioning system seems to be reduced, have the refrigerant charge checked (this includes checking for leaks) and recharged if necessary* **(see illustration).**
e) *Check that the drain tube from the front of the evaporator is clear* **(see illustration)** *– note that it is normal to have water dripping from this while the system is in use and when the vehicle is parked..*

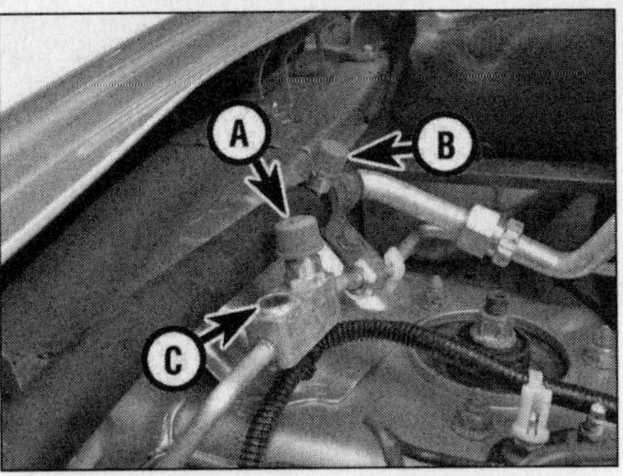

1.10a Air conditioning high-pressure service valve/port (A), low-pressure service valve/port (B) and sight glass (C)

1.10b Periodically check that air conditioning system evaporator drain tube is clear

If the air conditioning system is working properly, when the system is switched on with the engine running there should be an audible clunk as the compressor clutch engages. However, if the system is low on gas (low charge), the clutch will not engage.

Because of the complexity of the air conditioning system and the special equipment necessary to service it, in-depth troubleshooting and repairs are not included in this manual. For more complete information on the air conditioning system, refer to the Haynes *Air Conditioning Manual*. However, renewal procedures for the major components are included.

Precautions

Cooling system

Warning: DO NOT attempt to remove the radiator cap or expansion tank filler cap while the engine is hot, as there is a very great risk of scalding. If the filler cap must be removed before the system has fully cooled down (even though this is not recommended) the pressure in the cooling system must first be released. Cover the cap with a thick layer of cloth, and slowly unscrew it until a hissing sound can be heard. When the hissing has stopped, showing that pressure is released, slowly unscrew the filler cap further until it can be removed. At all times, keep well away from the filler opening.

Warning: Do not allow antifreeze to come in contact with your skin, or with the painted surfaces of the vehicle. Rinse off spills immediately with plenty of water. Never leave antifreeze lying around in an open container, or in a puddle in the driveway or on the garage floor. Children and pets are attracted by its sweet smell, but it is highly poisonous.

Warning: If the engine is hot, the electric cooling fan may start even if the engine is not running, so be careful to keep hands, hair and loose clothing well clear when working in the engine compartment.

Air conditioning system

Warning: The refrigerant is potentially dangerous, and should only be handled by qualified persons. If it is splashed onto the skin, it can cause frostbite – do not allow it to come in contact with skin or eyes. It is not itself poisonous, but in the presence of a naked flame (including a cigarette) it forms a poisonous gas. Uncontrolled discharging of the refrigerant is dangerous, illegal and damaging to the environment. Any work on the air conditioning system which involves opening the refrigerant circuit must only be carried out by an air conditioning specialist.

2 Cooling system hoses – disconnection and renewal

Note: *Refer to the precautions in Section 1 before starting work.*

1 If the checks described in Chapter 1 reveal a faulty hose, it must be renewed as follows.

2 Drain the cooling system (Chapter 1); the drained coolant may be re-used, if it is collected in a clean container.

3 Clean any dirt from the unions to be disconnected. Release the hose clips from the hose concerned **(see illustrations)**. The standard clips fitted at the factory are the spring type, released by squeezing their tangs together with pliers, at the same time working the clip away from the stub. Some clips have a locking device to hold the clip in the expanded position. Spring clips can be awkward to use, can pinch old hoses, and may become less effective with age, so may have been updated with worm-drive hose clips.

4 Diesel models have quick-release unions on the radiator top and bottom hoses; to disconnect these, pull out the wire retaining clip and pull the union off the stub **(see**

2.3a Most hose retaining clips are spring type – note paint marks to ensure correct realignment . . .

illustration). If the union is stiff, carefully work it loose by hand only – do not use any tools – but do not try to rotate it on the stub; there is a locating projection which engages with a slot in the union to ensure it is correctly positioned. The sealing O-ring must be renewed whenever the union is disturbed.

5 Unclip any wires, cables or other hoses which may be attached to the hose being removed. Make notes for reference when reassembling if necessary.

6 Note that coolant unions made of plastic are fragile; do not use excessive force when attempting to remove the hoses. If a hose proves to be difficult to remove, try to release it by rotating the hose ends before attempting to free it – if this fails, try gently prising up the end of the hose with a small screwdriver to break the seal. If all else fails, cut the hose with a sharp knife, then slit it so that it can be peeled off in two pieces. Although this

2.4 Pull out wire retaining clip, then pull union off radiator stub

2.9b . . . to release clip and secure hose

2.3b . . . release spring clips by using pliers to squeeze tangs together

may seem expensive if the hose is otherwise undamaged, it is preferable to buying a new radiator.

If a hose is stiff, use a little soapy water as a lubricant, or soften the hose by soaking it with hot water.

7 Before fitting a new hose, smear the stubs with liquid soap or rubber lubricant to aid fitting. Do not use oil or grease, which may attack the rubber.

8 Fit the hose clips over the ends of the hose, then fit the hose over its stubs. Work each hose end fully onto its stub, check that it is settled correctly and is properly routed, then slide each clip along the hose until it is behind the stub's flared end before tightening it securely.

2.9a To fasten spring clip with locking device, position clip, then release catch . . .

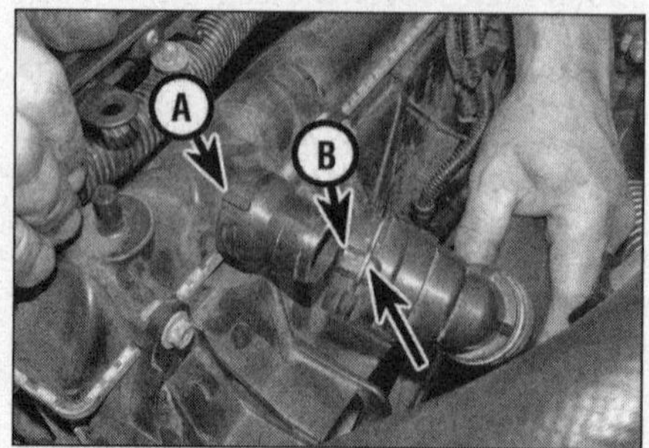

2.10 Press in clip, clean mating surfaces and press union on to stub so that projection (A) engages in slot (B)

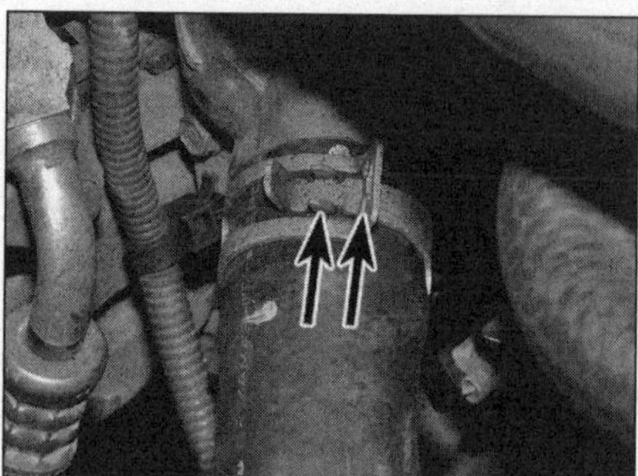

2.3c Some spring clips have locking device to hold clip expanded

9 Spring clips must have the ends squeezed together, and the clip positioned over the stub's flared end, then released; those with a locking mechanism must be released either by manipulation of the pliers or by levering with a screwdriver **(see illustrations)**. Do not overtighten screw-type clips, as this may damage the hoses and unions. When refitting hose clips, give some thought to how easy they will be to remove again future – try to make sure the screw fitting or spring tangs will be accessible.

10 The quick-release unions are fastened as follows. Check that a new O-ring has been fitted, and that the set ring is in place inside the union. Push in the wire retaining clip, seating it fully in its groove. Clean the stub and the mating surface inside the union, then smear clean coolant on the stub and press the union into place, aligning the slot in the union with the projection on the stub, until the retaining clip clicks into place **(see illustration)**. Pull on the union to check that the retaining clip has correctly locked into the groove on the stub.

11 Refill the cooling system (Chapter 1). Run the engine, and check that there are no leaks.

12 Recheck the tightness of the hose clips after a few hundred miles.

3 Thermostat – removal, testing and refitting

Note: *Refer to the precautions in Section 1 before starting work.*

Checking

1 As the thermostat ages, it may stick in the open or closed position. A thermostat which is stuck open will result in a very slow warm-up; a thermostat which is stuck shut will lead to rapid overheating.

2 Before assuming the thermostat is to blame for a cooling system problem, check the coolant level. If the system has not been properly filled, there may be an airlock in the system (see the coolant renewal procedure in Chapter 1).

3 If the engine seems to be taking a long time to warm up (based on heater output), the thermostat could be stuck open or missing.

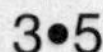

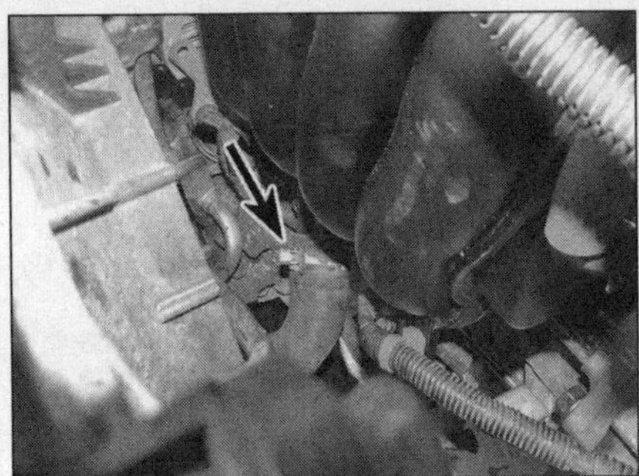
3.13 Disconnect radiator bottom hose from thermostat . . .

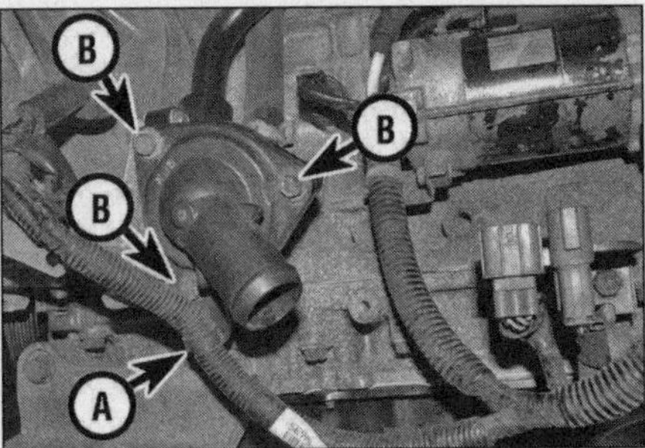

3.15 . . . release alternator wiring (A) and unscrew thermostat retaining bolts (B) to withdraw thermostat – petrol models

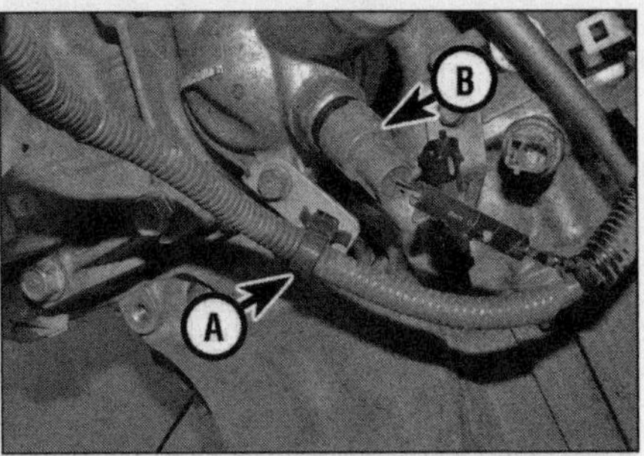

3.17 Release alternator wiring (A) and disconnect radiator fan switch wiring (B) . . .

4 Don't drive the vehicle without a thermostat – the engine management system's ECU will stay in warm-up mode for longer than necessary, causing emissions and fuel economy to suffer.

5 If the engine runs hot, use your hand to check the temperature of the radiator top hose. If the hose isn't hot, but the engine is, the thermostat is probably stuck closed. But again, this problem could also be due to an airlock.

6 If the radiator top hose is hot, it means that the coolant is flowing (at least as far as the radiator) and the thermostat is open.

7 To gain a rough idea of whether the thermostat is working properly, proceed as follows.

8 With the engine completely cold, start the engine and let it idle, while checking the temperature of the radiator top hose by hand. Periodically check the temperature indicated on the coolant temperature gauge – if overheating is indicated, switch the engine off immediately.

9 The top hose should feel cold for some time as the engine warms-up, and should then get warm quite quickly as the thermostat opens.

10 Precise testing is only possible after removing the thermostat as described below.

Removal

Note: *The thermostat is at the front of the engine, between the alternator and the starter motor. The most direct access is from underneath. If additional working space is required, remove the radiator and cooling fans (Section 5).*

11 Drain the cooling system (Chapter 1), saving the coolant if it is fit for re-use.

12 Remove the engine compartment under-shield (Chapter 11).

Petrol-engined models

13 Release the hose clip and disconnect the radiator bottom hose from the thermostat **(see illustration)**.

14 Unclip the alternator wiring guide from the thermostat.

15 Unscrew the three thermostat retaining bolts and withdraw the thermostat **(see illustration)**. If it is stuck, tap it with a soft-faced hammer to jar it loose. Be prepared for some coolant to spill as the seal is broken. Recover the O-ring.

3.18 . . . unscrew thermostat cover bolts to withdraw thermostat . . .

Diesel-engined models

16 Release the hose clip and disconnect the radiator bottom hose from the thermostat.

17 Unclip the alternator wiring guide from the bracket bolted to the thermostat cover disconnect the wiring from the radiator cooling fan switch in the thermostat cover **(see illustration)**.

18 Unscrew the two thermostat cover bolts and collect the wiring bracket. Detach the cover; if it is stuck, tap it with a soft-faced hammer to jar it loose **(see illustration)**.

19 Lift out the thermostat and recover the rubber seal **(see illustration)**.

Testing

20 If the thermostat remains in the open position at room temperature, it is faulty and must be renewed.

21 Check the temperature marking stamped on the thermostat **(see illustration)**. It should correspond with one of those given in the Specifications.

3.21 Thermostat opening or fully-open temperature is usually marked on thermostat end

3.19 . . . then renew thermostat rubber seal – diesel models. Note opening temperature marking

22 To test the thermostat fully, suspend it on a length of string in a pan of cold water, with a thermometer beside it. Ensure that the thermostat does not touch the bottom or sides of the container **(see illustration)**.

23 Heat the water and check the temperature at which the thermostat begins to open. Compare this value with that specified. Continue to heat the water until the thermostat is fully open; again, compare this value with that specified. When the thermostat is fully open, remove it from the water and measure the amount the valve has lifted. Allow the thermostat to cool down and check that it closes fully.

24 If the thermostat does not open and close as it should, then it must be renewed.

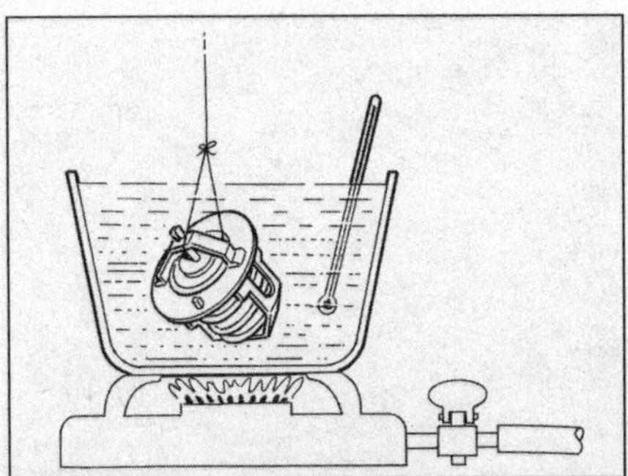
3.22 Testing the thermostat

3.25 Refitting the thermostat. Jiggle valve pin must be at top and projection on rubber seal must locate in housing as shown

Refitting

25 Refitting is a reversal of removal, but note the following additional points:

a) *Clean all mating surfaces thoroughly before reassembly.*
b) *Fit a new O-ring or rubber seal, as applicable.*
c) *On diesel-engined models, the thermostat should be fitted so that the jiggle valve/pin is at the top* ***(see illustration)****.*
d) *Tighten all bolts to their specified torques (where given).*

Thermostat housing

26 If it is necessary to remove the thermostat housing for any reason, access is best gained by removing the appropriate part of the intake manifold (Chapter 4A or 4B) and the radiator and cooling fans (Section 5).

4 Radiator and condenser cooling fans – testing, removal and refitting

Note: *Refer to the precautions in Section 1 before starting work.*

Testing

Note: *There are two cooling fan circuits – one for the radiator and one for the air conditioning condenser – but both are closely interconnected. The radiator fan is on the left-hand side, the condenser fan is on the right. The following procedures apply to both.*

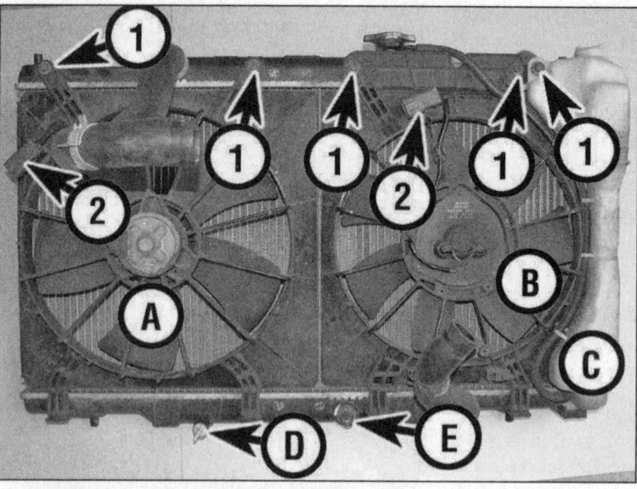

4.8 Radiator and cooling fan components – petrol models

A *Radiator cooling fan, with mounting bolts (1) and fan motor wiring plug (2)*
B *Air conditioning system condenser cooling fan, with mounting bolts (1) and fan motor wiring plug (2)*
C *Expansion tank, with mounting bolt (1)*
D *Radiator drain tap*
E *Radiator cooling fan switch*

1 To test a cooling fan motor, disconnect the two-pin electrical connector at the motor, and use bridging wires to connect the fan directly to the battery. If the fan still doesn't work, renew the motor. On petrol-engined models the fan motor connectors are clipped to the top of their respective shrouds; on diesel-engined models, the radiator fan wiring plug is at the bottom of its shroud, with the condenser cooling fan plug at the top – do not confuse these plugs with those for the bonnet alarm switch, the cooling fan switch or the air conditioning compressor clutch.

2 If the motor runs, check the fuse and relay (see Chapter 12), the cooling fan switch(es), the fan control relay (diesel-engined models), or the wiring which connects the components. **Note:** *All relays are mounted in the engine compartment main fuse/relay box.*

3 On petrol-engined models, only one radiator cooling fan switch is fitted – screwed into the bottom of the radiator. Diesel-engined models have a two-speed cooling fan, requiring two switches – a low-speed switch in the bottom of the radiator and a high-speed switch in the thermostat cover.

4 To test a radiator fan switch, remove the electrical connector and, using an ohmmeter, check for continuity across the switch terminals with the engine cold. The switch should not have continuity. Start the engine and allow the engine to reach normal operating temperature. Stop the engine and check for continuity again. The switch should show continuity when the coolant temperature reaches or exceeds the switch-on temperature. If the switch does not behave as described, renew it.

5 The air conditioning condenser fan is controlled by the ECU on petrol models, and by the cooling fan control relay on diesel models. If the condenser cooling fan fails to operate with the air conditioning on and all other checks have been completed, check for a low refrigerant charge or have the ECU diagnosed by a specialist.

Removal

Petrol models

6 Disconnect the battery (see *Disconnecting the battery*).

7 Remove the radiator (Section 5).

8 Unbolt the expansion tank and the cooling fans as required **(see illustration)**.

Diesel models

9 Disconnect the battery (see *Disconnecting the battery*).

10 Remove the engine compartment undershield (Chapter 11).

11 Release its retaining clips and remove the radiator grille top cover **(see illustration)**.

12 Disconnect the wiring for the bonnet switch and release the wiring harnesses from the various retaining clips on the radiator/bonnet lock support bracket **(see illustrations)**.

4.11 Removing radiator grille top cover

4.12a Disconnect bonnet switch wiring . . .

4.12b . . . and release wiring harnesses from retaining clips on radiator/bonnet lock support bracket

4.13a Unscrew mounting bolts . . .

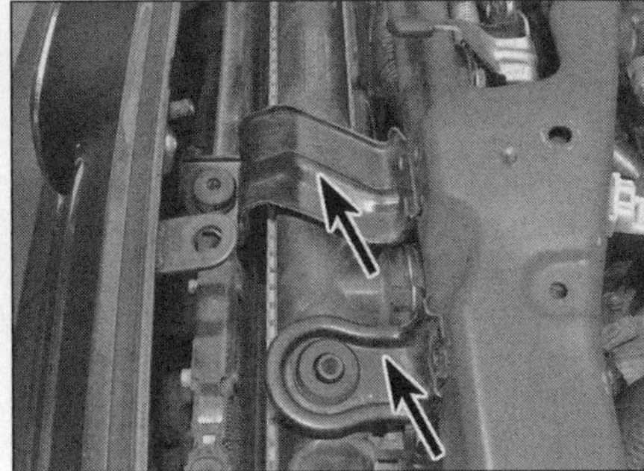
4.13b . . . to remove radiator top mounting brackets . . .

4.13c . . . air conditioning condenser mounting brackets . . .

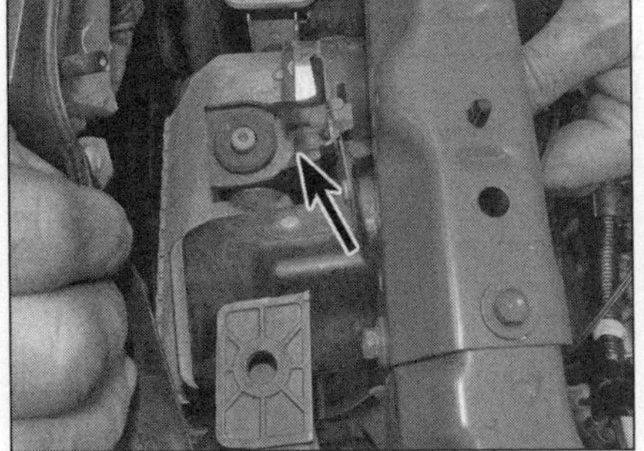
4.13d . . . and intercooler top mounting bracket

4.13e Unscrew four top mounting bolts (two at each end) . . .

13 Unscrew and remove the radiator top mounting bracket bolts, the condenser bracket mounting bolts and the intercooler mounting bracket bolt from the radiator/bonnet lock support bracket. Unscrew the four top mounting bolts and the single bolt at the bottom of the radiator/bonnet lock support bracket's vertical member. Lift out the radiator/bonnet lock support bracket (there is no need to disconnect the bonnet release

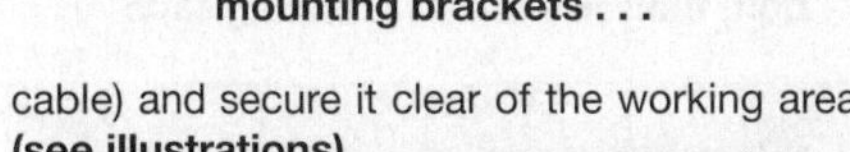

cable) and secure it clear of the working area **(see illustrations)**.

14 Disconnect the condenser fan motor wiring and release the wiring plugs from the cooling fan shroud. Unbolt the bracket securing the coolant pipe to the fan shroud, then unscrew the fan shroud's two upper mounting bolts and slacken its two lower mounting bolts (the mounting points are slotted). Lift out the condenser cooling fan assembly **(see illustration)**.

15 Disconnect the radiator fan motor wiring and release the wiring plug from the fan shroud. Unscrew the fan shroud's two upper mounting bolts and slacken its two lower mounting bolts (the mounting points are slotted). Lift out the radiator cooling fan assembly **(see illustrations)**.

Refitting

16 Refitting is a reversal of removal. Check for correct operation of the fans on completion.

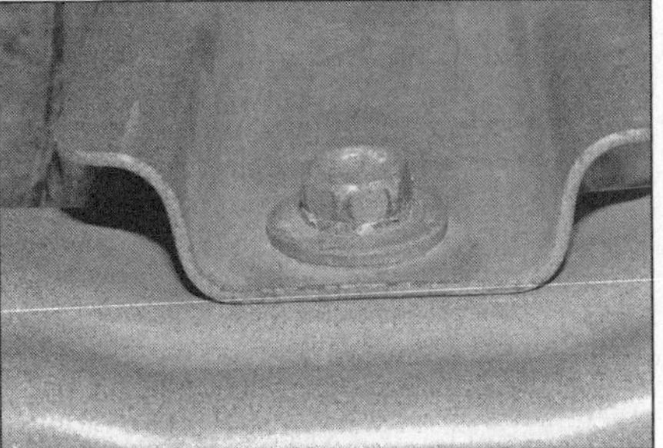
4.13f . . . and single bolt at bottom of radiator/bonnet lock support bracket vertical member . . .

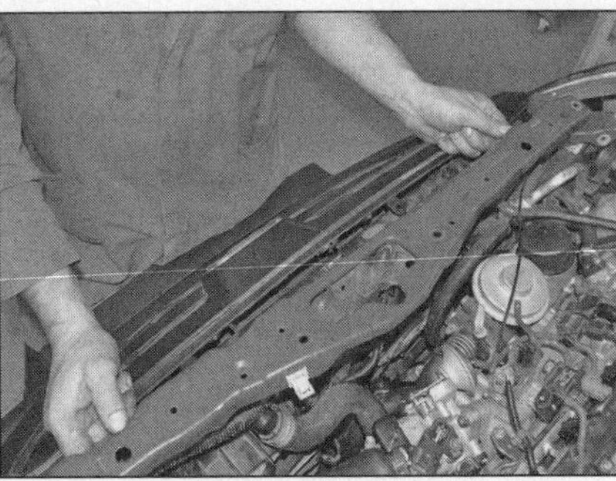
4.13g . . . to lift out radiator/bonnet lock support bracket

4.14 Unscrew air conditioning condenser cooling fan shroud's two upper mounting bolts to remove shroud

4.15a Disconnect radiator cooling fan motor wiring and release plug from fan shroud . . .

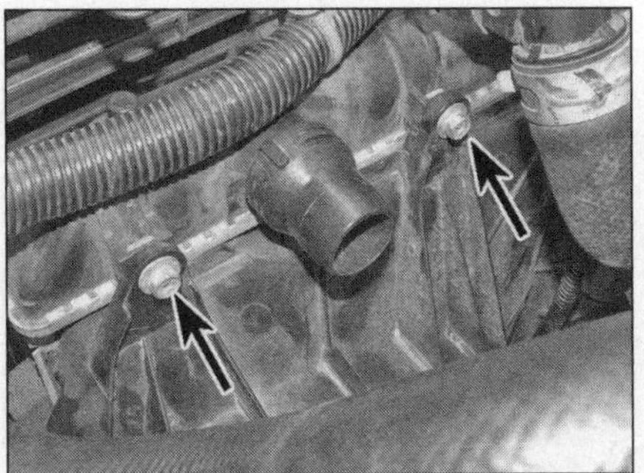
4.15b . . . unscrew fan shroud's two upper mounting bolts . . .

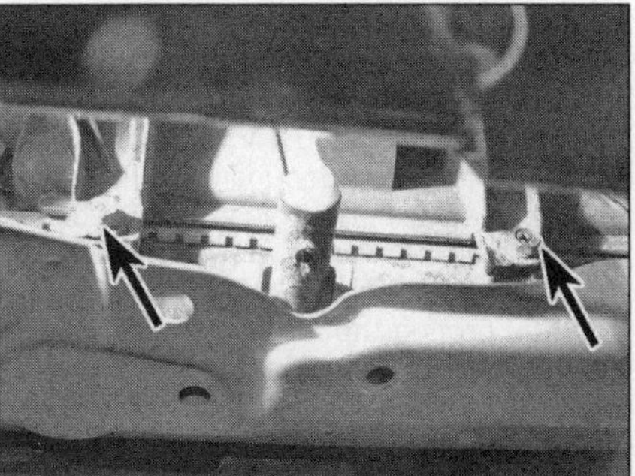
4.15c . . . and slacken two lower mounting bolts (mounting points are slotted)

5.3a Unscrew battery hold-down clamp bolt, then release its retaining clips . . .

5.3b . . . to remove the radiator grille top cover

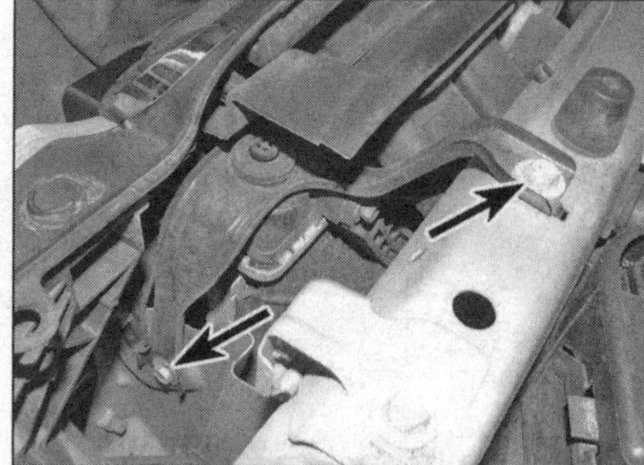
5.4a Unbolt and remove radiator top mounting brackets from left-hand . . .

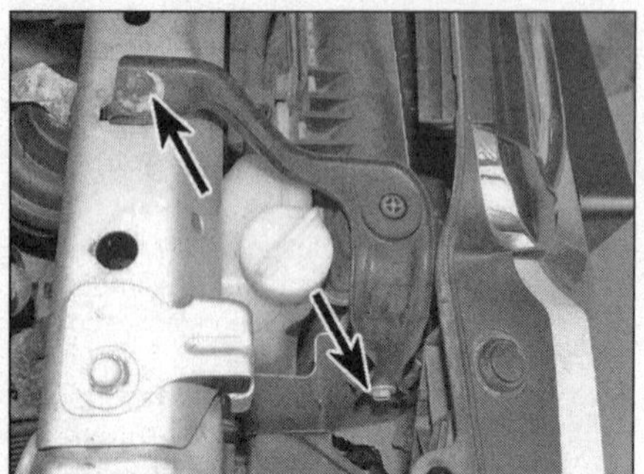
5.4b . . . and right-hand sides

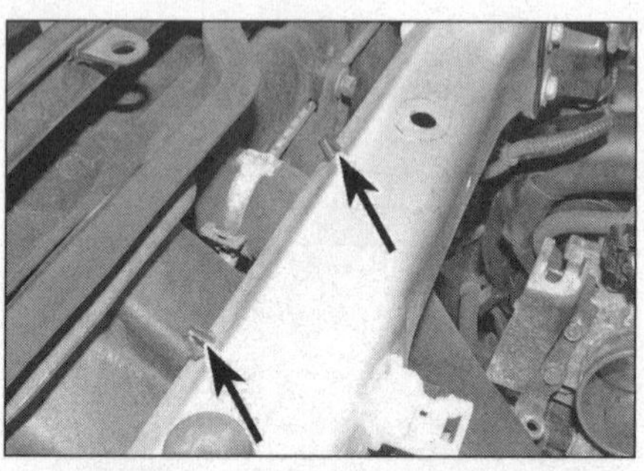
5.5 Release wiring harnesses from retaining clips on radiator/bonnet lock support bracket

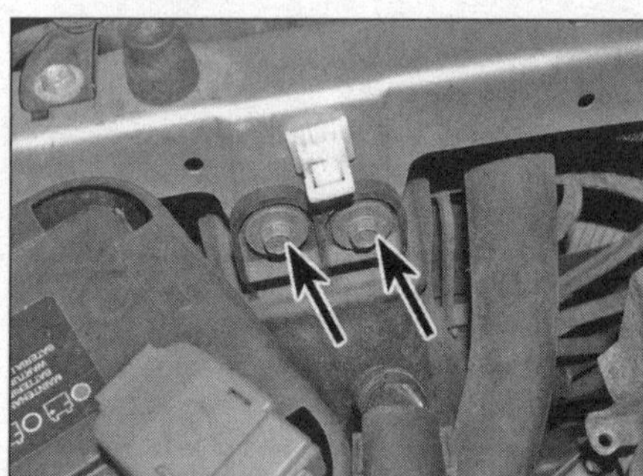
5.6a Unscrew two intake air duct mounting bolts

5 Radiator – removal and refitting

Note: *Refer to the precautions in Section 1 before starting work.*

Removal

1 Drain the cooling system (Chapter 1), saving the coolant if it is fit for re-use.

2 Remove the engine compartment under-shield (Chapter 11).

Petrol models

3 Unscrew the battery hold-down clamp bolt, then release its retaining clips and remove the radiator grille top cover **(see illustrations)**.

4 Unbolt and remove the radiator top mounting brackets **(see illustrations)**.

5 Disconnect the wiring for the bonnet switch (where fitted) and release the wiring harnesses from the retaining clips on the radiator/bonnet lock support bracket **(see illustration)**.

6 Unscrew and remove the intake air duct mounting bolts, the four radiator/bonnet lock support bracket top mounting bolts and the single bolt at the bottom of the radiator/bonnet lock support bracket's vertical member. Lift out the radiator/bonnet lock support bracket (there is no need to disconnect the bonnet release cable) and secure it clear of the working area **(see illustrations)**.

7 Disconnect the radiator top and bottom hoses.

8 Disconnect the condenser fan motor wiring and the radiator fan motor wiring. Release the wiring plugs from the cooling fan shrouds **(see illustrations)**.

Diesel models

9 Remove the condenser and radiator fan/shroud assemblies as described in Section 4.

10 Disconnect the radiator quick-release unions (Section 2).

11 Disconnect the two coolant hoses between the radiator and the expansion tank.

5.6b Unscrew two top mounting bolts at left-hand end (two at each end) . . .

5.6c . . . two top mounting bolts at right-hand end . . .

5.6d . . . and single bolt at bottom of radiator/bonnet lock support bracket vertical member . . .

5.6e . . . to lift out radiator/bonnet lock support bracket

All models

12 Disconnect the wiring from the radiator fan switch.

13 Lift out the radiator, noting that its lower pegs locate into rubber mountings. Tilt it to one side to avoid spilling coolant on the paintwork **(see illustration)**.

14 On petrol models, unbolt the expansion tank and the fan assemblies as required.

15 Use a soft brush and an airline or garden hose to clear the radiator matrix of leaves, insects, etc.

16 Leaks or damage should be repaired by a specialist, or the radiator should be renewed or exchanged for a reconditioned unit.

17 Examine the mounting rubbers for signs of damage or deterioration and renew if necessary.

Refitting

18 Refitting is a reversal of removal, noting the following points:

a) Guide the radiator onto its lower mountings, taking care not to damage the fins on the surrounding components ***(see illustration)****.*

b) On diesel-engined models, reconnect the quick-release unions as described in Section 2.

6 Expansion tank – removal and refitting

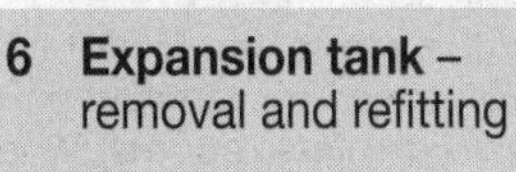

Note: *Refer to the precautions in Section 1 before starting work.*

Petrol-engined models

1 Remove the radiator as described in Section 5.

2 Unscrew the mounting bolt and release the expansion tank from its mountings. Unclip the overflow hose and withdraw the expansion tank.

3 Refitting is the reverse of removal.

Diesel-engined models

4 Unclip the steering fluid reservoir and secure it to one side.

5 Unbolt the expansion tank and its mounting bracket from the right-hand inner wing.

6 Have a container ready underneath the tank, then release the hose clip and disconnect the lower hose. Allow the coolant to drain.

7 Disconnect the two hoses at the front of the tank and release the overflow hose from the clips securing it to the bodywork. Remove the tank.

8 Refitting is the reverse of removal.

7 Water pump – inspection, removal and refitting

Note: *Refer to the precautions in Section 1 before starting work.*

5.8a Disconnect air conditioning condenser cooling fan motor wiring . . .

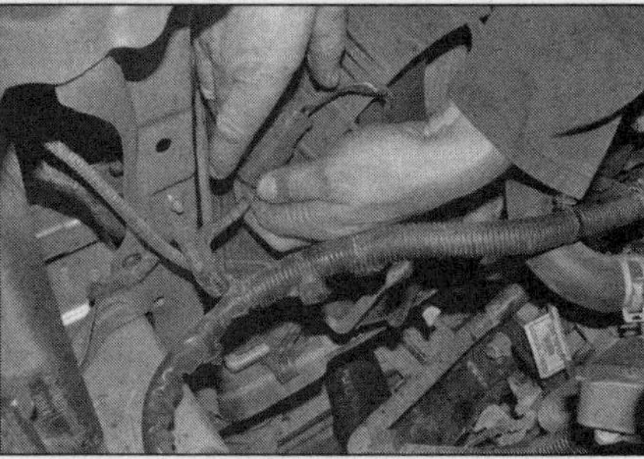

5.8b . . . and radiator cooling fan motor wiring – release wiring from cooling fan shrouds

5.13 Be careful not to damage fins when removing/refitting radiator

5.18 Ensure radiator bottom mounting pegs engage correctly in rubber mountings

Inspection

1 A water pump failure can cause serious engine damage due to overheating.

2 To check the pump, first remove the auxiliary drivebelt (Chapter 1A or 1B).

3 There are two weep (or vent) holes behind the water pump pulley. If a failure occurs in the pump seal, coolant will leak from these holes. Note however that a small amount of 'weeping' is normal.

4 An established coolant leak will usually show up as a powdery deposit under the holes.

5 If the pump bearings fail, there may be a howling or scraping sound from the pump while the engine is running. Check the rotation of the pulley: it should rotate smoothly and freely, without noise, stiffness or jerkiness. If the pump is defective it must be renewed.

Removal

6 Drain the cooling system (Chapter 1), saving the coolant if it is fit for re-use.

7 Remove the auxiliary drivebelt (Chapter 1A or 1B). Access will be improved if the drivebelt tensioner (and if applicable the idler pulley on diesel models) is also unbolted.

8 Remove the mounting bolts and detach the water pump from the engine. Prise the O-ring seal from the pump's groove.

9 It is not possible to overhaul the pump.

Refitting

10 Clean the bolt threads and the water pump housing and water pump mating surfaces.

11 Set a new O-ring in the groove of the pump mating surface **(see illustration)**.

12 Offer the pump up to the engine, fit the bolts and tighten them progressively to the specified torque **(see illustrations)**.

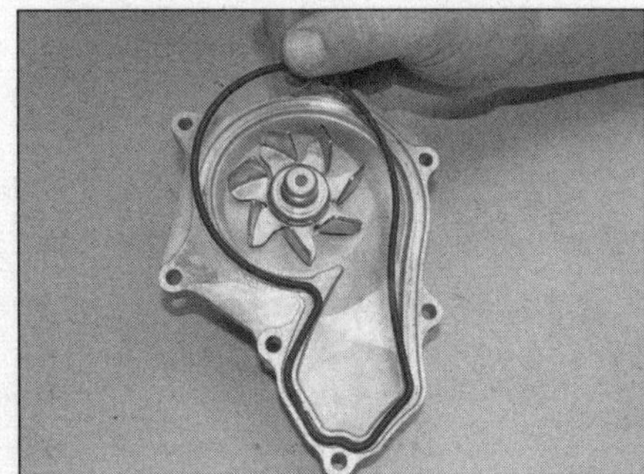

7.11 Fit a new O-ring in groove of water pump mating surface . . .

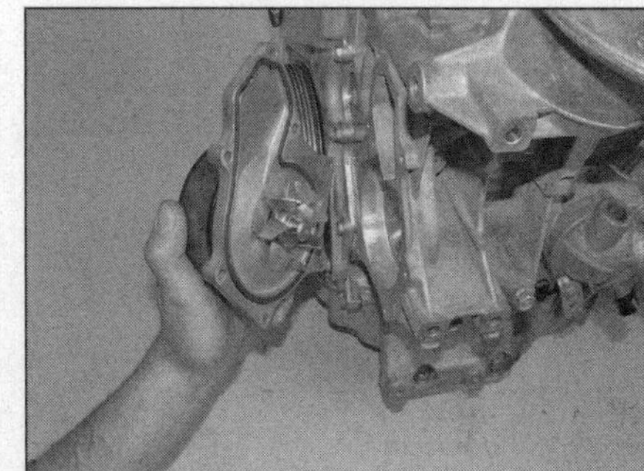

7.12a . . . and use grease to stick in place while refitting pump

7.12b Location of water pump mounting bolts – petrol models . . .

7.12c . . . and diesel models

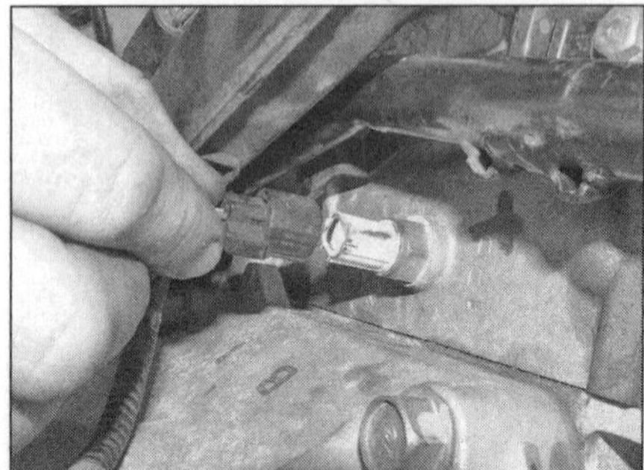

8.7 Engine coolant temperature sensor – petrol models

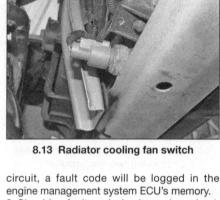

8.13 Radiator cooling fan switch

13 The remainder of refitting is a reversal of the removal procedure.

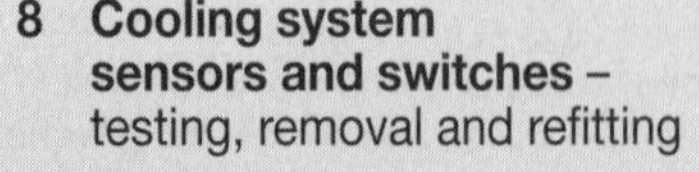

8 Cooling system sensors and switches – testing, removal and refitting

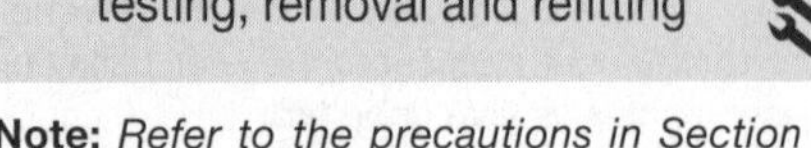

Note: *Refer to the precautions in Section 1 before starting work.*

Coolant temperature sensor

Testing

1 The coolant temperature sensor is located in the cylinder head, and is used by both the engine management system and the instrument panel temperature gauge. A faulty coolant temperature sensor is often the prime cause of poor running after a cold start, or poor fuel economy.

2 In the event of a fault in the sensor or its circuit, a fault code will be logged in the engine management system ECU's memory.

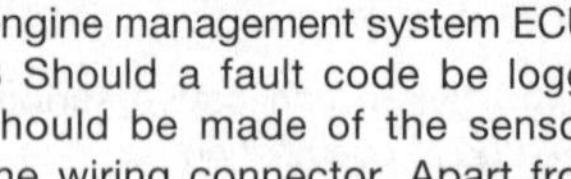

3 Should a fault code be logged, a check should be made of the sensor wiring and the wiring connector. Apart from testing by substitution with a new unit, further checks require the use of specialist test equipment.

Removal and refitting

4 Disconnect the battery (see *Disconnecting the battery*). On diesel models, remove the acoustic cover.

5 Drain the cooling system (partially, down to the level of the sensor) as described in Chapter 1.

6 On petrol models, remove the air cleaner assembly (Chapter 4A).

7 Disconnect the sensor **(see illustration)**, then unscrew and remove it from the cylinder head. Remove the O-ring.

8 Refitting is the reverse of the removal procedure. Fit a new O-ring and tighten the sensor to the specified torque.

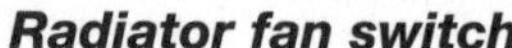

Radiator fan switch

Testing

9 Refer to Section 4.

Removal and refitting

10 Disconnect the battery (see *Disconnecting the battery*).

11 Remove the engine compartment undershield (Chapter 11).

12 Drain the cooling system as described in Chapter 1A or 1B.

13 Disconnect the wiring plug, then unscrew the switch from the radiator or thermostat housing and remove it **(see illustration)**. Recover the O-ring.

14 Refitting is the reverse of the removal procedure. Use a new O-ring and tighten the switch to the specified torque.

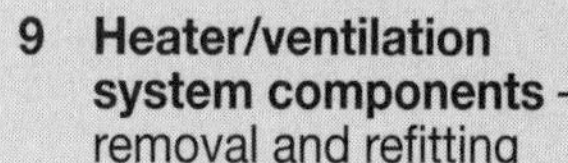

9 Heater/ventilation system components – removal and refitting

Side air vents

1 The facia panel side vents are clipped directly into the ends of the main facia panel. Wrap a flat-tipped screwdriver with protective tape and use a piece of card or a wad of cloth to prevent damage to the facia panel itself, then carefully prise up each vent at its side retaining clips **(see illustrations)**. When the side clips are released, lift the vent and disengage the two hooks along its upper edge. Refitting is a reversal of removal; ensure that the hooks and clips engage securely.

Centre air vents

2 Remove the two screws at the base of the panel **(see illustration)**.

3 Pull the panel outwards at the bottom, releasing the clips, then withdraw the panel and disconnect the hazard warning switch **(see illustrations)**.

4 Refitting is a reversal of removal.

Blower motor components

5 The blower motor is located behind the glovebox.

6 Remove the passenger's side under cover and the glovebox (Chapter 11).

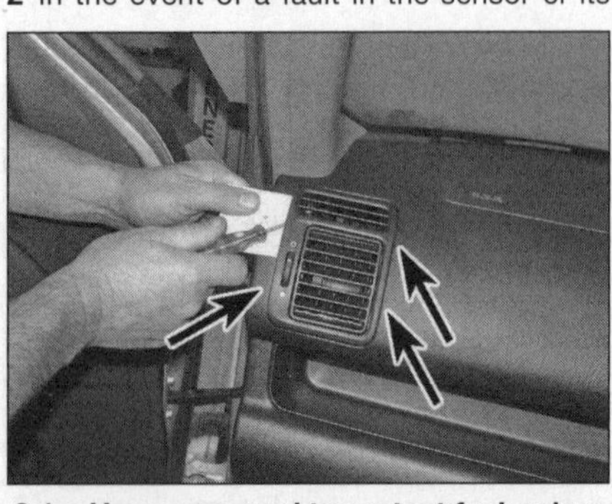

9.1a Use some card to protect facia when prising up side vents at points shown . . .

9.1b . . . lift vent (note clips at sides) to release hooks on upper edge

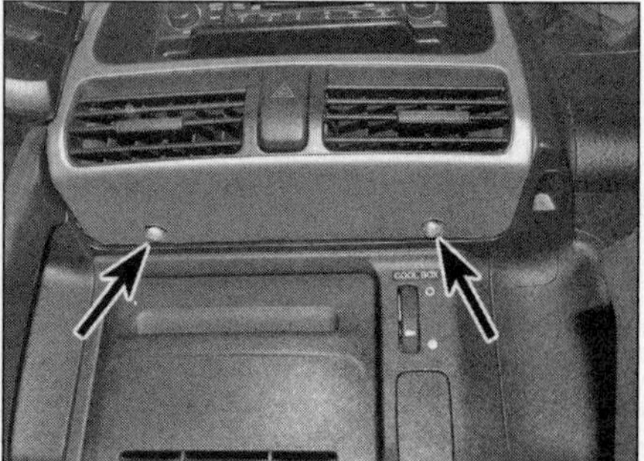

9.2 Remove two screws at base of centre air vent panel . . .

9.3a . . . gently pull panel out of facia to release clips . . .

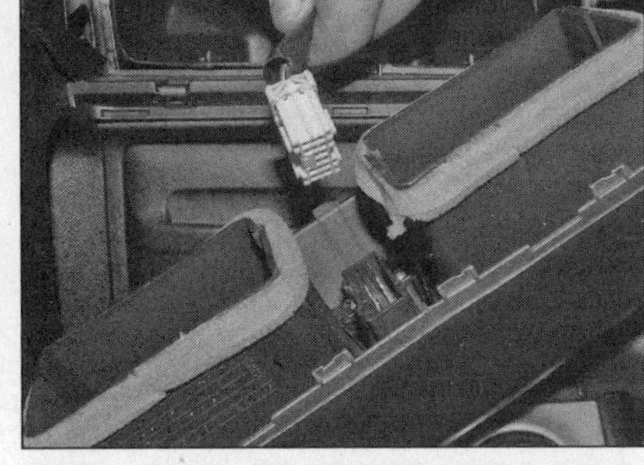
9.3b . . . then disconnect hazard warning switch wiring

9.8 Disconnect blower fan motor wiring plug . . .

9.9a . . . then undo three retaining screws . . .

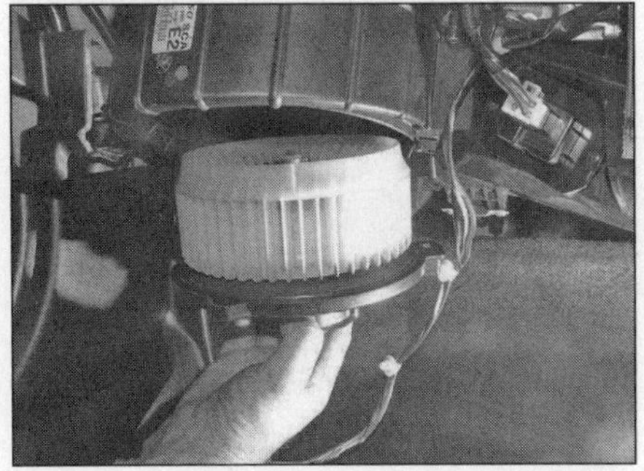
9.9b . . . and withdraw blower motor and fan from housing

9.12 Disconnect wiring plug from resistor pack . . .

7 More working room will be created by removing the engine management ECU (Chapter 4A or 4B).

Motor and fan

8 Disconnect the motor wiring plug **(see illustration)**.

9 Remove the three motor securing screws, and withdraw the motor and fan from the housing **(see illustrations)**.

10 Refitting is a reversal of removal.

Resistor pack

11 If the blower fan will only operate on its fastest speed, or not at all, the resistor pack may be faulty. Gain access as described in paragraph 6.

12 Disconnect the wiring plug from the resistor pack **(see illustration)**.

13 Remove the two mounting screws and withdraw the pack from the housing **(see illustration)**.

14 Refitting is a reversal of removal.

Recirculation motor

15 Gain access to the recirculation motor as described in paragraphs 6 and 7; in this case the ECU must be removed.

16 Disconnect the recirculation motor wiring plug. Release the wiring from the small bracket, then unbolt the ECU mounting bracket **(see illustrations)**.

17 Remove the three securing screws and withdraw the motor **(see illustration)**.

18 Refitting is a reversal of removal.

Complete housing

19 Remove the passenger's side under cover and the glovebox (Chapter 11). At the base of the glovebox aperture is a plastic cross-brace, which must be cut through at each end, between the moulded lines, to allow the blower motor housing to be removed **(see illustrations)**. Cut only the plastic, not the metal frame behind.

20 Release the relays from in front of the metal frame **(see illustrations)**.

21 Unscrew the four screws, two at each

9.13a . . . undo two retaining screws . . .

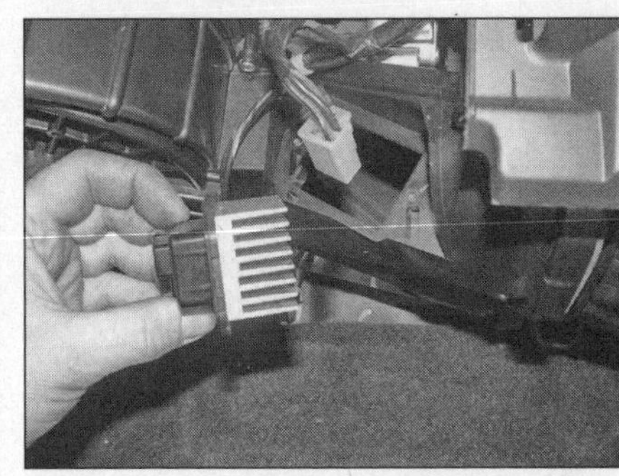
9.13b . . . and withdraw resistor pack from housing

9.16a Disconnect recirculation motor wiring plug and release wiring from bracket . . .

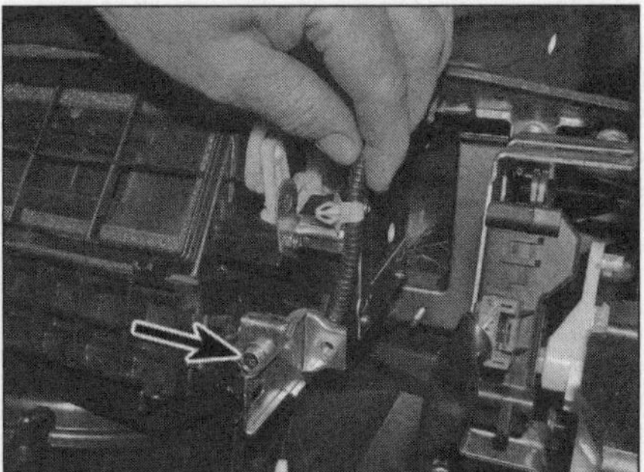
9.16b . . . unbolt ECU mounting bracket . . .

9.17 . . . then undo three screws to release recirculation motor

9.19a Cut through plastic cross-brace at each end, between moulded lines . . .

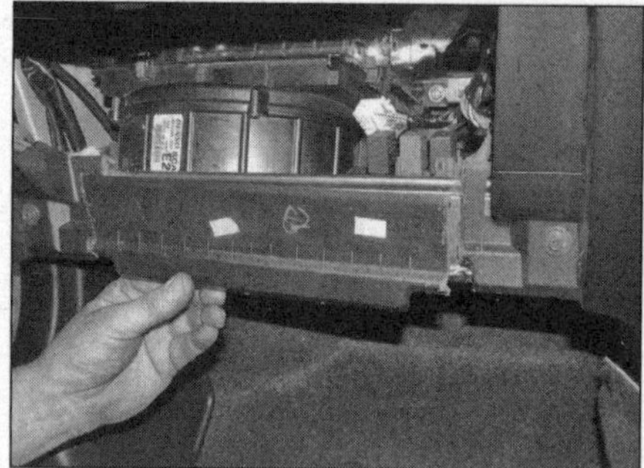

9.19b . . . and discard

9.20a Release relays from in front of metal frame . . .

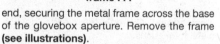

9.20b . . . by pushing up to release retaining clips

9.21a Unscrew four screws securing metal frame across base of glovebox aperture . . .

end, securing the metal frame across the base of the glovebox aperture. Remove the frame **(see illustrations)**.

22 Remove the engine management ECU as described in Chapter 4A or 4B.

23 Disconnect the wiring plugs from the blower motor, the resistor pack and the recirculation motor. Release the wiring from the clips and ties securing it to the blower motor housing **(see illustrations)**.

24 Fold the carpet towards the rear of the vehicle. The housing is fastened to the heater unit by two bolts and secured on the bulkhead mountings by two nuts and two bolts – unscrew these and withdraw the motor housing from under the facia **(see illustrations)**. Remove dead leaves and other rubbish from the space above and check that the seals are in good condition.

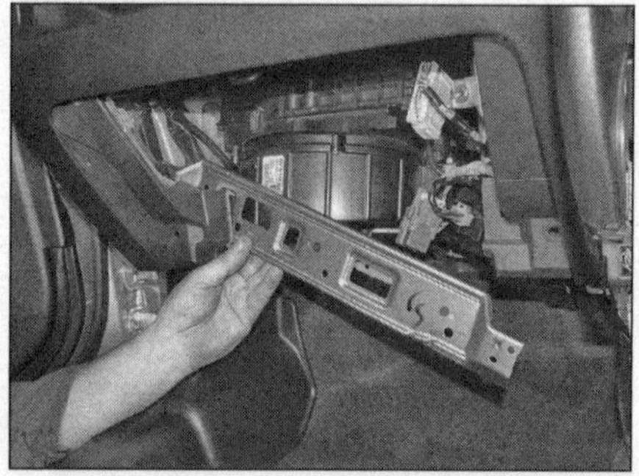

9.21b . . . and remove frame

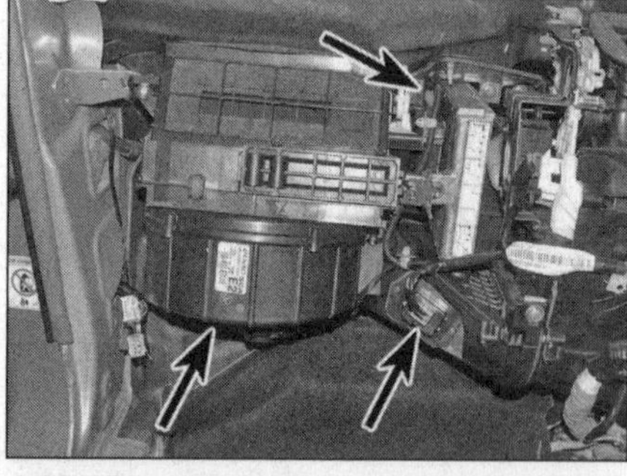

9.23a Disconnect wiring for blower motor, resistor pack and recirculation motor . . .

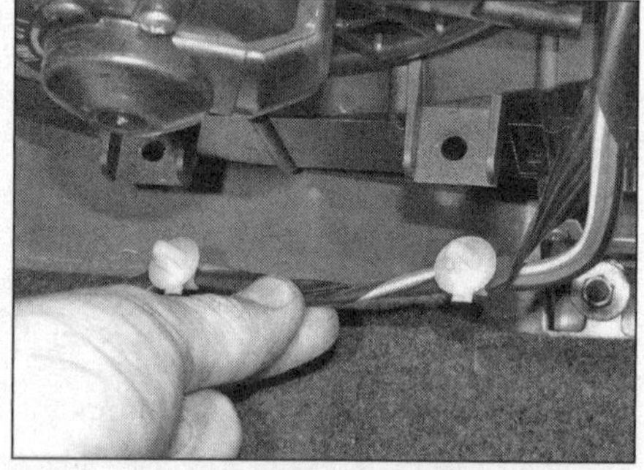

9.23b . . . and release wiring from clips and ties securing it to blower motor housing

9.24a Unscrew blower motor housing-to-heater unit bolts at front . . .

9.24b . . . and at rear, to release blower motor housing from heater unit . . .

9.24c . . . then unscrew bottom mounting nut from stud on bulkhead . . .

9.24d . . . and bolts at bottom . . .

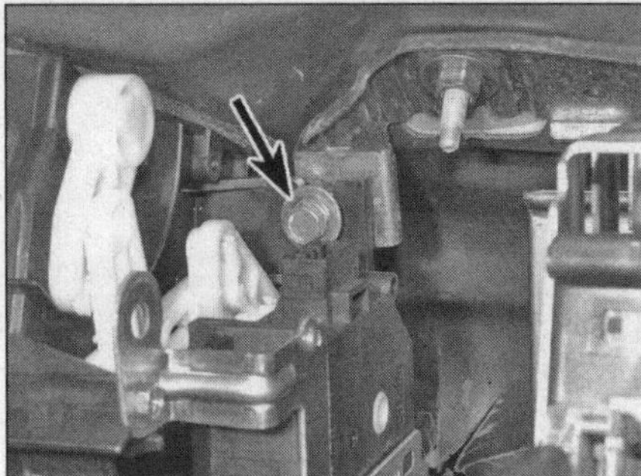
9.24e . . . and top of bulkhead mounting bracket

9.24f Unscrew mounting nut on left-hand side (door pillar bracket) . . .

9.24g . . . and withdraw blower motor housing

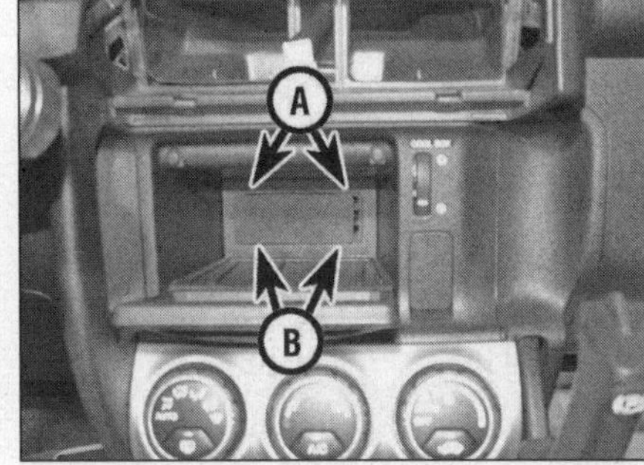

9.27a Carefully lever at points A first, then points B . . .

9.27b . . . to release panel from centre of dashboard pocket/cool box

25 Refitting is a reversal of removal.

Heater control panel

Note: *On vehicles with automatic air conditioning (climate control), this component is called the climate control unit (see Section 10).*

Removal and refitting

26 Remove the facia centre air vent panel, as described in paragraphs 2 and 3 above.

27 Open the lid of the dashboard pocket/cool box and, using a flat-tipped screwdriver and taking care not to damage the surface, prise out the upper edge of the panel at the centre of the pocket. With the two hooks on the upper edge released, release the two hooks on the lower edge and withdraw the panel **(see illustrations)**.

28 Undo the single retaining screw. Make up a hooked tool using welding rod or similar, engage it behind the screw hole and pull on the centre of the pocket to release the two clips on its top edge, the two clips on its bottom edge and the two clips on the driver's side. Withdraw the dashboard pocket/cool box from the facia **(see illustrations)**.

29 Undo the two retaining screws and carefully lever out the heater control panel to release the two retaining clips along its upper edge, followed by the two clips on its lower edge, then withdraw the heater control panel and disconnect its wiring to release it from the facia **(see illustrations)**.

30 The dials around the controls and the

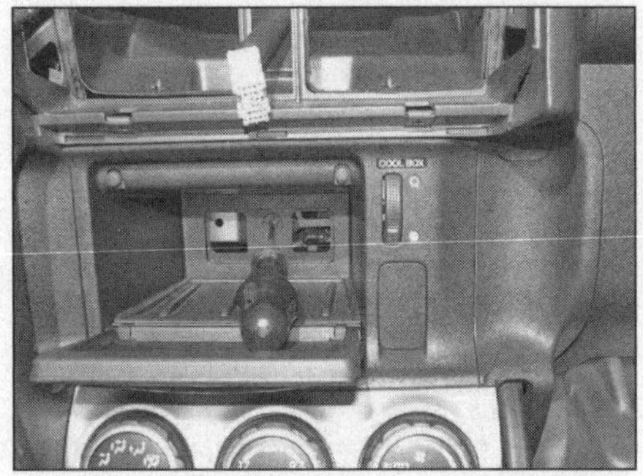
9.28a Unscrew retaining screw . . .

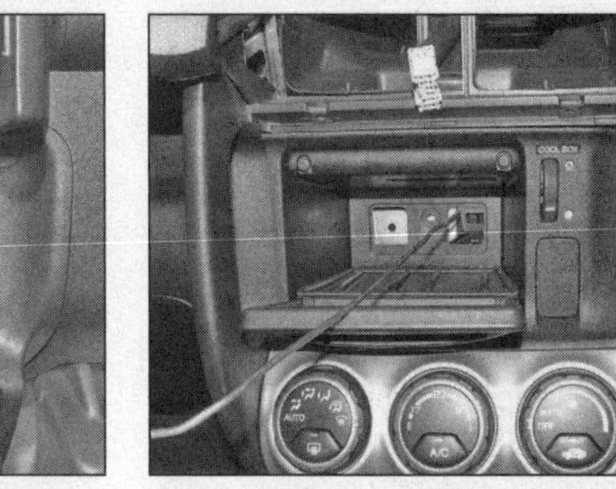
9.28b . . . then engage hooked tool behind pocket/box as shown . . .

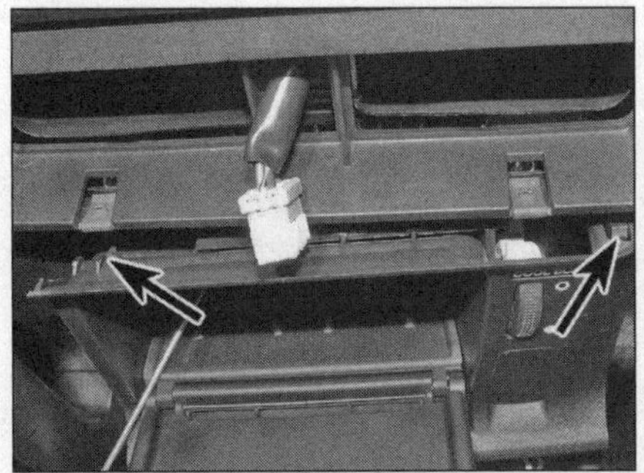
9.28c . . . and pull to release clips along top (bottom similar) edge . . .

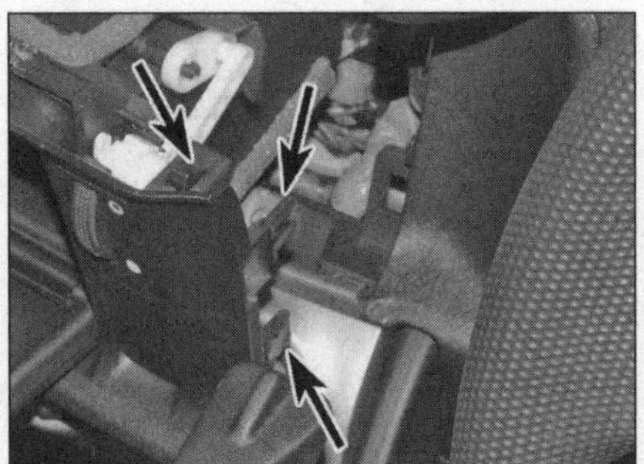
9.28d . . . and from driver's side edge, to withdraw dashboard pocket/cool box

9.29a Undo two retaining screws . . .

9.29b . . . and carefully lever out heater control panel to release retaining clip on right-hand end . . .

9.29c . . . and left-hand end of its upper edge, followed by two clips on its lower edge . . .

9.29d . . . then withdraw heater control panel and disconnect its wiring to release it from facia

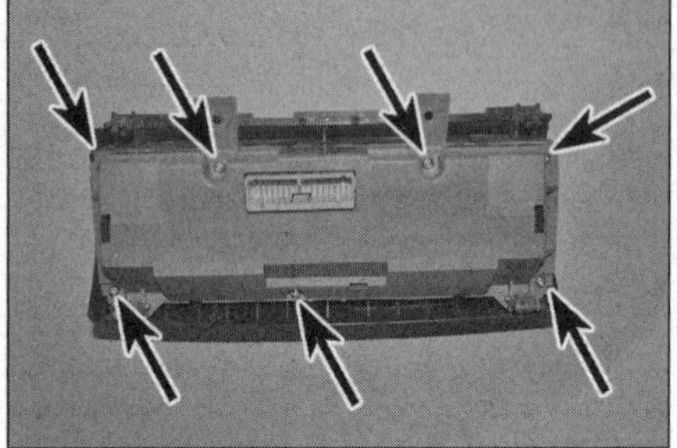

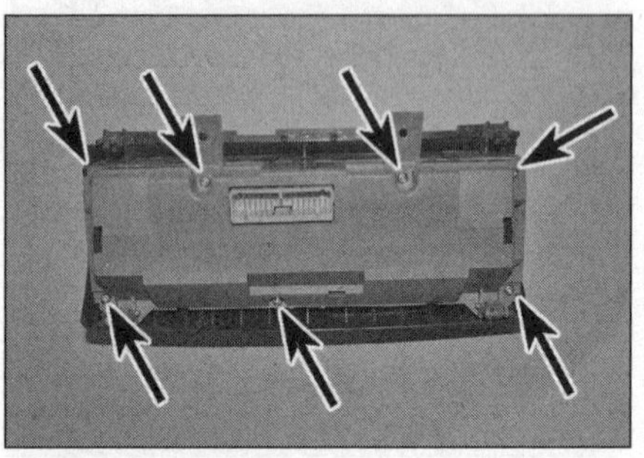

9.31a Undo retaining screws to separate heater control panel cover (and control unit) from panel . . .

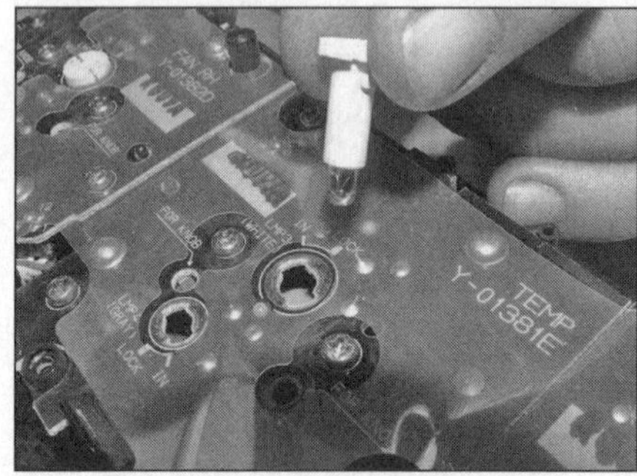

9.31b . . . turn illuminating bulbs one-quarter turn anti-clockwise to remove . . .

9.31c . . . and reverse to refit

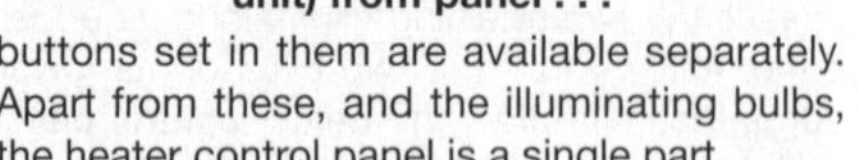

buttons set in them are available separately. Apart from these, and the illuminating bulbs, the heater control panel is a single part.

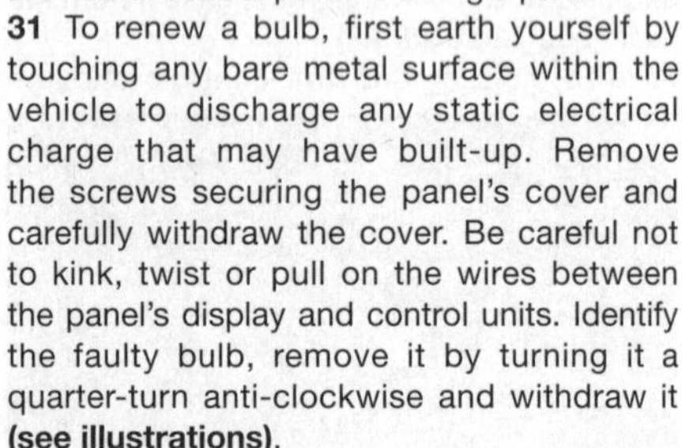

31 To renew a bulb, first earth yourself by touching any bare metal surface within the vehicle to discharge any static electrical charge that may have built-up. Remove the screws securing the panel's cover and carefully withdraw the cover. Be careful not to kink, twist or pull on the wires between the panel's display and control units. Identify the faulty bulb, remove it by turning it a quarter-turn anti-clockwise and withdraw it **(see illustrations)**.

32 Refitting is a reversal of removal.

Heater/ventilation and air conditioning self-diagnosis function

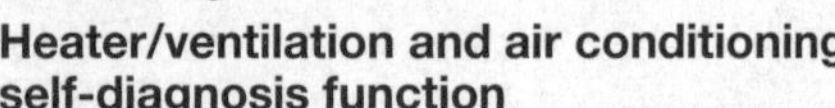

33 The electronic control unit mounted in the heater control panel has a self-diagnosis function, in which the system is continuously monitored for correct operation. Any detected faults are logged as fault codes which can be displayed as flashing signals using the following procedure. Any faults will have to be referred to a Honda dealer or specialist.

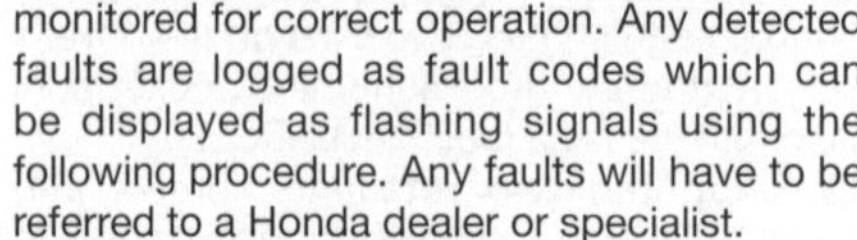

a) Switch the ignition off.

b) Switch off the fan switch, set the temperature control to the coldest setting (fully anti-clockwise) and set the mode control to face-level vents.

c) Switch on the ignition, press and hold the recirculation control button, then (within 10 seconds, while still holding down the recirculation control button), press the rear window demister button 5 times. The recirculation mode indicator in the button will blink twice, then self-diagnosis will begin. Release the buttons and watch carefully

d) If a fault code has been logged, the recirculation mode indicator will blink between one and thirteen times to indicate Diagnostic Trouble Codes (DTCs) 1 to 13. The signal will be repeated at 1.5-second intervals. If a fault has been found in the air conditioning system's evaporator temperature sensor circuit, the air conditioning system button's indicator will blink either fourteen or fifteen times to indicate DTCs 14 or 15. **Note:** *DTCs 1 to 6 will be found only on vehicles with automatic air conditioning (climate control).*

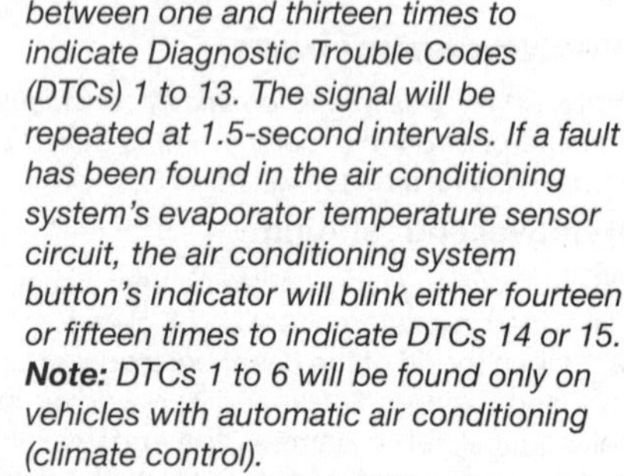

e) If no codes have been logged, the indicators will not blink.

f) Once self-diagnosis has been completed and any fault codes recorded, switch off the ignition to cancel the self-diagnosis function.

Heater unit

34 Have the air conditioning system discharged by a specialist. At the same time, have the evaporator connections at the bulkhead disconnected, then do not use the system until it has been reconnected and recharged. The evaporator connections are next to the heater pipes, and the pipe flange is secured by a single bolt to the evaporator core and by two nuts to the bulkhead **(see illustration)**.

35 Either drain the cooling system as described in Chapter 1, or clamp the heater hoses at their bulkhead connections.

36 Release the spring clips and disconnect the two heater hoses from their bulkhead connections **(see illustration)**. Mop-up any coolant spillage.

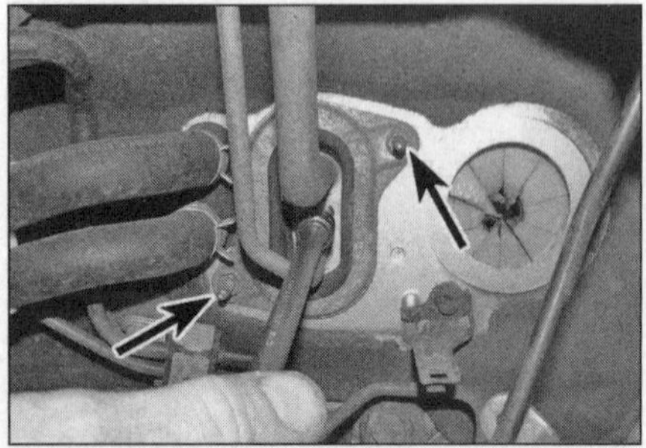

9.34 Unscrew bolt securing air conditioning system pipes to evaporator core – note nuts securing pipe flange to bulkhead

9.36 Disconnecting heater hoses from their bulkhead connections

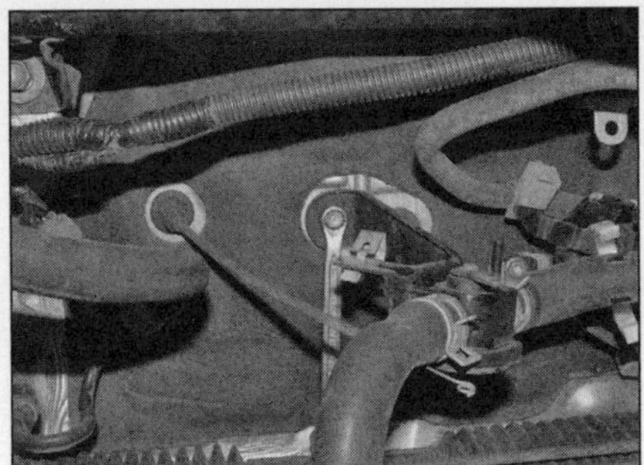

9.38a With cable disconnected, unbolt heater control valve from engine compartment bulkhead . . .

9.38b . . . to allow heater unit 8 mm mounting nut to be unscrewed

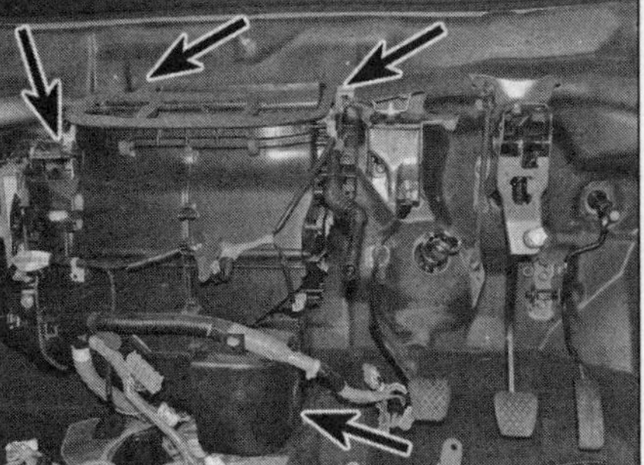

9.41a Disconnect wiring and release harnesses from heater unit – note mounting bolts arrowed

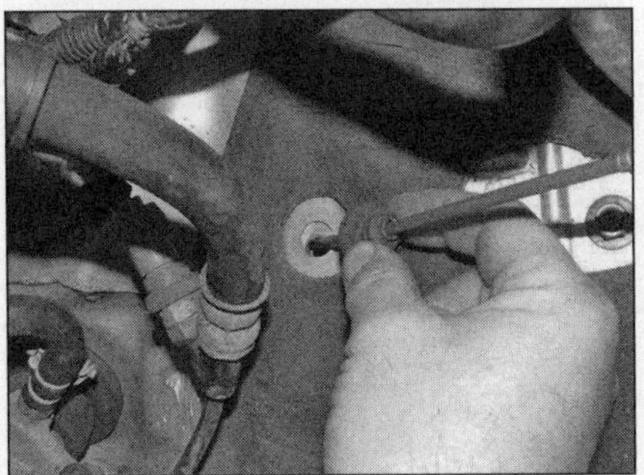

9.41b Release the cable grommet from the bulkhead

9.42a Unscrew mounting bolt from upper left-hand side . . .

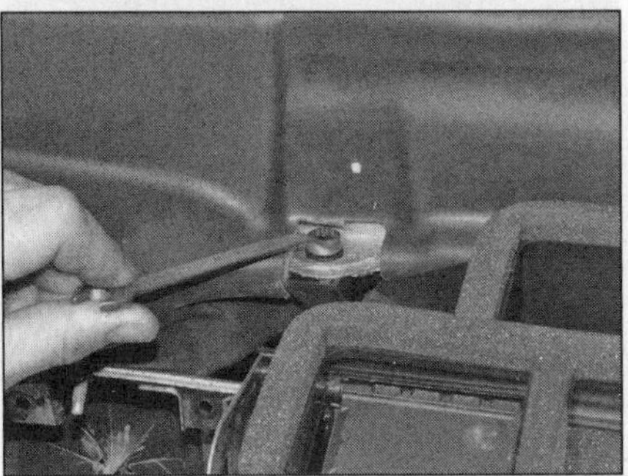

9.42b . . . from top left-hand side . . .

37 Disconnect the cable from the heater control valve and unbolt the valve's support bracket from the bulkhead (see paragraphs 52 to 53).

38 Unscrew and remove the heater unit mounting nut from the bulkhead **(see illustrations)**.

39 Remove the facia as described in Chapter 11.

40 Remove the engine management ECU as described in Chapter 4A or 4B.

41 Check around the heater unit and disconnect all the wiring plugs, noting their locations. Return to the engine compartment and release the control cable's grommet from the bulkhead **(see illustrations)**.

42 In addition to the blower motor housing's mounting nuts and bolts, the heater unit is secured by three bolts from the top, and a single bolt at the front at floor level. Remove the bolts, and with the help of an assistant, lift the heater unit slightly, and pull it away from the bulkhead. Note that, as this is done, the unit will separate itself from the drain tube in the floor at the front, and possibly from the twin-vent duct at floor level. Guide the control cable through the bulkhead aperture as the heater unit is removed. The heater pipes will be withdrawn through the bulkhead – recover the sealing grommet **(see illustrations)**.

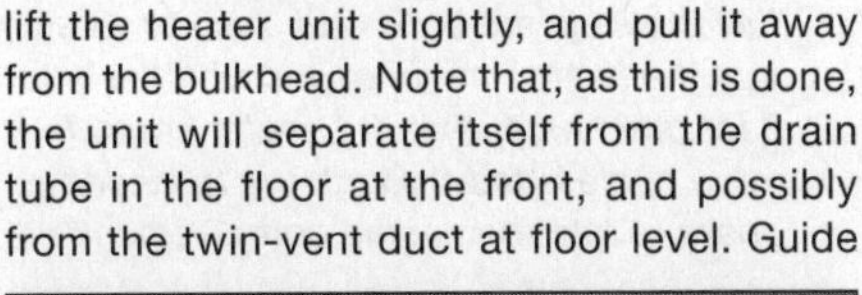

9.42c . . . from top right-hand side . . .

9.42d . . . and from bottom right-hand side

9.42e Heater unit can be removed complete with blower motor housing . . .

9.42f . . . or separately, if blower motor housing is removed first

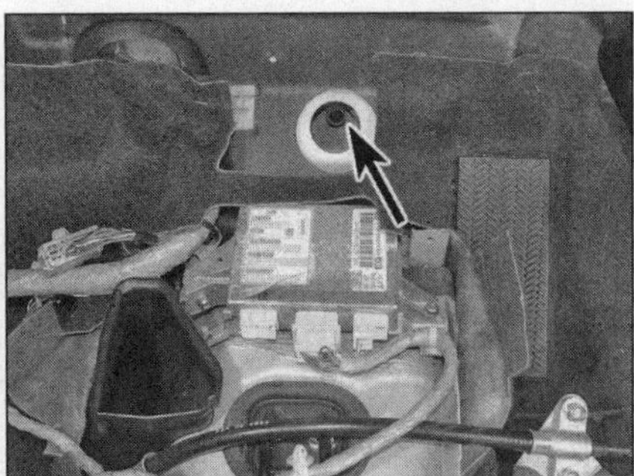

9.42g Note heater unit/evaporator drain tube protruding through bulkhead

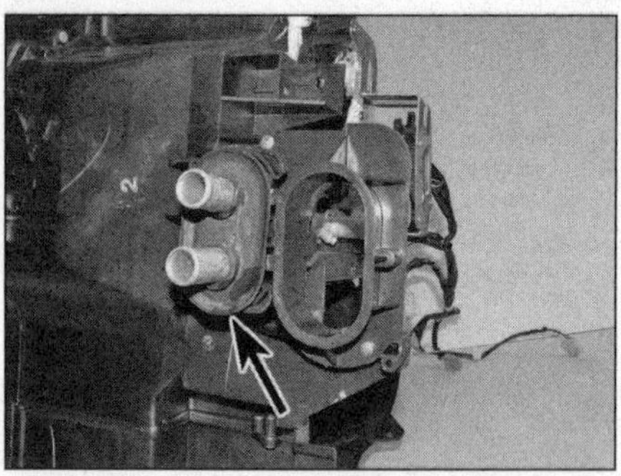

9.43a Ensure grommet is fitted correctly to heater pipes

9.43b If heater unit/evaporator drain tube is blocked or dislodged unbolt heat shield from engine compartment bulkhead . . .

9.43c . . . withdraw heat shield to reach drain tube (arrowed) . . .

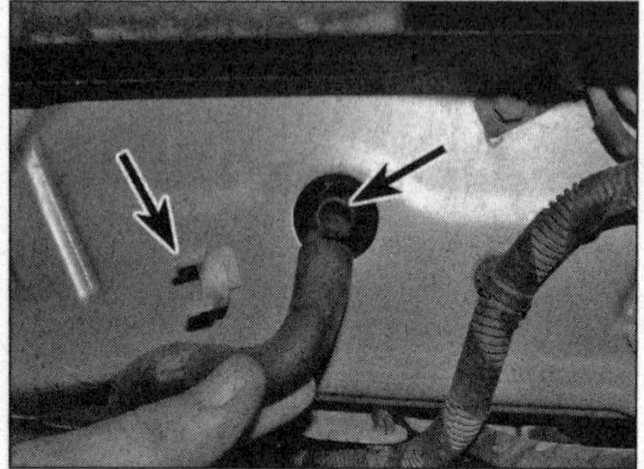

9.43d . . . connect drain tube to stub on heater unit and fit into clip provided

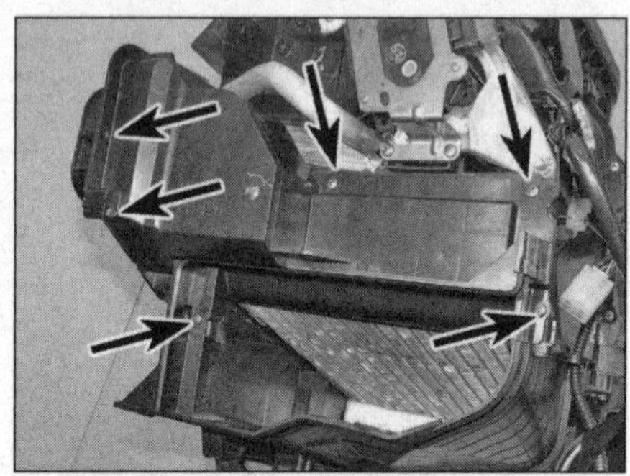

9.45a Undo six retaining screws from heater unit . . .

9.45b . . . withdraw expansion valve cover . . .

43 Refitting is a reversal of removal, noting the following points:

a) When offering the unit into place, make sure the grommet is fitted to the heater pipes, and that they fit properly into their holes in the bulkhead. Also ensure that the heater unit engages with the floor drain tube, that the heater control valve cable is fed through the bulkhead aperture into the engine compartment without being kinked or bent, and that the floor vent ducts are correctly fitted ***(see illustrations)****.*

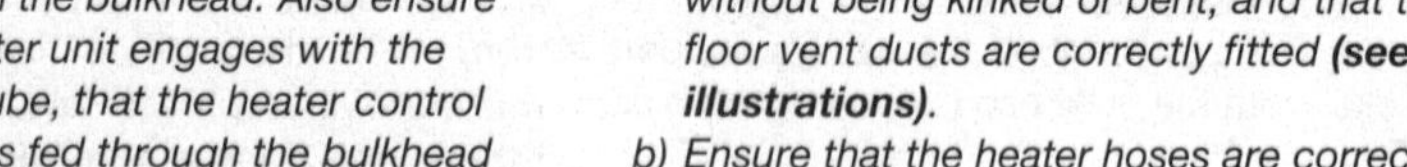

b) Ensure that the heater hoses are correctly reconnected.

c) Where applicable, have the air conditioning evaporator pipes reconnected (using new O-rings) and the system recharged by a specialist.

d) Either refill or top-up the cooling system (Chapter 1A, 1B or Weekly checks).

e) Reconnect and adjust the heater control valve cable as described later in this Section.

9.45c . . . and carefully withdraw evaporator from heater unit

9.46a Undo two screws from front . . .

9.46b . . . and single screw from rear . . .

9.46c . . . and remove heater pipe flange cover

Heater matrix

44 Remove the heater unit as described above.

45 Undo the six screws securing the expansion valve cover, and take off the cover. Withdraw the air conditioning system evaporator from the housing **(see illustrations)**.

46 Undo the three screws and take off the heater pipe flange cover **(see illustrations)**.

47 Taking care not to bend the heater pipes, withdraw the matrix from the housing **(see illustration)**. Be prepared for coolant spillage. Remove the sealing grommet.

48 If the matrix has been leaking, it may be possible for a radiator specialist to repair it; otherwise, a new matrix will be required.

49 Refitting is a reversal of removal.

Heater control valve

Note: *The heater control valve is located in the engine compartment, on the bulkhead just behind the engine. For diesel models*

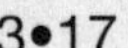

9.47 Carefully withdraw heater matrix from heater unit

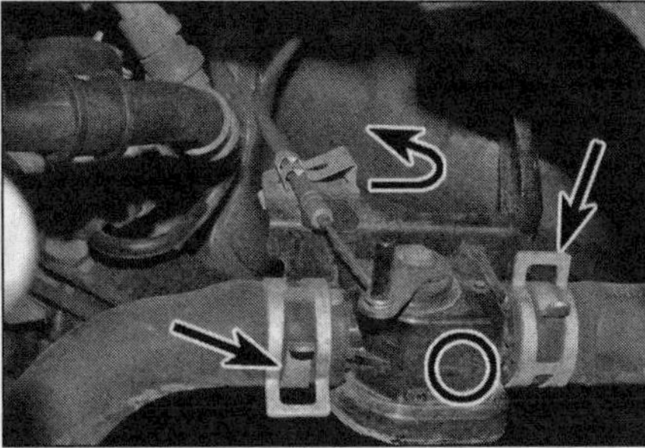

9.51 Disconnect heater hoses, release cable clamp as shown and note arrow marking on heater control valve

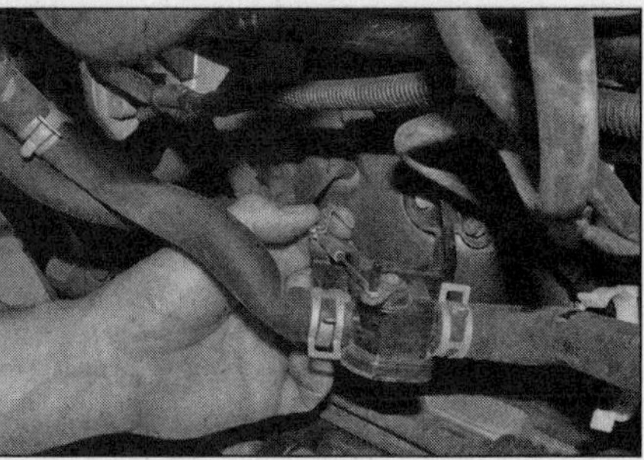

9.52 Disconnecting control cable inner wire from heater control valve – note valve in maximum heat position

access will be improved by the removal of the acoustic cover and the air cleaner assembly (Chapter 4B).

50 Either drain the cooling system as described in Chapter 1, or clamp the heater hoses either side of the valve.

51 Release the spring clip from the hose on either side, then disconnect the heater hoses from the valve **(see illustration)**. Note the arrow marking on the valve, showing the direction of coolant flow.

52 Release the cable clamp, then disconnect the cable inner wire from the heater control valve operating lever **(see illustration)**.

53 Unbolt the support bracket from the bulkhead, and remove the valve **(see illustration)**.

54 Refitting is a reversal of removal. Adjust the cable if necessary as described below.

Heater control valve cable

Removal and refitting

55 Disconnect the cable from the control valve as described above. Release the cable grommet from the bulkhead.

56 To disconnect the cable from the air mix control linkage on the driver's side of the heater unit, the facia must first be removed as described in Chapter 11, although someone with small hands might be able to reach it as outlined in paragraphs 60 and 61 below.

57 Withdraw the cable from the bulkhead.

58 Refitting is a reversal of removal. Adjust the cable as described below.

Adjustment

Note: *The procedure below will work for someone with small hands. We could not reach the cable and its fittings with the facia in place and concluded that the facia must first be removed as described in Chapter 11.*

59 Disconnect the cable inner wire from the heater control valve operating lever.

60 Remove the driver's side under cover and lower cover from the facia as described in Chapter 11.

61 Working in the driver's footwell, release the cable clamp and disconnect the cable from the air mix control linkage on the heater unit **(see illustration)**.

62 Set the temperature control to the coldest setting (fully anti-clockwise) with the ignition switched on.

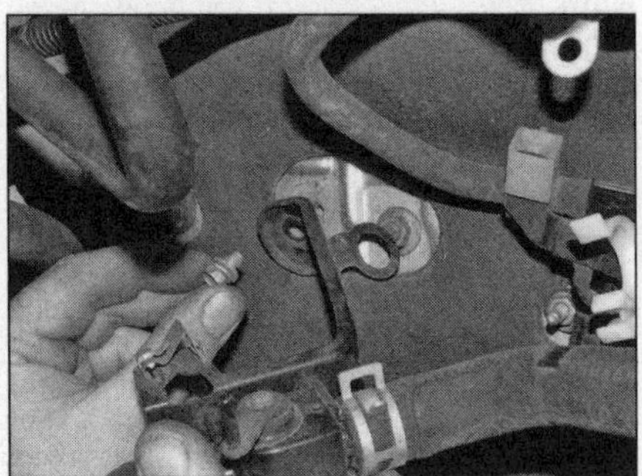

9.53 Unbolting heater control valve support bracket from engine compartment bulkhead

63 Reconnect the cable inner wire to the air mix control linkage. Push the cable outer sleeve against the stop on the side of the heater unit, then clip the cable into the clamp.

64 Back in the engine compartment, turn the valve operating lever to the fully-closed position (anti-clockwise, viewed from above).

65 Reconnect the cable inner wire to the fully-closed valve operating lever, then pull gently on the cable outer sleeve to take out any slack, and fit it into the cable clamp.

66 Check the operation of the heater temperature control on completion.

Air mix control motor

Note: *The procedure below will work for someone with small hands. We could not reach the cable and its fittings with the facia in place and concluded that the facia must first be removed as described in Chapter 11.*

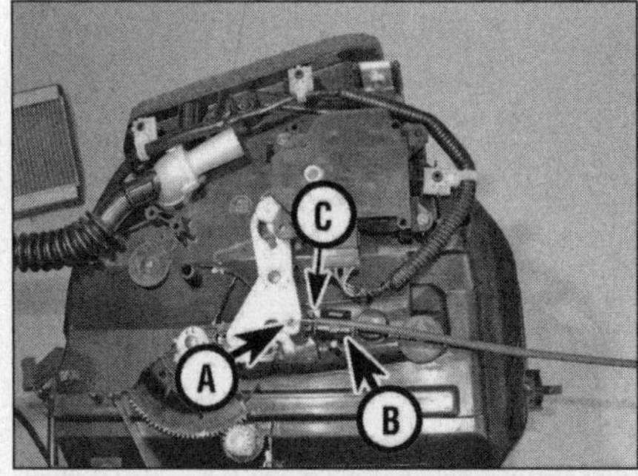

9.61 Heater control valve cable connected to air mix control linkage (A), and clamp (B)

Note cable outer sleeve abutted against stop (C) on heater unit

67 Remove the clutch pedal assembly (Chapter 6).

68 Reach up by the driver's side of the heater unit, and disconnect the air mix control motor wiring plug.

69 Undo the two retaining screws and withdraw the motor **(see illustration)**.

70 Refitting is a reversal of removal.

Mode control motor

71 Remove the engine management ECU as described in Chapter 4A or 4B.

72 Reach up by the passenger's side of the heater unit, and disconnect the mode control motor wiring plug.

73 Undo the three retaining screws and withdraw the motor **(see illustration)**.

74 Refitting is a reversal of removal.

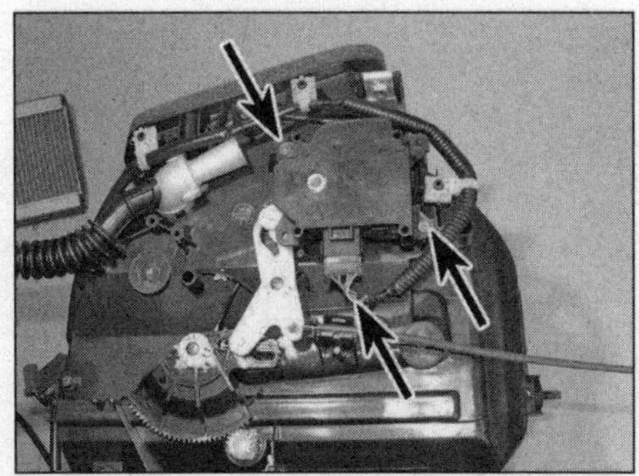

9.69 Heater unit air mix control motor wiring connector and mounting screws

9.73 Heater unit mode control motor wiring connector and mounting screws

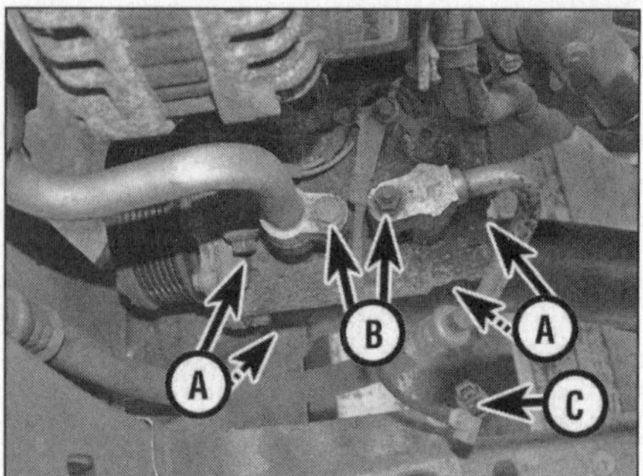

10.4 Air conditioning compressor mounting bolts (A), refrigerant line union fasteners (B) and compressor clutch wiring (C) – petrol models

10 Air conditioning system components – removal and refitting

Warning: Do not attempt to open the refrigerant circuit. Refer to the precautions in Section 1.

Compressor

1 If the compressor is being removed completely, have the air conditioning system discharged. Afterwards, the vehicle can still be driven, but make sure the air conditioning system stays switched off. If it is not being removed completely, do not disconnect the refrigerant pipes, and be careful not to strain them when the compressor is unbolted and moved aside.

2 Remove the auxiliary drivebelt and automatic tensioner (Chapter 1A or 1B). Also remove the engine compartment undershield (Chapter 11).

3 Remove the alternator as described in Chapter 5A.

4 Disconnect the wiring plug from the compressor **(see illustration)**.

5 Unscrew the bolt and nut and detach the air conditioning pipe unions from the compressor. Tape or plug the refrigerant apertures. Remove the seals and discard them.

6 Support the compressor, then unscrew and remove the mounting bolts and withdraw it from the engine compartment – take care not to damage the radiator fins **(see illustrations)**.

Note: *Keep the compressor level during handling and storage. If the compressor has seized, or if you find metal particles in the refrigerant lines, the system must be flushed out by an air conditioning specialist. Do not fit a new compressor to a system that may be contaminated.*

7 If you are installing a new compressor, refer to the manufacturer's instructions for adding refrigerant oil to the system.

8 Refitting is a reversal of removal, but renew the seals, smearing a little refrigerant oil on each, and tighten all bolts to the specified torque. On completion, have the air conditioning system evacuated, charged and leak-tested.

Evaporator

9 Have the air conditioning system discharged. At the same time, have the evaporator connections at the bulkhead disconnected, then do not use the system until it has been reconnected and recharged.

10 Remove the blower motor housing (Section 9).

11 Unbolt the engine management ECU mounting bracket **(see illustration)**.

12 Remove the six screws securing the expansion valve cover, and take off the cover. Withdraw the evaporator from the housing **(see illustrations)**.

13 Refitting is a reversal of removal. Use new O-rings on the evaporator connections, smearing a little refrigerant oil on each.

14 Have the system evacuated, charged and leak-tested by the specialist that discharged it.

Evaporator temperature sensor

Note: *The sensor is mounted at the rear of the heater unit, on the driver's side. If it cannot be reached as described below, the facia must first be removed (Chapter 11).*

15 Remove the driver's side under cover and lower cover from the facia, then remove the centre console (manual gearbox) or the facia lower centre section (automatic transmission), as described in Chapter 11.

16 Reach behind the facia brackets across the heater unit, and disconnect the sensor's wiring plug; it may be necessary to remove the heater control panel (Section 9) to reach it. Release the sensor wiring from the retaining bracket.

17 Reach up by the driver's side of the heater unit, rotate the sensor anti-clockwise and withdraw it **(see illustration)**.

18 Refitting is a reversal of removal.

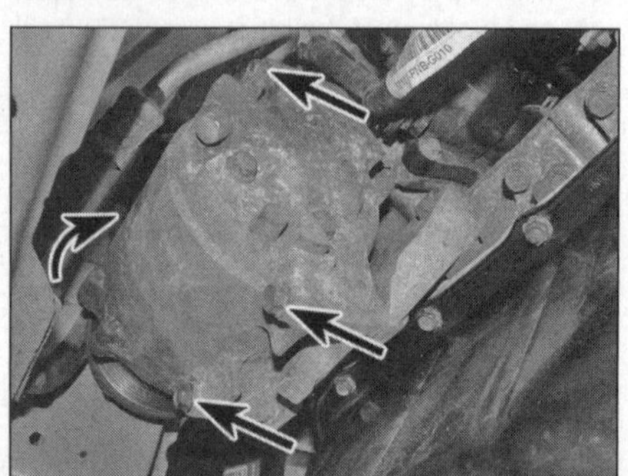

10.6a Air conditioning compressor mounting bolts – petrol models

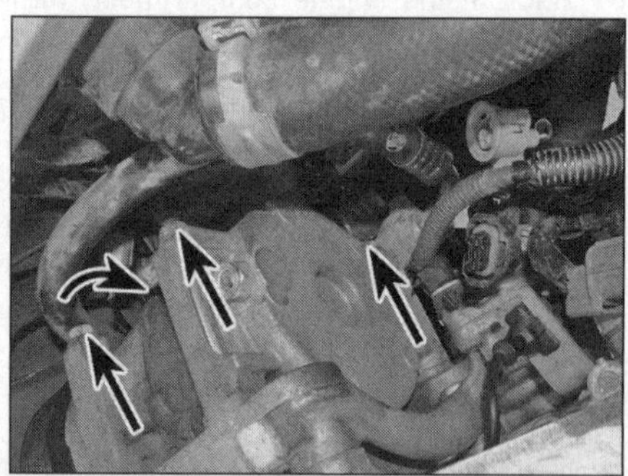

10.6b Air conditioning compressor mounting bolts – diesel models

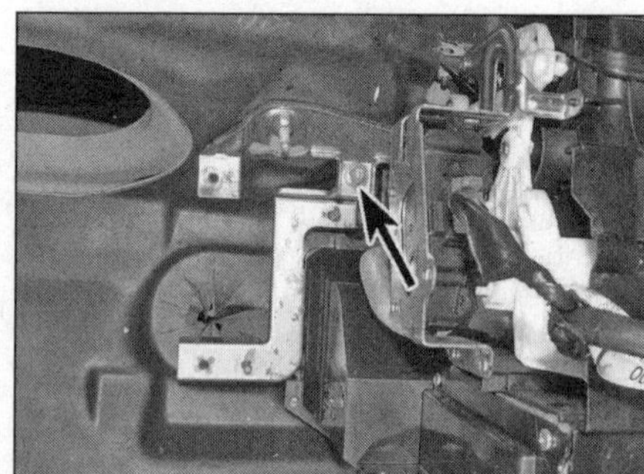

10.11 Unbolt ECU mounting bracket . . .

10.12a . . . remove six securing screws from heater unit . . .

10.12b . . . withdraw expansion valve cover . . .

10.12c . . . and carefully withdraw evaporator from heater unit

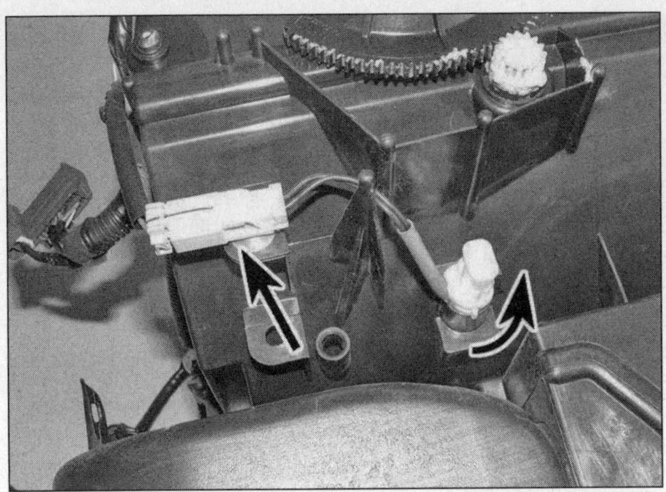

10.17 Rotate evaporator temperature sensor anti-clockwise to release from heater unit – note connector

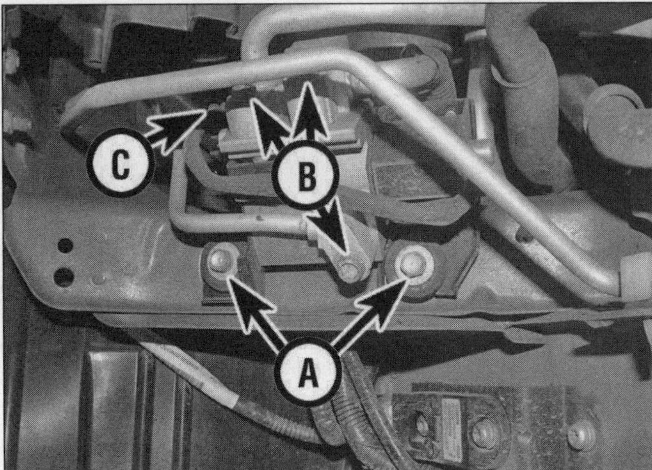

10.32 Air conditioning magnet valve mounting bolts (A), refrigerant line union bolts (B) and wiring connector (C) – diesel models

Condenser

19 If the condenser is being removed completely, the air conditioning refrigerant must be discharged. Afterwards, the vehicle can still be driven, but make sure the air conditioning system stays switched off.

20 Remove the front bumper (Chapter 11).

21 Unscrew the pipe union bolt(s) and separate the union(s) from the condenser. Recover the O-ring from each union.

22 On diesel models, unbolt the power steering fluid cooler and move it aside without disconnecting its hoses. Just beneath the fluid cooler, unscrew the union nut securing the receiver line (from the base of the condenser).

23 On all models, unscrew the mounting bracket bolt from each top corner. Lift out the condenser (taking care not to bend the receiver line, when applicable), noting that its lower pegs locate into rubber mountings.

24 Refitting is a reversal of removal. Use new O-rings if the pipes were disturbed, smearing a little refrigerant oil on each. On completion, have the system evacuated, charged and leak-tested by the specialist that discharged it.

Receiver/dryer desiccant

Note: *The receiver/dryer is an integral part of the condenser.*

25 Remove the condenser, as described above.

26 Unscrew the cap from the bottom of the receiver/dryer and withdraw it. Recover the O-rings.

27 Extract the filter and desiccant from the receiver/dryer.

28 Refitting is a reversal of removal, but renew the O-rings, smearing a little refrigerant oil on each. On completion, have the air conditioning system evacuated, charged and leak-tested by the specialist that discharged it.

Condenser cooling fan

29 Refer to Section 4.

Magnet valve

Note: *This component is found only on diesel-engined models.*

30 If the magnet valve is being removed completely, the air conditioning refrigerant must be discharged. Afterwards, the vehicle can still be driven, but make sure the air conditioning system stays switched off.

31 Remove the front bumper (Chapter 11).

32 Disconnect the valve's wiring plug. Unscrew the pipe union bolts and separate the three unions from the valve **(see illustration)**. Recover the O-rings.

33 Unscrew the mounting bolts and withdraw the magnet valve assembly. Detach the wiring connector clips and unbolt the mounting bracket from the valve, then withdraw the mounting collars and bushes.

34 Refitting is a reversal of removal. Use new O-rings, smearing a little refrigerant oil on each. On completion, have the system evacuated, charged and leak-tested by the specialist that discharged it.

Climate control unit

35 See Section 9, Heater control panel.

Self-diagnosis function

36 See Section 9.

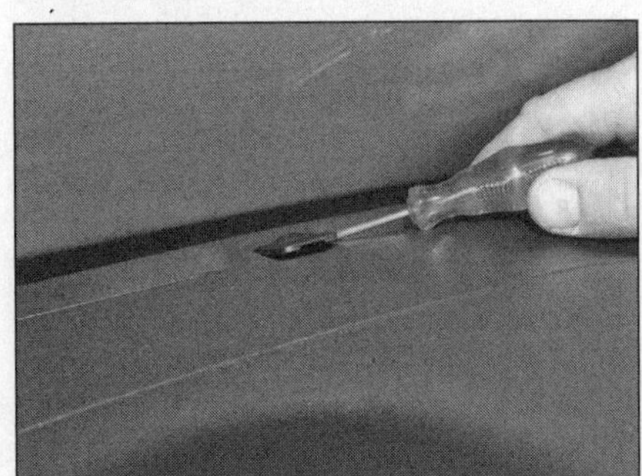

10.38 Carefully prise sunlight sensor out of facia

Sunlight sensor

37 Fitted only to models with climate control, the sun sensor allows the system to compensate for the additional cabin temperature generated in sunny conditions. It is located in the centre of the facia panel, just behind the windscreen.

38 Wrap a small flat-tipped screwdriver with protective tape and use a piece of card or a wad of cloth to prevent damage to the facia panel itself, then carefully prise up the sensor, noting its fitted orientation **(see illustration)**.

39 Disconnect the wiring plug from the sensor, and remove it completely. Make sure the plug doesn't fall back inside the facia.

40 Refitting is a reversal of removal. Ensure the sensor is fitted the right way round, with its wiring plug at the rear, facing into the vehicle **(see illustration)**.

Cabin temperature sensor

41 Fitted only to models with climate control, the sensor monitors cabin temperature so that the system can maintain the temperature selected. The sensor is located on the facia lower cover, to the left of the steering wheel, behind a small grille.

42 Remove the driver's side under cover and lower cover from the facia (Chapter 11). This includes disconnecting the sensor wiring and air hose.

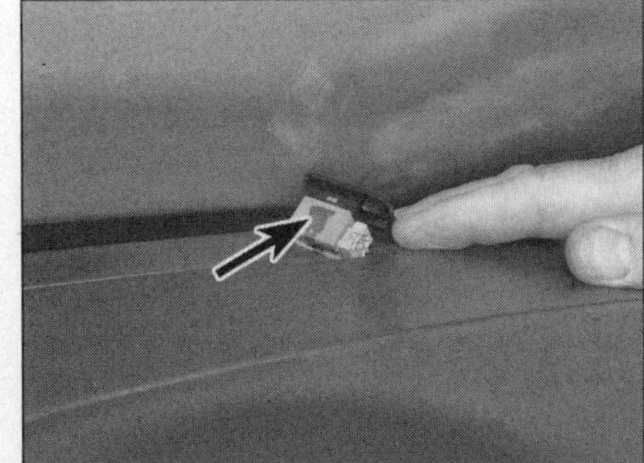

10.40 Install sunlight sensor with connector at rear

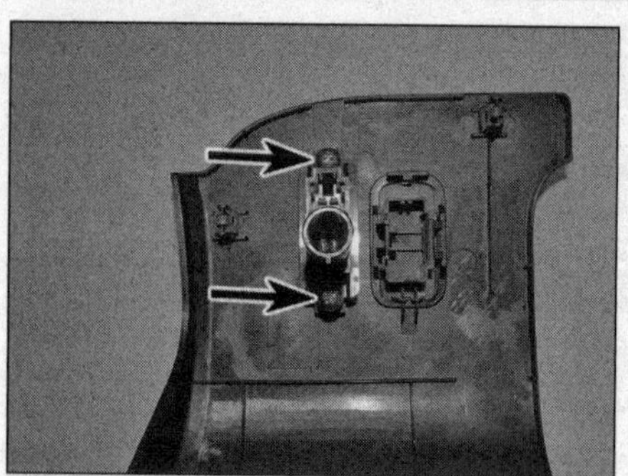

10.43 Undo two retaining screws to withdraw cabin temperature sensor

10.45 Location of outside air temperature sensor – diesel models

43 Undo the two retaining screws and withdraw the sensor **(see illustration)**.

44 Refitting is a reversal of removal.

Outside temperature sensor

45 The sensor is mounted behind the front bumper's lower air intake, on the left-hand side on petrol models, and on the right-hand side on diesel models **(see illustration)**. It is not fitted to petrol models without climate control.

46 Reach behind the grille, and unclip the sensor by pulling it sideways off its mounting bracket.

47 Disconnect the sensor wiring plug, and remove it.

48 Refitting is a reversal of removal.

Chapter 4 Part A:
Fuel and exhaust systems – petrol models

Contents

Degrees of difficulty

Easy, suitable for novice with little experience 

Fairly easy, suitable for beginner with some experience

Fairly difficult, suitable for competent DIY mechanic

Difficult, suitable for experienced DIY mechanic

Very difficult, suitable for expert DIY or professional 

Specifications

Fuel system data

Fast idle	1,600 ± 200 rpm
Fuel pressure	3.3 to 3.8 bar
Idle mixture CO content	0.1% maximum
Idle speed	See Chapter 1A
Injector resistance	10 to 13 ohms

Recommended fuel

Minimum octane rating	95 RON unleaded (UK unleaded premium). Leaded fuel must **not** be used

Torque wrench settings	Nm	lbf ft
Accelerator pedal mounting nuts	13	10
Air cleaner assembly and intake air duct fasteners	12	9
Air cleaner cover retaining bolts	See Chapter 1A	
Cable and wiring brackets-to-intake manifold bolts	12	9
Charcoal canister purge solenoid valve-to-throttle body screws	4	3
Clutch pedal position switch locknut	See Chapter 6	
Countershaft (output shaft) speed sensor mounting bolt (models with automatic transmission)	12	9
Crankshaft position (CKP) sensor mounting bolt	12	9
Electronic Control Unit (ECU) mounting bolt and nuts	10	7
Engine coolant temperature sensor	See Chapter 3	
Exhaust front pipe-to-centre section nuts*	33	24
Exhaust front pipe-to-manifold bolts*	22	16
Exhaust manifold cover bolts	22	16
Exhaust manifold nuts and bolts*	44	32
Exhaust manifold support bracket bolts	44	32
Exhaust rear silencer-to-centre section nuts*	22	16
Exhaust system heatshield mounting nuts	10	7
Fuel filler flap hinge bolts	10	7
Fuel pulsation damper-to-fuel rail – 2001 to 2004 models	22	16
Fuel pump/gauge sender unit locking ring – using special tool	93	69
Fuel rail mounting nuts	22	16
Fuel tank guard mounting bolts	10	7
Fuel tank mounting bolts	38	28
Idle air control valve screws	4	3
Intake air bypass control thermal valve:		
2001 to 2004 models	N/A.	
2005-on models (water outlet-to-cylinder head bolts)	12	9
Intake manifold cover bolts	See Chapter 1A	
Intake manifold mounting bolts and nuts	22	16
Intake Manifold Tuning (IMT) actuator valve-to-intake manifold bolts	10	7
MAP sensor screws	4	3
Power steering pressure switch	12	9
TDC (camshaft position) sensor retaining screw	12	9
Throttle body mounting bolts	22	16
Vehicle speed sensor mounting bolt (models with manual gearbox)	22	16
Water outlet-to-cylinder head bolts	See Chapter 2A	

** Use new fasteners.*

1 General information and precautions

General information

The fuel system consists of the fuel tank, located centrally on the underbody immediately in front of the rear axle, a fuel pump/gauge sender unit submerged in the tank, a fuel rail supplying four injectors (one per cylinder) and a fully-electronic multipoint sequential fuel injection system.

Fuel injection system

All petrol-engined models are equipped with Honda's Multi-Point Programmed Fuel Injection (PGM-FI) engine management system, in which information from various sensors is supplied to the engine management system's Electronic Control Unit (ECU), to enable the unit to determine the optimum settings for both fuelling and ignition timing. On models with automatic transmission, the system components and sensors are exactly the same, but because there are additional transmission control parameters and functions, the control unit is known by Honda as the Powertrain Control Module, or PCM. For simplicity, however, we shall refer to the control unit throughout as the ECU. The same control unit also manages aspects of the operation of the air conditioning system, especially on vehicles with automatic air conditioning (climate control) (see Chapter 3) and is linked to the ABS Electronic Control Unit (ECU) to play a part in the operation of the Vehicle Stability Assist (VSA) system (where fitted) – see Chapter 9. It also receives inputs from the power steering system and the alternator to enable it to compensate for the increased load placed on the engine – especially when cold – when the power steering system is being used or there is heavy demand from various electrical systems.

The ECU has a fail-safe function whereby if a signal from a sensor becomes abnormal, the ECU can ignore that signal and substitute a pre-programmed value that allows the engine to continue to run. There is also a back-up function which controls the injectors in the event of major system failure to permit minimal driving – a 'limp-home' mode. If a problem occurs with a component of the engine management system and/or transmission control system, the ECU has a self-diagnosis ability that enables it to store a code relating to that fault in its memory and to alert the driver to the fact that all is not well by illuminating the engine management Malfunction Indicator warning Lamp (MIL); for some systems (such as the automatic transmission), a supplementary warning will be given by flashing another indicator lamp. To filter out spurious indications for some self-diagnostic functions, the ECU stores the code whenever the fault occurs, but only illuminates the MIL if that fault occurs again after the ignition has been switched off and on again. If a fault ever occurs that causes a fault code to be logged so that the MIL illuminates consistently, the vehicle must be taken to a Honda dealer or other specialist so that dedicated electronic test equipment can be connected to the system via the diagnostic socket located under the driver's side of the facia. This will enable any fault codes stored to be read and, once the necessary corrective action has been taken, for the fault code(s) to be erased (refer to Section 10). **Note:** *The engine management Malfunction Indicator warning Lamp (MIL) in the instrument panel will illuminate when the ignition is first switched on as a check of its function. If the MIL lights while the vehicle is being driven, pull to the side of the road as soon as it is safe to do so and switch off the engine. Restart the engine (thus resetting the system) and watch the MIL; if it remains on, or comes back on while driving, the vehicle must be taken to a specialist as soon as possible for fault diagnosis and repair. If the vehicle has automatic transmission, the MIL's warning message may be reinforced by the instrument panel D indicator flashing as well.*

This Chapter deals with the fuel side of the system – refer to Chapter 5B for ignition-specific details and to Chapters 2A, 3, 4C, 7B and 9 as appropriate for other systems.

An electric fuel pump, filter gauze, pressure regulator and fuel gauge sender unit are located inside the fuel tank. Fuel is pumped from the fuel tank to the fuel rail, which is equipped with a pulsation damper to smooth out fluctuations in the flow of fuel. The system is 'returnless' – there is no return feed to the tank. Fuel vapours from the tank are stored in a canister at the rear of the tank, and supplied to the throttle body through a separate pipe.

Fuel delivery is by a multipoint sequential electronic fuel injection system, which essentially means it operates the four injectors separately, in firing order. Because each cylinder is equipped with its own injector, much better control of the fuel/air mixture ratio is possible. Various sensors are used to supply information relating to throttle butterfly position, engine coolant temperature, crankshaft angle, intake manifold pressure, atmospheric pressure, intake air temperature, vehicle speed and exhaust gas oxygen content. Information from these sensors is fed to the ECU, which then decides when to activate each injector. The system can alter fuel delivery to match the engine's needs under varying environmental and engine-load conditions. An Electrical Load Detector (ELD) built into the engine compartment main fuse/relay box monitors the demand on the alternator from the vehicle's other electrical systems and adjusts idle speed and fuelling accordingly to ensure smooth and consistent engine performance and response under all conditions.

Models from 2005 onwards are fitted with a drive-by-wire throttle – the Electronic Throttle Control System (ETCS). Instead of a conventional cable from the accelerator pedal to the throttle body a cable runs from the pedal to a throttle linkage/accelerator pedal position sensor mounted on the bulkhead. The throttle itself is electrically-controlled by the ECU. This ensures a more linear response to accelerator pedal inputs, particularly when pulling away. The control software works in conjunction with the engine management system to provide very smooth and responsive adjustments directly proportional to driver input. Furthermore, it forms an integral part of the VSA system (where fitted) as well as the automatic gearbox control software.

The large-capacity air cleaner housing used in the CR-V's induction system serves to muffle intake roar, and it also incorporates a Helmholtz chamber to damp unwanted resonances. CR-V drivers negotiating floods need to know that the engine's air intake is at the top of the radiator, next to the left-hand headlamp; do not drive through water deeper than the top of the bonnet's radiator grille opening, or allow a bow-wave of water to build up to that level.

i-VTEC and VTC systems

These systems are described and covered in Chapter 2A.

Intake Manifold Runner Control system

Because this system's function is so closely linked with that of the i-VTEC and VTC systems, it is described in Section 1 of Chapter 2A. Removal and refitting of the system's components is, however, covered in this Chapter.

Exhaust system

The exhaust system includes an exhaust manifold, primary and secondary oxygen sensors, a three-way catalytic converter, a centre section with silencer, and a rear silencer.

The catalytic converter is an emissions control device added to the exhaust system to reduce pollutants. Refer to Chapter 4C for more information regarding the catalytic converter and other emissions control components.

Precautions

Extreme caution should be exercised when dealing with either the fuel or exhaust systems. Fuel is a potentially-explosive liquid, and extreme care should be taken when dealing with the fuel system. The exhaust system is an area for exercising caution, as it will remain hot for some time after the engine is switched off. Serious burns can result from even momentary contact with any part of the exhaust system, and the fire risk is ever-present. The catalytic converter in particular runs at very high temperatures.

When removing the Electronic Control Unit (ECU), do not touch the terminals, as there is a chance that static electricity may damage the internal electronic components.

Warning: Many of the procedures in this Chapter require the disconnection of fuel lines, which will result in some fuel spillage. Before carrying out any operation on the fuel system, refer to the precautions given in Safety first! at the beginning of this manual, and follow them implicitly; also see the information on depressurising the fuel system given in Section 2. Petrol is a highly-dangerous and volatile liquid, and the precautions necessary when handling it cannot be overstressed.

- Petrol is extremely flammable – great care must be taken when working on any part of the fuel system. Do not smoke or allow any naked flames or uncovered light bulbs near the work area. Note that gas powered domestic appliances with pilot flames, such as heaters, boilers and tumble dryers, also present a fire hazard – bear this in mind if you are working in an area where such appliances are present. Always keep a suitable fire extinguisher close to the work area and familiarise yourself with its operation before starting work. Wear eye protection when working on fuel systems and wash off any fuel spilt on bare skin immediately with soap and water. Note that fuel vapour is just as dangerous as liquid fuel; a vessel that has just been emptied of liquid fuel will still contain vapour and can be potentially explosive.
- It is strongly advised that, wherever possible, the battery negative lead is disconnected whenever there is a danger of fuel spillage (see *Disconnecting the battery*). This reduces the risk of a spark causing a fire, and also prevents the fuel pump running, which could be dangerous if the fuel lines have been disconnected.
- When working with fuel system components, pay particular attention to cleanliness – dirt entering the fuel system may cause blockages which will lead to poor running.
- Electronic control units are very sensitive components, and certain precautions must be taken to avoid damage to these units as follows:

a) *When carrying out welding operations on the vehicle using electric welding equipment, the battery and alternator should be disconnected.*

b) *Although the underbonnet-mounted units will tolerate normal underbonnet conditions, they can be adversely affected by excess heat or moisture. If using welding equipment or pressure-washing equipment in the vicinity of an electronic unit, take care not to direct heat, or jets of water or steam, at the unit. If this cannot be avoided, remove the unit from the vehicle, and protect its wiring plug with a plastic bag.*

c) *Before disconnecting any wiring, or removing components, always ensure that the ignition is switched off.*

d) *Do not attempt to improvise ECU fault diagnosis procedures using a test lamp or multimeter, as irreparable damage could be caused to the unit.*

e) *After working on fuel injection/engine management system components, ensure that all wiring is correctly reconnected before reconnecting the battery or switching on the ignition.*

2.5 Slowly unscrew fuel pulsation damper from fuel rail to depressurise fuel system. Note rag placed to catch escaping fuel

2 Fuel system – depressurisation

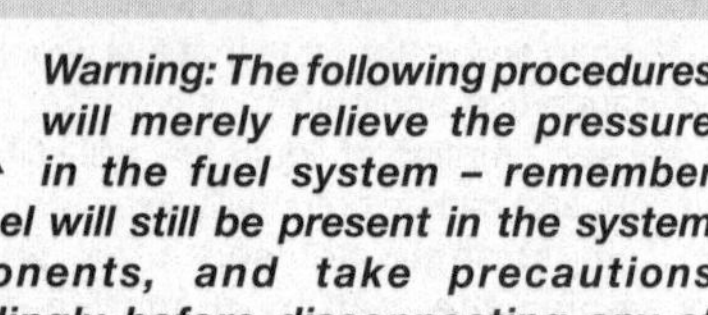

Warning: The following procedures will merely relieve the pressure in the fuel system – remember that fuel will still be present in the system components, and take precautions accordingly before disconnecting any of them.

Note: *Refer to the precautions in Section 1 before proceeding.*

1 Before working on any part of the fuel system, it is recommended that the residual fuel pressure is relieved. Even if the engine has been switched off for some time, there is a risk that, when fuel lines are disconnected, the residual fuel pressure will cause fuel to spray out. This is at best unpleasant and at worst a fire risk.

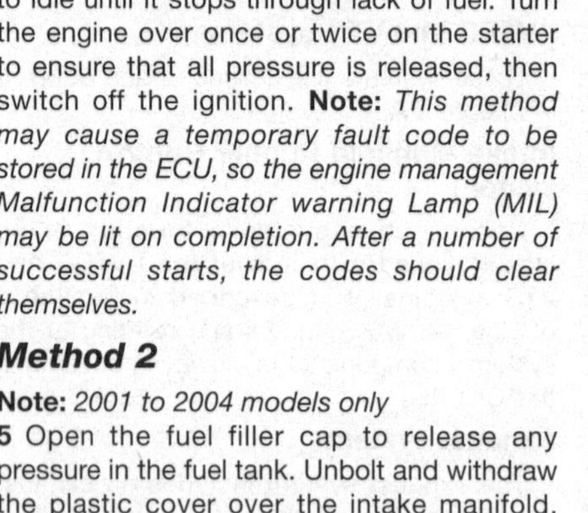

2 Whichever depressurisation method is used, plug the disconnected pipe ends to keep fuel in and dirt out.

3 Note that once the fuel system has been depressurised, it will take significantly longer to restart the engine.

Method 1

4 The simplest depressurisation method is to disconnect the fuel pump electrical supply. With the ignition switched off, remove the fuel pump fuse (typically, No. 17 in the passenger compartment fuse panel in the facia) or the PGM-FI main relay 2 (see Section 11), and open the fuel filler cap to release any pressure in the fuel tank. Start the engine and allow it to idle until it stops through lack of fuel. Turn the engine over once or twice on the starter to ensure that all pressure is released, then switch off the ignition. **Note:** *This method may cause a temporary fault code to be stored in the ECU, so the engine management Malfunction Indicator warning Lamp (MIL) may be lit on completion. After a number of successful starts, the codes should clear themselves.*

Method 2

Note: *2001 to 2004 models only*

5 Open the fuel filler cap to release any pressure in the fuel tank. Unbolt and withdraw the plastic cover over the intake manifold. Place a large rag around the fuel pulsation damper at the left-hand end of the fuel rail, ready to soak up any escaping fuel. Counterhold the hexagon on the end of the fuel rail with one open-ended spanner and slowly (to avoid a sudden release of pressure and to allow any fuel spray which may be expelled to be caught by the rag) unscrew the damper one full turn with a second spanner **(see illustration). Note:** *The damper's sealing washer must be renewed whenever the damper is removed or slackened.*

3 Accelerator pedal – removal and refitting

1 Remove the driver's side under cover and lower cover from the facia (Chapter 11).

2 Working in the driver's footwell, operate the accelerator pedal by hand, and unhook the throttle cable end fitting from the top of the pedal, sliding it out to the right **(see illustration).**

3 Unscrew the retaining nuts and remove the pedal assembly from the bulkhead **(see illustration).**

4 If the pedal is defective, the complete assembly will have to be renewed.

5 Refitting is a reversal of the removal operations. Adjust the throttle cable if necessary as described in Section 4.

4 Throttle cable – removal, refitting and adjustment

2001 to 2004 models

Removal

1 Unbolt and withdraw the plastic cover over the intake manifold, then undo its retaining screws and withdraw the cover over the throttle linkage **(see illustrations).**

2 Rotate the throttle quadrant to the fully-open position and disconnect the throttle cable inner wire from the quadrant; slowly allow the quadrant to return to the closed position **(see illustration).** Slacken the adjuster locknut and disengage the throttle cable outer from the bracket.

3 Trace the cable round to the bulkhead,

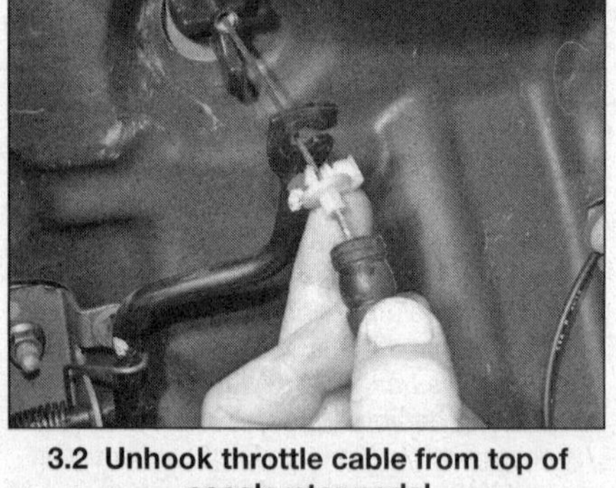

3.2 Unhook throttle cable from top of accelerator pedal

3.3 Unscrew two mounting nuts to remove accelerator pedal

4.1a Undo its retaining screws . . .

4.1b . . . and withdraw throttle linkage cover

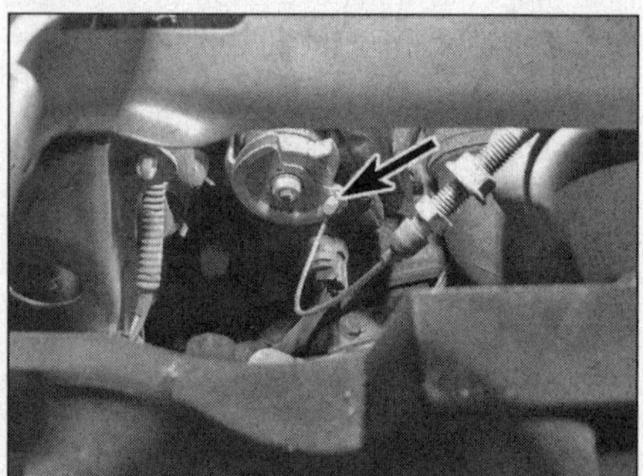

4.2 Disconnecting cable inner wire from throttle quadrant

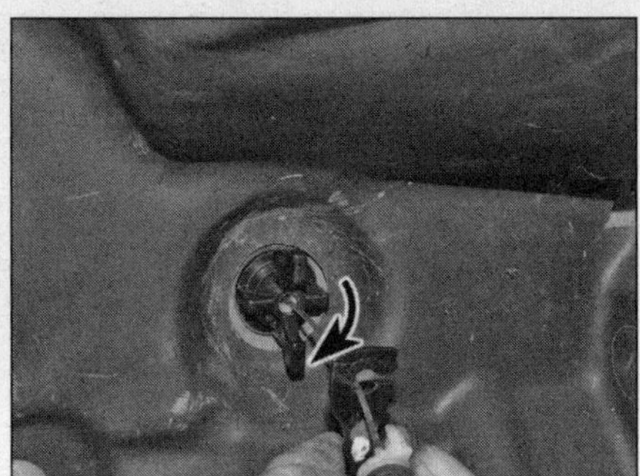
4.6 Fit cable grommet to bulkhead, then rotate quarter-turn clockwise to secure

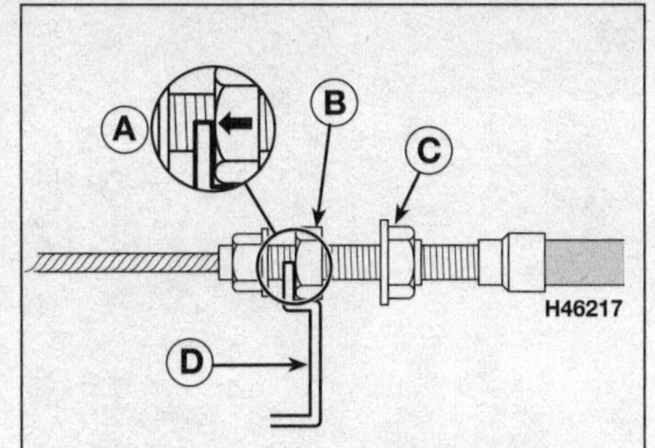

4.8 Throttle cable initial setting

A Adjust until no clearance exists here
B Adjuster nut
C Locknut
D Cable bracket

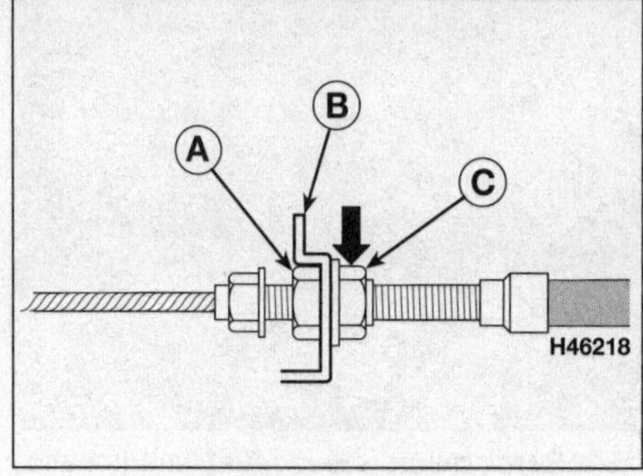

4.10 Throttle cable final setting

A Adjuster nut
B Cable bracket
C Locknut

releasing it from any clips, and noting how it is routed.

4 Disconnect the cable from the throttle pedal (Section 3).

5 Feed the cable back into the engine compartment, releasing the bulkhead grommet by rotating it one-quarter-turn anti-clockwise, then withdraw the cable.

Refitting

6 To refit the cable, feed it into place in the bulkhead and seat the grommet **(see illustration)**. Connect the cable to the upper end of the pedal; ensure that the nylon end fitting is correctly located in the pedal end.

7 Working in the engine compartment, run the cable back through the clips provided, ensuring that it is routed correctly with no tight turns or kinks, and that it is clear of any other hot or moving components.

8 Connect the cable inner wire end fitting into the throttle linkage quadrant, but position the cable outer on the bracket so that, when the quadrant is in the fully-closed position and there is no slack in the cable inner wire, the adjuster nut is held as shown, with no clearance between the adjuster nut and the bracket **(see illustration)**. Note that this means the cable will be sitting up from its normal position.

9 The engine should be fully warmed-up to normal operating temperature – if necessary, start the engine and leave it to idle until the radiator cooling fan has switched on and then off again. Switch off the ignition.

10 Once the position of the adjuster nut has been set, lift the cable off the mounting bracket, and fit it properly back down into place, so that the bracket is now between the adjuster nut and locknut **(see illustration)**.

11 Tighten the locknut up to the bracket, without disturbing the cable or the adjuster nut.

12 Without starting the engine, have an assistant depress the accelerator pedal fully, and check that the throttle quadrant opens fully. Similarly check that the quadrant returns to the idle position when the pedal is released.

13 On completion, refit all components removed for access.

Adjustment

14 To check the adjustment of the throttle cable, remove the rubber grommet from the throttle linkage cover and check that there is 10 to 12 mm deflection in the cable inner wire when the pedal is fully released **(see illustrations)**. If adjustment is required, proceed as follows:

15 Undo its retaining screws and withdraw the throttle linkage cover.

16 Slacken the cable adjuster locknut and turn the adjuster nut until the deflection is correct, then retighten the locknut without disturbing the cable or the adjuster nut **(see illustration)**.

17 Without starting the engine, have an assistant depress the accelerator pedal fully, and check that the throttle quadrant opens fully. Similarly check that the quadrant returns to the idle position when the pedal is released.

18 On completion, refit all components removed for access.

2005-on models

19 The procedure is similar to that described for earlier models, but note the following:

a) The throttle linkage is on the accelerator pedal position sensor mounted on the bulkhead.
b) There is no need to warm-up the engine (paragraph 9).
c) Cable deflection (paragraph 14) should be 15 to 18 mm.

5 Fuel lines and fittings – general information

Note: *Refer to the precautions in Section 1.*

1 Quick-release couplings are employed at several unions in the fuel feed and return lines.

2 Before disconnecting any fuel system component, relieve the pressure in the system as described in Section 2.

3 Some of the quick-release connections have a plastic cover which must be unclipped for access **(see illustration)**.

4 Release the protruding locking lugs on each fuel line union by squeezing them together

4.14a Remove rubber grommet from throttle linkage cover . . .

4.14b . . . and check that there is 10 to 12 mm deflection in cable inner wire

4.16 When cable deflection is correct, retighten locknut without disturbing cable or adjuster nut

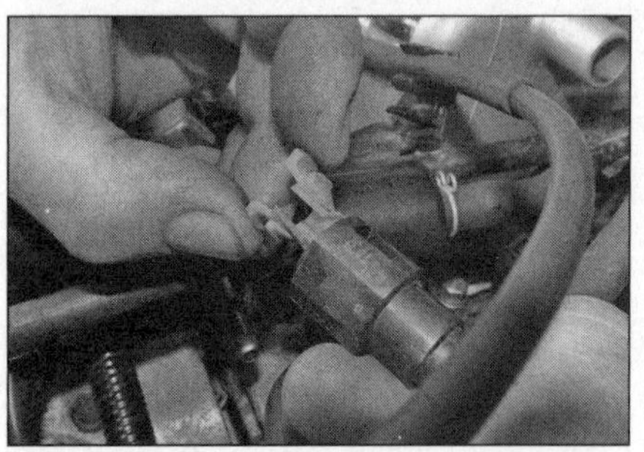

5.3 Some quick-release fuel unions have a removable insert – clean carefully and ensure it is correctly installed on refitting

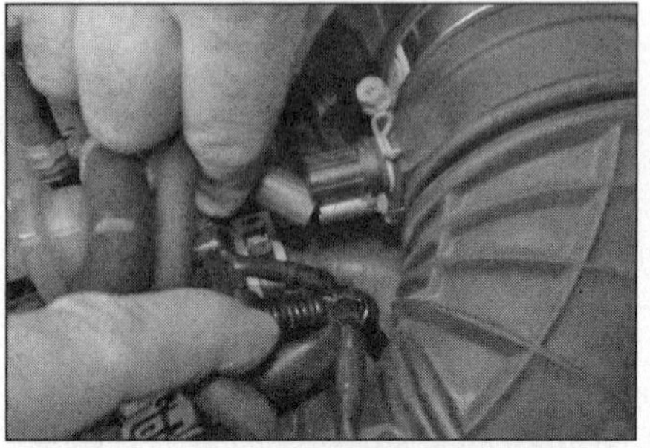

6.1c . . . and intake air bypass control thermal valve tube from air cleaner assembly's hose

and carefully pull the coupling apart. Use rag to soak up any spilt fuel. Some unions are colour-coded to aid correct refitting. Where both unions are the same colour, note which pipe is connected to which.

5 To reconnect one of these couplings, press

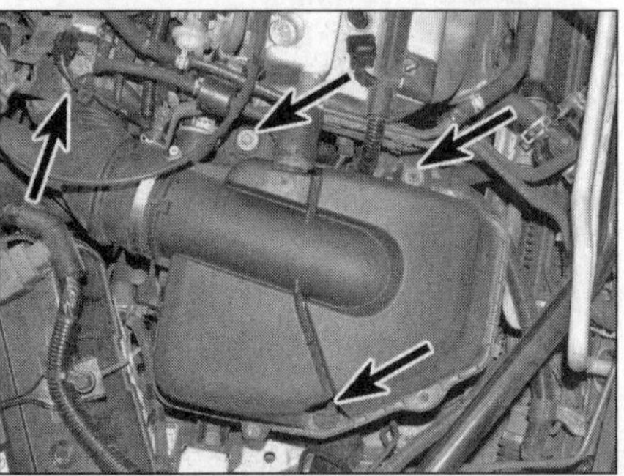

6.3a Location of air cleaner assembly mountings

6.3c . . . nut at rear mounting . . .

6.1a Disconnect breather hose from cylinder head cover . . .

6.2a Slacken clamp securing air cleaner assembly intake hose to throttle body . . .

the two halves together until they are locked. Switch the ignition on to pressurise the system, and check for any sign of fuel leakage around the disturbed coupling.

6 Always use genuine fuel lines and hoses when renewing sections of the fuel system.

6.3b Unscrew bolt from front mounting . . .

6.3d . . . and remove rubber blanking plug to unscrew mounting bolt next to battery

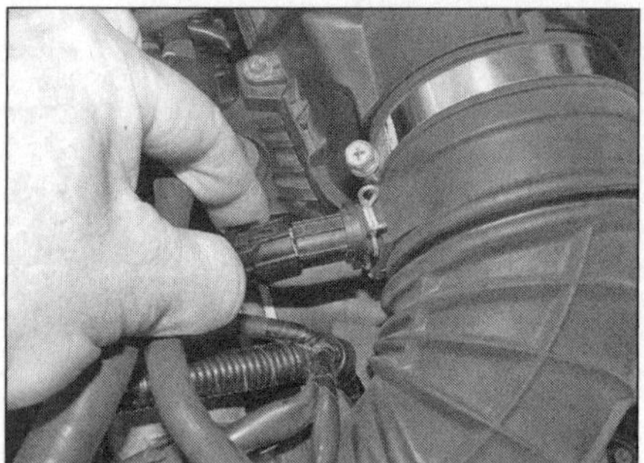

6.1b . . . and intake air temperature sensor wiring connector . . .

6.2b . . . and release intake hose from lower front of air cleaner assembly

Do not fit substitutes constructed from inferior or inappropriate material which could cause a fuel leak or a fire.

6 Air cleaner assembly and intake air duct – removal and refitting

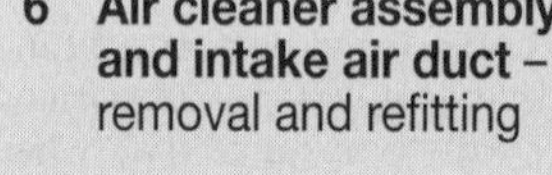

Air cleaner assembly

1 Disconnect the breather hose, the intake air temperature sensor wiring connector and the intake air bypass control thermal valve tube from the air cleaner assembly's hose **(see illustrations)**.

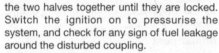

2 Slacken the clamp securing the air cleaner assembly intake hose to the throttle body and release the intake duct from the front of the air cleaner assembly **(see illustrations)**.

3 Unscrew the nuts and bolt securing the assembly, noting that the bolt next to the

6.4 Withdrawing air cleaner assembly

battery is concealed under a rubber blanking plug **(see illustrations)**.

4 Withdraw the air cleaner assembly and hose **(see illustration)**.

5 Refitting is a reversal of removal.

Intake air duct

6 Remove the air cleaner assembly as described above.

7 Unscrew the two mounting bolts and withdraw the duct **(see illustrations)**.

8 Refitting is a reversal of removal.

7 Fuel pump/ gauge sender unit – removal and refitting

Note 1: *Refer to the precautions in Section 1.*
Note 2: *The fuel pump/gauge sender unit locking ring and sealing ring must be renewed whenever they are disturbed.*

Removal

1 Depressurise the fuel system (Section 2).

2 Fold forwards the rear seats, and lift the floor carpet to expose the fuel tank access cover. Tape the carpet against the seats to prevent it from falling across the tank opening while work is in progress.

3 Unscrew the three screws securing the tank access cover to the vehicle floor, and lift it up – there's wiring attached to it **(see illustration)**.

4 Disconnect the fuel pump/gauge sender unit wiring plug, and move the access cover clear **(see illustration)**. Remove as much dust and dirt from the working area as possible; cleanliness is essential from now on.

5 Release the fuel hose fitting on the top of the fuel pump/gauge sender unit (Section 5), and disconnect it **(see illustration)**. Plug or tape the open ends.

6 The fuel pump/gauge sender unit is secured using a threaded plastic locking ring, which will be tight. Honda mechanics use a special three-legged gripping tool which engages the ribs on the locking ring's sides. We used a home-made alternative constructed from two strips of metal which fitted between the locking ring's ribs, two lengths of threaded rod and eight nuts. With care, it may be possible to unscrew the locking ring using slip-joint water pump pliers, an oil filter strap wrench, or even by tapping the locking ring round with a screwdriver, but care must be taken not to damage either the locking ring, the unit itself, or the tank **(see illustration)**.

7 Unscrew and remove the locking ring, then wipe around the tank's threaded neck to remove any dust or dirt remaining. Noting the reference mark on the top of the fuel pump/ gauge sender unit which aligns with similar marks on the tank, carefully lift the fuel pump/ gauge sender unit out of the tank. Lift the unit straight up, then turn it to keep the fuel level float from catching on the tank opening. Recover the sealing ring **(see illustrations)**. Unless refitting is to take place immediately, place a thin plastic sheet over the opening in the tank and tighten the locking ring over it to keep fuel vapour in and dirt out. This will also prevent distortion of the threads.

Dismantling and reassembly

8 Remove the fuel level sender unit, the sediment bowl and the fuel filter gauze from the fuel pump/gauge sender unit as described in Chapter 1A, Section 20.

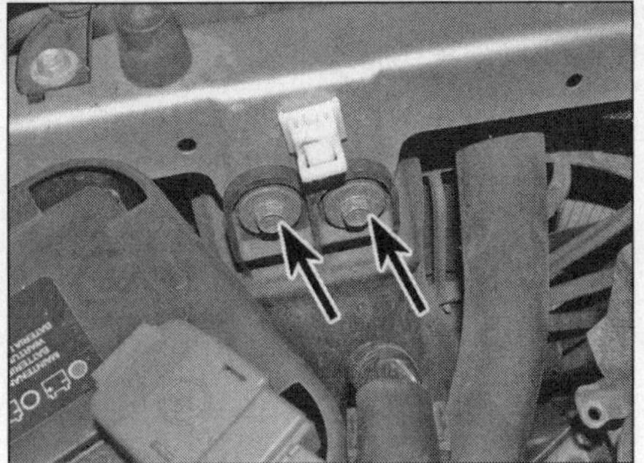

6.7a Unscrew two intake air duct mounting bolts . . .

6.7b . . . and withdraw intake air duct

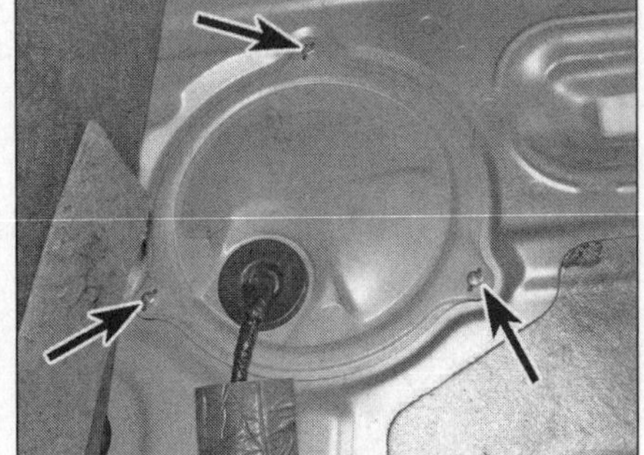

7.3 Unscrew three screws securing tank access cover to vehicle floor

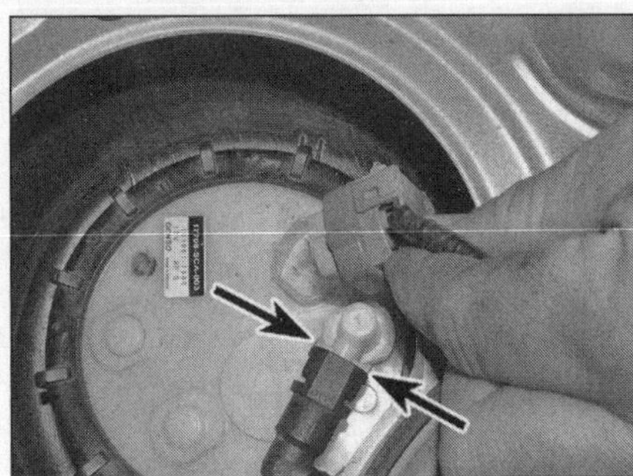

7.4 Disconnect fuel pump/gauge sender unit wiring plug and press in tabs . . .

7.5 . . . to release fuel hose fitting on top of fuel pump/gauge sender unit

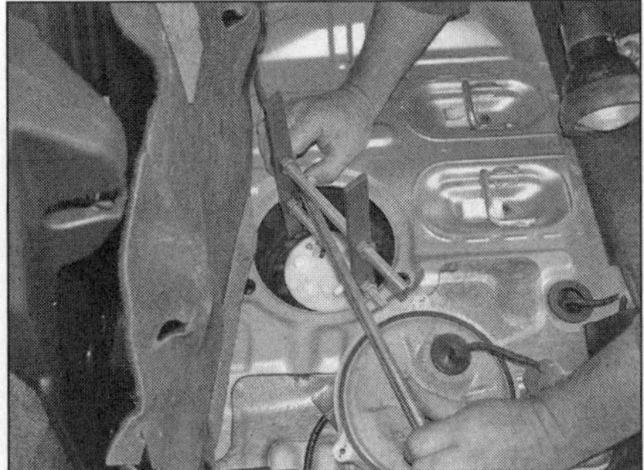

7.6 Using home-made tool to unscrew fuel pump/gauge sender unit locking ring

7.7a Lift fuel pump/gauge sender unit out of tank . . .

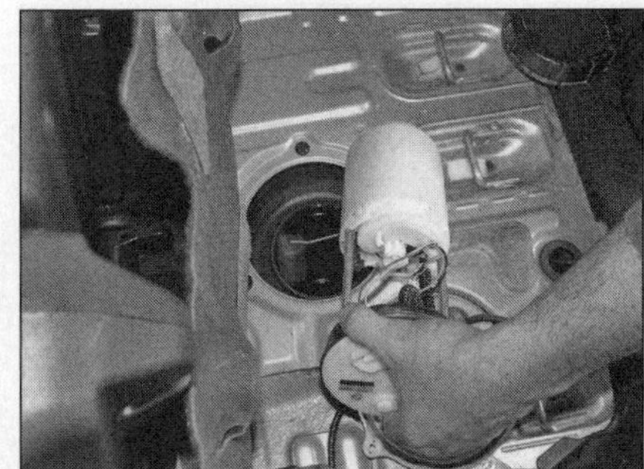

7.7b . . . then turn it to keep fuel level float from catching on tank opening

7.7c Temporarily refit locking ring to tank to prevent distortion of tank's threaded neck

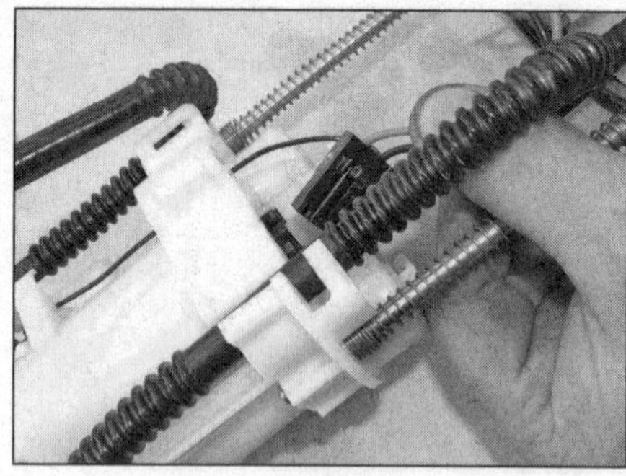

7.9a Disconnect fuel pump wiring plug . . .

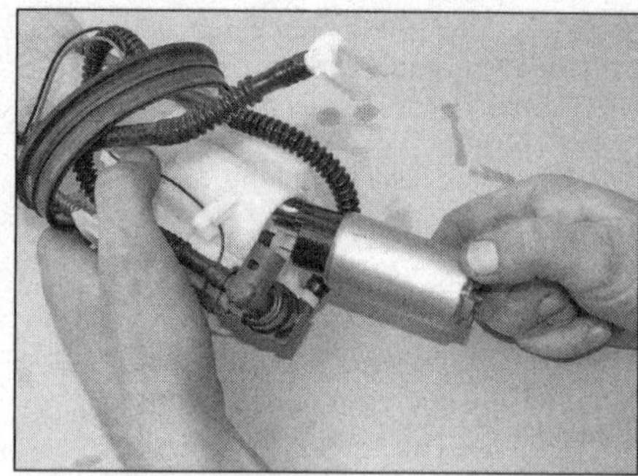

7.9b . . . and remove fuel pump

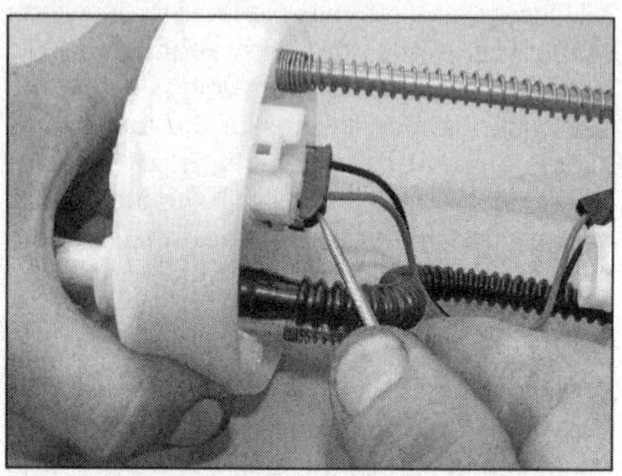

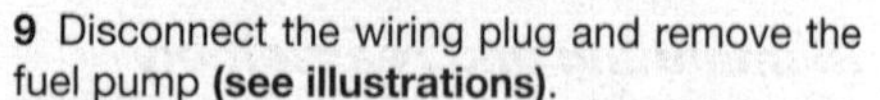

7.10 Depress its locking tab to release fuel pump wiring from unit

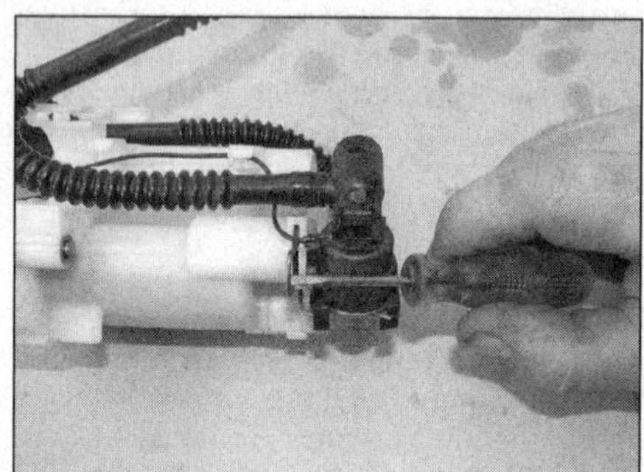

7.11a Extract the retaining clip . . .

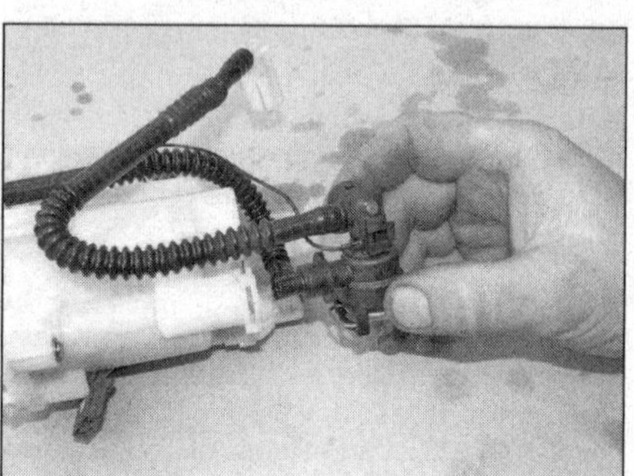

7.11b . . . to withdraw fuel pressure regulator

9 Disconnect the wiring plug and remove the fuel pump **(see illustrations)**.

10 Depress its locking tab to release the fuel pump wiring from the unit **(see illustration)**.

11 Extract the retaining clip and withdraw the fuel pressure regulator **(see illustrations)**.

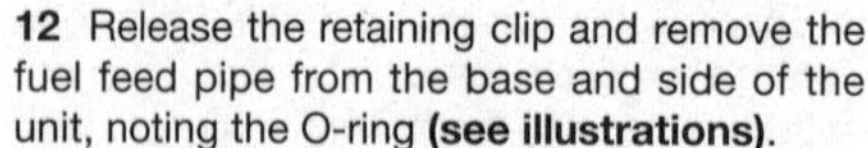

12 Release the retaining clip and remove the fuel feed pipe from the base and side of the unit, noting the O-ring **(see illustrations)**.

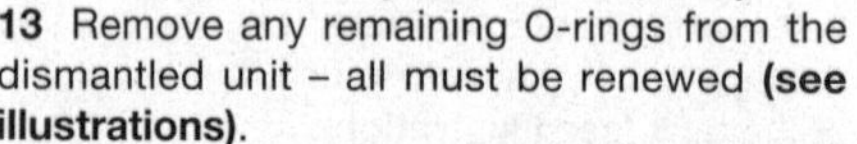

13 Remove any remaining O-rings from the dismantled unit – all must be renewed **(see illustrations)**.

14 On reassembly, fit the new sealing O-rings and lubricate them with clean fuel **(see illustrations)**.

15 When refitting the regulator, ensure that its retaining clip is correctly engaged in its slot **(see illustration)**.

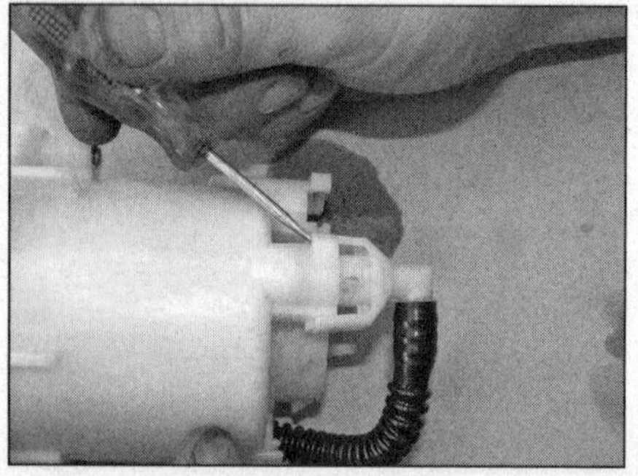

7.12a Release retaining clip . . .

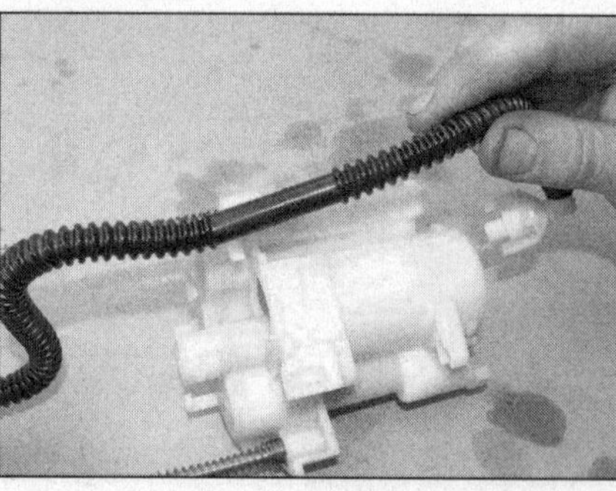

7.12b . . . to remove fuel feed pipe from unit

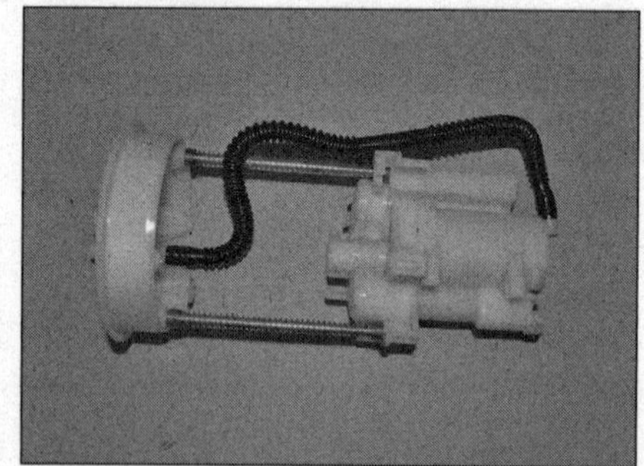

7.13a Fuel pump/gauge sender unit fully dismantled

7.13b Renew all sealing O-rings disturbed on dismantling . . .

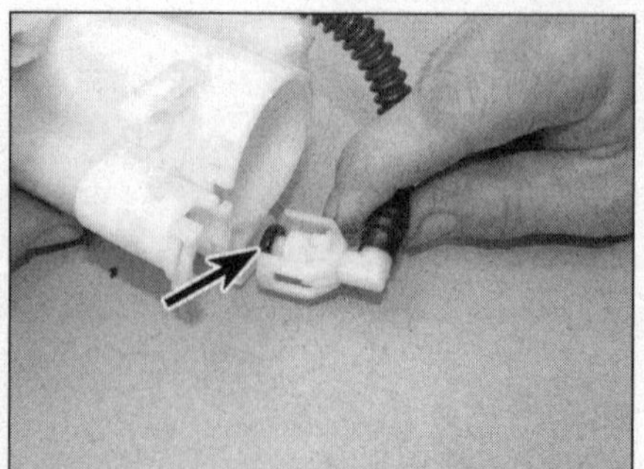

7.14a . . . including O-ring on fuel feed pipe . . .

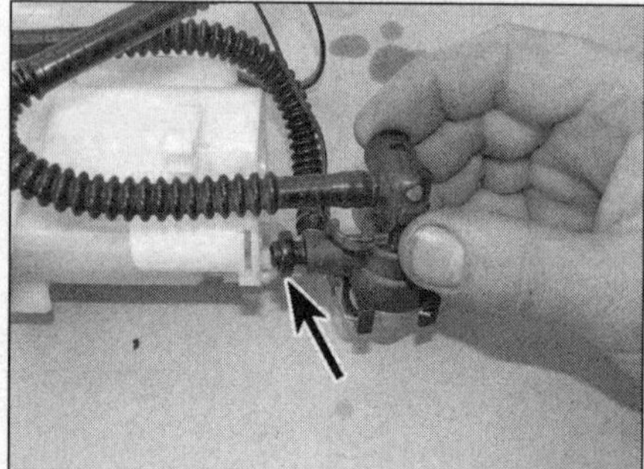

7.14b . . . on fuel pressure regulator . . .

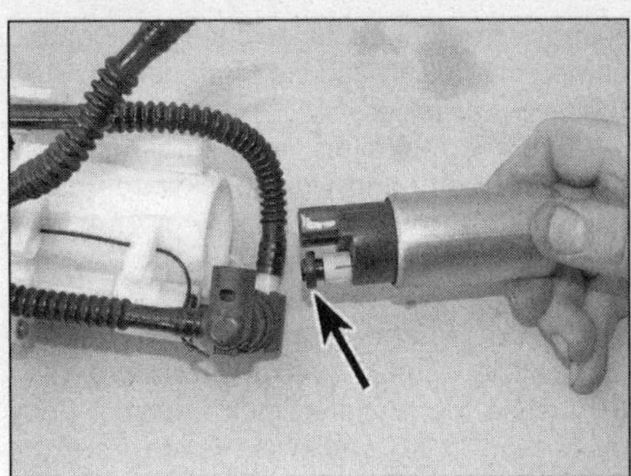
7.14c . . . and on fuel pump

7.15 Ensure fuel pressure regulator retaining clip is securely engaged in slot

7.16 Ensure that hoses and wiring are correctly located in clips provided

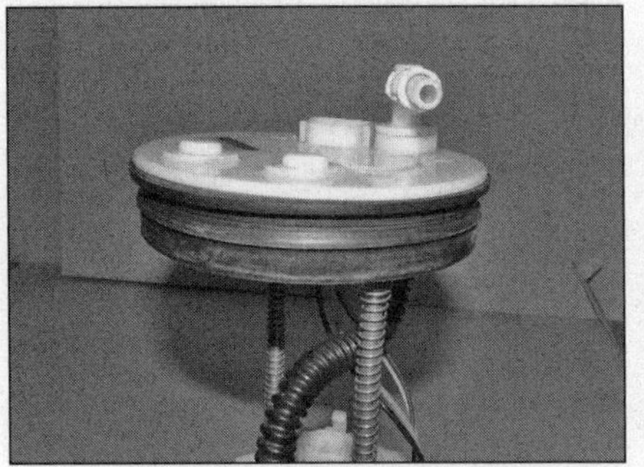
7.18 Fit new sealing ring to fuel pump/gauge sender unit . . .

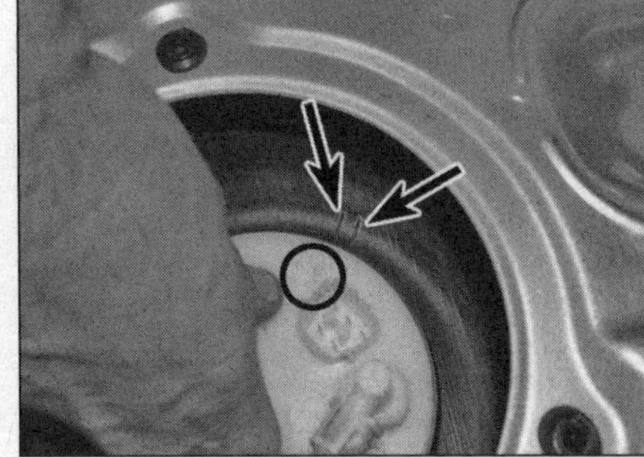
7.19 . . . and align reference mark on unit between marks on tank top surface

16 Ensure that hoses and wiring are correctly located in the clips provided **(see illustration)**.

17 Complete reassembly as described in Chapter 1A, Section 20.

Refitting

18 Fit the new sealing ring to the fuel pump/gauge sender unit **(see illustration)**.

19 Remove the old locking ring and discard it, then refit the unit to the tank, taking care not to catch the sender unit's float. Align the rib on top of the unit between the two ribs on the tank **(see illustration)**.

20 Fit the new locking ring to the fuel tank and tighten it securely.

21 Reconnect the fuel hose to the union on the top of the fuel pump/gauge sender unit, ensuring that the tabs click securely into position, and reconnect the wiring plug.

22 Start the engine and check for fuel leaks. If all is well, refit the access cover, carpet, and the rear seats.

8 Fuel tank – removal and refitting

Note: *Refer to the precautions in Section 1. The aid of one assistant, preferably two, will be required.*

Before removing the fuel tank, all fuel must be drained from it. Since a fuel tank drain plug is not provided, it is therefore preferable to carry out the removal operation when the tank is nearly empty.

Removal

1 Remove the fuel pump/gauge sender unit (Section 7).

2 Syphon or hand-pump the fuel from the tank into a suitable container.

3 Jack up the rear of the vehicle, and support it securely on axle stands (see *Jacking and vehicle support*).

4 Remove the exhaust centre section and rear silencer/tail pipe (Section 14).

5 Unbolt the charcoal canister cover and the canister itself. Disconnect hoses as necessary and secure the canister assembly clear of the working area (Chapter 4C).

6 Unbolt the fuel tank guard **(see illustrations)**.

7 Release the large hose clip and disconnect the filler hose from the tank **(see illustration)**. Disconnect the fuel vapour hose from the rear of the tank and unbolt the handbrake cable support brackets.

8 Disconnect the propeller shaft from the final drive unit (see Chapter 8), then unbolt and lower the final drive unit to provide sufficient clearance for the fuel tank to be removed; there is no need to disconnect the driveshaft(s) from the final drive unit.

9 Position a jack (and a large flat piece of wood, to spread the load) centrally under the tank, and just take its weight.

10 Taking care that the tank does not move, unscrew the four tank mounting bolts and remove the mounting straps **(see illustrations)**. Lower the tank a little and check that all hoses, etc, have been disconnected, and disconnect them as they become accessible.

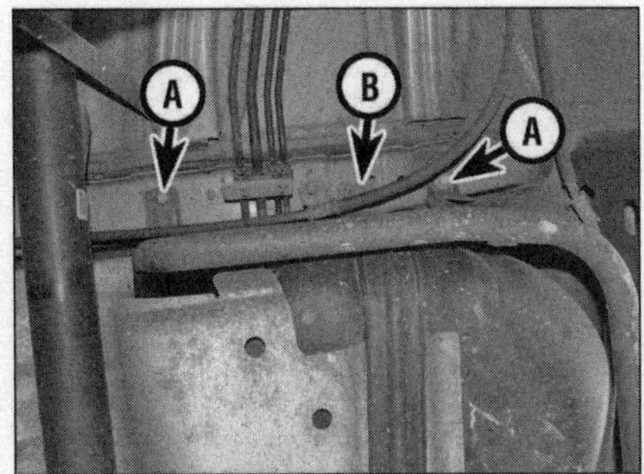

8.6a Fuel tank guard front mounting bolts (A), fuel tank front left-hand mounting bolt (B)

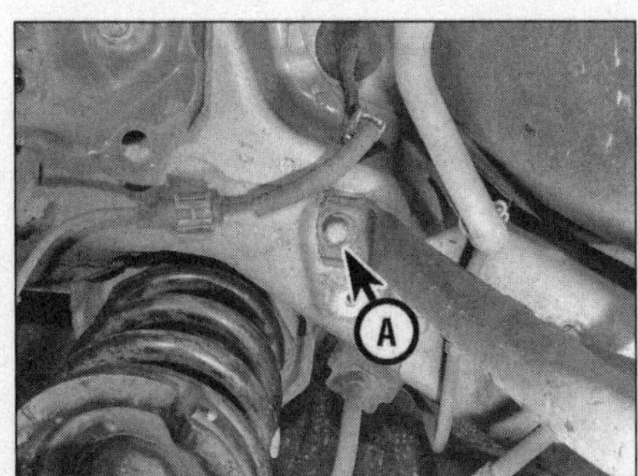

8.6b Fuel tank guard rear mounting bolt (A)

8.7 Fuel tank rear left-hand mounting bolt (B), fuel filler hose clip (C)

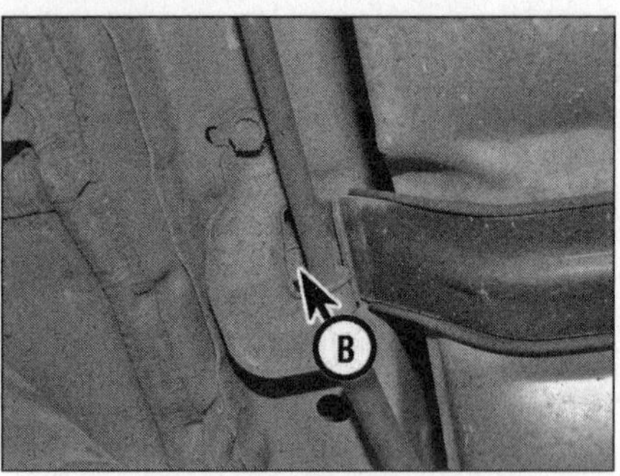

8.10a Fuel tank front right-hand mounting bolt (B)

11 With the aid of an assistant to steady the tank on the jack, lower the jack and remove the tank from under the vehicle. Note that the tank may 'stick' on the underseal. Try to keep the tank as level as possible, especially if it still contains fuel – if the tank tips, the fuel will run to one end and the tank may slide off the jack.

12 If the tank is contaminated with sediment or water, swill it out with clean fuel. The tank is injection-moulded from a synthetic material – if seriously damaged, it should be renewed. It may be possible to have small leaks or minor damage repaired – seek the advice of a specialist.

Refitting

13 Refitting is the reverse of the removal procedure. Check that there are no fuel leaks before taking the vehicle out on the road.

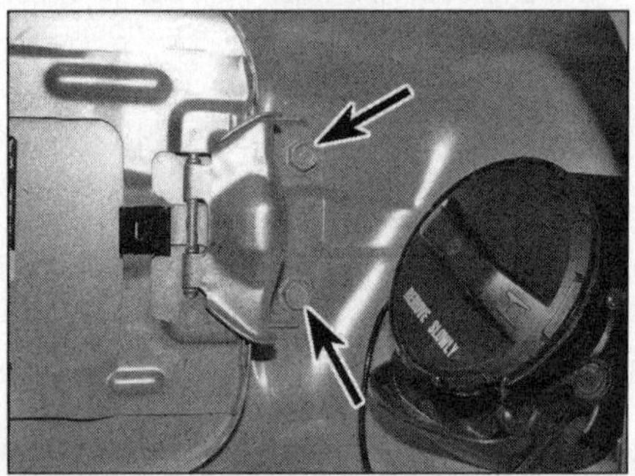

9.1 Fuel filler flap hinge bolts

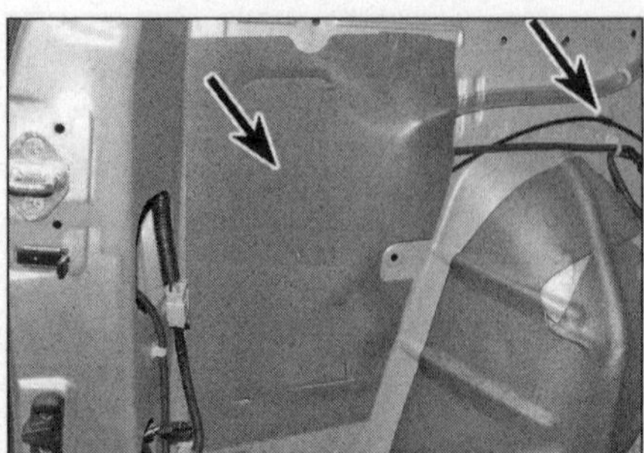

9.4b Remove luggage compartment left-hand side trim panel (note cable clip) and peel back sound insulation . . .

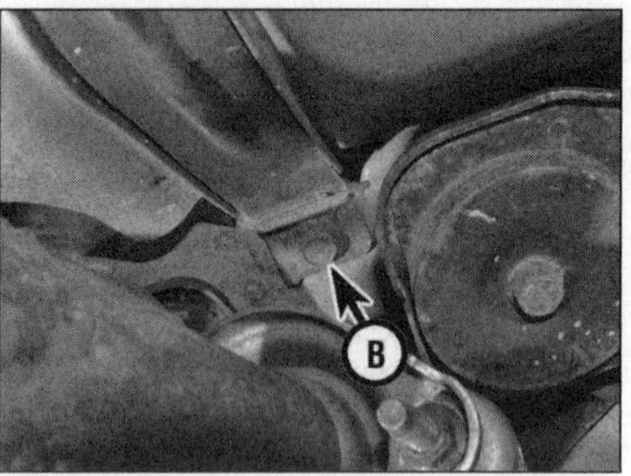

8.10b Fuel tank rear right-hand mounting bolt (B)

9 Fuel filler flap and cable – removal and refitting

Fuel filler flap

1 Unscrew and remove the two hinge bolts, and withdraw the flap from the vehicle **(see illustration)**.

2 Refitting is a reversal of removal. The position of the flap can be adjusted using the hinge bolts if necessary. Use touch-up paint as required on the hinge bolts and around the hinge.

Fuel filler flap release cable

3 Remove the driver's side under cover and lower cover from the facia, the driver's footwell side trim panel, the driver's door sill trim panel, the centre (B) pillar lower trim panel and the rear door sill trim panel (Chapter 11). Remove the rear seats, remove the luggage compartment left-hand side trim panel and lift the carpet as necessary.

4 Unscrew the filler flap release handle mounting bolts and work backwards along the length of the cable, releasing it from the securing clips and adhesive tape. Peel the sound insulation from the left-hand side of the luggage compartment to reach the inside of the fuel filler aperture **(see illustrations)**.

5 Release the filler flap lock from the body by turning it 90° clockwise (seen from the rear, inside the vehicle); the cable can then be removed completely **(see illustration)**. Renew any damaged clips and adhesive tape.

6 Refitting is a reversal of removal.

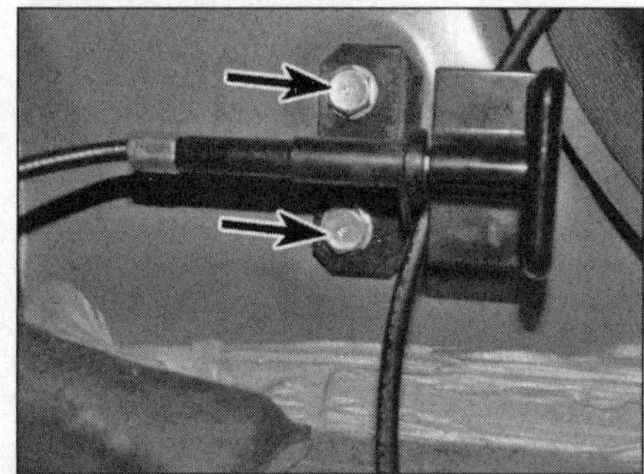

9.4a Unscrew filler flap release handle mounting bolts

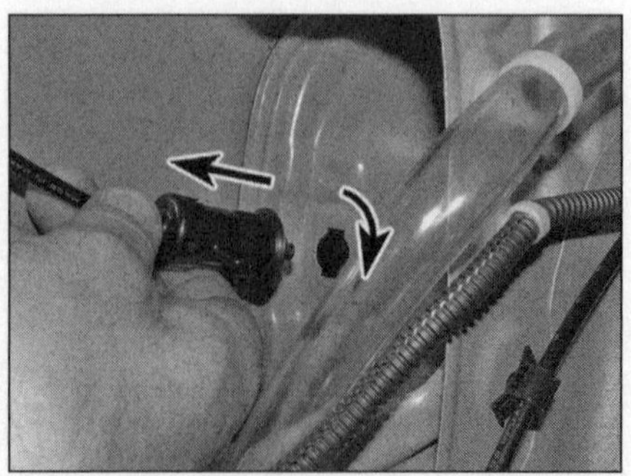

9.5 . . . to reach filler flap lock – turn 90° to release and withdraw from body

10 Fuel injection system – checking and fault code clearing

Note: *Refer to the precautions in Section 1.*

1 If a fault appears in the engine management system, first ensure that all the wiring connectors are secure and free of corrosion. Then ensure that the fault is not due to poor maintenance; ie, check that the air cleaner filter element is clean, that the valve clearances are correct, that the cylinder compression pressures are correct and that the engine breather hoses are clear and undamaged.

2 If these checks fail to reveal the cause of the problem, the vehicle should be taken to a specialist for testing. A diagnostic socket is incorporated in the wiring harness, into which dedicated electronic test equipment can be plugged – the connector is located under the driver's side of the facia **(see illustration)**. The test equipment communicates with the engine management system's Electronic Control Unit (ECU) and reads any fault codes stored in its memory.

3 Fault codes can only be extracted from the ECU using a dedicated fault code reader. It is unlikely to be cost-effective for the private owner to purchase a fault code reader, but a well-equipped local garage or auto-electrical specialist will have one.

4 Using this equipment, faults can be pinpointed quickly and simply, even if their occurrence is intermittent.

10.2 Engine management system's diagnostic socket is located under driver's side of facia, underneath fuse panel

5 The engine idle speed is not manually adjustable; an incorrect idle speed may be caused by leaking air or vacuum hoses, or a fault within the engine management system.

Clearing fault codes

6 Most of the components and sensors which make up the engine management system will log a fault code in the ECU memory in the event of a fault. When this happens, the Malfunction Indicator warning Lamp (MIL) on the instrument panel will come on. In some cases, the ECU will substitute its own default value instead of the correct sensor reading, and although it can still be driven safely, the vehicle will suffer driveability problems, often especially noticeable when cold.

7 Once the faulty component has been identified and the problem corrected (usually by fitting a new component), the fault code must be cleared. In some cases, this will happen automatically once the ignition has been switched on and off enough times.

8 To clear fault codes manually requires the use of a fault code reader tool as described above. However, on early (2001 to 2004) models, codes may also be cleared by the DIY mechanic, as follows.

9 With the ignition off, remove fuse No. 6 from the engine compartment main fuse/relay box for at least 10 seconds, then refit it. Switch the ignition on, and the fault should have cleared.

10 If the engine management Malfunction Indicator warning Lamp (MIL) remains on (or comes back on later), either the same fault still exists, or there is another faulty component triggering a different fault code. Check that any new components have been correctly fitted, and especially that their wiring plugs are clean and secure.

11 Fuel injection system components – removal and refitting

Note 1: *Refer to the precautions in Section 1 before proceeding.*

Note 2: *Before working on any part of the vehicle's electrical systems, it is advisable to disconnect the battery (see Disconnecting the battery).*

Accelerator pedal position sensor

Note: *This is fitted to 2005-on models only.*

1 Disconnect the throttle cable from the throttle linkage (Section 4).

2 Disconnect the wiring plug from the sensor, then unscrew the two mounting bolts and withdraw it. Unscrew the three bolts to separate the sensor from its bracket.

3 Refitting is a reversal of removal.

Barometric pressure sensor

4 The barometric pressure sensor is incorporated in the ECU to enable it to measure atmospheric pressure and adjust injector opening duration accordingly. The sensor is not available separately.

11.11 Crankshaft position sensor is fitted to engine's timing chain case, to rear of crankshaft pulley

Brake pedal position switch

5 Refer to Chapter 9.

Charcoal canister purge solenoid valve

6 Refer to Chapter 4C.

Clutch pedal position switch

Note: *The clutch pedal position switch is fitted to the clutch pedal assembly, above the clutch pedal (some models do not have this switch). If two switches are fitted, the interlock switch is mounted above the pedal position switch.*

7 Remove the driver's side under cover and lower cover from the facia (Chapter 11).

8 Disconnect the wiring plug from the top of the switch.

9 Unscrew the switch locknut, then unscrew and remove it from the bracket.

10 Refitting is a reversal of removal. Turn the switch clockwise until it just contacts the pedal arm, then turn it in an additional 3/4 to 1 turn. Tighten the locknut securely.

Crankshaft position (CKP) sensor

Note 1: *The crankshaft position sensor is fitted to the timing chain case, to the rear of the crankshaft pulley.*

Note 2: *For 2005-onwards models, Honda specify that their Honda Diagnostic System (HDS) tester must be used to clear old CKP data from the ECU memory and then to run a sequence during a road test to incorporate the new sensor data. If, on restarting the engine, it is found that disconnecting the crankshaft position sensor has caused a fault code to be logged so that the MIL illuminates, the vehicle must be taken to a Honda dealer or other specialist for this to be performed.*

11.18a Ignition coil relay (A), PGM-FI main relay 2 (B) and PGM-FI main relay 1 (C) are mounted to rear of ECU

11.13 Fit a new O-ring to the crankshaft position sensor

11 Jack up the front of the vehicle and securely support it on axle stands (see *Jacking and vehicle support*). Release the two securing clips and prise back the wheel arch liner section of the engine compartment undershield to reach the crankshaft pulley **(see illustration)**.

12 Disconnect the wiring plug, then unscrew the mounting bolt and remove the sensor from the engine. Recover the O-ring.

13 Refitting is a reversal of removal. Fit a new O-ring, lubricate it with engine oil and tighten the sensor mounting bolt to the specified torque **(see illustration)**.

14 The crankshaft position sensor's rotor is mounted on the crankshaft. It can be withdrawn once the timing chain case has been removed (Chapter 2A).

Electronic Control Unit (ECU)

Note 1: *The ECU contains the immobiliser coding which was programmed into it when the vehicle was new. If a new ECU is fitted, the immobiliser coding will have to be programmed into it by a Honda dealer before the vehicle will start.*

Note 2: *On 2005-on models, do not disconnect the ECU less than 15 minutes after the ignition was last switched off – the ECU will be in Self Shut Down (SSD) mode and must not be disconnected during this time or it may be damaged.*

15 Disconnect the battery (see *Disconnecting the battery*). This is essential when working on the ECU – if the unit's wiring connector is unplugged when the battery is still connected, this will almost certainly damage the unit.

16 Remove the passenger's side under cover and the glovebox from the facia (Chapter 11).

17 At the base of the glovebox aperture is a plastic cross-brace, which must be cut through at each end to allow the ECU to be removed (see Chapter 3, Section 9).

18 Release the relays from in front of the metal frame **(see illustrations)**.

19 Unscrew the four screws, two at each

11.18b Release relays from in front of metal frame by pushing up to release retaining clips

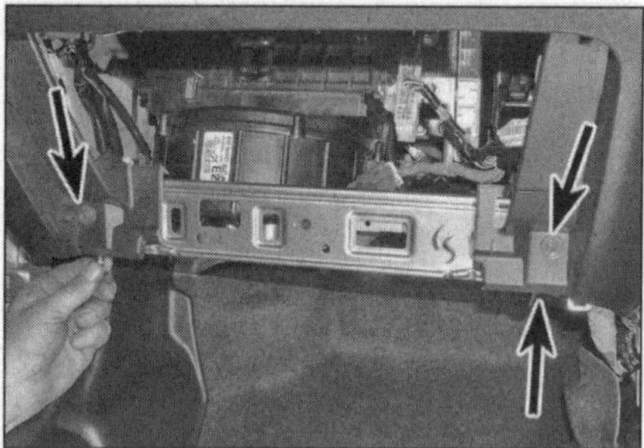
11.19a Unscrew four screws securing metal frame across base of glovebox aperture . . .

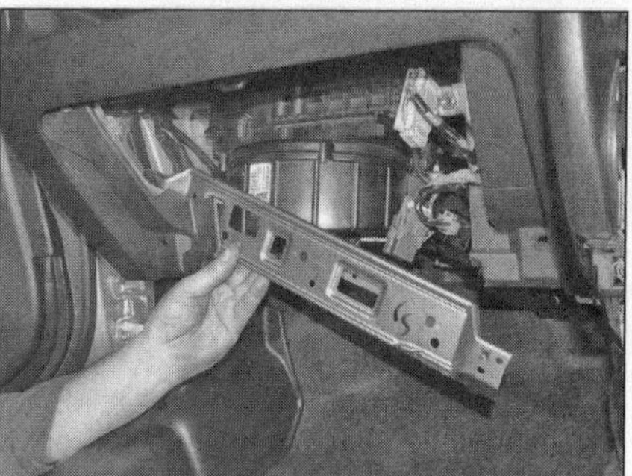
11.19b . . . and remove frame

11.20a Release large grey (main engine wiring harness) connector from ECU mounting bracket . . .

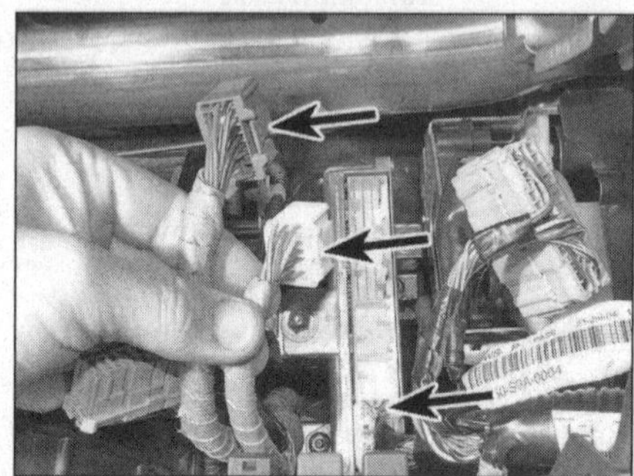
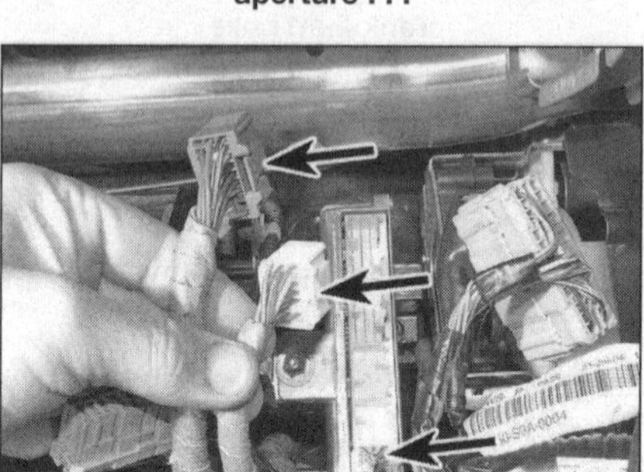
11.20b . . . then unplug connectors to disconnect ECU wiring

end, securing the metal frame across the base of the glovebox aperture. Remove the frame **(see illustrations)**.

20 Release the large grey wiring connector from the ECU mounting bracket, then unplug the connector(s) to disconnect the wiring from the ECU **(see illustrations)**.

21 Unscrew the ECU mounting bolt and nuts and withdraw the ECU **(see illustrations)**.

22 Refitting is a reversal of removal.

Coolant temperature sensor

23 Refer to Chapter 3.

Fuel filter

24 The fuel filter gauze is mounted in the base of the fuel pump/sender unit. Refer to Section 7 and to Chapter 1A.

Fuel injectors

25 Depressurise the fuel system (Section 2).

26 Unbolt and withdraw the plastic cover over the intake manifold.

27 Disconnect the wiring plugs from the fuel injectors and undo the bolt securing the earth lead to the intake manifold **(see illustration)**. Unclip the wiring conduit (and crankcase breather hose) from its support brackets on the fuel rail.

28 Disconnect the fuel feed hose from the fuel rail **(see illustration)**.

11.21a Unscrew ECU mounting bolt . . .

11.21b . . . mounting nut at upper right-hand side . . .

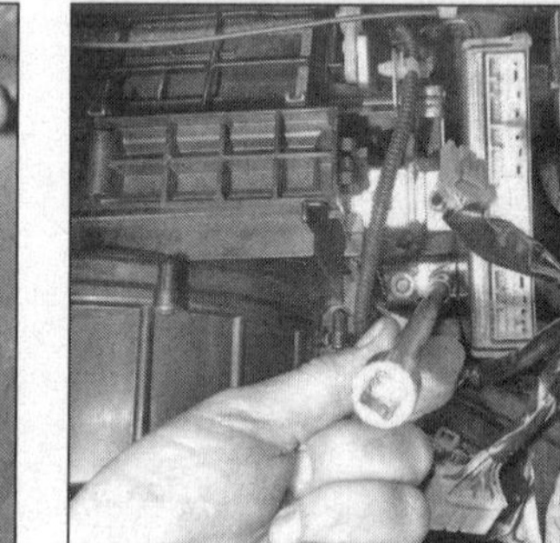
11.21c . . . and at lower left-hand side . . .

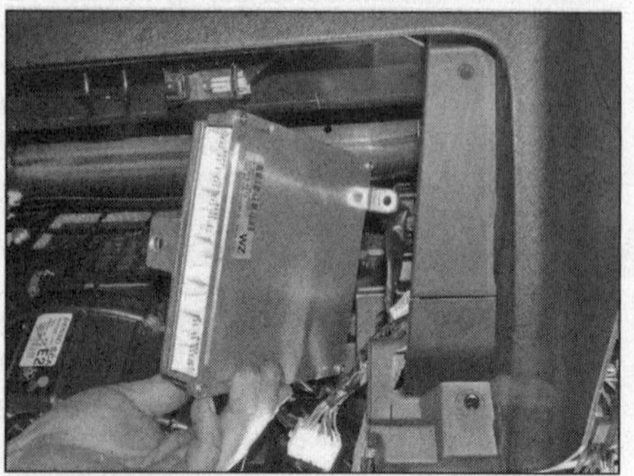
11.21d . . . then withdraw ECU

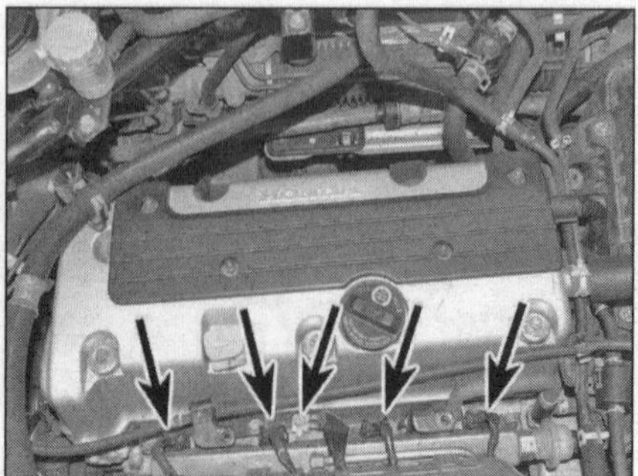
11.27 Disconnect fuel injector wiring and unbolt earth lead from intake manifold

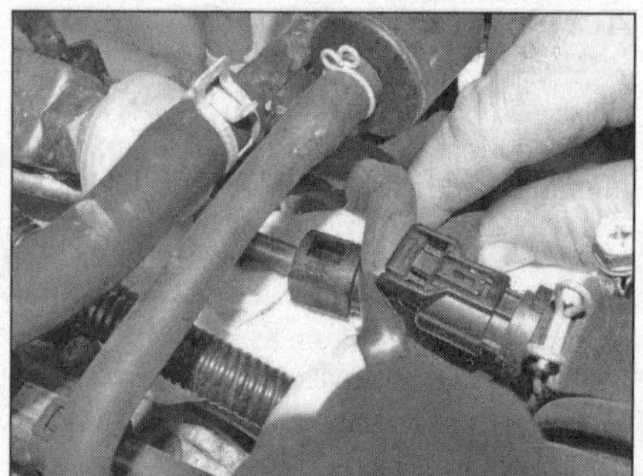
11.28 Disconnect fuel feed hose from fuel rail; be prepared for fuel spillage

29 Unscrew the two fuel rail mounting nuts **(see illustration)**.

30 Remove the fuel rail complete with injectors by pulling carefully and equally on both ends of the rail – there will be some resistance from the injector O-ring seals. Recover the O-ring seals if they become dislodged, and the small spacer from each mounting stud. Remove the rail to a clean working area.

31 Slide out the metal locking clip which secures each injector to the rail, then pull the injectors free, noting how they are fitted – again, there will be resistance from the O-rings. Remove and discard the upper, middle and lower O-rings from each injector – a new set should be obtained for refitting **(see illustration)**.

32 Refitting is a reversal of removal, noting the following points **(see illustrations)**:

a) *Use new O-ring seals, and coat them with clean engine oil.*
b) *The locating lug on each injector must fit between the ears provided in the fuel rail fitting.*
c) *On completion, switch on the ignition to pressurise the system, and check for leaks.*

Fuel pressure regulator

33 The pressure regulator is mounted in the base of the fuel pump/sender unit. Refer to Section 7.

Fuel pulsation damper

2001 to 2004 models

34 Unbolt and withdraw the plastic cover over the intake manifold.

35 Release the fuel pressure in the damper by slackening it as described in Section 2. When all fuel pressure is released, unscrew the damper and recover the sealing washer.

36 The damper is a sealed unit and must be renewed if faulty.

37 Refitting is a reversal of removal. Use a new sealing washer and tighten the damper to the specified torque while counterholding the fuel rail hexagon.

2005-on models

38 Unbolt and withdraw the plastic cover over the intake manifold.

39 Unscrew the bolt securing the injector wiring earth lead to the intake manifold, then unscrew the two fuel rail mounting nuts and lift the rail just enough to reach the damper.

40 Counterhold the hexagon on the fuel rail with one open-ended spanner and unscrew the damper with a second spanner.

41 The damper is a sealed unit and must be renewed if faulty.

42 Refitting is a reversal of removal. Use new sealing washer(s) and tighten the damper securely while counterholding the fuel rail hexagon.

Fuel shut-off (inertia) switch

Note: *This may not be fitted on some models.*

43 The fuel shut-off switch is a safety device which automatically cuts off the fuel supply in the event of a sudden impact or collision. The switch may occasionally be triggered in normal driving, for example when driving over badly-maintained roads.

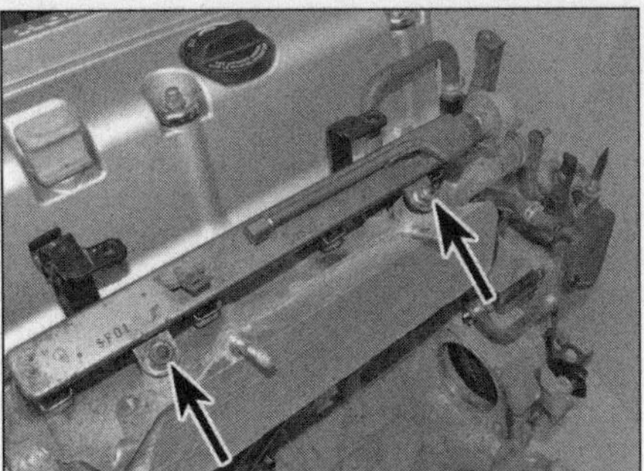

11.29 Unscrew two fuel rail mounting nuts

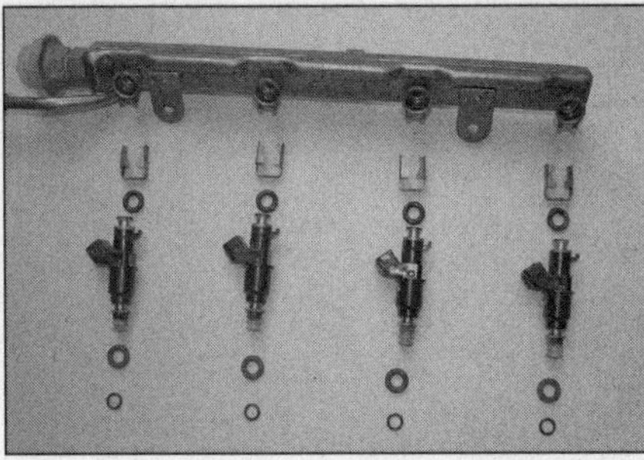

11.31 Slide out locking clip securing each injector to fuel rail. Remove and discard O-ring seals from each injector

44 The switch is located behind the glovebox, on the right-hand side. To reach it, open the glovebox, then press the two hooks, one on either side of the glovebox, forwards to release the stops, remove both hooks and allow the glovebox to swing down further.

45 To reset the switch after an impact or shock, depress the button on the top of the switch.

46 To remove the switch, disconnect the wiring plug on its base, then unscrew the mounting bolts and withdraw the switch.

47 Refitting is a reversal of removal.

Idle air control (IAC) valve

Note: *This is fitted to 2001 to 2004 models only.*

48 The idle air control valve is mounted on the underside of the throttle body, and is the primary means by which the ECU controls idle speed – as more air is allowed to bleed into the manifold, more fuel is supplied, and the idle speed rises. This type of valve can become sluggish in operation if carbon deposits build up in it.

49 Remove the throttle body as described below.

50 Undo the two mounting screws and withdraw the valve from the throttle body **(see illustration)**. Recover the O-ring. Check that the air and coolant passages in the throttle body and valve are clear. If there are carbon deposits, use carburettor cleaner to remove them, but take care not to damage the vane inside the valve and note the warnings given in paragraph 101.

51 Refitting is a reversal of removal. Use a new O-ring.

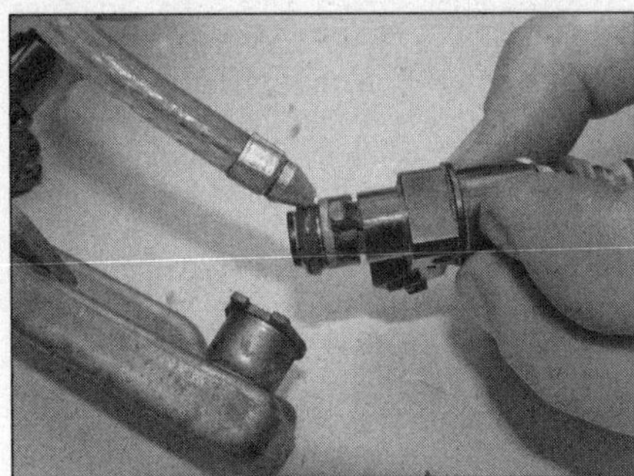

11.32a Fit new upper O-ring and smear with clean engine oil . . .

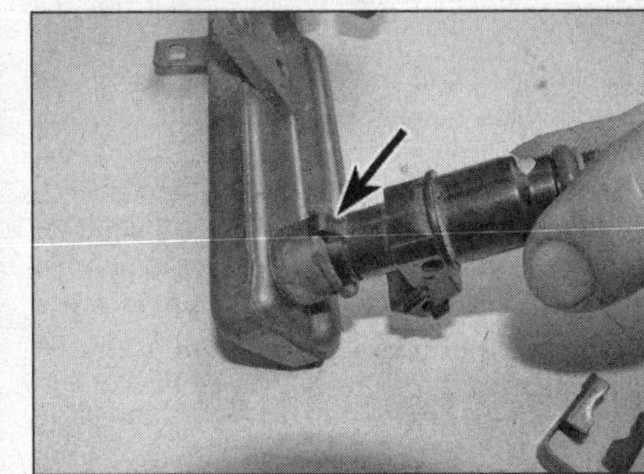

11.32b . . . refit injector to fuel rail so that locating lug engages as shown . . .

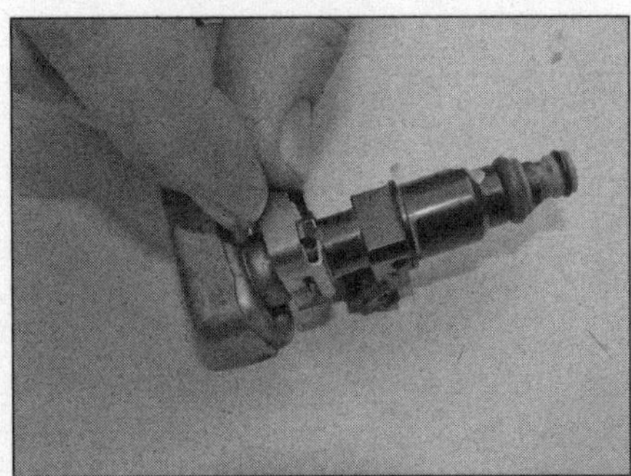

11.32c . . . then refit locking clip to secure injector to rail

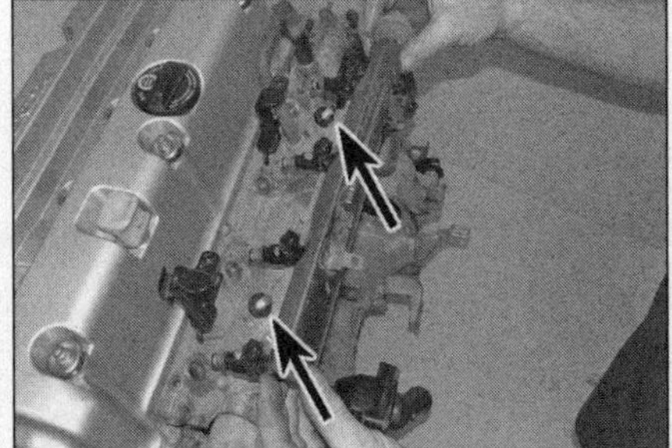

11.32d Refit fuel rail and injectors as an assembly. Note spacer on each mounting stud

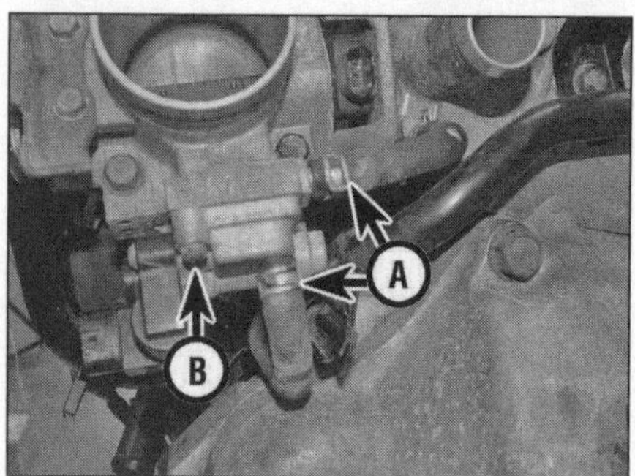

11.50 Idle air control valve coolant hoses (A) and mounting screw (B) on base of throttle body

11.55 Check carefully bearing on end of valve – renew O-ring (A). Note groove (B) which engages with stop in manifold

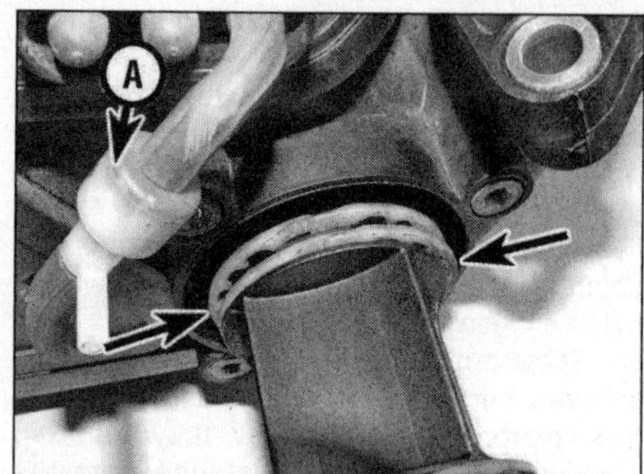

11.56a Squeeze together valve bearing elements to insert IMT actuator valve into manifold. Note location of IMT check valve (A)

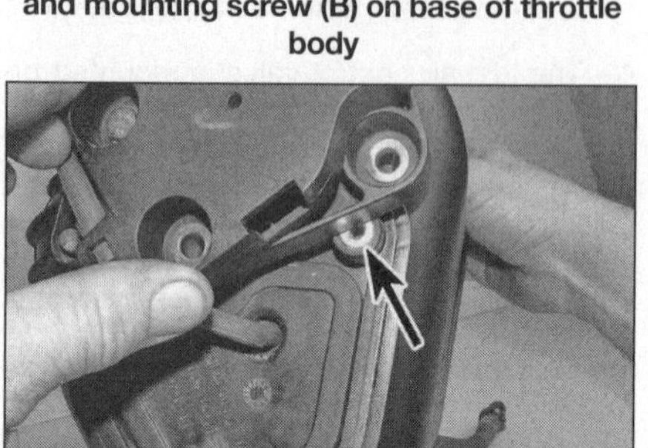
11.56b Position valve so that hole appears, then rotate to align mounting bolt holes and refit bolts

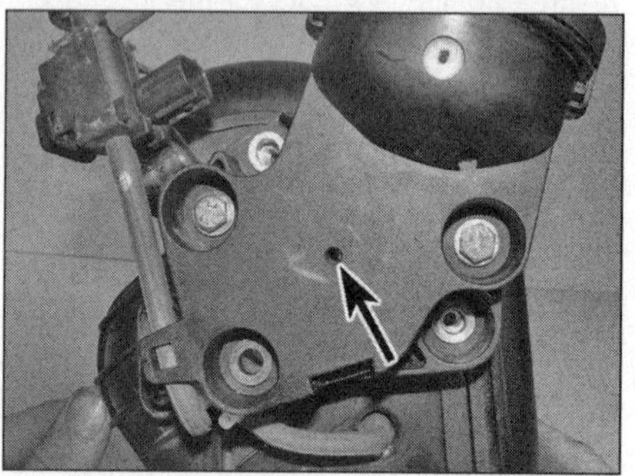
11.57 Insert split pin into actuator valve shaft to check valve operation

Intake Manifold Tuning (IMT)

Actuator valve

52 Remove the outer, black plastic intake manifold as described in Section 12.

53 Disconnect the vacuum hose from the valve.

54 Unscrew the three mounting bolts and withdraw the valve from the manifold. Recover and discard the sealing O-rings – these must be renewed whenever the valve is disturbed.

55 Check the valve for signs of wear or damage and renew it if necessary; remember that if the valve breaks up while the engine is running, the pieces will go straight into the engine. Check carefully the condition and security of the bearing on the end of the valve **(see illustration)**.

56 On reassembly, fit new sealing O-rings and carefully insert the valve into the manifold, squeezing together the valve bearing elements so that they do not snag on the manifold. Position the valve so that the hole appears as shown and ensure that the stop protruding from inside of the opposite end of the manifold has engaged with the groove in the end of the valve **(see illustrations)**. If the valve body does not mate easily with the manifold, do not force it; remove the valve and repeat the process to re-align the valve with the stop. When the valve is seated correctly and without force in the manifold, rotate it to align the mounting bolt holes, then refit and tighten securely the mounting bolts. Reconnect the vacuum hose.

57 To check that the valve is operating correctly, find a split pin of suitable-size and bend one leg at right-angles to the other to form a T-shaped tool. Insert the bent leg into the end of the valve's shaft **(see illustration)**. Apply suction to the valve hose and check that the split pin rotates smoothly and returns fully when the vacuum is released.

11.61 Disconnect IMT solenoid valve wiring and undo its mounting bolt

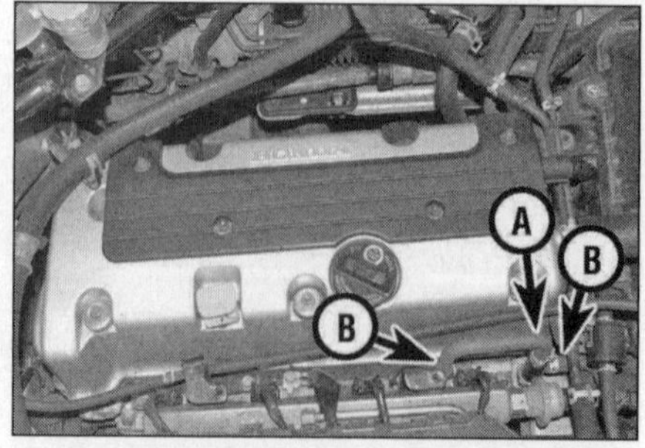

11.64 Remove intake manifold plastic cover to reach intake air bypass control thermal valve (A) and hose connections (B)

58 Refit the outer, black plastic intake manifold (Section 12).

Check valve

59 The valve is located in the vacuum line to the IMT solenoid valve, underneath the solenoid valve, at the right-hand end of the outer, black plastic intake manifold; it can be reached only after this has been removed, as described in Section 12 **(see illustration 11.56a)**. To test the valve, suck or blow through it in both directions. Air should flow in one direction only; if it flows in both directions, or in neither, the valve is faulty and must be renewed.

Solenoid valve

60 Unbolt and withdraw the plastic cover over the intake manifold.

61 Disconnect the IMT solenoid valve wiring and undo the solenoid mounting bolt **(see illustration)**. Disconnect the hoses from the valve and withdraw it.

62 Refitting is a reversal of removal.

Intake air bypass control thermal valve

Note: *For 2005-on models, the valve is only available with the cylinder head water outlet. Check parts availability before proceeding.*

63 The intake air bypass control thermal valve's passages are open when the engine coolant temperature is below 65°C, allowing air to pass from the air cleaner assembly-to-throttle body intake hose directly to the intake manifold, bypassing the throttle body. When the engine is warmed up to above this temperature, the valve closes and remains shut.

64 Unbolt and withdraw the plastic cover over the intake manifold **(see illustration)**.

65 Drain the cooling system as described in Chapter 1A.

66 On 2005-on models, remove the throttle body as described later in this Section.

67 Disconnect the two hoses from the intake air bypass control thermal valve unions. For 2001 to 2004 models, if the valve is available separately, it can be unscrewed from the water outlet at this point and renewed.

68 Disconnect the cooling system bypass hose and the radiator top hose from the water outlet at the left-hand front end of the cylinder head **(see illustration)**.

69 Unbolt the water outlet from the cylinder head; recover the O-ring. For 2005-on models, do not attempt to separate the valve from the outlet; for 2001 to 2004 models, check parts availability before unscrewing the valve.

70 Refitting is a reversal of removal. Use new O-rings on the water outlet and (if applicable) the valve.

Intake air temperature sensor

71 The intake air temperature sensor is mounted in the air cleaner assembly-to-throttle body intake hose, and informs the ECU of the temperature of the incoming air.

72 Disconnect the sensor's wiring plug, then remove the retaining clip and pull out the sensor, noting its sealing grommet **(see illustrations)**.

73 Refitting is a reversal of removal. Use a new grommet if necessary.

Intake Manifold Runner Control (IMRC) system

74 This system is described in Section 1 of Chapter 2A. Removal and refitting of the system's components is covered in this Section.

i-VTEC system components

75 Refer to Chapter 2A.

Knock sensor

76 Refer to Chapter 5B.

Manifold absolute pressure sensor

77 The sensor is mounted directly on top of the throttle body, and provides the ECU with information on pressure levels in the manifold. The ECU uses this to calculate the engine load, and the appropriate fuelling.

78 Disconnect the sensor wiring plug **(see illustration)**.

79 Undo the mounting screw and withdraw the sensor from the throttle body. Recover the O-ring.

80 Refitting is a reversal of removal. Fit a new O-ring.

Oxygen sensors

81 Refer to Chapter 4C.

Power steering pressure switch

82 The switch is mounted in the power steering line on the engine compartment bulkhead, and signals the ECU when the load imposed by the power steering pump is high. The ECU then increases idle speed to stop the engine stalling.

83 Disconnect the switch wiring plug, then unscrew the switch and withdraw it; plug or tape over the opening. Recover the O-ring or sealing washer **(see illustration)**.

84 Refitting is a reversal of removal. Fit a new O-ring or washer. On completion, top-up and bleed the power steering system (Chapter 10).

TDC (camshaft position) sensor

Note: *There are two identical camshaft*

11.68 Disconnecting cooling system bypass hose and radiator top hose from water outlet

11.78 Disconnecting MAP sensor wiring. Note mounting screw (arrowed)

position sensors fitted to the left-hand end of the cylinder head ***(see illustration)****. The rear sensor, detecting the position of the exhaust camshaft, is the TDC sensor.*

85 Remove the air cleaner assembly (Section 6).

86 Disconnect the sensor's electrical connector **(see illustration)**. Remove the retaining screw, and withdraw the sensor from the cylinder head; be prepared for slight oil loss. Remove the O-ring.

87 Refitting is the reverse of the removal procedure. Use a new O-ring.

88 The TDC position sensor's rotor is mounted on the exhaust camshaft. It can be withdrawn once the cylinder head cover has been removed (Chapter 2A).

Throttle actuator

Note: *This is fitted to 2005-on models only.*

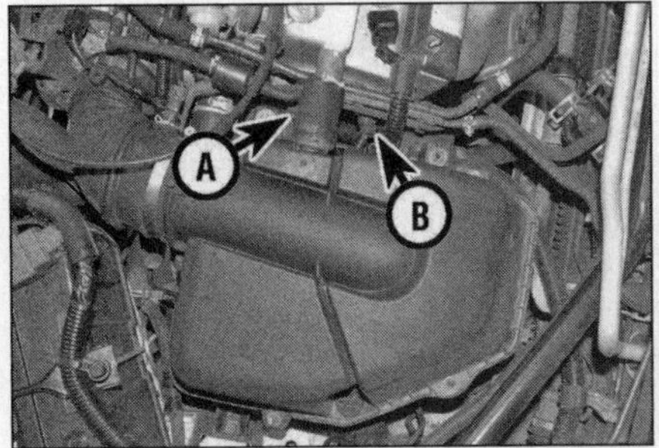

11.85 Front camshaft position sensor (A) serves i-VTEC/VTC system; rear sensor (B) is TDC sensor for engine management system

11.72 Intake air temperature sensor is mounted in air cleaner assembly-to-throttle body intake hose

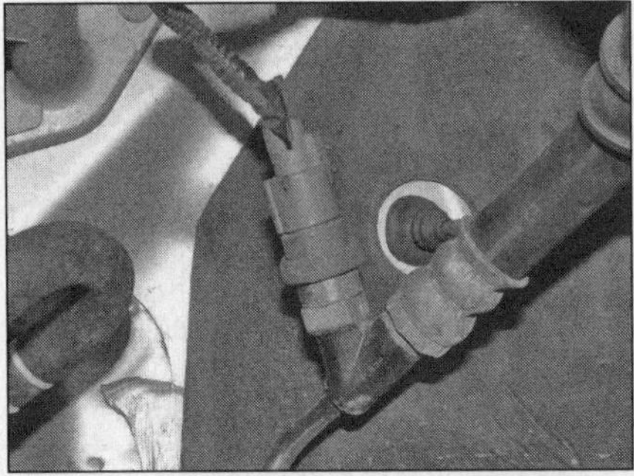

11.83 Power steering pressure switch is mounted in power steering line on engine compartment bulkhead

89 The throttle actuator is fitted to the throttle body; it is not available separately. In the event that a throttle actuator problem is suspected, the only solution is a new throttle body.

Control module

90 The module is located behind the glovebox, on the left-hand side. To reach it, open the glovebox, then press the two hooks, one on either side of the glovebox, forwards to release the stops, remove both hooks and allow the glovebox to swing down further.

91 To remove the module, depress the locking tab and unplug the connector to disconnect the module wiring, then unscrew the mounting bolts and withdraw the module.

92 Refitting is a reversal of removal.

Control module relay

93 The relay is located at the rear of the

11.86 Disconnecting camshaft position sensor's electrical connector

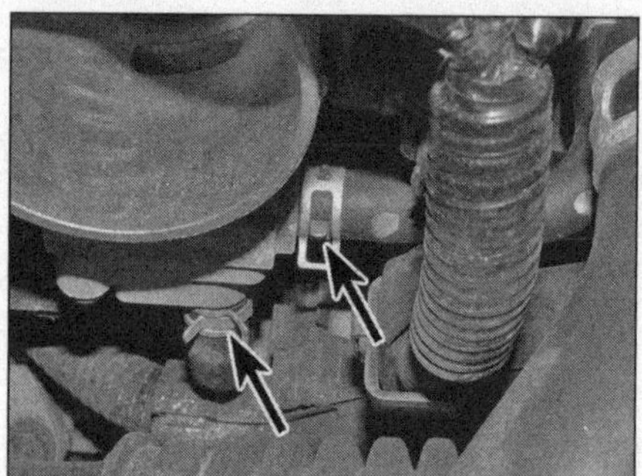
11.97 Disconnect cooling system bypass hoses from throttle body

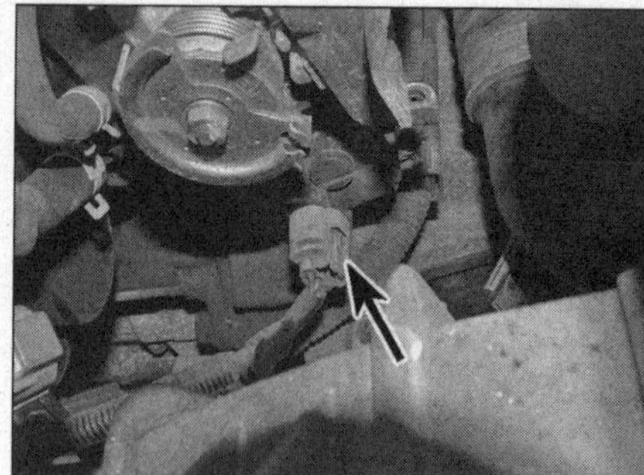
11.98a Disconnect idle air control valve wiring (where fitted) from throttle body . . .

11.98b . . . throttle position sensor wiring . . .

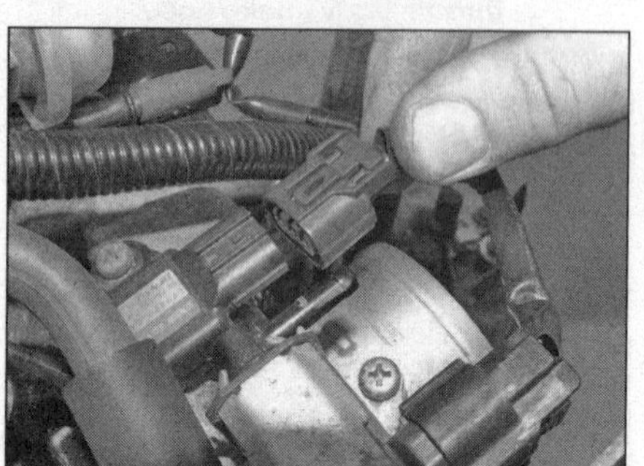
11.98c . . . MAP sensor wiring . . .

11.98d . . . and canister purge solenoid valve wiring and hose

engine compartment sub fuse/relay box A, which is mounted next to the main fuse/relay box and is furthest to the rear of the engine compartment.

Throttle body

Note: *If, on restarting the engine at the end of this procedure, it is found that disconnecting the throttle body and related components has caused the MIL to illuminate, the vehicle must be taken to a specialist for the fault code to be erased and for the engine idle characteristics to be cleared and relearned.*

Removal

94 Drain the cooling system as described in Chapter 1A. Alternatively, either clamp the hoses or be prepared for a small amount of coolant loss.

95 Disconnect the air cleaner assembly-to-throttle body intake hose from the throttle body as described in Section 6.

96 On 2001 to 2004 models, disconnect the throttle cable from the throttle linkage as described in Section 4.

97 Disconnect the cooling system bypass hoses from the throttle body **(see illustration)**.

98 Disconnect the wiring plugs from the idle air control valve (2001 to 2004 models), the throttle position sensor and (2005-on models) actuator, manifold absolute pressure (MAP) sensor and charcoal canister purge solenoid valve. Label the plugs if necessary, to ensure correct refitting. Disconnect the hose from the charcoal canister purge solenoid valve **(see illustrations)**.

99 Unscrew the four bolts (2001 to 2004 models) or the two bolts and two nuts (2005-on models) securing the throttle body to the intake manifold **(see illustrations)**. Ensure that nothing remains attached to it, then withdraw it. On 2001 to 2004 models, recover the seal from the throttle body and discard it; on 2005-on models recover and discard the gasket, withdraw the spacer, then recover and discard the seal between the spacer and intake manifold.

11.99a Unscrew the two upper bolts (2001 to 2004 models) . . .

11.99b . . . and two lower bolts securing throttle body to intake manifold

Cleaning

100 With the idle air control valve (2001 to 2004 models), the manifold absolute pressure (MAP) sensor and charcoal canister purge solenoid valve removed, check the throttle body for signs of wear or damage and renew it if necessary.

101 Check that the air and coolant passages in the throttle body are clear. If there are carbon deposits, use carburettor cleaner to remove them, but Honda state that only genuine Honda Carburetor Cleaner must be used, sprayed on to a paper towel so that the carbon can be wiped off the throttle butterfly and the interior of the throttle body. Do not spray carburettor cleaner directly on to the throttle body and do not clean the area around the throttle butterfly spindle's bearings, to avoid removing the molybdenum coating.

Refitting

102 Refitting is a reversal of removal, using new seals and gaskets. Adjust the throttle cable if necessary as described in Section 4.

Throttle position sensor

103 The throttle position sensor is fitted to the side of the throttle body, and signals the position of the throttle butterfly to the ECU. In the event that a throttle position sensor problem is suspected, consult a Honda parts specialist for advice, as it appears that the only solution is a new throttle body.

Vehicle speed sensor

Manual gearbox

104 The vehicle speed sensor is located on top of the gearbox, next to the gearchange cables and levers. The sensor should not be confused with the reversing light switch, which is also located on top of the gearbox, but does not have a separate mounting bolt **(see illustration)**. The sensor provides an electronic signal of vehicle speed which is used by the engine management ECU, the anti-lock braking system and the speedometer.

105 Remove the air cleaner assembly and intake air duct (Section 6).
106 Disconnect the wiring plug from the sensor.
107 Unscrew the sensor mounting bolt, then withdraw the sensor from the transmission. Remove the O-ring.
108 Refitting is a reversal of removal. Fit a new O-ring. Expect the sensor to twist as it meshes with the transmission gear, then turn it to align the mounting bolt hole.

Automatic transmission

109 The vehicle speed signal is provided by the output shaft speed sensor located at the top rear of the transmission, close to the engine. The sensor should not be confused with the mainshaft speed sensor, which is further to the left.
110 Proceed as described above for manual gearbox models.

VTC system components

111 Refer to Chapter 2A.

12 Intake manifold – removal and refitting

Note: *The intake manifold is composed of two parts: the outer black plastic section and the inner aluminium section fitted against the cylinder head. Many procedures involving the removal of the intake manifold will require only the removal of the outer section* ***(see illustration).***

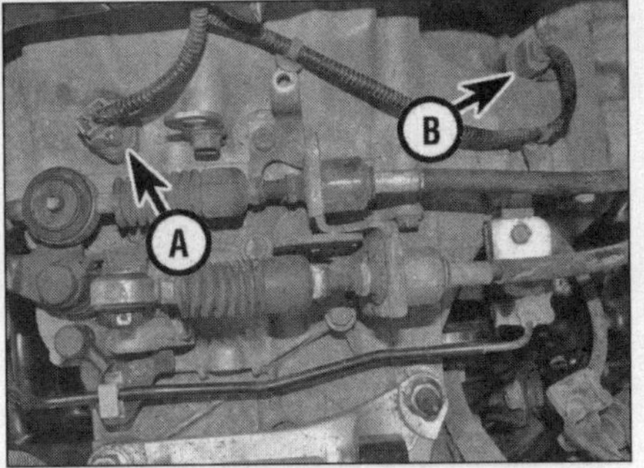

11.104 Do not confuse reversing light switch (A) with vehicle speed sensor (B)

Removal

1 Drain the cooling system (Chapter 1A).
2 Remove the air cleaner assembly and intake air duct (Section 6).
3 On 2001 to 2004 models, disconnect the throttle cable from the throttle linkage (Section 4). Release the cable from its guide bracket on the intake manifold.
4 If the injectors and fuel rail are to be disturbed, depressurise the fuel system (Section 2). Disconnect the fuel feed hose from the fuel rail.
5 Disconnect the charcoal canister and braking system vacuum hoses from their unions **(see illustration)**.
6 Disconnect the cooling system bypass hoses from the throttle body.
7 Disconnect the Positive Crankcase Ventilation (PCV) valve from the water pump housing **(see illustration)**.
8 Disconnect the IMT solenoid valve wiring and undo its mounting bolt.
9 Unscrew the battery hold-down clamp bolt, then release its retaining clips and remove the radiator grille top cover.
10 Disconnect the wiring for the bonnet switch (where fitted) and release the wiring harnesses from the retaining clips on the radiator/bonnet lock support bracket.
11 Remove the intake air duct mounting bolts and the radiator top mounting bracket bolts from the radiator/bonnet lock support bracket. Unscrew the four top mounting bolts and the single bolt at the bottom of the radiator/bonnet lock support bracket's vertical member. Carefully lift out the radiator/ bonnet lock support bracket (there is no need to disconnect the bonnet release cable) and secure it clear of the working area.
12 Disconnect the various wiring connectors from the throttle body components and free all wiring from the manifold **(see illustration)**.
13 Unscrew the three bolts and two nuts securing the outer manifold section to the inner section. Ensure that nothing remains attached to it, then withdraw the outer manifold **(see illustrations)**. Recover the seals from the outer manifold.
14 The inner manifold section can be removed with the injectors and fuel rail in place. Unscrew the five bolts and two nuts securing the inner manifold to the cylinder head and withdraw it **(see illustrations)**. Recover the manifold gasket.
15 Check the manifolds for any signs of splitting or cracking – this may be most

12.0 Intake manifold is in two parts: removal of outer, tubular black plastic section will be sufficient for most procedures

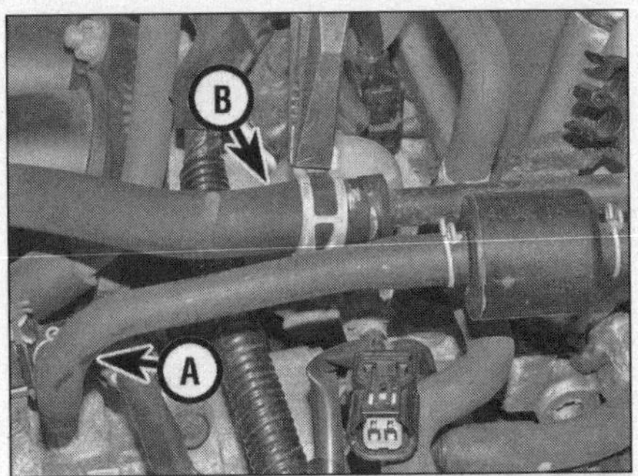

12.5 Disconnect charcoal canister (A) and braking system (B) vacuum hoses

12.7 Disconnect Positive Crankcase Ventilation (PCV) valve

12.12 Release wiring from outer, tubular black plastic section of intake manifold

12.13a Unscrew bolts and nuts securing outer intake manifold to inner intake manifold . . .

12.13b . . . and remove outer intake manifold

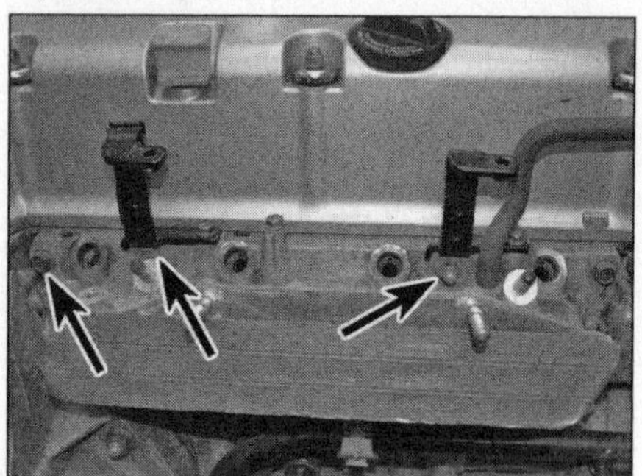
12.14a Unscrew two nuts and one bolt from above . . .

12.14b . . . and four bolts from below securing inner manifold to cylinder head

12.17 Always renew all seals and gaskets when refitting intake manifold(s)

evident around the mounting points. If either manifold is damaged, a new one will be needed, although small isolated cracks in the outer section may be repairable, either with sealant or with the help of a plastics repair specialist.

Refitting

16 Clean all mating faces prior to refitting, and wipe them dry. Fit a new inner manifold gasket over the studs, then slide on the inner manifold. Working in several stages and in a diagonal sequence from the centre outwards, tighten the mounting nuts and bolts to the specified torque.

17 Fit new seals to the outer manifold, then slide it onto the studs and into position **(see illustration)**.

18 Refit the outer manifold nuts and bolts, and working in several stages and in a diagonal sequence from the centre outwards, tighten them fully by hand. Once they are hand-tight, tighten the manifold nuts and bolts by a quarter-turn each at a time to the specified torque.

19 Further refitting is a reversal of removal.

13 Exhaust manifold – removal and refitting

Warning: Inspection and repair of exhaust system components should be done only after the system has cooled completely.

Removal

Note: *The manifold's nuts and bolts must be renewed irrespective of their apparent condition whenever they are disturbed, as must the gasket and the exhaust front pipe-to-manifold bolts and 'olive' gasket. Obtain new nuts, bolts and gaskets before starting work.*

1 Unbolt the steering hose clamp from the rear right-hand end of the cylinder head cover.

2 Unscrew the four nuts securing the ignition coil cover on top of the engine. Lift off the cover; be careful not to lose the separate spacer from each rear mounting stud. Disconnect the ignition coils and lift the large black plastic wiring conduit from its mountings; be careful not to lose the spacer from each mounting stud. Secure harness and conduit clear of the cylinder head.

3 Disconnect the i-VTEC solenoid valve and oil pressure switch connectors on the top of the i-VTEC solenoid valve assembly, then unbolt the assembly itself as described in Chapter 2A **(see illustration)**.

4 Unbolt and withdraw the cover from the exhaust manifold **(see illustration)**.

5 Jack up the front of the vehicle and support it on axle stands (see *Jacking and vehicle support*). Have a support (such as another axle stand or a small jack) ready to rest the front pipe on.

6 Unscrew the three bolts and withdraw the heat shield covering the right-hand driveshaft intermediate shaft **(see illustration)**.

7 Undo the two bolts securing the exhaust front pipe to the manifold. Recover the springs and the gasket.

8 Unbolt the manifold support bracket from the manifold and cylinder block **(see illustration)**.

9 Do not let the front pipe hang down unsupported, as this will strain the oxygen sensor wiring (as well as the pipe itself). Place an axle stand or another jack under the pipe.

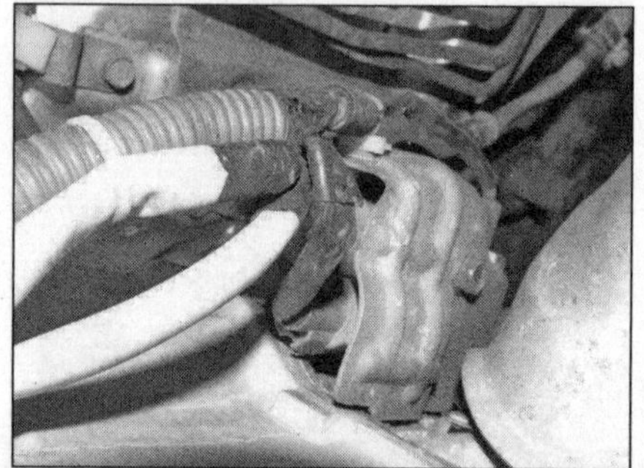
13.3 Remove i-VTEC solenoid valve assembly from right-hand rear end of cylinder head

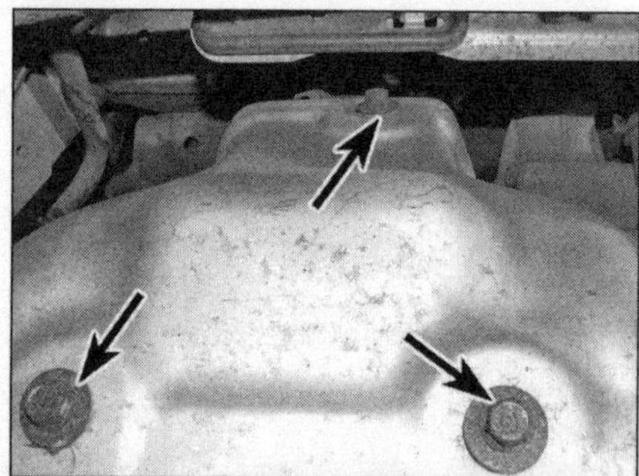
13.4 Unbolt and withdraw cover over exhaust manifold

13.6 Intermediate shaft support bearing heat shield bolts

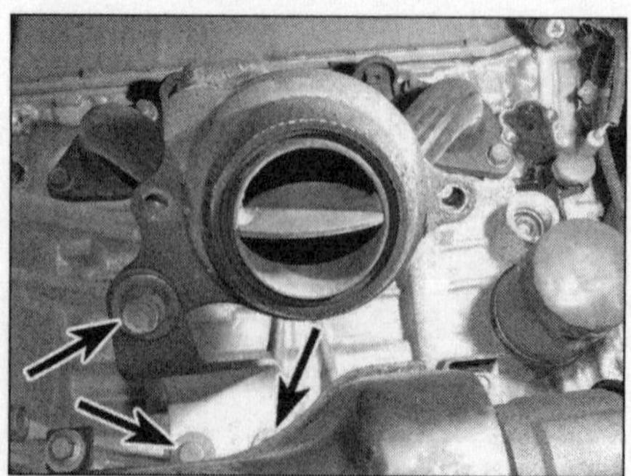
13.8 Undo bolts to remove exhaust manifold support bracket

13.11 Removing exhaust manifold

13.12a Always renew gasket when refitting exhaust manifold

13.12b Offer up manifold . . .

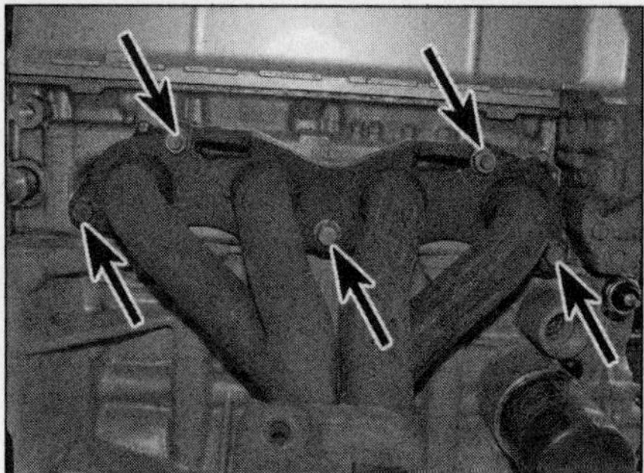

13.12c . . . and tighten nuts and bolts securely and evenly

10 Remove the three nuts and two bolts securing the manifold to the cylinder head. Use a wire brush and plenty of penetrating fluid first if they are rusty.

11 Withdraw the manifold from the studs, and remove it from the engine compartment **(see illustration)**. Recover the gasket.

Refitting

12 Refitting is a reversal of removal, using new gaskets, nuts and bolts. If the manifold studs came out with their nuts when unscrewed, fit new studs as well **(see illustrations)**. Tighten all fastenings progressively to the specified torques.

14 Exhaust system – general information, removal and refitting

Warning: Inspection and repair of exhaust system components should be done only after the system has cooled completely.

General information

1 The exhaust system consists of three sections: the front pipe and catalytic converter, the centre pipe and silencer, and the rear silencer.

2 The system is suspended throughout its entire length by rubber mountings.

3 If any section of the exhaust is damaged or deteriorated, excessive noise and vibration will occur.

4 Carry out regular inspections of the exhaust system, to check security and condition. Deteriorated sections should be renewed.

5 If the exhaust system components are extremely corroded or rusted together, it may not be possible to separate them. This often happens with the rear silencer, which rusts to the centre section – try twisting the pipes to separate them. Cut off the old components carefully with a hacksaw, and see if any corroded pipe can be removed (perhaps with a chisel) without damaging the remaining section.

Warning: Wear safety glasses to protect your eyes, and gloves to protect your hands.

6 Here are some simple guidelines to follow when repairing the exhaust system:

a) Work from the back to the front when removing exhaust system components.

b) Apply plenty of penetrating fluid to the flange nuts and bolts before unscrewing them. If possible, wire-brush any exposed threads to remove corrosion and dirt before trying to slacken the fasteners.

c) Use new nuts or bolts, gaskets and rubber mountings when installing exhaust system components.

d) Do NOT apply anti-seize compound or (copper grease) to the threads of exhaust system fasteners secured by self-locking nuts. Clean the threads as necessary and apply grease to prevent rust after the fasteners have been tightened securely.

e) The front pipe is secured to the manifold, and the rear silencer to the centre section, by two coil springs and bolts or nuts. When the bolts are tightened to the specified torque, the pressure of the springs will then be sufficient to make a leak-proof connection. Do not overtighten the bolts to cure a leak, or they may shear. Renew the gasket and the springs if a leak is found.

f) Be sure to allow sufficient clearance between newly-installed parts and all points on the underbody, to avoid overheating the floorpan, and possibly damaging the interior carpet and insulation. Pay particularly close attention to the catalytic converter and its heat shield.

Removal

Note: *The system's nuts and bolts must be renewed irrespective of their apparent condition whenever they are disturbed, as must the gaskets. Obtain new nuts, bolts and gaskets before starting work.*

7 Each exhaust section can be removed individually, or the complete system can be removed as a unit **(see illustration)**. Even if only one part of the system needs attention, in some cases it will be easier to remove the whole system and separate the sections on the bench.

8 To remove the system or part of the system, first jack up the front or rear of the vehicle, and support it on axle stands. Alternatively, position the vehicle over an inspection pit, or on vehicle ramps.

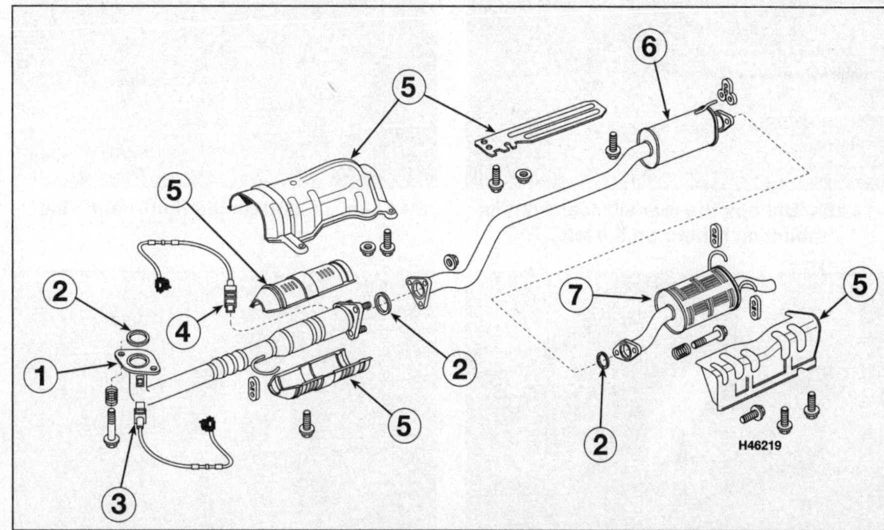

14.7 Typical exhaust system

1 *Front pipe and catalytic converter*
2 *Gasket*
3 *Primary oxygen sensor*
4 *Secondary oxygen sensor*
5 *Heat shield*
6 *Centre pipe and silencer*
7 *Rear silencer*

14.9 Trace oxygen sensor wiring, disconnect, and release wiring from clips or ties, so that it is free to be removed

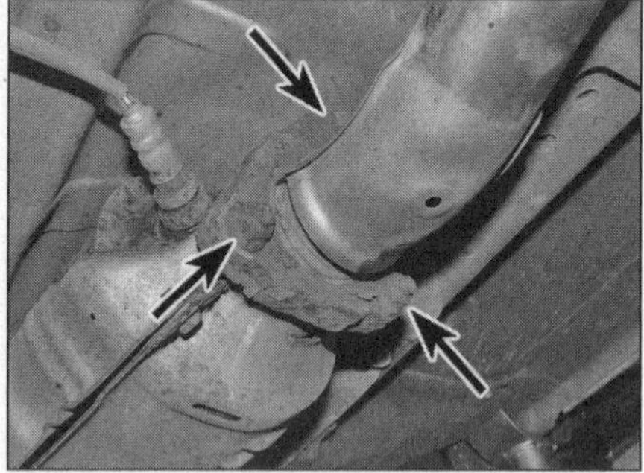
14.11 Unscrew three nuts from converter-to-centre section flange

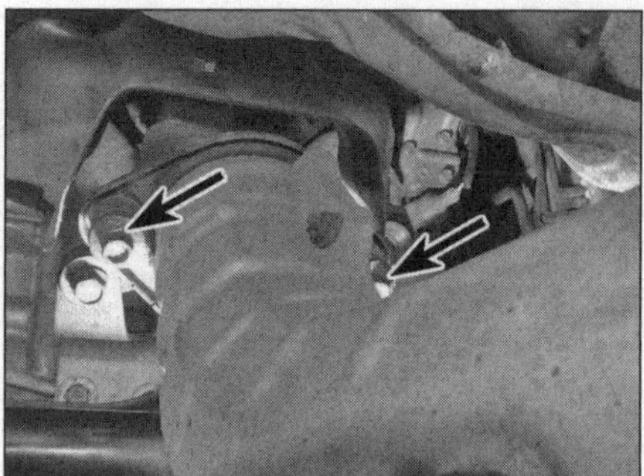
14.12 Remove two manifold-to-front pipe bolts to withdraw front pipe and catalytic converter

Front pipe and catalytic converter

9 Trace the wiring from both oxygen sensors to their connector plugs, and disconnect them. Release the wiring from any clips or ties **(see illustration)**.

10 Have a support (such as an axle stand or a small jack) ready to rest the front pipe on.

11 Unscrew and discard the three nuts from the joint behind the catalytic converter, and separate the converter flange from the centre section **(see illustration)**. Recover the gasket.

12 Undo the two bolts securing the front pipe to the manifold **(see illustration)**. Recover the springs and the 'olive' gasket.

13 Remove the front pipe and catalytic converter from underneath the vehicle. Take care that the converter is not dropped or roughly handled.

Centre pipe and silencer

14 Undo the two nuts securing the rear silencer to the centre section. Recover the springs, stud assembly and the 'olive' gasket.

15 Unscrew and discard the three nuts securing the centre pipe to the catalytic converter, and separate the joint. Recover and discard the 'olive' gasket – this and the flange nuts should be renewed when refitting.

16 Release the centre section from its mounting rubbers by pulling it forwards, then remove it from underneath the vehicle.

Rear silencer

17 Undo the two nuts securing the rear silencer to the centre section. Recover the springs, stud assembly and the 'olive' gasket.

18 Unhook the rear silencer from its mounting rubbers, and free it from the centre pipe **(see illustrations)**.

Complete system

19 Trace the wiring from both oxygen sensors to their in-line wiring plugs, and disconnect them. Release the wiring from any clips or ties.

20 Have a support (such as an axle stand or a small jack) ready to rest the front pipe on as required during removal.

21 Undo the two bolts securing the front pipe to the manifold. Recover the springs and the 'olive' gasket.

22 Free the system from its mounting rubbers, then remove it from underneath the vehicle.

Heat shields

23 The heat shields are secured to the underside of the body by nuts and bolts. Each shield can be removed once the relevant exhaust section has been removed. If a shield is being removed to gain access to a component located behind it, it may prove sufficient in some cases to remove the retaining nuts and bolts and simply lower the shield, without disturbing the exhaust system.

24 The catalytic converter has a two-part clam-shell shield around it, with a further shield above attached to the floor.

Refitting

25 Each section is refitted by reversing the removal sequence, noting the following points:

a) Ensure that all traces of corrosion have been removed from the flanges, and renew all gaskets, bolts and springs as applicable ***(see illustrations)****.*

b) The exhaust system nuts are all of self-locking type, and new ones should be used when refitting.

c) Inspect the rubber mountings for signs of damage or deterioration, and renew as necessary.

d) Prior to tightening the exhaust system fasteners, ensure that all rubber mountings are correctly located, and that there is adequate clearance between the exhaust system and underbody.

e) Tighten all bolts and nuts fully by hand, then by a quarter-turn each at a time to the specified torque.

14.18a Unhook the rear silencer from its mounting rubber on the left . . .

14.18b . . . and on the right-hand side

14.25a Fitting a new 'olive' gasket to manifold-to-front pipe joint . . .

14.25b . . . and to centre section-to-silencer joint

Chapter 4 Part B:
Fuel and exhaust systems – diesel models

Contents

Degrees of difficulty

Easy, suitable for novice with little experience 

Fairly easy, suitable for beginner with some experience

Fairly difficult, suitable for competent DIY mechanic

Difficult, suitable for experienced DIY mechanic

Very difficult, suitable for expert DIY or professional 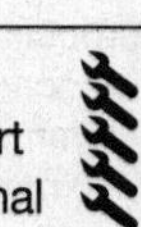

Specifications

General

Idle speed	See Chapter 1B
Fuel injection pressure	Up to 1600 bars

Torque wrench settings	Nm	lbf ft
Accelerator pedal mounting nuts	13	10
Acoustic engine cover retaining nuts	See Chapter 1B	
Air cleaner assembly mounting bolt	12	9
Air cleaner cover retaining bolts	See Chapter 1B	
Air intake passage-to-IMRC valve mounting bolts and nuts	22	16
Cable and wiring brackets-to-intake manifold bolts	12	9
Camshaft position sensor rotor-to-intake camshaft mounting bolt	See Chapter 2B	
Camshaft position sensor-to-cylinder head mounting bolt	12	9
Catalytic converter-to-exhaust centre section nuts*	33	24
Clutch pedal position switch locknut	See Chapter 6	
Crankshaft position (CKP) sensor mounting bolt	12	9
Electronic Control Unit (ECU) mounting bolts	12	9
Exhaust front pipe-to-catalytic converter nuts*	33	24
Exhaust front pipe-to-warm-up catalytic converter bolts	22	16
Exhaust manifold cover bolts	22	16
Exhaust manifold nuts*	44	32
Exhaust rear silencer-to-centre section nuts	22	16
Exhaust system heat shield mounting nuts	10	7
Fuel filler flap hinge bolts	10	7
Fuel filter water level switch	See Chapter 1B	
Fuel filter	See Chapter 1B	
Fuel gauge sender unit locking ring – using special tool	93	69
Fuel injector clamp bolts:		
Stage 1	5	4
Stage 2	Angle-tighten a further 90°	
Fuel pump mounting bolts	22	16
Fuel rail mounting nuts	22	16
Fuel return line-to-cylinder head cover mounting bolts	12	9
Fuel tank guard mounting bolts	10	7
Fuel tank mounting bolts	38	28
Fuel temperature sensor	12	9
High-pressure fuel pipe clamp bolt	12	9
High-pressure fuel pipe union nuts**	27	20
IMRC solenoid valve-to-intake manifold bolts	12	9
IMRC valve mounting bolts and nuts	22	16
Intake manifold support bracket bolts	22	16
Intake manifold mounting bolts and nuts	22	16
Intercooler top mounting bracket bolt	10	7
Manifold absolute pressure sensor-to-IMRC valve assembly	12	9
Mass airflow sensor-to-air cleaner cover screws	2	1
Turbocharger boost control solenoid-to-cylinder head cover mounting bolts	12	9
Turbocharger breather pipe union mounting nuts	12	9
Turbocharger coolant bypass pipe banjo union bolt	28	21
Turbocharger coolant bypass pipe union mounting flange bolts	12	9
Turbocharger intake pipe support bracket bolts:		
6 mm	12	9
10 mm	44	32
Turbocharger intake pipe-to-turbocharger flange nuts	22	16
Turbocharger mounting nuts	59	44
Turbocharger oil bypass pipe banjo union bolt	44	32
Turbocharger oil bypass pipe union mounting flange nuts and bolts	12	9
Turbocharger outlet elbow cover bolts	12	9
Turbocharger outlet elbow-to-turbocharger flange nuts	44	32
Turbocharger support bracket bolts	44	32
Turbocharger-to-intercooler (intake) pipe mounting bolts:		
6 mm	12	9
10 mm	44	32
Vacuum line assembly-to-intake manifold bolts	12	9
Vacuum line-to-cylinder head cover mounting bolts	12	9
Vehicle speed sensor mounting bolt	12	9
Warm-up catalytic converter-to-cylinder block/crankcase support bracket bolts	44	32
Warm-up catalytic converter-to-turbocharger flange nuts	44	32

* *Use new fasteners.*

** **Note:** *High-pressure pipes must be renewed whenever they are disturbed – ie, whenever the unions are slackened. See text for tightening sequence.*

1 General information and precautions

General information

The fuel system consists of the fuel tank, located centrally on the underbody immediately in front of the rear axle, and a hand primer and a filter assembly mounted on the engine compartment bulkhead and incorporating a fuel heater (controlled by a PTC element), a fuel temperature sensor and a water level switch. From the filter assembly, fuel is drawn to the fuel pump which is mounted on the left-hand end of the cylinder head and driven by gears from the exhaust camshaft. This is a tandem pump, combining a gear-type low-pressure lift pump to draw fuel from the tank via the hand primer and filter assembly, and a radial-piston high-pressure side which compresses the fuel ready for injection. Fuel at a pressure of up to 1600 bars is supplied to the fuel rail, which forms a reservoir of fuel common to all four injectors (hence the name 'common rail'). Rail pressure is controlled in the first instance by a fuel rail pressure control valve mounted on the pump, which regulates the quantity of fuel to the high-pressure side of the pump; the valve being opened by the engine management system's Electronic Control Unit (ECU) in response to signals from the fuel rail pressure sensor, and excess fuel being returned to the tank. A pressure-limiting valve mounted in the end of the fuel rail opens if rail pressure rises above the maximum permissible level, excess pressure again being returned to the tank. Solenoid-valve fuel injectors are connected to the fuel rail by short high-pressure lines and are opened by the ECU to spray fuel directly into the combustion chambers. A variable-nozzle turbocharger with intercooler is fitted.

Fuel injection system

All diesel-engined models are equipped with a second-generation version of the Bosch Electronic Diesel Control (EDC) engine management system, using EDC16C2 or C7 software, in which information from various sensors relating to engine coolant temperature, crankshaft angle, intake manifold pressure, atmospheric pressure, intake air temperature and vehicle speed is supplied to the engine management system's Electronic Control Unit (ECU), to enable the unit to determine the optimum settings for both fuelling and injection timing. The same control unit also manages aspects of the operation of the air conditioning system, especially on vehicles with automatic air conditioning (climate control) (see Chapter 3) and is linked to the ABS Electronic Control Unit (ECU) to play a part in the operation of the Vehicle Stability Assist (VSA) system (where fitted) – see Chapter 9. It also receives inputs from the power steering system and the alternator to enable it to compensate for the increased load placed on the engine when the power steering system is being used or there is heavy demand from various electrical systems. An Electrical Load Detector (ELD) built into the engine compartment main fuse/relay box monitors the demand on the alternator from the vehicle's other electrical systems and adjusts idle speed and fuelling to ensure smooth and consistent engine performance and response.

The ECU has a fail-safe function whereby if a signal from a sensor becomes abnormal, the ECU can ignore that signal and substitute a pre-programmed value that allows the engine to continue to run. There is also a back-up function which controls the injectors in the event of major system failure to permit minimal driving – a 'limp-home' mode. If a problem occurs with a component of the engine management system, the ECU has a self-diagnosis ability that enables it to store a code relating to that fault in its memory and to alert the driver to the fact that all is not well by illuminating the engine management Malfunction Indicator warning Lamp (MIL); for some systems (such as the ABS or VSA systems), a supplementary warning will be given by flashing another indicator lamp. To filter out spurious indications for some self-diagnostic functions, the ECU stores the code whenever the fault occurs, but only illuminates the MIL if that fault occurs again after the ignition has been switched off and on again. If a fault ever occurs that causes a fault code to be logged so that the MIL illuminates consistently, the vehicle must be taken to a specialist so that dedicated electronic test equipment can be connected to the system via the diagnostic socket located under the driver's side of the facia. This will enable any fault codes stored to be read and, once the necessary corrective action has been taken, erased. **Note:** *The MIL will illuminate when the ignition is switched on as a check of its function. If the MIL lights while the vehicle is being driven, pull to the side of the road as soon as it is safe to do so and switch off the engine. Restart the engine (thus resetting the system) and watch the MIL; if it remains on, or comes back on while driving, the vehicle must be taken to a specialist as soon as possible for fault diagnosis and repair. The glow plug warning lamp may also flash while the engine is running and the MIL is on. The glow plug warning lamp may also flash after the vehicle has run out of fuel, especially if air has entered the system so that the engine will not start even after the fuel tank has been refilled. In that case, once the engine has been restarted the warning lamp can be turned off by switching off the engine and then restarting it and switching it off at least three times in succession at intervals of approximately 30 seconds.*

The common rail injection system allows close regulation of injection pressure and timing to give optimum performance across all driving conditions. The fuel pump simply provides high-pressure fuel; the timing and duration of the injection is controlled by the ECU, based on the information received from the various sensors and is not adjustable in any way. The injection system interacts with the turbocharger to ensure optimum control over intake pressure, facilitating higher intake pressures at a lower speed, as well as better fuel economy and fewer harmful emissions through lean burn combustion.

A drive-by-wire throttle – the Electronic Throttle Control System (ETCS) – is fitted in place of a conventional cable. This ensures a more linear response to accelerator pedal inputs, particularly when pulling away. The control software works in conjunction with the engine management system to provide very smooth and responsive adjustments directly proportional to driver input. Furthermore, it forms an integral part of the VSA system (where fitted).

The large-capacity air cleaner housing used in the CR-V's induction system serves to muffle intake roar, and it also incorporates a Helmholtz chamber to damp unwanted resonances. CR-V drivers negotiating floods will need to know that the engine's air intake is next to the top of the intercooler, beside the left-hand headlamp; do not drive through water deeper than the top of the bonnet's radiator grille opening, or allow a bow-wave of water to build up to that level.

Intake Manifold Runner Control system

Because this system's function is so closely integrated with the design of the engine, it is described in Section 1 of Chapter 2B. Removal and refitting of the system's components is covered in this Chapter.

Turbocharger

A turbocharger increases engine efficiency by raising the pressure in the intake manifold above atmospheric pressure. Instead of the air simply being sucked into the cylinders, it is forced in. Additional fuel is supplied by the engine management system in proportion to the increased air intake.

Energy for the operation of the turbocharger comes from the exhaust gas. The gas flows through a specially-shaped housing (the turbine housing) and in so doing, spins the turbine wheel. The turbine wheel is attached to a shaft, at the end of which is another vaned wheel known as the compressor wheel. The compressor wheel spins in its own housing and compresses the inducted air on the way to the intake manifold.

The compressed air passes through an intercooler. This is an air-to-air heat exchanger, mounted with the radiator at the front of the vehicle. The purpose of the intercooler is to remove from the inducted air some of the heat gained in being compressed. Because cooler air is denser, removal of this heat further increases engine efficiency.

The turbocharger has adjustable guide vanes controlling the flow of exhaust gas into the turbine. The vanes are swivelled by the boost control solenoid valve, controlled by the engine management ECU. At lower engine speeds, the vanes close together, giving a smaller exhaust gas entry port, and therefore higher gas speed, which increases boost pressure. At high engine speed, the vanes are turned to give a larger exhaust gas entry port, and therefore lower gas speed, effectively maintaining a reasonably constant boost pressure over the engine rev range. This is known as a Variable Nozzle Turbocharger (VNT).

The turbocharger shaft is pressure-lubricated by an oil feed pipe from the main oil gallery. The shaft 'floats' on a cushion of oil. A drain pipe returns the oil to the sump. Similarly, the turbocharger has its own coolant feed from the main engine cooling system.

Exhaust system

The exhaust system includes an exhaust manifold, turbocharger, a four-way oxidation ('warm-up') catalytic converter, a front pipe with flexible section, a NOx-reducing catalytic converter, a centre section with silencer, and a rear silencer.

The catalytic converters are emissions control devices added to the exhaust system to reduce pollutants. Refer to Chapter 4C for more information regarding the catalytic converters and other emissions control components.

Precautions

General

Extreme caution should be exercised when dealing with either the fuel or exhaust systems. Fuel is a potentially-explosive liquid, and extreme care should be taken when dealing with the fuel system. The exhaust system is an area for exercising caution, as it will remain hot for some time after the engine is switched off. Serious burns can result from even momentary contact with any part of the exhaust system, and the fire risk is ever-present. The turbocharger and catalytic converters in particular run at very high temperatures.

When removing the Electronic Control Unit (ECU), do not touch the terminals, as there is a chance that static electricity may damage the internal electronic components.

Warning: Many of the procedures in this Chapter require the disconnection of fuel lines, which will result in some fuel spillage. Before carrying out any operation on the fuel system, refer to the precautions given in Safety first! at the beginning of this manual, and follow them implicitly.

- Diesel fuel may not be as flammable as petrol but nevertheless still requires respect – great care must be taken when working on any part of the fuel system. Do not smoke or allow any naked flames or uncovered light bulbs near the work area. Note that gas powered domestic appliances with pilot flames, such as heaters, boilers and tumble dryers, also present a fire hazard – bear this in mind if you are working in an area where such appliances are present. Always keep a suitable fire extinguisher close to the work area and familiarise yourself with its operation before starting work. Wear eye protection when working on fuel systems and wash off any fuel spilt on bare skin immediately with soap and water. Note that fuel vapour is just as dangerous as liquid fuel; a vessel that has just been emptied of liquid fuel will still contain vapour and can be potentially explosive.
- When working on diesel fuel system components, scrupulous cleanliness must be observed, and care must be taken not to introduce any foreign matter into fuel lines or components.
- It is strongly advised that, wherever possible, the battery negative lead is disconnected whenever there is a danger of fuel spillage (see *Disconnecting the battery*). This reduces the risk of a spark causing a fire.
- When carrying out welding operations on the vehicle using electric welding equipment, the battery and alternator should be disconnected.
- Although the underbonnet-mounted electronic units will tolerate normal underbonnet conditions, they can be adversely affected by excess heat or moisture. If using welding equipment or pressure-washing equipment in the vicinity of an electronic unit, take care not to direct heat, or jets of water or steam, at the unit. If this cannot be avoided, remove the unit from the vehicle, and protect its wiring plug with a plastic bag.
- Before disconnecting any wiring, or removing components, always ensure that the ignition is switched off.
- Do not attempt to improvise ECU fault diagnosis procedures using a test lamp or multimeter, as irreparable damage could be caused to the unit.
- After working on fuel injection/engine management system components, ensure that all wiring is correctly reconnected before reconnecting the battery or switching on the ignition.

Turbocharger

The turbocharger operates at extremely high speeds and temperatures. Certain precautions must be observed to avoid premature failure of the turbocharger or injury to the operator.

- Do not operate the turbocharger with its intake or outlet exposed. Foreign objects falling onto the rotating vanes could cause damage and (if ejected) personal injury.
- Do not race the engine immediately after start-up, especially if it is cold. Give the oil a few seconds to circulate.
- Always allow the engine to return to idle speed before switching it off – do not blip the throttle and switch off, as this will leave the turbocharger spinning without lubrication.
- Allow the engine to idle for several minutes before switching off after a high-speed run.
- Observe the recommended intervals for oil and filter changing, and use a reputable oil of the specified quality (see *Lubricants and fluids*). Neglect of oil changing, or use of inferior oil, can cause carbon formation on the turbocharger shaft and subsequent failure.

2 Fuel system – depressurising, priming and bleeding

Depressurising the fuel system

1 The low-pressure side of the fuel system, between the fuel tank and the pump, is under negative pressure while the engine is running. The high-pressure side of the system – the pump, the fuel rail, the injectors and the rigid high-pressure fuel pipes linking these components – can attain pressures of up to 1600 bars while the engine is running. Residual pressure may persist for some time after the engine is switched off.

2 There is no convenient method of depressurising the high-pressure side of the system. Do not attempt to 'depressurise' the system by disabling the fuel pump's supply and running the engine out of fuel – the pump and injectors rely on the lubrication offered by diesel fuel and will be irreparably damaged by being run dry. The only safe method of dealing with the residual pressure is to wrap a large rag around the first high-pressure fuel pipe union to be disconnected, ready to soak up any escaping fuel. Slowly (to avoid a sudden release of pressure and to allow any fuel spray which may be expelled to be caught by the rag) unscrew the union nut. When any hissing has stopped, indicating that all residual pressure has been released, unscrew the nut completely; be prepared for some loss of fuel.

Warning: Wear eye protection when disconnecting any part of the high-pressure side of the fuel system in this way.

Priming and bleeding

Warning: The following applies only to the low-pressure side of the fuel system, between the fuel tank and the pump. Do not attempt to disconnect any part of the high-pressure side of the system, between the fuel pump and the injectors, to bleed out trapped air.

3 Since the system is designed to be self-bleeding, it is not always necessary manually to prime and bleed the fuel system after working on the system components. Just starting the engine may be sufficient (although this may take longer than usual). Operate the starter in ten-second bursts only, with five seconds rest in between each operation. When the engine starts, run it at fast idle speed for a minute or so to purge any trapped air from the fuel lines. After this time, the engine should idle smoothly at a constant speed.

4 If a significant amount of work has been carried out on the fuel system, and the engine either won't start or idles roughly, then there is still some air trapped in the system.

5 To prime the system, operate the hand primer as many times as necessary (40 or 50 strokes) until the filter and hoses as far as the fuel pump are refilled with diesel fuel and the primer becomes hard **(see illustration)**. Start the engine and keep it running at a fast idle until it is running smoothly, then allow it to idle and check for signs of fuel leakage. If the engine does not start first time – do not operate the starter for more than 30 seconds at a time, or there is a risk of damage to the starter motor and to the common-rail injection system's fuel pump – operate the hand primer again until it becomes hard, then try again. Note that while the hand primer does become hard when used to pump fuel into the system, under normal circumstances it will be soft to the touch, as the lift pump draws fuel through the system from the fuel tank.

6 No bleed nipples being provided, the only way of bleeding the system is to disconnect the fuel feed hose from the fuel pump (Section 10) and to operate the hand primer until diesel fuel, free from air bubbles, appears from the end of the hose – direct the hose into a clean container and place plenty of rag to prevent any fuel from being spilled on to surrounding components. Reconnect the fuel feed hose to the fuel pump, operate the hand primer until it becomes hard, then try to start the engine again. Once the engine starts, keep it running at a fast idle until it is running smoothly, then allow it to idle and check for signs of fuel leakage.

2.5 Unclip fuel system hand primer and squeeze to prime low-pressure side of fuel system as far as fuel pump

7 If you have to resort to using the hand primer when no servicing work has been carried out, or if poor starting necessitates the use of the hand primer on a frequent basis, there is an air leak in the system. Refer to Section 9.

3 Throttle cable – removal, refitting and adjustment

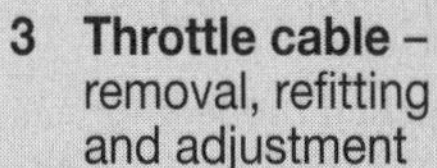

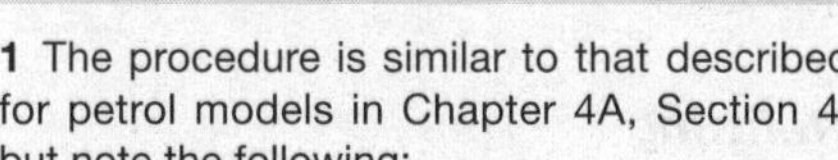

1 The procedure is similar to that described for petrol models in Chapter 4A, Section 4, but note the following:

a) The throttle linkage is on the accelerator pedal position sensor mounted on the bulkhead.

*b) Cable deflection (paragraph 14) should be 15 to 18 mm **(see illustration)**.*

3.1 Remove throttle linkage cover to check that deflection in cable inner wire is correct

4 Air cleaner assembly and intake air duct/resonator – removal and refitting

Note: *Whenever the air cleaner cover or the complete assembly is removed, pack the turbocharger air intake with clean rag to keep dirt out.*

Air cleaner assembly

1 Disconnect the mass airflow sensor wiring connector from the air cleaner assembly.

2 Slacken the clamp securing the air cleaner-to-turbocharger intake hose to the assembly's cover, disconnect the hose and release the intake duct from the lower front of the air cleaner assembly itself **(see illustrations)**.

3 Unscrew the bolt securing the assembly **(see illustration)**.

4.2a Slacken clamp securing air cleaner-to-turbocharger intake hose to cover . . .

4.2b . . . disconnect hose (and mass airflow sensor wiring)

4.3 Unscrew air cleaner assembly mounting bolt . . .

4.4 . . . and withdraw air cleaner assembly

4.8a Intake air duct/resonator mounting bolts – on battery tray mounting bracket . . .

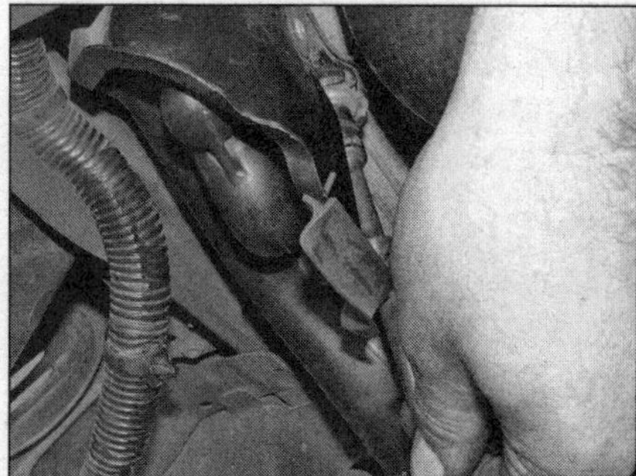

4.8b . . . and on intercooler mounting bracket

4 Withdraw the air cleaner assembly, easing it off the two mounting pegs at the bottom rear **(see illustration)**. If required, slacken the securing clamp and withdraw the air cleaner-to-turbocharger intake hose. As noted above, pack the turbocharger opening with clean rag.
5 Refitting is a reversal of removal.

Intake air duct/resonator

6 Remove the air cleaner assembly as described above.
7 Remove the battery and battery tray (see Chapter 5A).
8 Unscrew the two mounting bolts and withdraw the duct **(see illustrations)**.
9 Refitting is a reversal of removal.

5 Intercooler – removal and refitting

Note: *Whenever the intercooler or its hoses are removed, pack the turbocharger openings with clean rag to keep dirt out.*

Removal

1 Remove the air conditioning condenser and radiator cooling fan/shroud assemblies (Chapter 3).
2 Undo the two screws, release its retaining clips and remove the radiator grille.
3 Remove the intercooler mounting bracket **(see illustration)**.
4 Slacken the hose clips and disconnect the two air hoses from the intercooler, noting their fitted positions **(see illustrations)**.
5 Lift out the intercooler, taking care not to damage the fins **(see illustration)**.
6 If required, slacken the hose clips and disconnect the turbocharger outlet hose, then unbolt the turbocharger-to-intercooler (intake) pipe **(see illustrations)**.
7 Check inside the intercooler openings for significant amounts of oil. If present, this can be cleaned out with a suitable solvent – if contamination is bad, the whole intercooler should be washed out. The presence of oil indicates that the turbocharger oil seals have failed. The turbocharger should be removed for inspection (Section 15).
8 Use a soft brush and an airline or garden hose to clear the intercooler matrix of leaves, dead insects, etc.
9 Any damage should be repaired by a specialist, or the intercooler should be renewed or exchanged for a reconditioned unit.
10 Examine the mounting rubbers for signs of damage or deterioration and renew if necessary.

Refitting

11 Refitting is a reversal of removal. When reconnecting the turbocharger outlet hose, align the mark on the hose with the raised rib on the turbocharger body.

6 Fuel gauge sender unit – removal and refitting

Proceed as described in Section 7 of Chapter 4A, but note that diesel-engined models will have two quick-release fuel hose fittings on the top of the fuel gauge sender unit – one feed and one return. Mark or label these so that they do not get swapped over on refitting.

For diesel-engined models there is no fuel pump submerged in the tank, so there is only the fuel gauge sender unit; if this is faulty, it must be renewed complete.

7 Fuel tank – removal and refitting

Proceed as described in Section 8 of Chapter 4A, but note that diesel-engined models do not have a charcoal canister to remove, nor a fuel vapour hose to disconnect.

8 Electronic Diesel Control (EDC) system – checking and fault code clearing

1 Refer to Chapter 4A, Section 10. Note however that it is not possible to clear fault codes by removing the ECU fuse on these models.

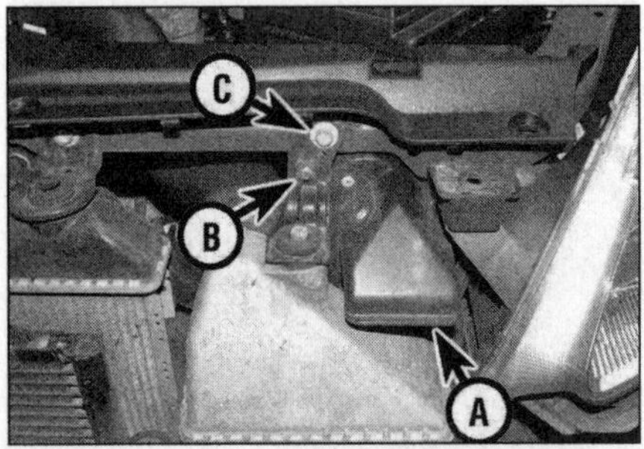

5.3 Engine air intake (A), intake air duct/resonator top mounting bolt (B), intercooler mounting bracket bolt (C)

5.4a Disconnect intercooler outlet hose from intake manifold air intake passage . . .

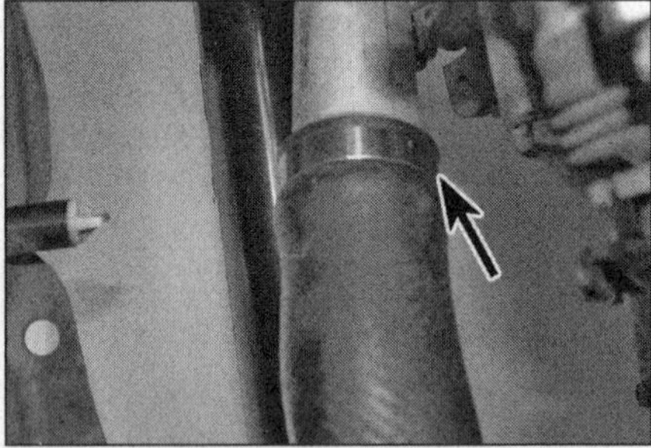

5.4b . . . disconnect intercooler intake hose from turbocharger-to-intercooler pipe . . .

5.5 . . . and remove intercooler

5.6a Undo bolts securing turbocharger-to-intercooler pipe to front . . .

5.6b . . . and rear of engine

9 Electronic Diesel Control (EDC) system components – removal and refitting

Note: *Refer to the precautions in Section 1 before proceeding.*

Accelerator pedal position sensor

1 Disconnect the throttle cable from the throttle linkage as described in Section 3.

2 Disconnect the wiring plug from the sensor, then unscrew the mounting bolts and withdraw the sensor **(see illustration)**. Unscrew the three bolts to separate the sensor from its mounting bracket.

3 Refitting is a reversal of removal.

Barometric pressure sensor

4 The barometric pressure sensor is incorporated in the ECU to enable it to measure atmospheric pressure and adjust injector opening duration accordingly. The sensor is not available separately from the ECU.

Brake pedal position switch

5 Refer to Chapter 9.

Camshaft position (CMP) sensor

Note: *The camshaft position sensor is fitted to the left-hand end of the cylinder head (underneath the large square-section black plastic wiring conduit), between the fuel pump and the EGR cooler bypass valve* ***(see illustration)****.*

6 Unscrew the four retaining nuts and remove the acoustic engine cover.

7 From the front left-hand end of the cylinder head, release the large square-section black plastic wiring conduit from its mountings and secure all wiring hoses and fuel lines clear of the cylinder head cover so that it can be lifted enough to provide access to the camshaft position sensor. If any wiring or hoses are disconnected to permit this, note them carefully.

8 Disconnect the sensor's electrical connector **(see illustration)**. Remove the mounting bolt, and withdraw the sensor from the cylinder head; be prepared for slight oil loss. Remove the O-ring.

9 Refitting is the reverse of the removal procedure, noting the following points:

a) Use a new O-ring and smear it with clean engine oil.

b) Tighten the bolt to the specified torque.

10 The camshaft position sensor's rotor is mounted on the intake camshaft. It can be withdrawn once the cylinder head cover has been removed (Chapter 2B).

Clutch pedal position switch

Note: *The clutch pedal position switch is fitted to the clutch pedal assembly, above the clutch pedal (some models do not have this switch). If two switches are fitted, the clutch interlock switch is mounted above the clutch pedal position switch.*

9.2 Accelerator pedal position sensor mounting bolts and wiring connector plug

11 Refer to Chapter 4A, Section 11.

Crankshaft position (CKP) sensor

Note: *The crankshaft position sensor is fitted to the front right-hand end of the engine's lower crankcase/main bearing ladder, buried behind the air conditioning compressor mounting bracket. It is visible from beneath, but a considerable amount of preliminary dismantling is required to reach it* ***(see illustration)****. Its pulse plate is bolted to the crankshaft right-hand web; the engine must be dismantled completely to reach it.*

12 Disconnect the battery (see *Disconnecting the battery*). This is essential before disconnecting the alternator wiring.

13 Unscrew the four retaining nuts and remove the acoustic cover. Remove the engine compartment undershield (Chapter 11).

9.8 Camshaft position sensor mounting bolt and wiring connector plug

9.19a Lubricate new sensor O-ring with engine oil . . .

9.6 Camshaft position sensor is fitted to left-hand end of cylinder head, between fuel pump and EGR cooler bypass valve

14 Remove the auxiliary drivebelt (Chapter 1B).

15 Remove the alternator (Chapter 5A).

16 Unscrew the air conditioning compressor's four mounting bolts. With the compressor unbolted, secure it clear of the working area without disconnecting or straining its wiring and pipes.

17 Unbolt the air conditioning compressor mounting bracket from the engine.

18 Disconnect the wiring plug, then unscrew the mounting bolt and remove the sensor from the engine. Recover the O-ring.

19 Refitting is a reversal of removal. Fit a new sealing O-ring, lubricate it with clean engine oil and tighten the sensor mounting bolt to the specified torque **(see illustrations)**.

20 Refit all components removed for access.

EGR control solenoid valve

21 Refer to Chapter 4C.

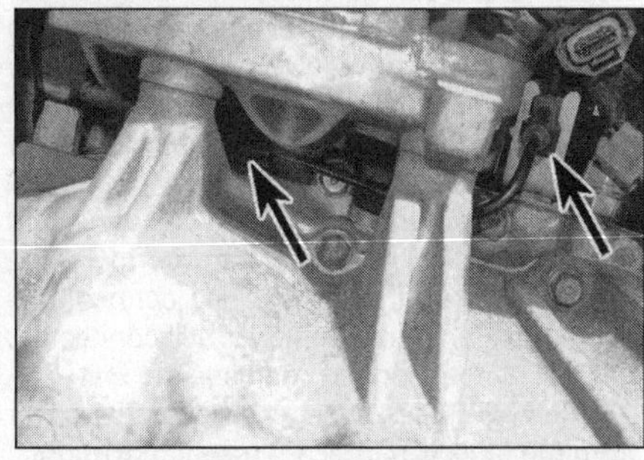

9.15 Crankshaft position sensor is behind air conditioning compressor mounting bracket – note sensor connector (arrowed)

9.19b . . . refit sensor, tighten bolt and route wiring as shown

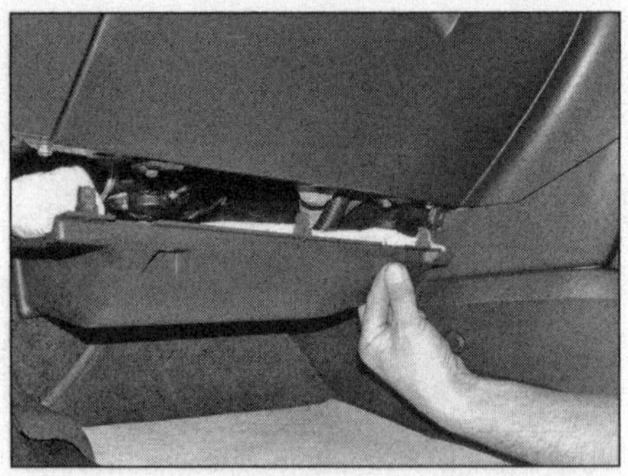

9.24 Remove passenger's side under cover from facia . . .

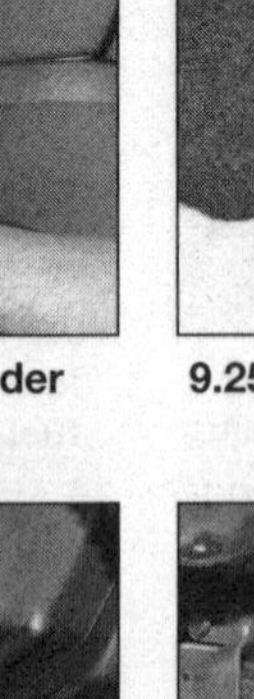

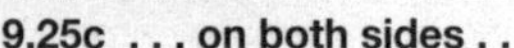

9.25c . . . on both sides . . .

EGR cooler bypass control solenoid valve

22 Refer to Chapter 4C.

Electronic Control Unit (ECU)

Note: *The ECU contains the immobiliser coding which was programmed into it when the vehicle was new. If a new ECU is fitted, the immobiliser coding will have to be programmed into it by a Honda dealer before the vehicle will start.*

23 Disconnect the battery (see *Disconnecting the battery*). This is essential when working on the ECU – if the unit's wiring connector is unplugged when the battery is still connected, this will almost certainly damage the unit.

24 Remove the passenger's side under cover from the facia (Chapter 11) **(see illustration)**.

25 Releasing their locking catches, unplug the connectors to disconnect the wiring from the ECU **(see illustrations)**.

9.37 Disconnecting fuel rail pressure sensor wiring from left-hand end of fuel rail

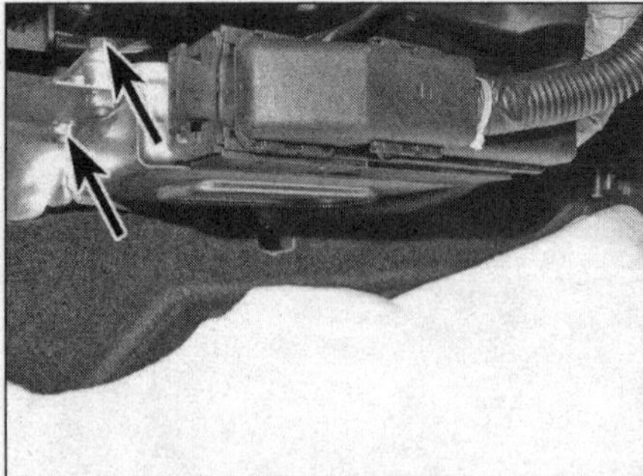

9.25a . . . to reach ECU – note two of ECU mounting bolts arrowed

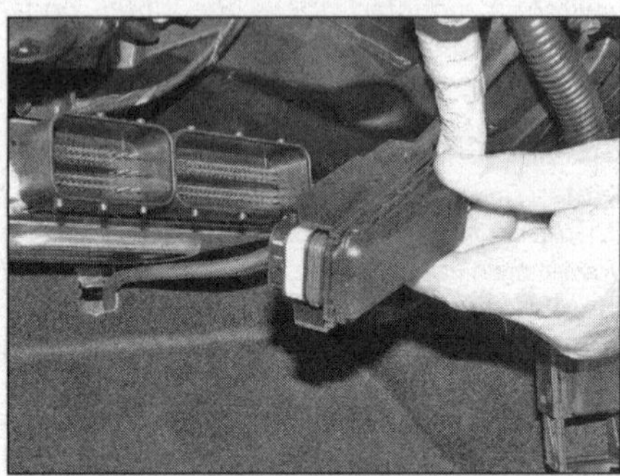

9.25d . . . to disconnect ECU wiring connector plug

26 Unscrew the two nuts and the bolt securing the ECU mounting bracket to the bulkhead.

27 Unscrew the ECU mounting bolts and withdraw the ECU.

28 Refitting is a reversal of removal.

Coolant temperature sensor

29 Refer to Chapter 3.

Hand primer

30 The hand primer is a rubber bulb fitted in the fuel feed line from the fuel tank to the fuel filter assembly and is clipped to the top of the filter, at the rear of the engine compartment **(see illustration 2.5)**.

31 Starting from the fuel gauge sender unit in the top of the fuel tank (see Section 7 of Chapter 4A), work forwards along the fuel feed line to the engine compartment and the filter assembly, then from there to the fuel pump; check with particular care all unions, mounting points and retaining clips and look for signs of wear or damage on the surface of the fuel lines. Leaks may be obvious from the presence of diesel fuel on the outside of the hoses and on surrounding components, but if no such signs can be seen it is possible, indeed more likely, that air is being drawn in through a defective seal or hose. The only (time-consuming and slow) remedy in such circumstances is to apply a coat of petroleum jelly (Vaseline) to each union in the system in turn to seal it temporarily against air ingress; if the problem then stops, you have found the leak and can take the necessary action to cure the fault.

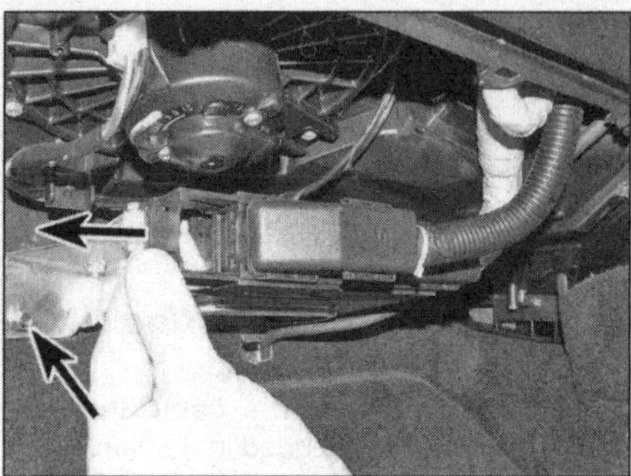

9.25b Slide out locking catches . . .

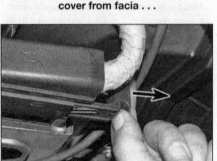

32 To remove the hand primer, unbolt and lift the filter assembly as necessary to reach the hoses to and from the primer. Clamp the fuel hoses using brake hose clamps; if such clamps are not available, unplug each hose in turn and plug it as quickly as possible to prevent diesel fuel from contaminating other components and to prevent dirt from getting into the fuel system – see Section 5 of Chapter 1B. Release the clips to remove the hand primer. Refitting is a reversal of removal.

Fuel filter

33 Refer to Chapter 1B.

Fuel filter water level switch

34 The switch is fitted to the base of the fuel filter and is removed and refitted as part of the fuel filter renewal procedure described in Chapter 1B.

Fuel heater

Note: *It was not clear at the time of writing whether the heater is available separately from the filter head. Check parts availability before proceeding.*

35 The heater is fitted to the fuel filter head **(see illustration 9.44)**, which is removed and refitted as part of the fuel filter water draining procedure described in Chapter 1B. The filter is secured by four small Torx screws.

Fuel rail pressure (FRP) sensor

Note: *It was not clear at the time of writing whether the sensor is available separately from the fuel rail. Check parts availability before proceeding.*

36 Unscrew the four retaining nuts and remove the acoustic engine cover.

37 The fuel rail pressure sensor is located in the left-hand end of the fuel rail. Disconnect the wiring plug from the sensor **(see illustration)**.

Warning: Before disconnecting any part of the high-pressure side of the fuel system, read the precautions concerning depressurising the fuel system given in Section 2 and take action accordingly.

38 Place a large rag around the sensor, ready to soak up any escaping fuel. Slowly (to avoid a sudden release of pressure and to allow any fuel spray which may be expelled to be caught by

9.40 Check whether fuel rail pressure control valve is available separately from fuel pump before removing

9.41 Fuel rail pressure control valve retaining screws and wiring connector plug, on side of fuel pump

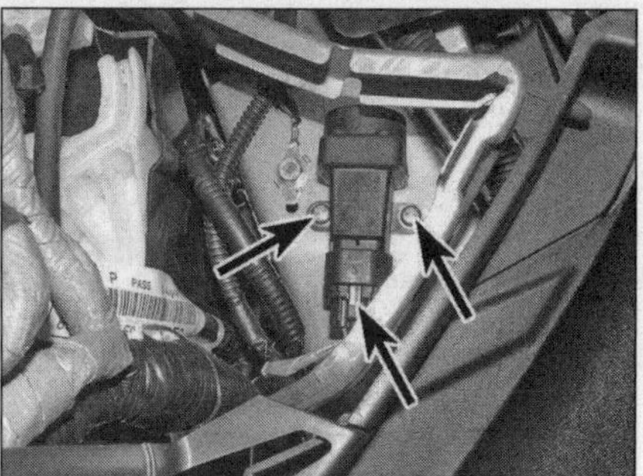

9.43 Fuel shut-off (inertia) switch is located behind glovebox – mounting bolts and wiring connector arrowed

9.44 Location of fuel temperature sensor (A). Note also fuel heater (B)

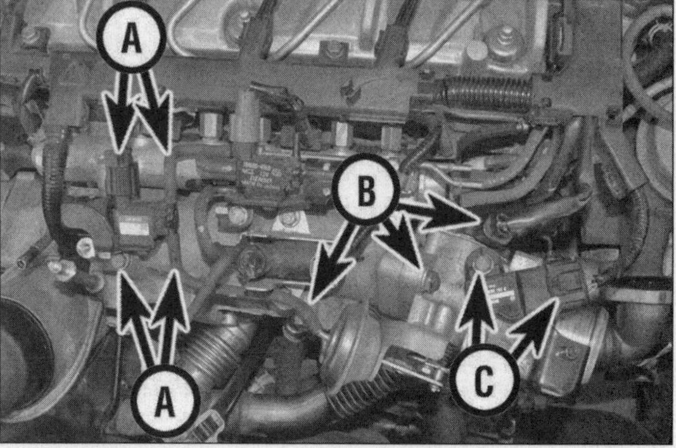

9.49 IMRC solenoid valve mounting bolt, hoses and wiring connector (A), IMRC valve upper mounting nut, hose and position sensor wiring connector (B), MAP/IAT No. 2 sensor wiring connector and mounting bolt (C)

the rag) unscrew the sensor one full turn using a suitable deep socket. When any hissing has stopped, indicating that all residual pressure has been released, unscrew the sensor from the rail; be prepared for some loss of fuel. Plug the rail opening to prevent contamination.

39 Refitting is a reversal of removal, tightening the sensor securely.

Fuel rail pressure control valve

Note: *At the time of writing it appeared that the control valve is not available separately from the fuel pump. Check parts availability before proceeding. Remember that the components are of Bosch manufacture and may be available through Bosch specialists.*

40 Unscrew the four retaining nuts and remove the acoustic engine cover. Although not strictly necessary, access is greatly improved by removing the air cleaner assembly as described in Section 4 **(see illustration)**.

41 Disconnect the control valve wiring plug, then undo the screws and detach the valve from the fuel pump **(see illustration)**.

42 Refitting is a reversal of removal, tightening the retaining screws securely.

Fuel shut-off (inertia) switch

43 Refer to Chapter 4A, Section 11 **(see illustration)**.

Fuel temperature sensor

44 The fuel temperature sensor is located in the fuel filter head and informs the ECU of the temperature of the incoming fuel; its resistance decreasing as the temperature of the incoming fuel increases. Disconnect the wiring plug from the sensor **(see illustration)**.

45 Using a suitable deep socket, unscrew the sensor from the filter head; be prepared for some loss of fuel. Plug the filter opening to prevent contamination.

46 Refitting is a reversal of removal. Fit a new sealing O-ring, lubricate it with clean diesel fuel to aid installation and tighten the sensor to the specified torque.

9.52 Unscrew bolts and nuts to remove air intake passage

Glow plug control module

47 Refer to Chapter 5C.

Intake Manifold Runner Control (IMRC) system

Solenoid valve

48 Unscrew the four retaining nuts and remove the acoustic engine cover.

49 Disconnect the valve's electrical connector and two vacuum hoses **(see illustration)**. Unscrew the mounting bolt, and withdraw the valve from the intake manifold.

50 Refitting is the reverse of the removal procedure.

Valve assembly

51 Unscrew the four retaining nuts and remove the acoustic engine cover.

52 Disconnect the intercooler outlet hose from the intake manifold air intake passage, then unscrew the mounting bolts and nuts and withdraw the air intake passage from the valve assembly. Recover and discard the gasket – a new one must be fitted on reassembly. Unscrew the bolt securing the intake manifold support bracket to the IMRC valve **(see illustrations 9.52 and 13.3b)**.

53 Disconnect the manifold absolute pressure sensor wiring plug (or remove the sensor, as

9.55 IMRC valve lower mounting bolts and nut

described below) and the IMRC valve position sensor wiring plug **(see illustration 9.49)**.

54 Disconnect the vacuum hose from the valve.

55 Unscrew the two mounting nuts and two mounting bolts and withdraw the valve from the intake manifold **(see illustration)**. Recover and discard the gasket – a new one must be fitted on reassembly.

56 The valve is available only as a complete assembly; do not attempt to dismantle it or to remove the valve position sensor **(see illustration)**.

57 Refitting is the reverse of the removal procedure, noting the following points:

a) Fit new gaskets to the valve and to the air intake passage.

b) Tighten all nuts and bolts to their specified torque wrench settings.

c) Ensure that all wiring plugs are securely reconnected.

9.56 IMRC valve is sealed – do not attempt dismantling or adjustment

Valve position sensor

58 The position sensor is fitted to the IMRC valve butterfly's spindle, and is not available separately. In the event that a position sensor problem is suspected, the only solution is a new IMRC valve assembly.

Manifold absolute pressure and intake air temperature #2 sensor

59 The manifold absolute pressure sensor is located on top of the IMRC valve assembly and provides the ECU with information on pressure levels in the manifold generated by the turbocharger. The sensor also incorporates an intake air temperature sensor, the resistance of which decreases as the temperature of the incoming air increases. The ECU uses these signals to calculate the engine load, and the appropriate fuelling, further to refine injector opening duration.

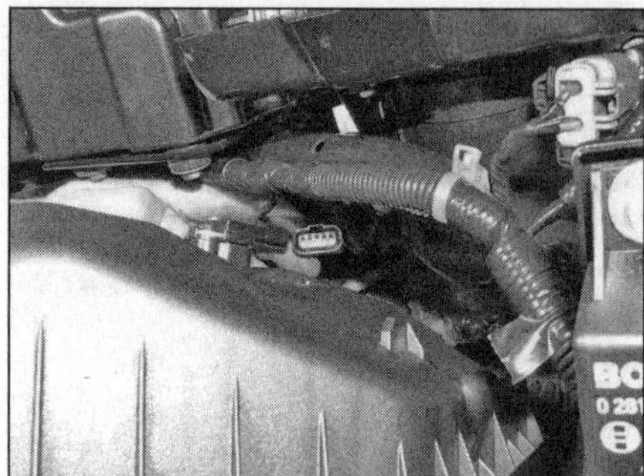

9.64 Disconnecting MAF/IAT No. 1 sensor wiring connector from top of air cleaner cover

60 Unscrew the four retaining nuts and remove the acoustic engine cover.

61 Disconnect the sensor wiring plug, then unscrew the mounting bolt and withdraw the sensor. Recover and discard the sealing O-ring – this must be renewed whenever the sensor is disturbed **(see illustration 9.49)**.

62 Refitting is a reversal of removal. Fit a new O-ring, lubricate it with clean engine oil to aid installation and tighten the mounting bolt securely; note the specified torque setting.

Mass airflow and intake air temperature #1 sensor

63 The mass airflow sensor is located in the air cleaner assembly cover and incorporates a hot-wire mass airflow sensor to send the ECU a constantly-varying (analogue) voltage signal corresponding to the volume of air passing into the engine, and an intake air temperature sensor, the resistance of which decreases as the temperature of the incoming air increases. The ECU uses these signals to calculate the mass of air entering the engine.

64 Remove the air cleaner cover, as described in Section 17 of Chapter 1B, disconnecting the mass airflow sensor wiring connector **(see illustration)**.

65 Undo the two screws and withdraw the sensor **(see illustration)**. Examine the seal, where fitted, and renew it if worn or damaged.

66 Refitting is a reversal of removal; tighten the mounting screws to the specified torque setting.

Reverse lockout solenoid

67 Refer to Chapter 7A.

Turbocharger boost control solenoid valve

68 Unscrew the four retaining nuts and remove the acoustic engine cover.

69 Disconnect the valve's electrical connector and two vacuum hoses. Unscrew the mounting bolts, and withdraw the valve from the cylinder head **(see illustrations)**.

70 Refitting is the reverse of the removal procedure.

Vehicle speed sensor

71 The vehicle speed sensor is located on the front of the gearbox, underneath the reversing light switch and behind the clutch slave cylinder hydraulic pipe **(see illustration)**.

9.65 MAF/IAT No. 1 sensor mounting screws on top of air cleaner cover

9.69a Turbocharger boost control solenoid valve wiring connector and vacuum hoses

9.69b Turbocharger boost control solenoid valve mounting bolts

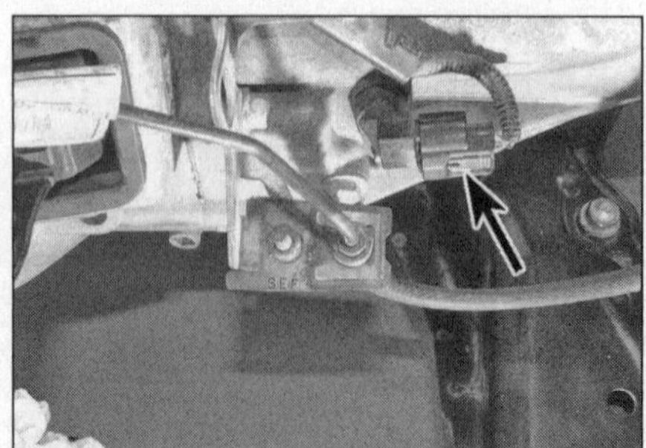

9.71 Vehicle speed sensor is located on gearbox front, behind clutch slave cylinder hydraulic pipe

The sensor should not be confused with the reversing light switch, which does not have a separate mounting bolt. The sensor provides an electronic signal of the vehicle speed, which is used by the engine management ECU and anti-lock braking system (ABS), as well as for the speedometer itself.

72 Jack up the front of the vehicle and support it securely on axle stands (see *Jacking and vehicle support*), then remove the engine compartment undershield (Chapter 11) to reach the sensor from underneath.

73 Disconnect the wiring plug from the sensor **(see illustration)**.

74 Unscrew the sensor mounting bolt, then withdraw the sensor from the transmission, noting the spacer under the bolt – there may be some resistance, both from the O-ring seal and from the sensor drive gear. Remove and discard the sensor's sealing O-ring; this must be renewed whenever it is disturbed.

75 Refitting is a reversal of removal, noting the following points:

a) *Clean the mating faces of the sensor and transmission, and fit a new O-ring. Expect the sensor to twist as it meshes with the transmission gear, then turn it to align the mounting bolt hole; do not forget the spacer.*

b) *Tighten the sensor mounting bolt securely, and ensure that the wiring plug is securely reconnected.*

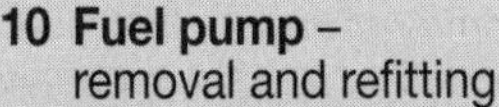

10 Fuel pump – removal and refitting

Caution: Be careful not to allow dirt into the fuel pump, fuel rail or injectors during this procedure.

Note: *Any rigid high-pressure fuel pipes disturbed must be renewed.*

Removal

1 Disconnect the battery negative lead, and position the lead away from the battery (see *Disconnecting the battery*).

2 Unscrew the four retaining nuts and remove the acoustic engine cover.

3 Remove the air cleaner assembly as described in Section 4.

4 Note the hoses' fitted positions and disconnect the fuel feed and return hoses from the fuel pump. Swiftly plug the hoses and cap the pump unions to prevent the loss of fuel and the entry of dirt into the system **(see illustrations)**.

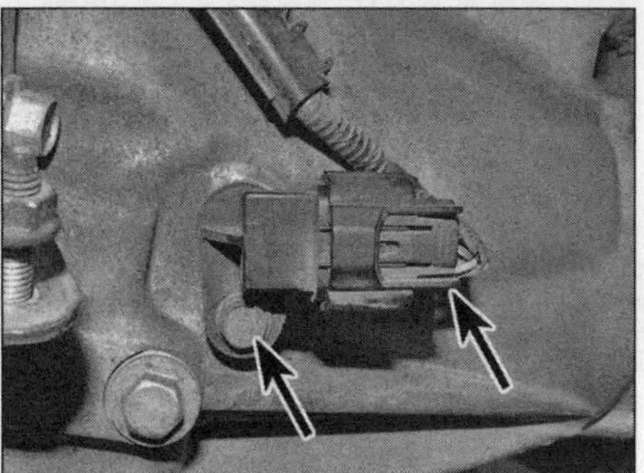

9.73 Vehicle speed sensor wiring connector and mounting bolt

5 Undo the two bolts securing the large square-section black plastic wiring conduit to the cylinder head cover and lift the other conduit off its brackets on the left-hand end of the cylinder head sufficiently to reach the fuel pump-to-fuel rail high-pressure fuel pipe union nut; if it is necessary to disconnect the wiring for the fuel rail pressure sensor, the fuel injectors and the glow plugs, and any vacuum hoses, to permit this, note them carefully and do not forget to reconnect them on reassembly **(see illustrations)**.

6 Make sure the areas around the high-pressure fuel pipe unions from the fuel pump to the fuel rail and from the fuel rail to the injectors are scrupulously clean and free from debris, etc. If possible, use a vacuum cleaner and a degreaser to clean the area.

Warning: Before disconnecting any part of the high-pressure side of the fuel system, read the precautions concerning depressurising the fuel system given in Section 2 and take action accordingly.

7 Place a large rag around the fuel pump-to-fuel rail high-pressure fuel pipe union nut near the centre of the fuel rail **(see illustration 10.5b)**, ready to soak up any escaping fuel. Slowly (to avoid a sudden release of pressure and to allow any fuel spray which may be expelled to be caught by the rag) unscrew the union nut. When any hissing has stopped, indicating that all residual pressure has been released, unscrew the nut from the rail; be prepared for some loss of fuel.

8 Counterhold the hexagon on the fuel pump union with one open-ended spanner and unscrew the fuel pump-to-fuel rail high-pressure fuel pipe union nut with a second spanner; be prepared for fuel spillage **(see illustration)**. Unscrew the high-pressure pipe retaining clamp bolt **(see illustration 10.5c)** and discard the high-pressure pipe – a new one must be fitted on reassembly. Swiftly cap the pump and rail unions to prevent the entry of dirt into either.

9 Disconnect its wiring and unbolt the fuel pump from the left-hand end of the cylinder head; be careful not to lose the connecting piece between the fuel pump drive shaft and the pump drive – this is easily lost as the

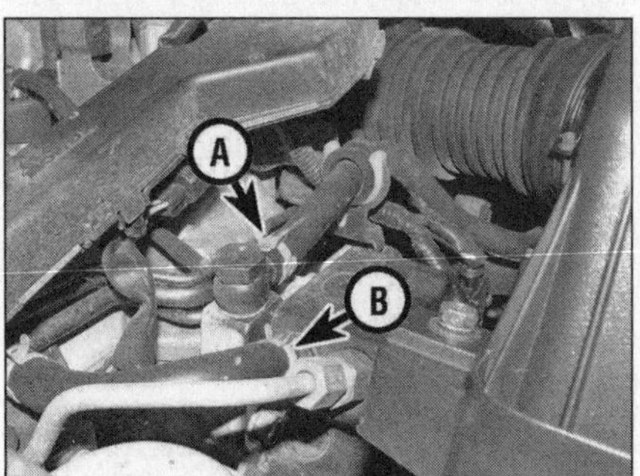

10.4a Disconnect fuel feed (A) and return (B) hoses from fuel pump . . .

10.4b . . . swiftly plug hoses and cap pump unions to prevent loss of fuel and entry of dirt into fuel system

10.5a Undo two bolts securing wiring conduit (A) and lift conduit off brackets on cylinder head left-hand end (B) . . .

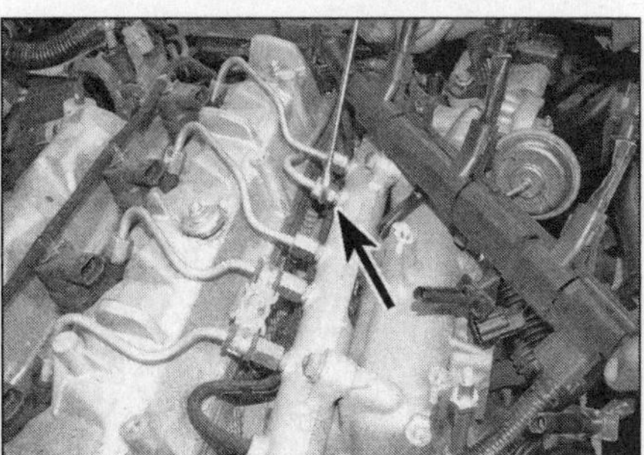

10.5b . . . then lift conduits sufficiently to unscrew fuel pump-to-fuel rail high-pressure pipe union . . .

10.5c . . . and undo high-pressure pipe retaining clamp bolt

10.8 Counterhold hexagon on union with one spanner and unscrew fuel pipe union nut with a second spanner

10.9a Release wiring from retaining bracket beneath fuel pump . . .

10.9b . . . disconnect wiring from fuel pump . . .

10.9c . . . and unbolt pump. Do NOT lose connecting piece (arrowed)

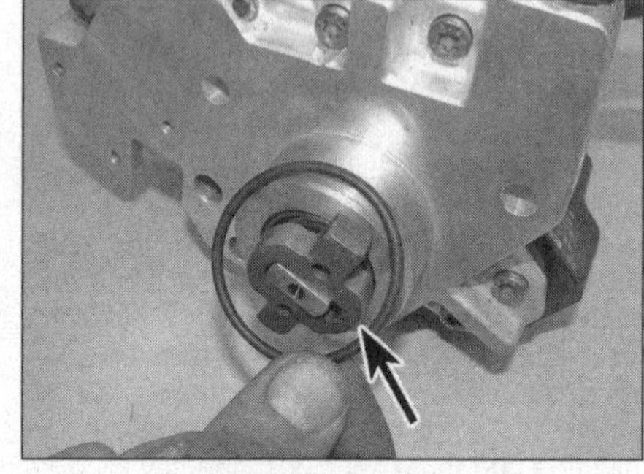

10.11a Refit connecting piece to pump drive and fit new O-ring . . .

10.11b . . . lubricate O-ring and refit pump, aligning connecting piece drive dogs with fuel pump driveshaft slots

pump is removed **(see illustrations)**. Remove and discard the pump's sealing O-ring; this must be renewed whenever it is disturbed.

10 It appears at the time of writing that no spare parts are available for the pump, though reconditioned units may be available. Check parts availability before proceeding, and remember that the components are of Bosch manufacture and so may be available through Bosch specialists.

Refitting

11 On refitting, wipe clean the mating surfaces of the cylinder head and fuel pump, fit a new O-ring to the pump mating surface, lubricate it with clean engine oil to aid installation and align the drive dogs on the pump connecting piece with the slots in the end of the fuel pump driveshaft **(see illustrations)**.

12 Offer up the pump and fit its mounting bolts, but tighten them by hand only at this stage **(see illustration)**. **Note:** *The fuel pump has no timing function, so its precise position, within the range of movement provided by the mounting bolts, is not important.*

13 Fit the new fuel pump-to-fuel rail high-pressure fuel pipe, settling it on the fuel rail union and retaining clamp bracket. Ensure that the pipe union seats correctly on that of the pump, then tighten the two union nuts as far as possible by hand **(see illustration)**.

14 Tighten the fuel pump mounting bolts to the specified torque wrench setting.

15 Using a crows-foot adapter, tighten the high-pressure fuel pipe union nuts to the specified torque wrench setting, fuel pump union first (counterholding the pump's hexagon), then the fuel rail union.

16 Fit the high-pressure fuel pipe retaining clamp rubber sleeve, check that the clamp fits correctly on its bracket without stressing the pipe, then refit the clamp bolt and tighten it to the specified torque wrench setting. **Note:** *If the retaining clamp strains the pipe away from its natural run, or if the retaining clamp and rubber sleeve are not fitted as described, stresses will be imposed on the pipe as the engine is running that will cause it to leak, or even break, in service.*

17 Refit the black plastic wiring conduit to the cylinder head cover and reconnect any hoses and wiring that were disconnected.

18 Reconnect the pump's wiring and the fuel feed and return hoses.

19 Refit the air cleaner assembly and reconnect the battery.

20 Prime the fuel system and start the engine, then thoroughly check for fuel leaks from the disturbed pipes/hoses before refitting the acoustic engine cover.

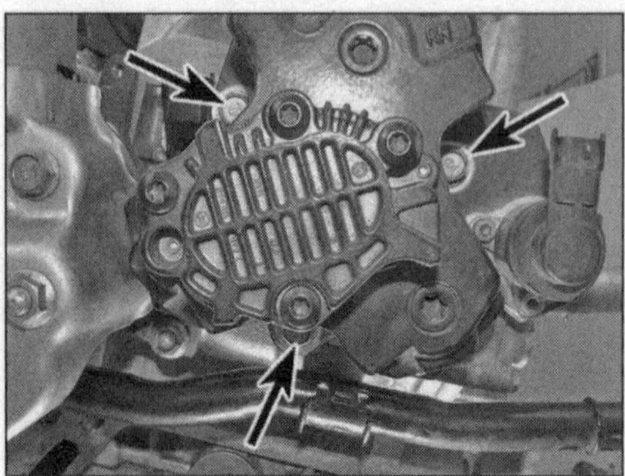

10.12 Refit pump mounting bolts, but do not tighten . . .

10.13 . . . until new fuel pump-to-fuel rail high-pressure fuel pipe has been fitted

11 Fuel (common) rail – removal and refitting

Caution: Be careful not to allow dirt into the fuel pump, fuel rail or injectors during this procedure.

Note: *Any rigid high-pressure fuel pipes disturbed must be renewed.*

Removal

1 Disconnect the battery negative lead, and position the lead away from the battery (see *Disconnecting the battery*).

2 Unscrew the four retaining nuts and remove the acoustic engine cover.

3 Unscrew the mounting bolts for the IMRC

11.8 Counterhold hexagon on injector body to prevent damage while slackening high-pressure fuel pipe union nut

11.10 . . . and withdraw fuel rail. Note fuel unions capped to exclude dirt

11.14 Reconnect the fuel return hose on refitting

solenoid valve, the EGR control solenoid valve, the EGR cooler bypass control solenoid valve, and the vacuum line assembly. Disconnect the vacuum hoses as necessary to release the assembly from the intake manifold **(see illustration 13.8a)**.

4 Undo the two bolts securing the large square-section black plastic wiring conduit to the cylinder head cover and lift the other conduit off its brackets on the left-hand end of the cylinder head sufficiently to reach the fuel rail high-pressure fuel pipe union nuts. Disconnect the wiring for the fuel rail pressure sensor, the fuel injectors and the glow plugs to permit this; if it is necessary to disconnect any other wiring, and any vacuum hoses, note them carefully and do not forget to reconnect them on reassembly **(see illustrations 10.5a and 10.5b)**.

5 Make sure the areas around the high-pressure fuel pipe unions from the fuel pump to the fuel rail and from the fuel rail to the injectors are scrupulously clean and free from debris, etc. If possible, use a vacuum cleaner and a degreaser to clean the area.

Warning: Before disconnecting any part of the high-pressure side of the fuel system, read the precautions concerning depressurising the fuel system given in Section 2 and take action accordingly.

6 Place a large rag around the fuel pump-to-fuel rail high-pressure fuel pipe union nut near the centre of the fuel rail **(see illustration 10.5b)**, ready to soak up any escaping fuel. Slowly (to avoid a sudden release of pressure and to allow any fuel spray which may be expelled to be caught by the rag) unscrew the union nut. When any hissing has stopped, indicating that all residual pressure has been released, unscrew the nut from the rail; be prepared for some loss of fuel.

7 Counterhold the hexagon on the fuel pump union with one open-ended spanner and unscrew the fuel pump-to-fuel rail high- pressure fuel pipe union nut with a second spanner; be prepared for fuel spillage **(see illustration 10.8)**. Unscrew the high-pressure pipe retaining clamp bolt **(see illustration 10.5c)** and discard the high-pressure pipe – a new one must be fitted on reassembly. Swiftly cap the pump and rail unions to prevent the entry of dirt into either.

8 Working in a similar fashion, first at the injector (and counterholding the injector hexagon to prevent damage to the injector), then at the rail, disconnect each fuel rail-to-fuel injector high-pressure fuel pipe in turn and discard them – all must be renewed on reassembly. Unbolt the retaining clamp securing Nos. 1 and 2 high-pressure pipes. Swiftly cap all injector and rail unions to prevent the entry of dirt into any of them **(see illustrations 11.8 and 13.9b)**.

9 Disconnect the fuel return hose from the fuel rail.

10 Unscrew and remove the two fuel rail mounting nuts, and withdraw the rail **(see illustration)**.

11 Store the fuel rail in clean conditions – take care that no dirt enters the pipe unions. If the pressure-limiting valve is thought to be faulty in any way, it must be checked by a Honda dealer or specialist.

12 As preparation for refitting, remove the fuel injectors, clean and check them as described in Section 12, fit new copper sealing washers and apply grease to their stems.

Refitting

13 On refitting, install the injectors in their original positions (see Section 12), and slacken the three fuel pump mounting bolts.

14 Wipe clean the mating surfaces of the cylinder head and fuel rail, refit the rail and tighten its mounting nuts to the specified torque wrench setting. Reconnect the fuel return hose **(see illustration)**.

15 Ensuring that each is fitted in its correct location, install the four new fuel rail-to-fuel injector high-pressure fuel pipes. Turn each injector as necessary to seat its pipe snugly at both end unions, then tighten both union nuts as far as possible by hand.

16 With all four pipes installed and the injectors aligned, refit the injector clamps and tighten the clamp bolts as described in Section 12. Refit the fuel return hose assembly.

17 Using a crows-foot adapter, tighten the high-pressure fuel pipe union nuts to the specified torque wrench setting, fuel injector union first (counterholding the injectors' hexagons to prevent damage), then the fuel rail union. Tighten securely the retaining clamp bolt securing Nos. 1 and 2 high-pressure pipes.

18 Fit a new fuel pump-to-fuel rail high-pressure fuel pipe and tighten its union nuts, and the pump mounting bolts and pipe retaining clamp, as described in paragraphs 13 to 16 of Section 10.

19 Refit the black plastic wiring conduit to the cylinder head cover and reconnect all hoses and wiring that were disconnected.

20 Reconnect the battery, prime the fuel system and start the engine, then thoroughly check for fuel leaks from the disturbed pipes/hoses before refitting the acoustic engine cover.

12 Fuel injectors – removal, testing and refitting

Caution: Be careful not to allow dirt into the fuel pump, fuel rail or injectors during this procedure.

Note: *The removal of the fuel injectors seems in itself a quite simple and straightforward procedure. However, not only is extraction of the fuel injectors quite likely to be extremely difficult, but all four fuel rail-to-injector high-pressure pipes and the four copper sealing washers must be renewed as a matter of course on reassembly, regardless of their apparent condition.*

Removal

1 See Section 11, paragraphs 1 to 5.

Warning: Before disconnecting any part of the high-pressure side of the fuel system, read the precautions concerning depressurising the fuel system given in Section 2 and take action accordingly.

2 Prise out the clips just far enough to release the unions, and disconnect the fuel return hose from the top of each injector **(see illustrations)**. Check the sealing O-ring at each union – if any are damaged, the complete return hose assembly must be renewed. If any of the clips were removed completely, they must be renewed as a matter of course.

3 Place a large rag around the first fuel rail-to-fuel injector high-pressure fuel pipe union nut at the fuel rail, ready to soak up

12.2a Prise out clips just far enough to release unions (removing clips completely means they have to be renewed) . . .

12.2b . . . and disconnect fuel return hose from top of each injector – check sealing O-ring

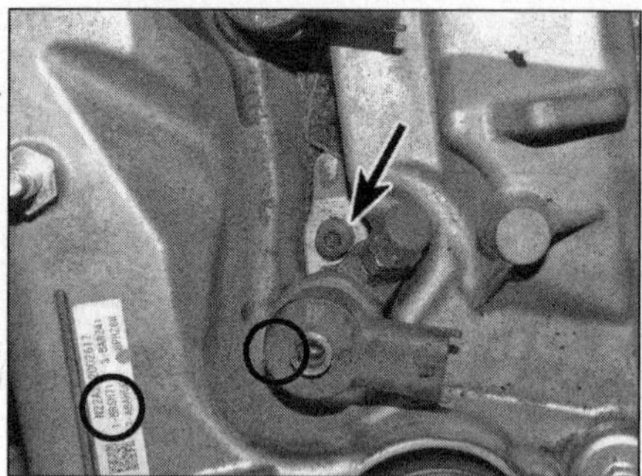

12.6a Unscrew clamp bolt to release injector (surroundings should be much cleaner than this) . . .

Note: *Injectors are coded to specific cylinders – see label and marking on top of injector.*

12.6b . . . then lift injector out of cylinder head . . .

12.6c . . . although some persuasion will be necessary in most cases

any escaping fuel. Slowly (to avoid a sudden release of pressure and to allow any fuel spray which may be expelled to be caught by the rag) unscrew the union nut. When any hissing has stopped, indicating that all residual pressure has been released, unscrew the nut from the rail; be prepared for some loss of fuel.

4 Counterhold the hexagon (but do not move it or the injector will be damaged) on the injector body with one open-ended spanner and unscrew the fuel rail-to-fuel injector high-pressure fuel pipe union nut with a second spanner; be prepared for fuel spillage **(see illustration 11.8a)**. Remove and discard the high-pressure pipe – a new one must be fitted on reassembly. Swiftly cap the injector and rail unions to prevent the entry of dirt into either.

5 Working in a similar fashion, first at the injector, then at the rail, disconnect each fuel rail-to-fuel injector high-pressure fuel pipe in turn and discard them – all must be renewed on reassembly **(see illustration 11.8b)**. Unbolt the retaining clamp securing Nos. 1 and 2 high-pressure pipes. Swiftly cap all injector and rail unions to prevent the entry of dirt into any of them.

6 Unscrew the Torx bolt securing each injector clamp, withdraw the clamps and remove the injectors **(see illustrations)**. If any of the injectors is found to be stuck, first try soaking it in penetrating fluid and leaving the vehicle for as long as possible for the fluid to act. If this does not work, it is always worth laying a thick blanket over the engine and turning it over on the starter motor to use compression to try to blow the injectors out. In most cases, though, it will be necessary to get the vehicle to a Honda dealer or diesel injection specialist for the injectors to be removed.

7 Once the injectors are removed, recover (noting which way up each is fitted) and discard the copper sealing washer under each – these must be renewed on reassembly. As each injector is removed, cover or plug its well with clean rag or similar to prevent dirt or other objects from dropping into the combustion chambers; be very careful to keep this in place all the time the injectors are removed so as not to allow dirt and debris to fall into the engine.

8 The injectors are coded to their respective cylinders; a label affixed to the cylinder head cover lists by cylinder the individual identification number marked on each injector's top surface. They must be refitted to their original positions – if the original number cannot be deciphered mark the injectors for identification, so they can refitted to their original locations **(see illustrations 12.14a and 12.14b)**.

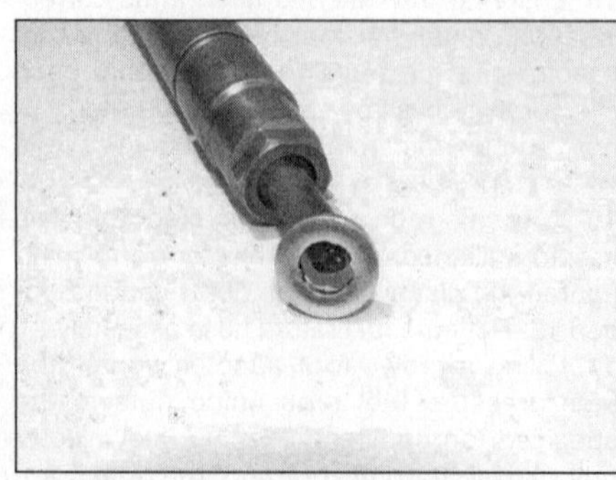

12.13a Fit new copper sealing washer . . .

9 Use a rag or paper towel to wipe clean each injector's stem; DO NOT clean the smaller-diameter injector nozzle. Do not attempt to dismantle the injectors or use any stronger cleaning methods on them. If any of the injectors require attention of any sort, this is a task for a Honda dealer or specialist. Take care not to drop the injectors, nor allow the needles at their tips to become damaged.

10 Thoroughly clean the injector wells – both the tubes in the cylinder head cover and the seatings in the cylinder head. Be very careful not to allow dirt and debris to fall into the combustion chambers. Use an electric torch to examine the condition of the seatings in the cylinder head – if any are damaged, burned, corroded or marked in any way they must be resurfaced.

Testing

11 Testing of the injectors requires the use of special equipment. If any injector is thought to be faulty have it tested and, if necessary, reconditioned by a Honda dealer or specialist.

Refitting

12 Remove the material covering or plugging the well and ensure that the injectors and seats in cylinder head are clean and dry. It's essential the sealing surfaces are dirt-free, otherwise leakage will occur. Check that each injector's clamp bolt threads are clean and dry.

13 Fit a new copper sealing washer to each injector, using a dab of grease to stick it in place and ensuring it is fitted the same way as noted on removal. It is advisable to coat the stem of each injector with suitable grease to make easier the task of removing them in the future. Special grease is available from some suppliers, but copper grease can also be used if nothing better is available. Do NOT grease the smaller-diameter injector nozzle **(see illustrations)**.

14 Fit each injector to its original cylinder, rotate it approximately into position and, ensuring that each is fitted in its correct location, install the new fuel rail-to-fuel injector high-pressure fuel pipe **(see illustrations)**.

12.13b . . . and grease injector stem to prevent sticking. Do NOT clean or grease smaller-diameter nozzle area indicated

12.14a To ensure injectors are refitted to original cylinders, check marking on top of injector . . .

12.14b . . . against label on cylinder head cover

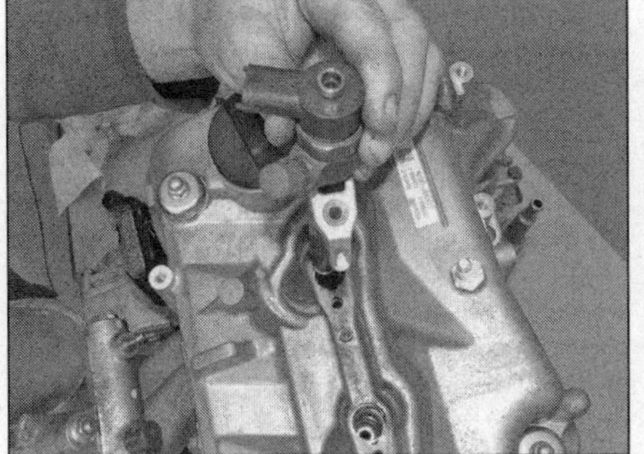
12.15a Injector clamps must engage as shown on flats of injector bodies . . .

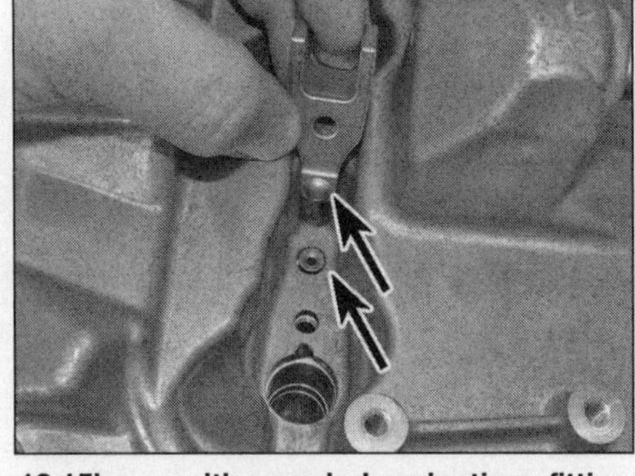
12.15b . . . with rounded projections fitting into locating dowels

12.15c Check threads are clean and dry before refitting clamp bolts

Turn each injector as necessary to seat its pipe snugly at both end unions, then tighten both union nuts as far as possible by hand.

15 When all four injectors and pipes are installed, refit the clamps; each has a rounded projection on its underside which fits into a locating dowel projecting from the cylinder head, through the cover, and its forked ends should engage the flats on the injector body. Fit each clamp bolt and tighten it to the specified Stage 1 torque wrench setting. Once the bolt has been tightened to the Stage 1 torque, tighten it through its specified Stage 2 angle. It is recommended that an angle-measuring gauge is used during this stage of tightening, to ensure accuracy, but a good alternative is to use a felt-tip pen, paint, typists' correction fluid or similar to make alignment marks between the bolt head and the clamp, the clamp mark being 90° (one-quarter-turn) after the bolt head mark. The Stage 2 fastening can then be achieved by tightening the bolt through one-quarter of a turn so that the mark on the bolt head now aligns with the corresponding mark on the clamp **(see illustrations)**.

16 Using a crows-foot adapter, tighten the high-pressure fuel pipe union nuts to the specified torque wrench setting, fuel injector union first (counterholding the injectors' hexagons to prevent damage), then the fuel rail union. Tighten securely the retaining clamp bolt securing Nos. 1 and 2 high-pressure pipes **(see illustrations)**.

12.15d Tighten clamp bolts to Stage 1 torque setting . . .

12.15e . . . then tighten through Stage 2 angle

12.16a Counterhold hexagon on injector body to prevent damage while tightening high-pressure fuel pipe union nut . . .

12.16b . . . then tighten fuel rail union nut

12.16c Do not forget to refit and tighten retaining clamp bolt securing Nos. 1 and 2 high-pressure pipes

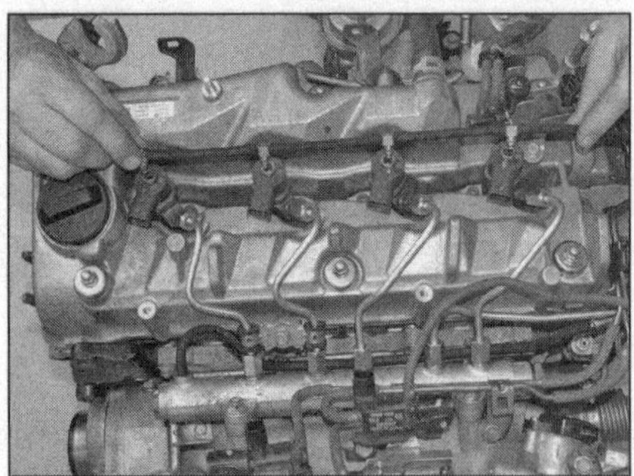
12.17a Fit fuel return hose assembly to tops of injectors . . .

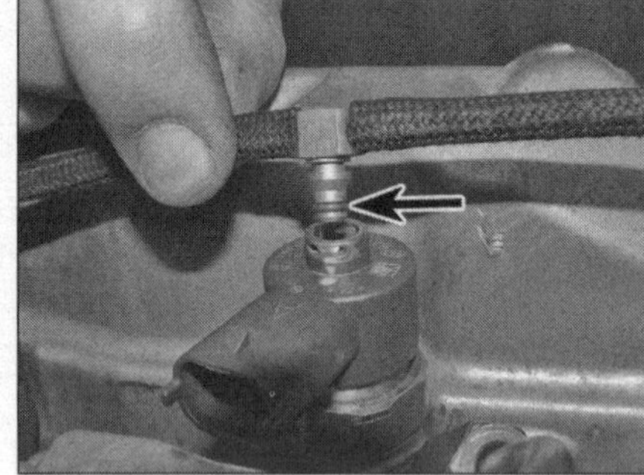
12.17b . . . ensuring that O-rings are sound and properly fitted . . .

12.17c . . . fit retaining clips (new if originals were removed completely on dismantling) . . .

12.17d . . . and press into place as shown . . .

12.17e . . . then reconnect return hose to return pipe

17 Fit the return hose assembly to the top of each injector and press in the clip to secure each union **(see illustrations)**.

18 Refit the black plastic wiring conduit to the cylinder head cover and reconnect all hoses and wiring that were disconnected.

19 Reconnect the battery, prime the fuel system and start the engine, then thoroughly check for fuel leaks from the disturbed pipes/ hoses before refitting the acoustic engine cover.

20 Honda specify that their Honda Diagnostic System (HDS) tester must be used, connected to the diagnostic socket under the driver's side of the facia, to run an Injector Quantity Adjustment (IQA) sequence whenever the injectors have been removed and refitted. The tester will recognise the original injectors and display the individual identification number marked on each injector's top surface. If it does not recognise an injector, for example when one has been renewed, a coding procedure will be instituted.

13 Intake manifold – removal and refitting

Removal

1 Disconnect the battery negative lead, and position the lead away from the battery (see *Disconnecting the battery*).

2 Unscrew the four retaining nuts and remove the acoustic engine cover.

3 Disconnect the intercooler outlet hose from the intake manifold air intake passage, then unscrew the bolt securing the intake manifold support bracket to the IMRC valve **(see illustrations)**.

4 Unscrew the dipstick tube mounting bolt and the nuts securing the short EGR pipe to the EGR valve and intake manifold **(see illustration)**.

5 Unscrew the nuts securing the EGR valve to the long EGR pipe and the three bolts securing the EGR valve to the cylinder head. Disconnect its vacuum hose and withdraw the

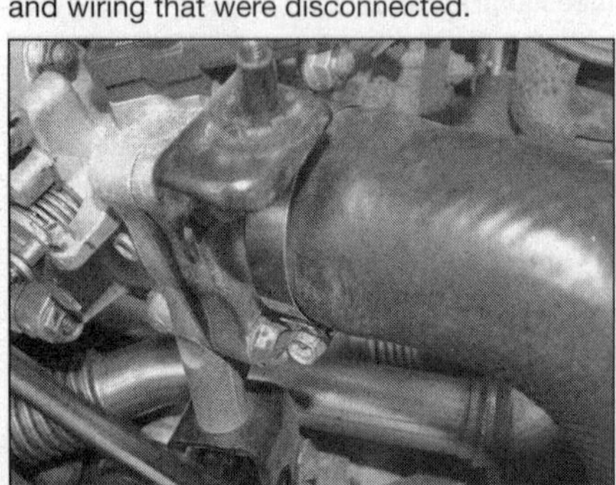
13.3a Disconnect intercooler outlet hose from intake manifold air intake passage . . .

13.3b . . . and unscrew bolt securing support bracket to underside of manifold

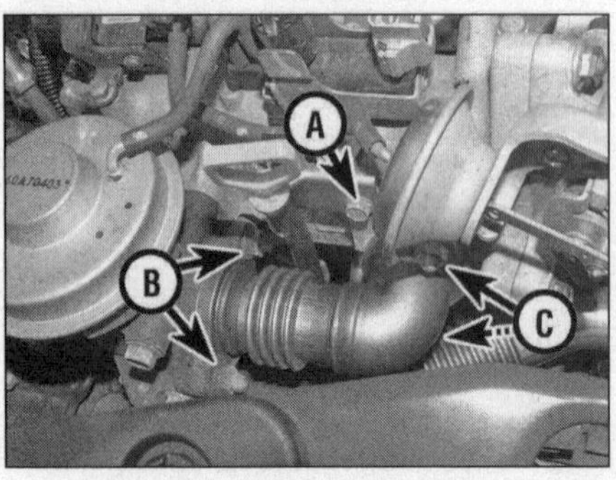

13.4 Unscrew dipstick tube bolt (A) and shorter EGR pipe nuts (B) and (C)

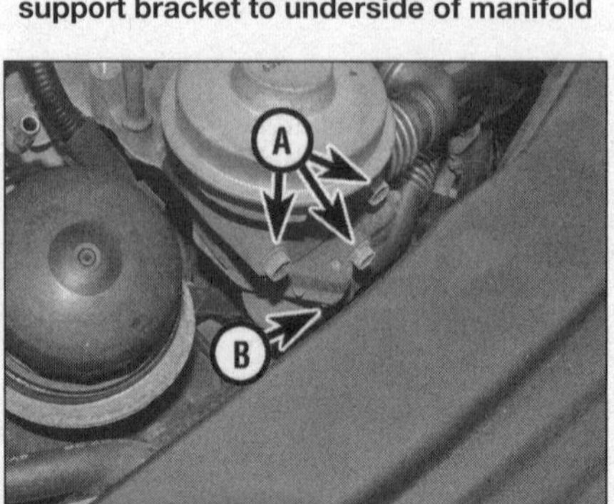

13.5a Unscrew bolts (A) securing EGR valve to cylinder head and nuts (B) . . .

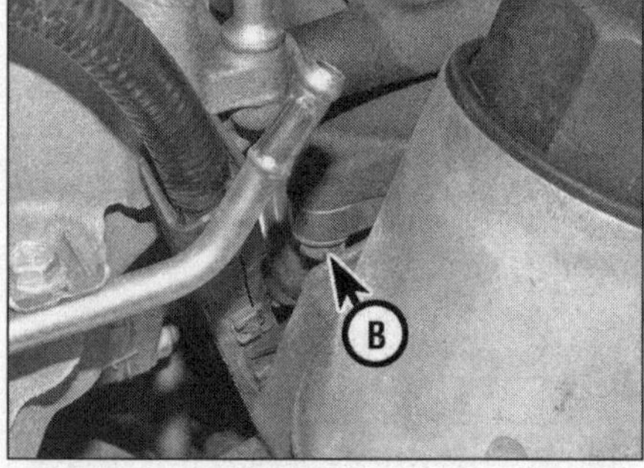

13.5b . . . securing EGR valve to long EGR pipe . . .

EGR valve and short EGR pipe together **(see illustrations)**. Recover all EGR component gaskets and discard them – new ones must be fitted on reassembly.

6 Remove the dipstick and dipstick tube **(see illustration)**. Recover and discard the sealing O-ring – a new one must be fitted on reassembly.

7 Disconnect the wiring for the IMRC solenoid valve, the EGR control solenoid valve, the EGR cooler bypass control solenoid valve, the manifold absolute pressure/intake air temperature No. 2 sensor and the IMRC valve position sensor. Release the wiring from any clips or ties **(see illustration)**.

8 Unscrew the mounting bolts for the IMRC solenoid valve, the EGR control solenoid valve, the EGR cooler bypass control solenoid valve, and the vacuum line assembly. Disconnect the vacuum hoses as necessary and remove the valve and line assembly from the intake manifold **(see illustrations)**.

9 Disconnect the wiring for the fuel rail pressure sensor, the fuel injectors and the glow plugs, then undo the two bolts securing the square-section black plastic wiring conduit to the cylinder head cover and lift the conduit off its brackets on the left-hand end of the cylinder head **(see illustrations)**.

Warning: Before disconnecting any part of the high-pressure side of the fuel system, read the precautions concerning depressurising the fuel system given in Section 2 and take action accordingly.

10 Disconnect and remove all five high-pressure fuel pipes, disconnect the fuel return hose from the end of the fuel rail, unscrew its mounting nuts and remove the fuel rail (see Section 11). Note that the high-pressure fuel pipes must be discarded – new ones must be fitted on reassembly.

11 Disconnect the coolant bypass hoses from each end of the pipe, then unbolt the bypass pipe from the intake manifold **(see illustrations)**.

12 Unscrew the three bolts and four nuts securing the manifold to the cylinder head and withdraw it **(see illustrations)**. Recover and discard the manifold gasket – this must be

13.5c . . . then disconnect EGR valve vacuum hose and withdraw valve and short pipe together

13.6 Remove the dipstick and tube

13.7 Disconnect wiring for IMRC solenoid valve (A), EGR control solenoid valve (B), EGR cooler bypass control solenoid valve (C), manifold absolute pressure/ intake air temperature No. 2 sensor (D) and IMRC valve position sensor (E)

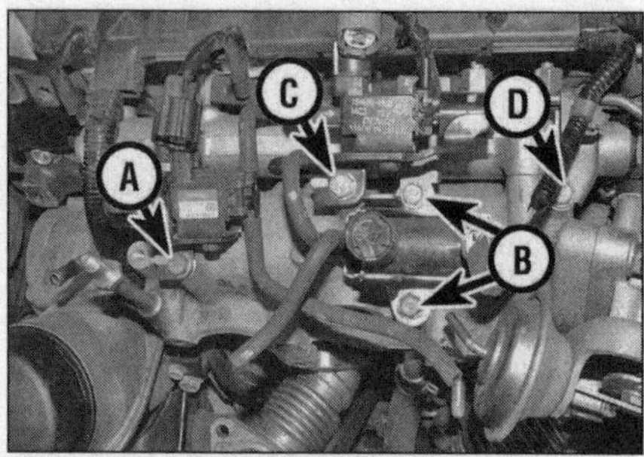

13.8a Unscrew mounting bolts for IMRC solenoid valve (A), EGR control solenoid valve (B), EGR cooler bypass control solenoid valve (C), and vacuum line assembly (D)

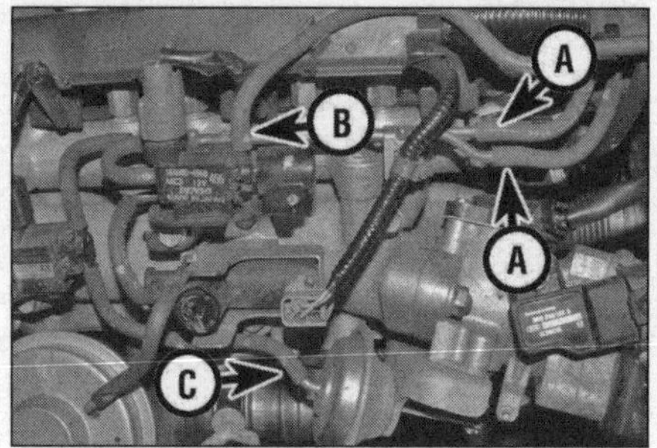

13.8b Disconnect vacuum hoses from vacuum line assembly (A), EGR cooler bypass control solenoid valve (B) and IMRC valve (C)

13.8c . . . then remove valve and line assembly from intake manifold

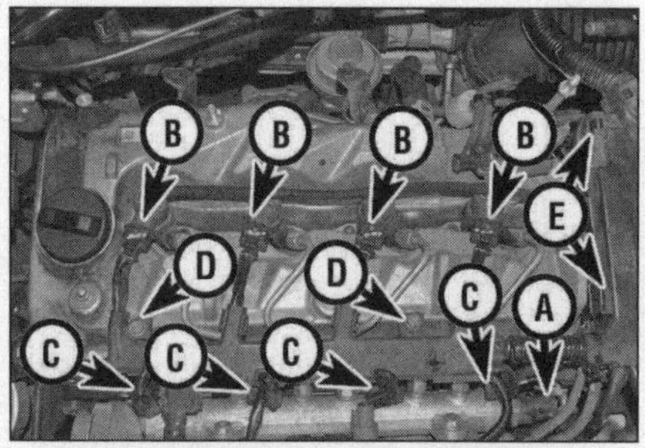

13.9a Disconnect wiring for fuel rail pressure sensor (A), fuel injectors (B) and glow plugs (C), then unbolt wiring conduit bolts (D) and release conduit from brackets (E)

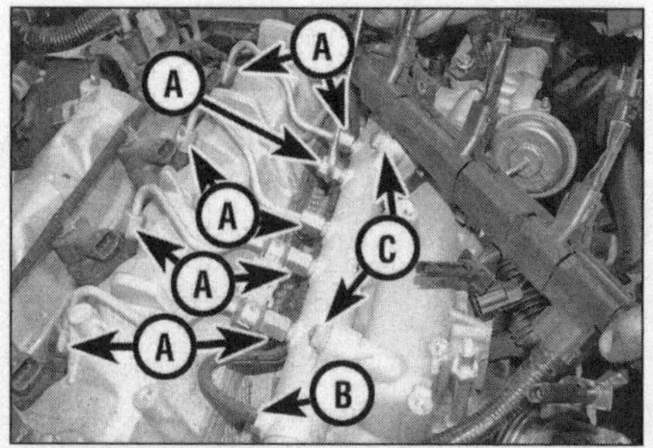

13.9b Disconnect and remove all five high-pressure fuel pipes (A), disconnect fuel return hose (B), unscrew fuel rail mounting nuts (C) . . .

13.9c . . . disconnect high-pressure fuel pipe from fuel pump (A) and unscrew pipe support bracket bolt (B) to remove fuel rail

13.11a Unscrew bolts (arrows) to release coolant bypass pipe from intake manifold . . .

13.11b . . . then disconnect hoses from each end of bypass pipe to remove

13.12a Unscrew three bolts underneath and four nuts (shown here) securing manifold to cylinder head . . .

13.12b . . . and withdraw intake manifold

13.14a Always renew manifold gasket to prevent air leaks . . .

13.14b . . . then refit intake manifold

renewed whenever it is disturbed to prevent any risk of air leaks.

13 Check the manifold for any signs of cracking or other damage – this may be most evident around the mounting points. If the manifold is damaged, a new one will be needed.

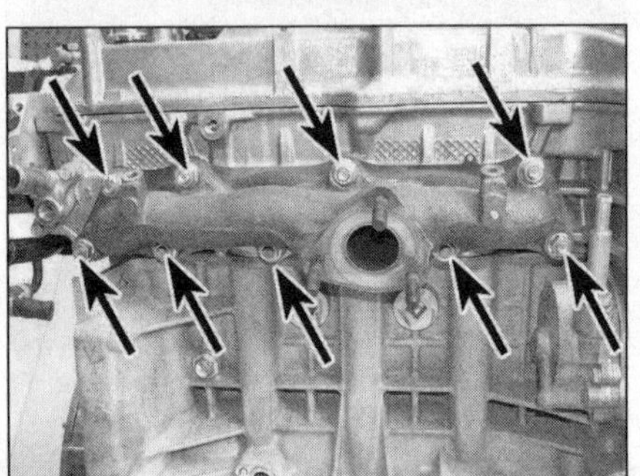
14.2 Unscrew exhaust manifold retaining nuts . . .

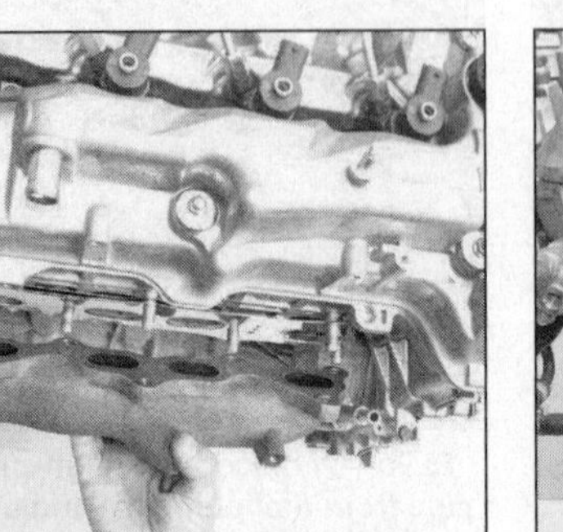
14.3 . . . to withdraw exhaust manifold

Refitting

14 Clean all mating faces prior to refitting, and wipe them dry. Fit a new manifold-to-head gasket over the studs, then slide on the manifold **(see illustrations)**. Working in several stages and in a diagonal sequence from the centre outwards, tighten the mounting nuts and bolts to the specified torque wrench setting.

15 Further refitting is a reversal of removal.

14 Exhaust manifold – removal and refitting

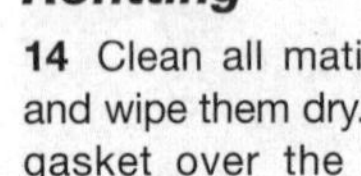

Removal

1 Remove the turbocharger (Section 15).

14.4 Always renew manifold gasket to prevent exhaust leaks

2 Unscrew and remove, then discard, the nine nuts securing the manifold to the cylinder head **(see illustration)**. Use a wire brush and plenty of penetrating fluid first if they appear to be rusty.

3 Withdraw the manifold from the studs, and remove it from the engine compartment **(see illustration)**. Recover the manifold gasket – a new one should always be used when refitting.

Refitting

4 Refitting is a reversal of removal, noting the following points **(see illustration)**:

a) Clean the manifold and cylinder head mating faces, and fit a new gasket.

b) It is recommended that new nuts are used as a matter of course – even if the old ones came off without difficulty, they may not stand being retightened. New components will be much easier to remove in future, should this be necessary.

c) If any of the manifold studs were removed, it's best to obtain new studs with the new nuts, rather than try to separate the old ones. The new studs can be fitted by tightening two nuts against each other on the stud, then using them to screw the stud into place – once this is done, the nuts can be unscrewed from each other, and removed.

d) Tighten the manifold nuts to the specified torque.

e) Refit the turbocharger as described in Section 15.

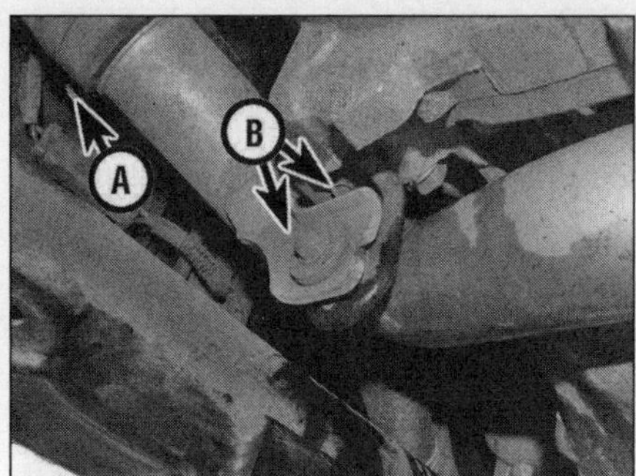

15.5a Slacken hose clamp (A) and unscrew mounting bracket bolts (B) at front . . .

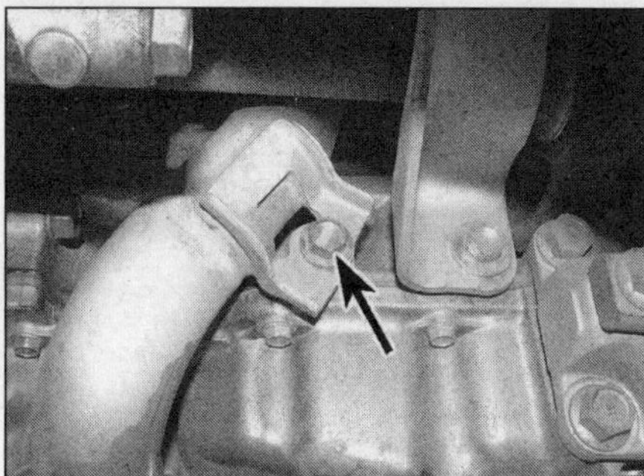

15.5b . . . and rear of turbocharger-to-intercooler pipe, remove pipe . . .

15.5c . . . and turbocharger outlet hose. Note raised rib to be aligned with hose mark on refitting

15.6 Unscrew three exhaust front pipe-to-catalytic converter nuts to remove front pipe completely

15.9 Disconnect breather hose from rear of cylinder head cover

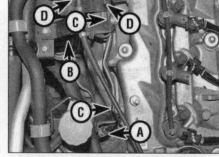

15.10a Disconnect vacuum pump vacuum hose (A), turbocharger vacuum hose (B), then undo vacuum line assembly bolts (C) and intake pipe support bracket bolts (D) . . .

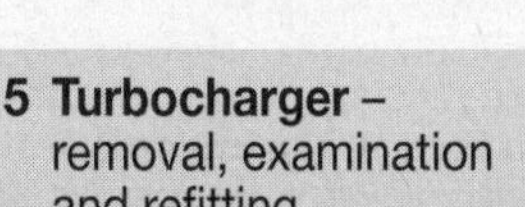
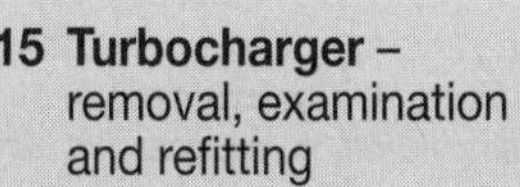
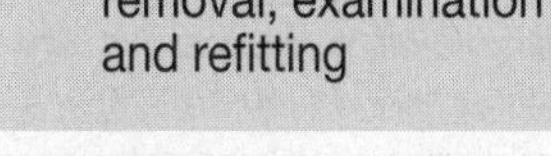

15 Turbocharger – removal, examination and refitting

Note: *Pack the turbocharger openings with clean rag to prevent dirt or other objects falling in.*

Removal

1 Unscrew the four retaining nuts and remove the acoustic engine cover.

2 Remove the air cleaner assembly and withdraw the air cleaner-to-turbocharger intake hose as described in Section 4.

3 Remove the engine compartment under-shield (Chapter 11).

4 Drain the cooling system (see Chapter 1B).

5 Slacken the hose clamps at each end and unbolt the turbocharger-to-intercooler pipe, then remove the turbocharger outlet hose **(see illustrations)**.

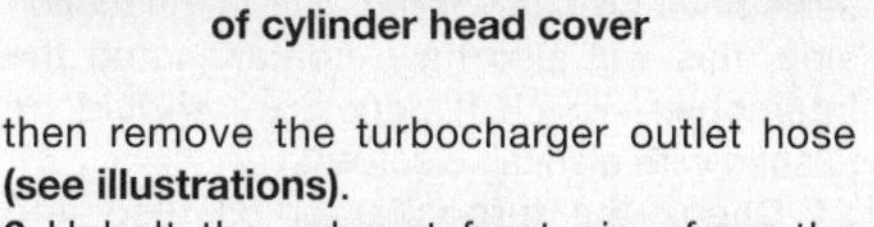

6 Unbolt the exhaust front pipe from the warm-up catalytic converter; recover the springs **(see illustration 16.5)**. Unscrew and discard the three front pipe-to-catalytic converter nuts, then withdraw the exhaust front pipe **(see illustration)**. Recover and discard both gaskets.

7 Unscrew the two bolts and withdraw the support bracket between the cylinder block/crankcase and the warm-up catalytic converter **(see illustration 16.6)**.

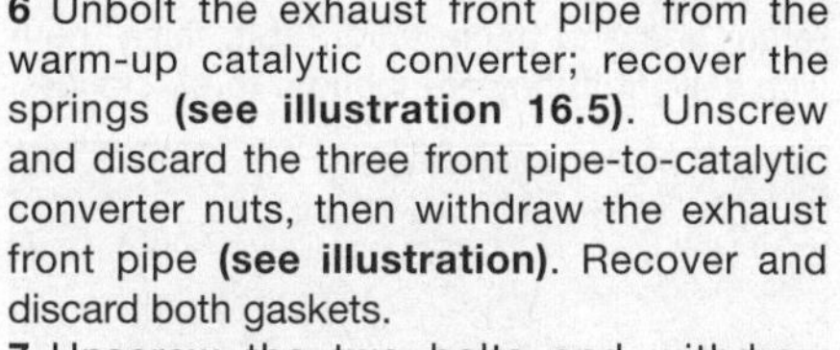

8 Unscrew the three retaining nuts and withdraw the warm-up catalytic converter **(see illustration 16.7)**.

9 Disconnect the breather hose from the rear of the cylinder head cover **(see illustration)**.

10 Unscrew the two bolts securing the vacuum line assembly to the rear of the cylinder head cover and the bracket supporting the air cleaner-to-turbocharger intake pipe, disconnect the vacuum hose from the vacuum pump and from the turbocharger, then withdraw the vacuum line assembly **(see illustrations)**.

11 Unbolt and withdraw the cover over the exhaust manifold **(see illustration)**.

12 Unscrew the turbocharger coolant line banjo union bolt and recover the sealing washers, then disconnect the coolant hose from the turbocharger union **(see illustrations)**.

13 Unscrew the two bolts and withdraw the support bracket between the cylinder block/crankcase and the turbocharger.

14 Unscrew the two nuts, two bolts and the banjo union bolt (recover the gaskets and sealing washers) to withdraw the turbocharger oil feed and return line **(see illustration)**.

15.10b . . . and withdraw vacuum line assembly

15.11 Unbolt and withdraw exhaust manifold cover

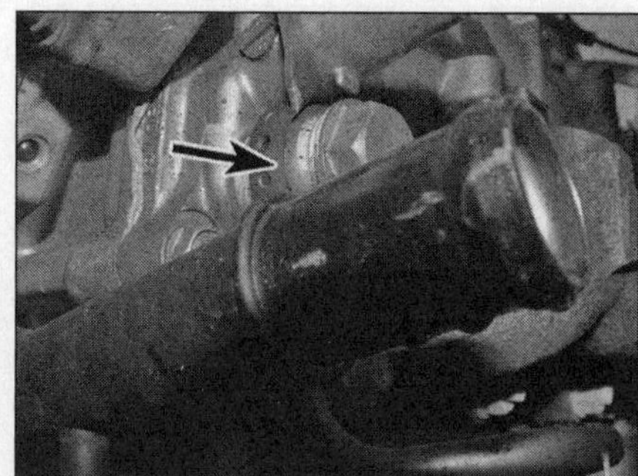

15.12a Unscrew turbocharger coolant bypass pipe banjo union bolt . . .

15.12b . . . and disconnect turbocharger coolant return hose

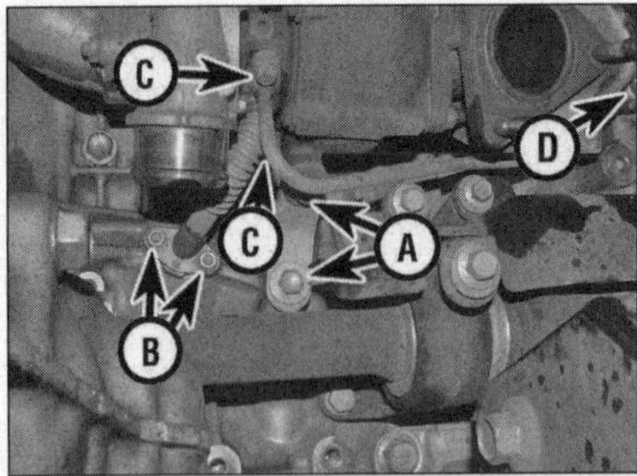

15.14 Unscrew two turbocharger support bracket bolts (A), nuts (B) and bolts (C) and banjo union bolt (D) to withdraw turbocharger oil feed and return line

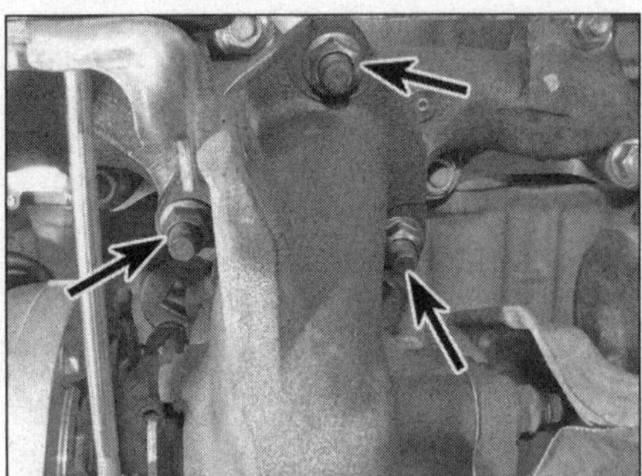

15.15a Unscrew three nuts . . .

15 Undo the three retaining nuts and withdraw the turbocharger assembly **(see illustrations)**. Recover and discard the gasket – this must be renewed whenever it is disturbed.

Examination

16 Unscrew the two bolts and withdraw the coolant pipe. Unscrew the two nuts and withdraw the breather hose assembly and undo the two nuts to remove the intake pipe. Unscrew the two bolts securing the turbocharger outlet elbow cover, then unscrew the three nuts and remove the outlet elbow itself. Recover and discard the gasket from each of these unions – all must be renewed whenever they are disturbed **(see illustrations)**.

17 With the turbocharger removed, inspect the housing for cracks or other visible damage.

18 Spin the turbine or the compressor wheel to verify that the shaft is intact and to feel for excessive shake or roughness. Some play is normal since in use the shaft is 'floating' on a film of oil. Check that the wheel vanes are undamaged.

19 The wastegate and actuator are integral with the turbocharger, and cannot be checked or renewed separately. Consult a Honda dealer or other specialist if it is thought that the wastegate may be faulty.

20 If the exhaust or induction passages are oil-contaminated, the turbocharger shaft oil seals have probably failed. (On the induction side, this will also have contaminated the intercooler, which if necessary should be flushed with a suitable solvent.)

21 Check the turbocharger oil feed and return line and banjo union bolt; flush them with solvent if they are thought to be clogged and blow them clear with an airline **(see illustration)**. Renew the oil feed and return line and banjo union bolt if there is the slightest doubt about their condition.

22 No DIY repair of the turbocharger is possible. A new unit may be available on an exchange basis.

23 On reassembly, refit the coolant pipe, breather, intake pipe and outlet elbow. Renew all gaskets and sealing washers and tighten all fasteners to the torque wrench settings specified. Plug or cover the turbocharger openings until the intake and outlet hoses are ready to be connected during the refitting procedure.

Refitting

24 Refitting is a reversal of removal, noting the following points **(see illustrations)**:

a) Ensure all mating surfaces are clean and dry.

b) Renew all sealing washers and gaskets.

15.15b . . . and remove turbocharger. Note openings taped to exclude dirt, etc.

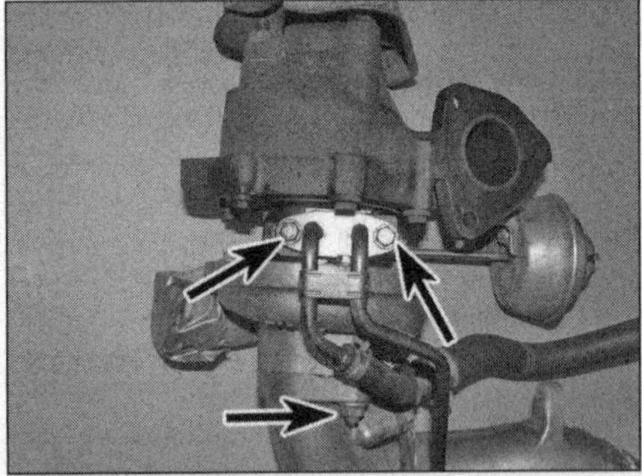

15.16a Unscrew bolts and nuts shown . . .

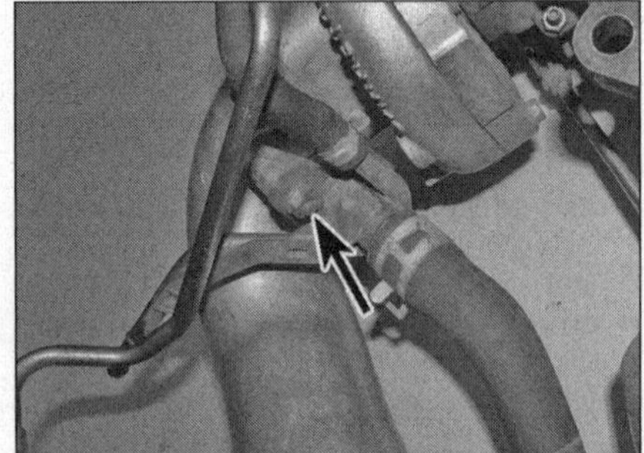

15.16b . . . to remove coolant, breather and intake pipes from turbocharger

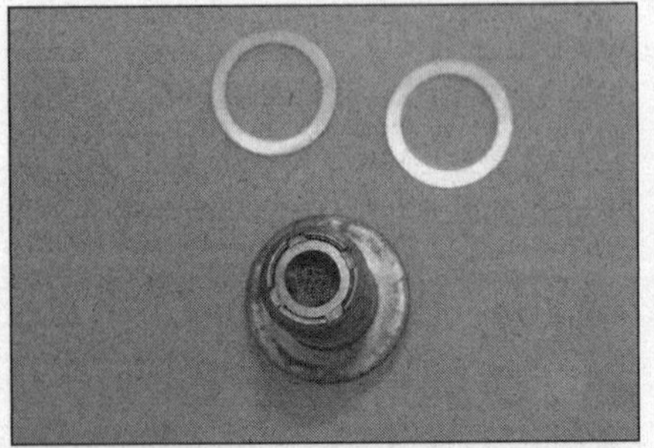

15.21 Check turbocharger oil feed banjo union bolt is clear – always renew sealing washers

15.24a Always renew turbocharger gasket to prevent leaks

15.24b Securely fasten turbocharger coolant return hose . . .

15.24c . . . and always renew sealing washers at coolant bypass pipe banjo union

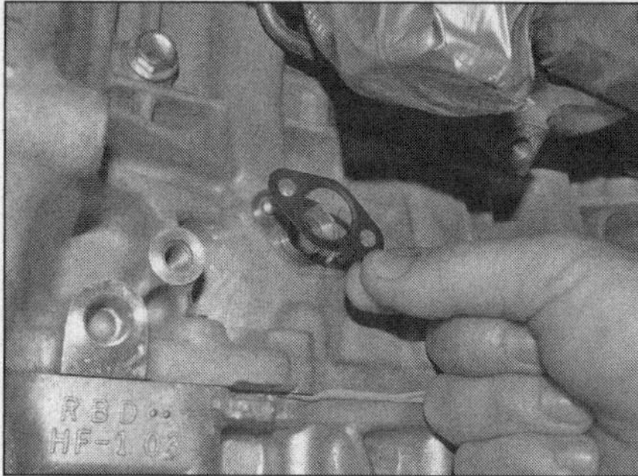

15.24d Fit new gasket to oil return line union on cylinder block . . .

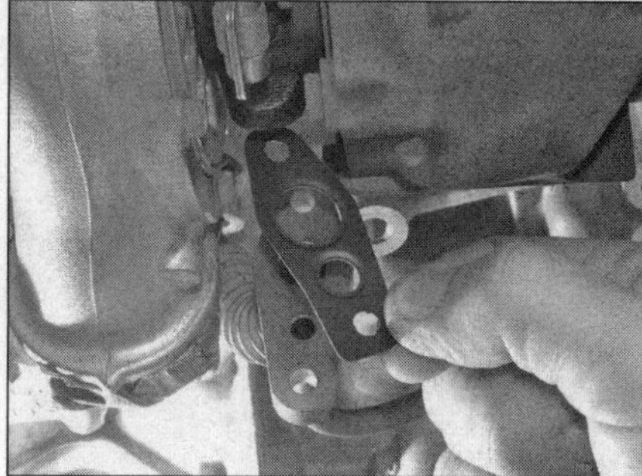

15.24e . . . and to turbocharger union

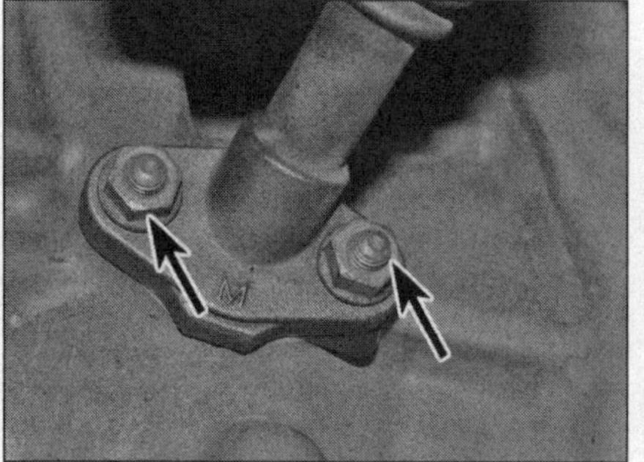

15.24f Tighten oil bypass pipe union mounting flange nuts . . .

15.24g . . . and bolts to specified torque setting

15.24h Prime turbocharger lubrication system by injecting as much oil as possible into feed line . . .

15.24i . . . then refit banjo union bolt with new sealing washers and tighten to specified torque setting

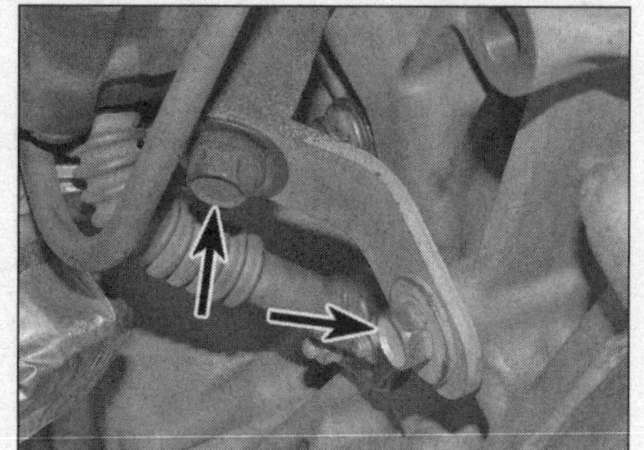

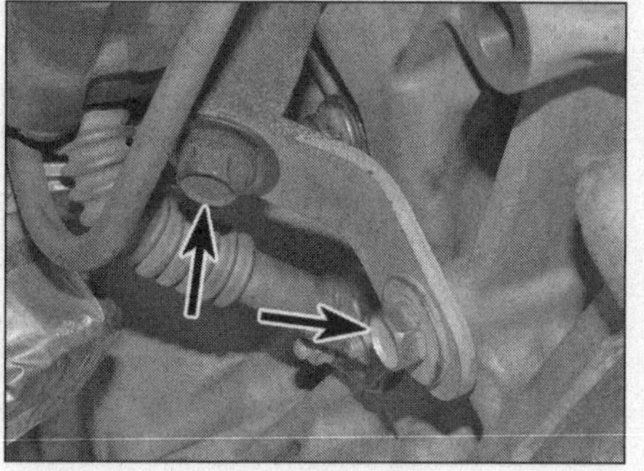

15.24j Refit turbocharger support bracket and tighten bolts

15.24k Leave turbocharger openings covered until ready to be reconnected

c) Tighten all fasteners to the specified torque wrench settings, where available.

d) When refitting the turbocharger oil feed and return line, prime the lubrication system by filling the pipe as much as possible with clean engine oil via the banjo union orifice.

*e) When reconnecting the turbocharger outlet hose, align the mark on the hose with the raised rib on the turbocharger body **(see illustration 15.5c)**.*

f) Tighten all hose clips securely, to avoid air leaks.

g) Fit new exhaust front pipe-to-catalytic converter nuts.

h) Refill the cooling system (Chapter 1B).

i) Start the engine, then thoroughly check for exhaust, oil and coolant leaks from the disturbed pipes/hoses before refitting the acoustic engine cover and engine compartment undershield.

16 Exhaust system – general information, removal and refitting

Warning: Inspection and repair of exhaust system components should be done only after the system has cooled completely. This applies particularly to the turbocharger and catalytic converters, which run at very high temperatures.

General information

1 Downstream of the turbocharger and four-way oxidation ('warm-up') catalytic converter, the exhaust system consists of four sections: the front pipe with flexible section, a NOx-reducing catalytic converter, the centre section with silencer, and the rear silencer.

2 The system is suspended throughout its entire length by rubber mountings; one on the front pipe, three on the centre section and two on the rear silencer **(see illustrations)**.

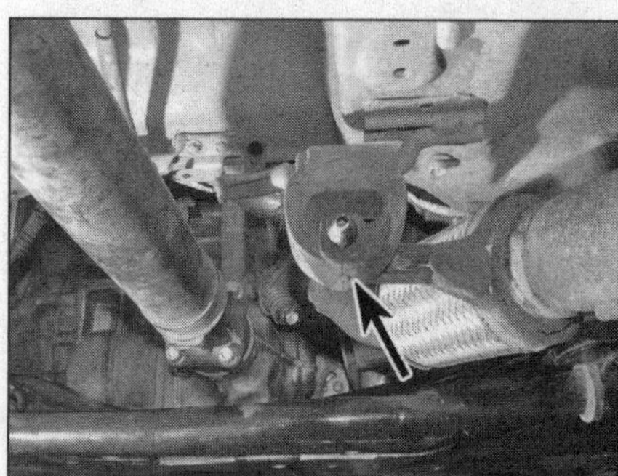

16.2a Exhaust system rubber mounting on front (flexible) section . . .

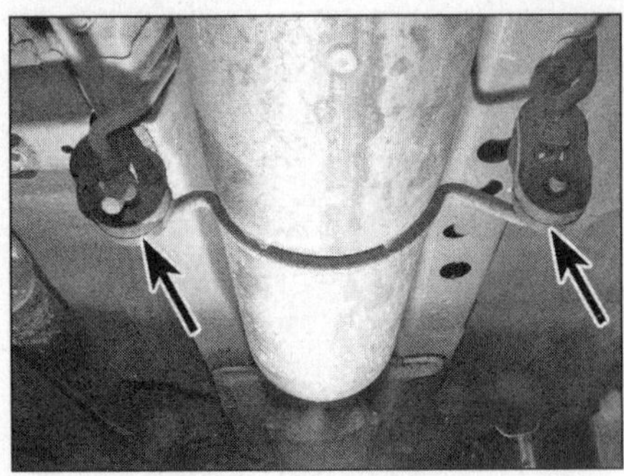

16.2b . . . at front and . . .

16.2c . . . rear of centre section . . .

16.2d . . . on the left of the rear silencer . . .

Removal and refitting

Note: *Some of the system's nuts (see Specifications) must be renewed irrespective of their apparent condition whenever they are disturbed, as must the gaskets. Obtain new nuts and gaskets before starting work.*

3 Although there are detail differences between the systems fitted to petrol- and diesel-engined models, basic working procedures are identical. Proceed as described in Section 14 of Chapter 4A, noting the torque wrench settings given in the Specifications Section of this Chapter **(see illustrations)**.

Warm-up catalytic converter

4 Have a support (such as an axle stand or a small jack) ready to rest the front pipe on as required during removal.

5 Unbolt and disconnect the exhaust front pipe from the warm-up catalytic converter. Recover the springs and the gasket, then unhook the front pipe's rubber mounting and rest the exhaust system on the support.

6 Unscrew the two bolts and withdraw the support bracket between the cylinder block/crankcase and the warm-up catalytic converter.

7 Unscrew the three retaining nuts and withdraw the warm-up catalytic converter **(see illustration)**. Take care that the converter is not dropped or roughly handled.

8 Refitting is the reverse of removal; ensure that all traces of corrosion have been removed from the flanges, and renew the gaskets **(see illustrations)**. Tighten the nuts to the torque wrench settings specified. Inspect the rubber mounting for signs of damage or deterioration, and renew as necessary.

16.2e . . . and on its right-hand side

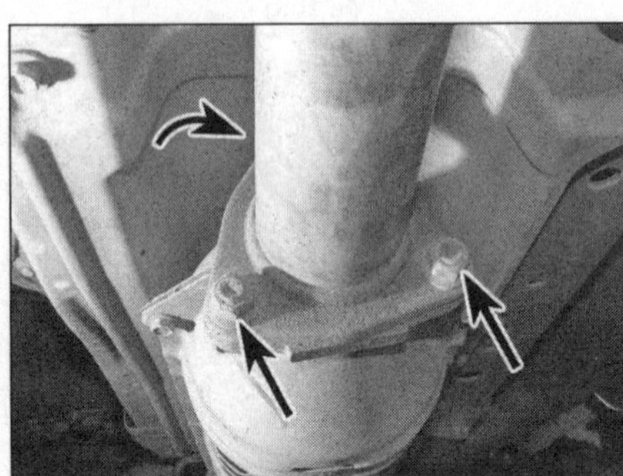

16.3a Catalytic converter-to-centre section nuts must be renewed whenever they are disturbed

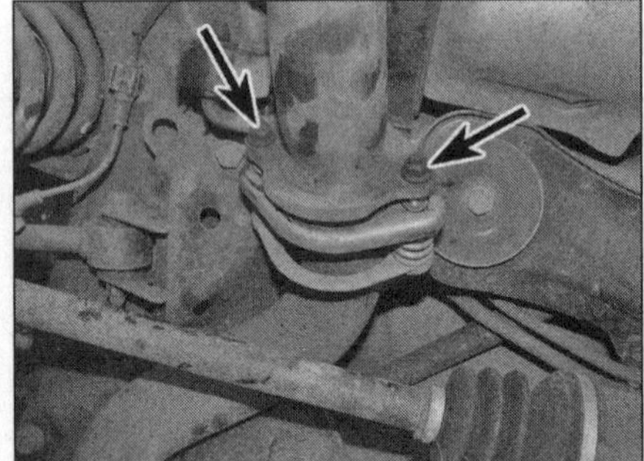

16.3b Do not overtighten exhaust rear silencer-to-centre section nuts – tighten evenly and let spring pressure make a leak-proof connection

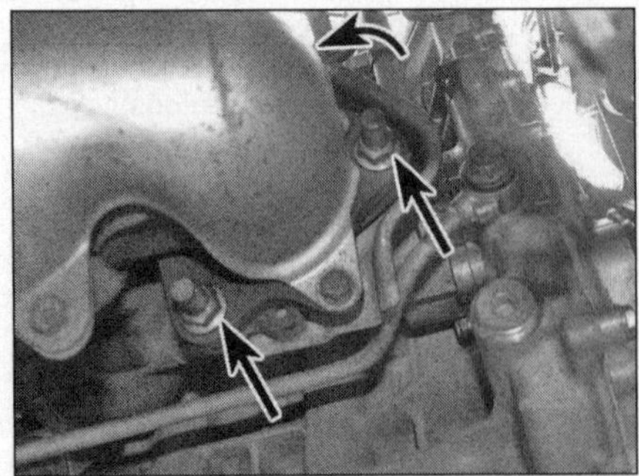

16.7 Unscrew warm-up catalytic converter mounting nuts to withdraw converter

16.8a Always remove old gasket – however sound it may seem . . .

16.8b . . . and fit new gasket to prevent exhaust leaks

Chapter 4 Part C: Emissions control systems

Contents

Degrees of difficulty

Easy, suitable for novice with little experience 	**Fairly easy,** suitable for beginner with some experience	**Fairly difficult,** suitable for competent DIY mechanic	**Difficult,** suitable for experienced DIY mechanic	**Very difficult,** suitable for expert DIY or professional

Specifications

Torque wrench settings

	Nm	lbf ft
Charcoal canister purge solenoid valve-to-throttle body screws	4	3
Exhaust Gas Recirculation (EGR) components:		
EGR control solenoid valve-to-intake manifold bolts	12	9
EGR cooler bypass control solenoid valve-to-intake manifold bolts	12	9
EGR valve, bypass valve, cooler and pipe mounting nuts and bolts	22	16
Intake manifold support bracket bolts	22	16
Oxygen sensors	44	32
Positive Crankcase Ventilation (PCV) valve assembly	44	32

1 General information

All models covered by this manual have various features built into their fuel and exhaust systems to help minimise harmful emissions.

The main features of these systems are as follows.

Crankcase emission control

Petrol-engined models

To reduce the emissions of unburned hydrocarbons from the crankcase into the atmosphere, a Positive Crankcase Ventilation (PCV) system is used which circulates fresh air from the air cleaner through the crankcase, where it mixes with blow-by gases and is then rerouted through a PCV valve to the intake manifold. The engine is sealed, and the blow-by gases and oil vapour are drawn from inside the crankcase, through an oil separator, into the intake tract, to be burned by the engine during normal combustion.

Under conditions of high manifold depression (idling, deceleration) the gases will be sucked positively out of the crankcase. Under conditions of low manifold depression (acceleration, full-throttle running) the gases are forced out of the crankcase by the (relatively) higher crankcase pressure; if the engine is worn, the raised crankcase pressure (due to increased blow-by) will cause some of the flow to return under all manifold conditions.

The main components of the system are the PCV valve and the hoses connecting the air cleaner with the engine and the valve with the intake manifold.

Diesel-engined models

To reduce the emission of unburned hydrocarbons from the crankcase into the atmosphere, the engine is sealed. Blow-by gases and oil vapour are drawn from inside the crankcase, through an oil separator and the cylinder head cover into the turbocharger. From the turbocharger, the gases enter the intake manifold to be burned by the engine during normal combustion. There are no restrictors in the system, since the minimal depression in the intake manifold remains constant during all engine operating conditions.

Evaporative emission control

Petrol-engined models only

The evaporative emission control (EVAP) system is used to minimise the escape of unburned hydrocarbons into the atmosphere. To do this, the fuel tank filler cap is sealed, and a charcoal canister is used to collect and store petrol vapours generated in the tank. When the engine is running, the vapours are cleared from the canister by an ECU-controlled electrically-operated purge valve, into the intake tract, to be burned by the engine during normal combustion. To enable this to happen, fresh air is drawn through the canister via a vent filter.

To ensure that the engine runs correctly when idling, the valve only opens when the coolant temperature is above 65°C and the engine is running under load; the valve then opens to allow the stored vapour to pass into the intake tract.

A two-way valve, mounted behind the fuel tank, regulates fuel vapour flow from the fuel tank to the charcoal canister, based on the pressure or vacuum caused by temperature changes. A liquid/vapour separator is fitted, mounted inside the fuel tank, to ensure that no liquid fuel is passed into the system.

Exhaust emission control

Petrol-engined models

To minimise the amount of pollutants which escape into the atmosphere, all models are fitted with a catalytic converter in the exhaust system. The system is of the closed-loop type, in which two heated oxygen sensors in the exhaust system provide the engine management ECU with constant feedback on the oxygen content of the exhaust gases.

This enables the ECU to adjust the mixture by altering injector opening time, thus providing the best possible conditions for the converter to operate.

The sensors upstream and downstream of the converter are known respectively as the 'primary' and 'secondary' sensors; the primary sensor is also referred to as the air/fuel ratio (A/F) sensor on 2005-on models. Both function in the same way, but the ECU monitors the signals from the secondary sensor and compares them with those of the primary sensor to determine whether the catalytic converter is working properly or not. The system functions in the following way:

The oxygen sensors (also known as lambda sensors) have built-in heating elements, activated by the ECU to quickly bring the sensor's tip to an efficient operating temperature. The sensor's tip is sensitive to oxygen, and sends the ECU a varying voltage depending on the amount of oxygen in the exhaust gases; if the intake air/fuel mixture is too rich, the exhaust gases are low in oxygen, so the sensor sends a voltage signal proportional to the oxygen detected, the voltage altering as the mixture weakens and the amount of oxygen in the exhaust gases rises. Peak conversion efficiency of all major pollutants occurs if the intake air/fuel mixture is maintained at the chemically-correct ratio for complete combustion of petrol – 14.7 parts (by weight) of air to 1 part of fuel (the stoichiometric ratio). The sensor output voltage alters in a large step at this point, the ECU using the signal change as a reference point, and correcting the intake air/fuel mixture accordingly, by altering the fuel injector opening time.

Diesel-engined models – catalytic converters

A close-coupled warm-up four-way oxidation catalytic converter and underfloor deNox catalytic converter contribute to low emissions performance. The warm-up catalytic converter is bolted directly to the turbocharger to ensure the quickest-possible warm-up time and maximum efficiency of its conversion of carbon monoxide and hydrocarbons to carbon dioxide and water. It also raises the temperature in the exhaust system to increase the efficiency of the underfloor catalytic converter in reducing the level of oxides of nitrogen (NOx) present in the exhaust gas.

Diesel-engined models – exhaust gas recirculation (EGR) system

The exhaust gas recirculation (EGR) system is designed to recirculate small quantities of exhaust gas into the intake tract, and therefore into the combustion process. This lowers peak combustion temperatures at the appropriate moments and so reduces the level of oxides of nitrogen (NOx) present in the exhaust gas which is released into the atmosphere. Exhaust gas recirculation under the control of the electrically-operated EGR valve increases intake air volume and reduces oxides of nitrogen and particulates. Water cooling of the exhaust gases prior to their recirculation helps to reduce the formation of oxides of nitrogen still further.

A passage in the exhaust manifold and through the cylinder head left-hand end allows exhaust gases to be fed to the EGR system components at the front of the cylinder head without using bulky external conduits and associated heat shielding. The volume of exhaust gas recirculated is controlled, via an electrically-operated solenoid valve, by the engine management ECU, which receives information on engine operating parameters from its various sensors.

The EGR system components are all located at the front of the engine under the intake manifold.

2 Catalytic converter – general information and precautions

On petrol-engined models, a three-way catalytic converter is incorporated into the front section of the exhaust pipe, whilst on diesel-engined models, a close-coupled warm-up four-way oxidation catalytic converter is bolted directly to the turbocharger and a NOx-reducing catalytic converter is fitted between the system's front and centre sections. Refer to Part A or B of this Chapter for removal procedures.

The catalytic converter is a reliable and simple device, which needs no maintenance in itself, but there are some facts of which an owner should be aware if the converter is to function properly for its full service life.

Petrol-engined models

a) DO NOT use leaded petrol – the lead will coat the precious metals, reducing their converting efficiency, and will eventually destroy the converter.
b) Always keep the ignition and fuel systems well-maintained in accordance with the manufacturer's schedule (see Chapter 1A).
c) If the engine develops a misfire, do not drive the vehicle at all (or at least as little as possible) until the fault is cured.

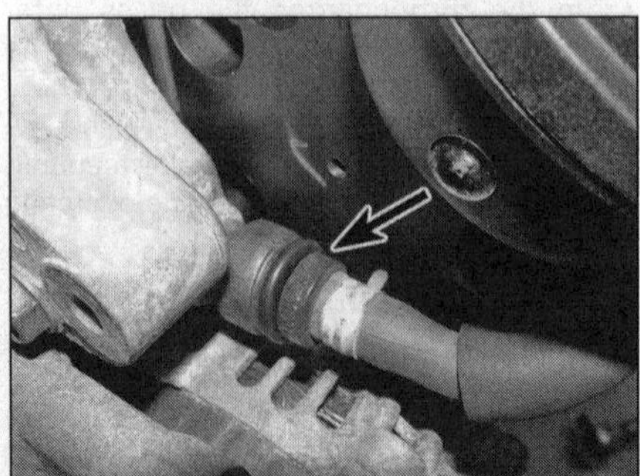

3.2 Positive Crankcase Ventilation (PCV) valve

d) DO NOT push – or tow-start the vehicle – this will soak the catalytic converter in unburned fuel, causing it to overheat when the engine does start.
e) DO NOT switch off the ignition at high engine speeds, ie, do not blip the throttle immediately before switching off.
f) DO NOT use fuel or engine oil additives – these may contain substances harmful to the catalytic converter.
g) DO NOT continue to use the vehicle if the engine burns oil to the extent of leaving a visible trail of blue smoke.
h) Remember that the catalytic converter operates at very high temperatures. DO NOT, therefore, park the vehicle in dry undergrowth, over long grass or piles of dead leaves, after a long run.
i) Remember that the catalytic converter is FRAGILE. Do not strike it with tools during servicing work.
j) In some cases, a sulphurous smell (like that of rotten eggs) may be noticed from the exhaust. This is common to many catalytic converter-equipped vehicles. Once the vehicle has covered a few thousand miles, the problem should disappear – in the meantime, try changing the brand of petrol used.
k) The catalytic converter used on a well-maintained and well-driven vehicle should last for between 50 000 and 100 000 miles. If the converter is no longer effective, it must be renewed.

Diesel-engined models

Refer to the information given in parts f, g, h, i, and k of the petrol engine information given above.

3 Crankcase emission control system – checking and component renewal

Checking

1 The components of this system require no attention other than to check that the hoses are clear and undamaged. To check the valve on petrol-engined models, pinch its hose lightly while the engine is idling; the valve should be heard to click shut. If not, check the valve's sealing grommet in the water pump housing, looking for signs of cracking, leaks or other damage. If the grommet seems sound, renew the valve.

Positive Crankcase Ventilation (PCV) valve

2 The valve is located on the front of the water pump housing, next to the intake manifold **(see illustration)**.

3 To remove the valve, disconnect its hose and unscrew it.

4 Refitting is the reverse of removal; tighten the valve to the specified torque wrench setting.

4.8a Unscrew charcoal canister cover mounting bolts at front and rear . . .

4 Evaporative emission control (EVAP) system – checking and component renewal

Checking

1 Poor idle, stalling and poor driveability can be caused by an inoperative canister vacuum valve, a damaged canister, split or cracked hoses, or hoses connected to the wrong fittings. Check the fuel filler cap for a damaged or deformed gasket.

2 Fuel loss or fuel odour can be caused by liquid fuel leaking from fuel lines, a cracked or damaged canister, an inoperative canister vacuum valve, and disconnected, misrouted, kinked or damaged vapour or control hoses.

3 Inspect each hose attached to the canister for kinks, leaks and cracks along its entire length. Repair or renew as necessary.

4 Inspect the canister. If it is cracked or damaged, renew it. Look for fuel leaking from the bottom of the canister. If fuel is leaking, renew the canister, and check the hoses and hose routing.

Component renewal

Charcoal canister

5 The canister is located underneath the vehicle, at the rear of the fuel tank on the left-hand side.

6 Chock the front wheels, select first or reverse gear (or P), then jack up the rear of the vehicle, and support it securely on axle stands (see *Jacking and vehicle support*).

7 Open the fuel filler cap to release any excess pressure in the fuel tank.

8 Unbolt the charcoal canister cover **(see illustrations)**.

9 Disconnect the two vapour hoses and the larger-diameter air vent hose from the canister **(see illustration)**. Label all hoses before disconnecting, to ensure correct refitting.

10 Unscrew the two mounting bolts and lower the canister from the underbody **(see illustration)**.

11 Refitting is a reversal of removal.

Charcoal canister purge solenoid valve

12 The canister purge valve is mounted in the engine compartment, on top of the throttle body.

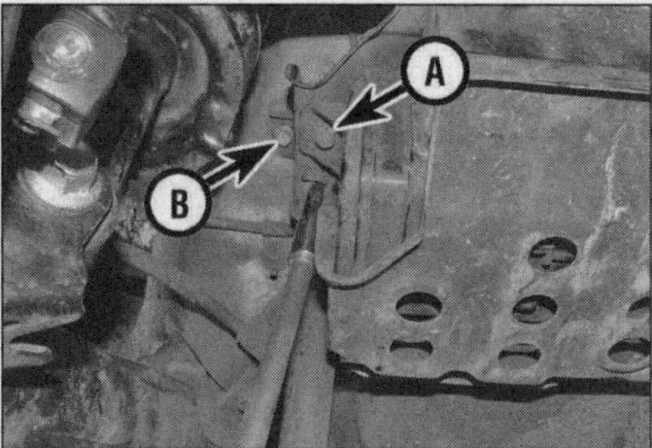

4.8b . . . and on left-hand side – note also canister mounting bolt (A) and canister mounting bracket bolt (B) . . .

13 Disconnect the hose and wiring plug from the valve **(see illustration)**.

14 Undo the mounting screws and withdraw the valve from the throttle body. Recover and discard the sealing O-ring – this must be renewed whenever the valve is disturbed.

15 Refitting is a reversal of removal. Fit a new O-ring, and tighten the mounting screws to the specified torque setting.

Charcoal canister two-way valve

16 The two-way is located underneath the vehicle, bolted to the canister mounting bracket, just above the canister itself.

17 Remove the charcoal canister, as described above.

18 Unbolt the canister mounting bracket from the underbody **(see illustration)**.

19 Disconnect the two vapour hoses from the valve **(see illustration)**. Label all hoses before disconnecting, to ensure correct refitting.

4.10 Unscrew two mounting bolts to remove charcoal canister

4.18 Unscrew mounting bolts to withdraw charcoal canister mounting bracket . . .

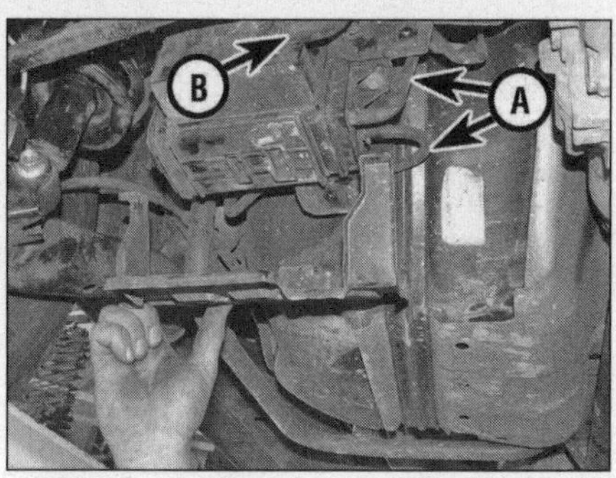

4.9 . . . remove cover and disconnect vapour hoses (A) and air vent hose (B)

20 Unscrew the single mounting bolt and withdraw the valve from the mounting bracket.

21 Refitting is a reversal of removal.

5 Exhaust emission control systems – checking and component renewal

1 Checking of the system as a whole entails a close visual inspection of all hoses, pipes and connections for condition and security. Apart from this, any known or suspected faults should be attended to by a Honda dealer or specialist.

Oxygen (lambda) sensors

Note: *The sensor is delicate, and will not work if it is dropped or knocked, if its power supply is disrupted, or if any cleaning materials are used on it.*

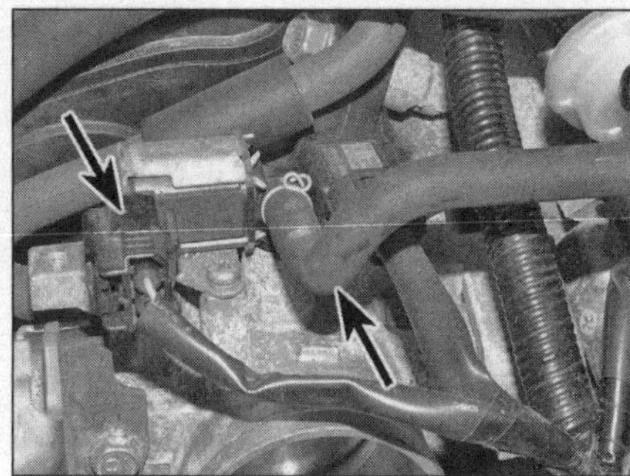

4.13 Disconnect canister purge solenoid valve wiring and hose

4.19 . . . disconnect two-way valve's vapour hoses and unscrew mounting bolt

5.4a Primary oxygen sensor (air/fuel ratio sensor) is at front of catalytic converter . . .

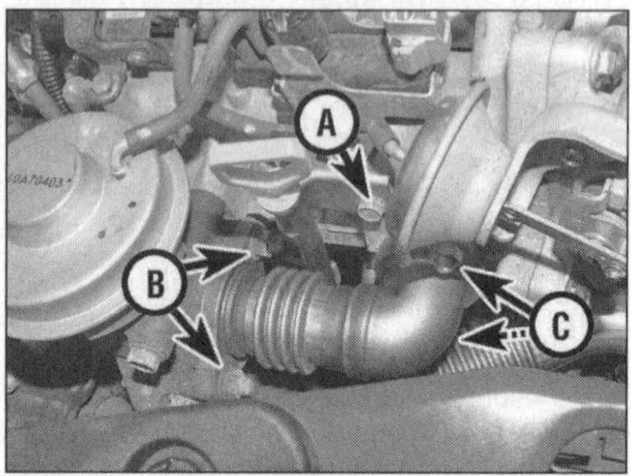

5.12 Unscrew dipstick tube mounting bolt (A) and shorter EGR pipe nuts (B) and (C)

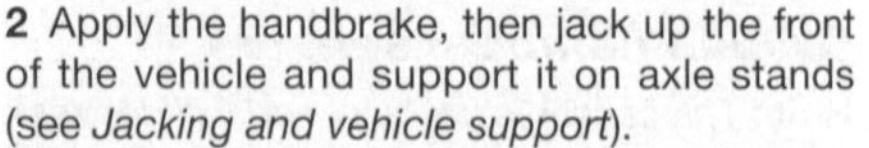

2 Apply the handbrake, then jack up the front of the vehicle and support it on axle stands (see *Jacking and vehicle support*).

3 Disconnect the sensor wiring connector, and release the wiring from any clips or ties.

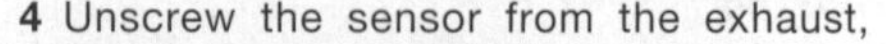

4 Unscrew the sensor from the exhaust,

5.13c . . . then disconnect EGR valve vacuum hose and withdraw valve and short pipe together

5.14b . . . until intake manifold support bracket is unbolted from manifold and from cylinder block

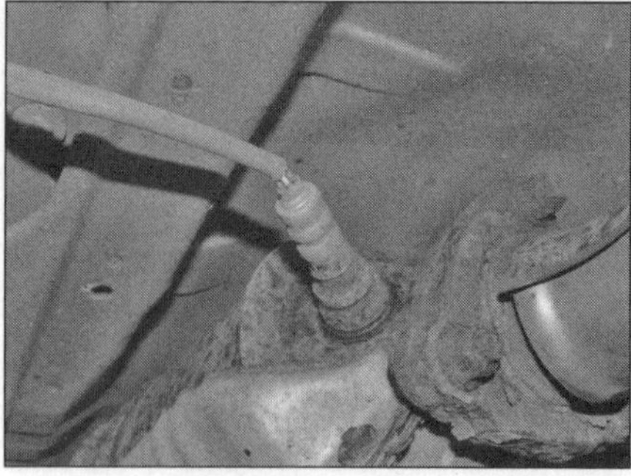

5.4b . . . secondary oxygen sensor is at rear

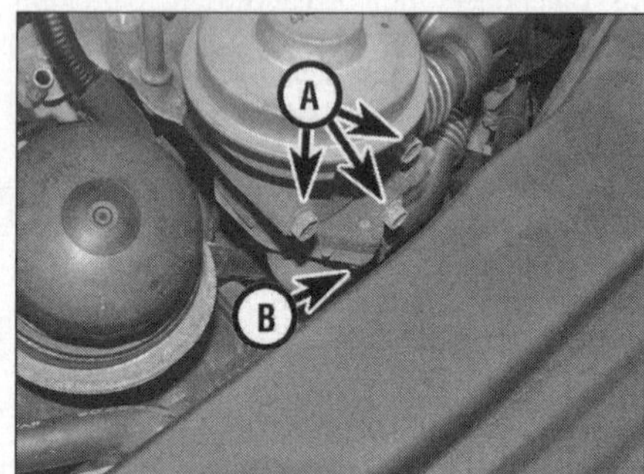

5.13a Unscrew bolts (A) securing EGR valve to cylinder head and nuts (B) . . .

and collect the sealing washer (if fitted) **(see illustrations)**.

5 On refitting, clean the sealing washer (where fitted) and renew it if it is damaged or worn. Apply a smear of anti-seize compound to the sensor's threads, then refit the sensor,

5.14a Long EGR pipe can be disconnected but cannot be removed . . .

5.14c Showing removal of long EGR pipe – here with EGR valve and short EGR pipe attached

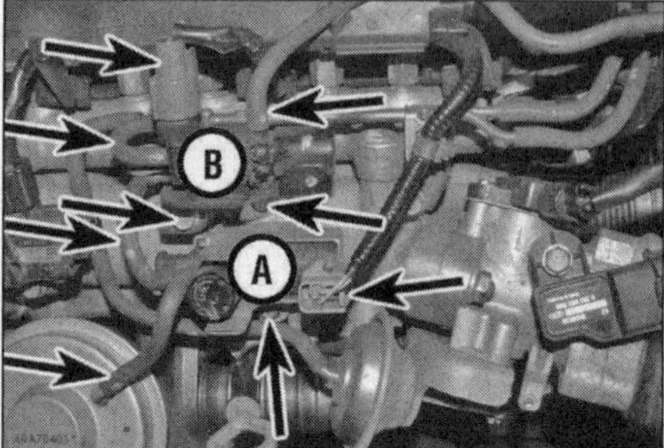

5.8 Mounting bolts, wiring connectors and vacuum hoses of control solenoid valve (A), cooler bypass control solenoid valve (B)

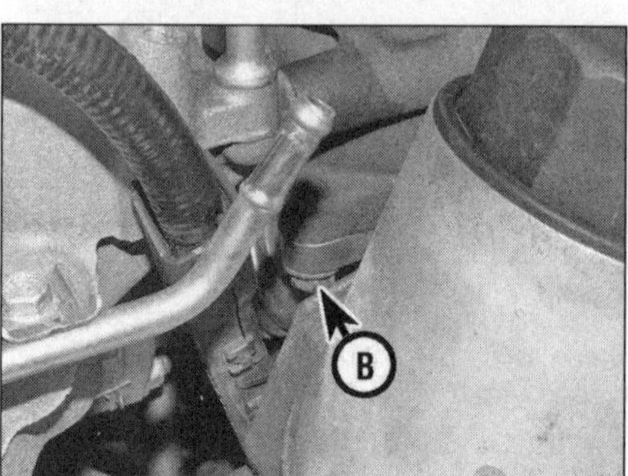

5.13b . . . securing EGR valve to long EGR pipe . . .

tightening it to the specified torque. Reconnect the wiring and secure with the clips or ties provided.

Catalytic converter(s)

6 Refer to Part A or B of this Chapter for renewal procedures and additional information.

Exhaust Gas Recirculation

Control solenoid valve

7 Unscrew the four retaining nuts and remove the acoustic engine cover.

8 Disconnect the valve's electrical connector and two vacuum hoses **(see illustration)**. Unscrew the mounting bolts, and withdraw the valve from the intake manifold.

9 Refitting is the reverse of the removal procedure.

Cooler and valve

10 Drain the cooling system (see Chapter 1B).

11 Unscrew the four retaining nuts and remove the acoustic engine cover.

12 Unscrew the dipstick tube mounting bolt and the nuts securing the short EGR pipe to the EGR valve and intake manifold **(see illustration)**.

13 Unscrew the nuts securing the EGR valve to the long EGR pipe and the three bolts securing the EGR valve to the cylinder head. Disconnect its vacuum hose and withdraw the EGR valve and short EGR pipe together **(see illustrations)**. Recover all EGR component gaskets and discard them – new ones must be fitted on reassembly.

14 Unbolt the intake manifold support bracket from the manifold and cylinder block. Unscrew the bolts and nuts and withdraw

5.15 Disconnect coolant bypass hose from EGR cooler

5.16 Unscrew bolts (A) securing EGR cooler to EGR cooler bypass valve. Note cooler mounting bolt (B)

5.17a Unscrew EGR cooler left-hand mounting bolt . . .

the long EGR pipe from the EGR cooler and EGR cooler bypass valve **(see illustrations)**. Recover and discard the gaskets – new ones must be fitted on reassembly.

15 Disconnect the coolant hose from the EGR cooler **(see illustration)**.

16 Unscrew the bolts securing the EGR cooler to the EGR cooler bypass valve and recover the gasket **(see illustration)**.

17 Unscrew the two bolts securing the mounting brackets at each end of the EGR cooler and remove the EGR cooler, pulling it directly to the front – a coolant stub is fitted deeply into a passage in the cylinder block; recover the O-ring sealing the stub union **(see illustrations)**.

18 Refitting is a reversal of removal; renew the sealing O-ring and all gaskets and tighten all fasteners to the torque wrench settings specified **(see illustrations)**. On completion, refill the cooling system, start the engine and check thoroughly for coolant and exhaust leaks before refitting the acoustic engine cover.

Cooler bypass control solenoid valve

19 Unscrew the four retaining nuts and remove the acoustic engine cover.

20 Disconnect the valve's electrical connector and two vacuum hoses **(see illustration 5.8)**. Unscrew the mounting bolt, and withdraw the valve from the intake manifold.

21 Refitting is the reverse of the removal procedure.

Cooler bypass valve

22 Unscrew the four retaining nuts and remove the acoustic engine cover.

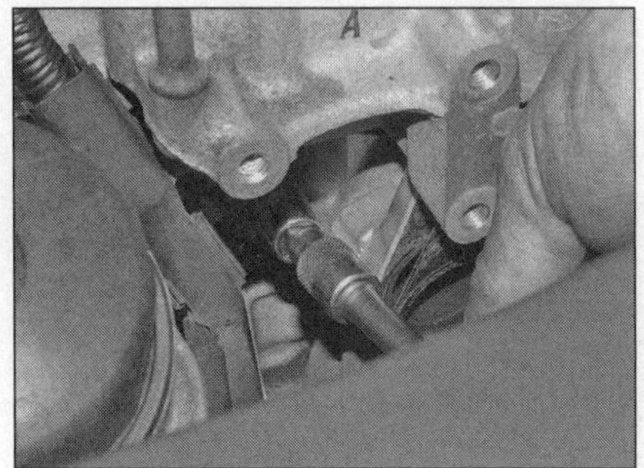
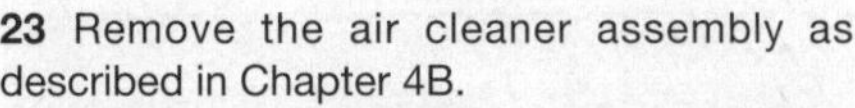
5.17b . . . right-hand mounting bolt . . .

5.17c . . . to withdraw EGR cooler. Note coolant stub projecting into cylinder block

23 Remove the air cleaner assembly as described in Chapter 4B.

24 Remove the battery and battery tray (see Chapter 5A).

25 Unscrew the bolts securing the long EGR pipe and the EGR cooler to the EGR cooler bypass valve **(see illustrations 5.25 and 5.16)**.

26 Unscrew the two nuts and one bolt and withdraw the EGR cooler bypass valve from the cylinder head **(see illustrations)**.

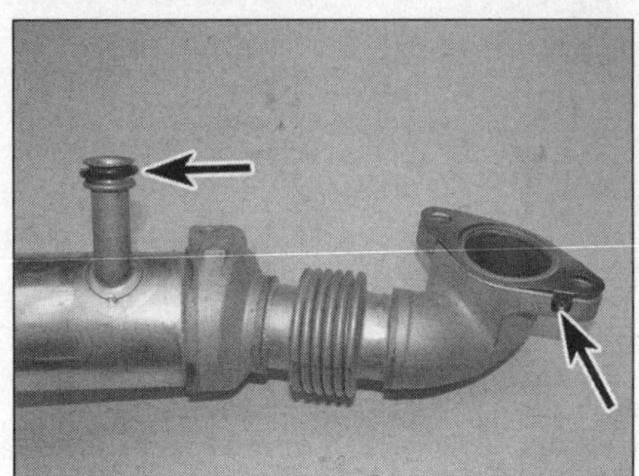
5.18a Renew sealing O-ring and gasket . . .

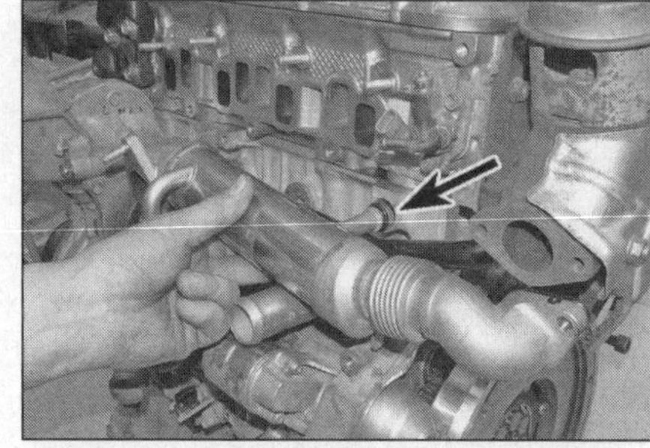
5.18b . . . and refit EGR cooler so that coolant stub enters passage in cylinder block . . .

5.18c . . . reconnect coolant hose to EGR cooler. Note right-hand mounting bolt

5.18d Fit new gaskets when refitting long EGR pipe . . .

5.18e . . . then refit intake manifold support bracket

5.25 Unscrew bolts securing long EGR pipe to EGR cooler bypass valve

5.26a Unscrew EGR cooler bypass valve mounting nuts and bolt . . .

5.26b . . . and slide valve off studs

5.27 Renew gasket when refitting EGR cooler bypass valve

5.29a Fit new gaskets to EGR cooler and intake manifold flanges . . .

5.29b . . . fit new gasket to EGR valve and refit short EGR pipe . . .

5.29c . . . then fit long EGR pipe, with new gasket . . .

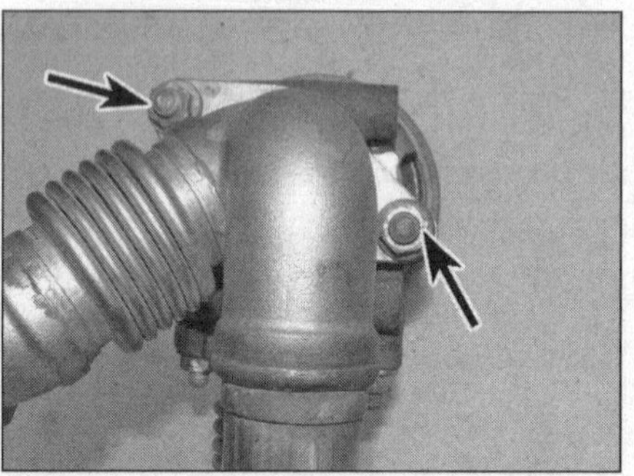
5.29d . . . and tighten flange nuts securely

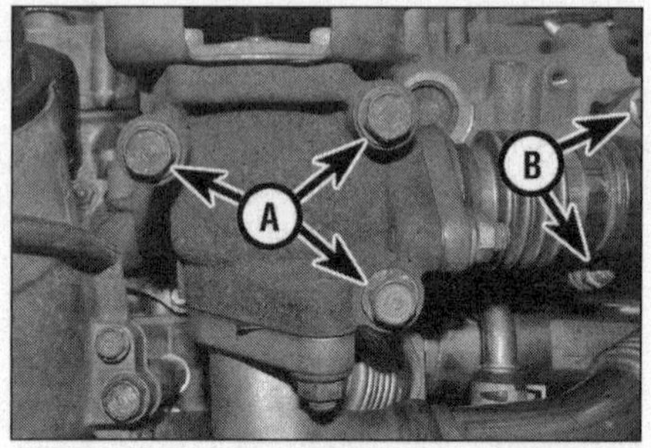

5.29e Tighten EGR valve-to-cylinder head bolts (A), short EGR pipe-to-intake manifold nuts (B) . . .

5.29f . . . and long EGR pipe-to-EGR cooler nuts

27 Refitting is a reversal of removal; renew all gaskets and tighten all fasteners to the torque wrench settings specified **(see illustration)**.

Valve

28 Proceed as described in paragraphs 11 to 13 above.

29 Refitting is a reversal of removal; renew all gaskets and tighten all fasteners to the torque wrench settings specified **(see illustrations)**.

Chapter 5 Part A: Starting and charging systems

Contents

Degrees of difficulty

Easy, suitable for novice with little experience	**Fairly easy,** suitable for beginner with some experience	**Fairly difficult,** suitable for competent DIY mechanic	**Difficult,** suitable for experienced DIY mechanic	**Very difficult,** suitable for expert DIY or professional

Specifications

Battery	**Petrol-engined models**	**Diesel-engined models**
BCI size code	057 (049 alternative)	096 (100 alternative)
Capacity ratings:		
@ 5-hour rate	36 Ah	N/Av.
@ 20-hour rate	45 Ah	74 Ah
Cold Cranking Amps (CCA) rating	330 (EN), 450 (SAE), 210 (DIN)	680 (EN)

Alternator	**Petrol-engined models**	**Diesel-engined models**
Manufacturer	Mitsubishi A2TB7591ZE	Mitsubishi
Output @ 13.5 V and normal engine temperature	90 A	105 A
Coil (rotor) resistance @ 20°C	1.84 to 2.10 ohms	2.5 ohms
Slip ring diameter:		
Standard	22.7 mm	14.4 mm
Minimum	21.7 mm	14 mm
Brush length:		
Standard	19 mm	10.5 mm
Minimum	5 mm	1.5 mm
Brush spring tension	3.3 to 4.1 N	3.3 to 4.1 N

Starter motor	**Petrol-engined models**	**Diesel-engined models**
Manufacturer	Denso	Mitsubishi M002T85672
Output	1.1 kW	2.0 kW
Commutator mica depth:		
Standard	0.5 to 0.8 mm	0.5 mm
Minimum	0.2 mm	0.2 mm
Commutator runout:		
Standard	0.02 mm maximum	0.05 mm maximum
Service limit	0.05 mm	0.10 mm
Commutator diameter:		
Standard	28 mm	31.9 to 32.1 mm
Minimum	27 mm	31.4 mm
Brush length:		
Standard	14 to 14.5 mm	18 mm
Minimum	9 mm	11 mm
Brush spring tension – Denso motors only	13.7 to 17.7 N	

Torque wrench settings

	Nm	lbf ft
Alternator mounting bolts – all models	22	16
Alternator pulley nut:		
Petrol-engined models	111	82
Diesel-engined models	110	81
Alternator wiring terminal nut:		
Petrol-engined models	8	6
Diesel-engined models	12	9
Battery hold-down clamp bolt	12	9
Battery tray and tray mounting bracket mounting bolts:		
6 mm	10	7
8 mm	22	16
Oil pressure warning light switch	18	13
Positive Crankcase Ventilation (PCV) valve	44	32
Starter motor mounting bolts:		
Upper (10 mm) mounting bolt	44	32
Lower (12 mm) mounting bolt	64	47
Starter motor wiring terminal nut:		
Petrol-engined models	9	7
Diesel-engined models	11	8

1 General information and precautions

General information

Because of their engine-related functions the charging and starting systems are covered separately from the body electrical devices such as the lights, instruments, etc, which are covered in Chapter 12. On petrol-engined models, refer to Part B of this Chapter for information on the ignition system, while for diesel-engined models refer to Part C for information on the preheating (glow plug) system.

The electrical system is of the 12 volt negative-earth type.

The battery may be of the low maintenance or maintenance-free (sealed for life) type and is charged by the alternator, which is belt-driven from the crankshaft pulley.

Charging system

The charging system includes the alternator, an internal voltage regulator, a charge indicator light, the battery, a fusible link and the wiring between all the components. The charging system supplies electrical power for the ignition system, the lights, the radio, etc. The alternator is driven by a drivebelt from the crankshaft pulley.

The alternator control system within the engine management system's Electronic Control Unit (ECU) controls the voltage generated at the alternator in accordance with driving conditions. Depending upon electric load, vehicle speed, engine coolant temperature, accessories (air conditioning system, radio, cruise control, etc) and the intake air temperature, the system will adjust the amount of voltage generated, creating less load on the engine.

The purpose of the voltage regulator is to limit the alternator's voltage to a preset value. This prevents power surges, circuit overloads, etc, during peak voltage output. An Electrical Load Detector (ELD) built into the engine compartment main fuse/relay box assists in monitoring the system and protecting components from excessive loads.

The charging system doesn't ordinarily require periodic maintenance. However, the auxiliary drivebelt, battery and wires and connections should be inspected at the intervals outlined in Chapter 1A or 1B.

The instrument panel warning light should come on when the ignition key is turned to the second position, but it should go off immediately after the engine is started. If it is slow to go out, or remains on, there is a malfunction in the charging system (see Section 4).

Starting system

The starting system consists of the battery, the starter motor, the starter solenoid and the wires connecting them.

The solenoid/starter motor assembly is installed at the front of the engine, next to the transmission bellhousing. The starter motor is of the pre-engaged type incorporating an integral solenoid. On starting, the solenoid moves the drive pinion into engagement with the flywheel ring gear before the starter motor is energised. Once the engine has started, a one-way clutch prevents the motor armature being driven by the engine until the pinion disengages from the flywheel/driveplate.

The starter on models equipped with automatic transmissions can only be operated when the selector lever is in P or N. On some models with manual gearboxes, the starter will operate only when the clutch pedal is fully depressed.

Precautions

Further details of the various systems are given in the relevant Sections of this Chapter. While some repair procedures are given, the usual course of action is to renew the component concerned.

It is necessary to take extra care when working on the electrical system to avoid damage to semi-conductor devices (diodes and transistors), and to avoid the risk of personal injury. In addition to the precautions given in *Safety first!* at the beginning of this manual, observe the following when working on the system:

a) *Be extremely careful when servicing engine electrical components. They are easily damaged if checked, connected or handled improperly.*
b) *Never leave the ignition switched on for long periods of time when the engine is not running.*
c) *Don't disconnect the battery leads while the engine is running.*
d) *Maintain correct polarity when connecting a battery lead from another vehicle during jump starting – see the Jump starting Section at the front of this manual.*
e) *Always disconnect the negative lead first, and reconnect it last, or the battery may be shorted by the tool being used to slacken the lead clamps.*

It's also a good idea to review the safety-related information regarding the engine electrical systems shown in the *Safety first!* section at the front of this manual, before beginning any operation included in this Chapter.

2 Battery – testing and charging

Testing

Standard and low maintenance battery

1 If the vehicle covers a small annual mileage, it is worthwhile checking the specific gravity of the electrolyte every three months to determine the state of charge of the battery. Use a hydrometer to make the check and compare the results with the following table.

Note that the specific gravity readings assume an electrolyte temperature of 15°C; for every 10°C below 15°C subtract 0.007. For every 10°C above 15°C add 0.007.

	Ambient temperature above 25°C	below 25°C
Fully-charged	1.210 to 1.230	1.270 to 1.290
70% charged	1.170 to 1.190	1.230 to 1.250
Discharged	1.050 to 1.070	1.110 to 1.130

2 If the battery condition is suspect, first check the specific gravity of electrolyte in each cell. A variation of 0.040 or more between any cells indicates loss of electrolyte or deterioration of the internal plates.

3 If the specific gravity variation is 0.040 or more, the battery should be renewed. If the cell variation is satisfactory but the battery is discharged, it should be charged as described later in this Section.

Maintenance-free battery

4 In cases where a 'sealed for life' maintenance-free battery is fitted, topping-up and testing of the electrolyte in each cell is not possible. The condition of the battery can therefore only be tested using a battery condition indicator or a voltmeter.

5 Models may be fitted with a 'Delco' type maintenance-free battery, with a built-in charge condition indicator. The indicator is located in the top of the battery casing, and indicates the condition of the battery from its colour. If the indicator shows green, then the battery is in a good state of charge. If the indicator turns darker, eventually to black, then the battery requires charging, as described later in this Section. If the indicator shows clear/yellow, then the electrolyte level in the battery is too low to allow further use, and the battery should be renewed. **Do not** attempt to charge, load or jump start a battery when the indicator shows clear/yellow.

All battery types

6 If testing the battery using a voltmeter, connect the voltmeter across the battery terminals. The test is only accurate if the battery has not been subjected to any kind of charge for the previous six hours. If this is not the case, switch on the headlights for 30 seconds, then wait four to five minutes before testing the battery after switching off the headlights. All other electrical circuits must be switched off, so check that the doors and tailgate are fully shut when making the test.

7 If the voltage reading is less than 12.2 volts, then the battery is discharged, whilst a reading of 12.2 to 12.4 volts indicates a partially-discharged condition.

8 If the battery is to be charged, remove it from the vehicle (Section 4) and charge it as described later in this Section.

Charging

Note: *The following is intended as a guide only. Always refer to the manufacturer's recommendations (often printed on a label attached to the battery) before charging a battery.*

3.2 Disconnecting battery negative (earth) terminal

3.3a Lift insulating cover (petrol models) . . .

3.3b Lift insulating cover (diesel models) . . .

3.3c . . . to disconnect battery positive terminal

Standard and low maintenance battery

9 Charge the battery at a rate of 3.5 to 4 amps and continue to charge the battery at this rate until no further rise in specific gravity is noted over a four hour period.

10 Alternatively, a trickle charger charging at the rate of 1.5 amps can safely be used overnight.

11 Specially rapid 'boost' charges which are claimed to restore the power of the battery in 1 to 2 hours are not recommended, as they can cause serious damage to the battery plates through overheating.

12 While charging the battery, note that the temperature of the electrolyte should never exceed 38°C.

Maintenance-free battery

13 This battery type takes considerably longer to fully recharge than the standard type, the time taken being dependent on the extent of discharge, but it can take anything up to three days.

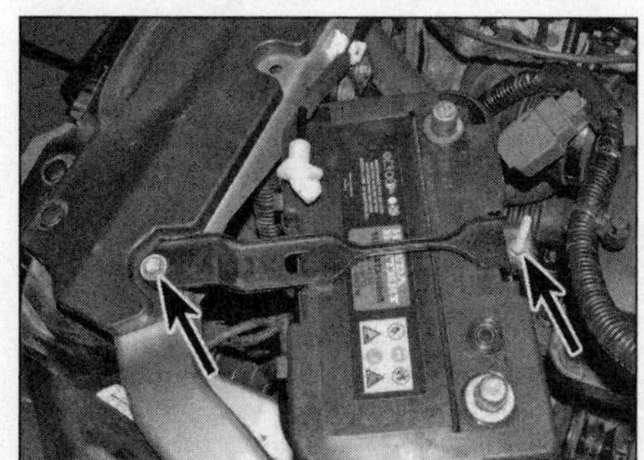

3.4a Battery fasteners (petrol models)

14 If the battery is to be charged from a fully-discharged state (condition reading less than 12.2 volts), have it recharged by your Honda dealer or local automotive electrician, as constant supervision during charging is necessary.

3 Battery and battery tray – removal and refitting

Battery

Note: *Refer to Section 1 of this Chapter before starting work.*

Removal

1 The battery is located on the left-hand side of the engine compartment.

2 Slacken the clamp nut and disconnect the clamp from the battery negative (earth) terminal **(see illustration)**.

3 Lift the insulating cover and disconnect the positive terminal lead in the same way **(see illustrations)**.

4 Unscrew the bolt and slacken the nut as necessary to unhook the battery hold-down clamp from the tray, then remove the battery clamp and the plastic sleeve (where fitted). Lift the battery out of the engine compartment **(see illustrations)**.

3.4b Battery fasteners (diesel models)

3.4c Unscrew battery hold-down clamp bolt, and slacken nut . . .

3.4d . . . to unhook hold-down clamp from tray . . .

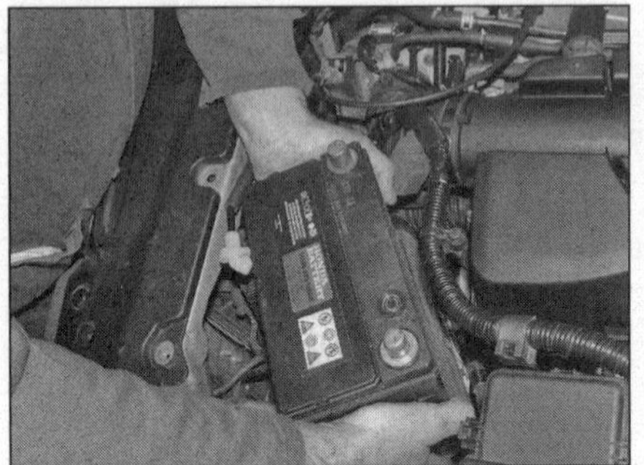
3.4e Removing the battery

3.6a Removing the plastic tray (petrol models)

Refitting

5 Refitting is a reversal of removal, but smear petroleum jelly on the terminals after reconnecting the leads, and always reconnect the positive lead first, and the negative lead last.

Battery tray

Removal

6 With the battery removed, lift out the plastic tray **(see illustrations)**.

7 On diesel-engined models, remove the air cleaner assembly and intake air duct/ resonator as described in Chapter 4B **(see illustrations)**. This is not absolutely necessary on petrol-engined models, but if the additional space is needed for other work, proceed as described in Chapter 4A.

8 On all models, release the wiring harnesses from the various retaining clips on the battery tray and the battery tray mounting bracket **(see illustration)**.

9 On petrol-engined models, unscrew the three upper retaining bolts, then slacken the two lower retaining bolts, and remove the battery tray **(see illustrations)**.

10 On diesel-engined models, unscrew the four retaining bolts and remove the battery tray **(see illustration)**.

11 On diesel-engined models, unscrew the two upper retaining bolts, then slacken the

3.6b When removing the plastic tray on diesel models . . .

3.6c . . . note pegs locating it on battery tray

3.7a On diesel models, air cleaner assembly is bolted to battery tray . . .

3.7b . . . and intake air duct/resonator is bolted to tray mounting bracket

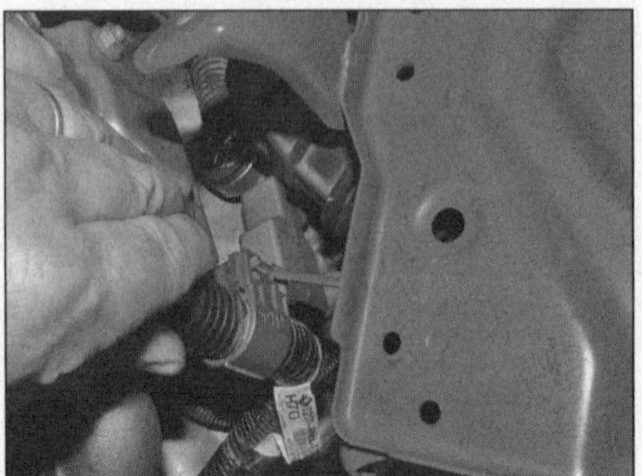
3.8 Unclip any wiring harnesses from battery tray

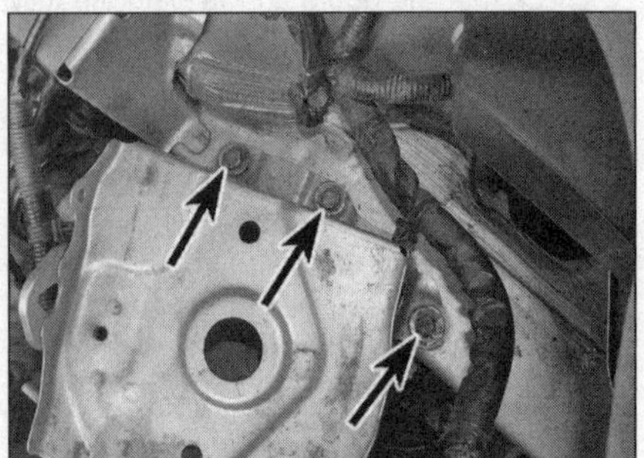
3.9a On petrol models, unscrew three bolts on top . . .

3.9b . . . then slacken two underneath . . .

3.9c . . . and lift out battery tray

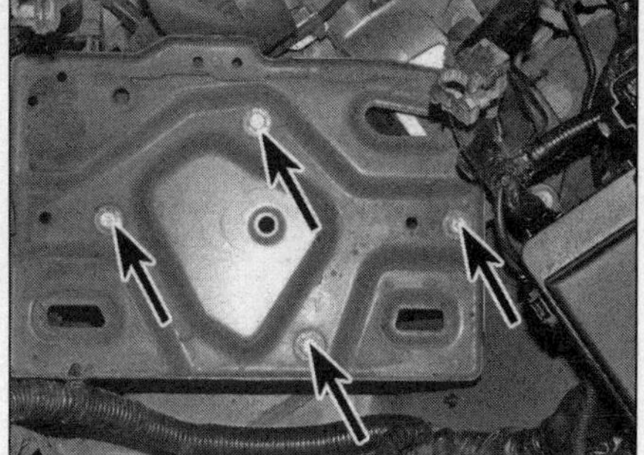

3.10 On diesel models, unscrew four bolts and remove battery tray . . .

two lower retaining bolts, and unbolt the clutch slave cylinder hydraulic line support bracket. Remove the battery tray mounting bracket **(see illustrations)**.

Refitting

12 Refitting is a reversal of removal. Ensure that the wiring harnesses are routed correctly and clipped back into the various locations on the battery tray and the battery tray mounting bracket.

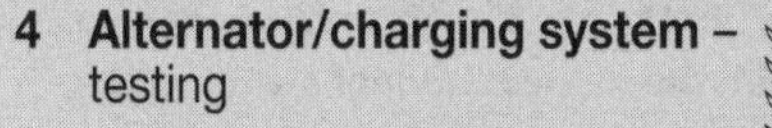

4 Alternator/charging system – testing

Note: *Refer to Section 1 of this Chapter before starting work.*

1 If the ignition warning light fails to illuminate when the ignition is switched on, first check the alternator wiring connections for security. If satisfactory, check that the warning light bulb has not blown, and that the bulbholder is secure in its location in the instrument panel. If the light still fails to illuminate, check the continuity of the warning light feed wire from the alternator to the bulbholder. If all is satisfactory, the alternator is at fault and should be renewed or taken to an auto-electrician for testing and repair.

2 If the ignition warning light illuminates when the engine is running, stop the engine and check that the drivebelt is correctly tensioned (see Chapter 1A or 1B) and that the alternator connections are secure. If all is so far satisfactory, have the alternator checked by an auto-electrician for testing and repair.

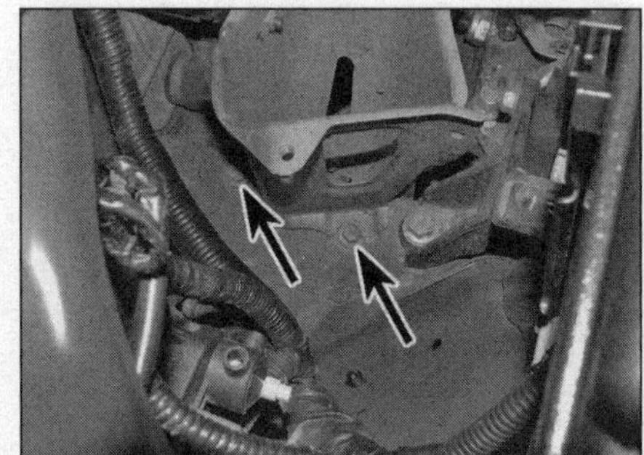

3.11a . . . unscrew two bolts on top . . .

3 If the alternator output is suspect even though the warning light functions correctly, the regulated voltage may be checked as follows.

4 Connect a voltmeter across the battery terminals and start the engine.

5 Increase the engine speed until the voltmeter reading remains steady; the reading should be approximately 12 to 13 volts, and no more than 14 volts.

6 Switch on as many electrical accessories (eg, the headlights, heated rear window and heater blower) as possible, and check that the alternator maintains the regulated voltage at around 13 to 14 volts.

7 If the regulated voltage is not as stated, the fault may be due to worn brushes, weak brush springs, a faulty voltage regulator, a faulty diode, a severed phase winding or worn or damaged slip-rings. The alternator should be renewed or taken to an auto-electrician for testing and repair.

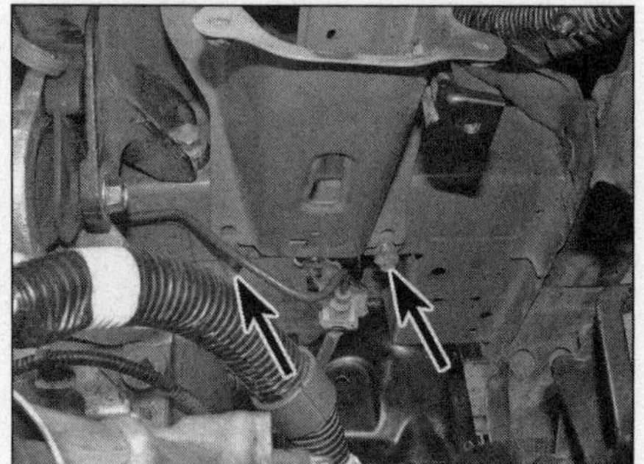

3.11b . . . and slacken two underneath to lift out tray mounting bracket

5 Alternator – removal and refitting

Petrol-engined models

Removal

1 Disconnect the battery negative and positive leads, and position the leads away from the battery (see *Disconnecting the battery*). This is essential before disconnecting the alternator wiring.

2 Unscrew the battery hold-down clamp bolt, then release its retaining clips and remove the radiator grille top cover **(see illustrations)**.

3 Unbolt and remove the radiator top mounting brackets **(see illustrations)**.

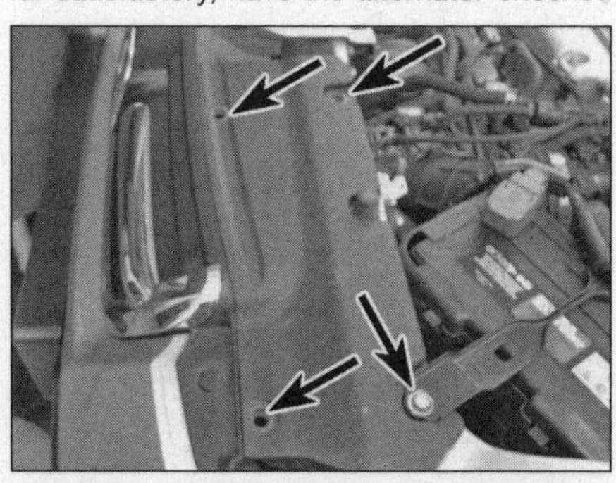

5.2a Unscrew battery hold-down clamp bolt, then release its retaining clips . . .

5.2b . . . to remove the radiator grille top cover

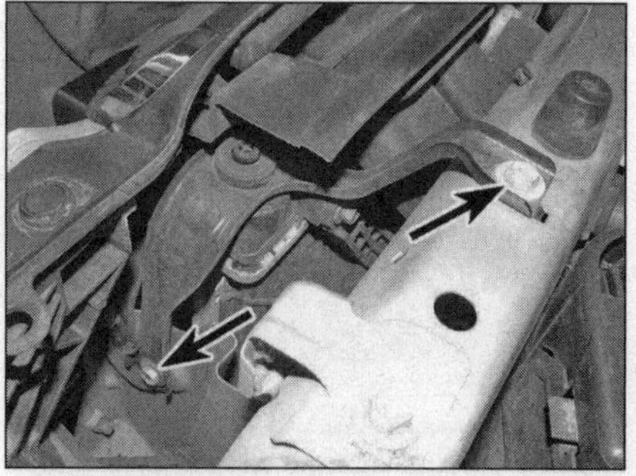

5.3a Unbolt and remove radiator top mounting brackets from left-hand . . .

5.3b . . . and right-hand sides

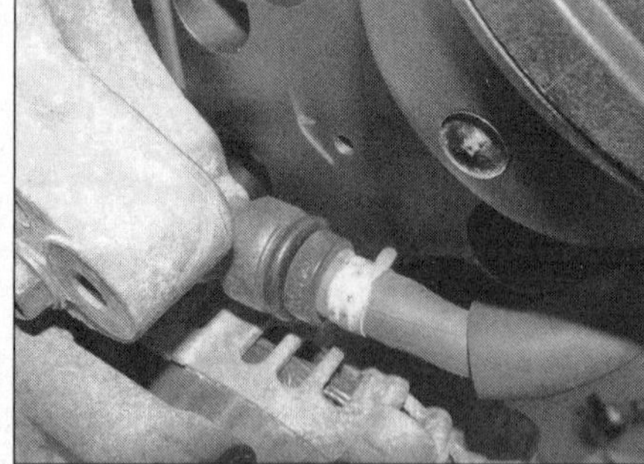

5.5 Disconnect PCV valve hose and unscrew valve from water pump housing

5.6 Unscrew three alternator mounting bolts

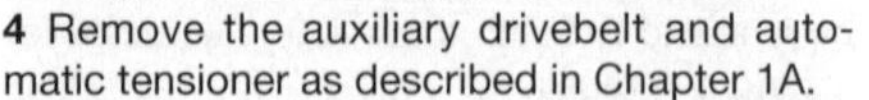

5.7 Pull back rubber cover and unscrew battery lead securing nut, unclip harness then disconnect (green) wiring plug

5.12 Removing radiator grille top cover

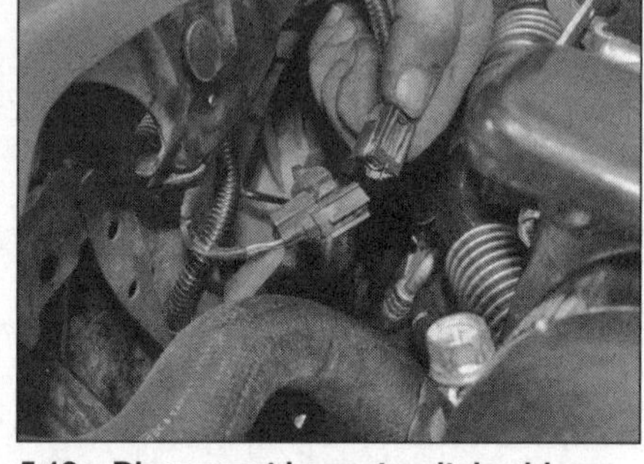

5.13a Disconnect bonnet switch wiring . . .

4 Remove the auxiliary drivebelt and automatic tensioner as described in Chapter 1A.

5 Disconnect its hose and unscrew the Positive Crankcase Ventilation (PCV) valve from the water pump housing **(see illustration)**.

6 Unscrew the three alternator mounting bolts and move it until the wiring terminals can be seen **(see illustration)**.

7 Peel back the rubber cover and unscrew the nut securing the battery lead to the alternator, then release the wiring harness from the retaining clip on the alternator. Unplug the connector to disconnect the (green) alternator wiring plug **(see illustration)**.

8 Manoeuvre the alternator out and withdraw it.

Refitting

9 Refitting is a reversal of removal; tighten all fasteners to the specified torque wrench settings. When refitting the PCV valve, apply a smear of sealant to the valve threads then refit the valve to the housing and tighten it to the specified torque (Chapter 4C). Ensure all wiring is correctly routed and the battery lead retaining nut is securely tightened.

Diesel-engined models

Note: *The alternator pulley incorporates a one-way over-run clutch mechanism, the function of which must be checked whenever the auxiliary drivebelt is removed, or if noise and vibrations are experienced which lead one to suspect a problem in the drivebelt components. See Section 14 of Chapter 1B.*

Removal

10 Disconnect the battery negative and positive leads, and position the leads away from the battery (see *Disconnecting the battery*). This is essential before disconnecting the alternator wiring.

11 Remove the auxiliary drivebelt and automatic tensioner as described in Chapter 1B. It is advisable to remove the engine compartment undershield so as to improve access to the various components that have to be removed or disconnected during this procedure.

12 Release its retaining clips and remove the radiator grille top cover **(see illustration)**.

13 Disconnect the wiring for the bonnet switch and release the wiring harnesses from the various retaining clips on the radiator/bonnet lock support bracket **(see illustrations)**.

14 Unscrew and remove the radiator top mounting bracket bolts, the air conditioning condenser bracket mounting bolts and the intercooler mounting bracket bolt from the radiator/bonnet lock support bracket. Unscrew the four top mounting bolts and the single bolt at the bottom of the radiator/bonnet lock support bracket's vertical member. Carefully lift out the radiator/bonnet lock support bracket (there is no need to disconnect the bonnet release cable) and secure it clear of the working area **(see illustrations)**.

5.13b . . . and release wiring harnesses from retaining clips on radiator/bonnet lock support bracket

5.14a Unscrew mounting bolts . . .

5.14b . . . to remove radiator top mounting brackets . . .

5.14c . . . air conditioning condenser mounting brackets . . .

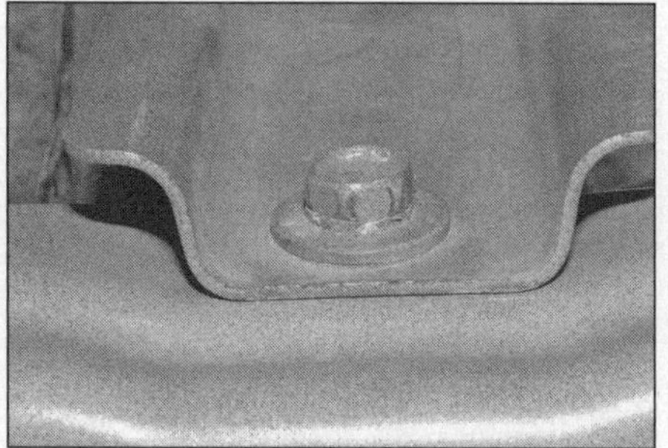

5.14f . . . and single bolt at bottom of radiator/bonnet lock support bracket vertical member . . .

15 Disconnect the air conditioning condenser cooling fan motor wiring and release the cooling fan motor and air conditioning compressor clutch wiring plugs from the cooling fan shroud. Unbolt the bracket securing the coolant pipe to the fan shroud, then unscrew

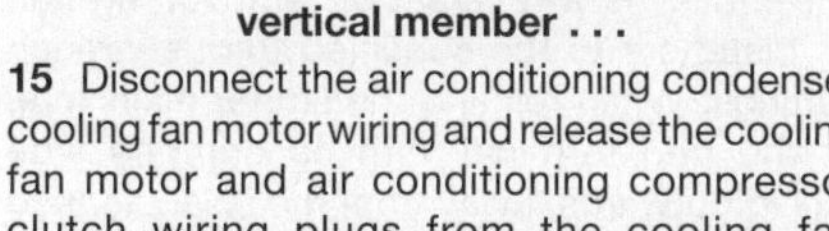

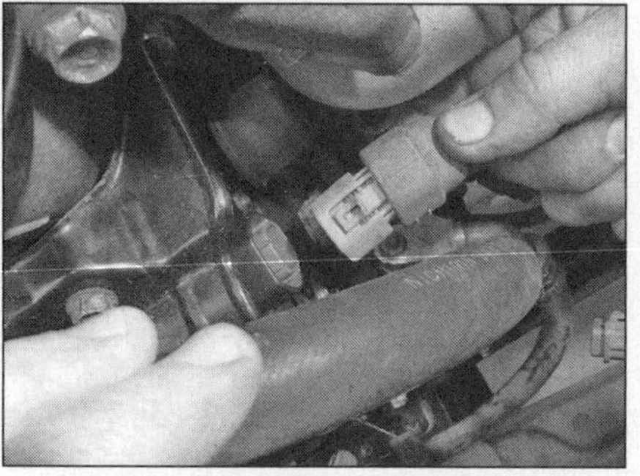

5.16a Unplug green connector to disconnect alternator wiring . . .

5.16c . . . and release wiring harness from retaining clip on alternator

5.14d . . . and intercooler top mounting bracket

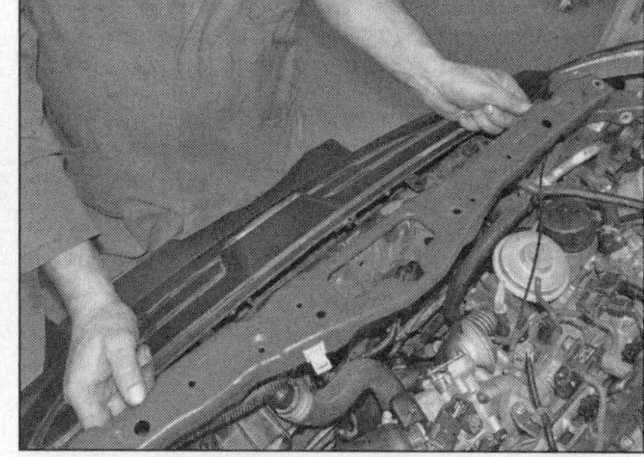

5.14g . . . to lift out radiator/bonnet lock support bracket

the fan shroud's two upper mounting bolts and slacken its two lower mounting bolts (the mounting points are slotted). Carefully lift out the air conditioning condenser cooling fan assembly **(see illustration)**.

16 Unplug the green connector to disconnect

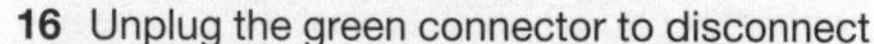

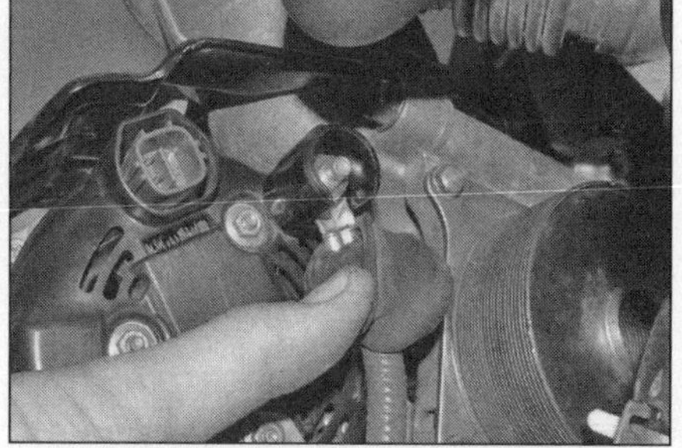

5.16b . . . peel back rubber cover and unscrew battery lead securing nut . . .

5.17 Four alternator mounting bolts also retain oil shield

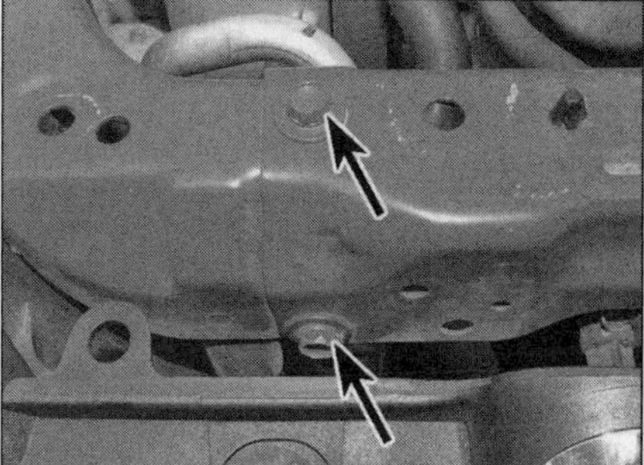

5.14e Unscrew four top mounting bolts (two at each end) . . .

5.15 Unscrew air conditioning condenser cooling fan shroud's two upper mounting bolts to remove shroud

the alternator wiring. Peel back the rubber cover and unscrew the nut securing the battery lead to the alternator, then release the wiring harness from the retaining clip on the alternator **(see illustrations)**.

17 Unscrew the four alternator mounting bolts and withdraw it, with the oil shield **(see illustration)**.

Refitting

18 Refitting is a reversal of removal; tighten all fasteners to the specified torque wrench settings. Ensure all wiring is correctly routed and the battery lead retaining nut is securely tightened.

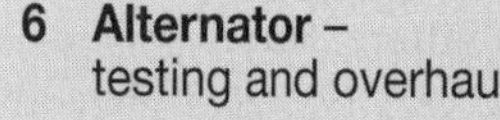

6 Alternator – testing and overhaul

If the alternator is thought to be suspect, it should be removed from the vehicle and taken to an auto-electrician for testing. Most auto-electricians will be able to supply and fit brushes at a reasonable cost. However, check on the cost of repairs before proceeding as it may prove more economical to obtain a new or exchange alternator.

7 Starting system – testing

Note: *Refer to Section 1 of this Chapter before starting work.*

1 If the starter motor fails to operate when

8.3 Peel back rubber cover and unscrew starter main wire securing nut . . .

8.4 . . . then disconnect starter solenoid wire

the ignition key is turned to the appropriate position, the following possible causes may be to blame:

a) The battery is faulty.

b) The electrical connections between the switch, solenoid, battery and starter motor are somewhere failing to pass the necessary current from the battery through the starter to earth.

c) The solenoid is faulty.

d) The starter motor is mechanically or electrically defective.

2 To check the battery, switch on the headlights. If they dim after a few seconds, this indicates that the battery is discharged – recharge (see Section 3) or renew the battery. If the headlights glow brightly, operate the ignition switch and observe the lights. If they dim, then this indicates that current is reaching the starter motor, therefore the fault must lie in the starter motor. If the lights continue to glow brightly (and no clicking sound can be heard from the starter motor solenoid), this indicates that there is a fault in the circuit or solenoid – see following paragraphs. If the starter motor turns slowly when operated, but the battery is in good condition, then this indicates that either the starter motor is faulty, or there is considerable resistance somewhere in the circuit.

3 If a fault in the circuit is suspected, disconnect the battery leads (including the earth connection to the body), the starter/solenoid wiring and the engine/transmission earth strap. Thoroughly clean the connections, and reconnect the leads and wiring, then use a voltmeter or test lamp to check that full battery voltage is available at the battery positive lead connection to the solenoid, and that the earth is sound. Smear petroleum jelly around the battery terminals to prevent corrosion – corroded connections are amongst the most frequent causes of electrical system faults.

4 If the battery and all connections are in good condition, check the circuit by disconnecting the wire from the solenoid blade terminal. Connect a voltmeter or test lamp between the wire end and a good earth (such as the battery negative terminal), and check that the wire is live when the ignition switch is turned to the 'start' position. If it is, then the circuit is sound – if not the circuit wiring can be checked as described in Chapter 12.

5 The solenoid contacts can be checked by connecting a voltmeter or test lamp between the battery positive feed connection on the starter side of the solenoid, and earth. When the ignition switch is turned to the 'start' position, there should be a reading or lighted bulb, as applicable. If there is no reading or lighted bulb, the solenoid is faulty and should be renewed.

6 If the circuit and solenoid are proved sound, the fault must lie in the starter motor. In this event, it may be possible to have the starter motor overhauled by a specialist, but check on the cost of spares before proceeding, as it may prove more economical to obtain a new or exchange motor.

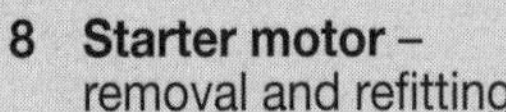

8 Starter motor – removal and refitting

Petrol-engined models

Removal

1 Disconnect the battery negative and positive leads, and position the leads away from the battery (see *Disconnecting the battery*). This is essential before disconnecting the starter wiring.

2 Access to the starter motor is only possible with the outer black plastic intake manifold removed as described in Chapter 4A.

3 Peel back the rubber cover and unscrew the nut securing the starter main wire, then disconnect it, noting which way round the ring terminal fits **(see illustration)**.

4 Disconnect the smaller solenoid wire from the starter **(see illustration)**.

5 Unscrew and remove the two mounting bolts, withdraw the starter motor from the bellhousing and remove it **(see illustrations)**. Note that the lower (front) mounting bolt is longer than the upper (rear) one.

Refitting

6 Refitting is a reversal of removal; tighten all fasteners to the specified torque wrench settings. When refitting the starter main wire, fit the ring terminal with its crimped side facing outwards, away from the solenoid **(see illustration)**. Ensure all wiring is correctly routed.

Diesel-engined models

Note: *If it is considered necessary to disconnect any coolant hoses to reach the starter mountings and/or connections, drain the cooling system first as described in Chapter 1B.*

Removal

7 Disconnect the battery negative and positive leads, and position the leads away from the battery (see *Disconnecting the battery*). This is essential before disconnecting the starter wiring.

8.5a Unscrew two mounting bolts . . .

8.5b . . . and remove starter motor (petrol models)

8.6 Fit starter main wire ring terminal with crimped side outwards, away from solenoid

8.15 Release wiring harness from brackets on front of engine and on starter

8 Remove the auxiliary drivebelt and automatic tensioner as described in Chapter 1B. It is advisable to remove the engine compartment undershield so as to improve access to the various components that have to be removed or disconnected during this procedure.

9 Release its retaining clips and remove the radiator grille top cover **(see illustration 5.12)**.

10 Disconnect the wiring for the bonnet switch and release the wiring harnesses from the various retaining clips on the radiator/bonnet lock support bracket **(see illustrations 5.13a and 5.13b)**.

11 Unscrew and remove the radiator top mounting bracket bolts, the air conditioning condenser bracket mounting bolts and the intercooler mounting bracket bolt from the radiator/bonnet lock support bracket. Unscrew the four top mounting bolts and the single bolt at the bottom of the radiator/bonnet lock support bracket's vertical member. Carefully lift out the radiator/bonnet lock support bracket (there is no need to disconnect the bonnet release cable) and secure it clear of the working area **(see illustrations 5.14a to 5.14g)**.

12 Disconnect the air conditioning condenser cooling fan motor wiring and release the cooling fan motor and air conditioning compressor clutch wiring plugs from the cooling fan shroud. Unbolt the bracket securing the coolant pipe to the fan shroud, then unscrew the fan shroud's two upper mounting bolts and slacken its two lower mounting bolts (the mounting points are slotted). Carefully lift out the air conditioning condenser cooling fan assembly **(see illustration 5.15)**.

13 Remove the oil pressure switch as described in Section 10.

14 Unscrew the mounting bolt at the oil level dipstick tube's upper end and withdraw the dipstick and tube. Remove and discard the small O-ring from the bottom end of the tube; this must be renewed whenever it is disturbed.

15 Release the wiring harness from the various retaining brackets on the front of the cylinder block/crankcase and on the starter itself; if necessary, unscrew the bracket securing bolts **(see illustration)**.

16 Peel back the rubber cover and unscrew the nut securing the starter main wire, then disconnect it, noting which way round the ring terminal fits, and disconnect the smaller solenoid wire from the starter **(see illustration)**.

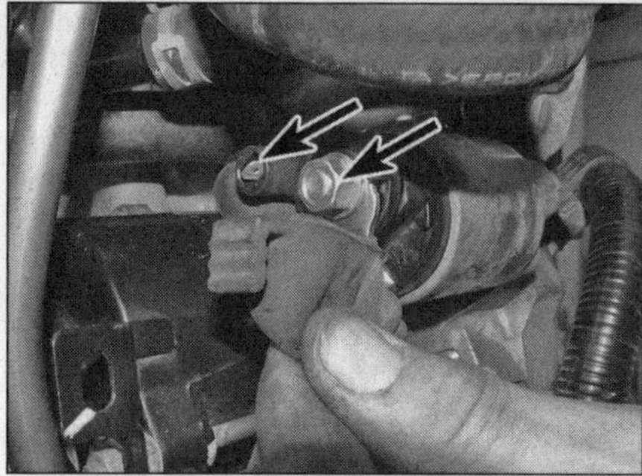

8.16 Peel back rubber cover and unscrew starter main wire securing nut to disconnect main wire, then disconnect starter solenoid wire

17 Unscrew and remove the two mounting bolts, withdraw the starter motor from the bellhousing and remove it **(see illustration)**. Note that the lower (front) mounting bolt is shorter than the upper (rear) one, which has been extended to make it slightly easier to reach.

Refitting

18 Refitting is a reversal of removal; tighten all fasteners to the specified torque wrench settings. When refitting the starter main wire, fit the ring terminal with its crimped side facing outwards, away from the solenoid. Ensure all wiring is correctly routed. Fit a new sealing O-ring to the dipstick tube. If any part of the cooling system was disconnected, refill the system as described in Chapter 1B.

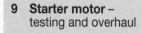

9 Starter motor – testing and overhaul

If the starter motor is thought to be defective, it should be removed from the vehicle and taken to an auto-electrician for assessment. In the majority of cases, new starter motor brushes can be fitted at a reasonable cost. However, check the cost of repairs first, as it may prove more economical to purchase a new or exchange motor.

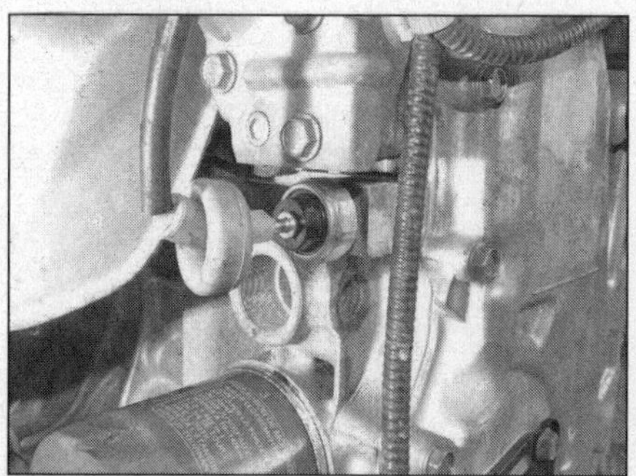

10.1 Oil pressure warning light switch (petrol models)

8.17 Starter mounting bolts – top bolt very difficult to reach

10 Oil pressure warning light switch – removal and refitting

Note: *Liquid gasket (Honda Part No. 08C70-K0234M, 08C70-K0334M, 08C70-X0331S or 08718-0001 or equivalent) must be available on reassembly.*

Removal

Petrol-engined models

Note: *Two oil pressure switches are fitted to the engine. The switch mounted at the right-hand rear end of the cylinder head serves the i-VTEC/VTC system.*

1 The switch is screwed into the rear right-hand end of the cylinder block, just above the oil filter **(see illustration)**.

2 Before working on any part of the vehicle's electrical systems, it is advisable to disconnect the battery negative (earth) lead (see *Disconnecting the battery*).

3 Unbolt the steering hose clamp from the rear right-hand end of the cylinder head cover.

4 Disconnect the wiring connector then unscrew the switch and remove it from the engine. Be prepared for oil spillage, and if the switch is to be left removed from the engine for any length of time, plug the switch aperture.

Diesel-engined models

5 The switch is screwed into the front of the cylinder block lower crankcase/bearing ladder, just below the starter motor and next to the dipstick tube **(see illustration)**.

10.5 Oil pressure warning light switch (diesel models)

6 Before working on any part of the vehicle's electrical systems, it is advisable to disconnect the battery negative (earth) lead (see *Disconnecting the battery*).

7 Jack up the front of the vehicle and support it securely on axle stands (see *Jacking and vehicle support*), then remove the engine compartment undershield (Chapter 11) to reach the switch from underneath.

8 Disconnect the wiring plug from the switch, then unscrew the switch and remove it from the engine. Be prepared for oil spillage, and if the switch is to be left removed from the engine for any length of time, plug the switch aperture.

Refitting

9 Ensure the switch threads are clean and dry; clean any old liquid gasket from the threaded hole. Apply a smear of liquid gasket to the switch threads then refit the switch and tighten it to the specified torque.

10 Reconnect the wiring connector.

11 The remainder of refitting is a reversal of removal. On completion check and, if necessary, top-up the engine oil as described in *Weekly checks*.

Chapter 5 Part B: Ignition system – petrol models

Contents

Degrees of difficulty

Easy, suitable for novice with little experience 	**Fairly easy,** suitable for beginner with some experience	**Fairly difficult,** suitable for competent DIY mechanic	**Difficult,** suitable for experienced DIY mechanic	**Very difficult,** suitable for expert DIY or professional 

Specifications

General

Firing order	1-3-4-2 (No. 1 cylinder at timing chain end)

Ignition timing

All models	8° ± 2° at idle (red pulley mark)

Torque wrench setting

	Nm	lbf ft
Knock sensor	31	23

1 General information

The PGM-FI engine management system provides complete control of the ignition timing by determining the optimum timing in response to engine speed, coolant temperature, throttle position, intake air temperature and intake manifold pressure. These parameters are relayed to the engine management system's Electronic Control Unit (ECU) by the crankshaft position and camshaft position (TDC) sensors, throttle position sensor, coolant temperature sensor and the Manifold Absolute Pressure (MAP) sensor. Ignition timing is altered during warm-up, idling and warm running conditions by the ECU.

A knock sensor is mounted on the cylinder block to inform the ECU when the engine is 'pinking'. Its sensitivity to a particular frequency of vibration allows it to detect the impulses which are caused by the shock waves set up when the engine starts to pink (pre-ignite). The knock sensor sends an electrical signal to the ECU which retards the ignition timing until the pinking ceases – the ignition timing is then gradually returned to the 'normal' setting. This maintains the ignition timing as close to the knock threshold as possible – the most efficient setting for the engine under normal running conditions.

The ignition system itself consists of the ignition switch, battery, four direct-ignition coils, and the spark plugs. The ignition system uses one coil for each cylinder, with each coil mounted on the relevant spark plug; there are no HT leads. The coils are triggered individually in firing order.

Precautions

The following precautions must be observed, to prevent damage to the ignition system components and to reduce risk of personal injury.

a) Ensure the ignition is switched off before disconnecting any of the ignition wiring.

b) Ensure that the ignition is switched off before connecting or disconnecting any ignition test equipment, such as a timing light.

c) Do not earth the coil primary or secondary circuits.

Warning: Voltages produced by an electronic ignition system are considerably higher than those produced by conventional ignition systems. Extreme care must be taken when working on the system with the ignition switched on. Persons with surgically-implanted cardiac pacemaker devices should keep well clear of the ignition circuits, components and test equipment

2 Ignition system – testing

1 The components of ignition systems are normally very reliable; most faults are far more likely to be due to loose or dirty connections, or to 'tracking' of HT voltage due to dirt, dampness or damaged insulation than to the failure of any of the system's components. Always check all wiring thoroughly before condemning an electrical component and work methodically to eliminate all other possibilities before deciding that a particular component is faulty.

Engine will not start

2 If the engine either will not turn over at all, or only turns very slowly, first check the battery and starter motor as described in Chapter 5A.

3 The anti-theft immobiliser system disables the fuel system when in operation, meaning that the engine will turn over as normal, but will not start. The immobiliser should be deactivated when a properly-coded ignition key is inserted into the ignition switch. If possible, substitute a spare key and recheck.

4 Check the fuses relating to the engine management system in the passenger compartment fuse panel (in the facia) and in the engine compartment fuse/relay box(es) – see Chapter 12.

5 Remove all four ignition coils and spark plugs (see Chapter 1A), then unbolt and withdraw the plastic cover over the intake manifold and disconnect all four injector connectors to disable them and prevent them from spraying fuel into the combustion chamber while work is in progress. Connect the ignition coils to their wiring, fit the spark plug to each coil and place the spark plugs so that each plug body is in firm contact with the metal of the cylinder head. Check for a good

5.1 Disconnecting knock sensor wiring plug – outer black plastic intake manifold removed

spark at each plug as an assistant cranks the engine on the starter motor. If there is no spark at all, the fault lies elsewhere in the system. If the spark is poor, intermittent or missing on one spark plug only, swap components until the source of the fault can be identified. Repairs are not possible; all that can be done is to substitute a known good component.

6 Ultimately, the vehicle should be referred to a Honda dealer or diagnostic specialist for testing. A diagnostic socket is incorporated in the engine management system wiring harness, into which dedicated electronic test equipment can be plugged – the connector is located under the driver's side of the facia (see Chapter 4A). The tester will locate the fault quickly and simply, alleviating the need to test all the system components individually, which is a time-consuming operation that carries a high risk of damaging the ECU. If necessary, the system wiring and wiring connectors can be checked as described in Chapter 12, ensuring that the ECU wiring connector is only unplugged with the battery disconnected.

Engine misfires

7 An irregular misfire suggests either a loose connection or intermittent fault in the primary circuit, or an HT fault between the coils and spark plugs.

8 With the ignition switched off, check carefully through the system, ensuring that all connections are clean and securely fastened.

9 Check that the HT coils and their associated wiring connections are clean and dry.

10 Regular misfiring of one spark plug may be due to a faulty spark plug, faulty injector, a faulty coil or loss of compression in the relevant cylinder. Regular misfiring of all the cylinders suggests a fuel supply fault, such as a clogged fuel filter or faulty fuel pump, especially if it occurs in conditions where fuel demand is high.

3 Ignition coils – removal and refitting

Removal

1 Proceed as described in Chapter 1A, Section 18, paragraphs 2 to 8.

Refitting

2 Proceed as described in Chapter 1A, Section 18, paragraphs 23 and 25.

4 Ignition timing – checking and adjustment

It is possible to check the ignition timing with the correct equipment, but even if all this is done/available, the ignition timing cannot be adjusted, and if it is out of specification, a new Engine Control Unit (ECU) will be needed.

If the timing is felt to be incorrect because the engine can be heard pinking, the knock sensor may be faulty (see Section 5).

If performance in general is down, carry out the primary operations listed in Chapter 1A, Section 2, before having the engine management system checked by a Honda dealer or diagnostic specialist.

5 Knock sensor – removal and refitting

1 The knock sensor is screwed into the front of the cylinder block, just next to the starter motor, behind the thermostat and below the intake manifold. Access is only possible with the outer black plastic intake manifold removed as described in Chapter 4A, though it may just be possible from below **(see illustration)**.

2 Before working on any part of the vehicle's electrical systems, it is advisable to disconnect the battery negative (earth) lead (see *Disconnecting the battery*).

3 Unclip the plug to disconnect the sensor wiring.

4 Unscrew the sensor and withdraw it.

5 Clean the sensor and engine block mating faces before fitting.

6 Refitting is a reversal of removal. It is critical for the correct operation of the sensor that it is tightened to the specified torque wrench setting on to a completely clean mating surface.

Chapter 5 Part C:
Preheating system – diesel models

Contents

Degrees of difficulty

Easy, suitable for novice with little experience 	**Fairly easy,** suitable for beginner with some experience	**Fairly difficult,** suitable for competent DIY mechanic	**Difficult,** suitable for experienced DIY mechanic 	**Very difficult,** suitable for expert DIY or professional 

Specifications

Torque wrench setting	**Nm**	**lbf ft**
Glow plugs	18	13

1 General information

Even with the advantages of precisely-metered air/fuel mixture and direct-injection engine configuration, diesel engines still require some assistance to start at low temperatures. Being compression-ignition engines, they require the injected fuel to be ignited by the air that is compressed and heated during the compression stroke. At low ambient temperatures and when the engine is cool, however, the fuel does not ignite properly or even at all; too much heat can be lost to the cold metal surrounding the combustion chamber. This is why glow plugs are used to assist starting. The preheating system is far more rapid in operation than that fitted to older diesel engine designs, and, if it is energised at all (the ECU will only switch it on at low temperatures), it can be so quick that it is virtually unnoticeable.

Preheating commences when the ignition is switched on; a warning lamp in the instrument panel informs the driver that preheating is taking place. The duration of the preheating period is governed by the Electronic Diesel Control (EDC) system's Electronic Control Unit (ECU), using information provided by the coolant temperature sensor (see Chapter 4B). The ECU alters the period during which the glow plugs are supplied with current to suit the prevailing conditions. While the warning lamp goes out when sufficient preheating has taken place to allow the engine to be started, power will still be supplied to the glow plugs until the engine starts (standby heating phase). If no attempt is made to start the engine, the power supply to the glow plugs is switched off to prevent battery drain and glow plug burn-out.

Once the engine is running and the ignition key is released, the post-heating phase starts. As the engine warms-up, the sheathed-element glow plugs continue to operate for up to three minutes to improve cold-running behaviour and to prevent the annoying diesel knock which used to accompany a cold start.

Apart from the battery, ignition switch, fuses and associated wiring, the preheating system consists of a relay – the control module – and four glow plugs, and is controlled by the Electronic Diesel Control (EDC) system control unit (ECU), using information provided by the coolant temperature sensor.

Note: *Apart from illuminating when the glow plug system is operating, the instrument panel glow plug warning lamp also serves to reinforce the messages of the engine management Malfunction Indicator warning Lamp (MIL). If a problem occurs with a component of the engine management system that causes a fault code to be logged so that the engine management Malfunction Indicator warning Lamp (MIL) illuminates, the glow plug warning lamp may also flash while the engine is running until the vehicle can be taken to a Honda dealer or other specialist for the fault code to be erased.*

Note: *The glow plug warning lamp may also flash after the vehicle has run out of fuel, especially if air has entered the system so that the engine will not start even after the fuel tank has been refilled. In this latter eventuality, once the engine has been restarted the warning lamp can be turned off by switching off the engine and then restarting it and switching it off at least three times in succession at intervals of approximately 30 seconds.*

2 Preheating system – testing

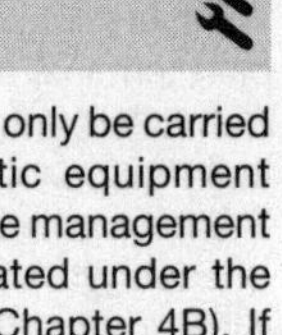

1 Full testing of the system can only be carried out using specialist diagnostic equipment which is connected to the engine management system diagnostic socket located under the driver's side of the facia (see Chapter 4B). If the preheating system is thought to be faulty, some preliminary checks of the glow plug operation may be made as described in the following paragraphs.

2 Connect a voltmeter or 12 volt test lamp between the glow plug supply cable and a good earth point on the engine.

Caution: Make sure that the live connection is kept well clear of the engine and bodywork.

3 Have an assistant activate the preheating system by turning the ignition key to the ON (II) position, and check that battery voltage is applied to the glow plug electrical connection. **Note:** *The supply voltage will be less than battery voltage initially, but will rise and settle as the glow plug heats up. It will then drop to zero when the preheating period ends and the safety cut-out operates.*

4 If no supply voltage can be detected at the glow plug, then the glow plug control module or the supply cable may be faulty.

5 To locate a faulty glow plug, first operate the preheating system to allow the glow plugs to reach working temperature, then disconnect the battery negative cable and position it away from the battery terminal (see *Disconnecting the battery*).

6 Unplug the connector to disconnect the supply cable from No. 1 glow plug. Measure

3.2 Grip lugs at end of connectors to pull them from glow plugs

3.3 Using a deep socket, unscrew and remove glow plugs

4.1 Glow plug control module is bolted next to engine compartment fuse/relay box

4.3 Unplug connector to disconnect control module wiring

the electrical resistance between the glow plug terminal and the engine earth. A reading of anything more than a few ohms indicates that the glow plug is defective.

7 If an ammeter is available, the current draw of each glow plug can be checked. After an initial surge of 15 to 20 amps, each plug should draw 12 amps. Any plug which draws much more or less than this is probably defective.

8 As a final check, remove the glow plugs and inspect them visually, as described in Section 3.

9 If no problems are found, take the vehicle to a Honda dealer for testing using the appropriate diagnostic equipment.

3 Glow plugs – removal, inspection and refitting

Removal

1 Unscrew the four retaining nuts and remove the acoustic engine cover. Before working on any part of the vehicle's electrical systems, it is advisable to disconnect the battery negative (earth) lead (see *Disconnecting the battery*).

2 Grip the lugs at the end of the connectors and pull them from the glow plugs **(see illustration)**.

3 Using a deep socket, unscrew and remove the glow plugs **(see illustration)**.

Warning: If the glow plug (preheating) system has just been energised, or if the engine has recently been running, the glow plugs may be extremely hot.

Inspection

4 Inspect the glow plugs for signs of damage. Burnt or eroded glow plug tips can be caused by a bad injector spray pattern. Have the injectors checked if this sort of damage is found.

5 If the glow plugs are in good condition, check them electrically, as described in Section 2.

6 The glow plugs can be energised by applying 12 volts to them to verify that they heat up evenly and in the required time. Observe the following precautions:

a) *Support the glow plug by clamping it carefully in a vice or self-locking pliers. Remember it will be red hot.*

b) *Make sure that the power supply or test lead incorporates a fuse or overload trip to protect against damage from a short-circuit.*

c) *After testing, allow the glow plug to cool for several minutes before attempting to handle it.*

7 A glow plug in good condition will start to glow red at the tip after drawing current for 5 seconds or so. Any plug which takes much longer to start glowing, or which starts glowing in the middle instead of at the tip, is probably defective.

Refitting

8 Thoroughly clean the glow plugs, and the glow plug seating areas in the cylinder head.

9 Apply a smear of anti-seize compound to the glow plug threads, then refit the glow plug and tighten it to the specified torque.

10 Reconnect the wiring to the glow plug. The connectors are a push-fit.

11 Refit the acoustic engine cover and tighten its retaining nuts.

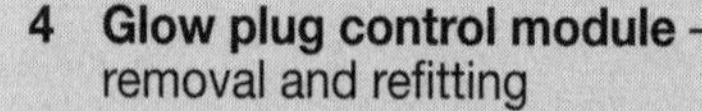

4 Glow plug control module – removal and refitting

Removal

1 The glow plug control module is located on the left-hand side of the engine compartment, bolted next to the engine compartment fuse/relay box **(see illustration)**.

2 Before working on any part of the vehicle's electrical systems, it is advisable to disconnect the battery negative (earth) lead (see *Disconnecting the battery*).

3 Unplug the connector to disconnect the control module wiring **(see illustration)**.

4 Unscrew the bolt and remove the control module.

Refitting

5 Refitting is a reversal of removal.

Chapter 6
Clutch

Contents

Degrees of difficulty

Easy, suitable for novice with little experience	**Fairly easy,** suitable for beginner with some experience	**Fairly difficult,** suitable for competent DIY mechanic	**Difficult,** suitable for experienced DIY mechanic	**Very difficult,** suitable for expert DIY or professional

Specifications

Friction plate	**Petrol-engined models**	**Diesel-engined models**
Friction material-to-rivet head depth:		
New	1.65 to 2.25 mm	1.0 mm
Service limit	0.7 mm	0.2 mm
Friction plate thickness:		
New	8.7 to 9.3 mm	8.68 to 9.53 mm
Service limit	6.0 mm	7.2 mm

Pressure plate	
Diaphragm spring finger height difference:	
Nominal	0.6 mm max.
Service limit	0.8 mm
Warpage of machined surface:	
Nominal	0.03 mm max.
Service limit	0.15 mm

Pedal	**Petrol-engined models**	**Diesel-engined models**
Height from floor	200 mm	198 mm
Disengagement height from floor	112 mm	112 mm
Stroke	125 to 135 mm	135 to 145 mm
Free play	6 to 17 mm	11 to 19 mm

Torque wrench settings	**Nm**	**lbf ft**
Master cylinder mounting nuts:		
Petrol-engined models	13	10
Diesel-engined models	12	9
Master cylinder pushrod locknut	18	13
Pedal interlock switch locknut	9	7
Pedal mounting bolt – diesel-engined models	22	16
Pedal position switch or adjuster bolt locknut	10	7
Pressure plate retaining bolts	25	18
Slave cylinder bleed nipple	8	6
Slave cylinder hydraulic line-to-gearbox support bracket bolts	10	7
Slave cylinder mounting-to-gearbox bolts	22	16

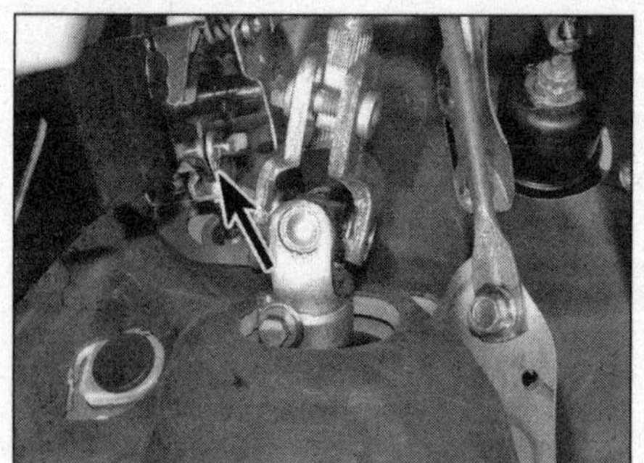
2.3 Prise out the spring locking clip from the master cylinder pushrod clevis pin

2.4 Two master cylinder mounting nuts and bolt securing clutch pedal assembly to bulkhead

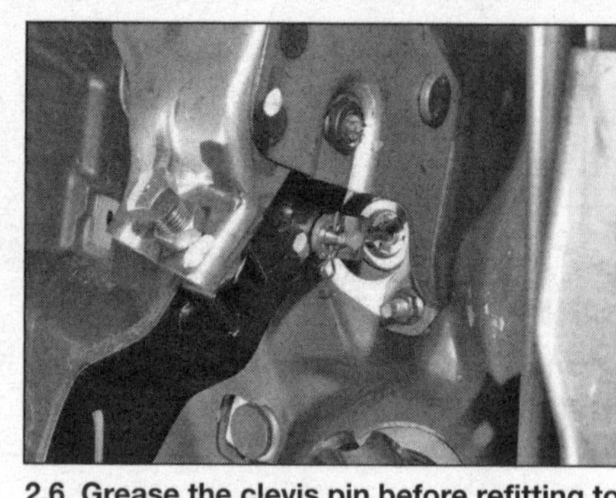
2.6 Grease the clevis pin before refitting to clutch pedal and master cylinder pushrod – secure with new clip

1 General information

The single dry plate clutch consists of a friction plate, a pressure plate assembly, a release bearing and the release fork lever; all of these components are contained in the large cast-aluminium alloy bellhousing, sandwiched between the engine and the gearbox. The clutch release mechanism is hydraulically-operated and so is self-adjusting and requires no manual adjustment to compensate for wear of the friction material.

The friction plate is fitted between the engine flywheel and the clutch pressure plate, and is allowed to slide on the gearbox input shaft splines. Friction lining material is riveted to both sides of the friction plate which, on all petrol-engined models, has a spring-cushioned hub to absorb transmission shocks and help ensure a smooth take-up of the drive. There is no spring-cushioned hub on the diesel-engined models, however, the flywheel being of the dual-mass type, built in two sections with internal torsion springs to take up transmission shocks.

The pressure plate assembly is bolted to the engine flywheel. When the engine is running, drive is transmitted from the crankshaft, via the flywheel, to the friction plate (these components being clamped securely together by the diaphragm spring in the pressure plate assembly) and from the friction plate to the gearbox input shaft.

The release bearing is located on a guide sleeve at the front of the gearbox, and the bearing is free to slide on the sleeve, under the action of the release fork lever which pivots on a ball-stud inside the bellhousing.

To interrupt the drive, the diaphragm spring's pressure must be relaxed. Depressing the clutch pedal pushes on the master cylinder pushrod which thus causes hydraulic pressure to force out the slave cylinder piston which bears on the end of the clutch release fork lever. The release fork acts on its pivot to press the release bearing against the pressure plate diaphragm spring fingers. As the centre of the spring is pushed in, the outside of the spring pivots out, so moving the pressure plate backwards and disengaging its grip on the friction plate.

Diesel-engined models are fitted with a Self-Adjusting Clutch (SAC). This is in fact something of a misnomer, as the clutches fitted to petrol-engined models are also self-adjusting, but the SAC device compensates for the effect of friction plate wear on clutch pedal load by altering the attitude of the diaphragm spring fingers by means of a sprung mechanism within the pressure plate cover. This ensures a consistent clutch pedal 'feel' over the life of the clutch, as opposed to the progressively-heavier effort required to depress the pedal of a conventional clutch as its friction plate wears. The pressure plate assembly, like that of a conventional unit, is riveted together and must not be dismantled; any fault with any part of the assembly can be rectified only by the renewal of the friction plate and pressure plate assembly as a set.

Note: *Due to the amount of work necessary to remove and refit clutch components, it is usually considered good practice to renew the clutch friction plate, pressure plate assembly and release bearing as a matched set, even if only one of these is actually worn enough to require renewal.*

2 Pedal – removal, refitting and adjustment

Note: *The master cylinder pushrod clevis pin locking clip must be renewed as a matter of course on reassembly.*

Removal

1 With reference to Chapter 11, remove the driver's side under cover and lower cover from the facia.

2 Where fitted, disconnect the clutch pedal position switch and clutch interlock switch connectors.

3 Prise out the spring locking clip from the master cylinder pushrod clevis pin **(see illustration)**. Pull out the clevis pin to the left, to disconnect the pushrod from the pedal.

4 Unscrew the two (master cylinder mounting) nuts and the bolt securing the pedal assembly to the bulkhead then manoeuvre the assembly out from underneath the facia **(see illustration)**. Do not attempt to dismantle the pedal assembly; if it is worn or damaged the complete assembly must be renewed – no individual components are available.

Refitting

5 Grease the pedal pivot and manoeuvre the pedal assembly into position, ensuring it is correctly engaged with the pushrod clevis. Refit the mounting nuts and bolt and tighten them to the torque wrench settings, where specified.

6 Grease the clevis pin, then press it back into the clutch pedal and master cylinder pushrod, then fit the new clip **(see illustration)**. Ensure that the clip is securely fastened.

7 Where relevant, reconnect the clutch pedal position switch and clutch interlock switch connectors, then check the pedal adjustments as described below.

8 Check the operation of the clutch pedal then refit the driver's side under cover and lower cover to the facia.

Adjustment

9 With reference to Chapter 11, remove the driver's side under cover and lower cover from the facia.

10 The height of the clutch pedal is the distance the pedal sits off the floor (remove any accessory floor mats), measured from the centre of the top surface of the pedal. If the pedal height is not as specified, it must be adjusted.

11 To adjust the clutch pedal, slacken the locknut on the clutch pedal position switch (or the adjuster bolt) and back the switch/bolt out until it no longer touches the pedal, then slacken the locknut on the clutch pushrod **(see illustrations)**. Turn the pushrod to adjust the pedal height. Also check the pedal stroke, which is the distance from the fully-released position to fully-depressed, and pedal free play, which is the distance the pedal can be depressed before it begins to exert pressure on the master cylinder piston. Some free play must exist or the release mechanism will be pressing constantly on the pressure plate spring fingers, resulting in clutch slip and premature clutch wear.

12 When all three adjustments are correct, tighten the pushrod locknut to the specified torque wrench setting.
13 Turn the switch/bolt clockwise until it just contacts the pedal arm, then turn it in an additional 3/4 to 1 turn. Tighten the locknut to the specified torque wrench setting.
14 If a clutch interlock switch is fitted (above the clutch pedal position switch), proceed as follows:
a) *On petrol-engined models, press the clutch pedal to the floor and then release it to 10 to 16 mm above the fully-depressed position. Check that the engine will start with the pedal at this height.*
b) *On diesel-engined models, press the clutch pedal to the floor and then release it to a height of 112 mm from the floor. Check that the switch is on with the pedal at this height.*
c) *On all models, if adjustment is required, slacken the switch locknut and turn the switch in or out as required. Tighten the locknut to the specified torque wrench setting.*
15 Check the operation of the clutch pedal then refit the driver's side under cover and lower cover to the facia.

3 Master cylinder – removal and refitting

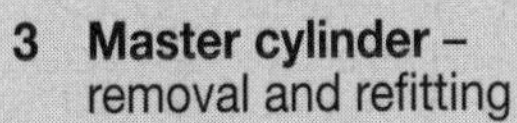

Warning: Hydraulic fluid is poisonous; wash off immediately and thoroughly in the case of skin contact, and seek immediate medical advice if any fluid is swallowed or gets into the eyes. Certain types of hydraulic fluid are inflammable, and may ignite when allowed into contact with hot components; when servicing any hydraulic system, it is safest to assume that the fluid is inflammable, and to take precautions against the risk of fire as though it is petrol that is being handled. Hydraulic fluid is also an effective paint stripper, and will attack plastics; if any is spilt, it should be washed off immediately, using copious quantities of fresh water. Finally, it is hygroscopic (it absorbs moisture from the air) – old fluid may be contaminated and unfit for further use. When topping-up or renewing the fluid, always use the recommended type, and ensure that it comes from a freshly-opened sealed container.

Note: *The master cylinder pushrod clevis pin locking clip, the hydraulic pipe union locking clip and O-ring and the master cylinder gasket must be renewed as a matter of course on reassembly.*

Removal

1 With reference to Chapter 11, remove the driver's side under cover and lower cover from the facia.
2 Prise out the spring locking clip from the master cylinder pushrod clevis pin **(see illustration 2.3)**. Pull out the clevis pin to the left, to disconnect the pushrod from the pedal.
3 Unscrew the two master cylinder mounting nuts **(see illustration 2.4)**.
4 Access to the master cylinder in the engine compartment is limited by various pipes, hoses and cables – where possible, unclip them to improve matters. Clamp the fluid supply hose from the reservoir, then release the spring clip, and pull off the hose – quickly turn the hose end upwards, to reduce fluid spillage. Take care not to drip hydraulic fluid onto paintwork or hot engine components.
5 Use a pair of pliers to squeeze together the ends of one of the tips of the U-shaped clip securing the hydraulic pipe union in the top of the master cylinder, then extract the clip and discard it. Unscrew the union nut and disconnect the hydraulic pipe from the master cylinder. Either plug or tape over the open connections.
6 Withdraw the master cylinder from the bulkhead **(see illustration)**. Recover and discard the gasket fitted behind the cylinder, and the O-ring fitted inside the hydraulic pipe connection – new ones should be used when refitting.

Overhaul

Note: *Check the availability of overhaul kits before dismantling the cylinder.*
7 Press the pushrod into the cylinder body and prise out the circlip.
8 Remove the stopper, then ease out the pushrod, and pull out the piston assembly. If necessary, use compressed air to force the piston from the cylinder body.
9 Carefully examine the bore of the cylinder for rust, scratches, gouges and general wear. If the bore is damaged, the complete cylinder must be renewed. If the bore is in good condition, thoroughly clean the assembly, and renew the seals as described below.
10 Take note of the seal orientation on the piston, and using a small screwdriver, lever the seals from the grooves on the piston.
11 Fit the new seals to the piston, ensuring the seal lips point towards the spring end of the piston. Smear the seals with the assembly grease supplied in the overhaul kit.

2.11a To adjust clutch pedal, slacken clutch pedal position switch (or adjuster bolt, shown here) locknut and back switch/ bolt out until it no longer touches pedal . . .

2.11b . . . then slacken the locknut and turn clutch pushrod to adjust

12 Insert the piston assembly into the cylinder, spring end first. Ensure the seal lips enter the cylinder bore without catching or folding back.
13 Compress the piston with the pushrod, fit the stopper, then secure with the circlip.

Refitting

14 With the new gasket fitted, position the master cylinder on the bulkhead and secure it temporarily in position.
15 Working in the passenger compartment, refit the mounting nuts and tighten them to the torque wrench setting specified.
16 Grease the clevis pin, then press it back into the clutch pedal and master cylinder pushrod and fit the new clip **(see illustration 2.6)**. Ensure that the clip is securely fastened.
17 Returning to the engine compartment, fit the new O-ring to the master cylinder hydraulic pipe connection, then reconnect the hydraulic pipe to the master cylinder and tighten the union nut. Fit the new U-shaped clip to secure the union nut and splay the clip end open to retain the clip.
18 Reconnect the fluid supply hose from the reservoir and secure it with the spring clip. Ensure that the clip's tabs are located clear of any other component.
19 Top-up the reservoir, then bleed the system as described in Section 5.
20 Check the operation of the clutch pedal then refit the driver's side under cover and lower cover to the facia.

3.6 Withdraw the master cylinder from the bulkhead

4.3a Unbolt the hydraulic pipe from gearbox . . .

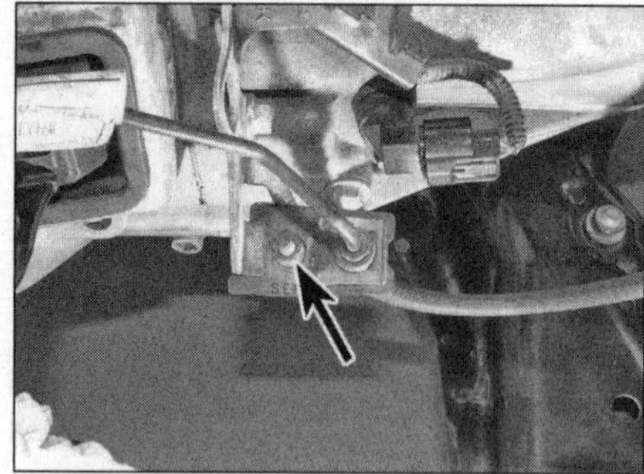

4.3b . . . as necessary to work on slave cylinder

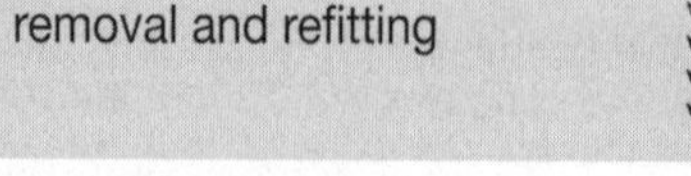

4 Slave cylinder – removal and refitting

Note: *Refer to Warning in Section 3.*

Note: *The slave cylinder pushrod clevis pin locking clip, the hydraulic pipe union locking clip and O-ring and the master cylinder gasket must be renewed as a matter of course on reassembl.*

Removal

1 With reference to Chapter 4A or 4B, remove the air cleaner assembly. Remove also the intake ducting as necessary to reach the slave cylinder.

2 Remove the battery. If the additional working space is required, remove the battery tray on petrol-engined models and the battery tray and tray mounting bracket on diesel-engined models (see Chapter 5A).

3 Unbolt the hydraulic pipe from the top of the gearbox as necessary to work on the slave cylinder **(see illustrations)**.

4 Unbolt the slave cylinder from the gearbox **(see illustrations)**.

5 Pull out the two roll-pins from beneath the hydraulic pipe union nut **(see illustration)**. Unscrew the union nut.

6 Anticipating some fluid spillage, disconnect the hydraulic pipe union from the slave cylinder, then recover and discard the O-ring – a new one must be used when refitting. Either plug or tape over the open connections to prevent fluid loss and the entry of dirt.

Overhaul

Note: *Check the availability of overhaul kits before dismantling the cylinder.*

7 Unclip the dust boot from the cylinder body, and pull out the pushrod. Extract the piston and spring. If necessary, use compressed air to force the piston from the bore. Recover the piston spring. **Note:** *On diesel-engined models, the one-way valve in the top of the slave cylinder body in line with the hydraulic pipe union is built into the cylinder body and cannot be dismantled. If the valve is faulty, the complete cylinder must be renewed.*

8 Carefully examine the bore of the cylinder for rust, scratches, gouges and general wear. If the bore is damaged, the complete cylinder must be renewed. If the bore is in good condition, thoroughly clean the assembly, and renew the seals as described below.

9 Note their fitted locations, then using a small screwdriver, prise the seals from the piston.

10 Fit the new seals to the piston, ensuring they are fitted as noted on removal. Coat the seals with assembly grease (supplied in the overhaul kit).

11 Insert the spring, large diameter end towards the cylinder bleed nipple, followed by the piston. Ensure the seal's lips enter the cylinder bore without catching or folding back.

12 Squeeze some brake assembly lubricant into the dust boot, then refit the boot and pushrod.

Refitting

13 On refitting, first pull back the slave cylinder's rubber dust boot and apply brake assembly lubricant to the pushrod, the end of the piston and the interior of the boot. Refit the boot and grease the tip of the pushrod; Honda recommend Urea Grease UM264 (Part No. 41211-PY5-305).

14 Engage the pushrod correctly on the clutch release fork lever, refit the slave cylinder mounting bolts and tighten them to the torque wrench setting specified.

15 Fit the new O-ring to the slave cylinder hydraulic pipe connection, then reconnect the hydraulic pipe to the slave cylinder. Ensure the hydraulic pipe is correctly routed and retained by all the necessary clips. Tighten the union nut and fit the roll-pins to secure it. Tighten any bolts disturbed securing the hydraulic pipe to the gearbox.

16 Top-up the reservoir, then bleed the system as described in Section 5. It may be necessary to limit the movement of the release fork lever to get all the air out of the system.

17 Check the operation of the clutch pedal then refit all components removed for access.

5 Clutch hydraulic system – bleeding

Note: *Refer to Warning in Section 3.*

1 If any part of the hydraulic system is dismantled, or if air has accidentally entered the system, the system will need to be bled. The presence of air is characterised by the pedal having a spongy feel and it results in difficulty in changing gear.

2 During the bleeding procedure, add only clean, unused hydraulic fluid of the recommended type; never re-use fluid that has already been bled from the system. Ensure that sufficient fluid is available before starting work.

3 To reach the slave cylinder bleed nipple, remove the battery tray on petrol-engined models and the battery tray and tray mounting bracket on diesel-engined models (see Chapter 5A). Remove also the air cleaner assembly and the intake ducting as necessary to reach the slave cylinder (Chapter 4A or 4B).

4 Check that the slave cylinder bleed nipple is closed. Remove the dust cap, and clean

4.4a Unbolt the slave cylinder from the gearbox – petrol-engined models

4.4b Unbolt the slave cylinder from the gearbox – diesel models

4.5 Pull out two roll-pins from beneath hydraulic pipe union nut

any dirt from around the bleed nipple **(see illustration)**.

5 It is recommended that pressure-bleeding equipment is used to bleed the system. Pressure-bleeding kits are usually operated by the reservoir of pressurised air contained in the spare tyre. However, note that it will probably be necessary to reduce the pressure to a lower level than normal; refer to the instructions supplied with the kit.

6 By connecting a pressurised, fluid-filled container to the brake fluid reservoir, bleeding can be carried out simply by opening the bleed nipple on the slave cylinder and allowing the fluid to flow out until no more air bubbles can be seen in the expelled fluid.

7 This method has the advantage that the large reservoir of fluid provides an additional safeguard against air being drawn into the system during bleeding.

8 Collect a clean glass jar, a suitable length of plastic or rubber tubing which is a tight fit over the bleed nipple, and a ring spanner to fit the nipple.

9 Fit the spanner and tube to the slave cylinder bleed nipple, place the other end of the tube in the jar, and pour in sufficient fluid to cover the end of the tube.

10 Connect the pressure-bleeding equipment to the brake fluid reservoir in accordance with the manufacturer's instructions.

11 Slacken the bleed nipple using the spanner, and allow fluid to drain into the jar until no more air bubbles emerge.

12 When bleeding is complete, tighten the bleed nipple, and disconnect the hose and pressure bleeding equipment.

13 Wash off any spilt fluid, check once more that the bleed nipple is tightened securely, and refit the dust cap.

14 Check the hydraulic fluid level in the reservoir, and top-up if necessary (see *Weekly checks*).

15 Discard any hydraulic fluid that has been bled from the system; it will not be fit for re-use.

16 Check the feel of the clutch pedal. If it feels at all spongy, air must still be present in the system, and further bleeding is required. Failure to bleed satisfactorily after a procedure may be due to worn master or slave cylinder seals.

17 On completion, refit all components removed for access.

6 Clutch assembly – removal, inspection and refitting

Warning: Dust created by clutch wear and deposited on the clutch components may contain asbestos, which is a health hazard. DO NOT blow it out with compressed air, or inhale any of it. DO NOT use petrol or petroleum-based solvents to clean off the dust. Brake system cleaner or methylated spirit should be used to flush the dust into a suitable receptacle. After the clutch components are wiped clean with rags, dispose of the contaminated rags and cleaner in a sealed, marked container.

Note: *Although some friction materials may no longer contain asbestos, it is safest to assume that they do, and to take precautions accordingly.*

Petrol-engined models

Removal

1 Unless the complete engine/transmission unit is to be removed from the vehicle and separated for major overhaul (see Chapter 2C), the clutch can be reached by removing the gearbox as described in Chapter 7A.

2 Before disturbing the clutch, check for paint marks showing the relationship of the pressure plate assembly to the flywheel. If none can be found, make your own using chalk, touch-up paint or a marker pen **(see illustration)**.

3 Working in a diagonal sequence, slacken the pressure plate bolts by half a turn at a time, until spring pressure is released and the bolts can be unscrewed by hand **(see illustration)**.

4 Prise the pressure plate assembly off its locating dowels, and collect the friction plate, noting which way round the friction plate is fitted.

Inspection

Note: *Due to the amount of work necessary to remove and refit clutch components, it is usually considered good practice to renew the clutch friction plate, pressure plate assembly and release bearing as a matched set, even if only one of these is actually worn enough to require renewal. It is also worth considering the renewal of the clutch components on a preventative basis if the engine and/or transmission have been removed for some other reason.*

5 When cleaning clutch components, read first the warning at the beginning of this Section; remove dust using a clean, dry cloth, and working in a well-ventilated atmosphere.

6 Check the friction plate facings for signs of wear, damage or oil contamination. If the friction material is cracked, burnt, scored or damaged, or if it is contaminated with oil or grease (shown by shiny black patches), the friction plate must be renewed. Measure the friction plate thickness and check the depth of the rivets below the friction material surface. If the friction plate thickness or the depth of any rivet is equal to, or less than, the service limit given in the Specifications, then the friction plate must be renewed.

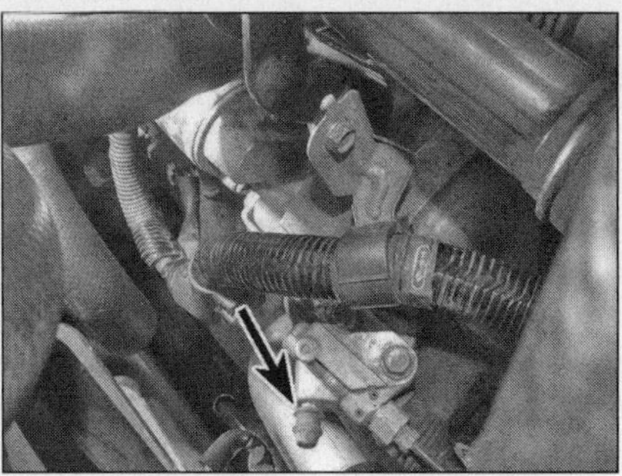

5.4 Before bleeding hydraulic system, remove dust cap and clean any dirt from around slave cylinder bleed nipple

7 If the friction material is still serviceable, check that the centre boss splines are unworn, that the torsion springs are in good condition and securely fastened, and that all the rivets are tight. If any wear or damage is found, the friction plate must be renewed.

8 If the friction material is fouled with oil, this must be due to an oil leak from the crankshaft left-hand oil seal, from the cylinder block-to-lower crankcase/main bearing ladder or the lower crankcase/main bearing ladder-to-sump intersections, or from the gearbox input shaft. Renew the seal or repair the joint, as appropriate, as described in the relevant part of Chapter 2 or 7, before installing the new friction plate.

9 Check the pressure plate assembly for obvious signs of wear or damage; shake it to check for loose rivets or worn or damaged fulcrum rings, and check that the drive straps securing the pressure plate to the cover do not show signs of overheating (such as a deep yellow or blue discoloration).

10 Check the diaphragm spring fingers for signs of wear or damage to their tips, where they contact the release bearing. The condition of the spring itself is assessed by comparing the heights of the tips of the spring fingers where the release bearing makes

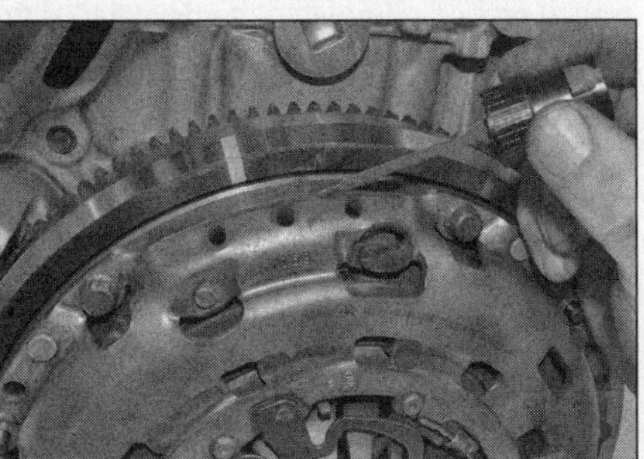

6.2 Before disturbing the clutch, paint marks showing the relationship of pressure plate assembly to flywheel

6.3 Working in a diagonal sequence, slacken the pressure plate bolts half a turn at a time

6.14 Fit friction plate so that spring hub assembly faces away from the flywheel – note dowels

contact. Either use a dial gauge clamped to the cylinder block/lower crankcase, zero the gauge on the lowest finger tip and check the height of the higher ones, or use feeler gauges and a flat surface (the release bearing or the centre part of a clutch aligning tool, for example). If any finger's height differs from the others by more than the specified service limit, or the diaphragm spring is worn or damaged, or if its pressure is in any way suspect, the pressure plate assembly should be renewed.

11 Examine the machined bearing surfaces of the pressure plate and of the flywheel; they should be clean, completely flat, and free from scratches or scoring. If either is discoloured from excessive heat, or shows signs of cracks, it should be renewed – although minor damage of this nature can sometimes be polished away using emery paper. Using a straight-edge and feeler blades check the pressure plate surface for warpage at several points around its diameter; if the warpage exceeds the specified limit the plate must be renewed.

12 Check that the release bearing contact surface rotates smoothly and easily, with no sign of noise or roughness. Also check that the surface itself is smooth and unworn, with no signs of cracks, pitting or scoring. If there is any doubt about its condition, the bearing must be renewed.

Refitting

13 On reassembly, ensure that the friction surfaces of the flywheel and pressure plate are completely clean, smooth, and free from oil or grease. Use solvent to remove any protective grease from new components.

14 Apply a thin smear of grease to the splines of the friction plate and the gearbox input shaft, and to the crankshaft pilot bush; Honda recommend Urea Grease UM264 (Part No. 41211-PY5-305). Fit the friction plate so that its spring hub assembly faces away from the flywheel (the thickness of the spring hub usually makes it impossible to fit it with the hub against the flywheel); there may also be a marking showing which way round the plate is to be refitted **(see illustration)**.

15 Refit the pressure plate assembly, aligning the marks made on dismantling (if the original pressure plate is re-used), and locating the pressure plate on its locating dowels. Fit the pressure plate bolts, but tighten them only finger-tight, so that the friction plate can still be moved.

16 The friction plate must now be centralised, so that when the gearbox is refitted, its input shaft will pass through the splines at the centre of the friction plate.

17 Centralisation can be achieved by passing a screwdriver or other long bar through the friction plate and into the hole in the crankshaft; the friction plate can then be moved around until it is centred on the crankshaft hole. Alternatively, a clutch-aligning tool can be used to eliminate the guesswork; these can be obtained from most accessory shops **(see illustration)**. A home-made alignment tool can be fabricated from a length of metal rod or wooden dowel which fits closely inside the crankshaft hole, and has insulating tape wound around it to match the diameter of the friction plate's splined centre.

6.17 Use a clutch-aligning tool to centralise friction plate on crankshaft

18 When the friction plate is centralised, tighten the pressure plate bolts evenly and in a diagonal sequence to the specified torque setting. Ensure the pressure plate is drawn squarely onto the flywheel, to prevent the pressure plate being distorted.

19 Refit the gearbox as described in Chapter 7A.

Diesel-engined models

Caution: Honda state that unless tools are used both on removing and installing the pressure plate assembly, it will be irreversibly damaged. We found, however, that careful, progressive and even slackening of the pressure plate mounting bolts allowed us to dismantle and rebuild the clutch without these special tools, and the setting procedure can also be carried out without them.

Removal

20 Refer to paragraphs 1 and 2.

21 If the pressure plate assembly is likely to be re-used and the special tools are available, fit the tool to the engine/gearbox mounting bolt holes (or to the pressure plate itself, as applicable) and tighten down the centre screw to compress the diaphragm spring and lock the mechanism.

22 Refer to paragraph 3. If the special tools are not being used, be careful to slacken the pressure plate bolts carefully, progressively and evenly. Keep your hands away from the Self-Adjusting Clutch (SAC) mechanism.

Caution: As the diaphragm spring pressure is relaxed, the mechanism's adjusting ring may spring into place. Ensure all fingers are clear of the area.

23 Refer to paragraph 4.

Inspection

Note: *Refer to note with paragraph 5. Owners should also note that it is considered good practice by many professionals to renew dual-mass flywheels as a matter of course whenever the clutch is renewed.*

24 Proceed as described in paragraphs 5 to 12 above. When checking the pressure plate assembly, check also the components of the Self-Adjusting Clutch (SAC) mechanism; if there is any sign of excessive wear or of damage to any part of this, then the complete pressure plate assembly must be renewed.

Refitting

25 Refer to paragraph 13. It is advisable to refit the clutch assembly with clean hands, and to wipe down the pressure plate and flywheel faces with a clean rag before assembly begins.

26 Refer to paragraph 14. Fit the friction plate with the greater projecting side of the hub facing away from the flywheel; there may also be a marking showing which way round the plate is to be refitted. On genuine Honda clutches the friction plate should be fitted with the TRANSMISSION SIDE marking facing towards the gearbox **(see illustration)**.

6.26 Fit friction plate with the TRANSMISSION SIDE marking facing towards gearbox

27 The Self-Adjusting Clutch (SAC)'s mechanism must now be reset before refitting the pressure plate. Note that a new pressure plate assembly may be supplied pre-set, in which case this procedure can be ignored; follow the instructions provided by the supplier carefully.

28 A large diameter bolt (M14 at least) long enough to pass through the pressure plate, a matching nut, and several large diameter washers, will be needed for this procedure. Mount the bolt head in the jaws of a sturdy bench vice, with one large washer fitted.

6.29 Washer should bear on centre ring of self-adjusting mechanism so it can be compressed . . .

6.30 . . . by tightening nut so that adjusting ring can be moved anti-clockwise until small coil springs are fully compressed

6.33a Hold adjusting ring and unscrew nut so adjusting ring is gripped in position, and pressure plate is ready to fit

6.33b Refit pressure plate assembly, aligning marks made on dismantling and locating pressure plate on dowels

6.33c Use a clutch-aligning tool to centralise friction plate on crankshaft

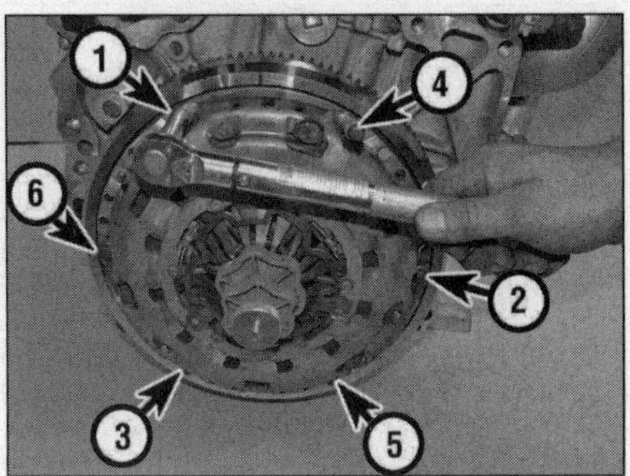

6.34 Tighten the pressure plate bolts evenly – in several stages, by half a turn at a time – and in a star pattern

29 Offer the pressure plate over the bolt, friction plate surface facing down, and locate it centrally over the bolt and washer – the washer should bear on the centre ring or hub **(see illustration)**.

30 Fit several further large washers over the bolt, so that they bear on the ends of the spring fingers, then add the nut and tighten by hand to locate the washers.

31 The purpose of the procedure is to turn the pressure plate's internal adjusting ring so that the three small coil springs visible on the pressure plate's outer surface are fully compressed. Tighten the nut just fitted until the adjusting ring is free to turn. Either push the adjusting ring with a screwdriver or use a pair of thin-nosed, or circlip, pliers in one of the windows in the top surface, opening the jaws of the pliers to turn the adjusting ring anti-clockwise, so that the springs are fully compressed **(see illustration)**.

32 Hold the adjusting ring in this position, then unscrew the centre nut. Once the nut is released, the adjusting ring will be gripped in position, and the screwdriver or pliers can be removed. Take the pressure plate from the vice, and it is ready to fit **(see illustration)**.

33 Refer to paragraphs 15 to 17 **(see illustrations)**. If the Honda special tools are available, fit the pressure plate compressor/flywheel holding tool to the engine/gearbox mounting bolt holes and the clutch alignment arbor and adapter to the pressure plate assembly to centralise the friction plate, then tighten down the compressor's centre screw to compress the diaphragm spring and lock the Self-Adjusting Clutch (SAC) mechanism.

34 When the friction plate is centralised, tighten the pressure plate bolts evenly – in several stages, by half a turn at a time – and in a star pattern to the specified torque setting **(see illustration)**. Ensure the pressure plate is drawn squarely onto the flywheel, to prevent the pressure plate being distorted and the setting of the Self-Adjusting Clutch (SAC)'s mechanism being lost.

35 Refit the gearbox as described in Chapter 7A.

Note: *The Self-Adjusting Clutch (SAC)'s adjusting ring should be heard moving into place when the diaphragm spring's pressure is relaxed for the first time. As soon as the transmission and clutch components have been refitted and the clutch hydraulic system has been (if necessary) bled, ensure that there is quiet as the clutch pedal is depressed for the first time; a 'buzz' should be heard as the mechanism rotates into place.*

7.3 Use a screwdriver to slip one leg of release fork spring clear of head of pivot

7 Release bearing and fork – removal, inspection and refitting

Note: *Refer to the warning concerning the dangers of asbestos dust at the beginning of Section 6.*

Removal

1 Unless the complete engine/transmission unit is to be removed from the vehicle and separated for major overhaul (see Chapter 2C), the clutch release mechanism can only be reached by removing the gearbox, as described in Chapter 7A.

2 Remove the release fork dust boot, noting how it is fitted.

3 Disengage the release fork spring from the ball-stud pivot. Either use a pair of pliers to compress together the ends of the spring inside the fork so that they can be slipped out of the retaining slots in the fork, or use the tip of a screwdriver to slip one leg of the release fork spring clear of the head of the pivot **(see illustration)**. Withdraw the release fork from the bellhousing, noting which way around the release fork and spring are fitted.

4 Slide the release bearing off the gearbox shaft guide sleeve and withdraw it.

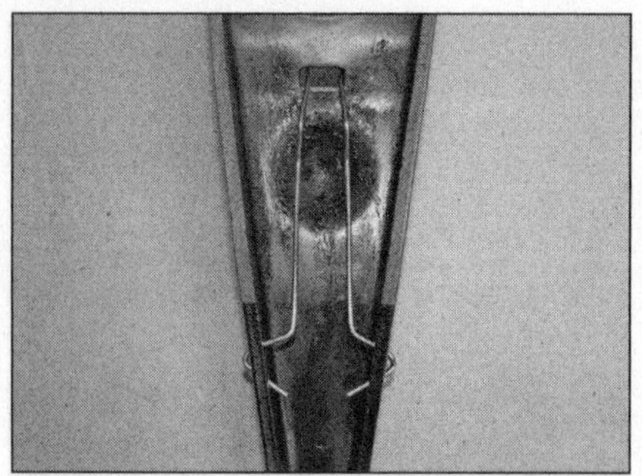

7.8 Fit spring to the release fork as shown

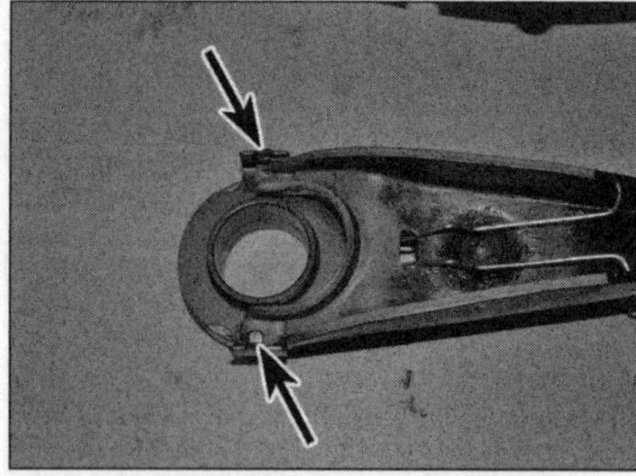

7.9a Engage tips of release fork behind retaining ears of release bearing's operating arms . . .

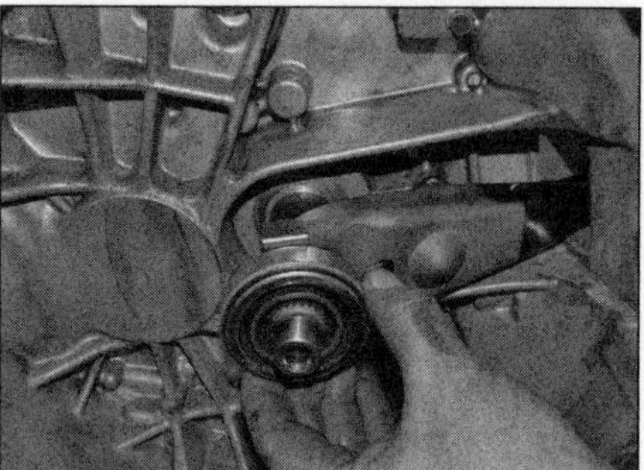

7.9b . . . then fit both together to gearbox shaft guide sleeve and aperture in bellhousing . . .

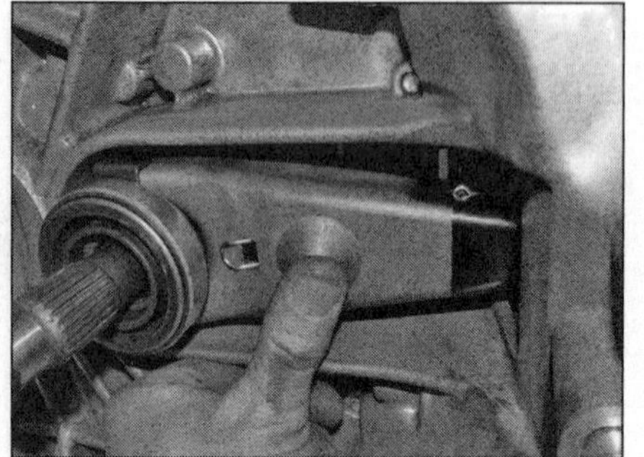

7.10a . . . then press release fork on to ball-stud pivot . . .

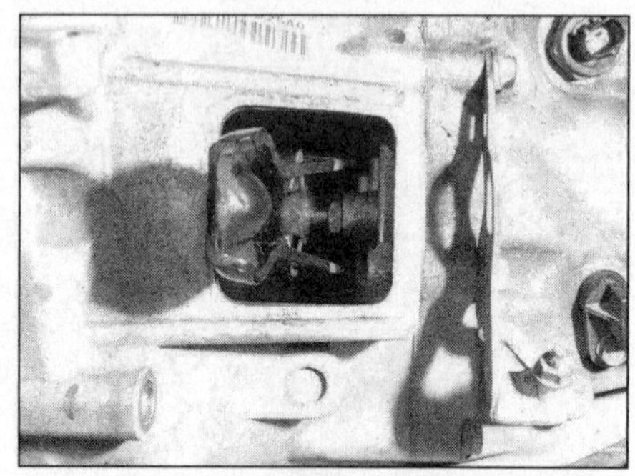

7.10b . . . so that spring clips over ball-stud's head

7.11 Ensure release fork dust boot seals fully around fork and in bellhousing aperture

Inspection

5 Check the release mechanism, renewing any component which is worn or damaged. Carefully check all bearing surfaces and points of contact.

6 When checking the release bearing itself, note that it is packed with grease and so should not be washed in solvent; wipe it clean with a paper towel or rag before examining it. Note also that it is often considered worthwhile to renew the release bearing as a matter of course. Check that the contact surface rotates smoothly and easily, with no sign of noise or roughness, and that the surface itself is smooth and unworn, with no signs of cracks, pitting or scoring. If there is any doubt about its condition, the bearing must be renewed.

Refitting

7 Ensure all components are clean and dry then grease sparingly the contact areas of the release fork (slave cylinder pushrod and ball-stud pivot), the bore of the release bearing and the gearbox shaft guide sleeve, and the splines of the friction plate and the gearbox input shaft; Honda recommend Urea Grease UM264 (Part No. 41211-PY5-305).

8 Fit the spring to the release fork **(see illustration)**.

9 Engage the tips of the release fork behind the retaining ears of the release bearing's operating arms, then offer up the two together so that the release bearing fits over the gearbox shaft guide sleeve and the release fork passes through the aperture in the bellhousing **(see illustrations)**.

10 Press the release fork on to its ball-stud pivot so that the spring clips over the ball-stud's head **(see illustrations)**.

11 Fit the release fork dust boot, ensuring that it seats correctly in the bellhousing aperture and seals fully around the fork **(see illustration)**.

12 Check the operation of the release mechanism then wipe off any surplus grease.

13 Refit the gearbox as described in Chapter 7A.

Chapter 7 Part A: Manual gearbox

Contents

Degrees of difficulty

Easy, suitable for novice with little experience	**Fairly easy,** suitable for beginner with some experience	**Fairly difficult,** suitable for competent DIY mechanic	**Difficult,** suitable for experienced DIY mechanic	**Very difficult,** suitable for expert DIY or professional

Specifications

General

Type:		
Petrol engine:		
2001 to 2003 models	Z2M1, five forward speeds and reverse. Synchromesh on all forward speeds	
2004-on models	PSB1, five forward speeds and reverse. Synchromesh on all forward speeds	
Diesel engine	MBE9, six forward speeds and reverse. Synchromesh on all forward speeds	
Reduction ratios:	**Z2M1 and PSB1**	**MBE9**
First	3.533 : 1	3.933 : 1
Second	1.769 : 1	1.892 : 1
Third	1.212 : 1	1.189 : 1
Fourth	0.921 : 1	0.928 : 1
Fifth	0.714 : 1	0.777 : 1
Sixth	N/A	0.653 : 1
Reverse	3.583 : 1	4.008 : 1

Lubrication

Recommended fluid	See *Lubricants and fluids* on page 0•16
Capacity	See Chapter 1A or 1B

Torque wrench settings

	Nm	**lbf ft**
Air cleaner assembly mounting bracket-to-cylinder head bolt	12	9
Air cleaner assembly mounting bracket-to-gearbox bolts	12	9
Coolant pipe bracket-to-cylinder head bolts	12	9
Earth lead-to-gearbox clamp bolt	10	7
Gear lever knob	8	6
Gearchange cable bracket-to-gearbox bolts	27	20
Gearchange cable guide-to-underbody bolts	10	7
Gearchange lever housing mounting bracket-to-floorpan bolts	22	16
Gearchange lever housing-to-mounting bracket bolts	22	16
Reverse lockout solenoid assembly bolts – diesel-engined models	12	9
Reversing light switch	29	21

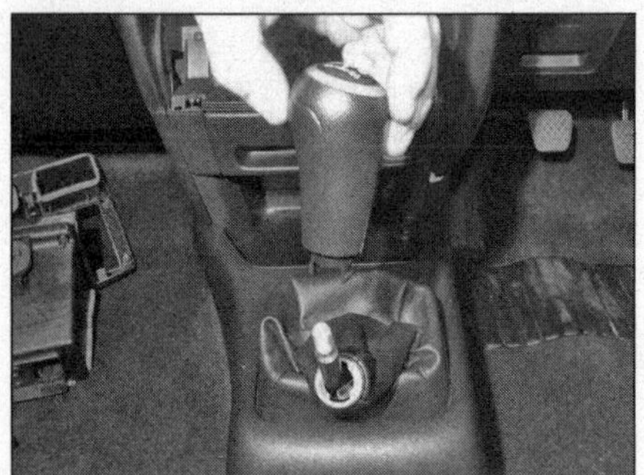

3.1 Unscrew the gear lever knob . . .

1 General information

The gearbox is contained in a cast-aluminium alloy casing bolted to the engine's left-hand end, and consists of the gearbox and final drive differential, with the four-wheel-drive system's transfer case (see Chapter 8) bolted to the rear of the assembly. The gearboxes fitted to petrol and diesel models are clearly different in detail, but similar enough in practice to be treated the same in this Chapter. However, their differences should be borne in mind when obtaining parts. The transmission type code and numbers are marked on a label on the front surface of the transmission casing (see *Vehicle identification*).

Drive is transmitted from the crankshaft via the clutch to the input shaft, which has a splined extension to accept the clutch friction plate, and rotates in ball-bearings. From the input shaft, drive is transmitted to the output shaft, which rotates in a roller bearing at its clutch end and a ball-bearing at its left-hand end. From the output shaft, the drive is transmitted to the differential crown wheel, which rotates with the differential case and planetary gears, thus driving the sun gears and front driveshafts. The rotation of the planetary gears on their shaft allows the inner roadwheel to rotate at a slower speed than the outer roadwheel when the vehicle is cornering. The drive is also transmitted, by means of a transfer drive gear bolted to the back of the differential crown wheel, to the transfer case.

The input and output shafts are arranged side-by-side, parallel to the crankshaft and driveshafts, so that their gear pinion teeth are in constant mesh. In the neutral position, the output shaft gear pinions rotate freely, so that drive cannot be transmitted to the crownwheel.

Gear selection is via a floor-mounted lever operating two cables. The selector linkage causes the appropriate selector fork to move its respective synchro-sleeve along the shaft, to lock the gear pinion to the synchro-hub. Since the synchro-hubs are splined to the output shaft, this locks the pinion to the shaft, so that drive can be transmitted. To ensure that gearchanging can be made quickly and quietly, a synchromesh system is fitted to all forward gears, consisting of baulk rings and spring-loaded fingers, as well as the gear pinions and synchro-hubs. The synchromesh cones are formed on the mating faces of the baulk rings and gear pinions.

On petrol-engined models a mechanical lockout ensures that the driver cannot change directly from top gear to reverse; on diesel-engined models, a reverse lockout solenoid assembly governed by the Electronic Diesel Control (EDC) system control unit (ECU) ensures that the driver cannot change directly from fifth gear to reverse gear instead of top. With this latter system, if you cannot select reverse at any time, first move the gearchange lever across to the first/second side of the gate, then try to select reverse. If this does not work, apply the handbrake and switch off the ignition, then depress the clutch pedal and select reverse before switching the ignition on again and starting the engine (keeping the clutch pedal depressed). If you need to use this latter procedure at any time to select reverse, the system may be developing a fault which will require the vehicle to be taken to a Honda dealer or other suitably-equipped specialist for the ECU's memory to be checked for fault codes and for the necessary action to be taken. Note that this system also operates the rear window wipers automatically (even if they are switched off) whenever reverse gear is selected while the windscreen wipers are switched on.

2 Driveshaft oil seals – renewal

1 Driveshaft oil seals are located at the sides of the gearbox, where the driveshafts are attached.

2 If leakage at the seal is suspected, raise the front of the vehicle and support it securely on axle stands (see *Jacking and vehicle support*). If the seal is leaking, lubricant will be found on the sides of the gearbox, below the seals.

3 Refer to Chapter 8 and remove the driveshaft(s).

4 Use a screwdriver or lever bar to carefully prise the oil seal out of the gearbox casing.

5 Remove all traces of dirt from the area around the oil seal aperture. Using a large section of pipe or a large deep socket (slightly smaller than the outside diameter of the seal) as a drift, fit the new oil seal. Ensure that the spring side of the seal faces into the gearbox casing. Drive it into the bore squarely and make sure it's completely seated. Coat the seal lip with gearbox lubricant.

6 Refit the driveshaft(s). Be careful not to damage the lip of the new seal.

7 Refill/top-up the gearbox with the specified type of fluid (see *Lubricants and fluids*) and check the fluid level as described in Chapter 1A or 1B.

3 Gearchange mechanism and cables – removal and refitting

Removal

1 Unscrew the gear lever knob **(see illustration)**.

2 Remove the the centre console as described in Chapter 11.

3 The two gearchange cables must now be detached. The inner cables are each secured by a split pin – note how all components are arranged, then straighten the pins and remove them, and separate the inner cables from the fittings on the gearchange lever and mechanism **(see illustrations)**. Discard the split pins – new ones should be used on refitting.

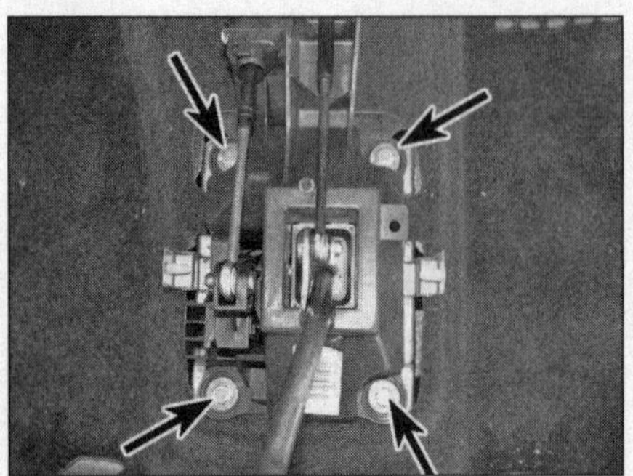

3.3a . . . and remove centre console to reach gearchange lever and mechanism

3.3b Inner cables are each secured by a split pin – remove pin to disconnect cable from gearchange mechanism . . .

3.3c . . . and from gearchange lever

3.4a Twist cable outer anti-clockwise and pull it out to the side . . .

3.4b . . . noting how moulded fitting locates in bracket in top of gearchange lever housing

3.4c Other cable is secured by a spring clip – unhook clip to separate cable from lever housing

3.10a Gearchange cable end fittings are secured to gearbox levers by a split pin and washers – petrol models

3.10b Gearchange cable end fittings are secured to gearbox levers by a split pin and washers – diesel models

3.10c Noting how washers are arranged, remove pins and disconnect cable ends . . .

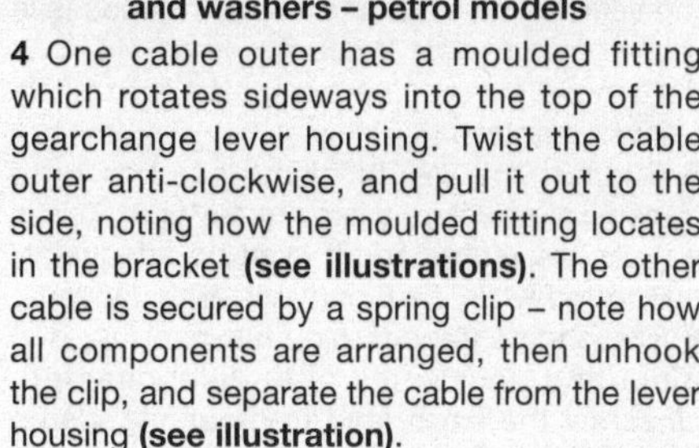

4 One cable outer has a moulded fitting which rotates sideways into the top of the gearchange lever housing. Twist the cable outer anti-clockwise, and pull it out to the side, noting how the moulded fitting locates in the bracket **(see illustrations)**. The other cable is secured by a spring clip – note how all components are arranged, then unhook the clip, and separate the cable from the lever housing **(see illustration)**.

5 Prise up the grommet sealing the cables into the floor. Check that the cables are free to be withdrawn into the engine compartment.

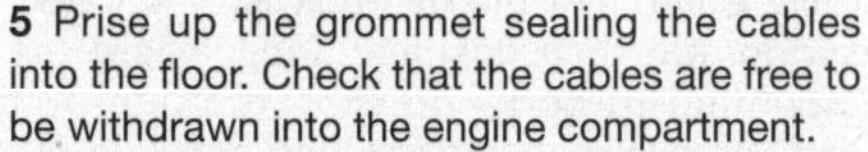

6 If required, unscrew the four bolts securing the gearchange lever housing to its mounting bracket **(see illustration 3.3a)**, then detach the lever housing from the mounting bracket. The mounting bracket is bolted to the floorpan; access to its mounting bolts will require the lifting of the floor carpet.

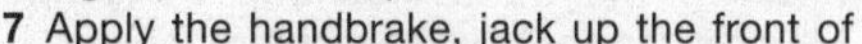

7 Apply the handbrake, jack up the front of the vehicle and support it securely on axle stands (see *Jacking and vehicle support*). Unbolt the guide bracket securing the cables to the underbody, just above the propeller shaft front universal joint.

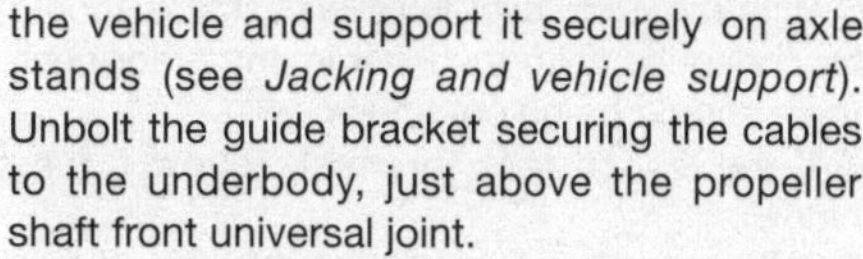

8 In the engine compartment, gain access to top of the gearbox by removing the air cleaner assembly and intake air duct/resonator as described in Chapter 4A or 4B.

9 If the additional working space is required, remove also the battery and battery tray (see Chapter 5A).

10 The gearchange cable end fittings are secured to the gearbox levers by a split pin and washers. Noting how these components are arranged, remove the pins and disconnect the cable ends **(see illustrations)**. Discard the split pins – new ones should be used on refitting.

11 The cable outers are secured to a bracket on top of the gearbox by two metal 'horse-shoe' clips. Pull these clips upwards to remove, then unhook the cables and withdraw them completely from the vehicle. Mark the cables for identification purposes, if they are to be refitted. Discard the clips – new ones should be used on refitting.

Refitting

12 Refitting is a reversal of removal, noting the following points:

a) Lightly grease the cable end fittings, at both the gearbox and gearchange lever/mechanism ends, when refitting; Honda recommend Urea Grease UM264 (Part No. 41211-PY5-305).

*b) Honda state that new split pins and horse-shoe clips must be used when refitting the cables **(see illustrations).***

c) Ensure that the cables are correctly refitted, and routed as before, with no sharp bends.

3.10d . . . do not forget washers under cable end fittings

3.12a New horse-shoe clips must be used when refitting cables . . .

3.12b . . . refit washers as noted on removal

3.12c Fit new split pins and spread ends securely . . .

3.12d . . . when refitting cables

d) Tighten the gearchange lever housing mounting bolts to the specified torque.

e) On completion, check that all gears can be selected properly before taking the vehicle out on the road.

4 Reversing light switch – testing and renewal

Testing

1 Before testing the reversing light switch, check the fuse (No. 10) in the passenger compartment fuse panel (see also the wiring diagrams in Chapter 12).

2 Put the gear lever in reverse, and turn the ignition switch to the ON (II) position. The reversing lights should go on. Turn off the ignition switch.

3 If the reversing lights don't go on, check the light bulbs in the tail light assembly (see Chapter 12). It's unlikely that both bulbs would fail at once, but it's still a possibility.

4 If the fuse and bulbs are both sound, the reversing light switch on the gearbox should be checked. On petrol-engined models it is located on top of the gearbox, next to the gearchange cables and levers, while on diesel-engined models, it is located at the front of the gearbox, behind the clutch slave cylinder hydraulic pipe. As required, gain access to the switch by removing the air cleaner assembly and intake air duct/resonator as described in Chapter 4A or 4B. On diesel models, if the additional working space is required, remove also the battery, battery tray and the battery tray mounting bracket (see Chapter 5A). Alternatively, jack up the front of the vehicle and support it securely on axle stands (see *Jacking and vehicle support*), then remove the engine compartment undershield (Chapter 11) to reach the switch from underneath.

5 The reversing light switch should not be confused with the vehicle speed sensor, which is also located in the top or front of the gearbox, but unlike the reversing light switch, has a separate mounting bolt **(see illustrations)**. Disconnect the switch wiring plug.

6 With the gear lever in reverse, there should be continuity; with the lever in any other gear, there should be no continuity.

7 If the switch fails this test, renew it (see below).

8 If the switch is OK, but the reversing lights aren't coming on, check for power to the switch. If voltage is not available, trace the circuit between the switch and the fuse panel. If power is present, trace the circuit between the switch and the reversing lights for an open-circuit condition.

Renewal

Note: *Liquid gasket (Honda Part No. 08C70-K0234M, 08C70-K0334M, 08C70-X0331S or 08718-0001 or equivalent) must be available on reassembly.*

9 If not already done, gain access to the switch as described in paragraphs 4 and 5 above. Before working on any part of the vehicle's electrical systems, it is advisable to disconnect the battery negative (earth) lead (see *Disconnecting the battery*).

10 A large deep socket or spanner will be needed to unscrew the switch.

11 Refitting is a reversal of removal. Apply a smear of liquid gasket to the switch threads, and tighten the switch to the specified torque. Test the operation of the lights on completion.

5 Reverse lockout solenoid – removal, testing and refitting

Note: *This component is found only on diesel-engined models. Liquid gasket (Honda Part No. 08C70-K0234M, 08C70-K0334M or 08C70-X0331S or equivalent) must be available on reassembly, in addition to new engine/transmission mounting fasteners and any other items (gaskets, seals, etc) found to be in need of renewal during the procedure.*

Removal

1 Remove the air cleaner assembly and intake air duct/resonator as described in Chapter 4B.

2 Remove the battery, battery tray and the battery tray mounting bracket (see Chapter 5A).

3 Apply the handbrake, jack up the front of the vehicle and support it on axle stands (see *Jacking and vehicle support*).

4 Remove the engine compartment under-shield (Chapter 11).

5 Support the weight of the gearbox on a transmission jack or a large trolley jack. This is a heavy assembly, and it must be adequately supported while the mountings are removed.

6 The engine/transmission left-hand (upper) mounting must now be disconnected. Unscrew the earth lead-to-mounting clamp bolt. Make sure the gearbox is adequately supported, then unscrew and discard the mounting-to-body bracket through-bolt and the two nuts and the bolt securing the mounting to the gearbox **(see illustrations)**. Remove the mounting; if necessary, unscrew the two studs from the top of the gearbox using a deep socket applied to the hexagon form on their upper ends.

7 Disconnect the solenoid wiring plug. Unscrew the three mounting bolts and withdraw the solenoid **(see illustration)**.

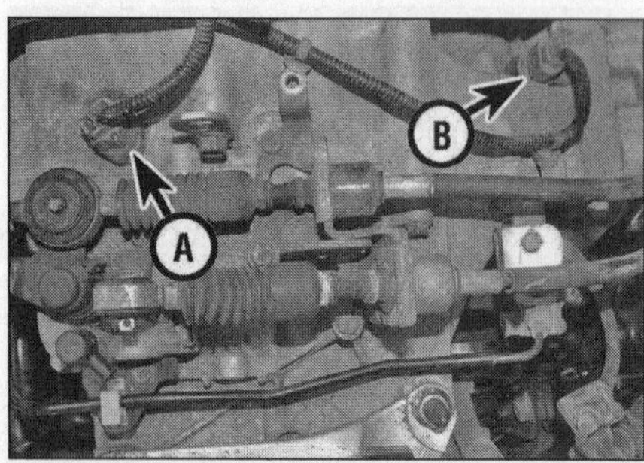

4.5a On petrol models, do not confuse reversing light switch (A) with vehicle speed sensor (B)

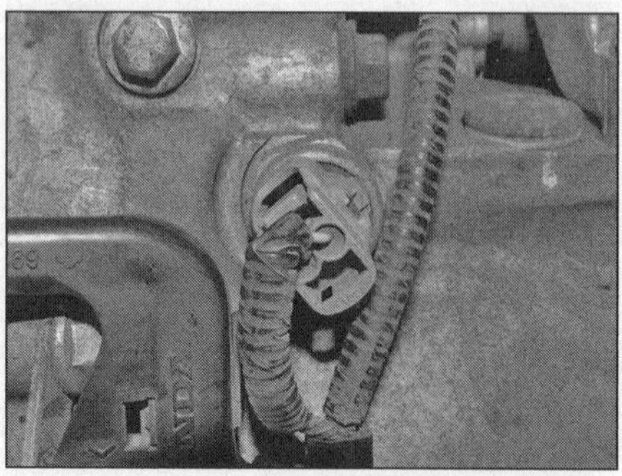

4.5b Reversing light switch – diesel models

5.6a To remove reverse lockout solenoid on diesel models the engine/transmission left-hand (upper) mounting . . .

Testing

8 Verify the state of the solenoid by checking whether it operates when it is energised by connecting the vehicle's battery across its terminals (battery negative (earth) lead to the solenoid's No. 1 terminal). If the solenoid does not operate as described, it must be renewed.

Refitting

9 Refitting is a reversal of removal, noting the following points:

a) Apply a smear of liquid gasket to the solenoid assembly's mating surface, then refit it to the gearbox, tightening the mounting bolts to the specified torque wrench setting.

b) Renewing the nuts, bolt and through-bolt as described in Chapter 2B, refit the engine/transmission left-hand (upper) mounting. Tighten all fasteners to the torque wrench settings specified.

c) Remove the jack, refit the engine compartment undershield (Chapter 11) and lower the vehicle to the ground.

d) Refit all components removed for access, as described in Chapters 5A and 4B.

e) On completion, check the operation of the system before taking the vehicle out on the road.

6 Gearbox – removal and refitting

Caution: The removal of the gearbox requires the removal first of the front suspension subframe. This leaves the engine hanging on a hoist in the engine compartment and located only by the engine right-hand mounting; great care will be required to minimise the risk of personal injury and of expensive component damage. Read through the procedure first to ensure that all the tools and equipment required are to hand. Note also that various engine mounting fasteners, driveshaft locking circlips, propeller shaft Torx bolts, etc, must be renewed as a matter of course whenever they are disturbed, in addition to any other items (gaskets, seals, etc) found to be in need of renewal during the procedure.

6.3 . . . then unbolt earth strap next to clutch slave cylinder

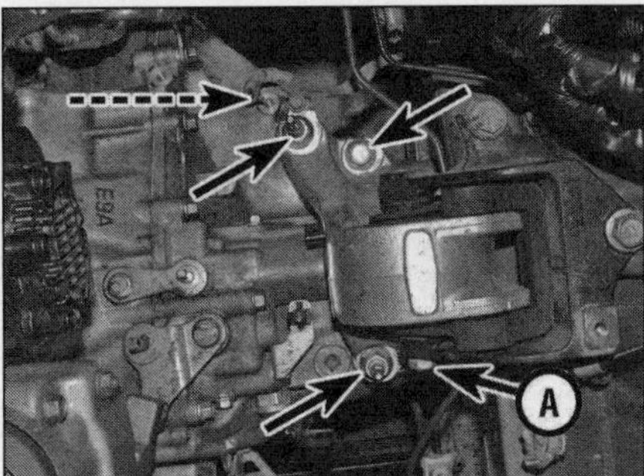

5.6b . . . must be dismantled – note mounting through-bolt (A), and disconnected earth lead

Removal

Petrol-engined models

1 Remove the air cleaner assembly and intake air duct as described in Chapter 4A.

2 Remove the battery and the battery tray as described in Chapter 5A **(see illustrations)**.

3 Unbolt the earth strap next to the clutch slave cylinder **(see illustration)**.

4 Drain the gearbox fluid as described in Chapter 1A.

5 Disconnect the wiring plugs from the reversing light switch and vehicle speed sensor (see illustration 4.5a).

6 Remove the split pin and washers securing the gearchange cable ends to the gearbox levers, and disconnect the cables (see Section 3). Unscrew the three bolts securing the gearchange cable bracket to the top of the gearbox, then secure the whole assembly to one side, taking care not to bend the cables **(see illustration)**.

7 Trace the clutch hydraulic line back from the slave cylinder to the master cylinder, and unbolt the pipe/union support bracket(s) securing the pipe or hose to the gearbox (see Chapter 6). Remove the two slave cylinder mounting bolts, and move the slave cylinder and hydraulic pipe/hose assembly clear of the gearbox **(see illustration)**.

Caution: Be careful not to bend or kink the clutch hydraulic pipe, and don't depress the clutch pedal while the slave cylinder is removed.

8 Unscrew the bolts securing the coolant pipe and the black plastic square-section wiring harness conduit to the left-hand end of the cylinder head. Slacken slightly the bolt securing the air cleaner assembly mounting bracket to the left-hand end of

5.7 Unscrew three mounting bolts to withdraw reverse lockout solenoid

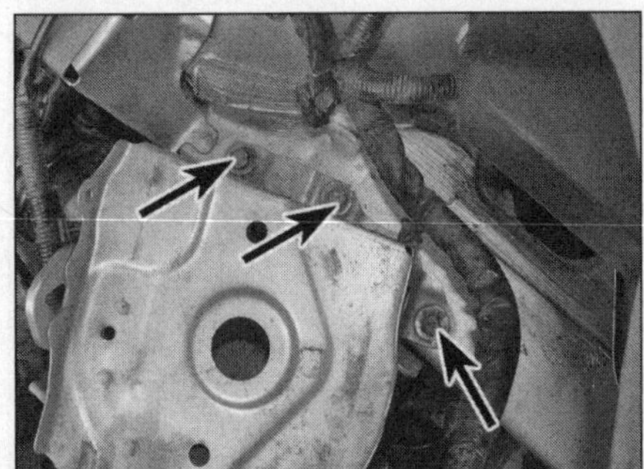

6.2a Undo battery tray upper mounting bolts . . .

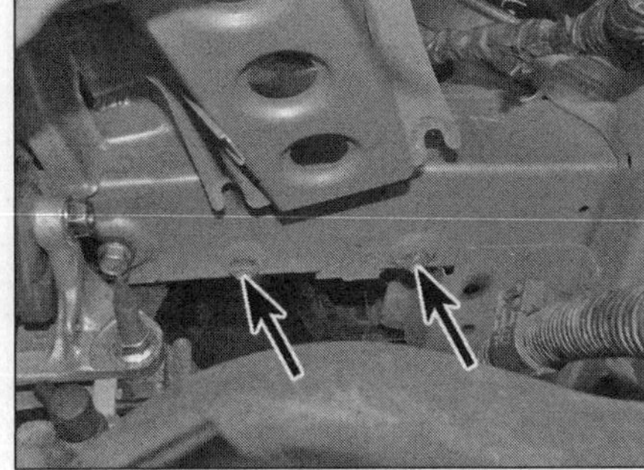

6.2b . . . and lower bolts to remove tray . . .

6.6 Disconnect gearchange cable ends from gearbox levers, and unbolt cable bracket from top of gearbox

6.7 Unbolt clutch hydraulic pipe/union support bracket(s) securing pipe or hose to gearbox

6.14 Unbolt and remove engine bellhousing (flywheel) cover plate

the cylinder head, then lower the coolant pipe slightly.

9 Support the gearbox end of the engine. This must be done from above, with an engine hoist/crane – supporting from below will be awkward, as the front suspension subframe must be removed late. Bolt a lifting eye to the left-hand end of the cylinder head, using one of the now-empty bolt holes.

10 Unscrew the two uppermost engine bellhousing-to-gearbox bolts.

11 Slacken the front wheel nuts, and if possible, also slacken both driveshaft nuts while the vehicle is still on the ground (see Chapter 8). Jack up the front of the vehicle, and support it on axle stands (see *Jacking and vehicle support*). Note that the vehicle must be raised sufficiently high for the gearbox to be lowered out and withdrawn from underneath. Remove the front wheels and the engine compartment undershield (Chapter 11).

6.23 Check components of rear mounting; renew any worn or damaged items before refitting gearbox

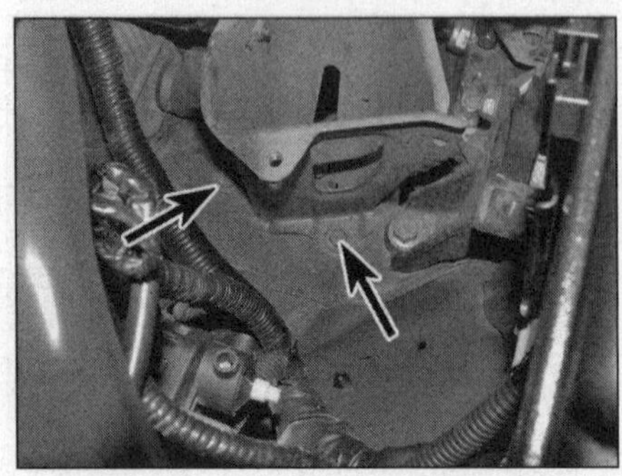

6.25a . . . unscrew upper mounting bolts . . .

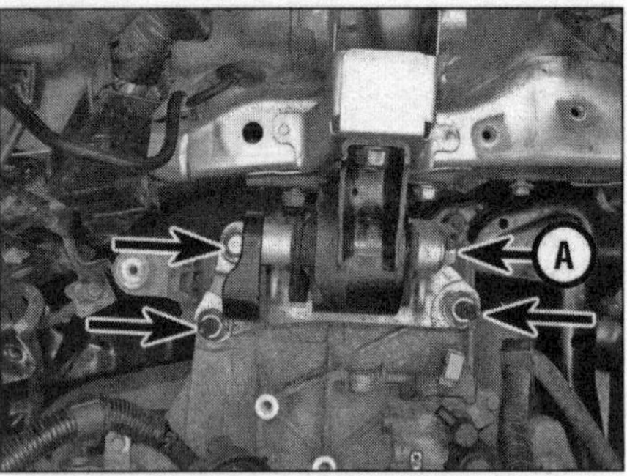

6.19 Unscrew engine/transmission left-hand mounting through-bolt (A), then unscrew two nuts and bolt, and remove mounting bracket from gearbox

12 Remove the driveshafts and intermediate shaft as described in Chapter 8.

13 Disconnect the propeller shaft from the transfer case as described in Chapter 8. Make sure that, once separated, the propeller shaft is either supported or tied up clear of the subframe – do not let it hang down unsupported.

14 Unbolt and remove the engine bellhousing (flywheel) cover plate **(see illustration).**

15 Unscrew the through-bolt from the engine/transmission front mounting (note that the nut is 'captive', with a tab that fits inside a loop on the subframe). Unscrew the three bolts securing the front mounting to the cylinder block and bellhousing, and remove it completely, with the wiring harness bracket.

16 Unscrew the three engine/transmission rear mounting-to-front suspension subframe bolts.

6.24 Remove intake air duct/resonator . . .

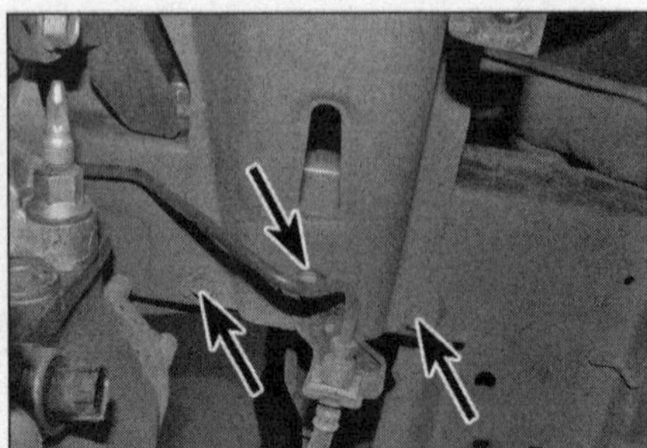

6.25b . . . lower bolts and clutch hydraulic line to remove battery tray mounting bracket

6.20 Unbolt air cleaner assembly mounting bracket from rear of gearbox

17 Remove the front suspension subframe as described in Chapter 10.

18 Support the weight of the gearbox on a transmission jack or a large trolley jack and a flat piece of wood. Have an assistant ready to support the gearbox as the jack is lowered. This is a heavy assembly, and it must be adequately supported while the mountings are removed.

19 The engine/transmission left-hand mounting must now be disconnected. Ensuring that the engine is securely supported, unscrew the engine/transmission left-hand mounting through-bolt, then unscrew the two nuts and bolt, and remove the mounting bracket from the gearbox **(see illustration).**

20 Unbolt the air cleaner assembly mounting bracket from the rear of the gearbox **(see illustration).**

21 Check round the gearbox that everything has been disconnected from it, and that there is nothing in the way which might hinder its removal.

22 Unscrew the remaining engine bellhousing-to-gearbox bolts, then carefully pull the gearbox away from the engine until the gearbox input shaft is clear of the clutch pressure plate. If necessary, carefully prise the gearbox away at first, to release the alignment dowels.

23 With the help of an assistant to guide the unit out, lower the gearbox on the jack until it can be removed from under the vehicle. Recover the two locating dowels, noting their fitted locations, and store them for safekeeping. Check the components of the engine/transmission rear mounting (see Chapter 2A) and renew any that are worn or damaged before refitting the gearbox **(see illustration).**

Diesel-engined models

24 Remove the air cleaner assembly and intake air duct/resonator as described in Chapter 4B **(see illustration).**

25 Remove the battery, battery tray and the battery tray mounting bracket as described in Chapter 5A **(see illustrations).**

26 Trace the clutch hydraulic line back from the slave cylinder to the master cylinder, and unbolt the pipe/union support bracket(s) securing the pipe or hose to the gearbox and battery tray mounting bracket (see Chapter 6).

6.26 Unbolt clutch hydraulic pipe/union support bracket(s) securing pipe or hose to gearbox

Remove the two slave cylinder mounting bolts, and move the slave cylinder and hydraulic pipe/hose assembly clear of the gearbox **(see illustration)**.

Caution: Be careful not to bend or kink the clutch hydraulic pipe, and don't depress the clutch pedal while the slave cylinder is removed.

27 Remove the split pin and washers securing the gearchange cable ends to the gearbox levers, and disconnect the cables (see Section 3). Unscrew the three bolts securing the gearchange cable bracket to the top of the gearbox, then secure the whole assembly to one side, taking care not to bend the cables **(see illustration)**.

28 Disconnect the wiring plugs from the reversing light switch, the vehicle speed sensor and the reverse lockout solenoid.

29 Unscrew the two uppermost engine bellhousing-to-gearbox bolts and secure the wiring harness bracket and the black plastic square-section wiring harness conduit clear of the gearbox **(see illustration)**.

30 Support the gearbox end of the engine. This must be done from above, with an engine hoist/crane – supporting from below will be awkward, as the front suspension subframe must be removed later. Bolt a lifting eye to the left-hand end of the cylinder head, using one of the now-empty bolt holes, but take care to avoid damaging the fuel lines and air hoses running around the end of the cylinder head.

31 Slacken the front wheel nuts, and if possible, also slacken both driveshaft nuts while the vehicle is still on the ground (see Chapter 8). Jack up the front of the vehicle, and support it on axle stands (see *Jacking and vehicle support*). Note that the vehicle must be raised sufficiently high for the gearbox to be lowered out and withdrawn from underneath. Remove the front wheels and the engine compartment undershield (Chapter 11).

32 Remove the intercooler pipe as described in Chapter 4B. Pack the turbocharger opening with clean rag to prevent dirt or other objects falling in.

33 Drain the gearbox fluid as described in Chapter 1B.

34 Remove the driveshafts and intermediate shaft (with the engine rear mounting) as described in Chapter 8.

6.27 Disconnect gearchange cable ends from gearbox levers, and unbolt cable bracket from top of gearbox

35 Disconnect the propeller shaft from the transfer case as described in Chapter 8. Make sure that, once separated, the propeller shaft is either supported or tied up clear of the subframe – do not let it hang down unsupported.

36 Unbolt the engine/transmission left-hand (lower) mounting both from the front suspension subframe and from the gearbox **(see illustrations)**.

37 Remove the front suspension subframe as described in Chapter 10.

38 Support the weight of the gearbox on a transmission jack or a large trolley jack and a flat piece of wood. Have an assistant ready to support the gearbox as the jack is lowered. This is a heavy assembly, and it must be adequately supported while the mountings are removed.

39 The engine/transmission left-hand (upper) mounting must now be disconnected.

6.29 Unscrew two uppermost engine bellhousing-to-gearbox bolts

Ensuring that the engine is securely supported, unscrew and discard the mounting-to-body bracket through-bolt and the two nuts and the bolt securing the mounting to the gearbox. Unscrew the earth lead-to-mounting clamp bolt. Unscrew the two studs from the top of the gearbox using a deep socket applied to the hexagon form on their upper ends and remove the mounting **(see illustration 5.6b)**.

40 Check round the gearbox that everything has been disconnected from it, and that there is nothing in the way which might hinder its removal.

41 Unscrew the remaining engine bellhousing-to-gearbox bolts **(see illustrations)**. Carefully pull the gearbox away from the engine until the gearbox input shaft is clear of the clutch pressure plate. If necessary, carefully prise the gearbox away at first, to release the alignment dowels.

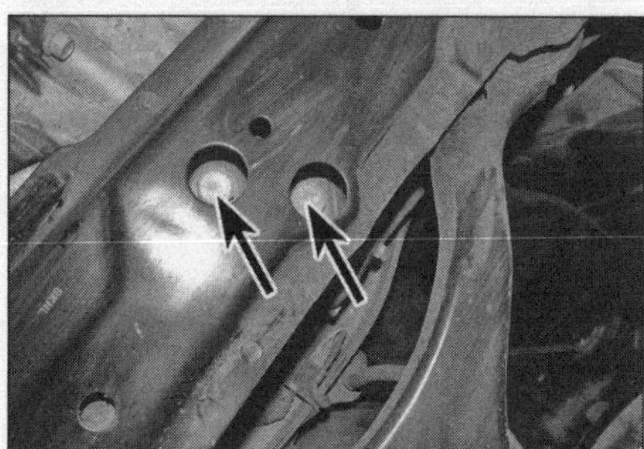

6.36a Unbolt engine/transmission left-hand (lower) mounting both from front suspension subframe . . .

6.36b . . . and from gearbox

6.41a Unscrew remaining engine bellhousing-to-gearbox bolts from front . . .

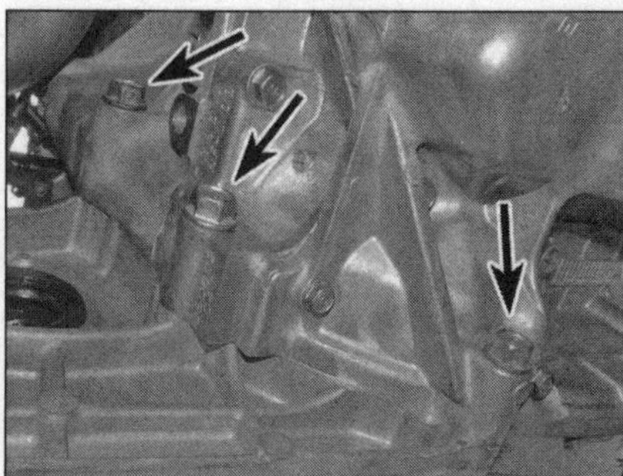

6.41b . . . and rear of engine/gearbox unit

42 With the help of an assistant to guide the unit out, lower the gearbox on the jack until it can be removed from under the vehicle. Recover the two locating dowels, noting their fitted locations, and store them for safekeeping.

Refitting

43 If removed, fit the clutch components (see Chapter 6). It is recommended that the clutch components and crankshaft pilot bush or bearing (Chapter 2A or 2B) are at least inspected, if not renewed, while the gearbox is removed.

44 Apply a thin smear of grease to the splines of the friction plate and the gearbox input shaft, and to the crankshaft pilot bush or bearing; Honda recommend Urea Grease UM264 (Part No. 41211-PY5-305).

45 Make sure the two locating dowels are installed in the bellhousing mating face.

46 Raise the gearbox on the jack, then slide it onto the engine so that the gearbox shaft enters the clutch. It may be necessary to 'wiggle' the gearbox slightly, to align the shaft splines with those of the clutch – if great difficulty is experienced when new clutch components have been fitted, it may mean that the clutch friction plate has not been centred (see Chapter 6). With the splines aligned, the gearbox should slide onto the two dowels, and fully up to the engine.

47 While your assistant holds the gearbox in place, insert two or three engine bellhousing-to-gearbox bolts initially, and tighten them fully by hand to hold the unit fully onto the dowels.

48 Further refitting is a reversal of removal, noting the following points:

a) As far as possible, fit all engine/gearbox mounting bolts hand-tight only at first. Delay fully tightening these bolts until the weight of the engine/transmission unit is resting on its mountings and note that, especially on diesel models, a particular sequence is to be followed to ensure that the unit is correctly settled on its mountings (see Chapter 2A or 2B).

b) Tighten all nuts/bolts to the specified torque wrench settings.

c) Lightly grease the gearchange cable end fittings and slave cylinder pushrod end when refitting.

d) Honda state that new split pins and horse-shoe clips should be used when refitting the cables.

e) Refill the gearbox with fluid as described in Chapter 1A or 1B.

f) Check the operation of the clutch, and bleed the system if necessary as described in Chapter 6.

g) As the front subframe was removed, have the front wheel alignment checked at the earliest opportunity.

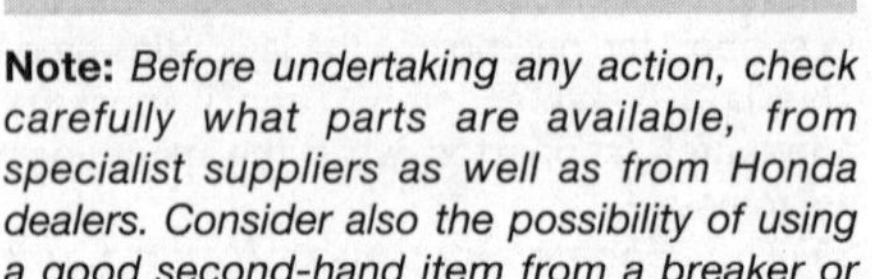

7 Gearbox overhaul – general information

Note: *Before undertaking any action, check carefully what parts are available, from specialist suppliers as well as from Honda dealers. Consider also the possibility of using a good second-hand item from a breaker or vehicle dismantler.*

Overhauling a manual gearbox is a difficult and involved job for the DIY home mechanic. In addition to dismantling and reassembling many small parts, clearances must be precisely measured and, if necessary, changed by selecting shims and spacers. Internal gearbox components are also often difficult to obtain, and in many instances, extremely expensive. Because of this, if the gearbox develops a fault or becomes noisy, the best course of action is to have the unit overhauled by a specialist repairer, or to obtain an exchange reconditioned unit.

Nevertheless, it is not impossible for the more experienced mechanic to overhaul the gearbox, provided the special tools are available, and the job is done in a deliberate step-by-step manner, so that nothing is overlooked.

The tools necessary for an overhaul include internal and external circlip pliers, bearing pullers, a slide hammer, a set of pin punches, a dial test indicator, and possibly a hydraulic press. In addition, a large, sturdy workbench and a vice will be required.

During dismantling of the gearbox, make careful notes of how each component is fitted, to make reassembly easier and more accurate.

Before dismantling the gearbox, it will help if you have some idea what area is malfunctioning. Certain problems can be closely related to specific areas in the gearbox, which can make component examination and renewal easier. Refer to the *Fault finding* Section of this manual for more information.

Chapter 7 Part B: Automatic transmission

Contents

Degrees of difficulty

Easy, suitable for novice with little experience 	**Fairly easy,** suitable for beginner with some experience	**Fairly difficult,** suitable for competent DIY mechanic	**Difficult,** suitable for experienced DIY mechanic	**Very difficult,** suitable for expert DIY or professional 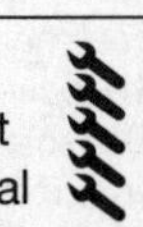

Specifications

General

Transmission code/designation:	
2001 to 2004 models	MRVA
2005-on models	PSB2
Reduction ratios:	
First	2.684
Second	1.534
Third	1.081
Fourth	0.695
Reverse	2.000

Lubrication

Recommended fluid	See *Lubricants and fluids*
Capacity	See Chapter 1A

Torque wrench settings

Torque wrench settings	Nm	lbf ft
Air cleaner assembly mounting bracket-to-cylinder head bolt	12	9
Air cleaner assembly mounting bracket-to-transmission bolts	22	16
Earth lead-to-transmission clamp bolt	10	7
Engine/transmission stiffener mounting bolts	12	9
Fluid filter mounting bolt	12	9
Selector cable bracket and cover to transmission and underbody	10	7
Selector lever mounting bolts	22	16
Torque converter-to-driveplate bolts	12	9
Transmission range switch and cover mounting bolts	12	9

1 General information

The automatic transmission fitted to the CR-V has four forward speeds (and one reverse). The automatic gearchanges are controlled electronically, including the kickdown function, which allows a lower gear to be selected when full acceleration is required. The transmission's control system employs 'fuzzy logic' to determine the gear change-up and change-down points. Instead of these being preset to different vehicle speeds, the system takes into account several influencing factors before deciding to change up or down. These factors include engine and vehicle speed, engine load, brake pedal position, throttle position, and the rate at which the throttle pedal position is changed. This results in an almost infinite number of change points, which the system can tailor to match the driving style, from sporting to economical. The transmission also features Grade Logic Control – a system that automatically changes down and holds a lower gear when the CR-V is climbing a steep hill – this reduces the gear-hunting that can occur as the driver changes throttle position in response to changing engine load.

The system is controlled by the Powertrain Control Module (PCM); this, however, is just the engine management system's Electronic Control Unit (ECU) described in Chapter 4A, differing only in its additional transmission control functions.

The automatic transmission consists of four main assemblies, these being the torque converter, which is directly coupled to the engine; the planetary gearbox, with its multi-disc clutches and brake bands; the final drive unit, which incorporates the differential; and the four-wheel-drive system's transfer case (see Chapter 8), which is bolted to the rear of the assembly. From the differential in the automatic transmission the drive is transmitted both to the front wheels and, by means of a transfer drive gear bolted to the back of the differential crown wheel, to the transfer case. All parts of the transmission are lubricated with automatic transmission fluid

(ATF), which should be changed at regular intervals as described in Chapter 1A.

A fluid cooler is fitted into the cooling system radiator's bottom hose so that fluid pumped via external hoses and metal pipes is cooled before being returned to the transmission.

The torque converter incorporates a lock-up feature, which eliminates any possibility of converter slip in the top three gears, to the benefit of performance and economy.

The selector lever features the usual P (Park), R (Reverse), N (Neutral), D (Drive), 2 (Second) and 1 (First) positions. D is the position for normal driving and features D3 mode; when driving in D with the engine cold, the transmission may delay changing up to help the engine warm-up more quickly. D3 mode allows automatic gearchanging using only the first three gears and the lock-up feature is restricted to third gear only; it is selected by pressing the D3 switch on the end of the selector lever; the system will allow D3 mode only when the ignition is switched on and position D is selected. A warning indicator in the instrument panel reminds the driver that D3 mode is selected; pressing the D3 switch again will deactivate D3. Position 2 locks the transmission in second gear, while position 1 locks it in first; exceeding the specified maximum allowable speeds in these positions (37 mph for position 1, 67 mph for position 2) will cause the system to cut off the fuel supply to the injectors to limit the engine's speed and protect it from over-revving. **Note:** *Apart from illuminating when the ignition is switched on as a check of its function, the instrument panel D indicator also serves to reinforce the messages of the engine management Malfunction Indicator warning Lamp (MIL). If a problem occurs with a component of the engine management system and/or transmission control system that causes a fault code to be logged so that the engine management Malfunction Indicator warning Lamp (MIL) illuminates, the D indicator may also flash while driving (with any position selected) until the vehicle can be taken to a Honda dealer or other specialist for the fault code to be erased.*

A safety interlock system is fitted, which requires that the transmission is placed in P before leaving the vehicle – the system prevents the ignition key being removed until P is selected. On next entering the vehicle, the transmission cannot be moved out of P unless the brake pedal is pressed (the accelerator pedal must be completely released), and the ignition switch is in positions II or III. Similarly, a reverse interlock prevents R being selected at speeds above 5 mph. An emergency override procedure is provided, as follows: Prise out the small blanking plug (the Shift Lock Release cover) at the bottom of the scale next to the selector lever. To release the transmission from P, check that the ignition is switched off, insert a screwdriver and push down on the shift lock release lever, then pull the selector lever towards you in the usual way and move it out of P. To release the reverse interlock, check that the ignition switch is in position I, insert a screwdriver and push down on the shift lock release lever, then pull the selector lever towards you in the usual way and move it from N to R, then to P. Remove the screwdriver and refit the Shift Lock Release cover, with the notch in the cover on the driver's side. **Note:** *If you need to use this latter procedure at any time, the system may be developing a fault which will require the vehicle to be taken to a Honda dealer or other specialist for the ECU's memory to be checked for fault codes and for the necessary action to be taken.*

Because of the need for special test equipment, the complexity of some of the parts, and the need for scrupulous cleanliness when servicing the transmission, the amount which the owner can do is limited. Repairs to the final drive differential are also not recommended. Most major repairs and overhaul operations should be left to a Honda dealer or specialist, who will have the necessary equipment for fault diagnosis and repair. The information in this Chapter is therefore limited to removal and refitting of the transmission as a complete unit.

In the event of a transmission problem occurring, consult a Honda dealer or transmission specialist before removing the transmission from the vehicle, since the majority of fault diagnosis is carried out with the transmission *in situ*.

2 Fault finding – general

Note: *Automatic transmission malfunctions may be caused by five general conditions: poor engine performance, improper adjustments, hydraulic malfunctions, mechanical malfunctions or malfunctions in the computer or its signal network. Diagnosis of these problems should always begin with a check of the easily-repaired items: fluid level and condition (see Chapter 1A), and selector cable adjustment (Section 3). Next, perform a road test to determine if the problem has been corrected or if more diagnosis is necessary. If the problem persists after the preliminary tests and corrections are completed, additional diagnosis should be done by a dealer service department or transmission specialist.*

Preliminary checks

1 Drive the vehicle to warm the transmission to normal operating temperature.

2 Check the fluid level as described in Chapter 1A:

a) If the fluid level is unusually low, add enough fluid to bring the level within the designated area of the dipstick, then check for external leaks (see below).

b) If the fluid level is abnormally high, drain off the excess, then check the drained fluid for contamination by coolant. The presence of engine coolant in the automatic transmission fluid indicates that a failure has occurred in the internal radiator walls that separate the coolant from the transmission fluid.

c) If the fluid is foaming, drain it and refill the transmission, then check for coolant in the fluid, or a high fluid level.

3 Check the engine idle speed. **Note:** *If the engine is malfunctioning, do not proceed with the preliminary checks until it has been repaired and runs normally.*

4 Inspect the selector cable linkage (see Section 3). Make sure that it's properly adjusted and that the linkage operates smoothly.

Fluid leak diagnosis

5 Most fluid leaks are easy to locate visually. Repair usually consists of renewing a seal or gasket. If a leak is difficult to find, the following procedure may help.

6 Identify the fluid. Make sure it's transmission fluid and not engine oil or brake fluid (automatic transmission fluid is typically a deep red colour).

7 Try to pinpoint the source of the leak. Drive the vehicle several miles, then park it over a large sheet of cardboard. After a minute or two, you should be able to locate the leak by determining the source of the fluid dripping onto the cardboard.

8 Make a careful visual inspection of the suspected component and the area immediately around it. Pay particular attention to gasket mating surfaces. A mirror is often helpful for finding leaks in areas that are hard to see.

9 If the leak still cannot be found, clean the suspected area thoroughly with a degreaser, then dry it.

10 Drive the vehicle for several miles at normal operating temperature and varying speeds. After driving the vehicle, visually inspect the suspected component again.

11 Once the leak has been located, the cause must be determined before it can be properly repaired. If a gasket is renewed but the sealing flange is bent, the new gasket will not stop the leak. The bent flange must be straightened.

12 Before attempting to repair a leak, check to make sure that the following conditions are corrected or they may cause another leak. **Note:** *Some of the following conditions cannot be fixed without highly specialised tools and expertise. Such problems must be referred to a transmission specialist or a dealer service department.*

Gasket leaks

13 Check the right-hand side cover periodically. Make sure the bolts are tight, no bolts are missing, the gasket is in good condition and the cover is not damaged.

14 If the leak is from the right-hand side cover area, the bolts may be too tight, the sealing surface of the transmission housing may be damaged, the gasket may be damaged or the transmission casting may be cracked or porous. If sealant instead of gasket material has been used to form a seal between the cover and the transmission housing, it may be the wrong sealant.

Seal leaks

15 If a transmission seal is leaking, the fluid level or pressure may be too high, the vent may be blocked, the seal bore may be damaged, the seal itself may be damaged or improperly installed, the surface of the shaft protruding through the seal may be damaged or a loose bearing may be causing excessive shaft movement.

16 Make sure the dipstick tube seal is in good condition and the tube is properly seated. Periodically check the area around the vehicle speed sensor for leakage. If transmission fluid is evident, check the O-ring for damage.

Housing leaks

17 If the housing itself appears to be leaking, the casting is porous and will have to be repaired or renewed.

18 Make sure the fluid cooler hose fittings are tight and in good condition.

Fluid comes out vent pipe or filler tube

19 If this condition occurs, the transmission is overfilled, there is coolant in the fluid, the housing is porous, the dipstick is incorrect, the vent is blocked or the drain-back holes are blocked.

Fault diagnosis

20 Should a fault be recognised by the engine management system's Electronic Control Unit (ECU), a fault code will be generated and stored in the unit's memory, and the D indicator on the instrument panel's transmission display will flash.

21 First ensure that all the system wiring connectors are securely connected and free of corrosion.

22 If these checks fail to reveal the cause of the problem, the vehicle should be taken to a Honda dealer for testing. A diagnostic socket is incorporated in the wiring harness, into which dedicated electronic test equipment can be plugged – the connector is located under the driver's side of the facia. The test equipment is capable of 'interrogating' electronically the ECU and reading any fault codes stored in its memory.

23 Fault codes can only be extracted from the ECU using a dedicated fault code reader. A Honda dealer will obviously have such a reader, but they are also available from other suppliers. It is unlikely to be cost-effective for the private owner to purchase a fault code reader, but a well-equipped local garage or auto-electrical specialist should have a compatible equivalent.

24 Using this equipment, faults can be pinpointed quickly and simply, even if their occurrence is intermittent. Testing all the system components individually in an attempt to locate the fault by elimination is a time-consuming operation that is unlikely to be fruitful (particularly if the fault occurs dynamically), and carries a high risk of damage to the ECU's internal components.

Clearing fault codes

Note: *If a fault code is logged in the engine management ECU's memory so that the engine management Malfunction Indicator warning Lamp (MIL) illuminates, the fault code must be cleared using a Honda PGM Tester or Honda Diagnostic System (HDS) tester, connected to the diagnostic socket under the driver's side of the facia, and the necessary action taken.*

25 Once the fault has been identified and the problem corrected (usually by fitting a new component), the fault code must be cleared. In some cases, this will happen automatically once the ignition has been switched on and off enough times – if the fault does not recur, it may clear itself.

26 To clear fault codes manually requires the use of a fault code reader tool as described above. However, on early (2001 to 2004) models, codes may also be cleared by the DIY mechanic, as follows. **Note:** *This procedure is not mentioned by Honda for 2005-onwards models.*

27 With the ignition off, remove fuse No. 6 from the engine compartment main fuse/relay box for at least 10 seconds, then refit it. Switch the ignition on, and the fault should have cleared.

28 If the engine management Malfunction Indicator warning Lamp (MIL) remains on (or comes back on later), either the same fault still exists, or there is another faulty component triggering a different fault code. Check that any new components have been correctly fitted, and especially that their wiring plugs are clean and secure.

3 Selector cable – renewal and adjustment

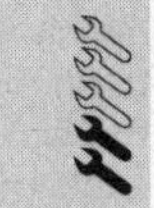

Note: *The selector cable end holder locking clip must be renewed as a matter of course on reassembly.*

Renewal

1 Remove the driver's side under cover and lower cover from the facia, the heater control panel (Chapter 3), the ashtray and stowage pocket from the facia lower centre section as described in Chapter 11, and the instrument panel surround as described in Chapter 12.

2 Move the selector lever to the R position.

3 Slide down the plastic locktab on the selector cable end holder. Pull out the ribbed horseshoe-shaped locking clip from the cable end holder and discard it – a new one must be used when refitting **(see illustration)**. **Note:** *Extract the locking clip using only a pair of needle-nosed pliers gripping the clip's centre; do NOT attempt to prise it out with a screwdriver, or the selector cable end holder may be damaged.*

4 Unhook the cable end fitting from the end holder.

5 Further down the cable, twist the moulded fitting a quarter-turn anti-clockwise so that the projecting tab is in the opening in the selector cable mounting bracket, then slide the cable out of the bracket **(see illustration)**. **Note:**

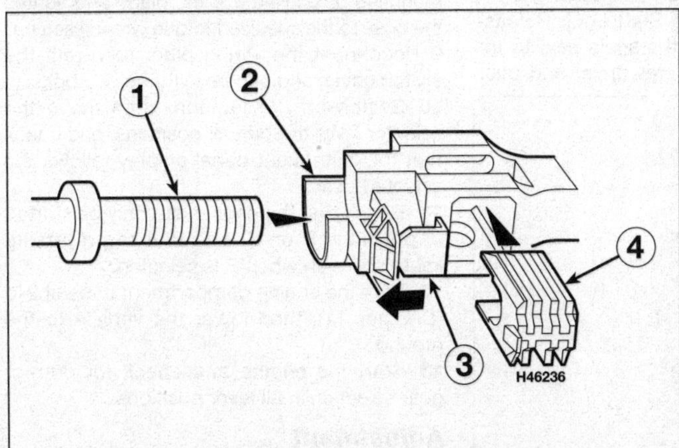

3.3 Disconnecting the selector cable end fitting

1 *Cable end fitting*
2 *Cable end holder*
3 *Plastic locktab*
4 *Locking clip*

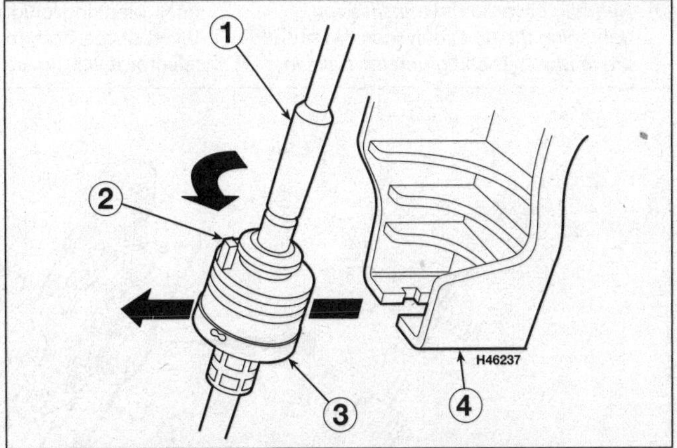

3.5 Disconnecting the selector cable outer

1 *Cable guide – do not twist here*
2 *Projecting tab*
3 *Moulded fitting – twist here*
4 *Cable mounting bracket*

Rotate ONLY the moulded fitting, NOT the cable guide projecting above the moulded fitting or the damper beneath it.

6 Just above the floor, release the selector cable from its clamp.

7 Apply the handbrake, jack up the front of the vehicle and support it securely on axle stands (see *Jacking and vehicle support*).

8 Unbolt the guide bracket securing the selector cable to the underbody, just above the propeller shaft front universal joint. Unclip the cable grommet from the floor.

9 Unbolt and remove the cover fitted over the transmission end of the cable, then unbolt the cable bracket.

10 Prise out the spring locking clip from the transmission selector lever clevis pin. Pull out the clevis pin to disconnect the cable end fitting from the lever.

11 Unbolt the selector cable bracket from the transmission, then remove the bracket from the cable. Remove the cable from the vehicle, taking care not to bend it any more than necessary.

12 Refitting is a reversal of removal, noting the following points:

a) *Feed the cable back into the vehicle through the grommet aperture in the underbody, taking care not to bend it any more than necessary.*
b) *Refit the cable at the transmission end, starting with the transmission selector lever in the R position.*
c) *Ensuring that the dot on the cable outer sleeve is facing downwards, refit the bracket to the cable and bolt the bracket back on to the transmission.*
d) *Grease the clevis pin, then press it back into the transmission selector lever and cable, and refit the spring locking clip, ensuring that the clip is securely fastened.*
e) *Once the cable is fully refitted at the transmission end, refit the remaining bracket. Tighten both cable brackets' mounting bolts to the specified torque wrench setting.*
f) *Refit the cover to the transmission, tightening the bolts only loosely until all are in place. Then tighten the bolts in sequence to the specified torque wrench setting – first the front bolt, then the lower bolt and finally the middle bolt.*
g) *Once the cable is back in the passenger compartment and secured into the clamp just above the floor, carry out the adjustment procedure described below.*

Adjustment

13 If not already done, proceed as described in paragraphs 1 to 5.

14 Switch on the ignition and check that the instrument panel is displaying R selected. If this is not the case, push the cable inner downwards until firm resistance is felt, then pull it back (pull only on the cable inner's end fitting, NOT on the cable guide projecting from the moulded fitting) one 'click' until R is displayed. Switch off the ignition.

15 Lock the selector lever in the R position by inserting a 6.0 mm pin (such as a drill bit) through the holes in the base of the selector lever housing and the selector lever.

16 Offer the selector cable's moulded fitting into the cable mounting bracket with the projecting tab opposite the opening in the mounting bracket. When the cable is slotted in correctly, twist the moulded fitting a quarter-turn clockwise to secure it. **Note:** *Rotate ONLY the moulded fitting, NOT the cable guide projecting above the moulded fitting or the damper beneath it.*

17 Being careful to keep these parts free of grease, slot the cable end fitting into the end holder.

18 Fit a new horseshoe-shaped locking clip into the cable end holder, then push up the plastic locktab to secure it.

19 Remove the 6.0 mm pin or drill bit from the selector lever housing and the selector lever, then switch on the ignition and check that the instrument panel display follows the selected gear.

20 Start the engine and check for correct gear selection in all lever positions.

21 Switch off the ignition and prise out the small blanking plug (the Shift Lock Release cover) at the bottom of the scale next to the selector lever. Insert a screwdriver and push down on the shift lock release lever to check that the selector lever can be moved out of positions P and/or R. Remove the screwdriver and refit the Shift Lock Release cover, with the notch in the cover on the driver's side.

22 On completion, refit all removed components, then take the vehicle for a road test.

4 Transmission range switch – renewal and adjustment

Renewal

1 Apply the handbrake, jack up the front of the vehicle and support it securely on axle stands (see *Jacking and vehicle support*). Remove the engine compartment undershield (Chapter 11). Before working on any part of the vehicle's electrical systems, it is advisable to disconnect the battery negative (earth) lead (see *Disconnecting the battery*).

2 Move the selector lever to the N position.

3 On the right-hand end of the transmission, unscrew the three bolts and take off the cover from the transmission range switch.

4 Disconnect the wiring plug on top of the switch, then unscrew the two mounting bolts and slide the switch off its shaft.

5 Before refitting the switch, ensure that the shaft on the transmission is in the N position – this should be the case if the selector lever inside the vehicle is also in the N position.

6 The switch has to be 'aligned with itself' before fitting – the centre part (which turns) has to align with the switch body. Using a 2.0 mm thick feeler blade across the face of the switch, align the two slots in the centre of the switch with the slot on the edge of the switch body, just below the wiring plug socket **(see illustration)**.

7 Keeping the switch aligned in this position, offer it carefully onto the transmission shaft.

8 With the feeler blade still holding the switch aligned, tighten carefully the two switch mounting bolts. Remove the blade and tighten the bolts to the specified torque wrench setting.

9 Reconnect the wiring plug, then refit the switch cover, and secure with the two bolts.

10 Switch on the ignition, then move the selector lever through all positions, and check that the instrument panel display follows the selected gear.

11 Check that the engine can only be started in positions P or N, and that the reversing lights come on when R is selected.

12 Refit the engine compartment undershield (Chapter 11), then lower the vehicle to the ground.

13 Start the engine and check for correct gear selection in all lever positions.

Adjustment

14 To adjust the switch, follow the renewal procedure, with the exception that the switch does not have to be removed – for adjustment only, the switch mounting bolts need only be slackened.

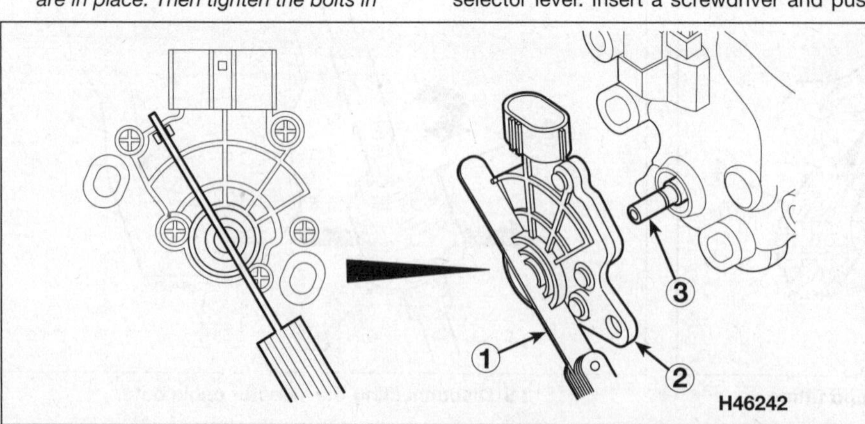

4.6 Align transmission range switch centre with slot on switch body, and refit

1 2.0 mm feeler blade *2 Transmission range switch* *3 Transmission shaft*

5 Selector lever and D3 switch - removal and refitting

Selector lever

1 Proceed as described in Section 3, paragraphs 1 to 5 inclusive. Before working on any part of the vehicle's electrical systems, it is advisable to disconnect the battery negative (earth) lead (see *Disconnecting the battery*).

2 Unplug the connector to disconnect the wiring from the selector lever and release the plastic tie securing the wiring harness.

3 Unscrew the three lever mounting bolts, then, taking care not to scratch any surrounding trim, remove the lever assembly.

4 Refitting is a reversal of removal, noting the following points:

a) Tighten the selector lever mounting bolts to the specified torque.

b) Reconnect and adjust the selector cable as described in Section 3.

Selector D3 switch

5 Remove the selector lever assembly as described above and in Section 3.

6 Release the wiring harness from the clamp on the selector lever bracket base and release the plastic tie securing the wiring harness.

7 Make a written note of exactly which colour wire goes to which terminal in the lever wiring connector. Prise up the locking tabs on the back of the lever wiring connector and remove the lock. Prising up each terminal's locking tab in turn, release all six wires from the connector.

8 Wrap the base of the selector lever knob and the selector lever with adhesive tape and use paint or typist's correction fluid to make marks showing the relationship of the knob to the lever that can be removed easily after reassembly. Remove the selector lever knob and push the D3 switch out of the knob. Using a small, thin-bladed screwdriver, depress the locking tabs in the D3 switch and release both of its wires.

9 Leaving their plastic sleeve in place, carefully pull the switch wires out of the selector lever.

10 Refit the selector lever knob and align the marks made on removal to ensure that it is correctly located; the opening for the D3 switch should be inclined by 50° towards the vertical axis of the lever.

11 Insert the new D3 switch's wires into the original plastic sleeve and tie a piece of string tightly around the sleeve to secure the wire terminals in the sleeve. Lubricate the sleeve with a squirt of water-dispersant lubricant.

12 Carefully pull the original plastic sleeve up through the selector lever towards the knob, drawing the new D3 switch's wires and new plastic sleeve up into place. When enough new switch harness has emerged, cut the string and fit the new switch's wires to the new D3 switch; either wire can be fitted to either terminal.

13 Press the new D3 switch into the end of the selector lever. Ensuring that each wire is returned exactly to the location noted on removal, refit all six wires to the lever wiring connector. Fasten the connector's locking tabs and lock to secure the wires in place.

14 Align the marks on the three plastic sleeves of the wiring harness, then secure them by fastening the plastic tie over the marks. Clamp the new D3 switch's harness 15 mm from the tie.

15 Refit the selector lever assembly as described above and in Section 3.

6 Interlock system - component renewal

1 The main components of the interlock system are as follows:

a) The Powertrain Control Module (PCM), which is the engine management system's Electronic Control Unit (ECU) – see Chapter 4A. Through its control of the ignition system, it is able to prevent the engine being started when this is inappropriate. The information it receives from the vehicle speed sensor enables it to control the reverse gear interlock, and it also receives a signal from the brake pedal position switch for the Park interlock system.

b) The brake pedal position switch – see Chapter 4A. This informs the ECU when the brake pedal is being pressed, for the Park interlock system.

c) The ignition switch/steering lock assembly – see Chapter 10. This contains the ignition key interlock and solenoid, which prevents the key being removed, and which only allows the selector lever to be moved out of P in switch positions II and III.

d) The shift lock solenoid – see below. Fitted to the selector lever assembly, this is what physically prevents the lever being moved into or out of positions P and R.

Shift lock solenoid

2 Remove the selector lever assembly as described in Section 5 and in Section 3.

3 The solenoid is fitted to the left-hand side of the selector lever assembly.

4 Release the wiring harness from the clamp on the selector lever bracket base and release the plastic tie securing the wiring harness.

5 Make a written note of exactly which colour wire goes to which terminal in the lever wiring connector. Prise up the locking tabs on the back of the lever wiring connector and remove the lock. Prising up each terminal's locking tab in turn, release all six wires from the connector.

6 Remove the selector lever cover and the shift lock solenoid. Note how its wiring harness is routed around the selector lever assembly before removing it.

7 Install the plunger and spring in the new solenoid. Fit the new solenoid so that the plunger tip engages with the tip of the shift lock stop, then install its wiring harness, routing it carefully as noted on removal.

8 Ensuring that each wire is returned exactly to the location noted on removal, refit all six wires to the lever wiring connector. Fasten the connector's locking tabs and lock to secure the wires in place.

9 Align the marks on the three plastic sleeves of the wiring harness, then secure them by fastening the plastic tie over the marks. Clamp the harness 15 mm from the tie.

10 Refit the selector lever cover.

11 Refit the selector lever assembly as described above and in Section 3.

7 Automatic transmission - removal and refitting

Caution: The removal of the transmission requires the removal first of the front suspension subframe. This leaves the engine hanging on a hoist in the engine compartment and located only by the engine right-hand mounting; great care will be required to minimise the risk of personal injury and of expensive component damage. Read through the procedure first to ensure that all the tools and equipment required are to hand. Note also that various engine mounting fasteners, driveshaft locking circlips, propeller shaft Torx bolts, etc, must be renewed as a matter of course whenever they are disturbed, in addition to any other items (gaskets, seals, etc) found to be in need of renewal during the procedure.

Removal

1 Remove the air cleaner assembly and intake air duct as described in Chapter 4A.

2 Remove the battery and battery tray as described in Chapter 5A, then unbolt the earth strap from the front of the transmission.

3 Drain the transmission fluid as described in Chapter 1A.

4 From the top of the transmission, unplug their connectors and free the wiring harnesses from the retaining brackets as necessary to disconnect the following:

a) Second clutch pressure switch.

b) Clutch pressure control solenoid valve A.

5 From the front of the transmission, unplug their connectors and free the wiring harnesses from the retaining brackets as necessary to disconnect the following:

a) Countershaft/vehicle speed sensor.

b) Mainshaft speed sensor.

c) Transmission range switch.

d) Third clutch pressure switch.

e) Shift solenoid wiring harness

f) Clutch pressure control solenoid valve B.

g) Clutch pressure control solenoid valve C.

6 At the front of the transmission, release the hose clips and disconnect the fluid hoses from the metal fluid pipes. Anticipate some fluid spillage as this is done – keep the hose ends turned upwards to reduce this, and either plug or tape over the open connections. Check for signs of fluid leakage at any of the hose or pipe unions and take the necessary action on refitting the transmission.

7 Unscrew the bolts securing the coolant pipe and the black plastic square-section wiring harness conduit to the left-hand end of the cylinder head. Slacken slightly the bolt securing the air cleaner assembly mounting bracket to the left-hand end of the cylinder head, then lower the coolant pipe slightly.

8 Support the transmission end of the engine. This must be done from above, with an engine hoist/crane – supporting from below will be awkward, as the front suspension subframe must be removed later. Bolt a lifting eye to the left-hand end of the cylinder head, using one of the now-empty bolt holes.

9 Slacken the front wheel nuts, and if possible, also slacken both driveshaft nuts while the vehicle is still on the ground (see Chapter 8). Jack up the front of the vehicle, and support it on axle stands (see *Jacking and vehicle support*). Note that the vehicle must be raised sufficiently high for the transmission to be lowered out and withdrawn from underneath. Remove the front wheels and the engine compartment undershield (Chapter 11).

10 Disconnect the selector cable from the transmission as described in Section 3; secure the cable clear of the transmission and subframe, taking care not to bend it any more than necessary. Note that while disconnecting the cable at its lower end only involves the work described in paragraphs 9 to 11 of Section 3, cable adjustment on refitting requires that the cable be disconnected at its upper end as well, so you should carry out the full procedure described in Section 3 from the start.

11 Unbolt and remove the engine bellhousing (torque converter) cover plate.

12 Before disturbing the torque converter, check for paint marks showing the relationship of the torque converter to the driveplate. If none can be found, make your own using chalk, touch-up paint or a marker pen. Unscrew and remove the eight torque converter-to-driveplate bolts, turning the engine using a socket on the crankshaft pulley bolt to bring each of the bolts into view.

13 Release the hose clip and disconnect the fluid hose from the fluid cooler metal fluid pipe. Anticipate some fluid spillage as this is done – keep the hose end turned upwards to reduce this, and either plug or tape over the open connections.

14 Remove the driveshafts and intermediate shaft as described in Chapter 8.

15 Disconnect the propeller shaft from the transfer case as described in Chapter 8. Make sure that, once separated, the propeller shaft is either supported or tied up clear of the subframe – do not let it hang down unsupported.

16 Unscrew the through-bolt from the engine/transmission front mounting (note that the nut is 'captive', with a tab that fits inside a loop on the subframe).

17 Unscrew the three engine/transmission rear mounting-to-front suspension subframe bolts.

18 Remove the front suspension subframe as described in Chapter 10.

19 Support the weight of the transmission on a transmission jack or a large trolley jack and a flat piece of wood. Have an assistant ready to support the transmission as the jack is lowered. This is a heavy assembly, and it must be adequately supported while the mountings are removed.

20 The engine/transmission left-hand mounting must now be disconnected. Ensuring that the engine is securely supported, unscrew the engine/transmission left-hand mounting through-bolt, then unscrew the two nuts and bolt, and remove the mounting bracket from the transmission.

21 Unscrew the two uppermost engine bellhousing-to-transmission bolts.

22 Check round the transmission that everything has been disconnected from it, and that there is nothing in the way which might hinder its removal.

23 Unscrew the two engine bellhousing-to-transmission bolts from the front of the engine/transmission.

24 Unbolt and remove the stiffener fitted between the engine and transmission. Unscrew the two engine bellhousing-to-transmission bolts from the rear of the engine/transmission.

25 Carefully pull the transmission away from the engine until the transmission is clear of the locating dowels. If necessary, push the torque converter back into the transmission – take care that it does not fall out as the transmission is lowered.

26 With the help of the assistant to guide the unit out, lower the transmission on the jack until it can be removed from under the vehicle. Recover the two locating dowels, noting their fitted locations, and store them for safekeeping. Either remove the torque converter (in which case be prepared for significant fluid spillage when the torque converter is removed, and the sealing O-ring must be renewed as a matter of course), or devise a method of keeping it inside the housing (such as bolting a metal strip across its face, secured through the bellhousing bolt holes).

27 If the transmission is being exchanged or renewed, unbolt the engine/transmission front and rear mountings and unbolt the air cleaner assembly mounting bracket from the rear of the unit. Check the components of the engine/transmission mountings (see Chapter 2A) and renew any that are worn or damaged before refitting the transmission.

Refitting

28 If removed, refit the engine/transmission front and rear mountings and the air cleaner assembly mounting bracket. Tighten the mounting bolts to the specified torque wrench settings.

29 If the torque converter was removed, refit it using a new O-ring seal. Have an assistant ready to keep the converter pressed into the housing as the transmission is refitted.

30 Make sure the two locating dowels are installed in the transmission mating face.

31 Raise the transmission on the jack, then slide it onto the engine so that the torque converter seats against the driveplate; align the marks made or noted on removal. It may be necessary to 'wiggle' the transmission slightly to align the two dowels with their locations in the engine belllhousing – with the dowels aligned, the transmission should slide fully up to the engine.

32 While your assistant holds the transmission in place, insert two or three engine bellhousing-to-transmission bolts initially, and tighten them fully by hand to hold the unit fully onto the dowels.

33 Further refitting is a reversal of removal, noting the following points:

a) *As far as possible, fit all engine/transmission mounting bolts hand-tight only at first. Delay fully tightening these bolts until the weight of the engine/transmission unit is resting on its mountings and note that a particular sequence is to be followed to ensure that the unit is correctly settled on its mountings (see Chapter 2A).*
b) *Tighten all nuts/bolts to the specified torque wrench settings.*
c) *When reconnecting the fluid hose to the fluid cooler metal fluid pipe, position the clip 2 to 4 mm from the hose end.*
d) *Before tightening the torque converter-to-driveplate bolts, align the marks made on dismantling.*
e) *Refer to Section 3 when reconnecting the selector cable, and adjust the cable as described.*
f) *When reconnecting the fluid hoses to the metal fluid pipes at the front of the transmission, position the clips 2 to 4 mm from the hose ends.*
g) *Refill the transmission with fluid as described in Chapter 1A. Note that the transmission may require more fluid than in a normal fluid change, since the torque converter may be empty (the converter is not drained during a fluid change).*
h) *On completion, start the engine. Allow the engine to reach its proper operating temperature with the transmission in P or N, then switch it off and check the fluid level. Road test the vehicle and check for fluid leaks.*
i) *After the road test, unscrew and discard the through-bolt of the engine/transmission front mounting and slacken the through-bolts of the rear and left-hand mountings, then retighten them to their specified torque wrench settings (see Chapter 2A); tighten first the left-hand mounting through-bolt, then the rear mounting through-bolt, and finally fit and tighten a new front mounting through-bolt on to its nut.*
j) *As the front subframe was removed, have the front wheel alignment checked at the earliest opportunity.*

Chapter 8
Driveshafts, propeller shaft & final drive

Contents

Degrees of difficulty

Easy, suitable for novice with little experience 	**Fairly easy,** suitable for beginner with some experience	**Fairly difficult,** suitable for competent DIY mechanic	**Difficult,** suitable for experienced DIY mechanic	**Very difficult,** suitable for expert DIY or professional 

Specifications

Transfer case

Reduction ratio	0.904 : 1
Lubrication	Shared with manual gearbox/automatic transmission
Recommended fluid	See *Lubricants and fluids* on page 0•16
Capacity	See Chapter 1A or 1B

Front driveshafts

Dynamic damper installed position:	
From outboard face of outboard joint to inboard face of damper:	
Petrol-engined models	297.5 to 301.5 mm
Diesel-engined models:	
Left-hand driveshaft	335 to 339 mm
Right-hand driveshaft	306.5 to 310.5 mm
Driveshaft length:	
From outboard face of outboard joint to inboard face of inboard joint:	
Petrol-engined models:	
Left-hand driveshaft	539 to 544 mm
Right-hand driveshaft	519 to 524 mm
Diesel-engined models:	
Left-hand driveshaft	519 to 524 mm
Right-hand driveshaft	529 to 534 mm
Lubrication:	
Inboard joint	150 to 160 g CV joint grease
Outboard joint	140 to 150 g CV joint grease

Rear driveshafts

Driveshaft length:	
From outboard face of outboard joint to inboard face of inboard joint:	
Left-hand driveshaft	641 to 646 mm
Right-hand driveshaft	692 to 697 mm
Lubrication:	
Inboard joint	96 to 123 g CV joint grease
Outboard joint	70 to 90 g CV joint grease

Propeller shaft

Maximum runout – measured at mid-point of front and rear section	1.5 mm

Final drive unit

Reduction ratio:	
Petrol-engined models with manual gearbox	5.062 : 1
Petrol-engined models with automatic transmission	4.562 : 1
Diesel-engined models	3.894 : 1
Recommended fluid	See *Lubricants and fluids* on page 0•16
Capacity	See Chapter 1A or 1B

Torque wrench settings

	Nm	lbf ft
Final drive unit front mounting-to-underbody bolts	49	36
Final drive unit front mounting-to-unit bolts	69	51
Final drive unit rear mounting bracket and damper bolts	54	40
Final drive unit rear mounting-to-subframe bolts	39	29
Final drive unit propeller shaft flange nut:*		
Early (2001 to 2004) models	118	87
Later (2005-on) models	147	108
Front driveshaft nut – seating surface lightly oiled*	245	181
Intermediate shaft support bearing heat shield bolts:		
Diesel-engined models	44	32
Petrol-engined models	22	16
Intermediate shaft support bearing-to-cylinder block/crankcase bolts	39	29
Propeller shaft centre support bearing bolts*	39	29
Propeller shaft guard bolts	22	16
Propeller shaft Torx bolts*	32	24
Rear driveshaft nut – seating surface lightly oiled*	181	134
Transfer case-to-gearbox/transmission mounting bolts	44	32

* *Use new fasteners.*

1 General information

From the (front) differential in the manual gearbox or automatic transmission the drive is transmitted both to the front wheels and, by means of a transfer drive gear bolted to the back of the (front) differential crown wheel, to the transfer case.

The front wheels are driven via conventional unequal-length driveshafts which have a constant-velocity (CV) joint at each end, splined into the (front) differential and wheel hubs; the inboard joints are tripod type, and the outboard joints are ball-and-cage type. The right-hand driveshaft is in two sections, and incorporates a support bearing; the inboard (intermediate) shaft is held in the transmission by the support bearing, which in turn is supported by a bracket bolted to the rear of the cylinder block.

From the transfer case, drive is taken to the rear wheels via a tubular propeller ('prop') shaft. The propeller shaft has a Hardy-Spicer-type universal joint (UJ) at each end, to cater for the varying angles between the transfer case and final drive unit caused by suspension movement, and a centre support bearing bolted to the body. Although both universal joints have sealed needle-roller bearings, none of these are available separately, nor is the centre support bearing; in the event of excessive wear or of damage to any of these components, the propeller shaft must be renewed as a complete assembly.

The final drive unit, comprising the Dual Pump system mounted in front of the (rear) differential, distributes drive from the propeller shaft to the rear wheels, via two driveshafts. The shafts are similar to those used at the front, having a CV joint at either end, and are splined into the (rear) differential and wheel hubs; again, the inboard CV joints are tripod type while the outboard CV joints are ball-and-cage. The final drive unit housing is of aluminium alloy, and is bolted to the rear underbody via a mounting secured by two large rubber bushes and a rear mounting with a damper assembly. A breather is located on the top of the housing.

The CR-V can be regarded as either a permanent four-wheel-drive vehicle, or as a front-wheel-drive vehicle with four-wheel-drive when needed. When used on-road it is effectively front-wheel-drive only, thanks to the Dual Pump system, which only transmits power to the rear wheels when the front wheels lose traction, and the speed of the front wheels exceeds that of the rear wheels.

The CR-V's Real Time four-wheel-drive system sends power to the rear wheels only when there is insufficient traction for the front wheels. The transmission consists of the conventional front-wheel-drive system, a transfer case that distributes drive to a propeller shaft running the length of the vehicle, a Dual Pump system, the rear differential, and the rear wheel driveshafts. The four-wheel-drive engages automatically and only when needed, requiring no intervention on the part of the driver for it to be engaged or disengaged; there are no warning lights or other indication of whether it is engaged or not. It delivers better acceleration and hill-climbing performance on slippery, and in particular snow-covered, surfaces, as well as smoother response and improved performance when accelerating around corners or turning out of slippery road junctions, and also in the wet on mountain hairpins.

The heart of the system is the Dual Pump unit. It consists of two hydraulic pumps, one driven by the front wheels via the propeller shaft and one driven by the rear wheels via the rear differential. A hydraulically-actuated multiplate clutch, similar to the clutches used in Honda automatic transmissions, connects the propeller shaft to the rear differential; no electronics are involved. All of these components are enclosed in the final drive unit.

When the CR-V is in motion with the front and rear wheels turning at the same speed, for example on dry tarmac, both pumps operate at the same speed. Hydraulic fluid circulates between the two pumps but no pressure is generated. In effect, the fluid fed by the front pump is absorbed by the rear pump. If the front wheels begin to turn faster than the rear wheels, as would be the case if they were spinning on snow or ice, the two hydraulic pumps turn at different speeds and hydraulic pressure proportional to the difference in their speeds of rotation is generated. The resulting hydraulic pressure opens a valve body and feeds pressure to the multiplate clutch, which connects the propeller shaft to the rear differential and thus transmits drive to the rear wheels. The greater the degree of front-wheel slippage, the greater the amount of torque fed to the rear wheels to re-establish overall traction. 2005-on models feature an additional one-way ball cam and pilot clutch system for faster and smoother response matching the best electronically-controlled four-wheel-drive systems.

The system provides two-wheel-drive when driving forwards or backwards at constant speed, under braking (unlike conventional four-wheel-drive systems, Real Time four-wheel-drive automatically disengages under braking, thereby allowing the ABS system to operate properly), if the fluid overheats (a thermal switch opens a pressure-relief valve, releasing the pressure to the clutch) and if fluid pressure becomes excessive (the pressure-relief valve opens, releasing the pressure to the clutch and preventing the rear-wheel-drive system components from experiencing excessive torque). It provides four-wheel-drive under starting and acceleration forwards or backwards and can do so under heavy engine braking.

The Real Time four-wheel-drive system is practically maintenance-free, requiring only a scheduled fluid level check and fluid change like the manual gearbox and automatic transmission.

2 Front driveshafts – removal and refitting

Note: *The driveshaft nuts and locking circlips, and the swivel hub balljoint locking clips must be renewed as a matter of course on reassembly.*

Removal

1 The driveshaft nut is tightened to an extremely high torque and in the interests of safety it is preferable, if possible, to slacken the nut with all four roadwheels on the ground. However, this cannot be done on vehicles with roadwheels which do not have detachable centre caps or covers, while on those which do, this means slackening the wheel nuts, jacking up the vehicle, taking off the wheel nuts and roadwheel to remove the centre cap or cover (carefully tap out the cap, taking care not to damage it), then refitting the roadwheel and nuts before lowering the vehicle to undo the driveshaft nut.

Warning: Before attempting to slacken the driveshaft nut, which is done up extremely tight, make sure the front of the vehicle is securely supported. Do not use poor-quality, badly-fitting tools for this task, due to the risk of personal injury.

2 Significant force will be required to slacken the nut, so be sure to use only good-quality, close-fitting tools. A long-handled 'breaker bar' will be needed, to provide the necessary leverage – if this is not available, slip a strong piece of metal pipe over the end of the socket handle. Wear gloves to protect your hands, should something slip.

3 If the vehicle is on the ground, proceed as follows:

*a) The driveshaft nut has a raised collar, part of which is punched into the driveshaft groove to stop the nut slackening accidentally. Using a hammer and suitable chisel, open out the staking so the nut can be unscrewed **(see illustration)**.*
b) Chock the roadwheel and have an assistant select top gear and apply the footbrake firmly to prevent the driveshaft/hub from turning.
c) Slacken the driveshaft nut and unscrew it until it is flush with the end of the driveshaft.
d) Slacken the roadwheel nuts.
e) Jack up the front of the vehicle and support it securely on axle stands (see Jacking and vehicle support).
f) Remove the roadwheel.

4 If the nut has to be slackened with the vehicle raised, proceed as follows:

a) Slacken the roadwheel nuts.
b) Jack up the front of the vehicle and ensure that it is very well supported, using well-placed, good-quality axle stands (see Jacking and vehicle support).
c) Remove the roadwheel.

2.3 Releasing the staking of a driveshaft nut

d) Release the staking of the driveshaft nut as described above.
*e) Have an assistant select top gear and apply the footbrake firmly to prevent the driveshaft/hub from turning. Alternatively, a tool can be fabricated from two lengths of steel strip (one long, one short) and a nut and bolt; the nut and bolt forming the pivot of a forked tool. Drill a hole in each tip of the fork and fit these over two opposite wheel studs so that the assistant can prevent the driveshaft/hub from rotating as shown **(see illustration 2.26)**.*
f) Slacken the driveshaft nut and unscrew it until it is flush with the end of the driveshaft.

5 Remove the engine compartment undershield (Chapter 11).

6 Drain the manual gearbox or automatic transmission fluid as described in Chapter 1A or 1B. If this is not done, be prepared for significant fluid spillage when the driveshafts are removed – put down plenty of rags or newspaper if necessary.

7 Unscrew the nut securing the anti-roll bar drop link to the suspension lower arm – use an Allen key to stop the drop link balljoint turning as this is done. Unhook the drop link from the lower arm.

8 Extract the locking clip (note which way round and how it is fitted), then unscrew the swivel hub balljoint castle nut. Using a balljoint separator tool (be careful – this carries the risk of damaging the balljoint's rubber boot) disconnect the lower arm from the swivel hub. Discard the locking clip – a new one should be used on refitting.

9 The splined outboard end of the driveshaft now has to be released from the hub. It's likely that the splines will be very tight (corrosion may even be a factor, if the driveshaft has not been disturbed for some time), and considerable force may be needed. Tap the end of the shaft with a plastic or hide mallet only – if an ordinary hammer is used, place a small piece of wood over the end of the driveshaft – and leave the old nut loosely in place on the end to avoid damaging the thread and tip of the driveshaft.

10 Once the driveshaft is released, remove the driveshaft nut and discard it – the nut is only intended to be used once.

11 Pull the disc/hub outwards, and turn it to allow the driveshaft to be withdrawn through the hub. It's helpful to have an assistant on hand here, to pull the swivel hub outwards and support the driveshaft outboard end, while you go on to release the driveshaft inboard end. Be careful not to damage the ABS wheel sensor, the tip of which protrudes on the inside of the swivel hub next to the bearing outer race.

Left-hand side

12 On the left-hand driveshaft, carefully lever the inboard end of the driveshaft from the gearbox/transmission, using a large screwdriver or lever bar positioned between the gearbox/transmission and the CV joint. The inboard end of the shaft is secured with a locking circlip, which must be released – do not pull on the shaft, as the inboard CV joint may separate. Support the CV joints and carefully remove the driveshaft from under the vehicle. To prevent damage to the driveshaft oil seal, hold the inboard CV joint horizontal until the driveshaft is clear of the gearbox/transmission **(see illustrations)**.

Right-hand side

13 The right-hand driveshaft may either be disconnected from the outboard end of the intermediate shaft or it may be removed complete with the intermediate shaft from the gearbox/transmission. In the first case, use a hammer and soft metal drift sharply to tap the inboard CV joint from the intermediate shaft. The internal locking circlip will be released, and the driveshaft may be withdrawn from the splines **(see illustrations)**. Support the CV joints and carefully remove the driveshaft from under the vehicle.

2.12a Lever the inboard end of the driveshaft out of the transmission

2.12b Keep the driveshaft horizontal as it is removed – do not bend the CV joints

2.13a Use a hammer and soft metal drift sharply to tap the inboard CV joint . . .

2.13b . . . to separate the right-hand driveshaft from the intermediate shaft

2.14a Intermediate shaft support bearing heat shield bolts – petrol models

2.14b Cylinder block/crankcase-to-warm-up catalytic converter support bracket . . .

2.14c . . . and intermediate shaft support bearing heat shield bolts – diesel models

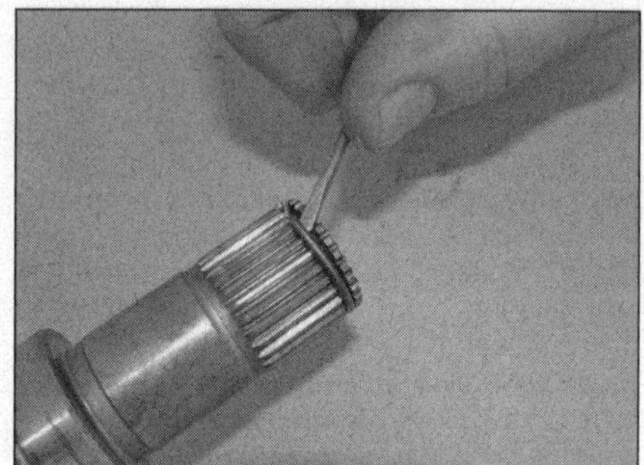

2.18 Always renew locking circlip on left-hand driveshaft inboard end

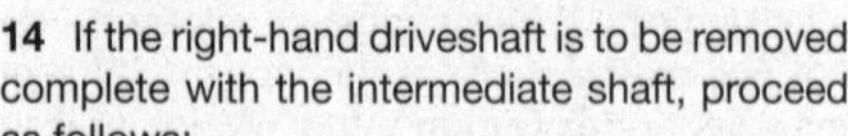

14 If the right-hand driveshaft is to be removed complete with the intermediate shaft, proceed as follows:

a) On all models, slacken the driveshaft in the hub (see paragraphs 9 to 11 above), but leave it in place (or support it by some other means) for the time being.

*b) On petrol-engined models, unscrew the three bolts and withdraw the heat shield covering the intermediate shaft **(see illustration)**. Unbolt the intermediate shaft support bearing from the cylinder block/crankcase (note that two of the bolts are shouldered to locate precisely the support bearing bracket).*

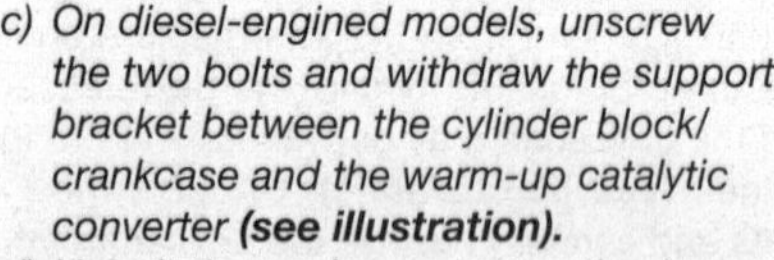

*c) On diesel-engined models, unscrew the two bolts and withdraw the support bracket between the cylinder block/crankcase and the warm-up catalytic converter **(see illustration)**.*

d) Unbolt the engine rear mounting torque rod from the front suspension subframe and the bracket on the lower crankcase/main bearing ladder/sump and withdraw the torque rod. Discard the bolts – these must be renewed as a matter of course, as described in Chapter 2B.

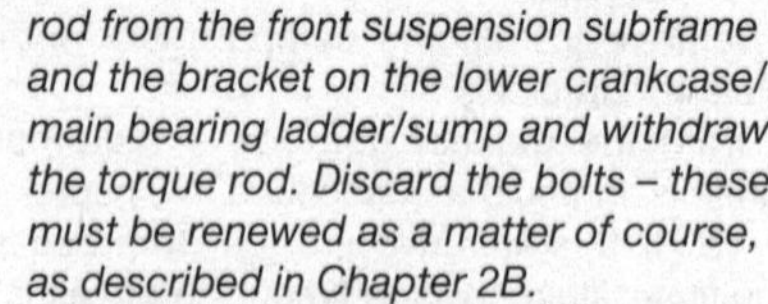

*e) Unscrew the three bolts and withdraw the heat shield covering the intermediate shaft **(see illustration)**.*

f) Unbolt the intermediate shaft support bearing from the cylinder block/crankcase (note that two of the bolts are shouldered to locate precisely the support bearing bracket).

g) On all models, to prevent damage to the driveshaft oil seal, hold the intermediate shaft horizontal until it is clear of the gearbox/transmission and remove the complete driveshaft from under the vehicle. Especially if the gearbox/transmission was not drained, be prepared for fluid spillage.

Both sides

15 When the driveshaft(s) is/are free, remove the locking circlip from its groove on the inboard end of the left-hand driveshaft and/or the outboard end of the intermediate shaft (if applicable), and discard it – a new one should be obtained for refitting.

Refitting

Both sides

16 Inspect the driveshaft oil seal for signs of damage, and renew it if necessary, as described in Chapter 7A.

17 Thoroughly clean (use solvent or carburettor cleaner, then dry them using compressed air) the points of contact between the driveshaft or intermediate shaft and the gearbox/transmission and hub, then lubricate the oil seal lips with a smear of grease. Wipe clean the ends of the driveshaft.

Left-hand side

18 Fit a new locking circlip to the groove on the inboard end of the driveshaft; rotate the circlip in its groove to check that it is fully-seated **(see illustration)**.

19 Taking care not to damage the oil seal as the shaft is offered up, fit the driveshaft inboard end into the gearbox/transmission, until the circlip is felt to engage. Pull gently on the inboard CV joint – not the shaft – to ensure that the circlip is correctly seated.

20 Wipe the wheel bearing's magnetic encoder clean of oil, grease, dust and any other foreign matter which might affect its operation, then refit the driveshaft fully into

2.20a Swing the hub assembly out to remove and refit front driveshaft

2.20b Apply a smear of oil to the seating surface of new driveshaft nut before fitting

the hub, taking care not to damage the ABS wheel sensor. Apply a smear of oil to the seating surface of the new driveshaft nut, then screw it into place, tightening it hand-tight only at this stage **(see illustrations)**.

Right-hand side

21 If the driveshaft alone was removed, leaving the intermediate shaft in place, fit a new locking circlip to the groove on the outboard end of the intermediate shaft; rotate the circlip in its groove to check that it is fully seated **(see illustration)**. Apply a thin smear of grease to the splines on the inside of the inboard CV joint, but then wipe the grease clear of every third spline and from the circlip groove just beyond the splines to ensure air is not trapped inside and can bleed out as the driveshaft is refitted. Refit the driveshaft as described in paragraphs 19 and 20 **(see illustration)**.

22 If the driveshaft was removed with the intermediate shaft, proceed as follows:

a) Offer up the intermediate shaft and driveshaft, keeping it as level as reasonably possible to prevent damage to the driveshaft oil seal. Insert the inboard end into the differential and the outboard end into the hub ***(see illustration)****.*

b) Refit the intermediate shaft support bearing to the cylinder block/crankcase, refit the bolts and tighten them to the specified torque wrench setting ***(see illustration)****.*

c) Refit the intermediate shaft heat shield and tighten the bolts to the specified torque wrench setting – tighten first the upper right bolt, then the lower right bolt and finally the left bolt.

d) On diesel-engined models, refit the engine rear mounting torque rod to the front suspension subframe and to the bracket on the lower crankcase/main bearing ladder/sump; tighten the new bolts to the torque wrench settings specified (see Chapter 2B).

e) On diesel-engined models, refit the support bracket between the cylinder block/crankcase and the warm-up catalytic converter; tighten the bolts to the torque wrench setting specified (see Chapter 4B).

f) Wipe the wheel bearing's magnetic encoder clean of oil, grease, dust and any other foreign matter which might affect its operation, then refit the driveshaft fully into the hub, taking care not to damage the ABS wheel sensor. Apply a smear of oil to the seating surface of the new driveshaft nut, then screw it into place, tightening it hand-tight only at this stage.

2.21a Always renew locking circlip on intermediate shaft outboard end . . .

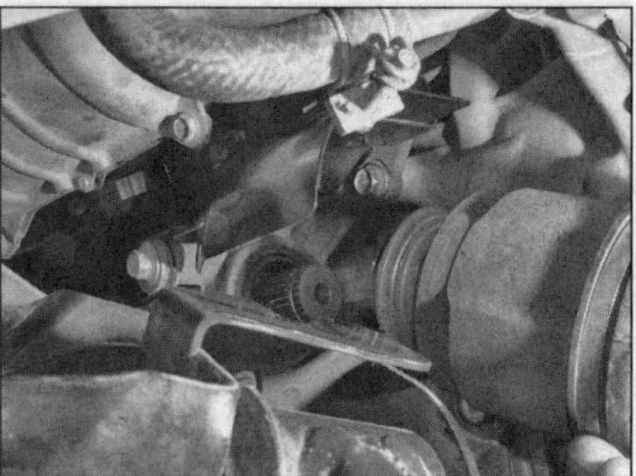

2.21b . . . before refitting right-hand driveshaft

2.22a Keep intermediate shaft level on refitting to avoid seal damage

2.22b Tighten intermediate shaft support bearing bolts as described

Both sides

23 Clean the swivel hub balljoint taper and its seat in the lower arm before fitting – it must be fitted dry.

24 Lever the lower arm downwards, then hook the outer end over the swivel hub balljoint stud and refit the balljoint castle nut **(see illustration)**. Carefully load the suspension with the vehicle's weight by using a jack applied to the lower arm (do not apply pressure to the balljoint stud), then tighten the nut initially to the Stage 1 (minimum) setting (see Chapter 10). From this point, tighten the nut only as required to align the locking clip holes (do not slacken to align), then fit a new pin from the centreline of the vehicle outwards to secure. The locking clip's free end must engage with the groove and one of the slots in the castle nut.

25 Reconnect the anti-roll bar drop link to the lower arm, and tighten the nut to the specified torque, holding the drop link balljoint with an Allen key as for removal.

26 Referring to the Warning earlier in this Section, tighten the new driveshaft nut to the specified torque **(see illustration)**.

27 Stake the driveshaft nut's collar into the groove in the end of the shaft **(see illustration)**.

28 Refit the engine compartment undershield (Chapter 11).

29 Refit the roadwheel, then lower the vehicle to the ground and tighten the wheel nuts to the specified torque.

30 Check and if necessary top-up the manual gearbox or automatic transmission fluid level, as described in Chapter 1A or 1B.

2.24 Prise down lower arm to refit swivel hub balljoint

2.26 Tighten new driveshaft nut to specified torque – note holding tool

2.27 Stake driveshaft nut's collar into groove in end of driveshaft

3 Rear driveshafts – removal and refitting

Note: *The following procedure assumes that it is quicker and easier to unbolt and lower the final drive unit than to disconnect the rear suspension arms to allow the rear hub carrier to be moved aside. Depending on the tools and facilities available and the work to be carried out, the DIY mechanic may prefer the latter option. Refer to the relevant Sections of Chapter 10 if this approach is adopted.*

Note: *The driveshaft nuts and locking circlips and the propeller shaft Torx bolts must be renewed as a matter of course on reassembly.*

Removal

1 Refer to Section 2, paragraphs 1 to 4, noting that the rear of the vehicle will need to be raised.

Warning: Before attempting to slacken the driveshaft nut, which is done up extremely tight, make sure the rear of the vehicle is securely supported. Do not use poor-quality, badly-fitting tools for this task, due to the risk of personal injury.

2 Working as described in Section 8, paragraphs 1 to 9, disconnect the propeller shaft from the final drive unit (Section 7), then unbolt and lower the final drive unit until the driveshaft(s) can be disconnected from the final drive unit.

3 With the final drive unit securely supported and the driveshaft either tied back to the rear suspension trailing arm lateral link or supported by an assistant, the splined outboard end of the driveshaft now has to be released from the hub. It's likely that the splines will be very tight (corrosion may even be a factor, if the driveshaft has not been disturbed for some time), and considerable force may be needed. Tap the end of the shaft with a plastic or hide mallet only – if an ordinary hammer is used, place a small piece of wood over the end of the driveshaft – and leave the old nut loosely in place on the end to avoid damaging the thread and tip of the driveshaft.

4 To release the driveshaft, have your assistant hold the driveshaft as level as reasonably possible to prevent damage to the CV joints and pull the driveshaft outboard CV joint – not the shaft – inwards to allow the driveshaft to be withdrawn through the hub, while you tap on the driveshaft outboard end. Be careful not to damage the ABS wheel sensor, the tip of which protrudes on the inside of the hub next to the bearing outer race.

5 Once the driveshaft is released, remove the driveshaft nut and discard it – the nut is only intended to be used once – and withdraw the driveshaft from under the vehicle, supporting carefully the CV joints. Remove the locking circlip from its groove on the inboard end of the driveshaft, and discard it – a new one should be obtained for refitting.

Refitting

6 Inspect the driveshaft oil seal for signs of damage, and renew it if necessary, as described in Section 9.

7 Refitting is a reversal of removal, noting the following points:

a) Thoroughly clean (use solvent or carburettor cleaner, then dry them using compressed air) the points of contact between the driveshafts and the final drive unit and hub, then lubricate the oil seal lips with a smear of grease.

b) Fit a new locking circlip to the groove on the inboard end of each driveshaft and wipe clean the ends of the driveshaft(s).

c) Wipe the wheel bearing's magnetic encoder clean of oil, grease, dust and any other foreign matter which might affect its operation, then refit the driveshaft fully into the hub, taking care not to damage the ABS wheel sensor. Apply a smear of oil to the seating surface of the new driveshaft nut, then screw it into place, tightening it hand-tight only at this stage.

d) Taking care not to damage the oil seal as the final drive unit is raised and each driveshaft is offered up, fit each driveshaft inboard end into the final drive unit, until the circlip is felt to engage. Pull gently on the inboard CV joint – not the shaft – to ensure that the circlip is correctly seated.

e) Tighten all fasteners to the torque wrench settings specified.

f) Refit the propeller shaft using the information in Section 7.

*g) Referring to the Warning earlier in this Section, tighten the new driveshaft nut to the specified torque wrench setting, then stake the driveshaft nut's collar into the groove in the end of the shaft **(see illustration 2.27)**.*

h) Refit the roadwheel, then lower the vehicle to the ground and tighten the roadwheel nuts to the specified torque.

i) On completion, refill the final drive with fluid, as described in Chapter 1A or 1B.

4 Driveshaft gaiters – renewal

Note: *The driveshaft locking circlips and the gaiter securing clips must be renewed as a matter of course on reassembly. These should be supplied with the joint/gaiter repair kit, which will also contain sufficient special CV joint grease for each joint. Check that all these are available before starting work, also any special crimping pliers or clip-tightening tool required to fasten the type(s) of gaiter securing clips.*

1 Remove the driveshaft as described in Section 2 or 3, as applicable.

2 Mount the driveshaft in a vice. The jaws of the vice should be lined with wood or rags to prevent damage to the driveshaft.

Inboard CV joints

Dismantling

3 If not already done, remove the locking circlip from its groove on the inboard end of the left-hand driveshaft and discard it – a new one should be obtained for refitting. Cut off or release both gaiter securing clips, and slide the gaiter towards the centre of the driveshaft **(see illustrations)**.

4 Scribe or paint alignment marks on the joint body and the driveshaft (and/or on the joint body and the tripod arms) so they can be returned to their original position, then slide the joint body off the tripod assembly and shaft **(see illustrations)**.

5 Scribe or paint alignment marks on each tripod arm and its respective roller bearing assembly so they can be returned to their original position, then slide the roller bearings off the tripod bearing assembly, noting

4.3a Cut off or release inboard joint gaiter securing clips, whichever is easiest . . .

4.3b . . . and discard them – they must be renewed

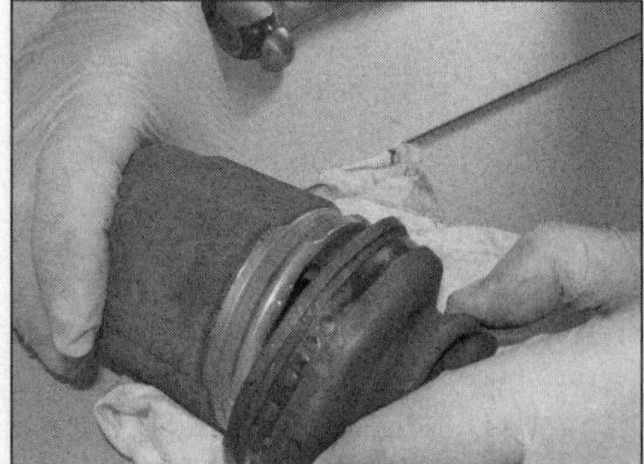

4.3c Slide the gaiter towards the centre of the driveshaft

carefully which way round they are fitted **(see illustrations)**.

6 Scribe or paint alignment marks on the driveshaft and the tripod body so they can be returned to their original position. Remove the circlip from the end of the driveshaft, then drive the tripod body off the driveshaft with a soft metal drift and a hammer **(see illustrations)**. Alternatively, use a puller to draw off the tripod body.

7 Slide the old gaiter off the driveshaft and discard it **(see illustration)**. If there is any chance it is to be re-used, wrap tape around the shaft splines and shoulder to protect the gaiter's sealing lip as it is removed.

Inspection

8 Clean up the driveshaft before fitting the new gaiter. If the gaiter has been split for some time, there is a danger that dust and dirt will have got into the joint, causing accelerated wear or damage in the joint. Simply packing it with grease and fitting a new gaiter will only delay the need for a new joint. If wished, there's nothing to lose by washing the joint clean in a suitable solvent, but let it dry completely before packing it liberally with fresh grease.

9 Clean the old grease from the joint body and the tripod assembly. Carefully dismantle each section of the tripod assembly, one at a time so as not to mix up the parts, and clean the needle bearings with degreaser. Blow each component dry with compressed air, if available.

Warning: Wear eye protection when using compressed air.

10 Inspect the roller bearings, tripod and joint body for scoring, pitting or other signs of abnormal wear or damage, which will necessitate the renewal of the complete joint.

Reassembly

11 Wrap the splines and shoulder of the driveshaft with tape to avoid damaging the new gaiter, then slide the gaiter and its small securing clip onto the driveshaft. Remove the tape **(see illustrations)**.

12 Aligning carefully the marks made on dismantling, slide the tripod body onto the

4.4a Scribe or paint alignment marks on joint body and driveshaft . . .

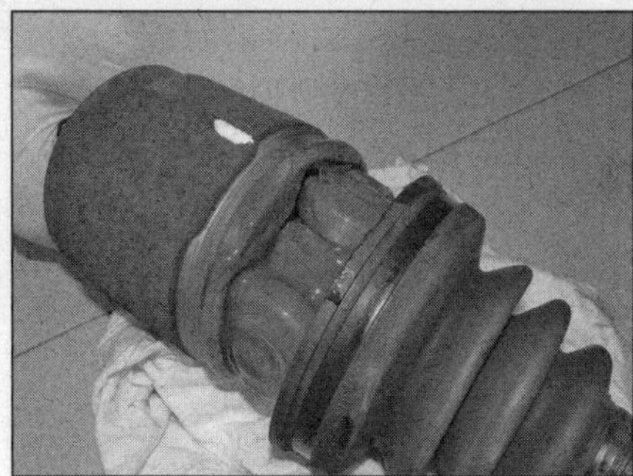

4.4b . . . before sliding joint body off tripod assembly and driveshaft

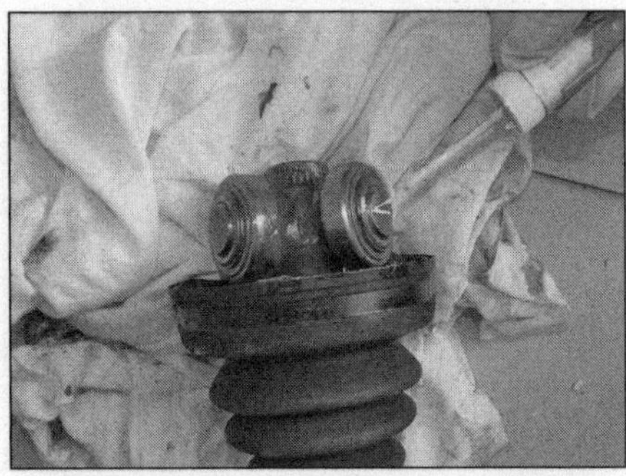

4.5a Scribe or paint alignment marks on each tripod arm and its roller bearing . . .

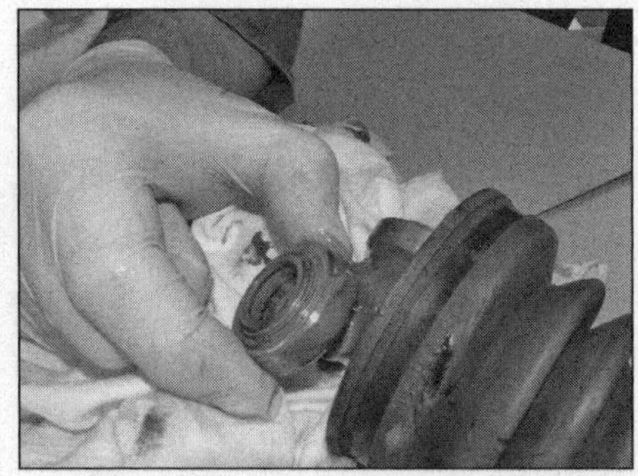

4.5b . . . then remove roller bearings, noting which way round they are fitted

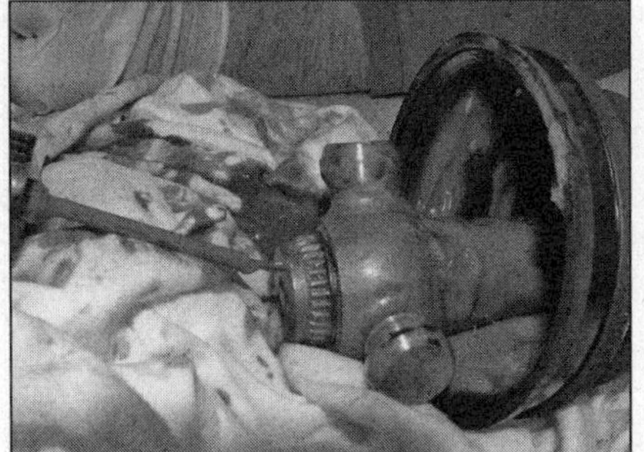

4.6a Scribe or paint alignment marks on tripod body and driveshaft . . .

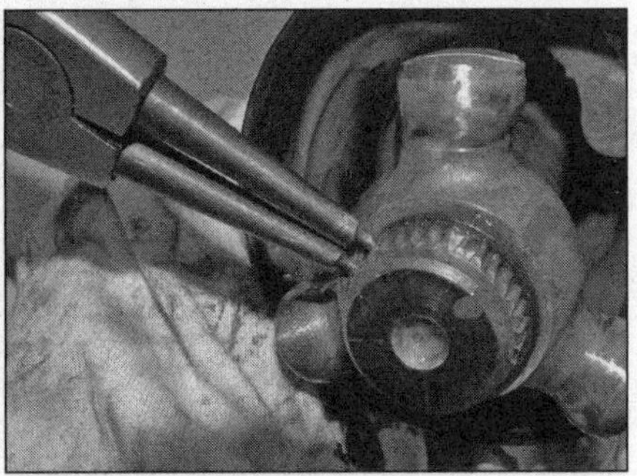

4.6b . . . remove circlip . . .

4.6c . . . and remove tripod body from driveshaft

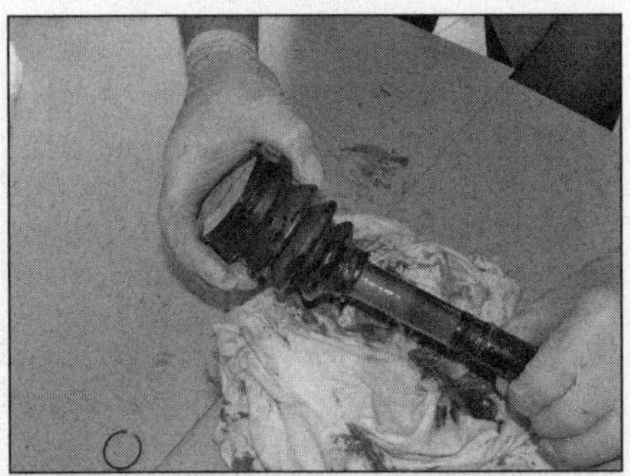

4.7 Slide the old inboard gaiter off driveshaft

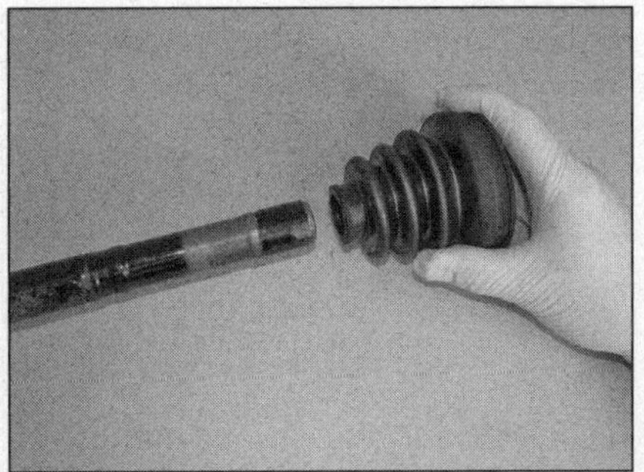

4.11a Tape driveshaft splines and shoulder to protect new gaiter as it is fitted . . .

4.11b . . . then remove tape

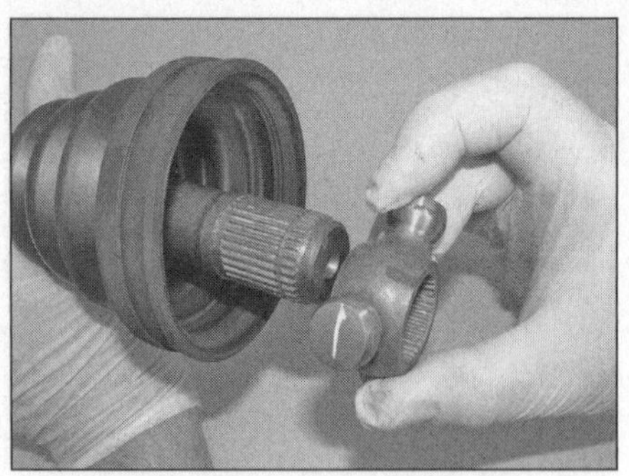
4.12a Align marks made on removal when sliding tripod onto driveshaft . . .

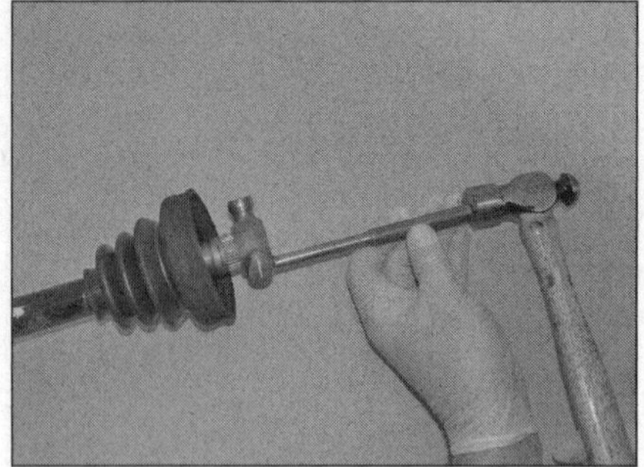
4.12b . . . and tap it home on the splines . . .

4.12c . . . until it contacts shoulder on driveshaft

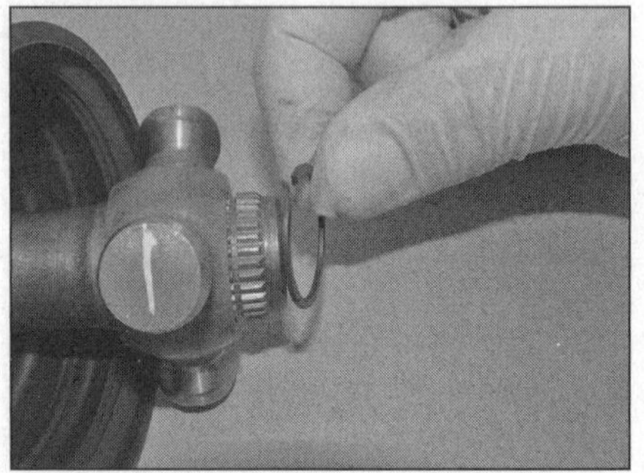
4.13a Fit new locking circlip . . .

4.13b . . . and rotate in its groove to check circlip is fully seated

driveshaft, and tap it home against the shaft shoulder with a soft metal drift and a hammer **(see illustrations)**.

13 Fit the locking circlip; always rotate such a circlip in its groove to check that it is fully seated **(see illustrations)**.

14 Apply a little CV joint grease to each tripod arm to hold the roller bearings in place when reassembling the tripod assembly **(see illustrations)**. Work some grease into each roller bearing, then use the marks made on dismantling to ensure that each roller bearing

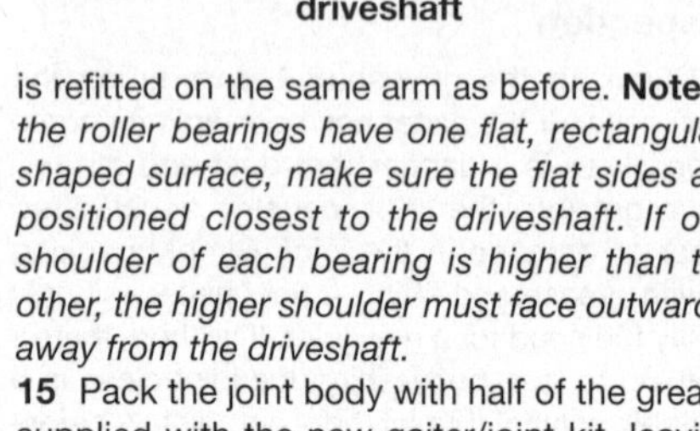
is refitted on the same arm as before. **Note:** *If the roller bearings have one flat, rectangular-shaped surface, make sure the flat sides are positioned closest to the driveshaft. If one shoulder of each bearing is higher than the other, the higher shoulder must face outwards, away from the driveshaft.*

15 Pack the joint body with half of the grease supplied with the new gaiter/joint kit, leaving the remainder for the gaiter. Aligning carefully the marks made on dismantling, slide the joint body on to the tripod assembly and shaft **(see illustrations)**.

16 Seat the gaiter in the groove in the driveshaft, then pack the remainder of the grease into the gaiter. Fit the gaiter into the groove in the joint body, compress the joint and lift the gaiter edges to release any trapped air. To check that the joint is correctly refitted, measure the driveshaft length from the outboard face of the outboard joint to

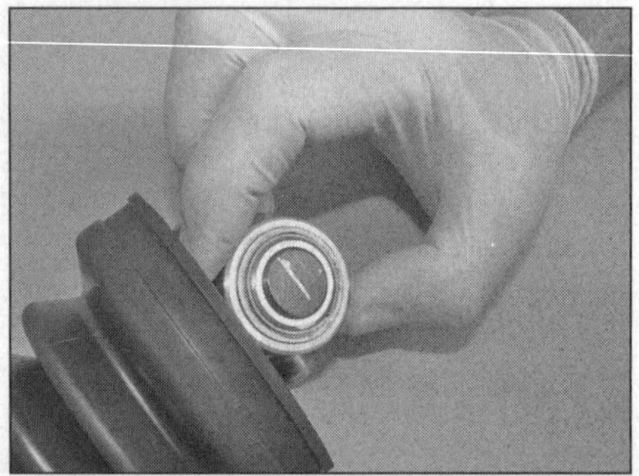
4.14a Ensure roller bearings are fitted correct way round . . .

4.14b . . . and align marks made on removal to ensure each is in original location . . .

4.14c . . . then keep driveshaft upright to stop roller bearings dropping off

4.15a Fill outboard joint body with half the supplied grease . . .

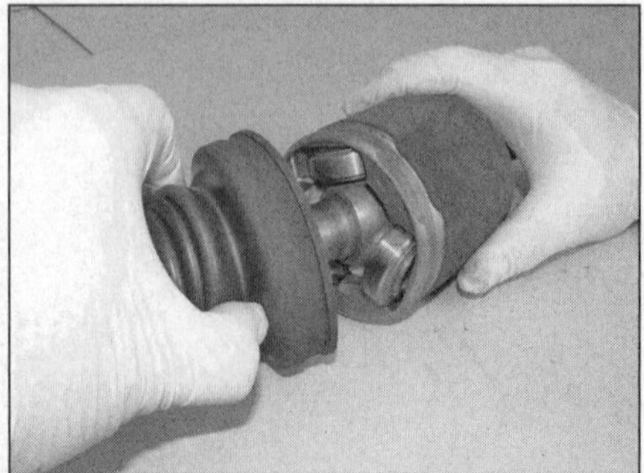
4.15b . . . then fit joint body onto driveshaft

4.16 Measure driveshaft length from outboard face of outboard joint to inboard face of inboard joint to check joint is correctly fitted

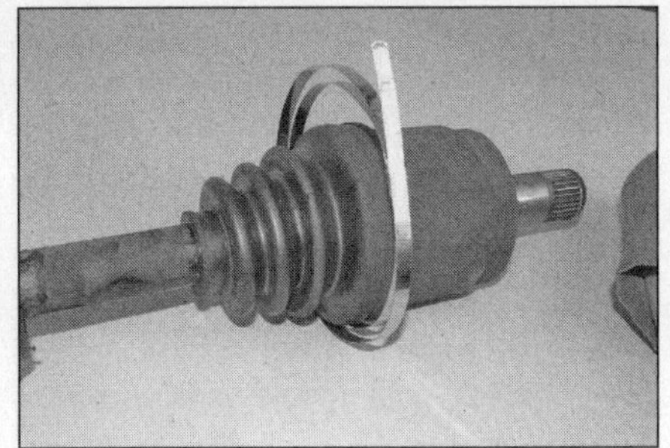

4.17a To fasten double-loop type of gaiter securing clip, place clip on gaiter, free end towards front of vehicle . . .

4.17b . . . pull up slack in clip by hand until tight . . .

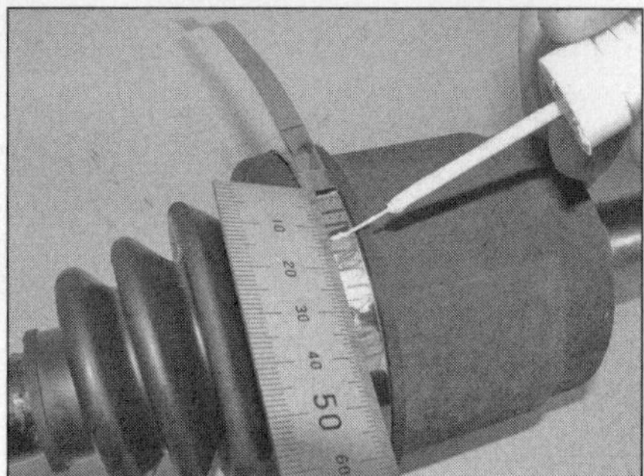

4.17c . . . mark clip 10 to 14 mm from fastening . . .

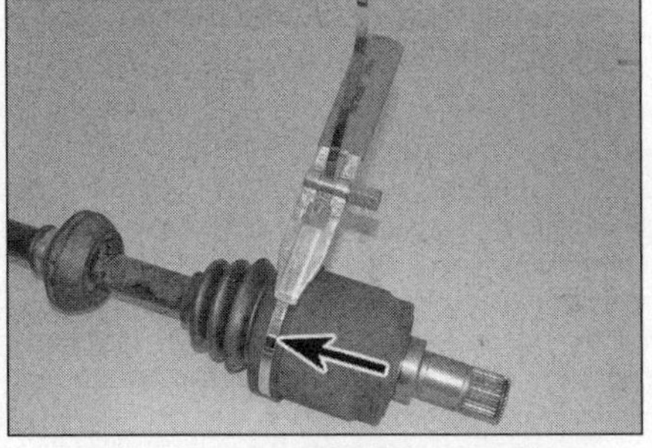

4.17d . . . fit free end into special clip-tightening tool and through tool's winding mandrel . . .

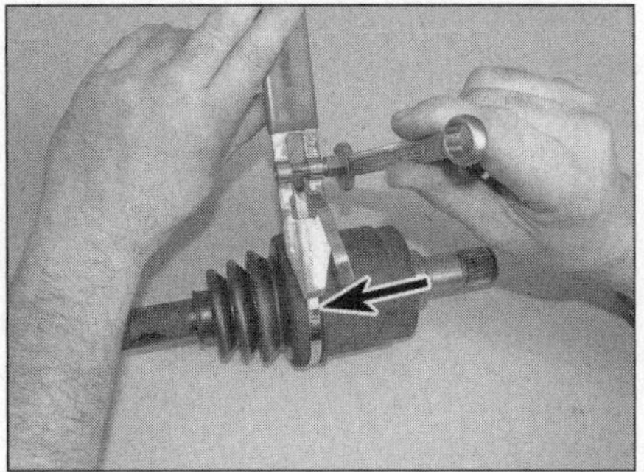

4.17e . . . then pull tight using spanner to tighten tool mandrel . . .

4.17f . . . until mark on clip meets edge of fastener . . .

the inboard face of the inboard joint; this should correspond to the value given in the Specifications Section of this Chapter **(see illustration)**.

17 Fit and tighten the new gaiter securing clips. A special pair of crimping pliers or clip-tightening tool will be needed for certain types of clip **(see illustrations)**.

18 Refit the driveshaft as described in Section 2 or 3, as applicable.

Outboard CV joints

Dismantling

19 Cut off or release both gaiter securing clips, and slide the gaiter towards the centre of the driveshaft **(see illustrations)**.

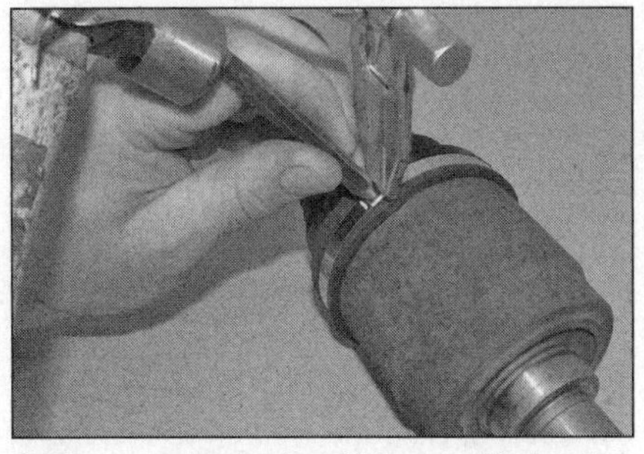

4.17g . . . raise tool until free end is bent at 90° to fastener and centre-punch fastener to secure . . .

4.17h . . . fold over the end and cut off surplus free end 5 to 10 mm from fastener. . .

4.17i . . . then flatten down to secure

4.17j Repeat the process on the other clip

4.19a Cut off or release outboard joint gaiter securing clips, whichever is easiest . . .

4.19b . . . and discard them – they must be renewed

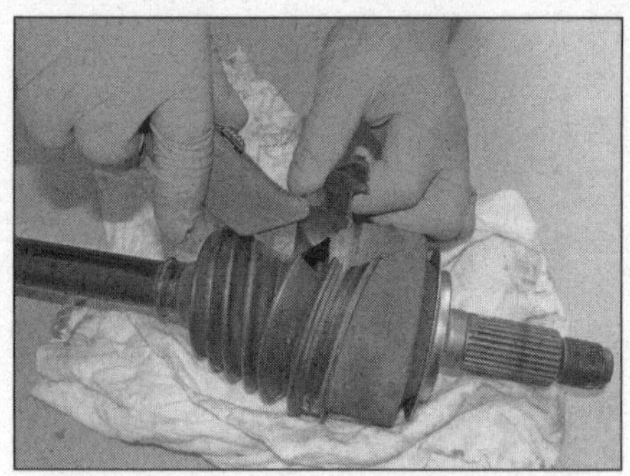
4.19c Gaiter can be cut off if not to be re-used

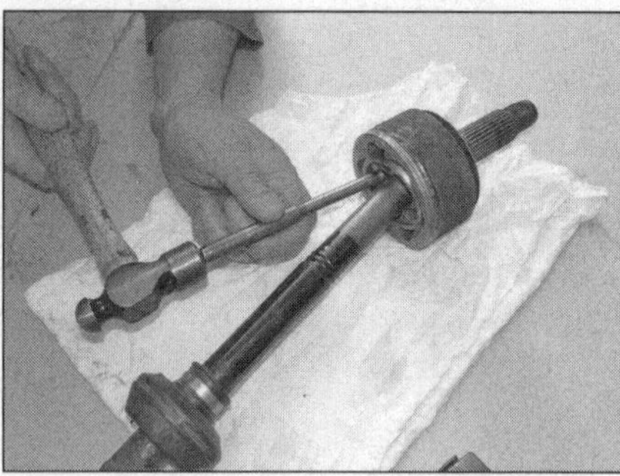
4.20 Drive outboard joint off driveshaft

4.24 Rotate joint to inspect bearing surfaces for signs of wear

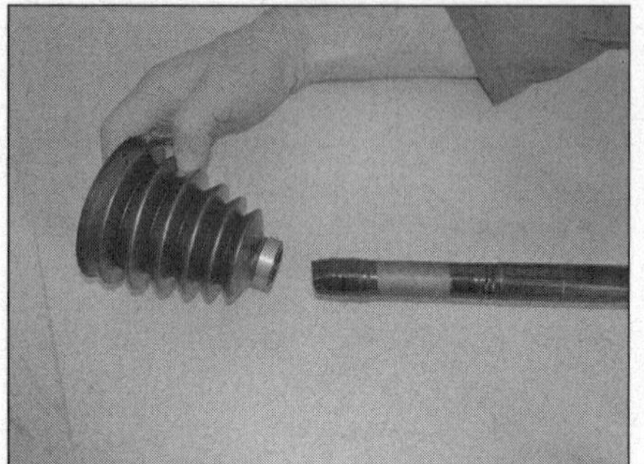
4.25a Tape driveshaft splines to protect new gaiter as it is fitted . . .

4.25b . . . then remove tape

20 The outboard joint is secured on the shaft by a locking circlip at its outboard end. Scribe or paint alignment marks on the joint body and the driveshaft so they can be returned to their original position, then use a hammer and soft metal drift sharply to tap the outboard joint off the shaft **(see illustration)**. Slide the old gaiter off the driveshaft and discard it. If there is any chance it is to be re-used, wrap tape around the shaft splines to protect the gaiter's sealing lip as it is removed.

21 Remove the circlip from the driveshaft outboard groove – a new one should be obtained for refitting.

4.26a Fit a new locking circlip into driveshaft groove . . .

4.26b . . . and the larger securing clip to the gaiter

4.27a Slide the outboard joint onto the driveshaft as far as circlip . . .

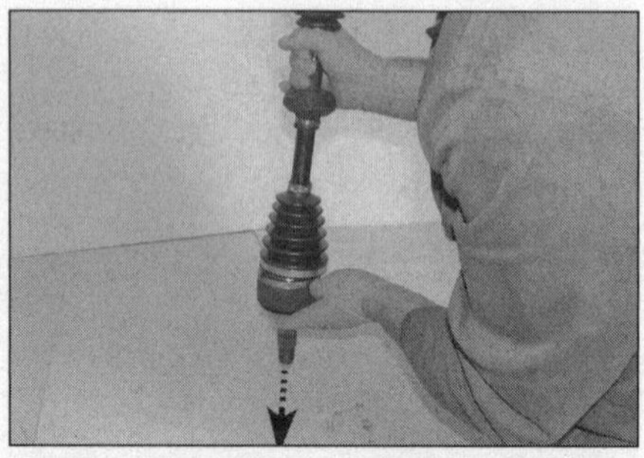
4.27b . . . and 'drop' driveshaft assembly on to hard surface to press joint over circlip. Do NOT hammer joint into place

Inspection

22 Refer to paragraph 8.

23 Thoroughly wash the joint in degreaser and blow it dry with compressed air, if available. **Note:** *Because the outboard joint can't be dismantled, it is difficult to wash away all the old grease and to remove the degreaser once it's clean. But it is imperative that the job be done thoroughly.*

Warning: Wear eye protection when using compressed air.

24 Bend the outboard joint at an angle to the driveshaft to expose the bearings, inner race and cage. Inspect the bearing surfaces for signs of abnormal wear or damage, which will necessitate the renewal of the complete joint **(see illustration)**.

Reassembly

25 Wrap the splines of the driveshaft with tape to avoid damaging the new gaiter, then slide the gaiter and its small securing clip onto the driveshaft. Remove the tape **(see illustrations)**.

26 Fit a new locking circlip to the groove at the end of the shaft, rotate the circlip in its groove to check that it is fully seated, then fit the larger gaiter clip to the gaiter **(see illustrations)**.

27 Aligning carefully the marks made on dismantling, slide the joint on to the end of the driveshaft and up to the locking circlip. To press the joint over the circlip, hold the driveshaft and joint vertically and 'drop' them from a height of about 10 cm on to a hard wooden surface **(see illustrations)**. **Note:** *Do NOT hammer the joint back on to the driveshaft as this may damage the components of the joints and driveshaft. If a clean wooden surface is not available, refit the driveshaft nut flush with the end of the driveshaft to protect the thread and tip of the driveshaft.* Once the joint is in position, pull on the joint to make sure the circlip has engaged. To check that the joint is correctly refitted, measure the driveshaft length from the outboard face of the outboard joint to the inboard face of the inboard joint **(see illustration 4.16)**; this should correspond to the value given in the Specifications Section of this Chapter.

28 Add the grease from the repair kit to the outboard joint – try to 'squirt' the grease into the centre, as this will distribute it around the ball-bearings. Work the grease around the joint's insides. Pack as much grease as possible into the joint, leaving the remainder for the gaiter **(see illustrations)**.

29 Seat the gaiter in the groove in the driveshaft, then pack the remainder of the grease into the gaiter. Fit the gaiter into the groove in the joint body, lifting the gaiter edges to release any trapped air. Tighten the gaiter clips, as described in paragraph 17 if appropriate **(see illustrations)**.

30 Refit the driveshaft as described in Section 2 or 3, as applicable.

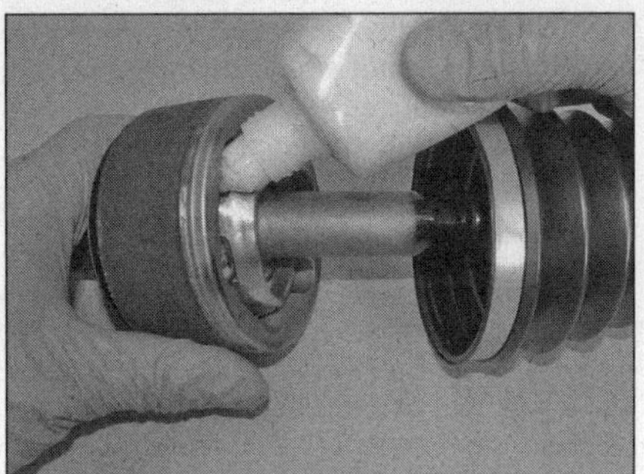

4.28a Squirt grease into centre of outboard joint, pack joint with grease . . .

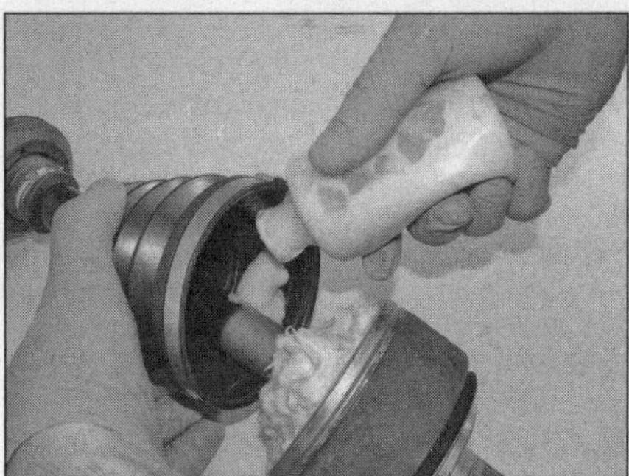

4.28b . . . and put remainder into gaiter

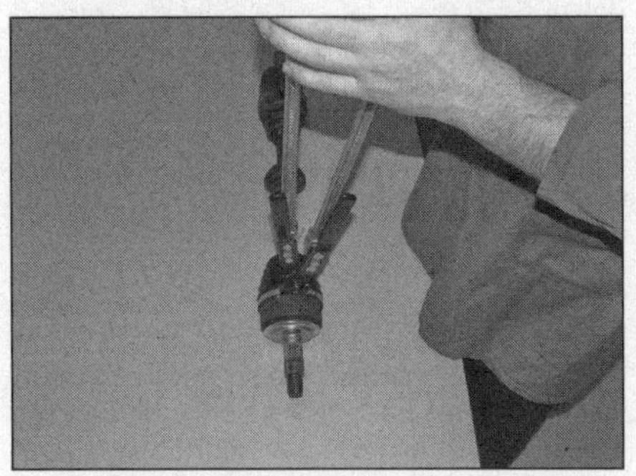

4.29a Ear-clamp type clips need special crimping pliers . . .

4.29b . . . to close fastening clamp to 3 mm maximum opening and 6 mm maximum height

5 Driveshaft overhaul – general

Note: *Before undertaking any action, check carefully what parts are available, from specialist suppliers as well as from Honda dealers. Consider also the possibility of using a good second-hand item from a breaker or vehicle dismantler.*

General

1 The road test and driveshaft gaiter checks carried out as part of the annual/12 500 mile service (see Chapter 1A or 1B) should give some indication of any possible faults in the driveshafts. Beyond this, wear or damage can be detected only by the removal and complete dismantling of a suspect driveshaft, as described in Section 4, so that the components can be cleaned and checked for signs of wear or damage.

2 If wear is apparent, the components concerned should be renewed. Check carefully what is available and consider the costs, in time and facilities as well as just the cost of parts. It would seem that both inboard and outboard joints can be purchased separately, with and/or without gaiter kits, but any damage to the shaft itself (for example, to the splines) means that the complete driveshaft assembly must be renewed.

Dynamic damper

Removal

3 Remove the driveshaft as described in Section 2 or 3, as applicable.

4 Remove the inboard joint as described in Section 4.

5 Measure the distance from the outboard face of the outboard joint to the inboard face of the damper; this should correspond to the value given in the Specifications Section of this Chapter **(see illustration)**.

6 Wrap tape around the shaft splines to protect the damper as it is removed **(see illustration)**.

7 Cut the damper securing clips and slide the damper off the shaft.

Refitting

8 Refitting is the reverse of removal, noting the following points:

a) Wrap tape around the shaft splines to protect the damper as it is installed.
b) Locate the damper on the shaft so that its inboard face is the specified distance from the outboard face of the outboard joint.
c) Fasten the damper securing clips as described in Section 4.

Intermediate shaft

Note: *A press will be required to remove and refit the support bearing. Failing this use a bolt, with several large washers and large sockets to extract the old bearing and to draw the new one into place.*

Note: *The support bearing and dust seal must be renewed as a matter of course, irrespective of their apparent condition, whenever they are disturbed.*

Dismantling

9 Remove the right-hand driveshaft and intermediate shaft as described in Section 2.

10 If not already done, use a hammer and soft metal drift sharply to tap the right-hand driveshaft's inboard CV joint from the intermediate shaft, then remove the locking circlip from its groove on the outboard end of the intermediate shaft and discard it – a new one should be obtained for refitting.

11 To check the bearing's condition, try to push and pull it up and down and from side-to-side on the shaft, and look for any sound or sign of movement. A further check can be made by spinning the bearing to check for any signs of rough or jerky rotation.

12 If the assembly is to be dismantled, use a flat-bladed screwdriver carefully to extract the old seal from the support bearing, noting its fitted depth and ensuring that the seal recess is not damaged in the process.

5.5 Measure distance from outboard face of outboard joint to inboard face of damper . . .

5.6 . . . and note which way round dynamic damper is fitted before releasing securing clips

13 Remove the retaining circlip using external circlip pliers.

14 To remove the bearing, press it off the shaft. Alternatively, clamp the shaft in a vice fitted with soft jaw covers to prevent damage to the shaft, then use a hammer and soft metal drift sharply to tap the support bearing off the intermediate shaft. Note however, that this latter method requires great care to avoid damaging the support bearing's support ring and shield fitted to the intermediate shaft.

15 Use internal circlip pliers to remove the circlip retaining the bearing inside the support, then press the bearing out of the support. Alternatively, use a bolt, with several large washers and large sockets to pull out the old bearing.

Inspection

16 Thoroughly clean the intermediate shaft components and check them for signs of wear or damage. Renew any worn or damaged component.

Reassembly

17 Press or draw the new bearing into the support until the retaining circlip can be refitted.

18 Press or tap the support bearing assembly on to the intermediate shaft until it locates against the shaft support ring and shield. Fit the retaining circlip to secure the assembly in position.

19 Apply a smear of grease to its sealing lips and press or tap the new dust seal on to the intermediate shaft and into the support bearing assembly.

20 Do not forget to fit a new locking circlip to the groove on the outboard end of the intermediate shaft before refitting the shaft to the vehicle (see Section 2).

6 Transfer case – removal and refitting

Note: *The propeller shaft Torx bolts and the transfer case O-ring must be renewed as a matter of course on reassembly.*

Removal

1 Drain the manual gearbox or automatic transmission fluid as described in Chapter 1A or 1B. If this is not done, be prepared for significant fluid spillage when the transfer case is removed – put down plenty of rags or newspaper if necessary.

2 Jack up the front and rear of the vehicle, and support securely on axle stands, as described in *Jacking and vehicle support*.

3 Unbolt the propeller shaft from the transfer case as described in the following Section. Make sure that, once separated, the propeller shaft is either supported or tied up – do not let it hang down unsupported.

4 Unbolt the transfer case and withdraw it from under the vehicle, noting the locating dowel pin; if this is loose it should be removed and kept with the transfer case to prevent its loss. Remove and discard the O-ring from the transfer case; this must be renewed whenever it is disturbed. Cover the open aperture in the gearbox/transmission to prevent the entry of dirt while the transfer case is removed.

Refitting

5 Before fitting, thoroughly clean (use solvent or carburettor cleaner, then dry them using compressed air) the points of contact between the transfer case and the gearbox/transmission. Similarly, clean the propeller shaft flange and the corresponding mating face on the transfer case.

6 Refitting is the reverse of the removal procedure, noting the following points:

a) Fit a new O-ring to the transfer case and apply a thin smear of grease.

b) Apply a smear of gearbox/transmission fluid to the teeth of the transfer drive and driven gears.

c) Fit the locating dowel pin to the gearbox/transmission.

d) Fit the mounting bolts to the transfer case and offer it up, then tighten the bolts to the specified torque wrench setting.

e) Align the reference marks made on removal when refitting the propeller shaft; tighten the Torx bolts to the specified torque wrench setting.

f) Refill the manual gearbox or automatic transmission with fluid, as described in Chapter 1A or 1B.

7 Propeller shaft – inspection, removal and refitting

Note: *Before undertaking any action, check carefully what parts are available, from specialist suppliers as well as from Honda dealers. Consider also the possibility of using a good second-hand item from a breaker or vehicle dismantler.*

Inspection

1 Wear in the universal joint needle roller bearings is characterised by vibration in the transmission, 'clonks' on taking up the drive, and in extreme cases, unpleasant metallic noises as the bearings break up (lack of lubrication).

2 To test the universal joints for wear with the propeller shaft in place, apply the handbrake, and chock the wheels.

3 Working under the vehicle, apply leverage between the yokes using a large screwdriver or a flat metal bar. Wear is indicated by movement between the shaft yoke and the coupling flange yoke. Check both universal joints in this way.

4 To check the centre support bearing, try to push and pull the propeller shaft up-and-down and from side-to-side at that point, and look for any sound or sign of movement. A further check can be made with the propeller shaft removed by spinning the bearing to check for any signs of rough or jerky rotation.

5 A dial gauge can be used, applied to the mid-point of the propeller shaft's front and rear sections (wiped clean of mud and dirt) while the shaft is slowly rotated, to check the shaft for truth. If runout is found to exceed the maximum value permissible at any point, the propeller shaft is bent or distorted.

6 If the shaft is distorted or damaged, or if a universal joint or the centre support bearing is worn, the complete shaft assembly must be renewed. No component parts are available with which it can be reconditioned.

Removal

Note: *It is considered good practice to renew highly-stressed fasteners such as the propeller shaft Torx bolts as a matter of course whenever they are disturbed. Honda states clearly that the propeller shaft centre support bearing bolts must be renewed. Owners are advised to err on the side of safety and renew both sets of bolts whenever they are disturbed.*

7 Jack up the front and rear of the vehicle, and support securely on axle stands, as described in *Jacking and vehicle support*.

8 If the original propeller shaft is to be refitted, make alignment marks on its front and rear flanges at the transfer case and the final drive **(see illustration)**.

9 Unscrew the Torx bolts securing the front universal joint to the transfer case flange **(see illustration)**.

10 Separate the front universal joint from

7.8 Paint alignment marks on propeller shaft and flanges to preserve balancing on refitting

7.9 Propeller shaft Torx bolts must be renewed as a matter of course whenever they are disturbed

the transfer case flange. If necessary, use a soft-faced mallet to tap the joint sideways to break it free of the transfer case flange. When the joint is free, refit a bolt loosely to support the front of the propeller shaft, to prevent any risk of damage to it; do not just allow the shaft to hang down to the ground.

11 Unscrew the two bolts securing the centre support bearing. Leave the bolts loosely in place to hold the propeller shaft for the time being.

12 Unbolt and withdraw the propeller shaft guard.

13 Unscrew the Torx bolts securing the rear universal joint to the final drive unit flange and separate the joint from the flange as described above.

14 With the aid of at least one assistant, remove the bolts and lower the complete propeller shaft assembly to the ground, keeping it as level as reasonably possible.

Refitting

15 Before fitting, clean the propeller shaft flanges and the corresponding mating faces on the transfer case and final drive unit – take care, however, that the alignment marks made prior to removal are not destroyed by this process.

16 With assistance, raise the complete propeller shaft assembly into position under the vehicle.

17 Offer up the rear universal joint to the final drive unit flange, check that the previously-made marks align, then fit the four new bolts and tighten them to the specified torque.

18 Locate the centre support bearing on the underbody, then fit the new bolts and tighten them to the specified torque.

19 Similarly, offer up the front universal joint to the transfer case flange, check that the previously-made marks align, then fit the four new bolts and tighten them to the specified torque.

20 Refit the propeller shaft guard and tighten the bolts to the specified torque.

21 On completion, lower the vehicle to the ground.

8 Final drive – removal and refitting

Note: *The propeller shaft Torx bolts and the driveshaft locking circlips must be renewed as a matter of course on reassembly. The aid of one assistant, preferably two, will be required.*

Removal

1 Drain the final drive fluid as described in Chapter 1A or 1B. If this is not done, be prepared for significant fluid spillage when the driveshafts are removed – put down plenty of rags or newspaper if necessary.

2 Unbolt the propeller shaft from the final drive unit as described in the previous Section. Make sure that, once separated, the propeller shaft is either supported by the propeller shaft guard or tied up – do not let it hang down unsupported.

3 On petrol-engined models, unbolt the charcoal canister cover and the canister itself. Secure the canister assembly clear of the working area, disconnecting hoses only as necessary to permit this (refer to Chapter 4C if required).

4 Support the weight of the final drive unit on a transmission jack or a large trolley jack. This is a heavy assembly, and it must be adequately supported while the mountings are removed.

5 Unbolt the damper and the left- and right-hand mounting brackets securing the rear of the final drive unit to the mounting above the rear suspension subframe **(see illustrations)**.

6 Remove the two bolts securing the final drive unit front mounting, and withdraw the large circular plate under each **(see illustrations)**.

7 Carefully lower the final drive unit on the jack until the breather tube can be disconnected from the top rear of the unit.

8 To disconnect the driveshafts, the inboard ends of which are each secured with a locking circlip which must be released, do not pull on the shafts, as the inboard CV joints may separate. Instead, taking care not to damage the shield fitted around each CV joint (a leverage point is provided at the bottom of the final drive unit casing boss surrounding each driveshaft oil seal; insert a large flat-bladed screwdriver and gently prise the driveshaft CV joints away at these points first), carefully use a large screwdriver or lever bar positioned between the final drive unit and the CV joint to lever out the inboard end of each driveshaft from the final drive unit until the locking circlip is felt to release.

Warning: When levering out the rear driveshafts, prevent any risk of personal injury and of expensive component damage by making sure that the final drive unit remains securely supported on the jack at all times.

9 Once both driveshaft locking circlips are released, lower the final drive unit on the jack until the driveshafts can be completely withdrawn. Note the following:

a) To prevent damage to the driveshaft oil seal, guide each inboard CV joint carefully, keeping the driveshaft as level as possible, until it is clear of the final drive unit.

b) As each driveshaft is disconnected from the final drive unit, have your assistant tie it back to the rear suspension trailing arm lateral link – do not let it hang down unsupported.

c) Lower the final drive and remove it from under the vehicle.

d) Remove the locking circlip from its groove on the inboard end of each driveshaft, and discard it – a new one should be obtained for refitting.

10 If required, the final drive front mounting can now be unbolted from the unit and the rear mounting can be unbolted from the subframe, for renewal. Tighten the mounting

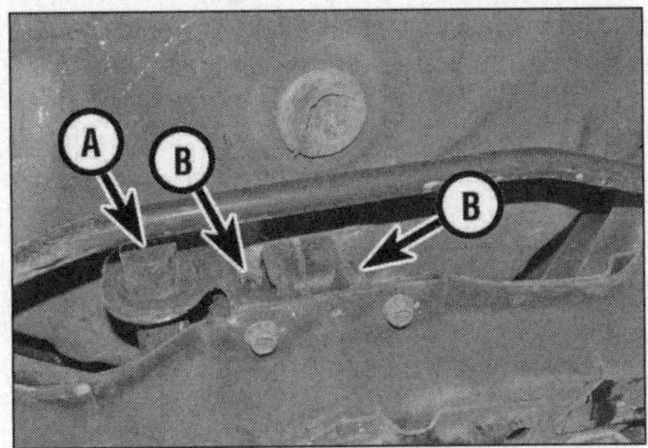

8.5a Unbolt damper (A) and mounting brackets (B) securing rear of final drive unit . . .

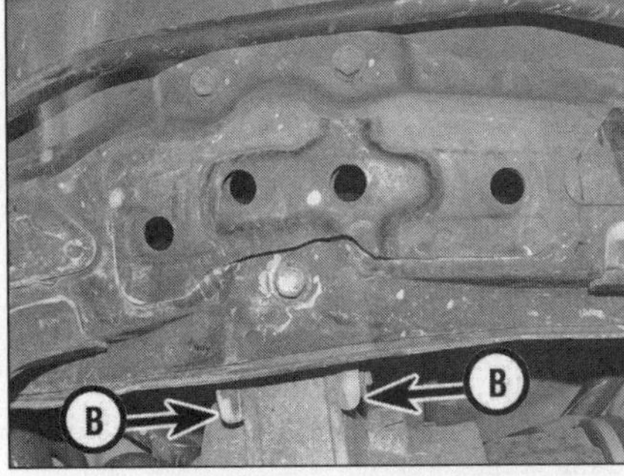

8.5b . . . to mounting above rear suspension subframe

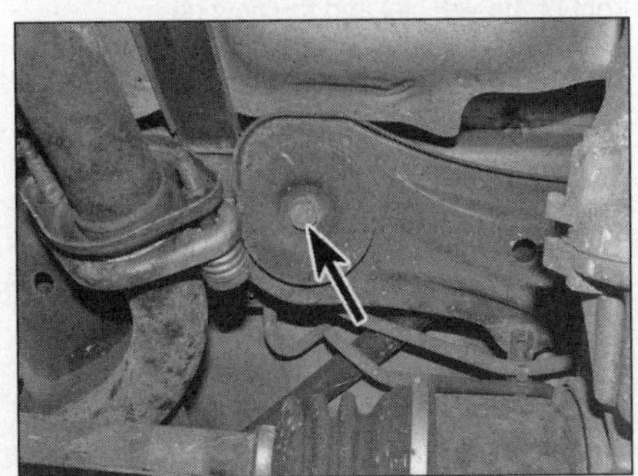

8.6a Final drive unit front mounting – right-hand side . . .

8.6b . . . and left-hand side

bolts to the specified torque wrench setting on completion.

11 Inspect the driveshaft oil seals for signs of damage, and renew them if necessary, as described in the following Section.

Refitting

12 Refitting is a reversal of removal, noting the following points:

a) *Thoroughly clean (use solvent or carburettor cleaner, then dry them using compressed air) the points of contact between the driveshafts and the final drive unit, then lubricate the oil seal lips with a smear of grease.*

b) *Fit a new locking circlip to the groove on the inboard end of each driveshaft; rotate the circlip in its groove to check that it is fully seated.*

c) *Taking care not to damage the oil seal as the shaft is offered up, fit the driveshaft inboard end into the final drive unit, until the circlip is felt to engage. Pull gently on the inboard CV joint – not the shaft – to ensure that the circlip is correctly seated.*

d) *Tighten all fasteners to the torque wrench settings specified.*

e) *Refit the propeller shaft using the information in Section 7.*

f) *On completion, refill the final drive with fluid, as described in Chapter 1A or 1B.*

9 Final drive oil seals – renewal

Driveshaft oil seals

1 Remove the final drive unit as described in Section 8.

2 Using a flat-bladed screwdriver, carefully extract the old oil seal, noting its fitted depth and ensuring that the oil seal recess is not damaged in the process.

3 Clean the oil seal recess. If the seal recess shows any sign of scoring or rough edges, clean it up now, or the new seal will also be damaged.

4 Lightly lubricate the new oil seal with Dual Pump System Fluid (DPSF), then press it into place using a suitable drift which bears on the seal edges. Press the seal in to the same depth as noted for the old seal; the left-hand seal should be flush with the edge of the final drive unit housing, while the right-hand seal is seated to a depth of 9 mm below the edge of the final drive unit housing.

5 Refit the final drive unit as described in Section 8.

Propeller shaft oil seal

Note: *While this can be renewed as described below, access would be easier and the necessary cleanliness easier to ensure if the final drive unit were first removed as described in Section 8 and the seal renewed on the bench. If this approach is adopted, slacken the flange nut as soon as the propeller shaft is disconnected, and tighten it at the same stage on refitting, while the final drive is bolted firmly in place on its mountings. In addition to the propeller shaft Torx bolts, the flange nut and the sealing O-ring must be renewed as a matter of course on reassembly.*

6 Unbolt the propeller shaft from the final drive unit as described in Section 7. Make sure that, once separated, the propeller shaft is either supported by the propeller shaft guard or tied up – do not let it hang down unsupported.

7 Obtain a strip of metal with two holes drilled to match the propeller shaft Torx bolt holes and bolt it to the final drive unit's flange with two of the used Torx bolts as a holding tool.

8 The flange nut has a raised collar, part of which is punched into the differential clutch assembly shaft groove to stop the nut slackening accidentally. Using a hammer and suitable chisel, open out the staking completely so the nut can be unscrewed.

9 First slacken the nut until the staked part clears the shaft groove, then tighten it again until the staked part aligns with the shaft groove. Carefully clean any dirt from the groove in the shaft (to prevent any risk of damage to the differential clutch assembly), then unscrew the nut.

10 Withdraw the spring washer, the back-up ring and the sealing O-ring, then draw off the drive flange. Discard the O-ring; this must be renewed whenever it is disturbed. Cover the open aperture in the final drive unit to prevent the entry of dirt while work is in progress.

11 Using a flat-bladed screwdriver, carefully extract the old oil seal, noting its fitted depth and ensuring that neither the oil seal recess not the shaft is not damaged in the process.

12 Clean the oil seal recess. If the seal recess shows any sign of scoring or rough edges, clean it up now, or the new seal will also be damaged.

13 Lightly lubricate the new oil seal with Dual Pump System Fluid (DPSF), then press it into place using a suitable drift which bears on the seal edges. Press the seal in to the same depth as noted for the old seal.

14 Refit the flange. Lightly lubricate the new O-ring with Dual Pump System Fluid (DPSF), then press it into place, followed by the back-up ring, the spring washer (convex surface to the front of the vehicle) and the new nut.

15 Hold the flange with the holding tool and tighten the nut to the specified torque wrench setting, then stake the nut's collar into the groove in the end of the shaft.

16 Reconnect the propeller shaft to the final drive unit as described in Section 7.

10 Transfer case and final drive overhaul – general information

Note 1: *Before undertaking any action, check carefully what parts are available, from specialist suppliers as well as from Honda dealers. Consider also the possibility of using a good second-hand item from a breaker or vehicle dismantler.*

Note 2: *A moaning/groaning noise when manoeuvring on full lock can be due to premature degradation of the final drive fluid. Since, however, this may be easily misdiagnosed as a steering rack problem, it may lead to unnecessary repairs. If this is suspected, the first course of action is to renew the fluid as described in Chapter 1A or 1B, using the latest specification of Honda Dual Pump fluid which is called Dual Pump Fluid II (DPF II) fluid – seek the advice of a Honda dealer's service department if in doubt.*

Overhauling such units is a difficult and involved job for the DIY home mechanic. In addition to dismantling and reassembling many small parts, clearances must be precisely measured and, if necessary, changed by selecting shims and spacers. Components are also often difficult to obtain and in many instances, extremely expensive. Because of this, if the transfer case or final drive develops a fault or becomes noisy, the best course of action is to have the unit overhauled by a specialist repairer, or to obtain an exchange reconditioned unit.

Nevertheless, it is not impossible for the more experienced mechanic to overhaul the transfer case or final drive, if the special tools are available and the job is done in a deliberate step-by-step manner so that nothing is overlooked.

The tools necessary for an overhaul include internal and external circlip pliers, bearing pullers, a slide hammer, a set of pin punches, a dial test indicator, and possibly a hydraulic press. In addition, a large, sturdy workbench and a vice will be required.

During dismantling, make careful notes of how each component is fitted, to make reassembly easier and more accurate.

If investigating the cause of a problem thought to be due to a fault in the Real Time system, especially in the switching in and out of four-wheel-drive by the Dual Pump arrangement, remember that these systems have proved themselves generally reliable; any perceived fault may be due to external factors such as low fluid level, incorrect fluid or poor fluid quality, rather than to a faulty component of the system. It is essential that only the specified fluid is used in the final drive unit and that this fluid is always changed at the recommended intervals (see Chapter 1A or 1B). If this advice is not followed, the fluid pumps, valves and clutch components may cease to function correctly, so that the system cannot work properly; ultimately, expensive repairs may be required. If a fault is encountered, especially if the vehicle's service history is in any way dubious, the first step is to have the final drive unit thoroughly flushed and to refill it with the correct fluid. The same principle applies to the transfer case, even though this shares lubricant with the manual gearbox or automatic transmission.

Chapter 9
Braking system

Contents

Degrees of difficulty

Easy, suitable for novice with little experience	**Fairly easy,** suitable for beginner with some experience	**Fairly difficult,** suitable for competent DIY mechanic	**Difficult,** suitable for experienced DIY mechanic	**Very difficult,** suitable for expert DIY or professional

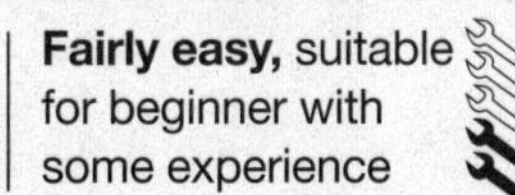

Specifications

General

Brake pedal:		
Free play	1.0 to 5.0 mm	
Height – with carpet removed and stop-light switch clear of pedal	173 mm	
Servo unit pushrod length – servo mating surface to clevis pin centre	116 mm	
Handbrake lever travel	5 to 9 clicks	
Front brakes:	**2001 to 2004 models**	**2005-on models**
Caliper piston diameter	57 mm	57 mm
Disc diameter	282 mm	300 mm
Disc thickness:		
Standard	23.0 mm	24.9 to 25.1 mm
Minimum	21.0 mm	23.0 mm
Disc maximum run-out	0.10 mm	0.10 mm
Disc maximum thickness variation (parallelism)	0.015 mm	0.015 mm
Pad friction material thickness:		
Standard	11.0 mm	10.5 to 11.5 mm
Minimum	1.6 mm	1.6 mm
Rear brakes:	**2001 to 2004 models**	**2005-on models**
Caliper piston diameter	38.1 mm	38.1 mm
Disc diameter	283 mm	305 mm
Disc thickness:		
Standard	9.0 mm	8.9 to 9.1 mm
Minimum	7.0 mm	8.0 mm
Disc maximum run-out	0.10 mm	0.10 mm
Disc maximum thickness variation (parallelism)	0.015 mm	0.015 mm
Pad friction material thickness:		
Standard	9.0 mm	8.5 to 9.5 mm
Minimum	1.0 mm	1.6 mm

General (continued)

	2001 to 2004 models	2005-on models
Handbrake:		
Drum inside diameter:		
Standard	170.0 mm	199.9 to 200.0 mm
Minimum	171.0 mm	201.0 mm
Shoe friction material thickness:		
Standard	3.2 mm	3.2 mm
Minimum	1.0 mm	1.0 mm
ABS wheel sensor-to-magnetic encoder air gap	0.5 to 1.5 mm	

Torque wrench settings

Torque wrench settings	Nm	lbf ft
ABS modulator-control unit mounting bolts	9	7
ABS wheel sensor retaining bolt	10	7
ABS wheel sensor wiring harness bracket retaining bolts	10	7
Bleed nipples	9	7
Brake disc retaining screws	10	7
Brake hose banjo union bolts	34	25
Brake hose support bracket retaining bolts	22	16
Brake pipe unions to master cylinder:		
Vehicles without VSA	15	11
Vehicles with VSA	22	16
Brake pipe-to-hose union nuts	15	11
Front brake disc shield retaining screws	6	4
Front caliper:		
Guide pins, guide pin bolts (see Section 8):		
8 mm bolt (separate guide pin)	34	25
Hexagon-headed guide pins	74	55
Mounting bracket-to-swivel hub bolts	108	80
Front suspension strut brace mounting nuts and bolts:		
6 mm	10	7
8 mm	22	16
Handbrake backplate-to-rear hub carrier retaining nuts:		
10 mm	38	28
16 mm	140	103
Handbrake cable end fitting-to-lever assembly 8 mm bolts	22	16
Handbrake cable support bracket 8 mm bolts	22	16
Handbrake cable support bracket-to-backplate 6 mm bolts	10	7
Handbrake equaliser cable guide-to-floor nuts	22	16
Handbrake equaliser cover-to-floor bolts	10	7
Handbrake lever mounting nut and bolts	22	16
Master cylinder fluid reservoir retaining bolt	3	2
Master cylinder mounting nuts	15	11
Rear caliper:		
Guide pin bolts	22	16
Mounting bracket-to-rear hub carrier bolts	55	41
Vacuum pump mounting bolts – diesel-engined models	22	16
Vacuum servo unit mounting nuts	13	10
Vacuum servo unit pushrod locknuts:		
'Star' locknut – servo end	22	16
Hexagon locknut – clevis end	15	11

1 General information

The braking system is of the servo-assisted, dual-circuit hydraulically-operated type, operating from a tandem master cylinder; in the event of hydraulic failure in one circuit, braking force will still be available at least two wheels.

All models have disc front and rear brakes; the front discs being ventilated while the rears are solid. An Anti-lock Braking System (ABS) is fitted as standard to all models, as is Brake Assist. All models are also equipped with one or two other traction-related systems, which rely on the ABS wheel sensors to operate – these being the Electronic Brake force Distribution (EBD) and Vehicle Stability Assist (VSA); refer to Section 19 for further information on the operation of these systems.

The front and rear disc brakes are actuated by single-piston sliding type calipers, which ensure that equal pressure is applied to each disc pad.

The handbrake is cable-operated, its shoes acting on drums formed inside the rear discs.

The vacuum servo unit uses intake manifold depression (generated only when a petrol engine is running) to boost the effort applied by the driver at the brake pedal and transmits this increased effort to the master cylinder pistons. Because there is no throttling of the intake manifold on a diesel engine, it is not a suitable source of vacuum for brake servo operation. Vacuum is therefore derived from a separate vacuum pump, which is bolted to the left-hand face of the timing chain case, at the rear right-hand end of the cylinder block. It is driven by the timing chain from the crankshaft.

Precautions

The vehicle's braking system is one of its most important safety features. When working on the brakes, there are a number of points to be aware of, to ensure that your health (or even your life) is not being put at risk.

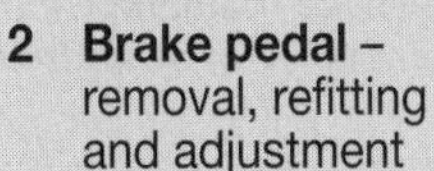

Warning: Brake fluid is poisonous. Take care to keep it off bare skin, and in particular not to get splashes in your eyes. The fluid also attacks paintwork and plastics – wash off spillages immediately with cold water. Finally, brake fluid is highly flammable, and should be handled with the same care as petrol.

- Make sure the ignition is off (take out the key) before disconnecting any braking system hydraulic union, and do not switch it on until after the hydraulic system has been bled. Failure to do this could lead to air entering the ABS modulator-control unit. If air enters the modulator-control unit pump, it will prove very difficult (in some cases impossible) to bleed the unit (see Section 5).
- When servicing any part of the system, work carefully and methodically – do not take short-cuts; also observe scrupulous cleanliness when overhauling any part of the hydraulic system.
- Always renew components in axle sets, where applicable – this means renewing brake pads, shoes, etc, on BOTH sides, even if only one set of pads is worn. In the instance of uneven brake wear, the cause should be investigated and fixed (the most likely causes being caliper bodies sticking on their guide pins or sticking caliper pistons).
- Use only genuine Honda parts, or at least those of known good quality.
- Although genuine Honda brake pads and shoes are asbestos-free, the dust created by wear of non-genuine parts may contain asbestos, which is a health hazard. Never blow it out with compressed air, and don't inhale any of it.
- DO NOT use petroleum-based solvents to clean brake parts; use brake cleaner or methylated spirit only.
- DO NOT allow any brake fluid, oil or grease to contact the brake pads or disc.

2 Brake pedal – removal, refitting and adjustment

Note: *The vacuum servo unit pushrod clevis pin locking clip must be renewed as a matter of course on reassembly.*

Removal

1 With reference to Chapter 11, remove the driver's side under cover and lower cover from the facia.

2 Disconnect the stop-light switch connector.

3 On the left-hand side of the pedal, pull out the spring clip, then withdraw the clevis pin from the right-hand side **(see illustration)**.

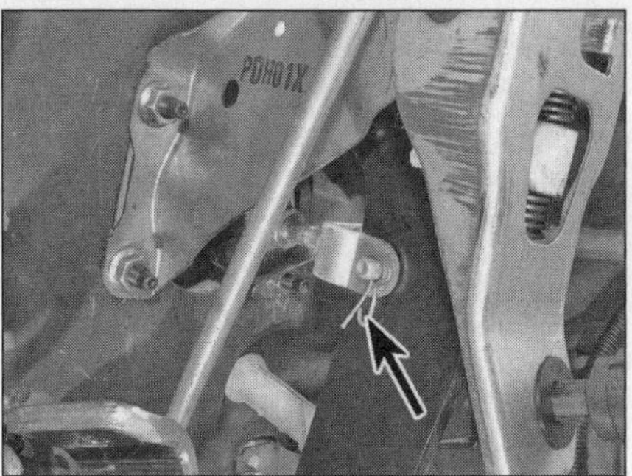

2.3 Pull out the spring clip on the left of the pedal

4 Unscrew the four (vacuum servo unit mounting) nuts and the bolt securing the pedal assembly to the bulkhead then manoeuvre the assembly out from underneath the facia **(see illustrations)**. Do not attempt to dismantle the pedal assembly; if it is worn or damaged the complete assembly must be renewed – no individual components are available.

Refitting

5 Grease the pedal pivot and manoeuvre the pedal assembly into position, ensuring it is correctly engaged with the pushrod clevis. Refit the mounting nuts and bolt and tighten them to the torque wrench setting, where specified.

6 Grease the clevis pin, then press it back into the brake pedal and servo pushrod, then fit the new clip **(see illustration 2.3)**. Ensure that the clip is securely fastened.

7 Reconnect the stop-light switch connector, then check the pedal adjustments as described below.

8 Check the operation of the brakes before taking the vehicle out on the road.

Adjustment

9 With reference to Chapter 11, remove the driver's side under cover and lower cover from the facia.

Pedal height

10 The height of the brake pedal is the distance the pedal sits off the floor, measured from the top surface of the pedal, with the carpet removed and the stop-light switch clear of the pedal; turn the stop-light switch anti-clockwise and pull the switch out until it no longer touches the pedal. Ensure that the pedal is not applying any pressure to the servo pushrod before measuring the pedal height. If the pedal height is not as specified, it must be adjusted.

11 To adjust the brake pedal height, slacken the locknut on the clevis end of the servo pushrod. Using pliers on the splined section of the pushrod, turn the pushrod to adjust the pedal height. When the adjustment is correct, tighten the locknut against the clevis to lock it **(see illustration)**.

12 Push the stop-light switch in to the pedal until its plunger is fully depressed against the nylon pad on the pedal arm, then turn it clockwise to lock it in position; this will automatically set the clearance between the switch body and the pad to 0.7 mm. Reconnect the switch wiring and check that the stop-lights illuminate when the pedal is depressed and that they go out as soon as it is released. Check the pedal free play as described below.

Pedal free play

13 The free play is the pedal slack, or the distance the pedal can be moved before it begins to have any effect on the brake system, measured at the pedal pad. If the pedal free play is not within the specified range, it must be reset.

14 Pedal free play is controlled by setting the stop-light switch, as described in paragraph 12 above. If correct pedal free play cannot be obtained with the stop-light switch correctly set, there must be a problem (such as worn pedal pivots or pushrod clevis and clevis pin) preventing this.

15 Check the operation of the brakes and stop-light switch, then refit the driver's side under cover and lower cover to the facia.

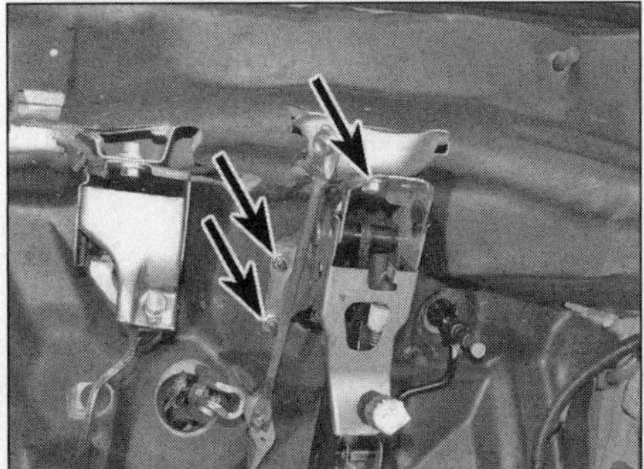

2.4a Vacuum servo unit mounting nuts and bolt – from the left

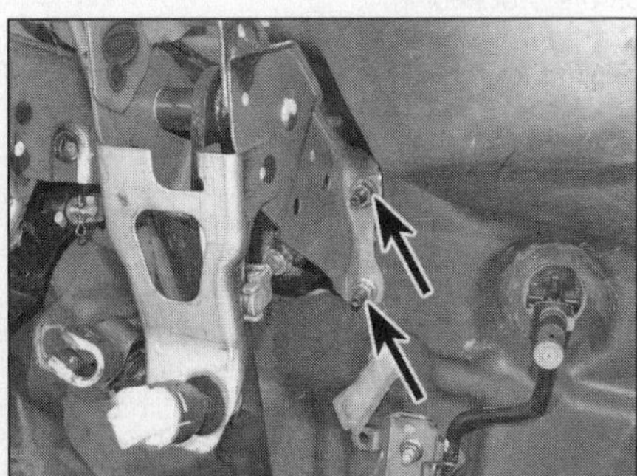

2.4b Vacuum servo unit mounting nuts – from the right

2.11 Brake pedal pushrod locknut (A) and splined section of pushrod (B)

3 Vacuum servo unit – testing, removal and refitting

Testing

1 To test the operation of the vacuum servo unit, depress the footbrake several times to exhaust the vacuum, then start the engine whilst keeping the pedal firmly depressed.

2 As the engine starts, there should be a noticeable 'give' in the brake pedal as the vacuum builds-up. Allow the engine to run for at least two minutes, then switch it off. If the brake pedal is now depressed it should feel normal, but further applications should result in the pedal feeling firmer, with the pedal stroke decreasing with each application.

3 If the vacuum servo unit does not operate as described, inspect its check valve as described in Section 4.

4 If the vacuum servo unit still fails to operate satisfactorily, the fault lies within the unit itself. Apart from external components, no spares are available, so a defective servo must be renewed.

Removal

Note: *The vacuum servo unit pushrod clevis pin locking clip must be renewed as a matter of course on reassembly.*

5 To remove the vacuum servo unit, first remove the brake master cylinder as described in Section 7.

6 Trace the vacuum hose from the vacuum servo unit to the fitting on the engine, and disconnect it. Release the hose from any clamps or ties securing it and note how it is routed.

7 Working in the passenger compartment, remove the driver's side under cover and lower cover from the facia (see Chapter 11).

8 On the left-hand side of the brake pedal, pull out the spring clip, then withdraw the clevis pin from the right-hand side **(see illustration 2.3)**.

9 Unscrew the four vacuum servo unit mounting nuts **(see illustrations 2.4a and 2.4b)**.

10 Return to the engine compartment and slide the vacuum servo unit straight out from the bulkhead until the studs clear the holes and withdraw the servo unit. Look carefully for any gaskets or seals which might be fitted; these must be renewed as a matter of course on refitting.

Refitting

11 If a new vacuum servo unit is being installed, the servo pushrod clearance must be set. This requires the use of special tools, so should be entrusted to a Honda dealer. If the original unit is being refitted, it can be assumed that the pushrod clearance is still correct.

12 Refitting is a reversal of removal, noting the following points:

a) Tighten the vacuum servo unit mounting nuts to the specified torque.

b) Grease the clevis pin, then press it back into the brake pedal and servo pushrod, then fit the new clip ***(see illustration 2.3)****. Ensure that the clip is securely fastened.*

c) After the final refitting of the master cylinder and brake hoses and pipes, bleed the brakes as described in Section 5.

d) Check and if necessary adjust the brake pedal height as described in Section 2.

4 Vacuum servo unit check valve – testing, removal and refitting

Testing

1 Examine the hose for signs of damage, such as splits at the ends, and renew if necessary. Check the valve is operating correctly by tracing the vacuum hose from the engine to the fitting on the vacuum servo unit and disconnecting the hose at the servo unit. With the engine idling, check that vacuum can be felt at the hose end. If not, remove the hose completely; the valve may be tested by blowing through it in both directions. Air should flow through the valve in one direction only – when blown through from the servo unit end of the valve. Renew the valve if this is not the case.

Removal

2 Trace the vacuum hose from the vacuum servo unit to the fitting on the engine, and disconnect it. Release the hose from any clamps or ties securing it and withdraw it, noting how it is routed.

3 The check valve is an integral part of the hose.

Refitting

4 Refitting is a reversal of removal. Ensure that the hose clips are secure, to prevent leaks. Check the operation of the brakes before taking the vehicle onto the road.

5 Hydraulic system – bleeding

Note: *Refer to the precautions in Section 1 before proceeding.*

Caution: Make sure the ignition is off (take out the key) before bleeding the system.

General

1 The correct operation of any hydraulic system is only possible after removing all air from the components and circuit; this is achieved by bleeding the system.

2 During the bleeding procedure, add only clean, unused hydraulic fluid of the recommended type; never re-use fluid that has already been bled from the system. Ensure that sufficient fluid is available before starting work.

3 If there is any possibility of incorrect fluid being already in the system, the system must be flushed completely with uncontaminated, correct fluid, and new seals should be fitted to the various components.

4 If air has entered the hydraulic system because of a leak, ensure that the fault is cured before proceeding further.

5 Park the vehicle on level ground, switch off the engine, remove the key, and select first or reverse gear (or P on automatic transmission models). Chock the wheels and release the handbrake.

6 Check that all pipes and hoses are secure, unions tight and bleed nipples closed. Clean any dirt from around the bleed nipples – if they have not been opened for some time, use a small wire brush to clean the threads, then apply a maintenance spray such as WD-40, and allow time for it to soak in. If a bleed nipple has seized, do not apply heat to it, as brake fluid is highly flammable.

7 Unscrew the master cylinder reservoir cap and top the master cylinder reservoir up to the MAX level line; refit the cap loosely. Remember to maintain the fluid level at least above the MIN level line throughout the procedure, or there is a risk of further air entering the system.

8 There is a number of one-man, do-it-yourself brake bleeding kits currently available from motor accessory shops. It is recommended that one of these kits is used whenever possible, as they greatly simplify the bleeding operation, and also reduce the risk of expelled air and fluid being drawn back into the system. If such a kit is not available, the basic (two-man) method must be used, which is described in detail below.

9 If a kit is to be used, prepare the vehicle as described previously, and follow the kit manufacturer's instructions. The procedure may vary slightly according to the type of kit being used; general procedures are as outlined below in the relevant sub-section.

10 Whichever method is used, the same sequence must be followed (paragraphs 11 and 12) to ensure the removal of all air from the system.

Bleeding sequence

11 If the system has been only partially disconnected, and the correct precautions were taken to minimise fluid loss, it should be necessary only to bleed that part of the system (ie, the primary or secondary circuit).

12 If the complete system is to be bled, then it should be done working in the following sequence:

a) Left-hand front brake.

b) Right-hand front brake.

c) Right-hand rear brake.

d) Left-hand rear brake.

Bleeding

Basic (two-man) method

13 Collect a clean glass jar, a length of plastic or rubber tubing which is a tight fit over the bleed nipple, and a ring spanner to fit the nipple. The help of an assistant will also be required.

14 Remove the dust cap from the first nipple in the sequence. Fit the spanner and tube to the nipple, place the other end of the tube in the jar, and pour in sufficient fluid to cover the end of the tube.

15 Ensure that the master cylinder reservoir fluid level is maintained at least above the MIN level line throughout the procedure.

16 Have the assistant fully depress the brake pedal several times to build-up pressure, then maintain it on the final stroke.

17 While pedal pressure is maintained, unscrew the bleed nipple (approximately one turn) and allow the compressed fluid and air to flow into the jar. The assistant should maintain pedal pressure, following it down to the floor if necessary, and should not release it until instructed to do so. When the flow stops, tighten the bleed nipple again. Have the assistant release the pedal slowly.

18 Repeat the steps given in paragraphs 16 and 17 until the fluid emerging from the bleed nipple is free from air bubbles. Remember to recheck the fluid level in the master cylinder reservoir every five strokes or so. If the master cylinder has been drained and refilled, and air is being bled from the first nipple in the sequence, allow approximately five seconds between strokes for the master cylinder passages to refill.

19 When no more air bubbles appear, tighten the bleed nipple securely, remove the tube and spanner, and refit the dust cap. Do not overtighten the bleed nipple.

20 Repeat the procedure on the remaining nipples in sequence until all air is removed from the system and the brake pedal feels firm.

Using a one-way valve kit

21 As their name implies, these kits consist of a length of tubing with a one-way valve fitted to prevent expelled air and fluid being drawn back into the system; some kits include a translucent container, which can be positioned so that the air bubbles can be more easily seen flowing from the end of the tube.

22 The kit is connected to the bleed nipple, which is then opened **(see illustration)**. The user returns to the driver's seat and depresses the brake pedal with a smooth, steady stroke and slowly releases it; this is repeated until the expelled fluid is clear of air bubbles.

23 Note that these kits simplify work so much that it is easy to forget the master cylinder reservoir fluid level; ensure that this is maintained at least above the MIN level line at all times.

Using a pressure-bleeding kit

24 These kits are usually operated by the reservoir of pressurised air contained in the spare tyre, although it may be necessary to reduce the pressure in the tyre to lower than normal; refer to the instructions supplied with the kit.

25 By connecting a pressurised, fluid-filled container to the master cylinder reservoir, bleeding can be carried out simply by opening each nipple in turn (in the specified sequence) and allowing the fluid to flow out until no more air bubbles can be seen in the expelled fluid.

26 This method has the advantage that the large reservoir of fluid provides an additional safeguard against air being drawn into the system during bleeding.

27 Pressure-bleeding is particularly effective when bleeding 'difficult' systems, or when bleeding the complete system at the time of routine fluid renewal.

All methods

28 When bleeding is complete and firm pedal feel is restored, wash off any spilt fluid, tighten the bleed nipples securely and refit their dust caps.

29 Check the hydraulic fluid level, and top-up if necessary (see *Weekly checks*).

30 Discard any hydraulic fluid that has been bled from the system; it will not be fit for re-use.

31 Check the feel of the brake pedal. If it feels at all spongy, air must still be present in the system, and further bleeding is required. Failure to bleed satisfactorily after several repetitions of the bleeding procedure may be due to worn master cylinder seals.

6 Brake pipes and hoses – renewal

Note: *Refer to the precautions in Section 1 before proceeding.*

1 If any pipe or hose is to be renewed, minimise fluid loss by removing the master cylinder reservoir cap and then tightening it down onto a piece of polythene (taking care not to damage the sender unit) to obtain an airtight seal. Alternatively, flexible hoses can be sealed, if required, using a proprietary brake hose clamp; metal brake pipe unions can be plugged (if care is taken not to allow dirt into the system) or capped immediately they are disconnected. Place a wad of rag under any union that is to be disconnected, to catch any spilt fluid.

2 If a flexible hose is to be disconnected, unscrew the brake pipe union nut before removing the horse-shoe clip which secures the hose to its mounting bracket **(see illustration)**.

3 To unscrew the union nuts, it is preferable to obtain a brake pipe spanner of the correct size (split ring); these are available from motor accessory shops. Failing this, a close-fitting open-ended spanner will be required, though if the nuts are tight or corroded, their flats may be rounded off if the spanner slips. In such a case, a self-locking wrench is often the only way to unscrew a stubborn union, but it follows that the pipe and the damaged nuts must be renewed on reassembly. Always clean a union and surrounding area before disconnecting it. If disconnecting a component with more than one union, make a careful note of the connections before disturbing any of them.

4 If a brake pipe is to be renewed, it can be obtained, cut to length and with the union nuts and end flares in place, from Honda dealers. All that is then necessary is to bend it to shape, following the line of the original, before fitting it to the vehicle. Alternatively, most motor accessory shops can make up brake pipes from kits, but this requires very careful measurement of the original to ensure that the new pipe is of the correct length. The safest answer is usually to take the original to the shop as a pattern.

5.22 Bleeding the brakes with a one-way valve kit

5 On refitting, do not overtighten the union nuts – it is not necessary to exercise brute force to obtain a sound joint.

6 Ensure that the pipes and hoses are correctly routed with no kinks, and that they are secured in the clips or brackets provided. In the case of flexible hoses, make sure that they cannot contact other components during movement of the steering and/or suspension assemblies.

7 After fitting, remove the polythene from the reservoir (or remove the plugs or clamps, as applicable), and bleed the hydraulic system as described in Section 5. Wash off any spilt fluid, and check carefully for fluid leaks.

7 Master cylinder – removal, overhaul and refitting

Note: *Refer to the precautions in Section 1 before proceeding.*

Removal

1 The master cylinder is located on the driver's side of the engine compartment, mounted on

6.2 Rear brake pipe-to-hose connection and mounting bracket – locking clip arrowed

7.3 Clutch master cylinder fluid reservoir mounting bolt

7.4a Front suspension strut brace mounting nuts – left-hand side

7.4b Front suspension strut brace left-hand mounting bolt

7.4c Front suspension strut brace right-hand mounting bolt

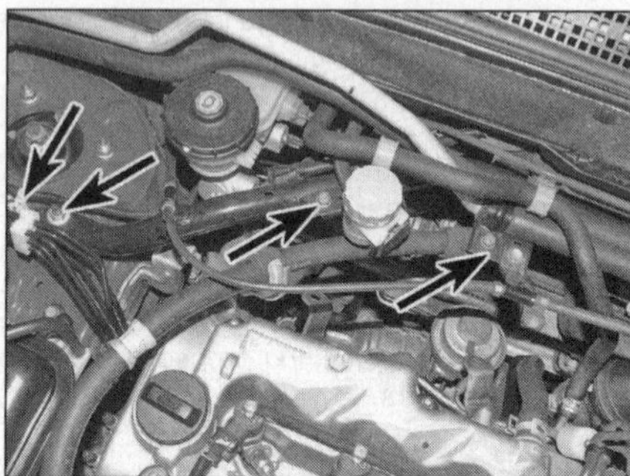
7.4d Front suspension strut brace mounting nuts – right-hand side. Note also items to be unbolted from brace on diesels

the vacuum servo unit. Access to the master cylinder in the engine compartment is limited by various pipes, hoses and cables – where possible, unclip them to improve matters.

2 On diesel-engined models, unscrew the four retaining nuts and remove the acoustic engine cover.

3 Unbolt any brackets and release any clamps or ties securing components or wiring harnesses, cables and hoses to the front suspension strut brace; on diesel-engined models, it may prove necessary also to unbolt the throttle linkage/accelerator pedal position sensor assembly and the fuel system hand primer (refer to Chapter 4B for details, if required). When unbolting the clutch master cylinder fluid reservoir, secure the reservoir upright clear of the working area; if care is taken, there is no need to disconnect its fluid hose **(see illustration)**.

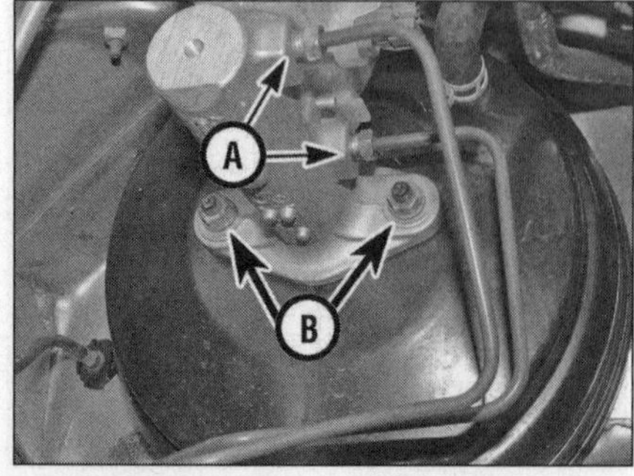

7.8 Master cylinder fluid unions (A) and mounting nuts (B)

4 Unscrew the nuts securing the brace to each front suspension strut top mounting, then unbolt the brace from the engine compartment bulkhead **(see illustrations)**.

5 Unscrew the master cylinder fluid reservoir cap. Remove as much fluid as you can from the reservoir before starting, using a syringe. If a syringe is not available, the fluid can be soaked out with clean paper towel. Take care not to drip hydraulic fluid onto paintwork or hot engine components.

6 Disconnect the brake fluid level sensor wiring plug from the side of the reservoir.

7 Slacken the two brake pipe union nuts on the side of the master cylinder. To prevent rounding off the corners on these nuts, the use of a brake pipe nut spanner which wraps around the nut is preferred. Place some absorbent rag or towel underneath, then pull the brake pipes away slightly from the master cylinder. Either plug or tape over the open connections to prevent contamination.

8 Unscrew and remove the two nuts attaching the master cylinder to the servo **(see illustration)**. Pull the master cylinder off the studs and out of the engine compartment. Again, be careful not to spill the fluid as this is done. Recover the master cylinder pushrod seal – a new one should be obtained for refitting.

Overhaul

Note: *Check availability of overhaul kits prior to dismantling the cylinder.*

9 Unscrew the reservoir retaining bolt. Wrap some clean rag or paper towel around the reservoir, then remove the reservoir from the cylinder. Recover the two grommets – new ones must be used on reassembly.

10 Hold the rear piston into the cylinder body, and extract the circlip.

11 Push the rear piston inwards, then extract the stop pin through the cylinder front port.

12 Remove the stopper, then ease out the piston assemblies. If necessary, use compressed air to force the piston from the cylinder body.

13 Carefully examine the bore of the cylinder for rust, scratches, gouges and general wear. If the bore is damaged, the complete cylinder must be renewed. If the bore is in good condition, thoroughly clean the assembly, and renew the seals as described below.

14 Take note of the seal orientation on each piston, and using a small screwdriver, lever the seals from the grooves on the pistons.

15 Smear the new seals with clean brake fluid, then fit them to the piston as noted on removal.

16 Apply a little of the assembly grease (which should be supplied in the overhaul kit) to the piston bodies and O-rings.

17 Insert the primary piston assembly into the cylinder, spring end first. Ensure the seal lips enter the cylinder bore without catching or folding back. Align the piston slot with the stop pin hole at the top of the cylinder.

18 Fit the secondary piston, and use it to push the primary piston in far enough to refit the stop pin, though the cylinder front port.

19 Push the rear piston inwards, fit the stopper, then secure with the circlip.

20 Using two new grommets, refit the reservoir and secure with the retaining bolt.

Refitting

21 Refitting is a reversal of removal, noting the following points.

22 Apply some of the overhaul kit's assembly grease to a new pushrod seal, and fit it to the rear of the cylinder.

23 Fit the master cylinder over the studs on the servo, and tighten the attaching nuts only finger-tight at this stage.

24 Thread the brake pipe fittings into the master cylinder. Since the master cylinder is still loose, it can be moved slightly in order for the fittings to thread in easily. Do not strip the threads as the fittings are tightened.

8.4 Unscrew and remove caliper bottom guide pin bolt or guide pin

8.5 Swing up caliper body and secure with piece of wire hooked around suspension strut

8.11 Using a piston retraction tool to push back caliper piston to make room for new brake pads

25 Fully tighten the mounting nuts and pipe unions to the specified torque.

26 Fill the master cylinder reservoir with fluid, then bleed the master cylinder and the brake system as described in Section 5. Check the operation of the brakes before taking the vehicle out on the road.

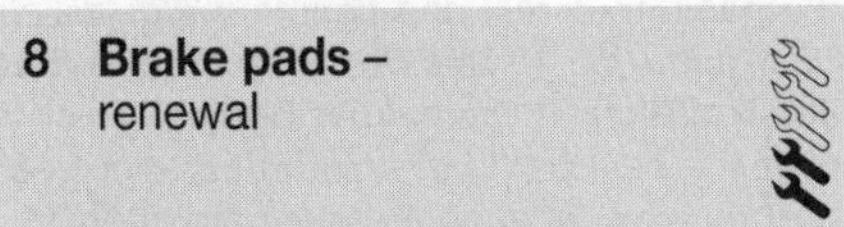

8 Brake pads - renewal

Note: *Refer to the precautions in Section 1 before proceeding.*

Front pads

Note: *Two types of front brake caliper are fitted to CR-Vs. Both are of the same kind (single-piston sliding type) and working procedures are essentially the same. The only difference lies in the fastening arrangements for the caliper body guide pins; one type uses separate bolts and guide pins, the other uses threaded guide pins.*

1 Chock the rear wheels and apply the handbrake lever fully, slacken the roadwheel nuts, then raise the front of the vehicle and support it securely on axle stands (see *Jacking and vehicle support*).

2 Remove the front wheels. Work on one brake assembly at a time, using the assembled brake for reference if necessary.

3 First, inspect the brake disc carefully as outlined in Section 10. If renewal is necessary, follow the information in that Section to remove the disc, at which time the calipers and pads can be removed as well.

4 Unscrew and remove the caliper bottom guide pin bolt or guide pin **(see illustration)**. If bolt and guide pin are separate, counterhold the guide pin if necessary by means of a slim open-ended spanner applied to the flats on its head while unscrewing the bolt. Carefully swing up the caliper body, ensuring that the pad springs do not fly off. Hold the pads and remove both pad springs. In theory, these should be discarded and renewed as a matter of course whenever they are disturbed.

5 With the springs removed, swing up the caliper body as far as possible (take care not to kink the brake flexible hose in so doing) and secure it with a piece of wire hooked around the suspension strut **(see illustration)**.

6 Remove both pads. If aftermarket pads have been fitted with no wear indicator tab on the inboard pads, note carefully which pad fitted where and, if they are to be refitted, ensure that each is refitted in its original location.

7 Noting their order of fitting, remove the shim(s) from the back of each pad. Two shims are used on the inboard pad (the larger one fits next to the pad), with one shim on the outboard pad.

8 Release the pad retainers from the top and bottom of the caliper mounting bracket, noting how they are fitted. If the retainers are in poor condition, it is recommended that new ones be used on refitting.

9 While the pads are removed, clean the caliper body and mounting bracket. This is best done using a brush together with spray or liquid brake cleaner, rather than dry brushing, which carries a greater risk of inhaling brake dust.

10 Check the disc and caliper, brake hose, piston dust seals and guide pin gaiters for any signs of damage. Move the caliper body in-and-out to check that it slides easily and smoothly on the guide pins; dismantle, clean and grease the guide pins and their bores if this is not the case (see Section 9).

11 If the pads are to be renewed, the caliper piston must be pushed back into the caliper body to make room for the increased thickness of the new pads. This may require considerable effort; to avoid the risk of scoring the piston or damaging the piston seals through using a G-clamp, sliding-jaw (water pump) pliers, or levers, use one of the many piston retraction tools that are widely available **(see illustration)**.

12 Pushing back the piston will cause the fluid level in the reservoir to rise, and possibly overflow. Make sure that there is sufficient space in the brake fluid reservoir to accept the displaced fluid, and if necessary, syphon some off first. Any brake fluid spilt on paintwork should be washed off with clean water, without delay – brake fluid is also a highly-effective paint-stripper.

13 Begin refitting by applying a little grease – either the grease supplied with the pad kit or copper-based brake grease – to the mating surfaces of the pad retainers, before fitting them to the caliper mounting bracket **(see illustrations)**.

14 Smear a little of the same grease on both

8.13a Thoroughly clean pad retainers . . .

8.13b . . . then smear on a little brake grease . . .

8.13c . . . and refit to caliper mounting bracket

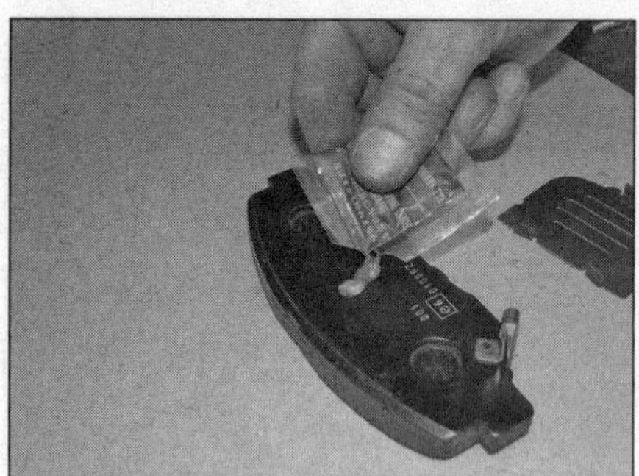

8.14a Smear a little grease on both sides of pad shims . . .

8.14b . . . before fitting to inboard pad

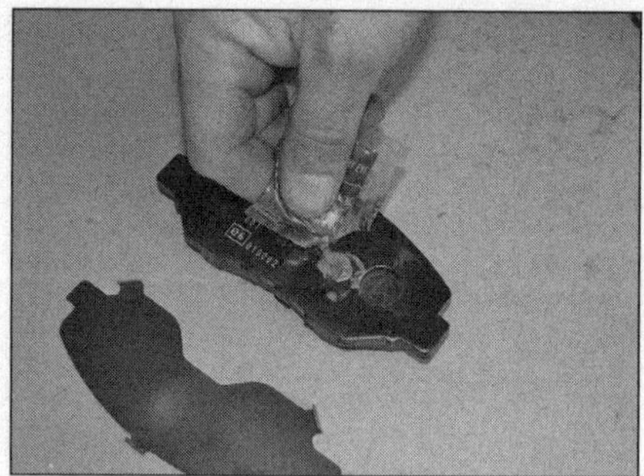

8.14c Apply grease to pad and shim . . .

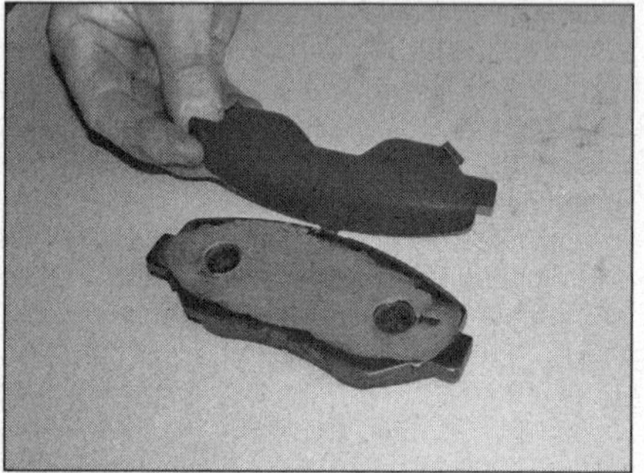

8.14d . . . before fitting shim to outboard pad

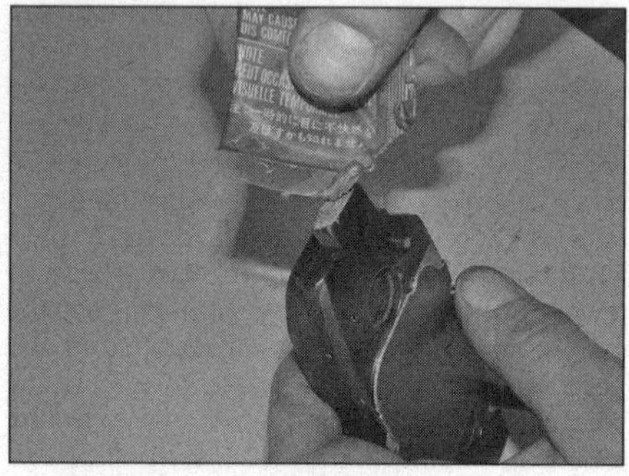

8.15a Grease edges of pad backing plates . . .

sides of the pad shims, then fit them into place **(see illustrations)**.

15 Apply a little of the same grease to the edges of the brake pad backing plates, and in particular the 'ears' which locate in the caliper mounting bracket – don't get any grease on the pad friction material **(see illustrations)**.

16 Fit the pads into the caliper mounting bracket, pressing them firmly into place with the friction material facing the disc **(see illustrations)**. The pad with the wear indicator tab is the inboard one.

17 Fit the pad spring ends securely into the pads **(see illustrations)**.

18 Holding the pads and springs in place, and being careful not to damage the guide pin gaiters, swing the caliper body down over the pads, then refit and tighten the guide pin bolt/guide pin to the specified torque **(see illustrations)**. If the caliper body will not fit over the new pads, the piston has not been pushed back far enough – see paragraph 11.

19 Depress the brake pedal several times to bring the pads into firm contact with the brake disc.

20 Repeat the above procedure on the remaining front brake caliper.

21 Refit the roadwheels, then lower the vehicle to the ground and tighten the wheel nuts to the specified torque.

8.15b . . . especially 'ears' which locate in caliper mounting bracket

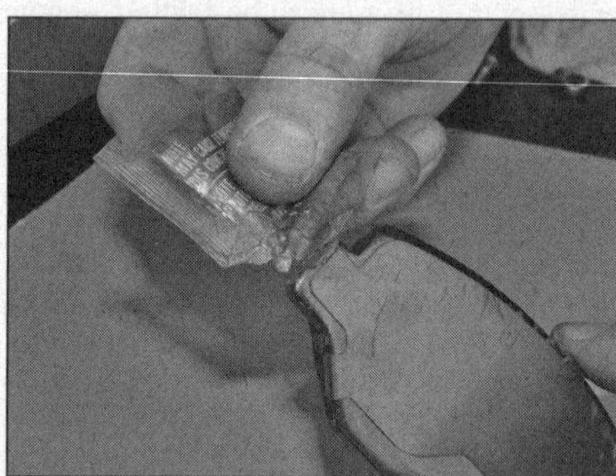

8.15c Greasing outboard pad backing plate

8.16a Don't get grease on pad friction material – which fits against disc . . .

8.16b . . . when fitting brake pads to caliper

8.17a Fit pad spring ends securely into pads . . .

8.17b . . . and hold in place when refitting caliper body

8.18a Swing caliper body down over pads . . .

8.18b . . . refit guide pin bolt . . .

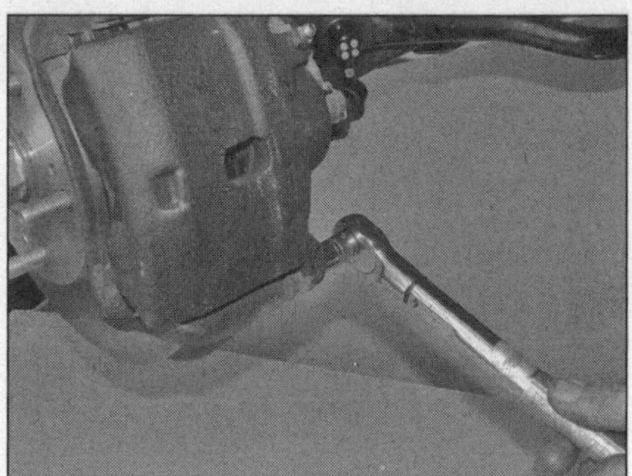

8.18c . . . and tighten to specified torque

22 Check the hydraulic fluid level as described in *Weekly checks*.

23 If new pads have been fitted, full braking efficiency will not be obtained until the friction material has bedded-in. Be prepared for longer stopping distances, and avoid harsh braking as far as possible for the first hundred miles or so after fitting new pads.

Rear pads

24 Rear pad renewal is similar to the front pad procedure, noting the following **(see illustrations)**.

a) Release the handbrake fully.

b) Unscrew and remove both caliper guide pin bolts, and remove the caliper body from its mounting bracket for access to the pads; note the pad spring inside the caliper body.

8.24a Unscrew and remove caliper guide pin bolts . . .

8.24b . . . unbolt brake hose support bracket from rear suspension hub carrier if required . . .

8.24c . . . and remove caliper body from mounting bracket to reach brake pads

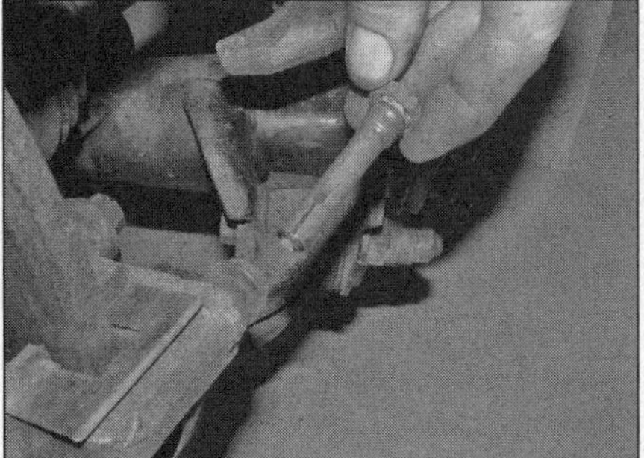

8.24d Dismantle and clean guide pins if caliper body is stiff to slide . . .

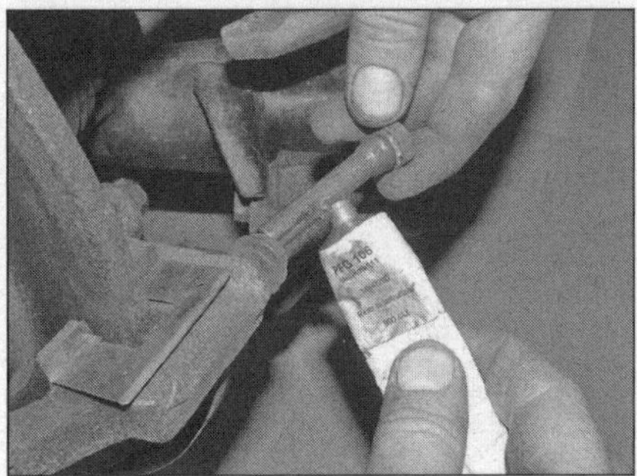

8.24e . . . and apply brake grease on reassembly

8.24f Using a piston retraction tool to push back caliper piston to make room for new brake pads

8.24g Thoroughly clean pad retainers before refitting . . .

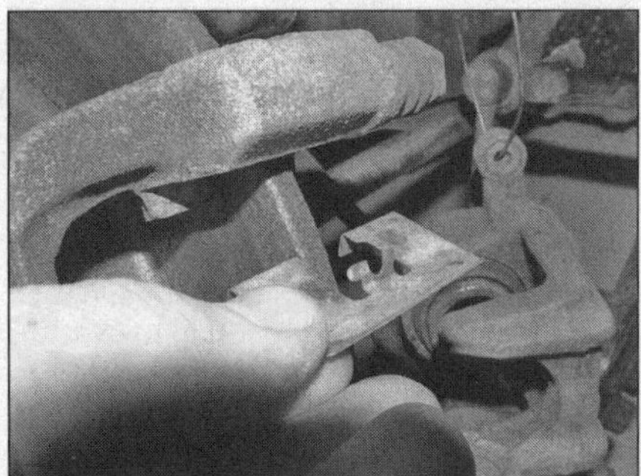

8.24h . . . ensure retainers are located correctly – they are different

8.24i Inboard pad has two shims . . .

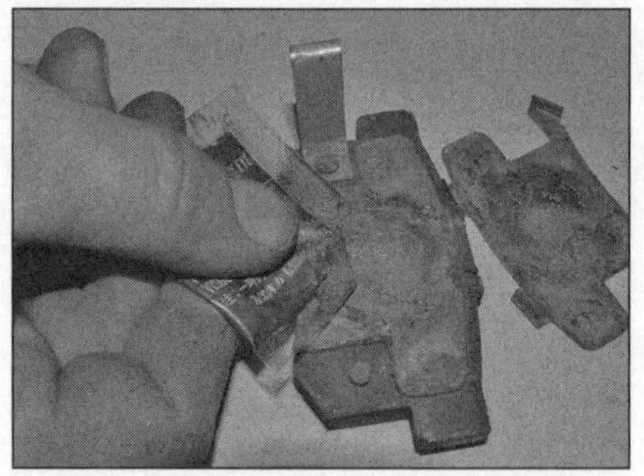
8.24j . . . smear on a little brake grease . . .

8.24k . . . on both sides of each shim . . .

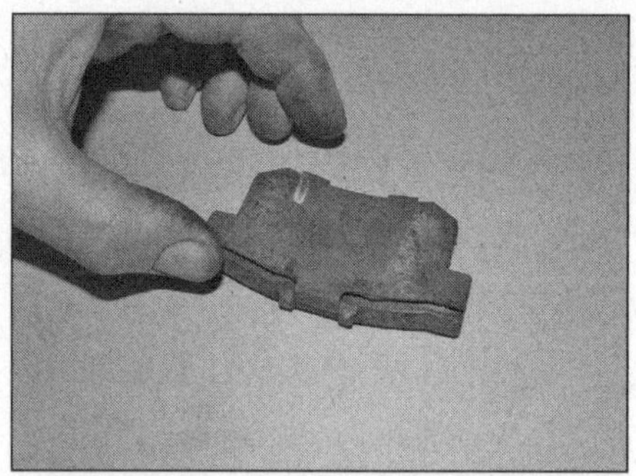
8.24l . . . then ensure shims are correctly located – outboard pad shown here

8.24m Grease edges of inboard pad backing plate . . .

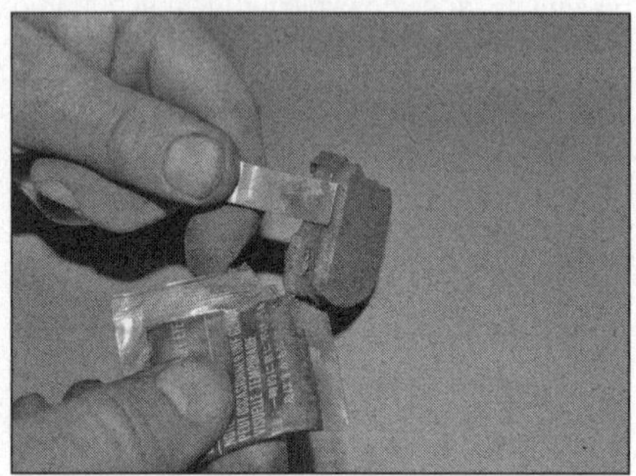
8.24n . . . especially 'ears' which locate in caliper mounting bracket

8.24o Refit pad with friction material against disc

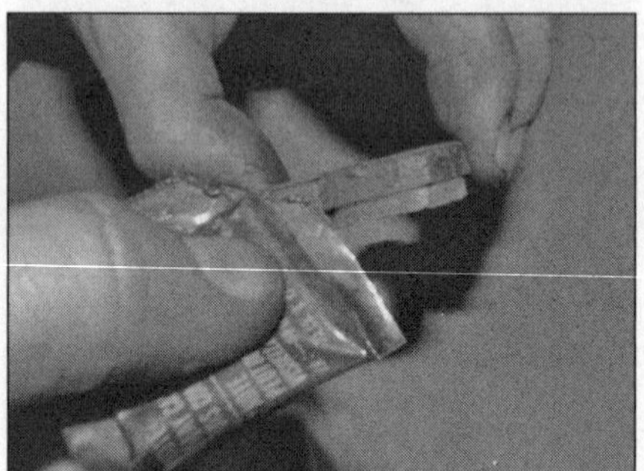
8.24p Grease edges of inboard pad backing plate . . .

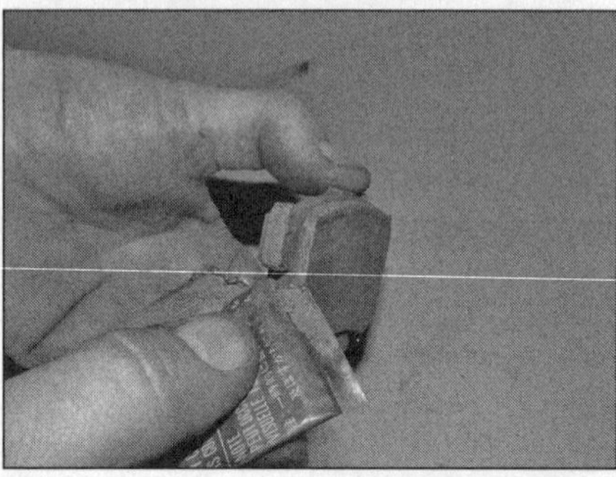
8.24q . . . and 'ears' which locate in caliper mounting bracket

8.24r Rear brake pads refitted to caliper mounting bracket

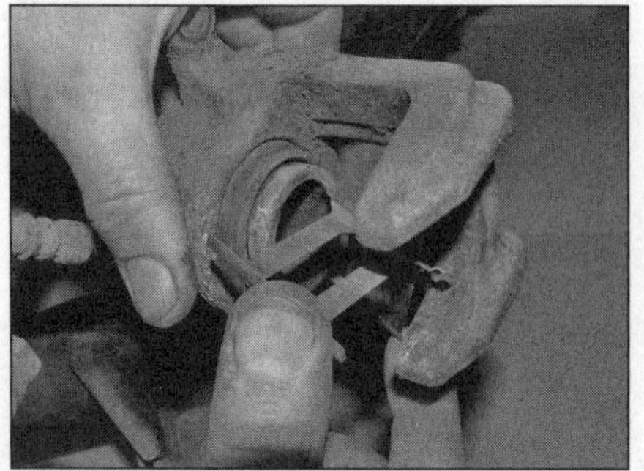
8.24s Fit pad spring into caliper body . . .

8.24t . . . so that locating tabs are engaged in caliper body inspection hole

8.24u Refit guide pin bolts and tighten to specified torque

c) When refitting, fit the pad spring to the caliper body, ensuring that it is the correct way round and that its locating tabs are securely engaged in the caliper body inspection hole.

9 Brake caliper – removal, overhaul and refitting

Note: *Refer to the precautions in Section 1 before proceeding.*

Removal

1 Slacken the relevant wheel nuts, chock

9.6 Unscrew bolts to remove caliper mounting bracket

the opposite wheels, then jack up either the front or rear of the vehicle and support on axle stands (see *Jacking and vehicle support*). Remove the appropriate roadwheel.

2 Clamp the brake hose, using a proper brake hose clamp if available (these are not expensive, and greatly reduce the risk of damaging the hose). In the absence of a proper clamp, use some self-locking pliers, but protect the hose by placing a couple of pieces of card in the plier jaws.

3 Wrap some clean rag or paper towel around the brake hose union on the caliper, then slacken the bolt.

4 Unscrew and remove both caliper guide pin bolts, then lift the caliper body off the pads. Remove both pads as described in Section 8.

5 Fully unscrew the union bolt, and disconnect the brake hose from the caliper body – anticipate a small amount of fluid spillage as this is done. Recover the sealing washers fitted either side of the hose end fitting – new washers should be used when reassembling.

6 Unscrew the two bolts securing the mounting bracket to the swivel hub, and remove the bracket **(see illustration)**.

Overhaul

Caution: As with all other work on the braking system, it is recommended that the calipers are overhauled in axle pairs – in other words, do not overhaul only one caliper at a time, as this may result in uneven braking.

Note: *Ensure that an appropriate caliper overhaul kit is obtained before starting work.*

7 With the caliper on the bench, wipe away all traces of dust and dirt, but avoid inhaling the dust, as it is may be a health hazard.

8 Using a small flat-bladed screwdriver, carefully prise the dust seal retaining clip (where fitted) out of the caliper body groove.

9 Withdraw the partially-ejected piston from the caliper body and remove the dust seal **(see illustration)**. The piston can be withdrawn by hand, or if necessary forced out by applying compressed air to the banjo union bolt hole.

Caution: The piston may be ejected with some force. Only low pressure should be required, such as is generated by a foot pump.

10 Extract the piston fluid seal using a blunt instrument such as a knitting needle or a crochet hook, taking care not to damage the caliper body bore.

11 Withdraw (as applicable) the guide pins and the guide pin rubber gaiters.

12 Thoroughly clean all components, using only methylated spirit, isopropyl alcohol or clean hydraulic fluid as a cleaning medium. Never use mineral-based solvents, such as petrol or paraffin, which will attack the hydraulic system rubber components. Dry the components immediately, using compressed air or a clean, lint-free cloth. Use compressed air to blow clear the fluid passages. Once the brake dust is removed, use a wire brush or similar to scrub clean and polish the points of contact on the caliper body and mounting bracket, removing all traces of rust and corrosion so that the pads are able to slide smoothly in the mounting bracket and the caliper body is free to slide smoothly on the mounting bracket. Flush or blow away any dust or rust particles created by this.

13 Check all components and renew any that are worn or damaged. Check particularly the cylinder bore and piston; if they are scratched, worn or corroded in any way, they must be renewed (note that this means the renewal of the complete assembly). Similarly check the condition of the guide pins and their bores; they should be undamaged and (when cleaned) a reasonably tight sliding fit in the mounting bracket bores. If there is any doubt about the condition of a component, renew it.

14 If the assembly is fit for further use, obtain the appropriate repair kit.

15 Renew as a matter of course all rubber seals, dust covers, dust seal retaining clips, gaiters, sealing washers and caps disturbed on dismantling; these should never be re-used.

16 Before commencing reassembly, ensure that all components are absolutely clean and dry.

17 Either lubricate the piston fluid and dust seals with the rubber grease supplied in the overhaul kit, or dip the piston and the new piston (fluid) seal in clean hydraulic fluid. Smear clean fluid on the cylinder bore surface.

18 Fit the new piston (fluid) seal, using only the fingers to manipulate it into the cylinder bore groove. Similarly lubricate and fit the new dust seal to the piston. Refit the piston to the cylinder bore using a twisting motion, ensuring that the piston enters squarely into the bore. Press the piston fully into the bore, then press the dust seal into the caliper body.

19 Install the dust seal retaining clip (where fitted), ensuring that it is correctly seated in the caliper body groove.

20 Apply the silicone grease supplied in the repair kit (or copper brake grease) to the guide pins. Fit the new rubber gaiters, ensuring that they are correctly located in the grooves on both the mounting bracket and, where applicable, the pins, then fit the pins (as applicable) to the mounting bracket.

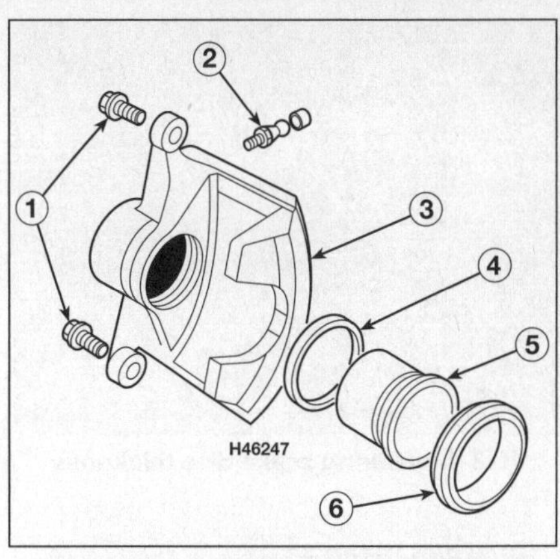

9.9 Typical front brake caliper exploded view

1 *Guide pin bolts*
2 *Bleed nipple*
3 *Caliper body*
4 *Piston seal*
5 *Piston*
6 *Dust seal*

Refitting

21 Fit the mounting bracket to the swivel hub and tighten the two mounting bolts to the specified torque wrench setting **(see illustration)**.

22 Using new sealing washers either side of the hose end fitting, reconnect the brake hose to the caliper body, tightening the bolt only hand-tight at this stage.

23 Holding the springs as described in Section 8, offer the caliper body into position over the pads, then refit the guide pin bolts and tighten them to the specified torque wrench setting.

24 Tighten the brake hose union bolt to the specified torque, then remove the brake hose clamp.

25 Bleed the brakes as described in Section 5. If the brake hose was clamped throughout, then only the disturbed caliper should require bleeding.

26 Depress the brake pedal several times to bring the pads into firm contact with the brake discs.

27 On completion, refit the wheel and lower the vehicle to the ground. Tighten the wheel nuts to the specified torque.

9.21 Tighten caliper mounting bracket bolts to specified torque

10.3 Measuring brake disc thickness

10.8a Unbolt brake hose support bracket from suspension components, if required . . .

10.8b . . . and suspend caliper on wire hook while work is in progress

10 Brake discs – inspection, removal and refitting

Note: *Refer to the precautions in Section 1 before proceeding.*

Inspection

1 Slacken the relevant wheel nuts, chock the opposite wheels, then jack up either the front or rear of the vehicle and support on axle stands (see *Jacking and vehicle support*). Remove the appropriate roadwheel. If working on the rear brakes, fully release the handbrake.

2 Slowly rotate the brake disc so that the full area of both sides can be checked; remove the brake pads, as described in Section 8, if better access is required to the inboard surface. Light scoring is normal in the area swept by the brake pads, but if heavy scoring is found, the disc must be renewed.

3 It is normal to find a lip of rust and brake dust around the disc's perimeter; this can be scraped off if required. If, however, a lip has formed due to wear of the brake pad swept area, the disc thickness must be measured using a micrometer **(see illustration)**. Take measurements at several places around the disc at the inside and outside of the pad swept area; if the disc has worn at any point to the specified minimum thickness or less, it must be renewed.

4 If the disc is thought to be warped, it can be checked for run-out, ideally by using a dial gauge mounted on any convenient fixed point, while the disc is slowly rotated. In the absence of a dial gauge, use feeler blades to measure (at several points all around the disc) the clearance between the disc and a fixed point such as the caliper mounting bracket.

5 If the measurements obtained are at the specified maximum or beyond, the disc is excessively warped, and must be renewed; however, it is worth checking first that the wheel bearing is in good condition (Chapters 1A or 1B and 10).

6 Check the disc for cracks, and for any other wear or damage. Renew the disc if necessary.

Removal

7 Remove the brake pads as described in Section 8.

8 If the caliper is to be overhauled, remove it as described in Section 9. If it is merely being removed to provide access to the discs, etc, unscrew the remaining guide pin or bolt (where applicable) and suspend the caliper body from the underbody or suspension using a wire hook; there is no need to disconnect the brake hose **(see illustrations)**. Unbolt the caliper mounting bracket.

9 If the same disc is to be refitted, use chalk or paint to mark the relationship of the disc to the hub.

10 Remove the two disc retaining screws – these may be tight, due to corrosion. If available, use an impact driver to remove the screws, or try tapping the end of the screwdriver to break the screw free **(see illustration)**. Sometimes, using a close-fitting screwdriver bit in a socket handle can provide greater leverage on a difficult screw than a screwdriver will.

11 With the screws removed, pull the brake disc from the hub – if it is tight, lightly tap its inboard face with a hide or plastic mallet. If you are trying to remove a rear brake disc/drum, check that the handbrake is fully released. While the handbrake shoes are unlikely to wear the disc/drum so much that a ridge forms against which the shoes lock when you try to pull off the disc/drum (as could be the case with normal rear drum brakes), it is worth trying the effect of backing off the handbrake adjustment (see Section 17) if the disc/drum is difficult to remove. If the disc is stuck fast, two M8 x 1.25 threaded holes are provided in the disc centre – screw two M8 bolts into these, and tighten them evenly to draw the disc off the hub. If the disc still will not move it is probable that a build-up of corrosion on its inboard surface is fouling the hub **(see illustrations)**. The application of heat may

10.10 Brake disc securing screws must be undone . . .

10.11a . . . to allow disc to be removed

10.11b If a disc is stuck, screw two M8 x 1.25 bolts into holes provided, and tighten evenly to draw disc off hub

10.11c If disc is stuck fast, problem is likely to be rust build-up of corrosion on its inboard surface fouling hub (arrows)

help, but take care to avoid damage to the bodywork and surrounding components if you have to resort to brute force and a heavy mallet. If severe corrosion does prove to be the cause of the problem, make sure all surfaces are scrubbed clean, back to the bare metal, and check that they are flat before the new disc is installed.

Refitting

12 Refitting is the reverse of the removal procedure, noting the following points:

a) *Ensure that the mating surfaces of the disc and hub are clean and flat. To reduce the risk of corrosion, apply copper grease to the hub before fitting the disc (ensure that the grease does not get on the disc friction surfaces).*

b) *If applicable, align the marks made on removal.*

c) *If a new disc has been fitted, use a suitable solvent to wipe any preservative coating from the disc before refitting the caliper* **(see illustration)**. *If working on the rear brakes, do not forget to clean and degrease the handbrake drum friction surface.*

d) *If the disc retaining screws suffered damage during removal, use new ones when reassembling. Apply a little copper grease to their threads, to prevent future corrosion problems.*

e) *Tighten the brake caliper mounting bracket bolts to the specified torque* **(see illustration).**

f) *Refit the caliper body and pads as described in Sections 8 and 9.*

g) *On completion, depress the brake pedal several times to bring the brake pads into firm contact with the discs.*

h) *If the work was carried out on the rear disc/drums, carry out the major handbrake adjustment as described in Section 17.*

i) *Refit the roadwheel, then lower the vehicle to the ground and tighten the wheel nuts to the specified torque.*

j) *As with new pads, if new discs have been fitted, full braking efficiency will not be obtained until the friction material has bedded-in. Be prepared for longer stopping distances, and avoid harsh braking as far as possible for the first hundred miles or so after fitting new brake components.*

10.12a Clean hub-disc mating surfaces before refitting - also degrease surface of new disc before fitting

10.12b Tighten brake caliper mounting bracket bolts to the specified torque wrench setting

11 Front brake disc shield - removal and refitting

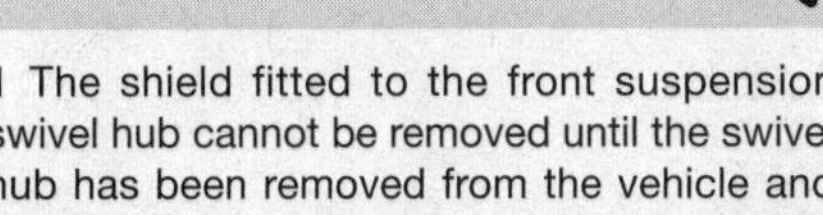

1 The shield fitted to the front suspension swivel hub cannot be removed until the swivel hub has been removed from the vehicle and the front hub has been pressed out; an action which will require the renewal of the wheel bearing. See Chapter 10.

2 Once the hub has been removed, unscrew the three retaining screws and withdraw the shield from the swivel hub; note the locating tab ensuring that the shield can be fitted correctly only one way **(see illustrations)**. If you have to tap it off because of corrosion, be careful to tap evenly all the way round to avoid distorting the shield.

3 Refitting is the reverse of removal; tighten securely the shield retaining screws.

12 Handbrake drum - removal, inspection and refitting

Note: *Refer to the precautions in Section 1 before proceeding.*

Removal and refitting

1 The handbrake drums are formed inside the rear discs. Removal and refitting are therefore as described in Section 10.

Inspection

2 Brush the dirt and dust from the disc/drum, taking care not to inhale it. Check it for signs of excessive wear or damage such as scoring grooves or cracks.

3 Examine the internal friction surface of the disc/drum. If deeply scored, or so worn that the disc/drum has become ridged to the width of the shoes, then both disc/drums must be renewed.

4 Regrinding of the friction surface may be possible, provided the maximum diameter given in the Specifications is not exceeded, but note that both rear disc/drums should be reground to the identical diameter.

13 Handbrake shoes - inspection and renewal

Note: *Refer to the precautions in Section 1 before proceeding.*

Inspection

1 Remove the brake disc/drum on the side concerned, as described in Section 10.

2 Remove all traces of brake dust from the brake disc/drum, backplate and shoes, but take care not to inhale the dust.

3 Measure the thickness of friction material remaining on each brake shoe at several points. If either shoe is worn at any point to the specified minimum thickness or less, all four shoes must be renewed as a set. Also, the shoes should be renewed if any are fouled with oil or grease, as there is no satisfactory way of degreasing friction material once contaminated.

4 If any of the brake shoes are worn unevenly or fouled with oil or grease, trace and rectify the cause before reassembly. If the shoes are to be renewed, proceed as described below. If all is well, refit the disc/drum as described in Section 10.

Renewal

Note 1: *All four rear brake shoes must be renewed at the same time, but to avoid mixing up parts, work on only one brake assembly at a time, using the other side as a guide.*

Note 2: *Honda state that if new handbrake shoes and/or rear disc/drums have been fitted, the new components must be bedded-in by*

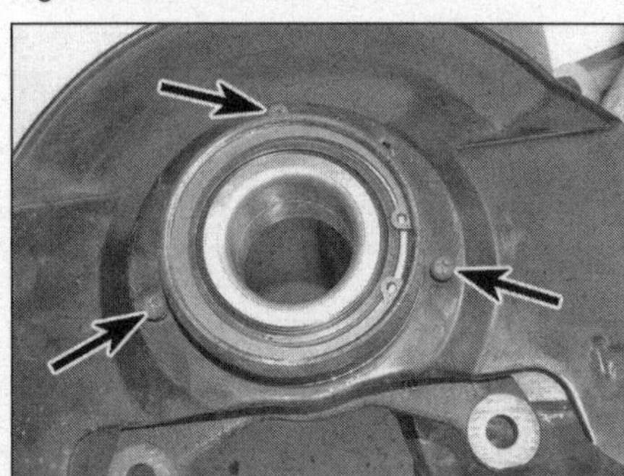

11.2a Front brake disc shield retaining screws

11.2b Note tab locating brake disc shield on swivel hub

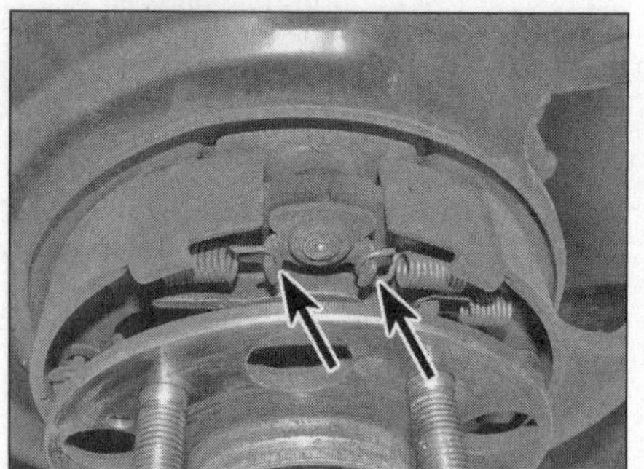
13.5 Unhook upper return springs . . .

13.6 . . . remove handbrake shoe retainer pin and spring . . .

13.8 . . . then unhook lower return spring

driving the vehicle at no more than 30 mph for a distance of one-quarter of a mile with the handbrake applied by two to four clicks. Stop the vehicle and wait for 5 to 10 minutes with the handbrake fully released to allow the disc/drums to cool. Repeat three more times (four times altogether), then carry out the major handbrake adjustment described in Section 17 again, as soon as the handbrake components have fully cooled down.

5 Unhook and remove the upper return springs **(see illustration)**.

6 Turn the end of each shoe retainer pin with pliers while pressing in the retainer spring, then withdraw the pin from the rear, and take off the springs **(see illustration)**.

7 Unhook the rod spring and remove the connecting rod.

8 Pull the shoes apart at the top and lower them until the lower return spring can be unhooked and the forward shoe and adjuster assembly can be removed **(see illustration)**.

9 Unhook the handbrake cable from the lever on the rearward shoe and remove the shoe.

10 Prise out the retaining clip and remove the wave washer and the pivot pin to separate the lever from the rearward shoe. Discard the retaining clip – a new one must be fitted on reassembly.

11 On reassembly, follow illustrations 13.11a to 13.11x for the brake shoe refitting procedure. Be sure to stay in order and read the caption under each illustration **(see illustrations)**.

13.11a Clean and apply brake grease to all . . .

13.11b . . . points of contact between handbrake shoes and backplate . . .

13.11c . . . and to mating surfaces of shoe anchor

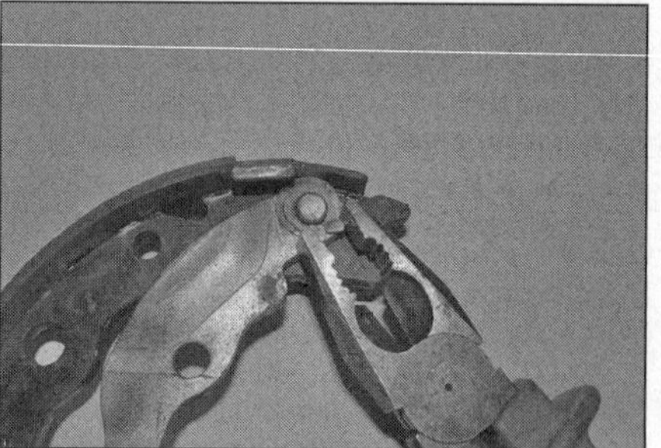
13.11d Refit lever pivot pin to rearward shoe, then wave washer and secure with new retaining clip, crimped as shown

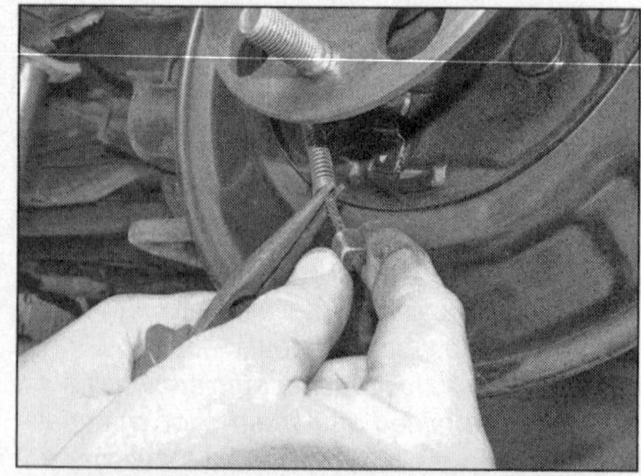
13.11e Compress return spring on handbrake cable . . .

13.11f . . . then connect cable inner wire end to lever . . .

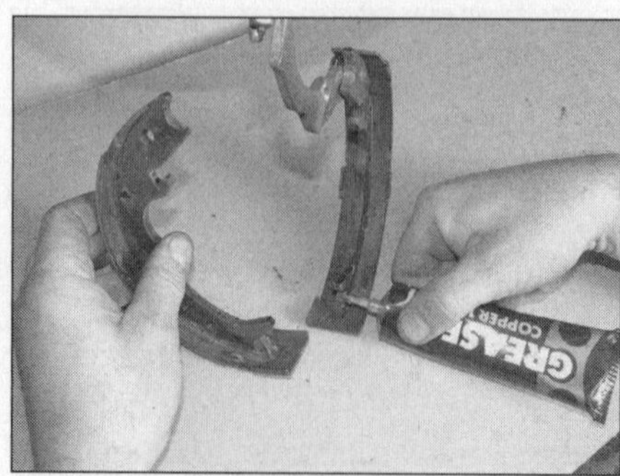

13.11g . . . apply grease to all points of contact . . .

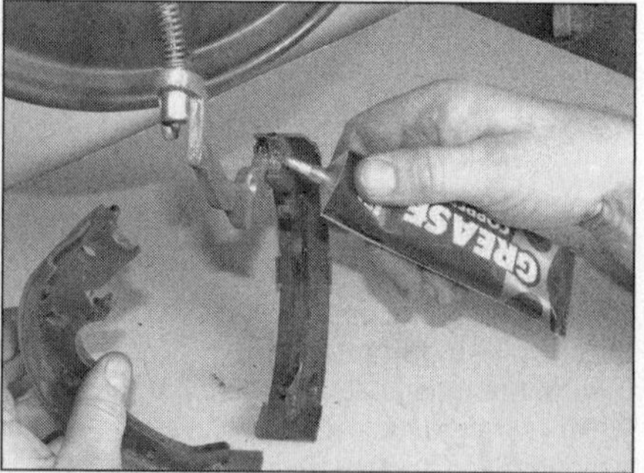

13.11h . . . and to lever pivot . . .

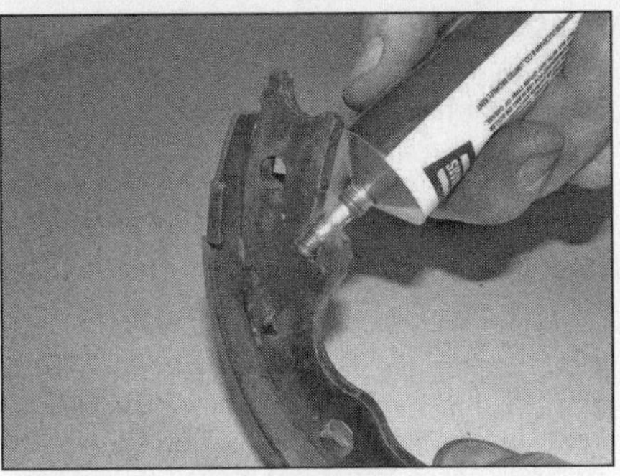
13.11i ... grease connecting rod slots on shoe ...

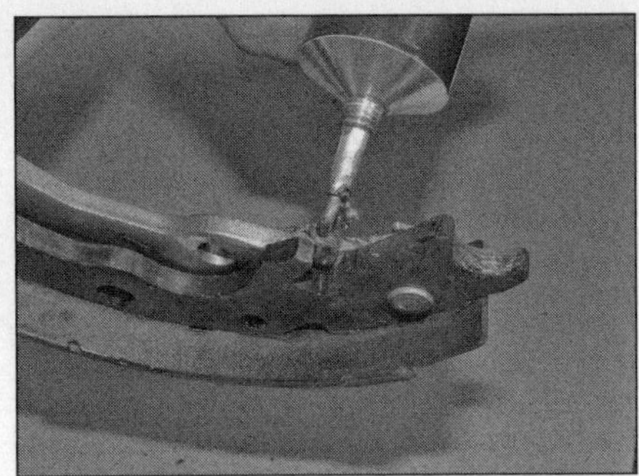
13.11j ... and on lever

13.11k Remove, clean and grease adjuster floating clevis

13.11l Remove, clean thread of adjuster clevis, grease, and screw in to shorten adjuster fully

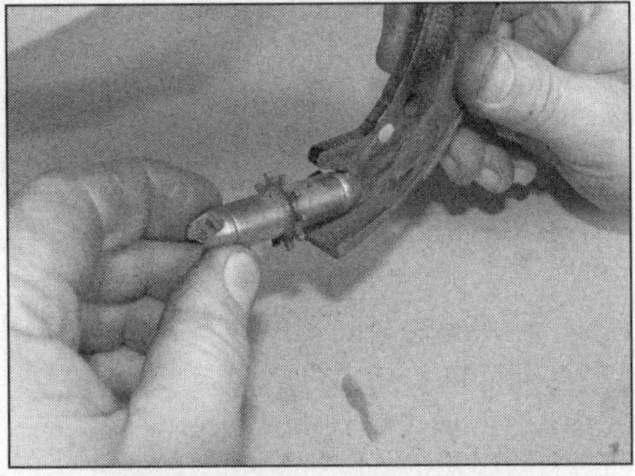
13.11m Fit adjuster assembly with threaded adjuster clevis pointing to rear of vehicle ...

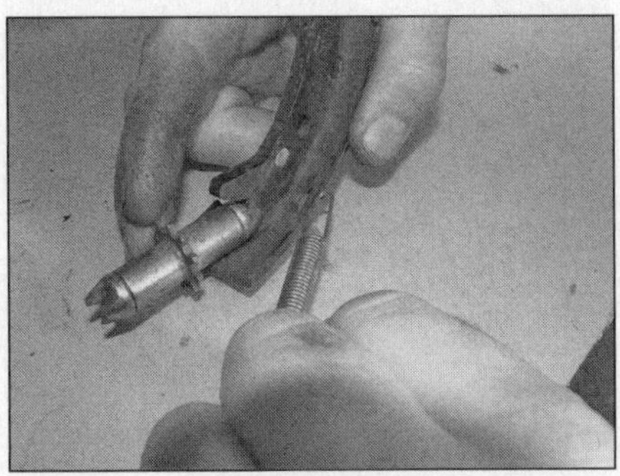
13.11n ... hook on lower return spring to rearward shoe ...

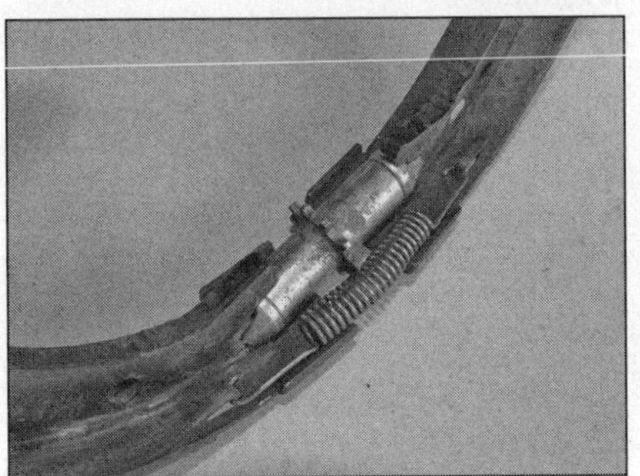
13.11o ... then refit forward shoe, with spring routed as shown

13.11p Hook connecting rod spring to rod with spring end pointing down ...

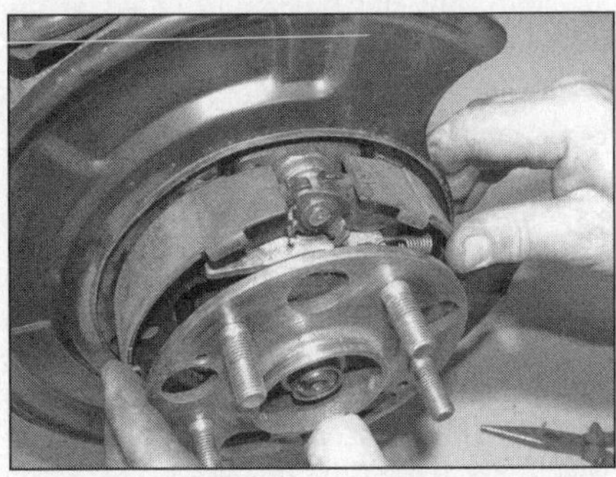
13.11q ... then refit forward shoe ...

13.11r ... refit handbrake shoe retainer pin to rearward shoe ...

13.11s ... press in on spring and turn pin to secure

13.11t Repeat same procedure ...

13.11u . . . to secure forward shoe

13.11w . . . and then onto shoe anchor

12 Refit the disc/drum as described in Section 10.
13 Carry out the major handbrake adjustment described in Section 17.
14 Carry out the procedure noted at the beginning of this Section to bed-in the new shoes.

14 Handbrake backplate – removal and refitting

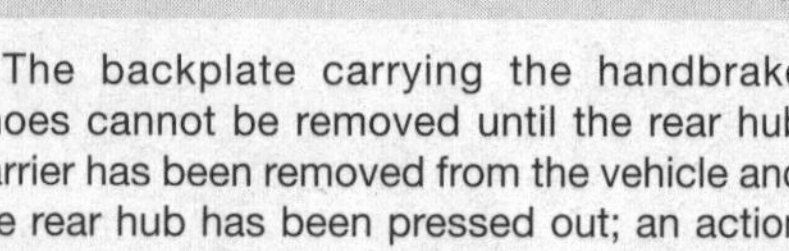

1 The backplate carrying the handbrake shoes cannot be removed until the rear hub carrier has been removed from the vehicle and the rear hub has been pressed out; an action which will require the renewal of the wheel bearing. See Chapter 10.
2 Once the hub has been removed, unscrew the two retaining nuts and withdraw the

13.11v Hook upper return spring onto forward shoe . . .

13.11x Hook upper return spring between rearward shoe and shoe anchor

backplate from the hub carrier. If you have to tap it off because of corrosion, be careful to tap evenly all the way round to avoid distorting the backplate.
3 Refitting is the reverse of removal; tighten the backplate retaining nuts to their specified torque wrench settings.

15 Handbrake cables – renewal

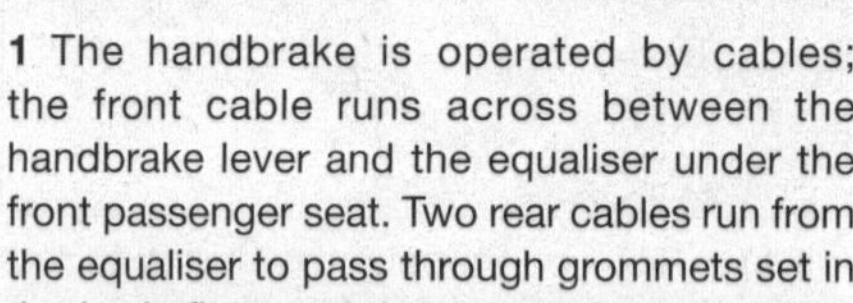

1 The handbrake is operated by cables; the front cable runs across between the handbrake lever and the equaliser under the front passenger seat. Two rear cables run from the equaliser to pass through grommets set in the body floor and then along the underbody to each rear brake assembly.

Front cable

2 To gain access to the front cable's end fittings, the handbrake lever must be unbolted; the cable can then be disconnected from the lever assembly. This entails a considerable amount of preliminary dismantling, as outlined in paragraphs 1 to 12 of Section 16.
3 Remove the front passenger seat (Chapter 11).
4 Working as described in Chapter 11, remove the passenger's footwell side trim panel, the front passenger door sill trim panel and the centre (B) pillar lower trim panel. Release the floor carpet from the fastener underneath the glovebox and peel it back clear of the front passenger footwell to reveal the handbrake front cable routing across the transmission tunnel and down across the footwell, under the ventilation system duct **(see illustrations)**.
5 Unbolt the support brackets securing the cable to the floor and release the cable from any clips or ties. Note how the cable is arranged and routed, for refitting.
6 Peel back the flap in the floor carpet under the front passenger seat, then undo the bolt and screw securing the handbrake equaliser cover to the floor.
7 Unhook the equaliser return spring.
8 Unscrew the handbrake adjuster nut on the equaliser.
9 The cable is secured by a spring clip to the support bracket bolted to the floor box member. Extract the clip, unbolt the support bracket and separate it from the cable **(see illustration)**.
10 Pull the cable forwards through the box member to release it from the equaliser, then withdraw the cable from the vehicle. If the ventilation duct prevents this, release its retaining clips until the cable can be pulled out from underneath.
11 Refitting is a reversal of removal, noting the following points:
a) Apply grease to all accessible handbrake pivots and linkages.
b) Ensure that the cable is correctly routed, with no sharp bends or kinks, and secured using all of the support brackets to the floor of the vehicle.
c) Carry out the major handbrake adjustment described in Section 17.

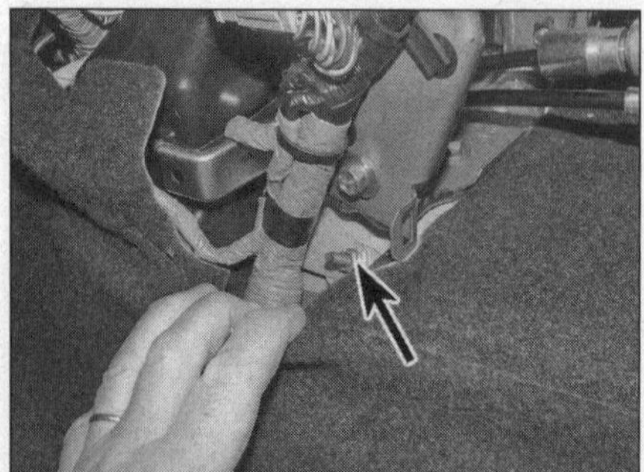
15.4a Release floor carpet from underneath the glovebox and peel it back clear of front passenger footwell . . .

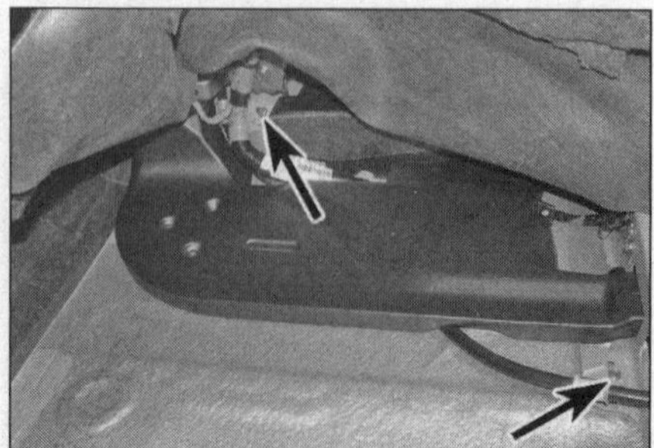
15.4b . . . to reveal handbrake front cable routing across transmission tunnel and footwell, under ventilation duct – note support brackets (arrows)

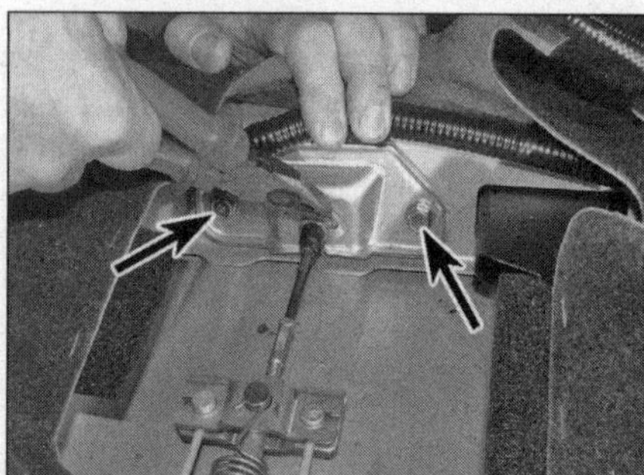
15.9 Extract clip, then unbolt support bracket to separate it from front cable

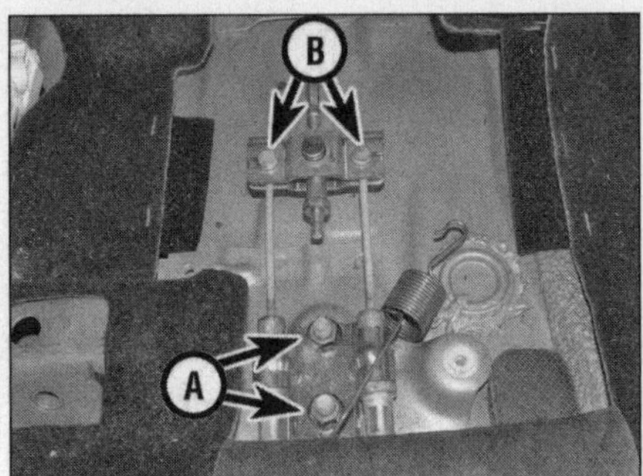

15.19 Unscrew cable guide plate securing nuts (A), then disconnect handbrake rear cable(s) from equaliser (B)

15.21a Handbrake rear cables each secured by brackets to underbody – here next to fuel tank . . .

15.21a . . . and here at rear suspension trailing arm front mounting

Rear cables

12 For preference, park the vehicle on level ground before starting. Chock the front wheels and select first or reverse gear (or P), slacken the roadwheel nuts, then raise the rear of the vehicle and support it securely on axle stands (see *Jacking and vehicle support*).

13 Remove the rear wheels. Work on one brake assembly at a time, using the assembled brake for reference if necessary.

14 Release the handbrake fully.

15 Move the front passenger seat fully forwards, then peel back the flap in the floor carpet under the seat.

16 Undo the bolt and screw securing the handbrake equaliser cover to the floor.

17 Unhook the equaliser return spring.

18 Unscrew the handbrake adjuster nut on the equaliser.

19 Unscrew the nuts securing the cable guide plate to release the cables from the floor, then disconnect the cable(s) from the equaliser **(see illustration)**.

20 Prise up the grommet sealing each cable into the floor and feed the cable down through the floor grommet. Check that the cable is free to be withdrawn from under the vehicle.

21 Working underneath the vehicle, unbolt the support brackets securing each cable to the underbody and releasing the cables from any clips or ties. Note how the cables are arranged and routed, for refitting **(see illustrations)**.

22 Unscrew the bolt securing the cable outer's end fitting to the handbrake backplate.

23 Remove the brake disc/drum on the side concerned, as described in Section 10.

24 Remove the handbrake shoes on the side concerned, as described in Section 13, to disconnect the cable inner wire end fitting from the handbrake mechanism.

25 Withdraw the cable from under the vehicle.

26 If either cable is stiff or jerky in operation, it must be renewed. Attempts to lubricate it (note that care must be taken to use only a lubricant which is compatible with the synthetic material sheathing the cable inner wire) may be apparently successful at first, when the cable is off the vehicle, but when the cable is refitted the cable will usually tighten up again. Renewal is the best course of action to ensure correct handbrake operation.

27 Refitting is a reversal of removal, noting the following points:

a) Apply grease to all accessible handbrake pivots and linkages.

b) Ensure that the cables are correctly routed, with no sharp bends or kinks, and secured using all of the support brackets to the underside of the vehicle.

c) Carry out the major handbrake adjustment described in Section 17.

16 Handbrake lever – removal and refitting

Removal

1 For preference, park the vehicle on level ground before starting. Chock the front wheels, engage a gear (or P) and release the handbrake.

2 Though not essential, access is greatly improved by removing the driver's side under cover and lower cover and the passenger's side under cover from the facia, and the front seat centre table (see Chapter 11).

3 Remove the facia centre air vent panel as described in Section 9 of Chapter 3.

4 Remove the dashboard pocket/cool box as described in Section 9 of Chapter 3.

5 Remove the heater control panel as described in Chapter 3.

6 On vehicles with a manual gearbox, unscrew the gear lever knob.

7 Remove the centre console (vehicles with a manual gearbox) or the facia lower centre section (vehicles with automatic transmission), as described in Chapter 11.

8 Reaching through the fuse panel aperture if necessary, disconnect the wiring plug from the handbrake warning light switch on the top right-hand side of the lever assembly **(see illustration)**.

9 Prise out the clip from the facia next to the handbrake lever **(see illustration)**.

10 Unscrew the two handbrake lever mounting bolts (one at the top, next to the handbrake warning light switch, and one at the bottom), and the retaining nut on its left-hand side **(see illustrations)**.

11 Withdraw the lever assembly until the cable outer's end fitting can be unbolted from the lever assembly **(see illustrations)**.

12 On the right-hand side of the lever assembly, pull out the spring clip, then

16.8 Handbrake warning light switch seen through fuse panel aperture. Note handbrake lever assembly top mounting bolt (arrow)

16.9 Prise out clip from facia next to handbrake lever

16.10a Reach in through fuse panel aperture to unscrew . . .

16.10b . . . handbrake lever assembly top mounting bolt

16.10c Handbrake lever assembly bottom mounting bolt . . .

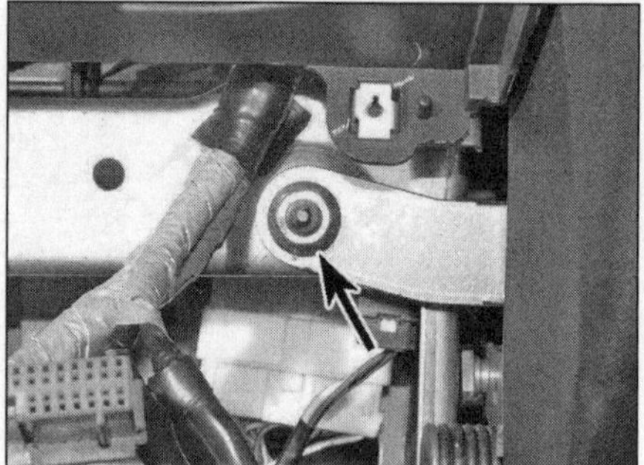
16.10d . . . and retaining nut on left-hand side

16.11a Withdraw handbrake lever assembly and turn onto one side . . .

16.11b . . . to unbolt cable outer's end fitting

16.12 Pull out spring clip and withdraw clevis pin to disconnect cable inner wire from lever assembly

withdraw the clevis pin from the left-hand side to disconnect the cable inner wire from the lever assembly **(see illustration)**.

13 Withdraw the lever assembly from the vehicle.

Refitting

14 Refitting is a reversal of removal. Grease the cable clevis pin and fittings and all sliding surfaces and pivots of the lever assembly. Tighten all fasteners to the torque wrench settings specified. Check the operation of the handbrake warning light switch as soon as possible before refitting too much of the facia components. Carry out the major handbrake adjustment described in Section 17.

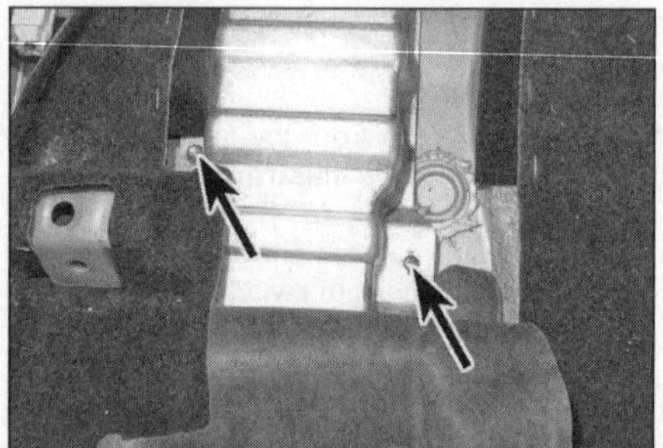
17.5a Peel back carpet flap under front passenger seat to reach handbrake cover (securing bolt and screw arrowed)

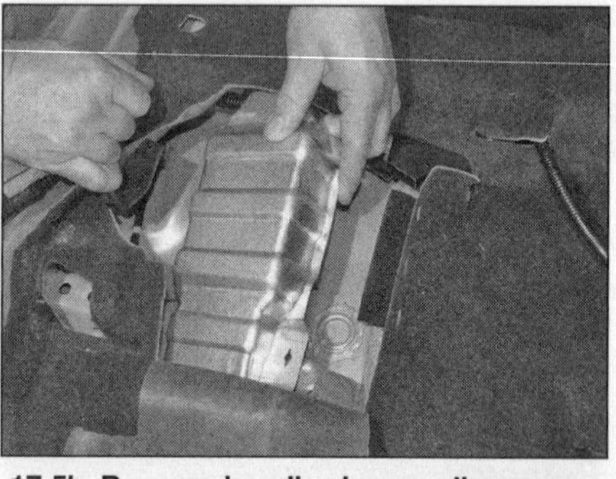
17.5b Remove handbrake equaliser cover

17 Handbrake – adjustment

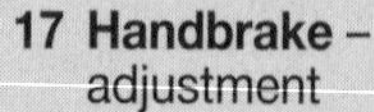

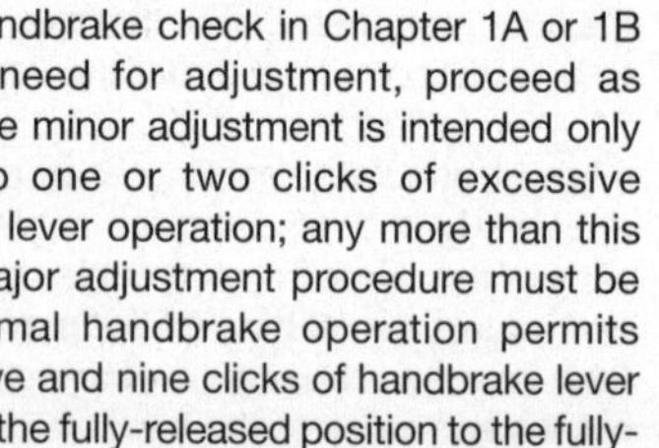

1 If the handbrake check in Chapter 1A or 1B reveals a need for adjustment, proceed as follows. The minor adjustment is intended only to take up one or two clicks of excessive handbrake lever operation; any more than this and the major adjustment procedure must be used. Normal handbrake operation permits between five and nine clicks of handbrake lever travel from the fully-released position to the fully-applied. If the lever travels ten or eleven clicks, perform the minor adjustment; if it travels twelve or more clicks, perform the major adjustment.

Minor adjustment

2 Chock the front wheels, then jack up the rear of the vehicle, and support it securely on axle stands (see *Jacking and vehicle support*).

3 Release the handbrake lever fully.

4 Move the front passenger seat fully forwards, then peel back the flap in the floor carpet under the seat.

5 Undo the bolt and screw securing the handbrake equaliser cover to the floor **(see illustrations)**.

6 Unhook the equaliser return spring **(see illustration)**.

17.6 Unhook handbrake equaliser spring

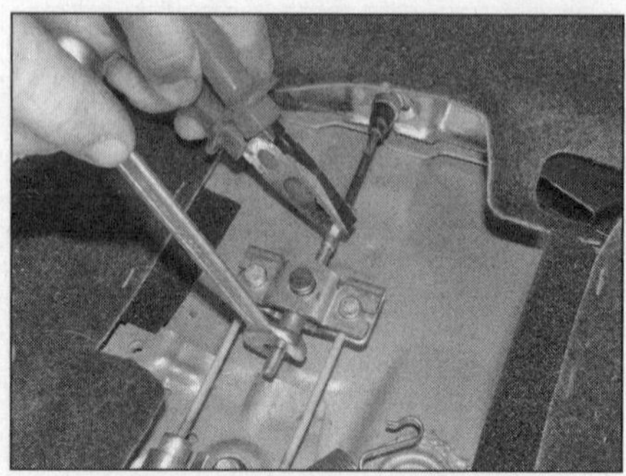
17.8 Adjusting the handbrake

7 Apply the handbrake lever by one click.
8 Tighten the handbrake adjuster nut on the equaliser until the rear wheels just start to drag **(see illustration)**.
9 Release the handbrake lever completely, and verify that the rear wheels are free to turn. Reset the adjuster nut accordingly if this is not the case.
10 Ensure that, by the time the handbrake lever is applied by 5 to 9 clicks, the rear wheels are completely locked.
11 Failure to adjust properly suggests that one or more of the handbrake cables may be binding. Examine and lubricate the cables and linkages as far as possible first. If necessary, new cables should be fitted as described in Section 15.
12 On completion, refit the return spring and equaliser cover. Refit (if completing the major adjustment) the rear roadwheels. Lower the vehicle to the ground and tighten the road wheel bolts to the specified torque wrench setting. Check carefully that the handbrake is working properly before taking the vehicle out on the road.

Major adjustment

Note 1: *This procedure is for normal maintenance, when handbrake lever travel exceeds twelve or more clicks, or after any kind of work has been carried out on the components of the handbrake itself.*
Note 2: *If new handbrake shoes and/or rear disc/ drums have been fitted, the new components must be bedded-in (see Section 13). This requires that the major handbrake adjustment be carried out before AND after the bedding-in. If this is not done, exactly as described, the handbrake will never be properly effective as its shoes only contact the drum when it is applied and never get a chance to bed-in in normal use.*
13 Chock the front wheels and select first or reverse gear (or position P), slacken the roadwheel nuts, then raise the rear of the vehicle and support it securely on axle stands (see *Jacking and vehicle support*).
14 Remove the rear wheels. Work on one brake assembly at a time, using the assembled brake for reference if necessary.
15 Release the handbrake fully.
16 Move the front passenger seat fully forwards, then peel back the flap in the floor carpet under the seat.
17 Undo the bolt and screw securing the handbrake equaliser cover to the floor.
18 Unhook the equaliser return spring.
19 Slacken fully the handbrake adjuster nut on the equaliser.
20 Prise out the rubber plug from the rear brake disc/drum **(see illustration)**.
21 Adjust the brake shoes by using a flat-bladed screwdriver to flick upwards the spokes on the adjuster assembly star wheel, thus turning the adjuster assembly until the shoes lock against the disc/drum, then turn it back eight clicks **(see illustration)**.
22 Repeat on the opposite brake.
23 When turning the disc/drum, the shoes should not rub; if they do, remove the disc/ drum and check the handbrake shoes (see Section 13). Remove all traces of brake dust and rust, check that the shoes are not sticking and take any action necessary, then refit the disc/drum. **Note:** *If this action is taken, do the same on the opposite side as well, whether it appears to need it or not, to ensure all components of the system are always maintained in the same condition.*
24 On completion, refit the rubber plugs, then carry out the minor adjustment procedure described above.

17.20 Prise out rubber plug from rear brake disc/drum . . .

17.21 . . . to carry out major handbrake adjustment

18 Braking system switches – testing, removal and refitting

Stop-light switch

Testing

1 To check the stop-light switch, push on the brake pedal and verify that the stop-lights come on.
2 If they don't, check the stop-light fuse (refer to the wiring diagrams at the end of Chapter 12). Also check the stop-light bulbs in both tail light assemblies – don't forget to check the high-level stop-light (also Chapter 12).
3 If the fuse and the bulbs are okay, locate the stop-light switch at the top of the brake pedal.
4 Disconnect the switch wiring plug.
5 Check for continuity across the switch terminals. When the brake pedal is depressed, there should be continuity; when it's released, there should be no continuity. If the switch doesn't operate as described, renew it.

Renewal

6 The stop-light switch is located on the pedal bracket behind the facia. Before working on any part of the vehicle's electrical systems, it is advisable to disconnect the battery negative (earth) lead (see *Disconnecting the battery*).
7 With reference to Chapter 11, remove the driver's side under cover and lower cover from the facia.
8 Disconnect the wiring connector plug from the switch.
9 Twist the switch body 45° anti-clockwise to disengage its bayonet fitting, and remove it from the pedal bracket.
10 Refitting is a reversal of removal, but adjust the switch as follows. Push the switch in to the pedal until its plunger is fully depressed against the nylon pad on the pedal arm, then turn it clockwise to lock it in position; this will automatically set the clearance between the switch and the pad to 0.7 mm. Reconnect the switch wiring and check that the stop-lights illuminate when the pedal is depressed and that they go out as soon as it is released **(see illustrations)**.

Brake pedal position switch

11 In addition to switching on the brake lights, the stop-light switch has a dual or triple role. As the brake pedal position switch, it informs the engine management system's ECU when the brakes are applied (which among other things, allows the ECU to implement fuel

18.10a Push stop-light switch in to pedal until plunger is fully depressed against nylon pad on pedal arm . . .

18.10b . . . then turn switch clockwise to lock; switch-to-pad clearance automatically set

injection cut-off, where applicable), and also serves the cruise control system, on models so equipped.

Handbrake warning light switch

Testing

12 Disconnect the wiring plug from the switch via the fuse aperture in the driver's side facia lower cover.

13 Connect a multimeter and check for continuity between the switch terminal and a good earth on the metal facia supports.

14 When the handbrake is released, there should be no continuity. Now apply the handbrake – continuity should be indicated. If this is not the case, the switch is faulty.

Renewal

15 The handbrake warning light switch is fitted to the top right-hand side of the handbrake lever assembly **(see illustration 16.8)**. If the switch is not working correctly the handbrake lever assembly must be removed to check the reason for the problem; see Section 16.

16 If the switch is not available separately, the handbrake lever assembly must be renewed.

Brake fluid level switch

Testing

17 Disconnect the wiring plug from the switch, which is located next to the reservoir mounting bolt.

18 Unscrew the reservoir cap for access to the fluid level float.

19 Connect a multimeter across the switch terminals, and check for continuity.

20 When the float is up, there should be no continuity. Now press the float down – continuity should be indicated. If this is not the case, the switch is faulty.

21 The brake fluid level float and switch are integral with the brake fluid reservoir, and are not available separately.

Renewal

22 Remove as much fluid as you can from the reservoir before starting, using a syringe. If a syringe is not available, the fluid can be soaked out with clean paper towel. Take care not to drip hydraulic fluid onto paintwork or hot engine components.

23 If not already done, disconnect the brake fluid level sensor wiring plug at the side of the reservoir, next to the reservoir mounting bolt.

24 Unscrew the reservoir front mounting bolt. Wrap some clean rag or paper towel around the reservoir, then release the hose clips, disconnect the two hoses, and remove the reservoir from the cylinder.

25 Refitting is a reversal of removal, noting the following points:

a) *Ensure the reservoir hose connections are securely remade.*

b) *On completion, refill the reservoir with fresh fluid, and bleed the brakes as described in Section 5.*

19 Anti-lock Braking System (ABS) – general information

All CR-Vs are equipped with ABS and, for optimum performance, Electronic Brake force Distribution (EBD) which adjusts front-to-rear brake effort to achieve maximum braking performance and stability. The system is a full-time four-channel type, offering individual speed control at each of the four wheels. In addition to the components of the non-ABS system, the system incorporates an ABS modulator-control unit and four roadwheel sensors. The modulator contains the hydraulic solenoid valves, an accumulator, and the electrically-driven pump, with an ABS Electronic Control Unit (ECU) forming an integral part of the modulator-control unit. Control of each wheel's speed is achieved through the modulator's solenoid valves, which switch the supply of brake fluid to each wheel's brake on and off.

The operation of the ABS system is entirely dependent on electrical signals. To prevent the system responding to any inaccurate signals, a built-in safety circuit monitors all signals received by the ECU; the ECU itself actually consists of two Central Processing Units (CPUs) – a main CPU and a sub-CPU, each one checking the other. If an inaccurate signal or low battery voltage is detected, the ABS system is automatically shut down, and the warning lamp on the instrument panel is illuminated to inform the driver that the ABS system is not operational. If the ABS warning lamp and the braking system warning lamp illuminate together (but the handbrake is fully released and the hydraulic fluid level is correct), the fault is serious enough to affect the operation of the Electronic Brake force Distribution function. Normal braking is unaffected, apart from the loss of EBD (which may result in premature rear wheel lock-up under braking).

If a fault does develop in the ABS system, the vehicle must be taken to a Honda dealer for fault diagnosis and repair. Check first, however, that the problem is not due to loose or damaged wiring connections, or badly-routed wiring picking up spurious signals from the ignition system.

Caution: The ABS and VSA systems base their operation on precise comparison of wheel speeds. Tyres of different size and construction to those fitted as original equipment may affect wheel speeds, causing these systems to function erratically. Always fit tyres of the recommended size and type (see Chapter 10, and the tyre information label on the driver's door pillar). If possible, it is best to renew all four tyres at the same time; if this is not possible or necessary, renew the two fronts or the two rears as a matched pair. Renewing just one tyre with one of a significantly different size will affect the operation of these systems, not to mention the negative consequences for the vehicle's handling and roadholding.

Anti-lock braking

The purpose of the system is to detect and counter any unacceptable acceleration or deceleration in any of the four wheels, relative to the vehicle speed and to the speeds of any of the other three wheels. The system will prevent wheel(s) locking-up by automatic release of the brake on the relevant wheel, followed by rapid reapplication of the brake.

The solenoids are controlled by the ECU, which receives signals from the wheel sensors. The sensors detect the speed of rotation of a magnetic encoder ring forming part of each wheel bearing. By comparing the speed signals from the four wheels, the ECU can determine when a wheel is decelerating at an abnormal rate, and can therefore predict when a wheel is about to lock. During normal operation, the system functions in the same way as a non-ABS braking system does.

When the system is in operation, the hydraulic fluid circulates through the caliper, the modulator accumulator and the master cylinder, flow being controlled by the modulator solenoid valves, under the control of the ECU. It has three modes of control; pressure intensifying, pressure retaining and pressure reducing.

If the ECU senses that a wheel is about to lock, the ABS system enters the pressure retaining mode. The ECU closes the relevant solenoid valves in the modulator; this isolates the brake on the wheel in question from the master cylinder, effectively sealing-in the hydraulic pressure.

If the speed of rotation of the wheel continues to decrease at an abnormal rate, the ABS system then enters the pressure reducing mode. The pump pumps hydraulic fluid back into the accumulator, releasing pressure on the brake. When the speed of rotation of the wheel returns to an acceptable rate, the pump stops and the solenoid valve opens, allowing hydraulic pressure to return and reapply the brake. This cycle can be carried out at up to 10 times a second.

The pressure intensifying mode is activated when the Brake Assist function determines that greater pressure is required. The valves are opened to allow hydraulic fluid to be pumped to a particular caliper or calipers, as the situation demands.

The action of the solenoid valves and pump creates pulses in the hydraulic circuit. When the ABS system is functioning, these pulses are deliberately allowed be felt through the brake pedal so that the driver knows that driving conditions are marginal.

ABS will not necessarily reduce braking distances under all conditions – especially on loose snow or gravel – the primary aim of the system is to help the driver retain steering control in emergency braking situations.

Electronic Brake Force Distribution

Electronic Brake force Distribution (EBD) adjusts front-to-rear brake effort to achieve maximum braking performance and stability.

On any vehicle, whether fitted with ABS or not, 90% of the actual braking is done by the front wheels, and under heavy braking, there is significant weight transfer to the front wheels. This situation is compounded if the vehicle is lightly loaded (without rear seat passengers or luggage), as the rear wheels will have very little weight over them. The EBD function is built into the system's software with the intention of limiting braking effort (fluid pressure) to the rear wheels, to prevent them locking prematurely under heavy braking, which might otherwise lead to the driver losing control of the rear of the vehicle. At the rear, a select-low braking strategy is also used to help maintain directional stability in slippery driving. In the event of a rear wheel beginning to lock up, triggering a pressure modulation at that wheel, brake pressure is also diminished at the adjoining wheel to help preserve the rear axle's lateral stability.

When the ABS is in operation, the brakes are operated in axle pairs, and the braking force is distributed between the front and rear axles as necessary, to maintain the stability of the vehicle. Distribution of the braking effort is dependent on direction of travel and the amount of braking effort being applied.

Brake Assist

Further security is provided by the Brake Assist system which monitors how rapidly the brake pedal is pressed, and determines whether an emergency stop is required – in this case, maximum braking effort is applied more quickly than the driver would normally be able to, unaided.

Vehicle Stability Assist

Optional on some models from 2005-onwards, standard on others, Honda's four-channel Vehicle Stability Assist (VSA) system is designed to assist the driver in maintaining control during cornering, acceleration and sudden manoeuvres by applying brake force to the right- or left-hand wheels as necessary and managing the throttle and ignition systems. The control software has been revised to complement the enhanced Dual Pump four-wheel drive system.

At its simplest level, VSA has a traction control function whereby it detects wheel slip under acceleration and coordinates the use of braking and retardation of the ignition to regain traction. In situations where the driven wheels are on surfaces with different levels of traction, such as a partially wet road surface, the system applies braking action to the wheel that's slipping, allowing the tyre with better grip to move the vehicle. In addition, the system reduces engine output to minimise wheelspin.

20.3 ABS modulator-control unit (orange) wiring plug – pull up its locking tab to disconnect unit's wiring

By monitoring input from a series of vehicle sensors, VSA calculates a predicted range of vehicle response while constantly monitoring the vehicle's actual response and the driver's control inputs. If the actual response is outside the predicted response range, as when cornering forces exceed the tyres' performance, VSA automatically intervenes with corrective action.

In the case of oversteer (which may lead to a spin), VSA applies braking to the outside front wheel to counter the yawing tendency. On the other hand, if understeer is detected, VSA applies braking to the inside rear wheel and reduces engine power to turn the vehicle back on to the intended course.

A facia-mounted switch to the side of the steering column is provided to disable the VSA, should the driver so wish. The VSA Activation Indicator lamp illuminates (steadily) a triangular symbol on the instrument panel to remind the driver that the system is switched off. Starting the engine will cause VSA to be switched back on, even if the driver had disabled it when the vehicle was used previously.

A VSA Activation Indicator lamp flashes a triangular symbol on the instrument panel while the system is in operation (and, as noted above, shines steadily if the system is switched off by the driver). If a fault occurs in the system, a VSA System Indicator lamp lights to show 'VSA' on the instrument panel. The VSA Activation Indicator lamp will also light to reinforce the message of the VSA System Indicator lamp. Both Indicator lamps illuminate when the ignition is switched on as a check of their function (have the vehicle checked by a Honda dealer if either does not, at any time). If the VSA System Indicator lamp lights while the vehicle is being driven, pull to the side of the road as soon as it is safe to do so and switch off the engine. Restart the engine (thus resetting the system) and watch the VSA System Indicator lamp; if it remains on, or comes back on while driving, the vehicle must be taken to a Honda dealer as soon as possible for fault diagnosis and repair.

20 Anti-lock braking system (ABS) components – removal and refitting

Note: *Refer to the precautions in Section 1 before proceeding.*

ABS modulator-control unit

Removal

1 The modulator-control unit is located in front of the front suspension right-hand strut mounting.

2 First disconnect the battery negative (earth) lead (see *Disconnecting the battery*). On diesel-engined models, unbolt the coolant expansion tank and move it to one side without disconnecting its hoses.

3 Pull up its locking tab and disconnect the unit's wiring connector plug **(see illustration)**.

4 Before removing the hydraulic unions from the unit, it is advisable to mark them for position, perhaps by attaching labels, or marked pieces of tape, to each pipe.

5 Slacken the hydraulic unions, then disconnect and unclip the pipes from the unit – avoid bending the pipes at all costs.

6 Unscrew the three bolts securing the unit's mounting bracket to the body, and lift it out **(see illustrations)**.

20.6a ABS modulator-control unit mounting bolt and nut – diesel models

20.6b On diesel models, unbolt coolant expansion tank to reach remaining mounting bolts

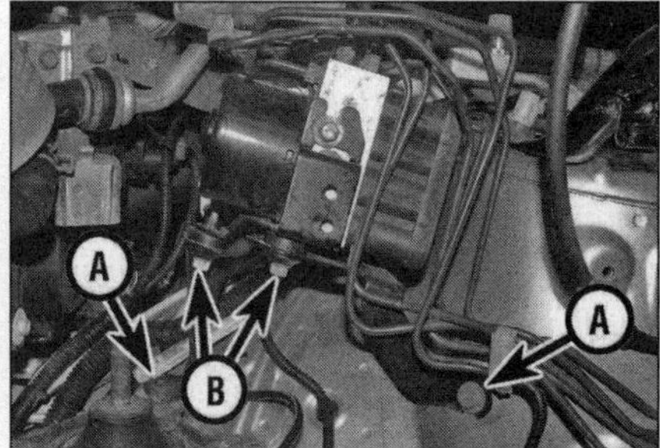

20.6c ABS modulator-control unit mounting bolts (A), unit-to-mounting bracket bolts (B) – petrol models

20.11a Location of ABS front wheel sensor on swivel hub

20.11b Location of ABS rear wheel sensor on rear hub carrier

20.13a Unbolting ABS wiring support bracket from front inner wheel arch . . .

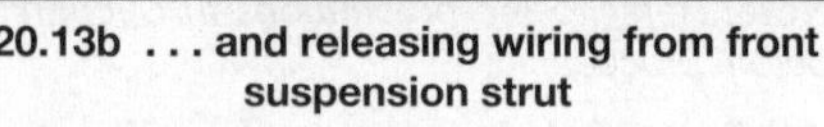

20.13b . . . and releasing wiring from front suspension strut

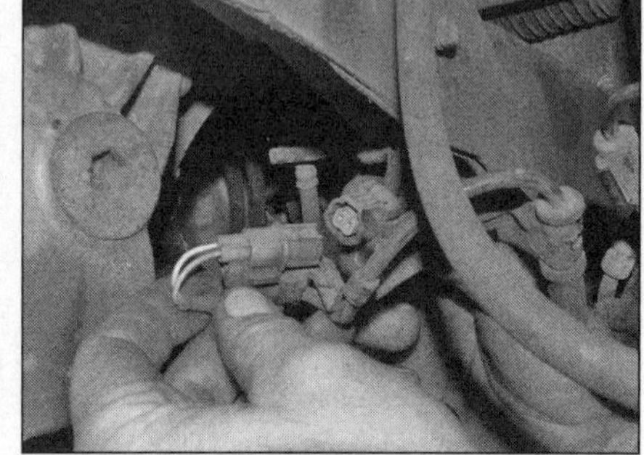

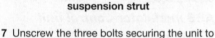

20.13c ABS components wiring connectors coloured orange for easy identification

20.13d Unbolt or unclip sensor wiring support brackets from rear suspension upper arm

7 Unscrew the three bolts securing the unit to its mounting bracket, and withdraw it.

Caution: Do not attempt to dismantle the modulator-control unit assembly. Overhaul of the unit is a complex job, and should be entrusted to a Honda dealer.

Refitting

8 Refitting is the reverse of the removal procedure, noting the following points:

a) Tighten the modulator-control unit mounting bolts securely.

b) Refit the brake pipes to the correct unions, and tighten the union nuts securely.

c) Reconnect the wiring plug securely.

d) Before reconnecting the battery, bleed the complete braking system as described in Section 5. Ensure the system is bled in the correct order, to prevent air entering the return pump.

ABS Electronic Control Unit

9 The ECU is an integral part of the modulator-control unit assembly, and cannot be renewed separately. If renewal is necessary, the modulator-control unit must be renewed as a complete assembly, as described above.

Wheel sensors

Note: *The sensor-to-magnetic encoder air gap should be checked whenever either the sensor or the wheel bearing is disturbed (see the relevant Sections of Chapter 10). This, however, requires the removal of the appropriate driveshaft.*

10 Slacken the relevant wheel nuts, chock the opposite wheels, then jack up either the front or rear of the vehicle and support on axle stands (see *Jacking and vehicle support*). Remove the appropriate roadwheel.

11 Thoroughly clean the inboard surfaces of the swivel hub/rear hub carrier and brake disc shield/handbrake backplate to enable the sensor to be identified and its bolt unscrewed. Trace the sensor wiring from the connector on the underbody to the sensor, noting how the wiring is routed for refitting; the front wheel sensors are at the front of the swivel hubs, while the rear wheel sensors are on top of each rear hub carrier **(see illustrations)**. Soak the head and bolt of the wheel sensor with plenty of penetrating fluid, and clean around the bolt and sensor before attempting removal. If the sensor is being re-used, take care when removing it, or it will suffer damage.

12 Unscrew the single mounting bolt, and carefully release the sensor from the swivel hub/rear hub carrier.

13 Trace the sensor wiring back from the sensor, freeing the wiring from any clips or ties. There's a wiring support bracket clipped to the front suspension struts, and another bolted in the inner wheel arches, to which the sensor wiring plug is clipped. At the rear, a wiring support bracket is bolted or clipped to the rear suspension upper arm **(see illustration)**. Once all the wiring has been detached, disconnect the wiring plug and remove the sensor.

14 Refitting is a reversal of removal, noting the following points:

a) Clean the sensor location in the swivel hub/rear hub carrier, and apply a little copper grease to make future removal easier.

b) Ensure that the wiring is routed as noted before removal, and secured with all necessary brackets, clips and ties.

c) Reconnect the wiring plug securely.

21 Vacuum pump (diesel engines) – removal and refitting

Note: *Liquid gasket (Honda Part No. 08C70-K0234M, 08C70-K0334M, 08C70-X0331S or 08718-0001 or equivalent) must be available on reassembly, in addition to a new auxiliary drivebelt, new cylinder head cover gaskets, vacuum pump O-rings and engine mounting fasteners and any other items (gaskets, seals, etc) found to be in need of renewal during the procedure.*

Note: *Honda state specifically that the timing chain is to be kept away from magnetic fields to prevent any chance of interference in the operation of the crankshaft position sensor.*

Removal

1 The braking system vacuum pump is bolted to the left-hand face of the timing chain case, at the rear right-hand end of the cylinder block. It is driven by the timing chain from the crankshaft. Unfortunately its mounting bolts are unscrewed from inside the timing chain case, thus necessitating a lot of

preliminary dismantling before the pump can be removed.

2 Remove the timing chain as described in Chapter 2B.

3 Referring as necessary to the relevant Sections of Chapters 4B and 4C, remove the exhaust pipe front (flexible) section and the warm-up catalytic converter, the exhaust manifold cover and the cover over the turbocharger outlet elbow.

4 Disconnect the vacuum hose from the pump.

5 Unscrew the vacuum pump mounting bolts **(see illustration)**.

6 Remove the pump. Withdraw and discard the two sealing O-rings from the pump mounting boss and flange; these must be renewed whenever the pump is disturbed **(see illustrations)**.

Refitting

7 Thoroughly clean the mating surfaces of the vacuum pump, the timing chain case, the cylinder head, the cylinder block and the sump. Clean any oil or old gasket material and sealant from the mating surfaces and from the bolt holes and threads. Be very careful not to allow dirt and debris to fall into the sump. Degrease the surfaces completely before applying sealant.

8 With the new O-rings fitted to the grooves in the pump boss and flange, and lubricated with a smear of grease, refit the pump and tighten its mounting bolts to the specified torque wrench setting **(see illustration)**.

9 The remainder of reassembly is the reverse of the removal procedure, referring to the relevant text for details where required.

21.5 Vacuum pump mounting bolts must be unscrewed from inside timing chain case – diesel models

21.6a Remove and discard O-ring from pump mounting boss . . .

21.6b . . . and from pump flange – renew whenever disturbed

21.8 Refitting vacuum pump – diesel models

22 Vacuum pump (diesel engines) – testing and overhaul

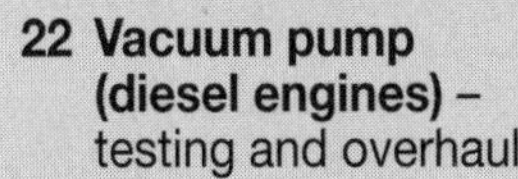

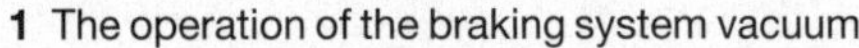

1 The operation of the braking system vacuum pump can be checked using a vacuum gauge. The pump should be capable of generating a vacuum of approximately 700 mm Hg.

2 Pump overhaul procedures are not given by Honda, which suggests that this may not be possible. Check for availability of spare parts before attempting to dismantle the pump.

Chapter 10
Suspension and steering

Contents

Degrees of difficulty

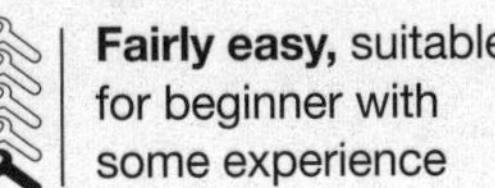

Easy, suitable for novice with little experience	**Fairly easy,** suitable for beginner with some experience	**Fairly difficult,** suitable for competent DIY mechanic	**Difficult,** suitable for experienced DIY mechanic	**Very difficult,** suitable for expert DIY or professional

Specifications

Wheel alignment and steering angles

Total toe:		
Front	0 ± 2.0 mm	
Rear:	**2001 to 2004 models**	**2005-on models**
Inspection values (toe-in)	2.0 ± 2.0 mm	1.0 ± 2.0 mm
Setting values (toe-in)	2.0 + 2.0 mm -1.0 mm	1.0 ± 1.0 mm
Camber angle:		
Front	0° 00' ± 45'	
Rear	-1° 00' ± 45'	
Castor angle	1° 45' ± 1°	
Turning angles:	**2001 to 2004 models**	**2005-on models**
Inward	39° 45' ± 2°	39° 00' ± 2°
Outward – reference value	32° 30'	32° 00'

Roadwheels

Type	Pressed-steel or aluminium alloy
Size:	
2001-2004 models	15 X 6 JJ or 16 X 6 JJ
2005-on models	16 X 6 1/2 JJ

Tyres

Pressures	Refer to the label on the driver's door pillar
Size:	
2001-2004 models:	
15-inch wheels	205/70R15 96T
16-inch wheels	205/65R16 95T
2005-on models	215/65R16 98T

Torque wrench settings

	Nm	lbf ft
Front suspension		
Anti-roll bar clamp bolts	22	16
Anti-roll bar drop link-to-lower arm flange nut	39	29
Anti-roll bar-to-drop link self-locking nut*	38	28
Lower arm-to-subframe bolts	83	61
Subframe damper mounting bolt – diesel-engined models	22	16
Subframe mounting bolts*	103	76
Subframe plate mounting bolt – diesel-engined models	10	7
Subframe rectifier mounting bolt – petrol-engined models	22	16
Suspension strut piston rod self-locking nut*	44	32
Suspension strut top mounting nuts	44	32
Suspension strut-to-swivel hub pinch-bolts and nuts*	157	116
Swivel hub balljoint castle nut:		
Nominal	59 to 69	44 to 51
Stage 1	59	44
Stage 2	Tighten until new clip can be inserted	
Rear suspension		
Anti-roll bar clamp bolts	22	16
Anti-roll bar drop link-to-trailing arm flange nut	38	28
Anti-roll bar-to-drop link self-locking nut:*		
Japanese-manufactured vehicles	29	21
UK-manufactured vehicles	38	28
Subframe damper mounting bolt	22	16
Subframe mounting bolts*	69	51
Suspension strut piston rod self-locking nut*	29	21
Suspension strut top mounting nuts	74	55
Suspension strut-to-trailing arm bolt	93	69
Trailing arm lateral link-to-subframe bolt	59	44
Trailing arm lateral link-to-trailing arm tubular section Torx bolts	Do not slacken	
Trailing arm-to-hub carrier front bolt	59	44
Trailing arm-to-hub carrier rear (toe-adjusting) bolt self-locking nut*	59	44
Trailing arm-to-underbody front mounting bolts	115	85
Upper control arm pivot bolts	93	69
Steering		
Power steering fluid cooler mounting bolt	10	7
Power steering fluid hose union bolts	11	8
Power steering fluid pipe union nuts:		
12 mm	17	13
14 x 1.5 mm	37	27
16 x 1.5 mm	28	21
Power steering hose clamp-to-cylinder head cover bolt:		
Diesel-engined models	12	9
Power steering pipe and hose support bracket bolts	10	7
Power steering pump pulley nut	64	47
Power steering pump-to-bracket mounting bolts	22	16
Steering column mounting nuts and bolts	16	12
Steering column universal joint pinch-bolts	28	21
Steering rack mounting bolts	62	46
Steering wheel bolt	39	29
Track rod end balljoint-to-swivel hub steering arm nuts	43	32
Track rod inboard ends-to-steering rack	54	40
Track rod outboard end balljoint locknuts:		
Petrol-engined models	44	32
Diesel-engined models	54	40
Roadwheels		
Roadwheel nuts	108	80

** Use new fasteners.*

1 General information

The CR-V has fully-independent front and rear suspension, by conventional coil springs and MacPherson struts, bolted to the swivel hub at the front and to the tubular trailing arm at the rear. Subframes are fitted front and rear, to provide mounting points for the suspension components.

At the front, the swivel hubs are attached to pressed-steel lower arms, which pivot on bonded-rubber bushes and are mounted on the subframe; the hubs run within non-adjustable bearings in the swivel hubs. An anti-roll bar is fitted, attached directly to the front subframe, with the bar ends attached to the lower arms by balljointed drop links.

At the rear, the rear hubs run within non-adjustable bearings in the rear hub carrier. The hub carriers are connected to the subframe and underbody via three link arms – two transverse, one trailing; it is the tubular trailing arm which provides location (at two mounting points) for the rear hub carrier. The trailing arm-to-hub carrier rear mounting bolt incorporates eccentrics at front and rear, to provide adjustment of the rear wheel toe setting. Although the trailing arm appears to have a flat, pressed-steel, lower transverse link bolted to its rear end, in fact Honda state that these bolts must **never** be slackened or otherwise disturbed, so the two are effectively a single component. The upper transverse link pivots on bonded-rubber bushes and is mounted on the subframe at its inboard end and on the rear hub carrier at its outboard end. An anti-roll bar is fitted, attached directly to the rear subframe, with the bar ends attached to the trailing arms by balljointed drop links.

The steering system comprises an impact-absorbing telescopic steering column, power-assisted steering rack and engine-driven fluid pump, with a fluid reservoir, fluid cooler (on diesel-engined models), and connecting pipes and hoses. The adjustable steering column has upper mountings which are designed to detach or deform in the event of a collision, allowing the column to collapse and reduce the risk of injuring the driver. The upper section of the column is splined to accept the steering wheel; the intermediate shaft is joined to the lower shaft by a universal joint, and a further universal joint at the base of the column joins it to the rack pinion shaft.

The steering rack, which is mounted on the engine compartment bulkhead, has both track rods mounted centrally on the rack – the long track rods and optimised steering geometry reduce the incidence of 'bump steer', which is especially useful off-road.

Power-assisted steering is standard on all models. The hydraulic steering system is powered by a vane-type pump, which is belt-driven off the crankshaft pulley; an automatic spring-loaded tensioner eliminates any need for drivebelt maintenance beyond a periodic check of its condition. Rotary movement of the steering wheel is transferred via the steering column to the valve unit mounted on the steering rack; depending on direction of rotation, fluid pressure is applied to one side of the valve or the other, to boost the turning force applied to the pinion, which in turn moves the rack left or right.

Seized nuts/bolts

When working on the suspension or steering system components, you may come across fasteners which seem impossible to loosen. These fasteners on the underside of the vehicle are continually subjected to water, road grime, mud, etc, and can become rusted or 'seized', making them extremely difficult to remove. To unscrew these stubborn fasteners without damaging them (or other components), first use a wire brush to clean exposed threads. Afterwards, apply lots of penetrating oil or a maintenance spray such as WD-40, and allow it to soak in for a while.

On stubborn screws, using a close-fitting screwdriver bit in a socket handle can provide greater leverage on a difficult screw than can a screwdriver, reducing the chance of chewing up the screw head.

With hexagon-headed fasteners such as nuts or bolts, hex (with six 'sides') ring spanners or sockets are preferable to bi-hex ones, as they are less likely to round off the corners – 'surface-drive' spanners and sockets are also available, which grip the flats, not the corners, of the fastener. Never use a tool which isn't a close fit, as it will slip if enough force is applied. If the fastener's corners have already been rounded-off, it can help to use a socket one size smaller (or try an imperial size), and tap it on using a hammer, to make a tight fit – in this case, a new fastener will clearly be needed.

Try turning the fastener in the tightening (usually clockwise) direction first – this may help to break it loose. If this produces a little movement, slacken then retighten the fastener several times, and slowly try to increase the range of movement until it will unscrew completely. Beware, however, that this approach may cause the fastener to shear off and risks damaging the component being secured.

Sometimes a sharp blow with a hammer and punch is effective in breaking the bond between threads, but care must be taken to prevent the punch from slipping off the fastener and ruining the threads. Impact drivers can also be successful in freeing a stubborn fastener, but make sure a close-fitting socket is used.

Heating the stuck fastener and surrounding area sometimes helps too, but isn't always recommended because of the obvious dangers associated with fire – take care if rubber or plastic components, or fuel/brake pipes, are close by. Heat may also ignite the penetrating oil or maintenance spray.

Long breaker bars will increase leverage, as will a strong piece of metal tubing slipped over the tool's handle to lengthen it; don't use an extension on a ratchet handle – the ratchet mechanism could be damaged. Wear gloves if a great amount of force is being applied – these will protect your hands if something 'lets go'. In extreme cases, the nut or bolt head may have to be cut off, if there's sufficient access.

Note: *Many of the suspension and steering components are secured in position with self-locking 'Nyloc' nuts, recognisable by having a plastic thread insert (often coloured blue). Whenever a self-locking nut is disturbed, it must be discarded and a new nut fitted.*

Warning: *Since most of the procedures that are dealt with in this Chapter involve jacking up the car and working underneath it, a good pair of axle stands will be needed. A trolley jack is the preferred type of jack to lift the car, and it can also be used to support other components during certain operations. Do not rely on a trolley jack alone to support the car, as they can 'creep' down – once the car is raised on the jack, place at least one axle stand underneath as a precaution.*

2 Front swivel hub – removal and refitting

Note: *The driveshaft nuts, the suspension strut pinch-bolts and nuts, and the swivel hub balljoint locking clips must be renewed as a matter of course on reassembly.*

Removal

1 Refer to Chapter 8, Section 2, paragraphs 1 to 4.

Warning: *Before attempting to slacken the driveshaft nut, which is done up extremely tight, make sure the front of the vehicle is securely supported. Do not use poor-quality, badly-fitting tools for this task, due to the risk of personal injury.*

2 Unbolt the brake hose support bracket and the brake caliper mounting bracket from the swivel hub (Chapter 9). Support the caliper while it is removed by suspending it from the underbody or suspension using a wire hook – do not let it hang down on its brake hose **(see illustrations)**.

3 Remove the brake disc as described in Chapter 9.

2.2a Unbolting brake hose support bracket

2.2b While detached, suspend caliper on wire hook from underbody or suspension

2.4 Releasing ABS wheel sensor wiring harness from swivel hub

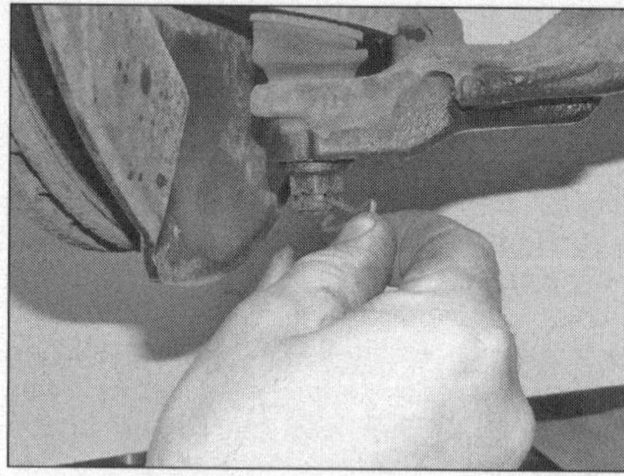
2.6 Extract locking clip from swivel hub balljoint castle nut

2.7a Release balljoint from lower arm using balljoint separator (take care not to damage rubber boot) . . .

2.7b . . . then prise lower arm down to separate it from swivel hub

4 Unscrew the ABS wheel sensor's mounting bolt, and carefully remove the wheel sensor from the front of the swivel hub (Chapter 9). Move the sensor clear of the working area – unclip the wiring harness as necessary, but it should not be necessary to disconnect it **(see illustration)**. While it is not advisable to disconnect unnecessarily the ABS wheel sensor wiring harness, in case a fault code is logged in the ECU's memory that causes the ABS warning lamp to light, if the sensor is locked in place with corrosion simply disconnect the ABS wheel sensor wiring harness and unclip it as necessary to remove the sensor with the swivel hub. If this method is followed, be careful not to damage the sensor tip during any of the succeeding work.

5 Unscrew the nut securing the anti-roll bar drop link to the suspension lower arm – use an Allen key to stop the drop link balljoint turning as this is done. Unhook the drop link from the lower arm.

6 Extract the locking clip (note which way round and how it is fitted), then unscrew the swivel hub balljoint castle nut **(see illustration)**. Discard the locking clip – a new one should be used on refitting.

7 The balljoint's taper can be released using a balljoint separator tool, but this carries the risk of damaging the balljoint's rubber boot – often, it is possible to release the taper by tapping the end of the lower arm with a hammer, but do not tap on the end of the balljoint pin unless the nut is in place to protect the pin's threaded end. Use a suitable lever to prise down the arm, and disconnect the lower arm from the swivel hub **(see illustrations)**.

8 The splined outboard end of the driveshaft now has to be released from the hub. It's likely that the splines will be very tight (corrosion may even be a factor, if the driveshaft has not been disturbed for some time), and considerable force may be needed. Tap the end of the shaft with a plastic or hide mallet only – if an ordinary hammer is used, place a small piece of wood over the end of the driveshaft – and leave the old nut loosely in place on the end to avoid damaging the thread and tip of the driveshaft.

9 Once the driveshaft is released, remove the driveshaft nut and discard it – the nut is only intended to be used once. As the driveshaft is disconnected, have your assistant hold it as level as reasonably possible to prevent damage to the CV joints – do not let it hang down unsupported.

10 Unscrew the two nuts from the pinch-bolts securing the lower end of the suspension strut to the swivel hub. Support the swivel hub, then tap the bolts through using a pin punch, noting which way round they are fitted (see Section 5, paragraph 5). Remove the swivel hub from under the vehicle **(see illustrations)**. Discard the pinch-bolts and nuts – new ones should be used on refitting.

2.10a Remove two strut-to-swivel hub pinch-bolts, noting direction of fitting . . .

2.10b . . . separate top of swivel hub from base of strut . . .

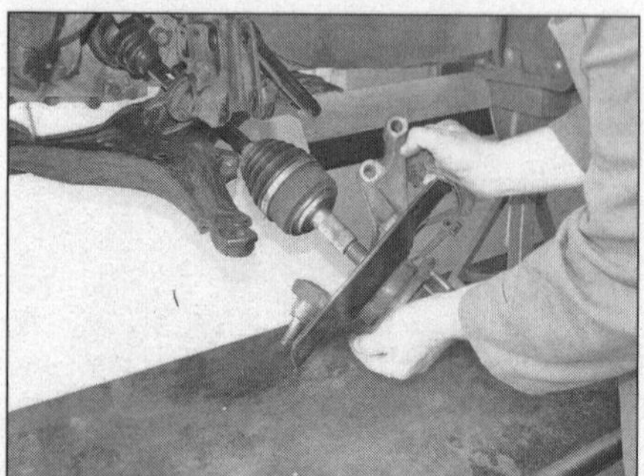
2.10c . . . and remove swivel hub

2.11a Fit new strut-to-swivel hub pinch-bolts and nuts front-to-rear or as noted on removal . . .

Refitting

11 Refitting is a reversal of removal, bearing in mind the following points:

a) Fit new pinch-bolts (front to rear, unless the opposite was noted on removal, in which case fit them as the originals were) and nuts to secure the suspension strut to the swivel hub. Tighten the nuts to the specified torque wrench setting ***(see illustrations)****.*

b) Thoroughly clean (use solvent or carburettor cleaner, then dry them using compressed air) the points of contact between the driveshaft and the hub.
c) Wipe the wheel bearing's magnetic encoder clean of oil, grease, dust and any other foreign matter which might affect its operation.
d) Fit the driveshaft fully into the hub. Apply a smear of oil to the seating surface of the new driveshaft nut, then screw it into place, tightening it hand-tight only at this stage.
e) Clean the swivel hub balljoint taper and its seat in the lower arm before fitting – it must be fitted dry. Lever the lower arm downwards, then hook the outer end over the balljoint stud and refit the balljoint castle nut. Carefully load the suspension with the vehicle's weight by using a jack applied to the lower arm (do not apply pressure to the balljoint stud), then tighten the nut initially to the Stage 1 (minimum) setting. From this point, tighten the nut only as required to align the locking clip holes (do not slacken to align), then fit a new clip from the centreline of the vehicle outwards to secure. The locking clip's free end must engage with the groove and one of the slots in the castle nut as shown **(see illustrations)**.
f) Reconnect the anti-roll bar drop link to the lower arm. While the suspension is still loaded with the vehicle's weight, tighten the nut to the specified torque, holding the drop link balljoint with an Allen key as for removal.
g) Tighten all brake component fixings to the specified torque.
h) If possible, do not fully tighten the driveshaft nut until the vehicle is resting on its wheels. Referring to the Warning earlier in this Section, tighten the new driveshaft nut to the specified torque (see Chapter 8). Stake the nut collar into the driveshaft groove **(see illustrations)**.
i) If applicable, refit the roadwheel, then lower the vehicle to the ground and tighten the wheel nuts to the specified torque.

3 Swivel hub balljoint – removal, overhaul and refitting

Removal and refitting

1 Refer to Sections 2 and 6, as appropriate.

Overhaul

2 The balljoint is an integral part of the swivel hub – if it is worn or damaged in any way the complete swivel hub must be renewed.

3 If the balljoint's rubber boot is damaged, a new one can be obtained from Honda dealers. Once the lower arm has been disconnected (refer to Section 6 for details), the old boot can be prised off. Wipe the balljoint clean (do not use excessive amounts of solvent), then pack it with fresh grease and fit the new boot, pressing it firmly into place until it is fully seated all the way round **(see illustrations)**. However, bear in mind

2.11b . . . then tighten to specified torque wrench setting . . .

2.11c Clean swivel hub balljoint taper and seat in lower arm before fitting – must be fitted dry

2.11d Load suspension with vehicle's weight by jacking up lower arm (not balljoint stud) . . .

2.11e . . . then tighten castle nut to Stage 1 (minimum) torque wrench setting . . .

2.11f . . . tighten further to align locking clip holes, then fit new clip so that free end engages groove and slots in castle nut . . .

2.11g . . . with clip inserted from centreline of vehicle outwards

2.11h Use fabricated tool as shown to prevent hub from rotating as driveshaft nut is tightened . . .

2.11i . . . and stake nut collar into driveshaft groove

3.3a Old balljoint boot can be prised off swivel hub

3.3b Clean and grease balljoint . . .

3.3c . . . then fit new boot, pressing firmly into place until fully seated all around

that if the boot has been damaged for some time, it is likely that dirt will have got into the balljoint, and a new balljoint may soon be needed.

4 Front wheel bearings – renewal

Note 1: *A press, a suitable puller, or a selection of large bolts, washers and other improvised tools will be required for this operation. Obtain a bearing kit before proceeding.*

Note 2: *Keep any magnetic tools well away from the new bearing's magnetic encoder, or it will not function correctly and the ABS system will be disabled. Similarly, keep it clean of oil, grease, dust and any other foreign matter which might affect its operation and be careful not to damage it as the new bearing is installed.*

1 With the swivel hub removed as described in Section 2, proceed as follows.

2 Securely support the swivel hub, on two metal bars for instance, with the inboard face uppermost then, using a metal bar or tube of suitable diameter, press or drive out the hub – we used a large bolt (the same diameter as the end of the hub's splined end) and a hammer **(see illustrations)**. Alternatively, use a puller to separate the hub from the bearing. Note that the bearing inner race will remain on the hub. Take care not to damage the brake disc splash shield.

3 With the hub removed, take off the disc shield, which is secured by three screws (see Chapter 9).

4 Use circlip pliers to extract the bearing circlip.

5 To remove the bearing itself first apply a generous amount of spray lubricant. Mount the swivel hub across two large blocks of wood, then drive the bearing out, using another old bearing, a socket or a large tube that will fit against the bearing's inner race **(see illustration)**.

6 The bearing inner race left on the hub must now be removed. To do this, preferably use a knife-edged bearing puller, but if this is not available, grip the hub flange in a vice, and drive the race off with a chisel, then a punch **(see illustrations)**. Tap the race at the top and both sides (turn the hub over in the vice) to stop it jamming as it comes off. Take care not to mark the hub bearing surface.

7 Using emery paper, clean off any burrs or raised edges from the hub and swivel hub, which might stop the components going back together.

8 On reassembly, note that the new bearing must be fitted with the brown ring of the magnetic encoder on the inboard side of the swivel hub, to fit against the ABS wheel

4.2a Using a hammer and large bolt . . .

4.2b . . . drive out the hub

4.5 Driving out the bearing, using a tube as a drift

4.6a Bearing inner race should be drawn off with a puller, if available . . .

4.6b . . . but other methods will work, with care

4.8 Ensure new bearing is fitted right way round (see text) . . .

4.9 . . . and draw into swivel hub using threaded rod, old bearing outer race, large washers and nuts, etc

sensor; the encoder should be easy to distinguish, as the opposite side of the bearing will have a black synthetic oil seal. Be careful not to mark or damage the encoder surface. Apply a light coat of lubricant to the inside of the swivel hub, and to the outside of the new bearing. Start fitting the bearing by offering it squarely into the swivel hub, then give it a few light taps with the hammer all round to locate it – keep the bearing square as this is done, or it will jam **(see illustration)**.

9 Fitting the bearing by tapping it in all the way with a hammer will probably damage it. We used a length of threaded bar (available from motor factors, DIY stores, etc), with a nut, some large washers and a drilled plate on the inside of the swivel hub. With the old bearing, another washer, and a nut on the outside, the whole assembly was mounted in a vice, and the nut tightened to press the new bearing in place. The actual method was to tighten the nut slightly, give the old bearing a few taps round its edge, tighten the nut some more, and so on until the bearing was fully home **(see illustration)**.

10 Fit the bearing circlip, ensuring that it locates fully into its groove all round. The old circlip can be re-used if it is undamaged, but if a new one is supplied with the bearing kit, it should be used **(see illustration)**.

11 Refit the brake disc shield, tightening its three screws securely **(see illustration)**.

12 The hub can be pressed into the new bearing using a very similar method to the one just used for the bearing **(see illustrations)**.

13 Wipe the magnetic encoder clean of oil, grease, dust and any other foreign matter which might affect its operation.

14 On completion, refit the swivel hub as described in Section 2.

5 Front suspension strut – removal, overhaul and refitting

Note: *Removal and refitting of the front suspension strut brace is described in Chapter 9, Section 7, paragraphs 2 to 4.*

Note: *The suspension strut pinch-bolts and nuts, and the track rod end balljoint split pin must be renewed as a matter of course on reassembly.*

4.10 Fit new retaining circlip to secure bearing

4.12a To refit hub to wheel bearing . . .

Removal

1 Slacken the relevant front wheel nuts, then jack up the front of the vehicle, and support securely on axle stands (see *Jacking and vehicle support*). Remove the roadwheel.

2 Extract the split pin from the steering track rod end balljoint nut (a new one will be needed when refitting). Unscrew the nut, but leave it attached by a couple of threads for now.

3 Disconnect the track rod end from the strut, either using a balljoint separator tool, or by tapping the end of the balljoint stud (use a block of wood and the still-fitted nut to protect the threads). When the balljoint separates, unscrew the nut completely, and move the track rod clear.

4 Unscrew the two bolts securing the ABS wiring harness and brake hose support brackets, and move the harness and hose clear of the strut.

5 Unscrew the two nuts from the pinch-bolts securing the lower end of the suspension strut to the swivel hub **(see illustrations 2.10a and 2.10b)**. Support the swivel hub, then remove the bolts; if necessary, tap them out using a pin punch. Note carefully which way round they are fitted.

6 Ensure that the strut is supported from below, then working in the engine compartment, slacken and remove the three suspension strut top mounting nuts **(see illustrations)**. Do not slacken the strut piston rod self-locking nut. Lower the strut (if necessary, press the lower arm down slightly) and withdraw it from under the wheel arch.

Overhaul

Note: *A spring compressor tool will be required for this operation.*

7 With the suspension strut resting on a bench, or clamped in a vice, fit a spring compressor tool, and compress the coil

4.11 Refit disc shield, ensuring locating tab is correctly aligned between swivel hub ribs

4.12b . . . use nut-and-rod method to draw hub into place

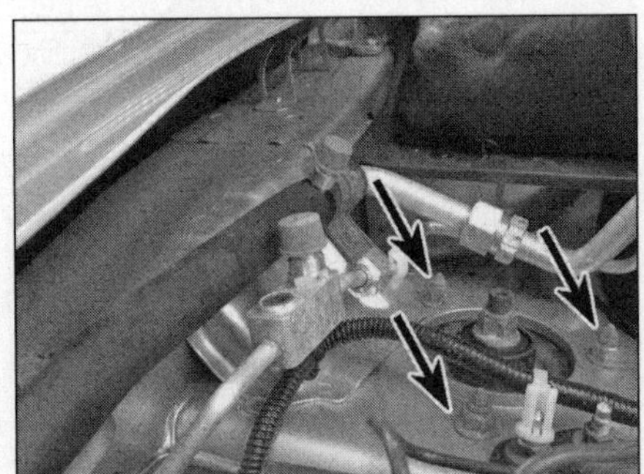

5.6a Unscrew and remove three strut top mounting nuts . . .

5.6b . . . and withdraw the strut

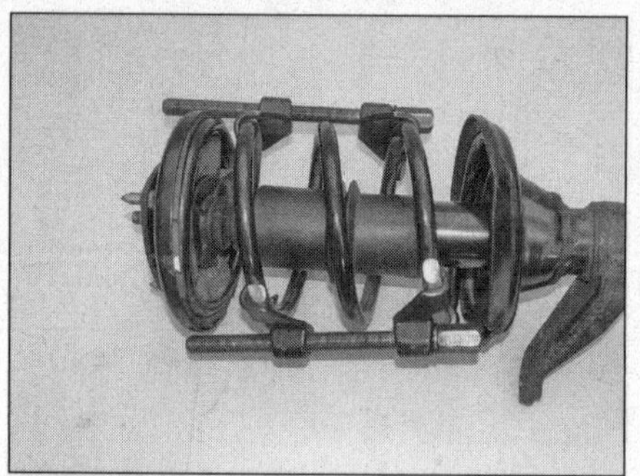
5.7 Fitting coil spring compressor – try to 'catch' as many coils as possible . . .

5.8 . . . then unscrew strut piston rod nut

5.9 Before dismantling strut, check for (paint) alignment marks

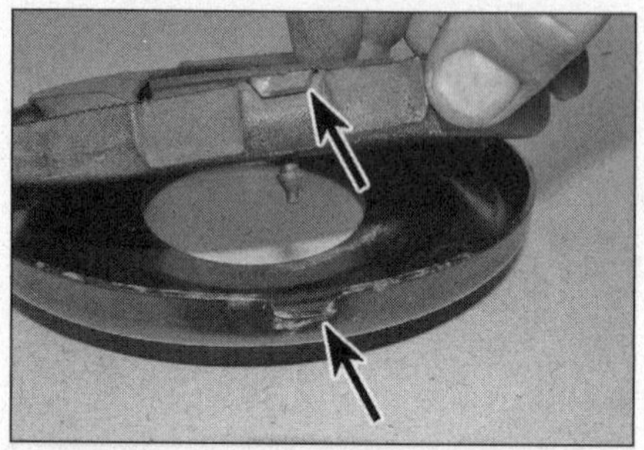
5.15a Fit strut spring mounting cushion to spring upper seat so that projection on cushion fits in cut-out on seat . . .

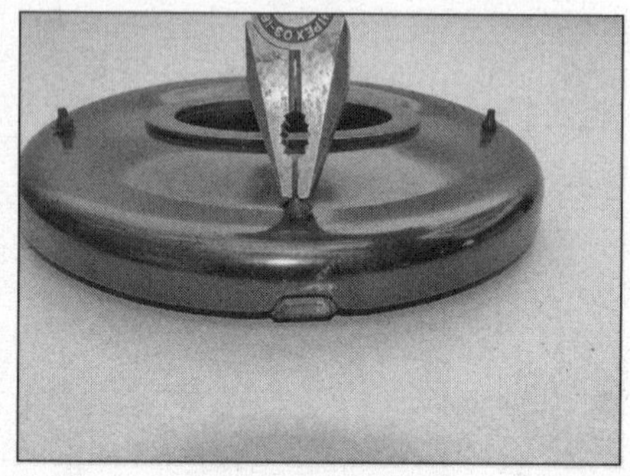
5.15b . . . then pull pegs through to secure cushion to seat . . .

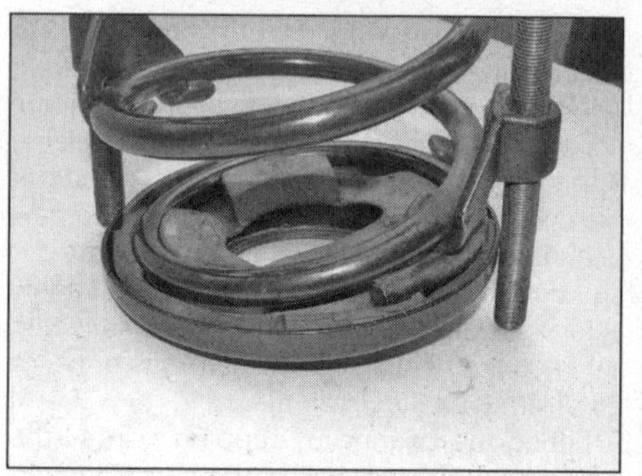
5.15c . . . and fit spring into groove in cushion

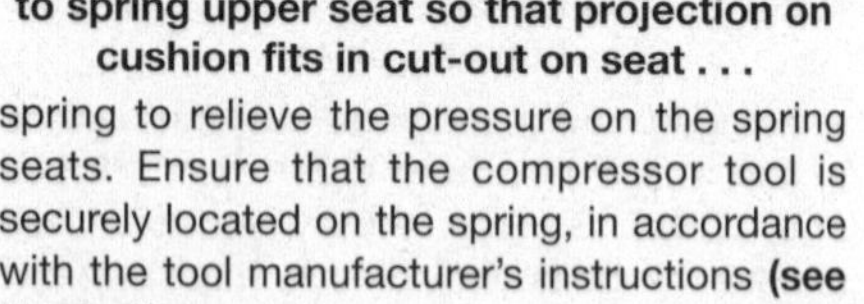
spring to relieve the pressure on the spring seats. Ensure that the compressor tool is securely located on the spring, in accordance with the tool manufacturer's instructions **(see illustration)**.

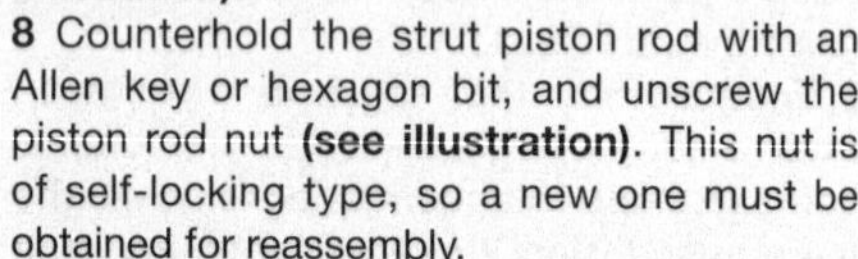
8 Counterhold the strut piston rod with an Allen key or hexagon bit, and unscrew the piston rod nut **(see illustration)**. This nut is of self-locking type, so a new one must be obtained for reassembly.

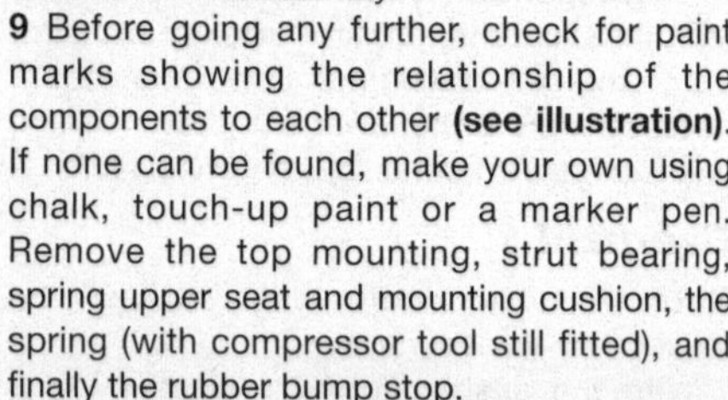
9 Before going any further, check for paint marks showing the relationship of the components to each other **(see illustration)**. If none can be found, make your own using chalk, touch-up paint or a marker pen. Remove the top mounting, strut bearing, spring upper seat and mounting cushion, the spring (with compressor tool still fitted), and finally the rubber bump stop.

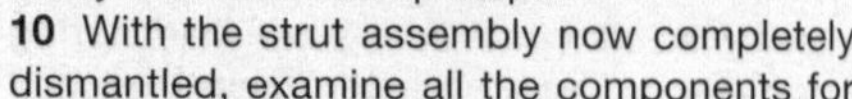
10 With the strut assembly now completely dismantled, examine all the components for wear, damage or deformation, and check the strut bearing for smoothness of operation. Renew any of the components as necessary.

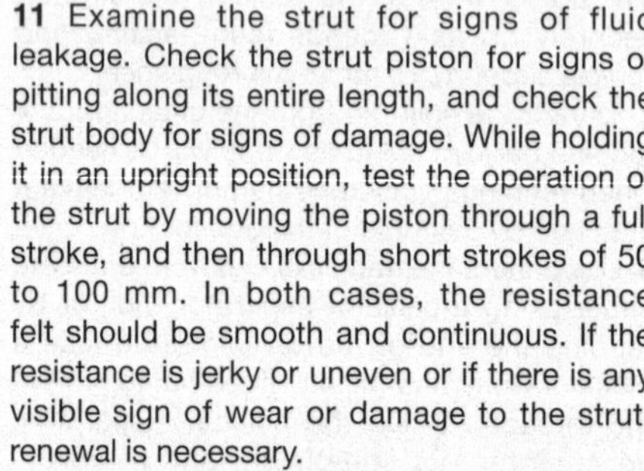
11 Examine the strut for signs of fluid leakage. Check the strut piston for signs of pitting along its entire length, and check the strut body for signs of damage. While holding it in an upright position, test the operation of the strut by moving the piston through a full stroke, and then through short strokes of 50 to 100 mm. In both cases, the resistance felt should be smooth and continuous. If the resistance is jerky or uneven or if there is any visible sign of wear or damage to the strut, renewal is necessary.

12 If any doubt exists as to the condition of the coil spring, carefully remove the spring compressors and check the spring for distortion and signs of cracking. Renew the spring if it is damaged or distorted, or if there is any doubt as to its condition.

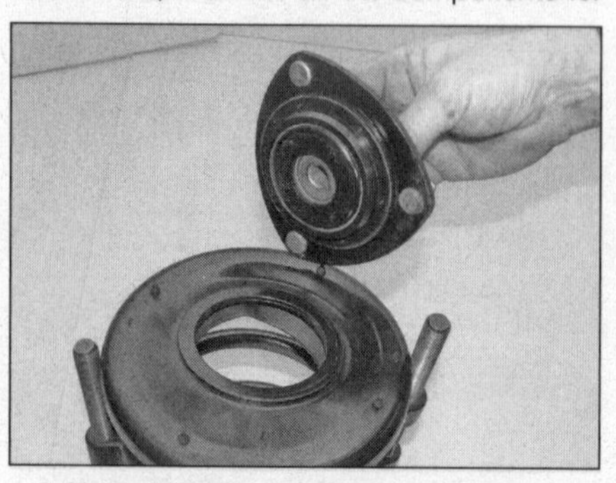
5.16 Refit top mounting plate and strut bearing

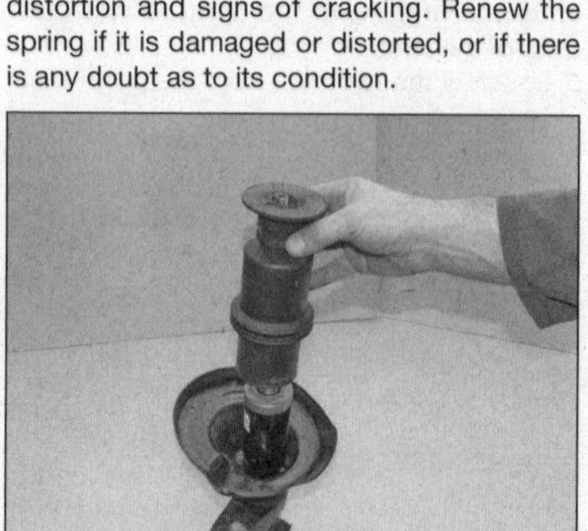
5.17 Slide rubber bump stop onto strut

13 Inspect all other components for damage or deterioration, and renew any that are suspect.

14 On reassembly, if the spring compressor tool has been removed from the spring or if new springs are being fitted, refit the compressor and compress the spring sufficiently to enable it to be refitted to the strut.

15 Fit the spring mounting cushion to the spring upper seat so that the projection on the cushion fits in the cut-out on the spring upper seat. Fit the spring (with compressor tool still fitted) to the cushion, so that the spring fits into the cushion groove – if the original components are being refitted, the original relationship should be easy to restore thanks to the marks left on the cushion **(see illustrations)**.

16 Refit the top mounting plate and strut bearing **(see illustration)**.

17 Slide the rubber bump stop onto the strut **(see illustration)**.

18 Slide the spring over the strut, and position it so that the lower end of the spring is resting against the stop on the lower seat **(see illustrations)**.

19 Check that the strut components are aligned as follows. At least three types of damper unit are fitted to CR-Vs; Type A (Part No. 51601 or 51602-S9A-G02), Type B (Part No. 51601 or 51602-S9A-G12) and the type fitted to the project vehicle (Part No. 51601 or 51602-S9A-G162). The part numbers are given on a yellow label stuck to the damper body under the bump stop.

a) On Type A dampers, the cut-out in the side of the spring upper seat must be at

5.18a Fit spring assembly to strut . . .

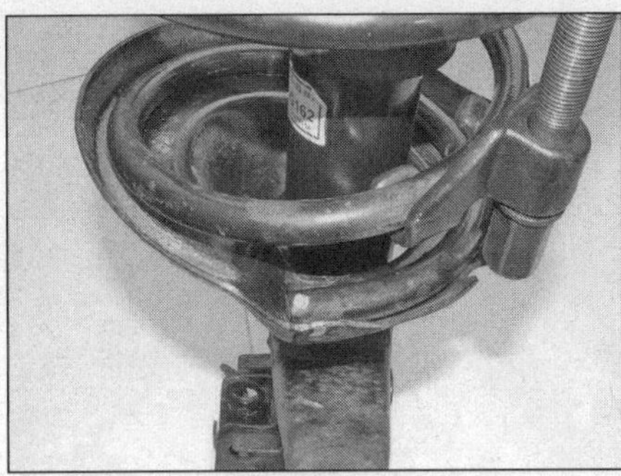
5.18b . . . so that spring lower end rests against stop on lower seat

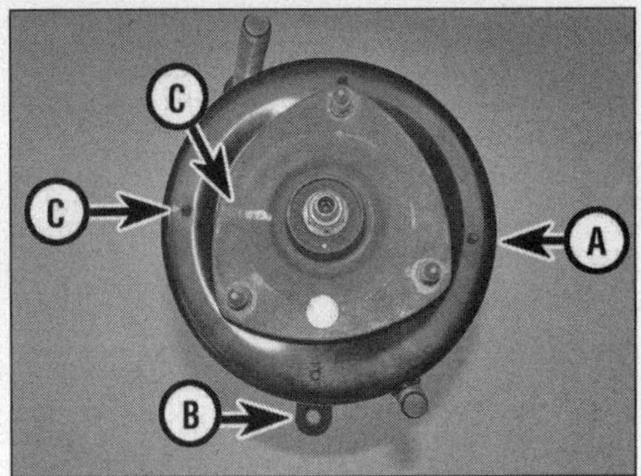

5.19 Cut-out in spring upper seat (A) must be at specified angle from steering arm (B) – left-hand strut shown – while arrow marks (C) on spring upper seat and top mounting plate must align, and point to outside of vehicle on refitting

115 ± 8° anti-clockwise from the steering arm on the left-hand strut, and 90 ± 8° clockwise from the steering arm on the right-hand strut.

b) *On Type B dampers, the cut-out in the side of the spring upper seat must be at 90 ± 8° anti-clockwise from the steering arm on the left-hand strut, and 90 ± 8° clockwise from the steering arm on the right-hand strut.*

c) *Information is not available for the third type of damper, but those on the project vehicle had their components located as described for Type B dampers* ***(see illustration)****.*

d) *On all models, note that the top mounting plate has an arrow marking on it which must align with that on the spring upper seat* ***(see illustration 5.19)****; both point to the outside of the vehicle on refitting the strut.*

20 Fit a new piston rod self-locking nut, and tighten it to the specified torque wrench setting; the easiest way of doing this is to use a reversible torque wrench (that can tighten left-hand threads) and a hexagon bit to tighten the piston rod while counterholding the nut with a spanner. Provided this final step is not forgotten, it may be easier to carry out when the strut is back in the vehicle **(see illustrations)**.

21 Slowly slacken the spring compressor tool to relieve the tension in the spring. Check that the ends of the spring locate correctly against the stops on the spring seats. If necessary, turn the spring and the upper seat so that the components locate correctly before the compressor tool is removed. Remove the compressor tool when the spring is fully seated.

Refitting

22 Refitting is a reversal of removal, bearing in mind the following points:

a) *Offer the strut up to the vehicle so that the steering arm is to the rear and the swivel hub brackets to the outside; the cut-out in the side of the spring upper seat must face to the inside (towards the engine). The arrow marks on the strut top mounting plate and spring upper seat should line up, and should both point to the outside of the vehicle.*

b) *Refit the strut top mounting nuts, but do not tighten them fully at this stage.*

c) *Refit the swivel hub to the strut and fit the new pinch-bolts and nuts; push the bolts through as noted on removal. Do not tighten the nuts fully at this stage.*

d) *Carefully load the suspension with the vehicle's weight by using a jack applied to the lower arm (do not apply pressure to the swivel hub balljoint stud), then tighten to their specified torque wrench settings the strut top mounting nuts, the piston rod self-locking nut (if not yet done) and the strut pinch-bolts and nuts* ***(see illustrations)****.*

e) *Clean the track rod balljoint taper and its seat in the strut before fitting – it must be fitted dry. Tighten the balljoint nut to the specified torque, then fit a new pin to secure.*

f) *Tighten all other fixings to the specified torque.*

5.20a Fit new piston rod nut . . .

5.22a Load suspension with vehicle's weight by jacking up lower arm (not balljoint stud) . . .

6 Front suspension lower arm – removal, overhaul and refitting

Removal

1 Slacken the front wheel nuts on the side concerned, then apply the handbrake, jack up the front of the vehicle, and support securely on axle stands (see *Jacking and vehicle support*). Remove the wheel.

2 Unscrew the nut securing the anti-roll bar drop link to the suspension lower arm – use an Allen key to stop the drop link balljoint turning as this is done. Unhook the drop link from the lower arm.

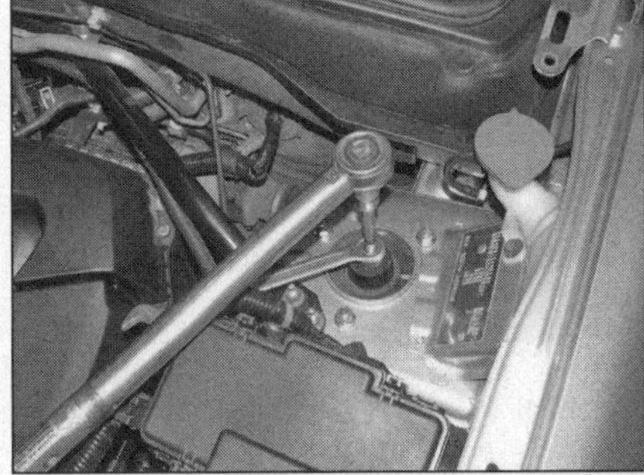
5.20b . . . and tighten to specified torque wrench setting

5.22b . . . then tighten strut top mounting nuts to specified torque wrench setting

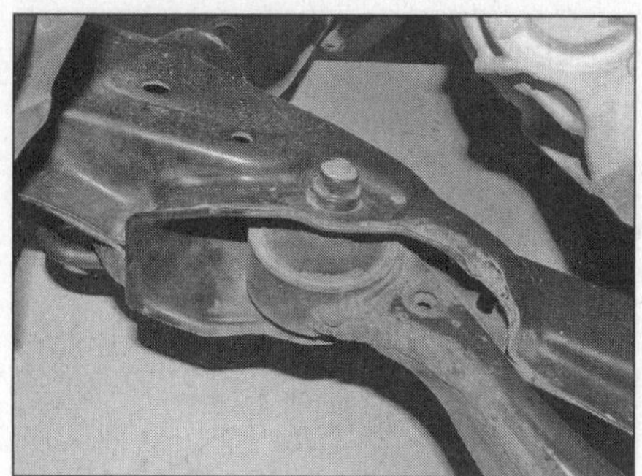
6.5a Lower arm front mounting bolt

6.5b Lower arm rear pivot bolt

3 Extract the locking clip (note which way round and how it is fitted), then unscrew the swivel hub balljoint castle nut **(see illustration 2.6)**. Discard the locking clip – a new one should be used on refitting.

4 The balljoint's taper can be released using a balljoint separator tool, but this carries the risk of damaging the balljoint's rubber boot – often, it is possible to release the taper by tapping the end of the lower arm with a hammer, but do not tap on the end of the balljoint pin unless the nut is in place to protect the pin's threaded end. Use a suitable lever to prise down the arm, and disconnect the lower arm from the swivel hub **(see illustrations 2.7a and 2.7b)**.

5 Unscrew and remove the lower arm front mounting bolt and rear pivot bolt, then remove the arm from under the vehicle **(see illustrations)**.

Overhaul

6 Overhaul is limited to renewing the bush at either end of the arm – if the arm has suffered damage (from, for example, careless jacking-up or off-road abuse), the arm is best renewed complete. It is advisable to consider renewing both arms in an axle set, rather than just one. Both bushes are available separately if the checks outlined in Chapter 1A or 1B have revealed play at either of these points, or if any other signs of wear or damage are discernible.

7 A press and adapters will be required for driving the bushes from the lower arms; measure carefully the exact fitted position of each bush in the lower arm before disturbing either and note that the rear bush is shouldered and so must be pressed out to the rear. In the absence of this tool, mount the arm in a vice, and make up your own puller, using a bolt, with several large washers and large sockets, or drive the bushes out using a suitable drift (such as a large socket). If the DIY approach fails, entrust bush renewal to a Honda dealer.

Refitting

8 Check the swivel hub balljoint rubber boot condition while the lower arm is removed (see Section 3).

9 Clean the swivel hub balljoint taper and its seat in the lower arm before fitting – it must be fitted dry. Offer the lower arm into position, taking care not to damage the balljoint boot as the lower arm is refitted.

10 Refit the two lower arm bolts, and tighten them by hand only at this stage.

11 Lever the lower arm downwards, then hook the outer end over the balljoint stud and refit the balljoint castle nut. Carefully load the suspension with the vehicle's weight by using a jack applied to the lower arm (do not apply pressure to the balljoint stud), then tighten the nut initially to the Stage 1 (minimum) setting. From this point, tighten the nut only as required to align the locking clip holes (do not slacken to align), then fit a new clip from the centreline of the vehicle outwards to secure. The locking clip's free end must engage with the groove and one of the slots in the castle nut as shown **(see illustrations 2.11c to 2.11g)**.

12 While the suspension is still loaded with the vehicle's weight, tighten the two lower arm bolts to the specified torque.

13 Refit the wheel, and lower the vehicle to the ground. Tighten the wheel nuts to the specified torque.

7 Front anti-roll bar, bushes and drop links – removal and refitting

Note: *As noted in Section 1, whenever a self-locking nut is disturbed, it must be discarded and a new nut fitted.*

1 Slacken the front wheel nuts, then jack up the front of the vehicle, and support it securely on axle stands (see *Jacking and vehicle support*). Remove the front wheels.

Bushes

2 If the bushes alone are to be renewed, working on one side at a time, unscrew the two bolts and remove the anti-roll bar mounting clamp, noting the arrow mark pointing to the front of the vehicle **(see illustrations)**. The bar can then be lowered slightly, and the bush removed (the bush is split for easy removal); note the paint marks on the arm, outboard of each bush.

3 Slip the new bush into place around the roll bar – if necessary, lubricate the bush with a little liquid soap first. Align the bush with the painted mark on the roll bar, to make initial fitting more accurate. No instructions are given as to whether the split in the bush goes to front or rear, but on both project vehicles, both bushes had the split at the front.

4 Refit the clamp, noting that it has an arrow marking which indicates the front of the vehicle. Slide the bush along the bar slightly if required, to bring the clamp bolt holes into alignment. Tighten the clamp bolts to the specified torque, front bolt first.

5 Repeat the procedure on the other side.

6 On completion, refit the wheels, then lower the vehicle to the ground and tighten the wheel nuts to the specified torque.

Drop links

7 Unscrew the nut at each end of the link – use an Allen key to stop the drop link balljoints turning as this is done. Remove the drop link from the lower arm and anti-roll bar, noting how it is fitted. Discard the self-locking nuts – new ones should be used when refitting **(see illustrations)**.

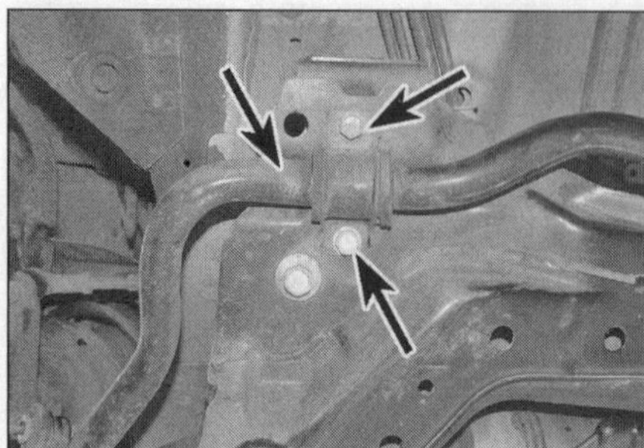
7.2a Front anti-roll bar mounting clamp and bolts on subframe. Note paint mark showing bush location . . .

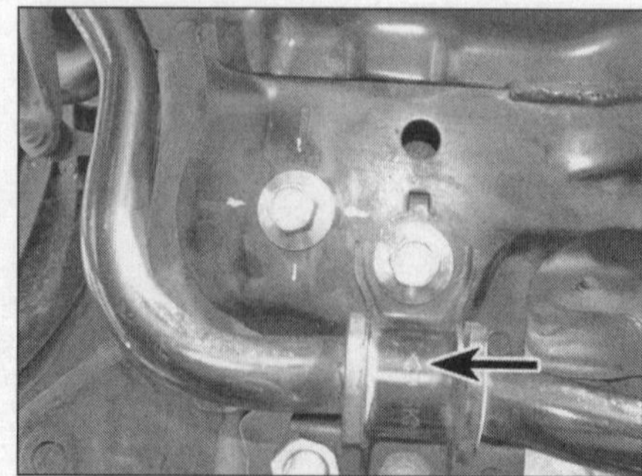
7.2b . . . and arrow mark on clamp pointing to front of vehicle

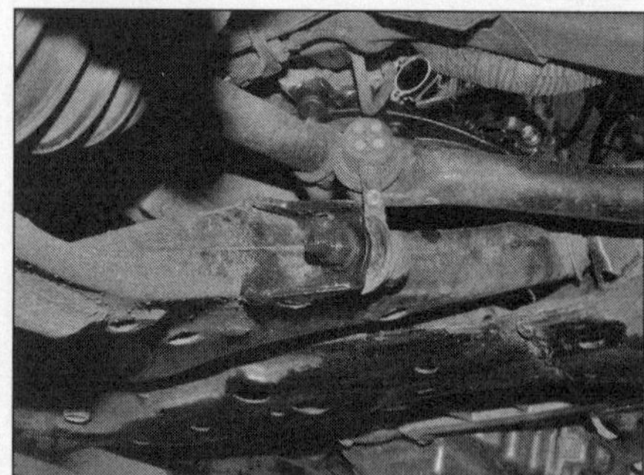
7.7a Apply penetrating fluid if nuts are rusted . . .

7.7b . . . before unscrewing nut securing anti-roll bar drop link to lower arm

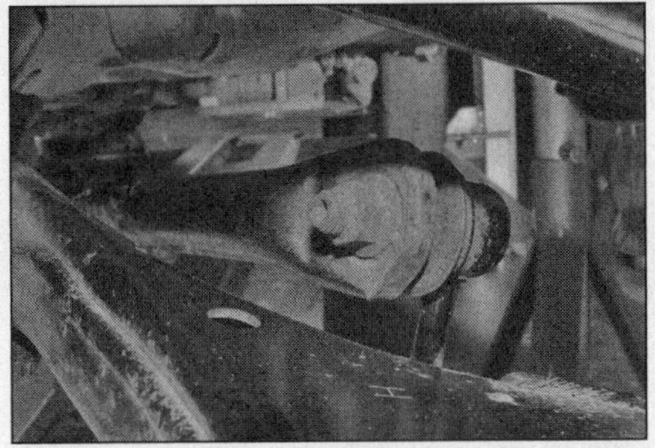

7.7c Self-locking nut securing drop link to anti-roll bar must be renewed whenever unscrewed

7.8a Front anti-roll bar drop link (note both nuts self-locking) – set balljoint pins to centre of their movement in all directions . . .

7.8b . . . refit drop link to anti-roll bar and suspension lower arm . . .

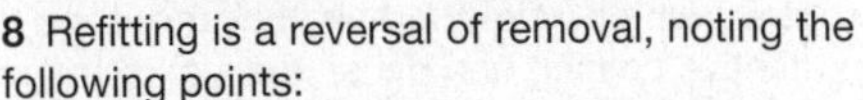

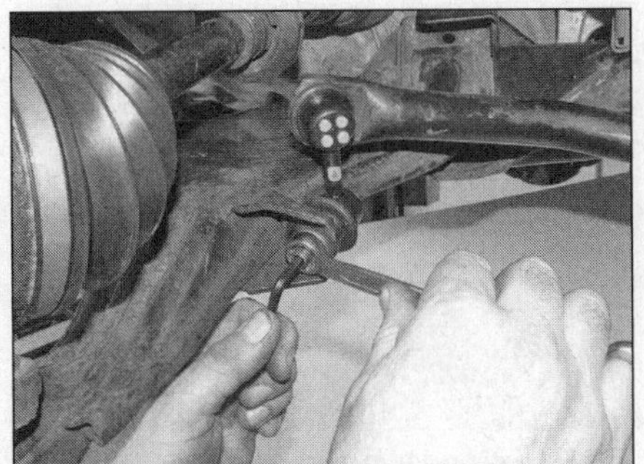

7.8c . . . tighten nut while counterholding balljoint pin . . .

7.8d . . . then tighten nut to specified torque wrench setting

8 Refitting is a reversal of removal, noting the following points:

a) *Set the balljoint pins to the centre of their movement in all directions* ***(see illustrations).***
b) *Use new self-locking nuts on the upper balljoint of the anti-roll bar drop links (see also note above).*
c) *Carefully load the suspension with the vehicle's weight by using a jack applied to the lower arm (do not apply pressure to the balljoint stud), then tighten the nuts to their specified torque wrench settings* ***(see illustrations).***
d) *On completion, refit the wheels, then lower the vehicle to the ground and tighten the wheel nuts to the specified torque.*
e) *After 5 minutes of driving, retighten the self-locking nuts to the specified torque.*

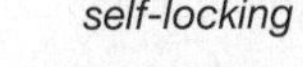

Anti-roll bar

9 The anti-roll bar is not symmetrical; before unbolting it, mark it with chalk, touch-up paint or a marker pen to ensure it is refitted the correct way round.

10 Unscrew the nut securing each of the two anti-roll bar drop links to the anti-roll bar or to the lower arm – use an Allen key to stop the drop link balljoint turning as this is done. Disconnect the drop links from the bar or lower arm. Discard the self-locking nuts – new ones should be used when refitting.

11 Unbolt the two anti-roll bar clamps, then remove the clamps and withdraw the bar from under the vehicle. If the drop links are still attached to the bar, they can be removed if required; all components are available separately if renewal is necessary.

12 Refitting is a reversal of removal, noting the following points:

a) *Ensure that the bar is fitted the correct way round.*
b) *Fit the bushes as described in paragraph 3.*
c) *Ensure that the clamps are refitted with their arrow markings facing forwards, and tighten the bolts to the specified torque wrench setting, front bolts first.*
d) *Refit and/or reconnect the drop links, as described in paragraph 8.*
e) *On completion, refit the wheels, then lower the vehicle to the ground and tighten the wheel nuts to the specified torque.*

8 Front suspension subframe – removal and refitting

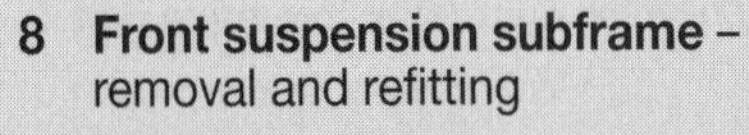

Caution: The removal of the front suspension subframe leaves the engine/transmission unit hanging on, and located by, only two of its normal four mountings; great care will be required to minimise the risk of personal injury and of expensive component damage. Read through the procedure first to ensure that all the tools and equipment required are to hand. Note also that the subframe bolts and rear mounting plates (diesel models only), various engine mounting fasteners, and the swivel hub balljoint locking clips, etc, must be renewed as a matter of course whenever they are disturbed, in addition to any other items (gaskets, seals, etc) found to be in need of renewal during the procedure.

Removal

1 Slacken the front wheel nuts. Jack up the front of the vehicle, and support it securely on axle stands located well clear of the subframe (see *Jacking and vehicle support*). Note that the vehicle must be raised sufficiently high for the subframe to be lowered and withdrawn from underneath. Remove the front wheels and the engine compartment undershield (Chapter 11).

2 Unscrew the nuts securing the anti-roll bar drop links to the suspension lower arms – use an Allen key to stop each drop link balljoint turning as this is done. Unhook the drop links from the lower arms.

3 Extract the locking clips (note which way round and how each is fitted), then unscrew the swivel hub balljoint castle nuts **(see illustration 2.6)**. Discard the locking clips – new ones should be used on refitting.

4 The balljoints' tapers can be released using a balljoint separator tool, but this carries the risk of damaging the balljoints' rubber boots – often, it is possible to release a taper by tapping the end of the lower arm with a hammer, but do not tap on the end of the balljoint pin unless the nut is in place to protect the pin's threaded end. Use a suitable lever to prise down the arms, and disconnect the lower arms from the swivel hubs **(see illustrations 2.7a and 2.7b).**

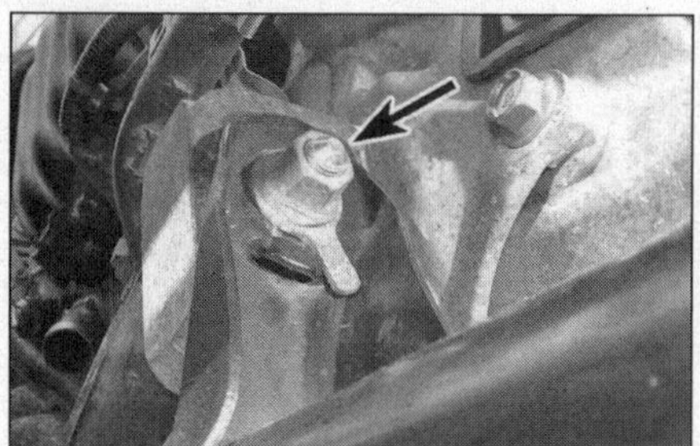

8.5a To remove subframe on petrol models, unbolt engine/transmission front mounting (note tab on nut should be fitted inside subframe loop) . . .

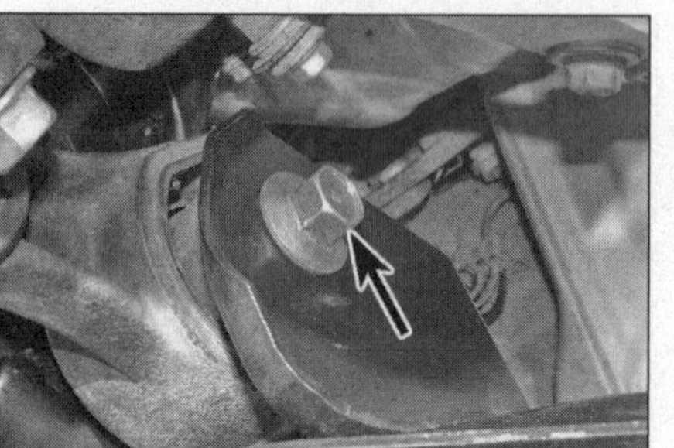

8.6a To remove subframe on diesel models, unbolt engine rear mounting through-bolt . . .

5 On petrol-engined models, unbolt the following:

a) *Unscrew the through-bolt from the engine/transmission front mounting (note that the nut is 'captive', with a tab that fits inside a loop on the subframe). Discard the bolt – this must be renewed as a matter of course, as described in Chapter 2A* ***(see illustration).***

b) *On models with automatic transmission, unscrew the transmission fluid filter mounting bolt from beside the engine/transmission front mounting.*

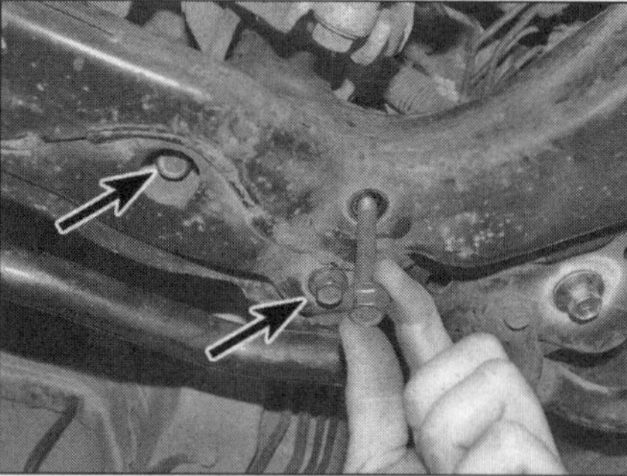

8.5b . . . and engine/transmission rear mounting-to-subframe bolts

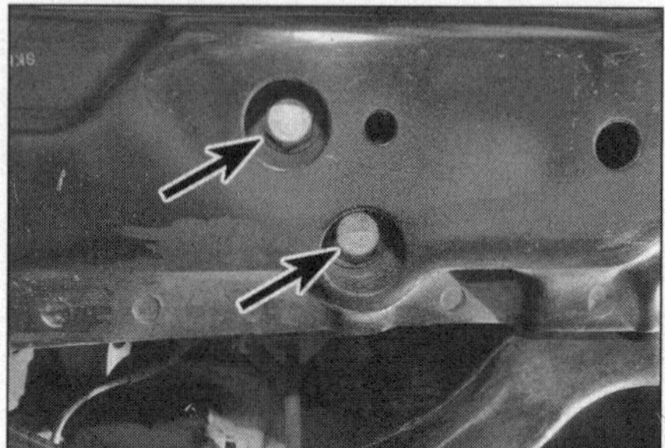

8.6b . . . and two engine/transmission left-hand (lower) mounting-to-subframe bolts

c) *On all models, unscrew the three engine/transmission rear mounting-to-subframe bolts* ***(see illustration).***

6 On diesel-engined models, unbolt the following:

a) *Unscrew the through-bolt from the engine rear mounting torque rod. Discard the bolt – this must be renewed as a matter of course, as described in Chapter 2B* ***(see illustration).***

b) *Unscrew the two engine/transmission left-hand (lower) mounting-to-subframe bolts. Again, discard the bolts, which must be renewed as a matter of course, as described in Chapter 2B* ***(see illustration).***

7 Check around the subframe to ensure that there are no brackets, hoses or harnesses still attached, or anything in the way which would prevent it from being lowered.

8 The subframe is secured to the body by four bolts **(see illustration)**. By the two rear bolts, there are alignment markings (two sets of double or triple lines, set at right angles to each other) stamped into the subframe to indicate the subframe's position relative to the centre of the head of the mounting bolt – mark the heads of both bolts in line with both sets of marks before unscrewing any of the bolts. If these are not clear, clean the area and make your own subframe-to-body marks with white paint or similar (do not use a sharp-pointed scriber, which might break the underbody protective coating and cause rusting) to mark the exact relationship of the subframe to the underbody. Seeing that holes have been made in the subframe and underbody next to each rear mounting point to allow the subframe

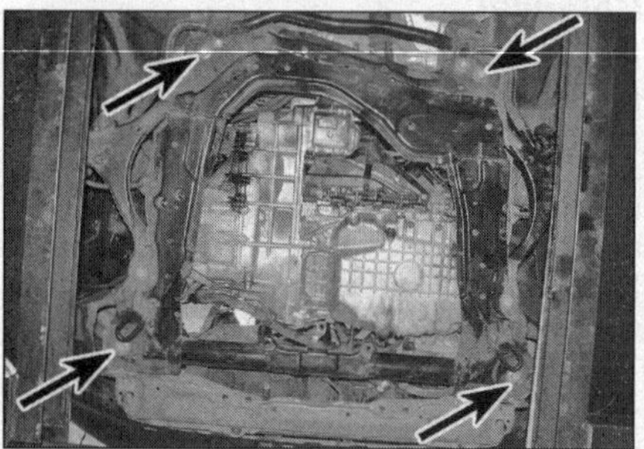

8.8a Front suspension subframe is secured by four bolts, which must be renewed on refitting

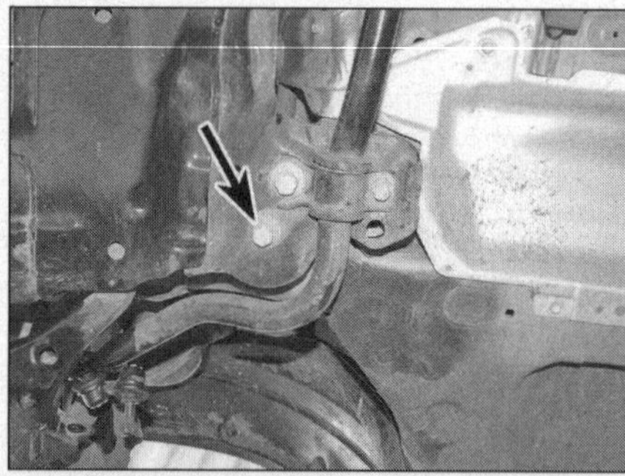

8.8b Rear right-hand mounting bolt

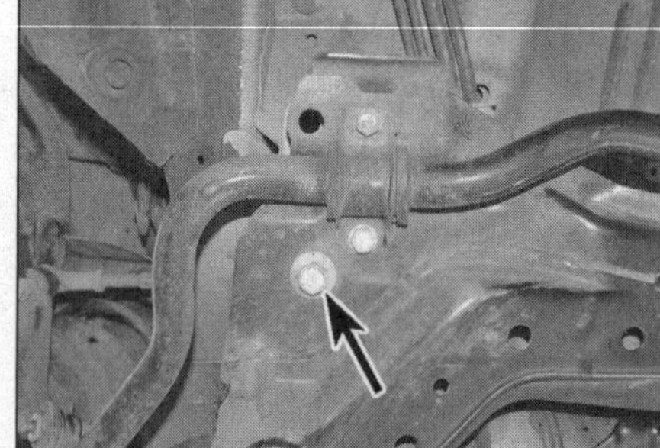

8.8c Rear left-hand mounting bolt

8.8d Front left-hand mounting bolt

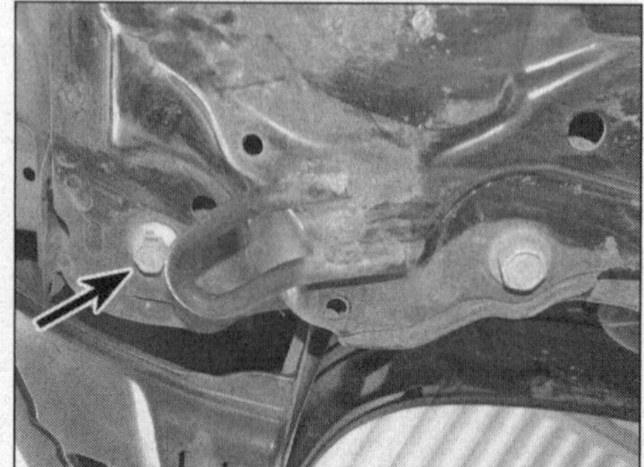

8.8e Front right-hand mounting bolt

8.8f Note alignment marks on subframe by rear bolts – enhance with paint if not clear enough . . .

to be located with tapered guides, we found two lengths of 16 mm threaded rod, passed them through both holes and secured them with nuts to provide a more positive means of alignment **(see illustrations)**.

9 Support the subframe with a transmission jack or a large trolley jack and a flat piece of wood. Have an assistant ready to support the subframe as the jack is lowered **(see illustration)**. Unscrew the subframe bolts.

10 Lower the subframe to clear the engine/transmission mountings, then withdraw it from under the vehicle.

11 Note that the four subframe bolts are only intended to be used once, and new ones should be obtained for refitting. On diesel-engined models, the plate bolted to the subframe top surface at each rear mounting must be renewed as a matter of course **(see illustrations)**. The front suspension lower arms, the rectifier (black rubber flap) and damper, where fitted, can be unbolted if required.

Refitting

Note: *It is essential that the subframe is re-aligned exactly on its mountings or the wheel alignment and steering geometry will be upset and will be difficult to set accurately.*

12 With the mounting plates renewed (diesel-engined models only), and any other items that were removed refitted, offer up the subframe and fit the new subframe bolts, tightening them only lightly at this stage.

13 The subframe must now be aligned on the underbody. If paint marks and/or guides have been made as suggested, use them to align the subframe precisely. If these were not used, you can align the subframe by eye, centring the subframe aligning holes on those of the underbody, and using the marks made on removal for assistance. Alternatively, you can align the subframe using a tapered drift (such as a clutch-aligning tool), or even a deep socket spanner of suitable size.

14 Once the subframe is aligned as precisely as possible, tighten its bolts to the specified torque wrench setting without disturbing its position. Recheck the alignment once all the bolts are securely tightened.

15 The remainder of refitting is a reversal of removal, noting the following points:

a) *Refit (or fit new, as directed in Chapter 2A or 2B, as applicable) the engine mounting bolts and tighten them to their specified torque wrench settings.*

b) *Clean the swivel hub balljoint tapers and their seats in the lower arms before fitting – they must be fitted dry. Lever each lower arm downwards, then hook the outer end over the balljoint stud and refit the balljoint castle nut. Carefully load the suspension with the vehicle's weight by using a jack applied to the lower arm (do not apply pressure to the balljoint stud), then tighten the nut initially to the Stage 1 (minimum) setting. From this point, tighten the nut only as required to align the locking clip holes (do not slacken to align), then fit a new clip from the centreline of the vehicle outwards to secure. The locking clip's free end must engage with the groove and one of the slots in the castle nut as shown* ***(see illustrations 2.11c to 2.11g)****.*

c) *Reconnect the anti-roll bar drop link to the lower arm. While the suspension is still loaded with the vehicle's weight, tighten the nut to the specified torque, holding the drop link balljoint with an Allen key as for removal.*

d) *Remember that, since the front suspension subframe has been disturbed, the wheel alignment and steering angles must be checked fully and carefully as soon as possible, with any necessary adjustments being made. This operation is best carried out by an experienced mechanic, using proper checking equipment; the vehicle should therefore be taken to a Honda dealer or similarly-qualified person for attention.*

9 Rear hub carrier – removal, overhaul and refitting

Note: *The driveshaft nut and trailing arm-to-hub carrier rear mounting (toe-adjusting) bolt's self-locking nut must be renewed as a matter of course on reassembly.*

Removal

1 Refer to Chapter, Section 3, paragraph 1.

Warning: Before attempting to slacken the driveshaft nut, which is done up extremely tight, make sure the rear of the vehicle is securely supported. Do not use poor-quality,

8.8g . . . or simply mark bolt area with paint as shown

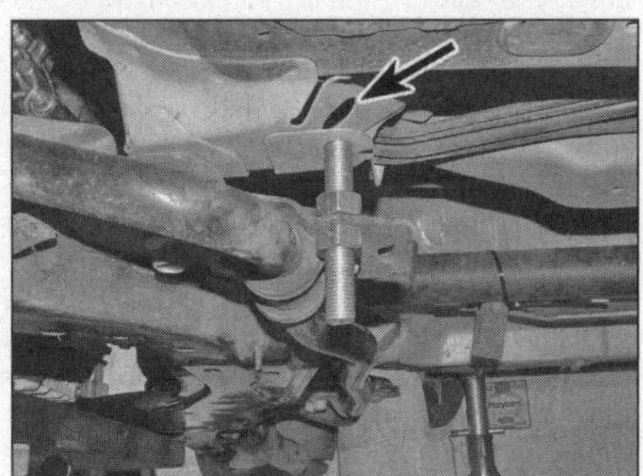

8.8h Make alignment guides from threaded rod and nuts . . .

8.8i . . . to fit though reference holes in subframe and underbody

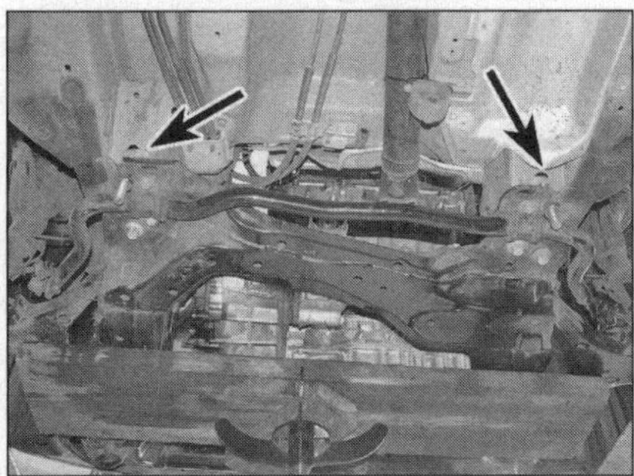

8.9 Lowering the subframe – note alignment guides clamped in place

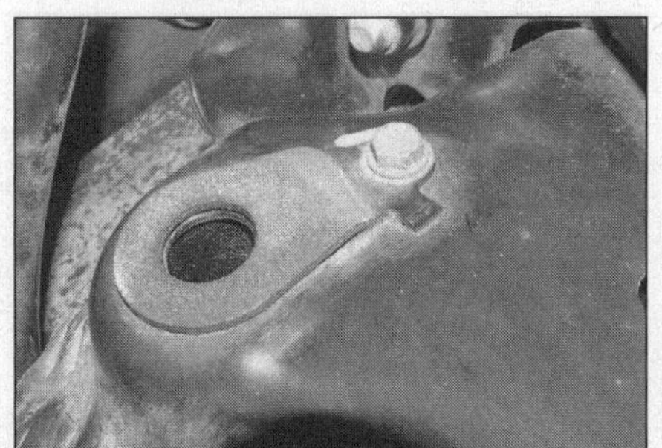

8.11a On diesel models, plates bolted to subframe top surface at each rear mounting . . .

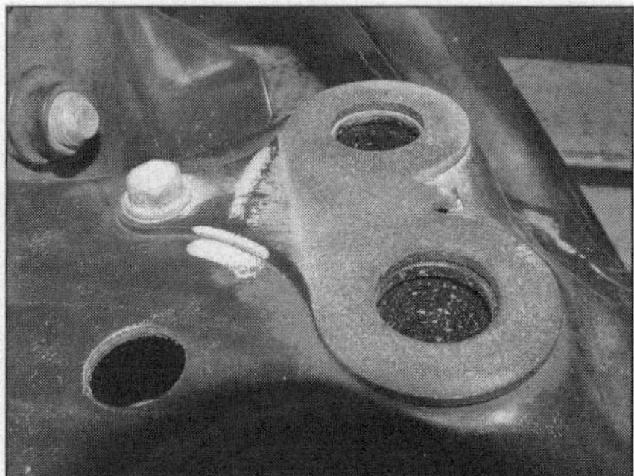

8.11b . . . must be renewed as a matter of course

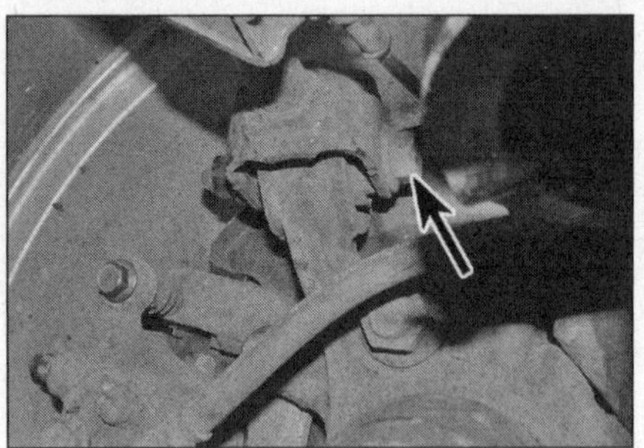

9.7 Unscrew upper control arm-to-hub carrier bolt and disconnect arm from hub carrier

9.8 Unscrew trailing arm-to-hub carrier front mounting bolt

badly-fitting tools for this task, due to the risk of personal injury.

2 Release the handbrake lever fully. Unbolt the brake hose support bracket and the brake caliper mounting bracket from the hub carrier (Chapter 9). Support the caliper while it is removed by suspending it from the underbody or suspension using a wire hook – do not let it hang down on its brake hose.

3 Remove the brake disc/drum as described in Chapter 9.

4 Remove the handbrake shoes as described in Chapter 9, to disconnect the cable inner wire end fitting from the handbrake mechanism. Unscrew the bolt securing the cable outer's end fitting to the handbrake backplate. Do not bend or kink the cable when tucking it away clear of the working area.

5 Unscrew the ABS wheel sensor's mounting bolt, and carefully remove the wheel sensor from the top of the hub carrier (Chapter 9). Move the sensor clear of the working area – unclip the wiring harness as necessary, but it should not be necessary to disconnect it. While it is not advisable to disconnect unnecessarily the ABS wheel sensor wiring harness, in case a fault code is logged in the ECU's memory that causes the ABS warning lamp to light, if the sensor is locked in place with corrosion simply disconnect the ABS wheel sensor wiring harness and unclip it as necessary to remove the sensor with the hub carrier. If this method is followed, be careful not to damage the sensor tip during any of the succeeding work.

6 Support the weight of the hub carrier – do not compress the suspension significantly – by placing a jack under the tubular section of the trailing arm (do not apply pressure to the flat, pressed-steel, lower transverse link).

7 Unscrew the upper control arm-to-hub carrier bolt and disconnect the arm from the hub carrier; tie it up clear of the working area **(see illustration)**.

8 Unscrew the trailing arm-to-hub carrier front mounting bolt **(see illustration)**.

9 Scrub clean the rear end of the trailing arm and the front of the trailing arm-to-hub carrier rear mounting. Use touch-up paint, typists' correction fluid or similar to mark the setting of the eccentrics on the head and nut of the trailing arm-to-hub carrier rear mounting (toe-adjusting) bolt, then unscrew the self-locking nut. Withdraw the mounting/adjusting bolt and its nut **(see illustrations)**. A new self-locking nut should be obtained for refitting.

10 The splined outboard end of the driveshaft now has to be released from the hub. It's likely that the splines will be very tight (corrosion may even be a factor, if the driveshaft has not been disturbed for some time), and considerable force may be needed. Tap the end of the shaft with a plastic or hide mallet only – if an ordinary hammer is used, place a small piece of wood over the end of the driveshaft – and leave the old nut loosely in place on the end to avoid damaging the thread and tip of the driveshaft.

11 Once the driveshaft is released, remove the driveshaft nut and discard it – the nut is only intended to be used once – and withdraw the hub carrier from under the vehicle. As the driveshaft is disconnected, have your assistant tie it back to the rear suspension trailing arm lateral link – do not let it hang down unsupported.

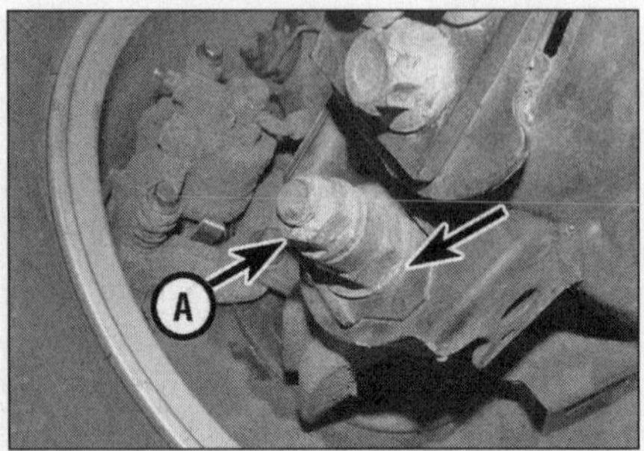

9.9a Unscrew self-locking nut (A) to dismantle trailing arm-to-hub carrier rear mounting – mark toe-adjusting eccentrics . . .

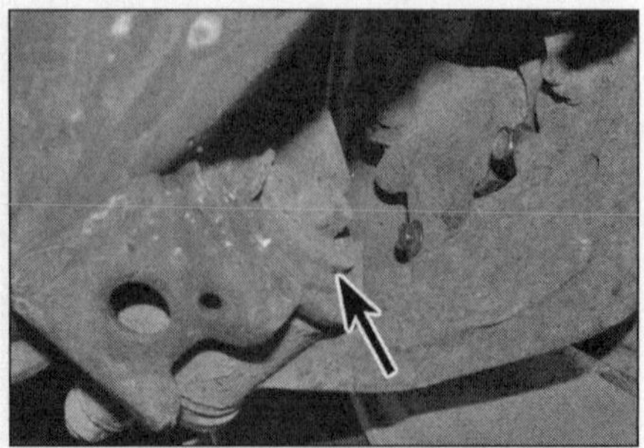

9.9b . . . (arrows) to ensure refitting in exact original positions to preserve toe setting

Overhaul

12 Whenever the hub carrier is removed, dismantle, clean thoroughly and grease, the trailing arm-to-hub carrier rear mounting (toe-adjusting) bolt and nut, so that rear wheel toe adjustment can be carried out with the minimum of difficulty.

13 The rear hub and wheel bearings should be removed and refitted as outlined in Sections 10 and 4.

14 Otherwise, overhaul is limited to renewing the bushes at the mounting points for the upper control and trailing arms. All are available separately if the checks outlined in Chapter 1A or 1B have revealed play at any of these points, or if any other signs of wear or damage are discernible.

15 A press and adapters will be required for driving the bushes from the hub carrier; measure carefully the exact fitted position of each bush in the hub carrier before disturbing either and check whether the bush is shouldered and so must be pressed out in one particular direction. In the absence of this tool, mount the hub carrier in a vice, and make up your own puller, using a bolt, with several large washers and large sockets, or drive the bushes out using a suitable drift (such as a large socket). If the DIY approach fails, entrust bush renewal to a Honda dealer.

Refitting

16 Refitting is a reversal of removal, noting the following points:

a) *Thoroughly clean (use solvent or carburettor cleaner, then dry them using compressed air) the points of contact between the driveshaft and the hub.*
b) *Wipe the wheel bearing's magnetic encoder clean of oil, grease, dust and any other foreign matter which might affect its operation, then refit the driveshaft fully into the hub, taking care not to damage the ABS wheel sensor. Apply a smear of oil to the seating surface of the new driveshaft nut, then screw it into place, tightening it hand-tight only at this stage.*
c) *Refit first the upper control arm to the hub carrier, tightening the bolt hand-tight only at this stage.*
d) *Refit the trailing arm-to-hub carrier front mounting bolt, tightening it hand-tight only at this stage.*
e) *Refit the trailing arm-to-hub carrier rear mounting (toe-adjusting) bolt and nut, aligning exactly the paint marks made on removal to restore the original toe setting. Until the rear wheel alignment has been checked, refit the old self-locking nut, tightening it hand-tight only at this stage.*
f) *Carefully load the suspension with the vehicle's weight by using a jack applied to the tubular section of the trailing arm (do not apply pressure to the flat, pressed-steel, lower transverse link), then tighten the bolts to their specified torque wrench settings.*
g) *Tighten all brake component fixings to the specified torque.*

h) If possible, do not fully tighten the driveshaft nut until the vehicle is resting on its wheels. Referring to the Warning earlier in this Section, tighten the new driveshaft nut to the specified torque (Chapter 8). Stake the nut collar into the driveshaft groove.

i) If applicable, refit the roadwheel, then lower the vehicle to the ground and tighten the roadwheel nuts to the specified torque.

j) Have the rear wheel alignment checked on completion. When the rear toe setting is accurately set, fit the trailing arm-to-hub carrier rear mounting (toe-adjusting) bolt's new self-locking nut and tighten it to the specified torque wrench setting.

10 Rear wheel bearings – renewal

Note 1: *A press, a suitable puller, or a selection of large bolts, washers and other improvised tools will be required for this operation. Obtain a bearing kit before proceeding.*

Note 2: *Keep any magnetic tools well away from the new bearing's magnetic encoder, or it will not function correctly and the ABS system will be disabled. Similarly, keep it clean of oil, grease, dust and any other foreign matter which might affect its operation and be careful not to damage it as the new bearing is installed.*

1 With the rear hub carrier removed as described in Section 9, proceed as described in Section 4. If the handbrake backplate hinders operations, remove it as described in Chapter 9.

2 On completion, refit the rear hub carrier as described in Section 9.

11 Rear suspension strut – removal, overhaul and refitting

Removal

1 Slacken the relevant rear wheel nuts. Chock the front wheels, select first or reverse gear (or P), then jack up the rear of the vehicle, and support securely on axle stands (see *Jacking and vehicle support*). Remove the rear roadwheel.

2 Unscrew the strut bottom mounting bolt, and separate the base of the unit from the trailing arm.

3 Open the rear door and tailgate, fold forwards the rear seats, then unclip the access panel from the luggage compartment side trim panel. Support the strut, then unscrew the two top mounting nuts, and withdraw the unit from the rear wheel arch **(see illustrations)**.

Overhaul

Note: *A spring compressor tool will be required for this operation.*

4 Refer to Section 5, paragraphs 7 to 14 but note the different components: remove the piston rod nut, followed by the top washer, top mounting plate with top and bottom bushes, dust cover, spring mounting cushion, the spring (with compressor tool still fitted), a flat washer, and finally the bump stop **(see illustration)**. **Note:** *The top mounting plate has a rubber bush in the top and bottom, which are actually separate, but usually remain attached during overhaul.*

5 Slide the bump stop onto the strut, followed by the flat washer **(see illustrations)**.

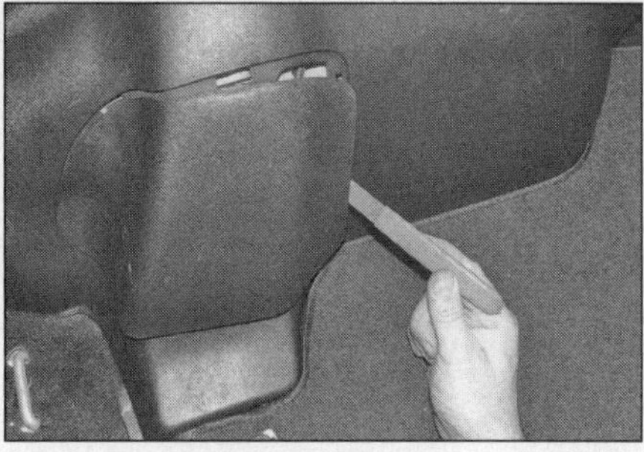

11.3a Fold forwards rear seats, then unclip access panel from luggage compartment side trim panel . . .

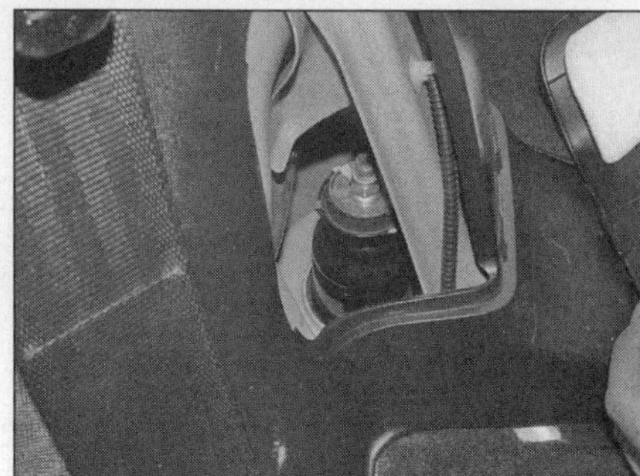

11.3b . . . to reach rear suspension strut top mounting . . .

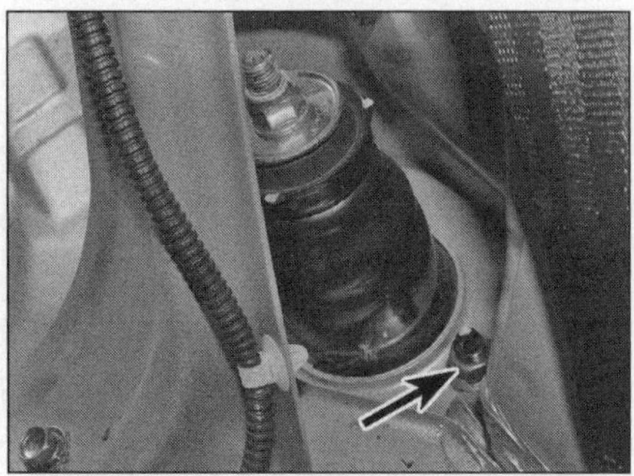

11.3c . . . and unscrew strut front . . .

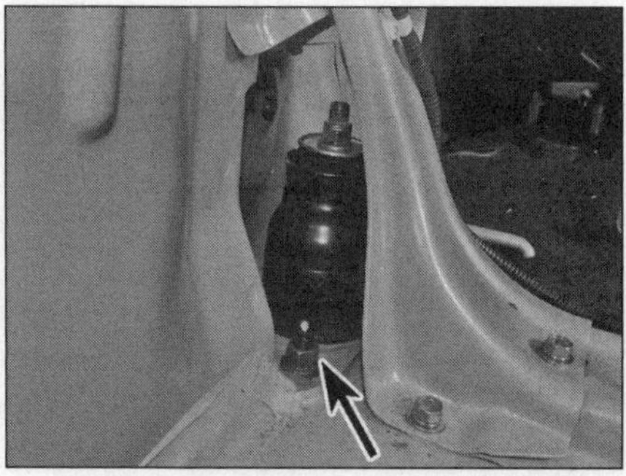

11.3d . . . and rear top mounting nuts

11.4a Fitting coil spring compressor – try to 'catch' as many coils as possible . . .

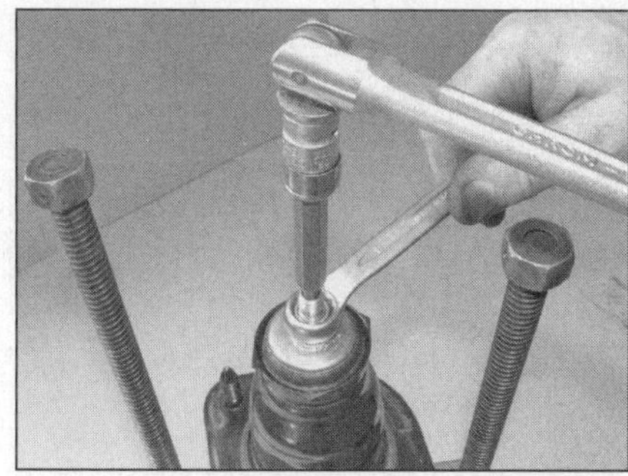

11.4b . . . then unscrew strut piston rod nut

11.5a Slide rubber bump stop onto strut . . .

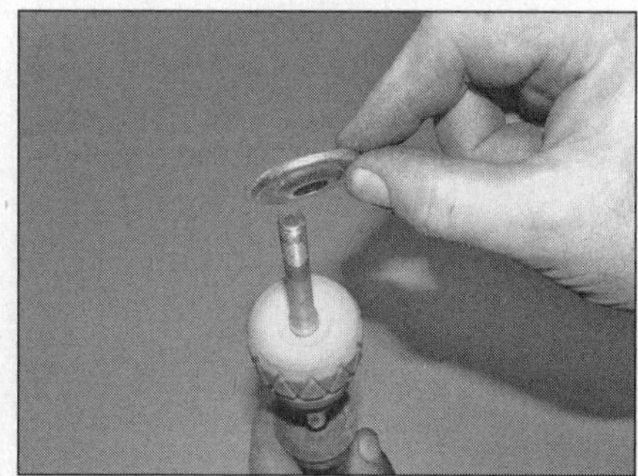

11.5b . . . followed by flat washer

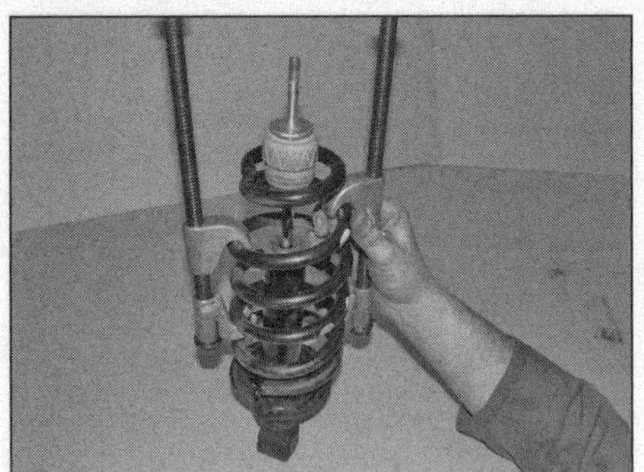
11.6a Fit spring to strut . . .

11.6b . . . so that spring lower end rests against stop on lower seat

11.7 Fit spring mounting cushion so spring fits cushion groove

11.8 Refit dust cover so that its locating projections fit into depressions in cushion

11.10 Heads of mounting plate's studs locate in recesses on top of dust cover. Small O mark (A) stamped in plate must face to inside of vehicle on refitting

6 Slide the spring (with compressor tool still fitted) over the strut, and position it so that the spring's bottom end is resting against the stop on the bottom seat **(see illustrations)**.

7 Refit the spring mounting cushion so that the spring fits into the cushion's groove – if the original components are being refitted, the original relationship should be easy to restore thanks to the marks left on the cushion **(see illustration)**.

8 Refit the dust cover so that its locating projections fit into the depressions in the cushion **(see illustration)**.

9 Fit the bottom bush to the underside of the top mounting plate, then fit the damper mounting collar and top bush into the recess in its upper surface.

10 Fit the top mounting plate and bushes, noting that the heads of the mounting plate's studs project from the underside of the plate, to locate in the recesses on top of the dust cover **(see illustration)**. Also, the small O mark stamped in the plate's top surface must face to the inside of the vehicle when the strut is refitted.

11 Refit the top washer and a new piston rod self-locking nut **(see illustrations)**.

12 Check that the strut components are aligned correctly. A line through the centres of the mounting studs should be 18 ± 3° clockwise from the axis of the strut's bottom mounting on the left-hand strut, and 18 ± 3° anti-clockwise from the axis of the strut's bottom mounting on the right-hand strut. Also, the small O mark stamped in the top mounting plate's top surface must face to the inside of the vehicle when the strut is refitted.

13 Tighten the new piston rod nut to the specified torque wrench setting; the easiest way of doing this is to use a reversible torque wrench (that can tighten left-hand threads) and a hexagon bit to tighten the piston rod while counterholding the nut with a spanner **(see illustration)**.

14 Slowly and evenly slacken the spring compressor tool to relieve the tension in the spring. Check that the ends of the spring locate correctly against the stops on the spring seats. If necessary, turn the spring and the upper seat so that the components locate correctly before the compressor tool is removed. Remove the compressor tool when the spring is fully seated.

Refitting

15 Refitting is a reversal of removal, noting the following points:

a) Offer the strut into position, with the small O mark stamped in the top mounting plate facing the inside of the vehicle, and loosely refit the two top mounting nuts. Guide the bottom end of the strut into

11.11a Refit top washer . . .

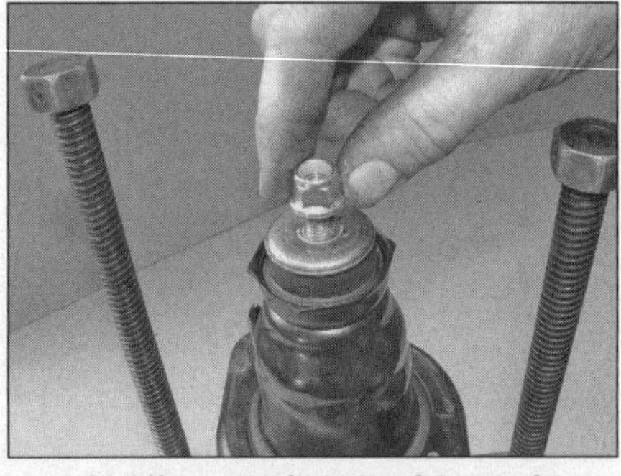
11.11b . . . and a new piston rod self-locking nut . . .

11.13 . . . and tighten to specified torque wrench setting

11.15a O mark (arrow) stamped in top mounting plate must face to inside of vehicle on refitting rear suspension strut

position on the trailing arm, then loosely refit the bottom mounting bolt **(see illustration)**.

b) Carefully load the suspension with the vehicle's weight by using a jack applied to the tubular section of the trailing arm (do not apply pressure to the flat, pressed-steel, lower transverse link).

c) Tighten the lower mounting bolt and the two upper mounting nuts to their specified torque wrench settings, then lower the jack **(see illustrations)**.

d) Refit the rear wheel, then lower the vehicle to the ground and tighten the wheel nuts to the specified torque.

12 Rear suspension upper arm – removal and refitting

1 Slacken the relevant rear wheel nuts, chock the front wheels, select first or reverse gear (or P), then jack up the rear of the vehicle and support it on axle stands (see *Jacking and vehicle support*). Remove the relevant rear roadwheel.

2 Support the weight of the rear hub carrier – do not compress the suspension significantly – by placing a jack under the tubular section of the trailing arm (do not apply pressure to the flat, pressed-steel, lower transverse link).

3 Remove (unclip or unbolt, depending on fasteners used) the ABS wheel sensor wiring harness support bracket from the upper arm.

4 Unscrew the arm pivot bolts and remove the arm from the vehicle **(see illustration)**.

5 The arm's inboard bush is not available separately; the arm must be renewed complete if it is bent, damaged or if the bush is worn or damaged. The outboard bush is available separately and is renewed as described in Section 9.

6 Refitting is a reversal of removal, noting the following points:

a) Fit the bolts hand-tight initially.

b) Carefully load the suspension with the vehicle's weight by using a jack applied to the tubular section of the trailing arm (do not apply pressure to the flat, pressed-steel, lower transverse link).

c) Tighten the nuts to the specified torque.

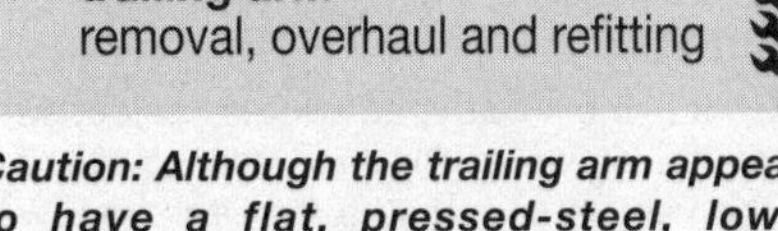

13 Rear suspension trailing arm – removal, overhaul and refitting

Caution: Although the trailing arm appears to have a flat, pressed-steel, lower transverse link bolted to its rear end, in fact Honda state that these bolts must never be slackened or otherwise disturbed.

Removal

1 Slacken the relevant rear wheel nuts. Chock the front wheels, select first or reverse gear (or P), then jack up the rear of the vehicle, and support securely on axle stands (see *Jacking and vehicle support*). Remove the rear roadwheel.

2 Remove the rear hub carrier as described in Section 9.

3 Support the weight of the trailing arm – do not compress the suspension significantly – by placing a jack under the tubular section of the trailing arm (do not apply pressure to the flat, pressed-steel, lower transverse link).

4 Unscrew the nut securing the anti-roll bar drop link to the trailing arm – use an Allen key to stop the drop link balljoint turning as this is done. Unhook the drop link from the arm.

5 Unscrew the strut bottom mounting bolt, and separate the base of the unit from the trailing arm.

6 Unscrew and remove the two trailing arm front mounting bolts from the underbody **(see illustration)**.

7 Unscrew the pivot bolt securing the trailing arm lower transverse link to the subframe **(see illustration)**, then lower the arm on the jack and remove it from under the vehicle.

Overhaul

8 Examine the rubber bushes for wear and damage, and check the arm for straightness, as it could have been bent by careless jacking-up; remove the shield over the lower transverse link to ensure that there is no hidden damage. If the checks outlined in Chapter 1A or 1B have revealed play at any of these points, or if any other signs of wear or damage are discernible, the component concerned must be renewed. At the time of writing, it does not appear that the trailing arm front mounting bushes are available separately, and therefore the complete trailing arm must be renewed if these are worn or damaged **(see illustration)**.

9 The pivot bush fitted to the lower transverse

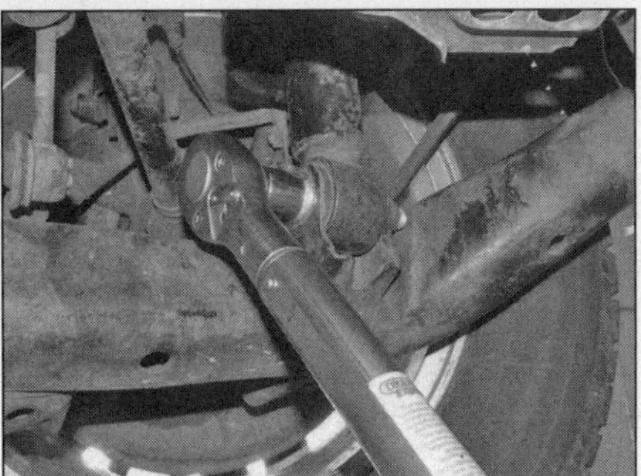

11.15b Tighten strut lower mounting bolt to specified torque wrench setting

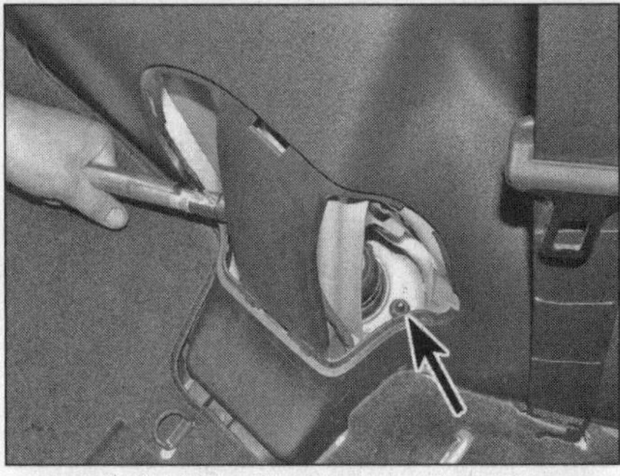

11.15c Then tighten strut top mounting nuts to specified torque wrench setting

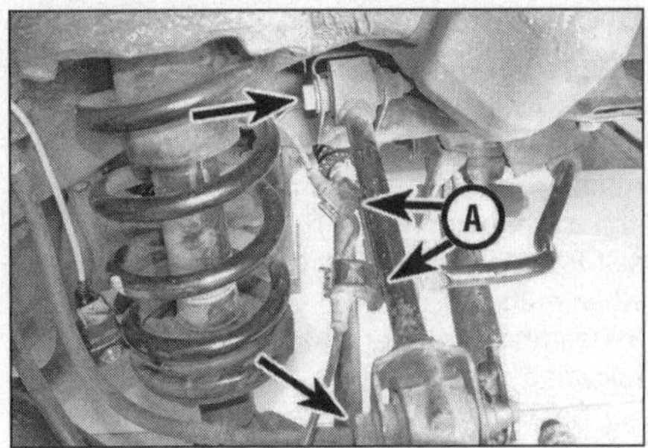

12.4 Upper control arm pivot bolts. Note ABS wheel sensor wiring harness support bracket fasteners (A)

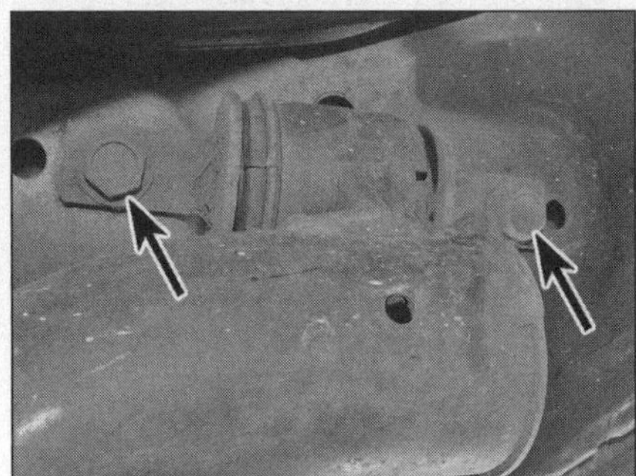

13.6 Rear suspension trailing arm front mounting bolts on underbody

13.7 Petrol models have mass damper fitted to pivot bolt securing trailing arm lower transverse link to subframe

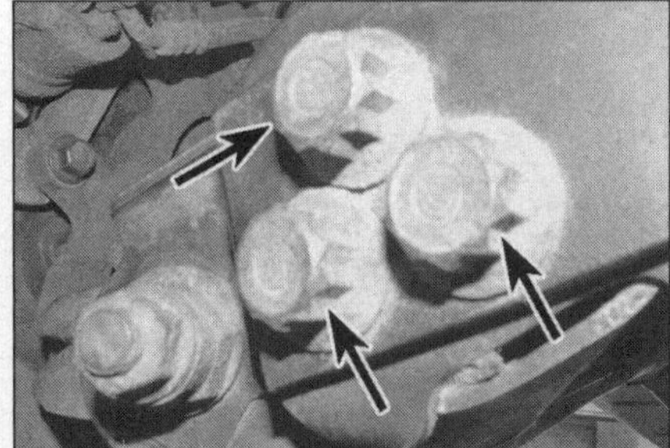

13.8 Do NOT disturb trailing arm lateral link-to-trailing arm tubular section Torx bolts

14.2 Rear anti-roll bar mounting clamp and bolts on subframe. Note paint mark showing bush location

link-to-subframe mounting is available separately. A press and adapters will be required for driving out the bush; carefully measure the exact fitted position of the bush before disturbing it and check whether the bush is shouldered and so must be pressed out in one particular direction. In the absence of this tool, mount the trailing arm in a vice, and make up your own puller, using a bolt, with several large washers and large sockets, or drive the bushes out using a suitable drift (such as a large socket). If the DIY approach fails, entrust bush renewal to a Honda dealer.

Refitting

10 Refitting is a reversal of removal, noting the following points:

a) Offer the arm into position, and loosely refit the three mounting bolts. Guide the bottom end of the strut into position on the trailing arm, then loosely refit the bottom mounting bolt. Reconnect the anti-roll bar drop link to the arm and refit the nut, tightened hand-tight only at this stage.

b) Carefully load the suspension with the vehicle's weight by using a jack applied to the tubular section of the trailing arm (do not apply pressure to the flat, pressed-steel, lower transverse link).

c) Tighten all nuts and bolts to the specified torque.

d) Refit the hub carrier as described in Section 9.

e) Refit the rear wheel, then lower the vehicle to the ground and tighten the wheel nuts to the specified torque.

14.7a Rear anti-roll bar drop link-to-bar connection

14 Rear anti-roll bar, bushes and drop links – removal and refitting

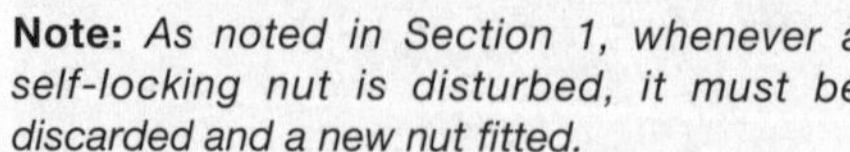

Note: *As noted in Section 1, whenever a self-locking nut is disturbed, it must be discarded and a new nut fitted.*

1 Slacken the rear wheel nuts. Chock the front wheels, select first or reverse gear (or position P), then jack up the rear of the vehicle, and support it securely on axle stands (see *Jacking and vehicle support*). Remove the rear wheels.

Bushes

2 If the bushes alone are to be renewed, working on one side at a time, unscrew the two bolts and remove the anti-roll bar mounting clamp **(see illustration)**. The bar can then be pulled away slightly, and the bush removed (the bush is split for easy removal); note the paint marks on the arm, inboard of each bush.

3 Slip the new bush into place around the roll bar – if necessary, lubricate the bush with a little liquid soap first. Align the bush with the painted mark on the roll bar, to make initial fitting more accurate.

4 Refit the clamp. Slide the bush along the bar slightly if required, to bring the clamp bolt holes into alignment. Tighten the clamp bolts to the specified torque.

5 Repeat the procedure on the other side.

6 On completion, refit the wheels, then lower the vehicle to the ground and tighten the wheel nuts to the specified torque.

Drop links

7 Unscrew the nut at each end of the link – use an Allen key to stop the drop link balljoints turning as this is done **(see illustrations)**. Remove the drop link from the trailing arm and anti-roll bar, noting how it is fitted. Discard the self-locking nuts – new ones should be used when refitting.

8 Refitting is a reversal of removal, noting the following points:

a) Set the balljoint pins to the centre of their movement in all directions.

b) Use new self-locking nuts on the upper balljoint of the anti-roll bar drop links (see also note above).

c) Carefully load the suspension with the vehicle's weight by using a jack applied to the tubular section of the trailing arm (do not apply pressure to the flat, pressed-steel, lower transverse link), then tighten the nuts to their specified torque wrench settings.

d) On completion, refit the wheels, then lower the vehicle to the ground and tighten the wheel nuts to the specified torque.

e) After 5 minutes of driving, retighten the self-locking nuts to the specified torque.

14.7b Rear anti-roll bar drop link-to-trailing arm connection

Anti-roll bar

9 The anti-roll bar is not symmetrical; before unbolting it, mark it with chalk, touch-up paint or a marker pen to ensure it is refitted the correct way round.

10 Unscrew the nut securing each of the two anti-roll bar drop links to the anti-roll bar or to the trailing arm – use an Allen key to stop the drop link balljoint turning as this is done. Disconnect the drop links from the bar or trailing arm. Discard the self-locking nuts – new ones should be used when refitting.

11 Unbolt the two anti-roll bar clamps, then remove the clamps and withdraw the bar from under the vehicle. If the drop links are still attached to the bar, they can be removed if required; all components are available separately if renewal is necessary.

12 Refitting is a reversal of removal, noting the following points:

a) Ensure that the bar is fitted the correct way round.

b) Fit the bushes as described in paragraph 3.

c) Refit the clamps and tighten the bolts to the specified torque wrench setting.

d) Refit and/or reconnect the drop links, as described in paragraph 7.

e) On completion, refit the wheels, then lower the vehicle to the ground and tighten the wheel nuts to the specified torque.

15 Rear suspension subframe – removal and refitting

Note: *The subframe bolts must be renewed as a matter of course on reassembly. The aid of an assistant will also prove useful in lowering the subframe.*

Removal

1 Chock the front roadwheels, select first or reverse gear (or P), then jack up the rear of the vehicle and ensure that it is very well supported, using well-placed, good-quality axle stands (see *Jacking and vehicle support*). Note that the vehicle must be raised sufficiently high for the subframe to be lowered and withdrawn from underneath.

2 Remove the rear wheels. Fit jacks, axle stands or blocks under the tubular section of the rear suspension trailing arm (do not apply pressure to the flat, pressed-steel, lower transverse link), to take the weight of the suspension; do not compress the suspension significantly.

3 Unbolt the final drive unit rear mounting from the subframe (Chapter 8).

4 Unscrew the pivot bolts securing the trailing arms' lower transverse links to the subframe (Section 13).

5 Unscrew the upper control arm inboard pivot bolts and release the arms from the subframe (Section 12).

6 Unscrew the nut securing each of the two anti-roll bar drop links to the anti-roll bar or to the trailing arm – use an Allen key to stop the drop link balljoint turning as this is done. Disconnect the drop links from the bar or trailing arm. Discard the self-locking nuts – new ones should be used when refitting.

7 If the anti-roll bar itself is likely to hinder removal of the subframe, unbolt it at this stage (Section 14). Otherwise it can remain on the subframe.

8 On petrol-engined models, unbolt the charcoal canister cover and the canister itself. Secure the canister assembly clear of the working area, disconnecting hoses only as necessary to permit this (refer to Chapter 4C if required).

9 With reference to Chapter 4A or 4B, remove the exhaust tail pipe/silencer. If it is decided simply to unhook the system from its mountings and allow it to hang down until there is sufficient clearance to remove the subframe (not recommended, especially on petrol-engined models which have no flexible section at the front), do not allow the exhaust to drop too far and support it carefully to ensure that there is no damage to any of the exhaust system's components. Disconnect or release the leads to the oxygen sensors, etc, to ensure that there is no damage caused to the wiring harnesses.

10 Check around the subframe to ensure that there are no brackets, hoses or harnesses still attached, or anything in the way which would prevent it from being lowered.

11 The subframe is secured to the body by four bolts **(see illustrations)**. Clean the area around each and make your own subframe-to-body marks with white paint or similar (do not use a sharp-pointed scriber, which might break the underbody protective coating and cause rusting) to mark the exact relationship of the subframe to the underbody. Holes have been made in the subframe at all four points, but corresponding holes have been made in the underbody only next to each rear mounting point to allow the subframe to be located with tapered guides. Fit two lengths of threaded rod through both holes and secure them with nuts to act as guides to correct location on refitting (see Section 8).

12 Support the subframe with a transmission jack or a large trolley jack and a flat piece of wood. Have an assistant ready to support the subframe as the jack is lowered. Unscrew the subframe bolts.

13 Lower the subframe to clear the engine/transmission mountings, then withdraw it from under the vehicle.

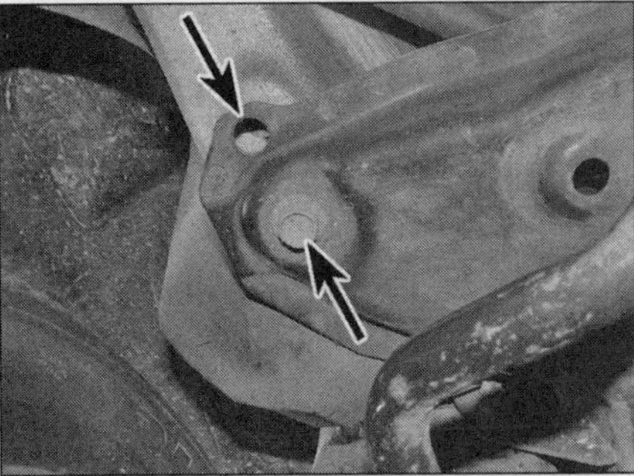

15.11a Rear suspension subframe is secured by four bolts: rear left-hand mounting . . .

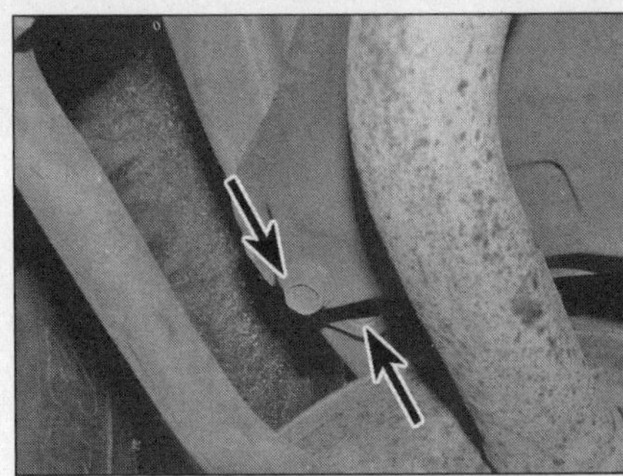

15.11b . . . and rear right-hand mounting bolt – note reference holes in subframe and underbody for alignment on refitting

15.11c Front right-hand mounting bolt

15.11d Front left-hand mounting bolt – all bolts must be renewed on refitting

14 Note that the four subframe bolts are only intended to be used once, and new ones should be obtained for refitting. The dampers, where fitted, can be unbolted if required.

Refitting

Note: *It is essential that the subframe is re-aligned exactly on its mountings or the wheel alignment and steering geometry will be upset and will be difficult to set accurately.*

15 With the any items that were removed refitted, offer up the subframe and fit the new subframe bolts, tightening them only lightly at this stage.

16 The subframe must now be aligned on the underbody. If guides have been made as suggested, use them to align the subframe precisely. If these were not used, you can align the subframe by eye, centring the subframe aligning holes on those of the underbody, and using the marks made on removal for assistance. Alternatively, you can align the subframe using a tapered drift (such as a clutch-aligning tool), or even a deep socket spanner of suitable size.

17 Once the subframe is aligned as precisely as possible, tighten its bolts to the specified torque wrench setting without disturbing its position. Recheck the alignment once all the bolts are securely tightened.

18 The remainder of refitting is a reversal of removal, noting the following points:

a) *Refit the final drive unit rear mounting, tightening its bolts to the specified torque wrench settings (Chapter 8).*

b) *Refit the trailing arms' lower transverse links to the subframe, tightening the bolts hand-tight only at this stage.*

c) *Refit the upper control arms to the subframe, tightening the bolts hand-tight only at this stage.*

d) *Carefully load the suspension with the vehicle's weight by using a jack applied to the tubular section of the trailing arm (do not apply pressure to the flat, pressed-steel, lower transverse link), then tighten the bolts to their specified torque wrench settings.*

e) *Reconnect the anti-roll bar drop links to the bar or trailing arms. While the suspension is still loaded with the vehicle's weight, tighten the nut to the specified torque, holding the drop link balljoint with an Allen key as for removal.*

f) *Refit the exhaust tail pipe/silencer as described in Chapter 4A or 4B and, where applicable, the charcoal canister (Chapter 4C).*

g) *Refit the roadwheels, then lower the vehicle to the ground and tighten the roadwheel nuts to the specified torque.*

h) *Remember that, since the rear suspension subframe has been disturbed, the wheel alignment must be checked fully and carefully as soon as possible, with any necessary adjustments being made. This operation is best carried out by an experienced mechanic, using proper checking equipment; the vehicle should therefore be taken to a Honda dealer or similarly-qualified person for attention.*

16.4 Disconnect the horn wiring plug from the steering wheel

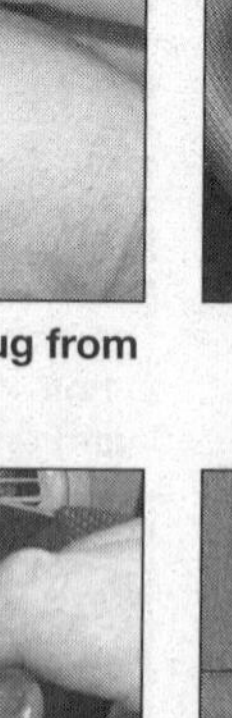

16.6 Make an alignment mark between steering wheel and column, to make refitting easier. Note holes threaded for steering wheel puller (but see Note in text)

16 Steering wheel – removal and refitting

Removal

1 Ensure that the front wheels are pointing in the straight-ahead position.

2 Switch off the ignition, disconnect the battery negative lead, and position the lead away from the battery (see *Disconnecting the battery*). Wait at least three minutes before proceeding. If this waiting period is not observed, there is a danger of accidentally activating the airbag(s).

3 Remove the airbag unit from the steering wheel as described in Chapter 12.

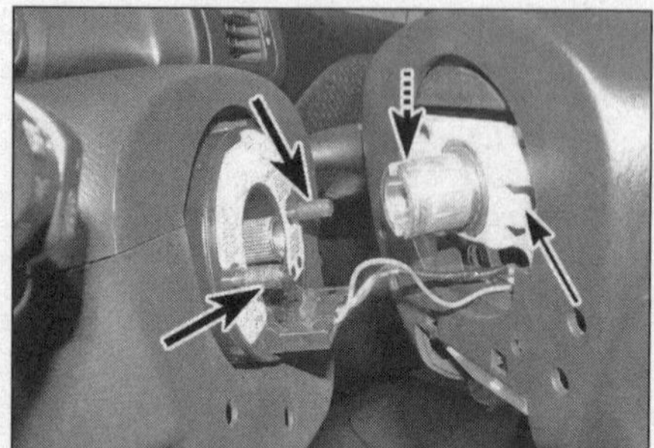

16.12 Airbag clock spring two locating pins must enter recesses on back of steering wheel

16.5 Unscrew the steering wheel bolt, while holding the wheel rim

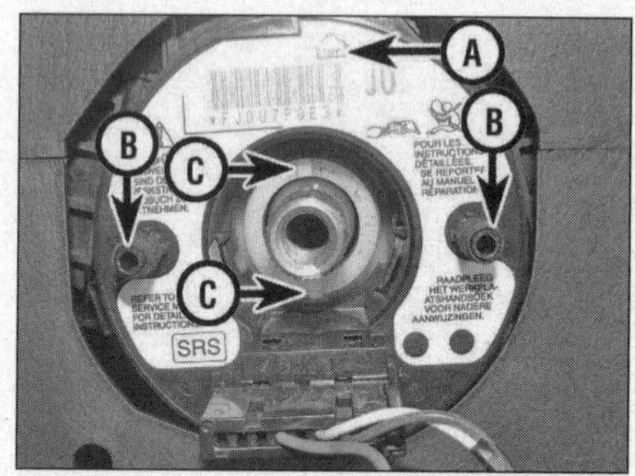

16.11 Airbag clock spring must be in central position, with arrow mark (A) pointing straight up and two locating pins (B) horizontal, and direction indicator self-cancelling tabs (C) should be vertical

4 Disconnect the horn wiring connector on the left-hand side of the wheel **(see illustration)**. Where applicable, also disconnect the switch wiring on the left and right-hand sides of the wheel, and the clock spring connector.

5 Prevent the steering wheel from turning by grasping the rim firmly, then unscrew and remove the steering wheel securing bolt. Do not rely on the steering column lock to prevent the wheel turning, as this may damage the lock **(see illustration)**.

6 If one is not already present, make an alignment mark between the steering wheel and the column, to make refitting easier **(see illustration)**.

7 Grip the steering wheel on each side (or top and bottom), then pull and withdraw it from the splines on the end of the column. Do not tap on the wheel or steering column to release the steering wheel.

16.13 Tighten steering wheel bolt to specified torque wrench setting

8 If the wheel proves difficult to remove, use a puller to release it from the splines. Two threaded holes are provided, which may be used with two bolts, a strong metal plate and a socket as a spacer, to free the wheel. **Note:** *If a puller or two bolts are used do NOT screw them into the wheel for more than five threads, or the clock spring will be damaged; fit nuts five threads up on the puller legs or bolts to ensure that they cannot be screwed in too deeply.*

Refitting

9 Make sure that the front wheels are pointing in the straight-ahead position.

10 If not already done, set the airbag clock spring to its central position, as described in Chapter 12.

11 The two direction indicator self-cancelling tabs should be in the vertical position, and the airbag clock spring's two locating pins should be horizontal **(see illustration)**.

12 Offer the steering wheel into position, ensuring that the recesses on the back of the wheel fit over the airbag clock spring's two pins and that the marks align that were made or noted on removal **(see illustration)**.

13 Refit the steering wheel securing bolt, and tighten to the specified torque – again, do not rely on the steering column lock to hold the wheel as the bolt is tightened **(see illustration)**.

14 The remainder of the refitting procedure is a reversal of removal. Ensure that the battery is still disconnected before refitting the airbag unit as described in Chapter 12.

17 Steering column – removal and refitting

Note: *Ensure that the front wheels are pointing in the straight-ahead position.*

Removal

1 Switch off the ignition, disconnect the battery negative lead, and position the lead away from the battery (see *Disconnecting the battery*). Wait at least three minutes before proceeding. If this waiting period is not observed, there is a danger of accidentally activating the airbag(s).

2 Remove the steering wheel as described in Section 16.

3 Remove the steering column shrouds (Chapter 11).

4 Remove the steering column switch assembly, and disconnect the three wiring plugs from the ignition switch and related components, as described in Chapter 12, Section 4.

5 Move the driver's seat fully to the rear, to allow maximum working area.

6 With reference to Chapter 11, remove the driver's side under cover and lower cover from the facia.

7 Detach the wiring harness from the column, noting how it is routed **(see illustration)**.

8 Working in the footwell, unscrew the upper pinch-bolt securing the column shaft to the universal joint **(see illustration)**. Note that the bolt-hole aligns with the flat machined in the column splines.

9 Unscrew the steering column's two upper mounting nuts and two lower mounting bolts, and lower the column assembly into the footwell. Pull the column rearwards to separate it from the universal joint, and it can then be removed from the vehicle **(see illustrations)**.

Inspection

10 Check the column for obvious signs of damage, then check the upper and lower bearings for play. Check the condition of the sliding bushes on the column adjustment linkage. The column is only available as a complete assembly.

Refitting

11 Refitting is a reversal of removal, noting the following points:

a) Align the upper pinch-bolt hole in the joint with the flat in the splines when refitting the column to the universal joint.

b) Tighten all fixings to the specified torque.

c) Ensure that the column wiring harness is routed correctly, and securely re-attached. Also ensure that all wiring connections are properly remade.

d) Refit the steering wheel as described in Section 16.

18 Ignition switch/steering lock – removal and refitting

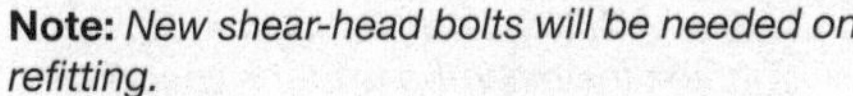

Note: *New shear-head bolts will be needed on refitting.*

Removal

1 Remove the steering column (Section 17).

2 Mount the column carefully in a vice.

3 Mark both bolts with a centre-punch (they are of shear-head type, so cannot be unscrewed), and drill them out with a 5 mm drill bit; be careful not to damage the switch body **(see illustrations)**.

4 Take off the ignition switch upper clamp, and remove the switch body.

Refitting

5 Refitting is a reversal of removal, noting the following points:

a) New shear-head bolts will be needed. Before tightening then fully, refit the switch hand-tight with the key removed, then insert the key and test the operation of the steering lock. When everything is working correctly, remove the ignition key and tighten the shear-head bolts until their heads snap off.

b) On completion, reconnect the battery and confirm correct switch operation.

17.7 Unclip the wiring harness from the steering column

17.8 Unscrew upper pinch-bolt securing universal joint to steering column

17.9a Unscrew upper nut and lower bolt each side . . .

17.9b . . . then lower steering column, and remove it

19 Steering rack – removal and refitting

Note: *A moaning/groaning noise when manoeuvring on full lock can be due to premature degradation of the final drive fluid. This may be easily misdiagnosed as a steering rack problem, and may lead to unnecessary repairs. If this is suspected, the first course of action is to renew the final drive fluid as described in Chapter 1A or 1B*

Note: *The track rod end balljoint split pins must be renewed as a matter of course on reassembly.*

Removal

1 Set the front wheels to the straight-ahead position, and engage the steering lock. The lock must be engaged, to prevent the column from turning during rack removal – which might otherwise cause damage to the airbag clock spring.

2 Switch off the ignition, disconnect the battery negative lead, and position the lead away from the battery (see *Disconnecting the battery*). Wait at least three minutes before proceeding. If this waiting period is not observed, there is a danger of accidentally activating the airbag(s).

3 Remove the steering wheel as described in Section 16.

4 Move the driver's seat fully to the rear, to allow maximum working area.

5 With reference to Chapter 11, remove the driver's side under cover and lower cover from the facia.

6 Working in the footwell, unscrew both pinch-bolts securing the universal joint to the steering column and to the rack pinion shaft. Noting which way round the joint is fitted,

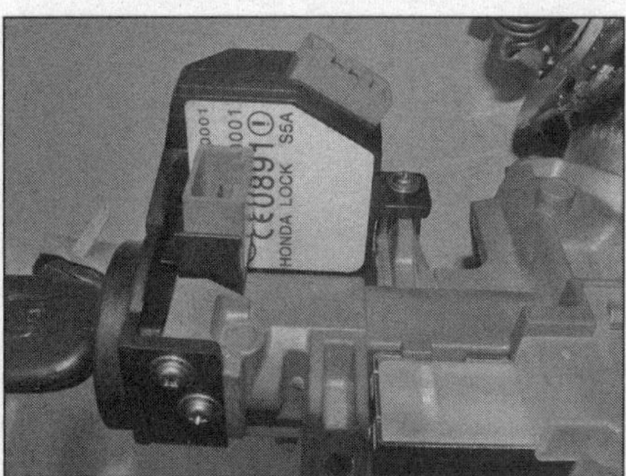

18.3a To remove ignition switch/steering lock from steering column . . .

18.3b . . . shear-head retaining bolts must be drilled out

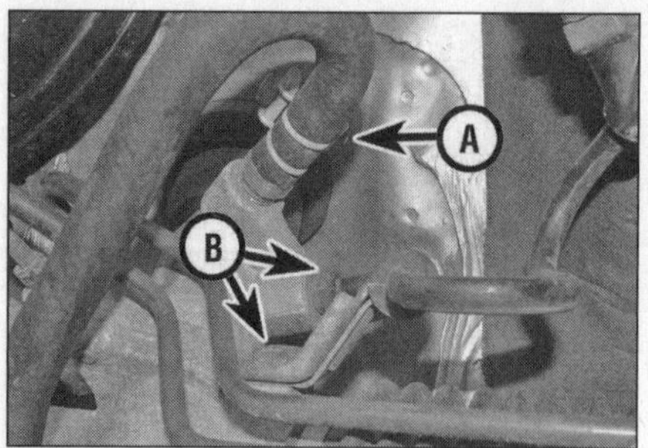

19.11a Slacken hose clamp (A) to disconnect fluid return hose from steering rack, then unscrew fluid pipe union nut and unbolt support bracket (B)

19.11b Unbolt hose support bracket from front of rack

either remove it or slide it up the column splines until it is clear of the rack pinion shaft splines, and secure it there with a rubber band. If a centre guide is fitted to the top of the pinion shaft, remove and discard it.

7 In the engine compartment, gain access to the steering rack by removing the air cleaner assembly and intake air duct/resonator as described in Chapter 4A or 4B.

8 Slacken the front wheel nuts, then jack up the front of the vehicle, and support it securely on axle stands (see *Jacking and vehicle support*). Remove the front wheels.

9 Extract the split pin from each track rod end balljoint nut (new split pins will be needed when refitting). Unscrew the nut, but leave it attached by a couple of threads for now.

10 Disconnect the track rod end from each strut, either using a balljoint separator tool, or by tapping the end of the balljoint stud (use a block of wood and the still-fitted nut to protect the threads). When the balljoint separates, unscrew the nut completely, and move the track rod clear. Secure both track rods to the steering rack so that they do not hinder removal.

11 Slacken the hose clamp securing the fluid return hose to the top of the rack. Wrap some absorbent cloth around the hose union, then disconnect it from the rack. If possible, plug or tape over the opened connection to reduce further fluid loss, and prevent the entry of dirt into the system. Unbolt the hose support bracket from the front of the rack **(see illustrations)**.

12 Unscrew the fluid pipe 14 mm union nut and unbolt the support bracket from the top of the rack, then disconnect the pipe from the rack, plugging or taping-over the opened connection to reduce further fluid loss and prevent the entry of dirt.

13 Unscrew the two steering rack-to-bulkhead bolts from the right-hand end of the rack, and recover the stiffener plate (where fitted) and the washers **(see illustration)**.

14 Unscrew the steering rack-to-bulkhead bolt and nut from the left-hand end of the rack, and recover the clamp **(see illustration)**.

15 Move the rack forwards to clear the bulkhead, then lower it at the pinion shaft end, to free the grommet (the grommet can also be 'helped' out from inside the vehicle, if necessary). When the pinion shaft is free of the bulkhead, twist the rack round so that the pinion shaft points vertically upwards. Remove the grommet from the pinion shaft housing.

16 Holding the rack and track rods together, and rotating it as necessary so that the pinion shaft clears the bodywork, manoeuvre the assembly out through the wheel arch aperture; the driver's side is probably easiest. As the rack is being removed, take great care not to damage the gaiters.

17 Recover and check the condition of the mounting components, particularly the pinion shaft grommet and the rack left-hand mounting rubber; renew any component that shows signs of wear or damage.

Refitting

18 Refitting is a reversal of removal, noting the following points:

a) Fit the left-hand mounting rubber to the rack, split or cut-out at the bottom.
b) Offer the rack carefully into position, again taking care not to damage any of the bulkhead hoses or components. Feed the pinion into the vehicle, and engage the grommet. To avoid water leaks into the passenger compartment in the future, check carefully that the grommet is correctly fitted all the way round.
c) Refit the two steering rack-to-bulkhead bolts to the right-hand end of the rack, with the washers and stiffener plate (where fitted); note that the stiffener plate must be fitted with its stamped arrow mark pointing upwards. Tighten the bolts hand-tight only at this stage.
d) Refit the mounting clamp – stamped arrow mark pointing upwards – to the left-hand end of the rack, with the bolt and nut. Tighten the bolt and nut hand-tight only at this stage.
e) Check that the rack is settled fully on its mountings, then tighten the left-hand bolt and nut (tighten them alternately, in two or more stages, working up to the specified torque setting), followed by the right-hand bolts.
f) Reconnect the fluid feed pipe and return hose to the rack and refit the support bracket; tighten all fasteners to their specified torque wrench settings.
g) Use new split pins when reconnecting the track rod ends. See Section 22.
h) When reconnecting the steering column universal joint, ensure that the lower (shorter, with a rounded collar) end fits on the pinion shaft and its bolt-hole aligns with the pinion shaft groove, while the upper (longer, flat U-shaped) end fits on the steering column and that its bolt-hole aligns with the flat in the column splines. Tighten the pinch-bolts to the specified torque.
i) On completion, top-up and bleed the power steering system as described in Section 26.
j) Have the front wheel alignment checked and if necessary adjusted as soon as possible.

19.13 Steering rack-to-bulkhead bolts – right-hand end

19.14 Steering rack-to-bulkhead bolt, nut and clamp – left-hand end

20 Steering rack rubber gaiters – renewal

The steering rack components are protected by two rubber gaiters; one at the left-hand end and one one-piece gaiter at the centre, covering the track rod connection. While the shorter gaiter can be slid off the rack left-hand end without too much trouble, this is not recommended due to the risk of getting dirt and debris in the rack's working parts; the gaiter should only be renewed once the rack has been removed. The centre gaiter can only be reached once the rack has been removed and dismantled to a considerable extent.

22.6a Extract split pin from balljoint nut and unscrew nut . . .

Dismantling the rack requires tools which will not be readily available to the DIY mechanic, so this work must be entrusted to a Honda dealer. Depending on the age and condition of the rack, it might be worth investigating the cost of a new or exchange rack in the event of new gaiters being needed.

21 Steering rack – overhaul and guide adjustment

Overhaul

1 Dismantling the rack requires tools which will not be readily available to the DIY mechanic, so this work must be entrusted to a Honda dealer. The cost and availability of parts might well render attempts at overhaul uneconomic. Depending on the nature of the problem, it might be worth investigating the cost of a new or exchange rack in the event of repairs being needed.

Guide adjustment

2 The CR-V has an adjustable guide (sometimes known as the 'slipper') fitted below the steering rack. If any unusual rattling or vibration is felt through the steering wheel when travelling over rough roads, it is possible that the noise could be the rack, rattling up and down inside the steering rack housing. The rack guide can be adjusted, to take out this vertical movement. This is not in itself a difficult operation, but special tools are required, and the job must be performed to a high level of accuracy – overtightening the adjuster will lead to stiff steering, which could be dangerous. It is therefore recommended that this job is entrusted to a Honda dealer.

22 Track rod end balljoint – removal and refitting

1 If the track rod end balljoint rubber boot is damaged, a new one can be obtained from Honda dealers. Once the track rod end has been disconnected (as described later in this Section), the old boot can be prised off. Wipe the balljoint clean (do not use excessive amounts of solvent), then pack it with fresh grease and fit the new boot, pressing it firmly into place until it is fully seated all the way round. However, bear in mind that if the boot has been damaged for some time, it is likely that dirt will have got into the balljoint, and a new track rod end may soon be needed.

22.6b . . . then release balljoint from strut using balljoint separator (take care not to damage rubber boot)

2 If the complete track rod end is to be renewed, proceed as follows:

Removal

Note: *The track rod end balljoint split pins must be renewed as a matter of course on reassembly.*

3 Slacken the relevant front wheel nuts. Apply the handbrake, then jack up the front of the vehicle, and support securely on axle stands (see *Jacking and vehicle support*). Remove the wheel.

4 Scrub clean the threads of the track rod using a wire brush and apply some lubricant. Hold the track rod end balljoint stationary with an open-ended spanner applied to its flats, and, using a suitable spanner, slacken by a quarter-turn the balljoint locknut.

5 Extract the split pin from the track rod end balljoint nut (a new split pin will be needed when refitting). Unscrew the nut, but leave it attached by a couple of threads for now.

6 Disconnect the track rod end balljoint from the strut, either using a balljoint separator tool, or by tapping the end of the balljoint stud (use a block of wood and the still-fitted nut to protect the threads). If the balljoint is to be re-used, take care not to damage the rubber boot when using the separator tool. When the balljoint separates, unscrew the nut completely, and move the track rod clear **(see illustrations)**.

22.6c With the balljoint separated, unscrew nut and move track rod clear

7 Unscrew the track rod end balljoint from the track rod, counting the number of turns necessary to remove it. If necessary, hold the track rod stationary with an open-ended spanner applied to its flats.

8 Carefully clean the balljoint/strut tapers and the track rod threads. Renew the balljoint if its movement is sloppy or too stiff, if it is excessively worn, or if it is damaged in any way; carefully check the stud taper and threads. If the balljoint rubber boot is damaged, it must be renewed as described above.

Refitting

9 Screw the track rod end balljoint on to the track rod the number of turns noted during removal.

10 Clean the balljoint and its seat in the steering arm before fitting – it must be fitted dry. Offer the balljoint into position, taking care not to damage the boot.

11 Tighten the balljoint nut to the specified torque. If the balljoint shank turns while the nut is being tightened, press down on the balljoint. The tapered fit of the shank will lock it and prevent rotation as the nut is tightened. Fit a new pin to secure, then tighten the balljoint locknut while holding the track rod stationary **(see illustrations)**.

12 Refit the roadwheel, then lower the vehicle to the ground, and tighten the wheel nuts to the specified torque.

22.11a On refitting, tighten balljoint nut to specified torque wrench setting . . .

22.11b . . . fit new split pin . . .

22.11c ... and spread ends as shown to secure

13 Have the front wheel alignment checked (see Section 27) at the earliest opportunity.

23 Track rods – removal and refitting

Note: *The track rod outboard end balljoint split pins and inboard end balljoint lockwashers must be renewed as a matter of course on reassembly.*

Removal

1 Set the front wheels to the straight-ahead position, and engage the steering lock. The lock must be engaged, to prevent the column from turning during track rod removal – which might otherwise cause damage to the airbag clock spring.

2 In the engine compartment, gain access to the steering rack by removing the air cleaner assembly and intake air duct/resonator as described in Chapter 4A or 4B.

3 Slacken the relevant front wheel nuts, then jack up the front of the vehicle, and support it securely on axle stands (see *Jacking and vehicle support*). Remove the wheel.

4 Scrub clean the threads of the track rod outboard end using a wire brush, and apply some lubricant. Hold the track rod end balljoint stationary with an open-ended spanner applied to its flats, and, using a suitable spanner, slacken by a quarter-turn the balljoint locknut.

5 Extract the split pin from the track rod outboard end balljoint nut (a new split pin will be needed when refitting). Unscrew the nut, but leave it attached by a couple of threads for now.

6 Disconnect the track rod outboard end balljoint from the strut, either using a balljoint separator tool, or by tapping the end of the balljoint stud (use a block of wood and the still-fitted nut to protect the threads). If the balljoint is to be re-used, take care not to damage the rubber boot when using the separator tool. When the balljoint separates, unscrew the nut completely, and move the track rod clear.

7 Unscrew the track rod outboard end balljoint from the track rod, counting the number of turns necessary to remove it. If necessary, hold the track rod stationary with an open-ended spanner applied to its flats.

8 Using a hammer and suitable punch, raise the flattened locking tab of the track rod inboard joint's lockwasher **(see illustration)**.

9 Hold the steering rack bracket with one open-ended spanner to prevent damage to the rack's components, and unscrew the track rod from the rack. Recover and discard the lockwasher – a new one should be used when refitting.

10 Carefully clean the balljoint/strut tapers and the track rod threads. Renew the track rod if its inboard balljoint's movement is sloppy or too stiff, if it is excessively worn, or if it is damaged in any way; carefully check the threads. If the balljoint rubber boot is damaged, the complete track rod assembly must be renewed; it is not possible to obtain the rubber boot separately.

Refitting

11 Refitting is a reversal of removal, noting the following points:

a) *Use a new lockwasher, and a new track rod outboard end balljoint split pin.*
b) *Fit the lockwasher with its radiused side facing outwards, towards the track rod.*
c) *Tighten securely the track rod; note the specified torque wrench setting.*
d) *Use a large pair of grips or a hammer and punch to flatten the lockwasher tab on to one of the flats on the steering rack bracket.*
e) *On completion, have the front wheel alignment checked at the earliest opportunity.*

24 Power steering pump – removal, overhaul and refitting

Note: *A new auxiliary drivebelt must be available on reassembly, in addition to a new pump feed hose union O-ring and any other items (gaskets, seals, etc) found to be in need of renewal during the procedure.*

Removal

1 Referring to Chapter 1A or 1B, remove the auxiliary drivebelt. Cover the components surrounding the pump with clean rag, etc, to keep power steering fluid from being spilled on to them.

2 Empty the contents of the power steering fluid reservoir into a suitable container. Position a container beside the pump, as close to it as possible.

3 Using pliers, release the spring clip securing the fluid intake hose from the reservoir, and disconnect it from the pump; direct the hose into the container to catch any fluid inside it. Clean the connections on the pump and hose, then plug them or tape over them to prevent dirt getting in.

4 Unscrew the bolts securing the feed hose union, disconnect the feed hose, and recover the O-ring. Again, direct the hose into the container to catch any fluid inside it. Clean the connections on the pump and hose, then plug them or tape over them to prevent dirt getting in. Discard the O-ring – a new one must be used on refitting.

5 Wipe up any spilled fluid and do not move the steering wheel while the pump is disconnected.

6 Unscrew its two mounting bolts and remove the steering pump **(see illustrations)**. If the pump is to be renewed, clamp it in a vice and unscrew the pulley retaining nut, using a forked tool that engages with the holes in the pulley to prevent it from rotating. Remove the pulley.

Overhaul

7 If the pump is thought to be defective, it must be dismantled and checked for wear or damage. Only O-rings and the bearings are

23.8 Track rod inboard ends – note lockwasher tabs (A) flattened on to steering rack bracket (B)

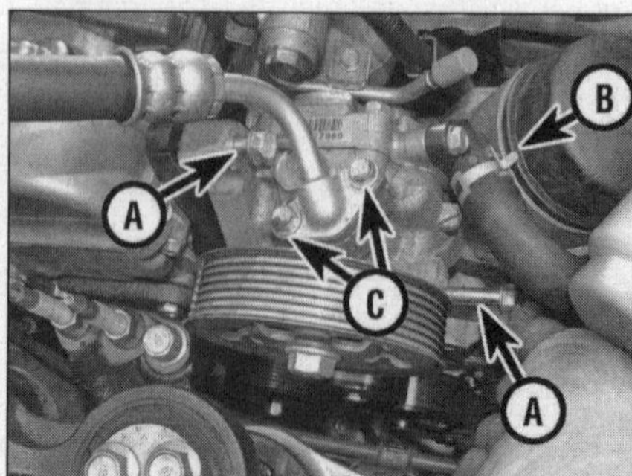

24.6a Power steering pump mounting bolts (A), fluid intake hose union (B), fluid feed hose union bolts (C) – diesel models

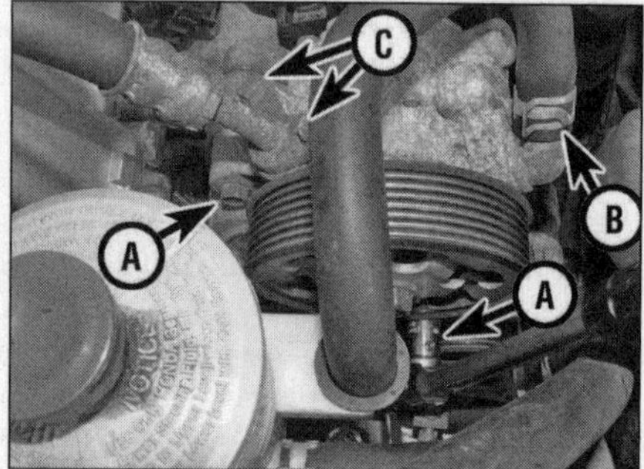

24.6b Power steering pump mounting bolts (A), fluid intake hose union (B), fluid feed hose union bolts (C) – petrol models

available separately; if any of the vanes, the rotor, the cam ring and any other component is worn or damaged, the pump must be renewed as a complete assembly. Since overhaul requires scrupulous cleanliness and some skill, it is recommended that the simplest course of action in most cases would be to renew the pump.

Refitting

8 Refitting is a reversal of removal, noting the following points:

a) Tighten all fasteners and unions to the specified torque.

b) When refitting the pump pulley, be careful to mount the pump in a vice fitted with soft jaw covers. Fit the pulley with its deeply-dished side over the pump body and refit the nut. Hold the pulley to prevent it from rotating and tighten the nut to the specified torque wrench setting.

c) Clean around the pump feed hose union, use a new O-ring, and tighten the union bolts to the specified torque.

d) Fit a new auxiliary drivebelt as described in Chapter 1A or 1B.

e) On completion, fill the fluid reservoir and bleed the system as described in Section 26.

25 Power steering fluid cooler – removal and refitting

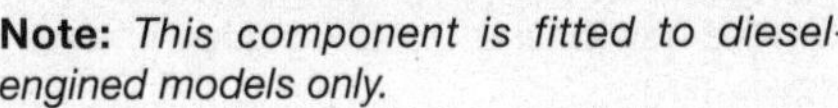

Note: *This component is fitted to diesel-engined models only.*

Removal

1 A loop of fluid pipe is fitted in the return line from the steering rack to the fluid reservoir, to help cool the fluid. The cooler is bolted to the right-hand inner wing panel, in front of the radiator and air conditioning condenser **(see illustration)**.

2 Remove the radiator grille and front bumper as described in Chapter 11.

3 Unclip the power steering fluid reservoir and empty its contents into a suitable container. Trace the return hose from the reservoir down to the fluid cooler, disconnect it and allow any fluid to drain into the container. Clean the connections on the cooler and hose, then plug them or tape over them to prevent dirt getting in.

4 Trace the return hose from the cooler back towards the steering rack and disconnect it either at the end of the cooler itself, or at the return hose-to-return pipe union next to the engine right-hand mounting. Again, direct the hose into the container to catch any fluid inside it. Clean the connections, then plug them or tape over them to prevent dirt getting in.

5 Unbolt the fluid cooler pipe mounting bracket from the wing. Taking care not to damage the pipes, withdraw the fluid cooler from the engine bay.

Refitting

6 Refitting is a reversal of removal. Ensure that all pipework is routed correctly, with no kinks which might restrict fluid flow, and with no risk of pipework coming into contact with hot or moving components. Tighten the fluid cooler mounting bolt to the specified torque wrench setting. On completion, refill the fluid reservoir, and bleed the system as described in Section 26.

26 Power steering fluid – draining, refilling and bleeding

Draining

1 Unclip and raise the fluid reservoir, then disconnect the return hose (not the fluid intake hose connected to the pump) and allow the reservoir's contents to drain into a suitable container.

2 Using a suitable length of hose or tubing if necessary, direct the return hose into the container. Start the engine and allow it to idle, turning the steering wheel several times from lock-to-lock. When fluid stops flowing from the hose, switch off the engine. Discard the used fluid and dispose of it safely with reference to *General repair procedures*.

3 Reconnect the return hose to the reservoir, fastening its clip securely.

Refilling

4 Fill the reservoir to the UPPER LEVEL mark with the specified type of fluid – refer to *Weekly checks* and *Lubricants and fluids*.

5 Have an assistant start the engine, while you keep watch on the fluid level. If the system has been drained, be prepared to add more fluid as soon as the engine starts – the fluid level is likely to drop quickly.

6 Start the engine and run it at a fast idle, turning the steering wheel several times from lock-to-lock; add fluid as necessary, but only up to the LOWER LEVEL mark. Once the fluid level has stabilised, switch the engine off, then check and top-up the fluid level to the UPPER LEVEL mark if necessary.

7 Restart the engine, and turn the steering onto full left-hand lock, holding it there for a few seconds, and then onto full right-hand lock; check all steering hose/pipe unions for signs of leakage. **Note:** *Do not hold the steering at full lock for more than 10 seconds at a time, otherwise the hydraulic system may be damaged.*

Bleeding

8 Following any operation in which the steering system fluid lines have been disconnected, the system must be bled to remove any trapped air. If the steering is noisy in operation, with clicking or hissing sounds emanating from the pump, especially when the steering is on full lock, it is likely that air is trapped in the system and must be bled out.

25.1 Power steering fluid cooler location – diesel models

9 With the front wheels in the straight-ahead position, check the steering fluid level in the reservoir and, if low, add fresh fluid until it reaches the UPPER LEVEL mark. Pour the fluid slowly, to prevent air bubbles forming and use only the specified fluid (refer to *Weekly checks*).

10 Start the engine and allow it to run at a fast idle. Check the hoses and connections for leaks.

11 Stop the engine and recheck the fluid level. Add more if necessary, up to the UPPER LEVEL mark.

12 Start the engine once more, and this time run it for about 2 minutes, turning the steering fully to the right and left several times. This should purge the system of all internal air. However, if air remains in the system (indicated by the steering operation being very noisy), leave the vehicle overnight and repeat the procedure again the next day.

13 Once all air is removed from the system, stop the engine, and check the fluid level as described in *Weekly checks*. Take the vehicle for a journey of a few miles, then recheck the fluid level with the system fully up to operating temperature – repeat the bleeding process completely if there is any suggestion that air is still present.

27 Wheel alignment and steering angles – general information

Caution: Accurate wheel alignment is essential for precise steering and handling, and for even tyre wear. Before carrying out any checking or adjusting operations, make sure that the tyres are correctly inflated, that all steering and suspension joints and linkages are in sound condition, and that the wheels are not buckled or distorted, particularly around the rims. It will also be necessary to have the vehicle positioned on flat, level ground, with enough space to push the vehicle backwards and forwards through about half its length.

Definitions

1 A vehicle's steering and suspension geometry is defined in four basic settings – all angles are expressed in degrees; the steering

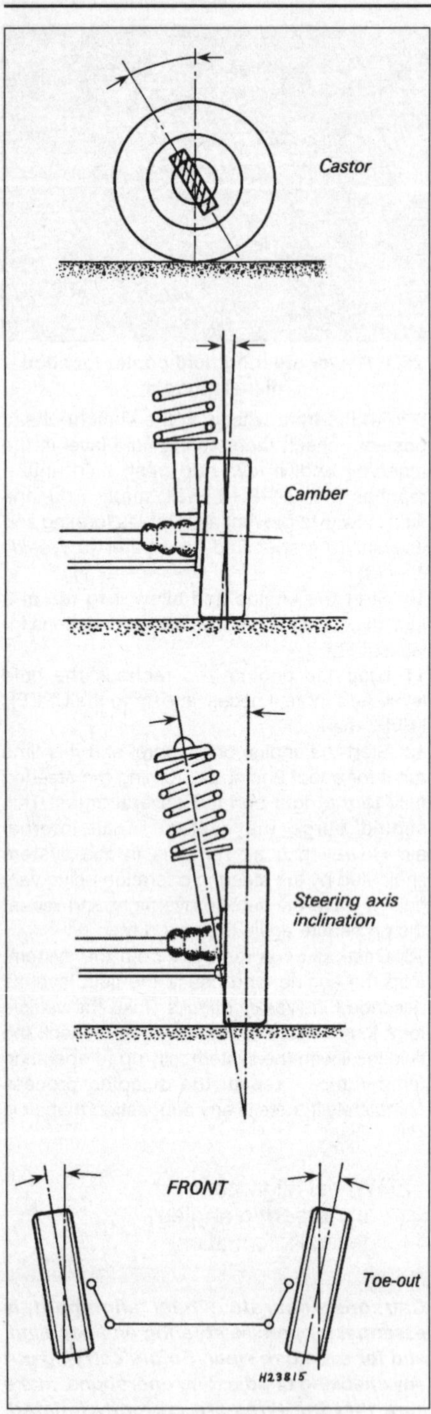

27.1 Front wheel alignment

axis is defined as an imaginary line drawn through the axis of the suspension strut, extended where necessary to contact the ground **(see illustration)**.

2 Camber is the angle between each roadwheel and a vertical line drawn through its centre and tyre contact patch, when viewed from the front or rear of the vehicle. Positive camber is when the roadwheels are tilted outwards from the vertical at the top; negative camber is when they are tilted inwards.

3 The front camber angle is adjustable, but only by slackening the front suspension strut-to-swivel hub pinch-bolts and moving the bottom end of the strut in or out within the limits of the slack present between the bolts and their holes in the strut and swivel hub. If this is insufficient, exchanging one or both of the front suspension strut-to-swivel hub pinch-bolts for smaller-diameter adjusting bolts gives ± 15' adjustment if one bolt is changed, ± 30' adjustment if both are changed. This is not considered a DIY operation, and should only be attempted if the proper tools are available. The rear camber angle is not adjustable (see paragraph 5).

4 Castor is the angle between the steering axis and a vertical line drawn through each roadwheel's centre and tyre contact patch, when viewed from the side of the vehicle. Positive castor is when the steering axis is tilted so that it contacts the ground ahead of the vertical; negative castor is when it contacts the ground behind the vertical.

5 Castor is not adjustable, and is given for reference only; while it can be checked using a castor checking gauge, if the figure obtained is significantly different from that specified, the vehicle must be taken for careful checking by a professional, as the fault can only be caused by wear or damage to the body or suspension components.

6 Steering axis inclination/SAI – also known as kingpin inclination/KPI – is the angle between the steering axis and a vertical line drawn through each roadwheel's centre and tyre contact patch, when viewed from the front or rear of the vehicle.

7 SAI/KPI is not adjustable, and is given for reference only.

8 Toe is the difference, viewed from above, between lines drawn through the roadwheel centres and the vehicle's centre-line. 'Toe-in' is when the roadwheels point inwards, towards each other at the front, while 'toe-out' is when they splay outwards from each other at the front.

9 The front wheel toe setting is adjusted by screwing the track rods in or out of their outboard end balljoints, to alter the effective length of the track rod assembly.

10 Rear wheel toe setting is also adjustable, by rotating eccentrics on the rear suspension trailing arm-to-rear hub carrier rear mounting bolt (see Section 9).

Checking – general

11 Due to the special measuring equipment necessary to check the wheel alignment, and the skill required to use it properly, the checking and adjustment of these settings is best left to an expert. Most tyre-fitting centres now possess sophisticated checking equipment.

Chapter 11
Bodywork and fittings

Contents

Degrees of difficulty

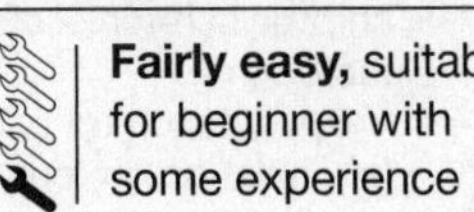

Easy, suitable for novice with little experience	**Fairly easy,** suitable for beginner with some experience	**Fairly difficult,** suitable for competent DIY mechanic	**Difficult,** suitable for experienced DIY mechanic	**Very difficult,** suitable for expert DIY or professional

Specifications

Torque wrench settings	**Nm**	**lbf ft**
Bonnet hinge bolts	10	7
Bonnet lock mounting bolts	10	7
Bumper mounting bolts	10	7
Centre table mounting nuts	22	16
Door and tailgate lock striker screws	18	13
Door hinge nuts and bolts (all)	29	21
Facia mounting bolts and nut	22	16
Front seat bolts	34	25
Luggage compartment cargo tie-down hook bolts	10	7
Rear seat bolts	22	16
Seat belts:		
Front seat belt height adjuster bolts	22	16
Inertia reel upper mounting bolt	10	7
All other seat belt mounting bolts	32	24
Spare wheel holder mounting nuts	39	29
Tailgate glass hinge and support strut fasteners	10	7
Tailgate hinge bolts:		
Hinge-to-body bolts	29	21
Hinge-to-tailgate bolts	30	22
Tailgate strut bolts:		
To body	5	4
To tailgate	10	7
Window regulator mounting bolts	10	7

1 General information

The body shell is made of pressed-steel sections, and is only available in a five-door version. Most body panel components are welded together. The front wings are bolted on, for easier accident repair.

Though the body is not 'fully' galvanised, all the outer panels and floor are, and high-strength steel is used extensively, giving a high degree of strength to the shell. Extensive use is made of plastic materials, mainly in the interior, but also in exterior components. The front and rear bumpers, and front grille, are injection-moulded from a synthetic material that is very strong and yet light. Plastic components such as wheel arch liners are fitted to the underside of the vehicle, to improve the body's resistance to corrosion.

2 Maintenance – bodywork and underside

The general condition of a vehicle's bodywork is the one thing that significantly affects its value. Maintenance is easy, but needs to be regular. Neglect, particularly after minor damage, can lead quickly to further deterioration and costly repair bills. It is important also to keep watch on those parts of the vehicle not immediately visible, for instance the underside, inside all the wheel arches, and the lower part of the engine compartment.

The basic maintenance routine for the bodywork is washing – preferably with a lot of water, from a hose. This will remove all the loose solids which may have stuck to the vehicle. It is important to flush these off in such a way as to prevent grit from scratching the finish. The wheel arches and underside need washing in the same way, to remove any accumulated mud which will retain moisture and tend to encourage rust. Strange as it sounds, the best time to clean the underside and wheel arches is in wet weather, when the mud is thoroughly wet and soft. In very wet weather, the underside is usually cleaned of large accumulations automatically, and this is a good time for inspection.

Periodically, except on cars with a wax-based underbody protective coating, it is a good idea to have the whole of the underside of the vehicle steam-cleaned, engine compartment included, so that a thorough inspection can be carried out to see what minor repairs are necessary. Steam-cleaning is available at many garages, and is necessary for the removal of the accumulation of oily grime, which sometimes is allowed to become thick in certain areas. If steam-cleaning facilities are not available, grease solvents are available which can be brush-applied; the dirt can then be simply hosed off. Note that these methods should not be used on cars with wax-based underbody protective coating, or the coating will be removed. Such cars should be inspected annually, preferably just prior to Winter, when the underbody should be washed down, and any damage to the wax coating repaired. Ideally, a completely fresh coat should be applied. It would also be worth considering the use of such wax-based protection for injection into door panels, sills, box sections, etc, as an additional safeguard against rust damage, where such protection is not provided by the vehicle manufacturer.

After washing the paintwork, wipe off with a chamois leather to give an unspotted clear finish. A coat of clear protective wax polish will give added protection against chemical pollutants in the air. If the paintwork sheen has dulled or oxidised, use a cleaner/polisher combination to restore the brilliance of the shine. This requires a little effort, but such dulling is usually caused because regular washing has been neglected. Care needs to be taken with metallic paintwork, as special non-abrasive cleaner/polisher is required to avoid damage to the lacquer finish – also note that many 'solid' colours are in fact lacquered ('clear over base') these days.

Always check that the door and ventilator opening drain holes and pipes are completely clear, so that water can be drained out. Brightwork should be treated in the same way as paintwork. Windscreens and windows can be kept clear of the smeary film which often appears, by the use of proprietary glass cleaner. Never use wax polish on the windscreen.

3 Maintenance – upholstery and carpets

Mats and carpets should be brushed or vacuum-cleaned regularly, to keep them free of grit. If they are badly stained, remove them from the vehicle for scrubbing or sponging, and make quite sure they are dry before refitting.

Cloth or velour seats and interior trim panels can be kept clean by wiping with a damp cloth. If they do become stained (which can be more apparent on light-coloured cloth or velour upholstery), use a little liquid detergent and a soft nail brush to scour the grime out of the grain of the material. Keep the headlining clean in the same way as the upholstery.

In the case of leather upholstery, a whole range of different products exist to clean, feed and generally restore the leather, and it is recommended that these are used exclusively. Ordinary detergents should be avoided, as they will prematurely dry out leather, causing it to crack and split.

When using liquid cleaners inside the vehicle, do not over-wet the surfaces being cleaned. Excessive damp could get into the seams and padded interior, causing stains, offensive odours or even rot.

If the inside of the vehicle gets wet accidentally, it is worthwhile taking some trouble to dry it out properly, particularly where carpets are involved. Do not leave oil or electric heaters inside the vehicle for this purpose.

4 Minor body damage – repair

Minor scratches

If the scratch is very superficial, and does not penetrate to the metal of the bodywork, repair is very simple. Lightly rub the area of the scratch with a paintwork renovator, or a very fine cutting paste, to remove loose paint from the scratch, and to clear the surrounding bodywork of wax polish. Rinse the area with clean water.

In the case of metallic paint, the most commonly-found scratches are not in the paint, but in the lacquer top coat, and appear white. If care is taken, these can sometimes be rendered less obvious by very careful use of paintwork renovator (which would otherwise not be used on metallic paintwork); otherwise, repair of these scratches can be achieved by applying lacquer with a fine brush. Also note that damage to the lacquer coat will show up worse if (white) polish residue collects in the chip or scratch – clean any suspected area thoroughly.

Apply touch-up paint to the scratch using a fine paint brush; continue to apply fine layers of paint (allowing each one time to dry) until the surface of the paint in the scratch is level with the surrounding paintwork. Allow the new paint at least two weeks to harden, then blend it into the surrounding paintwork by rubbing the scratch area with a paintwork renovator or a very fine cutting paste. Finally, apply wax polish.

Where the scratch has penetrated right through to the metal of the bodywork, causing the metal to rust, a different repair technique is required. Remove any loose rust from the bottom of the scratch with a penknife, then apply rust-inhibiting paint, to prevent the formation of rust in the future. Using a rubber or nylon applicator, fill the scratch with bodystopper paste. If required, this paste can be mixed with cellulose thinners, to provide a very thin paste which is ideal for filling narrow scratches. Before the stopper-paste in the scratch hardens, wrap a piece of smooth cotton rag around the top of a finger. Dip the finger in cellulose thinners, and quickly sweep it across the surface of the stopper-paste in the scratch; this will ensure that the surface of the stopper-paste is slightly hollowed. The scratch can now be painted over as described earlier in this Section.

Dents

If the dent is shallow, and the paint has not

been broken, it may be possible to have the dent repaired professionally, by one of the specialist mobile dent repair companies.

When deep denting of the vehicle's bodywork has taken place, the first task is to pull the dent out, until the affected bodywork almost attains its original shape. There is little point in trying to restore the original shape completely, as the metal in the damaged area will have stretched on impact, and cannot be reshaped fully to its original contour. It is better to bring the level of the dent up to a point which is about 3 mm below the level of the surrounding bodywork. In cases where the dent is very shallow anyway, it is not worth trying to pull it out at all. If the underside of the dent is accessible, it can be hammered out gently from behind, using a mallet with a wooden or plastic head. Whilst doing this, hold a block of wood firmly against the outside of the panel, to absorb the impact from the hammer blows and thus prevent a large area of the bodywork from being 'belled-out'.

Should the dent be in a section of the bodywork which has a double skin, or some other factor making it inaccessible from behind, a different technique is called for. Drill several small holes through the metal inside the area – particularly in the deeper section. Then screw long self-tapping screws into the holes, just sufficiently for them to gain a good purchase in the metal. Now the dent can be pulled out by pulling on the protruding heads of the screws with a pair of pliers.

The next stage of the repair is the removal of the paint from the damaged area, and from an inch or so of the surrounding 'sound' bodywork. This is accomplished most easily by using a wire brush or abrasive pad on a power drill, although it can be done just as effectively by hand, using sheets of abrasive paper. To complete the preparation for filling, score the surface of the bare metal with a screwdriver or the tang of a file, or alternatively, drill small holes in the affected area. This will provide a really good 'key' for the filler paste.

To complete the repair, see the section on filling and respraying.

Rust holes or gashes

Remove all paint from the affected area, and from an inch or so of the surrounding 'sound' bodywork, using an abrasive pad or a wire brush on a power drill. If these are not available, a few sheets of abrasive paper will do the job most effectively. With the paint removed, you will be able to judge the severity of the corrosion, and therefore decide whether to renew the whole panel (if this is possible) or to repair the affected area. New body panels are not as expensive as most people think, and it is often quicker and more satisfactory to fit a new panel than to attempt to repair large areas of corrosion.

Remove all fittings from the affected area, except those which will act as a guide to the original shape of the damaged bodywork (e.g. light units). Then, using tin snips or a hacksaw blade, remove all loose metal and any other metal badly affected by corrosion. Hammer the edges of the hole inwards, in order to create a slight depression for the filler paste.

Wire-brush the affected area to remove the powdery rust from the surface of the remaining metal. Paint the affected area with rust-inhibiting paint; if the back of the rusted area is accessible, treat this also.

Before filling can take place, it will be necessary to block the hole in some way. This can be achieved by the use of aluminium or plastic mesh, or aluminium tape.

Aluminium or plastic mesh, or glass-fibre matting is probably the best material to use for a large hole. Cut a piece to the approximate size and shape of the hole to be filled, then position it in the hole so that its edges are below the level of the surrounding bodywork. It can be retained in position by several blobs of filler paste around its periphery.

Aluminium tape should be used for small or very narrow holes. Pull a piece off the roll, trim it to the approximate size and shape required, then pull off the backing paper (if used) and stick the tape over the hole; it can be overlapped if the thickness of one piece is insufficient. Burnish down the edges of the tape with the handle of a screwdriver or similar, to ensure that the tape is securely attached to the metal underneath.

Filling and respraying

Before using this section, see the sections on dent, deep scratch, rust holes and gash repairs.

Many types of bodyfiller are available, but generally speaking, those proprietary kits which contain a tin of filler paste and a tube of resin hardener are best for this type of repair. A wide, flexible plastic or nylon applicator will be found invaluable for imparting a smooth and well-contoured finish to the surface of the filler.

Mix up a little filler on a clean piece of card or board – measure the hardener carefully (follow the maker's instructions on the pack), otherwise the filler will set too rapidly or too slowly. Using the applicator, apply the filler paste to the prepared area; draw the applicator across the surface of the filler to achieve the correct contour and to level the surface. As soon as a contour that approximates to the correct one is achieved, stop working the paste – if you carry on too long, the paste will become sticky and begin to 'pick-up' on the applicator. Continue to add thin layers of filler paste at 20-minute intervals, until the level of the filler is just proud of the surrounding bodywork.

Once the filler has hardened, the excess can be removed using a metal plane or file. From then on, progressively-finer grades of abrasive paper should be used, starting with a 40-grade production paper, and finishing with a 400-grade wet-and-dry paper. Always wrap the abrasive paper around a flat rubber, cork, or wooden block – otherwise the surface of the filler will not be completely flat. During the smoothing of the filler surface, the wet-and-dry paper should be periodically rinsed in water. This will ensure that a very smooth finish is imparted to the filler at the final stage.

At this stage, the 'dent' should be surrounded by a ring of bare metal, which in turn should be encircled by the finely 'feathered' edge of the good paintwork. Rinse the repair area with clean water, until all of the dust produced by the rubbing-down operation has gone.

Spray the whole area with a light coat of primer – this will show up any imperfections in the surface of the filler. Repair these imperfections with fresh filler paste or bodystopper, and once more smooth the surface with abrasive paper. If bodystopper is used, it can be mixed with cellulose thinners, to form a really thin paste which is ideal for filling small holes. Repeat this spray-and-repair procedure until you are satisfied that the surface of the filler, and the feathered edge of the paintwork, are perfect. Clean the repair area with clean water, and allow to dry fully.

The repair area is now ready for final spraying. Paint spraying must be carried out in a warm, dry, windless and dust-free atmosphere. This condition can be created artificially if you have access to a large indoor working area, but if you are forced to work in the open, you will have to pick your day very carefully. If you are working indoors, dousing the floor in the work area with water will help to settle the dust which would otherwise be in the atmosphere. If the repair area is confined to one body panel, mask off the surrounding panels; this will help to minimise the effects of a slight mis-match in paint colours. Bodywork fittings (e.g. chrome strips, door handles etc) will also need to be masked off. Use genuine masking tape, and several thicknesses of newspaper, for the masking operations.

Before commencing to spray, agitate the aerosol can thoroughly, then spray a test area (an old tin, or similar) until the technique is mastered. Cover the repair area with a thick coat of primer; the thickness should be built up using several thin layers of paint, rather than one thick one. Using 400-grade wet-and-dry paper, rub down the surface of the primer until it is really smooth. While doing this, the work area should be thoroughly doused with water, and the wet-and-dry paper periodically rinsed in water. Allow to dry before spraying on more paint.

Spray on the top coat, again building up the thickness by using several thin layers of paint. Start spraying at the top of the repair area, and then, using a side-to-side motion, work downwards until the whole repair area and about 2 inches of the surrounding original paintwork is covered. Remove all masking material 10 to 15 minutes after spraying on the final coat of paint.

Allow the new paint at least two weeks to harden, then, using a paintwork renovator or a very fine cutting paste, blend the edges of the

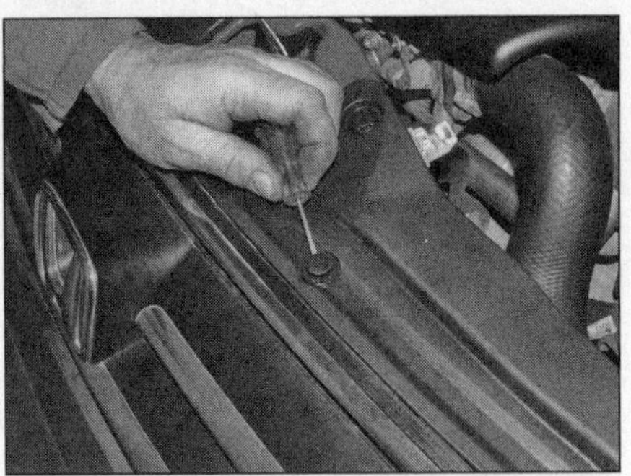
6.1a Release clips by prising out centre with small flat-tipped screwdriver . . .

6.1b . . . then withdraw clip centre and outer part together

6.1c Unscrew battery hold-down clamp bolt on petrol models, then release its retaining clips . . .

6.1d . . . to remove radiator grille top cover

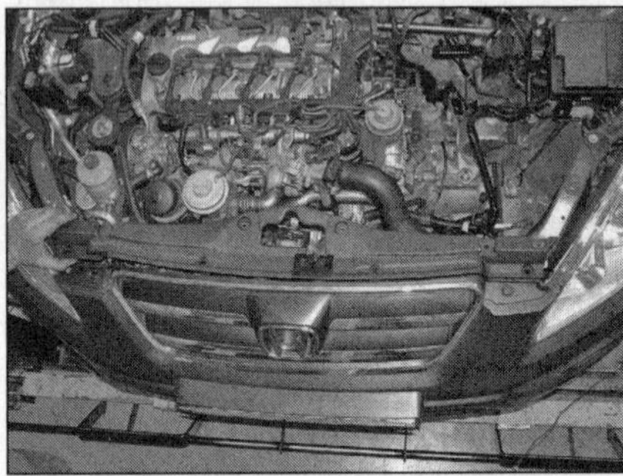
6.1e Removing radiator grille top cover – diesel models

paint into the existing paintwork. Finally, apply wax polish.

Plastic components

With the use of more and more plastic body components by the vehicle manufacturers (e.g. bumpers, spoilers, and in some cases major body panels), rectification of more serious damage to such items has become a matter of either entrusting repair work to a specialist in this field, or renewing complete components. Repair of such damage by the DIY owner is not really feasible, owing to the cost of the equipment and materials required for effecting such repairs. The basic technique involves making a groove along the line of the crack in the plastic, using a rotary burr in a power drill. The damaged part is then welded back together, using a hot-air gun to heat up and fuse a plastic filler rod into the groove. Any excess plastic is then removed, and the area rubbed down to a smooth finish. It is important that a filler rod of the correct plastic is used, as body components can be made of a variety of different types (e.g. polycarbonate, ABS, polypropylene).

Damage of a less serious nature (abrasions, minor cracks etc) can be repaired by the DIY owner using a two-part epoxy filler repair. Once mixed in equal, this is used in similar fashion to the bodywork filler used on metal panels. The filler is usually cured in twenty to thirty minutes, ready for sanding and painting.

If the owner is renewing a complete component himself, or if he has repaired it with epoxy filler, he will be left with the problem of finding a suitable paint for finishing which is compatible with the type of plastic used. At one time, the use of a universal paint was not possible, owing to the complex range of plastics encountered in body component applications. Standard paints, generally speaking, will not bond to plastic or rubber satisfactorily, but suitable paints to match any plastic or rubber finish, can be obtained from dealers. However, it is now possible to obtain a plastic body parts finishing kit which consists of a pre-primer treatment, a primer and coloured top coat. Full instructions are normally supplied with a kit, but basically, the method of use is to first apply the pre-primer to the component concerned, and allow it to dry for up to 30 minutes. Then the primer is applied, and left to dry for about an hour before finally applying the special-coloured top coat. The result is a correctly-coloured component, where the paint will flex with the plastic or rubber, a property that standard paint does not normally possess.

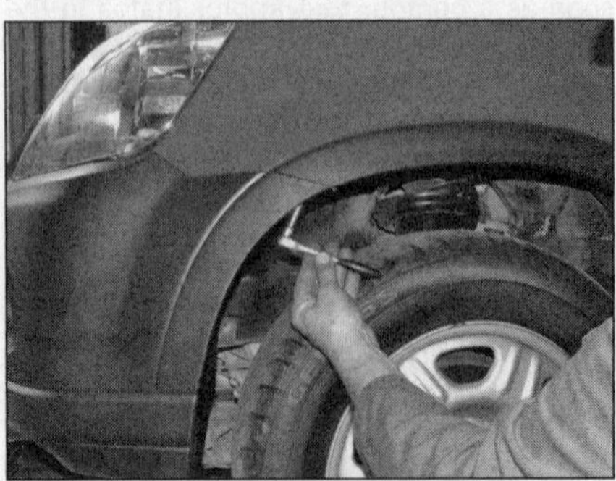
6.3a Removing bumper screw from wheel arch top . . .

5 Major body damage – repair

Where serious damage has occurred, or large areas need renewal due to neglect, it means that complete new panels will need welding-in, and this is best left to professionals. If the damage is due to impact, it will also be necessary to check completely the alignment of the body shell, and this can only be carried out accurately by a Honda dealer using special jigs. If the body is left misaligned, it is primarily dangerous, as the vehicle will not handle properly, and secondly, uneven stresses will be imposed on the steering, suspension and possibly transmission, causing abnormal wear, or complete failure, particularly to such items as the tyres.

6 Front bumper – removal and refitting

Note: *The front bumper and the wheel arch liner and engine compartment undershield are clipped together along the underside of the bumper and/or use the same mountings (depending on model year). Be careful you are undoing the appropriate fastener and check carefully that all fasteners for either component are released before applying pressure to remove it.*

Removal

1 Open the bonnet and, on petrol-engined models, unscrew the battery hold-down clamp bolt. Release its retaining clips to remove the radiator grille top cover **(see illustrations)**.

2 Release the two retaining clips, one at each end of the radiator grille **(see illustration 6.1b)**.

3 Remove the two bumper retaining screws at the front and top of each front wheel arch **(see illustrations)**.

4 The underside of the bumper is secured either by two mounting bolts at each end and two clips in the centre, or by six clips, along the bumper's bottom edge. Unscrew the mounting bolts and/or release the clips to free the bumper **(see illustrations 6.4 and 23.4a)**.

6.3b . . . and front mounting points

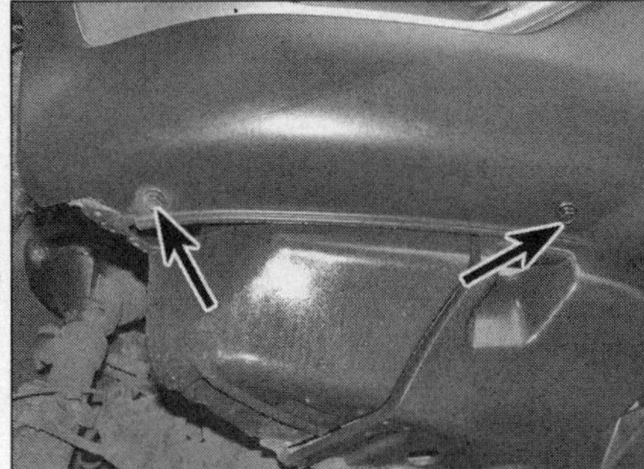

6.4 Remove two bolts or clips at each end

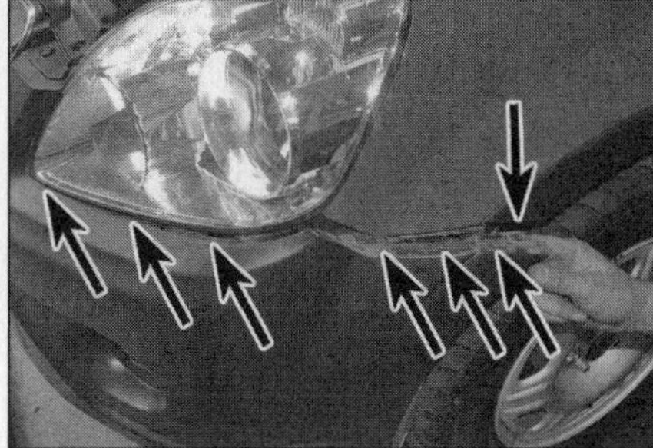

6.6 Pull bumper ends outwards to unclip, then down and forwards to release clips under headlights

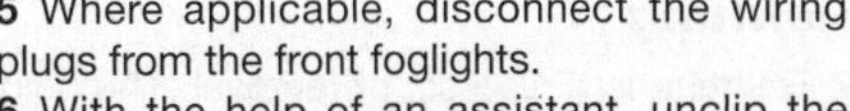

5 Where applicable, disconnect the wiring plugs from the front foglights.

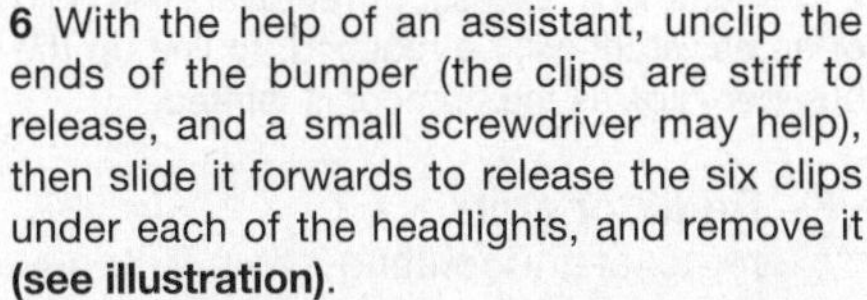

6 With the help of an assistant, unclip the ends of the bumper (the clips are stiff to release, and a small screwdriver may help), then slide it forwards to release the six clips under each of the headlights, and remove it **(see illustration)**.

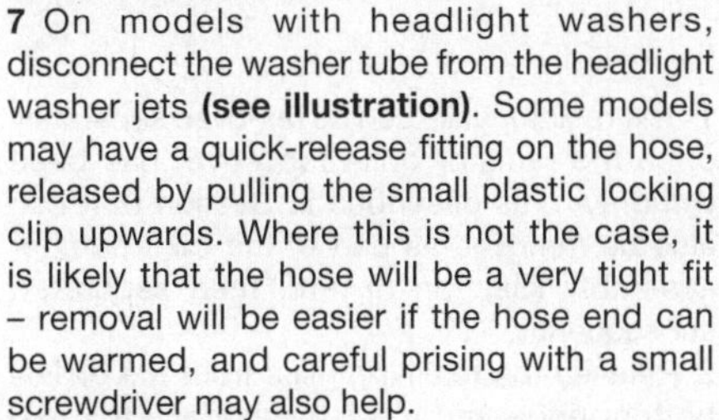

7 On models with headlight washers, disconnect the washer tube from the headlight washer jets **(see illustration)**. Some models may have a quick-release fitting on the hose, released by pulling the small plastic locking clip upwards. Where this is not the case, it is likely that the hose will be a very tight fit – removal will be easier if the hose end can be warmed, and careful prising with a small screwdriver may also help.

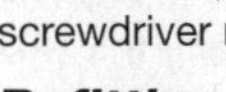

Refitting

8 Refitting is a reversal of removal. Again, the help of an assistant will be required, to line up the bumper clips as the bumper is refitted **(see illustration)**.

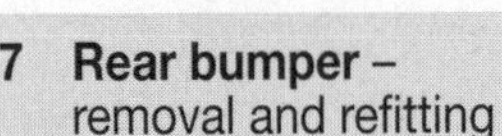

7 Rear bumper – removal and refitting

Removal

1 Open the tailgate, unscrew the bolt securing the body end of the tailgate strut and apply protective tape around the hinge side edge of the tailgate lower trim panel to prevent damage to it or to the bumper. Open the tailgate to give the maximum clearance between the tailgate lower trim and the bumper, then secure the tailgate in this position **(see illustrations)**.

2 Working underneath, carefully prise out the clip at the centre of the bottom edge of the bumper **(see illustration)**.

3 Carefully prise out the two bolt covers from the tailgate aperture at the top of the bumper – take care not to damage the paint. Remove the bolt behind each cover **(see illustrations)**.

4 Remove the bumper retaining screws at the rear of each rear wheel arch.

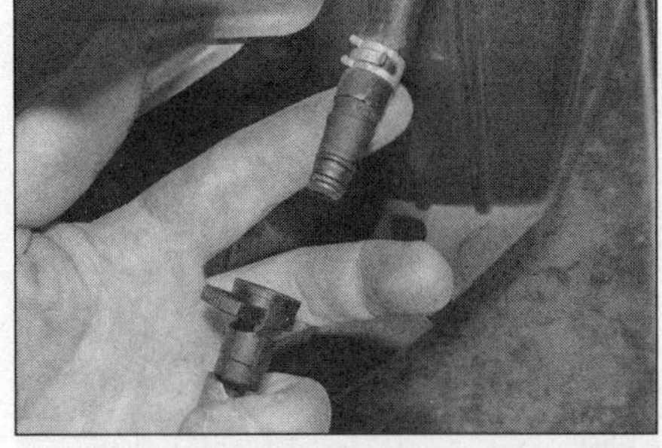

6.7 Pull small plastic locking clip upwards to release quick-release fitting on headlight washer tube hose

6.8 Ensure clips engage properly when refitting bumper

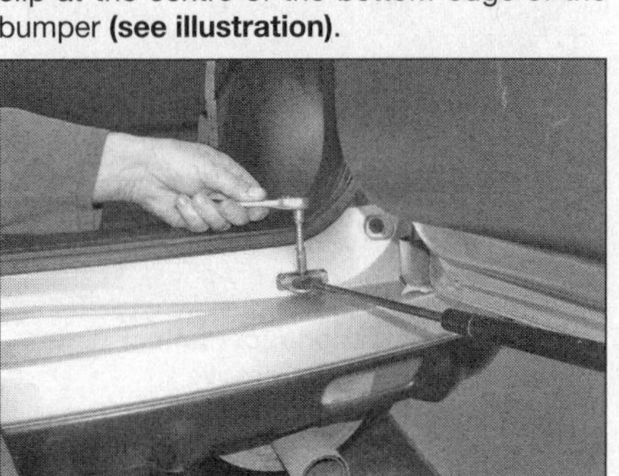

7.1a Open tailgate and unbolt strut . . .

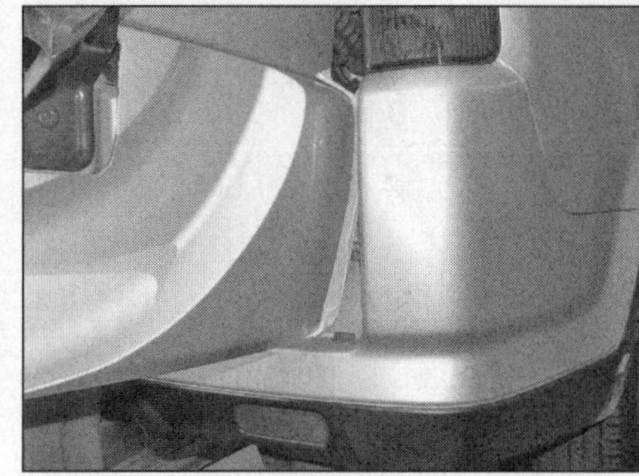

7.1b . . . then apply protective tape to prevent damage to paintwork

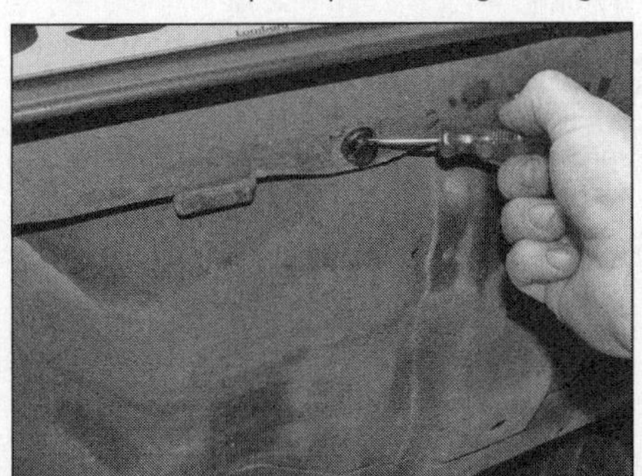

7.2 Release clip from centre of bumper underside

7.3a Take care to prevent damage to paintwork when removing covers . . .

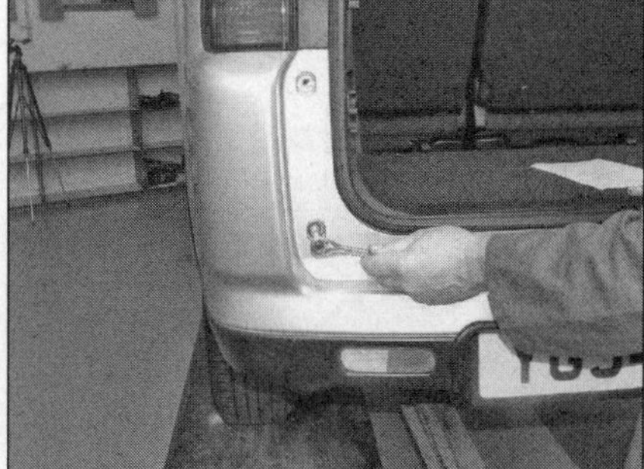

7.3b . . . then unscrew bumper mounting bolts

7.5 Undo screws and remove rear mudflaps

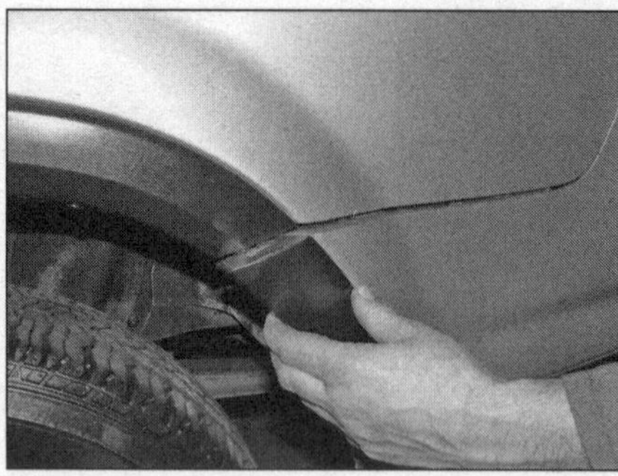
7.6a Pull bumper end outwards to release clips . . .

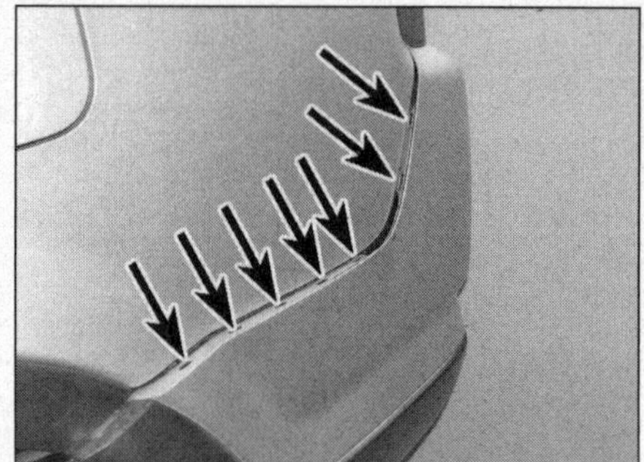
7.6b . . . seven along upper edge . . .

7.6c . . . and two at upper rear . . .

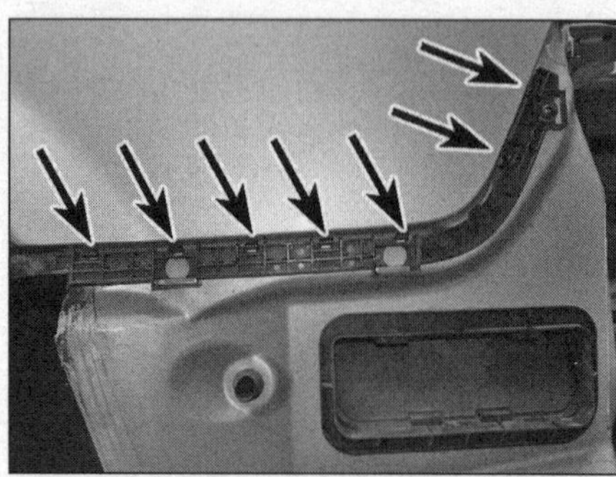
7.6d . . . which are easily broken

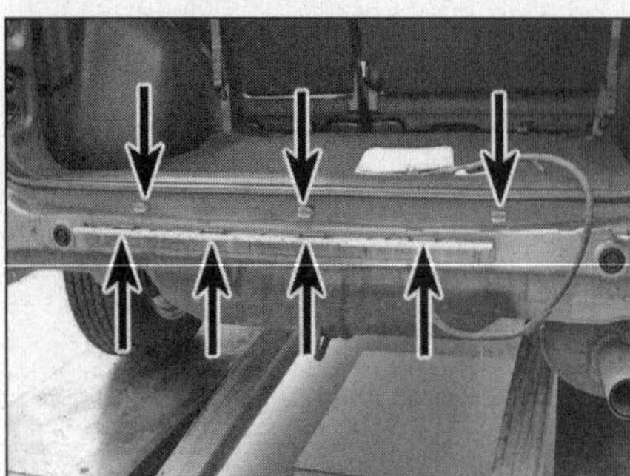
7.6e Remove bumper from rear mounting hooks and clips . . .

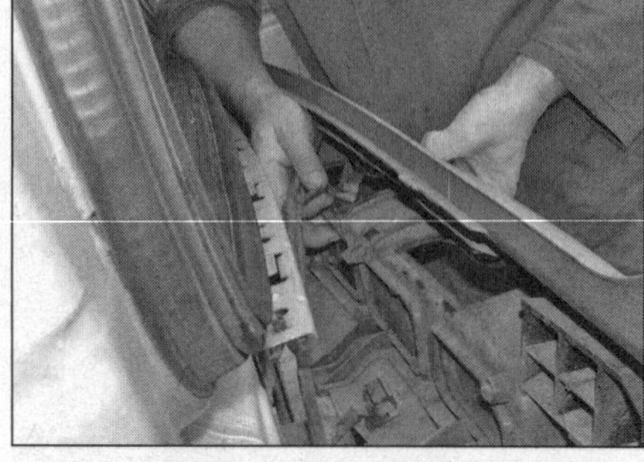
7.6f . . . and disconnect number plate wiring to remove

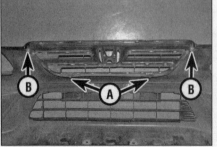

5 Undo the three retaining screws securing each rear mudflap **(see illustration)**.

6 With the help of an assistant, unclip the bumper ends by pulling them slightly outwards (the clips are stiff to release), and releasing the five hooks on each side securing the top edge of the bumper to the bodywork. Withdraw the bumper from the vehicle, releasing it from the hooks and clips along the rear of the vehicle and disconnecting the wiring for the number plate lights and, where fitted, the parking sensors **(see illustrations)**.

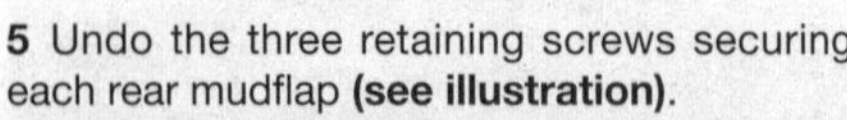

8.2 Release two clips (A) to remove radiator grille from front bumper. Later models also have two screws (B)

9.3 Unscrew bonnet retaining bolts

Refitting

7 Refitting is a reversal of removal. The help of an assistant will be required, to line up the bumper clips as the bumper is refitted.

8 Radiator grille – removal and refitting

1 The radiator grille can be removed separately once the radiator grille top cover has been withdrawn, as described in Section 6. It can also be removed as part of the front bumper assembly (Section 6), and then separated subsequently.

2 Release the retaining clips from the grille's bottom edge and, on later models, the two retaining screws at the grille's top corners, then separate the grille from the bumper **(see illustration)**. The badge, trim and cover plate can be removed as necessary, once their retaining screws and/or clips have been removed/released.

3 Refitting is a reversal of removal.

9 Bonnet – removal, refitting and adjustment

Removal

1 Open the bonnet, then, using a pencil or felt tip pen, mark the outline of each bonnet hinge relative to the bonnet, to use as a guide on refitting.

2 Have an assistant support the bonnet in its open position.

3 Unscrew the bonnet retaining bolts and carefully lift the bonnet clear **(see illustration)**. Store the bonnet out of the way in a safe place.

4 Inspect the bonnet hinges for signs of wear and free play at the pivots, and if necessary renew them. Each hinge is secured to the body by two bolts; mark the position of the hinge on the body then undo the retaining bolts and remove it from the vehicle **(see illustration)**.

Refitting and adjustment

5 Where removed, refit the bonnet hinges,

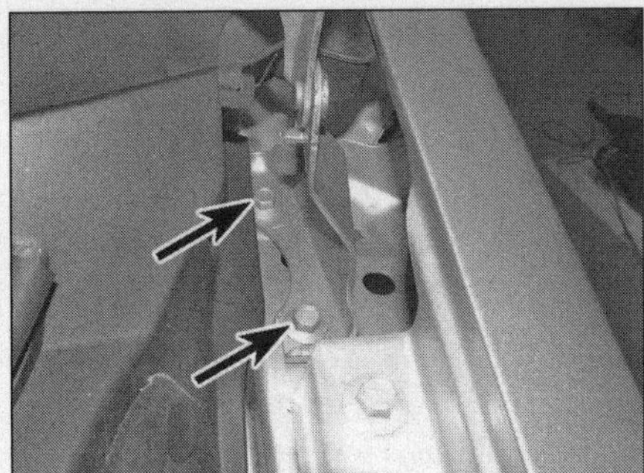
9.4 Slacken bonnet hinge bolts to adjust position of bonnet, if required

10.2a Unhook cable outer from slot in bonnet lock . . .

10.2b . . . and unhook cable end fitting

and align them with the previously-made marks. Tighten the bolts securely.

6 With the aid of an assistant, offer up the bonnet and loosely fit the retaining bolts. Align the hinges with the marks made on removal, then tighten the retaining bolts securely.

7 Close the bonnet, and check for alignment with the adjacent panels. If necessary, slacken the hinge bolts and re-align the bonnet. Adjust the height of the bonnet so that it is level with the surrounding front wings, by turning the rubber buffer at each front corner of the bonnet. Once the bonnet is correctly aligned, tighten the hinge bolts. Check that the bonnet fastens and releases satisfactorily.

10 Bonnet release cable – removal and refitting

Removal

1 Remove the right-hand wheel arch liner as described in Section 23.

2 Working in the engine compartment, unbolt the lock (Section 11) and lift the cable to release it from the locating slot in the bonnet lock, then unhook the cable end fitting **(see illustrations)**. Take care not to bend the cable as this is done.

3 Working as described in Section 27 of this Chapter, remove the driver's side under cover and lower cover from the facia and the driver's footwell side trim panel.

4 Unbolt the bonnet release handle from the body **(see illustration)**.

5 Working from the bonnet release handle through to the bonnet lock, release the cable from any clips or ties securing it and remove the sealing grommet from the bulkhead. Note how the cable is routed and withdraw it from the vehicle.

Refitting

6 Refitting is a reversal of removal. Ensure the cable is correctly routed and secured to all the relevant retaining clips. Before closing the bonnet, check the operation of the release lever and cable.

11 Bonnet lock – removal and refitting

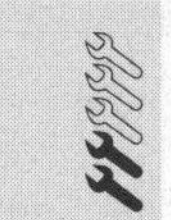

Removal

1 Open the bonnet, and disconnect the alarm switch wiring plug from the bonnet lock, then unclip the alarm wiring harness from the back of the lock assembly **(see illustration)**.

2 Lift the bonnet release cable to free it from the locating slot, then unhook the cable end fitting. Take care not to bend the cable as this is done.

3 Mark around the lock or make alignment marks between the lock and the body, to make refitting easier **(see illustration)**.

4 Unscrew and remove the bonnet lock mounting bolts, and withdraw the lock assembly from the vehicle.

Refitting

5 Refitting is a reversal of removal. Align the lock using the marks made on removal, and tighten the mounting bolts securely. Before closing the bonnet fully, check that the bonnet striker enters the lock centrally, and if necessary, adjust the lock position (by slackening the mounting bolts) to achieve satisfactory bonnet closing.

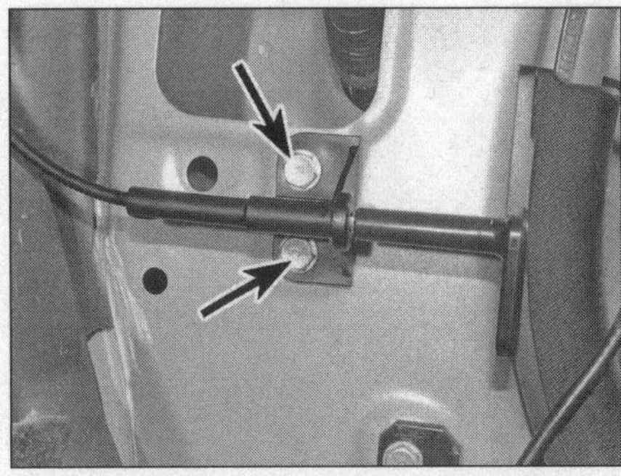
10.4 Unbolt bonnet release handle

12 Door – removal, refitting and adjustment

Removal

Front door

1 Locate the door wiring plug, then twist and disconnect it.

2 Unbolt the door check strap from the door pillar **(see illustration)**.

3 Have an assistant support the door, or rest

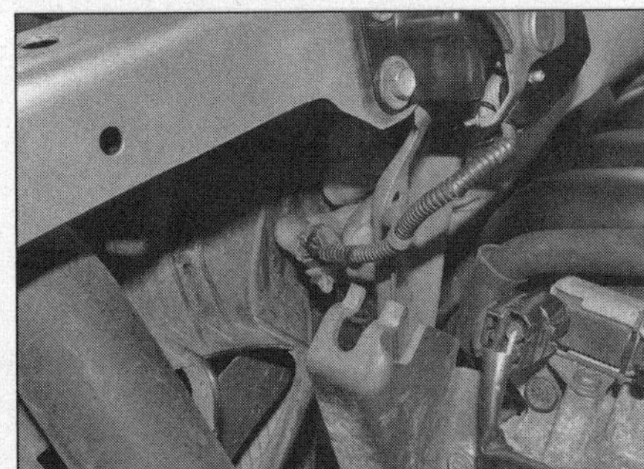
11.1 Disconnect alarm switch wiring from bonnet lock, then unclip alarm wiring harness

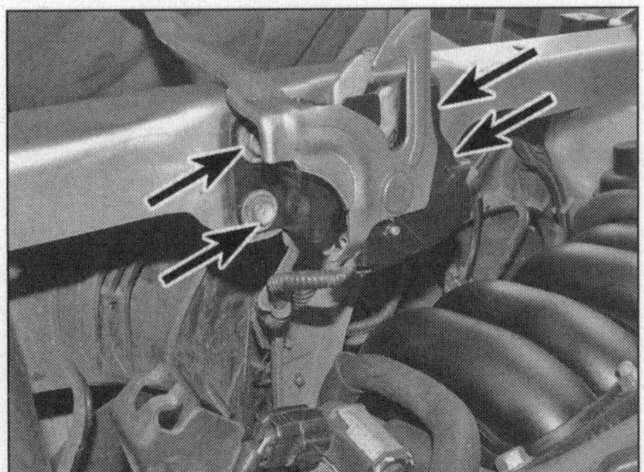
11.3 Mark around lock to ease refitting, then undo bonnet lock mounting bolts

12.2 Unbolt door check strap

12.4 Front door hinge bolts

12.7a Wiring for door electrical components is routed inside rubber boot – note arrow showing direction of fitting

12.7b Unclip rubber boot as door is removed . . .

12.7c . . . access to connector is behind B-pillar trim panel

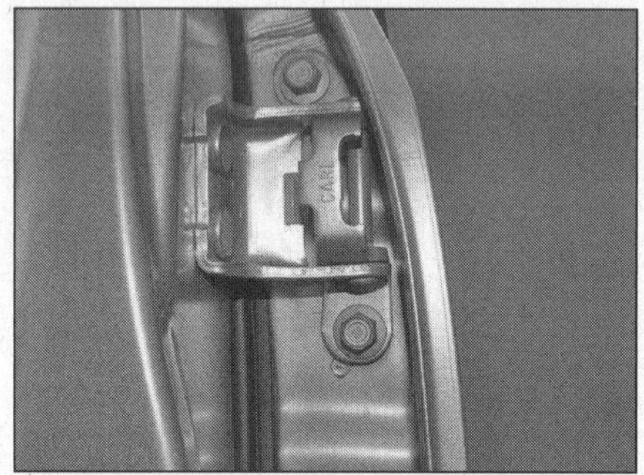

12.10a Rear door upper hinge

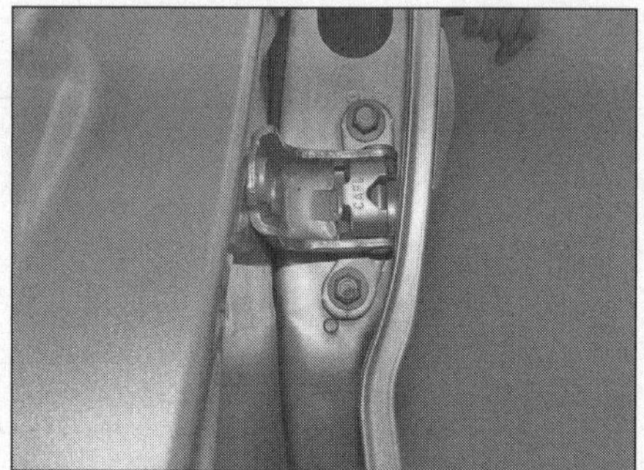

12.10b Rear door lower hinge

it on an axle stand – pad the top of the stand with cloth, to prevent damage to the paint.

4 Unscrew the upper and lower door-to-hinge bolts (two per hinge), and remove the door from the vehicle **(see illustration)**. Unclip the door wiring boot as the door is removed.

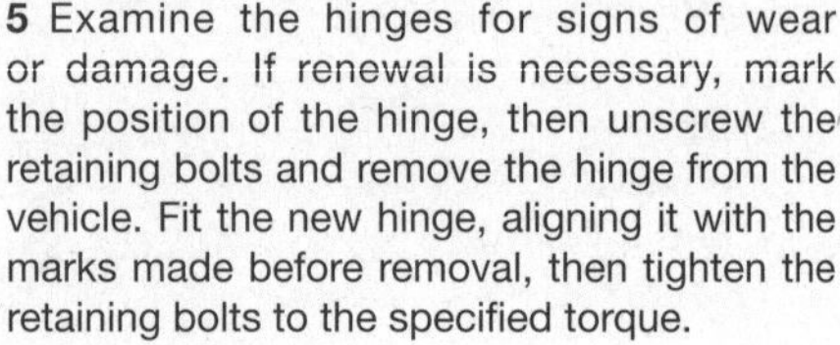

5 Examine the hinges for signs of wear or damage. If renewal is necessary, mark the position of the hinge, then unscrew the retaining bolts and remove the hinge from the vehicle. Fit the new hinge, aligning it with the marks made before removal, then tighten the retaining bolts to the specified torque.

Rear door

6 Remove the front seat belt as described in Section 26.

7 Locate the door wiring plug, then twist and disconnect it **(see illustrations)**.

8 Unbolt the door check strap from the door pillar.

9 Have an assistant support the door, or rest it on an axle stand – pad the top of the stand with cloth, to prevent damage to the paint.

10 Unscrew the upper and lower door-to-hinge bolts (two per hinge), and remove the door from the vehicle. Unclip the door wiring boot as the door is removed **(see illustrations)**.

11 Examine the hinges for signs of wear or damage. If renewal is necessary, mark the position of the hinge, then unscrew the retaining bolts and remove the hinge from the vehicle **(see illustration)**. Fit the new hinge, aligning it with the marks made before removal, then tighten the retaining bolts to the specified torque.

Refitting

12 Refitting is a reversal of removal, noting the following points:

a) Tighten the hinge bolts to the specified torque.

b) Check the door alignment and if necessary adjust as described later in this Section.

c) If the paintwork around the hinges has been damaged, paint the area with a suitable touch-in brush to prevent corrosion.

Adjustment

13 To adjust the door to compensate for general wear in the hinges, this is best done by adjusting the position of the lock striker **(see illustration)**.

14 If adjusting the door after removal, close the door and check that the gap between the door and surrounding bodywork is equal around the complete perimeter. If necessary, slight adjustment of the door position can be made by slackening the hinge retaining bolts and repositioning the hinge/door as necessary. Once the door is correctly positioned, tighten the hinge bolts to their specified torque. Check that the door striker engages centrally with the lock, and if necessary, adjust the position of the striker.

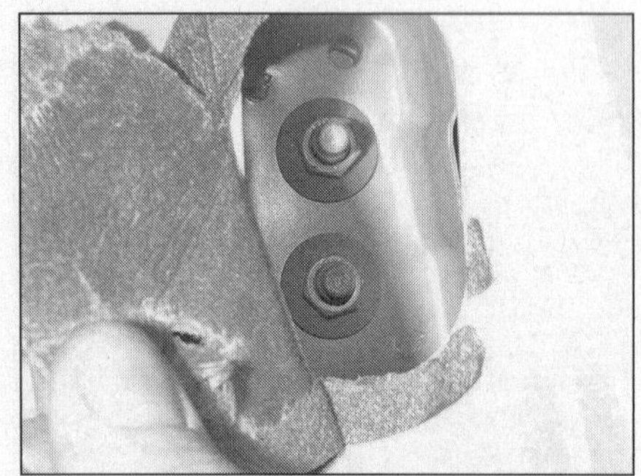

12.11 Access to rear door hinge nuts is behind B-pillar trim panel

12.13 Slacken screws and adjust door lock striker slightly if necessary

13 Door trim panel – removal and refitting

Removal

Front door

1 Insert a screwdriver with the tip wrapped in protective tape into the gap at the top of the panel in the centre of the inner handle and

13.1a Prise out panel at centre of door inner handle . . .

13.1b . . . and unscrew two screws behind

13.2a Pull out handle and unclip operating rod

13.2b . . . to release handle assembly

13.4a Undo screw at front . . .

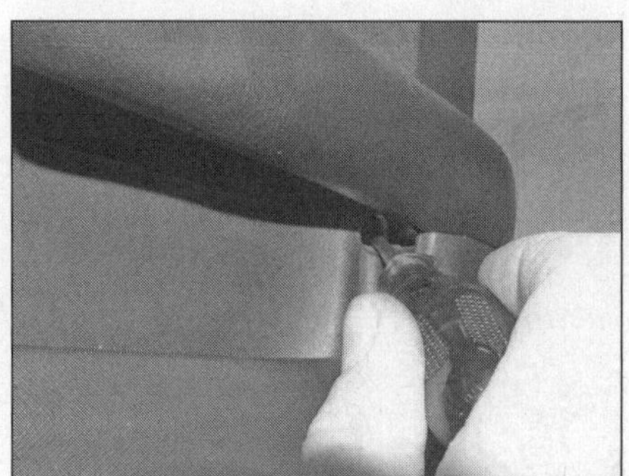
13.4b . . . and rear of armrest

prise out the panel until the hooks along its lower edge release **(see illustrations)**.

2 Undo the screws and withdraw the inner handle; disconnect the central locking switch wiring (where fitted). Release the clip and disengage the door lock operating rod, noting how it fits **(see illustrations)**.

3 Lower the window glass fully.

4 Undo the two screws from under the armrest **(see illustrations)**.

5 Remove the switch panel from the armrest as described in Section 4 of Chapter 12. Disconnect the switch wiring.

6 Carefully pull off the mirror inner trim panel by hand – pull the panel out at the rear edge, then prise it carefully inwards to disengage the two retaining clips **(see illustration 20.4)**.

7 Remove the door trim panel; a commercially-available forked trim removal tool is well worth the expense for this sort of operation. Failing this, use any strong flat-bladed tool that has rounded edges or is wrapped in protective tape to minimise damage to surrounding paintwork and trim.

8 Starting at the top front corner, release the clip by pressing in its centre, then work your way down the front edge (two clips), along the bottom (three clips) and up the rear edge (two clips) of the door trim panel **(see illustrations)**. Lift the panel at the rear to clear the door lock knob and withdraw the door trim panel.

9 If working on the driver's door, release the wiring for the various switches from the trim panel **(see illustration)**.

Rear door

10 Lower the window glass fully.

11 Insert a screwdriver with the tip wrapped in protective tape into the gap at the top of the panel in the centre of the inner handle and prise out the panel until the hooks along its lower edge release **(see illustrations 13.1a and 13.1b)**.

12 Undo the screws and withdraw the inner handle; release the clip and disengage the

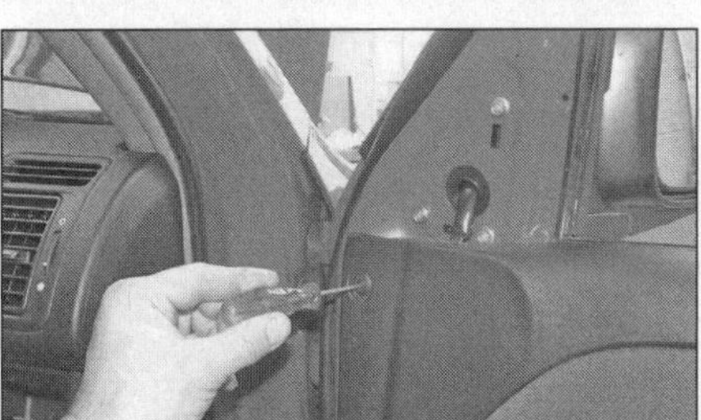
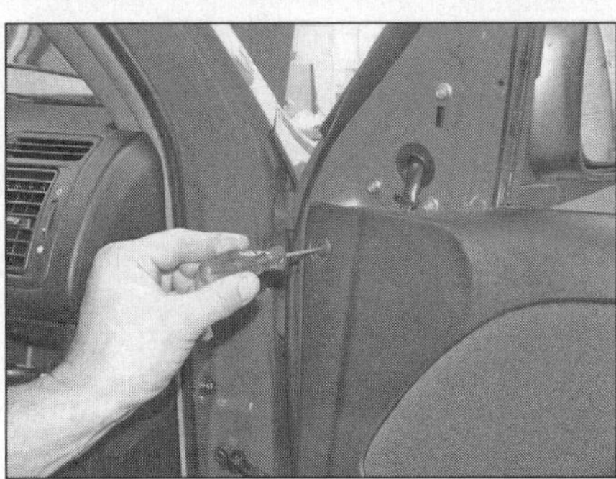
13.8a Press in centre of clip beneath mirror to release . . .

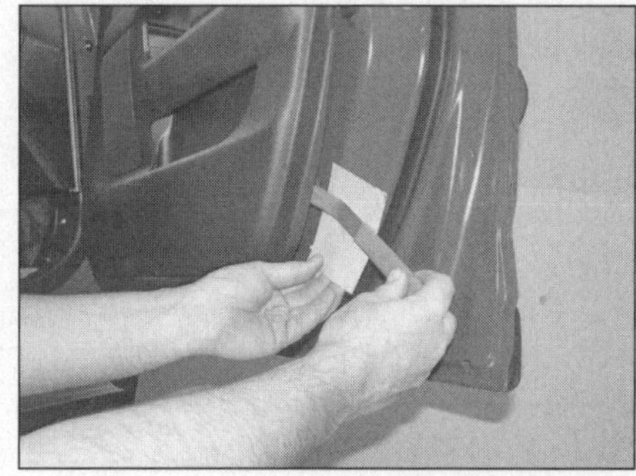
13.8b . . . then work around door trim panel releasing clips (without damaging paintwork) . . .

13.8c . . . which are located as shown

13.9 Withdraw panel and disconnect wiring to release

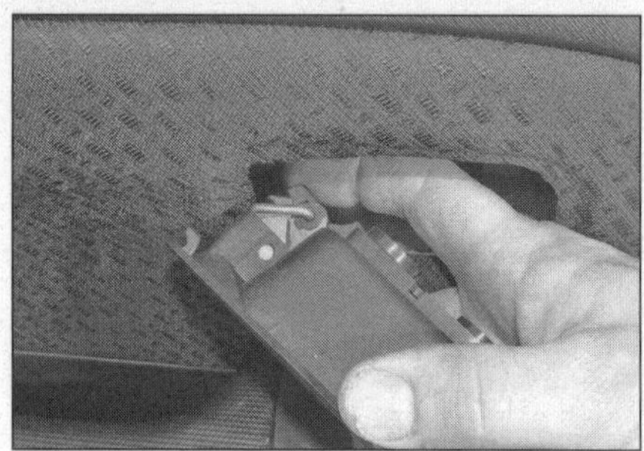
13.12 Pull out handle and unclip operating rod to release rear door inner handle assembly

13.13a Protect paintwork while prising out rear door trim panel . . .

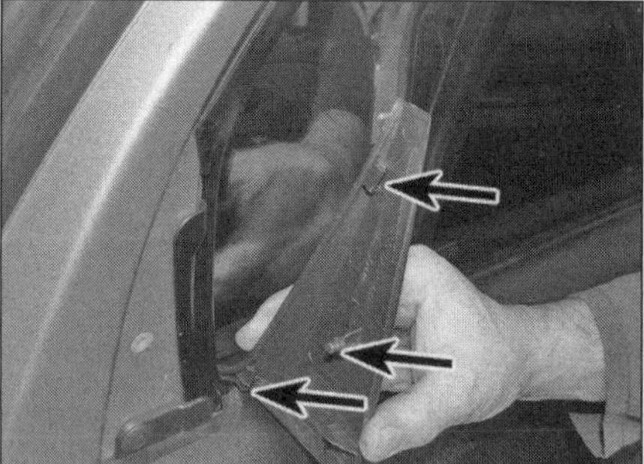
13.13b . . . which is retained by one clip and two hooks

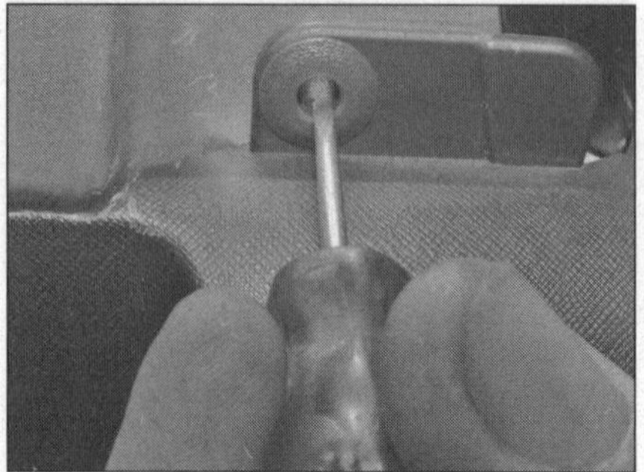
13.14 Press in centre to release clip in top rear corner of rear door trim panel

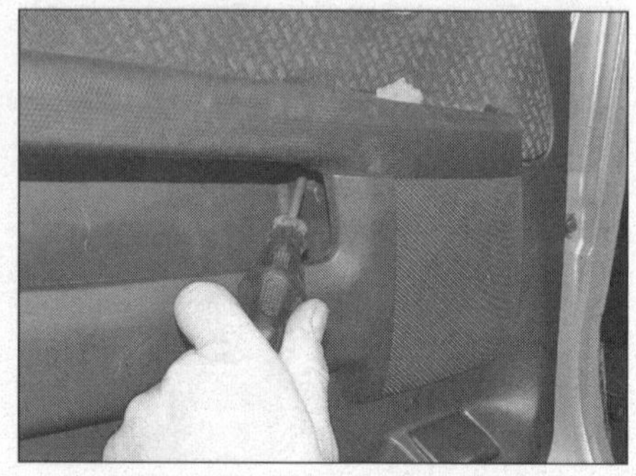
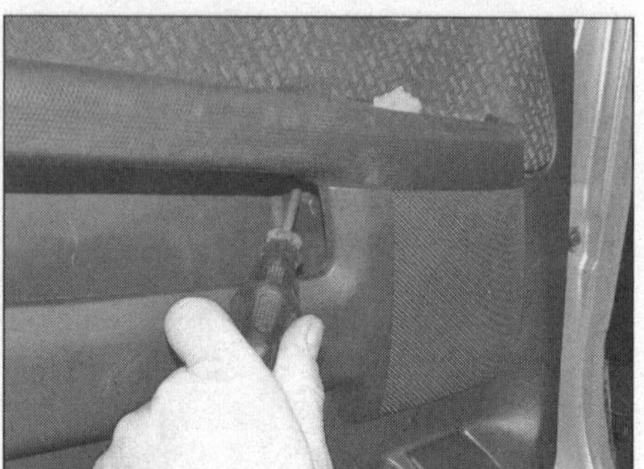
13.15a Undo screw at front . . .

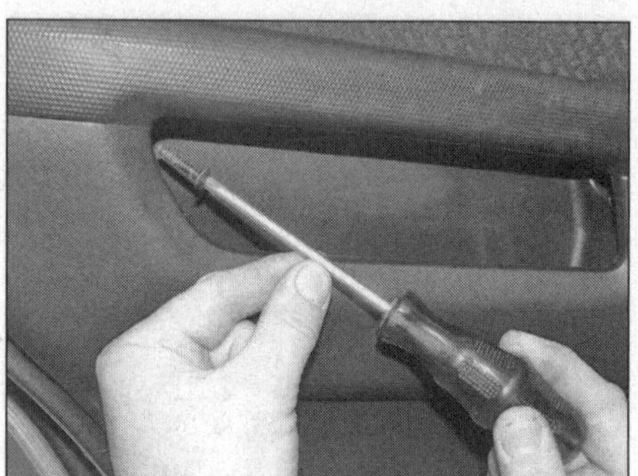
13.15b . . . and rear of armrest

door lock operating rod, noting how it fits **(see illustration)**.

13 Remove the triangular trim panel at the rear of the door by inserting a screwdriver with the tip wrapped in protective tape into the centre of the panel's rear edge, next to the retaining pin, prising the panel outwards without breaking the two hooks along its front edge, and then pushing the panel forwards to release the two hooks **(see illustrations)**.

14 Release the clip behind the trim panel by pressing in its centre **(see illustration)**.

15 Undo the two screws from under the armrest **(see illustrations)**.

16 Remove the switch panel from the armrest as described in Section 4 of Chapter 12. Disconnect the switch wiring.

17 Remove the door trim panel; a commercially-available forked trim removal tool is well worth the expense for this sort of operation. Failing this, use any strong flat-bladed tool that has rounded edges or is wrapped in protective tape to minimise damage to surrounding paintwork and trim.

18 Starting at the top front corner, work your way down the front edge (three clips), along the bottom (two clips) and up the rear edge (three clips) of the door trim panel. Lift the panel at the rear to clear the door lock knob and withdraw the door trim panel. Disconnect any wiring from the back of the panel **(see illustrations)**.

Door membrane

19 To access the door internal components, the plastic membrane must be removed **(see illustration)**.

20 On models with deadlocking ('super-locking'), disconnect the wiring plug then remove the screw securing the deadlocking control unit from the centre of the panel **(see illustration 18.4)**.

21 Prise out the clips, then carefully peel back the membrane. This sheet will be stuck on with a bead of mastic, which can be sliced though 'vertically' with a sharp knife, so that the membrane can be re-attached afterwards. Pull off the membrane and move it to a safe place, where it can be kept clean.

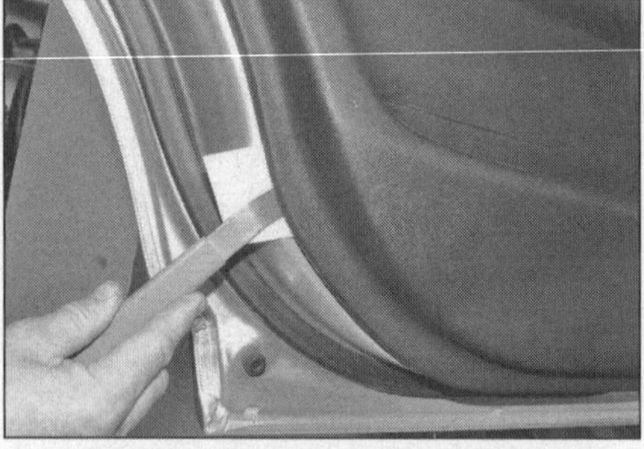
13.18a Work around door trim panel releasing clips (without damaging paintwork) . . .

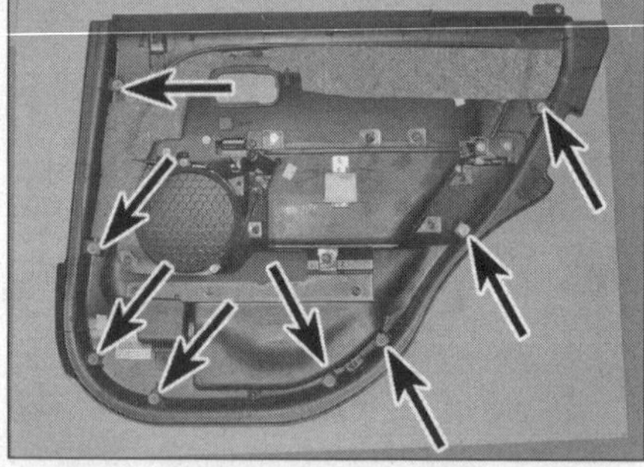
13.18b . . . which are located as shown . . .

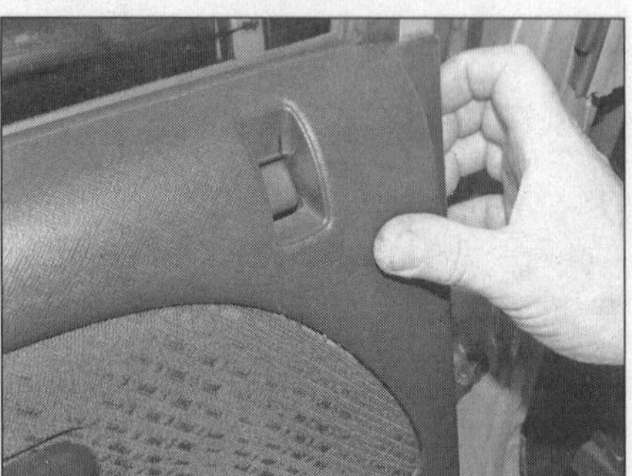
13.18c . . . lift door trim panel over locking button . . .

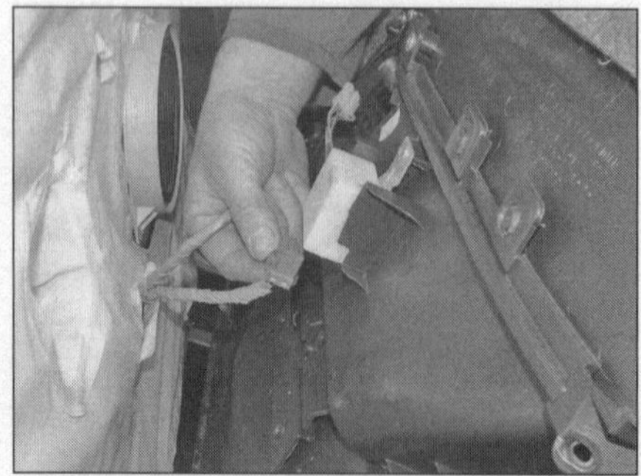
13.18d . . . then withdraw panel and disconnect wiring to release

Refitting

22 Refitting is a reversal of removal, noting the following points **(see illustrations)**:

a) *Check the door for any trim clips which might have been left behind by the panel as it was removed. If necessary, carefully prise these clips out of the door, and refit them to the panel – if this is not done, they will not re-engage properly when refitting the panel. If any clips have been broken, obtain new ones for refitting – take one of the good clips along to the dealer for matching.*

b) *Once the trim panel wiring has been reconnected, check the operation of the door electrical equipment as applicable, before clipping the panel back in place.*

c) *Similarly, check the operation of the inner handle, once the operating rod has been reconnected.*

14 Door handle and lock components – removal and refitting

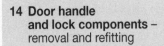

Note: *Details of the locks and mechanism actually fitted may vary, depending on specification (central locking or dead-locking/'super-locking') and lock component manufacture.*

Removal

Door inner handles

1 The inner handles are removed as part of the door trim panel procedure – refer to Section 13.

Front door outer handle and lock cylinder

2 Remove the door trim panel and membrane as described in Section 13, then temporarily reconnect the door window switch and close the window.

3 Where fitted, release the clip and detach the hook, then remove the lock rod protector between the door lock knob and the lock itself.

4 Disconnect the outer handle rod and (where fitted) the lock barrel rod **(see illustrations)**.

5 If working on the driver's door, pull away the window glass rear guide channel as necessary. If required (to release the operating rods), unscrew the bolt at the base of the window glass centre lower guide channel, then pull out the channel trim, and pull it downwards to remove it **(see illustrations)**.

6 Extract the retainer clip and remove the lock cylinder assembly **(see illustrations)**. **Note:** *Depending on specification (central locking or deadlocking/'super-locking') and lock component manufacture, it may not be possible to remove the assembly until the lock*

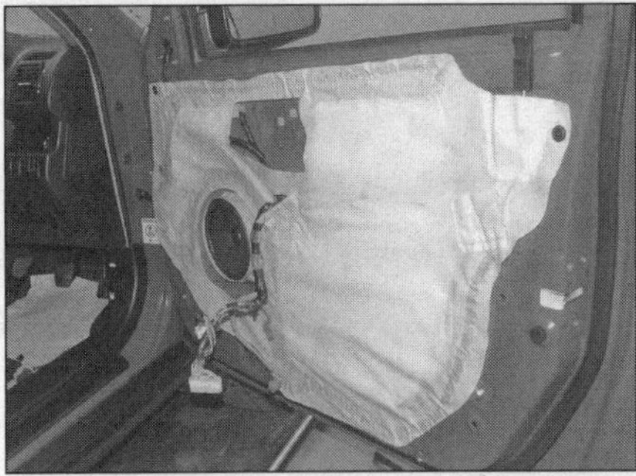

13.19 Plastic membrane must be peeled back to reach door components

13.22a Front door trim panel clip must be fitted as shown, then push in centre to secure clip

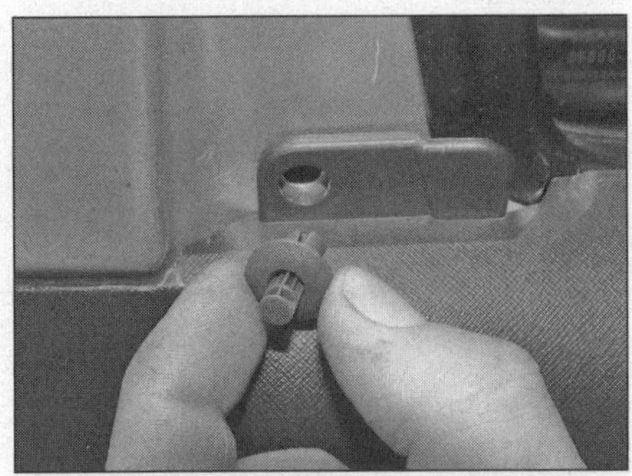

13.22b Rear door trim panel clip must be fitted as shown . . .

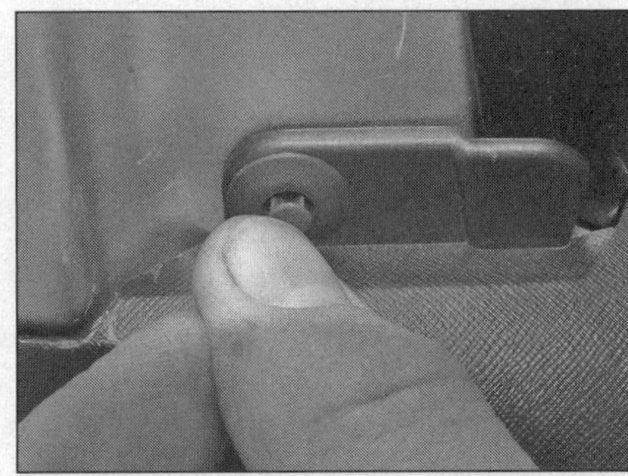

13.22c . . . then push in centre to secure clip

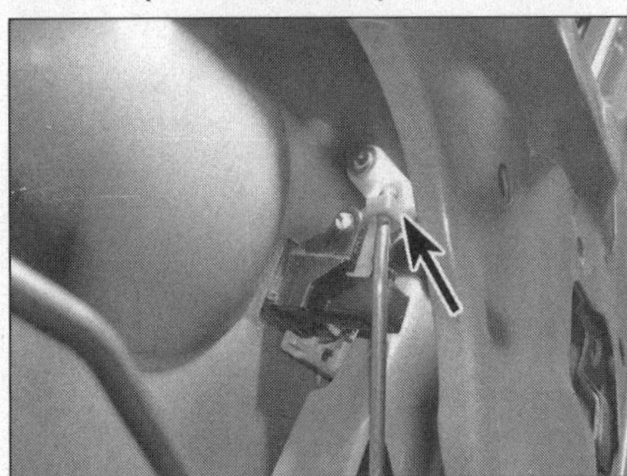

14.4a Release clip and disconnect operating rod(s) from outer handle

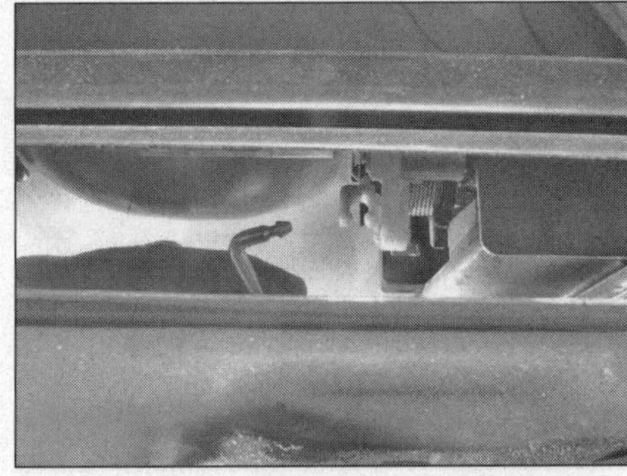

14.4b View from above (window glass removed) of operating rod and outer handle

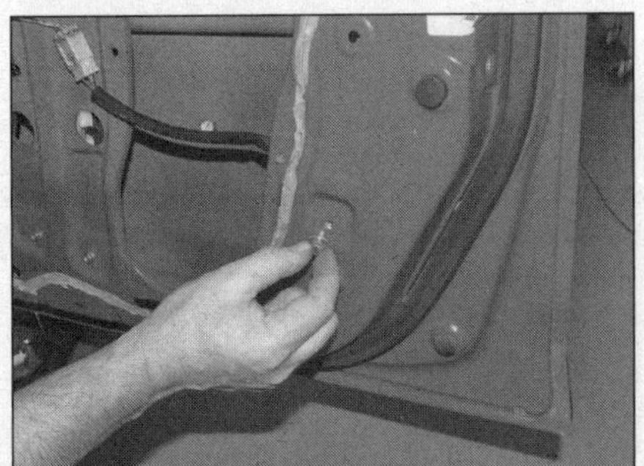

14.5a If required, undo mounting bolt . . .

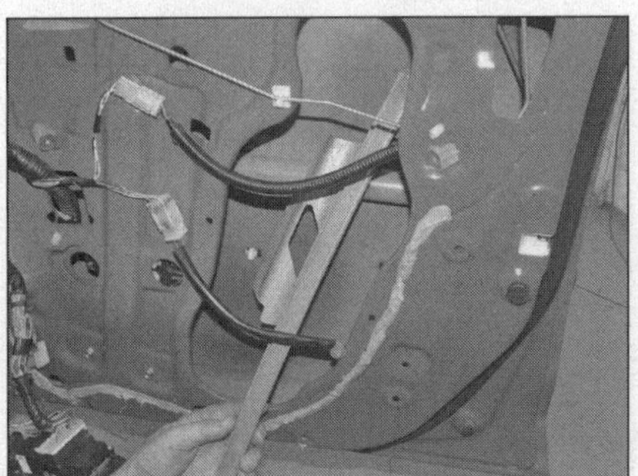

14.5b . . . and withdraw window glass centre lower guide channel . . .

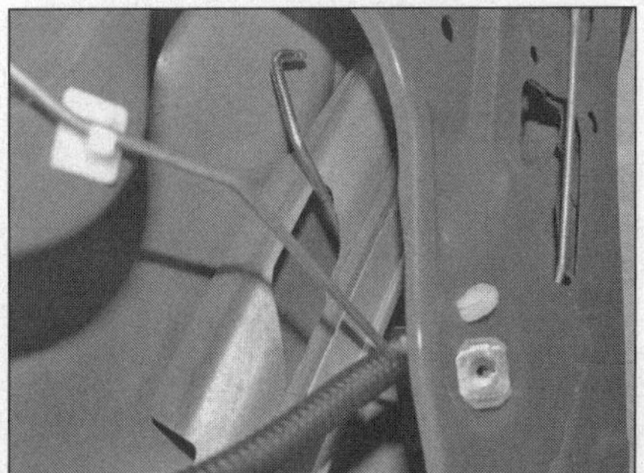

14.5c . . . to release door lock operating rods

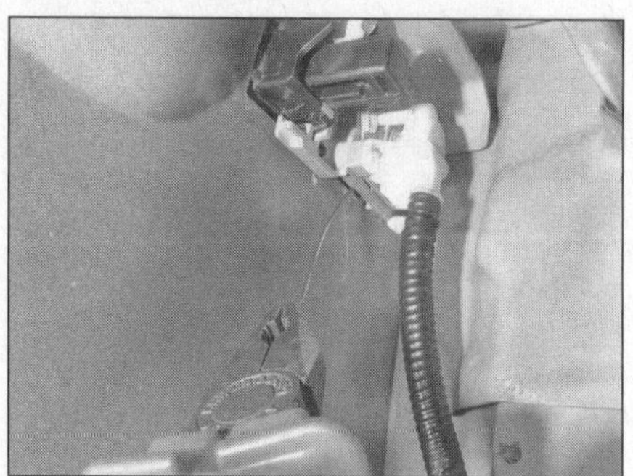

14.6a Make up suitable tool with hooked end to pull down retaining clip . . .

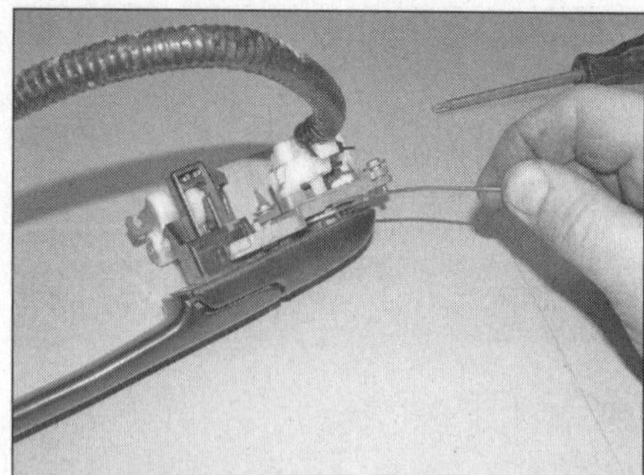

14.6b . . . shown here with handle removed from door for clarity . . .

14.6c . . . and with lock cylinder assembly removed

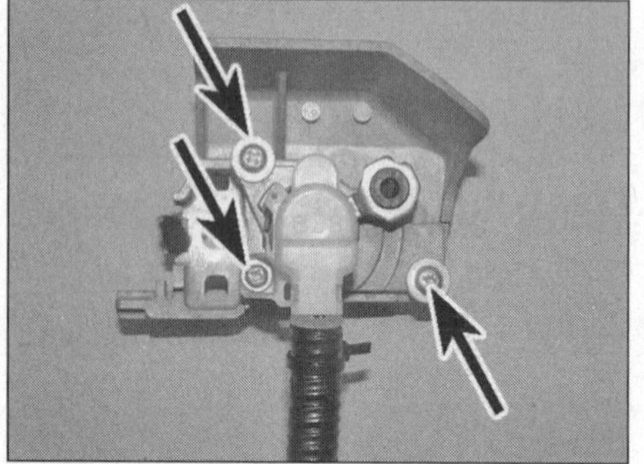

14.7 Undo screws to separate lock cylinder switch, lock cylinder and lock cover

14.8 Unscrew outer handle rear mounting bolt and withdraw lock protector

protector has been unbolts, as described in paragraph 8 below.

7 Where fitted, disconnect the wiring connector from the lock assembly and remove the lock cylinder switch. Unbolt the cover over the lock cylinder **(see illustration)**.

8 Unscrew the bolt and remove the protector over the lock **(see illustration)**.

9 Unscrew the outer handle mounting bolt and remove the spacer; withdraw the outer handle **(see illustrations)**.

Rear door outer handle

10 Remove the door trim panel and membrane as described in Section 13, then temporarily reconnect the door window switch and close the window.

11 Where fitted, undo the screws and release the hooks, then remove the lock rod protector between the door outer handle and the lock itself.

12 Noting their fitted positions, release the clip and unhook the longer rod from the door lock knob linkage, then unclip the two lock operating rods from the door **(see illustrations)**.

13 Remove the access cap fitted to the rear edge of the door and disconnect the outer handle operating rod **(see illustrations)**.

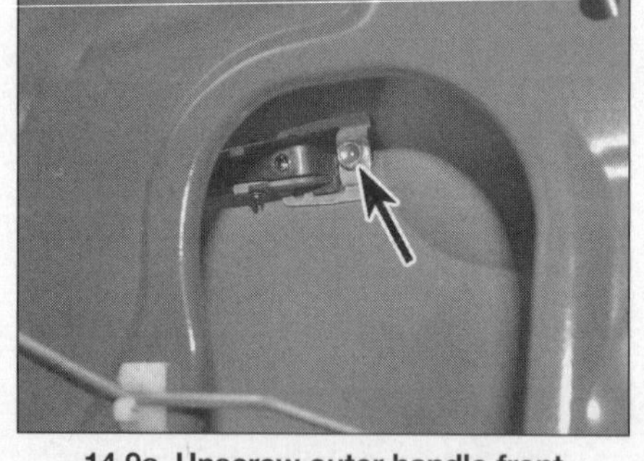

14.9a Unscrew outer handle front mounting bolt and withdraw spacer

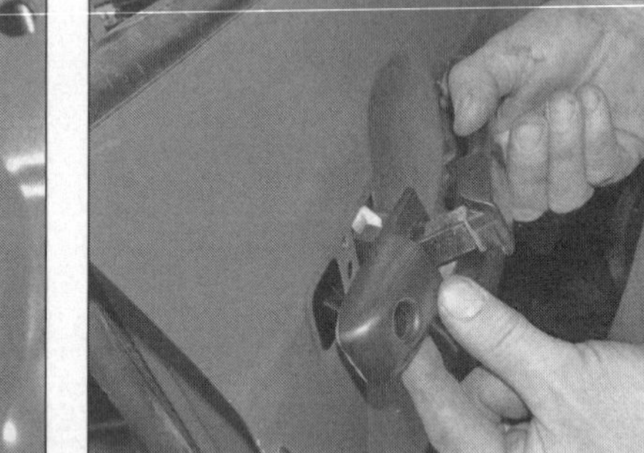

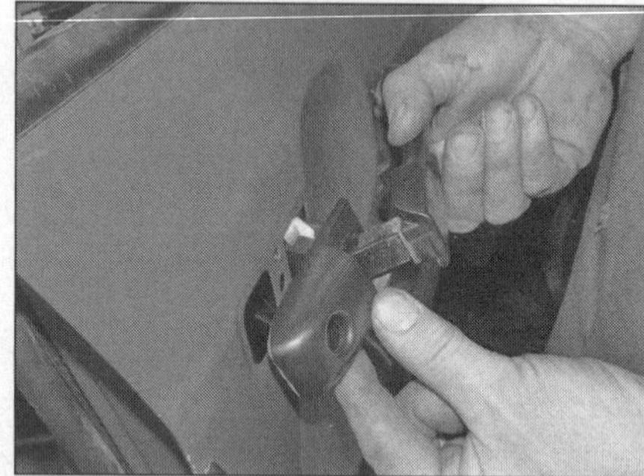

14.9b Operate door outer handle and manoeuvre . . .

14.9c . . . outer handle out of door

14.12a Release clip to disconnect rod from lock knob linkage . . .

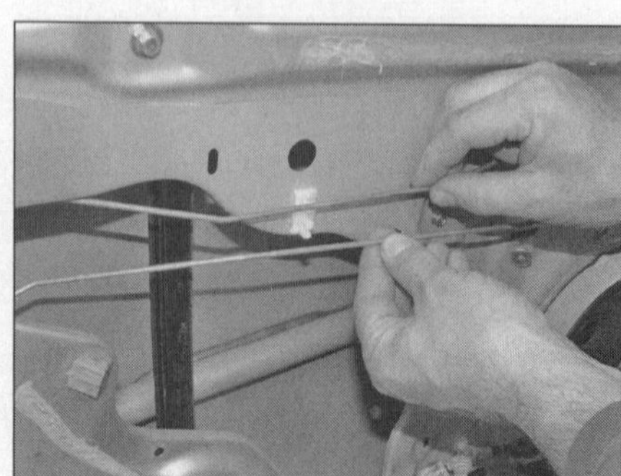

14.12b . . . then unclip lock operating rods from door

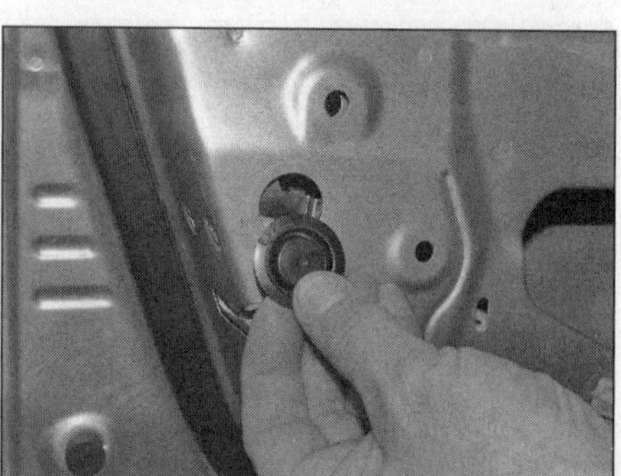

14.13a Prise out plastic cap, then . . .

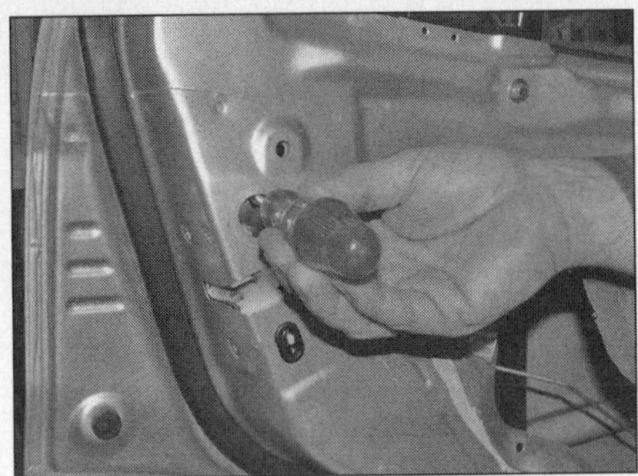

14.13b . . . working through access hole at rear . . .

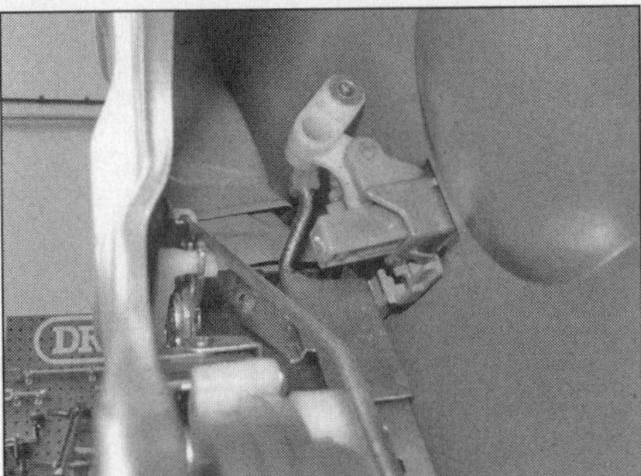

14.13c . . . release clip . . .

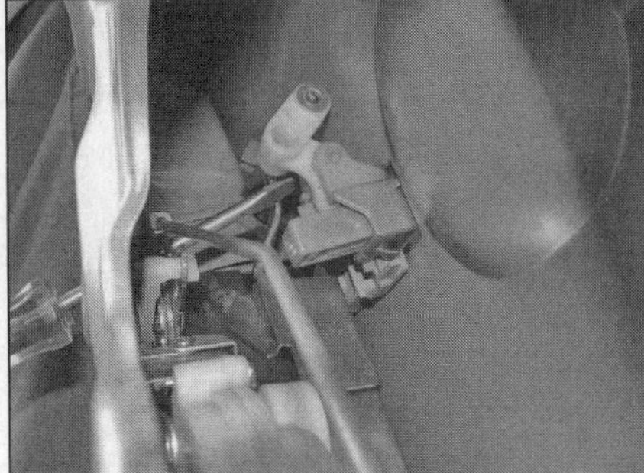

14.13d . . . and unhook lock operating rod from outer handle

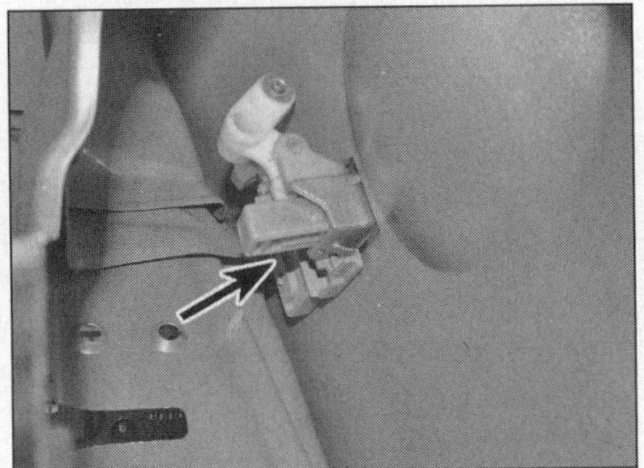

14.14 Unscrew outer handle rear mounting bolt and withdraw lock protector

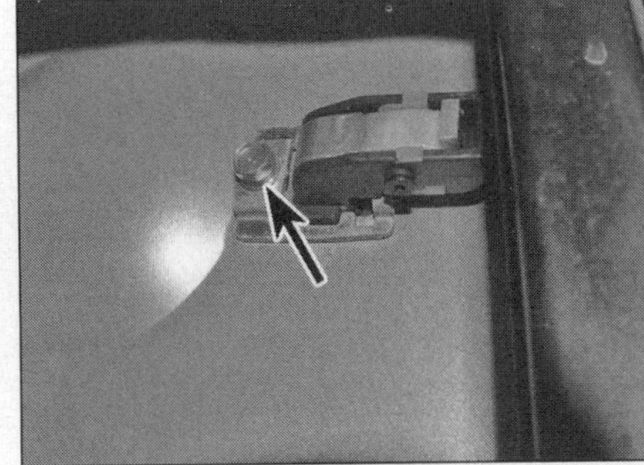

14.15a Unscrew outer handle front mounting bolt and withdraw spacer . . .

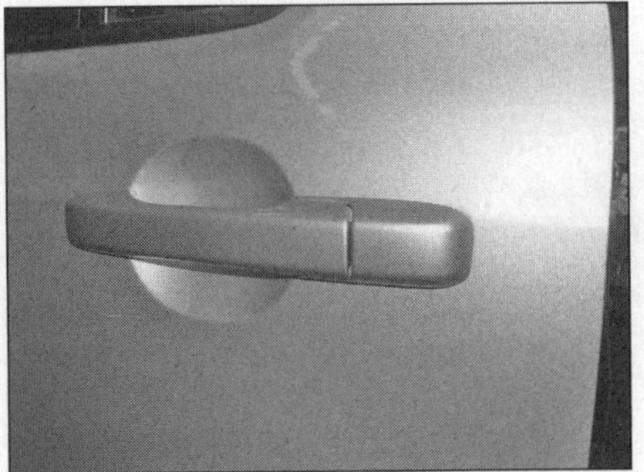

14.15b . . . then manoeuvre outer handle out of door

14 Unscrew the bolt and remove the protector over the lock **(see illustration)**.

15 Unscrew the outer handle mounting bolt and remove the spacer; withdraw the outer handle **(see illustrations)**.

Front door lock

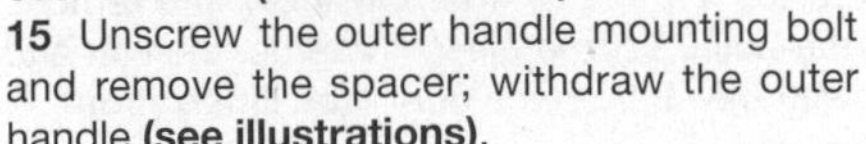

16 Proceed as described in paragraphs 2 to 5 inclusive.

17 Disconnect the lock motor wiring plug in the centre of the door, then trace the wiring back to the motor, unclipping it from the door **(see illustration)**.

18 Unclip the inner handle operating rod from the rod holder on the door.

19 Remove the three lock securing screws from the rear edge of the door, then move the lock assembly forwards and withdraw it from the door, taking care not to bend the still-attached operating rods **(see illustrations)**.

Rear door lock

20 Proceed as described in paragraphs 10 to 13 inclusive.

21 Disconnect the lock motor wiring plug in the centre of the door, then trace the wiring back to the motor, unclipping it from the door **(see illustrations)**.

22 Remove the three lock securing screws from the rear edge of the door, then move the lock assembly forwards and withdraw it from

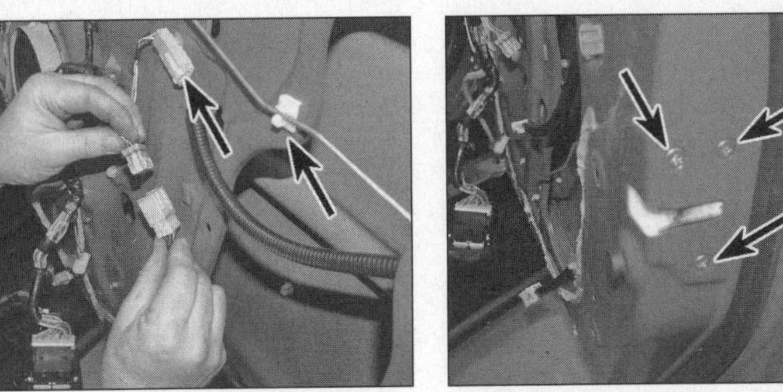

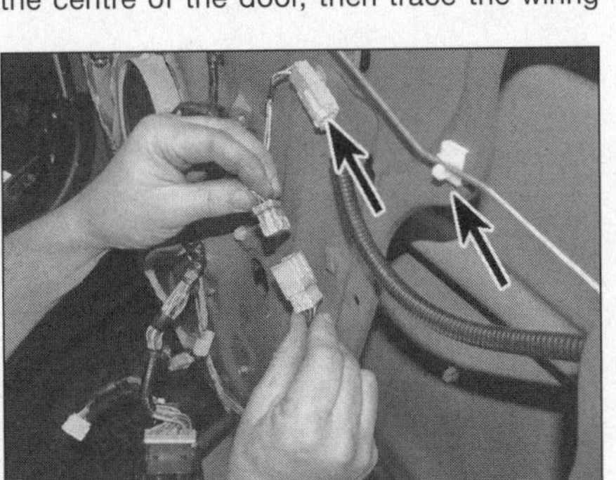

14.17 Disconnect lock wiring plugs, and unclip operating rod

14.19a Remove screws at rear edge of door . . .

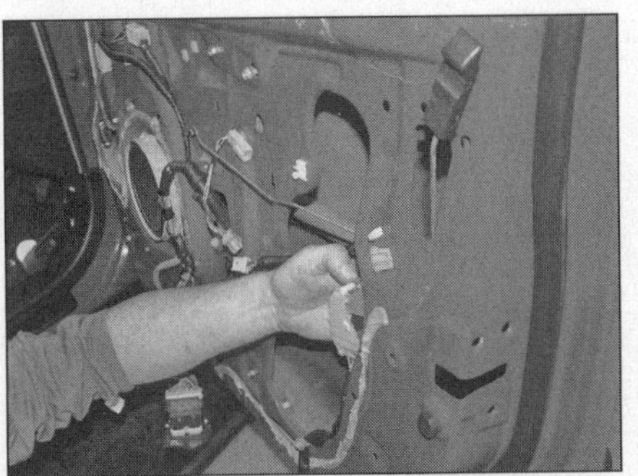

14.19b . . . to remove front door lock assembly

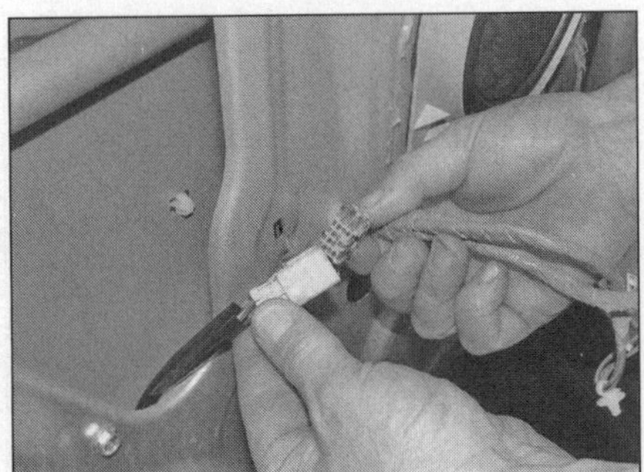

14.21a Disconnect door lock wiring connector . . .

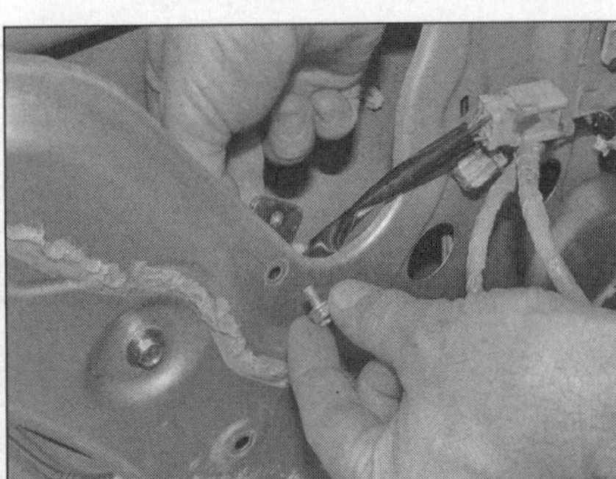

14.21b . . . then trace wiring back and unbolt it . . .

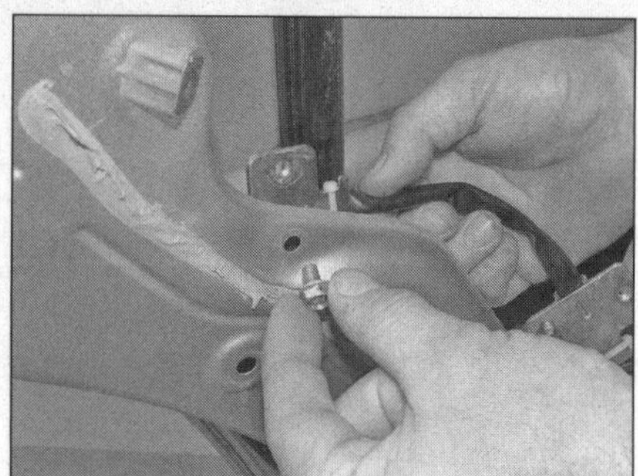

14.21c . . . to release it from door

the door, taking care not to bend the still-attached operating rods **(see illustrations)**.

Refitting

23 Refitting is a reversal of removal, noting the following points:

15.2 Door glass securing bolts, seen through door access holes

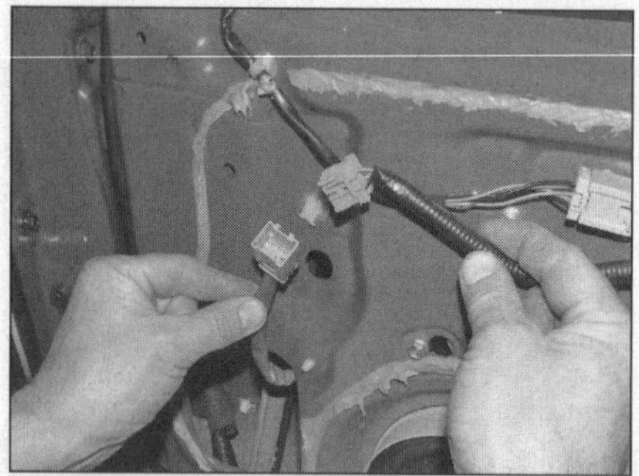

15.4 Disconnect front window motor wiring

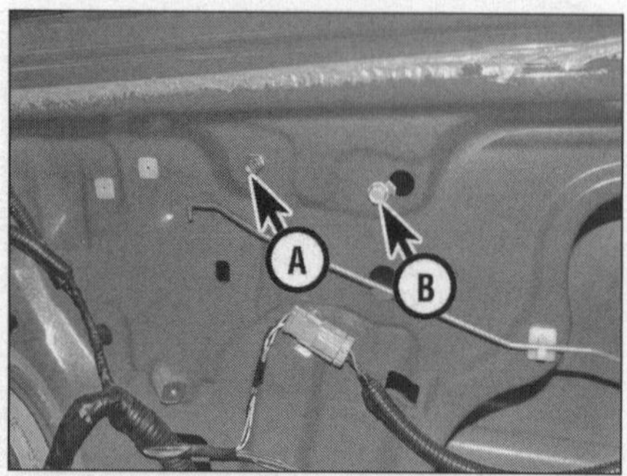

15.5b . . . unscrew regulator top mounting bolt (A), but only slacken bolt (B)

14.22a Remove screws at rear edge of door . . .

a) Ensure that all operating rods and wiring plugs are correctly and securely reconnected.
b) Lightly grease the operating rod sliding surfaces and pivots as necessary.
c) Check the operation of all components

15.3 Removing front door glass

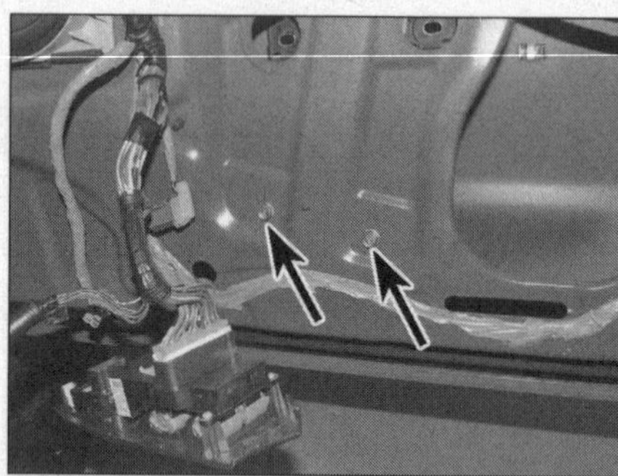

15.5a Remove regulator's two lower mounting bolts . . .

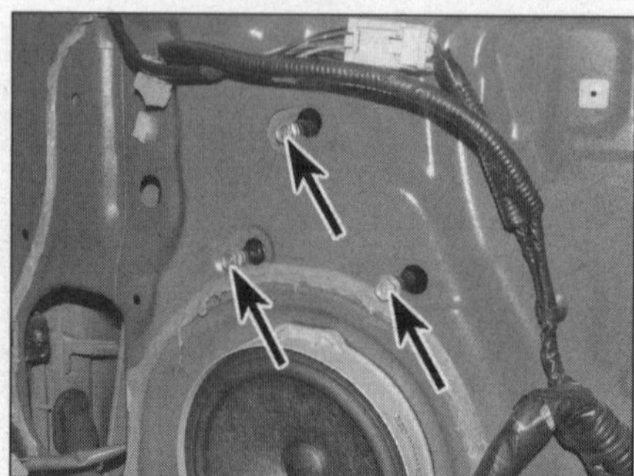

15.6a Slacken three motor mounting bolts . . .

14.22b . . . to remove rear door lock assembly

before refitting the membrane and door trim panel.

15 Door window glass and regulator – removal and refitting

Removal

1 Remove the door trim panel and membrane as described in Section 13.

Front glass

2 Temporarily reconnect the window switch, and lower the glass until the two securing bolts are visible in the door frame **(see illustration)**.

3 Have an assistant support the glass (take care – it's heavy), then unscrew and remove the bolts. Tilt the glass forwards, then lift and withdraw it from the door **(see illustration)**.

Front regulator/motor

4 To remove the regulator, first disconnect the motor wiring plug **(see illustration)**. Trace the wiring back towards the motor, and release the harness clip.

5 Unscrew and remove three of the regulator bolts – the fourth is on a slotted mounting, and need only be slackened **(see illustrations)**.

6 Similarly, the three motor mounting bolts need only be slackened, as they sit in slotted mountings. Withdraw the regulator and motor assembly from the door **(see illustrations)**.

Rear glass

7 Temporarily reconnect the window switch, and lower the glass until the two securing bolts are visible in the door frame.

15.6b . . . and remove motor/regulator assembly from front door

15.10 Peel back glass seal to undo screw underneath . . .

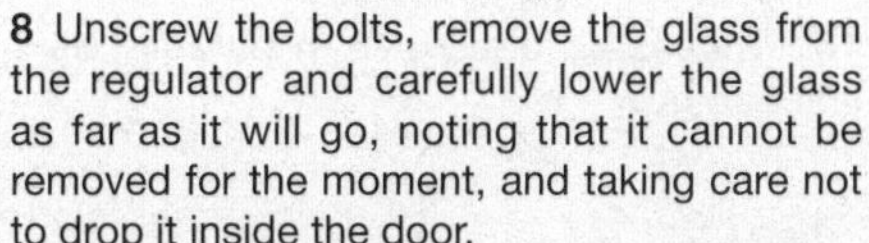

8 Unscrew the bolts, remove the glass from the regulator and carefully lower the glass as far as it will go, noting that it cannot be removed for the moment, and taking care not to drop it inside the door.

9 Starting at the top rear corner, carefully pull up and remove the door glass outer weatherstrip. Take care to ease the strip out slowly, as it can be bent if too much force is used, and the plastic clips are fragile. Also take care not to scratch the paint (it may be wise to apply a strip or two of masking tape along the top of the door first).

10 Peel back the door quarter glass seal at the top of the rear window guide channel and remove the screw underneath securing the centre guide channel's upper end **(see illustration)**.

11 Unscrew the guide channel's mounting bolts and withdraw the collar at the base of the guide channel **(see illustrations)**.

12 Pull the channel forwards to free the top end from the door frame and then upwards.

13 Withdraw the door quarter glass and seal as an assembly from the door.

14 Release the glass from the guide channel and carefully withdraw it completely from the door.

Rear regulator/motor

15 To remove the regulator, where applicable first disconnect the motor wiring plug, which is near the front of the door. Unclip the wiring harness from the door **(see illustration)**.

16 Unscrew and remove the regulator's single lower bolt, and unscrew the front upper bolt – the rear bolt is on a slotted mounting and need only be slackened. Similarly, the three motor mounting bolts need only be slackened, as they sit in slotted mountings **(see illustration)**.

17 Withdraw the regulator and motor assembly from the door.

Refitting

18 Refitting is a reversal of removal, noting the following points:

a) *Tighten all mounting bolts securely.*
b) *Lightly grease the regulator sliding surfaces as necessary.*
c) *Check the operation of all components before refitting the membrane and door trim panel.*

15.11a . . . then unscrew window glass centre guide channel middle mounting bolt . . .

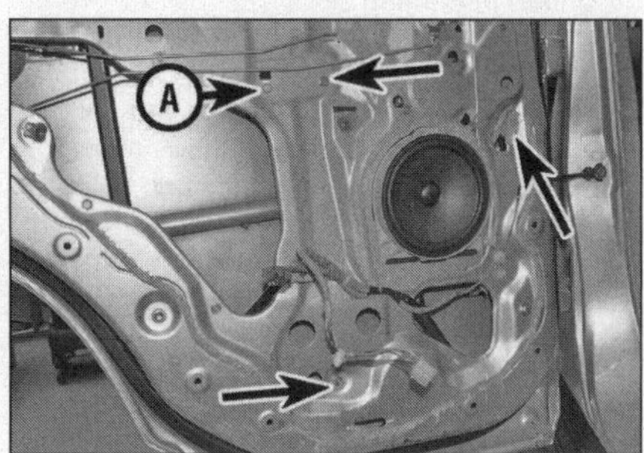

15.15 Rear window regulator mounting bolts (note bolt A need only be slackened) and motor wiring plug

16 Tailgate and support struts – removal and refitting

Tailgate

Removal

1 Locate the tailgate wiring plug, then twist and disconnect it.

2 Unbolt the tailgate support strut.

3 Have an assistant support the tailgate, or rest it on an axle stand – pad the top of the stand with cloth, to prevent damage to the paint.

4 Unscrew the upper and lower tailgate-to-hinge bolts, and remove the tailgate from the vehicle **(see illustration)**. Unclip the tailgate wiring boots and washer tube as the tailgate is removed.

5 Examine the hinges for signs of wear or damage. If renewal is necessary, mark the position of the hinge, then unscrew the retaining bolts and remove the hinge from the vehicle. Fit the new hinge, aligning it with the marks made before removal, then tighten the retaining bolts to the specified torque.

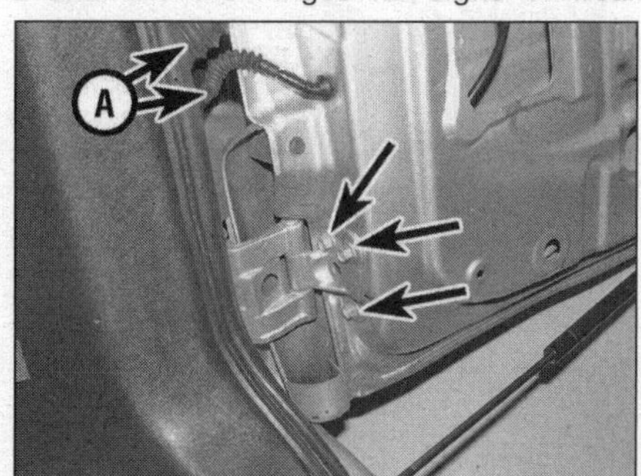

16.4 Tailgate hinge bolts. Note wiring boots (A)

15.11b . . . and lower mounting bolt

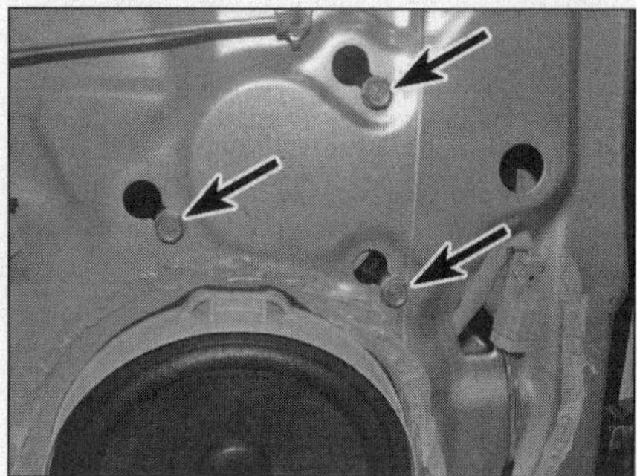

15.16 Rear window motor mounting bolts need only be slackened

Refitting

6 Refitting is a reversal of removal, noting the following points:

a) *Tighten the hinge bolts to the specified torque.*
b) *Check the tailgate alignment and if necessary adjust as described later in this Section.*
c) *If the paintwork around the hinges has been damaged, paint the area with a suitable touch-in brush to prevent corrosion.*

Adjustment

7 To adjust the tailgate to compensate for general wear in the hinges, this is best done

16.7 Slacken screws and adjust tailgate lock striker slightly if necessary

16.9 Tailgate strut-to-tailgate bolts

by adjusting the position of the lock striker **(see illustration)**.

8 If adjusting the tailgate after removal, close the tailgate and check that the gap between the tailgate and surrounding bodywork is equal around the complete perimeter. If necessary, slight adjustment of the tailgate position can be made by slackening the hinge retaining bolts and repositioning the hinge/tailgate as necessary. Once the tailgate is correctly positioned, tighten the hinge bolts to their specified torque. Check that the tailgate striker engages centrally with the lock, and if necessary, adjust the position of the striker.

Support strut

9 Open the tailgate, unscrew the bolt securing the body end of the tailgate strut and apply protective tape around the hinge side edge of the tailgate lower trim to prevent damage to the bumper. Open the tailgate to give the maximum clearance between the tailgate lower trim and the bumper, then secure the tailgate in this position. Unscrew the two mounting bolts and withdraw the support strut **(see illustrations 7.1a and 16.9)**.

10 Refitting is a reversal of removal.

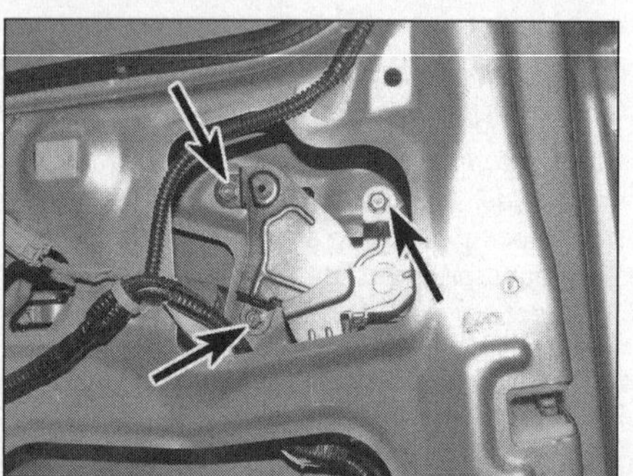

17.2 Tailgate stopper assembly mounting bolts

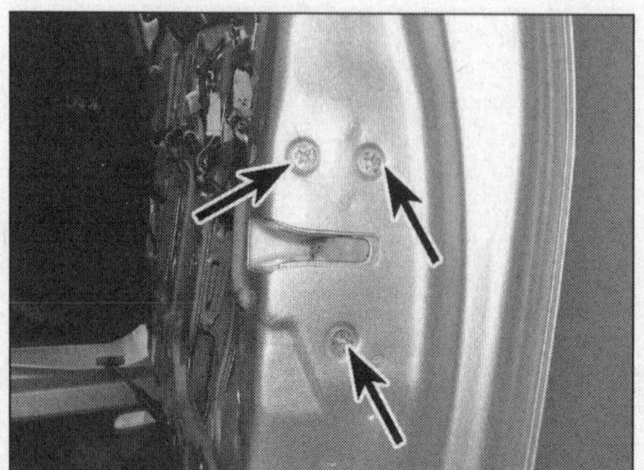

17.11 Remove screws at edge of tailgate to remove tailgate lock assembly

17 Tailgate lock components - removal and refitting

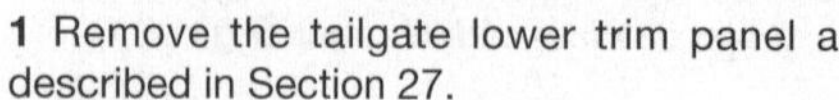

1 Remove the tailgate lower trim panel as described in Section 27.

Tailgate handle

2 Disconnect the lower end of the tailgate stopper operating rod from the lock assembly, then unscrew the mounting bolts and withdraw the tailgate stopper assembly **(see illustration)**.

3 Disconnect the lock cylinder operating rod and the tailgate glass opening rod from the tailgate lock cylinder.

4 Extract the retainer clip with a hooked tool and remove the lock cylinder from the tailgate handle.

5 Unscrew the bolt securing the lock cylinder protector and the tailgate handle. Unhook and release the protector.

6 Unscrew the remaining bolt securing the tailgate handle and remove the spacer. Pull out and withdraw the handle.

7 Refitting is a reversal of removal. Check the operation of the lock before refitting the tailgate trim panel.

Lock cylinder

8 Proceed as described in paragraphs 1 to 4 above.

9 Refitting is a reversal of removal. Check the operation of the lock before refitting the tailgate outer trim panel.

Lock

10 Disconnect the tailgate operating rod and cylinder rod from the lock assembly, then disconnect the wiring connector.

11 Undo the screws securing the lock and withdraw it through the aperture in the tailgate, taking care not to bend the operating rods **(see illustration)**.

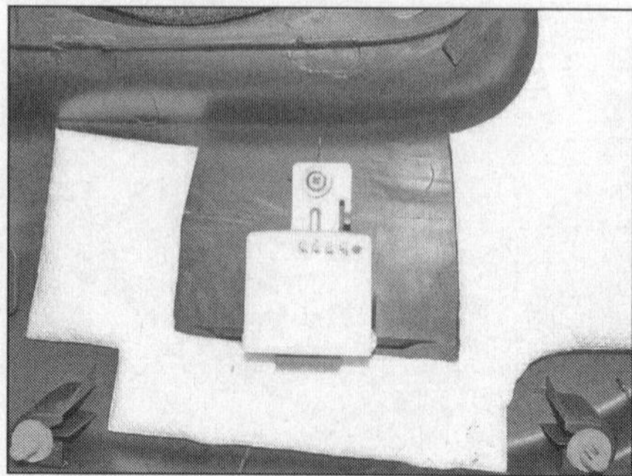

18.4 Deadlocking control unit

12 Refitting is a reversal of removal. Check the operation of the lock before refitting the tailgate trim panel.

Lock striker

13 Mark around the striker with paint (such as typist's correction fluid) to ensure it is accurately refitted.

14 Unscrew the two mounting screws, and withdraw the striker from the tailgate aperture **(see illustration 16.7)**.

15 Refitting is a reversal of removal. Align the striker with the previously-made marks, and tighten the screws to the specified torque.

Tailgate stopper assembly

16 Proceed as described in paragraphs 1 and 2 above.

18 Central locking components - general

1 The operation of the central locking is integrated into the door locks, and is controlled by the multiplex control unit, which is fitted behind the fusebox – refer to Section 3 of Chapter 12. If a fault occurs in the system, the vehicle should be taken to a Honda dealer who will have the special diagnostic equipment necessary to find the fault quickly.

Central locking switches

2 The central locking switches fitted to the two front door lock cylinders are removed as described in Section 14. The lock switches fitted to the rear doors and tailgate are part of the lock assemblies themselves. The central locking system switch fitted on 3-door model front door trim panels can be removed after taking off the door trim panel as described in Section 13 – the switch is screwed to the inside of the panel.

Remote receiver

3 The remote central locking receiver unit is mounted on the facia behind the heater control panel/climate control unit – remove the panel/unit as described in Chapter 3 for access. Disconnect the wiring plug, then unscrew the mounting bolt and remove the receiver unit from the facia.

Deadlocking control units

4 Each of the doors has a separate dead-locking (or 'super-locking') control unit fitted. When the deadlocking feature is activated, the inner door handles are effectively disconnected, meaning that a thief will still not be able to open a door, even after breaking a window. Remove the door trim panel as described in Section 13, then disconnect the deadlocking control unit wiring plug and remove the single mounting screw **(see illustration)**.

20.1 Interior rear view mirror base is bonded to windscreen

20.2a To refit, align mirror with base . . .

20.2b . . . 90° clockwise from slot . . .

20.2c . . . then rotate into correct position . . .

20.2d . . . and ensure mirror is locked correctly on base

20.4 Unclip mirror trim panel at front of door

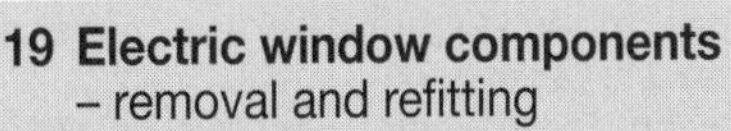

19 Electric window components – removal and refitting

Window switch

1 Refer to Chapter 12.

Window motor

2 The window motor is removed with the regulator assembly, as described in Section 15.

20 Mirrors and associated components – removal and refitting

Interior mirror

1 Remove the mirror by sliding the base downwards to release it from the base, which is bonded to the windscreen **(see illustration)**. Take care not to unbond the base from the windscreen.

2 On refitting, offer the mirror up to the base, aligned 90° clockwise from its slot. Engage the mirror onto the base, then twist it 90° anti-clockwise to secure **(see illustrations)**.

Door mirror assembly

3 Lower the window glass fully.

4 Carefully pull off the mirror inner trim panel by hand – pull the panel out at the rear edge, then prise it carefully inwards to disengage the two retaining clips **(see illustration)**.

5 Remove the door trim panel as described in Section 13.

6 Disconnect the mirror wiring plug at the top of the door – peel back the membrane as necessary to reach the connector **(see illustration)**.

7 Support the mirror, then unscrew the three mounting nuts and withdraw the mirror from the outside of the door **(see illustration)**.

8 Refitting is a reversal of removal. Check the mirror operation before refitting the door and mirror trim panels.

Door mirror glass

9 Push the glass fully into the housing at the top, so that the lower edge is sticking out. Insert a wide, flat-bladed tool (wrapped with tape to protect the housing) into the gap between the glass and mirror housing, and release the glass, which is secured to the centre pivot plate with two clips and a little mastic.

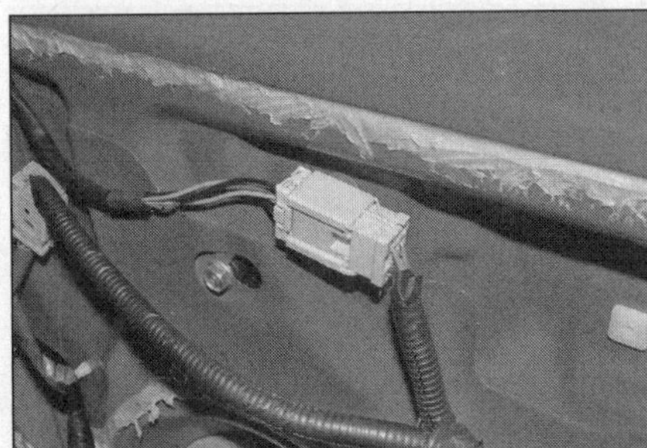

20.6 Remove door trim panel and membrane, then disconnect mirror wiring plug . . .

10 Disconnect the wiring connector from the mirror heating element, and remove the glass.

11 When refitting, align the glass with the two mounting clips, and push it evenly onto them – use a wad of cloth, and take care not to use excessive force, as the glass is easily broken.

Door mirror switch

12 Refer to Chapter 12.

Door mirror motor

13 With the mirror removed, separate the mirror body from the mounting plate by removing the three screws underneath.

14 The motor wiring plug will have to be cut off, to feed it back through the mirror body – leave plenty of wire attached to the plug, to reconnect the new motor to.

15 Unscrew the three motor mounting screws, then remove the motor, withdrawing the wiring through the mirror body.

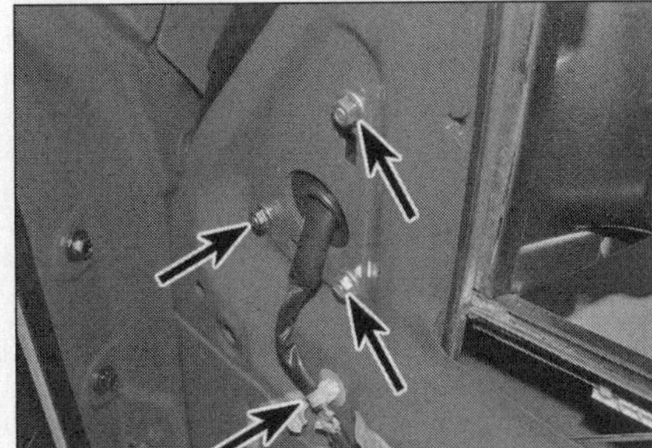

20.7 . . . unclip wiring harness from and unscrew three mounting nuts to withdraw mirror

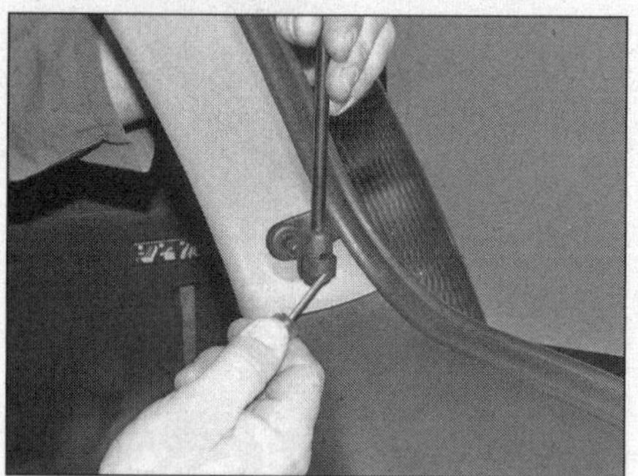

21.8 Prise out retaining clip to release tailgate glass support strut from mounting

16 Refitting is a reversal of removal. Feed the wiring through, then reconnect the wiring plug – it is recommended that the wires are soldered and properly insulated.

21 Windscreen, tailgate and fixed side window glass – general information

Windscreen and fixed side window glass

1 These areas of glass are bonded in position with a special adhesive. Renewal of such fixed glass is a difficult, messy and time-consuming task, which is beyond the scope of the home mechanic. It is difficult, unless one has plenty of practice, to obtain a secure, waterproof fit. In view of this, owners are strongly advised to have this work carried out by one of the many specialist windscreen fitters.

Tailgate glass

Removal

2 Remove both tailgate side trim panels.

3 Remove the high-level stop-light (Chapter 12).

4 Disconnect the wiring for the rear window demister, and release the wiring and retaining clips from the tailgate glass support strut brackets; on the right-hand side, release the wiring from the trim channel.

5 Have an assistant support the glass (take care – it's heavy), then unscrew and remove the Torx (size T30) bolt securing each tailgate glass support strut to the tailgate. Withdraw both support strut brackets from the tailgate.

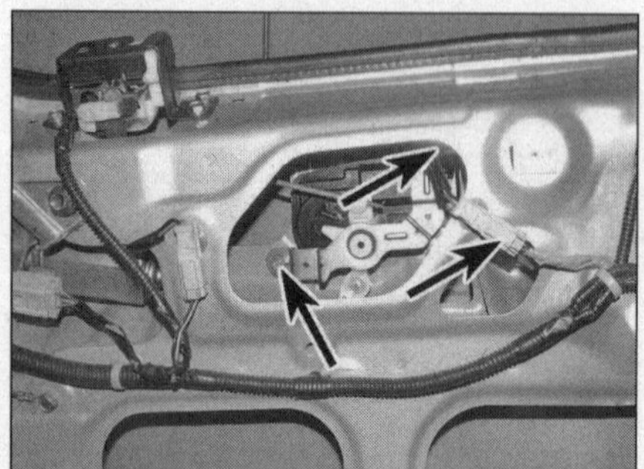

21.17 Tailgate glass actuator mounting bolts and wiring connector plug

21.9 Remove tailgate side trim panel to unbolt strut mounting from tailgate

6 Unscrew the hinge retaining nuts and withdraw the tailgate glass.

7 Refitting is a reversal of removal. To adjust the tailgate glass after removal, close the glass and check that the gap between the glass and tailgate is equal around the complete perimeter. If necessary, slight adjustment of the glass position can be made by slackening the hinge retaining nuts and repositioning the hinge/glass as necessary. Once the glass is correctly positioned, tighten the hinge nuts to their specified torque. Check that the tailgate glass striker engages centrally with the lock, and if necessary, adjust the position of the striker.

Tailgate glass support strut

8 The support struts alone can be removed by prising out their retaining clips to release them from their mountings **(see illustration)**.

9 To remove the strut completely, remove first both tailgate side trim panels. Disconnecting the wiring for the rear window demister if necessary, release the wiring and retaining clips from the tailgate glass support strut brackets **(see illustration)**.

10 Have an assistant support the glass (take care – it's heavy), then unscrew and remove the Torx (size T30) bolt securing each tailgate glass support strut to the tailgate. Withdraw both support strut brackets from the tailgate.

11 Unscrew and remove the Torx (size T30) bolt securing each tailgate glass support strut to the tailgate glass; collect the nut and seal from the other side of the glass and remove the strut (it is secured with double-sided adhesive tape).

21.19 Tailgate glass release button is mounted on inside of driver's door trim panel

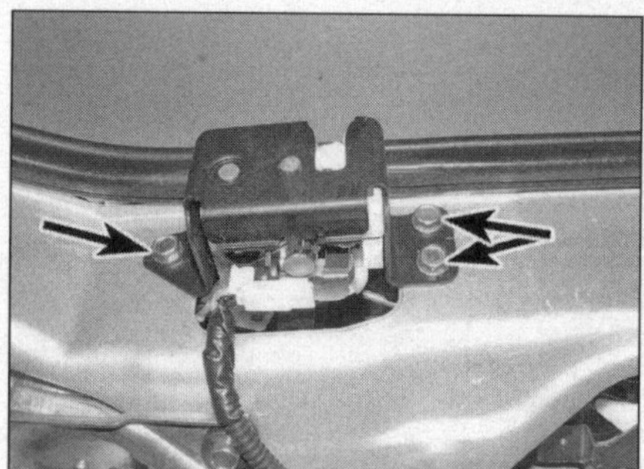

21.14 Tailgate glass lock mounting bolts

12 Refitting is a reversal of removal. Tighten the Torx bolts to their specified torque.

Tailgate glass opening mechanism

Tailgate glass lock

13 Remove the tailgate lower trim panel as described in Section 27.

14 Disconnect the wiring plugs, unscrew the mounting bolts and withdraw the lock **(see illustration)**.

15 Refitting is a reversal of removal. Check the operation of the lock before refitting the tailgate trim panel.

Tailgate glass actuator

16 Remove the tailgate lower trim panel as described in Section 27.

17 Disconnect the wiring plug and operating rods from the actuator, then unscrew the mounting bolts and withdraw the lock **(see illustration)**.

18 Refitting is a reversal of removal. Check the operation of the lock before refitting the tailgate trim panel.

Tailgate glass release button

19 Remove the driver's door trim panel as described in Section 13. The button is secured by two screws to the inside of the panel **(see illustration)**.

20 Refitting is a reversal of removal. Check the operation of the system before refitting the door trim panel.

22 Sunroof – general information

Due to the complexity of the sunroof mechanism, considerable expertise is needed to repair, renew or adjust the sunroof components successfully. Removal of the roof first requires the headlining to be removed, which is a complex and tedious operation, and not a task to be undertaken lightly. Therefore, any problems with the sunroof should be referred to a Honda dealer.

On models with an electric sunroof, if the sunroof motor fails to operate, first check the relevant fuse. If the fault cannot be traced and rectified, the sunroof can be opened and closed manually using a special cranked tool to turn the motor spindle (this tool is supplied with the vehicle, in the toolkit which is in the luggage compartment). To gain access to the motor, unclip the small round trim cover in front of the rear interior light. Insert the tool fully into the motor opening, and turn it to open or close the sunroof **(see illustrations)**.

23 Exterior fittings – removal and refitting

Engine undershield

1 The undershield is secured by a number of clips around the edge, by bolts and/or clips to the bottom edge of the front bumper and by two clips in each wheel arch. The clips are released by prising out their centres with a small flat-tipped screwdriver so that the clip centre and outer part can be withdrawn together.

2 Jack up the front of the vehicle, and support it on axle stands (see *Jacking and vehicle support*).

3 Start in the wheel arch; turn the steering to full lock and reach behind the wheel to release the two clips. Carefully disengage the undershield from the wheel arch liner itself; note the tab projecting from the undershield to link it to the wheel arch liner **(see illustrations)**.

4 Work along the bottom edge of the front bumper unscrewing the bolts and releasing the clips. Note that the outermost clip/bolt on each side secures the wheel arch liner itself. Release the clips along the rear edge of the undershield and withdraw it **(see illustrations)**.

5 Refitting is a reversal of removal. Ensure that the various panels are fitted together properly and that all clips and bolts are securely fastened **(see illustration)**.

Front wheel arch liners

6 Removing the wheel arch liners is much easier with the relevant wheel removed. Slacken the relevant wheel nuts, then jack up the front or rear of the vehicle, and support it on axle stands (see *Jacking and vehicle support*). Remove the wheel.

7 Remove the three screws from the mudflap at the rear of the wheel arch, and withdraw the mudflap.

8 Unscrew and remove the Torx (size T30) bolt securing the liner at the top of the wheel arch, and the screw at the front.

9 From under the front bumper release the clip(s) and unscrew the bolt(s) securing the bumper, undershield and wheel arch liner.

10 Work around the inside of the wheel arch liner, and prise out the clips (approximately seven in total) securing the liner to the wheel arch. It may be necessary to wipe the liner

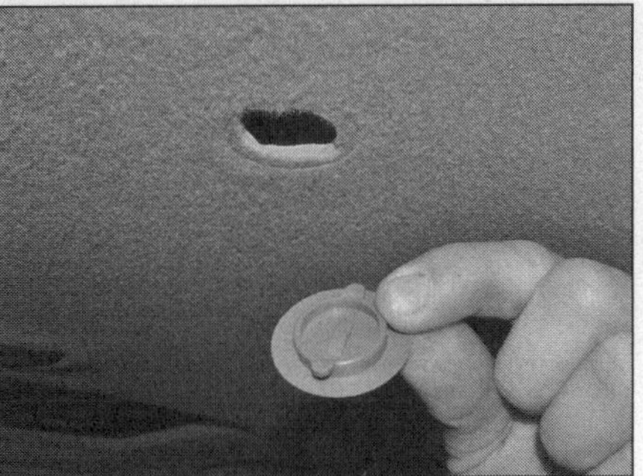

22.2a Unclip small round trim cover in centre of headlining . . .

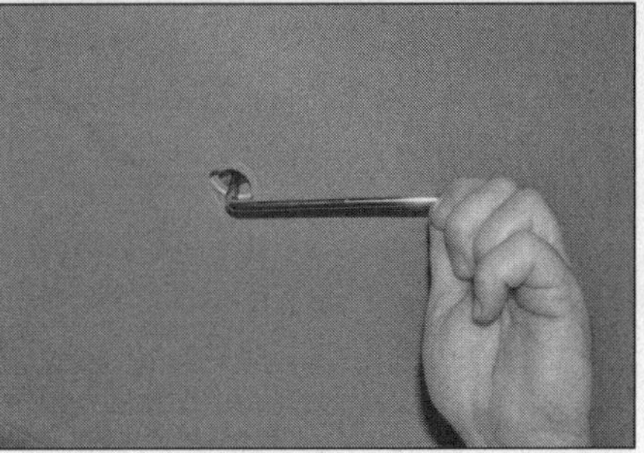

22.2b . . . and use special cranked tool from vehicle toolkit to close sunroof manually

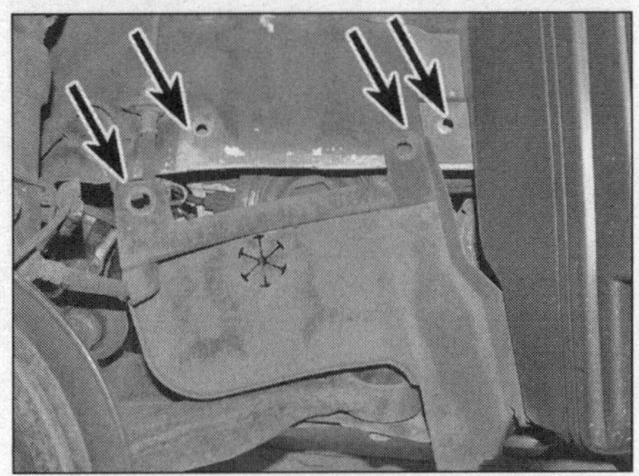

23.3a Start undershield removal by releasing clips in wheel arches . . .

23.3b . . . separate undershield tab from wheel arch liner . . .

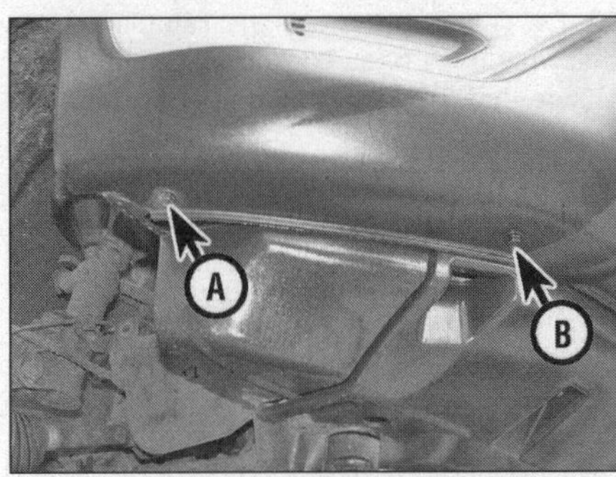

23.3c Wheel arch liner is secured by bolt (A), undershield by bolt (B)

23.4a Undershield is secured by two clips in centre – later models

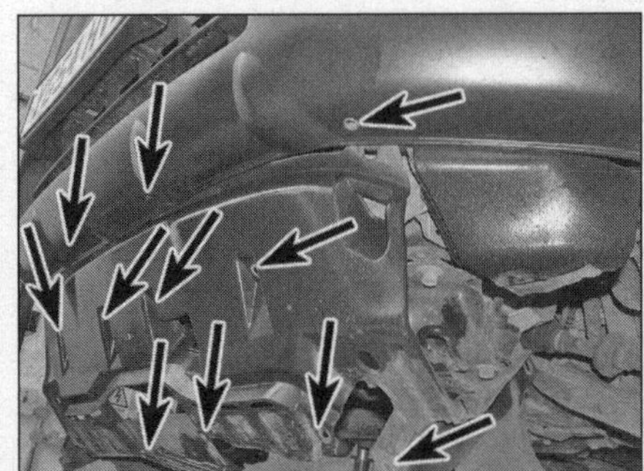

23.4b Locations of undershield retaining clips – petrol models

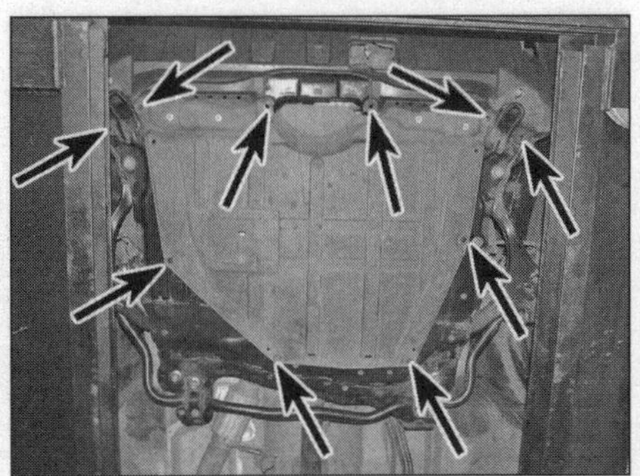

23.4c Locations of undershield retaining clips – diesel models

23.5 Ensure panels match correctly when refitting undershield

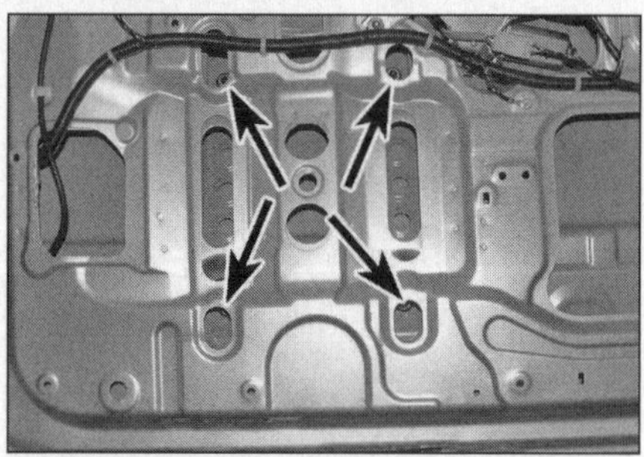
23.25 Spare wheel holder nuts are reached once tailgate interior lower trim panel has been removed

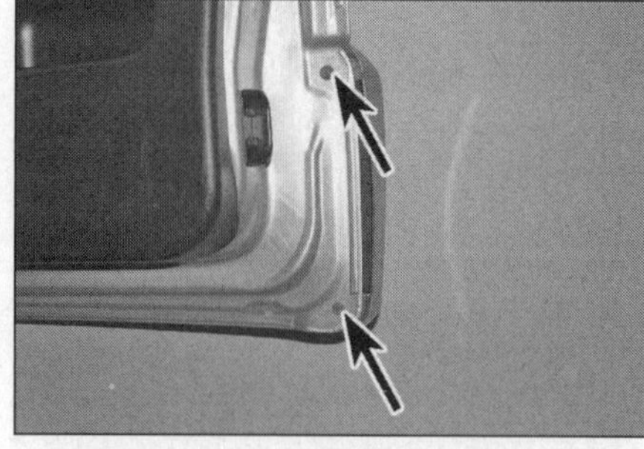
23.26 Tailgate exterior trim panel is secured by four nuts, two at each end of tailgate

23.29a Door exterior upper trim strip . . .

23.29b . . . is secured by clips on inside

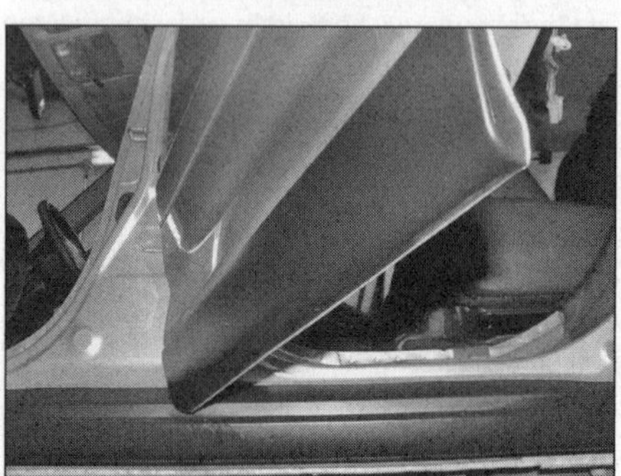
23.29c Door exterior lower trim strip . . .

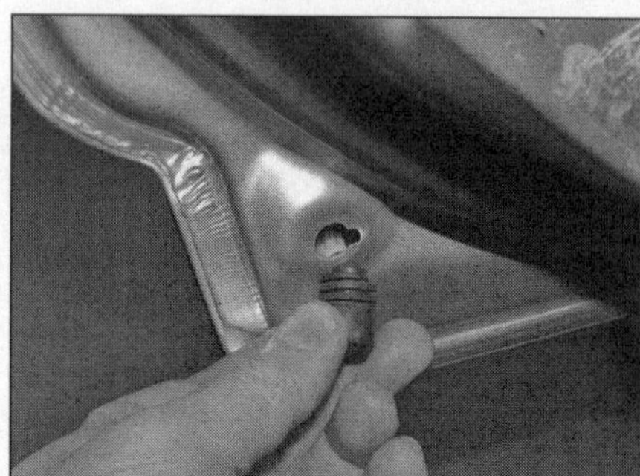
23.29d . . . is also secured by clips on inside, behind door stop rubber

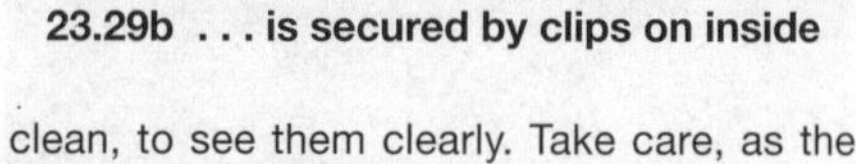

clean, to see them clearly. Take care, as the clips are easily broken.

11 With all the clips removed, release the liner and withdraw it from under the wheel arch.

12 On refitting, renew any retaining clips that may have been broken on removal, and ensure that the liner is securely fastened.

Front wheel arch trim

13 Remove the wheel arch liner as described above.

14 Carefully pull away the trim, releasing the five clips securing it to the body.

15 On refitting, renew any retaining clips that may have been broken on removal, and ensure that the trim and liner are securely fastened.

Sill trim

16 Remove the three screws from the mudflap at the rear of the front wheel arch, and withdraw the mudflap.

17 Carefully work along the length of the trim, pulling outwards to release the six clips.

18 Pulling back the wheel arch liner as necessary, slide the trim forwards to disengage it from the seven mounting clips; these will stay in the body.

19 On refitting, renew any retaining clips that may have been broken on removal, and ensure that the liner is securely fastened.

Rear wheel arch trim

20 Remove the bumper retaining screws at the rear of the rear wheel arch. Unclip the bumper ends by pulling them slightly outwards (the clips are stiff to release), and releasing the five hooks on each side securing the top edge of the bumper to the bodywork, then open the rear door.

21 Unscrew the four screws retaining the trim around the edge of the wheel arch.

22 Carefully pull away the trim, releasing the six clips securing it to the body.

23 On refitting, renew any retaining clips that may have been broken on removal, and ensure that the trim and bumper are securely fastened.

Tailgate trim panel

24 Remove the tailgate lower trim panel as described in Section 27.

25 Unscrew the spare wheel holder mounting nuts and withdraw the holder **(see illustration)**.

26 Unscrew the four bolts securing the trim panel to the tailgate **(see illustration)**.

27 Pull out the tailgate trim along its bottom edge to release the five clips. Working from the inside of the tailgate, release the five clips securing its upper edge and withdraw the trim.

24.2 Remove seat front mounting bolts and disconnect seat wiring connectors (passenger's seat)

28 On refitting, renew any retaining clips that may have been broken on removal, and ensure that the trim panels are securely fastened.

Body trim strips and badges

29 The various body trim strips and badges are held in position with a special adhesive tape and locating lugs **(see illustrations)**. Removal requires the trim/badge to be heated, to soften the adhesive, and then carefully lifted away from the surface. Due to the high risk of damage to the paintwork during this operation, it is recommended that this task should be entrusted to a Honda dealer.

24 Seats – removal and refitting

Note: *Refer to the airbag warnings in Chapter 12 if removing front seats with side airbags. Before disconnecting the battery, refer to Disconnecting the battery at the back of this manual.*

Removal

Front seats

1 On models with side airbags (identifiable by having an AIRBAG label on the side of the front seat), disconnect the battery negative lead, and wait for at least 3 minutes before proceeding (see *Disconnecting the battery*). If this precaution is not taken, there is a risk that the side airbags will fire when the seat wiring plug is disconnected.

2 Slide the seat fully to the rear. Unclip and remove the plastic end cap from the front of each seat rail **(see illustration 27.109a)**, then remove the two seat front mounting bolts **(see illustration)**.

3 Slide the seat fully forwards, then remove the plastic end cap(s) from the rear of each seat rail. Unscrew and remove the two seat rear mounting bolts **(see illustrations)**.

4 Tilt the seat backwards and disconnect the wiring plugs underneath for the side airbag, seat heating and seat belt buckle signalling, as applicable **(see illustration)**.

5 Carefully remove the seat from inside the vehicle, taking care not to damage the surrounding trim panels. The help of an assistant may be necessary, as the seat is heavy.

Rear seats

6 Remove the head rests. Fold the seat back forwards and slide the seat fully to the rear.

7 Unclip and remove the plastic end cap from the front of each seat mounting **(see illustrations)**.

8 Unlock the rear seat and fold it forwards. If the seat lock release strap is broken, pierce holes in the rear of the seat track covering 15 mm inside the track and insert a flat-tipped screwdriver that is at least 100 mm long to release the seat catch levers.

9 Unclip and remove the plastic end cap from the rear of each seat mounting **(see illustrations)**.

10 Unscrew and remove the seat mounting bolts.

24.3a Similarly unclip seat rail rear end caps . . .

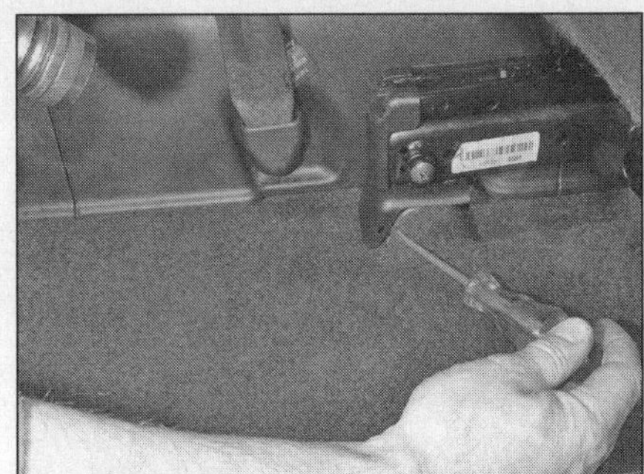

24.3b . . . take care not to mark cap if tools are used to release . . .

24.3c . . . rear outer rail caps are in two pieces

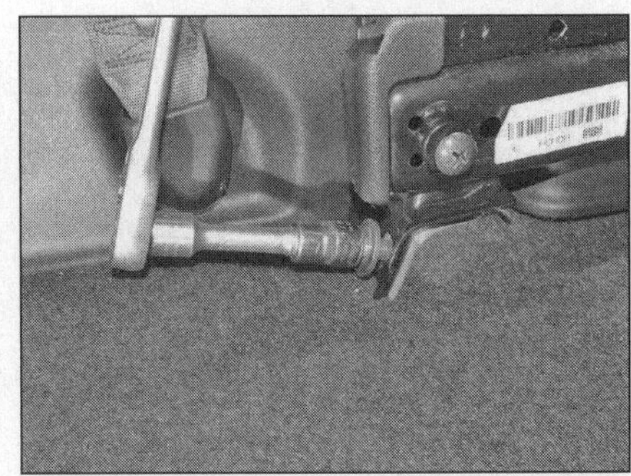

24.3d Unscrew seat rear mounting bolts

11 Carefully remove the seat from inside the vehicle, taking care not to damage the surrounding trim panels. The help of an assistant may be necessary, as the seat is heavy.

Refitting

12 Refitting is a reversal of removal, noting the following points:

a) Before reconnecting the front seat wiring, on models with side airbags,

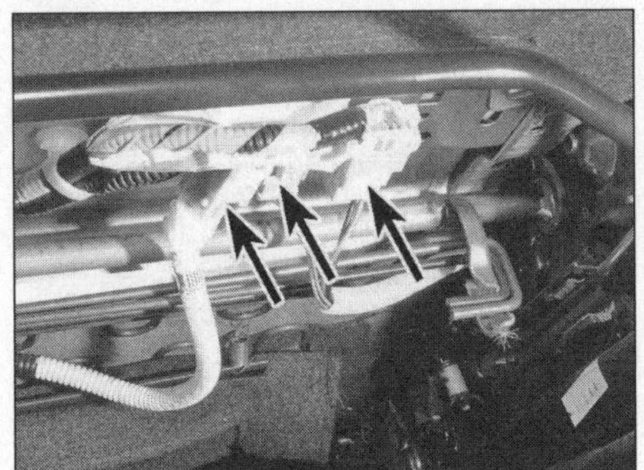

24.4 Disconnect driver's seat wiring connectors

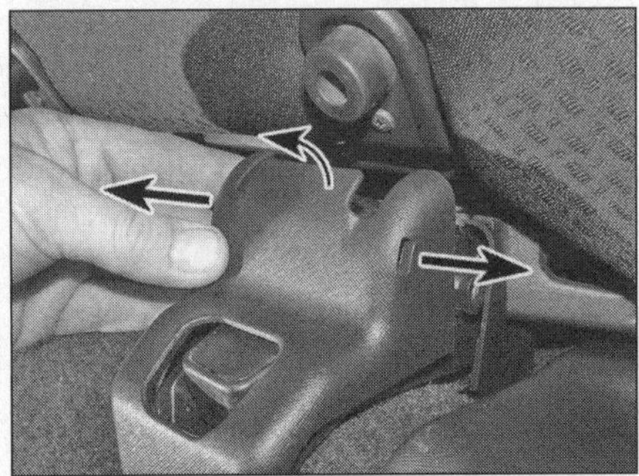

24.7a Unclip plastic end caps from front of each seat mounting . . .

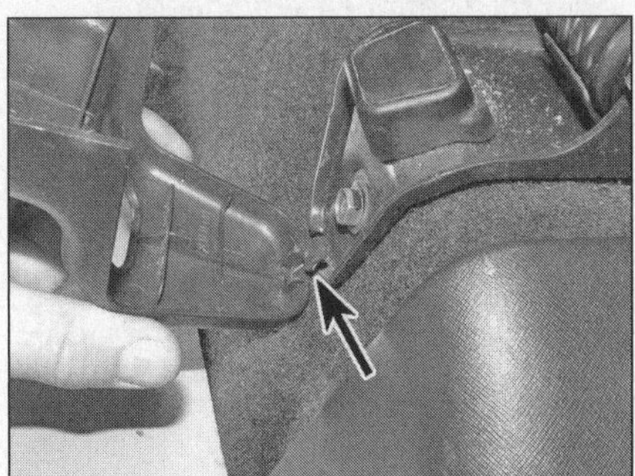

24.7b . . . and unhook from front mounting

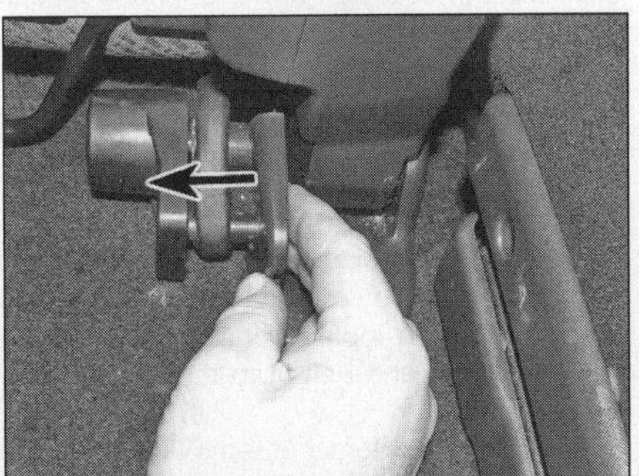

24.9a Unclip plastic end caps from rear of each seat mounting . . .

24.9b . . . inboard mounting shown here . .

24.9c . . . and outboard rear mounting

26.3 Unclip trim cover to unscrew front belt lower anchor bolt

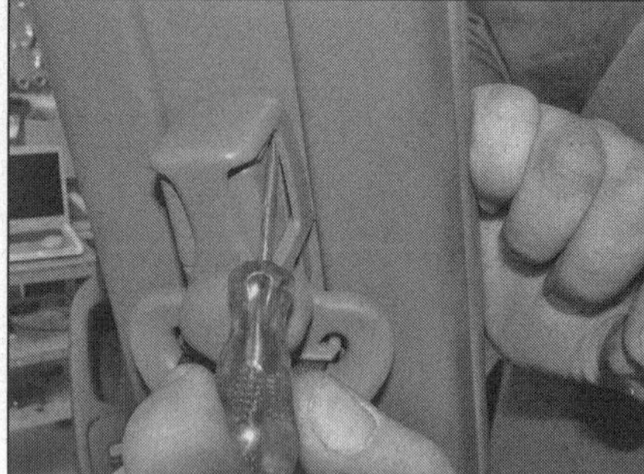
26.5a Unclip upper anchor trim cover on one side . . .

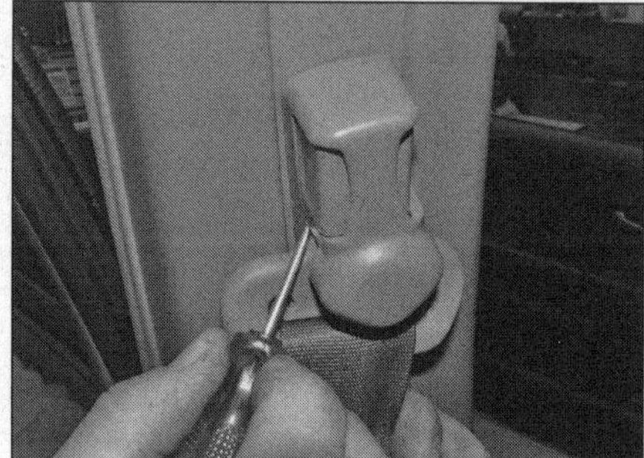
26.5b . . . then on the other . . .

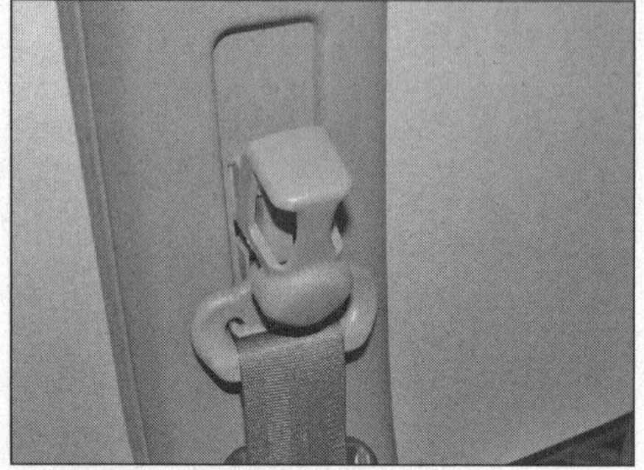
26.5c . . . and prise off upper anchor's plastic cover . . .

26.5d . . . to unscrew bolt and remove upper anchor

ensure that the battery is still disconnected.

b) Tighten the mounting bolts to the specified torque.

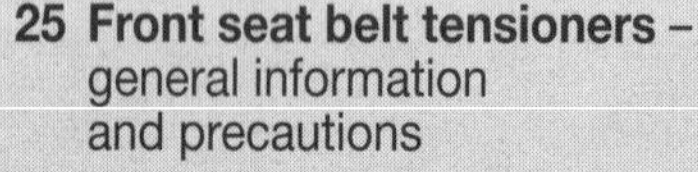

25 Front seat belt tensioners – general information and precautions

The front seat belt inertia reels are fitted with integral automatic belt tensioners (the rear seat belt inertia reels are not fitted with tensioners). The system is designed to instantaneously take up any slack in the seat belt in the case of a sudden frontal impact, therefore reducing the possibility of injury to the front seat occupants.

The seat belt tensioner is triggered by a frontal impact above a predetermined force. Lesser impacts, including impacts from behind, will not trigger the system. If the impact is sufficient to trigger the airbags, the seat belt tensioners will also be deployed.

When the system is triggered, the explosive gas in the tensioner mechanism retracts and locks the seat belt through a cable which acts on the inertia reel. This prevents the seat belt moving and keeps the occupant firmly in position in the seat. Once the tensioner has been triggered, the seat belt will be permanently locked and the assembly must be renewed.

Note the following warnings before contemplating any work on the front seat belts.

Warning: Do not expose the tensioner mechanism to temperatures in excess of 100°C.

• If the tensioner mechanism is dropped, it must be renewed, even it has suffered no apparent damage.

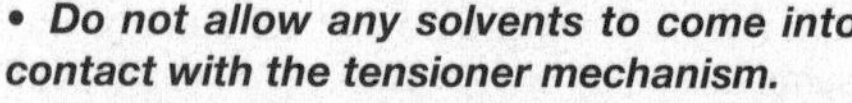
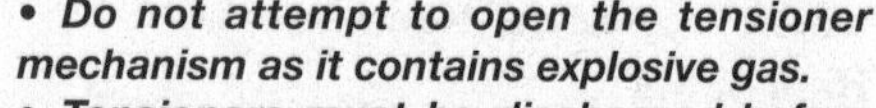

• Do not allow any solvents to come into contact with the tensioner mechanism.

• Do not attempt to open the tensioner mechanism as it contains explosive gas.

• Tensioners must be discharged before they are disposed of, but this task should be entrusted to a Honda dealer.

• Before removing the front seat belt inertia reels, the battery negative lead must be disconnected. Once disconnected, wait at least 3 minutes before proceeding, otherwise there is a risk that the tensioners will fire when the inertia reel wiring plug is disconnected. The battery must remain disconnected until after the tensioner wiring plug is reconnected.

26 Seat belt components – removal and refitting

Front seat belt

Note: *Refer to the warnings in Section 25.*

1 Disconnect the battery negative lead (see *Disconnecting the battery*). Wait at least 3 minutes before proceeding.

2 Slide the front seat fully forwards.

3 Unclip the seat belt lower anchor trim cover for access to the lower anchor bolt. Unscrew and remove the bolt, noting carefully how the washers and bushes are arranged **(see illustration).**

4 Remove the door sill and B-pillar lower trim panels as described in Section 27.

5 Unclip the seat belt upper anchor's plastic cover by spreading it apart and prising it off. Unscrew and remove the upper anchor bolt, again noting carefully how the washers and bushes are arranged **(see illustrations).**

6 Disconnect the tensioner wiring plug and release the wiring clip from the inertia reel.

7 Unscrew the inertia reel's upper mounting bolt and (larger) lower bolt (note that this has a spring-loaded locking collar) and remove the inertia reel and belt from the vehicle **(see illustration).**

8 Refitting is a reversal of removal, noting the following points:

a) Apply thread-locking fluid to the upper anchor bolt ***(see illustration).***

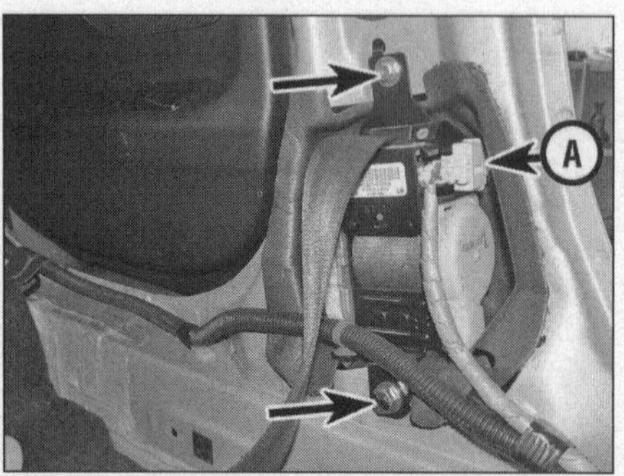

26.7 Front seat belt inertia reel mounting bolts and tensioner wiring plug (A)

26.8 Apply thread-locking fluid to upper anchor bolt

26.11a Remove height adjuster upper . . .

26.11b . . . and lower mounting bolts to remove adjuster from B-pillar

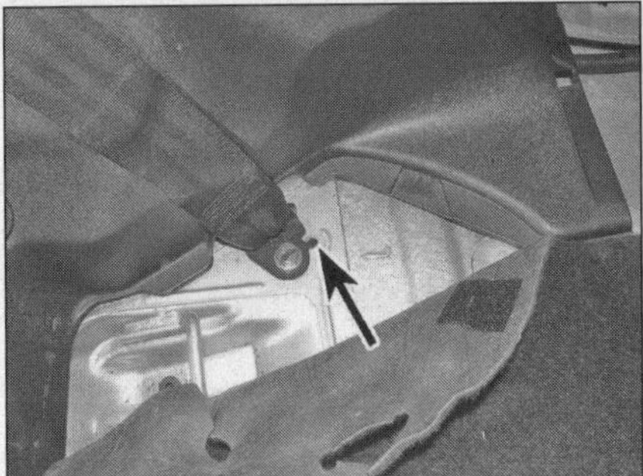

26.19 Rear side seat belt lower anchor on floor. Note lug locating anchor in place

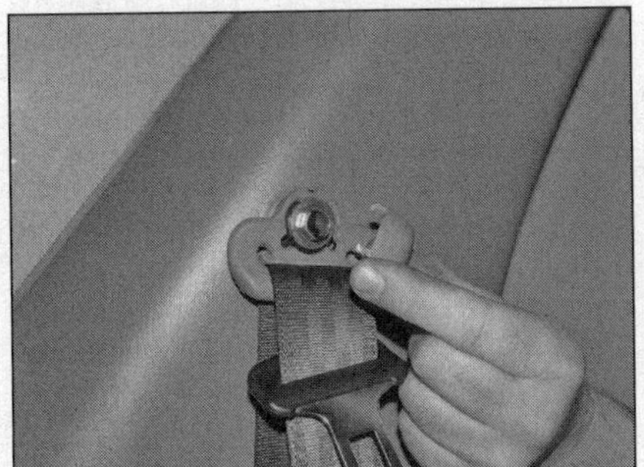

26.20a Unclip plastic cover from rear side seat belt's upper anchor . . .

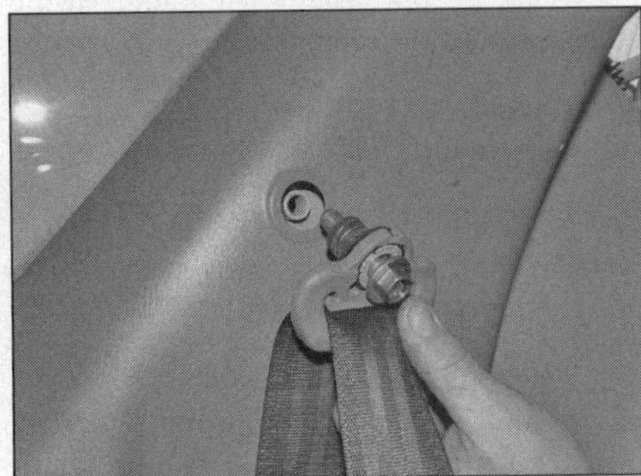

26.20b . . . and note arrangement of washers and bushes on bolt

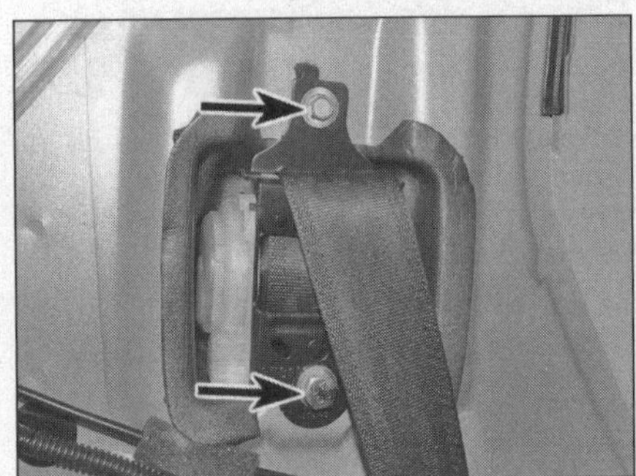

26.22 Rear side seat belt inertia reel mounting bolts

b) *Tighten all bolts to the specified torque, where given.*
c) *Ensure that the battery is still disconnected before reconnecting the tensioner wiring plug.*

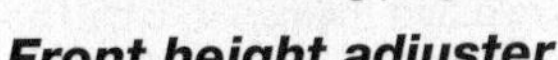

Front height adjuster

9 Unclip the seat belt upper anchor's plastic cover by spreading it apart and prising it off. Unscrew and remove the upper anchor bolt, again noting carefully how the washers and bushes are arranged.

10 Remove the B-pillar upper trim panel as described in Section 27.

11 Unscrew the height adjuster upper and lower mounting bolts, and remove the adjuster from the B-pillar **(see illustrations)**.

12 Refitting is a reversal of removal, noting the following points:

a) *Apply thread-locking fluid to the upper anchor bolt.*
b) *Tighten all bolts to the specified torque, where given.*

Front seat belt stalk

13 Remove the front seat as described in Section 24. Remove also the centre table and the underseat stowage box (where fitted).

14 Unclip and remove the plastic cover from the inner side of the seat.

15 Disconnect the wiring from the seat occupancy monitor and stalk buckle indicator (where applicable), and unclip the wiring from under the seat.

16 Unscrew the stalk mounting bolt, noting carefully how the washers are arranged, and remove the stalk from the seat.

17 Refitting is a reversal of removal. Engage the stalk's mounting lug into the hole on the seat frame, and tighten the mounting bolt to the specified torque.

Rear side belts

18 Fold forwards the rear seats.

19 Fold back the carpet as required to reach the seat belt lower anchor bolt, then unscrew and remove the bolt from the floor, noting how the lug on the anchor plate fits into the hole in the floor **(see illustration)**.

20 Unclip the seat belt upper anchor's plastic cover. Unscrew and remove the upper anchor bolt, again noting carefully how the washers and bushes are arranged **(see illustrations)**.

21 Remove the luggage compartment side trim panel as described in Section 27.

22 Unscrew the inertia reel's two mounting bolts, and remove the seat belt from the vehicle **(see illustration)**.

23 Refitting is a reversal of removal. Tighten all bolts to the specified torque.

Rear belt buckles

24 Access to the mounting bolts on the right-hand and centre seats can require the dismantling of the seats and the removal of the seat covering. This is not considered a DIY operation; for this reason, take the vehicle to a Honda dealer for work on the centre belt.

Rear centre belt

25 The belt's inertia reel is mounted above the headlining, the removal of which requires considerable skill and experience if it is to be carried out without damage, and is therefore not considered a DIY operation; for this reason, take the vehicle to a Honda dealer for work on the centre belt.

27 Interior trim and fittings – removal and refitting

General

1 The interior trim panels are secured by a combination of clips and screws, with plastic clips featuring heavily – these clips often get 'left behind' in the bodywork when the panels are removed, and should be prised out for refitting to the panels. Removal and refitting is generally self-explanatory, noting that it may be necessary to remove or slacken surrounding panels to allow a particular panel to be removed. The following paragraphs describe the removal and refitting of the major panels in more detail.

Door trim panels

2 Refer to Section 13.

Steering column shrouds

3 Working in the driver's footwell, remove the three screws from the lower shroud **(see illustration)**.

4 Unclip the upper shroud from the lower one, and withdraw it **(see illustrations)**.

5 Remove the lower shroud, manoeuvring it out past the column height adjuster lever, and over the ignition switch.

6 Refitting is a reversal of removal.

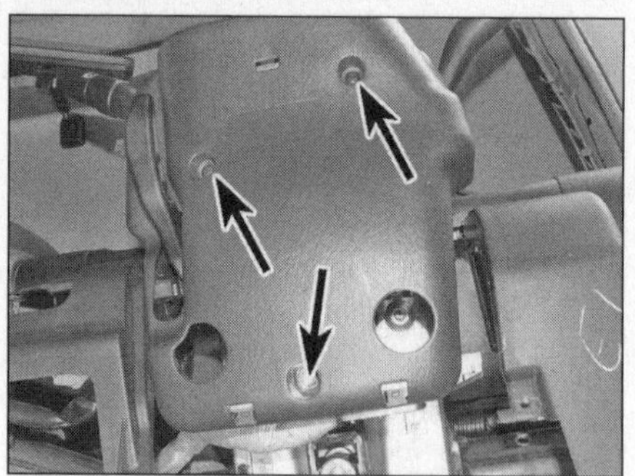
27.3 Unscrew three lower shroud screws under steering column

Driver's side facia under cover

7 Release the panel's lock knob by turning it through 90°.

8 Gently pull down at the rear to release the retaining clip, then pull the panel into the passenger compartment to release it from its bulkhead mounting.

9 Refitting is a reversal of removal.

Driver's side facia lower cover

10 Remove the driver's side under cover as described above.

11 Pull out the fuse panel's cover and open the driver's stowage pocket, then unscrew the single retaining screw behind each **(see illustrations)**.

12 Pull the bottom edge of the panel into the passenger compartment to release it from its eight mounting clips **(see illustrations)**.

13 Where fitted, disconnect the cabin temperature sensor wiring and air hose and the wiring for the switches mounted in the panel **(see illustrations)**.

27.4a Unclip upper shroud, then remove lower shroud . . .

14 Refitting is a reversal of removal. Ensure the sensor's air hose and all wiring plugs are securely refitted.

Facia lower centre section

Note: *This applies to vehicles with automatic transmission.*

15 Remove the passenger's side under cover from the facia, as described below.

16 Remove the heater control panel as described in Chapter 3, Section 9.

17 Open the centre stowage pocket and remove the ashtray; open the ashtray, then press down on the metal plate inside, and slide it out completely.

18 Unscrew the two mounting screws in the pocket opening, the third in the ashtray opening and the two mounting screws at the top edge of the centre section.

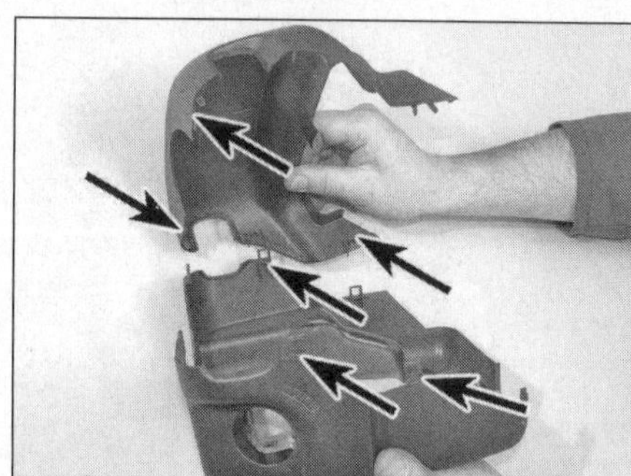
27.4b . . . noting how the two are clipped together

19 Release the single clip on each side of the centre section, at the front and near the floor.

20 Pull outwards, towards the driver's footwell, the part of the centre section covering the handbrake lever to release the two retaining clips.

21 Pull the centre section into the passenger compartment to release the remaining two clips and the passenger's side locating tab.

22 Disconnect the ashtray illumination bulbholder and the cigarette lighter wiring.

23 Refitting is a reversal of removal. Take care that the centre section's locating tabs slot together properly when it is refitted to the facia. Ensure that all wiring plugs are securely refitted.

Centre console

Note: *This applies to vehicles with manual gearboxes.*

24 Remove the passenger's side under cover from the facia and the centre table, as

27.11a Open driver's stowage pocket, then unscrew single retaining screw

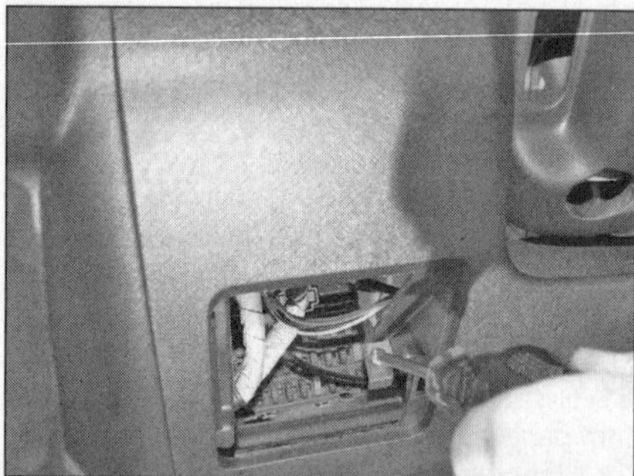
27.11b Remove fuse panel's cover, then unscrew single retaining screw

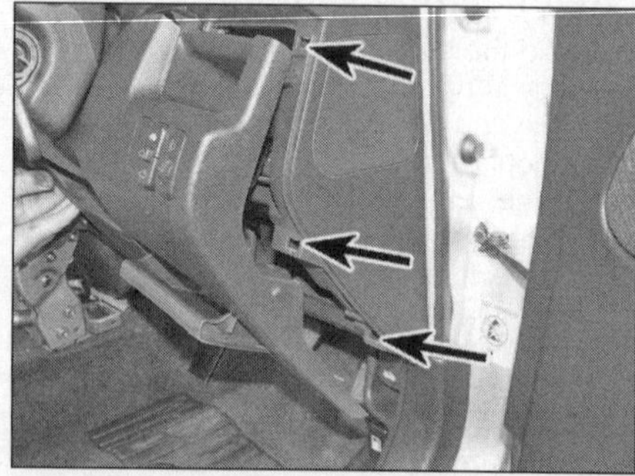
27.12a Pull driver's side lower cover away from facia to release retaining clips . . .

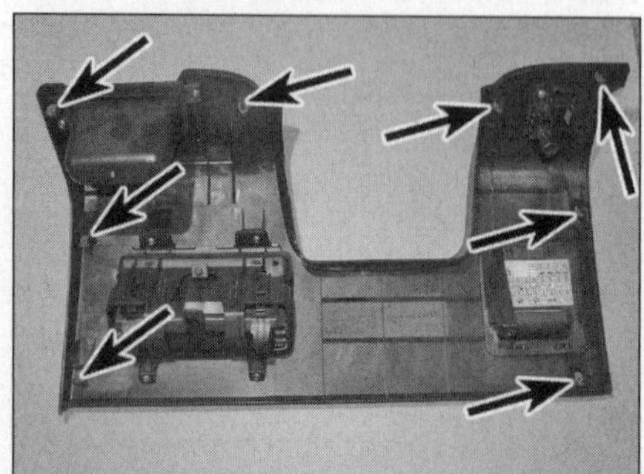
27.12b . . . noting location and type of clips used

27.13a Disconnect facia-mounted switches as lower cover is removed . . .

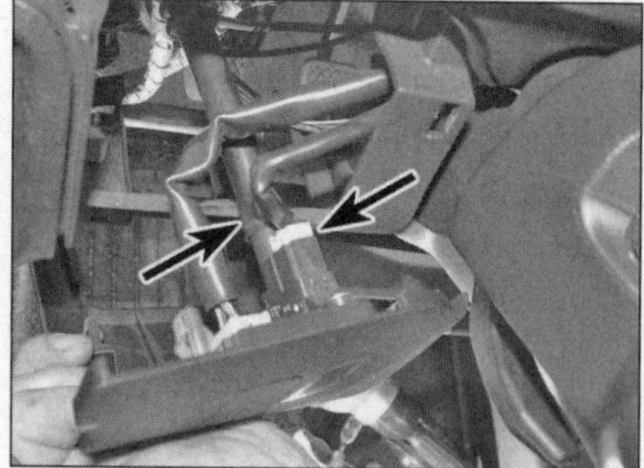
27.13b . . . including disconnecting cabin temperature sensor wiring and air hose

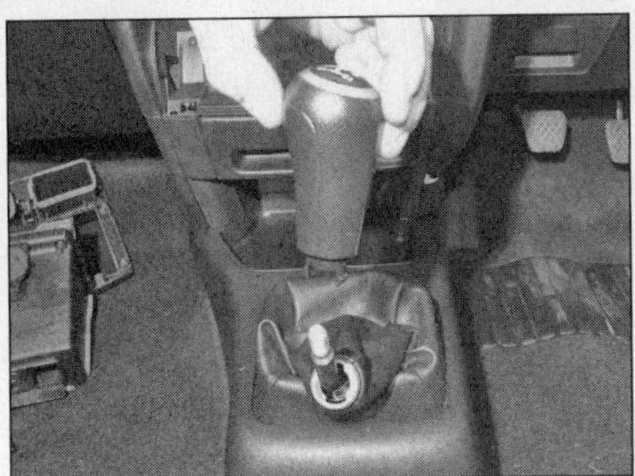
27.26 Unscrew gear lever knob . . .

27.27 . . . prise out covers on each side of storage tray . . .

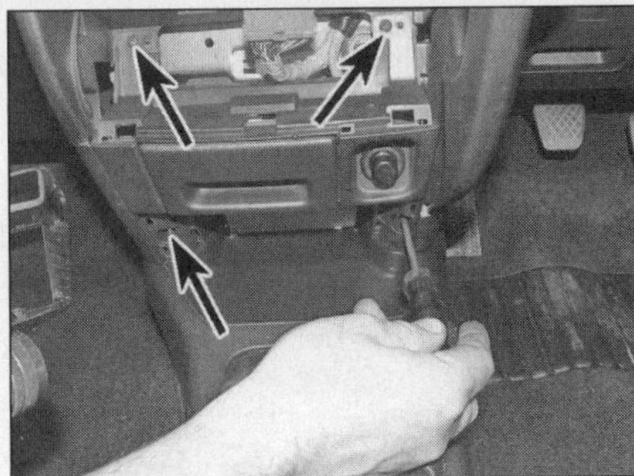
27.28a . . . and undo screws beneath, and at top of centre section . . .

described below. Slide both front seats fully to the rear.

25 Remove the heater control panel as described in Chapter 3, Section 9.

26 Unscrew the gear lever knob **(see illustration)**.

27 Remove the covers on each side of the storage tray immediately in front of the gear lever. Insert a screwdriver with the tip wrapped in protective tape into the gap on the inside edge of the covers to release the two hooks on each cover's outer edge, then remove both covers **(see illustration)**.

28 Unscrew the two mounting screws underneath those covers (beneath the cigarette lighter and ashtray), the two mounting screws at the top edge of the centre section, the screw on the passenger's side at the front, and the two screws, one on each side at the rear of the centre console. Release the two clips, one on each side at the front **(see illustrations)**.

27.28b . . . undo screw on passenger's side at front of centre console . . .

29 Pull outwards, towards the driver's footwell, the front lower part of the centre console to release the two retaining clips **(see illustration)**.

30 Pull the centre console into the passenger compartment to release the remaining three clips and the passenger's side locating tab **(see illustration)**.

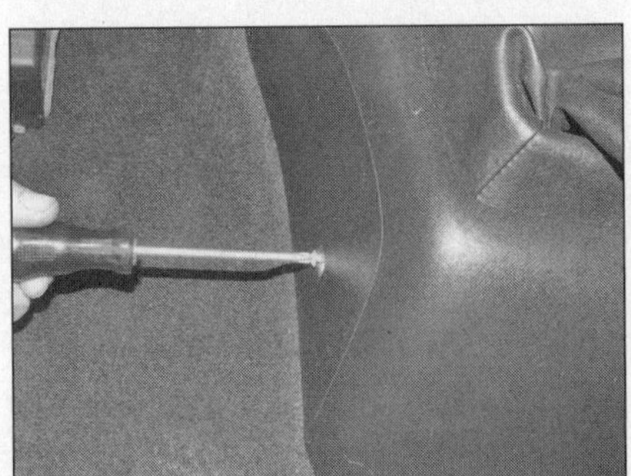
27.28c . . . screw on each side at rear of centre console . . .

31 Disconnect the ashtray illumination bulbholder and the cigarette lighter wiring and remove the centre console **(see illustrations)**.

32 If required, invert the centre console and

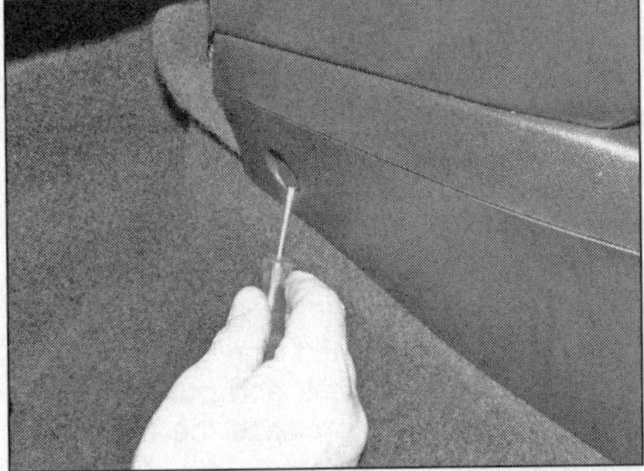
27.28d . . . take care not to mark centre console when releasing clips at front . . .

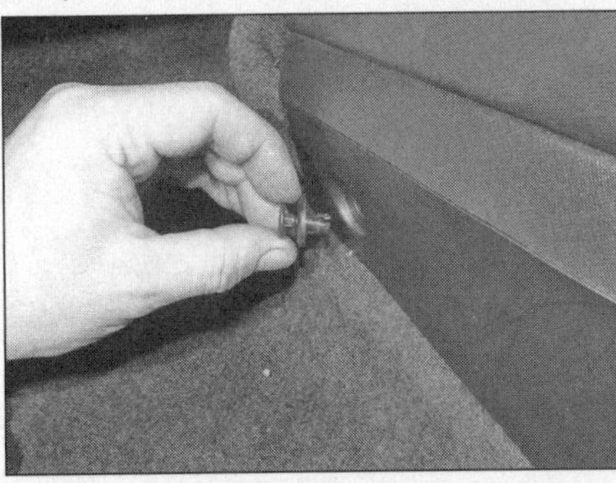
27.28e . . . remove fully to release centre console

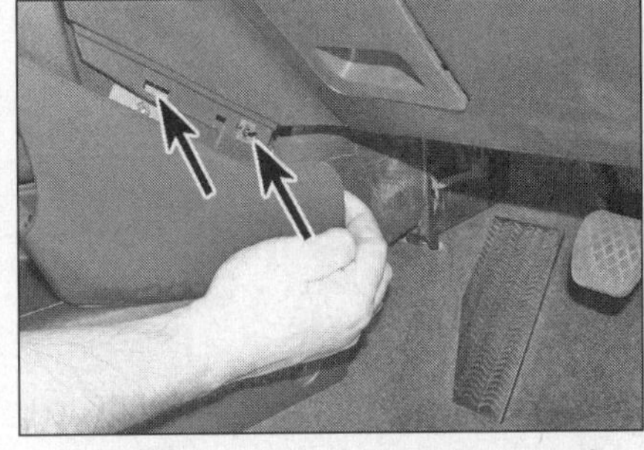
27.29 Pull front edge of centre console outwards to release retaining clips on driver's side . . .

27.30 . . . and release clips and locating tab on passenger's side

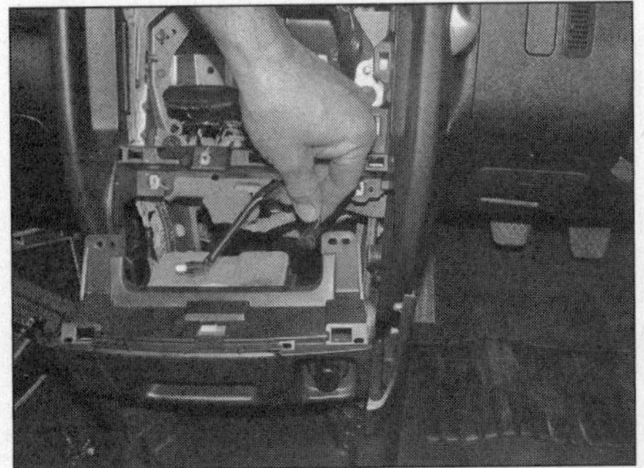
27.31a Disconnect ashtray illumination bulbholder and cigarette lighter wiring . . .

27.31b . . . and withdraw centre console

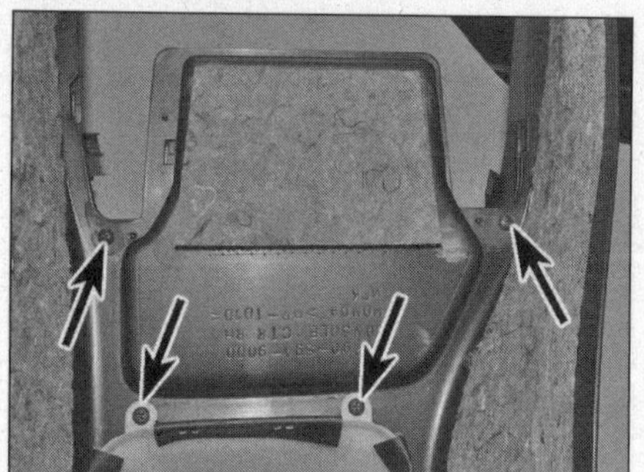
27.32a Undo screws to remove centre lower cover and . . .

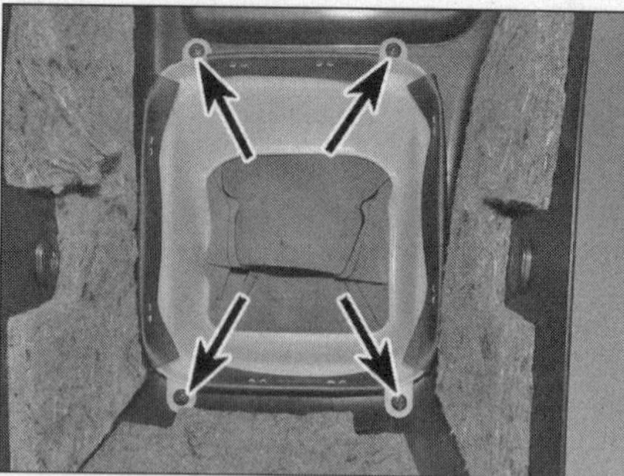
27.32b . . . gear lever gaiter from centre console

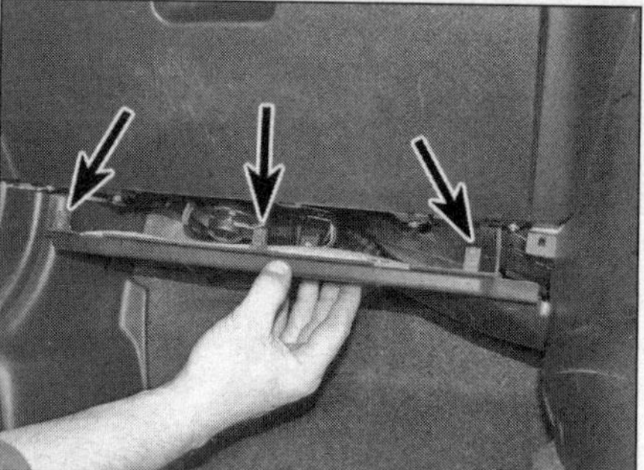
27.36a Pull down rear edge of passenger's side under cover to release clips . . .

27.36b . . . then pull to release from bulkhead mountings

remove the four screws to separate the centre lower cover and gear lever gaiter from the centre console **(see illustrations)**.

33 Refitting is a reversal of removal. Take care that the console's locating tabs slot together properly when the front and rear sections are each offered in place and when it is refitted to the facia. Ensure that all wiring plugs are securely refitted.

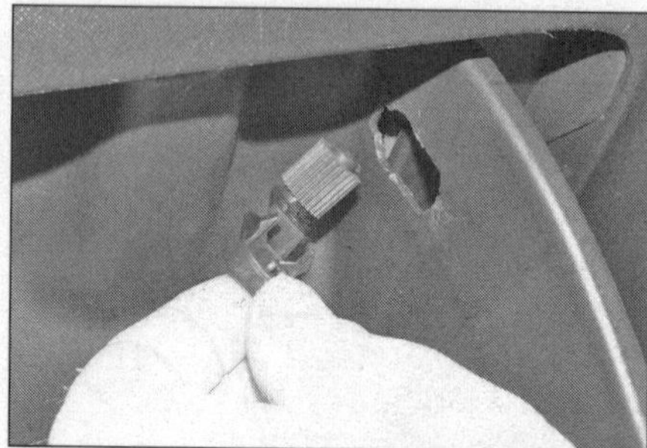
27.39 Open glovebox and press two hooks forwards to release stops, then remove both hooks

Facia centre air vent panel

34 Refer to Chapter 3, Section 9.

Facia dashboard pocket/cool box

35 Refer to the heater control panel removal procedure, in Chapter 3, Section 9.

Passenger's side facia under cover

36 Gently pull down the rear edge of the panel to release it from its three mounting clips, then pull the panel into the passenger compartment to release it from its two bulkhead mountings **(see illustrations)**.

37 Refitting is a reversal of removal.

Glovebox

38 Remove the passenger's side under cover from the facia as described above.

39 Open the glovebox, then press the two hooks, one on either side of the glovebox, forwards to release the stops, remove both hooks and allow the glovebox to swing down further **(see illustration)**.

40 Unscrew and remove the two glovebox hinge bolts from below **(see illustrations)**.

41 Lower out the glovebox and remove it from the facia, disconnecting the wiring.

42 Refitting is a reversal of removal.

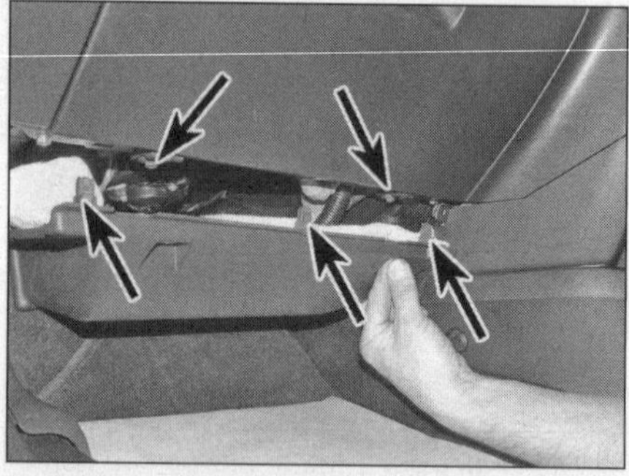
27.40a Remove passenger's side under cover from facia . . .

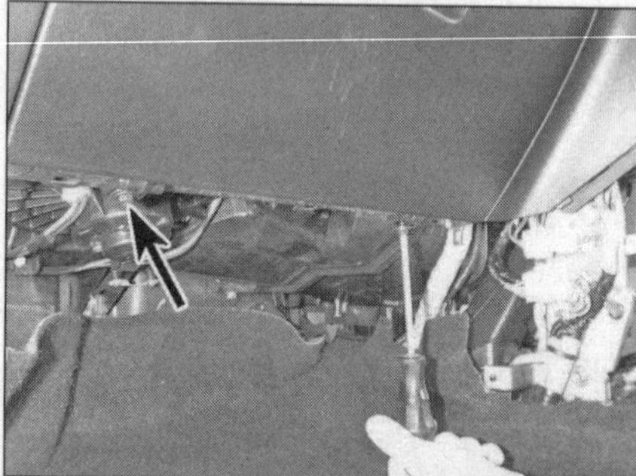
27.40b . . . to undo glovebox hinge bolts

A-pillar trim panels

43 The A-pillar trim panels are held in place by two clips along their length, and there are locating lugs at the top and bottom. Start at the top of the panel, and pull the panel towards the facia to release the clips **(see illustrations)**.

44 Lift the panel to free the lugs at the base from the facia, and remove it.

45 Refitting is a reversal of removal. Transfer any clips back onto the panel as necessary before refitting.

27.43a Removing an A-pillar trim panel

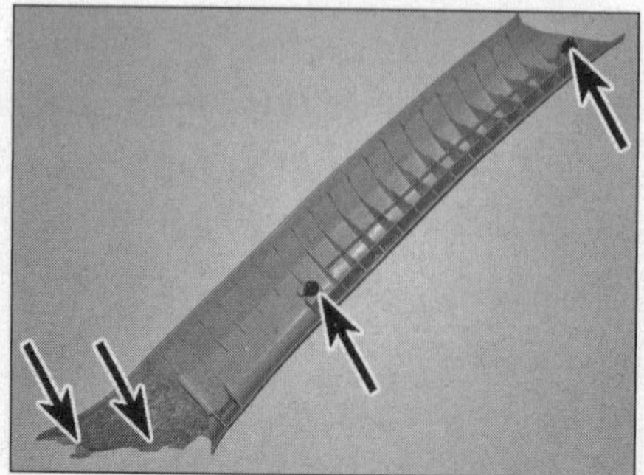
27.43b Showing A-pillar trim panel retaining clips and locating lugs

Front footwell side panels

46 Each panel is secured by two clips – starting at the rear, pull the panel outwards, towards its footwell, to release it **(see illustration)**.

47 If working on the driver's side, manoeuvre the panel to free it from the bonnet and fuel filler flap release levers, and withdraw it from the vehicle **(see illustration)**.

48 Refitting is a reversal of removal. Transfer any clips back onto the panel as necessary before refitting.

27.46 Removing driver's footwell side panel – work panel around bonnet and fuel filler flap release levers

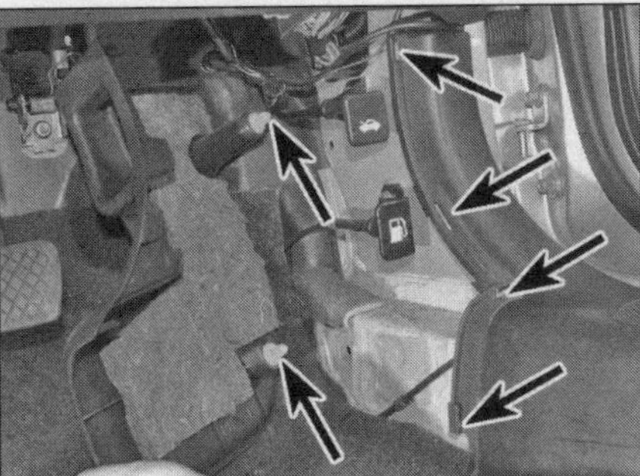
27.47 Showing footwell side trim panel retaining clips

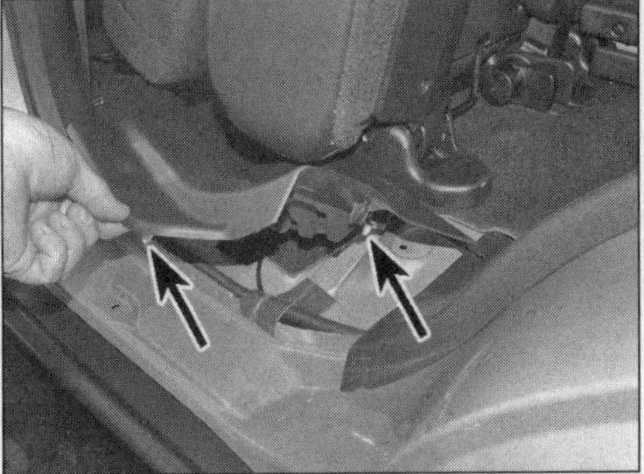
27.52a Removing rear door sill trim panel

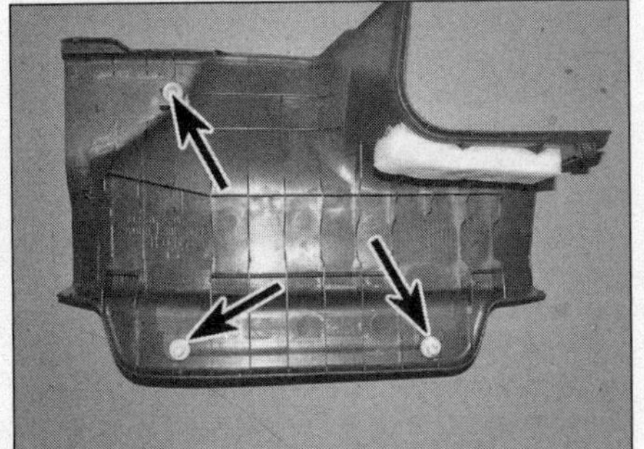
27.52b Showing rear door sill trim panel retaining clips

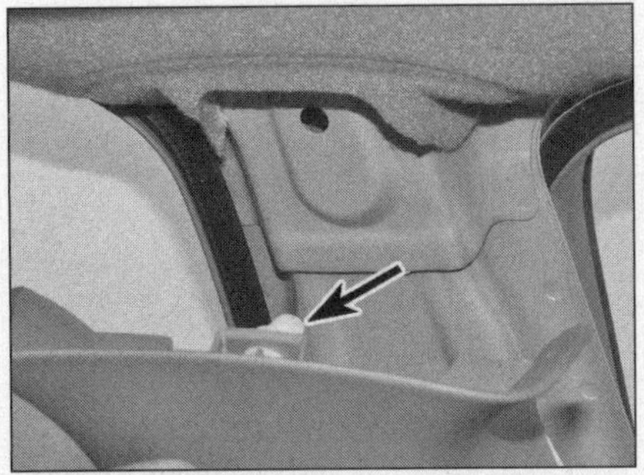
27.56a Pull B-pillar upper trim panel out at top to release clip . . .

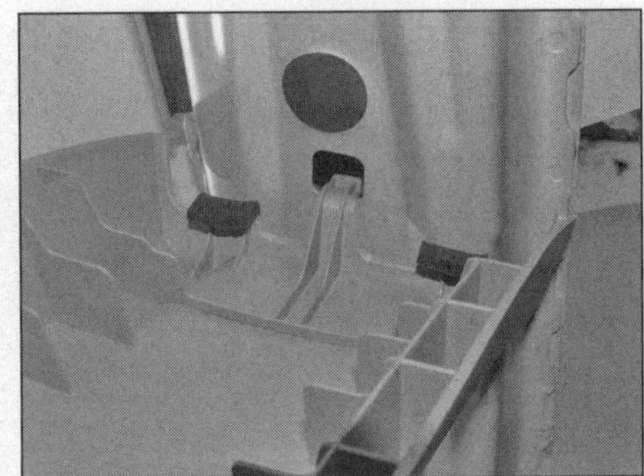
27.56b . . . then unhook panel's bottom mounting

Door sill trim panels

Front

49 The front sill trim panel is 'trapped' by the footwell side panel. Remove the footwell side panel first, as described above.

50 Starting at the front, pull upwards on the outer edge of the sill panel to release the three clips, then pull inwards on the bottom edge of the panel to release the two clips, and remove the panel from the vehicle.

51 Refitting is a reversal of removal. Transfer any clips back onto the panel as necessary before refitting.

Rear

52 Starting at the front, pull upwards on the outer edge of the sill panel to release the two clips, then pull upwards on the inner edge of the panel to release the single clip **(see illustrations)**. Remove the panel from the vehicle.

53 Refitting is a reversal of removal. Transfer any clips back onto the panel as necessary before refitting.

B-pillar trim panels

54 Detach the rubber weatherstrips from the B-pillar as necessary to free the edges of the trim panels.

Upper panel

55 Unclip the seat belt upper anchor's plastic cover by spreading it apart and prising it off. Unscrew and remove the upper anchor bolt, noting carefully how the washers and bushes are arranged.

56 Pull the trim panel out to release the clip at the top, then unhook it from its bottom mounting **(see illustrations)**.

57 Refitting is a reversal of removal. Apply thread-locking fluid to the seat belt upper anchor bolt, then tighten it to the specified torque.

Lower panel

58 Remove both front and rear door sill trim panels, as described above.

59 At the top of the panel, pull both sides outwards to release them **(see illustration)**.

60 At the bottom of the panel, pull it into the vehicle to release the two retaining clips.

61 Lift the panel, and pull it into the vehicle at the top **(see illustration)**.

62 Refitting is a reversal of removal. Transfer any clips back onto the panel as necessary before refitting.

C-pillar upper trim panels

63 Detach the rubber weatherstrip from the C-pillar as necessary to free the edges of the trim panels.

64 Unclip the seat belt upper anchor's plastic cover. Unscrew and remove the upper anchor bolt, noting carefully how the washers and bushes are arranged.

65 Pull the trim panel into the vehicle to release the two clips at the top. To free the bottom of the panel, pull out the luggage compartment side trim panel slightly where it overlaps, disengage the two hooks, then pull the C-pillar trim panel into the vehicle to release the two clips at the bottom **(see illustration)**.

66 Refitting is a reversal of removal. Tighten the seat belt upper anchor bolt to the specified torque.

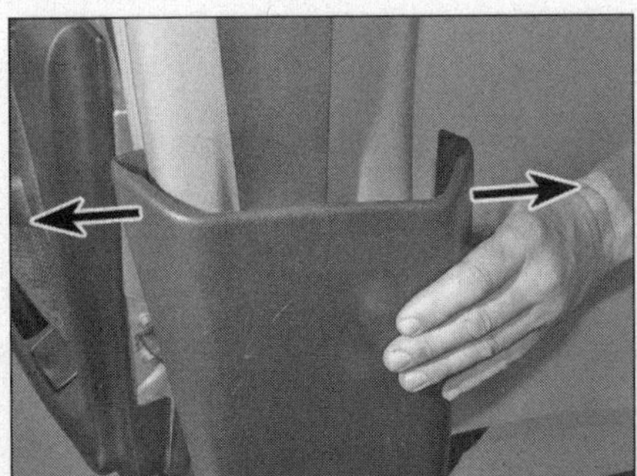
27.59 Pull both sides of B-pillar lower trim panel outwards at top to release clips . . .

27.61 . . . then release bottom clips and lift panel to withdraw

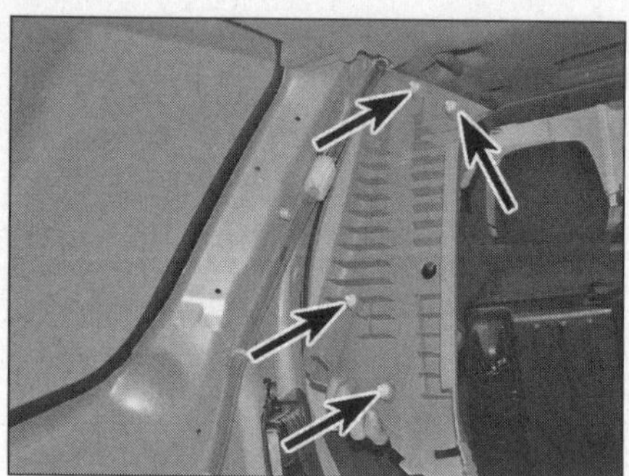
27.65 Showing C-pillar upper trim panel retaining clips

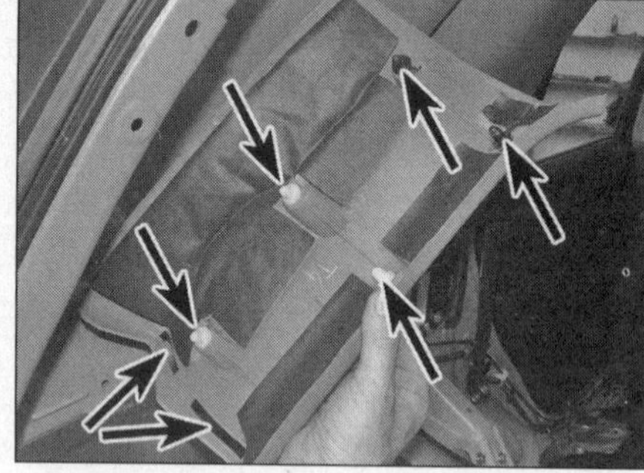
27.68 Showing D-pillar upper trim panel retaining clips and hooks

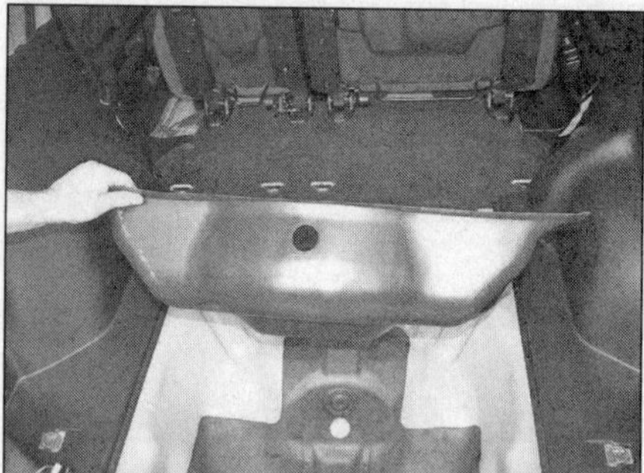
27.70 Removing underfloor/wet storage compartment liner

27.71a Remove jack and tools from luggage compartment right-hand side trim panel

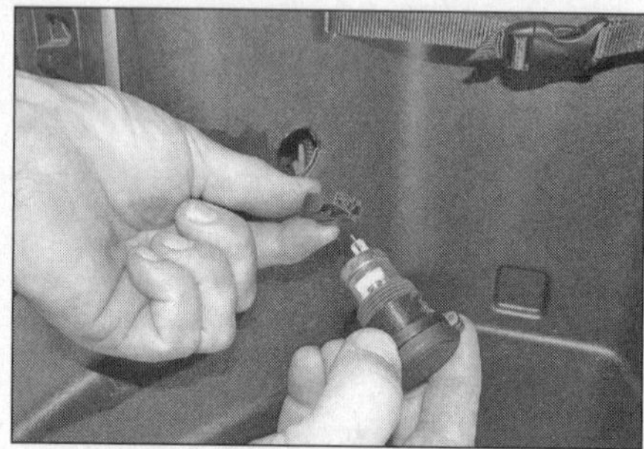
27.71b Prise out and disconnect rear accessory power socket from luggage compartment left-hand side trim panel

D-pillar upper trim panels

67 Detach the rubber weatherstrip from the tailgate opening as necessary to free the edges of the trim panels.

68 Starting at the top, pull the trim panel into the vehicle to release the five clips. To free the bottom of the panel, pull out the luggage compartment side trim panel slightly where it overlaps and disengage the two hooks **(see illustration)**.

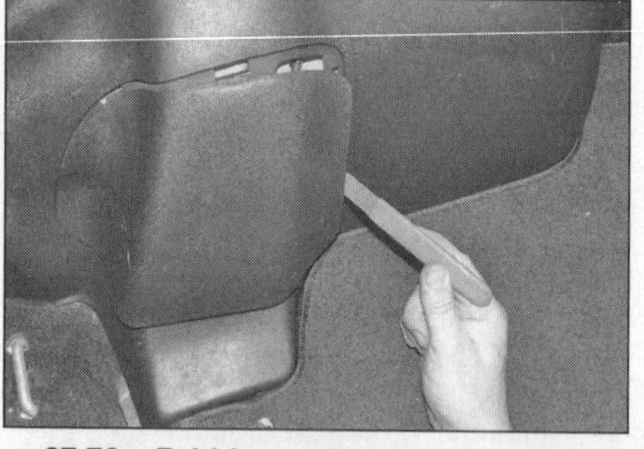
27.72a Fold forwards rear seats, then unclip access panel from luggage compartment side trim panel . . .

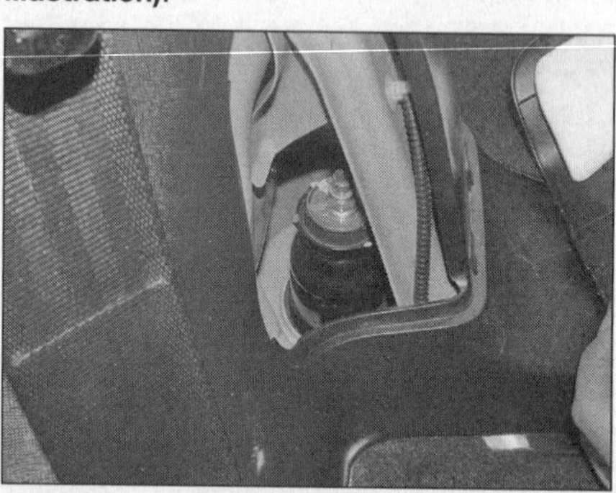
27.72b . . . and withdraw rear suspension strut access panel

27.73a Prise up cap and undo screw securing each cargo hook to side trim panel's upper edge . . .

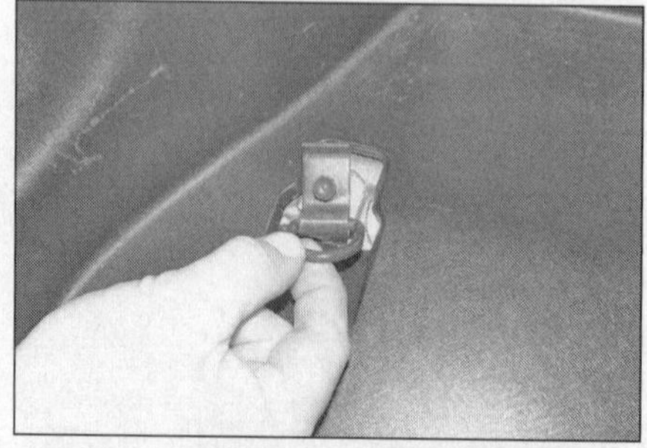
27.73b . . . if panel cannot be lifted over floor-mounted cargo hooks, unbolt them as well

69 Refitting is a reversal of removal. Transfer any clips back onto the panel as necessary before refitting.

Luggage area side trim panels

70 This is a very large panel, covering as it does the whole side of the vehicle, from the C-pillar rearwards, in one piece. First slide all the seats fully to the front, then fold forwards the rear seats and remove the luggage compartment cover (where fitted), the luggage compartment floor mat, the cargo floor lid/ picnic table, and the underfloor/wet storage compartment liner **(see illustration)**.

71 If working on the right-hand panel, open the cover and withdraw the vehicle jack and tools. If working on the left-hand panel, prise out and disconnect the rear accessory power socket **(see illustrations)**.

72 On either side, insert a screwdriver with the tip wrapped in protective tape into the gap on the front edge of the access panel to release the two hooks on the panel's rear edge, then remove the access panel **(see illustrations)**.

73 Prise up its cap and undo the screw securing each of the two cargo hooks to the side trim panel's upper edge. If the side trim panels cannot be lifted over the floor-mounted cargo tie-down hooks, unbolt them **(see illustrations)**.

74 Remove the relevant rear door sill trim panel, as described above.

75 Remove the tailgate sill trim panel, as described below.

76 Detach the rubber weatherstrip from the tailgate opening as necessary to free the edges of the trim panel.

77 Though not essential, it is helpful to unbolt the rear side seat belt lower anchor, and move it clear **(see illustration)**.

78 Slacken the screw at its centre to release the retaining clip securing the side trim panel to the floor **(see illustration)**.

79 Pull the panel inwards (into the vehicle) along its bottom edge to release the two clips at the rear, then pull further to release the clip further up and finally release the four clips along the panel's upper edge. Carefully disengage the side trim panel from the C- and D-pillar upper trim panels and withdraw it, clearing it from the seat belt, if still bolted in place **(see illustration)**.

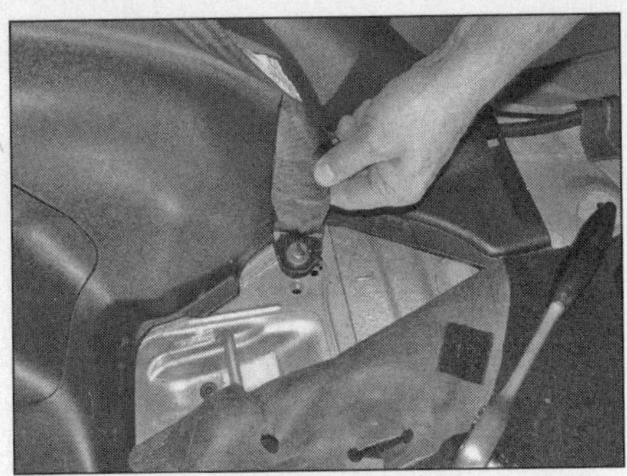

27.77 Unbolt rear side seat belt lower anchor, if seat belt hinders panel removal

27.78 Release clip securing luggage compartment side trim panel to floor

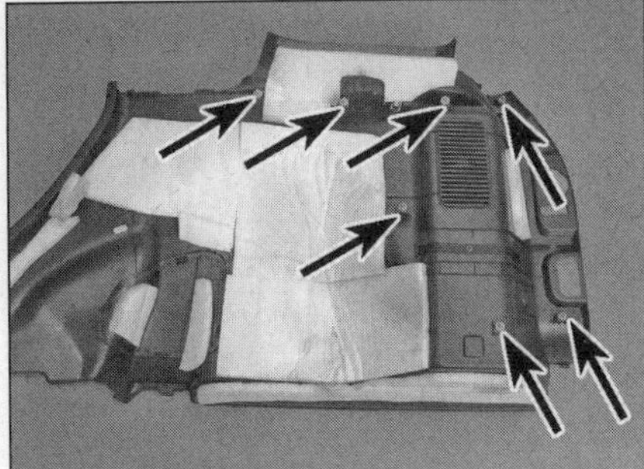

27.79 Showing luggage compartment side trim panel retaining clips and hooks

27.83 Push in central pin to release tailgate sill trim panel front lower clips

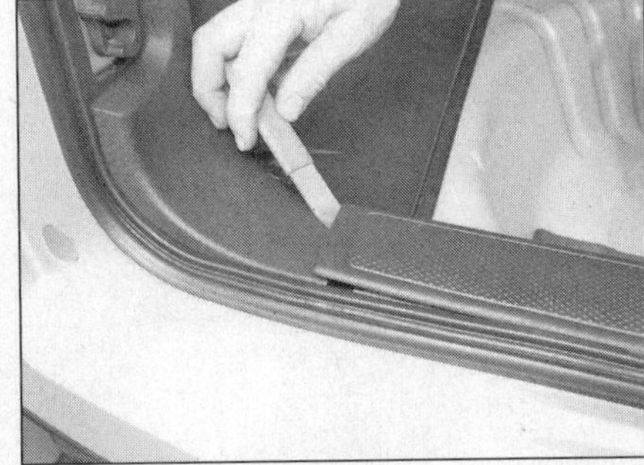

27.84a Prise up tailgate sill trim panel at one end . . .

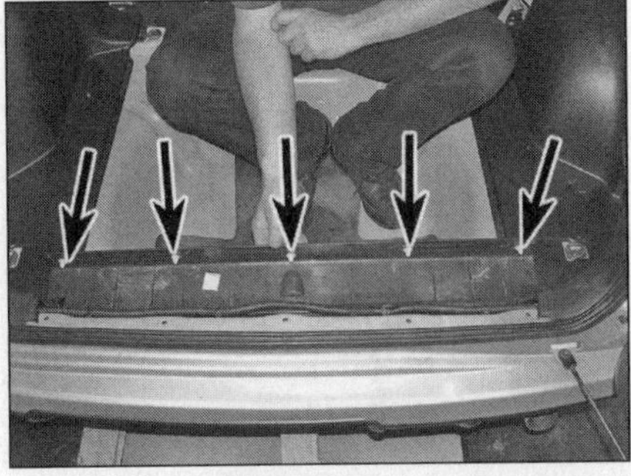

27.84b . . . and lift carefully to release five retaining clips

80 Refitting is a reversal of removal. Transfer any clips back onto the panel as necessary before refitting. Tighten the seat belt mounting bolt to the specified torque.

Tailgate sill trim panel

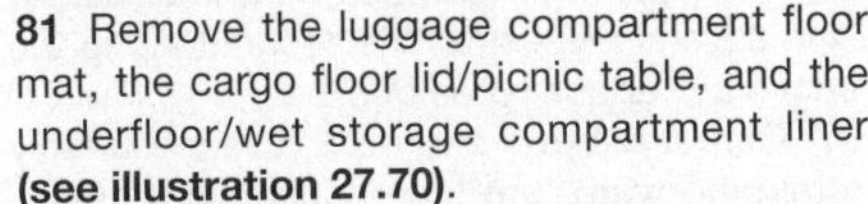

81 Remove the luggage compartment floor mat, the cargo floor lid/picnic table, and the underfloor/wet storage compartment liner **(see illustration 27.70)**.

82 Detach the rubber weatherstrip from the tailgate opening as necessary to free the edges of the trim panel.

83 Release the two clips on the front lower edge of the panel by pressing in their centres **(see illustration)**.

84 Prise up the panel at one end and pull it upwards along its length to release the five retaining clips **(see illustrations)**.

85 Refitting is a reversal of removal. Transfer any clips back onto the panel as necessary before refitting. To secure the two front lower clips, press the outer part of the clip into the hole, then insert the expander pin in the centre, and tap the pin in until it is just flush.

Tailgate trim panels

Upper trim panel

86 Open the tailgate, and taking care not to scratch the panels, prise one end of the tailgate upper trim panel to start releasing it. The panel has four clips along its length – once the end is free, gradually pull the panel down to release the clips and remove it **(see illustration)**.

87 Refitting is a reversal of removal. Note that the tailgate side trim panels (where removed) must be refitted before the upper trim panel.

Side trim panels

88 Remove the upper trim panel as described above.

89 Starting at the top, carefully prise the trim panel away to release its two retaining clips, then separate it from the lower panel; on the right-hand side, disengage the panel carefully from the support strut mounting **(see illustration)**.

90 Refitting is a reversal of removal. Note that the side trim panels should be fitted after the lower panel, and before the upper trim panel.

Lower trim panel

91 Because the tailgate upper and side trim panels overlap each other, to remove the main trim panel without risk of damage, the upper and side trim panels must be removed first, as described above.

92 Prise up its cap and undo the screw securing the cargo hook to the panel upper edge **(see illustrations)**.

93 Starting at the lower corners, prise out the panel – use a piece of card or similar to prevent damage to the surrounding paintwork and trim **(see illustration)**.

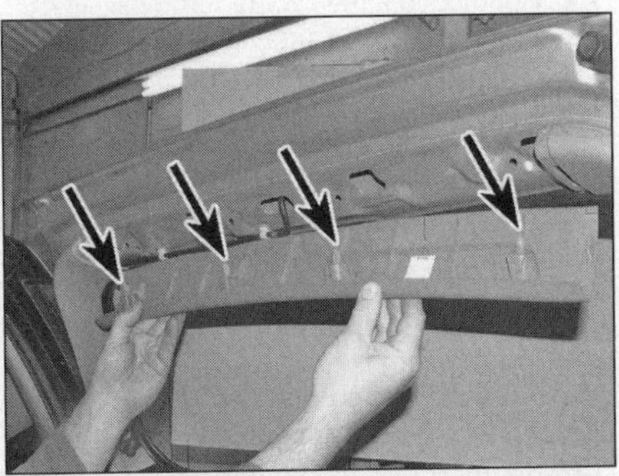

27.86 Showing tailgate upper trim panel retaining clips

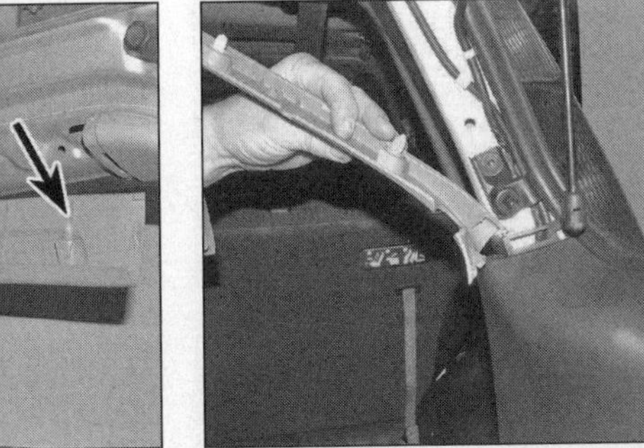

27.89 Removing a tailgate side trim panel

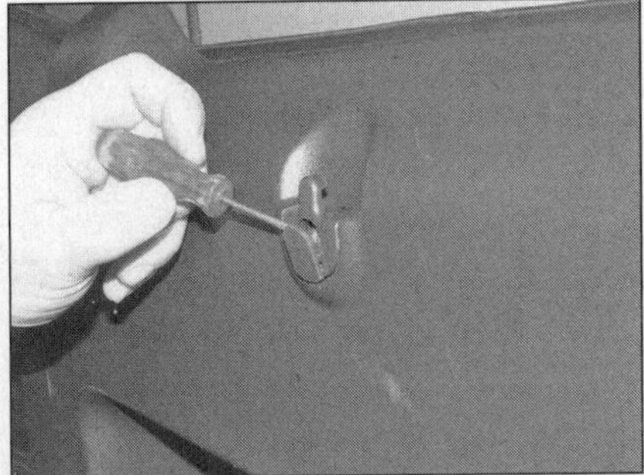

27.92a Prise up cap and . . .

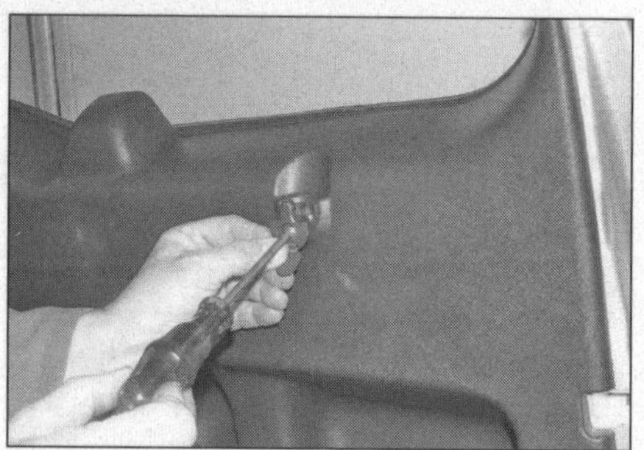

27.92b . . . undo screw securing cargo hook to tailgate lower trim panel's upper edge

27.93 Work around tailgate lower trim panel releasing clips (without damaging paintwork) . . .

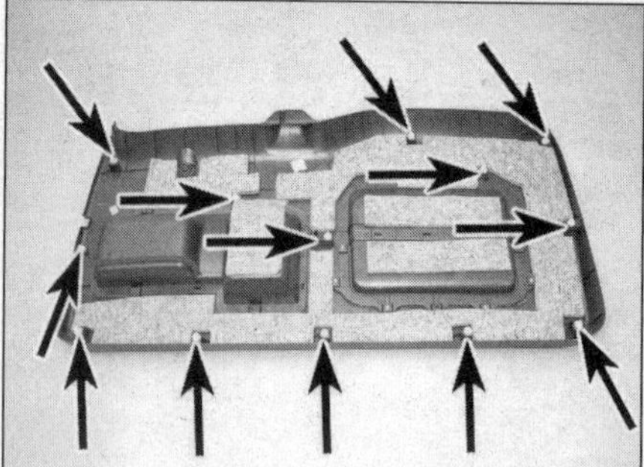

27.94a . . . which are located as shown . . .

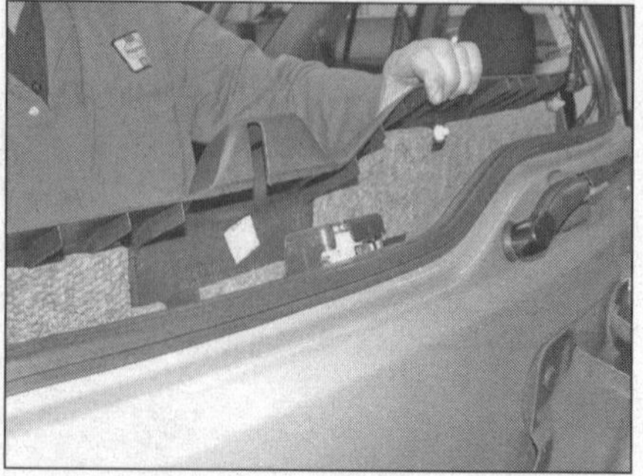

27.94b . . . lift tailgate lower trim panel over tailgate glass lock and withdraw it

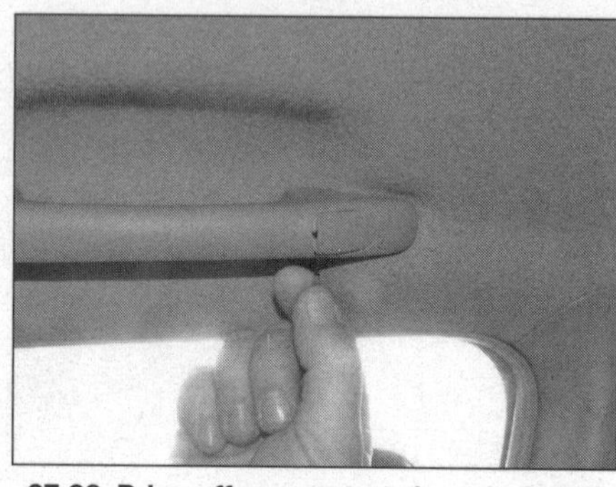

27.98 Prise off cover at each end of grab handle . . .

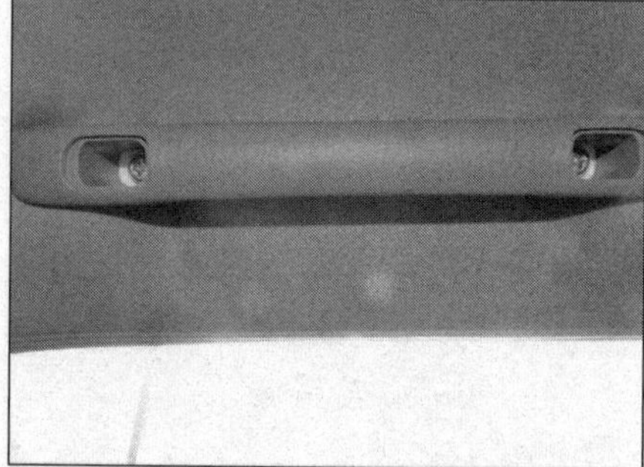

27.99 . . . for access to mounting screws

94 Pull the panel away from the tailgate along its bottom edge to release the five clips at the bottom, then pull further to release the five clips across the middle of the panel and finally release the three clips along the panel's upper edge. Carefully lift the trim panel over the tailgate glass lock and withdraw it **(see illustrations)**.

95 Refitting is a reversal of removal. Transfer any clips back onto the panel as necessary before refitting. Refit the lower panel first, followed by the side panels and finally the upper panel.

Carpets

96 The passenger compartment floor carpet is in several pieces, and is secured along the edges by various types of clips.

97 Carpet removal and refitting is reasonably straightforward, but time-consuming, due to the fact that all adjoining trim panels must be released, and the seats and centre console (where applicable) must be removed.

Grab handles

98 Fold the grab handle down, away from the roof, then carefully prise off the screw covers using a small screwdriver **(see illustration)**.

99 Unscrew and remove the single screw at each end of the handle, and remove it from the roof **(see illustration)**.

100 Refitting is a reversal of removal.

Sunvisors

101 Unclip the visor from the hook, then carefully prise off the cover from the mounting **(see illustration)**.

102 Carefully prise down the lower part of the mounting to release the clips so that the upper part of the mounting can be disengaged from the roof/headlining, then withdraw the visor **(see illustrations)**.

103 If required, the hook can be removed by twisting it anti-clockwise **(see illustration)**.

104 Refitting is a reversal of removal; press the mounting firmly into place to ensure that it is securely fastened **(see illustration)**.

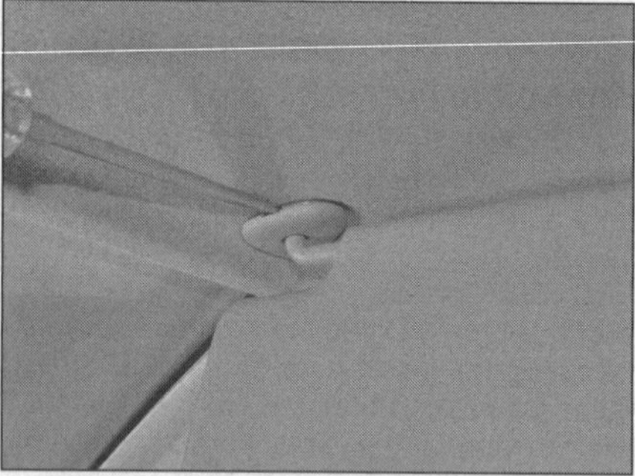

27.101 Carefully prise off cover from sunvisor mounting . . .

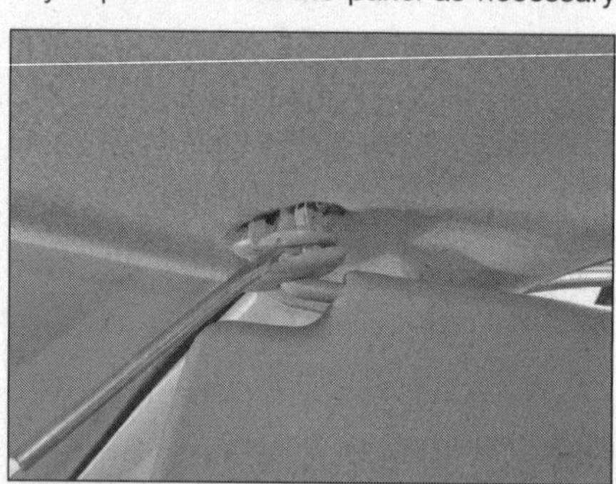

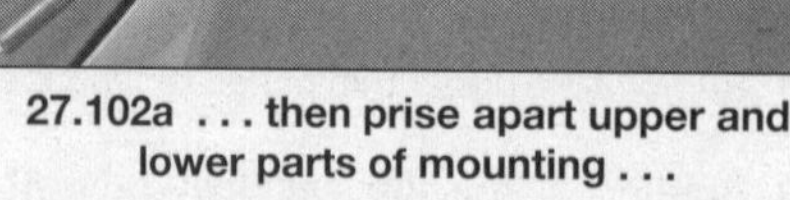

27.102a . . . then prise apart upper and lower parts of mounting . . .

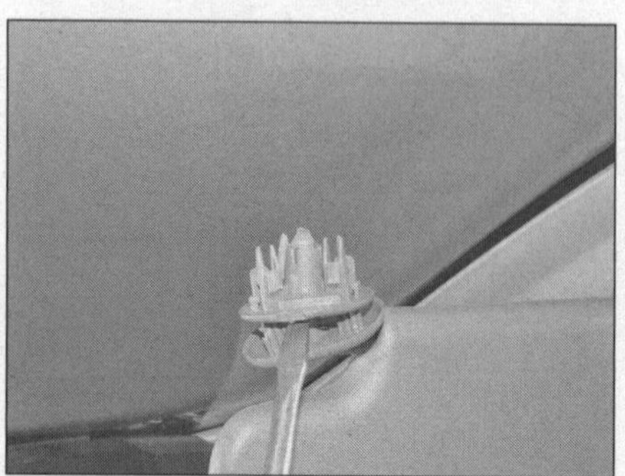

27.102b . . . so that clips release and sunvisor can be withdrawn

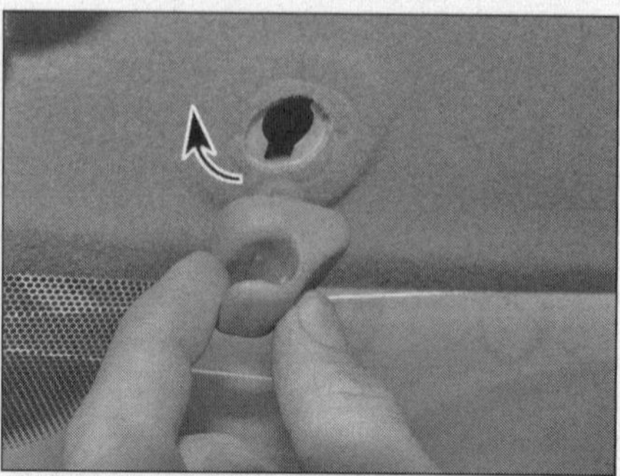

27.103 Rotate sunvisor hook through 90° to release, then withdraw

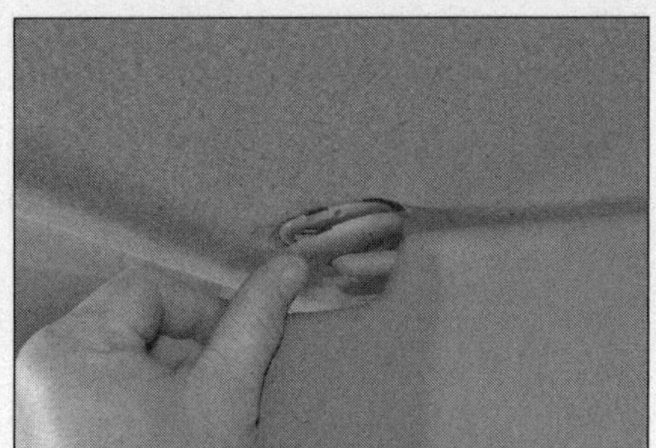

27.104 On refitting, press sunvisor mounting firmly into roof to ensure it is securely fastened

27.108a Undo retaining screw at front . . .

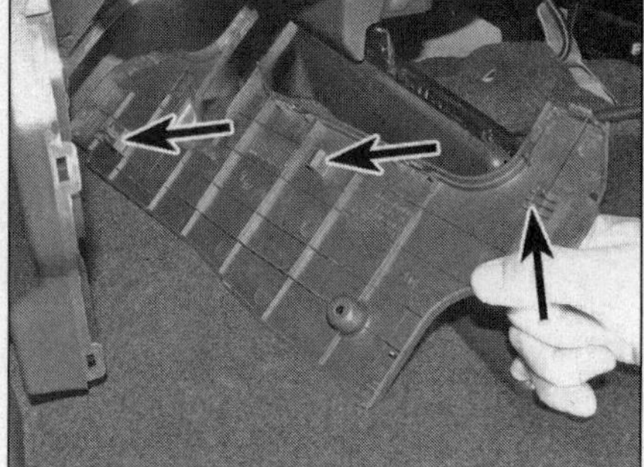

27.108b . . . then unclip and withdraw cover . . .

Headlining

105 The headlining is clipped to the roof, and can be withdrawn only once all fittings such as the grab handles, sunvisors, sunroof, A-, B-, C- and D-pillar trim panels, and associated components have been removed. The door, tailgate and sunroof aperture weatherseals will also have to be prised clear.

106 Note that headlining removal requires considerable skill and experience if it is to be carried out without damage, and is therefore best entrusted to an expert.

Centre table

107 Move the seats as necessary to obtain best access to the table mountings, then erect the table.

108 Undo the retaining screw at the front, then unclip and withdraw the cover **(see illustrations)**.

109 Unscrew the three mounting nuts (the front will require the removal of the plastic end cap from the front of the seat rail) and remove the table from the seat **(see illustrations)**. Remove the screws to dismantle the table inner cover and top from the frame, if required.

110 Refitting is a reversal of removal.

28 Facia panel assembly – removal and refitting

Note: *This is a complicated procedure – it is strongly recommended that this Section is read through thoroughly before starting work. The plastic facia panel is removed WITH the metal crossmember underneath it – if required, the panel can be separated from the crossmember after removal.*

Removal

Facia panel

1 Remove the ignition key, disconnect both battery leads, negative first (see *Disconnecting the battery*).

Warning: Wait at least 3 minutes before starting work. If this precaution is not observed, there is danger of activating the airbags and seat belt tensioners.

2 Referring to Section 27, remove the following trim panels:

a) Driver's side facia under cover.
b) Driver's side facia lower cover.
c) Passenger's facia side under cover.
d) Glovebox.
e) Facia lower centre section or centre console (as appropriate).
f) A-pillar trim panels.
g) Front footwell side panels.

3 Remove the steering wheel as described in Chapter 10.

4 Remove the steering column shrouds as described in Section 27.

5 Remove the steering column switch assembly, and disconnect the three wiring plugs from the ignition switch and related components, as described in Chapter 12, Section 4.

6 Remove the steering column as described in Chapter 10.

7 Remove the handbrake lever as described in Chapter 9. In addition to those components already removed, this involves removal first of the facia centre air vent panel, the dashboard pocket/cool box and the heater control panel, as described in Section 9 of Chapter 3.

8 On models with automatic transmission, disconnect the selector cable as described in Chapter 7B.

9 Working in the driver's footwell, look up under the facia, and disconnect the following (if necessary, attach labels for easier refitting):

a) All the wiring harness plugs at the right-hand end ***(see illustrations)****.*
b) Stop-light switch ***(see illustration)****.*
c) Clutch switch, where applicable (manual transmission models).
d) Unplug the relay from its bracket next to these connectors.
e) Fuse panel wiring plugs, as required;

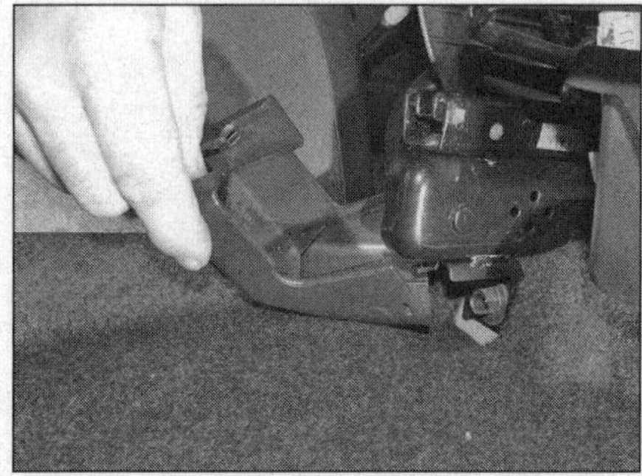

27.109a . . . unclip seat rail end cap . . .

27.109b . . . to reach centre table mounting nuts

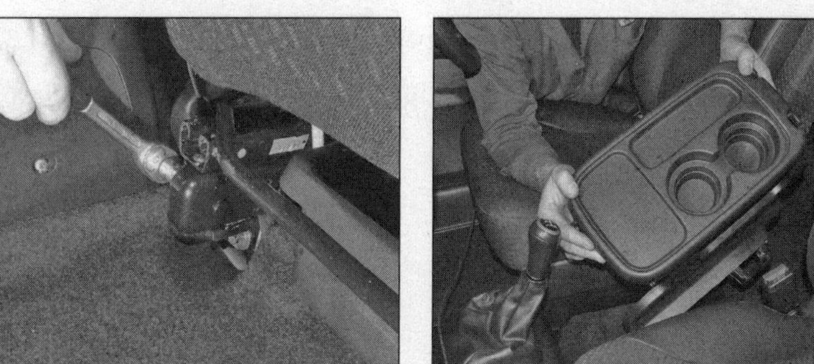

27.109c Unscrew mounting nuts . . .

27.109d . . . and withdraw centre table

28.9a Disconnect interior wiring harness connector . . .

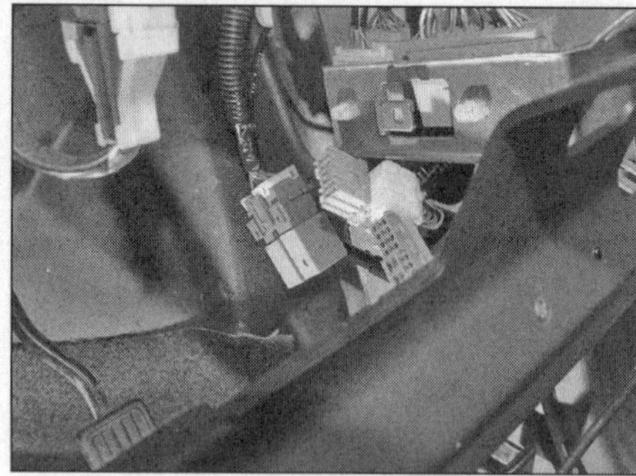

28.9b . . . and all other connectors at right-hand end of facia . . .

28.9c . . . and unplug relays

28.9d Disconnect stop-light switch

28.9e Release engine compartment wire harness connectors from above fuse panel . . .

28.9f . . . and disconnect wiring

unbolt the fuse panel for easier access, if required ***(see illustrations).***

10 Working around the centre part of the facia, at floor level, disconnect the following:

a) Detach the ventilation system floor vent ducts ***(see illustrations).***

b) All accessible wiring harness plugs ***(see illustrations).***

11 From the passenger footwell, disconnect all the wiring harness plugs, including the aerial lead, ECU wiring and main engine wiring harness connectors **(see illustrations).**

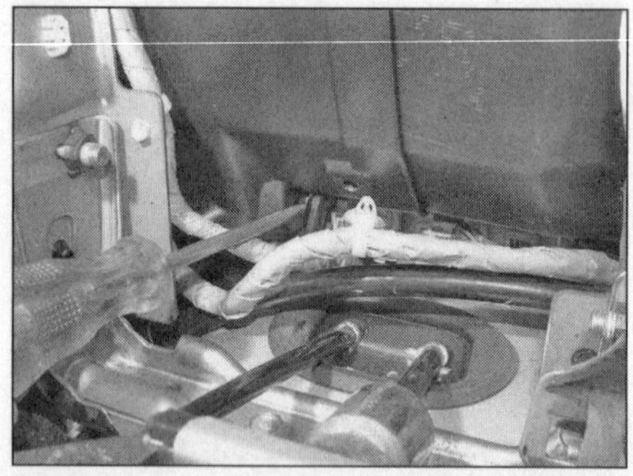

28.10a Unclip ventilation system duct . . .

28.10b . . . and withdraw

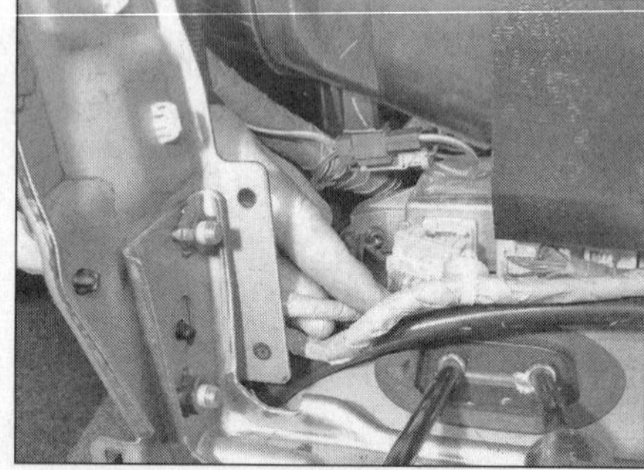

28.10c Disconnect airbag control unit wiring . . .

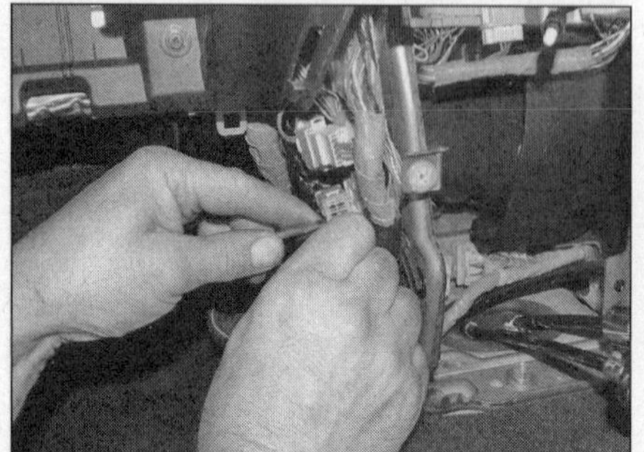

28.10d . . . release retaining clips where necessary . . .

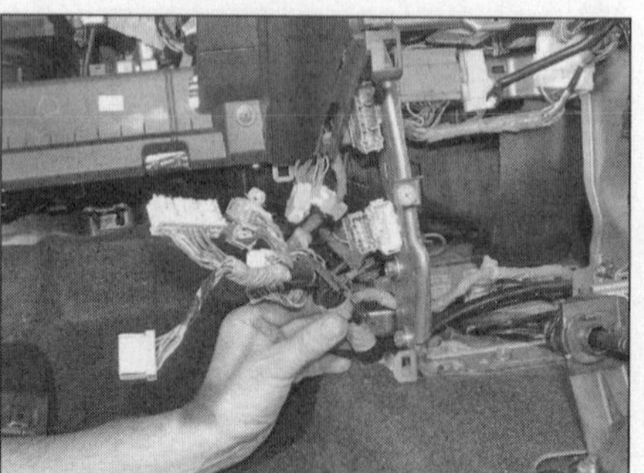

28.10e . . . and disconnect wiring from left-hand side of facia centre section . . .

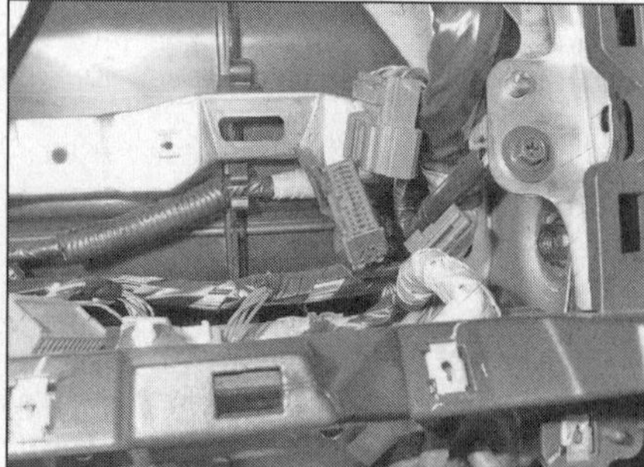

28.10f . . . in upper part of centre section . . .

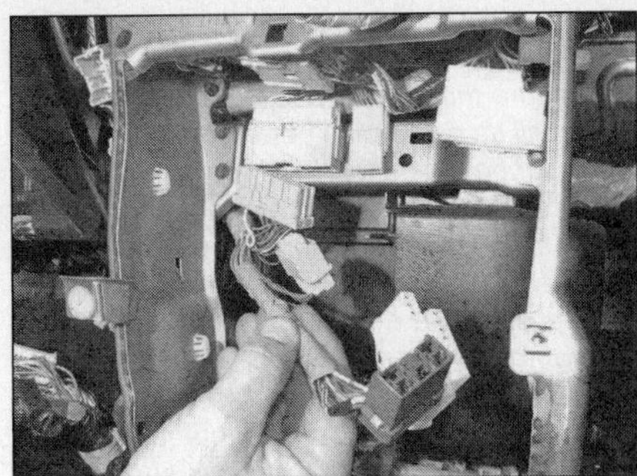
28.10g . . . and in lower part

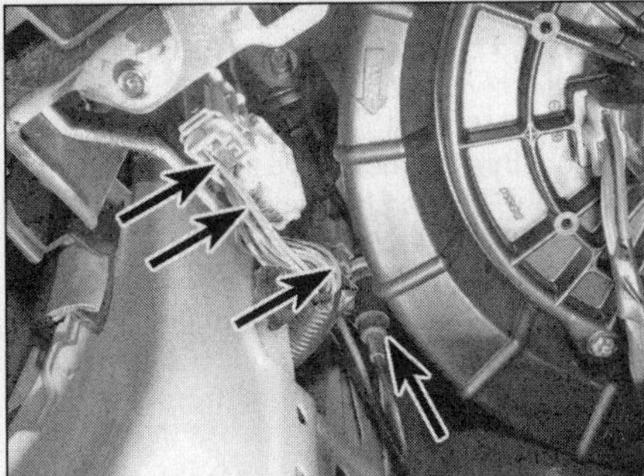
28.11a Disconnect connectors and aerial lead at left-hand end of facia . . .

28.11b . . . and unplug ECU wiring connectors

28.13a Open driver's door and prise off caps . . .

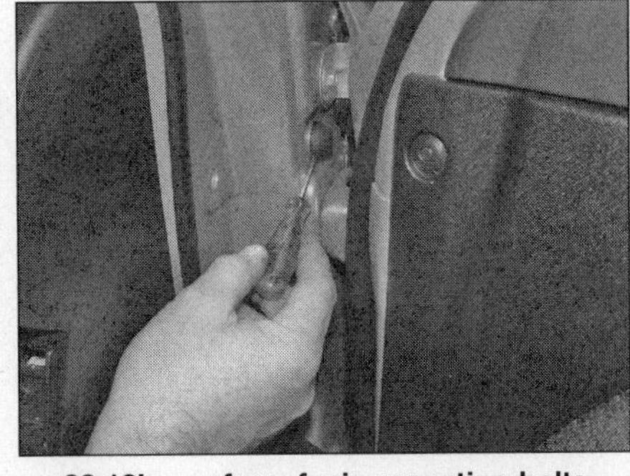
28.13b . . . from facia mounting bolts

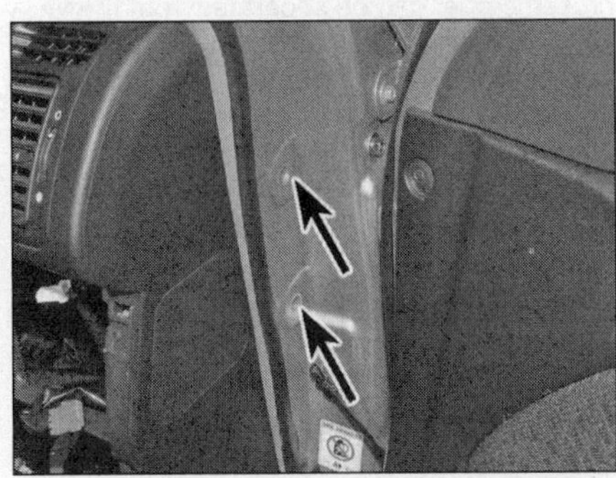
28.13c Two rearmost bolts are easy to reach . . .

12 Release all the disconnected wiring harnesses from its securing clips and ties – note how it is routed, for refitting.

13 Open the driver's door, and prise off the caps from the three bolts above the door check strap. Unscrew and remove the three bolts **(see illustrations)**.

14 Remove the passenger's side air vent from the facia as described in Section 9 of Chapter 3. Unscrew the facia mounting nut underneath **(see illustration)**.

15 Unscrew the two bolts securing the facia centre bracket to the floor, and slacken the four bolts securing the facia centre metal supports to the floor bracket **(see illustrations)**.

16 Make a final check that all the wiring has been disconnected, and that the facia panel is free to be removed.

17 With the help of an assistant, lift the facia at both ends to free it from the three guide pins along the windscreen lower edge and the two guide pins on the driver's end, unscrew the bolts to separate the facia centre section from the floor bracket, and remove the facia from the vehicle **(see illustrations)**.

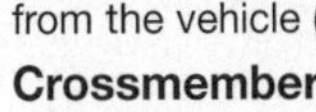

Crossmember

18 With the facia removed, the metal

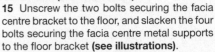

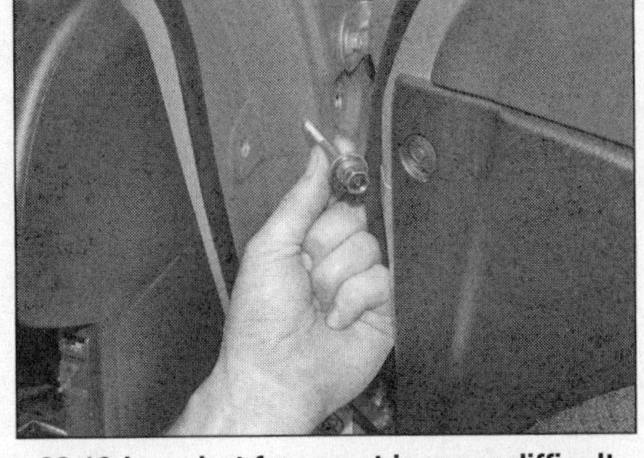
28.13d . . . but foremost is more difficult

28.14 Unscrew facia mounting nut behind passenger's side air vent

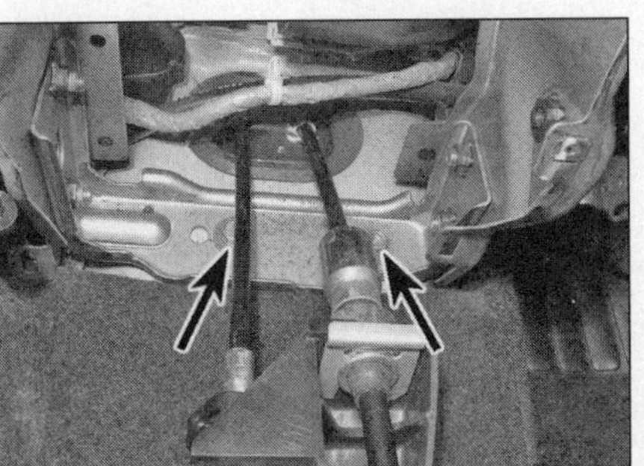
28.15a Unscrew bolts securing facia centre bracket to floor . . .

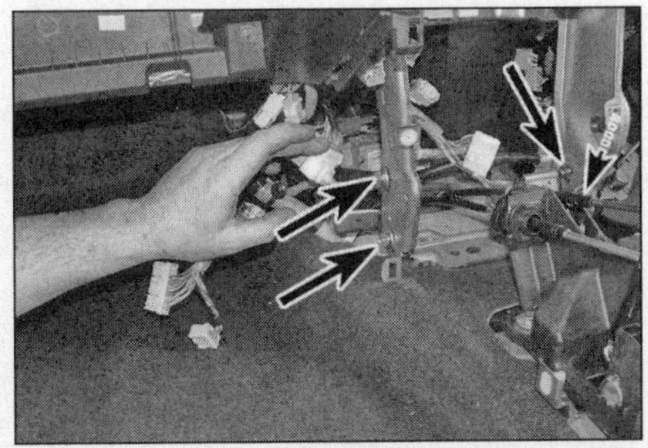
28.15b . . . and slacken four bolts arrowed – do not unscrew until facia is ready to be removed

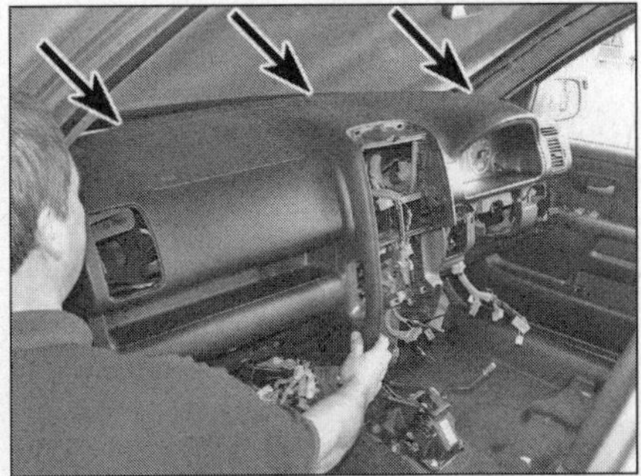
28.17a Lift facia off three guide pins . . .

28.17b . . . and dismantle centre section so facia can be removed

crossmember can be separated from the facia panel if required, as follows.

19 Remove the instrument panel and passenger airbag as described in Chapter 12.

20 On models with automatic air conditioning, remove the sunlight sensor as described in Chapter 3, Section 10.

21 On models with automatic transmission, remove the selector lever (Chapter 7B).

22 Unscrew the two bolts in the instrument panel aperture, the two in the glovebox opening, three in the centre section and one in front of the handbrake lever location.

23 Where applicable, detach the various wiring harnesses from the crossmember.

24 With the help of an assistant, and ensuring that the facia panel does not get damaged, separate the crossmember from the facia panel.

Refitting

25 Refitting is a reversal of the removal procedure, noting the following points:

a) *Assemble the centre floor bracket on to the metal supports but tighten the bolts only lightly at first.*

b) *Make sure the wiring is correctly routed and connected, and secure where necessary with cable-ties. Do not allow the wiring harness to get trapped or pinched during refitting.*

c) *Ensure that the facia is located correctly on all its guide pins before refitting the mounting fasteners. Tightening the foremost driver's side mounting bolt with a torque wrench is very difficult, given the lack of clearance with the door in place – ensure that the bolts and nut are all tightened securely.*

d) *When the facia is securely fastened and the centre floor bracket tightened down, unscrew one by one the bolts securing the centre metal supports to the bracket, apply thread-locking fluid, and tighten each to the specified torque.*

e) *On completion, check that all the electrical components and switches function correctly. As a precaution against the airbags being activated, make sure no one is sitting in the vehicle as the battery is being reconnected.*

Chapter 12
Body electrical systems

Contents

Degrees of difficulty

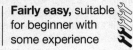

Easy, suitable for novice with little experience	**Fairly easy,** suitable for beginner with some experience 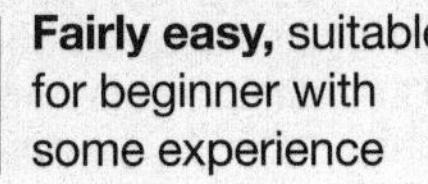	**Fairly difficult,** suitable for competent DIY mechanic	**Difficult,** suitable for experienced DIY mechanic	**Very difficult,** suitable for expert DIY or professional 

Specifications

System type .... 12 volt negative-earth

Bulbs	**Wattage**	**Type/fitting**
Cigarette lighter/ashtray illumination	N/Av.	Capless/wedge-base
Courtesy lights	8	SV8.5d 11 x 30 festoon
Direction indicators:		
Early models – front and rear	21	W3 x 16d capless/wedge-base
Later models:		
Front	21	Amber W3 x 16d capless/wedge-base
Rear	21	Amber Bau15s SCC
Direction indicator side repeaters	5	Amber W5W or W2.1 x 9.5d capless/wedge-base
Foglights:		
Front:		
Early models	51	HB4/P22d
Later models	55	H11/PGJ19-2
Rear	21	W21W or W3 x 16d capless/wedge-base (early models), Ba15s SCC (later models)
Glovebox light	3.4	Festoon
Hazard warning switch illumination	N/Av.	Integral with bulbholder
Headlights:		
Early models	60/55	H4/P43t
Later models:		
Dipped beam	55	H1/P14.5s
Main beam	55	H1/P14.5s
Heater control panel illumination:		
White	14V 60 mA	Integral with bulbholder
Grey	N/Av.	Integral with bulbholder
High-level stop-light	21	W21W or W3 x 16d capless/wedge-base

Bulbs (continued)	**Wattage**	**Type/fitting**
Instrument panel illuminating and indicator lights	1.4	Capless/wedge-base or integral with bulbholder
Luggage compartment light	8	SV8.5d 11 x 30 festoon
Number plate lights	5	W5W or W2.1 x 9.5d capless/wedge-base
Reversing lights	21	W21W or W3 x 16d capless/wedge-base (early models), Ba15s SCC (later models)
Sidelights	5	W5W or W2.1 x 9.5d capless/wedge-base
Spotlights:		
In roof console	8	W5W capless/wedge-base
No roof console	8	SV8.5d 11 x 30 festoon
Stop/tail lights	21/5	W3 x 16q capless/wedge-base

Torque wrench settings	**Nm**	**lbf ft**
Airbag components:		
Airbag control unit Torx bolts	10	7
Driver's airbag unit Torx bolts*	10	7
Passenger's airbag unit screws	10	7
Windscreen wiper arm nuts	18	13
Windscreen wiper motor and linkage mounting bolts	10	7
Tailgate wiper arm nut	9	7
Tailgate wiper motor bolts	10	7

* *Use new fasteners.*

1 General information and precautions

Warning: Before carrying out any work on the electrical system, read through the precautions given in Safety first! at the beginning of this manual.

The electrical system is of 12 volt negative-earth type. Power for the lights and all electrical accessories is supplied by a lead-acid battery which is charged by the alternator.

This Chapter covers repair and service procedures for the various electrical components not associated with the engine. Information on the battery, alternator, and starter motor can be found in Chapter 5A; the ignition system is covered in Chapter 5B and the preheating system in Chapter 5C.

All UK models are fitted with an alarm system incorporating an engine immobiliser. The system protects the doors, bonnet and tailgate, and certain models may also have ultrasonic protection for the whole interior, meaning that the alarm will sound if a thief breaks a window to gain entry. A transponder chip fitted to the ignition key automatically disarms the immobiliser when it is inserted into the ignition switch. For more information, refer to Section 19.

All models are fitted with airbags for the driver and front seat passenger, which are designed to prevent serious chest and head injuries during a frontal accident and side airbags, fitted into the front seat side cushions. Some 2005-on models are also fitted with side curtain airbags. For more information, refer to Section 20.

All models are fitted with a manually-controlled headlight levelling system, with a facia-mounted control. On position 0, the headlights are in their base (normal) position – from here, turn the control to lower the aim of the headlights according to the load being carried.

It should be noted that, when portions of the electrical system are serviced, the lead should be disconnected from the battery negative terminal, to prevent electrical shorts and fires (see *Disconnecting the battery*).

2 Electrical fault finding – general information

Note: *Refer to the precautions given in Safety first! and at the beginning of Chapter 5A before starting work. The following tests relate to testing of the main electrical circuits, and should not be used to test delicate electronic circuits (such as anti-lock braking systems), particularly where an electronic control unit is used.*

General

1 A typical electrical circuit consists of an electrical component, any switches, relays, motors, fuses, fusible links or circuit breakers related to that component, and the wiring and connectors which link the component to both the battery and the chassis. To help to pinpoint a problem in an electrical circuit, wiring diagrams are included at the end of this Chapter.

2 Before attempting to diagnose an electrical fault, first study the appropriate wiring diagram to obtain a more complete understanding of the components included in the particular circuit concerned. The possible sources of a fault can be narrowed down by noting whether other components related to the circuit are operating properly. If several components or circuits fail at one time, the problem is likely to be related to a shared fuse or earth connection.

3 The multiplex wiring system fitted to some circuits of this vehicle makes electrical fault finding less straightforward than on previous models. The multiplex module 'talks' to other parts of the vehicle's wiring, meaning that the same wire might be carrying different signals at any time – this can produce confusing test results, and there is even a risk of damage to the module itself through careless testing. For more information, see Section 3.

4 Electrical problems usually stem from simple causes, such as loose or corroded connections, a faulty earth connection, a blown fuse, a melted fusible link, or a faulty relay (refer to Section 3 for details of testing relays). Visually inspect the condition of all fuses, wires and connections in a problem circuit before testing the components. Use the wiring diagrams to determine which terminal connections will need to be checked, in order to pinpoint the trouble-spot.

5 The basic tools required for electrical fault finding include a circuit tester or voltmeter (a 12 volt bulb with a set of test leads can also be used for certain tests); a self-powered test light (sometimes known as a continuity tester); an ohmmeter (to measure resistance); a battery and set of test leads; and a jumper wire, preferably with a circuit breaker or fuse incorporated, which can be used to bypass suspect wires or electrical components. Before attempting to locate a problem with test instruments, use the wiring diagram to determine where to make the connections.

6 To find the source of an intermittent wiring fault (usually due to a poor or dirty connection, or damaged wiring insulation), a 'wiggle' test can be performed on the wiring. This involves wiggling the wiring by hand, to see if the fault occurs as the wiring is moved. It should be possible to narrow down the source of the fault to a particular section of wiring. This method of testing can be used in conjunction with any of the tests described in the following sub-sections.

7 Apart from problems due to poor connections, two basic types of fault can occur in an electrical circuit – open-circuit, or short-circuit.

8 Open-circuit faults are caused by a break somewhere in the circuit, which prevents current from flowing. An open-circuit fault will prevent a component from working, but will not cause the relevant circuit fuse to blow.

9 Short-circuit faults are caused by a 'short' somewhere in the circuit, which allows the current flowing in the circuit to 'escape' along an alternative route, usually to earth. Short-circuit faults are normally caused by a breakdown in wiring insulation, which allows a feed wire to touch either another wire, or an earthed component such as the bodyshell. A short-circuit fault will normally cause the relevant circuit fuse to blow.

Finding an open-circuit

10 To check for an open-circuit, connect one lead of a circuit tester or voltmeter to either the negative battery terminal or a known good earth.

11 Connect the other lead to a connector in the circuit being tested, preferably nearest to the battery or fuse.

12 Switch on the circuit, bearing in mind that some circuits are live only when the ignition switch is moved to a particular position.

13 If voltage is present (indicated either by the tester bulb lighting or a voltmeter reading, as applicable), this means that the section of the circuit between the relevant connector and the battery is problem-free.

14 Continue to check the remainder of the circuit in the same fashion.

15 When a point is reached at which no voltage is present, the problem must lie between that point and the previous test point with voltage. Most problems can be traced to a broken, corroded or loose connection.

Finding a short-circuit

16 To check for a short-circuit, first disconnect the load(s) from the circuit (loads are the components which draw current from a circuit, such as bulbs, motors, heating elements, etc).

17 Remove the relevant fuse from the circuit, and connect a circuit tester or voltmeter to the fuse connections.

18 Switch on the circuit, bearing in mind that some circuits are live only when the ignition switch is moved to a particular position.

19 If voltage is present (indicated either by the tester bulb lighting or a voltmeter reading, as applicable), this means that there is a short-circuit.

20 If no voltage is present, but the fuse still blows with the load(s) connected, this indicates an internal fault in the load(s).

Finding an earth fault

21 The battery negative terminal is connected to 'earth' – the metal of the engine/transmission unit and the vehicle body – and most systems are wired so that they only receive a positive feed, the current returning via the metal of the vehicle body. This means that the component mounting and the body form part of that circuit. Loose or corroded mountings can therefore cause a range of electrical faults, ranging from total failure of a circuit, to a puzzling partial fault.

22 In particular, lights may shine dimly (especially when another circuit sharing the same earth point is in operation), motors (eg, wiper motors or the radiator cooling fan motor) may run slowly, and the operation of one circuit may have an apparently-unrelated effect on another.

23 Note that on many vehicles, earth straps are used between certain components, such as the engine/transmission and the body, usually where there is no metal-to-metal contact between components, due to flexible rubber mountings, etc.

24 To check whether a component is properly earthed, disconnect the battery, and connect one lead of an ohmmeter to a known good earth point. Connect the other lead to the wire or earth connection being tested. The resistance reading should be zero; if not, check the connection as follows.

25 If an earth connection is thought to be faulty, dismantle the connection, and clean back to bare metal both the bodyshell and the wire terminal or the component earth connection mating surface. Be careful to remove all traces of dirt and corrosion, then use a knife to trim away any paint, so that a clean metal-to-metal joint is made.

26 On reassembly, tighten the joint fasteners securely; if a wire terminal is being refitted, use serrated washers between the terminal and the bodyshell, to ensure a clean and secure connection.

27 When the connection is remade, prevent the onset of corrosion in the future by applying a coat of petroleum jelly or silicone-based grease, or by spraying on (at regular intervals) a proprietary maintenance spray such as WD-40.

3 Fuses, relays and multiplex module – general information

Fuses

1 Fuses are designed to break a circuit when a predetermined current is reached, in order to protect the components and wiring which could be damaged by excessive current flow. Any excessive current flow will be due to a fault in the circuit, usually a short-circuit (see Section 2).

2 The main fuses are located either in the passenger compartment fuse panel, below and to the left of the steering column, or in the main fuse/relay box in the engine compartment. Depending on specification and equipment, some later models have more than one engine compartment fuse/relay box.

3 Release the fuse panel's cover by pulling it towards you **(see illustrations)**.

4 A blown fuse can be recognised from its melted or broken wire.

5 To remove a fuse, first ensure that the relevant circuit is switched off – for maximum safety, disconnect the battery (see *Disconnecting the battery*).

3.3a Removing passenger compartment fuse panel cover . . .

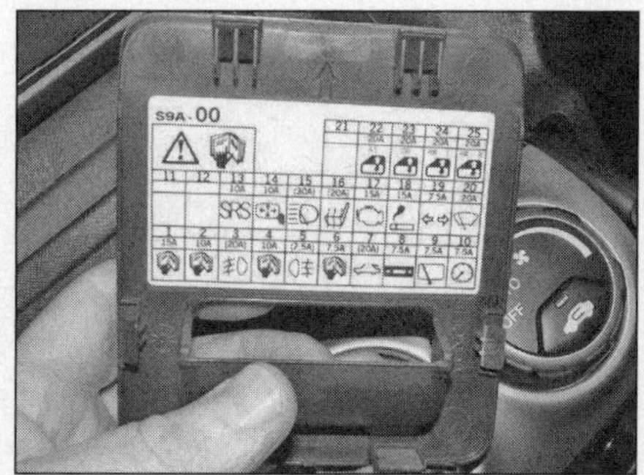

3.3b . . . shows fuse information printed inside

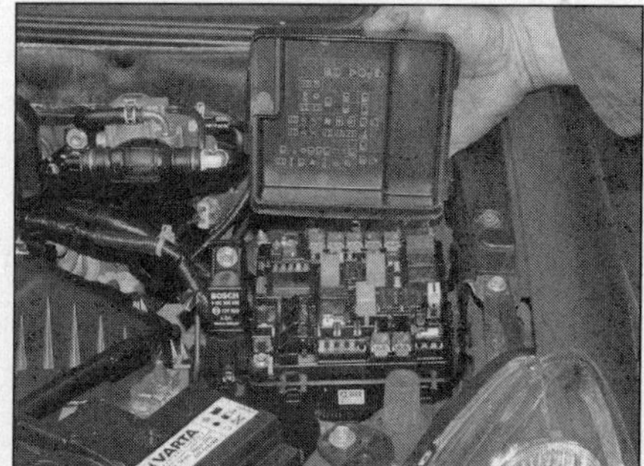

3.3c Engine compartment main fuse/relay box also has information printed inside lid

3.6 Pull out fuses using tool provided

6 Pull the fuse from its location, using thin-nosed pliers if necessary **(see illustration)**.

7 Before renewing a blown fuse, trace and rectify the cause, and always use a fuse of the correct rating. Never substitute a fuse of a higher rating, or make temporary repairs using wire or metal foil; more serious damage, or even fire, could result.

8 Note that the fuses are colour-coded as follows. Refer to the markings on the back of the fuse panel's cover for details of the circuits protected. Also note that the CR-V uses the later-type 'mini' fuses.

Colour	Rating
Brown	7.5A
Red	10A
Blue	15A
Yellow	20A
Clear or white	25A
Green	30A
Amber	40A

9 Some of the fuses located in the engine compartment main fuse/relay box are rated at 40 amps or more, and are secured by a small screw at each end – if any of these have blown, it indicates a serious wiring fault, which should be investigated **(see illustration)**. Just fitting a new fuse may cause further problems.

Relays

10 A relay is an electrically-operated switch, which is used for the following reasons:

a) A relay can switch a heavy current remotely from the circuit in which the current is flowing, allowing the use of lighter-gauge wiring and switch contacts.

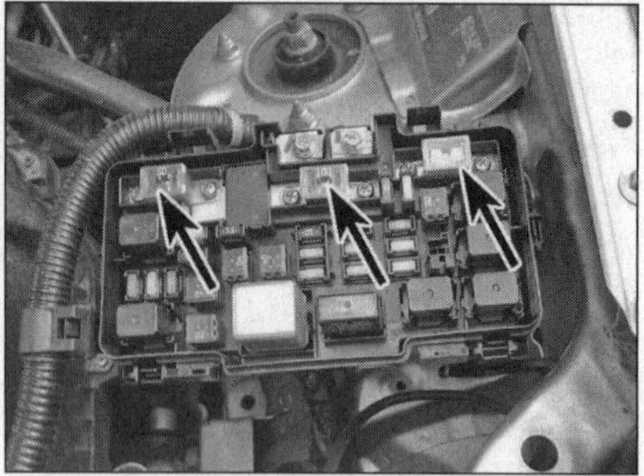

3.9 Heavy-duty fuses in engine compartment main fuse/relay box

b) A relay can receive more than one control input, unlike a mechanical switch.

c) A relay can have a timer function – for example, the intermittent wiper relay.

11 Most of the relays are located in the engine compartment main fuse/relay box. Others are behind the facia, either around the passenger compartment fuse panel or behind the glovebox.

12 To reach the relays behind the glovebox, open the glovebox then press the two hooks, one on either side of the glovebox, forwards to release the stops, remove both hooks and allow the glovebox to swing down further, then press the sides of the glovebox inwards and open the glovebox past its stops.

13 If a circuit or system controlled by a relay develops a fault, and the relay is suspect, operate the system. If the relay is functioning, it should be possible to hear it 'click' as it is energised. If this is the case, the fault lies with the components or wiring of the system. If the relay is not being energised, then either the relay is not receiving a main supply or a switching voltage, or the relay itself is faulty. Testing is by the substitution of a known good unit, but be careful – while some relays are identical in appearance and in operation, others look similar but perform different functions.

14 To remove a relay, first ensure that the relevant circuit is switched off. The relay can then simply be pulled out from the socket, and pushed back into position.

Multiplex module

15 This module, which is part of the passenger compartment fuse panel fitted below and to the left of the steering column, directly controls some of the vehicle's electrical functions:

a) Interior lighting, including battery saver function (the interior lights and chimes are automatically shut off after a predetermined period of inactivity).

b) Wipers and washers.

c) Lights-on, door-ajar, seat belt and ignition key-in warnings.

d) Central locking.

e) Interlock system

f) Instruments, warning lamps and gauges

g) Heating/ventilation and air conditioning compressor and fan control.

h) Rear foglight.

16 However, the module also communicates with the engine management's ECU, the instrument panel, air conditioning system, exterior lighting system and ABS – in fact, with most of the vehicle's major electrical systems.

17 Because the module is part of virtually every circuit on the vehicle, it must be considered during any diagnosis of a non-functioning electrical item. A Honda dealer can interrogate the module to determine the nature of most electrical faults, using a special tool.

4 Switches – removal and refitting

Note: *Before removing any switch, disconnect the battery negative lead, and position the lead away from the battery (also see Disconnecting the battery).*

Ignition switch/steering lock

1 Refer to Chapter 10.

Steering column switches

2 With reference to Chapter 11, remove the driver's side under cover and lower cover from the facia.

3 Remove the steering wheel (Chapter 10).

4 Remove the steering column shrouds (Chapter 11).

5 Either undo the single retaining screw and remove the steering column switch assembly, disconnecting the three wiring plugs from the ignition switch and related components, or undo the two screws securing each switch to the assembly and withdraw it, disconnecting

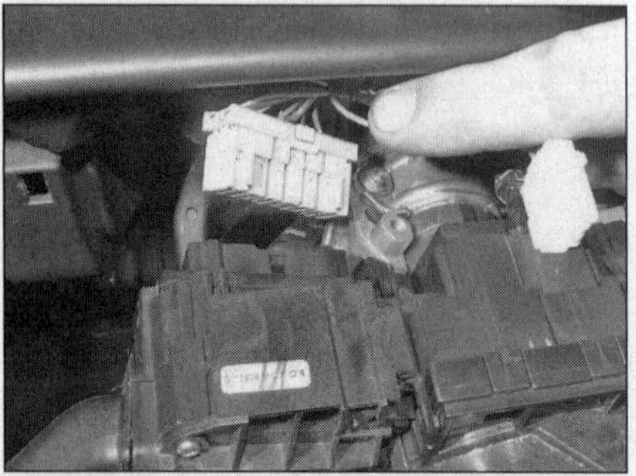

4.5a Unplug wiring connector behind switch assembly . . .

4.5b . . . undo two retaining screws . . .

4.5c . . . and carefully release switch retaining clip . . .

its wiring connector plug to do so **(see illustrations)**.

6 Refitting is a reversal of removal.

Hazard warning light switch

7 Remove the centre air vents panel, as described in Chapter 3, Section 9.

8 Release the retaining clips and push the switch out of the panel from behind **(see illustrations)**.

9 Refitting is a reversal of removal.

Fuel filler release

10 Refer to Chapter 4A.

Heated rear window switch

11 The switch is an integral part of the complete heater control panel/climate control unit. Refer to Chapter 3, Section 9.

Heater/ventilation controls

12 Refer to Chapter 3.

Facia-mounted switches

13 With reference to Chapter 11, remove the driver's side under cover and lower cover from the facia.

14 Release the retaining clips and push the switch out of the panel from behind **(see illustrations)**.

15 Refitting is a reversal of removal.

Door-mounted window switches

16 Insert a screwdriver with the tip wrapped in protective tape up through the hole under the armrest, and use it to push up the rear end of the switch panel from beneath. When the hook at the rear of the panel releases, pull it out along the edge of the panel, releasing the clips until the clip at the front tip of the panel can be released **(see illustrations)**.

17 Pull out the switch panel and disconnect its wiring plug **(see illustration)**.

18 The driver's door (master) switch appears to be an integral part of the panel. On all passenger doors, the switch itself can be removed from the switch panel by removing the two screws underneath **(see illustration)**.

19 Refitting is a reversal of removal.

4.5d ... to withdraw lighting switch ...

4.5e Procedure is the same to remove wash/wipe switch

4.8a Release retaining clips ...

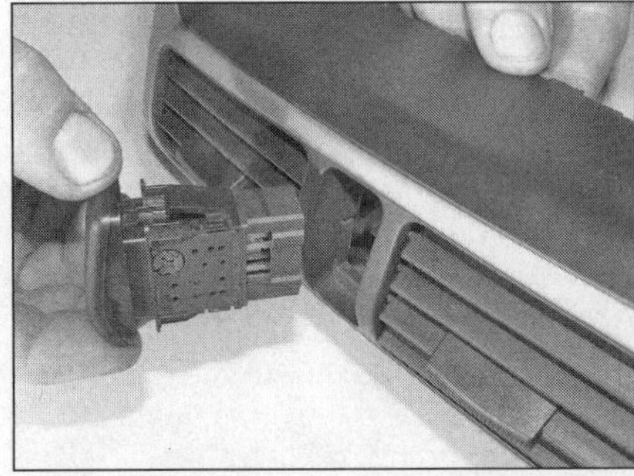

4.8b ... and push hazard warning switch out of centre air vents panel from behind

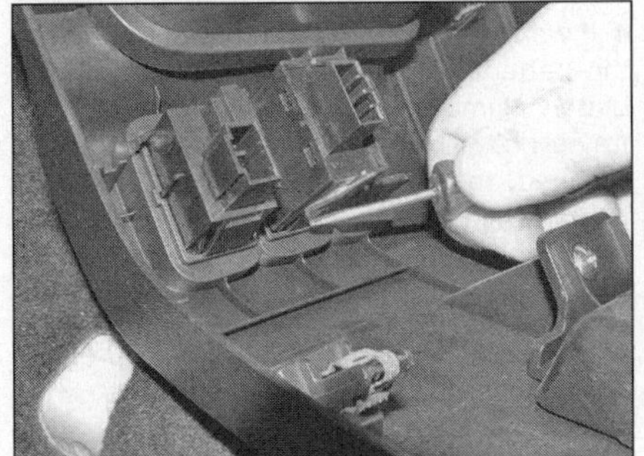

4.14a Release retaining clips ...

4.14b ... and push facia-mounted switches out of panel from behind

4.16a Insert a screwdriver up through hole under armrest ...

4.16b ... to push up rear end of switch panel from beneath. Release clips to remove ...

4.17 ... and disconnect switch wiring to withdraw

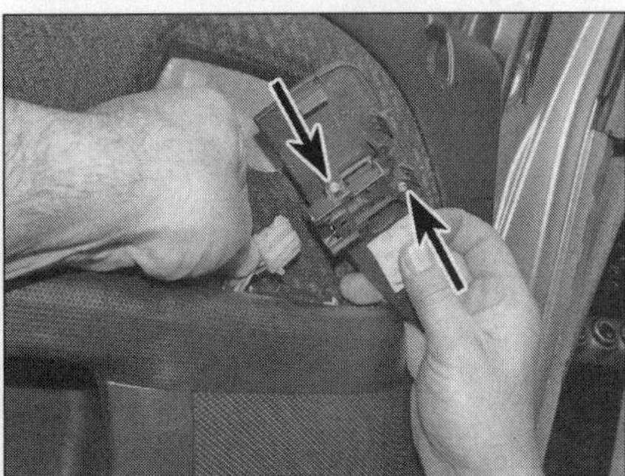

4.18 Undo two retaining screws to remove switch – passenger doors only

4.23 Prise open screw cap . . .

4.25 . . . withdraw switch and disconnect plug

Door-mounted mirror switch

20 The mirror switch is part of the driver's door master switch assembly. Proceed as described in paragraphs 16 to 19 above.

Handbrake-on warning switch

21 Refer to Chapter 9.

Fuel cut-off (inertia) switch

22 Refer to Chapter 4A or 4B.

Interior (courtesy) light switch

23 Open the relevant door, then prise back the screw cap from the switch **(see illustration)**.

24 Remove the mounting screw, and with- draw the switch from the door pillar **(see illustration)**.

25 Disconnect the switch wiring plug, and remove the switch **(see illustration)**.

26 These switches are simple 'plunger' types, and can sometimes suffer from corrosion, which causes them to stick, or have a bad

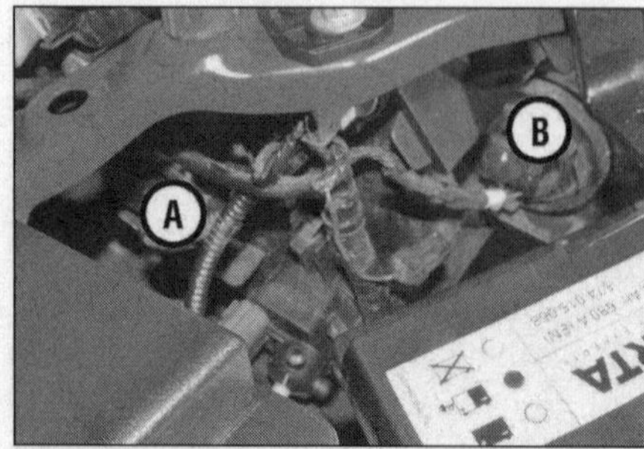

5.11 On later models, headlight dipped beam bulb (A) is outboard of main beam bulb (B)

4.24 . . . then remove mounting screw . . .

4.30 Slide back contact and undo screw to remove tailgate light switch

contact. It is worth applying a maintenance spray such as WD-40 to a defective switch, as this may be enough to restore its operation.

27 Note that the interior light switches itself off after a time, to save the battery – it will only 'reset' once the doors have been shut.

28 Refitting is a reversal of removal. Reconnect the switch wiring plug, and test the operation of the interior light before fitting the switch back into position.

Glovebox light switch

29 Refer to the bulb renewal procedure in Section 6.

Tailgate light switch

30 Open the tailgate, then remove the mounting screw from the tailgate switch **(see illustration)**. Withdraw the switch from the pillar and disconnect the switch wiring. Note that the luggage compartment light switches itself off after a time, to save the battery – it will only 'reset' once the tailgate has been shut.

Stop-light switch

31 Refer to Chapter 9.

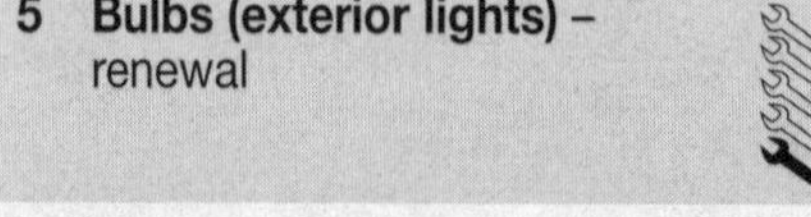

5 Bulbs (exterior lights) – renewal

1 Whenever a bulb is renewed, note the following points:

a) Ensure that the light is switched off, and also switch off the ignition (take out the key). For maximum safety, and particularly when changing the headlight bulbs, disconnect the battery negative lead (see Disconnecting the battery).

b) Remember that, if the light has just been in use, the bulb may be extremely hot.

c) Always check the bulb contacts and holder, ensuring that there is clean metal-to metal contact between the bulb and its live(s) and earth. Clean off any corrosion or dirt before fitting a new bulb.

d) Wherever bayonet-type bulbs are fitted, ensure that the live contact(s) bear firmly against the bulb contact.

e) Always ensure that the new bulb is of the correct rating, and that it is completely clean before fitting it; this applies particularly to headlight/foglight bulbs (see below).

Headlight

2 Models up to the end of 2004 (model year) had a single headlight bulb containing both main and dipped beam filaments. From 2005 onwards, headlights were fitted which use separate main and dipped beam bulbs. To make sure of purchasing the correct part, it is recommended that the old bulb is removed and taken with you for reference when buying a new one.

3 When handling a new bulb, try and hold it only by the metal body.

Avoid touching the glass with your fingers, as moisture and grease from the skin can cause blackening and rapid failure of this type of bulb. If the glass is accidentally touched, wipe it clean using methylated spirit.

4 If working on the bulb on the same side as the battery, it may be helpful to loosen the battery clamp, and slide the battery over in its tray slightly, to improve access. Ultimately, if required, remove the battery completely, as described in Chapter 5A.

2001 to 2004 models

5 Open the bonnet, identify the headlight bulb (it has a large round rubber cover on the back), then pull the wiring plug in the centre straight back to disconnect it.

6 Pull off the round rubber cover, using the tab provided (note that the cover is also marked with the word TOP, or an arrow).

7 Release the bulb's wire retaining clip by unhooking it sideways at the top, then pivot the clip down. Withdraw the bulb.

8 Install the new bulb, ensuring that its three locating tabs are correctly seated in the headlight cut-outs. Secure the bulb in position with the spring clip.

9 Refit the cover, then reconnect the wiring plug securely to complete.

10 Switch on the headlights, and check the operation on main and dipped beam.

2005-on models

11 Open the bonnet and identify the defective bulb – the main beam bulb is the inboard of the two **(see illustration)**.

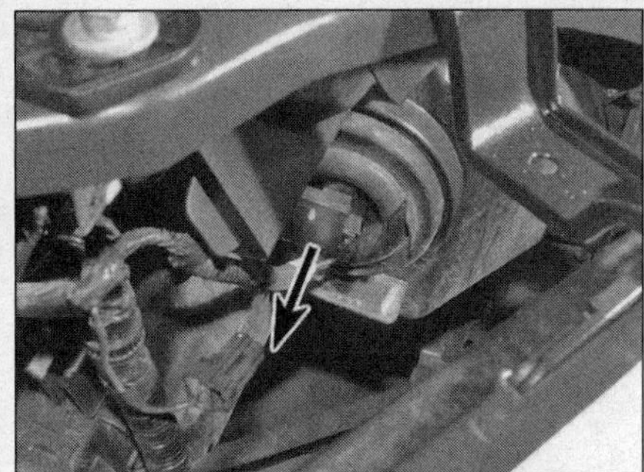
5.12 Disconnect main beam bulbholder wiring plug

5.13 Peel off rubber cover

5.14a Release spring clip securing bulb, and remove bulb . . .

5.14b . . . then separate bulb and bulbholder – do not touch glass

5.15a Fit new bulb and bulbholder into back of headlight . . .

5.15b . . . so that bulb fits into slot and projections on bulb flange fit into recesses . . .

12 Pull the wiring plug in the centre straight back to disconnect it **(see illustration)**.

13 Pull off the round rubber cover, using the tab provided (note that the cover is also marked with the word TOP, or an arrow) **(see illustration)**.

14 Release the bulb's wire retaining clip by unhooking it sideways at the top, then pivot the clip down. Withdraw the bulb and unplug the bulbholder **(see illustrations)**.

15 To fit the new bulb, offer it into the back of the headlight, ensuring that it fits correctly into the cutout provided and that the locating projections on the bulb flange engage with the recesses in the headlight, then secure it with the spring clip **(see illustrations)**.

16 Refit the rubber cover and push the wiring plug securely onto the new bulb to complete.

17 Switch on the headlights, and check the operation on main and dipped beam.

Sidelight

18 Open the bonnet, and identify the sidelight bulb – it is above the headlight/dipped beam bulb, with its own small wiring plug and bulbholder **(see illustration)**.

19 Twist the wiring plug and bulbholder a quarter-turn anti-clockwise, and withdraw it from the headlight **(see illustration)**.

20 Pull out the wedge-base bulb, then fit the new one by pushing it firmly into the bulbholder **(see illustration)**.

21 Offer the bulbholder into the headlight, then twist it a quarter-turn clockwise to secure.

22 Check the operation of the sidelights on completion.

Front direction indicator

23 Open the bonnet, and identify the direction indicator bulb (it is above the headlight/main beam bulb, inboard of the sidelight, with its own small wiring plug and bulbholder).

24 Twist the wiring plug and bulbholder a

5.15c . . . then secure with spring clip

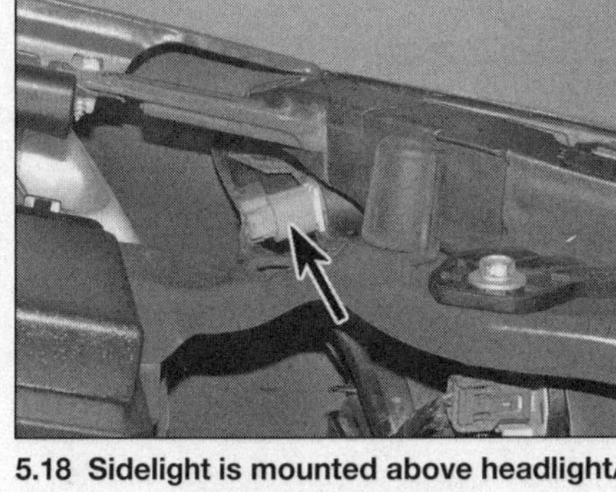
5.18 Sidelight is mounted above headlight/ dipped beam bulb

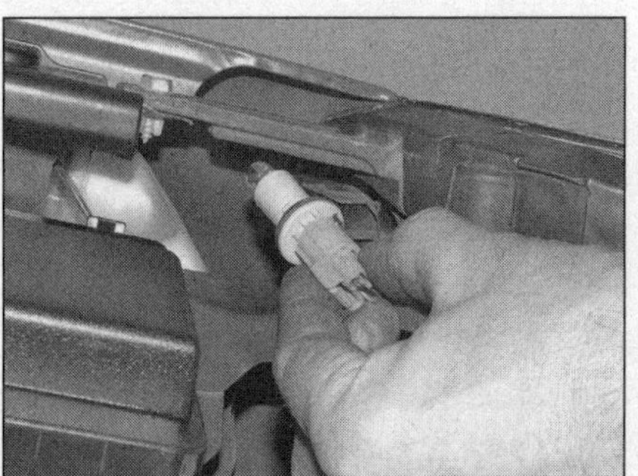
5.19 Twist and remove sidelight bulbholder . . .

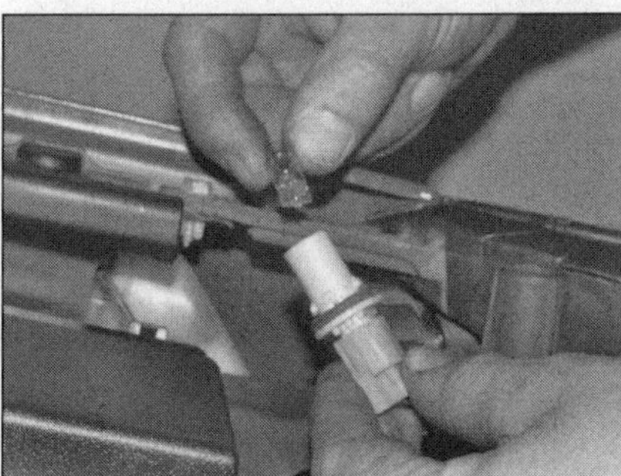
5.20 . . . then pull out wedge-base bulb

5.24 Twist and remove direction indicator bulbholder . . .

5.25 . . . then pull out wedge-base bulb

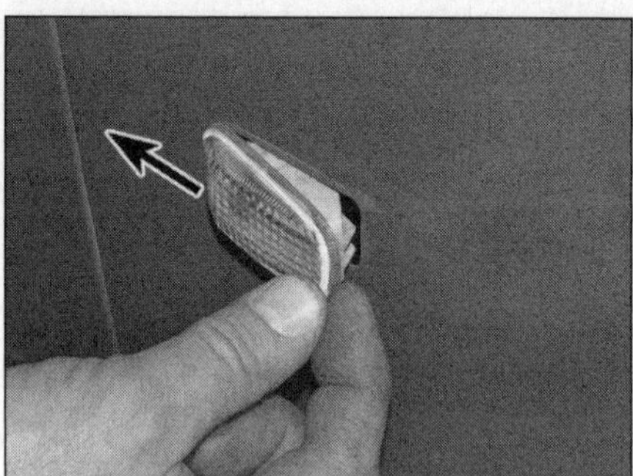
5.34 Push direction indicator side repeater to rear to release clip

quarter-turn anti-clockwise, and withdraw it from the headlight **(see illustration)**.

25 Pull out the wedge-base bulb, then fit the new one by pushing it firmly into the bulbholder **(see illustration)**.

26 Offer the bulbholder into the headlight, then twist it a quarter-turn clockwise to secure.

27 Check the operation of the direction indicators on completion.

Front foglight

28 Use a flat-tipped screwdriver to release the two clips on the underside of the front bumper, just in front of the access panel underneath the foglight.

29 Push the access panel inwards to release it and withdraw it.

30 Twist the wiring plug and bulbholder a quarter-turn anti-clockwise, and withdraw it from the foglight.

31 Squeeze the connector to release the locking tab and disconnect the wiring plug from the bulbholder.

32 Connect the wiring plug to the new bulb, ensure that it is fully engaged and refit the wiring plug and bulbholder to the foglight, turning it a quarter-turn clockwise to secure it.

33 Check the operation of the foglights, then refit the access panel and secure with the two clips.

Direction indicator side repeater

34 Wash the area around the side repeater to avoid grit scratching the paint. Push the light unit rearwards to compress its rear clip, then unhook the front end from the wing and withdraw it **(see illustration)**. Don't use any tools for this, otherwise there is a risk of damaging the paint – if tools must be used, it's worth applying some masking tape around the light first.

35 If the light unit is difficult to move, it may be easier, and carries less risk of damaging the wing, to remove the wheel arch liner (Chapter 11, Section 23), then reach inside and release the light unit from behind.

36 Twist the bulbholder anti-clockwise to release it, and pull out the wedge-base bulb **(see illustrations)**. Make sure that the bulbholder does not disappear back through the hole in the wing – tape it in place temporarily if necessary.

37 Refitting is a reversal of removal. Make sure that the light unit is refitted with the clip facing rearwards, and that it is clipped securely in place.

38 Check the operation of the lights on completion.

Rear lights

39 Open the tailgate. Wrap a small flat-tipped screwdriver with protective tape

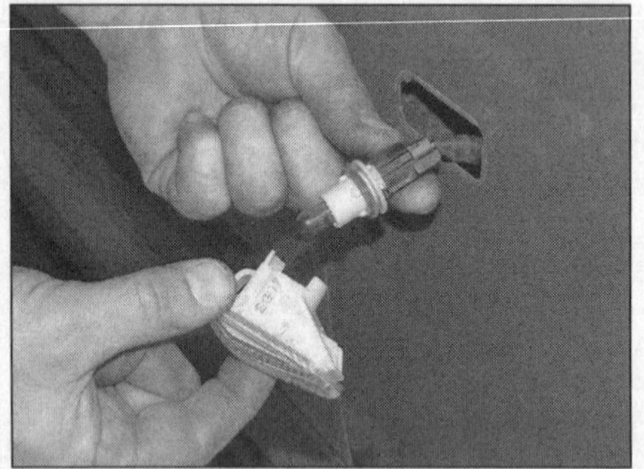
5.36a Twist and remove side repeater bulbholder . . .

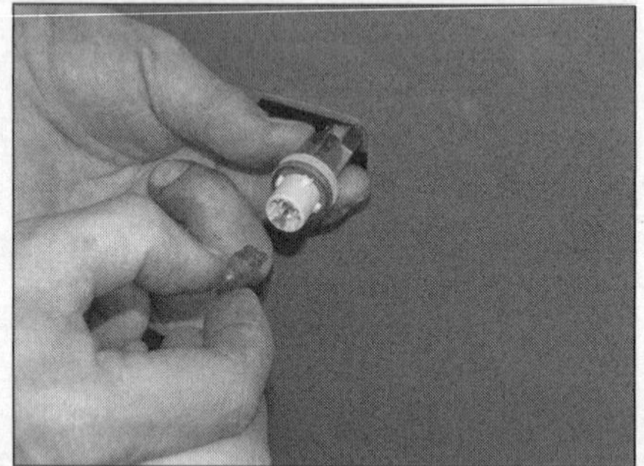
5.36b . . . then pull out wedge-base bulb

5.39a Taillight assembly is secured by two screws

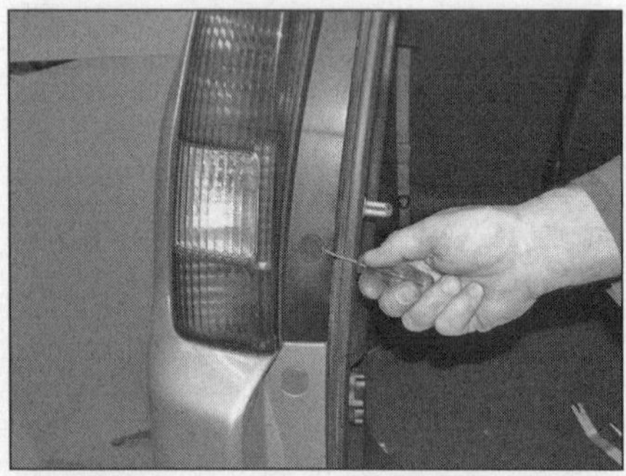
5.39b Carefully prise out cover over each screw . . .

5.39c . . . and undo mounting screws . . .

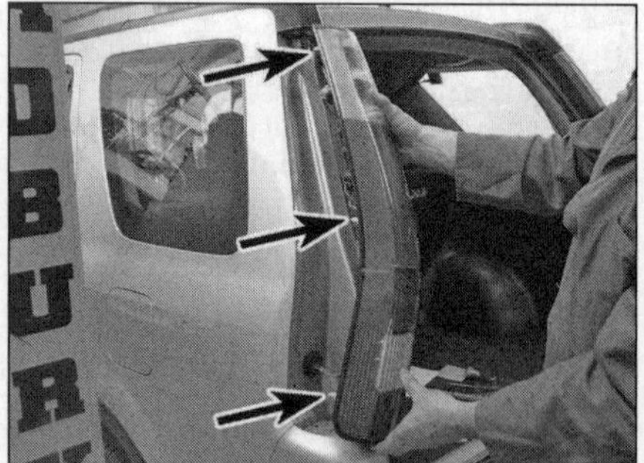
5.39d . . . to release taillight assembly

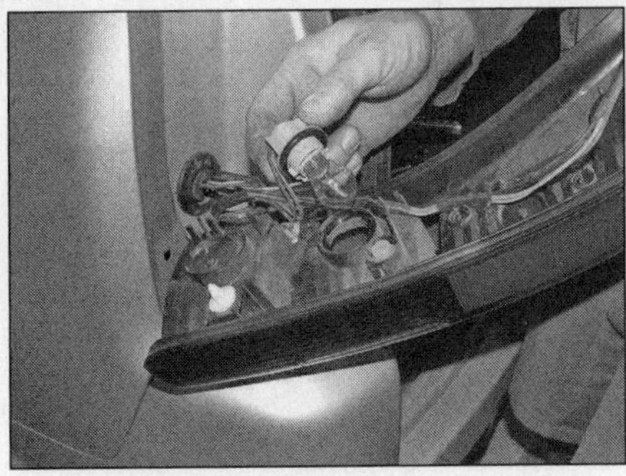
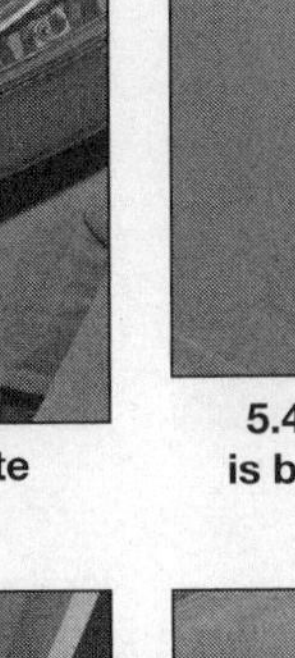

5.40 Twist and remove appropriate bulbholder . . .

5.41 . . . and remove bulb – this one is bayonet fitting (press and turn anti-clockwise to remove)

5.45 Carefully prise out number plate light lens . . .

5.46 . . . then pull out the wedge-base bulb

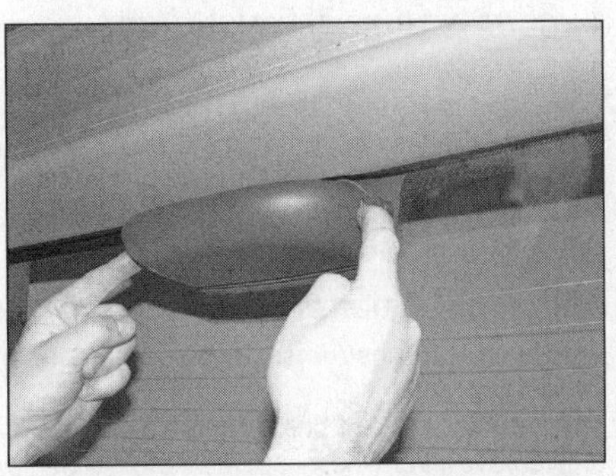

5.48 Press in clip at each end of high-level stop-light housing to release

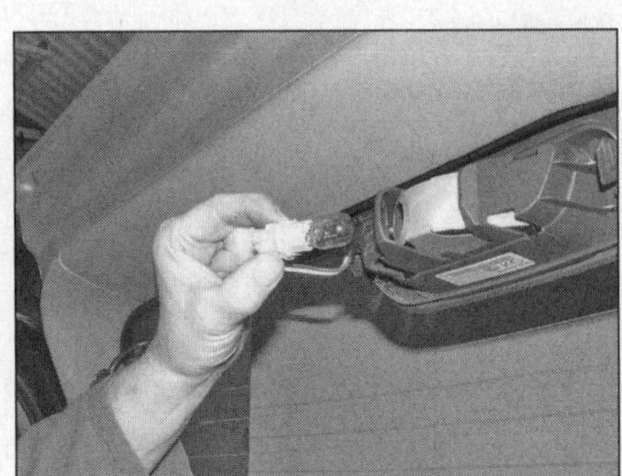

5.49 Twist and remove bulbholder . . .

and use a piece of card or a wad of cloth to prevent damage to the paintwork and trim itself, then carefully prise up the cover over the mounting screws at the top and bottom of each taillight assembly. Undo the two screws and remove the taillight assembly **(see illustrations)**.

40 Identify the defective bulb and remove the relevant bulbholder by turning it a quarter-turn anti-clockwise **(see illustration)**.

41 The bulbs are of the wedge-base type on early models (simply pull out the bulb, then fit the new one by pushing it firmly into the bulbholder) and of the bayonet-fitting on later models (press and turn them anti-clockwise to remove) **(see illustration)**.

42 Refit the bulbholder into the taillight assembly, then twist it a quarter-turn clockwise to secure.

43 Fit the taillight assembly to the body, aligning the clips on its outer edge with the slots in the bodywork, then push the assembly into place. Refit and tighten securely the two mounting screws and refit the screw covers.

44 Check the operation of the lights on completion.

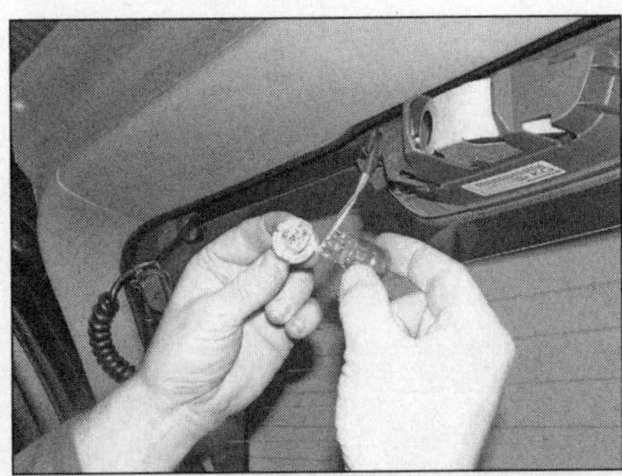

5.50 . . . then pull out wedge-base bulb

Number plate lights

45 Wrap a small flat-tipped screwdriver with protective tape and use a piece of card or a wad of cloth to prevent damage to the light, insert the screwdriver on the left edge of the lens and carefully prise out the light lens **(see illustration)**.

46 Pull out the wedge-base bulb, then fit the new one by pushing it firmly into the bulbholder **(see illustration)**.

47 Check that the light is working, then clip the lens back into place.

High-level stop-light

48 Open the tailgate, and press in the clip at each end of the housing to release it **(see illustration)**. Withdraw the housing from the tailgate.

49 Remove the bulbholder by turning it a quarter-turn anti-clockwise **(see illustration)**.

50 Pull out the wedge-base bulb, then fit the new one by pushing it firmly into the bulbholder **(see illustration)**.

51 Refit the bulbholder into the light assembly, then twist it a quarter-turn clockwise to secure.

52 Check that the light is working, then clip the housing back into place.

6 Bulbs (interior lights) – renewal

General

1 Refer to Section 5, paragraph 1. Remove light lenses by carefully prising them out using a small flat-tipped screwdriver or a nail file and levering on the edge of the lens, not on the surrounding housing.

Courtesy light (in headlining)

2 Carefully prise out the light lens at the rear edge, near each end **(see illustration)**.

3 Prise the festoon-type bulb from its spring contacts, and renew it **(see illustration)**.

4 Check the light's operation and clip the light lens back into place to complete.

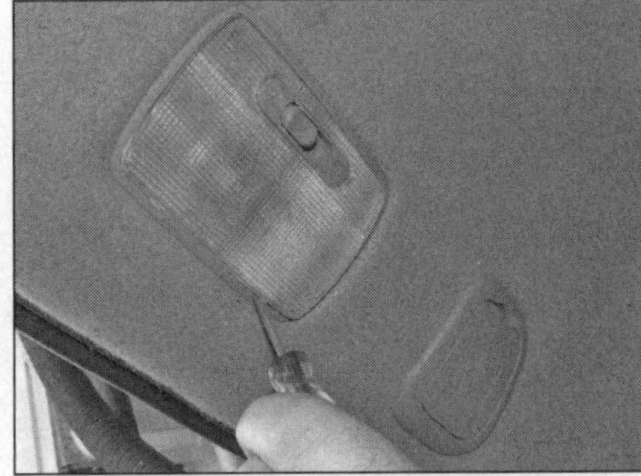

6.2 Prise out lens for access to bulb

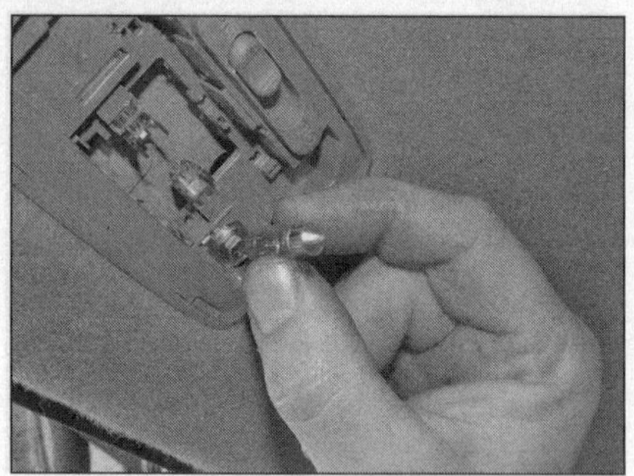

6.3 Removing festoon-type bulb (from rear interior light)

6.5 Prise out lens for access to bulb

6.6 Removing wedge-base bulb

Spotlights

In roof console

5 Carefully prise out the light lens at the front edge, in front of each spotlight **(see illustration)**.

6 Pull out the bulb (note that wedge-base bulbs are often a tight fit), and fit a new one, ensuring that it is securely refitted **(see illustration)**.

7 Check the light's operation and clip the light lens back into place to complete.

In headlining

8 Identify the defective bulb and very carefully prise out the light lens between the two spotlights, pushing on the lens opposite to the one being renewed.

9 Prise the festoon-type bulb from its spring contacts, and renew it.

10 Check the light's operation and clip the light lens back into place to complete.

Luggage compartment light

11 Carefully prise out the light lens at the front edge, near each end.

12 Prise the festoon-type bulb from its spring contacts, and renew it.

13 Check the light's operation and clip the light lens back into place to complete.

Instrument panel illumination

14 Remove the instrument panel as described in Section 10.

15 Twist the relevant bulbholder anti-clockwise and remove it from the rear of the panel. All bulbs are capless/wedge-base types, or integral with their respective bulbholders **(see illustrations)**.

16 Refit the instrument panel as described in Section 10.

Switch illumination

17 Most bulbs are integral with the switches, and cannot be renewed separately. However for some switches, such as the hazard warning switch, the bulbholder can be released by turning it through 90° and the bulb can be renewed separately, albeit all such bulbs are integral with their respective bulbholders **(see illustrations)**.

Glovebox illumination

18 Open the glovebox. The bulb is part of the switch assembly at the top of the glovebox aperture. Remove the two switch screws, then withdraw it and disconnect the wiring plug **(see illustration)**.

19 Prise the festoon-type bulb from its spring contacts, and renew it.

20 Refitting is a reversal of removal.

Heater control unit illumination

21 Refer to Chapter 3, Section 9.

Automatic transmission selector illumination

22 Refer to Chapter 7B, Section 5.

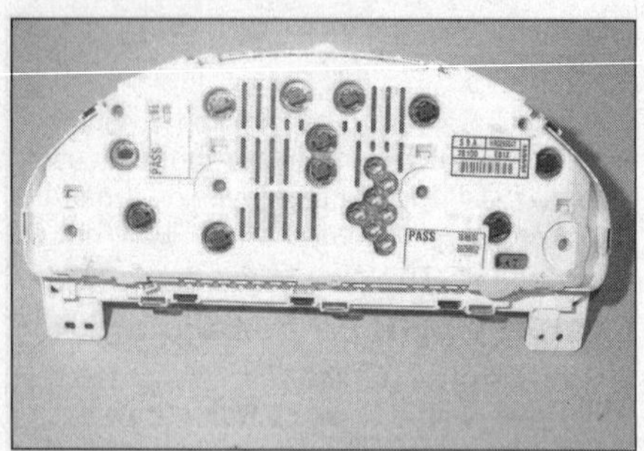

6.15a Instrument illuminating and warning lamps are fitted into back of instrument panel

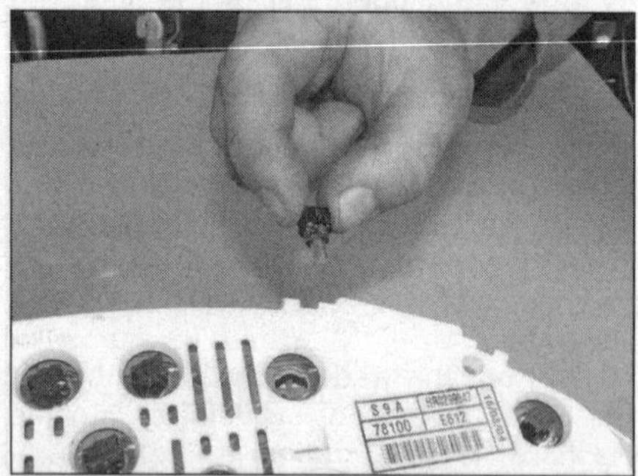

6.15b Twist and remove bulbholder . . .

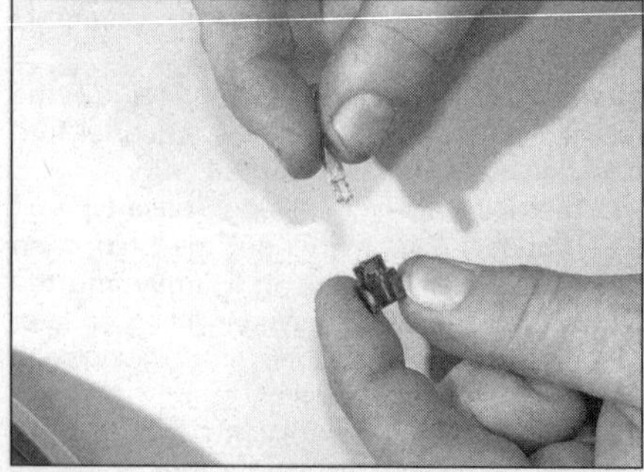

6.15c . . . then pull out wedge-base bulb

6.17a Where switches have separate illumination, twist and remove bulbholder

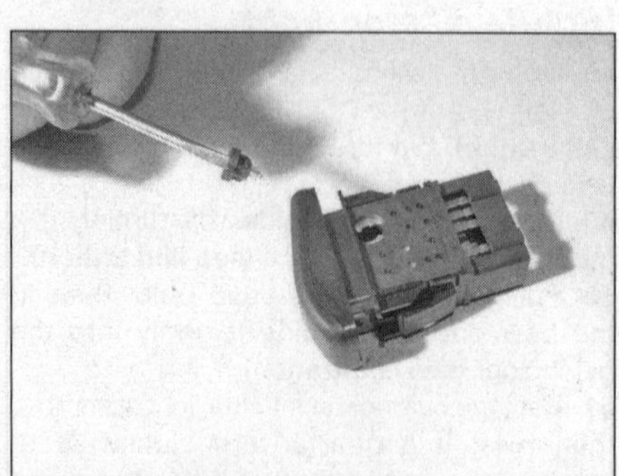

6.17b Bulbs are integral with bulbholders

6.18 Remove glovebox switch screws, then withdraw it to renew bulb

7.2 Remove two upper mounting bolts . . .

7.3 . . . and three lower mounting bolts

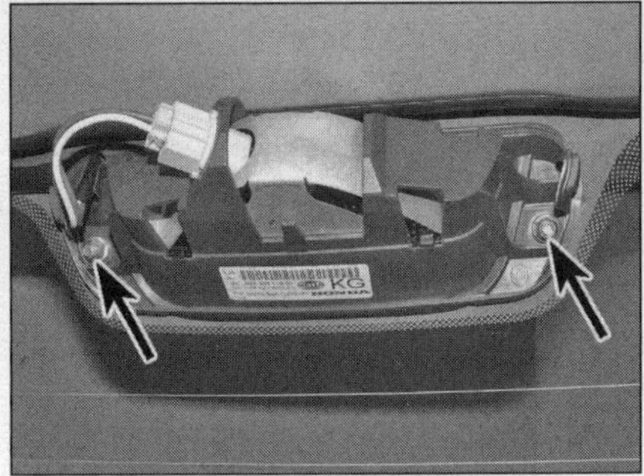

7.16 Unscrew two mounting nuts to remove high-level stop-light

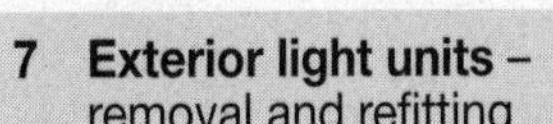

7 Exterior light units – removal and refitting

Headlight

1 Remove the front bumper as described in Chapter 11.

2 Unscrew the two upper mounting bolts **(see illustration)**.

3 Unscrew the three lower mounting bolts **(see illustration)**.

4 Partially withdraw the headlight, disconnecting the wiring plugs and bulbholders as they become more accessible, then remove it completely **(see illustration 9.3a)**.

5 The headlight mounting bracket can be unbolted from the bottom of the unit if required; it is retained by one bolt and a locating tab.

6 Refitting is a reversal of removal. On completion, check the light operation, and if necessary have the headlight beam alignment checked (see Section 8).

Sidelight

7 The front sidelight is integral with the headlight.

Front direction indicator

8 The front direction indicator is integral with the headlight.

Front foglight

9 Remove the front bumper as described in Chapter 11.

10 Unscrew the mounting bolts and screw and withdraw the foglight from the bumper.

11 Refitting is a reversal of removal. On completion, check the light operation.

Direction indicator side repeater

12 The side repeater is removed as part of the bulb renewal procedure in Section 5.

Rear lights

13 The taillight assembly is removed as part of the bulb renewal procedure described in Section 5.

Number plate light

14 Remove the bulb as described in Section 5, then unclip the light from the rear bumper by pushing it to the front. Disconnect the light's wiring and withdraw it.

15 Refitting is a reversal of removal. On completion, check the light operation.

High-level stop-light

16 Remove the bulb as described in Section 5, then disconnect the bulbholder wiring and unscrew the two mounting nuts to remove the light **(see illustration)**.

17 Refitting is a reversal of removal. On completion, check the light operation.

8 Headlight beam alignment – general information

All models are equipped with an electrical vertical beam adjuster unit – this can be used to adjust the headlight beam, to compensate for the relevant load which the vehicle is carrying. An adjuster wheel is provided on the facia – refer to the vehicle's handbook for further information.

Accurate adjustment of the headlight beam is only possible using optical beam-setting equipment, and this work should therefore be carried out by a Honda dealer or suitably-equipped workshop. Note that the headlight adjuster wheel should be set to its lowest position (0) before any adjustments are made.

For reference, the headlights can be finely adjusted by rotating the adjuster screws fitted to the top of each light unit, using a cross-head screwdriver. The screws are accessible through the top of the body front panel. The vertical adjustment screw is mounted at the inboard end of the headlight, on the adjuster motor. The horizontal adjustment screw is mounted at the outboard end of the headlight **(see illustrations)**.

9 Headlight adjuster components – removal and refitting

Adjuster switch

1 Refer to Section 4.

Adjuster motor

2 Remove the headlight as described in Section 7.

3 Twist the motor to free it, then gently pull

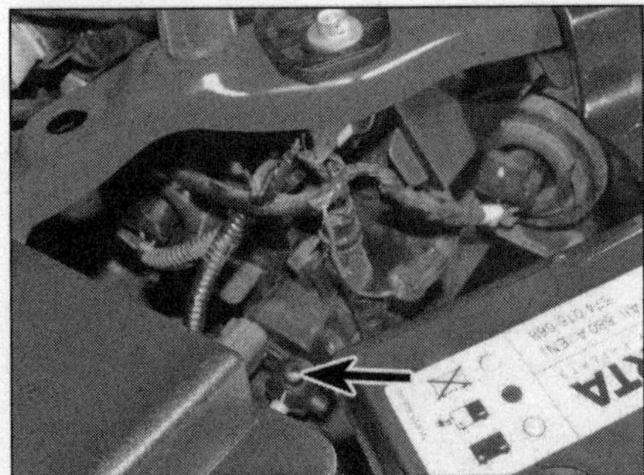

8.3a 2005-on headlight vertical adjuster location . . .

8.3b . . . bears directly on adjuster motor

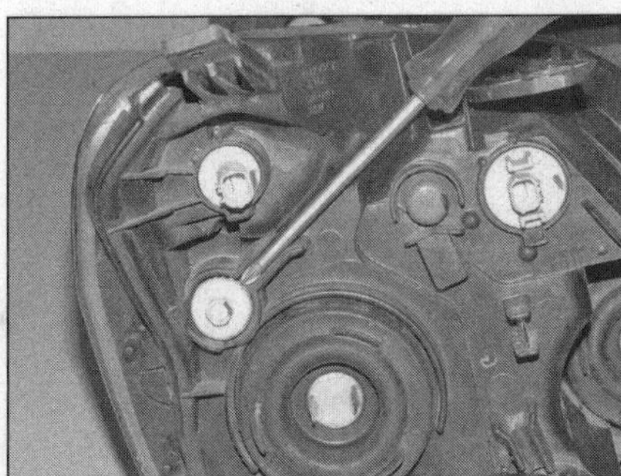

8.3c Horizontal adjuster is at an angle, beneath sidelight bulb

9.3a Disconnect the adjuster motor wiring plug

9.3b Removing the headlight adjuster motor

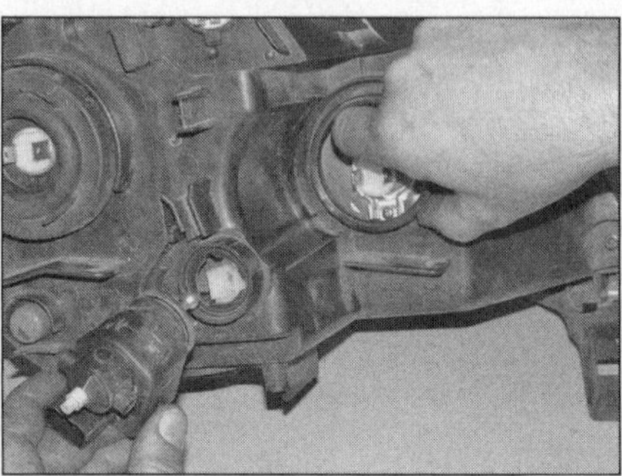
9.4 Hold the adjuster mechanism with a finger through the bulb hole when refitting

it from the headlight, to release the ball-and-socket joint **(see illustrations)**.

4 When refitting, remove the headlight bulb (or the main beam bulb on 2005-on models) and hold the adjuster mechanism with a finger as the ball-and-socket joint is reconnected **(see illustration)**.

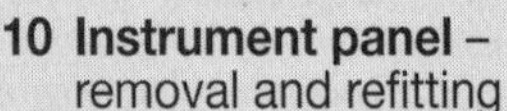

10 Instrument panel – removal and refitting

Removal

1 Ensure that the ignition is switched off (take out the key). Adjust the steering column to its lowest setting, using the lever underneath the steering wheel.

2 Remove the driver's side under cover and lower cover from the facia as described in Chapter 11, Section 27.

3 Remove the three screws from the steering column lower shroud, unclip the upper shroud from it, then work off the lower shroud (refer to Chapter 11, Section 27, if necessary).

4 The instrument panel surround must now be removed. The surround has two hooks and one clip at the top, and four clips along the bottom, and is released by gently pulling at the bottom edge **(see illustrations)**.

5 Remove the three instrument panel retaining screws (one at the top, and one on each lower corner), and withdraw the panel from the facia. Disconnect the two wiring plugs, and remove the panel completely **(see illustrations)**.

Refitting

6 Refitting is a reversal of removal.

Bulb renewal

7 Bulb renewal is covered in Section 6.

11 Horn(s) – removal and refitting

1 All models have two horns. On 2001 to 2004 models, they are mounted directly below the headlights; on 2005-on models they are mounted closer together, in front of the air conditioning system condenser **(see illustration)**.

2 On 2001 to 2004 models, remove the front bumper as described in Chapter 11. On 2005-on models the horns can be reached after the radiator grille has been removed (Chapter 11).

3 Disconnect the wiring plug from the horn.

4 Unscrew the mounting bolt, and remove the horn from the vehicle.

5 Refitting is a reversal of removal.

10.4a Unclip and remove the instrument panel surround by pulling on its bottom edge . . .

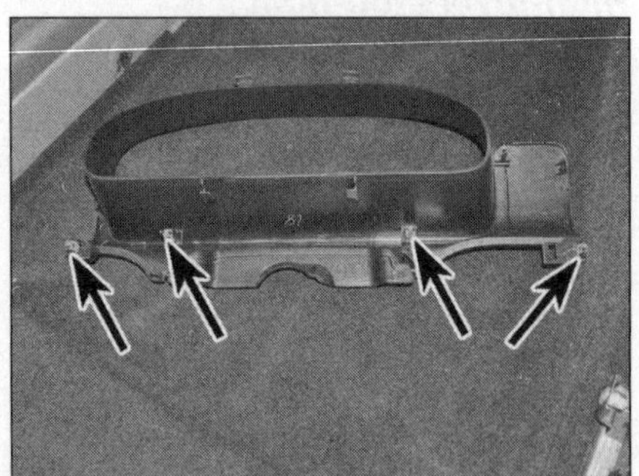
10.4b . . . to release four clips shown . . .

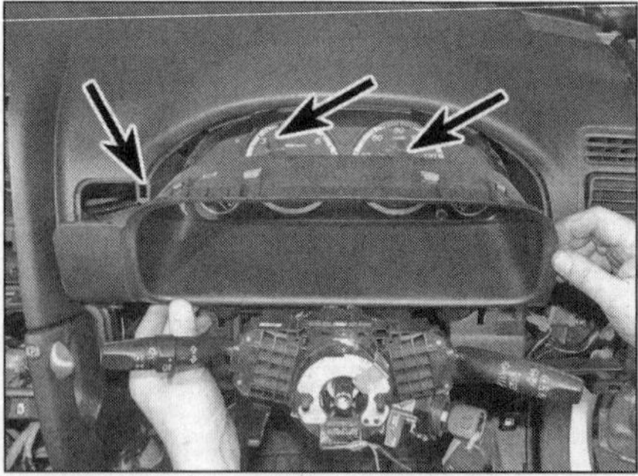
10.4c . . . then release upper hooks and clip to remove surround

10.5a Remove the three mounting screws . . .

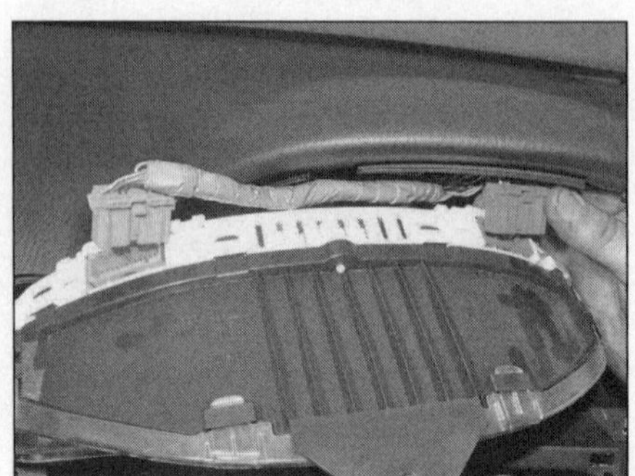
10.5b . . . then withdraw the panel and disconnect the two wiring plugs

11.1 Twin horns – with bumper removed – later models

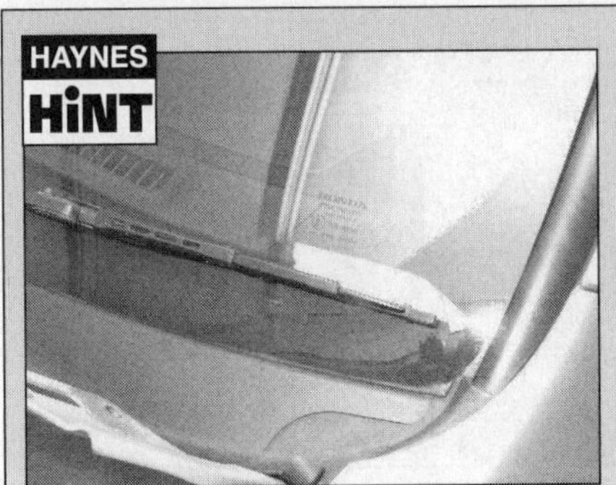
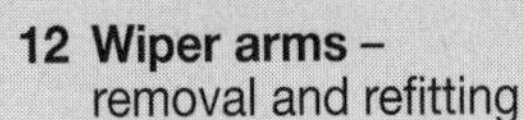

Stick a piece of masking tape along the edge of the wiper blade, to use as an alignment aid on refitting.

12 Wiper arms – removal and refitting

Removal

1 Operate the wiper motor, then switch it off so that the wiper arm returns to the park position **(see Haynes Hint)**.

Windscreen wiper arm

2 Unscrew the spindle nut **(see illustrations)**.

3 Lift the blade off the glass, and pull the wiper arm off its spindle **(see illustration)**. Note that on some models, the wiper arms may be very tight on the spindle splines – it should be possible to lever the arm off the spindle, using a flat-bladed screwdriver (take care not to damage the scuttle cover panel). In extreme cases, it may even be necessary to use a small puller to free the arm.

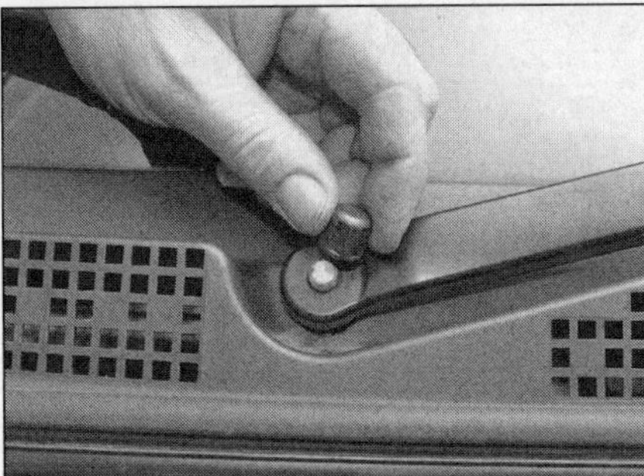

12.2 Unscrew wiper arm nut . . .

12.3 Pull wiper arm off splines

Tailgate wiper arm

4 Remove the cover, then unscrew the nut.

5 Lift the blade off the glass, and pull the wiper arm off its spindle. It should be possible to lever the arm off the spindle, using a flat-bladed screwdriver, but in extreme cases, it may even be necessary to use a small puller to free the arm.

Refitting

6 Ensure that the wiper arm and spindle splines are clean and dry, then refit the arm to the spindle. Where applicable, align the wiper blade with the tape fitted on removal.

7 Refit the spindle nut, tightening it securely, and clip the nut cover back into position.

13 Windscreen wiper motor and linkage – removal and refitting

Removal

1 Remove the wiper arms as described in Section 12.

2 Carefully prising out the clips along its length, peel off the rubber weatherstrip along the top edge of the windscreen scuttle panel. Disconnect the windscreen washer tube where it emerges from the scuttle panel **(see illustrations)**.

3 Carefully prise out the three clips from the front edge of the windscreen scuttle panel **(see illustrations)**.

4 Unclip the scuttle panel from the body along its front edge **(see illustrations)**.

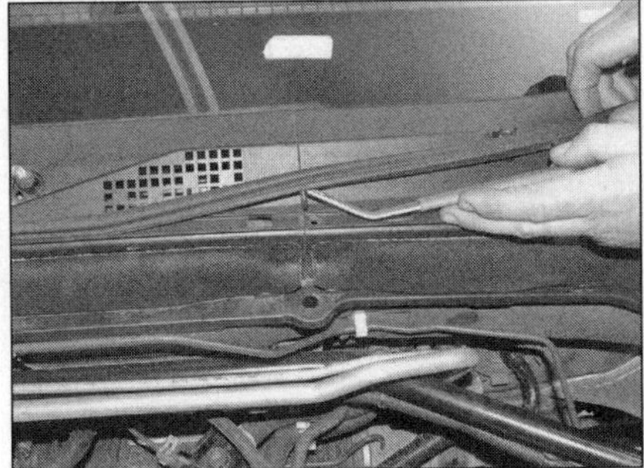

13.2a Carefully peel weatherstrip off scuttle panel . . .

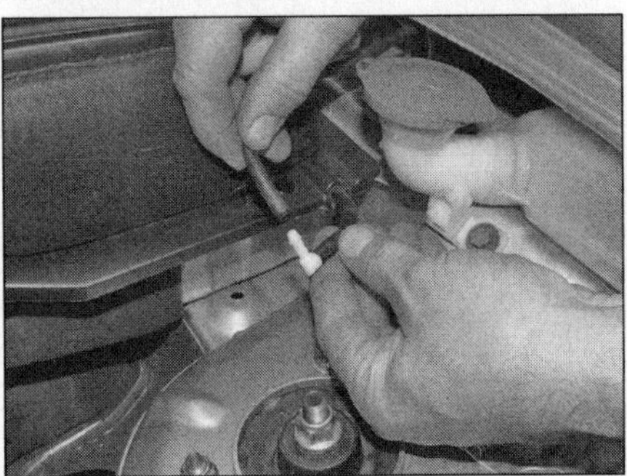

13.2b . . . and disconnect windscreen washer tube

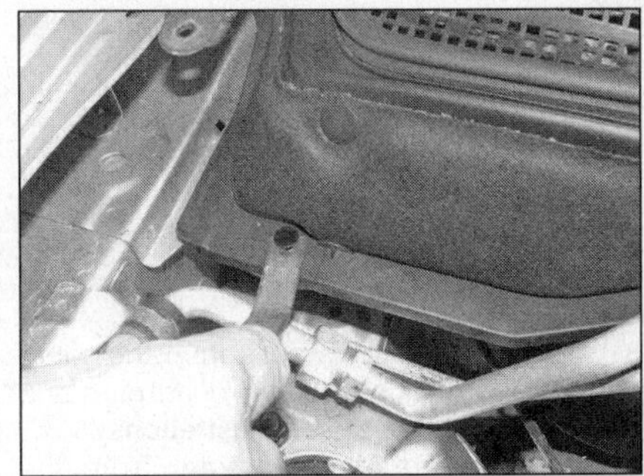

13.3a Prise out three clips . . .

13.3b . . . securing front edge of scuttle panel

13.4a Unclip front edge of scuttle panel . . .

13.4b . . . from body

13.5a Lift scuttle panel in the centre to bend it . . .

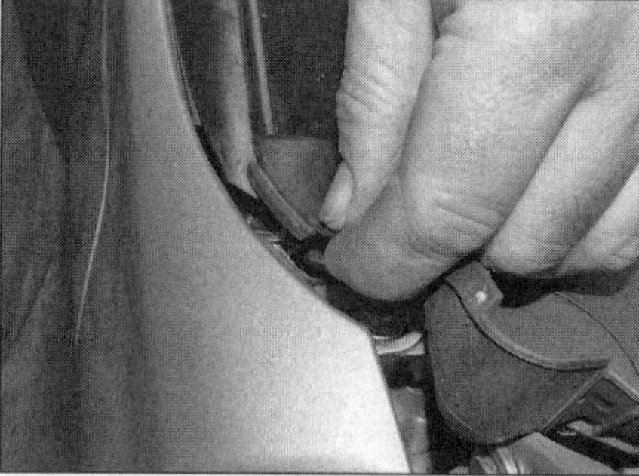

13.5b . . . so that rubber trim is released . . .

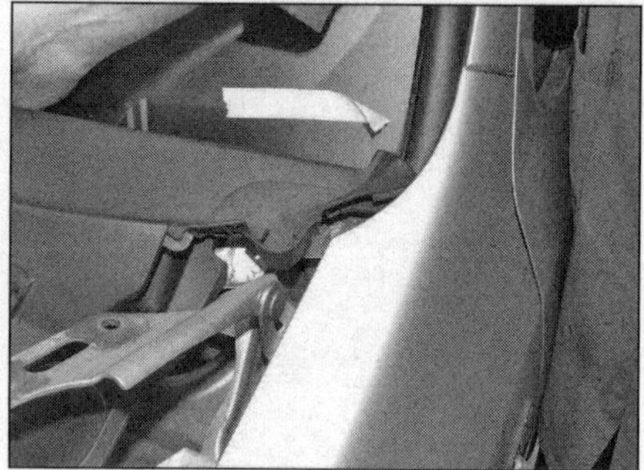

13.5c . . . at each end

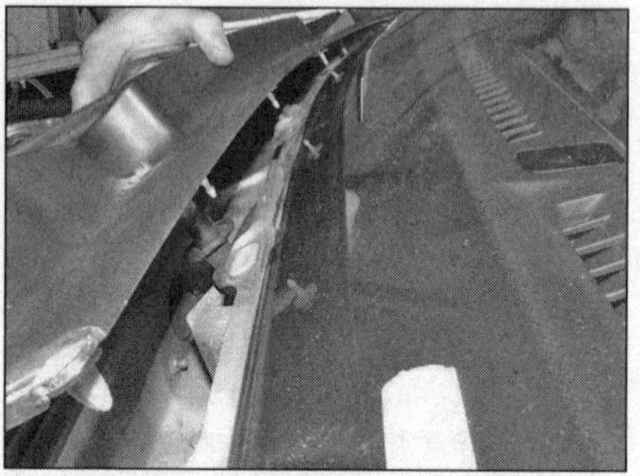

13.6 Release clips along rear edge to remove scuttle panel completely

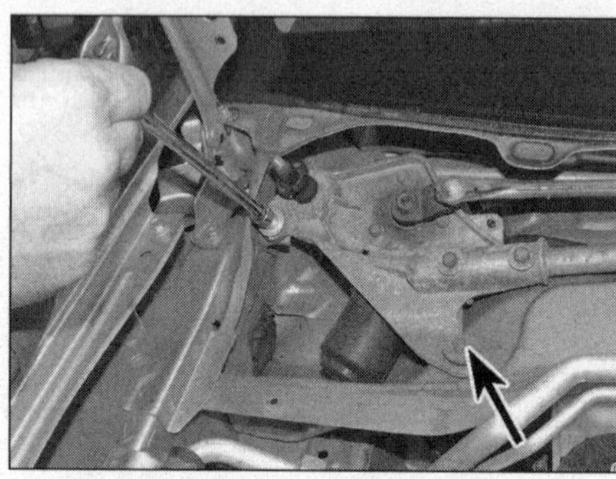

13.7a Wiper motor assembly has four mounting bolts – two on the driver's side . . .

13.7b . . . and two more in the centre of the vehicle

5 At each end of the panel, a rubber trim seals the panel to the windscreen and the wing – note how this rubber is fitted under the wing before removal. Lift the scuttle panel slightly in the centre, to bend it a little, and the end rubbers will release, allowing the panel to be removed **(see illustrations)**.

6 The scuttle panel's rear edge is secured under the windscreen by a row of eight clips – starting at one end, pull the panel forwards to release them **(see illustration)**.

7 The motor and linkage assembly is secured by four bolts – unscrew them and lift out the assembly **(see illustrations)**.

8 Unclip the wiring harness from the wiper motor, then disconnect the wiring plug and remove the assembly **(see illustrations)**.

9 Before separating the motor from the linkage, make an alignment mark between the linkage and the cranked arm attached to the motor, to show its parked position (typically, it will be horizontally aligned, along the axis of the motor frame).

10 Remove the spindle nut and washer, and separate the cranked arm from the motor. The other end of the cranked arm need not be detached, but for reference, it is on a ball fitting, which can be prised off if required.

11 Remove the three motor mounting bolts, and withdraw the motor from the wiper frame **(see illustration)**.

Refitting

12 Refitting is a reversal of removal, bearing in mind the following points:

a) Ensure that the motor arm is aligned in the 'parked' position (see paragraph 9) when refitting.

b) Where they have been disturbed, lightly grease the wiper linkage pivots.

c) Tighten all nuts and bolts securely.

d) Ensure that the scuttle panel is clipped back into place, and that the rubber trims at each end are tucked back under the wing correctly.

e) Test the motor's operation before refitting the wiper arms as described in Section 12.

14 Tailgate wiper motor – removal and refitting

Removal

1 Remove the tailgate wiper arm as described in Section 12.

2 Remove the tailgate lower trim panel as described in Chapter 11, Section 27.

3 Disconnect the motor wiring plug.

13.8a Release wiring from its clip then . . .

13.8b . . . disconnect wiper motor wiring plug

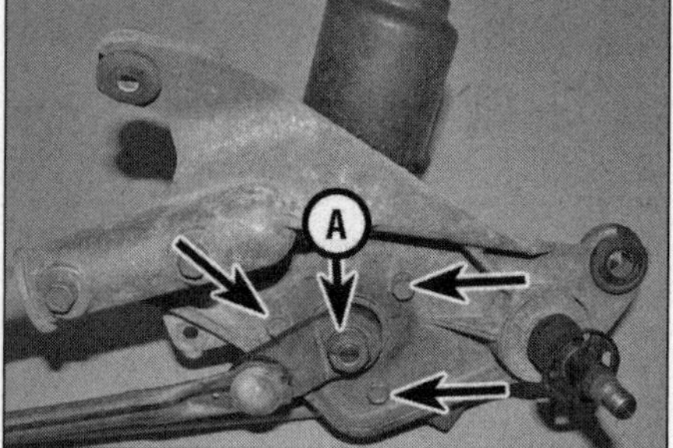

13.11 Unscrew spindle nut (A) to release linkage and three bolts to separate motor from linkage

4 Remove the three motor mounting bolts, and withdraw the motor from the tailgate **(see illustration)**.

Refitting

5 Refitting is a reversal of removal.

15 Windscreen/tailgate washer system components – removal and refitting

Washer fluid reservoir

Removal

1 Unscrew the single mounting bolt next to the reservoir filler neck and carefully disengage the filler neck from the reservoir **(see illustration)**.

2 Remove the front wheel arch liner as described in Chapter 11, Section 23.

3 Disconnect the wiring plug and washer tube from each of the two washer pumps – anticipate a small amount of fluid loss when the tubes are disconnected. Note the location of each washer tube, as they must be refitted to the correct pump.

4 Alternatively, the two pumps can be prised out of the reservoir, which means they can be left behind on the vehicle – however, the contents of the reservoir will be lost when the pumps are removed. Recover the rubber sealing grommet from each pump, and refit them to the reservoir.

5 Remove the reservoir mounting bolt, and lower the reservoir into the wheel arch to remove it.

Refitting

6 Refitting is a reversal of removal, noting the following points:

a) *If the pumps were removed, it may be helpful to apply a little liquid soap to the rubber sealing grommets to make refitting easier.*
b) *Make sure the washer hoses are securely reconnected to their original positions.*
c) *Refill the reservoir, then check the operation of the washers before refitting the wheel arch liner.*

Washer fluid pumps

Removal

7 The pumps are fitted into the washer reservoir. Remove the front wheel arch liner as described in Chapter 11, Section 23.

8 All models have two pumps – the inboard one is for the windscreen, with the outboard one for the tailgate. Where headlight washers are fitted, a third pump is fitted on its own next to the other two.

9 Disconnect the wiring plug and washer tube from the pump – anticipate a small amount of fluid loss when the tube is disconnected. If both pumps are being removed, note the location of each washer tube, as they must be refitted to the correct pump.

10 Prise the pump out of the reservoir, and remove it. If the rubber sealing grommet came out with the pump, refit it to the reservoir.

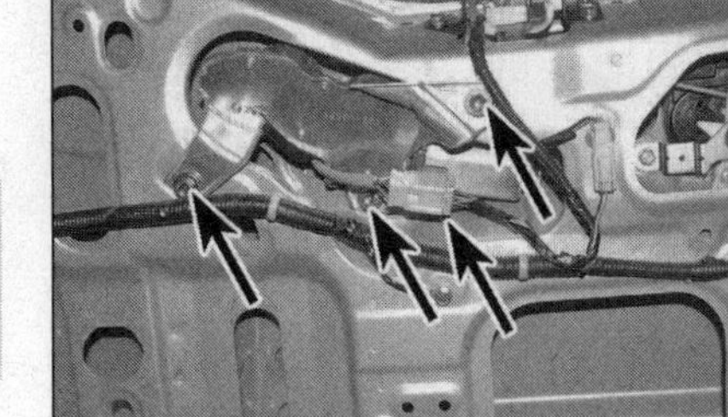

14.4 Tailgate wiper motor mounting bolts and wiring connector

Refitting

11 Refitting is a reversal of removal, noting the following points:

a) *It may be helpful to apply a little liquid soap to the rubber sealing grommets to make refitting easier.*
b) *Make sure the washer hoses are securely reconnected to their original positions.*
c) *Refill the reservoir, then check the operation of the washers before refitting the wheel arch liner.*

Windscreen washer jet

Removal

12 Remove the scuttle panel as described in Section 13. Working from the underside of the panel, release the retaining clips and push the jet out from behind **(see illustrations)**. Some models may have a quick-release fitting on the tube, released by pulling the small plastic clip upwards. Where this is not the case, it is likely that the tube will be a very tight fit – removal will be easier if the tube end can be warmed, and careful prising with a small screwdriver may also help.

Refitting

13 Refitting is a reversal of removal, but make sure that the fluid hose connections are securely remade. It may be helpful to apply a little liquid soap to the jet, to make fitting the tube easier.

Tailgate washer jet

Removal

14 Remove the tailgate upper and right-hand side trim panels as described in Chapter 11, Section 27. Remove also the tailgate lower trim panel if access is required to the washer tube's route up through the tailgate.

15.12a Use pliers to release washer jet clips . . .

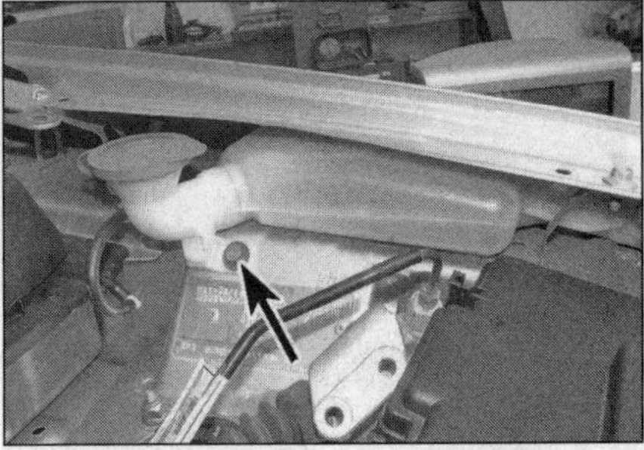

15.1 Undo filler neck mounting bolt to remove filler neck from washer fluid reservoir

15 The clip securing the back of the jet to the tailgate can be reached via one of the access holes in the tailgate. Release the clip, disconnect the washer tube (see note in paragraph 12 above, if required) and withdraw the jet.

16 The tailgate washer tube is routed down the passenger side of the vehicle, then across behind the front seats to the driver's side and down behind the luggage compartment side trim panel to the D-pillar. To gain access, remove the luggage compartment side trim panel and other trim panels as described in Chapter 11.

Refitting

17 Refitting is a reversal of removal.

Headlight washer jet

Removal

18 Remove the front bumper as described in Chapter 11.

19 Apply masking tape to the bumper, around the top part of the washer jet. Taking care not to damage the bumper or the cover, prise off the jet's top cover (which has two mounting legs) and remove it.

20 Remove the two jet body retaining screws now exposed in the bumper, and withdraw the jet body from inside.

Refitting

21 Refitting is a reversal of removal.

15.12b . . . then withdraw it from scuttle panel

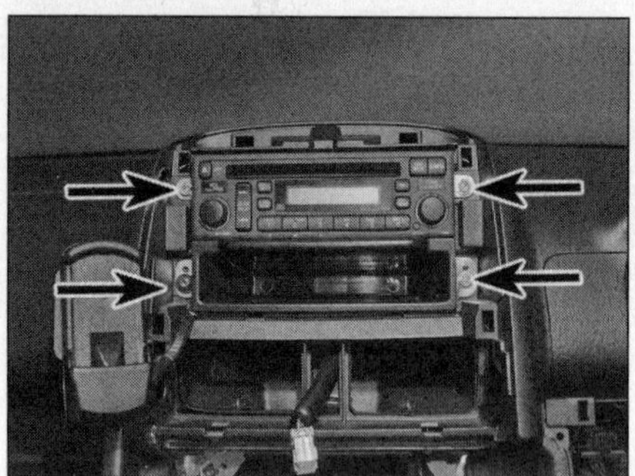

16.2a Remove mounting screws to extract audio unit . . .

16 Audio unit – removal and refitting

Removal

1 Remove the centre air vents panel, as described in Chapter 3, Section 9.

2 The whole unit can be removed by removing the four screws securing the metal mounting frame to the facia. Disconnect the unit's wiring and the aerial lead, then remove it **(see illustrations)**.

Refitting

3 Refitting is a reversal of removal. Refit the centre air vents panel as described in Chapter 3, Section 9.

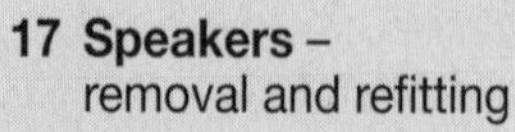

17 Speakers – removal and refitting

Removal

Front speakers

1 Remove the relevant door trim panel as described in Chapter 11, Section 13.

2 The speakers are clipped into the door. Insert a small screwdriver at the top to release the upper clip, then lift the speaker to unhook the two lower legs **(see illustration)**.

3 Withdraw the speaker from the door, and disconnect the wiring plug **(see illustration)**.

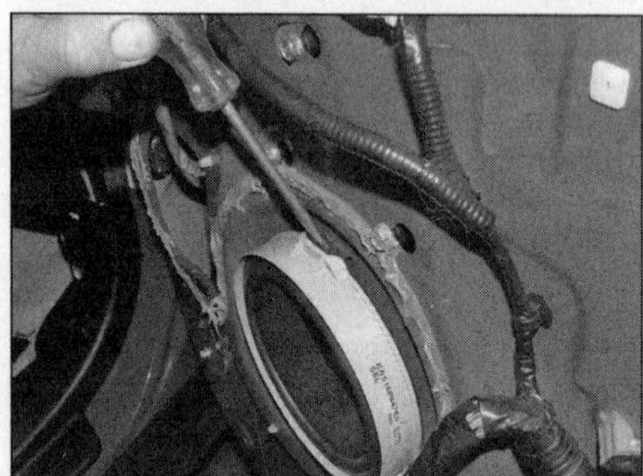

17.2 Use a small screwdriver to release upper clip . . .

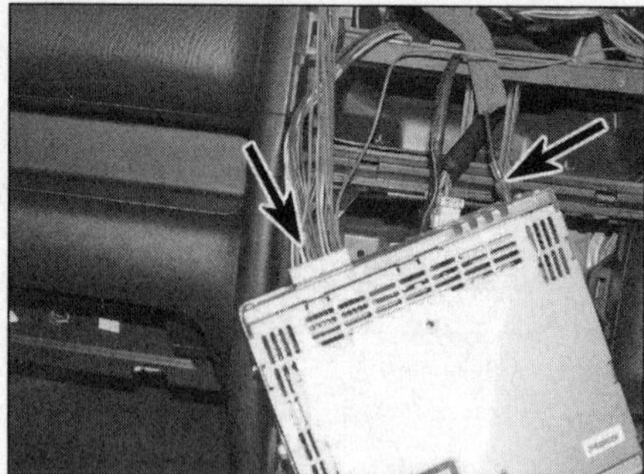

16.2b . . . then disconnect wiring plug and aerial lead to remove

Rear speakers

4 The rear speakers on 5-door models are removed in the same way as the front speakers.

Refitting

5 Refitting is a reversal of removal. Ensure that the speakers are securely clipped in place.

18 Radio aerial – removal and refitting

Removal

1 Access to the aerial is gained by removing the headlining, which requires the removal of all fittings such as the rear grab handles, B-, C- and D-pillar trim panels, and associated components as described in Chapter 11, Section 27. Release the headlining at the rear edge, and carefully pull it down for access to the aerial.

2 Disconnect the earth terminal spade connector, then pull the aerial lead from the base of the aerial.

3 Unscrew the mounting nut, and withdraw the aerial from the roof. Recover the rubber seal – if this has perished, use a new one when refitting.

Refitting

4 Refitting is a reversal of removal. Ensure that there is a good seal between the aerial and the roof, and good electrical connections on the base of the aerial, or reception will suffer.

17.3 . . . then lift speaker to unhook lower legs and disconnect wiring plug to remove speaker

19 Immobiliser system and alarm – general information

Immobiliser system

An engine immobiliser system is fitted as standard to all models, and the system is operated automatically every time the ignition key is inserted/removed.

The immobiliser system ensures that the vehicle can only be started using the original Honda ignition key. The key contains an electronic chip (transponder) which is programmed with a code. When the key is inserted into the ignition switch, it uses the current present in the reader coil (which is fitted around the switch) to send a signal to the immobiliser electronic control unit (ECU). The ECU checks this code every time the ignition is switched on. If the key code does not match the ECU code, the ECU will disable the fuel pump circuit (injection system on diesel models) to prevent the engine being started.

If the ignition key is lost, a new one can be obtained from a Honda dealer. They have access to the correct key code for the immobiliser system of your vehicle, and will be able to supply a new coded key.

If you have any spare keys cut, if they are not coded correctly, they will only open the doors, etc, and will not be capable of starting the engine. For this reason, it may be best to have any spare keys supplied by your Honda dealer, who will also be able to advise you on coding the keys.

Alarm system

Certain models are equipped with an anti-theft alarm system, in addition to the engine immobiliser. Various types of system may be fitted, depending on specification and market.

The anti-theft alarm system is automatically activated by the central locking system (manually, or via the remote control, where applicable). The alarm system uses the door lock cylinder/lock knob switches, and the tailgate and bonnet lock switches, to detect whether any of them is opened with the alarm set. A security control unit under the facia constantly monitors the switches – if any switch receives an earth signal, the alarm siren will be activated, and the indicators will flash.

This system (sometimes referred to as a 'perimetric' alarm, as it only protects the 'perimeter' of the vehicle) does not prevent a thief from gaining access to the inside of the vehicle by breaking a window – provided the doors, etc, are not opened, the alarm will not go off.

Later models may be fitted with an alarm featuring ultrasonic scanning of the whole inside of the vehicle – with this system, if the ultrasonic beam is broken by any movement inside the vehicle, the alarm will sound. Models with an ultrasonic alarm can be identified by the ultrasonic emitter and receiver grilles in the roof console.

Any faults with the system will most likely be related to the lock switches or associated wiring, which are covered in the relevant parts of Chapter 11. False alarms may also occur if the doors, bonnet or tailgate are not closing properly for any reason. On an ultrasonic alarm system, not closing a window or the sunroof properly may also set off the alarm, especially in windy conditions. Any persistent problems not explained by the above should be referred to a Honda dealer for diagnosis – for obvious security reasons, a more detailed description of the system is not included in this manual.

20 Airbag system – general information and precautions

General information

All models are fitted with a driver's airbag mounted in the steering wheel, and a similar airbag for the front seat passenger, mounted in the facia panel. These are designed to prevent serious chest and head injuries during a frontal accident (of sufficient force) within 30° from the left or right of the vehicle centre-line. Side airbags are also fitted into the front seat side cushions, to be triggered if there is an impact from the side of the vehicle. Some 2005-on models are also fitted with side curtain airbags. The control unit for the airbag system is located under the centre of the facia, and performs continual system diagnostics. Two crash sensors are located at the front of the vehicle, under each headlight, and a side impact sensor is located on the inside of the front door sill, in front of each B-pillar **(see illustrations)**.

The airbag system has an adaptive capability – it can adjust the level of protection according to circumstances, and to the number of passengers (or lack of them). If the system's crash sensors detect a less-severe impact, the front airbags may not fire at all. A seat occupancy sensor is fitted to the passenger seat, so the system knows when a front seat passenger is present – when the seat is empty, the passenger front and side airbags are disabled. The occupancy sensor forms part of the seat side cushion, and cannot be renewed separately.

The seat belt tensioners are also deployed in the event of an accident, and in fact can deploy independently at lower impact levels than the airbags.

The front seat side airbags offer greater passenger protection in a side impact. Although the side airbags are linked to the 'front' airbags, the side airbags will only deploy if the vehicle is struck from the side.

The airbags are inflated by a gas generator, which forces the bag out of the cover in the steering wheel, facia panel, or seat cushion.

20.1a Airbag crash sensor on the front inner wing

20.1b Side airbag crash sensor on the front sill

On the driver's airbag (which turns with the steering wheel) a 'clock spring' rotary connector ensures that a good electrical connection is maintained with the airbag at all times.

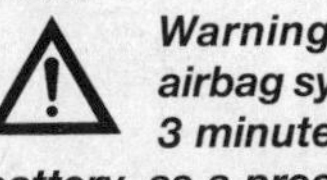

Warning: When working on the airbag system, always wait at least 3 minutes after disconnecting the battery, as a precaution against accidental deployment of the airbag unit. This period ensures that any stored energy in the back-up capacitor is dissipated. Do not use battery-operated radio key code savers, as this may cause the airbag to be deployed, with the possibility of personal injury.

Precautions

Warning: The following precautions must be observed when working on vehicles equipped with an airbag system, to prevent the possibility of personal injury.

General precautions

The following precautions must be observed when carrying out work on a vehicle equipped with an airbag:

a) Do not disconnect the battery with the engine running.

b) Before carrying out any work in the vicinity of the airbag, removal of any of the airbag components, or any welding work on the vehicle, de-activate the system as described in the following sub-section.

c) Do not attempt to test any of the airbag system circuits using test meters or any other test equipment.

d) If the airbag warning light comes on, or any fault in the system is suspected, consult a Honda dealer without delay. Do not attempt to carry out fault diagnosis, or any dismantling of the components.

Precautions when handling an airbag

a) Transport the airbag by itself, bag upward.

b) Do not put your arms around the airbag.

c) Carry the airbag close to the body, bag outward.

d) Do not drop the airbag or expose it to impacts.

e) Do not attempt to dismantle the airbag unit.

f) Do not connect any form of electrical equipment to any part of the airbag circuit.

Precautions when storing an airbag

a) Store the unit in a cupboard with the airbag upward.

b) Do not expose the airbag to temperatures above 80°C.

c) Do not expose the airbag to flames.

d) Do not attempt to dispose of the airbag – consult a Honda dealer.

e) Never refit an airbag which is known to be faulty or damaged.

De-activation of airbag system

The system must be de-activated as follows, before carrying out any work on the airbag components or surrounding area.

a) Remove the ignition key.

b) Switch off all electrical equipment.

c) Disconnect the battery negative lead (see Disconnecting the battery).

d) Insulate the battery negative terminal and the end of the battery negative lead to prevent any possibility of contact.

e) Wait for at least 3 minutes before carrying out any further work.

f) Ensure that the battery is still disconnected, before reconnecting any airbag wiring.

21 Airbag system components – removal and refitting

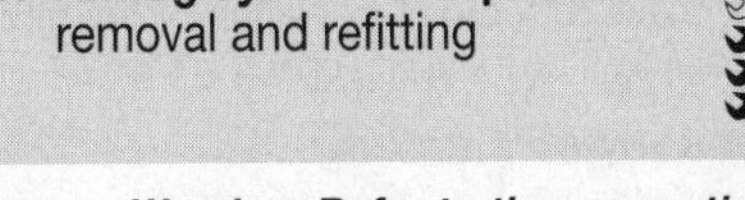

Warning: Refer to the precautions given in Section 20 before attempting to carry out work on the airbag components.

Driver's airbag

Removal

1 De-activate the airbag system as described in Section 20. The airbag unit is an integral part of the steering wheel centre pad.

2 Prise off the rectangular cover from the base of the steering wheel **(see illustration)**.

3 Disconnect the (yellow) airbag wiring plug by sliding back the spring-loaded locking sleeve **(see illustration)**.

4 Unscrew the two airbag mounting Torx bolts, using a T30 Torx bit. The bolts are located either side of the wheel, and are deeply recessed – look around the wheel rim to see them **(see**

21.2 Prise off the rectangular cover to disconnect the airbag plug

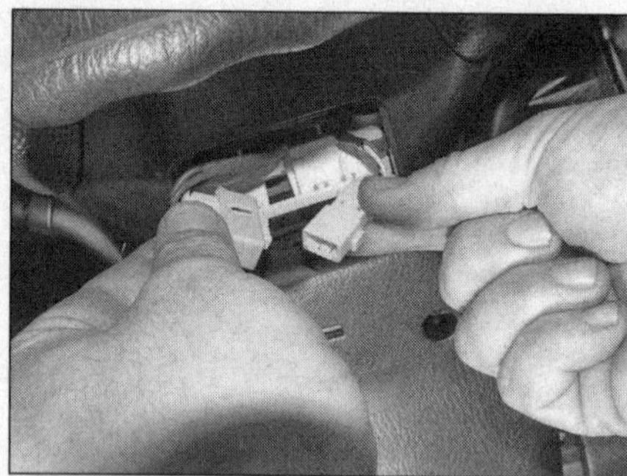
21.3 Slide back the locking sleeve, and disconnect the plug

21.4 Unscrew the airbag bolt on either side of the wheel

21.5 Removing the driver's airbag

illustration). The bolts may be quite tight – ensure that the right size of Torx bit is used.

5 When the bolts are loose, lift the airbag unit out of the steering wheel, feeding the wiring plug through as it is removed **(see illustration)**. Move the airbag to a safe place, and always keep the front facing upwards.

Refitting

6 Refitting is a reversal of removal. Feed the wiring back through the wheel, and (with the battery still off) connect the plug securely. Tighten the airbag mounting bolts, and clip on the wheel's lower cover to complete. Reconnect the battery and check for correct operation of the airbag warning light by switching on the ignition.

Passenger's airbag

Removal

7 De-activate the airbag system as described in Section 20.

8 Taking care not to mark the facia, prise out the access panel from the roof of the stowage tray above the glovebox.

9 Disconnect the (yellow) airbag wiring plug by sliding back the spring-loaded locking sleeve.

10 Remove the three mounting nuts securing the airbag unit to its mounting bracket.

11 Protect the top of the facia with strips of masking tape or some cloth. Using a wide-bladed tool, carefully prise the airbag at the sides to release the retaining tabs, and lift the unit out of the facia.

12 Move the airbag to a safe place, and always keep the front facing upwards.

Refitting

13 Refitting is a reversal of removal. Tighten the mounting nuts securely, and (with the battery still off), reconnect the airbag wiring plug. On completion, reconnect the battery and check for correct operation of the airbag warning light by switching on the ignition.

Airbag control unit

Removal

14 When a vehicle is involved in a heavy enough impact to set off the airbags, the event is logged in the airbag control unit. On some vehicles, even after new airbags are fitted, the 'event code' cannot be cleared from the airbag control unit (so the airbag warning light stays on), and a new control unit has to be fitted. Consult a Honda dealer for advice on this point.

15 Honda state that, before the control unit is removed, as well as disconnecting the battery and waiting three minutes, all the airbag and seat belt tensioner wiring plugs must be disconnected. This means disconnecting the driver's and passenger's airbags, the front seat wiring (models with side airbags), and the wiring plugs to the front seat belt inertia reels (refer to Chapter 11 for the last two).

16 Remove the centre console (vehicles with a manual gearbox) or the facia lower centre section (vehicles with automatic transmission), as described in Chapter 11, Section 27.

17 Fold down the carpet for access to the unit and disconnect the ventilation system floor vent ducts. Disconnect the three wiring plugs, noting their fitted locations, then remove the three Torx screws and withdraw the unit from the floor location **(see illustration)**.

Refitting

18 Refitting is a reversal of removal, bearing in mind the following points:

a) The battery must still be disconnected when reconnecting the airbag and seat belt tensioner wiring.
b) Make sure that the wiring connectors are securely reconnected.
c) Tighten the mounting screws securely.
d) On completion, reconnect the battery and check for correct operation of the airbag warning light by switching on the ignition.

Airbag clock spring (rotary connector)

19 Remove the driver's airbag as described previously in this Section.

20 Remove the steering wheel as described in Chapter 10.

21 Remove the steering column shrouds as described in Chapter 11, Section 27.

22 Trace the wiring harness from the front of the clock spring to the wiring plugs below at the top and bottom of the steering wheel – on most models, there will be two plugs to disconnect. The yellow plug underneath has a spring-loaded locking sleeve **(see illustrations)**.

23 Before removing the clock spring, note that it has an arrow marking on its front face – this should face upwards **(see illustration)**. If the same clock spring will be refitted, tape the unit so that it cannot turn once removed.

21.17 Airbag control unit is mounted on the floor under the facia

21.22a Disconnect the clock spring wiring plug on top . . .

21.22b . . . and the yellow plug underneath

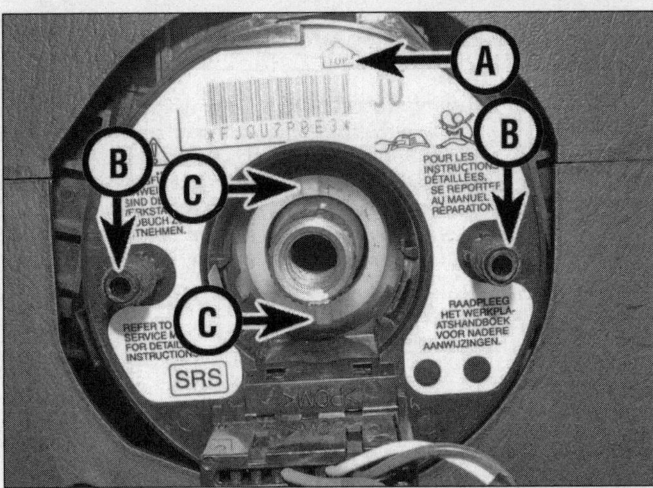

21.23 Airbag clock spring must be in central position, with arrow mark (A) pointing straight up and two locating pins (B) horizontal, and direction indicator self-cancelling tabs (C) should be vertical

24 When the wiring has been disconnected, carefully release the upper and lower tabs, and slide the clock spring off the steering column – feed its wiring through as it is removed, noting how it is routed.

25 Before fitting the clock spring, it must first be centred. If a new unit is being fitted, note that they are supplied set in the centre position. Similarly, if the old clock spring has not been turned while it was removed, this procedure can be omitted.

26 To centre the unit, gently turn the front face clockwise until it stops. Now turn the front face anti-clockwise by about 3 turns, and the arrow mark on its face should point straight up – this is the centre position. As a further reference, the two steering wheel locating pins on the front face should be horizontal.

27 With the front wheels still pointing straight ahead, offer the clock spring onto the steering column. Note that the direction indicator self-cancelling sleeve's two tabs should be aligned vertically.

28 Feed the clock spring wiring into position, making sure it is routed as before, and connect the wiring plugs. Secure the unit in place by pressing it home so that its upper and lower tabs locate properly.

29 Further refitting is a reversal of removal. On completion, reconnect the battery and check for correct operation of the airbag warning light by switching on the ignition.

Side airbags

30 The side airbags are located internally within the front seat backrests, and no attempt should be made to remove them. Any suspected problems with the side airbag system should be referred to a Honda dealer.

Side curtain airbags

31 The side curtain airbags are located internally behind the headlining in the centre and rear sides of the roof. The trim panels of vehicles with such equipment will be marked Side Curtain Airbag. No attempt should be made to remove them; any suspected problems with the side curtain airbag system should be referred to a Honda dealer.

Honda CR-V wiring diagrams

Diagram 1

Warning: This vehicle is fitted with a supplemental restraint system (SRS) consisting of a combination of driver (and passenger) airbag(s), side impact protection airbags and seatbelt pre-tensioners. The use of electrical test equipment on any SRS wiring systems may cause the seatbelt pre-tensioners to abruptly retract and the airbags to explosively deploy, resulting in potentially severe personal injury. Extreme care should be taken to correctly identify any circuits to be tested to avoid choosing any of the SRS wiring in error.
For further information see airbag system precautions in body electrical systems chapter.
Note: The SRS wiring harness can normally be identified by yellow and/or orange harness or harness connectors.

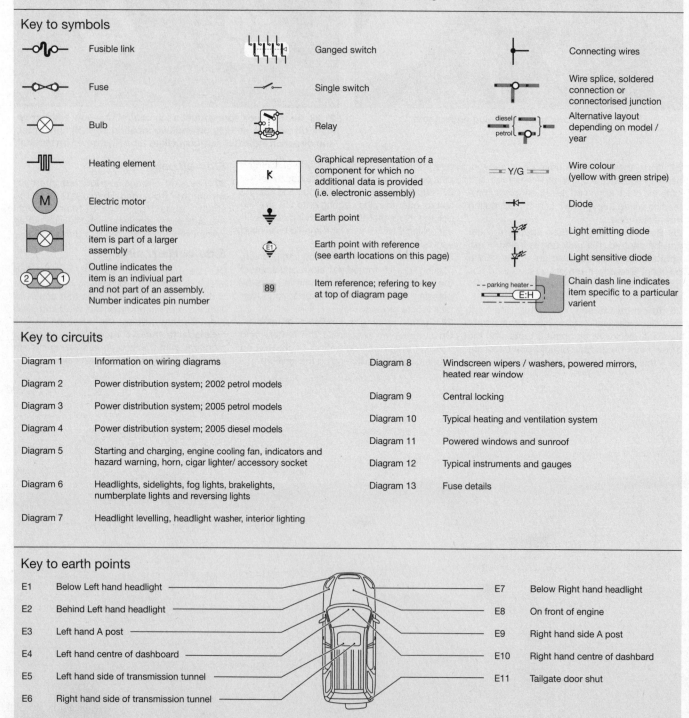

Key to symbols

- Fusible link
- Fuse
- Bulb
- Heating element
- M Electric motor
- Outline indicates the item is part of a larger assembly
- 2 1 Outline indicates the item is an indiviual part and not part of an assembly. Number indicates pin number
- Ganged switch
- Single switch
- Relay
- K Graphical representation of a component for which no additional data is provided (i.e. electronic assembly)
- Earth point
- E1 Earth point with reference (see earth locations on this page)
- 89 Item reference; refering to key at top of diagram page
- Connecting wires
- Wire splice, soldered connection or connectorised junction
- diesel / petrol Alternative layout depending on model / year
- Y/G Wire colour (yellow with green stripe)
- Diode
- Light emitting diode
- Light sensitive diode
- parking heater – E:H Chain dash line indicates item specific to a particular varient

Key to circuits

Diagram 1	Information on wiring diagrams
Diagram 2	Power distribution system; 2002 petrol models
Diagram 3	Power distribution system; 2005 petrol models
Diagram 4	Power distribution system; 2005 diesel models
Diagram 5	Starting and charging, engine cooling fan, indicators and hazard warning, horn, cigar lighter/ accessory socket
Diagram 6	Headlights, sidelights, fog lights, brakelights, numberplate lights and reversing lights
Diagram 7	Headlight levelling, headlight washer, interior lighting
Diagram 8	Windscreen wipers / washers, powered mirrors, heated rear window
Diagram 9	Central locking
Diagram 10	Typical heating and ventilation system
Diagram 11	Powered windows and sunroof
Diagram 12	Typical instruments and gauges
Diagram 13	Fuse details

Key to earth points

E1	Below Left hand headlight
E2	Behind Left hand headlight
E3	Left hand A post
E4	Left hand centre of dashboard
E5	Left hand side of transmission tunnel
E6	Right hand side of transmission tunnel
E7	Below Right hand headlight
E8	On front of engine
E9	Right hand side A post
E10	Right hand centre of dashboard
E11	Tailgate door shut

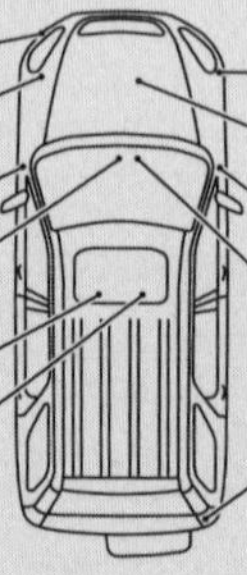

Diagram 2

Wire colours

B	Black	P	Purple
G	Green	R	Red
K	Pink	S	Grey
Lg	Light green	L	Blue
N	Brown	W	White
O	Orange	Y	Yellow
Lu	Light blue		

Key to items

1 Battery
2 Engine compartment fuse box
  a) radiator fan relay
  b) horn relay
  c) rear window heater window
  d) blower motor relay
  e) right headlight relay
  f) left headlight relay
  g) A/C compressor clutch relay
  h) A/C condenser fan relay
  m) ELD (electrical load device)
3 Passenger compartment fuse box
  a) taillight relay
  b) powered window relay
  c) starter 'enabled' relay
  d) multifunction control unit (MCU)
4 Engine compartment sub-fusebox A
5 Engine compartment sub-fusebox B
6 Ignition switch
7 Fuel injection system main relay No.1

H33856

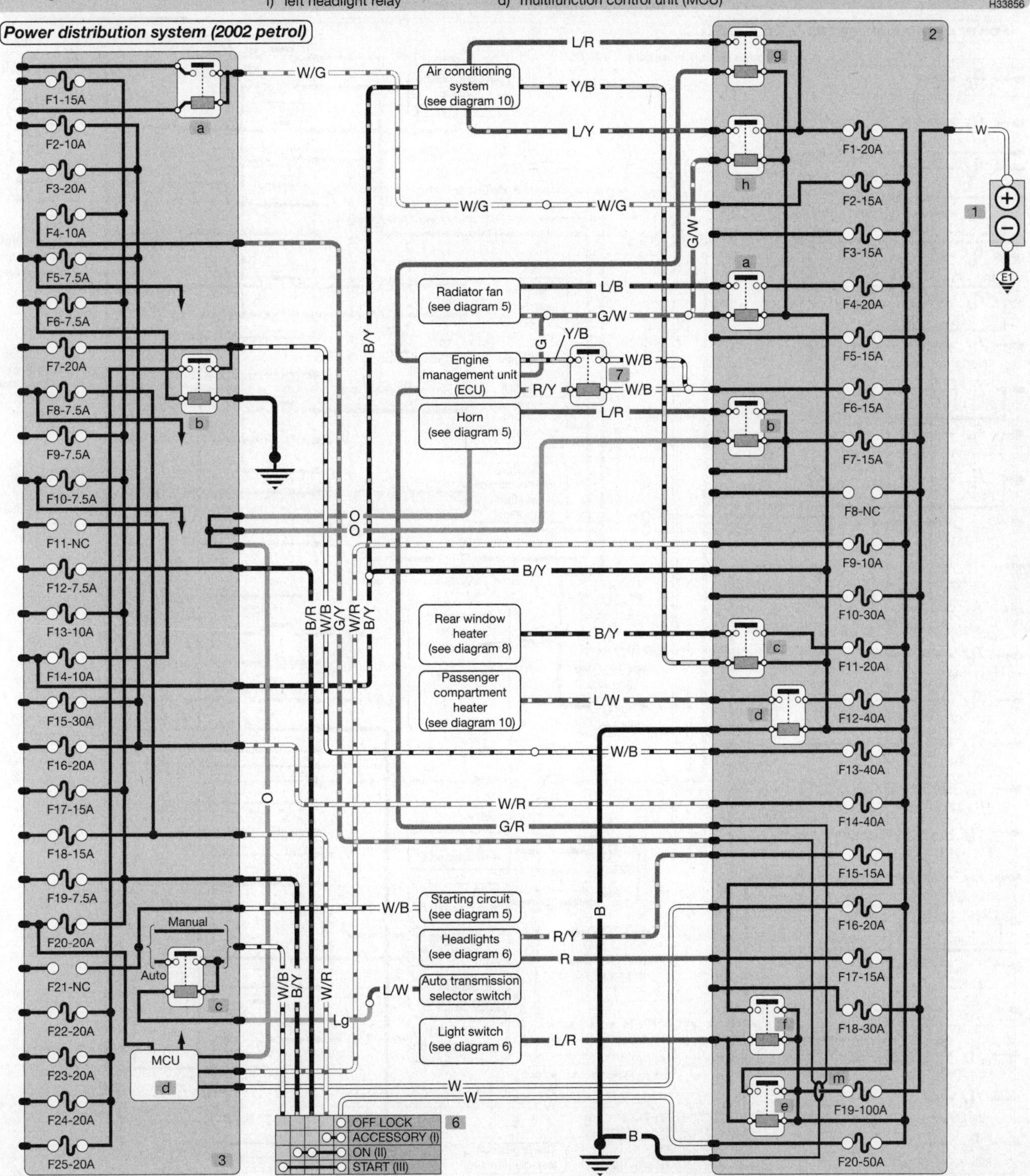

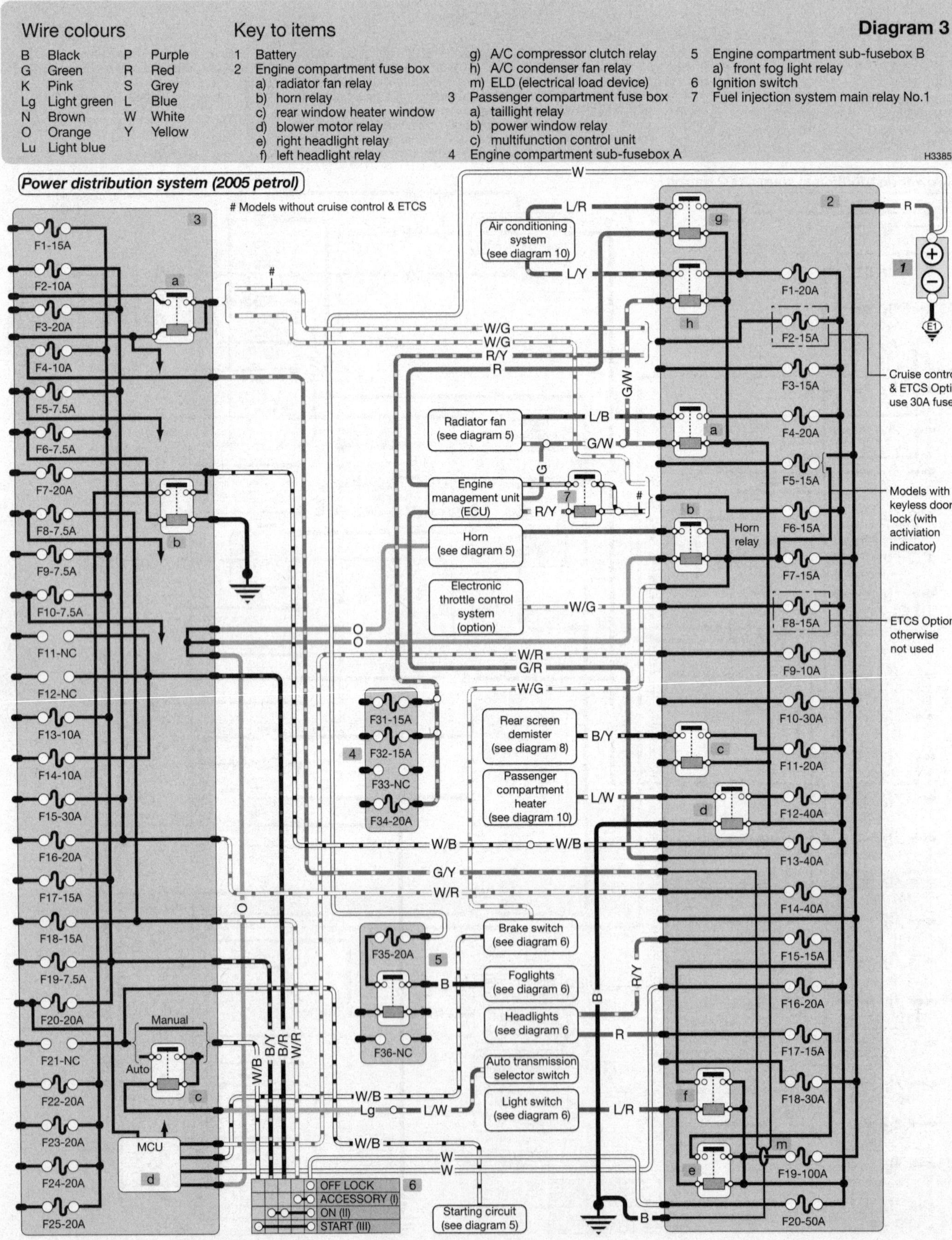

Wire colours
B Black
G Green
K Pink
Lg Light green
N Brown
O Orange
Lu Light blue
P Purple
R Red
S Grey
L Blue
W White
Y Yellow
Key to items
1 Battery
2 Engine compartment fuse box
a) radiator fan relay
b) horn relay
c) rear window heater window
d) blower motor relay
e) right headlight relay
f) left headlight relay
g) A/C compressor clutch relay
h) A/C condenser fan relay
m) ELD (electrical load device)
3 Passenger compartment fuse box
a) taillight relay
b) power window relay
c) multifunction control unit
4 Engine compartment sub-fusebox A
5 Engine compartment sub-fusebox B
a) front fog light relay
6 Ignition switch
7 Fuel injection system main relay No.1
Diagram 3
H33857
Power distribution system (2005 petrol)
Models without cruise control & ETCS
Air conditioning system (see diagram 10)
Radiator fan (see diagram 5)
Engine management unit (ECU)
Horn (see diagram 5)
Electronic throttle control system (option)
Rear screen demister (see diagram 8)
Passenger compartment heater (see diagram 10)
Brake switch (see diagram 6)
Foglights (see diagram 6)
Headlights (see diagram 6
Auto transmission selector switch
Light switch (see diagram 6)
Starting circuit (see diagram 5)
Horn relay
Cruise control & ETCS Option use 30A fuse
Models with keyless door lock (with activiation indicator)
ETCS Option otherwise not used
Manual
Auto
MCU
OFF LOCK
ACCESSORY (I)
ON (II)
START (III)
F1-15A
F2-10A
F3-20A
F4-10A
F5-7.5A
F6-7.5A
F7-20A
F8-7.5A
F9-7.5A
F10-7.5A
F11-NC
F12-NC
F13-10A
F14-10A
F15-30A
F16-20A
F17-15A
F18-15A
F19-7.5A
F20-20A
F21-NC
F22-20A
F23-20A
F24-20A
F25-20A
F31-15A
F32-15A
F33-NC
F34-20A
F35-20A
F36-NC
F1-20A
F2-15A
F3-15A
F4-20A
F5-15A
F6-15A
F7-15A
F8-15A
F9-10A
F10-30A
F11-20A
F12-40A
F13-40A
F14-40A
F15-15A
F16-20A
F17-15A
F18-30A
F19-100A
F20-50A
E1

Diagram 4

Wire colours

B	Black	P	Purple
G	Green	R	Red
K	Pink	S	Grey
Lg	Light green	L	Blue
N	Brown	W	White
O	Orange	Y	Yellow
Lu	Light blue		

Key to items

1 Battery
2 Engine compartment fuse box
- a) radiator fan relay
- b) horn relay
- c) rear window heater window
- d) blower motor relay
- e) right headlight relay
- f) left headlight relay
- g) A/C compressor clutch relay
- h) A/C condenser fan relay
- j) fuel heater relay
- k) front fog light relay
- l) fan control relay
- m) ELD (electrical load device)

3 Passenger compartment fuse box
- a) taillight relay
- b) powered window relay
- d) MCU (multifunction control unit)

6 Ignition switch

H33858

Power distribution system (2005 diesel)

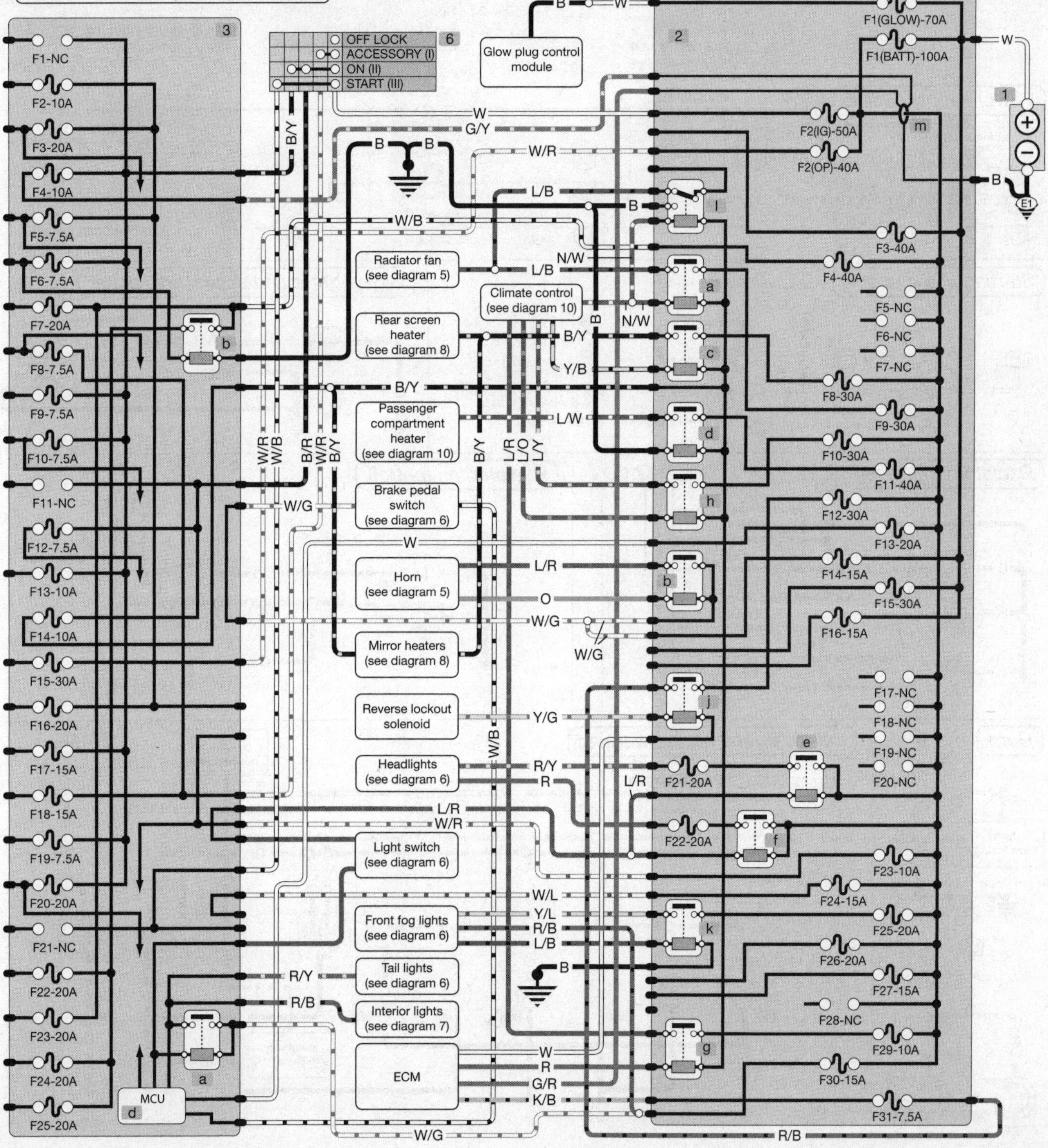

Diagram 5

Wire colours

B	Black	P	Purple
G	Green	R	Red
K	Pink	S	Grey
Lg	Light green	U	Blue
N	Brown	W	White
O	Orange	Y	Yellow
Lu	Light blue		

Key to items

2 Engine compartment fuse box
a) radiator fan relay
b) horn relay
h) A/C condenser fan relay
l) fan control relay
3 Passenger compartment fuse box
c) starter 'enabled' relay
10 Starter motor
11 Alternator
12 Audio unit
13 Instrument unit
14 Engine control unit
15 Radiator fan motor
16 A/C condenser fan motor
§17 Radiator fan switch (high)
18 Radiator fan switch (low)
19 Accessory socket
20 Cigar lighter
21 Rear accessory power socket relay
22 Horn switch
23 Steering column rotary joint
24 Horn
25 Rear LH light cluster
a) indicator
26 Rear RH light cluster
a) indicator
27 LH indicator repeater
28 RH indicator repeater
29 LH front light cluster
a) indicator
30 RH front light cluster
a) indicator
31 Indicator switch
32 Hazard warning switch
a) switch illumination
33 indicator relay

H33859

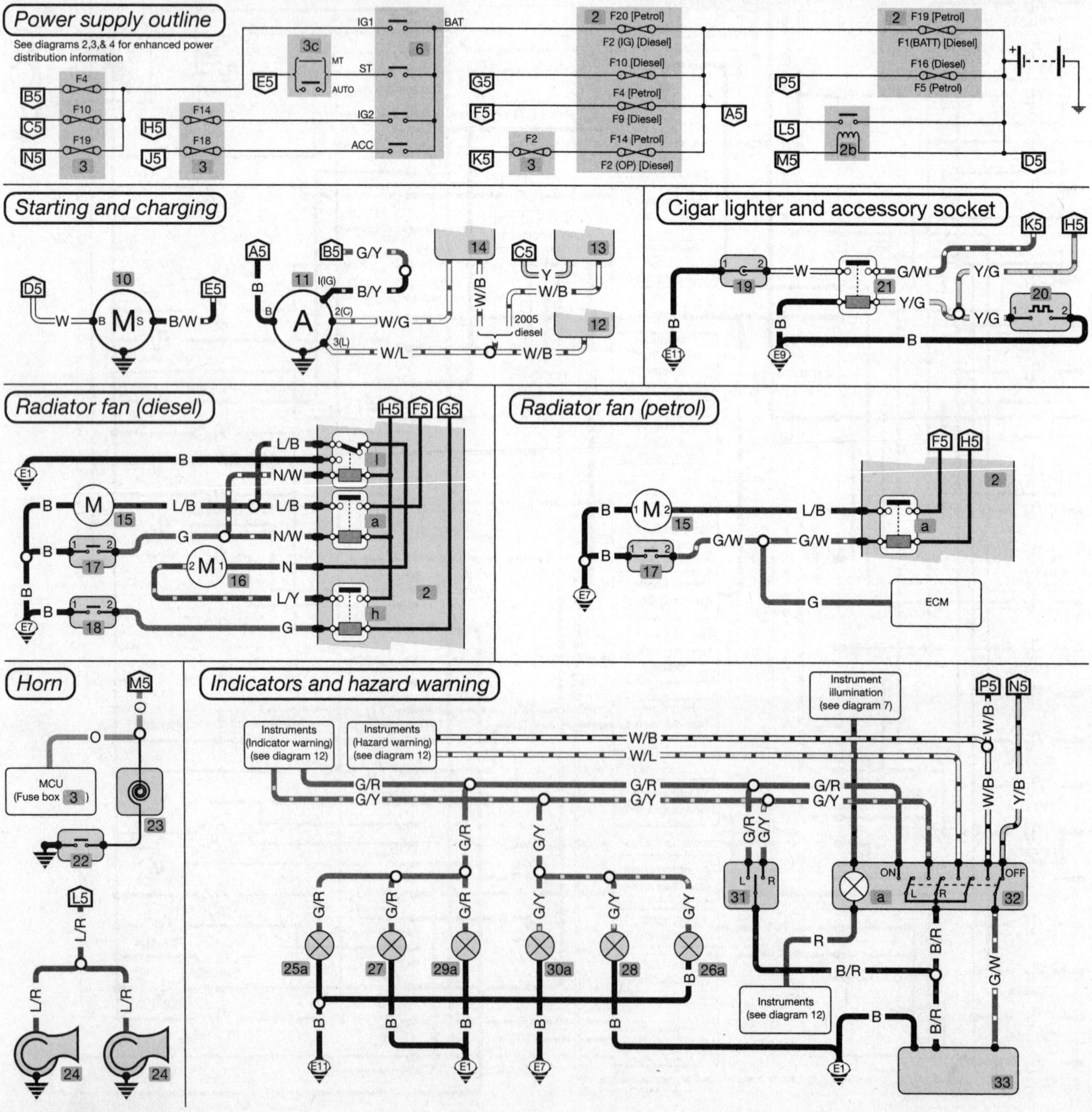

Power supply outline

See diagrams 2,3,& 4 for enhanced power distribution information

Starting and charging

Cigar lighter and accessory socket

Radiator fan (diesel)

Radiator fan (petrol)

Horn

Indicators and hazard warning

Diagram 6

Wire colours

B	Black	P	Purple
G	Green	R	Red
K	Pink	S	Grey
Lg	Light green	U	Blue
N	Brown	W	White
O	Orange	Y	Yellow
Lu	Light blue		

Key to items

2 Engine compartment fuse box
- e) RH headlight relay
- f) LH headlight relay
- k) front foglight relay

3 Passenger compartment fuse box
- a) tail light relay
- d) MCU (multifunction control unit)

6 Ignition switch

25 Rear LH light cluster
- b) tail light
- c) brake light
- d) reversing light

26 Rear RH light cluster
- b) tail light
- c) brake light
- d) reversing light
- e) fog light

29 LH front light cluster
- b) high beam headlight
- c) low beam headlight
- d) side light

30 RH front light cluster (as 29 above)

36 LH front fog light

37 RH front fog light

38 Number plate lights

39 High level brake light

40 Lighting combination switch
- a) headlight switch
- b) tail light switch
- c) passing switch
- d) rear fog light switch
- e) front fog light switch

41 Footbrake switch

42 Reversing switch (M/T)

43 Reversing relay (A/T)

44 Front fog light relay

H33860

Power supply outline

See diagrams 2,3,& 4 for enhanced power distribution information

IG1 6 BAT; F10 3; 3a; 2k; F20 [Petrol] F2 (IG) [Diesel]; F25 [Diesel]; 2 F2; F14 [Petrol] F2 (OP) [Diesel]; F3; F5 3; F17 [Petrol] F22 [Diesel]; 2e; F15 [Petrol] F21 [Diesel]; 2f; F19 [Petrol] F1(BATT) [Diesel]; F7 [Petrol] F14 [Diesel]; J6 K6 D6 E6 F6 G6 L6 B6 A6 C6 H6

Headlights, sidelights, front / rear foglights, brake lights, reversing lights & number plate lights

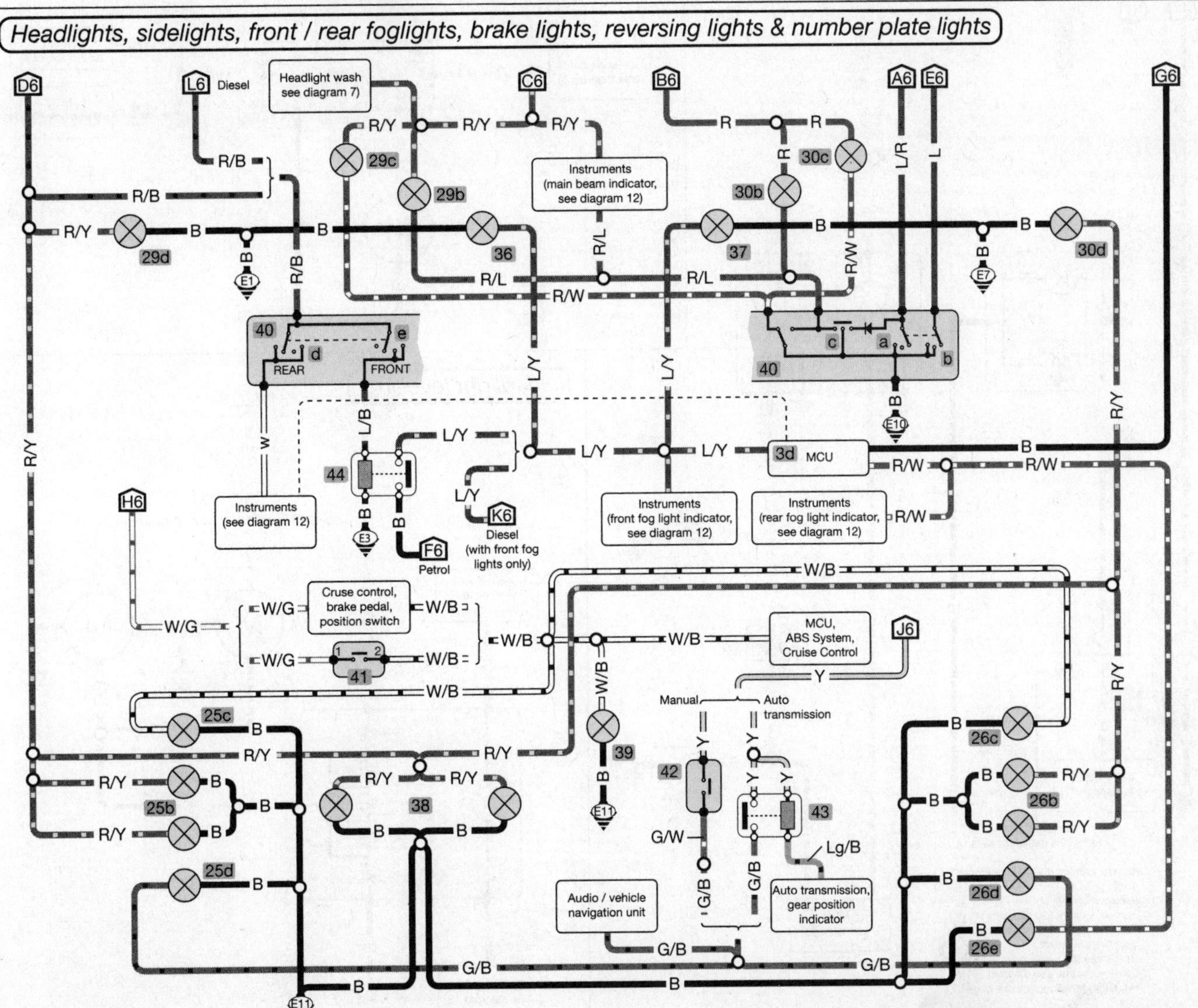

Diagram 7

Wire colours

B	Black	P	Purple
G	Green	R	Red
K	Pink	S	Grey
Lg	Light green	U	Blue
N	Brown	W	White
O	Orange	Y	Yellow
Lu	Light blue		

Key to items

2 Engine compartment fuse box
3 Passenger compartment fuse box
a) tail light relay
d) MCU (multifunction control unit)
6 Ignition switch
46 Glove box switch / lamp
47 Map lights / switches
48 Rear ceiling light / switch
49 Front ceiling light / switch
50 Sunroof open microswitch
51 Tailgate open microswitch
52 Diode
53 Headlight levelling switch
54 LH headlight adjuster motor
55 RH headlight adjuster motor
56 Headlight washer motor
57 Headlight washer control unit

H33861

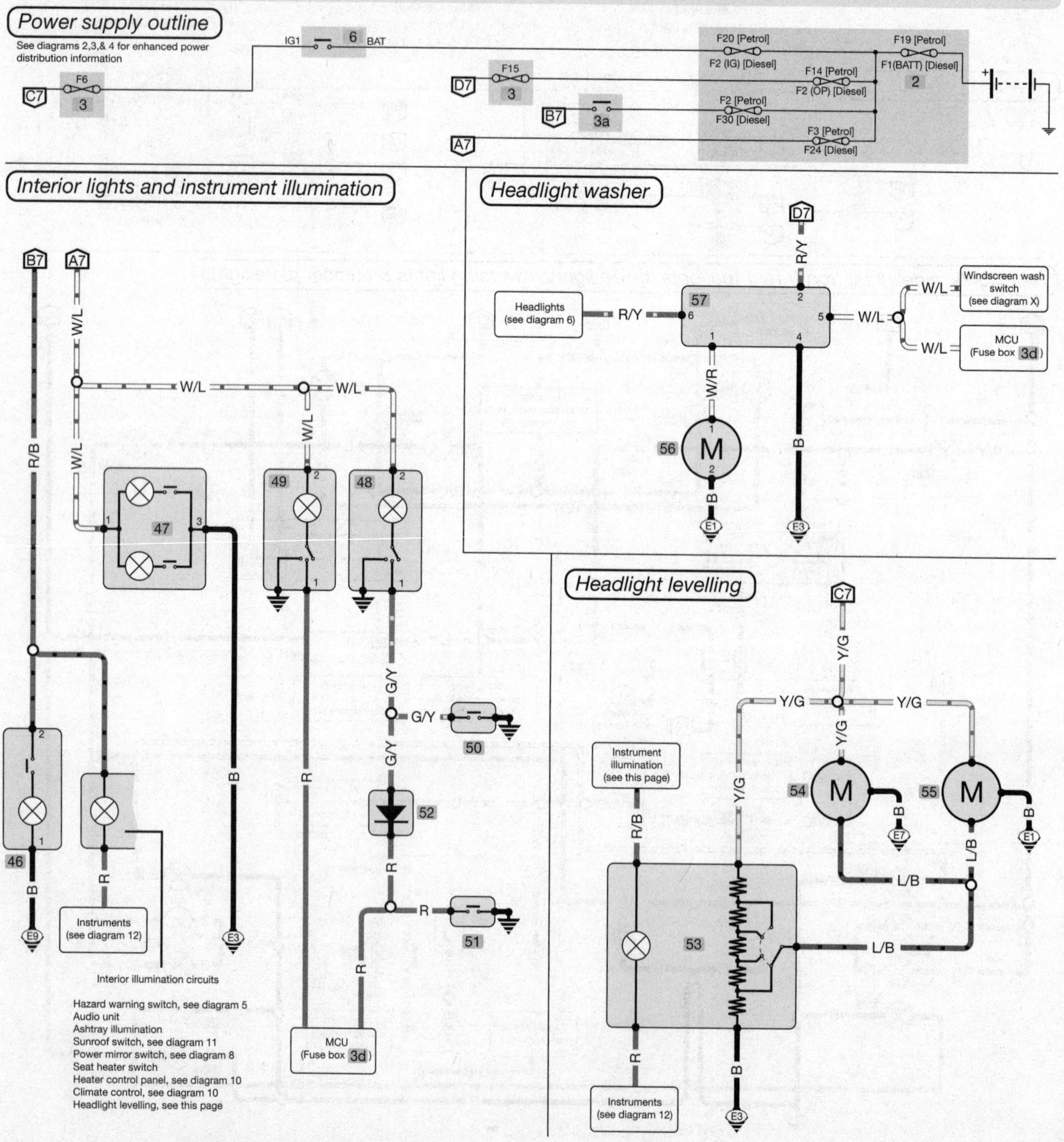

Diagram 8

Wire colours

B	Black	P	Purple
G	Green	R	Red
K	Pink	S	Grey
Lg	Light green	U	Blue
N	Brown	W	White
O	Orange	Y	Yellow
Lu	Light blue		

Key to items

2 Engine compartment fuse box
   c) rear screen heater relay
3 Passenger compartment fuse box
   d) MCU (multifunction control unit)
6 Ignition switch
60 Windscreen wiper/washer switch
   a) wash contact
   b) intermittent wipe contact
   c) lo speed contact
   d) hi speed contact
   e) mist contact
61 Windscreen wiper motor
62 Windscreen wash motor
63 Rear screen wiper/wash switch
64 Rear screen wiper motor
65 Rear screen wash motor
66 Rear wiper control unit
67 Rear window heating element
68 Noise condenser
69 Mirror control switch
   a) up/left contact
   b) left/down contact
   c) down/right contact
   d) mirror select contacts
   e) mirror heater switch
   f) indicator
   g) instrument illumination
70 RH mirror
   a) heating element
   b) up/down axis motor
   c) left/right axis motor
71 LH mirror
   (as 70 above)
72 Powered mirror heater relay
   (2005 models + diesel)

H33862

Power supply outline

See diagrams 2,3,& 4 for enhanced power distribution information

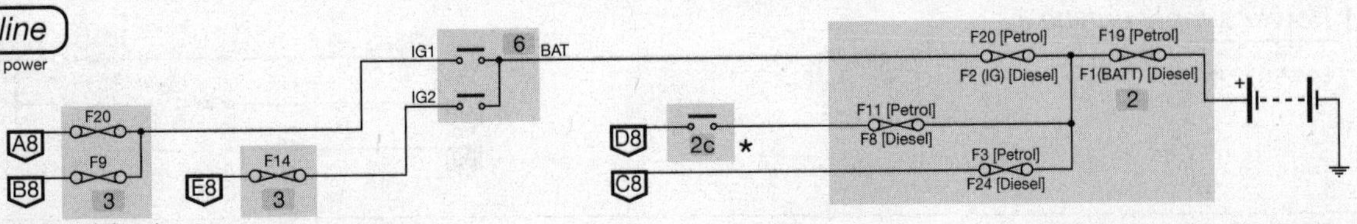

* Relay controlled by climate control / heater control panel

Front and rear windscreen wipers and washers

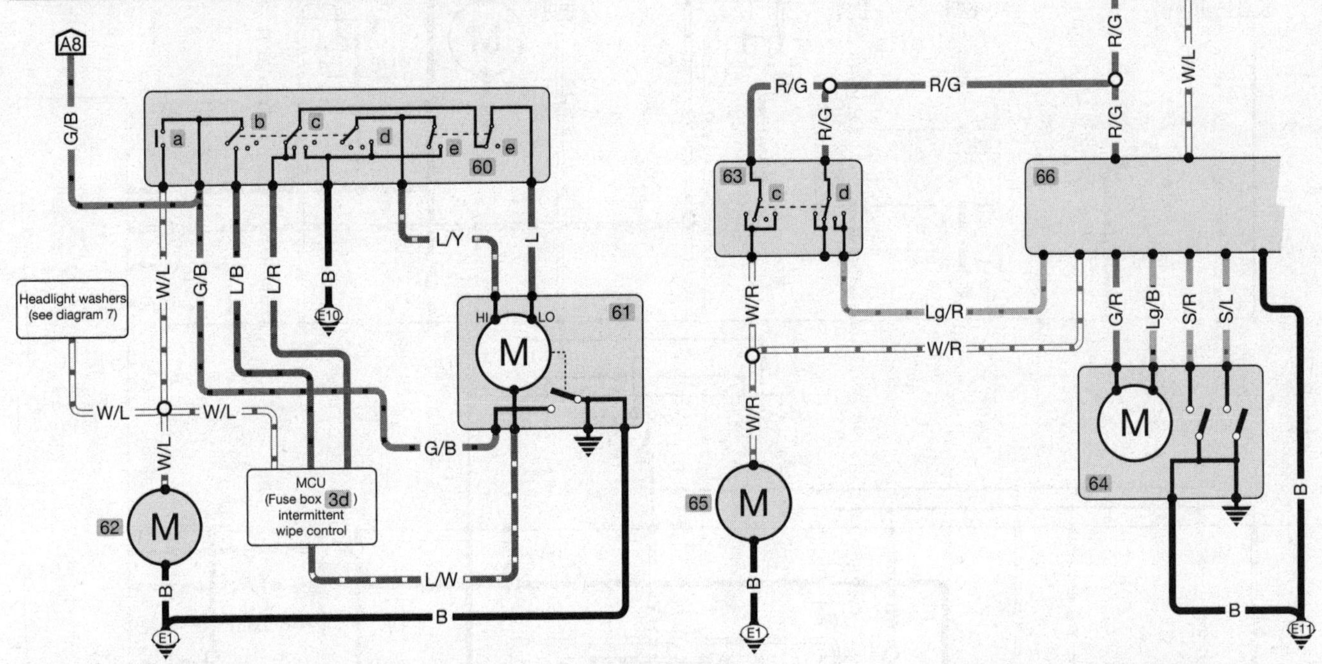

Headlight washers (see diagram 7)

MCU (Fuse box 3d) intermittent wipe control

Rear screen demister

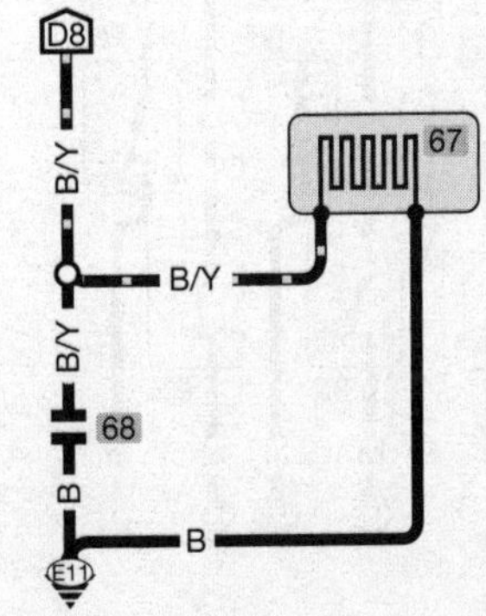

Powered mirrors

Petrol

Diesel + later models

	up	down	left	right
a	1	2	1	2
b	1	2	2	1
c	1	1	2	1

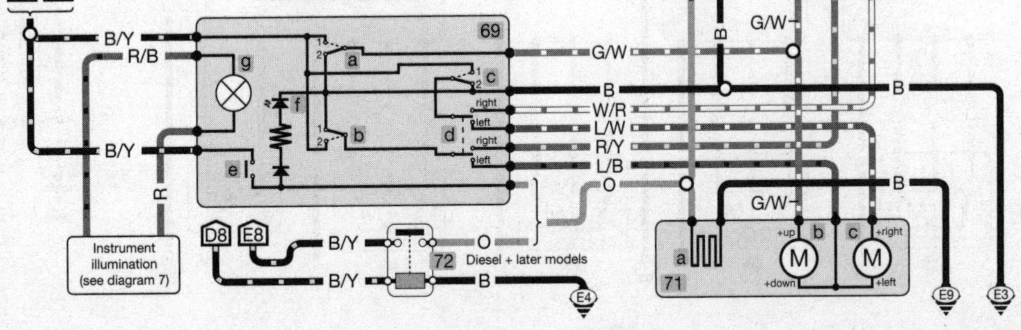

Instrument illumination (see diagram 7)

72 Diesel + later models

Diagram 9

Wire colours

B	Black	P	Purple
G	Green	R	Red
K	Pink	S	Grey
Lg	Light green	U	Blue
N	Brown	W	White
O	Orange	Y	Yellow
Lu	Light blue		

Key to items

2 Engine compartment fuse box
3 Passenger compartment fuse box
  d) MCU (multifunction control unit)
6 Ignition switch
76 Keyless receiver unit
77 Remote keyfob transmitter
78 Tailgate contact
79 Drivers door lock plunger switch
80 Hatch glass opener actuator
81 Drivers door key cylinder switch
82 Ignition 'key inserted' switch
83 Drivers door switch
84 Front passengers door switch
85 LH rear door switch
86 RH rear door switch
87 Front passenger door lock plunger switch
88 LH rear door lock plunger switch
89 RH rear door lock plunger switch
90 Tailgate lock knob switch
91 Drivers super locking control unit
92 Front passenger door super locking control unit
93 LH rear door super locking control unit
94 RH rear door super locking control unit
95 Drivers door super lock actuator
96 Front passenger door super lock actuator
97 LH rear super lock actuator
98 RH rear super lock actuator
99 Tailgate lock actuator

H33863

Power supply outline

See diagrams 2,3,& 4 for enhanced power distribution information

Typical central locking system

with super locking system

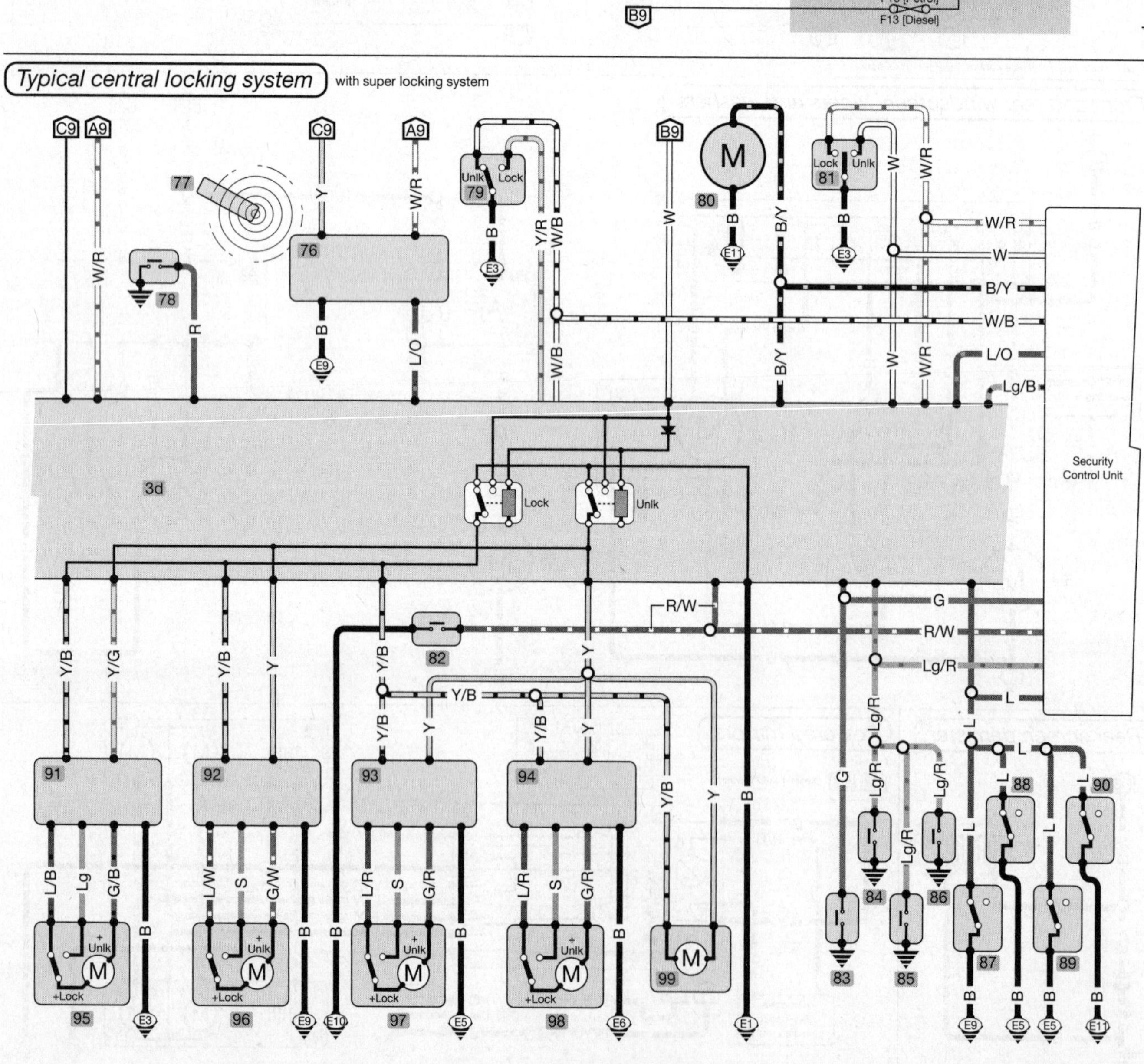

Diagram 10

Wire colours

B	Black	P	Purple
G	Green	R	Red
K	Pink	S	Grey
Lg	Light green	U	Blue
N	Brown	W	White
O	Orange	Y	Yellow
Lu	Light blue		

Key to items

2 Engine compartment fuse box
  d) blower relay
  g) A/C compressor clutch relay
  h) condenser fan relay
3 Passenger compartment fuse box
  d) MCU (multifunction control unit)
6 Ignition switch
103 Climate control or heating control panel
  a) instrument illumination
104 Recirculation control motor
105 Air mix control motor
106 Mode control motor
107 Blower speed control and switch
108 Sunlight sensor
109 Interior temperature sensor
110 Outside temperature sensor
111 Evaporator temperature sensor
112 Condenser fan motor
113 Thermal protector
114 Compressor clutch
115 A/C pressure switch
116 Blower motor

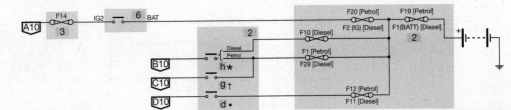

H33864

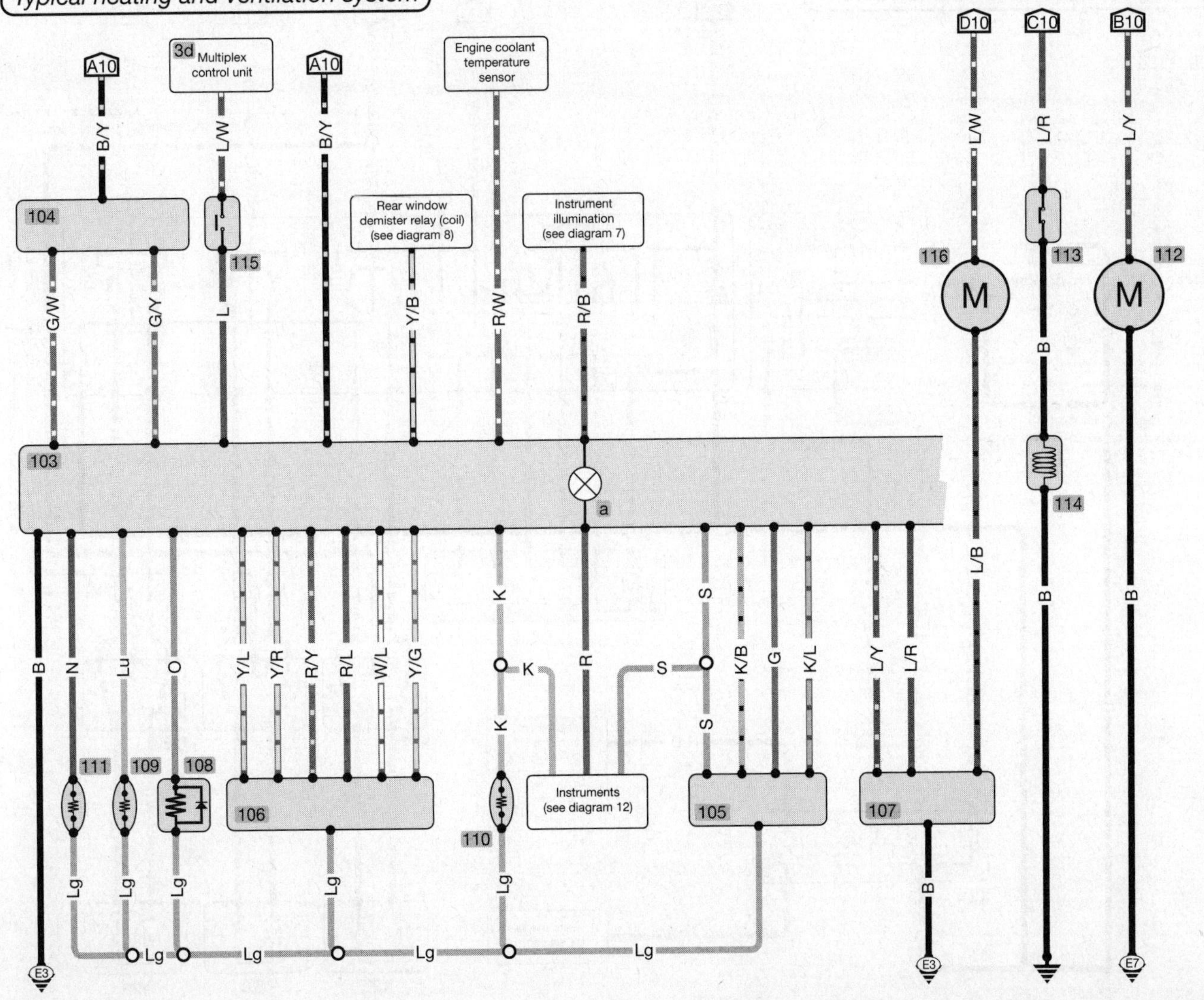

Diagram 11

Wire colours

B	Black	P	Purple
G	Green	R	Red
K	Pink	S	Grey
Lg	Light green	U	Blue
N	Brown	W	White
O	Orange	Y	Yellow
Lu	Light blue		

Key to items

2 Engine compartment fuse box
3 Passenger compartment fuse box
  b) powered window relay
6 Ignition switch
118 Sunroof open relay
119 Sunroof closed relay
120 Sunroof motor
  a) open/close limit switch
  b) open/tilt limit switch
  c) motor
121 Sunroof switch
  a) switch illumination
  b) open switch
  c) close switch
  d) tilt switch
122 Power window master switch
  a) drivers door window switch
  b) front passenger door window switch
  c) LH rear door window switch
  d) RH rear door window switch
  e) main switch
  f) power window control unit
  g) LED
123 Drivers window motor
  a) motor and protection
  b) detector circuit
124 Front passenger window switch
125 LH Rear window switch
126 RH Rear window switch
127 Front passenger window motor
128 LH Rear window motor
129 RH Rear window motor

H33865

Power supply outline

See diagrams 2,3,& 4 for enhanced power distribution information

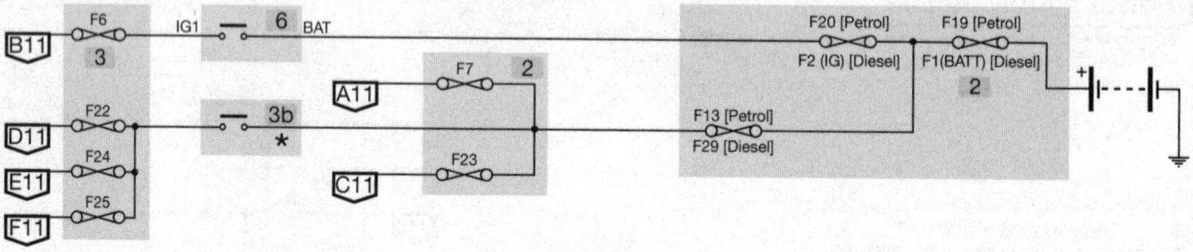

* Relay controlled by activation of ignition circuit

Typical powered windows and sunroof

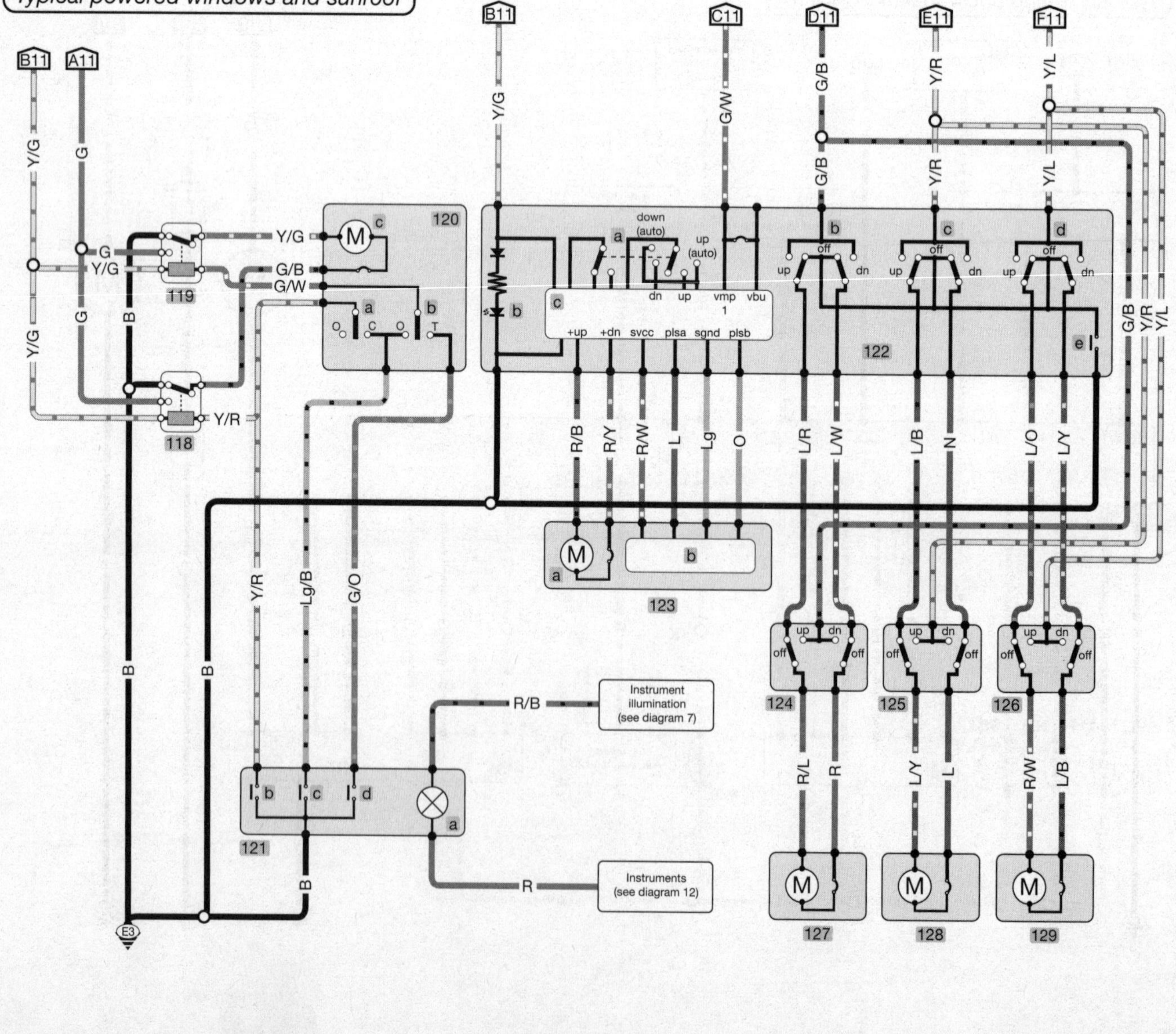

Diagram 12

Wire colours

B	Black	P	Purple
G	Green	R	Red
K	Pink	S	Grey
Lg	Light green	U	Blue
N	Brown	W	White
O	Orange	Y	Yellow
Lu	Light blue		

Key to items

2 Engine compartment fuse box
3 Passenger compartment fuse box
 d) Multifunction control unit (MCU)
6 Ignition switch
133 Instrument cluster
 a) seatbelt reminder light
 b) brake system light
 c) door indicator light
 d) tailgate indicator light
 e) charging system light
 f) low fuel indicator light
 g) ABS indicator light
 h) SRS indicator light
 j) rear fog light indicator light
 k) front fog light indicator light
 l) right turn signal indicator light
 m) left turn signal indicator light
 n) side airbag warning light
 o) cruise control system ight
 p) immobiliser light
 q) security indicator light
 r) malfunction indicator light
 s) oil pressure light
 t) hazard warning light
 u) high beam light
 v) trip/reset switch
 w) dash light dimmer
 x) dimmer electronics
 y) dash lights
134 Oil pressure switch
135 Vehicle speed sensor

H33866

Power supply outline

See diagrams 2,3,& 4 for enhanced power distribution information

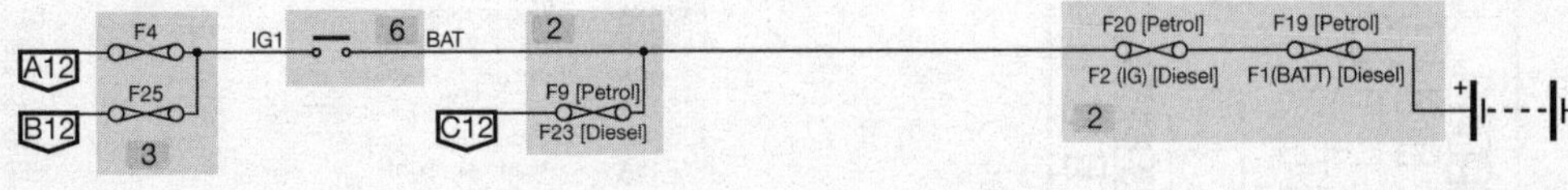

Typical instruments and gauges

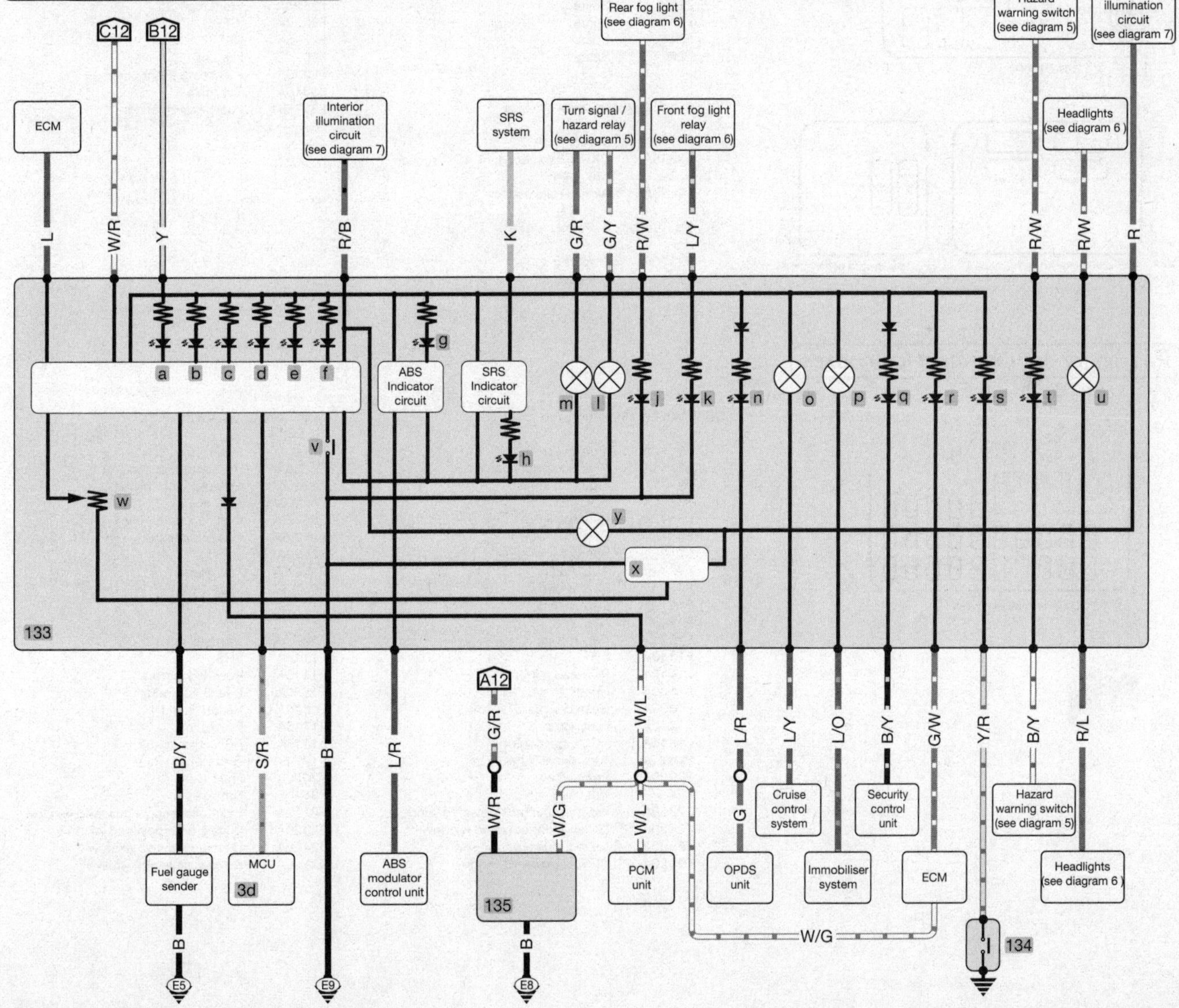

C12
B12
ECM
Interior illumination circuit (see diagram 7)
SRS system
Turn signal / hazard relay (see diagram 5)
Rear fog light (see diagram 6)
Front fog light relay (see diagram 6)
Hazard warning switch (see diagram 5)
Interior illumination circuit (see diagram 7)
Headlights (see diagram 6)
L
W/R
Y
R/B
K
G/R
G/Y
R/W
L/Y
R/W
R/W
R
a b c d e f g
ABS Indicator circuit
SRS Indicator circuit
h
m l j k n o p q r s t u
v
w
y
x
133
A12
B/Y
S/R
B
L/R
G/R
W/R
W/L
W/G
W/L
L/R
G
L/Y
L/O
B/Y
G/W
Y/R
B/Y
R/L
Cruise control system
Security control unit
Hazard warning switch (see diagram 5)
Fuel gauge sender
MCU
3d
ABS modulator control unit
135
PCM unit
OPDS unit
Immobiliser system
ECM
Headlights (see diagram 6)
W/G
134
B
B
B
E5
E9
E8

Note: On later models incandescent bulbs replaced by LED with series dropper resistor

Engine compartment fuse boxes

Diagram 13

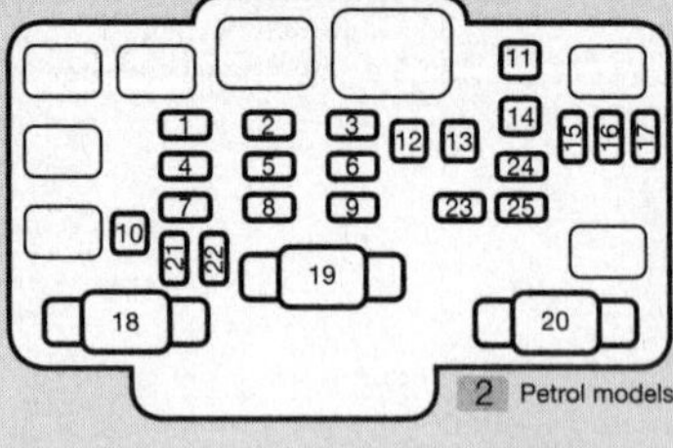

2 Petrol models

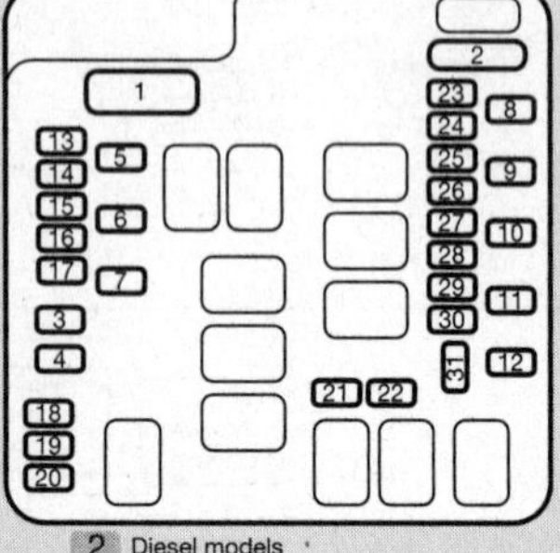

2 Diesel models

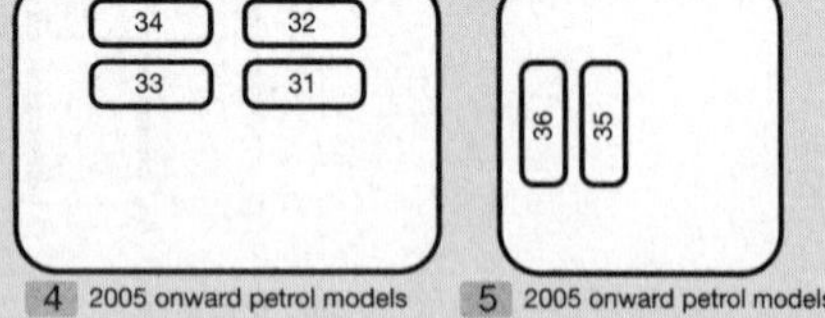

4 2005 onward petrol models 5 2005 onward petrol models

2 Main fusebox (Petrol models)

Fuse	Rating	Circuit
F1	20A	Condenser fan
F2	15A	Tail lights (early models)
	30A	Fuel injection (later models)
F3	15A	Interior light
F4	20A	Cooling fan
F5	15A	Hazard warning
F6	15A	Fuel injection ECU (early models)
		Tail lights (later models)
F7	15A	Horn, stop lights
F8	-	Not used (early models)
	15A	Drive by wire (later models)
F9	10A	Back up
F10	30A	ABS motor
F11	20A	Rear demister
F12	40A	Blower motor
F13	40A	Power window
F14	40A	Option
F15	15A	Left headlight
F16	20A	Door locks
F17	15A	Right headlight
F18	30A	ABS
F19	100A	Main fuse (battery)
F20	50A	Main fuse (ignition)
F21	-	Spare
F22	-	Spare
F23	-	Spare
F24	-	Spare
F25	-	Spare

4 Sub fusebox A (Petrol models)

Fuse	Rating	Circuit
F31	15A	Ignition coil
F32	15A	CKP sensor, ECM, FI, TDC sensor
F33	-	Not used
F34	20A	Air fuel ratio sensor

5 Sub fusebox B (Petrol models)

Fuse	Rating	Circuit
F35	20A	Front fog lights
F36	-	Not used

2 Main fusebox (Diesel models)

Fuse	Rating	Circuit
F1	70/100A	Battery/glow main fuse
F2	50/40A	Ignition/option main fuse
F3	40A	ABS
F4	40A	Power window
F5	-	Not used
F6	-	Not used
F7	-	Not used
F8	30A	Rear demister
F9	30A	Radiator fan
F10	30A	Condenser fan
F11	40A	Blower motor
F12	30A	Fuel heater system
F13	20A	Door locks
F14	15A	Horn, stop lights
F15	30A	ABS
F16	15A	Hazard warning
F17	-	Not used
F18	-	Not used
F19	-	Not used
F20	-	Not used
F21	20A	Left headlight
F22	20A	Right headlight
F23	10A	Back up
F24	15A	Interior light
F25	20A	Front fog light
F26	20A	IGP
F27	15A	IGP 2
F28	-	Not used
F29	10A	A/C compressor clutch
F30	15A	Tail lights
F31	7.5A	Fuel heater monitor

Passenger compartment fuse boxes

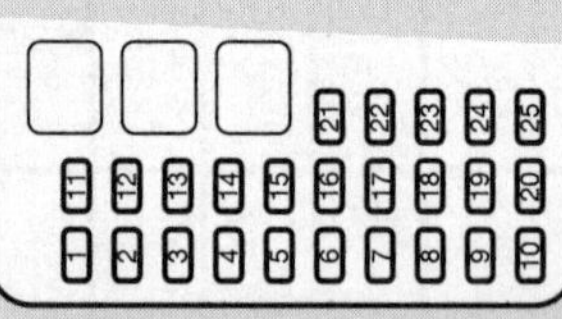

3 Petrol and diesel models

3 Main fusebox (Petrol models)

Fuse	Rating	Circuit
F1	15A	Ignition coil
F2	10A	Rear accessory socket
F3	20A	Front fog lights
F4	10A	ACC (IG)
F5	7.5A	Rear fog light
F6	7.5A	Power windows
F7	20A	Sunroof
F8	7.5A	ACC Radio
F9	7.5A	Rear wiper
F10	7.5A	Instruments
F11	-	Not used
F12	7.5A	Daytime lights
F13	10A	SRS
F14	10A	Powered mirrors
F15	30A	Headlight washer
F16	20A	Heated seats
F17	15A	Fuel pump
F18	15A	ACC cigar lighter
F19	7.5A	Turn signal lights
F20	20A	Front wiper
F21	-	Not used
F22	20A	Front passengers powered window
F23	20A	Drivers door powered window
F24	20A	LH rear powered window
F25	20A	RH rear powered window

3 Main fusebox (Diesel models)

Fuse	Rating	Circuit
F1	-	Not used
F2	10A	Rear accessory socket
F3	10A	Multiplex control unit
F4	10A	ACC (IG)
F5	7.5A	Multiplex control unit
F6	7.5A	Power windows
F7	20A	Sunroof
F8	7.5A	ACC Radio
F9	7.5A	Rear wiper
F10	7.5A	Instruments
F11	-	Not used
F12	7.5A	Daytime lights
F13	10A	SRS
F14	10A	Powered mirrors
F15	30A	Headlight washer
F16	20A	Heated seats
F17	15A	Fuel pump
F18	15A	ACC cigar lighter
F19	7.5A	Turn signal lights
F20	20A	Front wiper
F21	-	Not used
F22	20A	Front passengers powered window
F23	20A	Drivers door powered window
F24	20A	LH rear powered window
F25	20A	RH rear powered window

H33867

Dimensions and weights

Note: *All figures are approximate, and vary according to model. Refer to manufacturer's data for exact figures.*

Dimensions	**Early models**	**Facelift models**
Overall length – including spare wheel and cover	4575 mm	4615 mm (soft spare wheel cover) 4635 mm (hard spare wheel cover)
Overall width – excluding mirrors	1780 mm	1 85 mm (2050 mm, including mirrors)
Overall height – at kerb weight, excluding aerial and extra fittings	1710 mm	1710 mm (1835 mm, including aerial)
Wheelbase	2630 mm	2630 mm
Track:		
Front	1540 mm	1540 mm
Rear	1555 mm	1560 mm

Weights	**Early models**	**Facelift models**
Kerb weight:		
Petrol engine:		
Manual gearbox	1458 to 1542 kg	1502 to 1555 kg
Automatic transmission	1458 to 1542 kg	1526 to 1579 kg
Diesel engine	N/A	1622 to 1673 kg
Maximum permissible weight:		
Petrol engine:		
Manual gearbox	1930 kg	1990 kg
Automatic transmission	1960 kg	2020 kg
Diesel engine	N/A	2140 kg
Maximum permissible axle weight:		
Petrol engine:		
Front	960 kg	960 kg (manual) 980 kg (automatic)
Rear	1020 kg	1080 kg (manual) 1060 kg (automatic)
Diesel engine:		
Front	N/A	1090 kg
Rear	N/A	1070 kg
Maximum towing weight:		
Manual gearbox:		
Unbraked trailer	600 kg	600 kg
Braked trailer	1500 kg	1500 kg
Automatic transmission:		
Unbraked trailer	600 kg	600 kg
Braked trailer	1200 kg	1500 kg
Towbar maximum downward load*	60 kg	100 kg

* **Note:** *For trailer weights of less than 500 kg on early models, or 600 kg on facelift models, the towbar downward load should be 10% of that weight.*

Fuel economy

Although depreciation is still the biggest part of the cost of motoring for most car owners, the cost of fuel is more immediately noticeable. These pages give some tips on how to get the best fuel economy.

Working it out

Manufacturer's figures

Car manufacturers are required by law to provide fuel consumption information on all new vehicles sold. These 'official' figures are obtained by simulating various driving conditions on a rolling road or a test track. Real life conditions are different, so the fuel consumption actually achieved may not bear much resemblance to the quoted figures.

How to calculate it

Many cars now have trip computers which will display fuel consumption, both instantaneous and average. Refer to the owner's handbook for details of how to use these.

To calculate consumption yourself (and maybe to check that the trip computer is accurate), proceed as follows.

1. Fill up with fuel and note the mileage, or zero the trip recorder.
2. Drive as usual until you need to fill up again.
3. Note the amount of fuel required to refill the tank, and the mileage covered since the previous fill-up.
4. Divide the mileage by the amount of fuel used to obtain the consumption figure.

For example:

Mileage at first fill-up (a) = 27,903
Mileage at second fill-up (b) = 28,346
Mileage covered (b - a) = 443
Fuel required at second fill-up = 48.6 litres

The half-completed changeover to metric units in the UK means that we buy our fuel in litres, measure distances in miles and talk about fuel consumption in miles per gallon. There are two ways round this: the first is to convert the litres to gallons before doing the calculation (by dividing by 4.546, or see Table 1). So in the example:

48.6 litres ÷ 4.546 = 10.69 gallons
443 miles ÷ 10.69 gallons = 41.4 mpg

The second way is to calculate the consumption in miles per litre, then multiply that figure by 4.546 (or see Table 2).

So in the example, fuel consumption is:

443 miles ÷ 48.6 litres = 9.1 mpl
9.1 mpl x 4.546 = 41.4 mpg

The rest of Europe expresses fuel consumption in litres of fuel required to travel 100 km (l/100 km). For interest, the conversions are given in Table 3. In practice it doesn't matter what units you use, provided you know what your normal consumption is and can spot if it's getting better or worse.

Table 1: conversion of litres to Imperial gallons

litres	1	2	3	4	5	10	20	30	40	50	60	70
gallons	0.22	0.44	0.66	0.88	1.10	2.24	4.49	6.73	8.98	11.22	13.47	15.71

Table 2: conversion of miles per litre to miles per gallon

miles per litre	5	6	7	8	9	10	11	12	13	14
miles per gallon	23	27	32	36	41	46	50	55	59	64

Table 3: conversion of litres per 100 km to miles per gallon

litres per 100 km	4	4.5	5	5.5	6	6.5	7	8	9	10
miles per gallon	71	63	56	51	47	43	40	35	31	28

Maintenance

A well-maintained car uses less fuel and creates less pollution. In particular:

Filters

Change air and fuel filters at the specified intervals.

Oil

Use a good quality oil of the lowest viscosity specified by the vehicle manufacturer (see *Lubricants and fluids*). Check the level often and be careful not to overfill.

Spark plugs

When applicable, renew at the specified intervals.

Tyres

Check tyre pressures regularly. Under-inflated tyres have an increased rolling resistance. It is generally safe to use the higher pressures specified for full load conditions even when not fully laden, but keep an eye on the centre band of tread for signs of wear due to over-inflation.

When buying new tyres, consider the 'fuel saving' models which most manufacturers include in their ranges.

Driving style

Acceleration

Acceleration uses more fuel than driving at a steady speed. The best technique with modern cars is to accelerate reasonably briskly to the desired speed, changing up through the gears as soon as possible without making the engine labour.

Air conditioning

Air conditioning absorbs quite a bit of energy from the engine – typically 3 kW (4 hp) or so. The effect on fuel consumption is at its worst in slow traffic. Switch it off when not required.

Anticipation

Drive smoothly and try to read the traffic flow so as to avoid unnecessary acceleration and braking.

Automatic transmission

When accelerating in an automatic, avoid depressing the throttle so far as to make the transmission hold onto lower gears at higher speeds. Don't use the 'Sport' setting, if applicable.

When stationary with the engine running, select 'N' or 'P'. When moving, keep your left foot away from the brake.

Braking

Braking converts the car's energy of motion into heat – essentially, it is wasted. Obviously some braking is always going to be necessary, but with good anticipation it is surprising how much can be avoided, especially on routes that you know well.

Carshare

Consider sharing lifts to work or to the shops. Even once a week will make a difference.

Electrical loads

Electricity is 'fuel' too; the alternator which charges the battery does so by converting some of the engine's energy of motion into electrical energy. The more electrical accessories are in use, the greater the load on the alternator. Switch off big consumers like the heated rear window when not required.

Freewheeling

Freewheeling (coasting) in neutral with the engine switched off is dangerous. The effort required to operate power-assisted brakes and steering increases when the engine is not running, with a potential lack of control in emergency situations.

In any case, modern fuel injection systems automatically cut off the engine's fuel supply on the overrun (moving and in gear, but with the accelerator pedal released).

Gadgets

Bolt-on devices claiming to save fuel have been around for nearly as long as the motor car itself. Those which worked were rapidly adopted as standard equipment by the vehicle manufacturers. Others worked only in certain situations, or saved fuel only at the expense of unacceptable effects on performance, driveability or the life of engine components.

The most effective fuel saving gadget is the driver's right foot.

Journey planning

Combine (eg) a trip to the supermarket with a visit to the recycling centre and the DIY store, rather than making separate journeys.

When possible choose a travelling time outside rush hours.

Load

The more heavily a car is laden, the greater the energy required to accelerate it to a given speed. Remove heavy items which you don't need to carry.

One load which is often overlooked is the contents of the fuel tank. A tankful of fuel (55 litres / 12 gallons) weighs 45 kg (100 lb) or so. Just half filling it may be worthwhile.

Lost?

At the risk of stating the obvious, if you're going somewhere new, have details of the route to hand. There's not much point in achieving record mpg if you also go miles out of your way.

Parking

If possible, carry out any reversing or turning manoeuvres when you arrive at a parking space so that you can drive straight out when you leave. Manoeuvering when the engine is cold uses a lot more fuel.

Driving around looking for free on-street parking may cost more in fuel than buying a car park ticket.

Premium fuel

Most major oil companies (and some supermarkets) have premium grades of fuel which are several pence a litre dearer than the standard grades. Reports vary, but the consensus seems to be that if these fuels improve economy at all, they do not do so by enough to justify their extra cost.

Roof rack

When loading a roof rack, try to produce a wedge shape with the narrow end at the front. Any cover should be securely fastened – if it flaps it's creating turbulence and absorbing energy.

Remove roof racks and boxes when not in use – they increase air resistance and can create a surprising amount of noise.

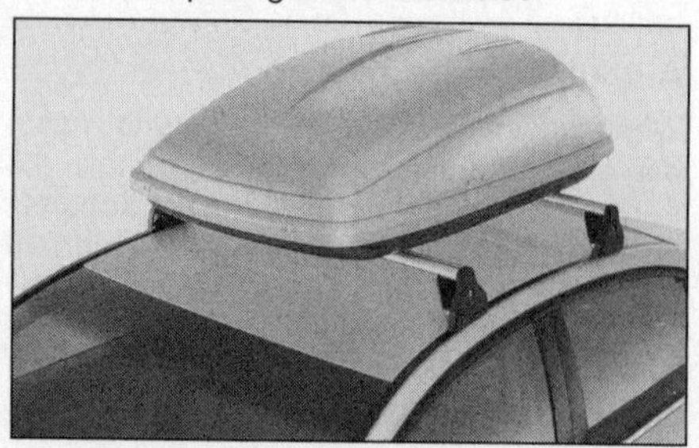

Short journeys

The engine is at its least efficient, and wear is highest, during the first few miles after a cold start. Consider walking, cycling or using public transport.

Speed

The engine is at its most efficient when running at a steady speed and load at the rpm where it develops maximum torque. (You can find this figure in the car's handbook.) For most cars this corresponds to between 55 and 65 mph in top gear.

Above the optimum cruising speed, fuel consumption starts to rise quite sharply. A car travelling at 80 mph will typically be using 30% more fuel than at 60 mph.

Supermarket fuel

It may be cheap but is it any good? In the UK all supermarket fuel must meet the relevant British Standard. The major oil companies will say that their branded fuels have better additive packages which may stop carbon and other deposits building up. A reasonable compromise might be to use one tank of branded fuel to three or four from the supermarket.

Switch off when stationary

Switch off the engine if you look like being stationary for more than 30 seconds or so. This is good for the environment as well as for your pocket. Be aware though that frequent restarts are hard on the battery and the starter motor.

Windows

Driving with the windows open increases air turbulence around the vehicle. Closing the windows promotes smooth airflow and reduced resistance. The faster you go, the more significant this is.

And finally . . .

Driving techniques associated with good fuel economy tend to involve moderate acceleration and low top speeds. Be considerate to the needs of other road users who may need to make brisker progress; even if you do not agree with them this is not an excuse to be obstructive.

Safety must always take precedence over economy, whether it is a question of accelerating hard to complete an overtaking manoeuvre, killing your speed when confronted with a potential hazard or switching the lights on when it starts to get dark.

Conversion factors

Length (distance)

Inches (in)	x 25.4	= Millimetres (mm)	x 0.0394	= Inches (in)
Feet (ft)	x 0.305	= Metres (m)	x 3.281	= Feet (ft)
Miles	x 1.609	= Kilometres (km)	x 0.621	= Miles

Volume (capacity)

Cubic inches (cu in; in^3)	x 16.387	= Cubic centimetres (cc; cm^3)	x 0.061	= Cubic inches (cu in; in^3)
Imperial pints (Imp pt)	x 0.568	= Litres (l)	x 1.76	= Imperial pints (Imp pt)
Imperial quarts (Imp qt)	x 1.137	= Litres (l)	x 0.88	= Imperial quarts (Imp qt)
Imperial quarts (Imp qt)	x 1.201	= US quarts (US qt)	x 0.833	= Imperial quarts (Imp qt)
US quarts (US qt)	x 0.946	= Litres (l)	x 1.057	= US quarts (US qt)
Imperial gallons (Imp gal)	x 4.546	= Litres (l)	x 0.22	= Imperial gallons (Imp gal)
Imperial gallons (Imp gal)	x 1.201	= US gallons (US gal)	x 0.833	= Imperial gallons (Imp gal)
US gallons (US gal)	x 3.785	= Litres (l)	x 0.264	= US gallons (US gal)

Mass (weight)

Ounces (oz)	x 28.35	= Grams (g)	x 0.035	= Ounces (oz)
Pounds (lb)	x 0.454	= Kilograms (kg)	x 2.205	= Pounds (lb)

Force

Ounces-force (ozf; oz)	x 0.278	= Newtons (N)	x 3.6	= Ounces-force (ozf; oz)
Pounds-force (lbf; lb)	x 4.448	= Newtons (N)	x 0.225	= Pounds-force (lbf; lb)
Newtons (N)	x 0.1	= Kilograms-force (kgf; kg)	x 9.81	= Newtons (N)

Pressure

Pounds-force per square inch (psi; lbf/in^2; lb/in^2)	x 0.070	= Kilograms-force per square centimetre (kgf/cm^2; kg/cm^2)	x 14.223	= Pounds-force per square inch (psi; lbf/in^2; lb/in^2)
Pounds-force per square inch (psi; lbf/in^2; lb/in^2)	x 0.068	= Atmospheres (atm)	x 14.696	= Pounds-force per square inch (psi; lbf/in^2; lb/in^2)
Pounds-force per square inch (psi; lbf/in^2; lb/in^2)	x 0.069	= Bars	x 14.5	= Pounds-force per square inch (psi; lbf/in^2; lb/in^2)
Pounds-force per square inch (psi; lbf/in^2; lb/in^2)	x 6.895	= Kilopascals (kPa)	x 0.145	= Pounds-force per square inch (psi; lbf/in^2; lb/in^2)
Kilopascals (kPa)	x 0.01	= Kilograms-force per square centimetre (kgf/cm^2; kg/cm^2)	x 98.1	= Kilopascals (kPa)
Millibar (mbar)	x 100	= Pascals (Pa)	x 0.01	= Millibar (mbar)
Millibar (mbar)	x 0.0145	= Pounds-force per square inch (psi; lbf/in^2; lb/in^2)	x 68.947	= Millibar (mbar)
Millibar (mbar)	x 0.75	= Millimetres of mercury (mmHg)	x 1.333	= Millibar (mbar)
Millibar (mbar)	x 0.401	= Inches of water (inH$_2$O)	x 2.491	= Millibar (mbar)
Millimetres of mercury (mmHg)	x 0.535	= Inches of water (inH$_2$O)	x 1.868	= Millimetres of mercury (mmHg)
Inches of water (inH$_2$O)	x 0.036	= Pounds-force per square inch (psi; lbf/in^2; lb/in^2)	x 27.68	= Inches of water (inH$_2$O)

Torque (moment of force)

Pounds-force inches (lbf in; lb in)	x 1.152	= Kilograms-force centimetre (kgf cm; kg cm)	x 0.868	= Pounds-force inches (lbf in; lb in)
Pounds-force inches (lbf in; lb in)	x 0.113	= Newton metres (Nm)	x 8.85	= Pounds-force inches (lbf in; lb in)
Pounds-force inches (lbf in; lb in)	x 0.083	= Pounds-force feet (lbf ft; lb ft)	x 12	= Pounds-force inches (lbf in; lb in)
Pounds-force feet (lbf ft; lb ft)	x 0.138	= Kilograms-force metres (kgf m; kg m)	x 7.233	= Pounds-force feet (lbf ft; lb ft)
Pounds-force feet (lbf ft; lb ft)	x 1.356	= Newton metres (Nm)	x 0.738	= Pounds-force feet (lbf ft; lb ft)
Newton metres (Nm)	x 0.102	= Kilograms-force metres (kgf m; kg m)	x 9.804	= Newton metres (Nm)

Power

Horsepower (hp)	x 745.7	= Watts (W)	x 0.0013	= Horsepower (hp)

Velocity (speed)

Miles per hour (miles/hr; mph)	x 1.609	= Kilometres per hour (km/hr; kph)	x 0.621	= Miles per hour (miles/hr; mph)

Fuel consumption*

Miles per gallon, Imperial (mpg)	x 0.354	= Kilometres per litre (km/l)	x 2.825	= Miles per gallon, Imperial (mpg)
Miles per gallon, US (mpg)	x 0.425	= Kilometres per litre (km/l)	x 2.352	= Miles per gallon, US (mpg)

Temperature

Degrees Fahrenheit = (°C x 1.8) + 32

Degrees Celsius (Degrees Centigrade; °C) = (°F - 32) x 0.56

** It is common practice to convert from miles per gallon (mpg) to litres/100 kilometres (l/100km), where mpg x l/100 km = 282*

Spare parts are available from many sources, including maker's appointed garages, accessory shops, and motor factors. To be sure of obtaining the correct parts, it will sometimes be necessary to quote the vehicle identification number. If possible, it can also be useful to take the old parts along for positive identification. Items such as starter motors and alternators may be available under a service exchange scheme – any parts returned should be clean.

Our advice regarding spare parts is as follows.

Officially-appointed garages

This is the best source of parts which are peculiar to your vehicle, and which are not otherwise generally available (eg, badges, interior trim, certain body panels, etc). It is also the only place at which you should buy parts if the vehicle is still under warranty.

Accessory shops

These are very good places to buy materials and components needed for the maintenance of your vehicle (oil, air and fuel filters, light bulbs, drivebelts, greases, brake pads, touch-up paint, etc). Components of this nature sold by a reputable shop are of the same standard as those used by the vehicle manufacturer.

Besides components, these shops also sell tools and general accessories, usually have convenient opening hours, charge lower prices, and can often be found close to home. Some accessory shops have parts counters where components needed for almost any repair job can be purchased or ordered.

Motor factors

Good factors will stock all the more important components which wear out comparatively quickly, and can sometimes supply individual components needed for the overhaul of a larger assembly (eg, brake seals and hydraulic parts, bearing shells, pistons, valves). They may also handle work such as cylinder block reboring, crankshaft regrinding, etc.

Tyre and exhaust specialists

These outlets may be independent, or members of a local or national chain. They frequently offer competitive prices when compared with a main dealer or local garage, but it will pay to obtain several quotes before making a decision. When researching prices, also ask what 'extras' may be added – for instance fitting a new valve and balancing the wheel are both commonly charged on top of the price of a new tyre.

Other sources

Beware of parts or materials obtained from market stalls, car boot sales or similar outlets. Such items are not invariably sub-standard, but there is little chance of compensation if they do prove unsatisfactory. In the case of safety-critical components such as brake pads, there is the risk not only of financial loss, but also of an accident causing injury or death.

Second-hand components or assemblies obtained from a vehicle breaker can be a good buy in some circumstances, but this sort of purchase is best made by the experienced DIY mechanic.

Vehicle identification

Modifications are a continuing and unpublicised process in vehicle manufacture, quite apart from major model changes. Spare parts manuals and lists are compiled upon a numerical basis, the individual vehicle identification numbers being essential to correct identification of the component concerned.

When ordering spare parts, always give as much information as possible. Quote the vehicle model, year of manufacture, chassis number/VIN and engine numbers as appropriate.

The *vehicle identification plate* is located under the bonnet, on the front suspension left-hand (as seen from the driver's seat) strut mounting **(see illustration)**. In addition to other information, it carries the Vehicle Identification Number (VIN), engine number, maximum vehicle weight information and the paint code. Further information is obtainable from any Honda dealer on quoting the vehicle's registration number and VIN.

The *Vehicle Identification Number (VIN)* is given on the vehicle identification plate. It is also stamped into the bulkhead at the rear of the engine compartment, and appears on a tag on the left-hand side of the facia, so that it can be seen through the bottom left-hand corner of the windscreen **(see illustrations)**.

Note: *It is often necessary to identify precisely the vehicle's model year (as opposed to date of sale, or of first registration). To establish this, find the tenth character of the VIN, which for the models covered in this manual should be the digit 2, 3, 4, 5 or 6, identifying respectively 2002, 2003, 2004, 2005 and 2006 models.*

The *engine number* is stamped on a flat surface (which may be painted red for easier identification) on the front of the cylinder block/crankcase next to the starter motor mounting.

The *transmission number* is marked on a label on the front surface of the transmission casing.

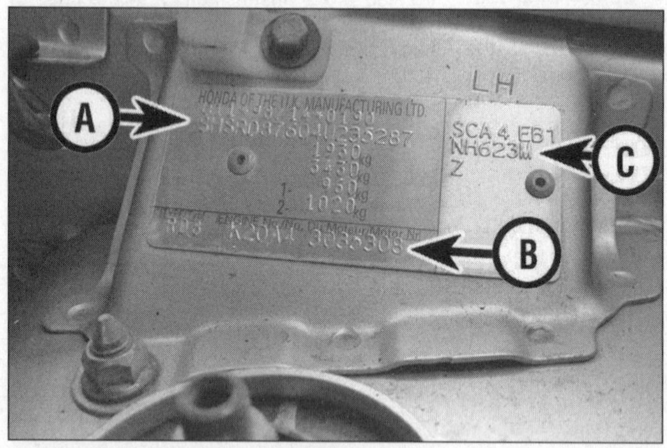

The vehicle identification plate is on the left-hand suspension strut mounting – note chassis number/VIN (A), engine number (B) and paint code (C)

The vehicle identification number (VIN) is stamped into the bulkhead

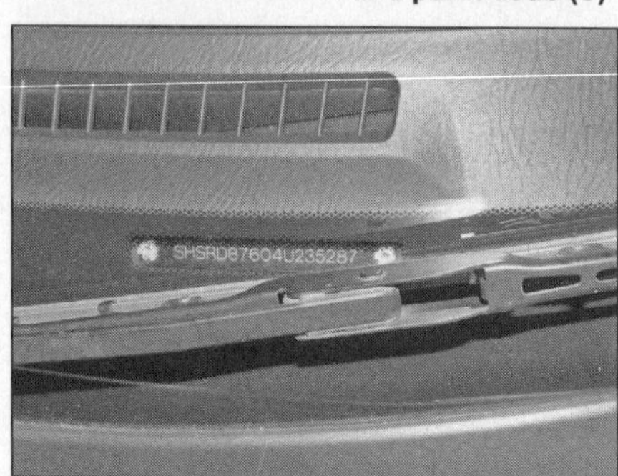

The VIN is also visible through the windscreen

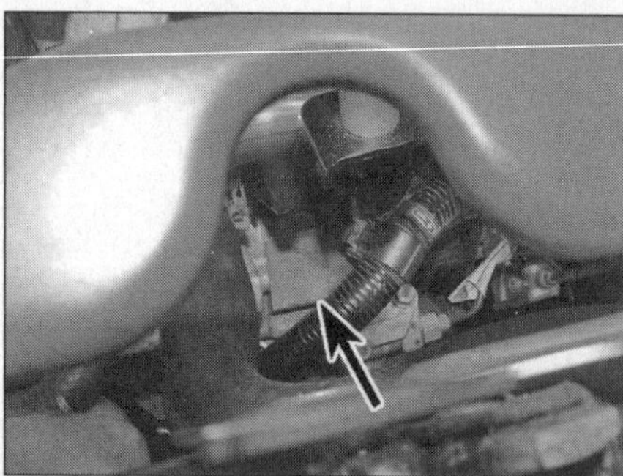
The engine number (seen here through bonnet lock) is stamped next to starter motor

Engine number (A), transmission identification label (B) – diesel models

Engine number location – petrol models

Transmission identification label – petrol models

The jack supplied with the vehicle's tool kit should only be used for changing the roadwheels – see *Wheel changing* at the front of this book. When carrying out any other kind of work, raise the vehicle using a hydraulic (or 'trolley') jack, and always supplement the jack with axle stands positioned under the jacking/support points. If the roadwheels do not have to be removed, consider using wheel ramps – if wished, these can be placed under the wheels once the vehicle has been raised using a hydraulic jack, and then lowered onto the ramps so that it is resting on its wheels.

Only ever jack the vehicle up on a solid, level surface. If there is even a slight slope, take great care that the vehicle cannot move as the wheels are lifted off the ground. Jacking up on an uneven or gravelled surface is not recommended, as the weight of the vehicle will not be evenly distributed, and the jack may slip as the vehicle is raised.

As far as possible, do not leave the vehicle unattended once it has been raised, particularly if children are playing nearby.

Before jacking up the front of the vehicle, ensure that the handbrake is firmly applied and chock behind the rear wheels. Place the jack head under one of the front jacking/support points on the door sill (these are elongated tabs on the base of the door sills at the front and rear, that may be indicated by an arrow mark in the underside of the body – the slotted jack head should locate on the tab). If the vehicle jack is not being used, place a block of wood with a slot cut to fit the tab between the jack head and the sill to prevent damage. Raise the vehicle to the required height and place an axle stand under the jacking/support point, or as close to this point as possible. Repeat, if desired, to raise the opposite side of the vehicle and bring it up level to the required height.

To raise the rear of the vehicle, chock the front wheels and engage a gear (or select P). Raise the vehicle in the same way, using one of the rear jacking/support points on the door sill, with a block of wood if necessary to prevent damage **(see illustration)**. Again, place axle stands as close to the rear jacking/support points as possible.

To raise one side of the vehicle, prepare it as described for front AND rear lifting. Place the jack head under the appropriate jacking/support point, then raise it first at the front, place an axle stand, then at the rear and place a second axle stand.

If a substantial jack is available – which it must be, as the weight of the whole front or rear end is being lifted at once, the jacking points at the front centre-point on the front suspension subframe (also indicated by an arrow marking moulded in the underside of the front bumper) and at the centre of the rear suspension subframe can be used **(see illustrations)**. Always place a flat piece of wood on the jack head, to spread the load and prevent damage to the subframe. Raise the vehicle to just above the required height (but be careful, especially at the rear, as there is a danger of the vehicle tipping sideways), then place axle stands under BOTH of the front or rear door sill jacking/support points, and lower the vehicle on to them.

DO NOT jack the vehicle under any other part of the sill, sump, floor pan, final drive or directly under any of the steering or suspension components.

NEVER work under, around, or near a raised vehicle, unless it is adequately supported on stands. Do not rely on a jack alone, as even a hydraulic jack could fail under load.

Jack head engaged on rear door sill jacking/support point

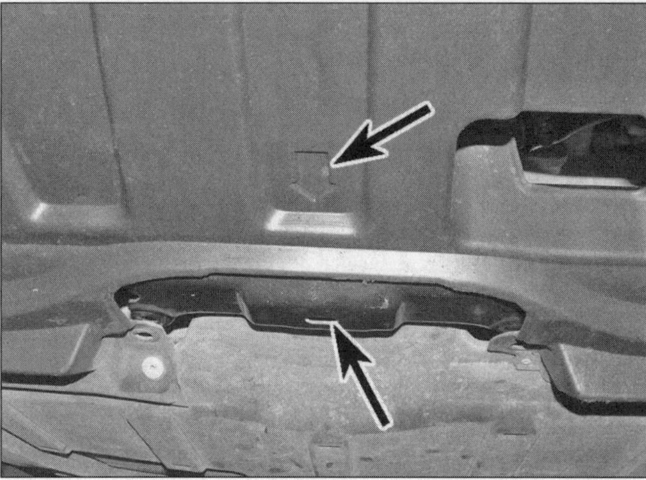

Front jacking point at front centre of front suspension subframe is indicated by arrow marking moulded in underside of front bumper

Rear jacking point is at centre of rear suspension subframe

Whenever servicing, repair or overhaul work is carried out on the car or its components, observe the following procedures and instructions. This will assist in carrying out the operation efficiently and to a professional standard of workmanship.

Joint mating faces and gaskets

When separating components at their mating faces, never insert screwdrivers or similar implements into the joint between the faces in order to prise them apart. This can cause severe damage which results in oil leaks, coolant leaks, etc upon reassembly. Separation is usually achieved by tapping along the joint with a soft-faced hammer in order to break the seal. However, note that this method may not be suitable where dowels are used for component location.

Where a gasket is used between the mating faces of two components, a new one must be fitted on reassembly; fit it dry unless otherwise stated in the repair procedure. Make sure that the mating faces are clean and dry, with all traces of old gasket removed. When cleaning a joint face, use a tool which is unlikely to score or damage the face, and remove any burrs or nicks with an oilstone or fine file.

Make sure that tapped holes are cleaned with a pipe cleaner, and keep them free of jointing compound, if this is being used, unless specifically instructed otherwise.

Ensure that all orifices, channels or pipes are clear, and blow through them, preferably using compressed air.

Oil seals

Oil seals can be removed by levering them out with a wide flat-bladed screwdriver or similar implement. Alternatively, a number of self-tapping screws may be screwed into the seal, and these used as a purchase for pliers or some similar device in order to pull the seal free.

Whenever an oil seal is removed from its working location, either individually or as part of an assembly, it should be renewed.

The very fine sealing lip of the seal is easily damaged, and will not seal if the surface it contacts is not completely clean and free from scratches, nicks or grooves. If the original sealing surface of the component cannot be restored, and the manufacturer has not made provision for slight relocation of the seal relative to the sealing surface, the component should be renewed.

Protect the lips of the seal from any surface which may damage them in the course of fitting. Use tape or a conical sleeve where possible. Lubricate the seal lips with oil before fitting and, on dual-lipped seals, fill the space between the lips with grease.

Unless otherwise stated, oil seals must be fitted with their sealing lips toward the lubricant to be sealed.

Use a tubular drift or block of wood of the appropriate size to install the seal and, if the seal housing is shouldered, drive the seal down to the shoulder. If the seal housing is unshouldered, the seal should be fitted with its face flush with the housing top face (unless otherwise instructed).

Screw threads and fastenings

Seized nuts, bolts and screws are quite a common occurrence where corrosion has set in, and the use of penetrating oil or releasing fluid will often overcome this problem if the offending item is soaked for a while before attempting to release it. The use of an impact driver may also provide a means of releasing such stubborn fastening devices, when used in conjunction with the appropriate screwdriver bit or socket. If none of these methods works, it may be necessary to resort to the careful application of heat, or the use of a hacksaw or nut splitter device.

Studs are usually removed by locking two nuts together on the threaded part, and then using a spanner on the lower nut to unscrew the stud. Studs or bolts which have broken off below the surface of the component in which they are mounted can sometimes be removed using a stud extractor. Always ensure that a blind tapped hole is completely free from oil, grease, water or other fluid before installing the bolt or stud. Failure to do this could cause the housing to crack due to the hydraulic action of the bolt or stud as it is screwed in.

When tightening a castellated nut to accept a split pin, tighten the nut to the specified torque, where applicable, and then tighten further to the next split pin hole. Never slacken the nut to align the split pin hole, unless stated in the repair procedure.

When checking or retightening a nut or bolt to a specified torque setting, slacken the nut or bolt by a quarter of a turn, and then retighten to the specified setting. However, this should not be attempted where angular tightening has been used.

For some screw fastenings, notably cylinder head bolts or nuts, torque wrench settings are no longer specified for the latter stages of tightening, "angle-tightening" being called up instead. Typically, a fairly low torque wrench setting will be applied to the bolts/nuts in the correct sequence, followed by one or more stages of tightening through specified angles.

Locknuts, locktabs and washers

Any fastening which will rotate against a component or housing during tightening should always have a washer between it and the relevant component or housing.

Spring or split washers should always be renewed when they are used to lock a critical component such as a big-end bearing retaining bolt or nut. Locktabs which are folded over to retain a nut or bolt should always be renewed.

Self-locking nuts can be re-used in non-critical areas, providing resistance can be felt when the locking portion passes over the bolt or stud thread. However, it should be noted that self-locking stiffnuts tend to lose their effectiveness after long periods of use, and should then be renewed as a matter of course.

Split pins must always be replaced with new ones of the correct size for the hole.

When thread-locking compound is found on the threads of a fastener which is to be re-used, it should be cleaned off with a wire brush and solvent, and fresh compound applied on reassembly.

Special tools

Some repair procedures in this manual entail the use of special tools such as a press, two or three-legged pullers, spring compressors, etc. Wherever possible, suitable readily-available alternatives to the manufacturer's special tools are described, and are shown in use. In some instances, where no alternative is possible, it has been necessary to resort to the use of a manufacturer's tool, and this has been done for reasons of safety as well as the efficient completion of the repair operation. Unless you are highly-skilled and have a thorough understanding of the procedures described, never attempt to bypass the use of any special tool when the procedure described specifies its use. Not only is there a very great risk of personal injury, but expensive damage could be caused to the components involved.

Environmental considerations

When disposing of used engine oil, brake fluid, antifreeze, etc, give due consideration to any detrimental environmental effects. Do not, for instance, pour any of the above liquids down drains into the general sewage system, or onto the ground to soak away. Many local council refuse tips provide a facility for waste oil disposal, as do some garages. If none of these facilities are available, consult your local Environmental Health Department, or the National Rivers Authority, for further advice.

With the universal tightening-up of legislation regarding the emission of environmentally-harmful substances from motor vehicles, most vehicles have tamperproof devices fitted to the main adjustment points of the fuel system. These devices are primarily designed to prevent unqualified persons from adjusting the fuel/air mixture, with the chance of a consequent increase in toxic emissions. If such devices are found during servicing or overhaul, they should, wherever possible, be renewed or refitted in accordance with the manufacturer's requirements or current legislation.

OIL CARE
FOLLOW THE CODE
OIL BANK LINE
0800 66 33 66
www.oilbankline.org.uk

Note: It is antisocial and illegal to dump oil down the drain. To find the location of your local oil recycling bank, call this number free.

The audio unit and navigation system fitted as standard equipment by Honda are each equipped with a built-in security code to deter thieves. If the power source to either unit is cut, its anti-theft system will activate. Even if the power source is immediately reconnected, the unit will not function until the correct security code has been entered. Therefore, if you do not know the correct security code for these units do not disconnect the battery negative terminal or remove either unit from the vehicle. **Note:** *Upon reconnection of the battery, the window system's control unit may need to be reset and the clock will need resetting.*

While it is advisable as a basic rule of safety to disconnect the battery negative (earth) lead before working on any part of any of the vehicle's electrical systems, several systems fitted to the vehicle require battery power to be available at all times, either to ensure their continued operation (such as the clock), or to maintain electronic memory settings which would otherwise be erased. Whenever the battery is to be disconnected, first note the following points, to ensure there are no unforeseen consequences:

a) *First, on any vehicle with central door locking, it is a wise precaution to remove the key from the ignition, and to keep it with you, so that it does not get locked in if the central locking engages when the battery is reconnected.*

b) *Ensure that you have a record of the anti-theft codes (where applicable) for components such as the audio and navigation systems and details of favourite radio stations preset into the audio system before disconnecting the battery. These will be erased on disconnection of the power supply to the system and must be re-entered manually once power has been restored.*

c) *During normal operation, the vehicle's engine control unit (ECU) learns and stores idling and other engine operating values in its memory. Whenever the battery is disconnected, this information is lost, and has to be re-learned. The ECU does this by itself, but until then, there may be surging, hesitation, erratic idle and a generally inferior level of performance. To allow the ECU to relearn these values, start the engine and let it run as close to idle speed as possible until it reaches its normal operating temperature, then run it for approximately two minutes at 1200 rpm. Next, drive the vehicle as far as necessary – approximately 5 miles of varied driving conditions is usually sufficient – to complete the re-learning process.*

d) *If the battery is disconnected while the alarm system is armed or activated, the alarm will remain in the same state when the battery is reconnected. The same applies to the engine immobiliser system. In some cases, the alarm may sound on reconnecting the battery – have the remote control ready to disarm the system.*

e) *If work is being carried out on the vehicle's airbag or seat belt tensioner systems, the battery should be reconnected last – ie, after all the airbag and belt tensioner wiring has been reconnected.*

Devices known as 'memory-savers' or 'code-savers' can be used to avoid some of the above problems. Precise details of use vary according to the device used. Typically, it is plugged into the cigar lighter socket, and is connected by its own wiring to a spare battery; the vehicle's battery is then disconnected from the electrical system, leaving the memory-saver to pass sufficient current to maintain audio unit security codes and other memory values, and also to run permanently-live circuits such as the clock.

Warning: Some of these devices allow a considerable amount of current to pass, which can mean that many of the vehicle's systems are still operational when the battery is disconnected. If a 'memory-saver' is used, ensure that the circuit concerned is actually 'dead' before carrying out any work on it!

Introduction

A selection of good tools is a fundamental requirement for anyone contemplating the maintenance and repair of a motor vehicle. For the owner who does not possess any, their purchase will prove a considerable expense, offsetting some of the savings made by doing-it-yourself. However, provided that the tools purchased meet the relevant national safety standards and are of good quality, they will last for many years and prove an extremely worthwhile investment.

To help the average owner to decide which tools are needed to carry out the various tasks detailed in this manual, we have compiled three lists of tools under the following headings: *Maintenance and minor repair*, *Repair and overhaul*, and *Special*. Newcomers to practical mechanics should start off with the *Maintenance and minor repair* tool kit, and confine themselves to the simpler jobs around the vehicle. Then, as confidence and experience grow, more difficult tasks can be undertaken, with extra tools being purchased as, and when, they are needed. In this way, a *Maintenance and minor repair* tool kit can be built up into a *Repair and overhaul* tool kit over a considerable period of time, without any major cash outlays. The experienced do-it-yourselfer will have a tool kit good enough for most repair and overhaul procedures, and will add tools from the *Special* category when it is felt that the expense is justified by the amount of use to which these tools will be put.

Maintenance and minor repair tool kit

The tools given in this list should be considered as a minimum requirement if routine maintenance, servicing and minor repair operations are to be undertaken. We recommend the purchase of combination spanners (ring one end, open-ended the other); although more expensive than open-ended ones, they do give the advantages of both types of spanner.

- ☐ *Combination spanners:*
  Metric - 8 to 19 mm inclusive
- ☐ *Adjustable spanner - 35 mm jaw (approx.)*
- ☐ *Spark plug spanner (with rubber insert) - petrol models*
- ☐ *Spark plug gap adjustment tool - petrol models*
- ☐ *Set of feeler gauges*
- ☐ *Brake bleed nipple spanner*
- ☐ *Screwdrivers:*
  Flat blade - 100 mm long x 6 mm dia
  Cross blade - 100 mm long x 6 mm dia
  Torx - various sizes (not all vehicles)
- ☐ *Combination pliers*
- ☐ *Hacksaw (junior)*
- ☐ *Tyre pump*
- ☐ *Tyre pressure gauge*
- ☐ *Oil can*
- ☐ *Oil filter removal tool*
- ☐ *Fine emery cloth*
- ☐ *Wire brush (small)*
- ☐ *Funnel (medium size)*
- ☐ *Sump drain plug key (not all vehicles)*

Repair and overhaul tool kit

These tools are virtually essential for anyone undertaking any major repairs to a motor vehicle, and are additional to those given in the *Maintenance and minor repair* list. Included in this list is a comprehensive set of sockets. Although these are expensive, they will be found invaluable as they are so versatile - particularly if various drives are included in the set. We recommend the half-inch square-drive type, as this can be used with most proprietary torque wrenches.

The tools in this list will sometimes need to be supplemented by tools from the *Special* list:

- ☐ *Sockets (or box spanners) to cover range in previous list (including Torx sockets)*
- ☐ *Reversible ratchet drive (for use with sockets)*
- ☐ *Extension piece, 250 mm (for use with sockets)*
- ☐ *Universal joint (for use with sockets)*
- ☐ *Flexible handle or sliding T "breaker bar" (for use with sockets)*
- ☐ *Torque wrench (for use with sockets)*
- ☐ *Self-locking grips*
- ☐ *Ball pein hammer*
- ☐ *Soft-faced mallet (plastic or rubber)*
- ☐ *Screwdrivers:*
  Flat blade - long & sturdy, short (chubby), and narrow (electrician's) types
  Cross blade – long & sturdy, and short (chubby) types
- ☐ *Pliers:*
  Long-nosed
  Side cutters (electrician's)
  Circlip (internal and external)
- ☐ *Cold chisel - 25 mm*
- ☐ *Scriber*
- ☐ *Scraper*
- ☐ *Centre-punch*
- ☐ *Pin punch*
- ☐ *Hacksaw*
- ☐ *Brake hose clamp*
- ☐ *Brake/clutch bleeding kit*
- ☐ *Selection of twist drills*
- ☐ *Steel rule/straight-edge*
- ☐ *Allen keys (inc. splined/Torx type)*
- ☐ *Selection of files*
- ☐ *Wire brush*
- ☐ *Axle stands*
- ☐ *Jack (strong trolley or hydraulic type)*
- ☐ *Light with extension lead*
- ☐ *Universal electrical multi-meter*

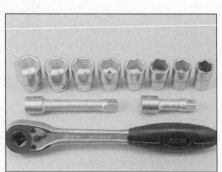

Sockets and reversible ratchet drive

Brake bleeding kit

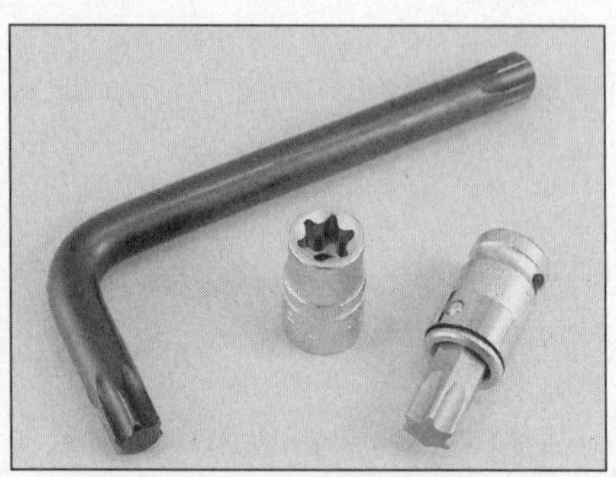

Torx key, socket and bit

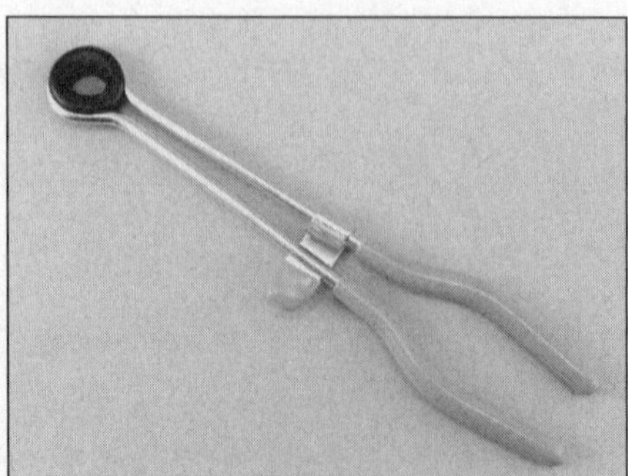

Hose clamp

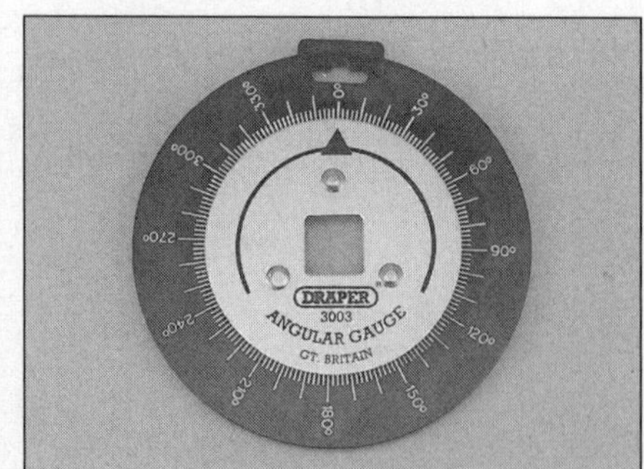

Angular-tightening gauge

Special tools

The tools in this list are those which are not used regularly, are expensive to buy, or which need to be used in accordance with their manufacturers' instructions. Unless relatively difficult mechanical jobs are undertaken frequently, it will not be economic to buy many of these tools. Where this is the case, you could consider clubbing together with friends (or joining a motorists' club) to make a joint purchase, or borrowing the tools against a deposit from a local garage or tool hire specialist. It is worth noting that many of the larger DIY superstores now carry a large range of special tools for hire at modest rates.

The following list contains only those tools and instruments freely available to the public, and not those special tools produced by the vehicle manufacturer specifically for its dealer network. You will find occasional references to these manufacturers' special tools in the text of this manual. Generally, an alternative method of doing the job without the vehicle manufacturers' special tool is given. However, sometimes there is no alternative to using them. Where this is the case and the relevant tool cannot be bought or borrowed, you will have to entrust the work to a dealer.

- ☐ *Angular-tightening gauge*
- ☐ *Valve spring compressor*
- ☐ *Valve grinding tool*
- ☐ *Piston ring compressor*
- ☐ *Piston ring removal/installation tool*
- ☐ *Cylinder bore hone*
- ☐ *Balljoint separator*
- ☐ *Coil spring compressors (where applicable)*
- ☐ *Two/three-legged hub and bearing puller*
- ☐ *Impact screwdriver*
- ☐ *Micrometer and/or vernier calipers*
- ☐ *Dial gauge*
- ☐ *Stroboscopic timing light*
- ☐ *Dwell angle meter/tachometer*
- ☐ *Fault code reader*
- ☐ *Cylinder compression gauge*
- ☐ *Hand-operated vacuum pump and gauge*
- ☐ *Clutch plate alignment set*
- ☐ *Brake shoe steady spring cup removal tool*
- ☐ *Bush and bearing removal/installation set*
- ☐ *Stud extractors*
- ☐ *Tap and die set*
- ☐ *Lifting tackle*
- ☐ *Trolley jack*

Buying tools

Reputable motor accessory shops and superstores often offer excellent quality tools at discount prices, so it pays to shop around.

Remember, you don't have to buy the most expensive items on the shelf, but it is always advisable to steer clear of the very cheap tools. Beware of 'bargains' offered on market stalls or at car boot sales. There are plenty of good tools around at reasonable prices, but always aim to purchase items which meet the relevant national safety standards. If in doubt, ask the proprietor or manager of the shop for advice before making a purchase.

Care and maintenance of tools

Having purchased a reasonable tool kit, it is necessary to keep the tools in a clean and serviceable condition. After use, always wipe off any dirt, grease and metal particles using a clean, dry cloth, before putting the tools away. Never leave them lying around after they have been used. A simple tool rack on the garage or workshop wall for items such as screwdrivers and pliers is a good idea. Store all normal spanners and sockets in a metal box. Any measuring instruments, gauges, meters, etc, must be carefully stored where they cannot be damaged or become rusty.

Take a little care when tools are used. Hammer heads inevitably become marked, and screwdrivers lose the keen edge on their blades from time to time. A little timely attention with emery cloth or a file will soon restore items like this to a good finish.

Working facilities

Not to be forgotten when discussing tools is the workshop itself. If anything more than routine maintenance is to be carried out, a suitable working area becomes essential.

It is appreciated that many an owner-mechanic is forced by circumstances to remove an engine or similar item without the benefit of a garage or workshop. Having done this, any repairs should always be done under the cover of a roof.

Wherever possible, any dismantling should be done on a clean, flat workbench or table at a suitable working height.

Any workbench needs a vice; one with a jaw opening of 100 mm is suitable for most jobs. As mentioned previously, some clean dry storage space is also required for tools, as well as for any lubricants, cleaning fluids, touch-up paints etc, which become necessary.

Another item which may be required, and which has a much more general usage, is an electric drill with a chuck capacity of at least 8 mm. This, together with a good range of twist drills, is virtually essential for fitting accessories.

Last, but not least, always keep a supply of old newspapers and clean, lint-free rags available, and try to keep any working area as clean as possible.

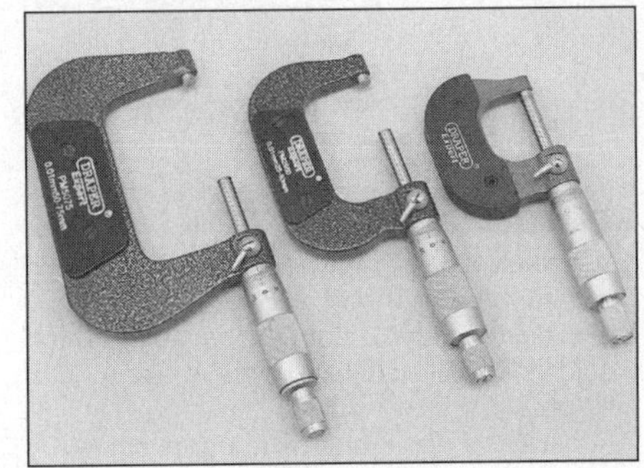

Micrometers

Dial test indicator ("dial gauge")

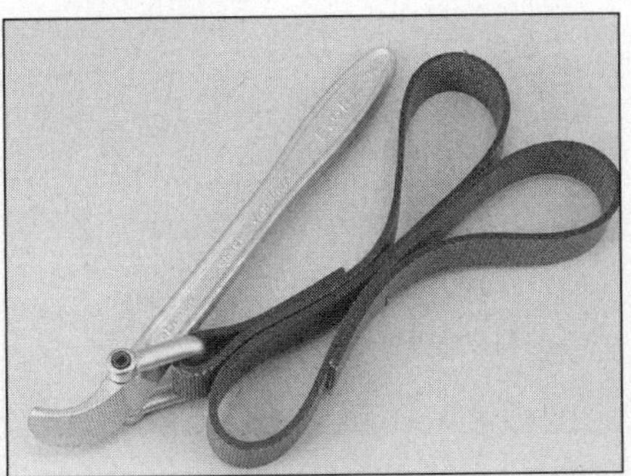

Strap wrench

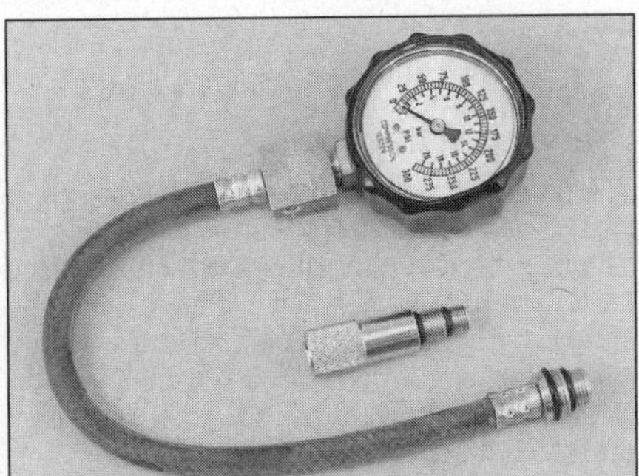

Compression tester

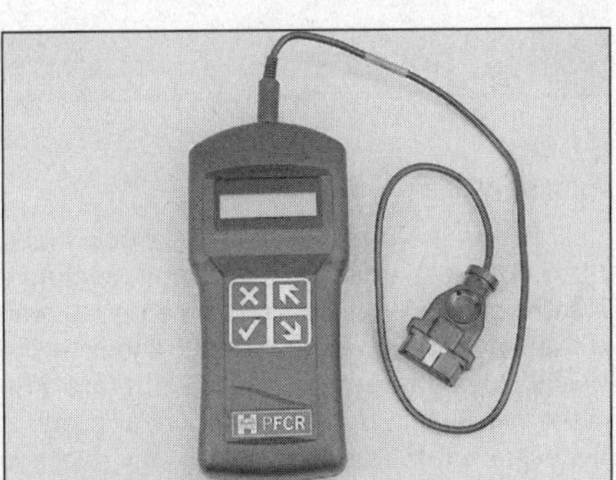

Fault code reader

MOT test checks

This is a guide to getting your vehicle through the MOT test. Obviously it will not be possible to examine the vehicle to the same standard as the professional MOT tester. However, working through the following checks will enable you to identify any problem areas before submitting the vehicle for the test.

It has only been possible to summarise the test requirements here, based on the regulations in force at the time of printing. Test standards are becoming increasingly stringent, although there are some exemptions for older vehicles.

An assistant will be needed to help carry out some of these checks.

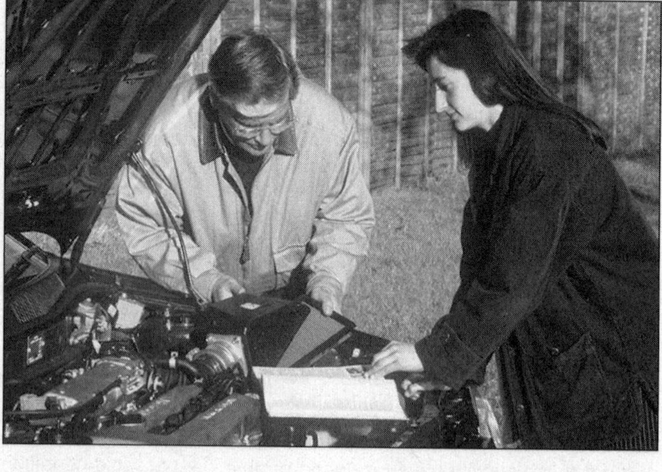

The checks have been sub-divided into four categories, as follows:

1 Checks carried out **FROM THE DRIVER'S SEAT**

2 Checks carried out **WITH THE VEHICLE ON THE GROUND**

3 Checks carried out **WITH THE VEHICLE RAISED AND THE WHEELS FREE TO TURN**

4 Checks carried out on **YOUR VEHICLE'S EXHAUST EMISSION SYSTEM**

1 Checks carried out FROM THE DRIVER'S SEAT

Handbrake

☐ Test the operation of the handbrake. Excessive travel (too many clicks) indicates incorrect brake or cable adjustment.

☐ Check that the handbrake cannot be released by tapping the lever sideways. Check the security of the lever mountings.

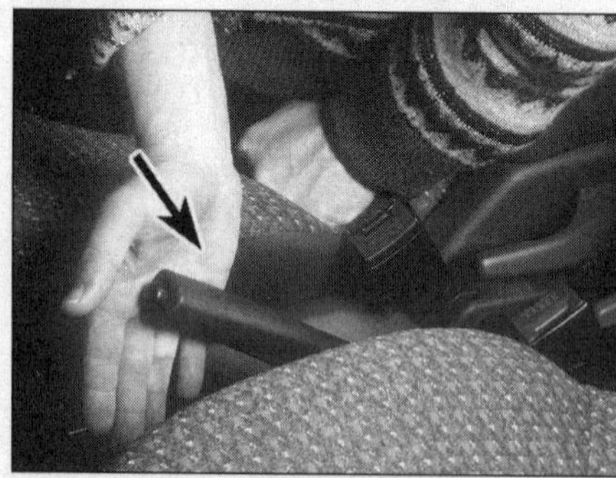

Footbrake

☐ Depress the brake pedal and check that it does not creep down to the floor, indicating a master cylinder fault. Release the pedal, wait a few seconds, then depress it again. If the pedal travels nearly to the floor before firm resistance is felt, brake adjustment or repair is necessary. If the pedal feels spongy, there is air in the hydraulic system which must be removed by bleeding.

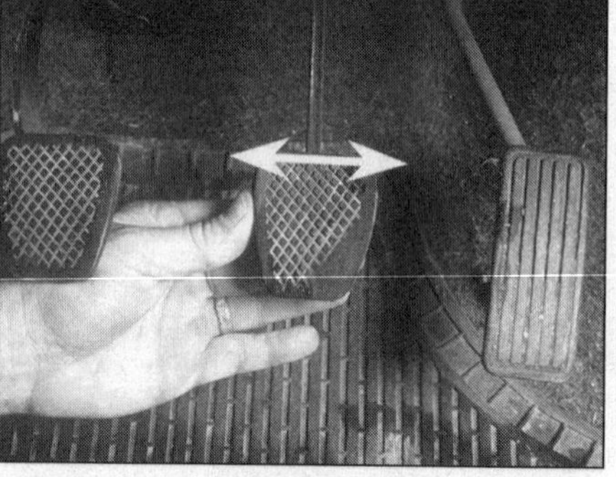

☐ Check that the brake pedal is secure and in good condition. Check also for signs of fluid leaks on the pedal, floor or carpets, which would indicate failed seals in the brake master cylinder.

☐ Check the servo unit (when applicable) by operating the brake pedal several times, then keeping the pedal depressed and starting the engine. As the engine starts, the pedal will move down slightly. If not, the vacuum hose or the servo itself may be faulty.

Steering wheel and column

☐ Examine the steering wheel for fractures or looseness of the hub, spokes or rim.

☐ Move the steering wheel from side to side and then up and down. Check that the steering wheel is not loose on the column, indicating wear or a loose retaining nut. Continue moving the steering wheel as before, but also turn it slightly from left to right.

☐ Check that the steering wheel is not loose on the column, and that there is no abnormal

movement of the steering wheel, indicating wear in the column support bearings or couplings.

Windscreen, mirrors and sunvisor

☐ The windscreen must be free of cracks or other significant damage within the driver's field of view. (Small stone chips are acceptable.) Rear view mirrors must be secure, intact, and capable of being adjusted.

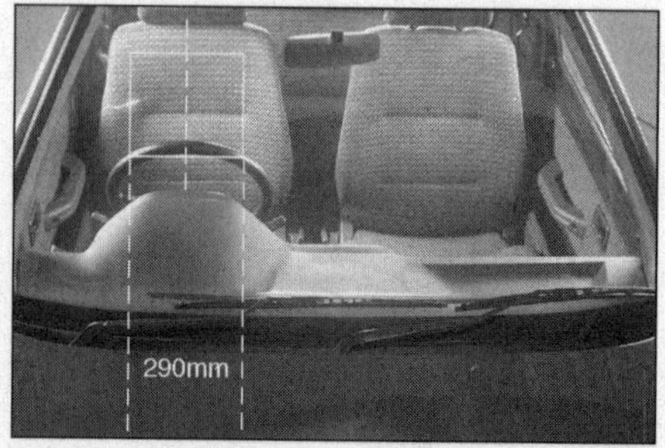

☐ The driver's sunvisor must be capable of being stored in the "up" position.

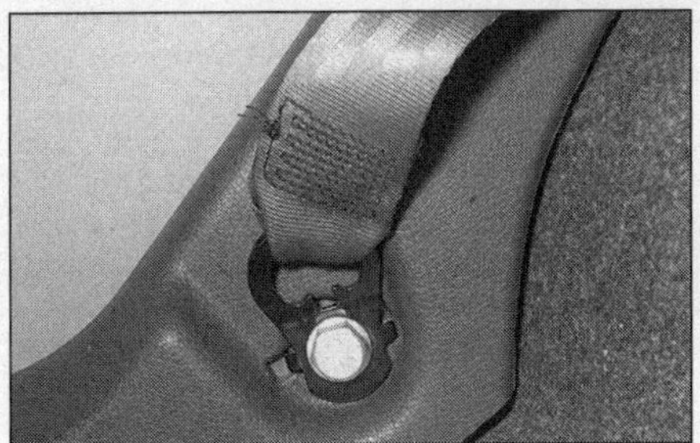

Seat belts and seats

Note: *The following checks are applicable to all seat belts, front and rear.*

☐ Examine the webbing of all the belts (including rear belts if fitted) for cuts, serious fraying or deterioration. Fasten and unfasten each belt to check the buckles. If applicable, check the retracting mechanism. Check the security of all seat belt mountings accessible from inside the vehicle.

☐ Seat belts with pre-tensioners, once activated, have a "flag" or similar showing on the seat belt stalk. This, in itself, is not a reason for test failure.

☐ The front seats themselves must be securely attached and the backrests must lock in the upright position.

Doors

☐ Both front doors must be able to be opened and closed from outside and inside, and must latch securely when closed.

2 Checks carried out WITH THE VEHICLE ON THE GROUND

Vehicle identification

☐ Number plates must be in good condition, secure and legible, with letters and numbers correctly spaced – spacing at (A) should be at least twice that at (B).

☐ The VIN plate and/or homologation plate must be legible.

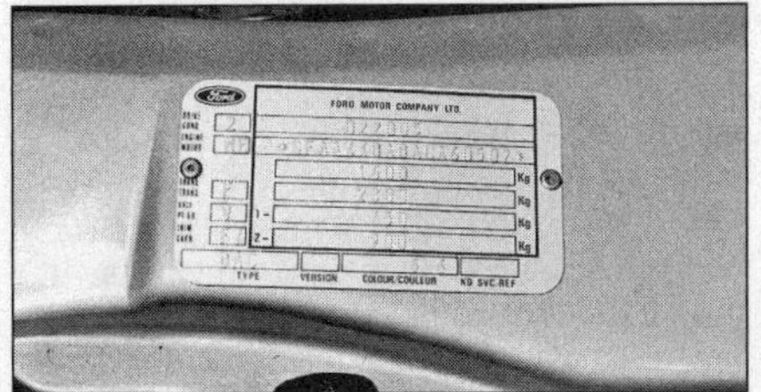

Electrical equipment

☐ Switch on the ignition and check the operation of the horn.

☐ Check the windscreen washers and wipers, examining the wiper blades; renew damaged or perished blades. Also check the operation of the stop-lights.

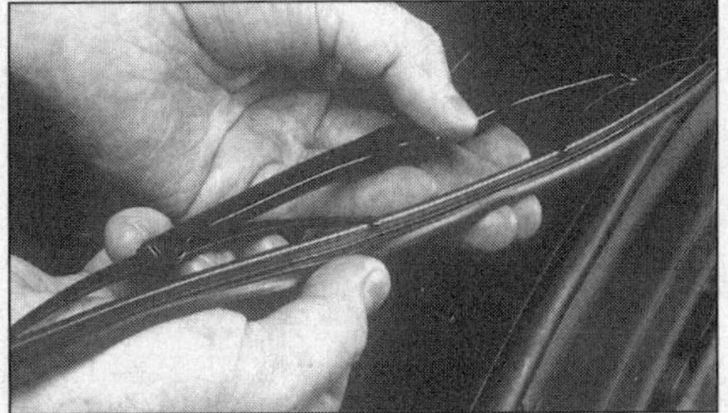

☐ Check the operation of the sidelights and number plate lights. The lenses and reflectors must be secure, clean and undamaged.

☐ Check the operation and alignment of the headlights. The headlight reflectors must not be tarnished and the lenses must be undamaged.

☐ Switch on the ignition and check the operation of the direction indicators (including the instrument panel tell-tale) and the hazard warning lights. Operation of the sidelights and stop-lights must not affect the indicators - if it does, the cause is usually a bad earth at the rear light cluster.

☐ Check the operation of the rear foglight(s), including the warning light on the instrument panel or in the switch.

☐ The ABS warning light must illuminate in accordance with the manufacturers' design. For most vehicles, the ABS warning light should illuminate when the ignition is switched on, and (if the system is operating properly) extinguish after a few seconds. Refer to the owner's handbook.

Footbrake

☐ Examine the master cylinder, brake pipes and servo unit for leaks, loose mountings, corrosion or other damage.

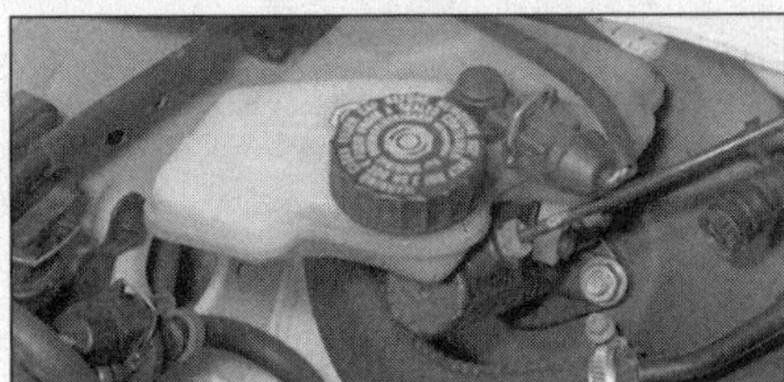

☐ The fluid reservoir must be secure and the fluid level must be between the upper (**A**) and lower (**B**) markings.

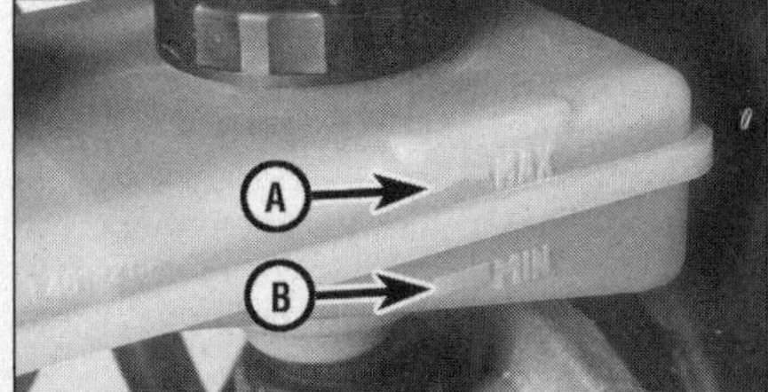

☐ Inspect both front brake flexible hoses for cracks or deterioration of the rubber. Turn the steering from lock to lock, and ensure that the hoses do not contact the wheel, tyre, or any part of the steering or suspension mechanism. With the brake pedal firmly depressed, check the hoses for bulges or leaks under pressure.

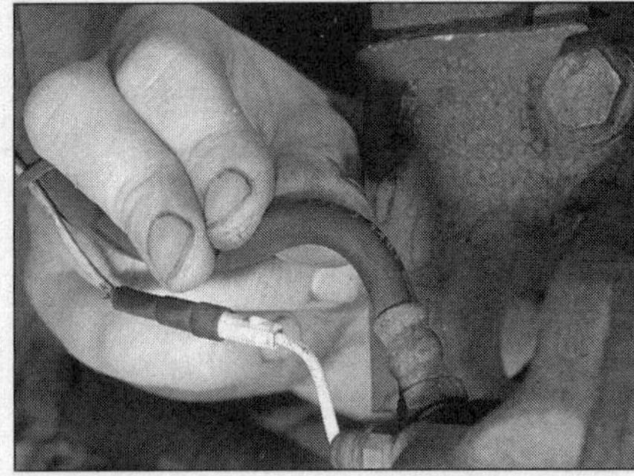

Steering and suspension

☐ Have your assistant turn the steering wheel from side to side slightly, up to the point where the steering gear just begins to transmit this movement to the roadwheels. Check for excessive free play between the steering wheel and the steering gear, indicating wear or insecurity of the steering column joints, the column-to-steering gear coupling, or the steering gear itself.

☐ Have your assistant turn the steering wheel more vigorously in each direction, so that the roadwheels just begin to turn. As this is done, examine all the steering joints, linkages, fittings and attachments. Renew any component that shows signs of wear or damage. On vehicles with power steering, check the security and condition of the steering pump, drivebelt and hoses.

☐ Check that the vehicle is standing level, and at approximately the correct ride height.

Shock absorbers

☐ Depress each corner of the vehicle in turn, then release it. The vehicle should rise and then settle in its normal position. If the vehicle continues to rise and fall, the shock absorber is defective. A shock absorber which has seized will also cause the vehicle to fail.

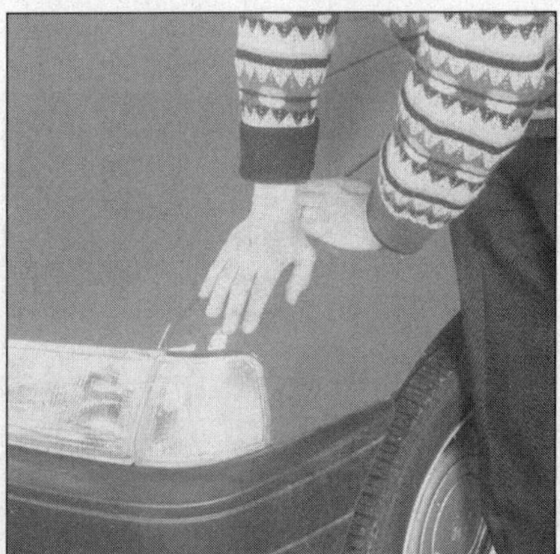

Exhaust system

☐ Start the engine. With your assistant holding a rag over the tailpipe, check the entire system for leaks. Repair or renew leaking sections.

3 Checks carried out WITH THE VEHICLE RAISED AND THE WHEELS FREE TO TURN

Jack up the front and rear of the vehicle, and securely support it on axle stands. Position the stands clear of the suspension assemblies. Ensure that the wheels are clear of the ground and that the steering can be turned from lock to lock.

Steering mechanism

☐ Have your assistant turn the steering from lock to lock. Check that the steering turns smoothly, and that no part of the steering mechanism, including a wheel or tyre, fouls any brake hose or pipe or any part of the body structure.

☐ Examine the steering rack rubber gaiters for damage or insecurity of the retaining clips. If power steering is fitted, check for signs of damage or leakage of the fluid hoses, pipes or connections. Also check for excessive stiffness or binding of the steering, a missing split pin or locking device, or severe corrosion of the body structure within 30 cm of any steering component attachment point.

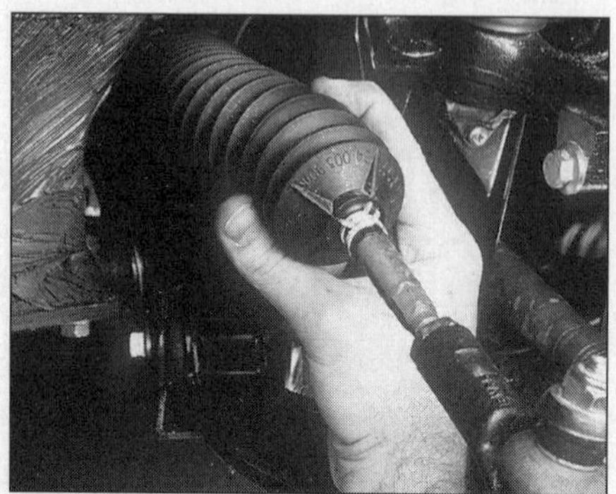

Front and rear suspension and wheel bearings

☐ Starting at the front right-hand side, grasp the roadwheel at the 3 o'clock and 9 o'clock positions and rock gently but firmly. Check for free play or insecurity at the wheel bearings, suspension balljoints, or suspension mountings, pivots and attachments.

☐ Now grasp the wheel at the 12 o'clock and 6 o'clock positions and repeat the previous inspection. Spin the wheel, and check for roughness or tightness of the front wheel bearing.

☐ If excess free play is suspected at a component pivot point, this can be confirmed by using a large screwdriver or similar tool and levering between the mounting and the component attachment. This will confirm whether the wear is in the pivot bush, its retaining bolt, or in the mounting itself (the bolt holes can often become elongated).

☐ Carry out all the above checks at the other front wheel, and then at both rear wheels.

Springs and shock absorbers

☐ Examine the suspension struts (when applicable) for serious fluid leakage, corrosion, or damage to the casing. Also check the security of the mounting points.

☐ If coil springs are fitted, check that the spring ends locate in their seats, and that the spring is not corroded, cracked or broken.

☐ If leaf springs are fitted, check that all leaves are intact, that the axle is securely attached to each spring, and that there is no deterioration of the spring eye mountings, bushes, and shackles.

☐ The same general checks apply to vehicles fitted with other suspension types, such as torsion bars, hydraulic displacer units, etc. Ensure that all mountings and attachments are secure, that there are no signs of excessive wear, corrosion or damage, and (on hydraulic types) that there are no fluid leaks or damaged pipes.

☐ Inspect the shock absorbers for signs of serious fluid leakage. Check for wear of the mounting bushes or attachments, or damage to the body of the unit.

Driveshafts (fwd vehicles only)

☐ Rotate each front wheel in turn and inspect the constant velocity joint gaiters for splits or damage. Also check that each driveshaft is straight and undamaged.

Braking system

☐ If possible without dismantling, check brake pad wear and disc condition. Ensure that the friction lining material has not worn excessively, (A) and that the discs are not fractured, pitted, scored or badly worn (B).

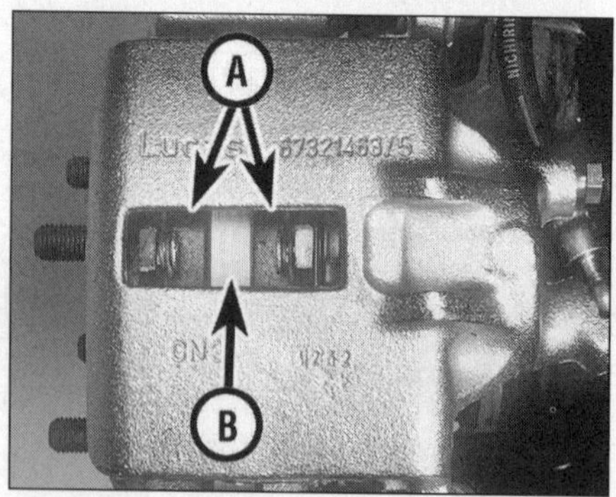

☐ Examine all the rigid brake pipes underneath the vehicle, and the flexible hose(s) at the rear. Look for corrosion, chafing or insecurity of the pipes, and for signs of bulging under pressure, chafing, splits or deterioration of the flexible hoses.

☐ Look for signs of fluid leaks at the brake calipers or on the brake backplates. Repair or renew leaking components.

☐ Slowly spin each wheel, while your assistant depresses and releases the footbrake. Ensure that each brake is operating and does not bind when the pedal is released.

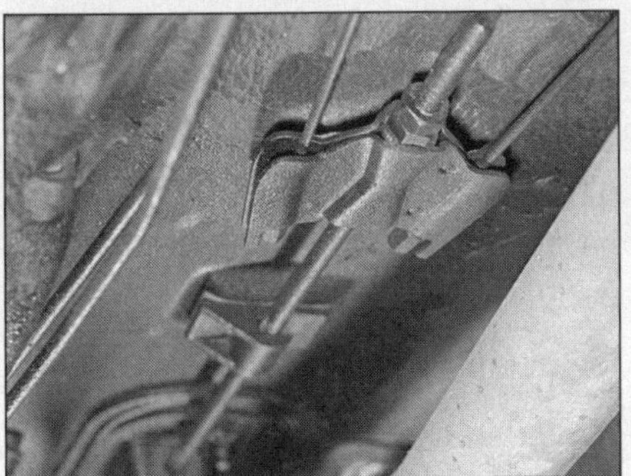

☐ Examine the handbrake mechanism, checking for frayed or broken cables, excessive corrosion, or wear or insecurity of the linkage. Check that the mechanism works on each relevant wheel, and releases fully, without binding.

☐ It is not possible to test brake efficiency without special equipment, but a road test can be carried out later to check that the vehicle pulls up in a straight line.

Fuel and exhaust systems

☐ Inspect the fuel tank (including the filler cap), fuel pipes, hoses and unions. All components must be secure and free from leaks.

☐ Examine the exhaust system over its entire length, checking for any damaged, broken or missing mountings, security of the retaining clamps and rust or corrosion.

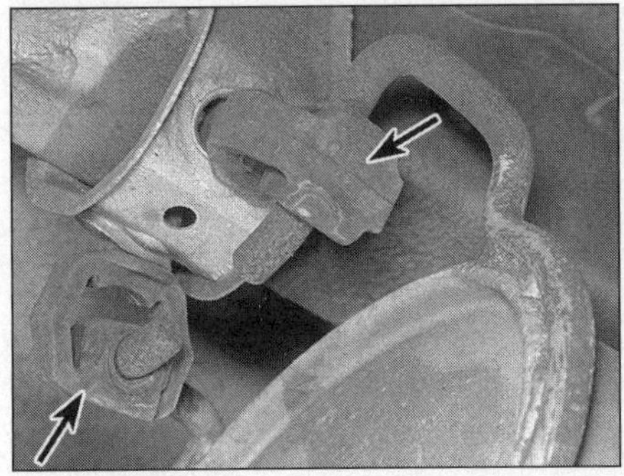

Wheels and tyres

☐ Examine the sidewalls and tread area of each tyre in turn. Check for cuts, tears, lumps, bulges, separation of the tread, and exposure of the ply or cord due to wear or damage. Check that the tyre bead is correctly seated on the wheel rim, that the valve is sound and properly seated, and that the wheel is not distorted or damaged.

☐ Check that the tyres are of the correct size for the vehicle, that they are of the same size and type on each axle, and that the pressures are correct.

☐ Check the tyre tread depth. The legal minimum at the time of writing is 1.6 mm over at least three-quarters of the tread width. Abnormal tread wear may indicate incorrect front wheel alignment.

Body corrosion

☐ Check the condition of the entire vehicle structure for signs of corrosion in load-bearing areas. (These include chassis box sections, side sills, cross-members, pillars, and all suspension, steering, braking system and seat belt mountings and anchorages.) Any corrosion which has seriously reduced the thickness of a load-bearing area is likely to cause the vehicle to fail. In this case professional repairs are likely to be needed.

☐ Damage or corrosion which causes sharp or otherwise dangerous edges to be exposed will also cause the vehicle to fail.

4 Checks carried out on YOUR VEHICLE'S EXHAUST EMISSION SYSTEM

Petrol models

☐ The engine should be warmed up, and running well (ignition system in good order, air filter element clean, etc).

☐ Before testing, run the engine at around 2500 rpm for 20 seconds. Let the engine drop to idle, and watch for smoke from the exhaust. If the idle speed is too high, or if dense blue or black smoke emerges for more than 5 seconds, the vehicle will fail. Typically, blue smoke signifies oil burning (engine wear); black smoke means unburnt fuel (dirty air cleaner element, or other fuel system fault).

☐ An exhaust gas analyser for measuring carbon monoxide (CO) and hydrocarbons (HC) is now needed. If one cannot be hired or borrowed, have a local garage perform the check.

CO emissions (mixture)

☐ The MOT tester has access to the CO limits for all vehicles. The CO level is measured at idle speed, and at 'fast idle' (2500 to 3000 rpm). The following limits are given as a general guide:

At idle speed – Less than 0.5% CO
At 'fast idle' – Less than 0.3% CO
Lambda reading – 0.97 to 1.03

☐ If the CO level is too high, this may point to poor maintenance, a fuel injection system problem, faulty lambda (oxygen) sensor or catalytic converter. Try an injector cleaning treatment, and check the vehicle's ECU for fault codes.

HC emissions

☐ The MOT tester has access to HC limits for all vehicles. The HC level is measured at 'fast idle' (2500 to 3000 rpm). The following limits are given as a general guide:

At 'fast idle' – Less then 200 ppm

☐ Excessive HC emissions are typically caused by oil being burnt (worn engine), or by a blocked crankcase ventilation system ('breather'). If the engine oil is old and thin, an oil change may help. If the engine is running badly, check the vehicle's ECU for fault codes.

Diesel models

☐ The only emission test for diesel engines is measuring exhaust smoke density, using a calibrated smoke meter. The test involves accelerating the engine at least 3 times to its maximum unloaded speed.

Note: *On engines with a timing belt, it is VITAL that the belt is in good condition before the test is carried out.*

☐ With the engine warmed up, it is first purged by running at around 2500 rpm for 20 seconds. A governor check is then carried out, by slowly accelerating the engine to its maximum speed. After this, the smoke meter is connected, and the engine is accelerated quickly to maximum speed three times. If the smoke density is less than the limits given below, the vehicle will pass:

Non-turbo vehicles: 2.5m-1
Turbocharged vehicles: 3.0m-1

☐ If excess smoke is produced, try fitting a new air cleaner element, or using an injector cleaning treatment. If the engine is running badly, where applicable, check the vehicle's ECU for fault codes. Also check the vehicle's EGR system, where applicable. At high mileages, the injectors may require professional attention.

Engine

- ☐ Engine fails to rotate when attempting to start
- ☐ Engine rotates, but will not start
- ☐ Engine difficult to start when cold
- ☐ Engine difficult to start when hot
- ☐ Starter motor noisy or excessively-rough in engagement
- ☐ Engine starts, but stops immediately
- ☐ Engine idles erratically
- ☐ Engine misfires at idle speed
- ☐ Engine misfires throughout the driving speed range
- ☐ Engine hesitates on acceleration
- ☐ Engine stalls
- ☐ Engine lacks power
- ☐ Engine backfires
- ☐ Oil pressure warning light on with engine running
- ☐ Engine runs-on after switching off
- ☐ Engine noises

Cooling system

- ☐ Overheating
- ☐ Overcooling
- ☐ External coolant leakage
- ☐ Internal coolant leakage
- ☐ Corrosion

Fuel and exhaust systems

- ☐ Excessive fuel consumption
- ☐ Fuel leakage and/or fuel odour
- ☐ Excessive noise or fumes from exhaust system

Clutch

- ☐ Pedal travels to floor – no pressure or very little resistance
- ☐ Clutch fails to disengage (unable to select gears)
- ☐ Clutch slips (engine speed rises, with no increase in vehicle speed)
- ☐ Judder as clutch is engaged
- ☐ Noise when depressing or releasing clutch pedal

Manual gearbox

- ☐ Noisy in neutral with engine running
- ☐ Noisy in one particular gear
- ☐ Difficulty engaging gears
- ☐ Jumps out of gear
- ☐ Vibration
- ☐ Lubricant leaks

Automatic transmission

- ☐ Fluid leakage
- ☐ General gear selection problems
- ☐ Transmission will not downshift (kickdown) with accelerator pedal fully depressed
- ☐ Engine will not start in any gear, or starts in gears other than Park or Neutral
- ☐ Transmission slips, shifts roughly, is noisy, or has no drive in forward or reverse gears

Transfer case

- ☐ Fluid leakage
- ☐ Noisy operation

Final drive

- ☐ Fluid leakage
- ☐ Noisy operation

Driveshafts and propeller shaft

- ☐ Vibration when accelerating or decelerating
- ☐ Clicking or knocking noise on turns (at slow speed on full-lock)

Braking system

- ☐ Vehicle pulls to one side under braking
- ☐ Noise (grinding or high-pitched squeal) when brakes applied
- ☐ Excessive brake pedal travel
- ☐ Brake pedal feels spongy when depressed
- ☐ Excessive brake pedal effort required to stop vehicle
- ☐ Judder felt through brake pedal or steering wheel when braking
- ☐ Brakes binding
- ☐ Rear wheels locking under normal braking

Suspension and steering systems

- ☐ Vehicle pulls to one side
- ☐ Wheel wobble and vibration
- ☐ Excessive pitching and/or rolling around corners, or during braking
- ☐ Wandering or general instability
- ☐ Excessively-stiff steering
- ☐ Excessive play in steering
- ☐ Lack of power assistance
- ☐ Tyre wear excessive

Electrical system

- ☐ Battery will not hold a charge for more than a few days
- ☐ Ignition/no-charge warning light stays on with engine running
- ☐ Ignition/no-charge warning light fails to come on
- ☐ Lights inoperative
- ☐ Instrument readings inaccurate or erratic
- ☐ Horn inoperative, or unsatisfactory in operation
- ☐ Windscreen/tailgate wipers failed, or unsatisfactory in operation
- ☐ Windscreen/tailgate washers failed, or unsatisfactory in operation
- ☐ Electric windows inoperative, or unsatisfactory in operation
- ☐ Central locking system inoperative, or unsatisfactory in operation

Introduction

The vehicle owner who does his or her own maintenance according to the recommended service schedules should not have to use this section of the manual very often. Modern component reliability is such that, provided those items subject to wear or deterioration are inspected or renewed at the specified intervals, sudden failure is comparatively rare. Faults do not usually just happen as a result of sudden failure, but develop over a period of time. Major mechanical failures in particular are usually preceded by characteristic symptoms over hundreds or even thousands of miles. Those components which do occasionally fail without warning are often small and easily carried in the vehicle.

With any fault-finding, the first step is to decide where to begin investigations. This may be obvious, but some detective work may be necessary. The owner who makes half a dozen haphazard adjustments or replacements may be successful in curing a fault (or its symptoms), but will be none the wiser if the fault recurs, and ultimately may have spent more time and money than was necessary. A calm and logical approach will be found to be more satisfactory in the long run. Always take into account any warning signs that may have been noticed in the period preceding the fault – power loss, high or low gauge readings, unusual smells, etc – and remember – failure of components such as fuses or spark plugs may only be pointers to some underlying fault.

The pages which follow provide an easy-reference guide to the more common problems which may occur during the operation of the vehicle. These problems and their possible causes are grouped under headings denoting various components or systems, such as Engine, Cooling system, etc. The general Chapter which deals with the problem is also shown in brackets; refer to the relevant part of that Chapter for system-specific information. Whatever the fault, certain basic principles apply. These are as follows:

• *Verify the fault*. This is simply a matter of being sure that you know what the symptoms are before starting work. This is particularly important if you are investigating a fault for someone else, who may not have described it very accurately.

• *Don't overlook the obvious*. For example, if the vehicle won't start, is there fuel in the tank? (Don't take anyone else's word on this particular point, and don't trust the fuel gauge either!) If an electrical fault is indicated, look for loose or broken wires before digging out the test gear.

• *Cure the disease, not the symptom*. Substituting a flat battery with a fully-charged one will get you off the hard shoulder, but if the underlying cause is not attended to, the new battery will go the same way. Similarly, changing oil-fouled spark plugs for a new set will get you moving again, but remember that the reason for the fouling (if it wasn't simply an incorrect grade of plug) will have to be established and corrected.

• *Don't take anything for granted*. Particularly, don't forget that a 'new' component may itself be defective (especially if it has been rattling around in the boot for months), and don't leave components out of a fault diagnosis sequence just because they are new or recently-fitted. When you do finally diagnose a difficult fault, you'll probably realise that all the evidence was there from the start.

Diesel fault diagnosis

The majority of starting problems on small diesel engines are electrical in origin. The mechanic who is familiar with petrol engines but less so with diesel may be inclined to view the diesel's injectors and pump in the same light as the spark plugs and distributor, but this is generally a mistake.

When investigating complaints of difficult starting for someone else, make sure that the correct starting procedure is understood and is being followed. Some drivers are unaware of the significance of the preheating warning light – many modern engines are sufficiently forgiving for this not to matter in mild weather, but with the onset of winter, problems begin.

As a rule of thumb, if the engine is difficult to start but runs well when it has finally got going, the problem is electrical (battery, starter motor or preheating system). If poor performance is combined with difficult starting, the problem is likely to be in the fuel system. The low-pressure (supply) side of the fuel system should be checked before suspecting the injectors and high-pressure pump. The most common fuel supply problem is air getting into the system, and any pipe from the fuel tank forwards must be scrutinised if air leakage is suspected. Normally the pump is the last item to suspect, since unless it has been tampered with, there is no reason for it to be at fault.

Engine

Engine fails to rotate when attempting to start

☐ Battery terminal connections loose or corroded (*Weekly checks*).
☐ Battery discharged or faulty (Chapter 5).
☐ Broken, loose or disconnected wiring in the starting circuit (Chapter 5).
☐ Defective starter solenoid (Chapter 5).
☐ Defective starter motor (Chapter 5).
☐ Starter pinion or flywheel ring gear teeth loose or broken (Chapters 2 and 5).
☐ Engine earth strap broken or disconnected.

Engine rotates, but will not start

☐ Fuel tank empty.
☐ Battery discharged (engine rotates slowly) (Chapter 5).
☐ Battery terminal connections loose or corroded (*Weekly checks*).
☐ Broken, loose or disconnected wiring in the ignition circuit – petrol-engined models (Chapters 1 and 5).
☐ Worn, faulty or incorrectly-gapped spark plugs – petrol-engined models (Chapter 1).
☐ Preheating system faulty – diesel-engined models (Chapter 5).
☐ Fuel injection or engine management system fault (Chapter 4).
☐ Ignition key not recognised by anti-theft system (Chapter 12)
☐ Major mechanical failure (e.g. camshaft drive) (Chapter 2).

Engine difficult to start when cold

☐ Battery discharged (Chapter 5).
☐ Battery terminal connections loose or corroded (*Weekly checks*).
☐ Worn, faulty or incorrectly-gapped spark plugs – petrol-engined models (Chapter 1).
☐ Preheating system faulty – diesel-engined models (Chapter 5).
☐ Fuel injection or engine management system fault (Chapter 4).
☐ Other ignition system fault – petrol-engined models (Chapters 1 and 5).
☐ Low cylinder compressions (Chapter 2).

Engine difficult to start when hot

☐ Air filter element dirty or clogged (Chapter 1).
☐ Fuel injection or engine management system fault (Chapter 4).
☐ Low cylinder compressions (Chapter 2).

Starter motor noisy or excessively-rough in engagement

☐ Starter pinion or flywheel ring gear teeth loose or broken (Chapters 2 and 5).
☐ Starter motor mounting bolts loose or missing (Chapter 5).
☐ Starter motor internal components worn or damaged (Chapter 5).

Engine starts, but stops immediately

☐ Loose or faulty electrical connections in the ignition circuit – petrol-engined models (Chapters 1 and 5).
☐ Vacuum leak at the throttle housing or intake manifold – petrol-engined models (Chapter 4).
☐ Blocked injector/fuel injection system fault – petrol-engined models (Chapter 4).

Engine idles erratically

☐ Air filter element clogged (Chapter 1).
☐ Vacuum leak at the throttle housing, intake manifold or associated hoses – petrol-engined models (Chapter 4).
☐ Worn, faulty or incorrectly-gapped spark plugs – petrol-engined models (Chapter 1).
☐ Uneven or low cylinder compressions (Chapter 2).
☐ Camshaft lobes worn (Chapter 2).
☐ Timing belt incorrectly fitted (Chapter 2).
☐ Blocked injector/fuel injection system fault (Chapter 4).

Engine misfires at idle speed

☐ Worn, faulty or incorrectly-gapped spark plugs – petrol-engined models (Chapter 1).
☐ Vacuum leak at the throttle housing, intake manifold or associated hoses – petrol-engined models (Chapter 4).
☐ Blocked injector/fuel injection system fault (Chapter 4).
☐ Uneven or low cylinder compressions (Chapter 2).
☐ Disconnected, leaking, or perished crankcase ventilation hoses (Chapter 4).

Engine (continued)

Engine misfires throughout the driving speed range

- ☐ Fuel filter choked (Chapter 1).
- ☐ Fuel pump faulty, or delivery pressure low (Chapter 4).
- ☐ Fuel tank vent blocked, or fuel pipes restricted (Chapter 4).
- ☐ Vacuum leak at the throttle housing, intake manifold or associated hoses – petrol-engined models (Chapter 4).
- ☐ Worn, faulty or incorrectly-gapped spark plugs – petrol-engined models (Chapter 1).
- ☐ Faulty ignition coil unit – petrol-engined models (Chapter 5).
- ☐ Uneven or low cylinder compressions (Chapter 2).
- ☐ Blocked injector/fuel injection system fault (Chapter 4).

Engine hesitates on acceleration

- ☐ Worn, faulty or incorrectly-gapped spark plugs – petrol-engined models (Chapter 1).
- ☐ Vacuum leak at the throttle housing, intake manifold or associated hoses – petrol-engined models (Chapter 4).
- ☐ Blocked injector/fuel injection system fault (Chapter 4).

Engine stalls

- ☐ Vacuum leak at the throttle housing, intake manifold or associated hoses – petrol-engined models (Chapter 4).
- ☐ Fuel filter choked (Chapter 1).
- ☐ Fuel pump faulty, or delivery pressure low – petrol-engined models (Chapter 4).
- ☐ Fuel tank vent blocked, or fuel pipes restricted (Chapter 4).
- ☐ Blocked injector/fuel injection system fault (Chapter 4).

Engine lacks power

- ☐ Timing belt incorrectly fitted or adjusted (Chapter 2).
- ☐ Fuel filter choked (Chapter 1).
- ☐ Fuel pump faulty, or delivery pressure low (Chapter 4).
- ☐ Uneven or low cylinder compressions (Chapter 2).
- ☐ Worn, faulty or incorrectly-gapped spark plugs – petrol-engined models (Chapter 1).
- ☐ Vacuum leak at the throttle housing, intake manifold or associated hoses – petrol-engined models (Chapter 4).
- ☐ Blocked injector/fuel injection system fault (Chapter 4).
- ☐ Brakes binding (Chapters 1 and 9).
- ☐ Clutch slipping (Chapter 6).

Engine backfires

- ☐ Timing belt incorrectly fitted or adjusted (Chapter 2).
- ☐ Vacuum leak at the throttle housing, intake manifold or associated hoses – petrol-engined models (Chapter 4).
- ☐ Blocked injector/fuel injection system fault (Chapter 4).

Oil pressure warning light on with engine running

- ☐ Low oil level, or incorrect oil grade (*Weekly checks*).
- ☐ Faulty oil pressure warning light switch (Chapter 5).
- ☐ Worn engine bearings and/or oil pump (Chapter 2).
- ☐ High engine operating temperature (Chapter 3).
- ☐ Oil pressure relief valve defective (Chapter 2).
- ☐ Oil pick-up strainer clogged (Chapter 2).

Engine runs-on after switching off

- ☐ Excessive carbon build-up in engine (Chapter 2).
- ☐ High engine operating temperature (Chapter 3).
- ☐ Fuel injection or engine management system fault (Chapter 4).

Engine noises

Pre-ignition (pinking) or knocking during acceleration or under load

- ☐ Ignition or engine management system fault (Chapters 1 and 5).
- ☐ Incorrect grade of spark plug – petrol-engined models (Chapter 1).
- ☐ Incorrect grade of fuel (Chapter 1).
- ☐ Vacuum leak at the throttle housing, intake manifold or associated hoses – petrol-engined models (Chapter 4).
- ☐ Excessive carbon build-up in engine (Chapter 2).
- ☐ Blocked injector/fuel injection system fault (Chapter 4).

Whistling or wheezing noises

- ☐ Leaking intake manifold or throttle housing gasket – petrol-engined models (Chapter 4).
- ☐ Leaking exhaust manifold gasket or pipe-to-manifold joint (Chapter 4).
- ☐ Leaking vacuum hose (Chapters 4, 5 and 9).
- ☐ Blowing cylinder head gasket (Chapter 2).

Tapping or rattling noises

- ☐ Worn valve gear or camshaft (Chapter 2).
- ☐ Faulty or damaged dual-mass flywheel – diesel-engined models (Chapter 2).
- ☐ Ancillary component fault (coolant pump, alternator, etc) (Chapters 3, 5, etc).

Knocking or thumping noises

- ☐ Worn big-end bearings (regular heavy knocking, perhaps less under load) (Chapter 2).
- ☐ Worn main bearings (rumbling and knocking, perhaps worsening under load) (Chapter 2).
- ☐ Piston slap (most noticeable when cold) (Chapter 2).
- ☐ Faulty or damaged dual-mass flywheel – diesel-engined models (Chapter 2).
- ☐ Ancillary component fault (coolant pump, alternator, etc) (Chapters 3, 5, etc).

Cooling system

Overheating

- ☐ Insufficient coolant in system (*Weekly checks*).
- ☐ Thermostat faulty (Chapter 3).
- ☐ Radiator core blocked, or grille restricted (Chapter 3).
- ☐ Electric cooling fan or thermoswitch faulty (Chapter 3).
- ☐ Pressure cap faulty (Chapter 3).
- ☐ Engine management system fault (Chapters 1 and 5).
- ☐ Inaccurate coolant temperature sensor (Chapter 3).
- ☐ Airlock in cooling system (Chapter 1).

Overcooling

- ☐ Thermostat faulty (Chapter 3).
- ☐ Inaccurate coolant temperature sensor (Chapter 3).

External coolant leakage

- ☐ Deteriorated or damaged hoses or hose clips (Chapter 1).
- ☐ Radiator core or heater matrix leaking (Chapter 3).
- ☐ Pressure cap faulty (Chapter 3).
- ☐ Coolant pump seal leaking (Chapter 3).
- ☐ Boiling due to overheating (Chapter 3).
- ☐ Core plug leaking (Chapter 2).

Internal coolant leakage

- ☐ Leaking cylinder head gasket (Chapter 2).
- ☐ Cracked cylinder head or cylinder bore (Chapter 2).

Corrosion

- ☐ Infrequent draining and flushing (Chapter 1).
- ☐ Incorrect coolant mixture or inappropriate coolant type (Chapter 1).

Fuel and exhaust systems

Excessive fuel consumption

- ☐ Air filter element dirty or clogged (Chapter 1).
- ☐ Fuel injection or engine management system fault (Chapter 4).
- ☐ Ignition system fault – petrol-engined models (Chapters 1 and 5).
- ☐ Tyres under-inflated (*Weekly checks*).
- ☐ Brakes binding (Chapters 1 and 9).

Fuel leakage and/or fuel odour

- ☐ Damaged or corroded fuel tank, pipes or connections (Chapter 4).

Excessive noise or fumes from exhaust system

- ☐ Leaking exhaust system or manifold joints (Chapters 1 and 4).
- ☐ Leaking, corroded or damaged silencers or pipe (Chapters 1 and 4).
- ☐ Broken mountings causing body or suspension contact (Chapter 1).

Clutch

Pedal travels to floor – no pressure or very little resistance

- ☐ Broken clutch cable – where applicable (Chapter 6).
- ☐ Air in clutch hydraulic system – where applicable (Chapter 6).
- ☐ Faulty clutch master or slave cylinder – where applicable (Chapter 6).
- ☐ Broken clutch release bearing or fork (Chapter 6).
- ☐ Broken diaphragm spring in clutch pressure plate (Chapter 6).

Clutch fails to disengage (unable to select gears)

- ☐ Clutch friction plate on transmission input shaft splines (Chapter 6).
- ☐ Clutch friction plate sticking to flywheel or pressure plate (Chapter 6).
- ☐ Faulty pressure plate assembly (Chapter 6).
- ☐ Clutch release mechanism worn or incorrectly assembled (Chapter 6).

Clutch slips (engine speed rises, with no increase in vehicle speed)

- ☐ Clutch friction plate linings excessively worn (Chapter 6).
- ☐ Clutch friction plate linings contaminated with oil or grease (Chapter 6).
- ☐ Faulty pressure plate or weak diaphragm spring (Chapter 6).

Judder as clutch is engaged

- ☐ Clutch friction plate linings contaminated with oil or grease (Chapter 6).
- ☐ Clutch friction plate linings excessively worn (Chapter 6).
- ☐ Clutch cable sticking or frayed – where applicable (Chapter 6).
- ☐ Faulty or distorted pressure plate or diaphragm spring (Chapter 6).
- ☐ Faulty or damaged dual-mass flywheel – diesel-engined models (Chapter 2).
- ☐ Worn or loose engine/transmission mountings (Chapter 2).
- ☐ Clutch friction plate hub or transmission input shaft splines worn (Chapter 6).

Noise when depressing or releasing clutch pedal

- ☐ Worn clutch release bearing (Chapter 6).
- ☐ Worn or dry clutch pedal bushes (Chapter 6).
- ☐ Faulty pressure plate assembly (Chapter 6).
- ☐ Pressure plate diaphragm spring broken (Chapter 6).
- ☐ Broken clutch friction plate cushioning springs (Chapter 6).
- ☐ Faulty or damaged dual-mass flywheel – diesel-engined models (Chapter 2).

Manual gearbox

Noisy in neutral with engine running

- ☐ Input shaft bearings worn (noise apparent with clutch pedal released, but not when depressed) (Chapter 7A).*
- ☐ Clutch release bearing worn (noise apparent with clutch pedal depressed, possibly less when released) (Chapter 6).
- ☐ Faulty or damaged dual-mass flywheel – diesel-engined models (Chapter 2).

Noisy in one particular gear

- ☐ Worn, damaged or chipped gear teeth (Chapter 7A).*

Difficulty engaging gears

- ☐ Clutch faulty (Chapter 6).
- ☐ Faulty or damaged dual-mass flywheel – diesel-engined models (Chapter 2).
- ☐ Worn or damaged gear linkage (Chapter 7A).
- ☐ Worn synchroniser units (Chapter 7A).*

Jumps out of gear

- ☐ Worn or damaged gear linkage (Chapter 7A).
- ☐ Worn synchroniser units (Chapter 7A).*
- ☐ Worn selector forks (Chapter 7A).*

Vibration

- ☐ Lack of oil (Chapter 1).
- ☐ Worn bearings (Chapter 7A).*

Lubricant leaks

- ☐ Leaking oil seal (Chapter 7A).
- ☐ Leaking housing joint (Chapter 7A).*
- ☐ Leaking input shaft oil seal (Chapter 7A).*

* *Although the corrective action necessary to remedy the symptoms described is beyond the scope of the home mechanic, the above information should be helpful in isolating the cause of the condition, so that the owner can communicate clearly with a professional mechanic.*

Automatic transmission

Note: *Due to the complexity of the automatic transmission, it is difficult for the home mechanic to properly diagnose and service this unit. For problems other than the following, the vehicle should be taken to a dealer service department or automatic transmission specialist. Do not be too hasty in removing the transmission if a fault is suspected, as most of the testing is carried out with the unit still fitted.*

Fluid leakage

☐ Automatic transmission fluid is usually dark in colour. Fluid leaks should not be confused with engine oil, which can easily be blown onto the transmission by airflow.

☐ To determine the source of a leak, first remove all built-up dirt and grime from the transmission housing and surrounding areas using a degreasing agent, or by steam-cleaning. Drive the vehicle at low speed, so airflow will not blow the leak far from its source. Raise and support the vehicle, and determine where the leak is coming from.

General gear selection problems

☐ Chapter 7B deals with checking and adjusting the selector cable on automatic transmissions. The following are common problems which may be caused by a poorly-adjusted cable:

a) Engine starting in gears other than Park or Neutral.
b) Indicator panel indicating a gear other than the one actually being used.
c) Vehicle moves when in Park or Neutral.
d) Poor gear shift quality or erratic gear changes.

☐ Refer to Chapter 7B for the selector cable adjustment procedure.

Transmission will not downshift (kickdown) with accelerator pedal fully depressed

☐ Low transmission fluid level (Chapter 1).
☐ Incorrect selector cable adjustment (Chapter 7B).

Engine will not start in any gear, or starts in gears other than Park or Neutral

☐ Incorrect selector cable adjustment (Chapter 7B).

Transmission slips, shifts roughly, is noisy, or has no drive in forward or reverse gears

☐ There are many probable causes for the above problems, but unless there is a very obvious reason (such as a loose or corroded wiring plug connection on or near the transmission), the vehicle should be taken to a dealer service department or automatic transmission specialist for the fault to be diagnosed. The transmission control unit incorporates a self-diagnosis facility, and any fault codes can quickly be read and interpreted by a dealer or specialist with the proper diagnostic equipment.

Transfer case

Fluid leakage

☐ Oil seal/O-ring leaking (Chapter 8).

Noisy operation

☐ Low fluid level (Chapter 1).
☐ Worn bearings/differential gears (Chapter 8).

Final drive

Fluid leakage

☐ Oil seal leaking (Chapter 8).

Noisy operation

☐ Low fluid level (Chapter 8).
☐ Worn bearings/differential gears (Chapter 8).

Note: *A moaning/groaning noise when manoeuvring on full lock can be due to premature degradation of the final drive fluid. Since, however, this may be easily misdiagnosed as a steering rack problem, it may lead to unnecessary repairs. If this is suspected, the first course of action is to renew the fluid as described in Chapter 1A or 1B, using the latest specification of Honda Dual Pump fluid which is called Dual Pump Fluid II (DPF II) fluid – seek the advice of a Honda dealer's service department if in doubt.*

HAYNES HiNT ***If investigating the cause of a problem thought to be due to a fault in the Real Time system, especially in the switching in and out of four-wheel-drive by the Dual Pump arrangement, remember that these systems have proved themselves generally reliable; any perceived fault may be due to external factors such as low fluid level, incorrect fluid or poor fluid quality, rather than to a faulty component of the system. It is essential that only the specified fluid is used in the final drive unit and that this fluid is always changed at the recommended intervals (see Chapter 1A or 1B). If this advice is not followed, the fluid pumps, valves and clutch components may cease to function correctly, so that the system cannot work properly; ultimately, expensive repairs may be required. If a fault is encountered, especially if the vehicle's service history is in any way dubious, the first step is to have the final drive unit thoroughly flushed and to refill it with the correct fluid. The same principle applies to the transfer case, even though this shares lubricant with the manual gearbox or automatic transmission.***

Driveshafts and propeller shaft

Vibration when accelerating or decelerating

- ☐ Worn driveshaft outboard constant velocity joint (Chapter 8).
- ☐ Bent or distorted driveshaft or propeller shaft (Chapter 8).
- ☐ Worn driveshaft inboard constant velocity joint (Chapter 8).
- ☐ Worn propeller shaft front and/or rear universal joint (Chapter 8).
- ☐ Worn propeller shaft centre support bearing (Chapter 8).

Clicking or knocking noise on turns (at slow speed on full-lock)

- ☐ Worn driveshaft inboard constant velocity joint (Chapter 8).
- ☐ Lack of driveshaft constant velocity joint lubricant, possibly due to damaged gaiter (Chapter 8).

Braking system

Note: *Before assuming that a brake problem exists, make sure that the tyres are in good condition and correctly inflated, that the front wheel alignment is correct, and that the vehicle is not loaded with weight in an unequal manner. Apart from checking the condition of all pipe and hose connections, any faults occurring on the anti-lock braking system should be referred to a Honda dealer for diagnosis.*

Vehicle pulls to one side under braking

- ☐ Worn, defective, damaged or contaminated brake pads on one side (Chapters 1 and 9).
- ☐ Seized or partially-seized brake caliper piston (Chapters 1 and 9).
- ☐ A mixture of brake pad friction materials fitted between sides (Chapters 1 and 9).
- ☐ Brake caliper mounting bolts loose (Chapter 9).
- ☐ Worn or damaged steering or suspension components (Chapters 1 and 10).

Noise (grinding or high-pitched squeal) when brakes applied

- ☐ Brake pad friction material worn down to metal backing (Chapters 1 and 9).
- ☐ Excessive corrosion of brake disc. May be apparent after the vehicle has been standing for some time (Chapters 1 and 9).
- ☐ Foreign object (stone chipping, etc) trapped between brake disc and caliper (Chapters 1 and 9).

Excessive brake pedal travel

- ☐ Faulty master cylinder (Chapter 9).
- ☐ Air in hydraulic system (Chapters 1 and 9).
- ☐ Faulty vacuum servo unit (Chapter 9).

Brake pedal feels spongy when depressed

- ☐ Air in hydraulic system (Chapters 1 and 9).
- ☐ Deteriorated flexible rubber brake hoses (Chapters 1 and 9).
- ☐ Master cylinder mounting nuts loose (Chapter 9).
- ☐ Faulty master cylinder (Chapter 9).

Excessive brake pedal effort required to stop vehicle

- ☐ Faulty vacuum servo unit (Chapter 9).
- ☐ Disconnected, damaged or insecure brake servo vacuum hose (Chapter 9).
- ☐ Primary or secondary hydraulic circuit failure (Chapter 9).
- ☐ Seized brake caliper(s) (Chapter 9).
- ☐ Brake pads incorrectly fitted (Chapters 1 and 9).
- ☐ Incorrect grade of brake pads fitted (Chapters 1 and 9).
- ☐ Brake pad friction material contaminated (Chapters 1 and 9).

Judder felt through brake pedal or steering wheel when braking

- ☐ Excessive run-out or distortion of discs (Chapters 1 and 9).
- ☐ Brake pad friction material worn (Chapters 1 and 9).
- ☐ Brake caliper mounting bolts loose (Chapter 9).
- ☐ Wear in suspension or steering components or mountings (Chapters 1 and 10).

Brakes binding

- ☐ Seized brake caliper(s) (Chapter 9).
- ☐ Incorrectly-adjusted handbrake mechanism (Chapter 9).
- ☐ Faulty master cylinder (Chapter 9).

Front or rear wheels locking under normal braking

- ☐ ABS system fault (Chapter 9).

Suspension and steering

Note 1: *Before diagnosing suspension or steering faults, be sure that the trouble is not due to incorrect tyre pressures, mixtures of tyre types, or binding brakes.*

Note 2: *A moaning/groaning noise when manoeuvring on full lock can be due to premature degradation of the final drive fluid. Since, however, this may be easily misdiagnosed as a steering rack problem, it may lead to unnecessary repairs. If this is suspected, the first course of action is to renew the fluid as described in Chapter 1A or 1B, using the latest specification of Honda Dual Pump fluid which is called Dual Pump Fluid II (DPF II) fluid – seek the advice of a Honda dealer's service department if in doubt.*

Vehicle pulls to one side

- ☐ Defective tyre (*Weekly checks*).
- ☐ Excessive wear in suspension or steering components (Chapters 1 and 10).
- ☐ Incorrect front wheel alignment (Chapter 10).
- ☐ Damage to steering or suspension components (Chapter 1).

Wheel wobble and vibration

- ☐ Front roadwheels out of balance (vibration felt mainly through the steering wheel) (Chapters 1 and 10).
- ☐ Rear roadwheels out of balance (vibration felt throughout the vehicle) (Chapters 1 and 10).
- ☐ Roadwheels damaged or distorted (Chapters 1 and 10).
- ☐ Faulty or damaged tyre (*Weekly checks*).
- ☐ Worn steering or suspension joints, bushes or components (Chapters 1 and 10).
- ☐ Wheel bolts loose (Chapters 1 and 10).

Excessive pitching and/or rolling around corners, or during braking

- ☐ Defective shock absorbers (Chapters 1 and 10).
- ☐ Broken or weak spring and/or suspension part (Chapters 1 and 10).
- ☐ Worn or damaged anti-roll bar or mountings (Chapter 10).

Wandering or general instability

- ☐ Incorrect front wheel alignment (Chapter 10).
- ☐ Worn steering or suspension joints, bushes or components (Chapters 1 and 10).
- ☐ Roadwheels out of balance (Chapters 1 and 10).
- ☐ Faulty or damaged tyre (*Weekly checks*).
- ☐ Wheel bolts loose (Chapters 1 and 10).
- ☐ Defective shock absorbers (Chapters 1 and 10).

Excessively-stiff steering

- ☐ Broken or incorrectly-adjusted auxiliary drivebelt (Chapter 1).
- ☐ Faulty power steering pump (Chapter 10).
- ☐ Lack of steering gear lubricant (Chapter 10).
- ☐ Seized track rod end balljoint or suspension balljoint (Chapters 1 and 10).
- ☐ Incorrect front wheel alignment (Chapter 10).
- ☐ Steering rack or column bent or damaged (Chapter 10).

Excessive play in steering

- ☐ Worn steering column intermediate shaft universal joint (Chapter 10).
- ☐ Worn steering track rod balljoints (Chapters 1 and 10).
- ☐ Worn rack-and-pinion steering gear (Chapter 10).
- ☐ Worn steering or suspension joints, bushes or components (Chapters 1 and 10).

Lack of power assistance

- ☐ Broken or incorrectly-adjusted auxiliary drivebelt (Chapter 1).
- ☐ Incorrect power steering fluid level (*Weekly checks*).
- ☐ Restriction in power steering fluid hoses (Chapter 1).
- ☐ Faulty power steering pump (Chapter 10).
- ☐ Faulty rack-and-pinion steering gear (Chapter 10).

Tyre wear excessive

Tyre treads exhibit feathered edges

- ☐ Incorrect toe setting (Chapter 10).

Tyres worn in centre of tread

- ☐ Tyres over-inflated (*Weekly checks*).

Tyres worn on inside and outside edges

- ☐ Tyres under-inflated (*Weekly checks*).

Tyres worn on inside or outside edges

- ☐ Incorrect camber/castor angles (wear on one edge only) (Chapter 10).
- ☐ Worn steering or suspension joints, bushes or components (Chapters 1 and 10).
- ☐ Excessively-hard cornering.
- ☐ Accident damage.

Tyres worn unevenly

- ☐ Tyres/wheels out of balance (*Weekly checks*).
- ☐ Excessive wheel or tyre run-out (Chapter 1).
- ☐ Worn shock absorbers (Chapters 1 and 10).
- ☐ Faulty tyre (*Weekly checks*).

Electrical system

Note: *For problems associated with the starting system, refer to the faults listed under 'Engine' earlier in this Section.*

Battery won't hold a charge for more than a few days

- ☐ Battery defective internally (Chapter 5).
- ☐ Battery terminal connections loose or corroded (*Weekly checks*).
- ☐ Auxiliary drivebelt worn or incorrectly adjusted (Chapter 1).
- ☐ Alternator not charging at correct output (Chapter 5).
- ☐ Alternator or voltage regulator faulty (Chapter 5).
- ☐ Short-circuit causing continual battery drain (Chapters 5 and 12).

Ignition/no-charge warning light stays on with engine running

- ☐ Auxiliary drivebelt broken, worn, or incorrectly adjusted (Chapter 1).
- ☐ Alternator brushes worn, sticking, or dirty (Chapter 5).
- ☐ Alternator brush springs weak or broken (Chapter 5).
- ☐ Internal fault in alternator or voltage regulator (Chapter 5).
- ☐ Broken, disconnected, or loose wiring in charging circuit (Chapter 5).

Electrical system (continued)

Ignition/no-charge warning light fails to come on

- ☐ Warning light bulb blown (Chapter 12).
- ☐ Broken, disconnected, or loose wiring in warning light circuit (Chapter 12).
- ☐ Alternator faulty (Chapter 5).

Lights inoperative

- ☐ Bulb blown (Chapter 12).
- ☐ Corrosion of bulb or bulbholder contacts (Chapter 12).
- ☐ Blown fuse (Chapter 12).
- ☐ Faulty relay (Chapter 12).
- ☐ Broken, loose, or disconnected wiring (Chapter 12).
- ☐ Faulty switch (Chapter 12).

Instrument readings inaccurate or erratic

- ☐ Faulty instrument panel/multifunction screen (Chapter 12).

Fuel or temperature gauges give no reading

- ☐ Faulty gauge sender unit (Chapters 3 and 4).
- ☐ Wiring open-circuit (Chapter 12).
- ☐ Faulty instrument panel/multifunction screen (Chapter 12).

Fuel or temperature gauges give continuous maximum reading

- ☐ Faulty coolant temperature sensor (Chapters 3 and 4).
- ☐ Wiring short-circuit (Chapter 12).
- ☐ Faulty instrument panel/multifunction screen (Chapter 12).

Horn inoperative, or unsatisfactory in operation

Horn operates all the time

- ☐ Horn push either earthed or stuck down (Chapter 12).
- ☐ Horn cable-to-horn push earthed (Chapter 12).

Horn fails to operate

- ☐ Blown fuse (Chapter 12).
- ☐ Cable or cable connections loose, broken or disconnected (Chapter 12).
- ☐ Faulty horn (Chapter 12).

Horn emits intermittent or unsatisfactory sound

- ☐ Cable connections loose (Chapter 12).
- ☐ Horn mountings loose (Chapter 12).
- ☐ Faulty horn (Chapter 12).

Windscreen/tailgate wipers failed, or unsatisfactory in operation

Wipers fail to operate, or operate very slowly

- ☐ Wiper blades stuck to screen, or linkage seized or binding (Chapters 1 and 12).
- ☐ Blown fuse (Chapter 12).
- ☐ Cable or cable connections loose, broken or disconnected (Chapter 12).
- ☐ Faulty relay (Chapter 12).
- ☐ Faulty wiper motor (Chapter 12).

Wiper blades sweep over too large or too small an area of the glass

- ☐ Wiper arms incorrectly positioned on spindles (Chapter 1).
- ☐ Excessive wear of wiper linkage (Chapter 12).
- ☐ Wiper motor or linkage mountings loose or insecure (Chapter 12).

Wiper blades fail to clean the glass effectively

- ☐ Wiper blade rubbers worn or perished (*Weekly checks*).
- ☐ Wiper arm tension springs broken, or arm pivots seized (Chapter 12).
- ☐ Insufficient windscreen washer additive to adequately remove road film (*Weekly checks*).

Windscreen/tailgate washers failed, or unsatisfactory in operation

One or more washer jets inoperative

- ☐ Blocked washer jet.
- ☐ Disconnected, kinked or restricted fluid hose (Chapter 12).
- ☐ Insufficient fluid in washer reservoir (*Weekly checks*).

Washer pump fails to operate

- ☐ Broken or disconnected wiring or connections (Chapter 12).
- ☐ Blown fuse (Chapter 12).
- ☐ Faulty washer switch (Chapter 12).
- ☐ Faulty washer pump (Chapter 12).

Washer pump runs for some time before fluid is emitted from jets

- ☐ Faulty one-way valve in fluid supply hose (Chapter 12).

Electric windows inoperative, or unsatisfactory in operation

Window glass will only move in one direction

- ☐ Faulty switch (Chapter 12).

Window glass slow to move

- ☐ Regulator seized or damaged, or in need of lubricant (Chapter 11).
- ☐ Door internal components or trim fouling regulator (Chapter 11).
- ☐ Faulty motor (Chapter 11).

Window glass fails to move

- ☐ Blown fuse (Chapter 12).
- ☐ Faulty relay (Chapter 12).
- ☐ Broken or disconnected wiring or connections (Chapter 12).
- ☐ Faulty motor (Chapter 11).

Central locking system inoperative, or unsatisfactory in operation

Complete system failure

- ☐ Blown fuse (Chapter 12).
- ☐ Faulty relay (Chapter 12).
- ☐ Broken or disconnected wiring or connections (Chapter 12).
- ☐ Faulty control unit (Chapter 11).

Latch locks but will not unlock, or unlocks but will not lock

- ☐ Faulty master switch (Chapter 12).
- ☐ Broken or disconnected latch operating rods or levers (Chapter 11).
- ☐ Faulty relay (Chapter 12).
- ☐ Faulty control unit (Chapter 11).

One solenoid/motor fails to operate

- ☐ Broken or disconnected wiring or connections (Chapter 12).
- ☐ Faulty solenoid/motor (Chapter 11).
- ☐ Broken, binding or disconnected latch operating rods or levers (Chapter 11).
- ☐ Fault in door latch (Chapter 11).

A

ABS (Anti-lock brake system) A system, usually electronically controlled, that senses incipient wheel lockup during braking and relieves hydraulic pressure at wheels that are about to skid.

Air bag An inflatable bag hidden in the steering wheel (driver's side) or the dash or glovebox (passenger side). In a head-on collision, the bags inflate, preventing the driver and front passenger from being thrown forward into the steering wheel or windscreen.

Air cleaner A metal or plastic housing, containing a filter element, which removes dust and dirt from the air being drawn into the engine.

Air filter element The actual filter in an air cleaner system, usually manufactured from pleated paper and requiring renewal at regular intervals.

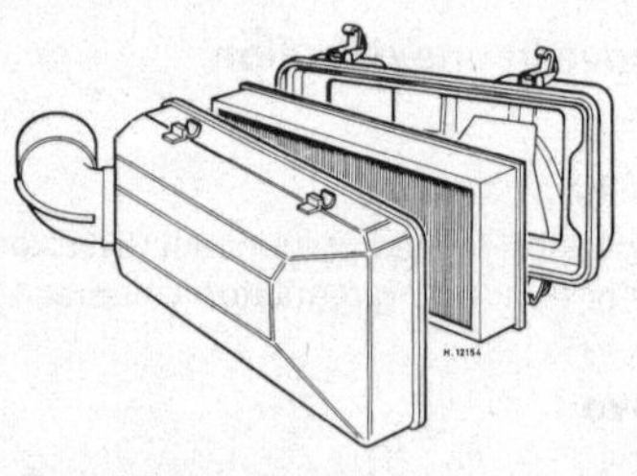

Air filter

Allen key A hexagonal wrench which fits into a recessed hexagonal hole.

Alligator clip A long-nosed spring-loaded metal clip with meshing teeth. Used to make temporary electrical connections.

Alternator A component in the electrical system which converts mechanical energy from a drivebelt into electrical energy to charge the battery and to operate the starting system, ignition system and electrical accessories.

Ampere (amp) A unit of measurement for the flow of electric current. One amp is the amount of current produced by one volt acting through a resistance of one ohm.

Anaerobic sealer A substance used to prevent bolts and screws from loosening. Anaerobic means that it does not require oxygen for activation. The Loctite brand is widely used.

Antifreeze A substance (usually ethylene glycol) mixed with water, and added to a vehicle's cooling system, to prevent freezing of the coolant in winter. Antifreeze also contains chemicals to inhibit corrosion and the formation of rust and other deposits that would tend to clog the radiator and coolant passages and reduce cooling efficiency.

Anti-seize compound A coating that reduces the risk of seizing on fasteners that are subjected to high temperatures, such as exhaust manifold bolts and nuts.

Asbestos A natural fibrous mineral with great heat resistance, commonly used in the composition of brake friction materials. Asbestos is a health hazard and the dust created by brake systems should never be inhaled or ingested.

Axle A shaft on which a wheel revolves, or which revolves with a wheel. Also, a solid beam that connects the two wheels at one end of the vehicle. An axle which also transmits power to the wheels is known as a live axle.

Axleshaft A single rotating shaft, on either side of the differential, which delivers power from the final drive assembly to the drive wheels. Also called a driveshaft or a halfshaft.

B

Ball bearing An anti-friction bearing consisting of a hardened inner and outer race with hardened steel balls between two races.

Bearing The curved surface on a shaft or in a bore, or the part assembled into either, that permits relative motion between them with minimum wear and friction.

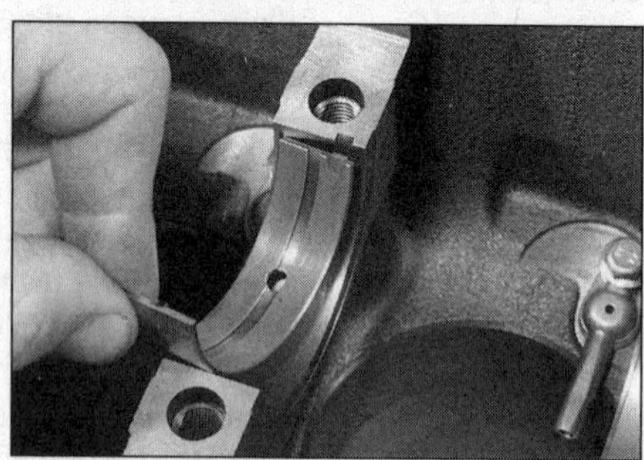

Bearing

Big-end bearing The bearing in the end of the connecting rod that's attached to the crankshaft.

Bleed nipple A valve on a brake wheel cylinder, caliper or other hydraulic component that is opened to purge the hydraulic system of air. Also called a bleed screw.

Brake bleeding Procedure for removing air from lines of a hydraulic brake system.

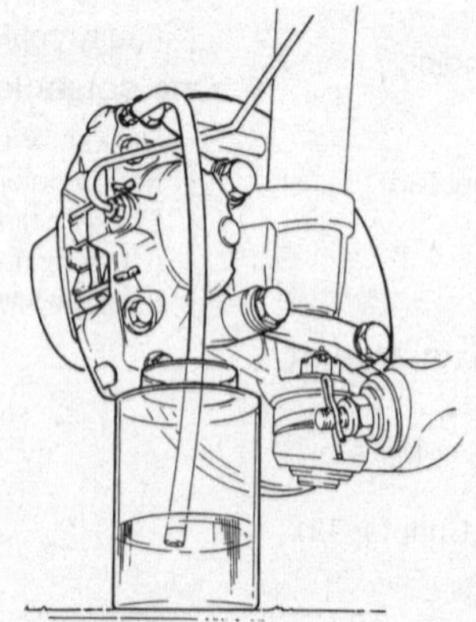

Brake bleeding

Brake disc The component of a disc brake that rotates with the wheels.

Brake drum The component of a drum brake that rotates with the wheels.

Brake linings The friction material which contacts the brake disc or drum to retard the vehicle's speed. The linings are bonded or riveted to the brake pads or shoes.

Brake pads The replaceable friction pads that pinch the brake disc when the brakes are applied. Brake pads consist of a friction material bonded or riveted to a rigid backing plate.

Brake shoe The crescent-shaped carrier to which the brake linings are mounted and which forces the lining against the rotating drum during braking.

Braking systems For more information on braking systems, consult the *Haynes Automotive Brake Manual*.

Breaker bar A long socket wrench handle providing greater leverage.

Bulkhead The insulated partition between the engine and the passenger compartment.

C

Caliper The non-rotating part of a disc-brake assembly that straddles the disc and carries the brake pads. The caliper also contains the hydraulic components that cause the pads to pinch the disc when the brakes are applied. A caliper is also a measuring tool that can be set to measure inside or outside dimensions of an object.

Camshaft A rotating shaft on which a series of cam lobes operate the valve mechanisms. The camshaft may be driven by gears, by sprockets and chain or by sprockets and a belt.

Canister A container in an evaporative emission control system; contains activated charcoal granules to trap vapours from the fuel system.

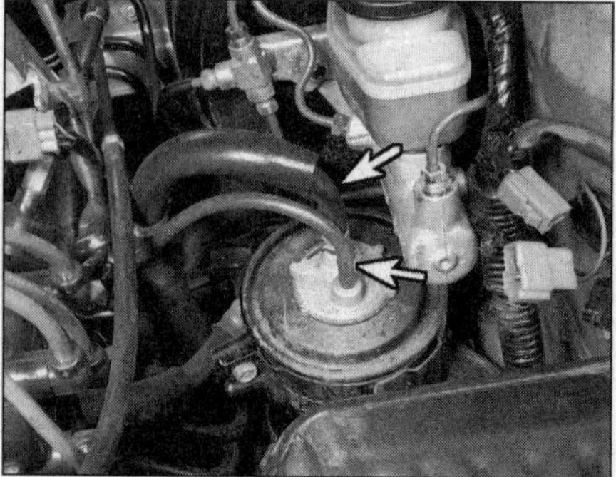

Canister

Carburettor A device which mixes fuel with air in the proper proportions to provide a desired power output from a spark ignition internal combustion engine.

Castellated Resembling the parapets along the top of a castle wall. For example, a castellated balljoint stud nut.

Castor In wheel alignment, the backward or forward tilt of the steering axis. Castor is positive when the steering axis is inclined rearward at the top.

Catalytic converter A silencer-like device in the exhaust system which converts certain pollutants in the exhaust gases into less harmful substances.

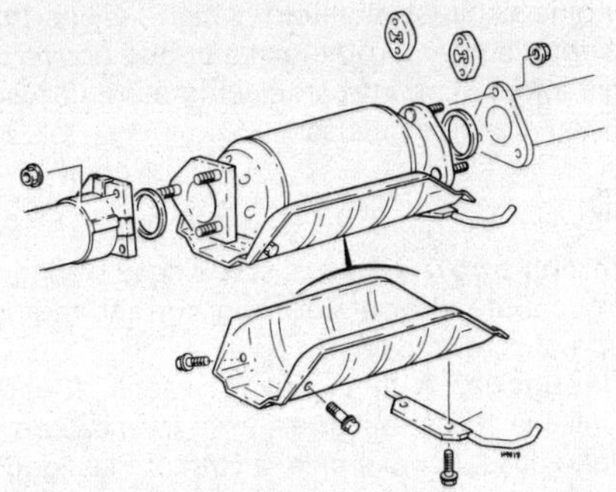

Catalytic converter

Circlip A ring-shaped clip used to prevent endwise movement of cylindrical parts and shafts. An internal circlip is installed in a groove in a housing; an external circlip fits into a groove on the outside of a cylindrical piece such as a shaft.

Clearance The amount of space between two parts. For example, between a piston and a cylinder, between a bearing and a journal, etc.

Coil spring A spiral of elastic steel found in various sizes throughout a vehicle, for example as a springing medium in the suspension and in the valve train.

Compression Reduction in volume, and increase in pressure and temperature, of a gas, caused by squeezing it into a smaller space.

Compression ratio The relationship between cylinder volume when the piston is at top dead centre and cylinder volume when the piston is at bottom dead centre.

Constant velocity (CV) joint A type of universal joint that cancels out vibrations caused by driving power being transmitted through an angle.

Core plug A disc or cup-shaped metal device inserted in a hole in a casting through which core was removed when the casting was formed. Also known as a freeze plug or expansion plug.

Crankcase The lower part of the engine block in which the crankshaft rotates.

Crankshaft The main rotating member, or shaft, running the length of the crankcase, with offset "throws" to which the connecting rods are attached.

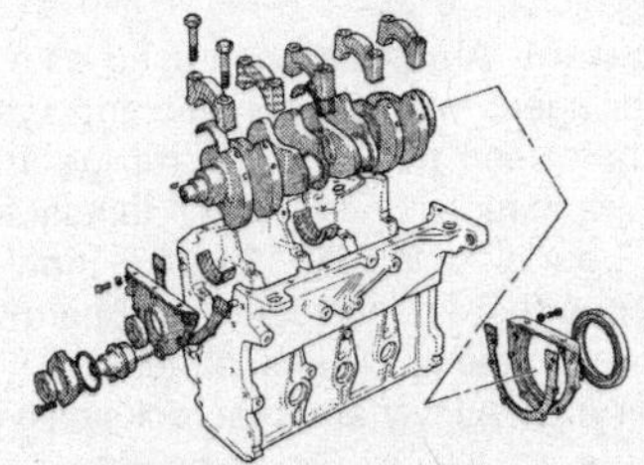

Crankshaft assembly

Crocodile clip See Alligator clip

D

Diagnostic code Code numbers obtained by accessing the diagnostic mode of an engine management computer. This code can be used to determine the area in the system where a malfunction may be located.

Disc brake A brake design incorporating a rotating disc onto which brake pads are squeezed. The resulting friction converts the energy of a moving vehicle into heat.

Double-overhead cam (DOHC) An engine that uses two overhead camshafts, usually one for the intake valves and one for the exhaust valves.

Drivebelt(s) The belt(s) used to drive accessories such as the alternator, water pump, power steering pump, air conditioning compressor, etc. off the crankshaft pulley.

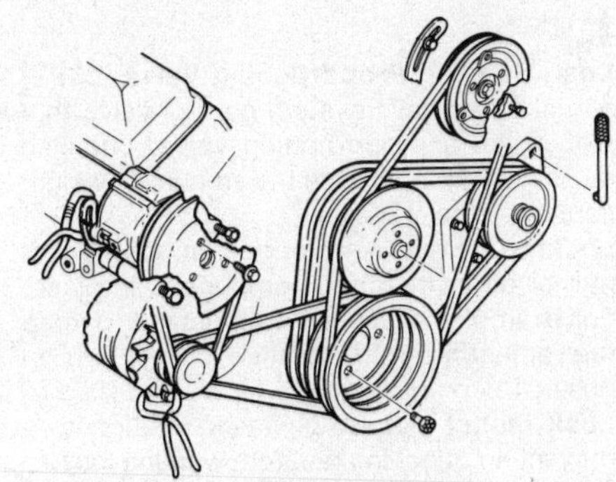

Accessory drivebelts

Driveshaft Any shaft used to transmit motion. Commonly used when referring to the axleshafts on a front wheel drive vehicle.

Drum brake A type of brake using a drum-shaped metal cylinder attached to the inner surface of the wheel. When the brake pedal is pressed, curved brake shoes with friction linings press against the inside of the drum to slow or stop the vehicle.

E

EGR valve A valve used to introduce exhaust gases into the intake air stream.

Electronic control unit (ECU) A computer which controls (for instance) ignition and fuel injection systems, or an anti-lock braking system. For more information refer to the *Haynes Automotive Electrical and Electronic Systems Manual.*

Electronic Fuel Injection (EFI) A computer controlled fuel system that distributes fuel through an injector located in each intake port of the engine.

Emergency brake A braking system, independent of the main hydraulic system, that can be used to slow or stop the vehicle if the primary brakes fail, or to hold the vehicle stationary even though the brake pedal isn't depressed. It usually consists of a hand lever that actuates either front or rear brakes mechanically through a series of cables and linkages. Also known as a handbrake or parking brake.

Endfloat The amount of lengthwise movement between two parts. As applied to a crankshaft, the distance that the crankshaft can move forward and back in the cylinder block.

Engine management system (EMS) A computer controlled system which manages the fuel injection and the ignition systems in an integrated fashion.

Exhaust manifold A part with several passages through which exhaust gases leave the engine combustion chambers and enter the exhaust pipe.

F

Fan clutch A viscous (fluid) drive coupling device which permits variable engine fan speeds in relation to engine speeds.

Feeler blade A thin strip or blade of hardened steel, ground to an exact thickness, used to check or measure clearances between parts.

Feeler blade

Firing order The order in which the engine cylinders fire, or deliver their power strokes, beginning with the number one cylinder.

Flywheel A heavy spinning wheel in which energy is absorbed and stored by means of momentum. On cars, the flywheel is attached to the crankshaft to smooth out firing impulses.

Free play The amount of travel before any action takes place. The "looseness" in a linkage, or an assembly of parts, between the initial application of force and actual movement. For example, the distance the brake pedal moves before the pistons in the master cylinder are actuated.

Fuse An electrical device which protects a circuit against accidental overload. The typical fuse contains a soft piece of metal which is calibrated to melt at a predetermined current flow (expressed as amps) and break the circuit.

Fusible link A circuit protection device consisting of a conductor surrounded by heat-resistant insulation. The conductor is smaller than the wire it protects, so it acts as the weakest link in the circuit. Unlike a blown fuse, a failed fusible link must frequently be cut from the wire for replacement.

G

Gap The distance the spark must travel in jumping from the centre electrode to the side electrode in a spark plug. Also refers to the spacing between the points in a contact breaker assembly in a conventional points-type ignition, or to the distance between the reluctor or rotor and the pickup coil in an electronic ignition.

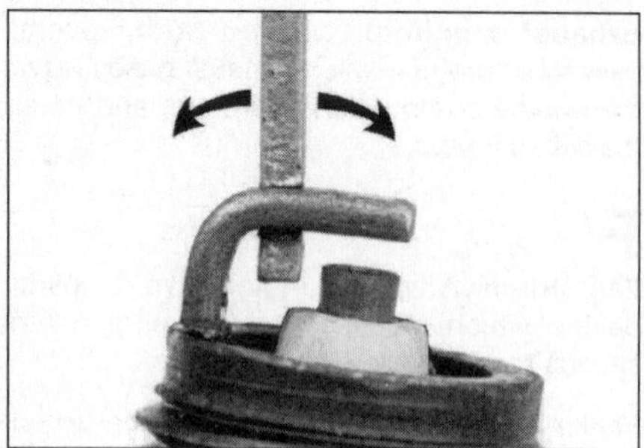

Adjusting spark plug gap

Gasket Any thin, soft material - usually cork, cardboard, asbestos or soft metal - installed between two metal surfaces to ensure a good seal. For instance, the cylinder head gasket seals the joint between the block and the cylinder head.

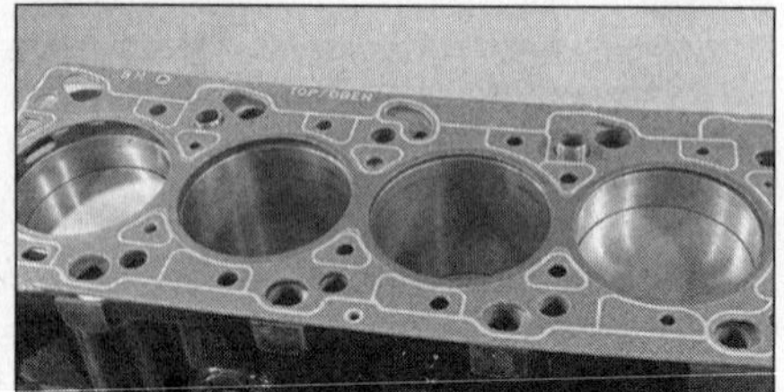

Gasket

Gauge An instrument panel display used to monitor engine conditions. A gauge with a movable pointer on a dial or a fixed scale is an analogue gauge. A gauge with a numerical readout is called a digital gauge.

H

Halfshaft A rotating shaft that transmits power from the final drive unit to a drive wheel, usually when referring to a live rear axle.

Harmonic balancer A device designed to reduce torsion or twisting vibration in the crankshaft. May be incorporated in the crankshaft pulley. Also known as a vibration damper.

Hone An abrasive tool for correcting small irregularities or differences in diameter in an engine cylinder, brake cylinder, etc.

Hydraulic tappet A tappet that utilises hydraulic pressure from the engine's lubrication system to maintain zero clearance (constant contact with both camshaft and valve stem). Automatically adjusts to variation in valve stem length. Hydraulic tappets also reduce valve noise.

I

Ignition timing The moment at which the spark plug fires, usually expressed in the number of crankshaft degrees before the piston reaches the top of its stroke.

Inlet manifold A tube or housing with passages through which flows the air-fuel mixture (carburettor vehicles and vehicles with throttle body injection) or air only (port fuel-injected vehicles) to the port openings in the cylinder head.

J

Jump start Starting the engine of a vehicle with a discharged or weak battery by attaching jump leads from the weak battery to a charged or helper battery.

L

Load Sensing Proportioning Valve (LSPV) A brake hydraulic system control valve that works like a proportioning valve, but also takes into consideration the amount of weight carried by the rear axle.

Locknut A nut used to lock an adjustment nut, or other threaded component, in place. For example, a locknut is employed to keep the adjusting nut on the rocker arm in position.

Lockwasher A form of washer designed to prevent an attaching nut from working loose.

M

MacPherson strut A type of front suspension system devised by Earle MacPherson at Ford of England. In its original form, a simple lateral link with the anti-roll bar creates the lower control arm. A long strut - an integral coil spring and shock absorber - is mounted between the body and the steering knuckle. Many modern so-called MacPherson strut systems use a conventional lower A-arm and don't rely on the anti-roll bar for location.

Multimeter An electrical test instrument with the capability to measure voltage, current and resistance.

N

NOx Oxides of Nitrogen. A common toxic pollutant emitted by petrol and diesel engines at higher temperatures.

O

Ohm The unit of electrical resistance. One volt applied to a resistance of one ohm will produce a current of one amp.

Ohmmeter An instrument for measuring electrical resistance.

O-ring A type of sealing ring made of a special rubber-like material; in use, the O-ring is compressed into a groove to provide the sealing action.

Overhead cam (ohc) engine An engine with the camshaft(s) located on top of the cylinder head(s).

Overhead valve (ohv) engine An engine with the valves located in the cylinder head, but with the camshaft located in the engine block.

Oxygen sensor A device installed in the engine exhaust manifold, which senses the oxygen content in the exhaust and converts this information into an electric current. Also called a Lambda sensor.

P

Phillips screw A type of screw head having a cross instead of a slot for a corresponding type of screwdriver.

Plastigage A thin strip of plastic thread, available in different sizes, used for measuring clearances. For example, a strip of Plastigage is laid across a bearing journal. The parts are assembled and dismantled; the width of the crushed strip indicates the clearance between journal and bearing.

Plastigage

Propeller shaft The long hollow tube with universal joints at both ends that carries power from the transmission to the differential on front-engined rear wheel drive vehicles.

Proportioning valve A hydraulic control valve which limits the amount of pressure to the rear brakes during panic stops to prevent wheel lock-up.

R

Rack-and-pinion steering A steering system with a pinion gear on the end of the steering shaft that mates with a rack (think of a geared wheel opened up and laid flat). When the steering wheel is turned, the pinion turns, moving the rack to the left or right. This movement is transmitted through the track rods to the steering arms at the wheels.

Radiator A liquid-to-air heat transfer device designed to reduce the temperature of the coolant in an internal combustion engine cooling system.

Refrigerant Any substance used as a heat transfer agent in an air-conditioning system. R-12 has been the principle refrigerant for many years; recently, however, manufacturers have begun using R-134a, a non-CFC substance that is considered less harmful to the ozone in the upper atmosphere.

Rocker arm A lever arm that rocks on a shaft or pivots on a stud. In an overhead valve engine, the rocker arm converts the upward movement of the pushrod into a downward movement to open a valve.

Rotor In a distributor, the rotating device inside the cap that connects the centre electrode and the outer terminals as it turns, distributing the high voltage from the coil secondary winding to the proper spark plug. Also, that part of an alternator which rotates inside the stator. Also, the rotating assembly of a turbocharger, including the compressor wheel, shaft and turbine wheel.

Runout The amount of wobble (in-and-out movement) of a gear or wheel as it's rotated. The amount a shaft rotates "out-of-true." The out-of-round condition of a rotating part.

S

Sealant A liquid or paste used to prevent leakage at a joint. Sometimes used in conjunction with a gasket.

Sealed beam lamp An older headlight design which integrates the reflector, lens and filaments into a hermetically-sealed one-piece unit. When a filament burns out or the lens cracks, the entire unit is simply replaced.

Serpentine drivebelt A single, long, wide accessory drivebelt that's used on some newer vehicles to drive all the accessories, instead of a series of smaller, shorter belts. Serpentine drivebelts are usually tensioned by an automatic tensioner.

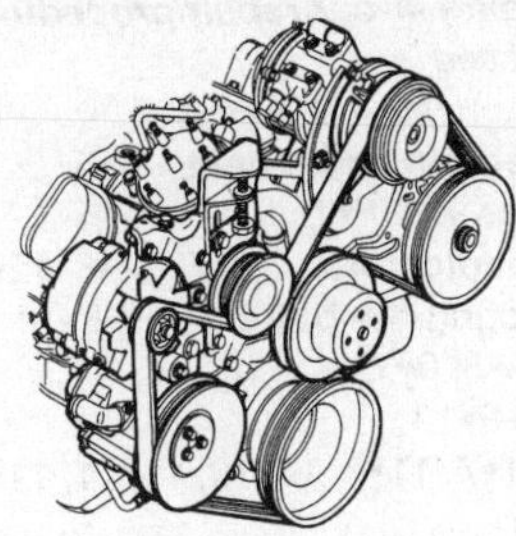

Serpentine drivebelt

Shim Thin spacer, commonly used to adjust the clearance or relative positions between two parts. For example, shims inserted into or under bucket tappets control valve clearances. Clearance is adjusted by changing the thickness of the shim.

Slide hammer A special puller that screws into or hooks onto a component such as a shaft or bearing; a heavy sliding handle on the shaft bottoms against the end of the shaft to knock the component free.

Sprocket A tooth or projection on the periphery of a wheel, shaped to engage with a chain or drivebelt. Commonly used to refer to the sprocket wheel itself.

Starter inhibitor switch On vehicles with an automatic transmission, a switch that prevents starting if the vehicle is not in Neutral or Park.

Strut See MacPherson strut.

T

Tappet A cylindrical component which transmits motion from the cam to the valve stem, either directly or via a pushrod and rocker arm. Also called a cam follower.

Thermostat A heat-controlled valve that regulates the flow of coolant between the cylinder block and the radiator, so maintaining optimum engine operating temperature. A thermostat is also used in some air cleaners in which the temperature is regulated.

Thrust bearing The bearing in the clutch assembly that is moved in to the release levers by clutch pedal action to disengage the clutch. Also referred to as a release bearing.

Timing belt A toothed belt which drives the camshaft. Serious engine damage may result if it breaks in service.

Timing chain A chain which drives the camshaft.

Toe-in The amount the front wheels are closer together at the front than at the rear. On rear wheel drive vehicles, a slight amount of toe-in is usually specified to keep the front wheels running parallel on the road by offsetting other forces that tend to spread the wheels apart.

Toe-out The amount the front wheels are closer together at the rear than at the front. On front wheel drive vehicles, a slight amount of toe-out is usually specified.

Tools For full information on choosing and using tools, refer to the *Haynes Automotive Tools Manual.*

Tracer A stripe of a second colour applied to a wire insulator to distinguish that wire from another one with the same colour insulator.

Tune-up A process of accurate and careful adjustments and parts replacement to obtain the best possible engine performance.

Turbocharger A centrifugal device, driven by exhaust gases, that pressurises the intake air. Normally used to increase the power output from a given engine displacement, but can also be used primarily to reduce exhaust emissions (as on VW's "Umwelt" Diesel engine).

U

Universal joint or U-joint A double-pivoted connection for transmitting power from a driving to a driven shaft through an angle. A U-joint consists of two Y-shaped yokes and a cross-shaped member called the spider.

V

Valve A device through which the flow of liquid, gas, vacuum, or loose material in bulk may be started, stopped, or regulated by a movable part that opens, shuts, or partially obstructs one or more ports or passageways. A valve is also the movable part of such a device.

Valve clearance The clearance between the valve tip (the end of the valve stem) and the rocker arm or tappet. The valve clearance is measured when the valve is closed.

Vernier caliper A precision measuring instrument that measures inside and outside dimensions. Not quite as accurate as a micrometer, but more convenient.

Viscosity The thickness of a liquid or its resistance to flow.

Volt A unit for expressing electrical "pressure" in a circuit. One volt that will produce a current of one ampere through a resistance of one ohm.

W

Welding Various processes used to join metal items by heating the areas to be joined to a molten state and fusing them together. For more information refer to the *Haynes Automotive Welding Manual.*

Wiring diagram A drawing portraying the components and wires in a vehicle's electrical system, using standardised symbols. For more information refer to the *Haynes Automotive Electrical and Electronic Systems Manual.*

Note: *References throughout this index are in the form* "**Chapter number**" • "**Page number**". *So, for example, 2C•15 refers to page 15 of Chapter 2C.*

Note: *References throughout this index are in the form* **"Chapter number" • "Page number"**. *So, for example, 2C•15 refers to page 15 of Chapter 2C.*

Note: *References throughout this index are in the form* **"Chapter number" • "Page number"**. *So, for example, 2C•15 refers to page 15 of Chapter 2C.*

Note: *References throughout this index are in the form* **"Chapter number" • "Page number"**. *So, for example, 2C•15 refers to page 15 of Chapter 2C.*

T

U

V

W